MALTA: THE SPITFIRE YEAR 1942

MALTA: THE SPITFIRE YEAR 1942

Christopher Shores and Brian Cull
with Nicola Malizia

GRUB STREET · LONDON

Published by
Grub Street
The Basement
10 Chivalry Rd
London SW11 1HT

Maps by Graeme Andrew

British Library Cataloguing in Publication Data
Shores, Christopher, *1937–*
Malta: the spitfire year 1942.
1. World War 2: Air operations 2. Malta
I. Title II. Cull, Brian III. Malizia, Nicola
940.5442

ISBN 0-948817-16-X

Edited by John Davies

Typeset by Pearl Graphics

Printed and bound in Great Britain by
Biddles Ltd, Guildford and King's Lynn

DEDICATION

The authors dedicate this book to the memory of the men and women of all nationalities who gave their lives in the Battle of Malta, 1940-1942, and to Philip Vella, first Honorary Secretary of the National War Museum Association of Malta, who died on 31 December, 1987.

CONTENTS

Maps 6

Introduction and Acknowledgements 10

Chapter 1: Opening Rounds of a New Year 17
Chapter 2: Nadir of the Hurricanes 67
Chapter 3: Spitfires at Last! 106
Chapter 4: 'Who Says a Wasp Can't Sting Twice?' 195
Chapter 5: Spring Attrition 252
Chapter 6: The June Convoys 317
Chapter 7: Summer Skirmishes 379
Chapter 8: Operation 'Pedestal' 448
Chapter 9: Autumnal Offensive 517
Chapter 10: The Last Blitz 576
Chapter 11: Aftermath 648

Appendices

I: Fighter Units Based on Malta 1942 673
II: RAF Fighter Squadron Code Letters, Malta 1942 673
III: Establishment of the First RDF Station 675
IV: 'Operation Hercules': The Proposed Axis Invasion of Malta — 15 August 1942 677
V: Italian and German Vessels Sunk at Palermo 679
VI: Mediterranean Odyssey 680
VII: Shot Down over Malta 683
VIII: Awaiting Transfer 684
IX: Spitfire Vc BR108 685
X: The Crash of Liberator AL516 686
XI: Lord Gort VC 687

Bibliography 686

Index 689

GOZO
COMINO
N
St Pauls Bay
Ghajn Tuffieha
Mosta
Naxxar
Sliema
French Creek
Fort Tigne
Fort St. Elmo
Manoel Island
Takali
Attard
VALETTA
Grand Harbour
Rabat
Qormi
Zabbar
Tarxien
Zebbug
Dingli
Luqa
Dingli Cliffs
Safi
Marsaxlokk Bay
Delimara Point
Hal Far
Kalafrana
FILFLA
Km 1 0 1 2 3 4 5
Miles 1 0 1 2 3
MALTA

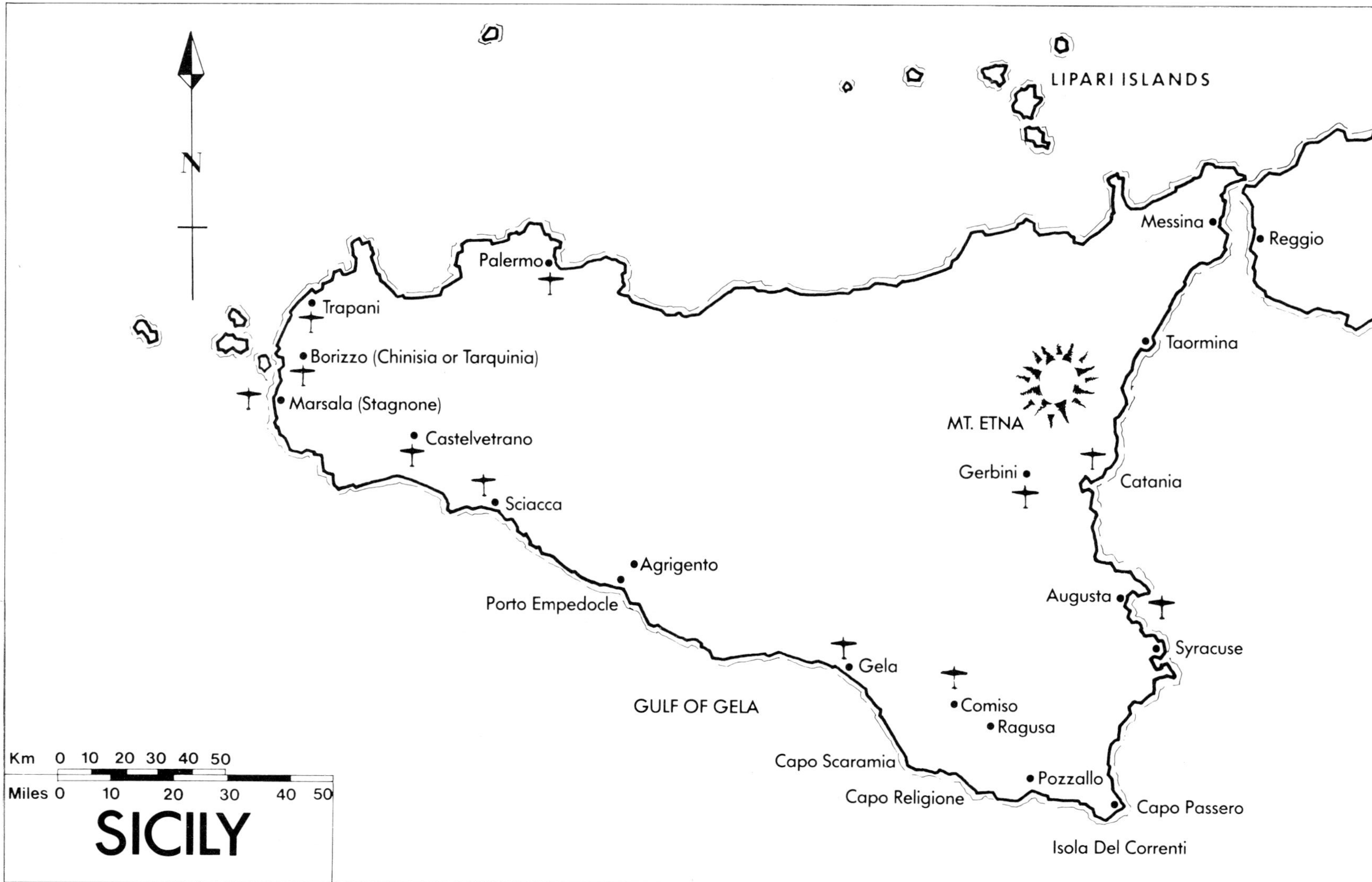
LIPARI ISLANDS
N
Palermo
Trapani
Borizzo (Chinisia or Tarquinia)
Marsala (Stagnone)
Castelvetrano
Sciacca
Agrigento
Porto Empedocle
Gela
GULF OF GELA
Comiso
Ragusa
Capo Scaramia
Capo Religione
Pozzallo
Capo Passero
Isola Del Correnti
Syracuse
Augusta
Catania
Gerbini
MT. ETNA
Taormina
Messina
Reggio
Km 0 10 20 30 40 50
Miles 0 10 20 30 40 50
SICILY

MEDITERRANEAN AREA

YUGOSLAVIA
BULGARIA
ADRIATIC SEA
ITALY
Bari
Naples
Brindisi
Taranto
ALBANIA
TURKEY
AEGEAN SEA
GREECE
Corfu
IONIAN SEA
Lipari Is
Athens
SICILY
C. Matapan
Gozo
MALTA
CRETE
Tobruk
Tripoli
Bardia
Benghazi
Cyrenaica
Sirte
LIBYA

INTRODUCTION AND ACKNOWLEDGEMENTS

Like most detailed campaign studies of this nature, work on this book has been going on for many years — certainly more than 15. Similarly, as with such books there remain some questions unanswered, and past experience dictates that as soon as it is published, some of those answers will appear! It remains the dilemma of authors such as us, when to draw the line and publish; it would be all too easy to go on researching indefinitely! However, if posterity is to be served, as we would wish, a time arises when the decision has to be taken to put together as complete a story as we reasonably can.

No sooner had the first volume of our history of the siege of Malta, *Malta: the Hurricane Years, 1940-41,* appeared, than certain new and additional information began to reach us. At the end of this introduction, and as a lead-in to the 1942 narrative, these additional facts are provided as an addendum for those readers who already own, or have read the earlier book.

During our researches for this book we have consulted Squadron Operational Record Books (Form 540 and 541), airfield records and various Command documents, first at the Air Historical Branch of the Ministry of Defence (Air) and in more recent years at the Public Record Office, Kew. For much of 1942 there are notable gaps and inaccuracies within certain of these official documents, 126 Squadron in particular failing to complete the monthly diary on several occasions, whilst for certain units such as 242, 601, 603 and 605 Squadrons, where only the air parties reached the Island, no formal records written at the time appear ever to have existed. It has taken many years of patient research to fill the gaps, and we have been particularly fortunate in obtaining, either directly or through intermediaries or families, the logbooks and/or diaries of a very considerable number of aircrew who served on Malta during 1942. These have been of the utmost assistance, and have included the following:–

Logbooks — J.L. Boyd, V.P. Brennan, C.A. Crombie, J.H. Curry, W.R. Daddo-Langlois, R.W. Elliott, R.C. Fumerton, A.P. Goldsmith, P.P. Hanks, A.C.W. Holland, P.B. Lucas, I. McKay, N. Macqueen, P.A. Nash, D.J. Neale, R. Noble, G.R. Nottage, N.M. Park, C.H. Parkinson, N.L. Pashen, J.A. Plagis, A.C. Rabagliati, J.D. Rae, L.S. Reid, W.T.E. Rolls, W.A.J. Satchell, R. Seed, M.C. Shipard, D.H. Smith, J.A. Smith, R.I.A. Smith, G.H. Williams, J.W. Yarra.

Diaries — C.H. Gates (USNR), A.P. Goldsmith, I. McKay, P.A.J. O'Brien, C.H. Parkinson, N.L. Pashen, J.A. Smith, J.W. Yarra.

Accounts based on logbooks and/or diaries — H.E. Duthie, I.R. MacLennan, R. Tilley, P. Wigley.

Confirmation of details — L.S. Nomis, A.F. Roscoe.

Amongst the pilots, Wg.Cdr. P.B. 'Laddie' Lucas, Sqn.Ldr. Rod Smith and the late Flt.Lt. Bill Rolls were particularly generous in their help and support; Rod Smith contributed not only a copy of his own logbook, but that of his brother Jerry and the latter's diary, kept up to the date on which he lost his life over the Island. Philip Wigley read and commented upon the initial chapters, and much assistance was also received from his fellow Hurricane pilots, Ron Noble and Judge Ian McKay. Others who were notably helpful were Archie Bartleman (who with his wife Freda, afforded wonderful hospitality to Brian Cull during a research trip to South Africa), the late Rod Carver, Joe Crichton, Reg Elliott, Fred Etchells, Paul Farnes, Gordon Farquharson, Dave Ferraby, Norris Ganes, Cyril Hone, Dave Howe, Cy King, Paddy O'Brien, Noel Ogilvie, George Powell-Shedden, the late Jack Satchell, Dr Felix Sauer, John Sherlock, John Thompson, Tommy Thompson, Peter Twiss, Arthur Varey and Innes Westmacott.

Mrs. Angela Dabourn was most generous in providing the logbook, diary and photograph collection of her late brother, Raoul Daddo-Langlois. She also acceeded to our suggestion that this collection and that of her late father, Wg.Cdr. Daddo-Langlois, should subsequently lodge at the Royal Air Force Museum, Hendon. Other relatives also assisted greatly, particularly Francis Rabagliati (brother of Sandy Rabagliati), Mrs Teresa McHan (widow of Richard McHan), the family of the late Nigel Park, the late Kenneth Cox and his widow Mrs Rosamund Hills (sister of the late Owen Berkeley-Hill), and John Berkeley-Hill (nephew); to all, our grateful thanks.

Thanks are also due to Sqn.Ldr. John Alton, Flt.Lt. Reg Townson and George Head. James A. Gray, adjutant of the Eagle Squadron Association, was instrumental in putting us in touch with Leo Nomis, Art Roscoe and Reade Tilley, all of whom have been most helpful. The Malta War Museum provided us with a taped interview with Hermann Harnisch, and subsequent correspondence proved most profitable in terms of both information and photographs.

Fellow historians, researchers and archivists who gave generously of their time and knowledge included Lex McAulay in Australia, who provided several logbook extracts from his fellow countrymen, together with photos, as did Paul Sortehaug in New Zealand. Russell Guest, Ray Sturtivant, Peter C. Smith, the late Allan Blythe, Andrew Stamatolpoulos, Chaz Bowyer and Tony Rogers also have our thanks.

As with the first volume, we received the most whole-hearted support from the Malta War Museum, and particularly from the late Philip Vella, his brief successor as Honorary Secretary of the Museum, the late Sqn.Ldr. Peter Durnford, and the current Secretary, Frederick Galea, to all of whom a great debt of gratitude is owed, as it is to John Agius and Louis Tortell. We also express our deepest thanks to our friend and colleague Winfried Bock, who with the assistance of Hans Ring provided the vast majority of the Luftwaffe material in the book, read and corrected each chapter, and considered and modified as necessary our comments and conclusions insofar as the German involvement was concerned. He was in effect a fourth full member of the team.

Clive Bassett telephoned unexpectedly one evening to offer photographs from an album he had acquired. Amongst the 'gems' therein was the best new illustration of George Beurling to appear for many years. The authors also offer their thanks for assistance received from the staff of the various official agencies consulted, including the Public Record Office, Air Historical Branch —

particularly Air Commodore Henry Probert and R.C.M. King Esq; the RAF Museum, Hendon, Deutsche Dienststelle (WASt), Berlin, and the Bury St. Edmunds Public Library.

As with other volumes we have produced, deadlines were met only with the administrative and material back-up of our good friend, Bruce Lander (who has recently had his own first aviation article published), and his colleague Eddie Pearson.

Nicola Malizia offers personal thanks for assistance in Italy to Ufficio Storico dello Stato Maggiore Aeronautica, Ufficio Propaganda e Fotografico dello SMAM, Ufficio Storico Marina Militare Italiana, Gen. SA Aldo Remondino, Gen. SA MOVM Giulio Cesare Graziani, Gen. SA Enrice Marescalchi, Gen. SA Giuseppe Pesce, Gen. SA Civello Luccioli, Gen. SA Luciano Nimis, Gen. DA Antonio Cumbat, First Ca. Giovanni Ambrosio, Fabio Bianchi, Richard Caruana, Ing. Dante Curcio, Girolamo Di Bella, Giorgio Di Giorgio, Stefano Doglio Niclot, Eduardo Ferri, Dott. Roberto Gentilli, Cesare Gori, Ing. Tullio Marcon, Giuseppe Mattesini, Sergio Mecchia, Nicola Patella, Prof. Nicola Pihnato, Karl-Heinz Schmeelke, Sergio Govi, Giulio Starna, Giovanni Terebindo and Achille Vigna.

Brian Cull adds his personal thanks to Stuart D. Bickel for photogaphic assistance and expertise, to his old mentor, Jack Lee, and to Val for her ever-present understanding and support.

A work such as this has required wide reading and reference to existing published material, much of which is warmly recommended to readers. A bibliography is provided at the end of the book.

Christopher Shores, Hendon, London
Brian Cull, Bury St Edmunds, Suffolk
Nicola Malizia, Rimini, Forli, Italy
August 1990

Additional and Corrected Information regarding
Malta: The Hurricane Years, 1940-1941

Page 39: The prisoner identified by his Italian captors as 'Captain Leslye' was, in fact, Flt.Lt. Leslie Gregory, pilot of Swordfish K8369; his crew — Corporal V.A. Kemp and AC1 F.C. Williams — were lost.
Page 67: AC1 Thomas 'Paddy' McCann, BEM — after he had received his award he was moved to Luqa, and early on the morning of 24 November 1941 was meeting a 40 Squadron Wellington returning from ops. During the servicing, the bombs doors were opened, and out fell a small bomb which was hung-up in the bomb bay. It exploded and killed McCann.
Page 158: Plt.Off. J.J. Walsh of 261 Squadron, who was shot down and wounded on 25 February, 1941, died on 2 March, 1941 (see also Pages 378 and 386).
Page 199: On 7 May, 1941 Beaufighters of 252 Squadron encountered an aircraft variously identified as a 'Ca 310' or an 'S.81'. In fact, this was an S.82 (MM609/9) of 149° Gruppo SA, flown by Serg. Aldo Pierano, which was shot down at 1550, eight miles south of Lampedusa. On board were 22 mechanics of 239ª Squadriglia on their way to North Africa, 13 of whom were lost as well as four of the crew; the pilot survived.
Page 205: On 10 May, 1941 Beaufighters of 252 Squadron strafed Catania airfield — in addition to the damage recorded, three He111 minelayers of 2/KG 4 were also damaged. This unit had undertaken minelaying duties throughout the Mediterranean during the period January–April 1941.
Page 205: Formation of 185 Squadron at Hal Far: 250 and 251 Squadrons had formed at Aqir, Palestine, on 1 April, 1941, and the first nine Tomahawks arrived for 250 Squadron on 28 April. Both squadrons were originally destined for Greece but events changed the move to Amriya, Egypt, ground personnel of both units travelling on 2 and 3 May, meeting 1430 Flight in Alexandria on the way.

Early on 6 May, ground personnel of 251 Squadron and 1430 Flight boarded HMS *Breconshire* in Alexandria, and sailed at midday together with the Mediterranean Fleet to meet 'Tiger' Convoy; *Breconshire* arrived in Marsamxett harbour on the 9th. 185 Squadron was formed at Hal Far on the 12th with pilots from 261, and ground personnel from 251 and 261 Squadrons and 1430 Flight.
Page 217: Comment on Plt.Off. John Pain's final recollections of conditions at Takali, by John Alton:

> 'I was particularly struck by the report of John Pain. I do not wish to be in any way critical, but I feel sure that there was plenty of sheet aluminium lying around to effect repairs without resorting to 50 Players' tins — and let me say, a packet of ten Players was a welcome find, never mind a 50s tin!
>
> 'The "bent wire for a ripcord handle" story surprised me, as knowing the construction of such things it seems impossible that the handle could come adrift. However, I can think of a possible souce of this story, and I can vouch for every word of it since it concerned me directly.
>
> 'Flt.Lt. MacLachlan was the sort of personality that inspired a sense of hero worship in every ground member, and perhaps this was why I was concerned in helping him to strap in his Hurricane for a scramble from Takali. Normally, as the line NCO, I would have taken up a position where I

could observe all aircraft starting up. Now, the safety harness in a Hurricane, and indeed in all British aircraft, comprised four stout woven straps, which passed over each shoulder and over the thighs, and were held in place by a cone-shaped stout pin which passed through eyelets in each strap. This pin was then secured in position by a lyre-shaped strong wire locking piece. Normally this was secured to the strap by a piece of chord.

'On the occasion of which I write, Mac drew my attention to the fact that it was missing. There was neither a spare pin nor another aircraft which could be robbed. I found a piece of fencing wire, and with Mac's help, pushed it through the locking piece, and with a grateful smile, he waved chocks away, and off he went. Of course, the correct pin would have been fitted before the next sortie."

Page 251/252: On 9 July seven Blenheims of 110 Squadron were despatched to raid Tripoli. The Fiat G.50bis fighters of 360ª Squadriglia, 155° Gruppo, 51° Stormo CT, had been moved there to intercept such raids, and on this occasion Serg.Magg. Aldo Buvoli and Mar. Francesco Faggiolo were patrolling at high level. Seeing the bombers, Buvoli dived to attack, claiming two shot down and chasing the others out to sea. Radio intercepts indicated that three more had crashed into the sea as a result of his attack, and he was credited with five victories. Four Blenheims in fact failed to return.

Later that day, Flg.Off. Warburton's Maryland was intercepted and damaged by a fighter identified as an MC200; this was probably a G.50bis of 51° Stormo flown by Mar. Faggiolo, who claimed a Maryland shot down.

Page 252: On 11 July in the combat between 10° Gruppo CT and 185 Squadron, Cap. Lucchini and Mar. Ferrulli were bounced at low level by eight Hurricanes, and the latter's aircraft was damaged. The top cover then claimed two Hurricanes shot down, jointly with 50° Stormo. Serg.Magg. Natale Fiorito crash-landed at base.

Page 267: On 28 July a Beaufighter was claimed shot down off Augusta by 4° Stormo pilots — Serg. Luigi Bignami, Serg. Patrizi and Serg. Valignani.

Page 274: Blenheim Z7503 GB-J of 105 Squadron, flown by Sqn.Ldr. G.E. Goode, which was shot down by AA fire during a raid on chemical works at Crotone, force-landed and the crew were captured. The IFF apparatus was recovered, and was the first such recovery by the Italians.

Page 287: When Ten. Col. Romagnoli was lost on 4 September, it is possible that four Hurricanes were claimed — one credited to Romagnoli by collision, two to Mar. Monterumici (one into the sea and one from which the pilot baled) and one to Mar. Migliorato. Later that day 4° Stormo claimed four more Hurricanes, and 54° Stormo claimed ten.

Page 312: The impression is given that one Albacore of 828 Squadron failed to reach Malta from *Ark Royal*. In fact, '5H' refused to start and later, when being lifted by crane, the hook broke and the aircraft was damaged beyond repair.

Page 326: In the account of the loss of four 830 Squadron Swordfish on the night of 11/12 November, the impression is given that the ASV Special Duties Flight Wellington also failed to return; this was not so.

Page 334: The impression is given that two of the Swordfish were flown by Lt. J.R.O. Stevenson and Sub Lt. R.E.F. Kerrison. In fact, Stevenson was Kerrison's observer.

Page 337: The two photographs on this page show Sgt. W.D. Greenhalgh's

Hurricane Z2491 HA-D of 126 Squadron, following its crash-landing on Comiso airfield on 24 November, 1941 and Sgt. Greenhalgh with a group of Italian pilots immediately after his capture.

Page 345: In the photograph of 249 Squadron pilots there is an unidentified pilot between Flg.Off. Davis and Flg.Off. Herrington — this is now believed to be Sgt. 'Skeet' Smith. Additionally, last on the right is not Sgt. 'Davies' but Sgt. Rist.

Sgt. W.D. Greenhalgh with his captors. *(Barbieri via Malizia)*

Hurricane Z2491 HA-D of 126 Squadron which force-landed at Comiso airfield on 24 November 1941, flown by Sgt. W.D. Greenhalgh, who was taken prisoner. *(G.F. Ghergo)*

Page 347: Two Blenheims of 18 Squadron were lost during a raid on Argostoli harbour; as recorded, it seems likely that one fell to Lt. Herbert Haas of I/NJG 2. Possibly the second fell to Lt. Peter Laufs of the same unit, who also claimed a twin-engined aircraft at approximately the same time, although identified as a Wellington.
Page 350: As recorded, Lt. Peter Laufs of I/NJG 2 claimed a Hurricane shot down. Laufs reported that his starboard engine was shot out by a Hurricane which then overshot as he turned with the dead engine, and it disintegrated under the power of the Ju88C's front armament. This was presumably Plt.Off. E.E. Steele's aircraft, which was also probably the machine claimed shot down by Maj. von Maltzahn of JG 53.
Page 355: 26th December 1941: In addition to the facts recorded, Sgt. D.T. Neale of 242 Squadron, flying Hurricane BE565, was also shot up by a Bf109 and belly-landed with a cannon shell splinter in his leg, obviously the second Hurricane claimed by the Luftwaffe (possibly by Maj. von Maltzahn).
Page 358: 29th December 1941: In addition to the RAF losses recorded, Flt.Lt. S.E. Andrews of 242 Squadron was also shot down and baled out into sea — he was rescued by HSL 128.
Page 360: The impression is given that the 40 Squadron Wellington detachment became 156 Squadron. In fact, the UK-based echelon became 156 Squadron, with the detachment becoming 40 Squadron.
Page 369-373: (Appendix III): It has now come to light that the names 'Faith', 'Hope' and 'Charity' — as used with regard to Gladiators of the Hal Far Fighter Flight — were in common usage as early as November 1941. On 27th of that month, Plt.Off. Charles Palliser of 249 Squadron recorded a flight in Gladiator 'Faith' in his logbook.
Page 372: The information regarding N5520 'Faith' credited to Arthur Coleman, in fact originated from research carried out by Richard Caruana, the eminent Maltese artist and illustrator.
Page 384: (Appendix V): The name of Flt.Lt. J.M.V. Carpenter, DFC, of 46/126 Squadron was omitted from the list of "RAF Pilots Claiming Five or More Victories Flying from Malta, 1940–41", he was credited with 5 during this period.

Chapter 1

OPENING ROUNDS OF A NEW YEAR

As the hands of the clock crept towards midnight, sheltering sentries on Takali airfield watched as a lone Ju88 swept over them in the bright moonlight. Unopposed, the German aircraft carried out half a dozen strafing attacks; by the time it had completed its last run over the airfield the witching hour had passed, and a new year had begun. It was 1942 — and for the Island of Malta the start of a critical phase in its history. Other bombers followed in the intruder's wake, their lethal loads falling on and around Takali, but there were no recorded fatalities amongst the civil or military populations. There were, however, many narrow escapes, as LAC Bill Metcalf noted in his diary:

> 'Two minutes after 1941 went out the New Year was brought in in real style by a blitz on Takali. Poor little "Spitcher" (*the airman's pet puppy*) was killed by the blast of a bomb which blew us all out of bed; window frames all over the billet and besides having the door hanging off its hinges, it made a mess of our happy home.'

When the sirens had warned of this latest intrusion into Malta's night skies, statisticians noted it was the 1175th air raid alarm since the very first some 18 months previous. These frequent — now almost nightly — raids caused relatively little military damage, and mercifully few casualties, but the constant drone of aircraft engines, the intermittent explosions of bombs, and the incessant barking of anti-aircraft guns did sap the will and morale of many of the tens of thousands — civilians and military personnel — crammed into shelters, cellars, caves and trenches, each defiantly trying to snatch a few hours of fitful sleep; even then however, some hardened souls somehow managed to sleep through the almost continuous commotion.

Occasionally Hurricanes would go up to challenge these night raiders, but without the benefit of AI (Airborne Interception) radar, pilots stood only a limited chance of success, although observers on the ground would sometimes be heartened by the sight of a flaming bomber falling through the darkened skies.

Throughout the latter part of 1941 the strength of the Island's forces had grown apace. As a base for destroyers, submarines, bombers and torpedo-carrying aircraft, it had been successful in taking a dreadful toll of Axis shipping plying across the Mediterranean from Italy and Greece, carrying supplies to Generaloberst Erwin Rommel's armies in Libya. In defence as well, the Island had gone from strength to strength until three full squadrons and one flight of Hurricanes were operational, joined before the year's end by elements of two more squadrons.

In North Africa, November and December 1941 had seen Operation 'Crusader' under way — the greatest British offensive of the war to date. Launched to secure the release of the port of Tobruk from its long-standing state of siege, and to exploit opportunities thereby raised, it had succeeded in pushing the Axis forces right out of the Libyan province of Cyrenaica. This success had been gained in no small measure due to the length of Rommel's lines of communication, and to the depredations on his supplies caused by Malta's diverse striking forces.

It was unfortunate for the forces of the British Commonwealth that 'Crusader' should have coincided with the arrival of winter on the Eastern Front in Russia. The onset of conditions there unsuitable for further major offensive action by the Wehrmacht or Luftwaffe, released air units available for relocation to the threatened Middle East.

While some units were despatched direct to Africa to bolster the growing strength of the Axis air forces there, the neutralization — and, indeed, possibly the occupation of Malta — was seen by the Germans as a priority task, and one which presaged any major prosecution of the Desert War. At this stage, Malta had been under virtual siege for 18 months — she was the British jewel in the hostile Mediterranean Sea, and a continual irritant to the Axis. From the beginning of the year, the British Chiefs-of-Staff fully realised the possibility of Malta being invaded, and directed that reinforcements for the garrison be sent from Alexandria in a forthcoming convoy. However, at this time neither Intelligence reports nor aerial reconnaissance of Sicilian air bases showed invasion to be imminent, although Axis plans were being devised for such a venture.

Indeed, Rommel was to write:

> 'With Malta in our hands, the British would have had little chance of exercising any further control over convoy traffic in the Central Mediterranean... It has the lives of many thousands of Germans and Italians on its conscience.'

To which his then Chief-of-Staff, Oberst Fritz Bayerlein, added:

> 'Until the air and naval base at Malta ceased to act as a thorn in the flesh of our rearward communications, there was no possibility of the situation at the front improving and therefore no prospect of the capture of the Nile Delta.'

An Italian political journalist, adopting a less stark and militaristic view, and with a hint of defeatism, painted a slightly different picture of the psychological effect Malta's strike force was having on crews of Axis convoys, when he wrote:

> 'Italy is like a man who has to cross a path on a more or less urgent errand, but who suspects that at any time he may be attacked without knowing by how many enemies and from which direction. He thinks of it and imagines that the assailants understand the advantage of sighting without being seen, of attacking and disappearing. He thinks all this and imagines that other men, ready to lend a hand in the assault, would jump upon him and then hastily vanish into the darkness.'

The Germans had returned with a more positive attitude. The damage caused by Malta's striking forces during the critical battles of late 1941 in North Africa had left them under no remaining misapprehension as to the Island's strategic importance. As already described by the authors in *Malta: The Hurricane Years, 1940-41*, II Fliegerkorps had been ordered to Sicily from the Eastern Front to neutralize this constant threat to Rommel's supply lines. While operations had at once begun in December, delays in arrival of several units, diversion to North Africa to ease the situation there, bad weather during the opening weeks of 1942, and particularly the need to train for the new duties involved, would delay the launching of full-scale offensive operations until the middle of March.

Generalleutnant Bruno Loerzer, himself a noted fighter pilot of the First War, had arrived with his Headquarters Staff from the Moscow region during December. Several of the units already forming part of II Fliegerkorps were in need of re-equipment and had returned to Germany first for this purpose. Other units, now to form part of his command, were already in Africa, or were based as far away as France, Belgium or Holland. As a result these units did not all arrive together, but trickled in as they were ready throughout December and January.

Initial contact with Malta's squadrons had been made on a small scale during mid December, but the first sustained attack had not been launched until the 19th of that month. Thereafter, for the remaining days of the year, the power of the raids made several times daily had shaken the defenders and inflicted heavy losses, particularly amongst aircraft on the ground.

The arrival of growing numbers of German units in Sicily had occasioned the re-location of some units of the Regia Aeronautica, but a substantial force of Italian aircraft remained based there, continuing their own operations. When at full strength — in excess of 400 combat aircraft — II Fliegerkorps in Sicily would comprise:

FIGHTERS

Stab/Jagdgeschwader 53 (Stab/JG 53) Maj. Günther von Maltzahn	Bf109F-4
I/Jagdgeschwader 53 (I/JG 53) Maj. Herbert Kaminski	Bf109F-4
II/Jagdgeschwader 53 (II/JG 53) Hpt. Walter Spies	Bf109F-4
III/Jagdgeschwader 53 (III/JG 53) Hpt. Wolf-Dietrich Wilcke	Bf109F-4
II/Jagdgeschwader 3 (II/JG 3) Hpt. Karl-Heinz Krahl	Bf109F-4
III/Zerstörergeschwader 26 (III/ZG 26) Hpt. Georg Christl	Bf110C, D and E
4/Nachtjagdgeschwader 2 (4/NJG 2) Hpt. Rolf Jung	Ju88C/Do17Z

The Bf109s were based at Comiso, Gela and San Pietro; II/JG 3 would arrive at Comiso on 18th January. Various Staffeln of JG 53 would intermittently operate from the neighbouring outpost island of Pantelleria. Both III/ZG 26 and 4/NJG 2 were based at Catania.

BOMBERS

Stab/Kampfgeschwader 54 (Stab/KG 54)	Ju88A-4
I/Kampfgeschwader 54 (I/KG 54)	Ju88A-4
Stab/Kampfgeschwader 77 (Stab/KG 77)	Ju88A-4
II/Kampfgeschwader 77 (II/KG 77)	Ju88A-4
III/Kampfgeschwader 77 (III/KG 77)	Ju88A-4
Küstenfliegergruppe 606 (KüFlGr 606)	Ju88A-4
Kampfgruppe 806 (KGr 806)	Ju88A-4
II/Stukageschwader 3 (II/StG 3)	Ju87D
III/Stukageschwader 3 (III/StG 3)	Ju87D

NB Prior to 13th January 1942 II and III/StG 3 had been designated I/StG 1 and II/StG 2.

RECONNAISSANCE

2/Fernaufklärungsgruppe 122 (2(F)/122)	Ju88D-1

RESCUE

Seenotdienststaffel 6 (Seenotst 6)	Do24T

The bombers and reconnaissance aircraft were based at Gerbini, Comiso, Catania, Gela and Trapani, the rescue machines at Syracuse and Augusta. Also attached to II Fliegerkorps were two specially-equipped Ju88s for RDF (Radio Direction Finding, as radar was then known) calibration and countermeasures, their main purpose being to locate the RDF installations on Malta. Specially trained German and Italian technicians would participate in these clandestine flights over and around the Island. Later the Germans would install powerful radar jamming equipment in Sicily in an attempt to neutralize the British RDF units. Although the jamming would prove effective, the British operators were ordered to continue scanning to give the impression nothing was amiss, and after a few days the jammers were switched off, without the Germans ever realizing how close they had been to achieving success.

The Regia Aeronautica in Sicily, under the command of Gen. D.A. Silvio Scaroni, was dispersed as follows:

FIGHTERS — Gen. B.A. Mario Piccinini — HQ, Palermo

54° Stormo CT — Col. Tarcisio Fagnani	Castelvetrano MC200, MC202, CR42
7° Gruppo CT — Magg. Albert Beneforti	Pantelleria
76ª Squadriglia — Cap. Valentino Festa	
86ª Squadriglia — Cap. Bruno Politi	
98ª Squadriglia — Cap. Saverio Gostini	
16° Gruppo CT — Magg. Francesco Beccaria	Castelvetrano

167ª Squadriglia — Cap. Pietro Garfagnoli
168ª Squadriglia — Cap. Luigi Lisardi
169ª Squadriglia — Cap. Antonio Lottero

377ª Squadriglia Aut CT — Ten. Giuseppe David	Re2000, Trapani

Squadriglie of CR42s and MC200s of 54° Stormo were detached from time to time to operate from the island of Pantelleria, mainly for convoy escort duties.

BOMBERS

9° Stormo BT — Col. Giovanni D'Auria	Z1007bis, Castelvetrano
29° Gruppo BT — Magg. Cesare De Porto	Chinisia
62ª Squadriglia — Cap. Aligi Selano	Chinisia
63ª Squadriglia — Cap. Vincenzo Pittaluga	Chinisia
33° Gruppo BT — Magg. Ercole Savi	Trapani
59ª Squadriglia — Cap. Eugenio Geymet	
60ª Squadriglia — Cap. Cesare Biancardi	
10° Stormo BT — Col. Ranieri Cupini	S.79 Sciacca Palermo
30° Gruppo BT — Magg. Giuseppe Noziglia	
55ª Squadriglia — Cap. Mario Franco	
56ª Squadriglia — Cap. Pietro Volenterio	
32° Gruppo BT — Magg. Albert Capitani	Chinisia
57ª Squadriglia — Cap. Massimo Marasco	
58ª Squadriglia — Cap. Gerardo De Caterina	
173ª Squadriglia Aut RST — Cap. Edoardo Agnello	CR25, Palermo

TORPEDO-BOMBERS

278ª Squadriglia Aut AS — Cap. Massimiliano Erasi	S.79, Pantelleria

MARITIME RECONNAISSANCE

83° Gruppo RM — Ten.Col. Adalberto Zanchi	Z501, Z506B, Augusta
170ª Squadriglia — Cap. Edoardo Gobbi	
184ª Squadriglia — Ten. Felice Bastianelli	
186ª Squadriglia — Cap. Antonio Blengini	
189ª Squadriglia — Cap. Alfredo Francine	
85° Gruppo RM — Magg. Gennaro Venditti	Z501, Z506B, Marsala
144ª Squadriglia — Cap. Antonio Baldassare	
197ª Squadriglia — Cap. Alfredo Francione	

OBSERVATION

76° Gruppo OA — Magg. Giovanni Ignaccolo	Ro37, Ca311, Palermo
30ª Squadriglia — Ten. Libero Ferrari	
40ª Squadriglia — Cap. Giovanni Laudano	
115ª Squadriglia — Cap. Vezio Vernesi	
with flights detached at Sciacca, Catania and Gela	

RESCUE

612ª Squadriglia Aut Socc — Ten. Alfio Giosue	Z506B, Marsala

In total there were about 50 bombers/torpedo-bombers, about 100 fighters and 60 reconnaissance/rescue aircraft. Small formations of S.79sil torpedo-bombers would also occasionally use Pantelleria as an advanced landing ground for operations directed against Malta or British convoys in the area. Two days into the new year six S.79sil from 280ª Squadriglia would arrive from Sardinia for such duties.

Although the units further to the west on Sardinia would not play a direct role in the assault on Malta, aircraft from the island did challenge Malta-bound convoys in the Western Mediterranean. At the turn of the year Aeronautica della Sardegna (Sardinia) boasted a strength of almost 200 operational aircraft:

FIGHTERS

24° Gruppo CT (354ª, 355ª, 370ª Squadriglia) based at Elmas, Monserrato and Alghero, with CR42s and G50bis.

BOMBERS

51° Gruppo Aut BT (212ª, 213ª Squadriglia) at Decimomannu with Z1007bis.

TORPEDO-BOMBERS

36° Stormo AS	S.84sil, S.79sil, Decimomannu
108° Gruppo AS (256ª, 257ª Squadriglia)	
109° Gruppo AS (258ª, 259ª Squadriglia)	
130° Gruppo Aut AS (280ª, 283ª Squadriglia)	S.79sil, Elmas

RECONNAISSANCE

65° Gruppo OA (28ª, 124ª Squadriglia OA)	Ro37bis, Villacidro
138ª Squadriglia RM	Z501, Olbia
146ª Squadriglia RM	Z506B, Elmas
188ª Squadriglia RM	Z501, Elmas
287ª Squadriglia RM	Z506B, Elmas

RESCUE

613ª Squadriglia Aut Socc	S. 66, Z506B, Elmas

To control the operations of II Fliegerkorps and seek to co-ordinate them with those of the Regia Aeronautica, and with other Luftwaffe units in Africa, the Headquarters and Staff of Luftflotte 2 had also been ordered to Sicily in late 1941, from the Southern Sector of the Eastern Front in Russia. The commanding officer, Feldmarschall Albert Kesselring, was at the same time designated Commander-in-Chief, South, with seniority over all other German forces in the Mediterranean area — the Deutsch Afrika Korps included. He at once issued categorical orders for the prosecution of the attacks on Malta. Priorities were to be:

i) destruction of all British aircraft, in the air or on the ground;
ii) destruction of the Island's radar system and anti-aircraft defences;
iii) blockade against all attempts at re-supplying the Island;
iv) heavy attacks on warships and harbour installations, using special PC1800/RS bombs as necessary;
v) mining of the approaches to all harbours, particularly that to Grand Harbour, with magnetic mines, which were to be dropped by parachute whenever necessary.

At this time, there was but one RDF unit available to the Axis, a German 'Freya' unit installed at Porto Palo, near Syracuse, operated by the Luftwaffe Luftnachrichten Regiment 200 under Oberst Rosenkranz. Until the installation of this 'Freya' the previous April, the Italians had relied upon a more basic means of locating and detecting British air and sea traffic — radio interception.

In 1936 Italy had established, at Valle Inviolata, near Rome, the 'Centro Radio Ricevente' unit to receive — but more importantly to intercept — radio signals, not only from her own newly-won North African empire, but from such far-flung locations as Tokyo and Buenos Aires, London and Seville. Following the country's entry into the war, the service was reorganized on a vast scale, with more powerful equipment being installed under the control of the air force; thus was born the Centro Radiointercettazione Regia Aeronautica (CRIRA).

Initial successes in this clandestine electronic war were partially achieved when British radio beams, used to guide Malta-bound aircraft flying from Gibraltar, were 'disturbed', resulting in crews losing their bearings over the Mediterranean during the 1000-mile flight. An early success occurred just before dawn on 13 September 1940, when an Overseas Air Delivery Unit (OADU) Blenheim landed on Pantelleria, some miles off course, the Radio Interception unit on the island claiming a share in its capture. It is not known what involvement the CRIRA contributed the following month — if any — when an aircraft carrying the British Foreign Secretary, Mr Anthony Eden, to the Middle East, was announced overdue at Malta. The pilot had 'missed' landfall and was heading for oblivion, but turned about in time and found the Island, landing with little fuel remaining.

Other developments in late 1940 had included not only the establishment of the primary Radio Interception unit on Pantelleria, but a secondary unit at Trapani (Sicily), on the nearby Monte Erice, connected with a CR42 fighter unit on the former island, its main function to attempt interception of Malta-bound transit aircraft. In comparison with anticipated results, little actual success was achieved. By mid 1941 a further CRIRA unit had been established at Palermo (Sicily), sited on nearby Monte San Pallagrino, capable not only of intercepting H/F radio emissions from Malta, but also of listening-in to signals and messages emanating from Malta's aircraft. However, the initial interception of coded words and phrases, such as 'Angels', 'Bandits' and 'Pancake', broadcast excitedly by airborne Hurricane pilots, made little sense, although the meaning of the ominous 'Tally Ho!' would soon become all too apparent!

Lacking radar technology, the Regia Aeronautica developed radio communications to an advanced art to provide at least partial intelligence of British aircraft in flight. Drawing upon the systems pioneered by the CRIRA, all communications between RAF aircraft and their ground bases were intercepted and carefully monitored, and thus was born 'Servizio Alfa' (Alfa Service). At airfields throughout Sicily, receiver-transmitter stations were set up in special vehicles, which were in direct vocal radio contact with fighters in the air, and via Morse-code transmission with the bombers.

By night this service monitored all radio traffic between the British ground control station on Malta and defending fighters, from the initial scramble to the order to open fire. At the point where night fighters were in position to attack, the service issued a three letter warning message to bombers, repeated insistently — for instance, 'ATA' or 'IRI'. For the fighters, when the CRIRA operator considered that the Italian aircraft had been 'hooked' by radar, the 'Servizio Alfa' transmitted the initial warning "Telemeter!". An imminent attack then brought the further alarm "Armata! Armata!", at which pilots were advised to execute violent evasive manoeuvres.

The system was soon discovered by the British, who resorted to many changes of radio channel, code words, etc, in an effort to outwit it. During the final assaults on Malta in October 1942, they were at last able to jam the transmissions, leaving the Italian night bombers without any warning of attack.

It was only after the setback at the Battle of Matapan on 28/29 March 1941, that the Italians began to take an interest in RDF. Off Matapan, the Italian Fleet had been close to annihilation by Admiral Cunningham's First Battle Squadron, when the use of ships' radar enabled the British force to sink three cruisers and two destroyers during a night action. Despite this, however, RDF would not be developed in Italy. It was left to the Germans to establish further units following the return of the Luftwaffe to Sicily at the end of 1941. By the following July, a second 'Freya' would be operating on Pantelleria, while a third unit on the nearby smaller island of Lampedusa was placed under the control of the Regia Aeronautica. Additionally, the Germans soon established units operating along the Libyan coast, at Tripoli, Benghazi and between Derna and Martuba.

Malta was well-served with four fully-operational RDF stations, including the first to be installed outside the United Kingdom. This was 241 AMES (Air Ministry Experimental Station) set up at Dingli Cliffs in 1939, and capable of plotting high-flying aircraft (see Appendix I). By mid 1941 four more units were operational — 242 AMES at Ghar Lapsi, 501 AMES at Tas-Silc, 502 AMES at Madliena, and 504 AMES also at Dingli. These units were each capable of locating and plotting medium- and low-flying aircraft. A GCI (Ground Control Interception) station was located near Salina Bay for more accurate controlling of RAF fighters, codenamed 'Gondar'. Two further RDF stations were under construction, including 521 AMES on the sister island of Gozo; these would come into operation during February 1942.

Malta also possessed its own RAF-manned tactical intelligence gathering unit, the 'Y' Service, the purpose of which was to intercept, analyse and interpret coded W/T (Wireless Telegraphy) and R/T (Radio Telephony) traffic of the Luftwaffe and Regia Aeronautica; information obtained in this way was often put to good use to the benefit of Malta's fighter pilots. But neither radar nor the 'Y' Service would be able to provide adequate warning of approaching raids at the height of the impending blitz, as will be seen.

However, undoubtedly the overriding advantage enjoyed by the British was represented by the Special Liaison Unit, based at the War HQ in Lascaris, responsible for receiving, distributing and ensuring the secrecy of 'Ultra' signals transmitted from England; these signals gave details of the majority of Axis naval and air movements in the Mediterranean theatre — the main reasons why Malta's striking forces were enjoying, and would continue to enjoy, such success in locating and attacking Axis convoys, so long as they could operate. Incredibly, by contrast, the main Axis intelligence came via the Italian Radio Interception service, which had broken the code used by the United States attache in Cairo, Colonel Fellers, who apparently sent meticulous reports to Washington on British plans and capability!

Air Vice-Marshal Hugh Pughe Lloyd, Air Officer Commanding Malta, presided over a relatively healthy fighter force, despite recent erosion of its numbers by the Bf109F pilots of JG 53. The Island could boast some 80 Hurricanes, a fighter which had proved capable of dealing with all Italian aircraft it had faced, except the Macchi 202. Indeed, since the outbreak of hostilities, Malta's fighter pilots had given a fine account of themselves, being credited with some 200 aerial victories during these 18 months, although losses had not been light — at least 90 Hurricanes had been destroyed whilst defending the Island, with over half that number of pilots losing their lives. Although the current Hurricanes were the latest Mark IIBs and cannon-armed IICs, they would be completely outclassed by their Luftwaffe adversaries from across the Malta

Channel. Spitfires were urgently needed if Malta was to survive, but these would not be forthcoming for some weeks.

On Malta the British had constructed three airfields. Takali, the main fighter base, was commanded by Wg.Cdr. W.A.J. Satchell, a former Battle of Britain squadron commander. His Wing Leader was another Battle of Britain veteran, Wg.Cdr. A.C. Rabagliati DFC, a pilot of Italo-Scottish ancestory; Alexander Coultate Rabagliati, known to his friends as 'Sandy', and by his pilots as 'Rags' or 'Ragbags', had successfully led 126 Squadron on the Island during the latter half of the previous year.

Luqa was the main bomber station, and was commanded by Grp.Capt. S.H.V. Harris. The remnants of the two Blenheim squadrons based there, loosely formed into a Wing, were overseen by Wg.Cdr. John Greenhalgh, one of the original 1940 Hurricane pilots. Wellington night bombers and ASV-equipped aircraft were also located there, as were the Maryland reconnaissance aircraft of 69 Squadron.

The third airfield, Hal Far, originally the Fleet Air Arm base, housed Hurricanes as well as a composite FAA torpedo-bomber squadron equipped with Swordfish and Albacore biplanes; it was commanded by Wg.Cdr. R. MacDougall. At the south-eastern tip of the Island, in Kalafrana Bay, the seaplane base no longer possessed a resident flyingboat squadron but was, nonetheless, frequented by visiting Sunderlands and Catalinas, as well as by BOAC flyingboats.

During the winter months BOAC operated five Short S.30 Empire flyingboats between Gibraltar and Egypt, with Malta as the staging post. Timed to arrive

Left: Wg.Cdr. A.C. 'Sandy' Rabagliati DFC — another Battle of Britain veteran and former commanding officer of 126 Squadron, was Wing Leader at Takali in early 1942. During 1941 he had been one of the top-scoring pilots on the Island. *(NWMA)* **Right:** Another notable Battle of Britain veteran on Malta at the start of 1942 was Sqn.Ldr. Stan Norris DFC, who led 126 Squadron until March. *(NWMA)*

Wg.Cdr. Jack Satchell DSO — a former Battle of Britain squadron commander who was station commander at Takali early in 1942, and who often flew operational sorties by both day and night. *(NWMA via Philip Dixon)*.

after dark to avoid detection and interception, they delivered/embarked passengers, stores and mail, refuelled and departed before dawn. At Kalafrana could also be found the sole surviving Swordfish floatplane of the Rescue Flight, an ex-Norwegian Naval Air Force Heinkel 115 'spyplane' — painted in spurious Luftwaffe markings for use on clandestine operations to the North African coast — and the launches of the Air Sea Rescue service. Currently this unit had on strength HSL107, one of the original craft, and recently-arrived HSL128 and HSL129, plus a few unarmed seaplane tenders and a pinnace or two; it was commanded by Flt.Lt. G.R. Crockett. By the turn of 1941 ASR craft had picked up 40 British, 11 Italian and two German airmen, and seven bodies.

At the beginning of the new year the strength of the RAF and FAA on Malta was:

FIGHTERS

126 Squadron	Sqn.Ldr. S.C. Norris DFC — Hurricane IIBs, Takali
185 Squadron	Sqn.Ldr. S.A.D. Pike — Hurricane IIB/Cs, Hal Far
249 Squadron	Sqn.Ldr. H.J.S. Beazley — Hurricane IIBs, Takali
242 Squadron (part)	Sqn.Ldr. W.G. Wells — Hurricane IICs, Hal Far
605 Squadron (part)	Sqn.Ldr. S.E. Andrews DFM — Hurricane IIBs, Hal Far
1435 Flight (formerly the MNFU)	Sqn.Ldr. I.B. Westmacott — Hurricane IIB/Cs, Takali

BOMBERS

18 Squadron 107 Squadron }	These detached Blenheim IV units were about to be disbanded, and their personnel were soon to depart for Egypt or the UK; 21 Squadron (also equipped with Blenheim IVs) was on its way from the UK to replace them.
104 Squadron (detachment)	With Wellington IIs was also about to depart for Egypt.
40 Squadron (detachment)	Wg.Cdr. L.J. Stickley DFC — Wellington ICs, Luqa
Special Duties Flight	Flt.Lt. A. Spooner DFC — Wellington VIIIs (ASV), Luqa
828 Squadron, FAA	Lt. G.M. Haynes — Albacores, Hal Far
830 Squadron, FAA	Lt.Cdr. F.E.H. Hopkins DSC — Swordfish, Hal Far

RECONNAISSANCE

69 Squadron	Wg.Cdr. J.N. Dowland GC — Marylands, PR Hurricanes, Luqa

An Allis-Chalmers towing-tractor with petrol bowser and Hurricane. *(Authors' collection)*

Recent arrivals for the reconnaissance unit were two well-worn PR Hurricanes and a specially modified PR Beaufighter (T4705) from 2 PRU, Egypt, on attachment to 69 Squadron for 'special tasks'. The Beaufighter was flown by Flt.Lt. Adrian Warburton DFC, a photo-reconnaissance 'ace' who had already built up quite a reputation flying from Malta. Painted dark-blue and stripped of some armour plating and armanent, T4705 was fitted with three 20-inch cameras; a second, similarly-modified Beaufighter would follow within two weeks. Two PR Mosquitos — the first in the Middle East — would soon arrive from England, but these were earmarked for Egypt; however, as will be seen, they did not reach their intended destination. More Marylands would be delivered by SAAF crews from the Middle East, bringing strength by the end of January to 14 of these aircraft.

The majority of successful search sorties undertaken by the Maryland crews were as a result of 'Ultra' intelligence, although the crews themselves — including the squadron commander — were completely unaware they were actually being directed to areas where convoys were known, or believed, to be present. To safeguard the security of 'Ultra' and to maintain this ultimate and complex bluff — arguably the war's greatest secret — AHQ was ordered to ensure that Axis convoys were first to be located by reconnaissance aircraft, prior to being attacked. In the coming twelve months, well in excess of 200 Axis merchant ships would fall victim to air or sea attacks in the Mediterranean, many of these delivered by Malta's strike force, the majority located as a result of 'Ultra'.

Thursday, 1 January

Following the welcoming-in of the New Year by the lone Luftwaffe intruder, New Year's Day proved relatively quiet and uneventful; perhaps there were too many muzzy heads from the night's celebrations on the various Sicilian airfields! There was one alert shortly before midday, when three Ju88s and about two dozen Bf109s approached the Island, bombs falling along the southern coast, damaging a number of fishing vessels. No Hurricanes were airborne.

Whatever the reason for the apparent inactivity, the brief respite was most welcome on Malta, where 126 Squadron bade farewell to one of its flight commanders when Flt.Lt. P.R. McGregor was posted to Hal Far, to take command of 185 Squadron vice Sqn.Ldr. Pike; McGregor was replaced by Flg.Off. L.D. Barnes, who was appropriately promoted.

Bombers were over the Island again after dark, bombs from one falling on the little town of Gzira, in the heavily-populated area around Grand Harbour, killing 27 civilians and wounding eight others. Amongst the fatalities were 50-year-old Dominic Spiteri and his eight children: Benedetta 15, Mary 12, 10 year-old twins Dominic and Carmela, Josephine 5, Vincenza 3, Emanuel 2, and seven month-old Alfred; the mother survived. This was the largest single-family tragedy during the raids but ironically, nearby on the same night, the Mifsud family suffered similarly when Mary, aged 36, and her six children — three boys and three girls — all perished.

Air Vice-Marshal Lloyd, who had been dining with squadron and flight commanders in a small restaurant in Valetta, had a narrow escape when a heavy bomb — described as a rocket bomb — exploded nearby, causing extensive damage. A number of night fighter Hurricanes were up, including one flown by Wg.Cdr. Bill Satchell, but no interceptions were made.

During the same night four Albacores set out to mine Zuara harbour on the Libyan coast, some 200 miles to the south, but only one succeeded in its task. The other three aircraft developed differing technical problems, which forced one to return early to Hal Far where, on approaching to land, it came under attack from a marauding Bf109, but was not hit. One Albacore failed to return, and Sub Lt. R.H. Pettit's machine was last seen with smoke issuing from its engine, heading for the Tunisian coast, where it force-landed; Pettit and his observer, Sub Lt. A.W.A. Capes were interned. Meanwhile, further to the east, between Misurata and Sirte, four Blenheims from Luqa raided Beurat-el-Hsum harbour, where they bombed and machine-gunned a number of small vessels, an 800-ton steamer being claimed damaged. Barracks and other buildings, as well as motor transport, were strafed as the bombers swept out to sea again, and crews observed many fires glowing in the darkness.

Friday, 2 January

Hurricane LE-X of 242 Squadron at Hal Far, displaying combat damage to the rear fuselage and starboard wing. *(NWMA)*

Sqn.Ldr. McGregor was soon in action with his new unit, for during the afternoon he led a scramble by ten Hurricanes from 185 Squadron to intercept an incoming raid, two formations totalling something over 15 German aircraft being engaged about ten miles north-east of Grand Harbour. McGregor and his No. 2, Sgt. Archie Steele, believed that they had jointly inflicted damage on a Ju88, while Sgt. J.R. Sutherland, in Z4104, chased a Bf109 back to Sicily and claimed to have damaged it; his own aircraft was hit however, and he suffered slight wounds. In Grand Harbour, the 10,000-ton commissioned auxiliary supply ship, HMS *Breconshire* — on her fourth supply run to the Island — sustained some damage during this raid, but was able to sail six days later.

By night, Hal Far and Luqa were the targets for an estimated 26 intruders, mostly Ju88s but including five Z1007bis of 9° Stormo BT. Flying throughout the night in relays, the Ju88s would dive on Luqa and drop a single bomb, climb and fly out to sea, only to return for another attack, until their bomb loads were exhausted. A number of Wellingtons were out on raids but three others — under repair at their dispersals — were hit and burnt out, including DV415 of the OADU. All hands were required to clear the rubble and hundreds of 'butterfly' bombs, and to fill-in bomb craters, before the Wellingtons returned; even the AOC and members of his staff lent a hand.

Four of the Wellingtons, one of which had to return early with an engine defect, had set out to raid Naples on the west coast of Italy, while two others bombed Tripoli. One of 40 Squadron's navigators, Plt.Off. John Tipton, explained the purpose of these missions:

> 'The Tripoli raids were against shipping which had arrived in the harbour and were often combined with a run up the coastal road to look for convoys. Other port attacks were similar except that the task at Naples and Brindisi were 'nuisance raids'. The purpose was mainly to fatigue workers and damage morale and so a single aircraft stayed over the port for two hours, the alert being maintained through the night (*similar to the Ju88's actions over*

Malta). The purpose could be achieved by keeping AA guns firing and when they paused a single bomb among the harbour shipping would start them up again. With luck some useful damage could be done.'

At sea two torpedo-armed Albacores, guided by an ASV-equipped Wellington of Special Duties Flight, attempted to attack a 5000-ton escorted merchantman but came under such intense AA fire — which damaged both aircraft — that results were not observed.

Saturday, 3 January

Daylight on the 3rd brought more sustained action when, at 0840, seven Hurricanes each from 126 and 249 Squadrons scrambled from Takali, led by Flt.Lt. Barnes; they were followed ten minutes later by eight more from 185 Squadron. Climbing to 20,000 feet, the leading pilot spotted over Luqa two or three Ju88s from KGr 806, with an escort provided by a dozen II/JG 53 Bf109s, some 5000 feet below. The unaccustomed height advantage was not to be wasted, and the Hurricane pilots made the best of this rare opportunity to dive on the bombers.

An ancient London open-top double-deck bus in use at Takali as a refuelling bowser for Hurricanes. *(via C. Bassett)*

Plt.Off. J.K. Russell of 126 Squadron attacked Oblt. Viktor Schnez's aircraft, which was heading westwards at 12,000 feet after having dropped its bombs, and he made a beam quarter attack, before being obliged to break away by a Messerschmitt. The following pilot, American Plt.Off. Ed 'Junior' Streets, attacked the same Junkers, and reported:

'On patrol with Red 1 — at about 18,000 feet saw one Ju88 over Luqa, also three or four 109s. Attacked Ju88 immediately after Yellow 2 delivered attack — followed enemy until all types baled out, firing all the time from quarter to astern until it span in and burned up; followed it down to 0 feet. Return fire from rear gunner until he baled out.'

All four of M7+AK's crew managed to bale out, and survived to be taken prisoner.

Meanwhile, another of 126 Squadron's American pilots, Plt.Off. Howard Coffin, a native of Los Angeles, attacked another of the bombers, but as he saw his fire hitting home he was set upon by a pair of the escort, which he mistakenly identified as Italian fighters, for he was to write:

> 'Shot down by two Macchis who hit me from behind just as I was closing in on a bomber for a squirt. They used cannon shells and almost blew my ship out of the sky; it was riddled with holes. I was hit in the arms and legs by shrapnel. Gas began pouring out of my tank and I was afraid it would catch on fire. When I pancaked a wheel came off and I crashed. I woke up twenty-four hours later. They had pulled a couple of pounds of shrapnel out of my legs and arms and I guess shot me full of dope because I felt all right. I tried to get up but my legs wouldn't work. The doctor came along — "Got a date in Valetta", I mumbled.'

Whilst Coffin was carrying out his crash-landing at Takali, the fighting raged overhead. A pilot of 249 Squadron, Plt.Off. J.G.K. Hulbert, had taken up the attack on the bomber damaged by Coffin, and opened fire at close range. Its port engine was already on fire when he attacked, and he was now able to gain strikes on the other, which then poured black smoke; the aircraft was last seen in a dive, and it was claimed as probably destroyed.

185 Squadron had no luck, and suffered the loss of Z5155 when Sgt. J.A. Westcott was shot down by a Messerschmitt, baling out over the Island with slight wounds; his Hurricane crashed near the Officers' Mess at Kalafrana.

This Wellington, Z1079 BL-F of 40 Squadron, is seen at Luqa on 3 January 1942. Five minutes after this photograph was taken the aircraft was destroyed by a strafing Bf109. *(AST)*

Another pilot of this unit reported seeing a German fighter 'blow up' when hit by AA fire and, in fact, Uffz. Werner Mirschinka of 4/JG 53, flying 'White 12', was lost. Luqa's guns also laid claim to damaging one of the bombers, but the airfield did not escape unscathed, for six Junkers dived out of the low cloud and rain and destroyed Wellington X9688, which had been left in the open due to a punctured tyre, while another Wellington, Z1079/BL-F, was destroyed at dispersal by a strafing Bf109. Bombs and shrapnel also totally destroyed an elderly Whitley bomber-transport, and damaged a second; these two aircraft, stranded at Luqa for almost two months awaiting an opportunity to return to England, had been on detachment from 138 Squadron, their duties to fly agents and supplies to Axis-occupied Yugoslavia. Unserviceability had delayed their departure; the Luftwaffe had now terminated the need.

After dark, German and Italian aircraft resumed bombing sorties to the Island, Luqa again being the main target. Here, Maryland BS776 was hit and burnt out, while two further Wellingtons (Z9042 and Z9045 of the OADU) were damaged beyond repair, as was Blenheim Z9818. One of 69 Squadron's PR Hurricanes (Z3123) was also damaged. During this raid working parties continued filling craters and clearing rubble, but a bomb exploded amongst one team, killing four airmen. A number of Hurricanes vainly attempted interceptions but only Flg.Off. A.R.F. Thompson briefly engaged a Ju88 in a head-on encounter, claiming some damage. Gunners on the ground blasted away at targets of opportunity, and reported one Junkers shot down and another probably so; one Ju88 (B3+CA of Stab I/KG 54) was reported damaged by anti-aircraft fire over Malta, the pilot being wounded.

Sunday, 4 January

Only one raid encroached upon Malta's airspace during the daylight hours of the 4th, when 30 bombers were reported heading for Luqa once again, the wailing sirens causing many to scurry for the safety of the shelters. This latest threat was met by three Hurricanes of 185 Squadron, two from 605 and one from 242, hastily scrambled from Hal Far, but these were at once engaged by ten escorting Bf109s of II/JG 53. During the ensuing brief skirmish strikes were claimed on a single Messerschmitt, while two Hurricanes suffered minor damage in return.

One Hurricane was credited to Ofw. Herbert Rollwage as his 13th victory — his first over Malta. AA gunners claimed another Junkers shot down into the sea and, indeed, Lt. Freidrich Muller's 7T+KH of KüFlGr 606 fell into the sea off the Sicilian coast with the loss of the crew.

Demonstrating Malta's continuing ability to strike hard at this time, despite the Luftwaffe's return, 11 Blenheims from 18 and 107 Squadrons set out from Luqa and Takali at 1535, to raid Castelvetrano airfield on the western spur of Sicily. There, reconnaissance aircraft had reported a concentration of aircraft, estimated at 75 multi-engined machines, identified as Ju52s and S.82s. Owing to waterlogging of many of Sicily's main airfields following severe storms, many transports and bombers had been forced to operate from Castelvetrano, and the British were not slow to seize upon this rare opportunity.

Following take off, one Blenheim developed engine trouble as its pilot struggled to gain height. Fearing a crash, the pilot ordered the bombload to be jettisoned — the Sergeant's Mess at Takali was narrowly missed! Arriving over Castelvetrano just after 1700, and apparently taking the defences by complete surprise, the remaining Blenheims, led by Sqn.Ldr. George Lerwill, bombed and strafed from low-level, the grounded aircraft being silhouetted against the skyline; only a single machine-gun opened up against the attackers, such was the surprise, the pilot of one Blenheim, Sqn.Ldr. T.A. Jefferson, receiving a slight leg wound as a result. The only enemy aircraft seen in the air were two unidentified fighters off the coast at 1655, and a little later a multi-engined aircraft four miles north of the airfield. None of these attacked or were attacked. Jubilant crews returned claiming at least 30 aircraft destroyed and many more damaged, Sgt. D.T. Bone's 18 Squadron sub-section alone accounting for 15 of these.

Close on the tails of the Blenheims, with the coming of darkness, followed the first of three Wellingtons — all that could be made available — two of these (from 104 Squadron) each carrying a 4000lb 'cookie' bomb. When they returned, they were rapidly refuelled, rearmed and re-crewed, and sent out again — then again, for a third time, adding to the mayhem and the confusion at Castelvetrano. After releasing their loads amongst the massed ranks of parked aircraft — a further 14 of which were claimed destroyed — the big bombers swept across the airfield, allowing the nose and turret gunners to relieve their pent-up feelings. Plt.Off. P.A. Huggins took his Wellington down to 800 feet, his gunners claiming at least two aircraft in flames. By now, however, the airfield's defences were ready and the alerted gunners claimed one of the raiders shot down. One Wellington, in fact, failed to return when Flt.Sgt. J.F. Lewthwaite's aircraft, Z9036, crashed near Castelvetrano with the loss of the crew; however, one of 4/NJG 2's Junkers night fighters was up, the unit's commander, Hpt. Jung, also claiming a twin-engined aircraft shot down, although this was identified as a Blenheim.

It was the Regia Aeronautica which had come off worst from these opportune attacks. Although losses were not as serious as claims would suggest, nonetheless five S.82s — four of these from 149° Gruppo Trasporti, the other from 146° Gruppo Trasporti — were destroyed, as were four Z1007bis of 9° Stormo BT, and a single CR42; the Luftwaffe suffered the loss of a Ju52/3m and a 'borrowed' S.82. However, no less than 42 other machines, mainly transports and bombers, were damaged — 22 S.82s, 15 Z1007bis, two FN305s (two-seater liaison aircraft), two CR42s and an MC200. There were eight fatalities, and a further seven persons were wounded during these attacks. Amongst supplies and stores lost were 115 drums of aviation fuel, while much motor transport and many buildings were damaged. The destruction and damaging of so many transport aircraft would seriously hinder the Axis air ferry service to North Africa — up to 500 soldiers a day were being airlifted across the sea at this time.

An immediate retaliatory raid was launched by the Luftwaffe, Takali again being selected as the target, as LAC Metcalf recorded:

> 'The "old sod" gave us what for at Takali. The third stick set the petrol bowser on fire and the Service Police kicked us out of bed and down the Madhouse shelter. Seven Hurricanes were damaged by bomb splinters, etc.'

There were no fatalities amongst Service personnel but three civilians were killed.

Monday, 5 January

Dawn saw the departure of HSL 128 from Kalafrana, to search for a 'fighter pilot' reported down in the sea but, presumably, as no fighter aircraft were missing, the skipper had been erroneously briefed and his actual task was to look for survivors of the missing Wellington. In the event the launch was recalled when strong winds caused high seas.

The storms which had raged over Sicily now struck Malta, and Takali was soon waterlogged and rendered unfit for flying. Operations from both Malta and Sicily were severely restricted, but the conditions did enable a heavily escorted, southward-bound, Italian convoy (codenamed 'M43') — comprising of six transports whose cargo included 54 urgently-needed tanks — to reach Tripoli unmolested. Although 'Ultra' intercepts had warned of its sailing, shortage of reconnaissance aircraft on Malta, and the atrocious weather conditions, allowed the convoy to near its destination before being located. Half a dozen Malta-based Wellingtons were belatedly despatched to bomb Tripoli harbour the following night, but no tangible results of the bombing were observed.

The PR Beaufighter had already completed a number of photo-reconnaissance sorties over various Sicilian airfields and harbours in the capable hands of Flt.Lt. Warburton, who was accompanied on these flights by a volunteer camera operator. Although attached to 69 Squadron, Warburton found himself under the direct control of Air Vice-Marshal Lloyd, who tended to dictate Warburton's role, and he in effect became the AOC's personal 'spy in the sky'.

Tuesday, 6 January

On the morning of the 6th Warburton was sent to Taranto to check on a convoy assembling there; low cloud forced him to fly round the harbour at 50 feet to count the ships, and he almost collided with a lighthouse. Apparently undaunted, he continued to circle, steel helmet perched on his head, cigarette dangling from his lips, and only set course for home when his camera operator, LAC Ron Hadden, reported that he had obtained photographs of all the vessels. The seaplane base was then visited, where a total of 23 machines were counted — nine Z501s and six Z506Bs afloat, three more on the slipway, and five small unidentified types ashore — before two fighters, hastily scrambled from a nearby airfield, pursued the Beaufighter out to sea; these were successfully evaded in the cloudy conditions, and Luqa safely reached. The photographs, when developed, revealed two battleships, a cruiser and the seaplane carrier *Giuseppe Miraglia*, seven destroyers and four MTBs, as well as the 13,000-ton liner *Victoria*, two smaller liners, a 5000-ton tanker and an assortment of 23 merchant vessels.

Wednesday, 7 January

Next day it was the turn of Sgt. McDonald's Maryland crew to search for a convoy believed to be steaming between Misurata and Tripoli. Having located it a few miles out from Tripoli, two fighters identified as Bf109s, attacked AH709; they were shaken off when the Maryland gained the safety of cloud, but not before the gunner, Sgt. Cameron, had fired off 200 rounds in defence.

Another Maryland crew subsequently spotted an estimated 10,000-ton merchant vessel with escorting destroyer, heading northwards. A few hours later, yet another Maryland crew sighted a smaller ship, believed to be part of a small convoy reported, via 'Ultra' intelligence, to be arriving off Kuriat Island that night. At dusk, an ASV Wellington from SD Flight set out and soon located two small merchantmen and two destroyers off Pantelleria.

In response to these sightings, an ASV Swordfish and three torpedo-carriers were promptly despatched from Malta, two of which — flown by Sub Lts. R.E.F. Kerrison and S.M.P. Walsh — carried out attacks on the northward-bound, 5741-ton *Perla*, some 20 miles south of Pantelleria; the freighter later sank, the crew having been taken off by the Italian torpedo-boat *Cascino*. Whilst the attack was in progress, a Ju88C night fighter of 4/NJG 2 was encountered by Lt. R.W. Slater's circling ASV aircraft, in which the squadron's observer CO, Lt.Cdr. Hopkins, was operating the radar. The exceedingly slow-flying Swordfish easily evaded the attack, and escaped in the darkness.

Three Albacores, summoned to join the attack, now arrived on the scene, and two of these, although under intense AA fire from the destroyers, succeeded in releasing their torpedoes at the other merchant ship. One missile reportedly hit amidships, and the vessel was observed to stop, enveloped in a cloud of smoke, while a destroyer was seen apparently going to her aid.

6-12 January, overview

Although there was little operational flying from and around Malta during the next few days, there was other aerial activity. On the 6th, a transit OADU Beaufighter, en route from Gibraltar, failed to arrive at Malta. Whether due to a navigational error, CRIRA interference from Sicily, or simply the inclement weather, in the early daylight hours the Beaufighter crew found themselves too near to the eastern tip of Sicily, and were fired upon by the defences; with a damaged engine, the pilot was obliged to ditch in the sea off Syracuse, from where he and his navigator were soon picked up to become prisoners.

Another OADU Beaufighter (T4887) failed to arrive next day; its crew also lost, it similarly strayed too near the Sicilian coast. When terra firma was sighted, a relieved Flt.Sgt. Jones made an immediate landing on the coast, only to discover landfall was at Magnisi, near Syracuse, and that he and Flt.Sgt. Bold, his navigator, had unwittingly become guests of the Regia Aeronautica. On this occasion the Italian Radio Interception service did claim responsibility for this success. T4887 was later flown to Guidonia airfield near Rome, where it was tested and evaluated, then issued to 235ª Squadriglia as a crew trainer, pending the proposed re-equipment of this unit with ex-Luftwaffe radar-equipped Do217J night fighters.

18 Squadron suffered the loss of two of its Blenheims on consecutive days during this relatively quiet period. Sgt. S.R. Baker's Z7652 failed to return from a maritime reconnaissance in the Cape Bon-Kerkenah Island area on the 7th; the cause of this aircraft's loss, in which the crew perished, is not known. Next day a section of Blenheims carried out an attack on the Italian steamer *Delia*, south of Kerkenah Island, one aircraft being hit by AA fire from an escorting torpedo-boat, *Calliope*, and ditching nearby; this crew were more fortunate and were picked up to become prisoners.

A transit aircraft was also lost on this date, when a Hudson bomber, which had arrived at Malta from Gibraltar, refuelled, and then departed for Egypt, but failed to reach its destination. Sgt. R.S. Jones, his three-man crew from 59 Squadron, and a civilian passenger, were presumed lost with AE539 in the depths of the Mediterranean.

The missing Hudson was one of a number of such aircraft, in flights of three or six, manned by crews from 53 and 59 Squadrons, on their way to reinforce that other beleaguered island, Singapore, en route via the Middle East, Northern India, Burma and Sumatra. Sgt. Jones' aircraft would be the first of a number of such losses. The skies to the west of Malta were becoming increasingly hazardous for transit aircraft, as testified two days later when a delivery Beaufighter, flying in from Gibraltar, was intercepted by a Bf110 from Sicily. On this occasion, however, the Beaufighter pilot managed to evade the attack and reached Malta safely.

Although there were no heavy raids on Malta during this period, individual aircraft continued to intrude, and when bombs fell on the settlement at Dingli, an elderly man lost his life; presumably the target had been the nearby military and RDF installations. A military shelter also took a direct hit, five airmen and a soldier being killed. Next day, bombs intended for Luqa airfield overshot their mark and smashed into Luqa village, where 15 houses were destroyed and five civilians killed outright; two others died later. Luqa village, for the obvious reason of its proximity to the airfield, suffered continually throughout 1942, and by the end of the year was almost completely flattened. AA gunners were credited with shooting down one of the raiders on this occasion, although again no losses were recorded.

During this relatively quiet period — although on the 14th there were 14 alerts within the space of 19 hours — there was little activity over the Island, other than the arrival and departure of transit aircraft, which continued to stage through on their way to other destinations. Some remained to reinforce the Island however, and new arrivals included the Blenheims of 21 Squadron, led by Wg.Cdr. W.R. Selkirk, which flew in from England, via Gibraltar, to replace the battle-weary survivors of the 18 and 107 Squadron detachments. The crews and aircraft of the former squadron now departed for the Middle East, while the latter detachment was disbanded. The surviving aircrew, numbering just 17, were flown to Gibraltar by Catalina flyingboat; none of the unit's few remaining Blenheims could be made serviceable, and these remained on the Island.

The Wellington IIs of 104 Squadron's detachment also departed at this time, although two of these bombers — capable of carrying the 4000lb bomb, which the Mark ICs were not able to do — were detached to operate with 40 Squadron, which was to remain for the time being. Meanwhile, on detachment from the Middle East came a flight of Blenheim IVF long-range fighter-bombers from 113 Squadron, each aircraft fitted with a 20mm cannon in the nose. So dire was the shortage of more suitable aircraft, such as Beaufighters, that the IVF crews were to operate these outmoded aircraft as long-range fighters, in an attempt to intercept Axis aircraft ferrying troops and supplies to North Africa from Sicily.

The second PR Beaufighter (T3301), flown by Flt.Lt. R.G.M. Walker, and carrying a spare pilot, Australian Plt.Off. Ben White, as well as a camera operator, arrived from 2 PRU, Egypt, on attachment to 69 Squadron. The arrival of this aircraft relieved some of the pressure on Flt.Lt. Warburton, who had already undertaken 12 photo-reconnaissance sorties in the few days he had been back on the Island.

605 Squadron — which received a new flight commander when newly-promoted Flt.Lt. Charles Palliser was posted in from 249 Squadron — and 242 Squadron were now considered fully operational as independent units, the latter squadron scrambling a flight of Hurricanes to intercept a small Luftwaffe fighter sweep during the 12th. Cloud and rain prevented any conclusive results, although strikes were claimed on two of the Messerschmitts, whilst in return one Hurricane was slightly damaged. Plt.Off. J.D. Tew Jr, yet another of the growing band of Americans on the Island, was unhurt and managed to land at Hal Far.

Tuesday, 13 January

Early in the morning, at 0730, Wg.Cdr. John Dowland, the Commanding Officer of 69 Squadron — who had been awarded the George Cross for bomb-disposal work in England in 1940 — undertook a special reconnaissance sortie to the Pantelleria-Cape Bon-Kerkenah Island area. Three hours into the search, which had been ordered as a result of 'Ultra' intelligence, an Italian convoy comprising six freighters with an escort of three destroyers, was located

Flt.Lt. Charles Palliser DFC, had served with 249 Squadron in England and had been posted out to Malta with the unit during 1941. He joined 605 Squadron as a flight commander during January 1942, and had been credited with a total personal score of five victories by the time he left the Island. *(NWMA)*

southward-bound. Having obtained photographs of the ships, Dowland straightaway set course for Malta. Just off Tigne Point, as the Maryland approached Luqa, two Bf109s pounced, inflicting damage as the turret gunner, Plt.Off. R.V. Gridley, doggedly fought back. It was believed by eye-witnesses that one of the attackers fell to his guns, but in fact no losses were admitted.

With fuel almost exhausted, Dowland — who had been shot down the previous November by Italian fighters while flying a PR Hurricane — flew the stricken Maryland over the Island and ordered his crew to bale out, but only the observer, Plt.Off. Arnold Potter, was able to do so, coming down safely on land. Dowland, desperately fighting the controls, ditched AH721 in the sea only a few yards offshore, but the heavy machine sank immediately. Despite the valiant efforts of a watching soldier, Gunner W. Izett, who dived into the rough, cold sea to help, both Dowland and Gridley were lost, the latter no doubt trapped in his turret. After about 20 minutes searching in vain, Izett was hauled out of the water in an exhausted condition.

The Wing Commander's body was later recovered, but there was no sign of the 20 year-old air gunner. Bob Gridley, who had flown during the Battle of Britain, had been with the unit since its formation on the Island some 15 months previously. He had married a young Maltese girl, Doris, who gave birth to a son a day or so after his death.

There followed a somewhat confusing series of engagements over the sea during the afternoon. At 1450, a second patrolling Maryland sighted a small formation of Blenheims approaching from the west on a delivery flight, closing in to act as a guide to them as they were still some distance from the Island.

Meanwhile, five Ju52/3m transports of the Luftwaffe's 4/KGrzbV 500 had departed Sicily to carry supplies to North Africa, escorted by eight Bf110s of III/ZG 26. This latter flight had been picked up by the Intelligence Service on Malta, either by radio intercept or via 'Ultra', and two Blenheim IVFs from the 113 Squadron detachment were despatched to make an interception (it seems unlikely that the presence of the strong escort was known to the authorities on Malta, given the vulnerability and small number of Blenheims involved).

The fighter Blenheim crews spotted the lumbering Junkers transports and Plt.Off. Rod Huggins closed on the tail of Fw. Karl-Heinz Stahnke's machine (DA+AE), but the gunners in the transport put up such a hail of fire that the Blenheim (Z7790) dived into the sea with its port engine ablaze, taking the pilot and his gunner to their deaths. It appears, meanwhile, that the escorting Bf110s had been drawn away prior to this attack, having sighted the delivery Blenheims, which they attacked. Claims for two Blenheims shot down were submitted by Lt. Alfred Wehmeyer and Fw. Otto Polenz although, in fact, the two aircraft attacked sustained only slight damage.

On arrival at Malta, the transit crews claimed that one of the attackers had fallen to their fire; it would seem that their gunners had hit 3U+DS, Uffz. Willi Jünger and his gunner, Uffz. Albert Wörner, both suffering wounds. On return to Sicily, Fw. Stahnke, the Junkers captain, claimed that his crew had shot down both Blenheim fighters, and subsequently the silhouettes of the two victories which they believed they had achieved were stencilled on the fin of their transport, in typical fighter pilot fashion! Shortly after this action another Maryland, on a special search to relocate the convoy spotted earlier in the day, was chased by two fighters, the identities of which the crew were unable to determine. In any event, the reconnaissance aircraft escaped without damage.

Earlier during the day, Flt.Lt. J.M.V. Carpenter of 126 Squadron, an experienced pilot with a number of victories to his credit, scrambled from Luqa to intercept an intruder. Over shipping south-east of Kalafrana, he encountered a lone twin-engined aircraft, which he identified as a Ju88, and during a brief head-on attack claimed to have inflicted some damage.

Somewhat later, at 1145, four of 21 Squadron's recently-arrived Blenheims made their first sorties, when they located and attacked a freighter of an estimated 5000 tons, 50 miles east of Kerkenah Island. As Flt.Lt. H.F. Dukes-Smith swept in at wave-top height, his starboard wing hit the mast of the ship which was, in fact, the much smaller 1325-ton Italian steamer *Brook*; the Blenheim (Z7342/H) plunged into the sea. A second Blenheim (Z7431/F), flown by New Zealander Sgt. Ken Coakley, was hit by AA fire from an escorting patrol vessel, *Zuri* and blew up; no members of either crew survived. Hits were also claimed on the freighter, for as the two surviving aircraft departed, clouds of smoke were seen billowing into the sky, but the damage inflicted was not serious.

A light raid was carried out on Hal Far by a small force of II/KG 77 Ju88s, where a Hurricane — Z2592 of 185 Squadron — was destroyed on the ground by a direct hit; there were a number of casualties, including two soldiers, while a civilian was killed at Siggiewi. AA gunners were successful in shooting down Oblt. Walter Biemer's 5 Staffel aircraft, 3Z+CN falling into the sea with the loss of Biemer, the Staffelkapitän, and his crew. On this occasion fighters made no contact.

During the day a Mosquito PR 1 (W4062), en route to Egypt via Malta, was

A group of 605 Squadron pilots seen outside their mess. Left to right are: Plt.Off. 'Sonny' Ormrod, Plt.Off. Ron Noble, Plt.Off. 'Chuck' Lester and Plt.Off. Joe Beckitt. *(R.F. Noble)*

shot up over Pantelleria and with one engine out, Plt.Off. Phil Kelley force-landed at Luqa, the aircraft hitting a patch of soft ground and suffering further damage; the navigator broke his thigh in the crash, and was removed to hospital. A second PR Mosquito arrived within a few days, ostensibly also for the use of 2 PRU in Egypt, but Air Vice-Marshal Lloyd had other ideas!

This would not be the first aircraft, or crew, to be 'shanghaied' on the authority of the AOC, who always considered his needs to be of greater priority than those of his neighbours in Cairo. Hence many a transit crew, under the impression they were 'simply' ferrying their aircraft to the Middle East when they departed Gibraltar would, on arrival at Malta, find themselves thrust into the front-line. This had been particularly true during the closing months of 1941, when the attrition suffered by the Island's Blenheim force was such that many untried and untested crews were lost on their first operational sortie, or within the first few days, when attacking heavily defended convoys, or other such targets. Lloyd later wrote:

> 'As reinforcement aircraft were passing through some would "accidentally", as it were, find their way into our pens and the older ones would be sent on "in exchange". This somewhat high-handed action was not confined to aircraft but also to the better and more experienced crews (*not always so, as indicated above*), particularly if they had friends on Malta or had volunteered to stay . . . I do not wish to give the impression that I knew nothing about the "wrangling". I did, and I openly connived with Cahill (*Grp.Capt. C.A. Cahill, one-time O/C Luqa, and subsequently with his successors*) and his squadron commander conspirators, but this sharp practice gave Malta a bad name in the Middle East. Several very rude signals came from that direction.'

To the Commander-in-Chief, Middle East, and to others in authority in Cairo, Air Vice-Marshal Lloyd was known as 'Sticky Fingers'!

Thursday, 15 January

At Luqa, command of 69 Squadron was taken by Wg.Cdr. Eric Tennant, who had served with the unit the previous year, and who was now posted back from AHQ. On the 15th, it was the turn of this unit to lose two aircraft. Firstly, Flt.Lt. E.J.A. Williams taxied his Maryland (AH288) into a bomb trolley loaded with four 250lb bombs — there was a mighty explosion, and he and two groundcrew personnel were killed.

The second Maryland — BS772 flown by Sgt. G.B. Parker, RAAF — was intercepted by two Bf110s of III/ZG 26 while returning from an afternoon reconnaissance mission. During a running fight which lasted some five minutes, hits were believed to have caused a fire in the port engine of one Messerschmitt, which was last seen going down at 700 feet, but the other continued to attack. The Maryland was badly hit, and with the hydraulic system shot away, Parker had to belly-land at Luqa, two of his crew sustaining injuries; the aircraft was too badly damaged to be repaired. Sgt. Jackson, the turret gunner, slightly wounded by machine-gun fire during the exchange and one of those injured in the subsequent crash, was credited with the possible destruction of one of the Bf110s. This was based mainly on the strength of a report from a ground witness, which suggested that an aircraft was believed to have crashed into the sea about eight miles from the Jordan Lighthouse.

Three Ju88s and nine Bf109s carried out a raid on Hal Far during the morning, where a Swordfish and a Skua were hit and set on fire; both were burnt out, and there were also a number of casualties on the airfield. Luqa was also hit, and here an unserviceable Blenheim (Z7760) was damaged beyond repair, while at the submarine base on Manoel Island (in Marsamxett Harbour), one of 10th Flotilla's craft, HMS *Uproar*, was damaged. As the raiders departed, Gozo came under attack from strafing Bf109s, the lighthouse receiving some attention, while at Nadur three Gozitans were killed.

After dark, torpedo-boats of the German 3rd Flotilla laid a barrage of 24 mines five miles east of Grand Harbour, while from Hal Far five Swordfish, including as ASV-equipped machine, set out to seek a supply ship reported by Sgt. Parker earlier in the day. At 0148 a ship was located 50 miles from Mahdia, and two of the biplanes carried out attacks, the crews claiming two probable hits when black smoke was seen gushing from the vessel. When last seen the ship was stationary, with her escort circling her.

Meanwhile further to the south, Plt.Off. McGrorie's lone 40 Squadron Wellington carried out a 'nuisance' raid on Tripoli, his crew's second such sortie on succcessive nights. Despite very bad weather — 10/10th cloud from 13,000 feet down to 4000 feet, and then more cloud and rain down to 1000 feet, with continuous electric storms and the temperature dropping to −15°C, the Wellington remained over the target area for two and a half hours; the AOC personally congratulated the crew on their return to Luqa.

The Hurricanes continued to go up after the swift Ju88s without undue success. The speed differential was marginal, while the armour of the Junkers was so effective that only cannon-armed IICs had any real chance of success. It was a frustrating but common experience for the pilots of the IIBs to struggle to within range of a fleeing bomber, only to fall back as the recoil of 12 .303 Brownings slowed their aircraft down without inflicting commensurate damage to the target. Flt.Sgt. Fred Etchells of 249 Squadron recalled:

'On several occasions, as I recall to my disgust, I saw an odd Ju88, unescorted, and just asking to be shot down, but with all power on, and nose down by 15°, it was able to increase distance between us.'

Etchells, who had been on the Island since the previous May, also summed up the defensive attitude of mind required to survive in the dangerous Malta skies at this time:

'In retrospect, I realise that Malta had to take a very low priority for good and modern fighters, and fear that a lot of our time was taken up by attempting to survive in well-used Hurricane Mk Is, and later Mk IIs, again very second hand... we were quite aggressive as a fighter squadron, but soon learned that it was more necessary to keep a good lookout behind and above than looking for victims, as the 109s in particular had many thousands of feet advantage over us, plus an enormous speed advantage.'

Flg.Off. (later Flt.Lt.) A.G.S. Anderson of 126 Squadron, who was a nephew of the great World War I 'ace', Capt. Albert Ball VC. *(J. Crichton)*

Friday, 16 January

During the afternoon of the 16th, 21 Hurricanes from 126, 242 and 249 Squadrons were sent off after an estimated 15 'bandits'. While patrolling in two formations at 12,000 feet and 16,000 feet, three Ju88s were seen way below, going west at about 8000 feet, with a close escort of two Bf109s. Despite the numerical and height advantage, the best that could be achieved was a few strikes on one bomber, which was credited as damaged to 126 Squadron's Flg.Off. Albert 'Andy' Anderson; a Nottingham man, Anderson was a nephew of the First War fighter ace, Captain Albert Ball VC.

The long and arduous oversea flight from Gibraltar to Malta was now being undertaken by ever more multi-engined aircraft, with Egypt, or perhaps India or the Far East, as their ultimate destination. This was fraught with danger for the mainly inexperienced crews, many of whom — during the first leg of the equally hazardous ferry flight from England to Gibraltar — were on their first 'operational' flight since leaving their OTU.

Firstly, assuming the aircraft had not violated Spanish airspace following take-off from Gibraltar's single runway, and had thereby avoided the wrath of the often itchy-fingered Spanish anti-aircraft gunners along the coast, or the patrolling Spanish Air Force fighters, there was the possibility of straying into Vichy-French controlled airspace along the North African coastline to contend with. Offenders faced the prospect of being intercepted by Vichy fighters, and perhaps forced down, or even shot down.

Next came the risk of being caught in daylight by Italian fighters from Sardinia, Sicily or Pantelleria; or the distinct possibility of running into patrolling Bf110s, Bf109s or Ju88Cs from Sicily. Indeed, Wellington DV417 was the most recent casualty, failing to arrive from Gibraltar on the 10th, the fate of its crew unknown. Sometimes luck favoured the transit crews; on one occasion a Blenheim was being stalked by a Bf110 of 7/ZG 26, flown by Uffz. Arno Frickmann; as the Zerstörer closed in on the tail of the wavetop-hugging bomber, Frickmann was unable to jettison his auxiliary fuel tanks, and was eventually forced to abandon the chase.

Finally, even if the transit crews had successfully avoided interception, the chance remained of being unwittingly 'guided' off course by the Regia Aeronautica's CRIRA. The consequence of this, at best, would be for the crews to become prisoners of war; at worst, to be shot down or for their aircraft to exhaust its fuel and eventually disappear into the depths of the Mediterranean.

However, a steady toll of these transit aircraft was also being taken by technical malfunctions — engine defects and suchlike — and, of course, by human error. When aircraft simply disappeared over the Mediterranean, the cause of the loss often remained a mystery. One such loss was Sgt. J.M. Brady's OADU Wellington (Z9043), which failed to arrive at Malta during the night of the 16th/17th. This may indeed have been the aircraft which crashed into a mountain near Bone (Algeria), with the loss of all aboard. It is possible that it had been intercepted and attacked by a Bf110 of III/ZG 26 — Fw. Günther Wegmann of this unit claiming a twin-engined aircraft shot down. On the same day, another Hudson en route to the Far East was lost when AE491 was forced to ditch in the Mediterranean; on this occasion Plt.Off. L.E. Cook's 59 Squadron crew survived.

Not so fortunate was Sgt. A.W. Story and his crew of V9126 — the third of the Singapore-bound Hudsons to be lost. Story's aircraft hit high ground as it was approaching to land at Luqa two days later, and crashed near Siggiewi; there was only one survivor. That same evening the pilot of Hudson AM945, Flg.Off. Bobby Richards, was just about to take-off from Luqa on the next leg of the flight — about an hour before nightfall — when a raid developed. As he taxied the Hudson down the runway, a stick of bombs fell close by, and shrapnel caused the starboard tyre to burst. His observer, Sgt. Arnold Longworth recalled:

'Bobby cut the engines as we swung across the runway on which we came to rest. Aircraft were lining up to take off and it was, therefore, necessary to move our aircraft. The four of us started to push with all our might, with the help of one engine, and much to our relief, airmen from their shelters along the runway came to assist, in spite of the enemy aircraft in the vicinity. With difficulty we managed to clear the runway to give enough space for the others to take off. This accomplished, we ran hell for leather for the shelter.'

The Hudson was soon repaired and departed the following evening. Before the month was out, a fourth Hudson of this unit (59 Squadron) would be lost when Flg.Off. D.J.R. Gee's aircraft (AM946) crashed into the sea off the coast of Spain, killing the crew. However, one aircraft which did arrive safely on Malta was the second PR Mosquito, Plt.Off. Walker landing W4063 at Luqa at first light on the 17th.

Saturday, 17 January

It was not, of course, only the RAF which suffered aircraft losses to non-operational causes; on the 17th, a Z1007bis of 212[a] Squadriglia, from the Sardinian base at Decimomannu, failed to return from a maritime patrol. The ASR unit at Elmas despatched a Z506B seaplane of 287[a] Squadriglia to search for the missing aircraft, the rescue crew sighting three survivors near wreckage at 1130. As the sea was too heavy for the Cant to alight, a nearby Vichy steamer, *Lillois*, was signalled to carry out the rescue.

In the late afternoon, Ju88s intruded over Malta together with the usual escort of Bf109s. A number of Hurricanes were led off after them by Wg.Cdr. Rabagliati, who caught up with one of the bombers, then followed it down to 1000 feet, where it dived away into cloud with its starboard engine stopped. The escorting fighters prevented Rabagliati from pursuing it, and he had to be content with just 'one damaged' to add to his impressive tally.

Flt.Lt. Warburton landed back at Luqa during the late afternoon from his second sortie of the day over Sicily, his Beaufighter slightly Flak-damaged near the cockpit and around the tail unit. His camera operator, LAC Norman Shirley, had obtained the specified photographs. These revealed large numbers of aircraft assembled at the various airfields: 71 aircraft at Palermo/Boccadifalco, 27 at Reggio di Calabria, 59 at Comiso, a further 42 at Gela, and 70 at Catania; only one could be seen at Gerbini due to poor visibility. The other PR Beaufighter, in the capable hands of either Flt.Lt. Walker or Flg.Off. White, was also fully active during this period, the roles of these skilled crews and the two comparatively fast and relatively manoeuvrable aircraft being of even greater importance considering the vulnerability of the ageing Marylands to the Messerschmitts.

Wellingtons from 40 Squadron which, during the past week, had carried out three raids on Tripoli harbour, once again turned their attention to Sicilian targets; a number of crews flew two sorties during an attack on Catania that night. Night fighters were about, and Lt. Felix-Dieter Schleif of 4/NJG 2 followed a Wellington back to Malta and manoeuvred into a favourable position, only to find that his guns would not fire. He tried again, stalking another bomber back to Luqa, but there his luck ran out, for the airfield guns caught him as he swept in at 600 feet, and the Junkers (R4+MM) fell in flames; Schleif and his crew were killed.

The Naval air strike force was also out again, an ASV-equipped Albacore shadowing a tanker and its two attendent destroyers, while awaiting the arrival of four torpedo-armed Swordfish and an accompanying ASV machine. The attack on the 7000-ton *Guilio Giordani* got under way at 0245, when she was about 40 miles from Lampedusa; three of the Naval pilots managed to release their torpedoes despite intense AA fire and a smoke-screen laid by the destroyer. An explosion and an orange flash were seen following Sub Lt. J.F. Wilson's attack, the ship being left stationary in the sea, but the actual damage sustained was less than that estimated.

Sunday, 18 January

The Wellingtons returned to Catania the following night, most crews undertaking second sorties, while some even returned for a third attack. This series of raids, organized and led by Sqn.Ldr. F.J. Steel, RNZAF, resulted in ten hours of almost continuous bombing. Not long before dawn during the final stages of the attack, a number of Wellingtons arrived over Catania just as landing lights were switched on to enable two Ju88s — probably returning night fighters, low on fuel — to land. Plt.Off. McGrorie followed them in and was able to drop a stick of bombs along the runway, from east to west, while the Junkers were landing; a violent red explosion was seen and the Wellington crew believed one of the aircraft appeared to run into the exploding bombs, while other aircraft were believed to have gone up in flames on the airfield.

Another of NJG 2's night fighters failed to return from a sortie, Lt. Herbert Haas having apparently repeated the fatal error committed by his colleague the previous night, by following a Wellington back to Luqa. Here, his 1 Staffel machine (R4+AH), also fell to the sharp-shooting airfield defenders, the 19 year-old Austrian and his crew, which included a war correspondent, perishing when the Junkers crashed.

The reason for this heavy assualt on Catania airfield — the Luftwaffe's main Sicilian bomber base — was the approach of British convoy 'MF3' from Alexandria, which comprised four cargo ships: *Ajax, Clan Ferguson, City of Calcutta* and the Norwegian *Thermopylae*, carrying much-needed foodstuffs, supplies and ammunition for Malta, and escorted by a strong Naval force. A patrol of Hurricanes of 30 Squadron, operating from LG05 near Sidi Barrani, was amongst the air escorts, and one of these, flown by Sgt. T.G. Paxton, intercepted a Ju88 shadower, which he promptly shot down; watchers aboard the *Carlisle* confirmed seeing the Junkers fall.

In the event the 6500-ton *Thermopylae*, loaded with 336 troops for the garrison, as well as ammunition, did not reach Malta for she developed engine defects and was ordered to make for Benghazi, escorted by the AA cruiser *Carlisle* and two destroyers. En route next day, a lone Ju88 spotted her when she was some 64 miles north-east of Derna and, following a skilfully placed salvo of bombs, the vessel caught fire; 30 of those aboard lost their lives.

A Beaufighter of 272 Squadron, despatched from Berka, arrived on the scene too late to assist; Plt.Off. Stephenson reported that the ship was burning fiercely. Owing to the danger of explosion threatened by the vast quantity of ammunition packed in her holds, *Thermopylae* was hastily abandoned. The escorting destroyer *Havock* picked up survivors in rather difficult conditions, the doomed freighter then being sent to the bottom by gunfire.

Two more Beaufighters — from 252 Squadron — were despatched from

Derna during the mid afternoon to patrol over the remaining ships of the convoy, during which several shadowers were sighted, Plt.Off. H.H.K. Gunnis (T4834) claiming one Ju88 shot down and two S.79s probably so. His companion, Plt.Off. C.H. Beet in T4833, was seen pursuing another Ju88, which Gunnis believed he probably destroyed, but his aircraft failed to return. Beet and his observer, Sgt. Gardner, were killed, presumably shot down by return fire.

The other three cargo vessels rendezvoused with the destroyers of Malta's Force 'K' and, despite heavy air attacks, were safely escorted to the Island. The supplies they brought provided a much needed supplement to others delivered during the previous week by the Glen Line supply ship *Glengyle*.

Monday, 19 January

A mini pre-emptive early morning strike was launched against Comiso airfield, home of the bombers of KG 77 and the fighters of JG 53. It was carried out by four bomb-carrying Hurricanes, led by Wg.Cdr. Rabagliati, which took off at 0730, each aircraft carrying eight 20lb fragmentation bombs. After releasing their bombs, Rabagliati, Sqn.Ldr. Beazley and Flt.Sgt. Etchells of 249 Squadron, and Plt.Off. Russell from 126 Squadron, proceeded to strafe aircraft and buildings. A fire was started and 65 drums of aviation fuel were burned, while two Ju88s were claimed probably destroyed. Sqn.Ldr. Beazley's aircraft (BV174) was hit by ground fire and he was subsequently forced to crash-land on Luqa on return.

Hurricane UP-H of 605 Squadron is seen force-landed at Hal Far. It has possibly suffered damage in action, for there are no patches over the wing gun ports, indicating that they have recently been fired. *(C.G. Jefford)*

Before midday Wg.Cdr. Rabagliati was off again, leading a patrol over the convoy now approaching Grand Harbour from the south-east, when he spotted and attacked a twin-engined aircraft which he initially identified as a Ju88; it was, in fact, Flt.Lt. Warburton's Beaufighter returning from a reconnaissance of the Cyrenaican coastline, the crew reporting being attacked five times by a Hurricane patrol, and also being fired upon by the ships! The attacks ceased on the colours of the day being fired by the Beaufighter, but a rather one-sided verbal 'dig' was later directed at Rabagliati when confronted by an eloquent and cool Warburton; according to Plt.Off. Ian 'Skip' McKay of 185 Squadron, the brief riposte went something like:

Warburton to Rabagliati:

> 'I don't mind, sir, that you don't know the colours of the day. You opened fire on me, I took evasive action, and I think it is rather a poor show that when inspecting my aircraft, I found only one bullet hole in my left aileron!'

The Wing Commander did not have too much to say in defence. In fact, this was not the first occasion on which Adrian Warburton's aircraft had been mistaken for that of an enemy. During his first tour of duty on Malta, when flying a 69 Squadron Maryland, he had been shot up by a Hurricane pilot, again in mistake for a Ju88, and been obliged to belly-land at Luqa; the Hurricane pilot involved in that incident was the current commander of 1435 Flight, Sqn.Ldr. (then Flg.Off.) Innes Westmacott.

Not so lucky was an 828 Squadron Albacore flying an anti-submarine patrol ahead of the convoy. A Bf109 — probably a JG 53 aircraft from Pantelleria, where such fighters had been sighted by a reconnaissance Hurricane — took the crew by surprise and shot down the biplane into the sea; the pilot, Sub Lt. P. Howson, suffered severe lacerations while L/Air. Stan Hedger, the TAG, sustained six wounds. However, they were picked up by an escorting destroyer and brought back to Malta.

The Albacore was the second FAA aircraft to be intercepted by Bf109s on this date. Earlier, two replacement Swordfish which were being ferried from Benina for 830 Squadron — one flown by one of the unit's experienced pilots, Sub Lt. Cedric Coxon, the other by a new pilot — were attacked while on their landing approach to Hal Far. Two Messerschmitts throttled back onto the tail of Coxon's V4586, bullets ripping into the top wing and the spar of the lower wing, the port ASV aerial and tailplane also being damaged. Return fire was not possible as the crew's luggage was stowed in the gunner's cockpit! As the German fighters passed over the top of the jinking Swordfish, Bofors' gunners on the airfield believed that they had hit one; two Hurricanes then appeared and gave chase, both 109s being claimed damaged by the pursuing pilots.

Shortly after midday, a 70 plus raid was plotted on the radar screens. The 'blips' represented hostile aircraft, including Ju88s from KüFlGr 606, a unit with special training in shipping attacks, which were making for the convoy while other bombers headed for the airfields. Hurricanes from 126, 242 and 249 Squadrons were patrolling over the convoy as the Junkers arrived. Sqn.Ldr. Norris of 126 Squadron, and his No 2, Sgt. Jack Mayall, were joined by Flt.Sgt. Etchells of 249 in attacking one of the bombers, but could only claim damage; Norris' aircraft was hit by return fire and he force-landed at Takali with a dead engine. Two others from his squadron, Flg.Off. Jack Kay and Plt.Off. Basil 'Rocky' Main, enjoyed greater success during a combined attack on another Ju88. Making several passes, the Hurricane pilots last saw their victim losing height at 2000 feet, with one engine stopped. They were credited with its probable destruction but this was undoubtedly Uffz. Waldemar Nicolay's 1 Staffel aircraft (7T+GH), which failed to return, reported by other crews to have been shot down by fighters. Main, an aggressive Canadian pilot, also claimed damage to another Ju88, one more being hit by Flg.Off. C.H. Baker.

Due to the prompt intervention of the Hurricanes, no co-ordinated attack could be made on the convoy by the raiders, and none of the ships were hit. Meanwhile, Flg.Off. Graham Leggett and Sgt. A.T. Branch of 249 Squadron were attacked from astern by three Bf109s over Luqa. Branch turned on the third of these, his fire striking its port wing and fuselage, but it escaped in cloud. He was then attacked by another, the starboard aileron control of his Hurricane being severed before he was able to evade its fire.

Although the ships escaped damage, both Takali and Hal Far airfields were bombed and strafed. At the latter one of the replacement Swordfish, its engine barely cooled after the flight from Benina, was destroyed. A mile to the north-east of Takali lay the ancient town of Mosta, famed for its awe-inspiring church which possesses the third largest unsupported dome in the world, its very location placing it in the firing line. During the raid, a number of bombs missed the airfield and exploded in and around the town, killing 13 civilians, including five members of the Bugeja family, while four more of the seriously injured later died.

On Takali airfield, where four airmen were killed when their rock shelter received two direct hits, a Hurricane was destroyed and two Blenheims badly damaged. One of these had been set on fire by a near miss, but two airmen sheltering nearby, LACs Bill Metcalf and 'Curly' Revell, rushed to the aircraft and, climbing aboard, removed its ammunition and wireless sets before the fire tender arrived. Cpl. David Louttit, who earlier had helped extinguish two burning petrol bowsers and thereby prevented flames from reaching nearby aircraft, promptly got to work. A small amount of fuel had remained in the Blenheim's tanks and a bomb splinter had severed a fuel line, allowing petrol to run out which had ignited into a mass of flame all around the aircraft.

With his bare hands Louttit stuffed rags into the broken pipe to prevent further spread of the escaping petrol. He then carried empty containers to the aircraft, unscrewed the drainage plugs of the tanks and drained off the remaining fuel. The fire was then extinguished before the Blenheim could be totally destroyed. At one time he was spraying foam on the flames while standing on a burning wing above the fuel tank, and would only leave this highly-dangerous position on specific orders from his officer. He was awarded the BEM for his actions.

While these raids were in progress, low-flying German fighters hunted for targets of opportunity, stafing anything that moved. Two Messerschmitts came across the submarine *Unbeaten* as it approached the entrance to Grand Harbour, on its return from a successful sortie during which it had sunk a German submarine, *U-374. Unbeaten* was strafed but little damage was inflicted. Malta's 10th Submarine Flotilla had, during the past months, achieved many successes; Lt.Cdr. M.D. Wanklyn's *Upholder* alone was credited with sinking in excess of 100,000 tons of Axis shipping before she was lost in April. Another of the Flotilla, *Utmost* commanded by Lt.Cdr. R.D. Cayley, although with only a modest number of sinkings to its credit, had the distinction of having rescued the crew of a transit Blenheim, which had been compelled to ditch en route to Malta.

After dark on the 19th, half a dozen Wellingtons continued the assault on Catania airfield, each aircraft making two sorties. At least one of the bombers was hit by Flak — the airfield gunners claiming to have shot one down — but all returned safely to Luqa. Results of such night attacks were never easy to assess by the returning crews, unless spectacular explosions or blazing aircraft and buildings could be observed. In fact little damage was caused during the majority of night raids except, of course, to the morale of those within the periphery of the target area.

A group of pilots of 126 Squadron. Left to right: Plt.Off. Howard Coffin, Flt.Lt. 'Banger' Barnes, Plt.Off. Jack Grant, Plt.Off. 'Andy' Anderson, Flg.Off. John Kay, Plt.Off. Joe Crichton and Plt.Off. David Steadman. *(J. Crichton)*

Tuesday, 20 January

With daylight on the 20th it was the turn of four Blenheims from 21 Squadron to strike in the opposite direction, two aircraft attacking ground targets along the Tripoli-Zuara road, then strafing Zuara airfield, where a Caproni transport was machine-gunned; the other two Blenheims bombed buildings further along the Cyrenaican coast at Homs, also strafing four lorries encountered. Little opposition from ground defences was met. Meanwhile, further to the south-west, Sgt. McDonald's Maryland (AR714), patrolling between Cape Bon and Kerkenah Island, was chased by a Ju88 which closed in to about 300 yards but apparently did not open fire before the Maryland entered cloud; the turret gunner, Sgt. Cameron, managed to get in a burst before the action terminated.

Wednesday, 21 January

Malta saw the resumption of heavy air raids next day when, during the morning, 14 Ju88s bombed Hal Far, escorting Bf109s also strafing. Three Hurricanes on the airfield were badly damaged by shrapnel, and there were a number of casualties. This raid was not intercepted, nor was an afternoon repeat attack, since the three airfields were waterlogged following torrential rain.

Thursday, 22 January

Thursday heralded better weather. While Hal Far was still unfit for flying, conditions at Takali were improving, and Luqa was serviceable. The first raid approached just after 1100, three Hurricanes from 126, six from 242 and seven from 249 being scrambled. Flt.Lt. Nigel Kemp led the 242 Squadron contingent, his flight struggling to catch up with the other ten Hurricanes, Sqn.Ldr. Beazley at their head.

Three Ju88s from I/KG 54, and five escorting fighters — identified by the RAF pilots as MC202s, but in all probability Bf109s — were sighted at 10,000 feet, ten miles east of Kalafrana. In the ensuing skirmish, Kemp was able to claim one of the escorts as probably destroyed, while Sgt. Jock Gardiner damaged one of the bombers. The leading formation of Hurricanes then became embroiled, Plt.Off. Main attacking another Ju88 and seeing smoke pour from both its engines. His own aircraft received hits in the engine from the rear gunner, and he was forced to break away. A third bomber was claimed damaged by Plt.Off. Joe Crichton (Z2481) of 126 Squadron, shared jointly with two pilots from 249 Squadron, Flt.Lt. C.C.H. Davis and American Plt.Off. Don Tedford. Following debriefing, it was decided that two of the bombers had possibly been too severely damaged to regain their bases in Sicily; but only Oblt. Hans Schumacher's B3+GH failed to return, probably the victim of Main's attack.

At 1400 there was another scramble, five aircraft from 242 Squadron giving cover to six from 249 and a further two from 126. When just south of Filfla, the latter spotted three Ju88s and 12 fighters, again tentatively identified as Macchis; meanwhile to the south-west, the top cover saw two more bombers and three fighters at 12,000 feet. Plt.Off. Paddy Kee, leading the 242 Squadron flight, engaged the escort and claimed one damaged, while Australian Sgt. Tony Boyd went after the bombers, later noting in his logbook:

> 'Saw six E/A and left formation to attack. Shot all ammo into a Ju88, stbd engine caught fire. Claim one Ju88 destroyed.'

The entry was then altered to read 'probable', and this was allowed but one

Plt.Off. (later Flt.Lt.) 'Paddy' Kee of 126 Squadron — another who had flown during the Battle of Britain. *(J. Crichton)*

suspects Boyd considered his victim — in this, his first combat — to have fallen.

As the Hurricanes drifted back to Takali, the airfield gunners, ever-fearful of being surprised by strafing Messerschmitts, mis-identified the returning fighters and opened up, hitting Sgt. Donald Neale's aircraft (BE346), before the mistake was realised. The 19 year-old Londoner, with much of his Hurricane's tail unit shot away, struggled to keep the stricken aircraft under control as he attempted to make a circuit of the airfield, but it spun-in and crashed; Neale died instantly. A second Hurricane had also been hit but Sgt. R.V. Harvey managed to land his damaged aircraft without further incident.

During these raids a number of the bombers, having evaded the defending fighters and heavy AA fire, succeeded in plastering Hal Far yet again. Here several aircraft were riddled by shrapnel, one Hurricane sustaining severe damage.

The Wellington night-bombing force, seeking some form of retribution, raided Tripoli, eight aircraft bombing the harbour over a period of two hours, 10½ tons of bombs being dropped. Hits were claimed on a naval vessel at Karamanli Mole, and on a Flak-ship, both of which were reported burning throughout the night. On approaching Tripoli, one Wellington crew reported sighting an enemy warship some 80 miles out to sea; two Blenheims were promptly despatched from Malta but failed to locate it. Another Wellington — 'Q' flown by Plt.Off. McGrorie — was chased by a Ju88C night fighter, the pilot managing to evade during a 300 mph dive, only to find another, or possibly the same aircraft, in the Luqa circuit on his return. The airfield guns kept the intruder at bay however, allowing the Wellington to get down safely.

Friday, 23 January

Two of 69 Squadron's reconnaissance aircraft came under attack during the 23rd, the first of these, Sgt. R.C. Mackay's Maryland (BS762), being intercepted during the early afternoon as the aircraft approached Malta when returning from a sortie to Corfu island, off the north-west coast of Greece. Cloud again prevented the Messerschmitt pilot from being able to carry out an effective attack, while Sgt. Haines, the turret gunner, fired a few bursts in return. Flg.Off. White's Beaufighter similarly escaped into cloud when attacked by a Bf110 off Palermo.

While two Hurricanes patrolled over Luqa in the afternoon, ten others from 126 and 249 Squadrons practised tactics, but were soon called into action when a dozen 'hostiles' were reported approaching Kalafrana. Five Ju88s and many Bf109s were seen, Flt.Sgt. Etchells claiming possible damage to one bomber, while Flg.Off. Kay attacked a fighter which emitted smoke, but he was chased away by others before he could ascertain results. Flg.Off. Baker claimed damage to another twin-engined aircraft, which he identified as a Do215 — but was possibly an escorting Bf110 from III/ZG 26. Both Luqa, where another Maryland (AH385) was hit and destroyed, and Hal Far, were heavily raided, resulting in both airfields again being pitted with bomb craters.

Those in command on Malta were well aware of the reasons for these current heavy attacks on the airfields, for information gleaned from 'Ultra' had warned of an impending Italian naval operation to get a vital convoy through to Tripoli. During recent fighting in Libya, the British 8th Army's latest push had succeeded in capturing Benghazi (again) as well as considerable Axis forces in the Bardia-Sollum-Halfaya area. However, the bulk of Rommel's Deutsch Afrika Korps was intact at El Agheila, although short of supplies, armour and transport. Urgent requests to Rome were promptly met when convoy 'T18' put to sea from Messina. Four freighters — *Monviso, Monginevro, Pisani* and *Ravello*, laden with equipment, including 71 tanks and much motor-transport, supplies and reinforcements — departed Messina to rendezvous with the 13,000-ton liner-cum-troopship *Victoria*, once the pride of the Italian merchant fleet and now carrying 1300 Panzer troops. In the event, *Ravello* was forced to return to port with a damaged rudder. For such a vitally-important convoy a strong naval escort was provided, comprising the battleship *Caio Duilio*, three cruisers from 13th Cruiser Squadron, plus 14 destroyers and two MTBs.

On this occasion, there was not a great deal that could be done to interfere with this convoy as far as Malta was concerned, due to the diminution in the Island's strike force; Swordfish, Albacores, Blenheims and Wellingtons combined, totalled less than 30 serviceable aircraft, added to which weather conditions were worsening steadily, gale force winds prevailing. In view of these limitations, a small force of Desert-based strike and reconnaissance aircraft had been assembled on the newly-captured airfield at Berka, near Benghazi; here were nine reconnaissance Blenheims of 203 Squadron, two ASV-equipped Wellingtons, nine strike Blenheims of 55 Squadron, together with eight Albacores from 826 Squadron, and three new-to-the-area Beaufort torpedo-bombers of recently re-equipped 39 Squadron; this unit also had a Maryland available for reconnaissance duties. Further to the east at Benina were 13 more bomber-Blenheims, drawn from 11 and 14 Squadrons, while at Fuka two newly-arrived Fortress I four-engined bombers of 220 Squadron were made available. Additionally, two flights of Wellingtons from 38 Squadron (18 aircraft), stood by at El Adem; two of these aircraft had been modified to carry torpedoes.

It was supposed the convoy would give Malta a wide berth in an attempt to avoid detection and consequential attack from that quarter, and should therefore come within range of these units on the eastern coast of the Gulf of Sirte.

The initial sighting of this formidable armada had been made during the night of the 22nd/23rd by Flt.Lt. Spooner's crew aboard an ASV-equipped Wellington VIII of the Special Duties Flight, in spite of ice forming on the array of radar aerials along the aircraft's upper fuselage. A large cruiser or battleship, an estimated 25,000-ton liner, and about five escorting warships were reported before severe icing caused the radio to pack up; in an effort to keep the convoy under surveillance, the Wellington became lost over the vast expanse of sea. It was only a chance interception of a signal from the radar site near Kalafrana which enabled the exhausted crew to find their way home after an outstanding 13-hour flight.

At 1310 on the 23rd a Blenheim departed Luqa to search for signs of the convoy, which was assumed by now to be within range of Malta's strike aircraft; unbeknown to AHQ Malta, a Blenheim of 203 Squadron from the mainland had earlier reported sighting a battleship, two cruisers and seven destroyers on a northerly course, 185 miles north-north-west of Benghazi. An hour later the same crew reported a further three cruisers and four destroyers on a southerly course. The two Fortresses were promptly despatched — for their first operational missions in the Mediterranean theatre — departing Fuka at 1205, their primary target the battleship. Reports of other sightings were late in being received owing to W/T malfunctions in the searching aircraft; there was much confusion, and it was not known whether there were one or two convoys, or in which direction it or they were heading!

Once it was conclusively established that the battleship was on a southerly course, other Blenheims and the Maryland were despatched to locate and shadow until dusk, when it was intended that a strike would be launched. This plan was partially upset when the Malta-based Blenheim crew located the convoy but incorrectly indicated its position 50 miles too far west! On receipt of the accurate position, an attempt was made to redirect the striking forces. Four Blenheims and three Albacores, delayed by refuelling problems at Berka, were contacted, but W/T failure prevented communication with the aircraft already airborne, which in the event was fortunate, as the one aircraft which received the amended position failed to find the target, while most of the others succeeded and delivered attacks!

As implied, it would be a number of hours following the initial sighting before the first attack on the convoy was launched by a lone Fortress between 1615 and 1625, the other having failed to locate the ships; near misses on the battleship and another vessel were claimed. Within ten minutes three Blenheims from Berka swept in from the north-west, releasing their bombs from low-level but failing to score any hits.

About an hour later, Flt.Lt. A.M. Taylor led in the three torpedo-carrying Beauforts for 39 Squadron's first such operation, the aircraft attacking individually as opportunities arose. Seemingly indifferent to the fierce AA barrage from the warships, and selecting *Victoria* as their target, Taylor (flying N1033) and his wingmen, Flg.Off. A.O.S. Jepson (W6518) and Plt.Off. K.R. Grant (N1093), each successfully launched their missiles. The troopship sustained her first hit at 1730 then, 12 minutes later, as she attempted a manoeuvre to starboard, was struck by a second torpedo close to her stern. Two destroyers rushed to assist but their offer was declined, and she was able to continue on course unaided.

Four Blenheims despatched from Malta were unable to locate the convoy, but it was soon re-sighted by the crew of one of the North African-based Blenheims of 203 Squadron, which proceeded to shadow the ships. However, this aircraft — V5738/A flown by Plt.Off. S.A. Langston — was spotted by one of the patrolling Ju88Cs of 4/NJG 2; although chased by the Junkers, Langston was able to evade by climbing into cloud. Not so fortunate was a second aircraft from this unit, Flg.Off. Campbell's V5861/Z failing to return, having run foul of another Ju88C flown by Lt. Georg Wiedow, who mistakenly identified his victim as a Beaufighter; the Blenheim was forced to ditch in the sea, although the crew survived to be rescued.

The next assault on the convoy was made by five vulnerable Albacores of 826 Squadron, which arrived just after 1830 led by Lt. J.D. Jackson, whose aircraft carried the Observer CO, Lt.Cdr. J.W.S. Corbett. The slow-flying torpedo-bombers were soon spotted by the Ju88Cs, two of which attempted to get on the tail of Lt. H.M. Ellis' biplane as he made his run-in on the damaged *Victoria*. Despite shrapnel damage to his aircraft from bursting AA shells, and the attention of the German fighters, Ellis steadfastly held course and released his torpedo from close range; it struck home below the troopship's forward funnel. As he pulled away from the attack, Ellis' aircraft was pursued by Ofw. Hermann Sommer's heavily-armed Junkers, further damage being inflicted. In fact, Sommer claimed the Albacore (which he, too, mis-identified as a Swordfish) as his 13th victory, but Ellis succeeded in reaching Berka.

Not so fortunate was Jackson, his aircraft being shot down by AA fire immediately after the torpedo had been released, his target also being the troopship. The two Naval officers and their TAG, L/Air. W.H. Budgen, were later picked up by an Italian hospital ship. Another of the Albacore pilots, Sub Lt. J.M. Brown, claimed that he had attacked and possibly hit one of the destroyers, a "violent explosion" being seen, but there was no report of damage to any of the escorts. The graceful *Victoria*, however, slipped beneath the waves within half an hour, with the loss of 391 of her passengers and crew.

There would be no respite for the convoy with the coming of darkness. Seven bomber Wellingtons from Malta, having been guided to the area by a shadowing ASV Wellington, commenced their attack just before 2130. Hits were somewhat optimistically claimed on a merchantman and a cruiser, but none of the ships actually sustained any damage. Shortly after this a lone 38 Squadron Wellington appeared, the only one of those initially despatched from El Adem to find the convoy. Following ineffectual bombing, Sgt. Donohue took his aircraft (X9690/W) down to 500 feet, allowing his gunners the somewhat doubtful privilege of being able to blast away at the ships from low-level and close range. Nevertheless, in this fashion, three destroyers and a large freighter were machine-gunned, and although Donohue got away with this daring action (particularly as his aircraft was the sole target for all the gunners) his bravery was in vain; damage inflicted on the ships was minimal. Some way behind came another solitary 38 Squadron machine, W5624/J flown by Sgt. Thompson, having been delayed some two hours in taking off due to technical problems. His attack similarly had little effect, apart from keeping the ships' gunners on constant alert.

Meanwhile, an ASV Swordfish set out from Hal Far to take over surveillance of the convoy. It was soon followed by a mixed formation of torpedo-carrying biplanes — six Swordfish and two Albacores — led by Lt.Cdr. Hopkins' ASV-equipped aircraft (flown by Lt. Slater), from which he was to control and co-ordinate the strike. Hopkins had briefed his crews to seek out the troopship, news of its demise not yet having reached Malta.

Taking off in driving rain from an unlit Hal Far, the strike aircraft rendezvoused some miles out to sea, but then two Swordfish promptly developed engine trouble and turned back. The others became scattered in the atrocious conditions, which forced four more Swordfish and an Albacore to abort and head back to the Island. This left only Hopkins' unarmed Swordfish and one Albacore to continue the search. After about two and a half hours of battling against the elements, the convoy was located some 80 miles east of its estimated position, but by now fuel was too low to allow the Albacore crew — Sub Lt. P.F. Laidler and Sub Lt. T.D. Roberts — to carry out an attack and have a chance of getting back to Malta. The CO decided, now that the convoy's actual position had been established, to return to the Island and assemble another strike force.

Landing just after 1200, the tenacious Hopkins was back in the air within half an hour, this time with Sub Lt Coxon as his pilot, leading four Swordfish and an Albacore. The latter was soon forced to turn back, a Swordfish then also losing formation, leaving just three torpedo-carriers and the CO's aircraft to reach the convoy shortly after 0500. Sub Lts. C.V. Shute and W.E.F. Elliott went after the leading merchant ship, both claiming possible hits but, in fact, both missed. The third pilot failed to find a target, and returned with his torpedo.

When Malta was finally reached, the Swordfish had been airborne for six and a half hours, and Lt.Cdr. Hopkins personally for almost twice that amount of time. He would be awarded an immediate DSO, while the successful Lt. Ellis of 826 Squadron, whose torpedo finally put paid to *Victoria*, received the RAF's DFC, one of the few Naval officers to gain this award. It was made on this occasion as 826 Squadron had been flying under the command and control of the RAF. Flt.Lt. Taylor, leader of the Beaufort flight, was also awarded a DFC.

Saturday, 24 January

The surviving ships of the convoy reached Tripoli during the afternoon of the 24th, unhindered by further air attack although searched for by a Fortress. A threat did manifest itself however, in the form of a Royal Navy submarine which, having gained position to make an attack on *Monviso*, only narrowly missed this choice target. As feared, the British would pay dearly for their inability to prevent these supplies from reaching their destination.

Confident in the knowledge that reinforcements had safely reached Africa in the form of tanks, motor transport, troops and supplies — even though many of the new Panzer crews were still literally 'drying out' after their enforced submergence in the Mediterranean — Generaloberst Rommel now decided to extend the tentative reconnaissance-in-force, which he had launched two days earlier, into a full offensive. With lines of communication stretched alarmingly, troops in need of rest and replenishment, and with the demands of the new Far Eastern war fronts making themselves felt on the resources available, the Commonwealth forces were taken by surprise, and rapidly fell back to the Gazala area where a new line was to be held.

Whilst Rommel had fuel sufficient only for two weeks' intensive operations, he was confident the Luftwaffe would fulfil its promise to keep him supplied; had not the Ju52s been able to ferry enough fuel from Italy to meet daily requirements, units of his air force would soon have been grounded.

The afternoon of the 24th saw a resumption of action over Malta, a major interception being attempted at 1325 as raiders approached the Island, heading for the airfields at Luqa and Hal Far once again. Four Hurricanes from 126 Squadron, six from 242 and five more from 249 took off from Takali, led by Wg.Cdr. Satchell, followed by eight others from 185 Squadron, Wg.Cdr. Rabagliati at their head. One pilot of the 249 Squadron flight, Plt.Off. H.H. Moon, became separated and joined forces with the Hal Far Hurricanes, which intercepted three Ju88s (from III/KG 77) and eight Bf109s at 17,000 feet, south of their airfield.

Sgt. Garth Horricks, a Canadian from Toronto, attacked one bomber, chased it towards Luqa and shot out its port engine; he was credited with its probable destruction. This was possibly Lt. Ernst Fischer's 8 Staffel machine which crashed at Castelvetrano with the loss of all on board. Meanwhile, Moon gained hits on another Junkers but his own aircraft suffered damage, and he was forced to make a dead-stick landing at Luqa. Wg.Cdr. Satchell engaged in a dogfight with a German fighter but was unable to achieve any hits.

The Hurricanes had been unable to prevent a further damaging attack on Luqa, where Wellington Z8959, Maryland AH404 and a Hurricane were destroyed; a second Maryland (AH358) was damaged beyond repair and two Wellingtons, two Hurricanes and a Blenheim sustained less serious damage. A group of 1435 Flight pilots and ground personnel, over from Takali, had lucky escapes when bombs exploded nearby, thus nearly wiping out the Island's night fighter force at one blow; shaken and shocked, the airmen returned to their home airfield. During this raid Hal Far was also hit hard, two Hurricanes being badly damaged there.

To help offset recent FAA aircraft losses, four Albacores were ferried from the Desert immediately. However, one of these crashed at Gazala en route to Berka airfield, the departure point for the long sea flight to Malta. Only one of the remaining three eventually reached the Island and of the missing aircraft, that crewed by Lt. V.N.S. Davies and Sub Lt. A.D. Maher, both recipients of the DSC, was presumed to have crashed into the sea with the loss of both airman; the other aircraft, completely off course, ditched in the waters of Noto Bay off the eastern coast of Sicily, from where the crew were picked up to become prisoners, and from where their Albacore (T8941) was recovered more or less intact. With the non-arrival of these two aircraft at Malta, the ASR launch HSL 129 and the Rescue Flight Swordfish floatplane were ordered out from Kalafrana, but both returned having sighted neither survivors nor wreckage.

A number of delivery aircraft arrived safely from Gibraltar during the day, although one Blenheim crew did report a brief skirmish with a Z506B when nearing the Island. However, gunners aboard the Cant seaplane — a machine from 186ª Squadriglia — believed they had shot down the British plane.

Presumably they thought the Blenheim had fallen into the sea, whereas the pilot had evaded the attack and reached the comparative safety of cloud, before continuing to Malta.

Earlier in the month Sqn.Ldr. Westmacott, commander of 1435 Flight, had suggested to the AOC that, as Hurricanes were experiencing great difficulty in catching the fast Ju88s over Malta, his pilots might carry out night intruder sorties over Sicily in an effort to catch the returning bombers over their own airfields. He pointed out that there were hundreds of discarded long-range fuel tanks on the Island, of the type used by Hurricanes when ferrying from carriers. If fitted to the Flight's aircraft these would give the Hurricanes sufficiently increased endurance to enable intruder sorties to be undertaken. Air Vice-Marshal Lloyd enthusiastically agreed, particularly as he was also aware of an agent, operating in Sicily, who desperately required money and certain supplies to be dropped by air. Could Westmacott help, now that he had the means and the required authority, enquired the AOC.

With the aid of able ground staff, Sqn.Ldr. Westmacott got down to work and devised a cylinder, fitted with a small parachute, which could be released via the Hurricane's flare tube. After several practice drops, Westmacott felt confident such tasks could be carried out when required. The responsibility for these early secretive flights would fall upon Westmacott personally, but a number of other senior and experienced pilots also became involved later, including Wg.Cdr. Satchell, Wg.Cdr. Hugh Dawson, a former Hornchurch Wing Leader who had recently arrived on Malta, and 1435 Flight's Flt.Lt. Don Stones.

Following practice flying with the cumbersome long-range tanks fitted, which restricted manoeuvrability, Westmacott declared his unit ready to commence intruder operations as from the night of the 24th/25th; thus five Hurricanes set out after dark to patrol over the Sicilian airfields at Comiso and Catania. After half an hour over Comiso Flg.Off. F.R.W. Palmer saw a Ju88 take off and promptly attacked; he reported that it disintegrated in the air. A second Junkers was then seen taxying on the airfield, and this was also attacked and claimed damaged. None of the other pilots saw any suitable targets.

Sunday, 25 January

The defending fighters were hit hard next day, however, when a maximum effort was called for to provide cover for two empty supply ships, *Glengyle* and her companion, *Rowallan Castle*, which were now departing the Island with an escort of destroyers from Force 'K'. They were to rendezvous with the incoming *Breconshire* — making her seventh dash to Malta from Alexandria, carrying petrol, food and ammunition — when the two escort forces would exchange charges.

To ensure minimum interference as the eastward-bound ships left Grand Harbour, Flt.Lt. Peter Thompson led off four Hurricanes from 185 Squadron, closely followed by three more from 242 Squadron, while eight others from Takali (drawn equally from 126 and 249 Squadrons) provided top cover; three of the latter were forced to return early. As the ships passed Delimara Point, the northern promontory of Marsaxlokk Bay, four Ju88s and a dozen Bf109s were seen approaching. Thompson led his flight after the bombers and just had time to fire at the nearest machine, seeing pieces fly off, before disaster — in the guise of the escorting Messerschmitts — struck.

Bouncing the top cover, Major von Maltzahn's JG 53 Staff flight of five Bf109s

Commanders of Jagdgeschwader 53 at Comiso, January 1941. Playing scat are, left to right, Hpt. Wolf-Dietrich Wilcke, Kommandeur of III Gruppe, Maj. Gunther von Maltzahn, Geschwader Kommodore, and Hpt. Herbert Kaminski, Kommandeur of I Gruppe. Watching are Hpt. Heinze, Lt. Franz Schiess and Maj. Beyschlag. *(von Maltzahn via J. Prien/W. Bock)*

rapidly shot down three of the five Hurricanes, before diving to attack those at lower level. The action took place over Kalafrana, where an armourer, LAC Philip Chandler, noted:

> 'A real dogfight between Hurricanes and Messerschmitts right overhead. Saw four fighters come down and three pilots bale out. Can't say which side they belonged to. One machine was flying itself round and round, upside down, and at last landed upside down and burned. That pilot did not get out.'

Chandler's observations were not quite accurate, for the crashing Hurricane had been abandoned by its pilot, one of the three who had baled out. However, Plt.Off. John Russell, a 22 year-old Hitchin man, who had shared in bringing down Oblt. Schnez's Ju88 earlier in the month, was killed when his aircraft (Z2827) fell into the sea. 126 Squadron lost two more aircraft, Plt.Off. C.A. Blackburn (BD828) baling out wounded, and Flg.Off. Anderson (BG765) followed suit; one of these two came down over the Island while the other, having abandoned his aircraft over Hal Far, drifted out to sea from where he was soon recovered by a rescue launch from Kalafrana. The other pilot of the top cover to be shot down, Plt.Off. C.F. Sluggett in Z5147, a Canadian with 249 Squadron, also drifted down safely to terra firma.

Three Hurricanes of the lower flight sustained damage and all three crash-landed, two at Takali, the other at Hal Far; Flt.Lt. Thompson was slightly injured while the other two — Plt.Off. C.R. Morrison-Jones and Flt.Sgt. C.T. Alpe, both from 242 Squadron, were unhurt. Two more Hurricanes were also hit in this extremely successful action by the German pilots, only Plt.Off. Kee (242 Squadron) managing to make any form of claim against the attackers. The Luftwaffe pilots accurately claimed eight Hurricanes shot down, two of these being credited to Major von Maltzahn, for his 54th and 55th victories, while Lt.

Franz Schiess, Lt. Joachim Louis and Lt. Karl-Heinz Preu each claimed one; the identities of the other three claimants (who are believed to have been from I or II/JG 53) are not known. Freiherr Günther von Maltzahn later recalled:

> 'I drew towards them (*the Hurricanes*) from behind with my five aircraft (*of Stab/JG 53*). Then, coming at them from the rear from out of the sun in wide curves, I set up the first attack against the five Hurricanes. This worked out well. We came in unnoticed, with me attacking the Hurricane laying on the extreme left (*probably Plt.Off. Russell's aircraft*). She was hit, went down immediately, and broke up in flames into the sea. Whereupon I collected together my flight and set up a second attack. The Hurricanes increased speed over the land and tried to climb above us. I allowed a little time in order to let my planes end their attack.
>
> 'Just then I saw two of the somewhat higher situated Hurricanes had curved around, apparently in order to position themselves behind us. But they didn't do this, though — on the contrary, they flew towards land. As a result, I was able to push forward with the second attack without any harassment. Again I fixed my sights on the plane laying on the extreme left, thus allowing my comrades also to get going once more. Again the Hurricane received a direct hit. The pilot baled out. I saw him immediately afterwards, falling away from me over my cabin roof. At the same time two other Mes were attacking two enemy planes, which were likewise shot down and broke in flames on the land. So that was three brought down.
>
> 'The third attack I set up against the large squadron of 12 (*sic*) Hurricanes, of which two had already peeled off inland. Bringing in my aircraft from behind, I once more directed my attack on the left-hand plane. Now a real hurly-burly broke out, in the course of which I was no longer able to make out the fate of the shot-down plane. For sure, though, a further Hurricane was brought down by Lt. Louis. The other planes went into a nosedive in order to break away from us.
>
> 'They succeeded in this, except that they then had the bad luck to come into contact with the fighter escort of our bombers which were just then flying a mission over Malta. As a result, two Hurricanes were shot down which, in their turn, plunged burning into the sea. Two more went down in a spin, trailing black smoke, but unfortunately it was not possible to observe their crash. On the other hand, Lt. Preu pursued a Hurricane as far as the immediate vicinity of the coast, where he caught her and dealt with her at a height of 600 metres. That was the eighth shooting-down.
>
> 'We must put it down to good luck that we came out of this combat completely unharmed, and returned to base without a single casualty.

Hal Far was the selected target for the Ju88s during this raid, while Bf109s strafed at low-level. One more Hurricane was destroyed on the ground and an older Mark I (Z4315) was seriously damaged; this latter aircraft would be cannibalized for spares. Two other aircraft were badly damaged during the attack, but there were no further serious casualties.

Another transit aircraft failed to reach Malta from Gibraltar when Flt.Lt. Duncan was obliged to force-land Wellington Z9098 at Cekhira, on the Tunisian coast; he and his crew were interned. Following little activity over Malta during the daylight hours of the 26th, Wellingtons paid a further visit to Tripoli — the seventh night raid on this harbour in the past three weeks — and on this occasion

Lt. Joachim Louis of Stab/JG 53 climbs out of his Bf109F-4, after a sortie over Malta. *(Louis via J. Prien/W. Bock)*

two CR42s were seen, but these failed to intercept and all the bombers returned safely. Night fighter Ju88Cs of 4/NJG 2 also unsuccessfully attempted to intercept the bombers, but suffered a major loss when the aircraft flown by Lt. Peter Laufs — victor of 12 noctural combats — crashed onto the slopes of Mount Etna on return, killing him and his crew.

Tuesday, 27 January

Just as dawn was breaking on the morning of the 27th, the roar of a Merlin engine could be discerned at Hal Far as a patched-up Fulmar staggered up into the darkened sky; the aircraft, N4001, a survivor of the long-defunct 800X Flight (see *Malta: The Hurricane Years, 1940-41*), was piloted by Sub Lt. Coxon, with Sub Lt. David Kinghorn in the rear seat. They had been granted permission to fly the redundant machine, which had been fitted with a Hurricane long-range fuel tank, to Derna; in the event, they eventually arrived at El Adem where the Fulmar was refuelled, ready to continue the flight to RNAS Dekheila, near Cairo, which was reached without undue concern.

With the coming of daylight, Blenheims of 21 Squadron were sent off to search for another convoy, Sqn.Ldr. C.A. White leading a sweep from the east of the Gulf of Gabes, to Zuara. Some 20 miles off Zaezis, a freighter of an estimated 5000 tons was located, escorted by a destroyer and three CR42s of 160° Gruppo Aut. CT. As White manoeuvred his formation, seeking an opportunity to strike, one of the patrolling fighters, flown by Serg. Antonio Crabbia, broke away and latched onto two of the Blenheims, forcing the formation to scatter and, hence, the leader to call off the attack. Both Plt.Off. Booth's Z7288/S and Sgt. G.R. Cameron's Z7341/X were hit; the latter aircraft had its cupola shot away, Sgt. George Hancock, the Welsh air gunner, narrowly escaping injury.

During mid morning Hurricanes led by Wg.Cdr. Rabagliati again patrolled over the converging convoys; a number of Ju88s and Bf109s were seen carrying out attacks on the escorting warships, of which none were hit, while the attackers departed with the arrival of the Hurricanes. German records show that a reconnaissance Ju88D of 2(F)/122 from Trapani, F6+KK flown by Lt. Fritz Freesman, was lost some 300 km south-east of Cape Passero. It is possible that this aircraft may have been hit by the guns of the convoy's escort; alternatively it may have been lost due to technical problems. II Fliegerkorps suffered further losses when two Bf109s of II/JG 3 crashed shortly after take off — apparently following a collision — one coming down at Comiso, the other at Sciacca; both Uffz. Edmund Mächer of 6 Staffel and Uffz. Heinrich Raben of 5 Staffel were injured.

Half an hour before dusk Hurricanes of 1435 Flight at Takali were preparing to take off for night flying practice, prior to further operations over Sicily. Just as the first aircraft, flown by Plt.Off. A.S. Mackie, got into the air, six Bf109s swept in over a hill from the direction of Rabat, three of them going after this Hurricane. There followed a brief exchange of fire — onlookers thought one of the Messerschmitts fell into the sea — but Z3571/J was hit and crashed; the Scots pilot was severely wounded and later died in hospital. Following this harrowing experience, the unit carried out its practice flying at various times throughout daylight hours, and was never again caught in such a manner.

Undaunted by this event, seven Hurricane pilots set off individually for Sicily at intervals, the first departing at 1725. Sgt. J.E. Wood patrolled a line between Catania and Comiso, commencing at 1925. When over the latter airfield, he saw a Ju88 take off and quickly closed to within 50 yards before he shot it down in flames. Oblt. Wolfhelm Dronke's 5/KG 77 machine crashed near the airfield resulting in the deaths of two of the crew, including Dronke, the Staffelkapitän; the two survivors were both injured.

About two hours later, one of the Flight's New Zealand pilots, Plt.Off. Jack Grant, reported seeing a twin-engined biplane flying south of Augusta with its cabin lights on, and claimed to have shot this down into the sea in flames. From the reported activity of vessels in the area, noted next day by a reconnaissance aircraft, it was assumed that some person or persons of importance had been aboard; Italian records, however, apparently fail to mention any such combat or loss. Possibly the unfortunate victim was a communications or training machine or even a civil aircraft. Sqn.Ldr. Westmacott's Hurricane was slightly damaged by Flak during his one hour patrol; he decided to circle Mount Etna for a break, only to have his aircraft hit by a rifle bullet fired by an unseen hand from the darkness below.

On the conclusion of this successful night, marred as it had been by the death

Two Bf109Fs of II/JG 53 escorting a Ju88 to Malta early in 1942. *(Dr Felix Sauer)*

of Alex Mackie, Sqn.Ldr. Westmacott was gratified to receive, on behalf of his Flight — incidentally on this occasion, referred to as the MNFU, the unit's former identity — a message of congratulations from the obviously delighted AOC; the signal read:

> 'My heartiest congratulations on the splendid performance of all pilots of the MNFU on night of 27th/28th January. A brilliant performance of which you may feel justly proud. Well done.'

Wellingtons were also out over Sicily during the night, the Luftwaffe's main bomber base at Catania being specially targeted, where four Ju88s were slightly damaged by shrapnel and debris, and three Luftwaffe and two Italian personnel sustained injuries. Bombs also fell near the airfields at Gerbini and Comiso, but no damage resulted.

Wednesday, 28 January

At first light on the 28th a delivery Blenheim, having completed the long flight from Gibraltar, spun in on approach to Luqa; the aircraft (Z9836) was destroyed but the crew survived. A little later one of 69 Squadron's attached PR Hurricanes, in the hands of Sgt. R. Ballantine, set out for a sortie over Southern Italy. Here his aircraft, Z3173, was hit by AA fire near Catanzaro, and Ballantine was forced to bale out, coming down near Marcellinara where he was taken prisoner.

Hal Far was on the receiving end of a sharp raid by three Ju88s and a number of Bf109s, the latter strafing the airfield. Although the gunners believed that they had shot down one of the bombers into the sea, all actually returned to Sicily; one Hurricane (BG752) was destroyed on the airfield during the attack.

Raiders operating over Malta during the night of the 28th/29th included four Z1007bis from the newly-arrived, specially-trained 210ª and 211ª Squadriglia, 50° Gruppo BT, flying from Castelvetrano. Another new night bombing unit to arrive was 221ª Squadriglia, 55° Gruppo BT, equipped with seven BR20Ms, which had made its debut over the Island a few nights earlier. To accommodate these units at Castelvetrano, the day-bomber Z1007bis of 9° Stormo had departed for the mainland.

Thursday, 29 January

Tripoli was still receiving regular attention from Malta's remaining small force of bombers, albeit on a very limited scale, since the British were only too well aware of the importance of the harbour's facilities to the success of Rommel's latest thrust. Wellingtons attacked during this night, and again on the next night, while by day on the 29th Wg.Cdr. Selkirk led five 21 Squadron Blenheims to the area. Their brief was to bomb the nearby coastal town of El Zauir but they made the wrong landfall, and alternative targets — buildings along the road east of Tripoli — were attacked instead. Flt.Lt. Edwin Fox's aircraft (Z7271/J), following closely on the leader's tail, was hit by debris from exploding bombs, crashed and blew-up; all three of the crew were killed.

There was a small raid on Malta during the day, bombs being scattered over a wide area, some falling on the village of Qrendi where a satellite airfield was under construction nearby. In the village three houses were partly demolished, and two civilians lost their lives. One bomber jettisoned its load over Gozo, where 49 year-old Carmela Grech and her four children were killed. The guns were credited with damaging one of the raiders.

As the month drew to a close, the Navy's torpedo-carriers, despite their depleted numbers, gained a further success on the night of the 29th/30th. While Wellingtons bombed Tripoli, Flt.Lt. Spooner's Special Duties Flight ASV-equipped Wellington (the crews of such aircraft often included an FAA observer or signalman) had located yet another small convoy off the Cyrenaican coast some 70 miles north-west of Tripoli, which included a 5628-ton Italian freighter, *San Giovanni Battista*. Four Swordfish were called in, claiming two hits on the freighter, and a possible third, but the aircraft crewed by Sub Lt. Wilson and Lt. J.R.O. Stevenson was shot down by intense AA fire from the escort. Flt.Lt. Anthony Spooner, observing the action from his Wellington, later wrote:

> 'One FAA officer who flew with us two or three times was Lieutenant Stevenson. And we were helping the FAA on an attack when "Steve's" own Swordfish was shot down. We got word of this and managed to locate him in the water. However, the remains of the convoy went steaming away, abandoning him in the dark waters a hundred miles or more from any possible aid. It was sad that all we could do for this brave and likeable man was to fly low over the sea as slowly as we dared and to attempt to drop through our hatch a few supplies and a Very-light pistol and cartridges wrapped up in our Mae Wests. We had earlier flown alongside an enemy destroyer and tried to get this to turn back and go to Steve's rescue by dropping flame floats in a line. Not surprisingly, the destroyer merely fired at us.'

Stevenson and his pilot were not rescued. The victim of the attack, *San Giovanni Battista* was last seen down by the stern, belching black smoke. Next day, a reconnaissance crew reported that the ship was still on fire; however, she did reach the sanctuary of harbour, but would never put to sea again.

Night 30/31 January

A second Italian cargo ship was attacked the following night by four Albacores from Malta, when it was found heading northwards some ten miles off Cape

Bon. At least one torpedo was claimed to have struck home, the ship apparently being left with a list to port.

The month ended with another relatively successful intrusion into the night skies above Sicily by the Hurricanes; on this occasion Flg.Off. Denis Winton, one of the longest-serving fighter pilots still operational on Malta, engaged a Ju88 over Comiso. Firing from long range before his target was lost in the darkness, he considered he had at least damaged it. Wg.Cdr. Satchell, ever keen to be involved in the action, also took one of the night fighter Hurricanes to intrude over Sicily, but was recalled when the weather closed in.

January overview

A number of stalwarts were advised of awards during the month, DFCs being announced for Flt.Lt. Thompson of 185 Squadron, Flt.Lt. Palliser of 605, Flt.Lt. Carpenter of 126, and for one of the earliest of the night fighters, Flt.Lt. Ernest Cassidy. In the New Year's Honours List, Air Vice-Marshal Lloyd had been made a Companion of the Bath (CB) in recognition of his services to Malta. Luqa received a new commander during the month, when Grp.Capt. J.S. Chick MC, AFC (who had been quite a notable fighter 'ace' of the First War) took over from Grp.Capt. Harris.

Plt.Off. T.C. Worrall (left) and Plt.Off. Howard Coffin of 126 Squadron. Coffin was one of the first American fighter pilots to serve on Malta. *(J. Crichton)*

During the month Rome radio had intensified the war of nerves with broadcasts directed at the Maltese population — in a further attempt to undermine morale — inferring that as an invasion had not been forthcoming, "other methods" would be tried. The natural consequence of such threats ensured rumours of possible gas attack or bacteriological warfare, or the use of new secret weapons, to circulate around the Island.

The weather throughout January had been poor; indeed, the end of the month found both Hal Far and Takali waterlogged to the point of unserviceability, only Luqa providing runways fit for use. As implied, similar conditions in Sicily had restricted Axis activity over the Island, and had certainly played their part in delaying the major assault which was daily anticipated. Nonetheless, Malta had experienced more than 100 attacks during the month — over 1800 tons of bombs being dropped by Axis bombers during at least 150 sorties. Some 800 of these missiles had landed on the three airfields, where more than 50 aircraft had been destroyed or seriously damaged.

Such a rate of attrition was very difficult to support, but was something which could be ameliorated during the unexpected period of delay before the Luftwaffe appeared in full force. Priority attention was therefore given to drawing up plans for the better dispersal of aircraft around the airfields, and for an intensive programme of building work to produce blast and splinter-proof pens for them.

To construct dozens of such pens around the periphery of each of the main bases was a herculean labour, but the AOC was inspired to appeal to the Army for help, since few airmen could be spared from their servicing duties. The response was immediate and overwhelming, since the soldiers could be freed for much of the day from the essential inaction of their defensive roles. Up to 3000 men were provided at once, while the Navy, not to be outdone, contributed all its available personnel not engaged in priority duties. Hundreds of Maltese civilians also volunteered their assistance. In a matter of weeks, structures would spring up in profusion as land was requisitioned around Luqa, Takali and Hal Far. Levelled or filled as necessary by the hard sweat of manual labour — there were no bulldozers on the Island — 84 large pens, suitable for Wellingtons and Marylands, more than 200 smaller versions for the Hurricanes and Fleet Air Arm aircraft, and others to house petrol bowsers, control vans, and even the steamrollers so vital to keep the runways repaired, were constructed.

Initially the pens were built from sandbags and rubble, but this method was soon superceded by the use of discarded four-gallon petrol cans — which were available in vast quantities; these were filled with earth or limestone rubble, and were built into walls 10-14 feet high. This proved a much less easy task than it may sound. To house a Wellington, for instance, required no less than 60,000 such cans to construct three walls, each 90 feet long and 14 feet high. The walls were built with 12 cans at the base, tapering to two at the top, all wired together for stability. It was estimated that it took 200 men working 18 hours to produce one such structure!

The sense of urgency which had been engendered was such that work continued virtually around the clock and in all weathers, the men employed barely pausing even for air raids, which began to intensify as the programme proceeded. Air Vice-Marshal Lloyd subsequently recorded:

'The soldiers made by far the greater proportion of the pens... There were some 1500 of them working on the aerodromes and sometimes as many as 3000. We wanted all the help we could get in addition to that provided by the civilians. Everyone made pens. Every contribution — even for an hour a day — was gratefully acknowledged.

'Officers, clerks, photographers, storemen, wireless operators, aircrew, in fact, anyone with a few hours to spare would arrive with their sandwiches and work for an hour or so, regardless of the weather or the enemy. My HQ, for example, provided a daily working party of 53 officers and men for 3½ months.'

Another duty for which the Army provided vital assistance was in the clearance of shrapnel, rubble and unexploded bombs from the airfields following raids, and above all, the filling-in of bomb craters. At Luqa, this task was handled by men of 2nd Royal West Kents and 4th Buffs, while at Takali, soldiers of 8th Manchesters and 2nd Royal Irish Fusiliers undertook similar duties, as did 2nd Devons at Hal Far. Immediately the all-clear sounded, hundreds of troops would swarm over each airfield armed with buckets and spades, picks, earth pounders and rollers, the work of debris clearance and repair beginning at once.

At Luqa, Wg.Cdr. George Powell-Shedden DFC, formerly commander of the MNFU, now served as Wing Commander Operations, and control of airfield serviceability was one of his duties. Having organized the clearance and repair of the damage, one of his roles was the final inspection of the runways to ensure that they had been adequately repaired — a function which won for him the lighthearted title — "Wing Commander Bombholes"! He recalled:

'There were only a few bomb-disposal men on the Island so I frequently checked out any unexploded bombs — DA (delayed-action) bombs either went off in 30 minutes or in 24 hours. I would wipe the fuse to check whether dud or DA — if DA I would walk away slowly, when I really wanted to run! On one occasion I stalked a suspected DA while trying to make up my mind whether or not to remain another five minutes. On another, when the first butterfly bombs* fell on Luqa, I was on duty, found some and phoned the Bomb Disposal Unit for advice, to be assured they were perfectly safe. So I picked up about 18 of them, and took them to the Bomb Disposal quarry — where I was informed they were highly dangerous!'

Wg.Cdr. Powell-Shedden discovered that around ten per cent of all bombs falling on Luqa were duds. Frequently the guiding fins had fallen off, so that instead of landing on the nose where the fuse was located, they hit the ground on their sides and split open. He also noted that despite the construction of the pens many aircraft were still being damaged by splinters and debris flying through their open fronts. He subsequently suggested to the AOC that a redesign be undertaken to resolve the problem.

A pen of similar width but twice the length was constructed, with an access in one of the long walls. The aircraft was then shunted into the fully-enclosed half, substantially safer from the effects of blast (see diagram). He was to oversee the reconstruction of many pens at Luqa to this improved design.

* Butterfly bomb: weighing 2kg, the cylindrical 3½ inch bomb had wings which opened on release, allowing it to spin down, thereby triggering the fuse which was often set for delayed-action.

Chapter 2

NADIR OF THE HURRICANES

126 Squadron Hurricane at Takali after suffering damage from an exploding bomb. *(J. Crichton)*

The month of February opened with high winds and torrential rain, which effectively put a stop to all flying. The weather continued to be kind to the defenders for the next two weeks — low cloud and almost continuous rain restricting the intensity of air raids, allowing the authorities to take stock of their perilous situation. Aviation fuel was beginning to run low, while the shortage of .303 ammunition for the Hurricanes, and shells for the anti-aircraft guns, was causing concern. Above all, the shortage of fighters following the devastating losses in the air and on the ground during the previous four weeks provoked even greater anxiety.

By the beginning of the month only 28 Hurricanes remained serviceable. Many of the damaged machines had been cannibalized to keep others operational; lack of spares was also becoming a major problem. When Air Vice-Marshal Lloyd appealed to HQ, Middle East for Spitfires and more Albacores, he was advised that it was intended that five squadrons of Spitfires and one of Hurricane IIC night fighters would soon be despatched to Malta. It was implied, however, that two Kittyhawk squadrons might have to be substituted for two of the Spitfire squadrons. Meanwhile, 201 Group would attempt to fly two Albacores per night to Malta, commencing on the night of 8/9 February; each aircraft was to be fitted with a saddle tank in the rear cockpit, and a torpedo-type tank between the undercarriage legs, to give as much range as possible.

Monday, 2 February

The skies cleared sufficiently on the second day of the month to allow three Ju88s to sneak in during the early afternoon, and attack Hal Far. Little damage resulted, although one Hurricane — Z2509 of 605 Squadron — was destroyed on the ground. Two aircraft from this unit had been scrambled on the approach of the bombers, Plt.Off. O.O. Ormrod and Sgt. A.S. Wilson intercepting a single Junkers at 10,000 feet, south of the airfield. They claimed to have inflicted severe damage before it escaped in cloud, reporting that the rear gunner had almost certainly been killed, but not before both Hurricanes had been hit by his accurate return fire.

With the onset of darkness, the raiders returned, an estimated 20 aircraft roaming over the Island. Hal Far was again the main target, but the bombing similarly had little effect, although a number of parked aircraft sustained slight damage from bomb fragments and debris. One of the Junkers did, however, gain a success when it dived out of low cloud over Kalafrana, where the pilot spotted a Sunderland flyingboat on the slipway. By chance, this aircraft had just been brought out of its hangar when the raid commenced, preparatory to the continuation of its flight to Alexandria. The 230 Squadron machine, W3996, had arrived the previous night from Gibraltar, carrying Air Marshal Sir Peter Drummond amongst its passengers. Fortunately, the crew and passengers had not yet embarked, for one of the bombs aimed at the 'boat shattered its tail and rear fuselage. AA gunners claimed a raider probably shot down.

Hurricanes from 1435 Flight continued their series of successful intruder sorties over southern Sicily, Flt.Lt. Don Stones strafing a military car near Modica, setting it on fire. Another of the pilots, Flg.Off. Thompson, spotted an aircraft off Gela, which he identified as a Cant Z506B floatplane; he reported that after he had shot off one float, it spun into the sea near Licata harbour. An aircraft with its lights on was spotted in the distance by Wg.Cdr. Satchell, but these were quickly extinguished on the approach of the Hurricane, and the aircraft was subsequently lost in cloud.

Malta's depleted striking force also continued to make its presence felt. During the day, five Blenheims bombed and strafed traffic on the road west of Buerat (Cyrenaica), and claimed damage to a number of motor vehicles. By night, five Wellingtons set out to bomb Naples, while another was briefed to carry out a lone 'nuisance' sortie over Palermo. The Naval airmen were also active, four Albacores attacking a large supply ship estimated to be of about 8000 tons, off the Tunisian coast. Two hits were claimed and a violent explosion observed on the 6142-ton Italian freighter *Napoli*, the crippled vessel being taken in tow by the escorting MTB *Orsa*. When three miles off Ras el Mahedia, south-east of Sousse, this choice target was spotted by a prowling Royal Navy submarine, HMS *Umbra*, and was promptly torpedoed. This third torpedo strike proved decisive, for the ship was abandoned and the surviving crew taken aboard the attendant *Orsa*. Air reconnaissance next morning showed that *Napoli* had been beached.

Tuesday, 3 February

Two Staffeln of Ju88s, with the usual fighter escort, swept in to raid Hal Far and Kalafrana during the morning of the 3rd, meeting a patrol of Hurricanes. Two of the bombers were claimed damaged during the brief skirmish, AA gunners claiming hits on a third. A single raider dived from cloud and scattered more than 100 incendiaries in the Kalafrana area, one of which pierced the hull of BOAC's flyingboat 'Clare', which had just arrived. A fire broke out in her cabin but this was speedily extinguished by the men of the ASR unit, led by the Airways station superintendent, Mr Peter Armour, and Flight Steward Victor Mansell; the 'boat was hastily repaired and succeeded in getting away at dusk, its passengers including the stranded Air Marshal Drummond.

These unarmed flyingboats faced constant dangers and hazards, not least of which was that all landings and take-offs at Kalafrana were of necessity made at night. Capt. J.C. Harrington made many such flights:

> 'Alighting was tricky. There was nearly always a raid on, and we were just one more in the crowd of aircraft over the Island. Down at Kalafrana they put a single light out for us when they could, but usually there were too many Huns about and we had to come down in total darkness. Taking-off was just as bad. There was no waiting for the air raid to finish; you just took off when you were ready and hoped for the best.'

Among the numbers of the delivery aircraft arriving on Malta from Gibraltar during the day were four Beaufighters, one of which had been involved in a combat en route. When some 55 miles from Pantelleria, an Italian trimotor aircraft had been spotted flying at 1000 feet, and was identified as an S.79 bomber by the Beaufighter pilot, Sqn.Ldr. Peter Ruston. He attacked from astern, closing to 250 yards, and saw fragments fall off the starboard engine. The aircraft was last seen by the Beaufighter crew just above the sea, serious damage subsequently being claimed. In fact, the aircraft was an S.82 transport (MM60395) of 607ª Squadriglia Trasporti, on its way to Castelvetrano (Sicily) from Tripoli carrying a considerable number of civilians.

In an effort to alert the attacker to their non-combatant status, several of the terrified passengers held up their children at the cabin windows but tragically four women, a child and a male civilian were killed, together with one military passenger; nine other people suffered wounds, including a baby of just seven months. The pilot, Ten. Vimercati, was obliged to seek the safety afforded by nearby Pantelleria Island, and skilfully landed the severely damaged machine. One small girl, who had lost both parents during the attacks, was subsequently befriended by personnel of the 54° Stormo CT, who cared for her for a week until alternative arrangements could be made.

Italian reports of this tragic incident indicated that all four Beaufighters attacked, whereas it seems the sole aircraft carried out four passes. The survivors, understandably distressed and shocked, vehemently protested that the attackers (*sic*) could not have failed to have seen the children at the cabin windows of their unarmed aircraft. Whether such a display through the portholes of an aircraft in flight, and in the heat of action, would have been possible for the Beaufighter pilot to notice is considered extremely doubtful.

The black-painted Hurricane night fighters went out over Sicily again after dark, including one flown by Wg.Cdr. Satchell who, however, was forced to return almost at once due to a faulty radio. Changing to another aircraft, he set out once more for Comiso airfield but failed to locate any worthwhile targets, whilst at the same time experiencing heavy AA fire; his Hurricane collected some shrapnel from near-misses. In the area of Comiso he saw only a single motor car, which was duly strafed. Meanwhile, one of the flight commanders, Flt.Lt. Stones, had the task of dropping a container of messages to the agent based in eastern Sicily, the dropping zone being sited halfway up Mount Etna. On returning from one of these nocturnal sorties, another pilot crashed Hurricane Z3570 on landing at Takali, but was unhurt.

Wednesday, 4 February

The first serious engagements of the month for Malta-based units were to occur on the 4th, when several raids were made on the Island, culminating in a heavy bombing attack on Takali. At 1225, four Hurricanes from 249 Squadron and two from 126 Squadron scrambled after Ju88s south of Kalafrana. One of these bombers was attacked jointly by a section from the former unit, Flt.Lt. Davis gaining hits on both engines, before Sqn.Ldr. Beazley and Plt.Off. Tedford joined in, the Junkers finally escaping in cloud. This was possibly an aircraft of 2/KGr 806 which crash-landed at Scalea; one crew member was injured.

Plt.Off. Joe Crichton, a Canadian member of 126 Squadron. *(J. Crichton)*

Meanwhile, six Blenheims from 21 Squadron had been despatched to carry out a low level attack on shipping in Palermo harbour, on the northern coast of Sicily. Shortly before 1115, as the formation approached the coastline from the north, skimming low over the waves, the wrong landfall was unwittingly made with disastrous results. Without warning, high ground was suddenly encountered and the bombers were forced to bank to climb over this. As they did so, the wingtip of the leading machine, Wg.Cdr. Bill Selkirk's Z9806, was seen to clip the water and the Blenheim cartwheeled into the sea; only Sgt. Sydney Phillips, the gunner, survived to become a prisoner.

Due to the navigational error which had been made, the remaining five Blenheims missed their target, the crews seeking instead opportune alternatives. A 'goods train' was seen and attacked near Carini, nine miles west of Palermo, as was a rail bridge at Scoppe, but the formation then flew into an area of cloud-covered hills. Three of the bombers were not seen again by those aboard the two surviving aircraft, who reported on return that the missing aircraft must have presumably flown into the hillsides.

The Italian account of this raid contained some important differences. The bombers, which they incorrectly identified as Wellingtons, had attacked a passenger train — not a goods train — in the small station of Santa Flavia, near Palermo, four passengers being killed. Anti-aircraft gunners then claimed three of the attackers shot down, one near Prizzi, another at Palazzo Adriano, the third near Santo Stefano Quisquina. One of these, Z9812 flown by Plt.Off. F.J. Workman, crash-landed, both the observer and gunner being killed; apparently the badly-injured Australian pilot was captured whilst attempting to complete the destruction of his aircraft; he died two days later in hospital. There were no survivors from the other two aircraft — Z7341 piloted by Sgt. Matthew Houston, an Irishman from County Antrim, and Z9824, flown by New Zealander Flt.Sgt. Jack Ibbotson.

From Malta, at 1350, six of 249 Squadron's Hurricanes took off to cover the returning Blenheims, three more from 126 and two from 242 Squadrons providing support. During the operation, Flt.Lt. Carpenter spotted a lone Ju88 at 6000 feet over Kalafrana — obviously a reconnaissance machine — which he attacked and claimed damaged before it disappeared in cloud.

An hour later another scramble was ordered, 11 Hurricanes from the same three squadrons taking off, but failing to make contact with the bombers which commenced to bomb Takali. Serious damage was caused to airfield buildings, and there were a number of casualties. One section of Hurricanes was bounced by Bf109s — probably from II/JG 53 — and all three were shot down; Z4003 and Z4016 of 249 Squadron fell into the sea, with the loss of both Plt.Off. John Hulbert and Sgt. Hugh McDowall, while 126 Squadron's Plt.Off. 'Rocky' Main was killed in BV167. The only damage noted by the Luftwaffe was to a 5 Staffel Messerschmitt, which sustained slight shrapnel damage from an AA burst over Valetta.

Four Hurricanes, two Swordfish and HSL 129 were sent out to search for the missing pilots, the launch heading for a point four miles south-south-east of Benghaisa Point. Near Filfla two Messerschmitts of 6/JG 53 swooped on the rescue craft, killing AC Gerry King who was manning the front turret. During a second pass the skipper, Flt.Lt. Victor Nicolls, was mortally wounded, while the aft-turret gunner, LAC Tom Griffith, was hit in the left side and thigh; nonetheless, he continued to man his gun but fell during the third attack. The coxswain, Cpl. Theo Nielsen, was also killed and his deputy wounded, although the latter managed to get the badly damaged launch back to Kalafrana. Silent spectators gathered as HSL 129 limped slowly into view, engines faltering and backfiring, and the foward gun cupola splashed with blood from the dead gunner. The launch would be out of action for a month, and with HSL 128 also temporarily unserviceable, HSL 107 was recalled from its station at St Paul's Bay.

The Wellingtons headed south again that night, seven aircraft from 40 Squadron attacking vehicles located south of Tripoli. One bomber was intercepted by a Ju88 on the return flight but the gunners drove it away, claiming probable hits. This may have been an aircraft of 8/KG 77 (3Z+ES), flown by Lt. Eberhard Dammbrück on a bombing sortie to the Island, which failed to return to its base at Comiso; on this occasion, no claims were submitted by Malta's defences.

Air-Sea Rescue launch HSL 129 after it had been strafed by a pair of Bf109s of 6/JG 53 off Filfla on 4 February 1942. Flt.Lt. Victor Nicolls and three of his crew were killed during this attack, but the craft was repaired and put back into service. *(NWMA)*

Thursday, 5 February

A delivery Wellington, on the last leg of the long flight from Gibraltar, was caught at daybreak on the 5th off Sicily by two Bf109s, and sustained damage before the pilot managed to evade; the gunners put up a spirited defence, claiming strikes on one of the assailants. Later in the day, a reconnaissance Maryland was similarly intercepted by two Messerschmitts but escaped undamaged. A further pair of Bf109s carried out a surprise strafe of Kalafrana seaplane base, catching the He115 'spyplane' (BV187) at its moorings, where it was set alight and damaged beyond repair. Plt.Off. McKay noted:

> 'Two 109s did some low flying attacks and set fire to the Heinkel 115 which sunk. It was really quite a sight to see them come down. They were going at least 400 (mph) when they went over. The Bofors opened up but they didn't touch them.'

Nonetheless, the defending AA gunners did claim hits on one of the attackers.

Friday, 6 February

During the morning the Dockyard and submarine base were subjected to heavy air attack, Junkers bombers from both KG54 and KG77 taking part. Bombs fell in the Sliema area, causing about 25 casualties and considerable damage to civilian property. Hurricanes were scrambled but failed to make any interceptions. The guns, however, were more successful on this occasion,

One of the many Bofors light anti-aircraft guns which provided close protection of the airfields and other key installations. These weapons extracted a considerable toll of low-flying raiders during 1942. *(NWMA)*

shooting down Fw. Claus Ahrens' 2/KG 54 aircraft (B3+CK), from which three of the crew baled out to become prisoners; a II/KG 77 bomber was also hit and seriously damaged, but got back to Sicily on one engine. Hal Far was attacked during the early afternoon by bombers and fighters, during which one of the Messerschmitts was claimed shot down by the ground defences, although no such loss was recorded. The airfield was rendered temporarily unserviceable due to the large number of bomb craters, shrapnel and debris, while an Albacore was destroyed at its dispersal.

From Palermo Boccadifalco airfield (Sicily), two pairs of twin-engined CR25s from 173ª Squadriglia took off to escort the German steamer *Achaja*, a task in which they were assisted by a dozen MC200s of 54° Stormo from Pantelleria. During the course of these patrols the Fiat flown by Ten. Pietro Rindone encountered a Blenheim, which was at once attacked, only for the pilot to find that his fixed forward-firing guns were jammed. He manoeuvred to enable his dorsal-turret gunner, Serg.Arm. Vito Trentadue, to open fire and the Blenheim was claimed probably shot down.

It seems probable that the CR25 crew had engaged a Blenheim from 21 Squadron, since three of these aircraft were on a sweep of the area off Buerat, searching for shipping. Four Blenheims had been despatched from Luqa following a report from a reconnaissance crew that two small merchant ships had been observed discharging their cargos into smaller vessels at Buerat el Hsum, but one aircraft had been forced to return early. Apparently the ships were not located but AHQ did announce a claim for an 'S.82' shot down — possibly the Blenheim crew believed that they had brought down Ten. Rindone's aircraft in return.

As Sqn.Ldr. Stewart led the trio of Blenheims back towards Malta at the end of this sortie, they fell foul of marauding Bf109s, believed to have been aircraft of Stab and II/JG 53. All three Blenheims were quickly shot down into the sea not far from Filfla, with the loss of all the crews. Losses were:-

Z7308	Sqn.Ldr. Russell Stewart RNZAF, and crew
Z9822	Plt.Off. Jim Grieve and crew (the body of his gunner was later recovered from the sea)

A pair of twin-engined Fiat CR25 reconnaissance-fighters of 173ª Squadriglia Autonomo RST on Palermo airfield. These aircraft were mainly employed as escort for Axis convoys plying between Sicily and North Africa, engaging RAF aircraft on several occasions. *(G. Garello via N. Malizia)*

Z9725 Flt.Sgt. Gordon Cameron RNZAF, and crew (the bodies of his observer and gunner were later recovered from the sea)

It is believed that one of these aircraft was shot down by Major von Maltzahn, and another by Lt. Herbert Soukop of 6 Staffel. These losses, added to the seven aircraft and crews lost during the previous three weeks, seriously weakened 21 Squadron as an effective strike force.

Shortly before midnight Sqn.Ldr. Westmacott set course for eastern Sicily, a package containing 500,000 Lire for the agent stowed in the Hurricane's flare tube. As he approached the dropping zone on the north-eastern slopes of Mount Etna, the weather closed in and, as the whole area was shrouded in low cloud, the mission was necessarily abandoned. Undeterred, Westmacott cruised over the darkened landscape looking for suitable targets to attack, and soon spotted an electric train when just south of Taormina, his cannon-shells causing a "spectacular display of blue-white flashes" as he strafed.

Meanwhile, four Albacores had spotted a northwards-bound Italian freighter, *Monviso*, with an escort comprising the destroyer *Da Noli* and a torpedo boat, about five miles off Cape Bon. An attack was made during which two torpedoes were believed to have struck home, as columns of smoke were seen following the attack, and the destroyer appeared to be going to *Monviso*'s aid; there were, however, no confirmatory reports of any damage to the ship.

Two hours later an ASV Wellington made contact with another convoy, this one southward-bound some 30 miles from Cape Turgeunes. Two Swordfish were called in to attack the fully-laden tanker *Rondine*, which was heading for Tripoli, escorted by the destroyer *Premuda* and four torpedo-boats. The escort had already warded off an attempted attack by a British submarine whilst off Trapani, and now their withering fire shot down Sub Lt. M. Swithinbank's aircraft, he and his observer, Sub Lt. R.A. Thomas, both being killed. The surviving crew returned to report having seen a violent explosion and a fire following their attack but, in fact, as with the night's earlier action by the Albacores, there was no tangible success.

Saturday, 7 February

Messerschmitts remained active over the Island on the 7th and when, at 1120, newly-promoted Flt.Lt. Ben White returned from a photographic-

An 828 Squadron Albacore at Hal Far, loaded with a torpedo, ready for takeoff. For many months these obsolescent aircraft provided the main 'teeth' of Malta's night striking force. *(NWMA)*

reconnaissance sortie over Sicily, he found a pair of Bf109s waiting, which proceeded to attack his Beaufighter (T3301) as it approached to land at Luqa. The pilot and the camera operator, LAC Shirley, were both wounded when their aircraft was hit and set on fire. Despite his severe wounds, Shirley managed to extinguish the flames and, following the crash-landing, to drag his wounded pilot clear. For this action, Norman Shirley was unusually (for he was not officially aircrew) awarded an immediate DFM.

A little over an hour later one of 69 Squadron's Marylands approached Luqa at the end of a sortie to Tripoli, and this aircraft was also attacked by a pair of Messerschmitts. Fire was effectively returned by the turret gunner, Sgt. Cameron, which not only enabled the pilot, Sgt. McDonald, to land safely, but also possibly resulted in one of the attackers being shot down.

Another Bf109 — or the same one — was claimed possibly shot down as it swept in at low level, victim of the submarine *Upright*, at anchor in Grand Harbour. The fighter was seen determinedly chasing the Maryland and Lewis gunner Able Seaman Fred Woolley, aided by Able Seaman Charlie Sprott, got in an accurate burst at the Messerschmitt. They were confident that their fire went home and reported that their victim was seen trailing smoke; the victory was duly symbolized on the submarine's 'Jolly Roger'.

Although rescue launch HSL 107 was sent out to look for signs of the ditched aircraft, it was soon recalled when further German fighters appeared on the horizon, particularly as the promised Hurricane escort failed to arrive. Later, with the coming of dusk, HSL 107 again put to sea to continue the search but no sign of pilot or wreckage was found.

However, a tangible success was gained by Hal Far's AA gunners when they caught a low-flying Bf109 of 6/JG 53 as it swept in to strafe parked Hurricanes; Ofw. Otto Göthe died when 'Yellow 4' crashed to earth, as recorded by Plt.Off. McKay:

> 'About eleven o'clock two 109s shot-up Luqa and were just on their way to shoot-up the Hurricanes on the line at Hal Far but the Bofors hacked one down. The tail was shot off and it went straight in about 300 miles per hour. The pilot (what was left of him) was scraped up.'

Able Seamen Fred Wooley (left) and Charlie Sprott of submarine HMS *Upright*, with the Lewis gun with which they claimed to have shot down a strafing Messerschmitt Bf109 on 7 February, whilst their vessel was anchored in Grand Harbour. *(Authors' collection)*

Hurricanes were sent up from Takali, led by Wg.Cdr. Rabagliati, to meet and escort another returning Maryland, these driving away yet a further pair of Messerschmitts which attempted to intercept. During all this fighter activity around the Island two delivery Wellingtons managed to slip into Luqa, unobserved and unhindered, but a third (Z9037) failed to arrive from Gibraltar, its fate unknown. Three Ju88s also managed to avoid the fighter patrols during the afternoon, and caused considerable damage to Hal Far, where an already damaged Albacore was completely destroyed and eight airfield personnel were injured.

After dark Sqn.Ldr. Westmacott departed for Sicily in his Hurricane and, on this occasion, managed to make a successful drop to the agent, who subsequently reported safe receipt of the container stuffed with 500,000 Lire, but said he had experienced great difficulty in extracting the money! On the return flight Westmacott spotted a truck near Catania airfield, which he duly strafed. Whilst he had been away raiders had again been active over Malta, with Hal Far, Kalafrana and the Safi dispersal area all being hit; Blenheim Z9712 and a Wellington (DV453 of the OADU) were destroyed at Safi. One Ju88 was illuminated by the searchlights, as 'Skip' McKay noted:

> 'He jettisoned his bombs right over our Mess at Marsaxlokk and as luck would have it, one dropped on the Mess and one right beside it. Joe Beckitt and Sonny (*Ormrod*) were in the bar at the time and that is the only room that was unhurt, the floors coming down in all the others. S/L McGregor, Ron Noble and 'Wiggles' (*Wigley*) were outside and, of course, lying flat. They had just left the dining room to get some lamps, seeing the lights had gone out, or they all would have been killed.'

With the successful conclusion to Westmacott's clandestine sortie, so began a series of such flights which would continue over the next ten months at monthly intervals, only terminating when the agent was ultimately caught (and subsequently executed). During this period not only money but clothes, batteries and even a bicycle were dropped to the agent, albeit via a proper underwing container which had been fitted in place of one of the long-range fuel tanks. The majority of these flights would be made by Wg.Cdr. Dawson in his personalized, black painted Hurricane, which bore the legend 'Dawson's Folly'.

Sunday — Tuesday 8-10 February

Six alerts during the hours of daylight on the 8th brought a single scramble at 0850 by four 126 Squadron Hurricanes. A little later Sqn.Ldr. Norris crash-landed at Luqa with the engine of his Hurricane on fire, having been hit by return fire from a reconnaissance Ju88 which his section had intercepted, and which was itself claimed damaged.

The dire winter weather continued to restrict operations, although Takali suffered another severe raid on the 9th, when six civilians, a soldier and an airman were killed. Hurricane Z5326/F, flown by Plt.Off. James Stuart of 249 Squadron, was lost and the pilot killed, when it dived into the ground at Takali during an air test and burst into flames. Additionally, a reconnaissance Maryland returning from a sortie to Pantelleria was intercepted by a Bf109 and a Bf110; the pilot, on this occasion, easily escaped these in the cloudy conditions and returned safely to Malta.

The weather was even worse on the 10th, when four Ju88s braved a raging storm to penetrate the defences in an attempt to bomb Luqa. With the crews unable accurately to pin-point the target, bombs aimed in the general direction of the airfield fell on nearby Qormi village instead, where 16 civilians were killed and a further 28 injured.

Wednesday, 11 February

Not until the 11th was any serious engagement recorded, when a substantial force of Hurricanes — drawn from 126 and 249 Squadrons at Takali, and 242 and 605 Squadrons at Hal Far — was led off by Wg.Cdr. Rabagliati at 1015 to provide cover for the cruiser *Cleopatra* and her escorting destroyer *Fortune* which were approaching Malta on transfer to the Island's Force 'K'. Twenty-five minutes after take off the Hurricanes had reached 16,000 feet and were eight miles north of Gozo when, some 10,000 feet below, a formation of six Ju88s with four escorting Bf109s were seen, heading towards Sicily. Rabagliati led the Takali Hurricanes down in a steep diving attack on the bombers, personally opening fire on Ofw. Heinz Bösch's 3Z+JR of 7/KG 77, seeing many strikes. His No 2, the American Plt.Off. Coffin, closely followed him down:

> 'My stomach went tight as we came on them. Rags (*Wg.Cdr. Rabagliati*) started to take his man apart with short deadly bursts and then the other 88 was round on my tail. His bullets ripped through my port wing. I began to shake and I froze to my stick... I was suddenly clear and steady again. I came up in a half-roll and the 88 dove (*sic*) under me. Rags led him away and then I had a chance to get square on his tail; I gave him a long burst and he slid off and began spinning down in flames.'

It seems likely that Coffin's victim was actually the same aircraft as attacked by

Plt.Off. Bill Hollis Hallett, native of Bermuda, in the cockpit of 126 Squadron's Hurricane HA-E, 'Death Warmed Up'. *(J. Crichton)*

Close-up of the 'Death Warmed Up' insignia on the nose of Hurricane HA-E. *(J. Crichton)*

his leader, which also came under further attack from Plt.Off Noel MacGregor, who recalled:

> 'Had good long bursts from very close range at Ju88, recording hits. Self hit in starboard wing and aileron by rear gunner, and attacked by 109 but evaded. Ju88 afterwards confirmed destroyed.'

Meanwhile, Flg.Off. Kay and Sgt. Ted Copp were attacking another Junkers, apparently an aircraft of KGr 806, which subsequently crash-landed at Catania, badly damaged by fighter attack. Kay's aircraft also sustained damage from return fire but he landed safely. The Hal Far Hurricanes, which had covered the attack on the bombers, had now become embroiled with the escorting Bf109s, Flt.Lt. Rhys Lloyd claiming one probably shot down while other pilots claimed strikes on two more.

The 60 miles across the Malta Channel to Sicily must have seemed more like 600 miles to the desperate crew aboard Ofw. Bösch's crippled Junkers, as the pilot struggled to keep the aircraft flying before finally losing the battle when it splashed into the sea. Bösch and one of his crew died in the crash but the other two, although both injured, were picked up by rescue craft from Sicily. This unfolding drama was not, however, witnessed by the Hurricane pilots and consequently only a claim for the aircraft's probable destruction was submitted by them on return.

Confirmation of the bomber's loss was soon forthcoming, however, via the RAF's 'Y Service' — the intelligence gathering unit responsible for intercepting Axis W/T and R/T traffic — which subsequently reported that intercepts indicated that neither the Ju88 nor the Bf109 had reached their respective bases, and that two more bombers had been damaged.

The Hurricanes, however, had been too late to prevent a determined attack on the Naval vessels, *Cleopatra* sustaining some damage from a near miss which killed eight and seriously wounded 11 more of her crew. II Fliegerkorps also suffered the loss of a Ju87B (KZ+25), flown by Obgfr. Heinrich Kron of ErgSt/StG 1, the newly-arrived Stuka Geschwader's operational training unit, which may have been shot down by the warships.

From Malta two of the remaining Blenheims of 21 Squadron attacked a 200-ton schooner 100 miles south-west of Lampione, in the Gulf of Gabes, while two others bombed and strafed a similar vessel nearby. As the small formation approached Malta on the return flight, they were intercepted by Bf109s from 8/JG 53. Three of the Blenheims managed to evade their attackers, but Z9823 was shot down into the sea by Oblt. Hans-Joachim Heinecke for his 17th victory; Plt.Off. D.F.W. Parrish and his crew were lost.

Four Ju88 night bombers achieved a resounding success when bombs hit the Grand Harbour area around midnight — the destroyer *Maori* received a direct hit, the bomb exploding in her engine room which caught fire; she blew up at 0210. Most of the skeleton crew aboard managed to escape — some being rescued by two Maltese police constables, PCs J. Meli and V. Gili — shortly before the explosion, and only one sailor lost his life although eight were injured. However, blast and debris killed two men and injured six others on another nearby destroyer, HMS *Decoy*. Elsewhere, air-dropped mines caused damage to the submarine base at Manoel Island, while bombs also fell on Hal Far airfield where a Swordfish was severely damaged. Many delayed-action bombs were located, Sqn.Ldrs. H.B.H. Dickinson and W.R. Hardeman and their respective teams of bomb disposal volunteers, aided by similar groups of Army and Navy personnel, being kept constantly busy.

Thursday, 12 February

With the coming of dawn on the 12th three delivery Beaufighters had just reached a point between Pantelleria and Malta, when Bf109s from III/JG 53 approached, obviously scrambled when tell-tale blips appeared on German radar screens. One Beaufighter was shot down into the sea by Lt. Herbert Schramm — his 39th victory — the crew of T4879 being lost with their aircraft. A little later a second Beaufighter was lost when eight such aircraft, which had arrived and refuelled at Malta during the hours of darkness, departed for Egypt and were intercepted by a pair of far-ranging Bf110s from III/ZG 26. Lt. Alfred Wehmeyer, another Luftwaffe 'Experte', raised his score to ten by despatching T4915 into the depths of the Mediterranean; again there were no survivors. Coincidentally, both German pilots identified their victims as Blenheims — probably an indication of the level of visibility during this winter period.

During the late morning ten Hurricanes from 605 Squadron, joined by two others from 185, were scrambled from Hal Far, Sqn.Ldr. Andrews at their head. Two Bf109s were seen at sea level, but these were not attacked as it was assumed that they were decoys for others higher up. Then, when about 20 miles north of Grand Harbour, a lone Ju88 and a Do24T flyingboat with escorting Messerschmitts appeared — possibly searching for the crews of aircraft lost the previous day. Plt.Off. 'Chuck' Lester was the first to spot the Ju88 — 3Z+DD of 7/KG 77, flown by the Staffelkapitän, Oblt. Herbert Loerz — and gave chase, followed by Plt.Offs. Wigley (Z3757/R) and McKay (LE-U), the latter recording:

> 'Chuck, "Wiggles" and I were weaving and we saw it first and immediately turned towards it and then the rest turned. It fired a white and green recognition cartridge to make us think it was friendly but turned and started off out to sea. Everyone pulled the tit, put on full revs and gave chase.
>
> "Wiggles" and Chuck were a bit above and a little ahead and got there first. "Wiggles" attacked first then Chuck and then I opened up. I could see my bullets enter the rear turret and rip the fuselage. I almost shot Chuck down 'cause on his attack he went down and then came up right in my sight (50 yards) and I was firing but stopped in time. He had one bullet in his port aileron. Everyone had a shot. Sonny Ormrod finished it off with cannon and it went straight in (three jumped).'

Plt.Off. Ormrod then attacked the flyingboat and observed hits, before his own aircraft sustained slight damage from return fire, forcing him to break away. The unit's newly-promoted flight commander, Flt.Lt. George Allen, was seen scrapping with two of the escort, one of which it was believed he may have damaged, before he was shot down by another, possibly that flown by Major von Maltzahn of JG53; Allen was seen to bale out of Z2527 and it was thought at the time that he had been picked up by the ASR Dornier, an aircraft from Seenotst 6, but this was not the case. Two Messerschmitts attacked Lester but his aircraft was not hit, and he claimed one damaged as it overshot, while McKay crashed on landing at Takali due to a broken wheel.

Between 0818 and 1351 there were six alerts, and an estimated 100 plus raiders caused much havoc and destruction at Hal Far (where a Swordfish and a Hurricane were damaged, the former seriously) and at Luqa. The Docks area also came under heavy attack, while indiscriminate bombing destroyed a number of houses at Paola where several streets were blocked by debris and much panic resulted. There were 31 known fatalities, including three soldiers, with a further six civilians reported missing; about 100 more were injured. Many houses were also demolished in Luqa village, while Tarxien similarly suffered much damage.

Flt.Lt. Cecil Baker of 126 Squadron, another pilot who lost his life in Malta's defence. *(J. Crichton)*

40 Squadron despatched six Wellingtons to raid Catania airfield that night, following which many large fires were reported, while a number of aircraft — presumably Ju88s — had been observed landing during the series of attacks. Some of the bombing was woefully off target, bombs falling on the little towns of Biancavilla and Santa Maria di Licodia, some 20 miles to the north, where six civilians were killed and eight others were injured.

Friday, 13 February

Friday saw 69 Squadron's reconnaissance aircraft at the centre of the action again when a Maryland flown by Plt.Off. T.M. Channon, returning from patrolling between Pantelleria and Cape Bon, was intercepted by two Bf109s as it approached Luqa. The Messerschmitts, believed to be from Stab II/JG 3, closed to within 40 yards during their first pass, seriously damaging the Maryland and killing the turret gunner, Sgt. A.C. Moore; the second gunner, Sgt. R.J. Watson, was wounded in several places. Despite the rear cockpit becoming filled with smoke and flames, Watson, painfully disregarding his wounds, succeeded in removing his dead comrade from the turret and manning the guns himself, in time to fire an accurate burst into the second fighter as it came in for another pass; the crew reported that this aircraft appeared to crash into the sea in flames.

With the fortuitous departure of the other Messerschmitt, Sgt. Watson was able to divert his attention to his perilous surroundings, and attempted to quell the flames by throwing out items which were ablaze; the dead gunner's clothing was on fire and in extinguishing this, Watson sustained severe burns. He was barely conscious when his pilot eventually crash-landed the burning Maryland (AH733), which was damaged beyond repair. For his gallant actions, Watson received an immediate DFM.

As to the fate of the Messerschmitt claimed shot down during this action, apparently the crew were mistaken in their belief that it fell into the sea. It seems likely that this was Lt. Karl-Heinz Ponec's 'Black 3', which crashed on the Sicilian coast at Agrigento, the pilot being killed.

Friday the 13th was almost the undoing of Flt.Lt. Warburton for whilst being pursued by four MC202s over Taranto, the Beaufighter's port engine failed due to an oil leak. Regardless of his predicament, not only did he shake off the Macchis but he then proceeded to photograph Messina before heading back to Malta.

A much-needed supply convoy was on its way from Alexandria and, during the day, eight Beaufighters of 252 Squadron flew in from North Africa to provide long-range cover to the ships as they approached Malta. Due to an error in navigation, the Beaufighters at first missed the Island and flew towards Sicily, the leader, Flt.Lt. A.S. Malcolm, only realising the mistake when Bf109s were seen taking off! The formation veered away rapidly, turned south, and eventually landed at Luqa shortly after a raid by Ju88s, Ju87s and Bf109s.

The Grand Harbour area was the main target for this latest assault, one bomb hitting the Governor's headquarters, Valetta Palace; although damage was not severe, General Dobbie wisely ordered his staff to vacate the building and set up shop at his residence at San Anton. Fierce resistance by the defending AA gunners resulted in claims being submitted for the shooting down of a Ju88, a Ju87 and a Bf109, with a second Ju88 probably destroyed. Records certainly confirm the loss of the Ju87 — again an aircraft (KZ+27) of Stukageschwader I's ErgStaffel — which crashed in the sea off Valetta, taking Gefr. Eugen Koretschek and his gunner to their deaths.

Earlier in the day, a trio of bomb-carrying Bf109s of the newly-formed 10(Jabo) Staffel of JG 53 carried out a surprise raid on Takali; although the pilots had received very little in the way of bombing-technique training, they nonetheless accurately placed their bombs on various buildings, causing much damage, as Bill Metcalf noted:

> 'What a hell of a day it has been too. In Takali's share this morning the M/T section was wrecked and the pottery badly knocked about by blast. Five casualties including Cpl. Barfoot of our Armoury Section.'

At 2230 that night three torpedo-armed Albacores followed an ASV-equipped machine flown by Lt. R.L. Williamson with Lt. Haynes, the CO, operating the radar, to intercept a west-bound convoy of two freighters south-east of Sousse. These were the German *Atlas* and the Italian *Ariosto*, escorted by the destroyer *Premuda* and a torpedo-boat, all of which had been spotted earlier in the day by a Maryland. At the approach of the biplanes, the destroyer laid an effective smoke-screen, thereby frustrating a co-ordinated attack.

Only one pilot was able to manoeuvre his aircraft into a position to launch its torpedo, successfully gaining a hit on the Italian ship which, billowing clouds of smoke, was left stationary in the water. Three hours later the Royal Navy submarine *P38* delivered the 'coup-de-grace'. Unbeknown to British intelligence, *Ariosto* was carrying 294 British prisoners-of-war taken during the battles in Cyrenaica, and many of these were lost when the ship went down; 158 men perished out of a total complement of 410 prisoners and crew aboard.

Saturday, 14 February

By the 14th the British supply convoy (codenamed MW9) had come within range of Sicilian-based aircraft and, during the afternoon, the crew of a reconnaissance Z1007bis reported seeing 18 merchant vessels (!), three cruisers and four destroyers. In fact, there were just two freighters, the 7798-ton *Rowallan Castle* and *Clan Chattan* (7762 tons); a third, *Clan Campbell*, had twice been severely damaged by bombs the previous day, and had consequently been despatched to make for the nearest Allied port — Tobruk. The escort of three cruisers, including the AA cruiser *Carlisle*, and 16 destroyers (clearly these had been mis-identified as merchant vessels by the Italian reconnaissance crew), was provided by Admiral Sir Philip Vian's Force 'B'.

From Malta a convoy of four empty supply ships — codenamed ME10 — comprising *Ajax*, *Breconshire, Clan Ferguson* and *City of Calcutta*, escorted by the cruiser *Penelope* and six destroyers from Force 'K', was to rendezvous with the incoming convoy. Escorts were to be exchanged and each convoy would then continue on its separate way — the supply convoy to Malta, the empty ships to Alexandria.

Meanwhile, Convoy MW9 was shadowed all day and from 1345 to 1700 was subjected to high-level and dive-bombing. The first attack was made by five Ju88s, which disabled *Rowallan Castle* with a near-miss at 1514, the destroyer *Zulu* going to her aid. The crippled ship was taken in tow but she was badly damaged, and progress was agonizingly slow. *Clan Chattan* did not escape the onslaught and received a direct hit in her after hold, and caught fire. As she was carrying much ammunition which started to explode, orders were given to abandon ship.

Shortly after this attack four Beaufighters arrived from Malta and, at 1554, they spotted a shadowing Z506B. Sgt. C.H. Mulholland (T4651/C) led the chase, followed closely by Australian Sgts. G.D.S. Rignall (T4717/V) and Easton Thwaites (T4893/A), and Sgt. G.A. Jackson (an American, in T4830/F). All four carried out attacks on the 186ª Squadriglia machine, claiming strikes on its wings and fuselage and forcing it down to sea level. It was thought that sufficient damage had been inflicted for it to be unlikely that the floatplane could regain its base at Augusta and AHQ, Malta subsequently credited the pilots jointly with its destruction. However, regain its base it did, and with comparatively little damage, the Cant's gunner claiming one of the attacking 'Blenheims' shot down!

The Beaufighters returned to continue patrolling over the convoy, until fuel exhaustion forced them to depart just before 1700. Within minutes, as if by design, two S.79sil torpedo-bombers approached but launched their missiles ineffectively at long-range. They were followed closely by 11 Ju88s which attempted to attack the crippled *Rowallan Castle (Clan Chattan* had already sunk following her abandonment), but intense and accurate fire by ships of Force 'B' kept them away from their intended target. By 2000 however, Admiral Vian realised that the stricken vessel could not make sufficient speed to reach Malta safely and following the evacuation of the crew, ordered *Zulu* to put a torpedo in her.

All did not auger well for Malta, and the situation was soon to become desperate.

Further to the south, as Force 'K' and the convoy of empty ships headed eastwards to the rendezvous point, bombers — reported to be Ju88s — carried out an ineffective attack. *Penelope*'s gunners, and those aboard *Ajax*, combined to shoot down one of the attackers which witnesses claimed fell in flames, blew up on impact and disappeared beneath the waves. As Fliegerkorps II records do not show any such loss, the aircraft concerned may well have been S.79sil of 278ª Squadriglia. Eight such torpedo-carriers had been despatched from Pantelleria to attack the convoy, but had been unable to locate it; one aircraft failed to arrive at Catania where the remainder of the squadriglia subsequently landed, its fate unknown.

From Taranto the battleship *Duilio* had put to sea flying the flag of Ammiraglio (Admiral) Carlo Bergamini, together with two cruisers and seven destroyers, while Ammiraglio Angelo Perona set out from Messina with an additional two cruisers and four destroyers, to hunt for Force 'B' and the convoy. Without the benefit of shipborne radar, and in the murky conditions prevailing, these warships were unable to locate the British formation. As the Italian forces withdrew and headed back to their respective bases, the destroyer *Carabiniere* was torpedoed by the Royal Navy submarine *P 36*; its prow was blown off and the ship required to be towed back to Messina.

Sunday, 15 February

The aftermath of the convoy actions brought one of the most active days of the month for the RAF, when four raids kept the Island on constant alert for a record 19 hours 59 minutes, commencing at 0800. Luqa was effectively raided 15 minutes later by seven Ju88s of II/KG 77, where two Wellingtons were burnt out (DV454 and DV482 of the OADU), including an ASV-equipped Mk VIII. Two more were damaged, as were two Blenheim IVFs and three of 252 Squadron's Beaufighters, one of which — T4834 — was damaged beyond repair. Anti-aircraft gunners put up a spirited defence, shooting down Lt. Waldemar Stadermann's 6 Staffel aircraft in flames, two of the crew baling out over the sea — from which only the observer was recovered — while the pilot and the other member of the crew perished in the wreck of 3Z+FP, which fell near Zurrieq. Light AA claimed a second bomber down into the sea, and a third was seen heading northwards with one engine on fire.

There followed a lull before the next raid, allowing the remaining five 252 Squadron Beaufighters to leave for Egypt on completion of their convoy duties, each aircraft carrying a fitter as a passenger. As they cleared the Island more hostile aircraft were plotted, and instructions were at once radioed for them to land again. Fortunately the radios of two aircraft were still tuned to Malta frequencies and the pilots responded at once, touching down just before the first bombs fell. The other three crews, however, failed to receive the message and set course for the south-east, but two miles out they were attacked by some 15-25 Bf109s of II/JG 3 and while two of the Beaufighters escaped, Sgt. Clive Mulholland's T4651/C was shot down by Uffz. Vogel; all three on board were lost.

An hour later Wg.Cdr. Satchell and Wg.Cdr. Rabagliati took of at the head of a force of Hurricanes from 242 Squadron and 1435 Flight on the approach of further raiders. Three Ju88s and five Bf109s were seen low down over the sea, heading for Sicily, and a diving attack was made on the fighters as Jack Satchell recalled:

> 'We were well out over the sea when I saw two 109s flying very low in approximately the same direction as ourselves. I called to "Ragbags" (*Rabagliati*) to take over the lead and dived flat out to attack the second 109 — they were flying in line astern. They were flying extremely low and I fired my cannons — and missed — but I saw the shells strike the water in front of the 109, and so did the pilot, who took such violent evasive action that he dipped his wingtip into the sea and, of course, crashed. I remember on my Combat Report claim I entered: "one 109 — frightened to death", and was duly credited.'

This latest claim brought Wg.Cdr. Satchell's total to five 'confirmed', three of which had been credited during the Battle of Britain, while Wg.Cdr. Rabagliati increased his own tally to 16 when he claimed a second Bf109 shot down. He reported that two of the Messerschmitts, flying in line astern, attacked him but the leading aircraft overshot, allowing him to turn about and attack the second. He believed his quick burst probably killed the pilot, and reported the fighter turned over and dived into the sea. It seems likely that both Satchell and Rabagliati attacked the same aircraft, believed to have been from II/JG 3, the pilot apparently being rescued from the sea.

At midday the two Beaufighters which had so narrowly escaped the Bf109s took off again, although Bf110s were known to be about. A promised Hurricane escort was not forthcoming, and although 15 minutes into the flight ten Zerstörer were seen, these were evaded as the Beaufighters sped away from the Island at low-level. When some 50 miles onwards, Flt.Lt. Malcolm (T4840/P) and Sgt. Granville Jackson (T4830/F) climbed their aircraft up to 200 feet, and almost immediately espied a Z506B skimming the wavetops. Rapidly turning on this, Jackson carried out three passes, his flight commander making six separate attacks, following which fuel was seen to stream from the ruptured tanks located in the Cant's floats, and with both outer engines stopped — oil from which enveloped Malcolm's windscreen — the Italian was lost to sight; Sottoten. Giulio Paccalegna perished with his crew aboard MM45323 ('10') when the 170ª Squadriglia machine crashed into the sea. The sole survivor, Naval Sottoten. Vasc. Emilio Pellegrini, was rescued by an aircraft from 171ª Squadriglia later in the afternoon.

Meanwhile, as the Beaufighters continued on their way eastwards, the American Sgt. Jackson now leading, a pair of twin-engined aircraft dived out of the sun from 2000 feet and promptly shot Jackson's aircraft into the sea. The two attackers broke steeply back as though to intercept the other Beaufighters, but Flt.Lt. Malcolm was able to evade and escape, and after a further three hours safely reached his destination. At the time it was believed the attackers were Bf110s but they were probably Ju88Cs of 2/NJG 2, Fw. Vincenz Giessubel of this unit claiming a Beaufighter shot down around this time.

Shortly after the two Beaufighters had departed Malta, a 69 Squadron Maryland followed suit. At 1715, as the time for its return from the reconnaissance sortie approached, Sqn.Ldr. Beazley led off a mixed formation of a dozen Hurricanes including two from 605 Squadron and others flown by 1435 Flight pilots, to cover its arrival. Flying south to the rendezvous point, the Hurricanes failed to find the Maryland, so turned north but were then 'jumped' by a Schwarm of Bf109s which were escorting a small number of Ju88s. Several pilots engaged the Messerschmitts, Flg.Off. Peter Rathie (1435 Flight) claiming damage to one, but Plt.Off. Peter Lowe of 605 Squadron was shot down when his aircraft (BG755) was hit by a Messerschmitt which dropped out of low cloud cover, the Hurricane diving straight into the sea. His victor was probably Major von Maltzahn, who claimed two Hurricanes during this fight (his 58th and 59th victories). His second 'victory' may have been as a result of carrying out another diving attack on the other 605 Squadron Hurricane, LE-H flown by Plt.Off. Wigley, who recalled:

> 'On the return to Malta, a 109F (*probably the same one*) attacked me off Delimara Point in similar fashion but was spotted in time, out-turned and seen off by the light AA guns on the Point.'

The Maryland, AH714 flown by Sqn.Ldr. W.E.M. Lowrey, then arrived in the area — late because it had suffered the failure of one engine. At once four Messerschmitts attacked — probably those which had just been engaged with the Hurricanes. Lowrey evaded by entering cloud but when the aircraft emerged it was again attacked, taking strikes in the starboard wing, engine and fuel tank. Both gunners returned fire, Sgt. N.E. Rasmussen claiming strikes on one, Sgt. Durrant then hitting a second which dived away vertically at 2000 feet; they were each credited with the probable destruction of their opponents. When within sight of Luqa, two more Bf109s — or two of the original four — attacked again, the damaged starboard engine sustaining further strikes. Hurricanes then arrived however, and drove one of the attackers away; the other German pilot, obviously more determined, pursued the crippled Maryland low over Kalafrana and with the last of the fuel draining from the punctured tanks, Lowrey ditched his aircraft in Kalafrana Bay. Although the observer, Flg.Off. J.E. Bosley, broke his arm, the other three survived the crash unhurt. The Messerschmitt pilot attempted to strafe the floating wreck but AA fire kept him at a distance. Seaplane Tender 338 was on the scene within minutes, the four airmen being promptly hauled aboard.

The crew of another Maryland (AH725) were not so fortunate. Flt.Lt. R.J.S. Wootton was flying the aircraft back to Malta after repairs in Egypt when fighters — possibly the same Messerschmitts — attacked and shot it down into the sea as it approached the Island. HSL 107 was immediately sent out to investigate, but was recalled after two hours due to rough seas; there were no survivors. One of these two Marylands undoubtedly fell to Oblt. Heinecke of 8/JG 53, although he identified his victim as a Beaufort.

An evening raid in the Valetta area was devastating — a Ju88 dropped a stick of bombs along Kingsway, the main street in the ancient, fortified city. One bomb fell on the Regent Cinema, packed with civilians and service personnel. Official reports mentioned up to 75 fatalities, 52 of whom were servicemen; many more were injured. Seven BR20Ms of the newly-arrived 220ª Squadriglia carried out their first raid with the onset of darkness. Crews reported heavy AA fire but no night fighters, and all got back without incident.

Monday, 16 February

Shortly before dawn, Albacores from 828 Squadron approached a northward-bound force of warships, 160 miles east-south-east of Cape Passero — four cruisers and nine destroyers, some of the Italian vessels which had been hunting for Convoy MW9, which had been located and shadowed by an ASV Wellington. Whilst Lt. Haynes controlled the attack in an ASV Albacore, Lt. P.C. Whitfield led four torpedo-carriers in for a surprise strike against the cruisers, the destroyers hastily but belatedly laying a smoke screen. Hits were claimed on two of the cruisers and a destroyer and it was reported that one cruiser appeared to be on fire aft, with oil pouring out into the sea. As if to add substance to these somewhat over-optimistic claims, the shadowing Wellington reported four red glows in the sea following the attack, while Intelligence sources subsequently suggested that only three of the four cruisers reached Taranto. Despite the 'evidence', Italian records noted the only casualty during these operations was the destroyer *Carabiniere*, which had been torpedoed by submarine *P 36*, as earlier recorded!

Oblivious to the drama on the seas north of Malta were the crew and passengers of a Sunderland of 10 RAAF Squadron, flown by Flt.Lt. Daggs, which arrived off the Island during the early hours of the morning. On board were a mixed bag of British and Commonwealth reinforcement fighter pilots, amongst whom the most prominent was a short, stocky Canadian, Sqn.Ldr. Stan Turner DFC. A veteran of the fighting over France, Britain and the Channel, he was credited with some ten victories. Others who would make names for themselves in the coming months included Flt.Lt. P.B. 'Laddie' Lucas, Flg.Off. Raoul Daddo-Langlois (a Channel Islander who was known, for obvious reasons, as 'Daddy-Longlegs'!), Canadian Plt.Off. R.W. 'Buck' McNair, Rhodesian Flg.Off. G.A.F. 'Buck' Buchanan, while newly-commissioned Plt.Off. Jeff West, a New Zealander, had been awarded a DFM for three victories, gained mainly whilst flying as No 2 to the legendary Wg.Cdr. Douglas Bader. Another of the group was Australian Sgt. A.P. 'Tim' Goldsmith, who recorded of the final leg of the flight:

> 'At about 4.30 in the morning I made my way to the Flight Deck to see what our position was. Standing in the cockpit behind the skipper I could see several searchlights about 40 miles north of us: "Where are the searchlights?" I asked him.
>
> "Malta" he replied.
>
> "Well, why aren't we headed that way?"
>
> "Because there's a bleeding air raid on, chum, and we don't want the bleeding machine smashed around our bleeding ears!"
>
> 'Feeling rather squashed I clambered back to the gunners' hatch to watch the proceedings... For two hours our machine circled north of the Island until the All Clear was given to us by wireless, just as dawn broke.'

Although the new arrivals swelled the ranks of fighter pilots available, and allowed some of those time-expired to depart, it was the rapidly diminishing number of Hurricanes which caused gravest concern. Following a raid on Luqa and Takali later in the day — when a Wellington and the PR Mosquito were both damaged — fewer than a dozen Hurricanes could be made serviceable and ready for operations.

However, some respite was forthcoming when the weather again intervened, and over the next four days gale force winds and torrential rain severely restricted flying activities. Takali and Hal Far were flooded and became temporarily unserviceable, 249 Squadron moving its Hurricanes to Luqa as a result. The newly-arrived Sqn.Ldr. Turner now took command of this unit, vice Sqn.Ldr. Beazley, who was to depart for the Middle East. Stan Turner was a tough, no-nonsense character — nicknamed 'Bull' — of whom one pilot wrote:

> 'Turner is not precisely a man of refinement and hardly ever uses polite language when he utters an opinion on something. It is not easy to discuss things with him or to contradict him. After he has drunk a few glasses he would scare off a regiment of Polish infantry.
>
> 'When he was with the Canadians of 242 Squadron (*in France and the UK before his posting to Malta*) he did not hesitate to bring out his revolver in cafes and fire at glasses placed on the counter. He fought magnificently in France, before he was more or less abandoned with his pals in the debacle. They continued to fight, stealing fuel and arming themselves with machine guns.'

The three remaining Beaufighters of the 252 Squadron detachment, damaged during the previous day's raid on Luqa, had been sufficiently patched up to make the flight to Egypt. Surviving serviceable Wellingtons of 40 Squadron's detachment also started flying out, others following as and when they could be made airworthy. This small force had undertaken 73 sorties in a month. In his farewell to the unit, Air Vice-Marshal Lloyd said that he believed no other squadron had operated at such rates and under such conditions. During its short stay on the Island, more targets had been attacked than the number of nights it was there — something in excess of 160. Amongst the awards made to members of its crews, air gunner Flt.Lt. J.S. Reeves received a DFC for shooting down two enemy fighters whilst flying from Malta, including one which had attacked his aircraft when he was engaged machine-gunning targets on the ground. 40 Squadron's place would be taken by a detachment from 37 Squadron, due to arrive within the next few days.

Tuesday, 17 February

There was much consternation on Malta during the early hours of the 17th, when five delivery aircraft failed to arrive from Gibraltar. A number of Wellingtons, including 17 aircraft of 458 (RAAF) Squadron, had left Gibraltar in flights of three or four. A sudden deterioration in the weather as the bombers neared Sardinia — resulting in the worst gales since the beginning of the war — combined with probable faulty navigation (and the possible intervention of the CRIRA), was responsible for a number of aircraft passing to the north of Sicily.

The Controller on Malta succeeded in guiding four of these wayward Wellingtons toward safe landings at Luqa, whilst a fifth was 'talked' in from somewhere near Naples! Another — AD649 — overshot when attempting to land and crashed, although the crew survived. Amongst the missing aircraft, AD539 of 458 Squadron, carrying the commanding officer, Wg.Cdr. N.G. Mulholland, was intercepted by a Ju88C night fighter flown by Oblt. Jung and shot down into the sea some 30 miles from Malta; Flg.Off. J. Willis-Richards, the Squadron Gunnery Leader, was the only survivor from this aircraft.

A second Wellington (DV497 of the OADU) was brought down near Modica by another German night fighter pilot, Lt. Robert von Keudell (flying R4+AM), but he failed to return from the sortie and was presumed shot down by return fire; five members of the Wellington crew were rescued from the sea near the island of Delle Correnti, Syracuse, and became prisoners. Another bomber was hit by AA fire and force-landed near Castelvetrano airfield, the all-New Zealand crew being captured, while a similar fate befell the crew of the fourth Wellington (DV458 of 21 OTU) when it force-landed off the North African coast; they were interned by the Vichy French. The fifth aircraft missing on this disastrous night, Hudson AE603 of the OADU, crashed into the sea near Villa Corrente island.

During the following night (17th/18th), six Beaufighters led by a Belgian, Plt.Off. Charles Delcour, arrived safely and without incident from Gibraltar; they flew on to Egypt as soon as they had refuelled.

Wednesday, 18 February

There were few encounters between opposing aircraft during this period of inclement weather, although Ju88 reconnaissance aircraft were as vigilant as their opposite numbers from 69 Squadron; consequently, the radar screens were seldom void of custom. At 0920 on the morning of the 18th a number of 605 Squadron Hurricanes were scrambled, followed by two pilots from 185 Squadron; this latter pair — Sgt. R.J.F. Ellis in HA-C, and Sgt. C.L. Hunton (Z2840/T) — intercepted a lone reconnaissance machine over Grand Harbour, which they claimed to have probably destroyed between them. Later in the day a Blenheim of 21 Squadron on a reconnaissance flight off Sicily was chased by Italian fighters, the pilots of which believed — incorrectly — that they had damaged it before it made good its escape.

Friday, 20 February

A number of Ju88s individually intruded over Malta two days later and although several interceptions were made by the Hurricanes, they could not prevent bombs falling on Takali and Kalafrana, and the Dockyard area. At 0930 Plt.Off. Phil Wigley encountered a Ju88:

> 'Intercepted a Ju88 at about 10,000 feet over Filfla Island south of Malta. Fortunately my aircraft (LE-M) was armed with 20mm cannon and hits were scored on the fuselage and port engine before it reached cloud cover — it was later revealed that the 88's radar plot abruptly disappeared and a "probably destroyed" was awarded. In view of the known hitting power of 20mm ammunition, this seemed to be a fair decision.'

Wigley may, indeed, have accounted for 7T+FH of 1/KüFlGr 606, in which

Flt.Lt. Don Stones DFC, a successful fighter pilot of the 1940 period, who joined the Malta Night Fighter Unit when he first reached the Island in 1941, but later served with 605 Squadron. He is seen here (left) with Flt.Lt. (later Sqn.Ldr.) 'Laddie' Lucas. *(Daddo-Langlois Collection)*

Uffz. Hermann Ehehalt and his crew perished, reported shot down by fighters. Alternatively the Junkers may have fallen foul of other Hurricanes, for just over one and a half hours later, Plt.Off. Ron Noble (BG756) led six more Hurricanes of 605 Squadron after another Ju88 which was intercepted at 10,000 feet, Noble and Plt.Off. McKay (BE583) carrying out attacks and claiming its probable destruction before this, too, was lost in cloud. A little later Flt.Lt. Stones fired at another — or the same — Ju88 at long range, but this similarly evaded in the prevailing conditions.

Due to an incident in a Valetta night club which upset the Provost Marshal, 605 Squadron's Sqn.Ldr. Andrews found himself relieved of his command; he was speedily posted to the Middle East, and Flt.Lt. Don Stones assumed temporary command.

Saturday, 21 February

During the early hours of the 21st another Sunderland — T9046 of 95 Squadron flown by Flt.Lt. W. Bocock — arrived from Gibraltar following an 11-hour flight carrying ten more new fighter pilots, including Sqn.Ldr. R.I. Chaffe, posted in to take command of 185 Squadron; an experienced New Zealander, Flt.Lt. Keith Lawrence, a Battle of Britain veteran with a number of victories to his credit, would also be posted to 185 Squadron as a flight commander; Flt.Lt. W.C. 'Bud' Connell, a Canadian who would take command of a flight in 126 Squadron; ex-Eagle Squadron pilot Plt.Off. Richard 'Sandy' McHan, and Sgt. Gordon Tweedale, an Australian who would soon make a name for himself.

The flyingboat was to leave again that night with a number of time-expired personnel, and was being prepared for departure when a Bf109 swept in at low level, guns blazing — damage was caused to the starboard wing and tail section. A second fighter was only prevented from attacking by the intense light AA fire. The damage was deemed repairable, but rough seas caused the 'boat to keel over, and despite attempts to put her right, part of the starboard wing eventually broke off below water; T9046 subsequently sank during a storm two days later.

Intruders got through during the day to bomb both Hal Far — where a Swordfish was destroyed — and Luqa. At this latter airfield five Wellingtons under repair were further damaged by blast and shrapnel, as were two Hurricanes, one of which (BG744) was written off; one of the irreplaceable and indispensable steamrollers — vital for runway repairs — was damaged, as were two petrol bowsers. Between raids, various delivery aircraft crept in to Luqa unmolested, but with fatigued crews; one OADU Hudson (AE582) crashed on landing.

That night (21st/22nd), Albacores from 828 Squadron operated between Pantelleria and the Cyrenaican coast on a shipping search. Not far out from Malta, Lt. Whitfield's ASV machine crashed into the sea following engine failure and quickly sank, taking the trapped observer, Sub Lt. Freddie Bedford, down with it. Whitfield and his TAG were later rescued from their dinghy. Meanwhile, a 400-ton tanker had been found further south without the aid of the ASV aircraft, and was attacked; Sub Lt. J.B. Blakeley's crew claimed a hit and a large flash was seen.

The vanguard of 37 Squadron's detachment — six Wellingtons — arrived safely during the night after their long flight from Shallufa (Egypt), to be followed by seven more next day.

Sunday, 22 February

At 1135 eight Hurricanes from 126 and 249 Squadrons were scrambled on the approach of three Ju88s — from LG1's newly-arrived detachment — and their escort from II/JG 3, which were encountered at 16,000 feet over Filfla. Plt.Off. Streets of 126 Squadron saw strikes on the bomber he attacked but was chased away by the escort, while Flt.Lt. Barnes, his flight commander, put a burst into a Bf109, seeing pieces fly off before he was attacked by others and had to break away.

Plt.Off. Moon (249 Squadron) attacked the right-hand Junkers of the trio but saw no results, his own aircraft sustaining damage. His No 2, Sgt. Branch, pursued the same bomber, closing from 300 to 75 yards but the tail of his Hurricane was hit — possibly by a Bf109 — while Sgt. A.G. Cairns' aircraft also suffered damage when he attacked another Ju88. Sqn.Ldr. Turner and Flt.Sgt. Etchells each reported strikes on the Bf109s with which they became entangled. In return, Uffz. Leopold Münster claimed one of the Hurricanes shot down for his 10th victory — possibly Sgt. Branch's aircraft — while another Messerschmitt returned to Sicily with fairly substantial damage.

It was the turn of 185 Squadron two hours later, seven Hurricanes going off to intercept another small formation of Ju88s, escorted on this occasion by Bf109s from 9/JG 53, one of which Sgt. Sutherland (BD826/A) shot down in the ensuing scrap — Uffz. Walter Schwartz's fighter ('White 10') crashed on the Island at Wied is-Sewda, near Qormi; Schwartz died in the cockpit. However, the squadron lost its new CO in this fight when Sqn.Ldr. Ron Chaffe was shot down in Z3452 on his first operational flight from the Island. It was believed that he had been so intent on getting his first victory, a Messerschmitt which he was seen chasing out to sea, that he did not see his attackers and was forced to bale-out. He was observed at the time of the action in his dinghy four to five miles south of Delimara Point, but was not subsequently found by the rescue services.

Flt.Lt. Lloyd led three others off to carry out a search for their commanding officer, but to no avail. Two pilots from JG 53's 9 Staffel were each credited with a Hurricane shot down during the fight, Ofw. Heinz Hipper for his eighth victory, Uffz. Max Nairz for his second; it seems likely both had attacked Chaffe's aircraft. Hipper's aircraft had exhausted its fuel by the time he reached the Sicilian coast, and he attempted an emergency landing on the beach near Scoglitti but his Messerschmitt crashed and he was killed; whether this aircraft had been hit by Chaffe during the combat is not known.

At Luqa as a result of these raids, five of the newly-arrived 37 Squadron Wellingtons were damaged by shrapnel, together with an ASV aircraft of the Special Duties Flight, while a previously damaged Maryland was burnt out. Hal Far, which had already been raided during the night — when an Albacore had been damaged by debris — was again heavily attacked, two more of the newly-arrived Albacores and a Swordfish being destroyed; another two of each type were seriously damaged and three others peppered by shrapnel.

The reason for this punishing assault on the Navy's strike aircraft soon became clear when two Italian air-escorted convoys were reported at sea bound for Tripoli, one having sailed from Messina, the other from Corfu (Greece). There was little the Malta forces could do to interfere with their progress except hope that submarines from 10th Flotilla might achieve success; African-based aircraft also vainly attempted small-scale attacks. One of the submarines, *P38*, was depth-charged by the torpedo-boat *Circe* and forced to the surface, where she was attacked by a destroyer — *Usodimare* — and was then bombed and strafed by a CR42; 20 minutes later her bows lifted high out of the water and she sank with the loss of all hands.

Fliegerkorps II's resources were also stretched at this time, 4/NJG 2's Ju88Cs being required to carry out frequent convoy protection patrols, air ferry escorts and anti-submarine sorties. Currently down to six serviceable aircraft, 4 Staffel soon returned to Germany to re-equip but in the meantime selected Bf110 crews from III/ZG 26 aided with convoy escort duties, some flying Do17Z-3 night fighters in this role. For the Bf110s properly to fulfil the escort role it was necessary for each aircraft to carry two 200-gallon jettisonable underwing fuel tanks, which increased flying time to five and a half hours.

Two delivery aircraft were lost during the day, including a Wellington (Z8952) of the OADU, proceeding from Gibraltar as part of a flight of six such aircraft; this aircraft may have been shot down by a Bf110 of 8/ZG 26 flown by Oblt. Peter Habicht, who tentatively identified the machine which he claimed at 1442 as a 'Boeing'. However, for the Wellington to have been his victim it would have to be assumed that it had been greatly delayed for some reason, or was seeking to take advantage of the poor weather conditions.The other machine which failed to arrive at Malta was one of two reinforcement Albacores despatched from El Adem to strengthen 828 Squadron; Sub Lts. J.S. Pagdin and J. Buscall DSC (the observer), an 821 Squadron crew, were lost. Among the delivery aircraft which did arrive safely from Gibraltar during the day were three night-fighter Beaufighters (minus their radar equipment). On approaching Lampedusa a number of CR42s attempted an interception; only by diving to sea level were the unarmed Beaufighters able to escape. Once refuelled, they departed for Egypt.

21 Squadron flew its last operational sorties from the Island during the day, when a Blenheim carried out a reconnaissance of the Djerba-Kuriat area. The surviving aircraft flew out to Egypt next day, where the squadron would finally be disbanded on 4 March.

Monday, 23 February

There were six raids on the Island during the day, involving an estimated 100 attackers. At 0915 Flt.Lt. Lloyd, temporarily in command of 185 Squadron, led off ten Hurricanes to escort a Maryland setting out to continue the search for Sqn.Ldr. Chaffe's dinghy. As the Hurricanes climbed, they were attacked by two Bf109s and broke formation. Two Ju88s and four more fighters were then seen approaching from the south-east and were individually engaged by the Hurricanes. Sgt. Horricks (Z5140/C) attacked one bomber and saw his fire hitting home, before he broke away to take on a Bf109; this was attacked at close range, many strikes being observed on its cockpit hood, starboard wing and engine. He was credited with its probable destruction. Flt.Lt Lloyd (BG769/J) got in several bursts at one of the Junkers, gaining strikes on the wing roots, rear fuselage and starboard engine, which began to stream smoke. This aircraft (B3+KH) was similarly considered unlikely to have reached its base (although in fact it did, crash-landing at Catania). Newly-commissioned Plt.Off. Archie Steele (HA-B) chased a Bf109 down from 10,000 feet to sea level, claiming that several bursts of machine-gun fire had hit the fleeing fighter, while Sgt. D.E. Eastman's adversary was last seen streaming white smoke. Sgt. Sutherland force-landed HA-A at Hal Far due to engine failure, his aircraft escaping damage.

During the next raid heavy AA fire hit B3+CH, a Ju88 of I/KG 54 which fell in flames into the sea between Filfla and the coast. Sgt. Tim Goldsmith witnessed its final plunge:

> 'The starboard motor burst into flames and two or three seconds later the whole wing broke off. The bomber flicked over, spun and crashed in flames... There were no survivors.'

Two Americans of 126 Squadron, seen outside the great church at Mosta; Plt.Off. Ed Streets (left) and Plt.Off. 'Junior' Steele would both be killed in the defence of Malta. *(J. Crichton)*

He was wrong, however; Obgfr. Günther Meister died in the crash but two seriously injured members of the crew were picked up from the sea; the body of a third was also recovered. Bf109s were again encountered during the early afternoon by Hurricanes searching for Sqn.Ldr. Chaffe's dinghy, one of which Sgt. Boyd of 242 Squadron (in LE-P) claimed shot down:

> 'Did search for dinghy, then joined remainder of squadron to intercept a 6 plus. Saw E/A and peeled off alone to attack as others did not see them. Fired short burst at one 300 yds from astern. Saw no results. Then got into position under a second and fired 4 second burst from stern quarter below. Obviously got him. Two others in line of fire. Cannon fire whizzing by so returned to 0 feet. Sgt. Gardiner shot at one on my tail.'

Other pilots confirmed that the pilot of a Bf109 attacked by Sgt. Boyd was seen to bale out. This was undoubtedly Gefr. Otto Butschek of 10(Jabo)/JG 53, who failed to return in 'White 4', colleagues reporting seeing his aircraft fall to a Hurricane; a second Messerschmitt was claimed damaged by 126 Squadron's Scot, Sgt. 'Jock' Gardiner.

All three airfields had come under attack during these raids. At Luqa two of the OADU Wellingtons which had arrived the previous day (Z8367 and Z8388) were destroyed, as was an unserviceable Blenheim (Z7420), while a Hurricane was badly damaged. Another Hurricane (BG754) was damaged beyond repair at Takali, where the pilots' dispersal hut was hit by a bomb-carrying Bf109, as LAC Bill Metcalf recorded:

> 'Today the pilots' dispersal hut was hit and Plt.Off. Macnamara was killed; four more injured. We were all leaning against the wall when the ME (*Messerschmitt*) dropped a bomb but he had to give a burst of cannon fire, which told us what to expect. We all dived for the hole and just made it. Truscott, who was the only chap behind me, was badly hurt.'

Although Plt.Off. Thady Macnamara of 242 Squadron was the only fatality, Flt.Lt. Lloyd and Plt.Off. A.C. Smith both sustained wounds during this incident, as did three airmen and a civilian. To take command of 185 Squadron came Sqn.Ldr. Edward Mortimer-Rose, who had briefly commanded 249 Squadron at the end of 1941, but who had been shot down on Boxing Day and had suffered a bullet wound to one heel.

A belated strike was launched against the ships of the two Italian convoys which, by now, had reached the Tripoli area; three Albacores and three Swordfish, all armed with torpedoes, were despatched with the coming of

A quartet of 185 Squadron pilots relax in the sun; from left, Plt.Off. 'Skip' McKay, Flt.Lt. Rhys Lloyd, Sqn. Ldr. E.B.B. Mortimer-Rose and Flt.Lt. Keith Lawrence. *(R.F. Noble)*

darkness. One Swordfish crashed on take-off — without injury to the crew — and an Albacore was forced to return with engine trouble. The remaining Swordfish sighted two or three merchant ships and a number of destroyers off Tripoli; the warships immediately laid an effective smoke screen, thus only Sub Lt. M. Holdsworth was able to make an attack. His aircraft was promptly shot down by AA fire from the destroyers, the pilot and his observer (Sub Lt. N.V. Clark) perishing. The 37 Squadron detachment could muster but one solitary Wellington to aid the FAA's attack on Tripoli, Flg.Off. C.P.T. Halliwell arriving over the port in DV421/W to find the area thick with haze and smoke. Unable to see any shipping, he dropped his bombs on harbour installations.

I/LG 1 despatched a number of Ju88s into the darkened skies above Malta, individual aircraft orbiting Luqa and Hal Far, releasing bombs at opportune moments. Hurricanes were sent up and one intercepted Lt. Georg Sattler's aircraft; unable to shake off the night fighter despite a series of violent manoeuvres, Sattler was only able to evade due to the speed of his bomber and set course for Sicily. The Hurricane pursued the fleeing Junkers northwards, almost as far as Catania, but was unable to close.

Tuesday, 24 February

At 1510 radar screens picked up the 'blips' of approaching aircraft and eight Hurricanes from 249 Squadron were scrambled, these separating into pre-

Left: Plt.Off. Don Tedford, an American pilot of 126 Squadron who was shot down and killed by Lt. Franz Schiess (**right**) of Stab/JG 53 on 24 February 1942 for his 16th victory of an eventual total of 67). *(NWMA)*

arranged pairs. Sqn.Ldr. Turner and his No 2, the American Plt.Off. Don Tedford, were vectored to the reported height of four 'hostiles' but were unable to see them. The Controller informed Turner that they were dead ahead, but had apparently confused the two plots on the radar. The four 'hostiles' — Bf109s from Stab/JG53 — were in fact behind, and the Hurricanes were consequently 'bounced'. Tedford's BG771 was shot down into the sea by Lt. Schiess (his 16th victory), while Turner's aircraft (Z3580) took hits in the engine — which caught fire — and the cockpit, one bullet clipping his goggles. Unable to open the damaged hood to bale out, the slightly wounded Turner dived his aircraft steeply, whereby the flames were extinguished enabling him to make a wheels-up landing at Luqa. What the irascible Canadian later said to the unfortunate Controller has not been recorded! Howard Coffin noted in his diary of his missing countryman:

> 'P/O Tedford, one of the four Americans on this bloody island, shot down and last seen to have crashed in the sea. Words cannot express how I feel at this moment. I've lost a buddy and the air force has lost a wizard pilot'.

Apparently Don Tedford had called Control to say he was wounded and was baling out. When Coffin heard the news he — according to his own account — took off without permission to search for him:

> 'Nobody ever blamed me for leaving my post of duty that day. At Takali I managed to get a plane into the air that was no good for fighting but was serviceable for patrol, and went looking for Tedford. I searched the sea until dark. I found no signs of life down below.'

The airfields were again attacked, one grounded machine being destroyed, and there were a number of RAF casualties. A bomb hit a shop in Valetta and three civilians were buried under the rubble. Two were recovered without much difficulty but the third remained buried for ten hours before being rescued.

For the next week or so there was a slackening in the intensity of the raids, partly due to further storms and torrential rains. This allowed some of the new pilots to familiarize themselves with local surroundings — essential to improve their chances of survival in combat, and to sharpen and refresh their reflexes for the coming fight. Whilst the Luftwaffe's respite was most welcome, all felt this was but a temporary pause — the lull before the storm.

Wednesday 25 — Thursday 26 February

Flg.Off. Daddo-Langlois, posted to 185 Squadron, damaged Hurricane UP-P when he crash-landed at Hal Far while on the 25th, two Ju88s carried out a sneak raid on Takali, suddenly appearing from out of cloud. Two patrolling Hurricanes from 605 Squadron, flown by Flt.Lt. Stones and newly-attached Flt.Lt. Lucas, intercepted one Junkers, Stones getting in a burst which caused it to jettison its bombs; these hit a farm house, injuring an occupant. Sqn.Ldr. Westmacott was also airborne, meeting the same pair of bombers which he chased back towards Sicily, but he was unable to close on them.

Luqa was the target for a similar raid the following morning, an OADU Wellington (Z9025) being severely damaged and a Hudson less so, while two of the precious petrol bowsers went up in flames; one soldier was wounded. During a lull between raids, two tour-expired FAA officers, Lt. Bill Garthwaite and Lt. Tony Gillingham, departed Hal Far in the sole-surviving Fulmar (N1931) —

following the example of Coxon and Kinghorn the previous month — their destination Egypt, which they duly reached via El Adem. The somewhat adventurous flight was successfully accomplished.

Small formations — between three and six Wellingtons — continued the series of night raids on Tripoli. These attacks were generally ineffective, however, as smoke screens appeared to be ever-present, preventing accurate bombing of the ships known to be unloading in the harbour. However, on the night of the 26th/27th, one crew raiding the harbour reported a violent explosion following their attack and a ship was set on fire, the hulk continuing to burn for the next week, serving as a beacon. Night fighters were out and about on this occasion, a Wellington being intercepted by a twin-engined aircraft (probably a Ju88C) when some 15 miles from Malta. The bomber pilot dived his heavy machine to 1000 feet, losing his pursuer in the darkness. The following night two unidentified fighters were seen over the target area but these did not attack the Wellingtons.

Friday, 27 February

The last engagements of the month occurred on the 27th, when a small number of Hurricanes from 126, 185 and 605 Squadrons intercepted two Ju88s from KGr 806 and three escorting Bf109s over Grand Harbour during the afternoon; newly-arrived Flt.Lt. Connell led the trio of 126 Squadron aircraft, his first operational flight from the Island, but only Plt.Off. Coffin was able to make a

Three stalwarts of 185 Squadron in early 1942; from left, Flt.Lt. Rhys Lloyd, Plt.Off. 'Skip' McKay (Canadian) and Flt.Lt. Keith Lawrence (New Zealander). *(R.F. Noble)*

claim, the American now showing a hint of confidence:

> 'Intercepted three 109s and two 88s... Had three second burst at one 109. Damage claimed. The 109s aren't so hot when you can see them.'

Meanwhile, Plt.Off. Ormrod of 185 Squadron caught Lt. Wilhelm Schmidt's Junkers (M7+DK) and shot it up so thoroughly that he considered it unlikely to have got back to Sicily; in fact, it failed to return but was reported by the Luftwaffe to have fallen to AA fire. However, on this occasion, the guns claimed only to have damaged one of the attackers and it would seem likely that Schmidt's aircraft fell to Ormrod's shooting. Another of the unit, Plt.Off. McKay in Z2840/T, tangled with one of the escort south of Kalafrana, claiming damage to his opponent's aircraft.

Four delivery aircraft failed to reach Malta during the day, including Wellingtons (Z9097, BB475 and DV510) from a flight of six OADU aircraft (one of which was hit by AA fire from Messina, being forced to ditch near Cape Peloro); the all-Canadian crew were rescued from the sea. One of six Beaufighters, also flying in from Gibraltar — T4894 flown by a Belgian pilot, Plt.Off. Christian Deffontaine — was shot down by a Bf109 when some 30 miles from Malta; both pilot and navigator perished.

The biggest disappointment, however, was the non-arrival of another batch of aircraft from the west. Rumour was rife on Malta — Spitfires were on their way, some said. Old sweats had heard it all before — seeing would be believing! This time though, the optimists were about to be rewarded. Spitfires were on their way, but due to technical problems with the experimental auxiliary fuel tanks fitted to each aircraft, it would be another week before they actually arrived.

Air Vice-Marshal Lloyd, perhaps more so than most others, was bitterly disappointed and signalled the AOC-in-C accordingly, outlining the current grave situation:

> 'Daylight attacks on aerodromes very serious. Little work being done owing to continuous alerts. Much minor damage to aircraft sufficient to make them unserviceable for night operations. They are repaired next day and then hit again. Deliveries are serious problem as they are damaged if they stay here during day. The longer they stay, the more the damage. Have 17 Wellingtons in this category, including those damaged in landing on arrival here with further minor damage due to air action. To avoid this, Wellingtons are passed through same night as arrival with relief crews. This is difficult with continuous intruder raids, but we can take it. Must have more fighters as soon as possible. Delay in Spitfires is annoying...'

At this time, trials were underway in Britain with both Hurricanes and Spitfires, to test the possibility of air-towing such aircraft from Gibraltar to Malta as an alternative means of reinforcing the Island. Wellingtons were employed as tugs. In the hands of skilled test pilots these trials proved relatively straightforward, and both types were successfully towed; whether ordinary Service pilots could have coped is a matter of conjecture. In the event the scheme was never adopted.

Saturday, 28 February

The month ended with the loss of a further two delivery Wellingtons; one crashed in the sea off Pantelleria, the other landed at Pachino, near Syracuse —

Plt.Off. G.A. Kennedy RNZAF, and his crew were taken prisoner after they had managed to destroy various pieces of equipment aboard their aircraft. The Luftwaffe also suffered two non-operational losses on the 28th, when a pair of Bf109Es from III/ZG 26 — apparently made available to the unit owing to the shortage of Zerstörer aircraft — collided and crashed into the sea some 140 km north-west of Trapani. Lt. Hans-Günther Haumann lost his life in 3U+G2, while the pilot of 3U+G3, Uffz. Willi Jünger — who had been wounded in combat with Blenheims a few weeks earlier — was rescued in an injured condition.

During February there had been 235 alerts culminating in 222 attacks on Malta. An estimated 990 tons of bombs had fallen on the Island during the month.

Sunday, 1 March

March came in traditionally — like a lion — although in 1942 it was not to go out like a lamb! On the first day of the month there was a midday scramble involving five Hurricanes from 242 Squadron and four from 605, followed by another four from 185, which intercepted the usual trio of Ju88s — aircraft from 8/KG 77 — with their escort comprising Bf109s from II and III/JG 53. The two formations clashed over Benghaisa at 14,000 feet, the Hurricanes of 605 Squadron for once evading the escort, Flt.Lt. Stones and Flt.Sgt. D.J. Howe each inflicting considerable damage to the bombers they attacked; Oblt. Erich Behr crash-landed his damaged aircraft at Donna Fugata on return, resulting in its total destruction with all members of the crew sustaining injuries. A second Junkers flown by Uffz. Heinrich Gassmann crashed near Santa Cruse and was also totally destroyed; the injured pilot was the only survivor from this aircraft. Immediately after the attack on the Ju88, Howe's aircraft (Z3756) was hit and the Canadian baled out, breaking a leg when coming down at Marsaxlokk.

Another of the 605 Squadron pilots, Plt.Off. Lester, managed to manoeuvre onto the tail of one unsuspecting Bf109 and launched an attack; as a result, Fw. Alexander Kelhbuth of 5 Staffel subsequently force-landed his damaged fighter at Syracuse, where he was injured and his aircraft suffered further severe damage. A second Messerschmitt — from 6 Staffel — bellied-in at Comiso in a damaged state; this possibly resulted from combat with a 242 Squadron Hurricane, flown either by American Plt.Off. Jimmy Tew or Canadian Sgt. Ray Harvey, both of whom failed to return. The 28 year-old Tew died when Z2824 was shot down into the sea, while Harvey attempted to abandon his burning aircraft at low level. He was killed when Z4002 hit the sea five miles off Delimara Point; apparently he had unfastened his seat straps ready to bale out and his body, which was later recovered by HSL 107, had been thrown clear.

One of these Hurricanes fell to Lt. Hermann Münzert of 9/JG 53 for his 14th victory. Flt.Lt. Stones and Plt.Off. Wigley took off to search for the missing pilots, but only Flt.Sgt. David Howe survived this clash with the Bf109s. These latest losses emphasised just how desperately Spitfires were needed; only a handful of Hurricanes now remained available.

On the night of the 1st/2nd, during a further raid on Tripoli, the Wellingtons of 37 Squadron achieved another tangible success. Six aircraft led by the commanding officer Wg.Cdr. R.R. Nash, flying as second pilot to Flt.Lt. Macfarlane, successfully bombed the harbour and, in spite of the usual dense smoke screen, an explosion was observed amongst the assembled shipping; the

5324-ton Italian freighter *Monginevro* was hit and damaged. It seems probable that Sgt. L.G. Fuller's well-aimed stick of bombs caused the initial damage when he attacked from 7500 feet. His HEs fell in the centre of Main Quay and started two orange-coloured fires, which could be seen when the aircraft left the target area. When Flg.Off. C.I.L. Boyd arrived some time later the fires were still visible and he dropped his bombs in the same area.

Monday, 2 March

Hal Far and Luqa were both on the receiving end of raids during the daylight hours of the 2nd, and although Hurricanes were up they could not prevent the five Ju88s of KüFlGr 606 from releasing their bombs over the target area, a number of which also fell on Floriana, as recorded in an official report:

> 'Two bombs of heavy calibre hit a block of buildings overlooking the Grand Harbour midway through the afternoon... The buildings collapsed and trapped a number of persons who were standing in the entrance of a shelter. Casualties were not light... Some corpses were recovered only after 48 hours.'

Later in the day six Bf109 Jabo from 10/JG 53 raided Luqa, the pilots reporting bombs falling amongst aircraft and on a fuel dump, while three Ju88s of II/KG 77 attacked Safi and another from I/KG 54 bombed Kalafrana. During the late evening two replacement Swordfish left El Adem for Malta, but failed to arrive. It was assumed that Sub Lts. S.W. Chapman/P.F.C. Brown, an 815 Squadron crew in V4590, and Sub Lts. J.A.K. Watson/T.H. Greet from 821 Squadron (V4592), missed the Island and crashed into the sea when fuel became exhausted. Almost as many of the Navy's biplane torpedo-bombers were being lost in these ferrying accidents as on operations from Malta.

Darkness brought much activity over both Malta and Sicily; Luqa was again raided, this time by eight Ju88s of KGr 806 and III/KG 77, and another Maryland was burnt out, while Kalafrana was severely damaged when two Ju88s (one each from KüFlGr 606 and KGr 806) found their target. However, the guns gained a further success, shooting down the KGr 806 machine (M7+CH) into the sea; there were no survivors from Lt Heinz Jesek's crew.

Shortly before the first intruders appeared over Luqa, ten Wellingtons from 37 Squadron had departed to carry out a raid on Palermo harbour, the first aircraft lifting off at 2100, each crew briefed to attack individually. Here, earlier in the day, Flt.Lt. Warburton had spotted and photographed three large, fully-laden ships in harbour, which were presumed about to depart for Tripoli. Towards the end of his reconnaissance, two formations of five and seven Messerschmitts were seen attempting to intercept but these were evaded. Life was becoming very difficult for the reconnaissance crews, as on the previous day Warburton's Beaufighter had again been hit by Flak whilst over Palermo.

On this occasion, the smoke screen over Palermo proved ineffective and the Wellington crews were able to see many ships in the harbour. At the start of the attack two Wellingtons arrived over the target area together, Sqn.Ldr. E.C.C. Tomkins, the raid leader (with Wg.Cdr. Nash as second pilot) and Sgt. Fuller simultaneously bombing shipping at the south end of the North Mole. Their bombs found a target in the shape of the 6600-ton German freighter *Cuma*, loaded with tanks and ammunition, and she was soon on fire. Other bombers followed, guided by the blazing ship, and nearby a second German freighter,

Rhur (5945 tons) was also hit and rapidly settled on the bottom, while the Italian torpedo-boat *Partenope* was badly damaged. Elsewhere in the harbour the Italian steamer *Securitas* (5365 tons) was hit, while other vessels suffered less serious damage. There were also many casualties amongst naval persons and civilian dockyard workers, including a number of fatalities.

On returning to Luqa, Sqn.Ldr. Tomkins' Wellington overshot the runway and was badly damaged, but six other crews set out individually for a second attack, once their aircraft had been refuelled and rearmed. The first aircraft of the second wave departed Luqa at 0115, the last leaving the target area at 0514, the crew reporting many large fires blazing in the harbour. Somewhat surprisingly, no enemy aircraft were encountered at all during the seven hours the raid was in progress, while anti-aircraft fire was noted to be fairly light and inaccurate. All the Wellingtons returned safely, although Italian AA gunners claimed to have shot down one of the attackers.

Tuesday, 3 March

Flt.Lt. Warburton was back over Palermo early in the morning to survey the night's work — he reported two '6000-ton' heavily-laden ships sunk in harbour; a third — a smaller vessel of about 2000 tons — was also confirmed sunk. A pair of Bf109s then appeared and harried the Beaufighter, but Warburton was able to reach the sanctuary of nearby cloud. On re-emerging, he was chased back to Malta by four others but managed to lose these in cloud north of Gozo.

Eleven Hurricanes were scrambled after six Ju88s of KGr 806 during the early afternoon, Sqn.Ldr. Wells of 242 Squadron leading; an earlier raid on Safi by four Bf109 Jabo had not been intercepted. Two of the bombers were claimed damaged before the escort forced the Hurricanes away. Bombs fell on Luqa where a 37 Squadron Wellington was hit and burnt out. Meanwhile, six bomb-carrying Bf109s of 10/JG 53 also attacked Hal Far. During a later raid by two Ju88s of I/KG 54, Luqa was again the main target and this time two more of 37 Squadron's machines were damaged, as were two ASV Wellingtons and Flt.Lt. Warburton's Beaufighter. Manoel Island submarine base also came under attack, while one of the craft — *P39* — was strafed by a single Bf109 as she entered harbour, a line of bullets striking along the casing but failing to puncture the pressure hull; however, the vessel would require some repair.

Wednesday, 4 March

Gallant firefighters at Palermo Harbour were, meanwhile, losing their 24-hour battle to quell the internal fires now raging within, and consuming *Cuma*, and at 0730 on the morning of the 4th, her plates glowing white hot, the freighter blew-up, projecting scraps of tank track, unexploded shells and other debris for up to a mile, thereby causing many casualties. The explosion also shattered the damaged *Securitas*, which now sank. Nearby, a small tanker and three other small ships were damaged by blast and debris, while a total of 29 other vessels, ranging from the 6835-ton freighter *Gino Allegri* to the 22-ton motorized fishing boat *La Nuova Annunziata*, suffered varying degrees of damage. A torpedo-boat — *Abba* — was amongst the casualties, as were the destroyers *Vivaldi* and *Maloncello, Folgore* and *Freccia*. During the raid, and as a consequence of the subsequent explosion, at least 30 military persons and civilians were killed with a further 255 injured (see Appendix V).

Sqn.Ldr. Tomkins and Sgt. Fuller received immediate awards of the DFC and

DFM respectively, in recognition of their achievements. Sgt. Len Fuller, an Australian, had previously gained fame in an unusual, if not unique, incident in his home country. There, as a trainee pilot, his Anson had collided with another, the two aircraft interlocking with Fuller's on top of the other. All occupants of the two aircraft baled out with the exception of Fuller, who successfully belly-landed this strange 'piggy-back' combination.

A dozen or so Hurricanes — more or less equally drawn from 185, 242 and 605 Squadrons — were scrambled during the early afternoon of the 4th, five Ju88s and escorting Bf109s being met north of St Paul's Bay. Sqn.Ldr. Wells of 242 Squadron set the port engine of one Junkers on fire, this same aircraft coming under attack from his No 2, Sgt. Gardiner. Newly-promoted Flt.Lt. Kee went after another bomber, and saw pieces fall off its port wing as he attacked, while Plt.Off. Noble (605 Squadron) gained strikes on the tailplane, fuselage and one engine of his target before his own aircraft (Z2414/E) was hit by return fire. Yet another Junkers was damaged by 185 Squadron's Flt.Sgt. Jack Fletcher (BD826/A); strikes were observed on the rear-gunner's turret and on the fuselage, but the German doggedly returned fire, damaging the Canadian pilot's Hurricane.

Two of the escorting I and III/JG 53 Messerschmitts were also claimed damaged, one by Plt.Off. M.W. Kidson of 242 Squadron, who saw pieces fly off his victim's tail unit, forcing it into a shallow dive; it seems likely that this was an aircraft of 3 Staffel which crash-landed at Gela, severely damaged. Similarly, a 7 Staffel machine returned to Gela in a badly damaged condition, probably as a result of an engagement with Sgt. Wilson (Z3757/R).

This was one of the few occasions when Malta's Hurricanes came off better in clashes with the Messerschmitts, for two other Bf109s failed to return to their base. An aircraft from 5 Staffel — one of three engaged by Plt.Off. 'Sonny' Ormrod (BG711/G) — was hit in the engine and the pilot, Uffz. Benedikt Wegmann, was forced to crash-land 'Black 3' on rocks at the Pembroke Ranges; he was not seriously injured and was soon on his way to hospital. AA gunners accounted for the other Bf109 shot down, a damaged 2 Staffel machine force-landing in the sea; the uninjured pilot was later picked up by a rescue craft from Sicily. A few days later Ormrod cycled from Marsaxlokk, where a number of pilots were billeted (Ormrod was personally staying with the Smith family, owners of the Honeymoon Hotel at Marsaxlokk Quay) to Mtarfa Hospital near Takali, a good 15 miles distant, to visit Wegmann with whom he became quite friendly.

At Takali, as a result of this latest raid, two Marylands had been hit by shrapnel while a 37 Squadron Wellington was burnt out at Luqa; another aircraft was damaged beyond repair and four others were peppered by shrapnel and debris. Luqa was also later visited by a relay of night bombers, Ju88s being reported over the airfield from dusk to dawn. Clearly the Luftwaffe was determined to prevent further raids on Palermo harbour, but one of the intruders was intercepted by a Hurricane from 1435 Flight, Sgt. Jimmy Wood catching 7T+JK of 2/KüFlGr 606 which was illuminated by searchlights. He closed to within 50 yards and opened fire with dramatic effect. The Junkers fell in flames near Siggiewi, Uffz. Albert Degenhardt and his crew being killed.

Thursday, 5 March

Just before midday six 242 Squadron Hurricanes intercepted five Ju88s of II/KG 77 and their escort, comprised of ten Messerschmitts, north of Grand Harbour;

On the night of 4/5 March 1942, Sgt. Jimmie Wood in a Hurricane of 1435 Flight shot down an intruding Ju88 of 2/KüFlGr 606. Uffz. Albert Degenhardt and his crew died in 7T+JK, the wreckage of which is seen here after crashing on the Island. *(Authors' collection)*

Sgt. Boyd (LE-P) reported:

> 'I attacked rear three in turn, causing black smoke pouring from engines of two and strikes seen on third. 1st one attacked slowed up and lost height. Jumped by Me's throughout and lost P/O Kidson.'

Boyd was credited with two of the bombers damaged, one of which was from 4 Staffel, in which the observer was wounded. The escorting fighters shot down Plt.Off. Marcus Kidson's Hurricane (Z2402) into the sea; he was killed. It is believed that he may have intercepted a Do24T rescue flyingboat just before being shot down, this machine returning to Syracuse with a dead crew member aboard.

Luqa was again heavily hit during the raid, another Wellington being totally destroyed; one more Wellington, a Maryland and two unserviceable Blenheims were damaged. The German bombers were back after dark, yet another Wellington being hit and burnt out, while a further one was damaged, as was another Blenheim.

Friday, 6 March

Midway through the afternoon of the 6th, eight Hurricanes from 185 Squadron were scrambled, Bf109s being encountered west of Filfla. Flt.Lt. Stones (BG770/D) attacked one Messerschmitt and got in a long burst, raking it from nose to tail before losing sight of it. Shortly afterwards, a parachute was reported coming down to the north of the Island and on the strength of this sighting, Don Stones was credited with the destruction of the fighter. About an hour later, four bomb-carrying Bf109s from 10(Jabo)/JG 53 swept in over Takali at low level; sharp-shooting Bofors gunners hit Oblt. Hermann Raab's 'Yellow 4', the pilot baling out and coming down near Mosta, while his aircraft crashed near Rabat.

The defence of Malta was now about to take a new turn, for the aircraft carrier *Eagle* was again on its way from Gibraltar, carrying aboard 16 Spitfire Vb (Trop)s for the Island. In preparation for this historic and much-anticipated event there had been considerable movement of pilots between the squadrons following the recent spate of new arrivals aboard the Sunderlands. 249 Squadron was to be the first unit to re-equip and in consequence, most of the remaining Hurricane pilots were now posted to the other units — mainly 126 Squadron — while those recently-arrived pilots with Spitfire experience were concentrated in 249 Squadron.

The arrival of the Spitfires was in the nick of time, for the Island's defences had almost ceased to exist. Since the beginning of February, 17 of the remaining stock of Hurricanes had been destroyed in the air or on the ground, while at least 14 more had been damaged; current availability was just 21 machines. Worse still, the Island's air striking force had all but been annihilated — nine Blenheims, some dozen of the Fleet Air Arm's torpedo-bombers, and no less than 19 Wellingtons (including transit and ASV aircraft) had been lost to one cause or another with at least 35 more bombers damaged. The reconnaissance force, too, had suffered severely with six Marylands destroyed and others damaged. Indeed, at least 75 aircraft from the Island's garrison and in transit had been destroyed in the five week period, with more than 60 others damaged — a rate of loss more than three times that suffered by the Sicily-based Axis air forces during the same period! The Germans had thus clearly and rapidly achieved their primary objective — to prevent ships and aircraft based at Malta from interfering with the supply route to Africa.

By early March the risk to BOAC's flyingboats, combined with constant delays due to bad weather, made it uneconomical to airlift supplies to Malta or to the Middle East via Malta. Consequently, the flyingboats were withdrawn from this service and sent back to the West African route. An attempt had been made to re-establish a direct Britain-Egypt service over France and the Mediterranean using two converted American B-24 Liberator bombers, the only aircraft then available able to make the flight without an intermediate refuelling halt. The first of these (G-AGDR) flown by Capt. Humphrey Page, having successfully and uneventfully accomplished the first flight to Egypt, fell foul of Polish-flown Spitfires when returning to England and was shot down into the sea

A Fairey Albacore torpedo-bomber of 828 Squadron blazes at Hal Far following a strafing attack by Bf109s. Aircraft dispersed on all three Malta airfields were vulnerable to attack until sufficient blast pens could be constructed. *(NWMA)*

off Eddystone, with the loss of all passengers and crew. Amongst them was Lt.Col. Townsend Griffiss of the USAAF; he was the first US serviceman to die in the line of duty in Europe.

With Malta seemingly no longer viable as a staging post en route to Cairo, the needs of the Island became even more desperate. Vital stores such as ammunition and spare parts still had to be ferried in, and would continue to arrive either by submarine or by air transport. The latter was shared between RAF transport aircraft and the merchant air service, flying to the Island from east and west; a night service was inaugurated from Cairo three times a week, and another from Britain at whatever irregular intervals could be managed, usually shuttling via Gibraltar. Initially the latter route was flown by a converted military flyingboat, operating out of Poole Harbour (Dorset), by way of Gibraltar with a load of six passengers and a ton of mail and freight; the arrival of prompt air-mail was, and remained, an important morale booster for the garrison.

Chapter 3

SPITFIRES AT LAST!

Plt.Off. Jeff West (left) and Plt.Off. 'Buck' McNair, both of 249 Squadron, awaiting the arrival of the first Spitfires on 7 March 1942. *(Daddo-Langlois Collection)*

> 'When the time came — 7 am on the second day out — everyone was keyed up and expectant and most of us were wondering if the Spitfires would really get off the deck quite OK... All the aircraft were lined up waiting and everyone was in their cockpits half an hour before the first Blenheim, which was to lead us there, arrived. The Blenheim was sighted and the ship turned into wind. The first motor started and was run up. Suddenly the naval controller gave "Chocks Away" and Sqn.Ldr. Grant opened his throttle and went roaring down the deck. He lifted off the end, sank slightly below the level of the deck, and sailed away, gaining altitude, proving that a Spitfire can take off an aircraft carrier. All the aeroplanes got off within the hour and we turned back to Gibraltar. I was not going as my aircraft was u/s. I was to go back to Gib and come out with the next lot of Spitfires.'

So wrote a young Australian pilot, Sgt. Jack 'Slim' Yarra, recalling the historic morning of Saturday, 7 March 1942, as the first fighter Spitfires (as opposed to the photographic-reconnaissance version) to see service outside the United Kingdom at last headed for their destination. Although there had been much anticipated apprehension amongst the pilots, all the launches had gone smoothly, but such take-offs were not straightforward, as recalled by one pilot:

'On a Spit, unlike a Hurricane, you could not use partial flap for take-offs or landings. To overcome this and to facilitate take-offs from the carrier, small blocks of wood were cut to make an angle of about 15°, so before we took-off we dropped our flaps and as mechanics held the blocks of wood in place — I think there were two on each flap — we closed our flaps which wedged the wood between the flaps and the wing. After take-off, we lifted our undercarriages and climbed to a couple of thousand feet, then dropped our flaps to allow the blocks of wood to drop out, and then quickly raised our flaps again.'

As the 15 Spitfires — allotted the R/T call-sign 'Exile' — droned towards the Island which was to be their new base, guided by four Blenheims from 1442 Flight from Gibraltar, a number of Ju52/3m transports were seen in the distance; one or two pilots broke away and gave chase, but without result. Towards the end of the four-hour flight, the Spitfire pilots were welcomed by the soon-to-be-familiar voice of Grp.Capt. A.B. Woodhall — 'Woody' to all on Malta — the Senior Controller, calling over the R/T: "Hello, Exile boys! Keep your present course. Watch out for 109s below", as he gave them clearance to land at Takali.

The Spitfires had been expected for some time — so what had delayed their arrival? The 16 pilots who had been briefed to fly them from the carrier had initially forgathered at Portreath, Cornwall, where they had all undertaken some air experience of flying long-range Spitfires (aircraft fitted with a 45-gallon slipper tank beneath the fuselage). They were to be led by Sqn.Ldr. Stan Grant, a newly-promoted Battle of Britain veteran, already with at least three victories to his credit. The fresh-faced Grant "is a very young chap to be in charge, but looks pretty capable", opined Yarra on first making his acquaintance. Grant's lieutenant in this venture was Flt.Lt. Philip 'Nip' Heppell DFC, also with at least three victories, while experienced pilots included Plt.Off. Peter Nash, a former *Times* reporter (two victories).

The party had departed England, bound for Gibraltar, on 10 February aboard the 5000-ton *Cape Hawke*, a vessel which left much to be desired in comfort and facilities, greatly to the ire of Yarra in particular:

'The conditions are not fit for animals to live in. The beds are lousy and all the condensation from the roof falls on us when we sleep.'

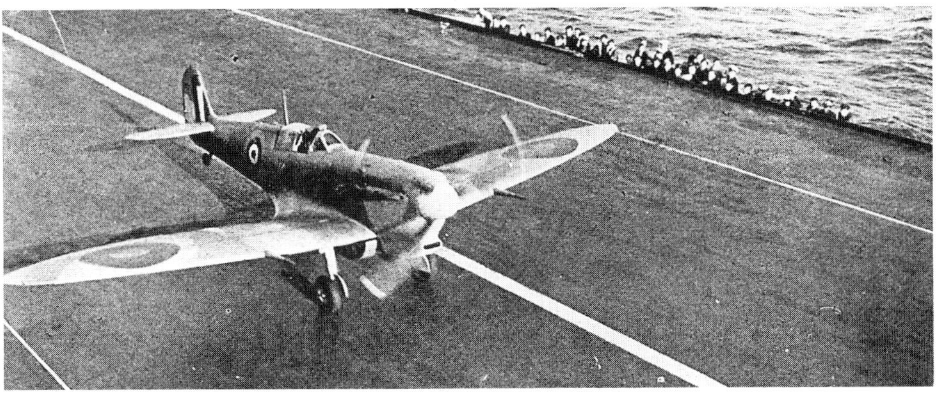

Sqn.Ldr. Stan Grant guns the first Spitfire down the deck of HMS *Eagle* on 7 March 1942, on the way to Malta. The long-range 'slipper' tank can be seen beneath the wing centre section. *(Authors' Collection)*

Top: The first Spitfire from HMS *Eagle* about to touch down at Takali. Note the Blenheim in the right background. **Above:** Safely down! *(J. Crichton)*

On arrival at Gibraltar on the 22nd, after a very rough crossing of the Bay of Biscay, Yarra added in his diary:

> 'Arrived today after the worst sea trip I've ever done in my life. It was absolutely shocking and after this war is over there are going to be some pretty stories told of how the invincible (*sic*) British Government looks after their troops. How in hell do they ever expect to win a war when they treat their fighting men like cattle? The Government spares no expense on machines of war, but when it comes to the men who run the machines the cheapest is too good for them, in the eyes of the crowd who are running this war. This may seem rather hard but it is perfectly right, and I am getting sick of seeing Churchill stick his bowler hat up on his cane so the populace hail him as their saviour, and think we are winning the war. The sooner the people of England realise that we are losing this damned war so far, the better it will be for everyone.'

A 'cri de coeur' which servicemen of all generations may well have echoed!

On arrival at the famous 'Rock', the group were to board the carrier *Eagle*, where they found their 16 Spitfire Vb (Trop)s in the hangar, hidden from the eyes of potential Axis agents and sympathizers in nearby Spain. These aircraft had been carried in crates aboard *Cape Hawke*, but now were hoisted aboard the carrier partly assembled — with wings attached and undercarriage lowered — for final assembly. Each was fitted with a 90-gallon slipper overload tank to enable it to complete its long flight. Comfort aboard the carrier for the NCO pilots was again noticeable by its absence, as Flt.Sgt. David Ferraby recalled:

'At least on *Cape Hawke* we had our wooden bunks, but on *Eagle* the crew and us had to doss down wherever we weren't in the way. The spot I picked for my bedding was on top of a wire mesh lock-up store in the hangar, with blokes assembling Spits all night long.'

At this stage, Sqn.Ldr. Grant was introduced to Flt.Lt. Norman Macqueen and Flg.Off. Norm Lee, both of whom had been flown to Gibraltar from Malta, and who were to join his party at the expense of two of the less-experienced pilots, Sgt. M. Irving Gass and Sgt. H.J. Fox RCAF. The final 16 selected for this epic flight now comprised Sqn.Ldr. Grant, Flt.Lts. Heppell and Macqueen, Flg.Off. Lee and Plt.Off. Nash, Flt.Sgts. Ferraby and Ian Cormack, and Sgt. John Tayleur (all British); four Australians — Plt.Offs. Ken Murray and Jim Guerin, Sgts. Paul Brennan and Yarra; two New Zealanders — Sgts. Ray Hesselyn and Bob Sim; and two Rhodesians — Plt.Offs. John Plagis (of Greek ancestry) and Doug Leggo. The 16 brand-new Spitfires were AB262, 264, 329-338, 341, 343, 344, 346.

After four days at Gibraltar the carrier sailed on the night of 26 February, escorted by Vice-Admiral Sir Neville Syfret's Force 'H' — the battleship *Malaya*, a cruiser (*Hermione*), nine destroyers and the elderly training carrier *Argus*. The latter had embarked nine Fulmars from 807 Squadron to provide air cover, and nine ASV-equipped Swordfish (812 Squadron) for anti-submarine purposes, while *Eagle* also carried two Sea Hurricanes of 813F Squadron for CAP (Combat Air Patrol) duties, as well as a few ASV Swordfish.

The next day dawned clear and with a favourable wind. Preparations for take-off were made, but as the pilots added a last polish to the perspex cockpit hoods and rear-view mirrors, the Engineering Officer reported that all was not well. Instead of feeding fuel into the engines, the auxiliary fuel tanks were syphoning it out into the airstream! There was no way that the 700-mile flight could be undertaken until this defect had been remedied. In the face of the extreme displeasure of *Eagle's* Captain Lachlan Mackintosh, the EO insisted, and a return to Gibraltar had to be made.

Here an expert had to be rushed out from England to sort out the problem, while the pilots continued to live on the carrier in considerably more salubrious and acceptable conditions than on the despised *Cape Hawke*! At last, on 5 March, the carrier set sail again and Operation 'Spotter' was underway.

Early on the morning of the 7th, therefore, Gibraltar-based 1442 Flight despatched, at half-hourly intervals, eight Blenheims to rendezvous with the carrier — half to lead the Spitfires to Malta, the remainder as reserves should any of the first four have to abort. Consequently, as recorded, Sqn.Ldr. Grant, Flt.Lts. Heppell and Macqueen led off 15 serviceable aircraft in three flights of five each, while the disappointed Yarra and the unserviceable 16th aircraft (AB333) returned with *Eagle* to Gibraltar once more.

On approaching Malta, the Spitfire pilots found Hurricanes in the air, patrolling to cover their arrival and landing at Takali, but of the Luftwaffe there was no sign. Sgt. Hesselyn was initially unable to lower his undercarriage and was obliged to let the others land first; he eventually got down without damage to his aircraft. As his first impression of the Island, Johnny Plagis noted:

'Land of burnt-out Wimpeys (*Wellingtons*) and bowsers!'

Even as the Spitfires were being stripped of their long-range tanks and full servicing was begun — to prepare them for their introduction to operations — more reinforcements flew in to Takali in the shape of four AI radar-equipped Beaufighter IF night fighters; these powerful machines had been detached from 89 Squadron at Abu Sueir, Egypt. Like the Spitfires, they had been the first of their type to operate outside the United Kingdom when they had arrived in North Africa earlier in the year. Led to the Island by a 252 Squadron Beaufighter flown by Flg.Off. A.D. Frecker, they were initially attached to 1435 Flight. The four crews were:

X7750	Flt.Lt. G. McL. Hayton/Plt.Off. N.H. Josling
X7756	Plt.Off. P.G. Oakes/Sgt. J. Walsh
X7648	Plt.Off. E.G. Daniel/Sgt D. Gosling
X7586	Sgt. R.A. Miller/Sgt. F.J. Tearle

With the arrival of the Beaufighters, a call went out for suitably experienced ground personnel at Luqa to come forward; six men who had previously worked on Beaufighters were located and drafted into 1435 Flight, to assist with the servicing of the night fighters.

The first the new arrivals were to see of the Luftwaffe was a raid by 27 aircraft on all three airfields that evening between 1515 and 1910, but all the indications were that the Germans were as yet unaware of these formidable new reinforcements. At Hal Far a single Hurricane (Z2819) of 185 Squadron was destroyed on the ground, while elsewhere a gun emplacement was hit, killing eight soldiers from 10th HAA and seriously wounding five others. One intruder attacked a bus carrying 37 Squadron's maintenance crews as it trundled along the Naxxar to Luqa road; two anti-personnel bombs were dropped, one falling just in front of the bus, the other just behind. The vehicle was riddled by splinters and hardly an occupant escaped injury, one of whom, AC Jim Asquith, later died.

During one of these attacks a Bf109 was claimed damaged by a Hurricane pilot; Oblt. Otto Böhmer, Staffelkapitän of 6/JG 53, returned to Sicily with his aircraft slightly damaged and himself slightly wounded, although he reported that his aircraft had been hit by AA fire. With its leader thus incapacitated, command of 6 Staffel now temporarily passed to Oblt. Belser of 8 Staffel.

At last light seven Wellingtons in transit landed at Luqa following the long flight from Gibraltar, whilst two Royal Navy transport submarines silently glided into the Manoel Island base, delivering quantities of aviation fuel.

Axis bombers were back that night to raid Luqa and Hal Far again, one Wellington of 37 Squadron being burnt out and four others, plus a Beaufighter, sustaining slight damage at the former airfield where nine airmen were wounded; two civilians were also killed and three others wounded, whilst the guns claimed the probable destruction of a Ju88 in return.

There were no raids at all during the daylight hours of the 8th, the only excitement occurring when eight 242 Squadron Hurricanes went out to escort in three delivery Blenheims. These were located some 30 miles west of Gozo, and were guided to Luqa without event.

Following the arrival of the Spitfires, they and their pilots were amalgamated into 249 Squadron, still under the command of Sqn.Ldr. Stan Turner, who now found himself not only with Sqn.Ldr. Grant as his supernumery, but with no less than four relatively-experienced Flight Lieutenants — Heppell and Macqueen joining Lucas and Connell, the latter having just joined the unit from 126 Squadron.

Although things were comparatively quiet on Malta, offensive action was pending. 'Ultra' had provided information to the high command that a convoy of five merchantmen (in fact, there were only four Italian freighters — *Giordani, Ravello, Lerici* and *Unione*) and eight destroyers (in fact, five destroyers and two torpedo boats) was sailing from Italy to North Africa. Malta had been requested to despatch a reconnaissance aircraft to enable an actual sighting to be made to allow an attack, but the Maryland was delayed for five hours by the damaged state of Luqa's runway following the latest air raid, and when it did at last get away the crew searched too far to the north, failing to see anything.

With the advent of darkness on the 8th, an ASV-equipped Swordfish located a large merchant vessel some 24 miles from Pantelleria at 1935, which was attacked by an accompanying torpedo-armed Swordfish; no result of the attack was observed but one-and-a-half hours later three Albacores attacked the same freighter. Two probable hits were claimed, although without actual success.

Between 2318 and 0642 an estimated 19 raiders were plotted on Malta's radar screens; these included seven BR20Ms of 55° Gruppo BT, bombs falling near all the airfields. Around midnight Sqn.Ldr Westmacott of 1435 Flight was scrambled in Hurricane Z4004/L, and was brought in behind a Ju88 by Ground Control. However, conditions were hazy and he pursued the intruder south for about 40 miles before finally opening fire, but then lost sight of his opponent. He then spotted what appeared to be a flame on the water, but did not think it was the Junkers; nonetheless, he was credited with its probable destruction by a generous IO.

It seems that the same aircraft — believed to have been a Ju88C night fighter (R4+V8) of I/NJG 2 — was then attacked by one of the newly-arrived Beaufighters, X7586 crewed by Sgts. Miller and Tearle. At 0100 they reported shooting down a Junkers in flames into the sea off the Sicilian coast, about seven miles east of Catania; Oblt. Heinz Schulz and his crew were killed. The Beaufighter was then vectored onto another 'hostile' which was tentatively identified as an He111, and hits were gained on this before the cannons ceased to operate. Miller was credited with damaging the Heinkel, possibly an aircraft of 4/KG 26.

Meanwhile, as Wellingtons of 37 Squadron were taking-off from Luqa — destined to raid Sicily — Flg.Off. C.I.L. Boyd's DV483, when about two-thirds the way down the runway, collided with Flt.Sgt. S.J. Kozlowski's Z9038; both aircraft caught fire and mines aboard exploded. Canadian Stan Kozlowski and two of his crew were killed instantly, the remaining three being injured as were Boyd and three of his crew, one of whom later succumbed to his wounds. Sqn.Ldr. Robert Hill, Luqa's Medical Officer, was swiftly on the scene with Signals Officer Flt.Lt. Ernest Williams. Even as the mines and bombs began to explode, and bombs began falling from Axis raiders, this intrepid duo — joined by LACs Cyril Boarman and Hyman Sumray — managed to extricate four members of the crews from the wreckage; all four rescuers were subsequently each awarded the George Medal, while a Military Medal went to the NCO in charge of the fire-fighting party, Sgt. J.S. Dewhurst.

Monday, 9 March

At 0700, Wg.Cdr. Rabagliati led seven 242 Squadron Hurricanes off to escort an incoming transit Blenheim, during which Sgt. Tony Boyd (in Z2961/K) saw an aircraft approaching him from behind:

> 'I turned slowly, thinking it was a Hurricane. By the time I realised (*it was a Bf109F*) he was 400 yards ahead. Gave him a futile burst. Followed another plot. No interception.'

An hour later more Blenheims were met and guided to Malta by Hurricanes of 185 Squadron, this time without incident.

The Luftwaffe returned at 1030, three Ju88s and nine 109s approaching the Island. Nineteen Hurricanes were scrambled at 1035 (seven/605, four/185 and eight/242), again led by Wg.Cdr. Rabagliati. The raiders were encountered east of Delimara but no conclusive actions ensued. Two Junkers were claimed damaged however, one by Flt.Sgt. Fletcher (Z2414/E) of 185 Squadron, the other by four pilots of 242 Squadron (Flt.Lts. Kemp and Kee, Plt.Off. Morrison-Jones and Sgt. H. Hale). 605 Squadron's Flt.Lt. Stones (BG770/D) attacked another but with unobserved results, then claimed strikes on one of the escorting fighters. Another Messerschmitt was claimed damaged by Plt.Off. Ormrod (BG711/G), while Rabagliati (Z4005/S) saw pieces break away from the tail of the one he attacked, then reported flames from its engine; he was awarded a probable. In return for all these claims, Sgt. Finlay's Hurricane sustained damage, the slightly wounded pilot nonetheless landing safely.

The Germans were back in greater strength soon after midday, 18 Ju88s and 26 Bf109s raiding Luqa, Safi and Hal Far between 1220 and 1550, and Messerschmitts strafing Hal Far where a number of aircraft were damaged on the ground. Twenty-one Hurricanes were scrambled, but only six aircraft of 126 Squadron which went off at 1500 led by Sqn.Ldr. Norris actually made contact, intercepting four Ju88s and six of the escort as the raiders swept out to sea.

Sgt. Tweedale chased a Ju88 to within ten miles of the Sicilian coast and claimed to have shot it down. Having used all his ammunition against this aircraft he was unable to defend himself when attacked by Bf109s, his Hurricane being badly shot up. He received a piece of shrapnel in one heel but was able to reach base safely;his injury would keep him hospitalized for almost three weeks.

Flg.Off. Anderson also attacked one of the bombers, seeing an explosion inside the aircraft after which it was seen to dive steeply; this was credited as destroyed. He then attacked two Messerschmitts but without results. Another bomber was claimed damaged by Plt.Off. Steele, who then attacked a Bf109 which he believed was shot down, while Flg.Off. Ron West reported strikes on two Junkers he attacked. Escorting fighters were also engaged by Plt.Off. Bill Hollis Hallett (from Bermuda), who claimed a probable and a damaged, while Sqn.Ldr. Norris led Plt.Offs. Joe Crichton (BG792) and Coffin in an attack on another bomber; serious damage was believed inflicted upon this machine which was last seen diving towards the sea with the starboard engine on fire. Coffin's Hurricane was hit in the engine by return fire and he was obliged to crash-land at Luqa, his aircraft sustaining serious damage and subsequently being written-off; the American suffered a slight head injury which required a stitch, and a cut above one eye.

Messerschmitt pilots of 2/JG 53 were just leaving the Sicilian coast when they spotted a Ju88 heading north pursued by a Hurricane some 400 yards behind and below, with two more off to its right. Lt. Gunther Hess dived down, attacking the last of the three Hurricanes and claiming it shot down. Fw. Hans Stockman got behind one of the other two (possibly Tweedale), but could not shoot at first for fear of hitting the Ju88, which was directly ahead. Swinging to the left, he then opened fire and saw hits, but was at that moment attacked by another Hurricane (possibly that flown by Steele), his aircraft being hit in the cooling system as a result of which he was obliged to ditch in the sea.

It seems likely that Anderson and Tweedale — if not the others — had attacked the same bomber, for the only Ju88 shot down was B3+KH of I/KG 54, in which Lt. Herbert Müller and his crew were lost. During the day's fighting at least five Hurricanes were claimed by the Luftwaffe fighters, two being credited to 9/JG 53's Ofw. Werner Stumpf for his 26th and 27th victories and one to that unit's Uffz. Gerhard Beitz for his first success; another was claimed by Lt. Louis of Stab I/JG 53. Fw. Stockmann had taken to his dinghy, and after a night at sea was to be rescued next day by a Seenotst 6 Do 24, recorded as that unit's 2299th rescue since March the previous year!

A third intrusion was plotted at 1615 when a single reconnaissance Ju88 appeared, soon to be followed by an estimated dozen bombers with Messerschmitt escort; again Hal Far, Luqa and Safi were attacked. No Hurricanes were available on this occasion, but guns managed to shoot down Oblt. Gerhard Becker's Ju88 of 6/KG 77; Becker, the Staffelkapitän, and his gunner baled out into the sea but were not picked up; the observer was killed when 3Z+LP crashed on Hal Far airfield, while Uffz. Walter Kunzi, the W/T operator, survived to be taken prisoner.

During the last major clash between the opposing fighters prior to the arrival of the first Spitfires, Uffz. Gerhard Beitz of 9/JG 53 claimed his first and only victory over the Island, on 9 March 1942. At far left is Ofw. Werner Stumpf who also claimed two Hurricanes during this fight, while next to him is the Staffelkapitän, Oblt. Franz Götz, who is congratulating Beitz. Behind and to Beitz's left are Uffz. Max Nairz, an unknown, and Lt. Wolf Schaller. *(G. Beitz via J. Prien/W. Bock)*

During the three raids Luqa suffered the loss of five Wellingtons destroyed or seriously damaged, including DV421 of the OADU, while one other was less seriously damaged; the 37 Squadron detachment effectively ceased to exist. Following the latest raid, AHQ assessed the day's claims as:

Hurricanes:	one Ju88 and two Bf109s shot down; one Bf 109 probable; seven Ju88s and two Bf109s damaged
AA guns:	one Ju88 shot down; one Bf109 damaged

Throughout the day aircraft of 69 Squadron had continued to search for an Axis convoy, and this time were successful — but not in finding the vessels which were the substance of the 'Ultra' report. Instead they reported a northbound convoy of four merchantmen (the returning *Giordani, Ravello, Lerici* and *Unione*) escorted by three destroyers and three torpedo boats, about 200 miles south-east of Malta. The southbound convoy also comprised four freighters (*Nino Bixio, Giuliani, Allegri* and *Monreale*), but enjoyed a close escort of five destroyers and two torpedo boats, with a covering force further off which

Remains of Ju88A 3Z+LP of 6/KG 77, shot down by anti-aircraft fire during a raid on Hal Far on 9 March 1942. *(K. Cox)*

included three cruisers and five more destroyers.

This more important southbound convoy was eventually sighted off the North African coast by a Western Desert Air Force reconnaissance aircraft, and consequently a force of eight Beauforts of 39 Squadron was despatched from Bu Amud to attack, proceeding alone when the proposed escort of Beaufighters failed to rendezvous with them. At 1640 the torpedo-bombers, led by Flt.Lt. Taylor in L8923, intercepted the wrong convoy — the northbound one — 170 miles north-east of Tripoli, finding it under escort by three Ju88s and at least one Bf110.

One torpedo was launched at the largest freighter, others at the escorting warships. Although the Beauforts escaped damage from the AA barrage they then came under attack by the air escort. Sgt. Frank White, gunner in Flg.Off. Derek Bee's W6506, claimed one attacking Ju88 shot down, while Sgt. Holland in Flg.Off. Tony Leaning's L9876 got a "good burst" at the Bf110 and claimed damage; one Beaufort was slightly damaged in the exchange. Hits were claimed on a merchant vessel, a cruiser and a destroyer, the latter believed sunk, but in fact no damage at all had been inflicted!

After dark a force of Desert-based Wellingtons (from 70 Squadron) were sent out to continue attacks on the convoy but three only were able to release their bombs on the ships, the single possible hit which was claimed actually doing no damage. It was then the turn of the Fleet Air Arm strike force from Malta. Three Swordfish went off at 1930, one returning early, but near Pantelleria two hours later the other two sighted yet another small convoy, the crews reporting one freighter and three destroyers; the escort, in fact, comprised the destroyer *Usodimare* and the torpedo-boat *Polluce*. An effective smoke-screen was at once laid by the destroyer, hence only one Swordfish was able to carry out an attack on the heavily-laden *Luciano Manara*, albeit without result.

Back at Hal Far three Albacores had been ordered off to the same area but one of these struck the airfield boundary wall on take-off, and was seen heading out to sea at low altitude. Fearing that it had come down in the sea, HSL 107 was at once despatched from Kalafrana but, in fact, the torpedo-bomber had only lost its tail wheel and completed its sortie, although it did crash-land on return; the crew were unhurt. The trio of Albacores came across *Luciano Manara* and her escort, releasing flares as the destroyer again began laying a smoke-screen.

One Albacore dived to 50 feet, its torpedo being released at 600 yards; although the missile was seen to be running well, smoke prevented further observation. The second aircraft went down to 30 feet before launching, the crew reporting with confidence that they had hit the merchantman. Indeed, the freighter sustained damage to her bow, and she had to be towed back to Palermo — the only actual success of the night's attacks.

Whilst Malta's puny strike force was away, Axis bombers headed towards the Island in pairs or trios, the first Ju88s arriving at about 2200. For the next eight hours a total of 17 Ju88s of I/KG 54 and III/KG 77 operated overhead, dropping in excess of 60 medium-sized bombs and 170 anti-personnel missiles on the three airfields; a direct hit on a hangar at Takali was claimed, other explosions being reported at Luqa and Hal Far. Six BR20Ms of 55° Gruppo BT also raided various targets in the Luqa and Hal Far area, during which Ten. Spartaco Zappi's aircraft developed engine trouble and the pilot was obliged to return early; an emergency landing was made near Agrigento.

One of the first Spitfires to arrive — AB264 — carrying 249 Squadron's code letters GN; the serial appears to have been repainted in unusual (and unofficial) white paint, instead of its normal black. *(NWMA)*

Tuesday, 10 March

At last, on the morning of 10 March, came the moment for the Spitfires' debut over Malta. This was made at 1020 when seven aircraft took off in company with eight 126 Squadron Hurricanes from Takali and four of 185 Squadron from Hal Far, causing Plt.Off. McKay to have noted in his diary:

> 'The Spitfires have arrived and are now doing top cover for us which is a great help. It rather shakes you to see one on your tail 'cause they look so much like a 109'.

The objective of the scramble was to intercept an incoming raid of nine Ju88s, of which three crossed the coast to bomb Luqa where a Wellington of 37 Squadron was destroyed; there were now no such aircraft available for operations. The Spitfires climbed to 19,000 feet, three led by Sqn.Ldr. Turner and four by Flt.Lt. Heppell, while Sqn.Ldr. Norris led four of the Hurricanes to 18,000 feet; the other eight stayed below cloud.

On reaching altitude, Heppell's section saw below them the Ju88s and their escorts, and at once 'bounced' the unsuspecting Messerschmitts. Heppell, in AB262/B, fired a long burst at one which was seen to crash into the sea; this was Fw. Heinz Rahlmeier's 'Black 11' of 8/JG 53, in which the pilot was killed. Other

A group of 249 Squadron's first Spitfire pilots. Left to right: Flg.Off. Raoul Daddo-Langlois, Flg.Off. Norman Lee, Sgt. Paul Brennan, Sgt. Ray Hesselyn and Flt.Lt. 'Laddie' Lucas. *(NWMA)*

Messerschmitts were attacked by Plt.Offs. Nash (AB335/F) and Plagis (AB346/K), and Flg.Off. Daddo-Langlois (GN-D), the first two claiming probables; Plagis attacked one on Nash's tail, while Daddo-Langlois claimed one damaged, having knocked pieces off its tail. Flt.Lt. Lucas (GN-A) chased another without success.

A number of the Hurricanes also became engaged in the battle, Plt.Off. Hollis Hallett claiming damage to one of the escorts, while Plt.Off. McKay (UP-F) reported strikes on one of the bombers, but Sgt. Jack Mayall was shot down; his Hurricane (Z5140/C) crashed near Qormi, and the Australian was killed. Records would suggest that he was the 24th victim of Hpt. Karl-Heinz Krahl, Kommandeur of II/JG 3. A second Hurricane was caught in the landing circuit by a Messerschmitt of III/JG 53, Flg.Off. Ron West being obliged to crash-land, surviving unhurt.

Attempts to intercept two more raids during the mid part of the day failed, during the second of which the Hal Far Officers' Mess and Quarters were hit, an RN officer and two soldiers being injured. Finally, at 1632, 40 more Axis aircraft were plotted approaching to attack Luqa and Hal Far — Ju88s of I/KG 54, II and III/KG 77 and LG 1 taking part. 242 Squadron scrambled eight Hurricanes, and 185 three more, while four Spitfires were also sent off; the 185 Squadron trio engaged six Bf109s over Filfla and claimed two damaged, by Plt.Off. Noble (UP-N) and Plt.Off. Steele. Three pilots of 242 Squadron attacked one of the bombers, Flt.Lt. Kee, Plt.Off. Morrison-Jones and Sgt. Boyd (HA-F) each claiming strikes, the latter noting:

> 'I attacked the Ju88 after Flt.Lt. Kee had caused explosion with cannons. I followed it ten miles using all ammo and causing smoke from both engines. Claim 1/3 of it.'

Meanwhile the Spitfires attacked two more Ju88s, both of which Flt.Lt. Macqueen and Flg.Off. Buchanan (AB262/B) claimed damage. However, Spitfire AB343 flown by Plt.Off. Ken Murray, a 20 year-old Australian from Toorak, Victoria, was attacked by Bf109s and shot down, apparently by Fw. Hans Schade of 8/JG 53 for his 13th victory — the first of the Spitfires to be lost.

Murray baled out at high altitude, but his parachute failed to open properly — initially his colleagues believed that he had been shot whilst descending — and he sustained severe injuries on striking the ground, dying in hospital that evening; his Spitfire crashed and burnt out near Dingli.

Since it was at first believed that Murray had come down in the sea, three Spitfires went out to cover him while HSL 107 was despatched to pick him up. During the subsequent search Flg.Off. Buchanan was attacked by Bf109s and suffered superficial wounds to his right leg when AB262/B was hit, necessitating an emergency landing at Takali. Three Messerschmitts also attempted to strafe the launch, but were held at bay by escorting Hurricanes until it was recalled.

During the afternoon raid only one Ju88 had actually been hit, a 4/KG 77 machine returning damaged following fighter attack, with two wounded on board; an aircraft from 2/KG 54 also crash-landed at Gerbini on return, reportedly due to undercarriage malfunction. OKW claimed five British aircraft shot down during the day, with a further six destroyed on the ground. One of the former may have been a transit Beaufighter (T4896), which failed to arrive from Gibraltar.

Wednesday, 11 March

Shortly before dawn two Swordfish arrived at Hal Far following a flight of over seven hours from El Adem, the latest of the reinforcements for 828 Squadron; two others failed to arrive. V4369 was flown by Sub Lt. E.D. Dunkerley and carried Lt.Cdr. N.C. Manley-Cooper of 821 Squadron as navigator, who recalled:

> 'It was a long journey, and very warm and tiring — Dunkerley went to sleep twice and I had to wake him up! At first the aircraft were able to keep in touch by W/T but near the end of the trip we encountered heavy rain and we parted company. We were then instructed to delay our arrival as there was an air raid in progress, but after flying around for a while we were allowed to land quite safely.
>
> 'This extraordinary exercise was only partially successful, unfortunately. Bertie Birse (*Sub Lt. S.W. Birse*) found himself over what turned out to be Sicily and tried to land on a German airfield before realizing his mistake. Another blew up over the coast at Tobruk, probably due to a spark catching an overfilled saddle tank.
>
> 'Afterwards, the survivors were flown back to Cairo in an RAF Wellington.'

There was only one raid during the day, when at 1135 two Ju88s of 5/KG 77 and six Bf109s approached the coast. The Ju88s turned back without bombing, and one crashed on landing at Comiso where it was completely destroyed; Fw. Otto Grams and his crew perished. Sixteen Hurricanes (four/185, twelve/126) and four Spitfires scrambled, the latter in pairs led by Sqn.Ldr. Grant and Flt.Lt. Connell, and a number of dogfights ensued. For 185 Squadron, Plt.Off. Ormrod (Z2840/T) claimed a Bf109 damaged, while Plt.Off. Noble (Z4942/Y) was jumped by another but was not hit; he fired at this with cannon from 500 yards but observed no result.

Sqn.Ldr. Grant (AB262/B) attacked two Bf109s at 10,000 feet over Grand Harbour; one was seen going down inverted towards the sea and he was credited with its probable destruction. Flt.Lt. Connell (AB335/F) and Sgt. Hesselyn

Plt.Off. Ron Noble of 185 Squadron in another of his squadron's gun pits, manning a pair of Lewis machine guns. Off-duty pilots took turns to man these guns during air raids. *(P. Wigley)*

(AB346/K) engaged three of the escort. Connell reported gaining strikes on one with a deflection shot, which he claimed damaged; in return he received a bullet hole in his own aircraft, two feet behind the cockpit. Hesselyn's reflector sight and R/T failed, which effectively put him out of the fight; the fourth member of the quartet, Flt.Sgt. Ferraby (AB341/E), also engaged a fighter but did not observe any results.

At midnight a single Ju88C of I/NJG 2 released six 50 kg bombs and 72 incendiaries over Valetta. Just over four hours later a second aircraft from this unit dropped two 50 kg bombs and a further 72 incendiaries on Hal Far; six explosions and fires were observed by the German crew but, in fact, little material damage was caused.

Thursday, 12 March

At 1100 six Hurricanes of 242 Squadron were scrambled after six Ju88s of II/KG 77 and escorting Bf109s; Sgt. George Mulloy claimed one of the escort damaged, but that was the only success reported. Meanwhile, Takali was raided by four of the bombers half an hour later, where seven Hurricanes were slightly damaged by debris and splinters; an unserviceable Wellington of 37 Squadron was burnt out at Luqa. Three Ju88s again bombed Takali at 1635 — one Hurricane, one Spitfire and one Blenheim were slightly damaged, and four airmen were wounded. At Luqa an unserviceable Wellington — Z1043 of 37 Squadron — was burnt out.

With the onset of darkness, nine bombers — including four BR20Ms of 55° Gruppo — raided the Kalafrana area. One hangar was hit, a Sunderland and one of the precious HSLs being damaged. Three Hurricanes of 1435 Flight and Beaufighter X7750 were scrambled, and at 2345 the latter intercepted a Ju88. Flt.Lt. Gil Hayton, a former Battle of Britain Spitfire pilot, and his radar operator, Plt.Off. Norman Josling (who had flown as an air gunner in Fairey Battles in France during 1940, and had been credited with probably shooting down two German aircraft), claimed severe damage to the intruder. It would seem that their victim was actually shot down, Uffz. Horst Ehler's 7T+AH of 1/KüFlGr 606 failing to return.

Malta's first successful Beaufighter night fighter crew who served with the detachment from 89 Squadron which joined 1435 Flight. Flt.Lt. Gil Hayton (right) was a New Zealander; he is seen here with his radar operator, Flg.Off. Norman Josling. *(P. Sortehaug)*

Friday, 13 March

Friday brought a further raid on Takali, one Hurricane and a petrol bowser being burnt out. Thirteen Hurricanes were scrambled but they missed the bombers and were themselves attacked by numerous Bf109s, although no claims or losses resulted. However, AA gunners claimed damage to one Ju88 and, in fact, the pilot of a 6/KG 77 bomber, Uffz. Rudolf Gösch, was wounded over

Flt.Lt. Gil Hayton's Beaufighter, X7750 'B', at Takali. *(Daddo-Langlois Collection)*

Takali but managed to fly back to Comiso safely.

At Luqa, through the efforts of toiling groundcrews, one Wellington of 37 Squadron had been made serviceable, and Flt.Sgt. Ellison and crew were briefed to attack Tripoli harbour. Over the target area dense haze obscured shipping in the harbour, a result of which was that the bombs were aimed at Spanish Quay, but with little effect.

Saturday, 14 March

Saturday heralded not only further action for the Spitfires of 249 Squadron, but a change in command for Sqn.Ldr. Turner handed the reins to Sqn.Ldr. Grant. The Canadian was promoted to take command of the Takali Wing from Wg.Cdr. Rabagliati, who departed that evening — tour expired — in an Egypt-bound Wellington.

The first intrusion of the morning, at around 0830, by a reconnaissance Ju88 and two escorting Bf109s of 3/JG 53 was not countered by the fighters; however, AA gunners on Gozo claimed the Junkers damaged and one of the escorts shot down and, indeed, their fire struck one of the fighters. Lt. Walter Seiz's Messerschmitt took a direct hit and smashed into that ('Yellow 8') flown by Uffz. Heinrich Blum; Seiz was able to bale out but the unlucky Blum crashed to his death.

Another raid was reported at 1030, as three Ju88s of II/KG 77 and an estimated 20 Bf109s approached, while 15 more Messerschmitts were noted to be on a sea search, obviously looking for the missing pilots. The raiders bombed Hal Far, the crews reporting one big fire on the taxying ground, while other bombs were seen to explode amongst buildings and aircraft in dispersal areas; one Hurricane was destroyed and three more, plus a Swordfish, were damaged.

To intercept this raid four Spitfires had been sent up, and these encountered a trio of Bf109s orbiting Gozo, apparently part of the sea search party. Flt.Lt. Macqueen dived on one, attacking from 275 to 50 yards, and fired all his ammunition, reporting strikes along the fuselage. The Messerschmitt pilot took no evasive action, continuing a slow climbing turn as the Spitfire broke away in front of it. Macqueen believed that it dived into the sea and its destruction was later confirmed by intelligence sources. This would appear to have been an aircraft of 7/JG 53, from which Uffz. Adolf Jennerich baled out. The skipper of HSL 107 was refused permission to go out when the Messerschmitt was seen to fall in flames a mile outside Kalafrana Bay, due to the threat posed by the presence of large numbers of other Bf109s at low level.

During mid-afternoon no less than 29 Messerschmitts were reported off the coast, searching and patrolling, accompanied by a Do24 which was seen to alight on the sea. Whether this was the rescue of Seiz or Jennerich is not known, for both were safely plucked from the water and were soon on their way back to Sicily. Two further Bf109s seen orbiting Gozo were chased by Flt.Lt. Lucas (GN-G) and Flg.Off. Daddo-Langlois at about 1535, the former seeing strikes on the fuselage and tail of the one he attacked before others drove him away; Daddo-Langlois experienced an oil leak which prevented him from attacking. Fw. Josef Kroschel of 8/JG 53 claimed a Spitfire at this time for his first victory, possibly believing that he had shot down Lucas' aircraft as the latter dived away.

Between 1550 and 1750 an estimated 16 Bf109s were reported patrolling to the west and south-west of the Island. Taking off again, Lucas (GN-G) and Daddo-Langlois firstly escorted a Maryland departing on a reconnaissance sortie, then once more two Messerschmitts were encountered. Lucas fired all his ammunition at one and saw hits on the fuselage, reporting a trail of black smoke as the German dived away; again he could claim only a damaged.

Shortly before darkness set in, two Axis flyingboats and three Bf109s were reported off the coast to the south-west — obviously still searching for the missing Uffz. Blum — but these were allowed to complete their task without further interference.

Sunday, 15 March

On Sunday three Ju88s with fighter escort raided Luqa and Valetta shortly before lunchtime; eight persons were killed, including two soldiers. Four Spitfires, led by Flt.Lts. Connell and Heppell, and seven Hurricanes (four/185, three/242) were up and intercepted the raid in low cloud. 'Nip' Heppell claimed a Bf109 damaged after seeing his cannon shells strike the underside of its fuselage, and from which his No 2 saw pieces fall off into the sea; he then attacked a Ju88 and a second Bf109 but without result.

One of the bombers was attacked by Plt.Off. Jeff West and Sgt. Tayleur, who jointly claimed some damage before being driven away by the escort. The Hurricanes also engaged, Plt.Off. Noble (Z2840/T) claiming a Bf109 damaged when he saw strikes near the cockpit and on the fuselage, while Plt.Off. Wigley (BG711/G) attacked another, but without apparent result. Sgt. Boyd (HA-H) reported:

> 'Mixed it with two Me's at 14,000 feet, then ten more appeared so lost height. I was climbing at 4,000 feet and saw one Ju88 over Grand Harbour, 2,000 feet above me. Chased it halfway to Sicily; two long bursts at 400 yards. Being still alone, broke off and returned while possible'.

At 1320 three Ju88s and seven Bf109s raided Zabbar, and were met by four Spitfires; Flt.Lt. Connell (AB346/K) claimed one bomber probably destroyed, and it seems likely that this was an aircraft of 3/KGr 806 (M7+ML) which failed to return from an operational sortie to Malta, Uffz. Rudolf Alex and his crew being reported missing. Three more Ju88s and six Bf109s approached at 1735, while 19 Bf109s patrolled just off the coast. Six Spitfires and eight Hurricanes (four/126 and four/185, led by Wg.Cdr. Satchell) were up, and Plt.Off. Allardice led Sgts. Bates, Eastman and Horricks of the latter unit to attack the port Ju88 of the formation some ten miles off Delimara. No return fire was experienced and it was believed the rear gunner was killed; however the bomber escaped serious damage.

Wg.Cdr. Satchell and Plt.Off. McHan (the American MNFU pilot, flying a

126 Squadron machine, HA-M) claimed damage to another Junkers, while fellow American Plt.Off. Coffin attacked the centre and starboard bombers in turn, but had to break away when a Messerschmitt dived on his tail. Wg.Cdr. Satchell attacked this and reported that pieces fell off its tail unit while the engine appeared to catch fire; it was last seen diving towards the sea and was claimed destroyed.

Ofw. Werner Stumpf of 9/JG 53, seen after claiming his 28th victory on 15 March 1942 — his fourth over Malta.

During the day Ofw. Werner Stumpf of 9/JG 53 and Oblt. Belser of 8 Staffel were each credited with Spitfires shot down, their 28th and 21st victories respectively, but no RAF losses were suffered. A total of over 130 Luftwaffe sorties had been directed against the Island during ten alerts. At Luqa, five civilians and a soldier had been killed, 17 civilians and seven soldiers injured, while at least a further 16 civilians had been injured elsewhere. AA gunners claimed damage to three Ju88s and two Bf109s.

Many miles to the east of Malta, a combined Naval and RAF one-day operation — codenamed MF 8 — was carried out against the Italian island of Rhodes, the object of which was to reduce the scale of air attack on Malta by drawing Axis air strength away from Sicily. The Navy's contribution to the operation was two cruisers — *Dido* and *Euryalus* — and six destroyers, which were to bombard shipping, seaplanes, harbour installations, M/T repair shops, oil storage tanks and aircraft hangars; the large Alliotti flour mills were also earmarked for destruction. Ten Beaufighters of 252 Squadron, operating from Edcu and Cyprus, were to provide long-range fighter protection, while four Hurricanes of 127 Squadron, also operating from Cyprus, were to provide air support nearer to that island.

Seven Wellingtons drawn from 37 and 40 Squadrons started the ball rolling by bombing Calato airfield between 0020 and 0135, when fires and explosions were observed, then three Wellingtons of 70 Squadron bombed and machine-gunned Lindos airfield, while four more from 148 Squadron raided Maritza airfield. Nine Blenheim crews of 14 Squadron then attacked Candia but had difficulty in seeing results owing to poor visibility. Whilst the air attacks were in progress, the Naval guns opened fire, the cruisers firing 150 rounds each with the destroyers contributing a further 100 rounds apiece, during which the flour mills received direct hits and several fires were started. Four long-range Albacores of 821 Squadron flew over the target areas to drop flares, but illumination was difficult owing to low cloud, reported as 10/10th at 1500 feet.

An unfortunate incident during the bombing raids occurred when bombs fell on the neutral Turkish mainland at Milas; several people were killed and property was damaged. 205 Group denied that any of its Wellingtons were responsible — although the Beaufighters lost their way when returning to Cyprus and did overfly Turkish territory — nonetheless, an apology and indemnity was made to the Turkish Government. Later, however, information received by Intelligence sources from a Yugoslav patriot leader stated that a German aircraft dropped bombs on Turkey that night; apparently even the pilot's name and unit was known! If this was correct, it would have been unlikely that the presence of this aircraft was a coincidence. It was concurred that details of the proposed raid had been leaked to the Axis, and that the bombing was done deliberately to damage British relationships with Turkey.

However, the main objective of the operation — the reduction of air pressure against Malta from Sicily — failed, and attacks against the Island continued to intensify.

Monday, 16 March

Monday began badly with the non-arrival of a transit aircraft from Gibraltar; the fate of Liberator AL577 and its crew are unknown, but it was presumed to have fallen into the sea. No interceptions of raiders were recorded on this day, despite 16 separate raids against Island targets, a listing of these indicating the level of constant attacks Malta was now enduring:-

0733: Seven Ju88s of I/KG 77 raided Luqa
0915: Six Ju88s of II/KG 77 attacked Sliema
1305: One Ju88 of LG 1 bombed Valetta
1320: Six Ju88s of III/KG 77 raided Luqa
1402: Two Ju88s of LG 1 attacked Takali
1412: Two Ju88s of LG 1 attacked Luqa
1420: Three Ju88s of LG 1 raided Safi
1505: Six Ju88s of II/KG 77 attacked Takali
1625: Five Ju88s of II/KG 77 raided Sliema
1720: Six Ju88s of III/KG 77 raided Luqa
1740: Three Ju88s of LG 1 attacked Safi
1835: Two Ju88s of LG 1 attacked Safi
1840: Two Ju88s of LG 1 raided Luqa
1840: One Ju88 of LG 1 bombed in Paola-Vittoriosa area
1842: Two Ju88s of LG 1 raided Takali

The only defiant response Malta could make was to despatch two repaired Wellingtons under cover of darkness to attack Catania. Over the target area Flg.Off. Halliwell and Flt.Sgt. Ellison encountered low cloud, and were unable to locate the airfield; they released their bombs on Flak concentrations. The next two days were to be marked by some heavy fighting over the Island, however.

Tuesday, 17 March

Between 0730 and 0945, 23 Ju88s struck at Luqa, where four Wellingtons (X9886 of 37 Squadron, Z9039 and DV493 of the OADU and Z1164 of 15 OTU) were destroyed and five other aircraft damaged, including a Spitfire and the Mosquito of 69 Squadron. A petrol bowser was burnt out, two civilians killed and three injured. Bombs also fell on Sliema, Tigne and Cospicua, where 23 more civilians and two policemen were killed and 40 civilians seriously injured.

Left: Plt.Off. Bob Sergeant (left) and Sgt. Paul Brennan of 249 Squadron. The Australian Brennan was particularly successful, gaining some 12 victories over Malta. **Right:** Sqn.Ldr. Stan Grant, 249 Squadron's first commanding officer after the arrival of the Spitfires, had already seen considerable action over England and Western Europe. He would return to Malta later in 1942 for a second tour as a Wing Leader. Here he lends a hand at dispersal pen building — a regular off-duty pursuit for all personnel on the Island. *(Daddo-Langlois Collection)*

Four Spitfires and 11 Hurricanes (seven/126 and four/605) were scrambled. The Spitfires climbed to 20,000 feet where six Ju88s and some Bf109s were seen 10,000 feet below. Sgt. Brennan (AB346/K) and Sgt. Tayleur were approached by two Bf109s, but Tayleur's aircraft then went into an uncontrollable dive as his seat had come off its hinges and jammed the control column; he had fallen to 8000 feet before he was able to get it back into place and pull out. Brennan, meanwhile, attacked a Messerschmitt from dead astern, closing from 150 to 100 yards and seeing strikes on the fuselage behind the cockpit, and on the port wing root. It turned on its back and went down, initially being credited as damaged. The claim was later upgraded, Brennan's logbook entry stating:

'Shot down one, confirmed as destroyed. My first.'

The Hurricanes, led by Sqn.Ldr. Wells of 242 Squadron, went after five Ju88s and ten Bf109s at 15,000 feet, as the bombers began their dives. Wells and Sgt. Hale each claimed one damaged and Sgt. Mulloy claimed strikes on two more, while Plt.Off. McHan (LE-E), again flying with the unit, reported:

'Attacked Ju88 from front and below. (*It*) almost dropped bombs on me!'

Flt.Lt. Kemp attacked four Messerschmitts diving on a Hurricane, seeing strikes on one of these, but none of these combats was conclusive. Following this raid, one Ju88 of 6/KG 77 crash-landed at Comiso on return, possibly due to damage sustained.

At 0955, seven more Ju88s and four Bf109s crossed the coast, a further four Spitfires led by Flt.Lt. Heppell attempting to intercept. Unable to gain position, Heppell told the others to dive for home, which they did, led by Sgt. Tayleur. Flt.Sgt. Ian Cormack in AB330 failed to pull out and was killed when his aircraft crashed straight into the sea off Filfla; it was presumed that he had blacked out. During the afternoon and early evening, an estimated 56 raiders approached at intervals, including 25 bombers (five of which were alleged to have been He111s), attacking all three airfields and Grand Harbour. At Takali two Hurricanes were damaged and two civilians killed. A dozen Hurricanes of 126 and 185 Squadrons, with two Spitfires as top cover, were scrambled.

Plt.Off. Steele and Sgt. Sutherland of 185 Squadron jointly claimed a Ju88 damaged; the latter then attacked a Bf109 and saw strikes between its engine and cockpit; an He111 was claimed damaged by 126 Squadron's Flt.Lt. Baker, while Sqn.Ldr. Grant and Plt.Off. Plagis (AB335/F), flying the Spitfires, each claimed damage to Messerschmitts. AA gunners reported one Ju88 shot down and another damaged. A Ju88 of 3/KüFlGr 606 (7T+BL) crash-landed on return to Catania, and was totally destroyed; Obfw. Wilhelm Heipe and his crew were all injured. However, Luftwaffe records imply this loss was caused by a landing accident and not due to enemy action.

During the day a 69 Squadron Maryland had located a convoy of two merchant vessels escorted by a cruiser, six destroyers and at least one Bf110, 200 miles east of Kalafrana. With the onset of dusk five Albacores were sent out, but failed to find the ships; at 2230 three Swordfish — one with flares and two with torpedoes — found a transport, estimated at 2000 tons, with an escort of two E-boats 25 miles from Tripoli. The torpedo-carriers became separated and only one attacked, Sub Lt. Cyril Shute hitting the 1778-ton German *Achaja*, which was set ablaze fore and aft. Return fire shot down the Swordfish, both Shute and his observer, Sub Lt. G.L. Hillary, being lost; the blazing *Achaja* ran into a minefield and was also lost. The second ship, the ex-Yugoslav *Salona*, was trailing some miles to the south and escaped detection.

Two more Swordfish and four Albacores then sighted two further merchant vessels and their escorts 45 miles from Lampedusa at 0232. One Swordfish and one Albacore attacked, claiming one certain and one possible hit on the 6837-ton Italian *Giuliani*, although no damage was actually inflicted. The other aircraft failed to attack due to bad visibility and low cloud.

Wednesday, 18 March

Wednesday saw the disbandment of both 242 and 605 Squadrons (the ground echelons of these squadrons had arrived in the Far East and had subsequently been lost with the fall of Java), all pilots of the former unit being absorbed into 126 Squadron (including Sqn.Ldr. Wells) while all members of the latter became part of 185 Squadron.

Lt. Hermann Neuhoff's Bf109F 'White 2' of III/JG 53, heads towards Malta early in March 1942. The rudder carries 36 white victory bars, the last eight recently claimed over North Africa. *(Neuhoff via J. Prien/W. Bock)*

It was again a day of heavy combat, which began around 0900 when two Bf109s crossed the coast at low level, covered by four more higher up. This marauding pair strafed the Gozo ferry boat *Royal Lady*, which had just docked at Marfa with 209 passengers aboard. Fortunately, only one civilian and two soldiers were wounded. Lunchtime was interrupted by four Spitfires scrambling to intercept five Bf109s patrolling off the coast, while another four Spitfires took off to escort a returning Maryland, but instead engaged two Messerschmitts at sea level south of Delimara. Plt.Off. McNair attacked one which Wg.Cdr. Turner then fired at, reporting damage, while McNair attacked and claimed damage to the other.

At 1425 Maryland AH294 of 69 Squadron, flown by Sgt. Graham Parker RAAF, was intercepted six miles off Benghaisa Point whilst returning from another sortie, and was shot down by Uffz. Michael Beikiefer of 6/JG 3; there were no survivors. The bombers were back during the early evening, 24 Ju88s of I/KG 54, KüFlGr 606 and KGr 806, in five waves with large fighter escort, bombing the airfields; in excess of 14 tons of bombs were dropped. Returning bomber crews estimated that 14 twin-engined aircraft had been badly damaged in these attacks, but were wildly optimistic in their claims. At Hal Far one Albacore was destroyed and several others hit by debris, while a hangar was almost demolished, and at Luqa three damaged Wellingtons were destroyed.

Four Spitfires and 11 Hurricanes (four/126, seven/185) were scrambled to meet this raid, but at 12,500 feet the Spitfires were jumped by four Bf109s. Plt.Off. Harry Fox's AB334/J was hit and the 20 year-old Liverpudlian baled out into the sea and was lost. Flt.Lt. Macqueen attacked a Bf109 which he believed had just shot down Fox, opened fire from 100 yards whereupon it smoked, shed pieces, and dived into the sea close to where Fox's Spitfire had splashed, about three miles off Wied iz-Zurrieq. The pilot of < 2, Lt. Kurt Lauinger of Stab

III/JG 53, was later picked up by HSL 107, wounded and with a broken leg. Although he claimed that he had shot down a Spitfire, claims were also submitted by other returning pilots of III/JG 53, one by Lt. Jurgen Harder (his 11th), and one by Lt. Ernst Kläger (his 10th).

Two Hurricanes were also claimed by pilots of III Gruppe, one each by Ofw. Stumpf (his 29th) and Lt. Neuhoff (38th) and, indeed, Plt.Off. 'Chuck' Lester (Z2840/T) and Sgt. George Mulloy (Z5213), both of 185 Squadron, were shot down. The Australian Lester was severely wounded and crashed into the sea, from where he was picked up by HSL 128 within the hour, but of Mulloy no sign could be found despite two searches. Of the fight and the shooting down of his close friend, Plt.Off. McKay of 185 Squadron noted in his diary:

> 'We climbed out over Gozo and then the Me109s started to bother us. We then had to turn and go back across the Island after the 88s. We did this by going straight for a minute then turning around after the 109s. We eventually did get to the 88s and some of us had a squirt at them. The 109s were coming down on us all the time and it was damn dangerous to fly straight and level for any length of time. Hal Far was bombed — and Luqa — so Don Stones, Fletcher and I came back and landed at Takali.
>
> 'We then heard that "Chuck" Lester had been jumped by four 109s and, not having any ammunition left, had to go down to sea level to get away from them, but one got him eventually through the leg and he hit the sea and was thrown out. The next thing he remembered is he was holding on to his dinghy but couldn't get into it 'cause both his legs were u/s.
>
> 'He is pretty badly shaken up. He has a compound fracture in one leg and a cannon shell in the other, and his face is badly bruised. It is amazing how he ever got out of his aircraft; he was going at least 220 (*mph*) when he hit the water.'

Other claims during these actions were submitted by Flg.Off. Lee and Sgt. Berchamps of 249 Squadron, who reported damaging a Ju88 and a Bf109 respectively; Flt.Lt. Stones (Z4942/GL-Y) of 185 Squadron attacked the same Ju88 as Lee and saw strikes, then attacked two others without result, while Flt.Sgt. Fletcher (BG770/UP-D) reported seeing strikes on the port engine of the Ju88 he attacked. Immediately following this action, HSL 107 was sent out to search for the downed pilots, escorted by two Spitfires. Bf109s were encountered and one was claimed damaged by Plt.Off. Bob Sergeant.

At 1830 Takali was again raided, this time by seven Ju88s; the airfield was rendered temporarily unusable due to cratering, and two Hurricanes were destroyed; another and two unserviceable Spitfires were damaged, while a Beaufighter was also damaged. Additionally, a petrol bowser containing 800 gallons of fuel was set ablaze and a tractor was destroyed. AA gunners claimed two of the raiders damaged, while on return to Catania a Ju88 of I/KG 54 crashed, apparently due to engine failure; the pilot of B3+EH, Lt. Klaus-Dieter Herberg, was killed although the three members of his crew managed to bale out safely.

At the end of this day's raids 37 Squadron's detachment had virtually ceased to exist. Of the 15 Wellingtons which had originally flown into Luqa, 11 had by now been destroyed, two of them in accidents. Two reinforcement aircraft had arrived but both of these had been destroyed. All that remained was one serviceable and three badly damaged aircraft. The lone airworthy survivor was, therefore, flown back to Egypt, Wg.Cdr. Nash and several other crews following in a departing Sunderland, while the remaining crews and ground personnel would evacuate aboard HMS *Carlisle*.

That night (18th/19th), two Swordfish and two Albacores set off on a shipping search in the Tripoli-Lampedusa area, but one of the former returned early with engine trouble, crashed on landing and burst into flames; the crew escaped unhurt. When the second Swordfish developed similar trouble, all three aircraft returned.

Thursday, 19 March

The day was marked by a single raid on Takali by an estimated 15 Ju88s (including aircraft of II/KG 77 and KüFlGr 606) and a dozen Bf109s, which destroyed Beaufighter X7648 of the night fighter detachment as it was under repair. Another Beaufighter, two Hurricanes and a Spitfire were damaged. At Luqa Z9035, an unserviceable delivery Wellington from 15 OTU, was also burnt out, while the Polish submarine *Sokol* — attached to the 10th Flotilla — was strafed by four Bf109s of II/JG 53 as it was making for Grand Harbour from Lazaretto Creek. The Messerschmitt pilots believed they had killed or wounded about 20 of the crew who were seen on the deck, but no casualties were in fact suffered. Although hit by eight 20mm cannon shells, little damage was inflicted. One of the raiders, a Ju88 (7T+AL) of 3/KüFlGr 606, was hit by AA splinters and a member of the crew was killed. A second Junkers, its crew briefed to attack a target south of Rabat, failed to regain its base; it was reported to have crashed near Comiso on return, Fw. Hubertus Hermann and his 7/KG 77 crew perishing.

The crew of a delivery Blenheim which arrived during the day reported seeing another such aircraft — which turned out to have been V6394 — crash into the sea about 30 miles off Cape Bon, apparently as a result of engine failure. Although the point of entry was circled for ten minutes, no survivors were seen. Other arrivals included six Beauforts of 22 Squadron, led by Sqn.Ldr. J.A. Bateson, which were on their way to Ceylon via Egypt; a seventh aircraft had been lost en route (Plt.Off. W.A. Thornton RAAF, and crew), while one section of three had been attacked by Bf110s. These managed to escape after Plt.Off. J.C. White's AW389 had been damaged and his air gunner, Sgt. Macaskell, wounded in the shoulder. This aircraft crashed on landing at Luqa, but the crew survived unhurt. Another crew reported sighting a dinghy with two occupants some 20 miles from Galite Island. Next day the six surviving aircraft flew on to Egypt.

A further arrival at this time was another photo-reconnaissance Spitfire (BP895) which was also on its way to Egypt, in the hands of Sgt. Leslie Colquhoun, a former member of 603 Squadron. On this occasion Air Vice-Marshal Lloyd actually requested permission from AHQ, Middle East, to retain both aircraft and pilot, and this was granted. The need for this aircraft was heightened by the departure of Flt.Lt. Warburton, who left for Egypt in his Beaufighter (on completion of his tour) with Cpl. Ron Hadden and LAC Norman Shirley, both of whom sported their newly-awarded DFMs; Adrian Warburton now proudly wore the ribbon of the DSO next to his double DFC. During his three months back on the Island, Warburton had flown 43 sorties and survived many close encounters. On one occasion he had passed above Catania's

Left: Flt.Lt. (later Wg.Cdr.) Adrian Warburton DFC, the photographic-reconnaissance 'ace' of 69 Squadron. **Right:** Warburton's stalwart camera operator, LAC (later Cpl.) Norman Shirley of 69 Squadron, who was awarded a DFM although not officially aircrew.

main runway at below hangar height, his Beaufighter sustaining damage from machine-gun fire. One bullet literally parted Shirley's hair as he operated the camera, slicing a groove through the top of his helmet!

With nightfall, motor-boats of the German 3rd MTB Flotilla laid a further 93 mines to the east and west of Grand Harbour, while six BR20Ms of 55° Gruppo BT bombed the Island's airfields between 0150 and 0305. Flt.Lt. Hayton was up again to intercept in his Beaufighter (X7750), claiming severe damage to one of the bombers and in fact his shooting had again been lethal, Sottoten. Girolamo Biundo's aircraft failing to return with the loss of all the crew.

Friday, 20 March

The day began normally enough, an estimated total of 20 Ju88s (II/KG 77 and LG 1) and 60 Bf109s appearing at intervals between 0810 and 1310, bombs falling on Valetta, Sliema, St Julians, Hamrun, Zeitun, Grand Harbour and the submarine base at Manoel Island. Two Ju88s of LG 1 were responsible for the latter attack, each releasing SC 1800 rocket-assisted bombs, one of which was reported to have hit the Governor's Palace. In fact, little damage of note was caused but six civilians and two soldiers were killed, 41 other persons suffering injuries.

Four Spitfires and a dozen Hurricanes went off at 0805, and Plt.Off. McNair of 249 Squadron encountered a Bf109. Firing at the German fighter as it turned, McNair saw pieces fall off and it went down in a spiral dive, pouring clouds of smoke; a splash was seen in the sea south of Delimara. There is little doubt that this was 'White 4' of 7/JG 53, in which Uffz. Josef Fankhauser was killed. However, Plt.Off. 'Douggie' Leggo was lagging behind when a Bf109 came out of the sun, and shot him down from 50 yards range; AB337 crashed in a field near Qrendi, the pilot being killed. Claims for Spitfires were submitted by Lt. Neuhoff (his 39th) and Lt. Kläger (11th), both of III/JG 53. Doug Leggo's grieving fellow Rhodesian, Johnny Plagis, recorded:

> 'Swear to shoot down ten for Doug — I will too, if it takes me a lifetime.'

Meanwhile, the AA defence also claimed a Ju88 and a Bf109 shot down and four Ju88s damaged. While no Ju88 was reported lost in these morning raids, a Bf109 of 6/JG 3 flown by Uffz. Michael Beikiefer may have been hit, for it crashed near Gela, the pilot being killed, although Luftwaffe records would suggest the loss was due to technical failure.

At the beginning of March, OKW had sanctioned new tactics for the assault on Malta in view of the increasing losses being suffered by individual or small formations of aircraft. Now RAF fighters were to be attacked on the ground at Takali in a surprise raid; the bases at Luqa, Hal Far and Kalafrana were also to be raided, while the docks and harbour installations at Valetta naval base were again to be targeted.

It was planned that two or three Staffeln of Messerschmitts should be sent over half an hour before the main attack was due in an attempt to get the defending fighters into the air; the intention was to make them use their ammunition and fuel, and force them to land prior to the arrival of the bombers. More Bf109s would then arrive and circle the airfields to pick off any Spitfires and Hurricanes entering the landing circuit. This particular tactic was to be adhered to for several weeks, during which period a number of British fighters would be destroyed or damaged in the act of touching down, while others ran out of fuel and crash-landed, often closely pursued by Bf109s. Indeed, this became perhaps the greatest danger that was to bedevil the defending fighter pilots.

Commencement of these attacks was delayed until photo-reconnaissance aircraft could confirm that the Spitfires and Hurricanes were mainly concentrated at Takali, and sufficient bomber crews were available to carry out the proposed mass formation raids. Feldmarschall Kesselring called for every aircrew with night flying experience to participate, and by the evening of the 20th the Luftwaffe was ready to strike. As dusk fell the Island's radar screens showed large numbers of aircraft assembling over Sicily and heading towards Malta. By 1830 the vanguard of some 63 Ju88s, drawn from II and III/KG 77, I/KG 54, KüFlGr 606 and KGr 806, began crossing the coast, escorted by Bf110s of III/ZG 26, Ju88Cs of I/NJG 2 and a few Bf109s. No defending fighters rose to oppose the aerial armada, but AA gunners claimed four Ju88s shot down and another damaged. Although an aircraft of KüFlGr 606 crash-landed at Catania, 40% damaged, there were no other recorded losses.

Takali was rendered unserviceable following this onslaught, when in excess of 114 tons of bombs were directed at the airfield. German crews reported good accuracy, with explosions seen among quarters, hangars and aircraft blast pens; it was believed a fuel dump was also set ablaze. A number of aircraft were damaged, including the Station Flight Magister (N5428), which was written-off. A petrol bowser, an ammunition lorry and a nearby aircraft caught fire, but the fires were quickly tackled by teams led by Flt.Sgt. Hugh Stammwitz, Cpl. Tom Barkas and LAC Harry Venn, in spite of heavy bombing. When the extinguishers were empty, these three continued to put out incendiaries, even though many were explosive; each was awarded a BEM for his actions.

Bombs fell on Naxxar, Mosta, Zebbug and Attard during this raid, ten civilians being killed, but the Luftwaffe particularly concentrated on what they believed was an underground hangar on the edge of Takali airfield. Photographs taken by reconnaissance aircraft revealed "a ramp on the airfield's boundary, leading downward. Beside it was a huge heap of earth and rock." The Germans were well-aware that just such an impregnable facility had been constructed by their Italian allies on nearby Pantelleria island, but at Takali there was no such hangar.

The British authorities, however, had sought to foster the belief that such a construction did exist, as Wg.Cdr. Jack Satchell confirmed:

> 'We encouraged the Germans into believing in the existence of an underground hangar. What happened was that we tried to cleave the rock, which caved in. On realizing the impracticability of the project, we painted half-open hangar doors and put in the opening all our broken-down Hurricanes and Spitfires, mocked up with pieces of wood and sacking. The Hun plastered hell out of them; we did not mind!'

However, on the periphery of the aerodrome four caves had indeed been cut out of the rock, and these accommodated the Station Orderly Room, the Equipment Section, Station Armoury and a fuel dump. The openings were covered by a double stone wall; the large quantity of loose rock excavated was heaped up in the open outside the caves. This mass of rock cuttings, clearly visible from the air, had obviously given the Germans the impression of an underground hangar.

To deal with such a difficult — albeit non-existent — target, a number of Ju88s were armed with the special PC 1800 RS armour-piercing bombs. Known to the Luftwaffe as 'Panther' bombs, the 2057kg Raketensatz (rocket-assisted) PC 1800 was fitted with cordite candles to give greater velocity and to increase penetration. It was claimed to be capable of penetrating rock or concrete to a depth of 45 feet.

The Naval air strike force was out again after dark, three Albacores locating a small convoy 23 miles off Messina. Two torpedoes were released at the lone freighter but results were not observed due to intense and accurate AA fire from the two escorting destroyers. Neither the Axis vessel nor the attacking biplanes suffered any damage.

Saturday, 21 March

The Luftwaffe's all-out assault on Takali was repeated during the morning, a total of 106 Ju88s (plus one Bf110 for observation duties), escorted by large numbers of Bf109s — over 200 aircraft in all — appearing between 0845 and 1015. The airfield was again heavily cratered (182 tons of bombs being released here), and many delayed-action bombs were dropped in the first example of 'carpet-bombing' the Island had experienced. Despite a complete lack of opposition in the air, only two persons were killed and seven injured on this occasion, the AA claiming one bomber shot down and two damaged, but without actual effect.

Soon after the bombers had departed, eight Bf110s of III/ZG 26 appeared overhead to bomb and strafe Hal Far, under an umbrella of some 35 Bf109s. Two Hurricanes, two Beauforts and a Spitfire were damaged, but six of 185 Squadron's Hurricanes were up, led by Sqn.Ldr. Mortimer-Rose, now recovered from his wounds and returned to action at the head of this unit. Called in to defend their airfield, they slipped past the escorting Bf109s and dived out of the sun in a perfect 'bounce' onto the tails of the Zerstörer, just as these crossed the coast at St Paul's Bay. Mortimer-Rose (in Z2961/K) opened fire and claimed two shot down in flames into the sea at once. The rest broke off and headed for Sicily, the Hurricanes in hot pursuit. Plt.Off. Beckitt (BN120/H) and Plt.Off. Allardice (BG711/G) pursued one and soon caught up with it; Joe Beckitt:

> 'Fired at second last e/a in formation — hits on fuselage and tail — smoke and sparks — last seen losing height over the sea. Saw another 110 go into the sea about five miles off St Paul's Bay.'

Reported Phil Allardice:

> 'I first sighted the bandits about 2000 feet above to port... I turned and dived to port as they came down and gave some short bursts from astern, scoring hits on one bomber from 200 yards. As we went out over St Paul's Bay I could not close, so I turned my attention to another bomber which was below me at about 50 feet. At the same time I saw two other Hurricanes making attacks on another bomber still further to port at same level. I did quarter attacks and then sat behind him giving long bursts until ammo ran out. I saw pieces fall off the fuselage, clouds of smoke and a/c staggered badly and my a/c covered in oil. When later seen e/a was very low and flying erratically.'

They were jointly credited with the destruction of this aircraft, while a fourth was claimed shared by Plt.Off. Ormrod (BG769/J) and Plt.Off. Wigley (BG770/D). Sgt. Ray Hesselyn of 249 Squadron was visiting Hal Far when the attack took place, and wrote:

> 'Eight Me110s came out of the sun in a shallow dive... but all the bombs fell short and none hit the aerodrome. The Me110s machine-gunned the aerodrome as they passed over... saw four Hurricanes diving out of the sun onto the tails of the bombers, which were straggled out line abreast. The Hurricanes opened fire as the bombers crossed the coast, apparently taking the 110s by surprise. It was point blank range, and almost simultaneously four of the 110s dived seawards. Two of them burst into flames, flicked over and fell straight into the drink. The other two lazily rolled on their backs and then dropped straight into the sea. The remaining four 110s at once broke, and began weaving, each steering a different course for home. Splitting up, the Hurricanes gave chase to the 110s, shooting down two more before returning to base.'

Yet, despite this apparent eye witness report of the destruction of at least four and possibly six of the Zerstörer, available German records indicate but a single loss — 3U+FT of 9 Staffel, together with the crew (Lt. Hans Hufnagel and Uffz. Emil Camler). However, it seems likely that two others may also have been lost, although it would seem that the crews may have survived. Of the apparent lack of admission of more than the one loss in German records, Phil Wigley comments:

> 'It is significant that none was reported by the German authorities to have been damaged, and that no Me110 was ever seen over the island again by day, although apparently there were occasional glimpes of them elsewhere (at night near Lampedusa, escorting convoys). Consequently, one is led to believe that the 110s had sustained serious losses and that the German records do not present the exact picture — there must have been a good

reason for the virtual non-appearance of these aircraft over Malta after 21st March.'

Messerschmitt Bf110 3U+JR of III/ZG 26 on a Sicilian airfield. Aircraft from this unit carried out a fighter-bomber raid on Takali on 21 March 1942, but suffered at the hands of defending 185 Squadron Hurricane pilots. *(via N. Malizia)*

TABLE 1

Operation 'Picket I'

9 Spitfires from HMS *Eagle* (it had been the intention to fly off 16 Spitfires but Blenheim escort for second flight failed to arrive)

Sqn.Ldr. E.J. Gracie DFC	BP844	Sgt. G.S. Bolton, RNZAF	
Flt.Lt. H.A.S. Johnston	BP850	Sgt. W.L. Miller, RNZAF	
Plt.Off. M.A. Graves		Sgt. W.H.L. Milner	
Plt.Off. D.W. McLeod, RCAF (US)		Sgt. J.W. Yarra, RAAF	AB333
Plt.Off. J.E. Peck, RCAF (US)			

As the engagement with the Bf110s was underway, the first elements of the second delivery of Spitfires were winging their way from *Eagle* — Operation 'Picket I' (see Table 1 above). Led by Sqn.Ldr. E.J. 'Jumbo' Gracie DFC, they included amongst their number Sgt. Yarra who, it will be recalled, had been forced to return to Gibraltar earlier in the month when his Spitfire proved to be unserviceable. Yarra recorded:

> 'The morrow dawned and the weather was lousy. Foggy and raining with a ceiling of 1000 feet. However we decided to take off and attempt the trip if the Blenheims found us. At 9am the first Blenheim arrived and we started to get off. I was the third man off. When my turn came I taxied into position. I was rather keyed up and my nerves were taut as stay-wires, but as soon as I opened the throttle I lost all my tautness and got that queer kick one always gets when opening up on the world's best fighter aircraft. The old Merlin sounded very sweet that morning as I raced down that little deck and lifted

off the end. At that moment the fact that we had 700 miles to travel over water, and hostile water at that, mattered not the slightest. All that mattered was that I was in the air again after nearly three weeks on the ground. We formed up on the leader and began our 700 mile trip. We were right down on the deck all the way, flying through rainstorms and patches of thick mist. We made one attempt to get above the overcast, but as this was unsuccessful we remained on the deck for the remainder of the way. I had trouble with my air pressure all the way. The release valve was not working and I had to keep the pressure down.'

Due to the adverse weather, not all the guiding Blenheims rendezvoused with the carrier and as a result, only nine of the 16 Spitfires aboard were launched before the ships had to turn back; that flown by Sgt. G.S. Bolton almost stall-turned into the sea on take-off, but the New Zealander managed to regain control. During the operation two Italian submarines — *Moncenigo* and *Dandolo* — were in the area, the former manoeuvring into a favourable position to fire two torpedoes at the escorting carrier *Argus*, which was again providing the fighter cover for the laden *Eagle*; both missiles missed their mark.

Meanwhile, the Spitfires droned on towards Malta, Yarra's diary continuing:

'As we were passing Pantelleria we sighted a squadron of CR42s (biplane fighters) but, as they did not interfere, we were quite happy to let them alone. We could not afford to use up vital petrol dog-fighting. After three hours flying I was very much in need of a cigarette but, as I could not find any matches, I had to forego the pleasure. I could see smoke coming from various other cockpits as the boys were enjoying their smokes. When we were 30 minutes from Malta we tightened up our formation a little and began to keep a good lookout for hostile aircraft. Suddenly Malta showed up on the horizon dead ahead. I, for one, was very pleased, as we had been flying for four hours and we were very tired. Just then I happened to look around and spotted a twin-engined machine approaching from the starboard quarter astern. I immediately thought Me110 and broke away to do a head-on attack. Just as I was about to fire I recognised it as a Beaufort. I very nearly squirted at that guy. He would have been a little brassed if I had! We landed at Takali and put the aircraft away. I then went up to the Mess to get a drink and find out how the rest of the boys were. I learned that Mac, Fox, Leggo and Murray were all dead and that, out of the 15 Spitfires they had brought, only two were left.'

The newly-arrived pilots — amongst whom were two Americans, Plt.Offs. Jimmy Peck and Don McLeod — were swiftly greeted to a display of German might, for at 1435 the third major raid to be centred on Takali within 24 hours began — 70 Ju88s with a large fighter escort bombing the airfield, while bombs also fell on Rabat, Mosta, Boschetto, Gzira, Tigne, Attard and Birkirkara. At Rabat, a large bomb fell just outside the front door of the Point de Vue Hotel which had been requisitioned to billet RAF officers stationed at nearby Takali, where a number of officers were gathered; six were killed outright, including four fighter pilots — Flt.Lt. Cecil Baker and Plt.Off. Bill Hollis Hallett of 126 Squadron, and Flg.Off. John Booth and Plt.Off. Jimmy Guerin of 249 Squadron. Additionally, the American Plt.Off. Eddie 'Junior' Streets, also of 126 Squadron, lost a leg and was blinded, and succumbed to his injuries in hospital.

Left: Sqn.Ldr. (later Wg.Cdr.) E.J. 'Jumbo' Gracie DFC, led the second delivery of Spitfires to Malta, and then commanded 126 Squadron. He later became Wing Commander at Takali, where he was a great inspiration to all serving under him. *(R.F. Noble)*. **Right:** One of the most successful of the Australian pilots to serve on Malta was Sgt. Gordon Tweedale, who flew with 126 and 185 Squadrons on Hurricanes before losing his life in action. *(L. McAuley)*

Once again there were no fighters up to intercept, but the AA claimed three Ju88s shot down and three others damaged; on this occasion the gunners' claiming proved to be more accurate. The bombers attacked in waves, usually diving down to 6000 feet but in some instances even lower, some releasing one large and ten smaller bombs, whilst others dropped two large bombs fastened together with a stout chain. Oblt. Rolf Kreig dived his KüFlGr 606 machine down to about 3000 feet, but was hit by Bofors fire, 7T+FH crashing in the middle of the runway; Kreig was killed but his crew managed to bale out to become prisoners. LAC Jim Somerville recalled:

> 'It was during the first wave of the afternoon attack that I brought a member of a Jerry bomber into a slit trench after he had baled out over Takali. When the all-clear went, some Maltese farmers appeared on the scene bearing all manner of wicked-looking farm implements. Just then an officer and a squad of soldiers came down the hill towards us. Go with the soldiers, I advised the Jerry. He gave me one of his medal ribbons.'

A second bomber — 3Z+FN of 5/KG 77 flown by Fw. Herbert Witt — lost a wing practically overhead, and crashed on the perimeter of the airfield. Two figures were observed to leap out, but came crashing to earth without parachutes. Whether they had forgotten to clip on their chest packs in the panic to abandon the stricken aircraft, or decided a freefall was preferable to death in the inevitable crash, was not clear. A third aircraft — from KGr 806 — was also hit and crash-landed at Catania on return, 30% damaged. A Bf109 of 4/JG 3 also crashed about ten miles south of San Pietro during the day, Uffz. Wolfgang

Buttstadt being injured; the reason for this crash is not known.

The results of the two raids were to damage Takali so severely that returning Luftwaffe crews reported that the base looked as if it had been subjected to volcanic eruption! Air Vice-Marshal Lloyd had to agree that it resembled a First War battlefield, and it was feared that it would remain unserviceable for at least a week. However, troops worked all through the night and the next day, and by the evening of the 22nd all serviceable Spitfires and Hurricanes were able to be flown over to Luqa. A reservoir on the edge of the airfield had also been destroyed, and millions of gallons of water lost — a severe blow to riverless Malta; as a result part of the airfield was temporarily flooded.

On the airfield itself two Spitfires, four Hurricanes, a Beaufighter, a Maryland and a Wellington had been destroyed, while five Spitfires, 15 Hurricanes, three Beaufighters, two Blenheims and a Maryland were damaged. The destroyed Maryland had only just been repaired following a crash-landing two weeks earlier, and was being prepared for a test flight at the time. Although a large number of Hurricanes were recorded as being destroyed or damaged, Lloyd indicated in his memoirs that most of these aircraft had been irreparably damaged in earlier raids, and had been placed in pens as decoys, so that actual losses were not as bad as they at first seemed — though serious enough by all accounts!

Around the Takali area, Mosta had been particularly hard-hit; 35 houses were demolished, 31 civilians killed and 80 injured. Two bombs had hit the entrance and emergency exit of a shelter in Gafsa Street, where many of the casualties were suffered. It seems that crews of LG 1 had been briefed to bomb Mosta in the belief that flying personnel and dock workers were billeted there. At Saqqajja, Rabat, several homes and a hotel were destroyed and eight persons killed; at Sliema 19 houses were damaged, with two persons killed; at Attard six houses were damaged, with one killed and two injured. A bomb also fell on the St Agatha Internment Camp where Maltese sympathisers of the Italian Fascist regime were imprisoned; here two internees were killed.

The new Spitfires and their pilots were intended to re-form 126 Squadron in a similar manner to that which had occurred with 249 Squadron earlier in the month. While Sgt. Yarra went to rejoin his colleagues in the latter unit, Sqn.Ldr. Gracie now became commanding officer of 126 Squadron vice Sqn.Ldr. Wells, who was posted to Takali Headquarters on promotion to Wing Commander. The few remaining Hurricane pilots of the unit who were not already due for a rest (their numbers reduced by the deaths in the Rabat Mess that day) were posted to Hal Far to join 185 Squadron, which was now the sole remaining day Hurricane unit on the Island.

Because of the losses of Spitfires to date, however — four had been lost in the air and two destroyed on the ground — 249 and 126 Squadrons were going to have to share the remaining aircraft. This left the two units with a preponderance of pilots to aircraft, while 185 Squadron was very low on pilots. Consequently after about a week, a 'trawl' was made of the Spitfire pilots to establish who had Hurricane experience.

The arrival of the new Spitfires and new faces brought with it a debate on tactics. Initially it had been policy to send up the Spitfires as cover to the Hurricanes, their task to hold off the Messerschmitts while the latter sought to deal with the Ju88s. Experience had shown however that the Hurricane IIBs were too slow and too lightly-armed to have great effect against the swift, heavily-armed bombers. Few cannon-armed IICs now remained, and of those that did, most had had two of their four cannons removed to increase their speed although thereby reducing their fire-power by half.

249 Squadron's initial experience had been to lose as many of their own aircraft to the Bf109s as they were able to claim — hardly a profitable ratio, given the circumstances. The case was put that II Fliegerkorps would be harder hit by bomber losses than by the loss of fighters, while Malta would be better-served if fewer bombers got through. It was agreed, therefore, that in future both Spitfires and Hurricanes would concentrate their efforts against the bombers, and avoid the escorting fighters wherever possible.

Albacore X8942/5B of 828 Squadron which was forced to ditch in bad weather on return from a seven hour flight on 22 March; only the pilot survived. *(R. Sturtivant)*

Sunday, 22 March

Sunday began badly. An ASV Albacore (X8942/5B) out on a midnight search for shipping, returned in the early hours in bad weather having sighted nothing. It was forced to ditch off Zonqor Point at the end of a seven-hour flight, only Lt. R.D. Head, the pilot, managing to swim ashore; Sub Lt. B.W. Rivers and L/Air. W.P. Tuttle were both drowned.

At 0950 a raid by six Ju88s and 20 Bf109s was reported coming in, making for Luqa and Takali. Seven Hurricanes of 185 Squadron from Hal Far were all that could be scrambled, Plt.Off. Allardice, Plt.Off. Wigley (BG770/D) and New Zealander Sgt. Robb attacking three Ju88s over the sea south of the Island; each claimed hits on a Junkers, but Phil Allardice (BG711/G) failed to return, apparently shot down by return fire, although Lt. Rudolf Müller of 8/JG 53 claimed a fighter which he identified as a Spitfire. Recalled Phil Wigley:

> 'The Ju88s got away quite easily — they had jettisoned their bomb loads just as we attacked and by diving away at full power they lived to fight another day. It was clear we needed the faster Spitfire and 20mm cannon to deal with the 88 and 109F, although the Hurricane was very much of a menace to the slower Ju87. P/O Allardice was definitely shot down by cross-fire from one of the Ju88 rear-gunners. We were both attacking two of the 88s at the same time — there were no 109s anywhere in sight at the time.'

Luqa suffered heavily during this raid, where Maryland AR712 and an unserviceable Wellington were both destroyed, and two damaged Blenheims were again hit and further damaged; two soldiers were killed while seven more servicemen and nine civilians were injured.

The Saga of Convoy MW10

Meanwhile, even as the 'Picket I' Spitfire delivery was underway from the west, from the eastern end of the Mediterranean a substantial convoy had put to sea carrying 26,000 tons of urgently-needed supplies for the Island. Known as MW10, the convoy comprised three merchantmen — *Clan Campbell* (17,500 tons), *Talabot* (17,000 tons) and *Pampas* (15,500 tons) — plus the navy supply vessel *Breconshire*, on her eighth sortie to Malta. The latter's cargo was typical — comprising 5000 tons of fuel oil, 176 tons of kerosene, 150 tons of .303 ammunition, 100 crates of 500lb bombs, 100 crates of 3-inch AA ammunition, 650 tons of grain and 690 tons of coal.

This body of ships had sailed from Alexandria early on the 20th to rendezvous with the escort of four cruisers, 16 destroyers and six submarines, under the command of Rear Admiral Vian. Force 'K' at Malta was to sortie with the cruiser *Penelope* and a destroyer (*Legion*), to meet the incoming force. Initial air cover was provided by Kittyhawks of 3 RAAF Squadron from their desert base at Gambut, these fighters being fitted with long-range tanks for the purpose.

Throughout the first day (the 20th) the ships seemed to have escaped detection — although, in fact, they had been spotted by an Axis submarine — but shortly before dusk, half an hour after the last of the escorting fighters had departed, a formation of five Ju52/3m transports appeared quite by chance, flying between Crete and Cyrenaica. Skirting the convoy out of range of the guns, they obviously gave the alarm and in short order a pair of S.79sil trimotors from 205ª Squadriglia AS on Rhodes — flown by Cap. Ettore Sondalini and Sottoten. Normanno White — approached and launched two torpedoes from long range and without effect.

Within 12 hours of sailing, Vian had received a signal from *P.36*, one of the submarines scouting well ahead, that elements of the Italian fleet had departed Taranto. This was a formidable force commanded by Ammiraglio (Admiral) Angelo Iachino, comprising the battleship *Littorio*, cruisers *Gorizia, Trento* and *Giovanni Delle Banda Nere*, and ten destroyers — a squadron which far outgunned the British escorting force. It was provided with air cover by units of 4ª Squadra from Puglia, and by four Ju88s and eight Bf110s. The Axis also put all their anti-shipping bomber units on priority alert in Crete, Sicily and Cyrenaica. The Regia Aeronautica made immediate re-locations as follows:—

130° Gruppo Aut. AS moved its S.79sil from Elmas (Sardinia) to Catania, while 278ª Squadriglia AS transferred its S.79sil from Catania to Castelvetrano. Meanwhile, 36° Stormo AS's S.84sil flew from Sardinia to Sciacca, Sicily, and 279ª Squadriglia AS arrived in Cyrenaica with its S.79sil from Naples/ Capodichino; while 205ª Squadriglia AS transferred its S.79sil from Rhodes to Heraklion, Crete. To the total of 132 Italian torpedo-carrying strike aircraft, the Luftwaffe had available 124 more (mostly Ju88s) 40 of them bombers of II Fliegerkorps.

In an attempt to subdue the threat from airfields located on Crete and in Southern Greece, it had been intended that Desert-based Blenheims and Wellingtons would carry out a series of raids. Thus, early on the morning of the

20th, five Blenheims of 14 Squadron were briefed to attack Heraklion, but two of these crashed immediately after taking off, killing two of the crew members and injuring the other four; a third aircraft returned after an hour owing to instrument trouble. The other two aircraft, in spite of bad visibility, reached the target area and dropped a paltry eight 250lb bombs without results being observed.

That night two Wellingtons of 104 Squadron, five of 108 Squadron and seven of 148 Squadron, took off to attack Heraklion again, and also Eleusis and Hassani aerodromes, near Athens. The weather proved hopeless operationally — 9/10th cloud and severe electric storms — and results were negligible; eight aircraft turned back on account of the weather, three bombed Heraklion, two bombed Sitia (nearby), and one bombed Hassani.

On the following night (21st/22nd) the crews of five Wellingtons of 37 Squadron, seven of 38 Squadron and five of 108 Squadron, were briefed to attack the same three aerodromes. Two of this force were prevented from taking off by engine trouble, and weather again forced seven to abandon the task. Of the six that reached Crete, one bombed Heraklion, two bombed Tymbaki airfield, one bombed Rettimo landing ground, and two released their loads over the southern coast of the island. Two others bombed their allotted target at Hassani, on the mainland.

One further similarly futile attempt was made to disrupt flying from the main Cretan airfields on the night of the 23rd/24th. This raid comprised five Wellingtons of 37 Squadron, four of 38 Squadron, two of 104 Squadron and three of 148 Squadron; four aircraft aborted due to hazy conditions, the others bombing without tangible results.

Meanwhile, by the morning of the 22nd, Beaufighters of 252 and 272 Squadrons from Gambut had taken over protection of the convoy, but were unable to distract a shadowing Ju88. At 0930 the escorting Beaufighters had just reached the limit of their range and had turned for base. At this point four S.79sil of 279ª Squadriglia, led by Cap. Giulio Marini, swept in to attack. Although the crews claimed two hits, all the torpedoes missed. Ten. Gugliemo Ranieri's aircraft failed to return, while that flown by Ten. Andrea Dell'Anna was seriously damaged. Behind them came four more torpedo-bombers from 284ª Squadriglia from Cyrenaica, led by Cap. Oscar Pegna, these crews optimistically claiming hits on two cruisers and a merchant vessel!

There were no further attacks during the morning, although an S.79 and a Cant Z506B were observed shadowing. Shortly after 1330, a Ju88 flew over the convoy following which a line of red flares were seen dropping ahead of the leading ships, apparently to signal their position to the approaching Italian warships, the first of which was sighted at 1410. Leaving just the AA cruiser *Carlisle* and six destroyers to cover the convoy — two of the latter at once making smoke to conceal the transports — Admiral Vian headed straight for the Italians at full speed, his ships in five parallel columns. The Italian vessels turned broadside and opened fire from long range; there followed 15 tense minutes before the British closed range sufficiently to reply. After a brief exchange, the Italians turned away, and at 1515 Vian's force was able to turn back to the convoy. The first round had definitely gone to the Royal Navy.

As this naval action had been taking place, the convoy had again been attacked from the air, this time by Ju88s and S.79s, a dozen of the latter from 278ª and 280ª Squadriglia having weathered atrocious conditions on the flight from Sicily. Their crews claimed hits on four transports and a cruiser but again no damage was actually caused, although *Breconshire* was straddled by bombs from the German aircraft, and there were several near misses. However, by the time the attackers withdrew some of the destroyers had expended up to 60% of their AA ammunition.

The ships' gunners had indeed thrown up a ferocious barrage; Sottoten. Gaetano Marietta's 280ª Squadriglia machine was badly hit and ditched in the sea off Catania on return, the crew perishing. A second aircraft from this unit was similarly hit and ditched off the Eolie group of islands; Sottoten. Giovanni Scalia's crew managed to scramble into their life-raft, but one of the flight engineers, 1° Av.Mot. Vito Bonfiglio, climbed back into the aircraft to retrieve the compass. As he did so, a large wave engulfed the raft with the loss of all aboard; Bonfiglio survived alone to be rescued by a Cant floatplane next day. A third 280ª Squadriglia aircraft, flown by Ten. Emilio Juzzolino, crashed into a mountainside near Catania on return, all the crew being killed. It was surmised that the machine had been damaged, for every S.79 returning from this sortie exhibited damage of some sort.

The warships had hardly regained their positions around the convoy than the 35,000-ton *Littorio* appeared on the horizon, her nine 15-inch and twelve 6-inch guns offering a broadside which outweighed the combined firepower of Vian's entire force! While an Ro43 spotter biplane, launched from one of the cruisers, endeavoured to control the accuracy of the battleship's fire, Vian again led his modest force in an aggressive charge at the threat, the division leaders creating smoke to make it difficult for the Italian gunners to see the results of their salvoes, and hazardous for Iachino to reach the transports, his main quarry. A number of skirmishes followed as individual Italian warships attempted to break through the protective screen. Vian's flagship, *Cleopatra*, was hit by a 6-inch shell from *Banda Nere*, 15 of the crew being killed, while *Euryalus* was slightly damaged by splinters from a 15-inch shell from the battleship.

At about 1800 *Littorio* and the two heavy cruisers almost got through, but the situation was saved by the arrival of *Penelope* from Malta. Joined by *Euryalus*, they attacked the battleship which was hit by a 6-inch shell between her after funnels, causing a fire. At the same time *Cleopatra* aimed three torpedoes at her which only narrowly missed. It was enough; the Italians withdrew. Although three destroyers had also suffered some damage during the action, it was a resounding triumph against odds for Admiral Vian.

The merchant vessels, meanwhile, had veered from their course to avoid the battle, being forced further south. As a result they were now way behind schedule, since it was necessary for them to reach Malta early next morning to avoid being caught in daylight by the full force of the Axis units from Sicily. The convoy commodore, Captain Colin Hutchinson, was well aware of this predicament, but could do little to ameliorate it, particularly when at 1700 a force of Ju88s from Stab/KG 77 attacked. By now, however, the weather had deteriorated, a near gale force wind from the south-east whipping up the sea. In such conditions, and in the face of intense AA fire, the attacking force could achieve no more than some near misses. The Junkers' gunners strafed the ships as they passed overhead after their dives, while it was believed one or two were shot down. By 1900 both they and the Italian fleet had gone.

The Luftwaffe did suffer a serious loss during this attack when Maj. Arved Cruger, the Geschwaderkommodore, and his crew were lost in 3Z+AA. The ships' gunners believed that they had shot down five attacking aircraft during the day, including one by *Breconshire* and an S.79 by *Euryalus*. Given the losses of the Italian torpedo-bomber units, their claims were remarkably accurate on this occasion.

Even as Force 'K' had set out from Malta to join Vian's force, all available FAA torpedo-bombers on the Island had been ordered to prepare to attack the Italian warships. At 1755, therefore, Lt.Cdr. Hopkins led off his five Albacores, escorted for the initial part of their flight by three Spitfires that had been made serviceable, flown by Sqn.Ldr. Gracie of 126 Squadron, and Flt.Lt. Macqueen and Plt.Off. R.W. James of 249 Squadron. No sooner were they on their way when two Bf109s attempted to intercept out of the setting sun, one diving onto Gracie's tail. Macqueen turned towards this, but then saw the other Messerschmitt firing at an Albacore and attacked this instead, sending it down in a shadow dive. James reported that he saw the aircraft turn on its back at 50 feet above the sea, and Macqueen then observed a splash; on the basis of this circumstantial evidence he was credited with the destruction of the German fighter.

By now low on fuel the Spitfires turned back, leaving the biplanes to their fate, but after a further two hours these were recalled. On learning of the despatch of the torpedo-bombers, Admiral Vian had advised Malta that the presence of British aircraft over the battle zone "might confuse the issue"; his decision probably saved the lives of most, if not all, of those Naval aircrews involved.

Acting upon Admiral Vian's outlined operational plans, Captain Hutchinson (the convoy commodore) decided the best chance his ships now had of reaching Malta was to proceed individually through the night, making the best speed they could raise, with the escorts split between them so far as was possible. *Clan Campbell* was at greatest risk, being the slowest vessel in the convoy. It would be touch and go, for there were about 240 miles to cover in some 13 hours of darkness, which required an average speed of 19 knots if Grand Harbour was to be reached by sunrise. The heavy seas running made this an outside chance, but with luck, all four vessels could be within range of fighter cover from Malta by daybreak on the 23rd.

Breconshire, the fastest of the four, surged ahead joined by the AA cruiser *Carlisle* and two destroyers and by 0645 they were within 35 miles of Malta — but no fighter escort appeared, only a Z506B which commenced to shadow them and report their location. A call for help was at once transmitted to Malta, but within five minutes of the floatplane's appearance, a single Ju88 dived steeply out of cloud, its bombs narrowly missing *Breconshire*. Soon after 0800 another Ju88 attempted to attack, but was driven off by the AA barrage and was last seen trailing black smoke. By 1300, Malta's hills were at last sighted and the crews thought their ordeal to be virtually over, when three bomb-carrying Bf109s (piloted by Oblt. Werner Langermann [Staffelkapitän], Lt. Max Lange and Uffz. Dr. Felix Sauer) dived out of cloud, hitting *Breconshire* with three 110kg bombs — a remarkable virtuoso performance by the pilots of 10/JG 53! One bomb struck aft, one level with No 1 Hold, and one close to the bridge. Although badly damaged, with the engineroom rapidly flooding, none of the explosives aboard were set off; she still had a fighting chance of survival.

Oblt. Langermann had initially set off at the head of four Jabo Messerschmitts from Gela to seek shipping, and had escorted two Ju88s on the way. Six miles south-west of Kalafrana the small formation had been sighted by a lone Hurricane of 185 Squadron, flown by Sgt. Horricks. Unable to get at the bombers because of the escort, Horricks closed in on one of the latter, and gained strikes on the cockpit of Uffz. Hermann Katthagen's 'White 9', then on its engine and starboard wing; the Messerschmitt flicked over and went down vertically into the sea; Katthagen was killed. Despite this loss, the remaining pilots had carried on to achieve their successful attack on *Breconshire*.

Before anything much could be done to fight the fires aboard *Breconshire*, a further lone Ju88 screamed out of the clouds, and although believed to have been hit repeatedly by AA fire from the destroyer *Southwold*, released three 220kg bombs which narrowly missed the transport. Within minutes another pair of Junkers arrived and while one was driven off, the other released two bombs which exploded directly beneath her, and seemed to lift her half out of the water. Still she did not sink, but now she drifted helplessly towards a minefield on Zonqor Beacon. She was attacked three more times in the next half hour, but no further damage was inflicted.

At this stage *Breconshire* was only nine miles from the entrance to Grand Harbour, and here the cruiser *Penelope* attempted to come to her aid and provide a tow, but this proved impracticable. Throughout the late morning and afternoon a succession of warships took turns in providing protection for the stricken vessel as some 10-15 German aircraft made individual attacks. During this period *Breconshire* was not hit again and finally, shortly before sunset, a Beaufighter appeared overhead, circled twice, and left to continue its patrol. This was recorded as the only friendly aircraft seen by the crew all day — not, as will be recounted shortly, because they were not in the air and doing the best job they could.

Meanwhile, further from the Island, the unfortunate *Clan Campbell* had been caught in broad daylight whilst still 20 miles out, and sank following several direct hits scored by Ju88s, and by a torpedo hit. Her Dutch skipper, Captain J.F. Vooght, and five of the crew were lost, the remainder being rescued by the destroyer *Eridge*. Meanwhile, the remaining two transports (*Pampas* and *Talabot*) reached Malta safely, the latter being strafed by four Messerschmitts as she entered the harbour, four of her AA gunners suffering wounds. Apparently disdainful of the hostile activity in the air, a huge crowd lined the battlements to cheer the vitally-needed ships to anchor.

Despite not being seen by *Breconshire's* long-suffering crew, Malta's fighters had spent a busy day. Dawn had found a record 14 Spitfires and 11 Hurricanes made ready for action, and these were split between defence of the Island and convoy protection. Operating in pairs at approximately half-hourly intervals over the ships, encounters were reported during the day with at least 60 Ju88s and 25 Bf109s.

The first such engagement occurred at 0910 when a pair of 185 Squadron Hurricanes attacked a Ju88 two miles south of Kalafrana at 1000 feet. Sgt. Horricks (Z2961/K) and Sgt. Eastman attacked in turn, and the bomber was last seen very low, flying at about 100 mph, with the starboard engine apparently stopped; this may have been an aircraft of KüFlGr 606, which returned in a damaged state. At about the same time two Spitfires of 126 Squadron, flown by Flt.Lt. 'Tim' Johnston and Plt.Off. Mike Graves, were patrolling over the incoming ships when they saw gunfire. They investigated and observed a lone Ju88, which fired a recognition flare of three red stars — presumably the crew thought the approaching fighters were Messerschmitts. Johnston attacked and hit the starboard engine, but the Junkers succeeded in climbing and reaching cloud, the Spitfires following. It was soon located and Johnston again attacked and saw white smoke stream from both engines, and three objects fall away from the fuselage — probably the crew baling out into the sea. The stricken bomber spiralled into low cloud, following which burning petrol was seen on the sea. This was almost certainly Obgfr. Hans Spix's F6+CH of 1(F)/122, which failed to return.

Just over an hour later, Flt.Lt. Lawrence and Sgt. Broad (GL-U) of 185 Squadron encountered an aircraft they identified as an He111, five miles east of Kalafrana, at 5500 feet. Ernie Broad recorded:

> 'Got burst in head on. The e/a then did a diving turn and released bombs. I then did a beam attack as the e/a turned, seeing strikes on the port engine. E/a then flew east gradually losing height. I did a rear quarter attack seeing strikes along fuselage. E/a flying very slowly and I was able to do another beam attack at 500 feet, when I saw the e/a dive into the sea.'

The bomber — believed actually to have been a Ju88 — was also attacked by Lawrence, and they were jointly credited with its destruction. Members of the crew were seen to scramble into their dinghy. This was believed to have been an aircraft (7T+KK) of 1/KüFlGr 606, in which Lt. Walter Kipfmuller and his crew were reported missing.

There were several skirmishes in the early afternoon, most Ju88s escaping serious damage by seeking sanctuary in the heavy cloud. At 1300 two 185 Squadron pilots — Plt.Off. Wigley (BG770/GL-D) and Flt.Sgt. Fletcher — claimed damage to a bomber, while shortly afterwards Sqn.Ldr. Mortimer-Rose and Sgt. Eastman of this unit joined two Spitfires, flown by Flt.Lt. Macqueen and Plt.Off. Sergeant, in claiming damage to three more bombers. Two other Spitfires patrolled four miles east of Grand Harbour where a further pair of Junkers were intercepted, Plt.Off. Plagis (BP846) and Plt.Off. Peck each claiming one damaged. Another pair of Hurricanes, meanwhile, caught two more Ju88s north of Zonqor Point, Plt.Off. Beckitt claiming strikes on the fuselage and starboard engine of one, while Plt.Off. Noble (BG769/GL-J) used all his ammunition on another, also claiming damage to this. He then chased a further Junkers and forced it to jettison its bombs.

An aircraft of 3/KG 54 (B3+LL flown by Lt. Hermann Janzik) failed to return from a sortie over the sea off Malta; reportedly, it fell to four Spitfires. Meanwhile, amongst the bombers returning damaged from these encounters was one of II/LG 1 in which the gunner had been wounded; in another, flown by Lt. Gerd Stamp, the hydraulics had been damaged by fire from the ships' AA, and the aircraft was then pursued northwards by Hurricanes until Messerschmitts arrived and drove them off. On arrival at Catania, Stamp crash-landed the bomber, almost colliding with a concrete wall; he and his crew survived unhurt.

Flt.Lt. Johnston of 126 Squadron was up again during the early afternoon, once more with Plt.Off. Graves. They spotted three Ju88s of 3/KGr 806 about five miles off Kalafrana, and chased these southwards out to sea. Graves carried out a quarter attack on one, then turned and made a head-on pass, gaining strikes on the cockpit and both engines. Just as the bomber rolled over on its back and dived into the sea, six Beaufighters of 272 Squadron approached from the east, having been despatched from Gambut to provide air cover for the convoy which they had been unable to locate. The formation leader, Flg.Off. Derek Hammond, seeing the Spitfires in hot pursuit of the bombers, ordered Flt.Lt. G.L. Campbell's section to prevent their escape to the west.

The trio of Beaufighters quickly caught up with the remaining two Junkers and Campbell himself attacked in a dive, but missed as his intended target took violent evasive action. Behind him came Sgt. George Tuckwell, who got a clear shot at the bomber, two bursts hitting the port wing which forced the pilot to change direction back towards Malta. Tuckwell fired again, and the Junkers exploded into a mass of orange flames, burning debris fluttering into the sea. The other bomber managed to escape in cloud but M7+DL and M7+GL, flown by Lt. Hermann Damaske and Fw. Herbert Augustin respectively, were lost in this engagement; there were no survivors from either aircraft.

Even as these actions were taking place just off the coast, other air fights were ensuing over Admiral Vian's warships further to the east, as these withdrew back towards Alexandria. As the ships came within patrol range of Gambut, Beaufighters of the other squadron — 252 — were again out to give cover, and these engaged in several interceptions, mainly of 'shadowers'. On the first occasion, Sgt. A.G.G. Machin (T4877) made two astern attacks on an He111, following which it dived away steeply, trailing black smoke from its port engine. A little later Plt.Off. Ian Maclean (T4883) and Sgt. Abdul Ydlibi (T4839) came across another Heinkel and pursued this almost to Crete, claiming severe damage. A third bomber, this time a Ju88, was engaged by Sgt. Cripps (T4884), who claimed damage before it escaped in cloud, but Sgt. Tom Shaw's T4866/Y was intercepted by a Bf109 (from JG 27) and had its hydraulic system damaged, crash-landing at Gambut on return as a result.

252 Squadron subsequently received a signal from 201 Group:

> 'Two merchant ships of convoy reached Malta safely, third, although damaged, anchored outside Valetta harbour expects berth today, assisted by tugs. Arrival of these ships in spite of heavy enemy air and sea opposition will greatly help and hearten defenders of Malta'.

201 Group itself received a congratulatory signal from the Commander-in-Chief, Mediterranean:

> 'We are most grateful for the prodigious efforts put out by 201 Group which played such a large part in ensuring safety of convoy and escort under most difficult conditions.'

The escort was not home yet, however, and during the late afternoon three S.79sil of 205ª Squadriglia from Heraklion, (led by Ten.Col. Ettore Muti) sighted the warships, awaited favourable light, and attacked. Although the crews believed that all torpedoes had run true, no hits were actually gained, while AA fire damaged the leader's aircraft.

On Malta at the end of this hectic day, although no losses had been suffered, only five fighters remained fully serviceable. A fierce resumption of attacks could be expected on the morrow, particularly on Grand Harbour where the two freighters now lay at anchor. By a tremendous overnight effort, the hard-working ground crews had a total of 18 Spitfires and Hurricanes airworthy by dawn next day, aided during the night by the unloading of a number of Merlin engines and other aircraft spares from the two ships, mainly by the efforts of RAF personnel, including aircrew.

Tuesday, 24 March

At first light on Tuesday, the tug *Beryl* arrived and endeavoured to take *Breconshire* in tow, but this proved beyond her capability in the high sea then running. The captain of the destroyer *Southwold* then signalled that he would shoot a line across the vessel's stern and take off the 60-70 passengers she had on board; but while manoeuvring into position to do this, the destroyer struck a mine which exploded under her engine room, causing a number of casualties. A second tug — *Ancient* — then arrived and took the damaged *Southwold* in tow, but the tightening of the cable was sufficient to break the damaged vessel's back, and she remained held together only by her upper deck plating. *Ancient* continued the attempt to rescue her but Bf109 fighter-bombers and Ju88s then appeared, whereupon she rolled over and sank. *Breconshire* was also attacked, but missed — but there were to be no more attacks on her that day, for the Luftwaffe now concentrated its effort against the two freighters in Grand Harbour.

About 200 more sorties were flown by Ju88s, Ju87s — the Stukas recently arrived from Africa for the task — and escorting Bf109s against *Pampas* and *Talabot*, but both escaped damage although much property around the harbour was demolished. Hal Far and Luqa were also attacked, the former airfield suffering considerable damage, whilst the Governor's Palace was hit as well. The day saw 30 service and 35 civilian casualties as a result of these raids.

The first interceptions were reported soon after 1040, when two Spitfires of 126 Squadron flown by the American pair, Plt.Offs. Peck and McLeod, attacked two Bf109 Jabo as they approached Kalafrana Bay. McLeod reported:

> 'First sighted 2 e/a at 8000 feet below going in direction of Kalafrana Bay. Immediately dived to attack and taking one on the left — P/O Peck the one on the right — opened fire with 5 second burst from dead astern. The 109 was enveloped in white smoke (apparently glycol) and started in gliding turn to left. E/a on my right did sharp turn in front of me. I used rest of my ammo on beam attack. On breaking from this attack I saw first e/a attacked by me diving straight into the sea, a mass of flames and black smoke'.

Peck's victim gave him some trouble before it, too, went down. Apparently McLeod called on the R/T to the effect:

> 'Hello Peck, Mac here, I've knocked mine down, do I have to come and help you with yours?'

Peck's reply, not surprisingly, was said to be unprintable! The identities of their victims, presumably fighter-bomber pilots from 10/JG 53, have not been established.

Within an hour some 40 Ju88s and 25 Bf109s appeared, heading for the Grand Harbour in the most damaging raid of the day. Six Hurricanes and three Spitfires challenged the raiders, but the only claim was for a Messerschmitt damaged by Flg.Off. Buchanan of 249 Squadron, while the AA gunners claimed one Ju88 shot down and two damaged. Sgt. Bolton's 126 Squadron Spitfire was attacked by three Bf109s, obliging the New Zealander to crash-land the damaged machine at Luqa, although escaping personal injury.

Between 1420 and 1800, 30 more Ju88s, 30 Ju87s and 25 Bf109s again approached, four Spitfires and four Hurricanes being scrambled. At about 1510, the 126 Squadron pair, Flt.Lt. Johnston and Plt.Off. Graves, were engaged by

Bf109s and became separated. Evading his assailants, Johnston then saw bombs exploding on Hal Far, which was under attack by Ju87Ds of III/StG 3. He attacked one of these, opening fire from 100 yards and seeing vivid flashes as his cannon shells struck the fuselage. White smoke streamed from the underside and he pulled to one side, but as he did so his Spitfire was hit by three bullets in the leading edge of his port wing, which punctured the tyre. He attacked again with a further three-second burst from the port quarter, whereupon the Stuka began to lag and streamed glycol from the engine. Believing that the damaged dive-bomber would not be able to make it back to Sicily, Johnston broke away and headed back to Luqa where he was twice attacked by Bf109s as he attempted to land, but was not hit. His No 2, Mike Graves, had landed before him, not having seen the Stukas.

Witnesses on the ground stated that two Ju87s had been shot down during this raid, but records indicate that only Uffz. Hans Bretschneider (who was killed) and his gunner (who was taken prisoner) of 7 Staffel, in T6+BM, failed to return. AA gunners claimed two Stukas shot down and it seems likely that Bretschneider's aircraft was hit by ground fire and by Flt.Lt. Johnston (who was credited with its probable destruction). Neither the pilots of the two 249 Squadron Spitfires up at the time, nor those flying the Hurricanes, engaged in any conclusive actions.

On the ground Sgt. Tim Goldsmith of 185 Squadron had a grandstand view of the dive-bombing of Hal Far, as he was sheltering in the entrance to the Operations Room with Sgt. Ernie Broad when the attack began, and graphically recorded:

> 'Puffs of brown smoke from Delimara Point across the bay indicated that the 3.7"'s were going into action before their bark floated across to us, but we still could not see the bandits. Suddenly I looked straight above, then clutched Ernie's arm: "Look there's a Hurricane coming straight down with its undercart lowered". Ernie took a swift look: "Hurricane be buggered — that's a flaming Stuka!".
>
> 'Suddenly we could see them all. About a dozen Ju87s were diving on Hal Far from three directions, while roughly 20 more upstairs were queuing up waiting for their turn. Above them Me's laced the sky and then we heard the rattle of machine-gun fire. Apparently the Hurricanes (*sic*) were there, too! Then all hell broke loose as the sharp, fast explosions from surrounding Bofors guns mixed with the crash of the heavies, both overridden by the high-pitched scream of falling bombs.
>
> 'We leaped down the Operations burrow like a couple of rabbits just as two terrific explosions above indicated a very near miss. The raid continued for 15-20 minutes, winding up with some strafing by three enemy fighters. We came forth blinking in the sunlight to survey the results. The Officers' Mess had been flattened altogether with part of the Airmens' Quarters. On the other side of the drome a Swordfish blazed furiously inside its dispersal bay. The wreckage of a Stuka (*Bretschneider's T6+BM*) smouldered in the centre of the field, the pilot smouldering with it. The gunner (*Uffz. Ferdinand Burger*) had managed to bale out, I learned later, and was taken prisoner by the crew of a Bofors gun, near which he had landed.
>
> 'It was not until we had looked around and taken all this in that we noticed two craters where the nearby air raid shelter had been. Apparently the two

> eggs which landed just after we leaped for shelter had caused the damage. Together with the others, we raced for spades and shovels and set to work excavating, or rather exhuming. Several hours later, when the job was completed, 23 bodies had been recovered. In addition, five badly injured airmen had been transferred to hospital. Three of these later died.'

During this raid Sqn.Ldr. Mortimer-Rose had been manning the twin-Browning .303 machine-guns which one of the armourers had erected near to the dug-out, when three bombs fell very close to him. He was buried in debris up to his waist and his ear drums were pierced, but the first thing he said to his rescuers was:

> 'The F-----s have stopped my gun!'

Having been safely extricated from the site, Mortimer-Rose then cycled to the sick quarters, from where he was taken to hospital.

Left: Flg.Off. Raoul Daddo-Langlois of 185 Squadron was posted to 249 Squadron on the arrival of the first Spitfires. *(Daddo-Langlois Collection)*. **Right:** Sqn.Ldr. E.B.B. 'Morty' Mortimer-Rose, commander of 185 Squadron, with his twin-Browning anti-aircraft post. During one raid on Hal Far three bombs landed close by this gun pit and he was buried up to his waist in debris. *(NWMA)*

Shortly after this devastating attack, at around 1700, Sgt. Broad was one of a section of four from 185 Squadron to scramble on the approach of a further raid. Eight Ju88s were encountered and Plt.Off. Beckitt led a diving attack, observing strikes on two bombers at which he fired, one of which Broad then attacked and damaged further, before being driven away by a Bf109. Plt.Off. Noble (Z2961/K) and Flt.Sgt. Fletcher jointly attacked another and hit the starboard engine, which began smoking; Noble fired at two more which were seen to jettison their bombs, but his own aircraft was hit eight times by one of the rear gunners. He managed to get down safely, as did two other Hurricanes similarly damaged. One of the bombers attacked may have been 3Z+CT of 9/KG 77, which failed to return, and was reported down in the sea about 20 miles south of Comiso; Lt. Heinz-Karl Müller and his crew did not survive.

By the end of the day Malta was again down to nine serviceable fighters!

Far to the east Admiral Vian's force was still struggling to reach Alexandria when dawn broke. At 0755 a pair of S.79sil from 41° Gruppo sighted the warships which their crews reported were under escort by a Sunderland flyingboat and three fighters. Evading these, they carried out an attack without material result. It is probable that Ten. Giorgio Tourn's aircraft was hit by AA fire, for it force-landed in the sea during the return flight, the crew being seen to get into their life-raft by those in Sottoten. Monterumici's aircraft, which circled overhead for a time. Three more aircraft were sent out from Gadurra (Rhodes) to relieve Monterumici, but the rescue service was unable to find any trace of the missing crew.

During the night of the 24th/25th Luqa was again raided, a Beaufighter and a Blenheim being seriously damaged. However, the raid did not prevent a Wellington from the Middle East sneaking in undetected, ostensibly loaded with urgently-needed supplies. But when these were inspected and subsequently reported to the AOC, an incensed Lloyd signalled the guilty despatchers in Cairo:

> 'The Wellington which arrived night 24th/25th from Middle East brought 750lbs of NAAFI goods, chief items of which were soap, toothpaste, razor blades and Brylcreem. Consider this absolutely reprehensible when we have a/c (*aircraft*) grounded for lack of so many spare parts which your MPO (*Movements Officer*) is well aware of. For example, four Hurricanes are grounded for lack of Colbert rivets. We are fighting for our existence here and Brylcreem is the last thing we need.'

Wednesday, 25 March

The tugs *Ancient* and *Robust* again went out to the stricken *Breconshire*'s aid early on the 25th, and this time succeeded in getting tow lines secured, whilst three destroyers provided cover. By 1000 they had got her almost to the entrance to Marsaxlokk Bay, and by midday she had been secured to a buoy in this harbour. There were, however, no unloading facilities here, although all those aboard were evacuated to the Island. It was decided that *Plumleaf*, a Reserve Fleet oiler, should secure alongside during the night and take off as much oil as possible. This achieved, it was surmised *Breconshire* could be towed into Grand Harbour to discharge the remainder of her cargo.

Rather surprisingly there was little hostile activity over Malta until mid afternoon, when at least 30 Ju88s, 25 Ju87s of III/StG 3 and 13 Bf109s of II/JG 3 were reported over the Island from 1540 to 1725. The Ju87s attacked *Breconshire* but failed to hit her. Grand Harbour was repeatedly attacked and while again civilian property suffered much damage, *Pampas* and *Talabot* escaped. However, the Power Station was severely damaged and the Pump Room demolished, and seven soldiers, two Polish sailors and four civilians were killed, and 16 other persons injured. Luqa was also bombed, a delivery Blenheim being damaged and 30 persons injured.

To meet these raids eight Hurricanes of 185 Squadron, four Spitfires of 249 Squadron and two of 126 Squadron got into the air, and a number of claims were made, primarily against the Ju87s. Sqn.Ldr. Grant and Plt.Off. Plagis each claimed a Stuka shot down, the latter also claiming strikes on a second before his Spitfire (BP850) was attacked and damaged by Fw. Max Fischer of Stab II/JG 3, claimed as his first victory; Fischer's joy was short-lived, however, for Grant was soon on the tail of the Messerschmitt and shot it down into the sea off Gozo. The German managed to bale out and was later rescued by a Do24 from Sicily.

Flg.Off. Lee gained strikes on another Ju87, while Plt.Off. Nash (AB335/F) initially claimed a probable, only to have this upgraded to a confirmed victory; he noted:

> '30+ Ju87s. Terrific!! Ju87 probable. A marvellous party! We caught them over Grand Harbour. Hurricanes also got some!!'

The two 126 Squadron Spitfires were flown by the inseparable American duo, Plt.Offs. Peck and McLeod, the former claiming a Ju87 damaged, while Don McLeod believed he had shot down a Bf109:

> 'Six Spitfires took off on interception; while flying at 16,000 feet in vicinity of GH, several 109s were spotted below. We dived to attack; 109s were in line astern and turning to left. I opened fire at about 200 yards, closing to 150, with three second burst. E/A suddenly did violent down snap. At this time I was engaged by another 109 which opened fire on me from my right front quarter. I did a head-on attack on this e/a, finishing my ammo. P/O Nash, who was in attack with me, saw first 109 attacked going straight into the sea.'

It seems likely that McLeod had actually attacked a Messerschmitt of 4/JG 3 flown by Lt. Rudolf Wicklaus, who was wounded (but succeeded in returning to Sicily) and that the aircraft witnessed by Nash falling into the sea was that shot down by Sqn.Ldr. Grant. The Hurricane pilots reported engaging 20 plus Ju87s over Kalafrana Bay at 6000 feet, and claimed one Ju87 shot down — shared by Plt.Offs. Ormrod and Wigley (Z4005/GL-S) — and two probables, one of which was shared by Sgt. Eastman, and the New Zealand pair, Sgts. Wilson and Robb. The other was credited to Sgt. Horricks; he attacked it from astern and saw strikes on its radiator and engine, following which it went into a dive; he attacked another and reported the rear gunner killed, then hit a third in the starboard wing. Yet another Stuka was claimed damaged during a joint attack by Flt.Lt. Lloyd and Plt.Off. Milburn. Despite all the claims, III/StG 3 lost only T6+CC, piloted by Lt. Klaus Heemann, which fell into the sea about five miles east off Marsaxlokk, while Uffz. Georg Claus, the gunner in another aircraft, was wounded.

During the day six Beaufighters of 272 Squadron had been ordered to Malta from Gambut to provide cover for *Breconshire*, since it was assumed she was still drifting out at sea. These aircraft ran into a violent electrical storm and became separated, being forced to turn back. Half of them force-landed at various locations in the desert, one coming down behind enemy lines. The formation leader, Flg.Off. Derek Hammond, spotted this and attempted to land nearby, only to damage his own aircraft in the attempt. He tried again and this time was successful, taking aboard the crew and getting off again. He then strafed the abandoned aircraft causing it to catch fire, to prevent it falling into Axis hands. Hammond was later awarded a DFC for this act.

In Grand Harbour an extremely serious situation was developing, meanwhile. Thanks in no small part to recent inclement weather, *Pampas* and *Talabot* had escaped damage for two days — days in which the unloading of the vital cargoes should have been completed. Instead, work on them had been proceeding at quite a leisurely pace, with no apparent sense of urgency.

Late that evening, Wg.Cdr. Powell-Shedden was scanning the harbour through binoculars when he realised that work on the ships had ceased. Properly alarmed, he telephoned Air Vice-Marshal Lloyd to report this, adding that as the cloud lifted, the ships would most surely be sunk. According to Powell-Shedden, Lloyd replied:

'Nonsense! They are being unloaded!'

Unconvinced, Powell-Shedden then telephoned the Harbour Master who confirmed that work had ceased for the night. At once he re-called Lloyd to advise him that he had been mis-informed, and to volunteer to organize men to carry out nocturnal unloading. Again the AOC insisted that the ships were indeed being unloaded!

Powell-Shedden drove to the docks to see for himself and found that, as he feared, no unloading was taking place. Returning to Luqa, he again telephoned the AOC, but the latter was now in bed and allegedly retorted:

'Shut up and go to bed!'

Really disturbed now by this apparent apathy, he telephoned the Governor, who was also in bed, reportedly receiving a similar negative response:

'Nothing can be done tonight!'

Thursday, 26 March

Sure enough, during the morning the clouds did lift and the sharp eyes of German reconnaissance crews soon spotted the anchored freighters, the first raiders approaching at 1220. A total of 24 Ju88s and 20 Ju87s were reported over Grand Harbour, *Talabot* at No 6 Buoy suffering a direct hit by a heavy calibre bomb about ten minutes into the attack. This penetrated the engine room and exploded, causing fires to start. The tug *Ancient* and two fire floats went to her aid, pumping water and foam into the engine room, but further bombs then put *Ancient* and the floats out of action, and it seems that *Talabot* was herself hit again. Fires in the ammunition holds caused further explosions, and it was decided to scuttle the ship to prevent a major conflagration; only 972 of her 8956 tons of cargo had been unloaded at this stage!

At around 1430 *Pampas* was sunk at Ras Hanzir. Initially a stick of bombs fell close by, then half an hour later a large bomb penetrated her funnel and exploded; the engine room flooded and she started to go down rapidly by the stern, while fires broke out. Eight Maltese dock labourers in No 4 hold were killed. Despite this, Lt. J. Dixon, in charge of operations to unload her, encouraged his men to fight the fires, and unload what could be saved. But at the moment of attack only 799 tons of cargo (out of her 7462 tons) had been taken off this ship!

These were not to be the only losses during this devastating raid, for the destroyer *Legion* was sunk in French Creek by a direct hit which killed 11 men; the oiler *Plumleaf*, which had been transferring fuel from *Breconshire* was driven aground also in French Creek; and the submarine *P 39* was sunk at Marsa. Casualties included six service personnel and four civilians.

The initial bomber formation was engaged by seven Hurricanes, which had taken off at 1210. Sqn.Ldr. Gracie of 126 Squadron, flying one of the Hurricanes on this occasion, attacked a Ju88 at point-blank range, last seeing this going out to sea very slowly; he broke away only when his own aircraft was hit by return fire. Plt.Off. Crichton, flying a cannon-armed IIC (HA-A), claimed another Junkers damaged:

> 'Intercepted 88s over Grand Harbour. Full deflection shot at 88, only time I flew a Hurry with two cannons; saw strikes when guns jammed, less than 15 rounds from each. P/O McKay saw 88 with starboard engine on fire at about 1000 ft headed downwards towards sea. F/L Anderson also saw it.'

At 1355 four Spitfires — the only fighters available — scrambled to engage the second formation, which comprised an estimated 15 Ju87s of III/StG 3 and three Ju88s of I/KG 54, with escorting Bf109s. Sgt. Brennan attacked the trio of Ju88s as they dived in formation, seeing cannon strikes on one, which turned away. Flt.Lt. Connell (GN-M), who was leading the formation, claimed to have shot the tail off a Ju88 but this was probably the same aircraft as that attacked by Brennan which Plt.Off. McNair then attacked, reporting that it went down disintegrating into the sea half a mile off Xlendi Bay, Gozo. Amazingly the four crewmen survived and were seen scrambling into their dinghy, from which they were later rescued by the local police. 'Bud' Connell then joined McNair in attacking the Stukas, the latter claiming one of these probably destroyed, this subsequently being upgraded to a confirmed victory.

The fourth member of the section, Flt.Lt. Johnston of 126 Squadron (in BP850), attacked a Ju87 with a two-second burst from dead astern at 150 yards range but it disappeared into cloud. He then attacked a second with a four-second burst, and saw black smoke pouring from the belly; he claimed this as a probable, but like McNair's claim, this, too, was later upgraded. Finally, he attacked a third, seeing strikes on its fuselage and wings followed by jets of white vapour. At that point his Spitfire was hit twice, once in the oil tank and once in the spinner. He promptly headed for Takali, but as a Bf109 was overhead as he approached, he went instead to Luqa, and landed there. Lt. Joachim Kirschner of 5/JG 3 claimed a Spitfire shot down for his first victory, one of two he was to claim over Malta.

The second major series of assaults came in between 1630 and 1857. Twenty-four Ju88s, 18 Ju87s and at least six Bf109s were reported over Grand Harbour and Kalafrana, while three Do24s and three Bf109s searched near Gozo for Rothmann and his crew. In Marsaxlokk Bay a lone Ju88 dived out of the evening sun onto *Breconshire*, and although seen to be repeatedly hit by AA fire, following which flames and smoke reportedly streamed from its engines, it released four bombs, all of which hit the vessel. One exploded in No 4 hold, two abreast the bridge and one in No 5 hold. Captain Hutchinson, who had been ashore, rushed out to his ship in an RAF launch, while the fire-fighting tugs *Robust, Swona* and *Beryl* sped to her aid with all haste. Most of the fires were extinguished after several hours effort, but *Breconshire* had now settled in the water. Next morning, with the fires having erupted again and with ammunition starting to explode in her holds, the stricken vessel rolled over onto her port side; members of her crew, watching from outside the hangars on Kalafrana's south slipway, gave their ship a traditional farewell cheer as she finally heeled over and settled down.

Meanwhile, four Spitfires and six Hurricanes had been scrambled to meet these attacks, Plt.Off. Steele of 185 Squadron, flying a cannon-armed IIC, caught one Ju88, seeing the starboard engine catch fire and the fuel tank explode after his attack from 100 yards. He reported this aircraft down in the sea, the crew being seen scrambling into their dinghy. This was probably B3+KH of I/KG 54, flown by Lt. Johannes Rothmann.

The other Hurricane pilots engaged mainly Ju87s, Flt.Sgt. Fletcher gaining strikes on the fuselage of one, chasing it into cloud before making a second attack, leaving it smoking; he then claimed damage to a Bf109. North-east of Grand Harbour Sgt. Broad damaged another Ju87 with a short burst, before being forced to break away with a Messerschmitt on his tail. Having evaded this, he attacked a second Stuka head-on, claiming some damage to this also. Plt.Off. Noble (Z2698/L) fired at two Ju88s and two Ju87s, believing that he probably caused some damage to all four, while Sgt. Goldsmith (Z3993/X) recorded:

> 'Ju88s intercepted dive-bombing *Breconshire* in Kalafrana (*sic*) harbour. Fired at two, hitting one. Fired 2000 rounds. Also intercepted Ju87s over Grand Harbour. Attacked two, hitting both. One lost height, smoking. Jumped by 109s.'

As the four Spitfires approached a formation of Ju88s, Plt.Off. McHan, flying AB346/K of 249 Squadron, found himself targeted by the AA guns, his aircraft being peppered by shrapnel; he managed to reach Takali and land safely. The other three engaged the bombers, four of which were claimed damaged — one each by Flt.Lt. Connell (GN-L) and Flg.Off. Buchanan, the other two being credited to Plt.Off. McNair — before the escorting fighters forced them away. A Ju88 (M7+AA) of 3/KGr 806 crash-landed at Comiso on return, having been damaged by fighter attack, during which the rear-gunner (Obfw. Gustav Reimers) had been killed.

Flg.Off. 'Buck' Buchanan of 249 Squadron, a Rhodesian and former policeman, who was one of the first pilots to gain notable success over Malta with the Spitfire. *(P.B. Lucas via NWMA)*

During this series of raids the AA gunners optimistically claimed two Ju88s and a Ju87 shot down, and one Ju87 damaged. One gun crew had a narrow escape when bomb-carrying Bf109s were manoeuvring to attack the ships, but were apparently so harassed by the gunners that, after winging down behind a ridge too low for the guns to get at them, the pilots let go their bombs to overshoot the mark. The four bombs, all with delayed action fuses, hit the rocky foreshore just in front of one of the light gun sites, re-bounded to a height of some 30 feet over the gun, struck the ground again near the men's billet and then rolled down the hill where, to everyone's relief, they went off doing no harm at all!

With the loss of *Pampas* and *Talabot*, the obligatory official enquiries began, with the obvious questions being asked: why had these two vessels been moored at anchor on arrival instead of close to the cliffs, where ships had generally been moored in the past, and where they were protected from attack from one direction and well-covered by the guns from others? Why had so little of the cargo been unloaded? These were the questions many were asking, amongst them Capt. George Hogan of 1/Hampshires:

> 'To some who watched the course of events at the time it seemed there was a certain amount of lethargy and lack of urgency in getting the cargoes out. It was as though the 16,418 tons tightly packed in the two merchantmen were considered to be in the larder and completely safe.
>
> 'Moreover, instead of getting everything out then sorting it, there was much shifting and selecting below decks to get out first what was considered to be most urgent.'

In fairness, it must be stressed that unloading had, indeed, started at once, with the benefit of low cloud cover that lasted for 36 hours. But whilst Governor Dobbie had given orders that they be unloaded by Maltese labour, no orders had been given for work to continue at night! Had there been some dispute over the level of overtime payment for night workers? In Singapore only weeks before, Governor Shenton Thomas and various committees had failed to agree on how much should be spent on local labour to construct defences, with the result that they had not been completed. Even in times of crisis, tired and fraught minds can be diverted by such apparent trivia. Ironically Dobbie, as GOC Malaya in 1937, had successfully argued for more money to be allocated for the defence of Singapore.

This suggestion, however, is disputed by John Agius, a Maltese civil servant then working for the RAF, who recalls:

> 'The arrival of *Talabot* and *Pampas* on 23rd March in very stormy weather made berthing a difficult operation. The crews of both ships were completely worn out and the ships had a lot of damage from near misses.
>
> 'I remember ships anchored in the middle of the harbour, and to off load a ship, cargo had to be hauled from the holds onto a lighter, the lighter then was towed to the quayside and off loaded either to stores, or to transport to be stored elsewhere. Lighters were few — many had been sunk, the same applied to tug boats; wharves and quaysides were very badly damaged. The storehouses were equally damaged. Plus all this, the stevedores had to work under air attack and in complete darkness. Naturally those persons down in the holds were not very happy. It was not a case of danger money. It was a case of real danger every single minute.
>
> 'I know of a case of some watchmen who worked in military stores close to the harbour. The stores were blitzed, those watchmen were buried under debris and they were not extricated until some two months later. Naturally these stories went round and made one think.
>
> 'We in Malta were not trade union minded at the time. I have seen many persons, both English and Maltese, who were literally afraid during air attacks. Others were afraid but did not show it. I have spoken to a number of

men who told me: "Yes, we were afraid while waiting for an air attack to develop but when we went into action then fear disappeared."

'My own view is that Dobbie could not have done any better, but then everybody is wise after the event. Who wasn't busy and worn out during those times?'

In the event, Air Vice-Marshal Lloyd advised the Prime Minister of the loss of the vessels and urged that Dobbie be relieved. Churchill later wrote:

> 'Disturbing news arrived about General Dobbie. Up to this moment he had been magnificent, and from all parts of the Empire eyes were turned on him — a Cromwellian figure at the key point. But the long strain had worn him down. I received the news with very deep regret, and I did not at first accept what I was told. However, a successor had to be chosen. I felt that in Lord Gort, the Governor of Gibraltar, would be found a warrior of the truest mettle.'

It would however, be several more weeks before Churchill acted. Lloyd later recorded:

> 'The odds against our survival now seemed almost insuperable. There must always be a sense of tragedy when a heroic defence is finally crushed by sheer weight of numbers, but it was a grim and murderous reflection at the time that it was not the fighting which had brought us to our present pass but sheer ineptitude, lack of resolution and bomb-stunned brains incapable of thought. For three whole nights two fully loaded merchant ships had lain in the Grand Harbour and not one bomb had been thrown there during that time; indeed, on two of the nights, because of low cloud, such an event seemed highly improbable. Yet — and this is my point — only 807 (*sic*) tons was unloaded, nearly half of them by a few enterprising airmen, including some aircrew.'

However, information supplied to the AOC was clearly in error, for on the day of their arrival a total of 539 tons of cargo had been unloaded from the two vessels (*Pampas* 209 tons; *Talabot* 330 tons); next day a further 310 tons was unloaded from *Pampas*, 497 tons from *Talabot*; then, before the ships were hit on the 26th, the stevedores had unloaded an additional 280 tons from *Pampas*, making her total 799 tons, and from *Talabot* a further 145 tons, bringing her total to 972 tons.

Despite this apparent disaster, however, all was not entirely lost, for work on the three sunken vessels continued as they had only settled in comparatively shallow waters. During the coming weeks no less than 3100 tons of cargo was salvaged from *Pampas* alone, with a further 80 tons from *Talabot*. It even proved possible to pump out several hundred tons of oil from *Breconshire*'s capsized hull.

If Wg.Cdr. Powell-Shedden's recollection of the events of the night of 25/26 March are correct, Air Vice-Marshal Lloyd does not appear blameless, and indeed his recorded comments verge on hypocrisy when seen in this light. In the event, Lloyd would in due course be saddled with a less than sympathetic replacement, for Field Marshal Lord Gort VC, had little time for the RAF which he felt had let down badly his Expeditionary Force in France in 1940. He doubted the air force's ability to achieve anything much of a concrete nature, and was to prove far from the most co-operative of Governors.

Friday, 27 March

Following the attacks on the ships there was some reduction in activity for a few days. Few interceptions were attempted while efforts were made to restore some semblance of numerical strength to the weakened fighter defences. During the daylight hours of the 27th there were seven alerts but no interceptions. Only one significant raid developed, when an estimated 38 bombers appeared over Grand Harbour and the airfields; one aircraft was slightly damaged at Hal Far, where eight casualties were suffered, the AA defences claiming damage to a single Bf109 in return. An aircraft of 10/JG 53 force-landed on the beach near Donnalucata due to engine failure; it was written off although the pilot, Uffz. Dr. Felix Sauer, was unhurt.

Uffz. Dr Felix Sauer's 'White 3' of 10(Jabo)/JG 53 on the beach near Donnalucata, Sicily, after force-landing on return from a flight over Malta on 27 March 1942. *(Dr Felix Sauer)*

The day was marked by a limited, but valuable and morale-boosting reinforcement, however — not from the usual, carrier-borne direction, but by the arrival of ten cannon-armed Hurricane IICs of 'A' Flight, 229 Squadron, from El Firdan. These were led by the unit's New Zealand-born commander, Sqn.Ldr. D. Kain, and the flight commander, Flt.Lt. P.C.P. Farnes DFM, a veteran of the fighting in France and the Battle of Britain in 1940, with at least eight victories to his credit; he had been with the unit for only one month, and had been promoted to flight commander on arrival. One other Hurricane failed to complete the trip, Plt.Off. Len Malthus being obliged to turn back when he discovered his aircraft had a faulty fuel pump. The Hurricanes had been escorted in two flights from Gambut by a Beaufort of 39 Squadron and a Blenheim of 203 Squadron (see Table 2 below).

TABLE 2

10 Hurricane IICs of 229 Squadron from Middle East

Sqn.Ldr. D. Kain	Flt.Sgt. R.L.K. Carson, RCAF
Flt.Lt. P.C.P. Farnes DFM	Flt.Sgt. J.K. Fullalove
Plt.Off. D.J. Carter, RCAF	Sgt. R.V. Potts
Plt.Off. E. Andrews	Sgt. J.B. Pauley, RAAF
Plt.Off. A.S.C. Lumsden	Sgt. N.L. Vidler, RAAF

NB: Plt.Off. L.G. Malthus, RNZAF, was forced to turn back with fuel problems.

Saturday, 28 March

Saturday brought only one interception when, just after midday, Sqn.Ldr. Grant led three other Spitfires — flown by Flg.Off. Lee, Plt.Offs. Plagis (AB346/K) and Nash (AB335/F) — to intercept a lone reconnaissance Ju88 some 20 miles north of Grand Harbour; all four attacked, three firing all their ammunition, while the fourth suffered a cannon failure. Recorded Nash:

> 'All attacked him from less than 50 yards but he wouldn't go down. He jettisoned bombs in the sea.'

Following the attack both engines of the Junkers streamed smoke, Lee continuing to follow for some 25 miles northwards, hoping to see it crash. He then realised that his own aircraft had been hit in the engine by the rear gunner, and warily turned back. The four were credited with the probable destruction of the bomber, but it would seem to have safely regained its base.

Sunday, 29 March

This day saw the arrival of the balance of the second batch of Spitfires from *Eagle* — codenamed Operation 'Picket II' (see Table 3 below) — Flt.Lt. A.R.H. Barton leading in seven more most-welcome Spitfires, all arriving safely, although several pilots had reported seeing up to 30 CR42s patrolling off Pantelleria as they passed. The operation was not entirely uneventful, however. The old carrier *Argus* was again accompanying *Eagle* to provide cover for her, carrying aboard a number of Fulmars of 807 Squadron. At 1215 Yellow Section were on patrol when they were vectored onto a Ju88, both Fulmars attacking this shadower — and coming off worse! Lt. P.R. Hall's aircraft was hit in the windscreen, engine and wing, whilst Sub Lt. P.E. Palmer's was hit in both wings; no damage to the Junkers was noted.

TABLE 3

Operation 'Picket II'

7 Spitfires from HMS *Eagle* (balance of Picket I)

Flt.Lt. A.R.H. Barton	Sgt. E.A. Crist, RCAF
Plt.Off. J. Bailey	Sgt. W.G. Dodd, RCAF
Plt.Off. J.H.E. Bisley, RAAF	Sgt. P.A. Schade
Sgt. G.A.J. Ryckman, RCAF	

The arrival of the latest batch of Spitfires did not go unnoticed by the Germans and soon after midday nine Ju88s approached the Island, crossing the coast singly or in pairs, to attack and depart under cover of the cloud which again persisted. Four Spitfires and four Hurricanes were scrambled, Flt.Lt. Johnston and Plt.Off Peck of 126 Squadron climbing to 17,000 feet, then being vectored onto an intruder 2000 feet below. Johnston dived from the port beam, but held his fire at the last moment, as he thought the aircraft might be a PR Mosquito. Peck, however, saw it for what it was — a Ju88 in desert camouflage — and gained strikes on its starboard engine before it escaped into cloud. AA guns also claimed a Ju88 probably destroyed during one of the incursions.

Monday, 30 March

In the early hours of the 30th, Blenheim Z6238 en route from Gibraltar became lost — possibly aided by CRIRA transmissions. It force-landed in Sicily, near Donnalucata, where it was captured intact, the crew being made prisoners. For the second day in succession there were no raids on Malta but again reconnaissance aircraft were around. At 1350 Flt.Lt. Macqueen and Flg.Off. Daddo-Langlois (GN-A) scrambled after one of these, chasing it to within a few miles of the Sicilian coast. Daddo-Langlois used all his ammunition from 250 yards range without noticing any significant results, while Macqueen also attacked; he claimed damage to the fleeing bomber, and this may well have been an aircraft of 5/LG 1 which ditched in the sea east of Catania with engine damage, Uffz. Heinz Pfeiffer and two of his crew being killed. Luftwaffe records, however, put this loss down to an accident.

The weather remained poor, which may have contributed to the loss of three more delivery aircraft during the day. One OADU Beaufort (N1034) failed to arrive from Gibraltar, in which Sgt. C.E. Johnson and his crew were reported missing; a second Beaufort (AW201) crashed on arrival at Luqa, with the deaths of three of the crew. Of a flight of three Wellingtons due in from Gibraltar, BB511 also failed to arrive, its fate and that of Plt.Off. Gerald Featherstone and his crew, unknown. The Regia Aeronautica also suffered a loss when, at 1250 a Cant Z506B of 146ª Squadriglia RM left Elmas (Sardinia) on a special mission to search for the British convoy, and did not return. Another, from 287ª Squadriglia RM, went out on a similar sortie at 1305, and this, too, failed to return; Sottoten. Achille Bigoni and his crew were reported missing, but it transpired that the first aircraft, captained by Sottoten. Claudio Cerretti, had only put down with engine problems and returned to base several days later.

Tuesday, 31 March

The last day of the month began with a raid when the first intruders approached — again in cloud — at 0650. Ju88s and Bf109s continued to appear in small numbers throughout the day, until 1515. Two of 185 Squadron's Hurricanes were scrambled, but were surprised by four Bf109s, Plt.Off. Archie Steele being shot down in Z5302, crashing to his death in a field near Tas-Silc. 69 Squadron's PR Mosquito (W4063) had recently been repaired and Plt.Off. Phil Kelley set off in this for a sortie to Tripoli, but was recalled soon after take-off due to the presence of fighters in the area. As he came in to land, two Bf109s attacked, Kelley crash-landing the damaged aircraft; neither the pilot nor Sgt. Pike, the navigator, were injured but the Mosquito was burnt out.

During the day another delivery aircraft from Gibraltar — Hudson V9025 — crashed on landing at Luqa, the crew being killed. AA gunners claimed a Bf109 shot down, adding two Ju88s at 1950 when a force of these bombers — estimated at 20 strong — made a late evening attack on Grand Harbour, Hal Far and Luqa. Naval AA also claimed damage to two Ju88s, but could not prevent the wrecked *Talabot* taking another hit. Four cannon-armed Hurricanes of 185 Squadron were also up in the dusk, aided by searchlights. It was a moonlit night and the Hurricane pilots each attacked a bomber, six in all being seen; Plt.Off. Ormrod damaged one but the guns of Plt.Off. Wigley's Z2396/HA-D jammed after firing a single round each — probably due to faulty oversized ammunition. Sgt. Eastman (GL-W) saw a Ju88 being attacked by two Hurricanes — probably the same one — and attacked from 100 yards. He then attacked another, making two passes and closing to 100 yards, claiming damage, but Sgt. Horricks made the evening a success by claiming another as probably shot down after he had inflicted serious damage.

On the ground at Luqa, as a result of the raid, Blenheim V6434 of OADU was destroyed, while at Hal Far a Swordfish and an Albacore were burnt out. By now 828 and 830 Squadrons were so reduced in strength that, while they retained their separate indentities for personnel and administrative matters, for operational purposes they were combined as the Naval Air Squadron, Malta.

During the month the Island had suffered 186 alerts which had brought 1230 incursions by Ju88s, Ju87s and Bf109s. The defending fighters had claimed 31 shot down, 20 probables and 65 damaged, for the loss of ten Hurricanes and four Spitfires; the guns had claimed a further 28 destroyed, three probables and 31 damaged, while Naval AA added one further probable and four damaged to the tally. 69 Squadron had flown a total of 47 reconnaissance sorties, including six by Spitfires.

As March drew to a close, the Island's commanders' anxieties were increased when 'Ultra' traffic referred to the arrival in Rome of a senior German paratroop commander, one who had participated in the invasion and capture of Crete; this was General Kurt Student. Furthermore, there were indications that paratroop units were being moved from the Eastern Front. Intelligence also indicated an intention by Hitler that Malta be seized during April to safeguard the sea lanes for supplies for Rommel's forthcoming North African offensive.

The Luftwaffe build-up in Sicily was now at its height. On the last day of March the Joint Intelligence Sub-Committee of the Chiefs-of-Staff warned that as Malta was so severely weakened by bombing, it must be assumed that invasion was imminent. However, there was as yet no evidence that Fliegerkorps XI — the command which had carried out the landings on Crete — had arrived in Sicily, nor were any transport aircraft or troop-carrying gliders included in the German arrivals.

Wednesday, 1 April

On this note Malta's defenders entered April, but began the month with a day which proved fairly costly for the Luftwaffe. However, the first loss was suffered by the RAF when BP906, a long-range photo-reconnaissance Spitfire IV, failed to arrive from Gibraltar; it force-landed in Vichy-controlled territory, where the pilot was interned.

It was 249 Squadron's day to man the Spitfires, but the first sorties were made by three Hurricanes of 229 Squadron on their first misson over the Island. On arrival at Malta, Sqn.Ldr. Kain had reported sick and was deemed unfit for further operational flying, which effectively put Flt.Lt. Farnes in charge; he now led off two of the unit's NCO pilots at 1045 to intercept Ju88s, but though Sgts. Pauley and Potts each made attacks, no results were noted.

Approximately 50 Ju88s and Ju87s, with an escort of similar strength, raided Hal Far, Valetta and the Dockyard, during which at least 20 civilians were killed. At Hal Far, 35 year-old LAC Albert Osborne led a party to extinguish the flames of a burning aircraft, when the fuel tank exploded; he was injured and almost overcome by fumes, but recovered sufficiently to return to the fire. As he attempted to put water over a number of torpedoes which were in danger of being 'cooked-off', one exploded and he was killed. The loss of this airman was particularly felt, for he had been a man of great courage who, on previous occasions, had accomplished numerous acts of gallantry, with scant regard to his own safety.

On one occasion Osborne had rendered safe a torpedo hung below a burning aircraft, working only three feet from the main fuel tank; had extinguished a burning aircraft during a heavy raid; attempted to save another burning aircraft, and removed torpedoes from the vicinity; assisted in saving the pilot of a burning aircraft, then extinguished the flames; saved a further aircraft from destruction by fire; attempted, for six hours, to extricate airmen from a bombed shelter, despite bombing and danger from falling masonry; and during the same day had fought fires in two aircraft, saving one of these, and freeing the parachute of a burning flare, thereby allowing the pilot to taxi clear. Not for nothing did Air Vice-Marshal Lloyd refer to him as "one of the bravest airmen it has been my privilege to meet." Osborne received the posthumous award of the George Cross.

There were several air raids during the afternoon, all of which were effectively intercepted. At 1315 Sqn.Ldr. Grant led off six Spitfires which engaged four Bf109s, apparently on a reconnaissance flight. One broke away as the Spitfires turned towards them, Plt.Off. Plagis in AB335/F giving chase, the appropriate log-book entry merely stating:

> 'Chased and shot down Me109 south-east of Grand Harbour'.

It would seem that his victim was one of III/JG 53's leading pilots, Fw. Hans Schade of 8 Staffel, a 13-victory 'Experte'; his aircraft crashed into the sea and he was posted as missing.

Thirty-five minutes later, just as Grant's flight had landed, four were immediately scrambled again with Grant still at their head. This time they encountered 15 escorted Ju88s of I and II/KG 77, diving through the AA barrage to get at them. Some way behind followed six Hurricanes of 185 Squadron. Plt.Off. Plagis noted:

> 'Shot down Ju88 bomber quarter mile north-west of Grand Harbour. Also shared a probably destroyed Ju88 with Hurricane.'

In fact Plt.Off. 'Skip' McKay (GL-Z), celebrating his 21st birthday, recorded sharing a Ju88 with fellow 185 Squadron pilot, Plt.Off. Beckitt (Z4942/Y); presumably all three attacked the same bomber. Meanwhile, Plt.Off. Peter Nash (GN-Z) attacked another of the bombers, which he claimed to have hit in the fuel tanks; he reported that it flicked onto its back in flames and spiralled into the sea. On the ground at Takali, other pilots of 249 Squadron were watching, Sgt. Ray Hesselyn reporting:

> 'We saw Pete's (*victim*) burst into flames and head straight for the sea, sending up a column of water as it crashed.'

Claims for bombers damaged were submitted by Sqn.Ldr. Grant, and by two of the Hurricane pilots — Plt.Off. Noble (HA-S) and Flt.Sgt. Fletcher (GL-W) — the latter believing his victim was probably destroyed. Another of the Spitfire pilots, Flg.Off. Norm Lee, was shot up by Messerschmitts as he attacked a bomber, force-landing at Takali with a shell splinter in his ankle. His probable victor was Oblt. Belser of 8/JG 53, who claimed a Spitfire shot down for his 22nd victory. During this raid, ever-defiant AA gunners enthusiastically if somewhat over-optimistically claimed two Ju88s and three Ju87s shot down! A Ju88 of

4/KG 77, flown by Uffz. Martin Leps, crashed on returning to Comiso, three of the crew (including Leps) being injured; they reported having been hit by AA fire.

At 1630 a Do24 flyingboat was seen five miles north-east of Grand Harbour, under an umbrella of Bf109s apparently searching for Fw. Schade. Four Spitfires and one Hurricane were sent off to investigate, and Plt.Off. Plagis — on his third sortie of the day in AB335/F — claimed one of the Messerschmitts shot down into the sea six miles north of Grand Harbour. Sgt. Hesselyn also claimed a fighter shot down, Sqn.Ldr. Grant and Flg.Off. Buchanan each claiming one damaged. Reported Hesselyn:

> 'Stan (*Grant*) led us down until we were directly behind the enemy and about 5000 feet above. Then he told us to go in and take our pick. I chose the one on the extreme right, and as I dived on him I could see the rest of the boys going in, line abreast. I quickly caught my 109, but I was coming in too fast, and overshot him. However, I got a good bead on the one ahead. It was a lovely break. This 109 was turning at the time, and I had him dead in my sights. Opening fire from about 50 yards, I gave him a four-second burst. He flipped on his back immediately and went straight in. I was as excited as hell. I told everybody, including Woody, that I had shot down my first, screaming over the R/T.'

Hesselyn began circling the Messerschmitt down in the sea but was attacked by two more, streams of tracer just missing his port wing. On landing he discovered that in his excitement he had pressed the wrong firing button, using only his four .303 Brownings to shoot down the German fighter, rather than his cannons! It would seem that he or Plagis — or more likely both of them — had shot down Uffz. Gerhard Kitzenmaier's 'Black 5' of 5/JG 53.

No sooner were the Spitfires down than another raid began approaching, some 70 plus including an estimated 54 Ju87s, making for the Dockyard and Hal Far. Two Hurricanes of 229 Squadron had been sent up at 1700 to cover the returning Spitfires, and these were joined by five more such aircraft from 185 Squadron at 1800, and then by five Spitfires half an hour later. The defenders encountered formations of Ju87s and Ju88s — and their escorts — over Grand Harbour; six of the Stukas were claimed shot down, including two claims made by the AA gunners, five more as probables and three damaged, as follows:

	249 Squadron
Plt.Off.Nash	one Ju87 destroyed
Plt.Off. Plagis	one Ju87 destroyed
Sgt. Hesselyn	one Ju87 destroyed
Sqn.Ldr. Grant	one Ju87 probable, one Ju87 damaged
Flg.Off. Buchanan	one Ju87 probable
	185 Squadron
Flt.Sgt. Fletcher	one Ju87 destroyed, one Ju87 probable
Sgt. Boyd	one Ju87 probable
Plt.Off. McKay	one Ju87 damaged
	229 Squadron
Sgt. Pauley	one Ju87 probable, one Ju87 damaged

AA guns

two Ju87s destroyed, one Bf109 destroyed

Plt.Off. Plagis (AB335/F) reported setting his victim's engine on fire, whereupon it spun down in flames, while Plt.Off. Nash (GN-W) saw his target blow up and fall into the sea; Sgt. Hesselyn wrote:

> 'We each got onto a bomber's tail. Pete (*Nash*) was slightly ahead of me, and I could see him firing before I opened up. His shells were striking and suddenly his 87 blew up. I had no time to see any more. I was within 100 yards of my 87, and, pressing the right gun-button this time, I gave him everything I had. In a couple of seconds he burst into flames and dived into the drink.'

Left: Plt.Off. Peter Nash of 249 Squadron was one of the more successful of the early Spitfire pilots. *(P.B. Lucas via NWMA)*. **Right:** Sgt. Tony Boyd of 242 and 185 Squadrons, one of Malta's most famous Hurricane pilots. This popular Australian was involved in many combats before his death in action, and was awarded the DFM. *(P. Wigley)*

Hurricane pilot Sgt. Tony Boyd (GL-M) recorded:

> 'Attacked Ju87 — probable. Had dogfight with it, several bursts, left it pouring white smoke from port side. Also attacked two Me109s (shot up).'

Plt.Off. McKay's Hurricane (GL-Z) was also hit and damaged by a Bf109 following his combat with the Stuka:

'I had a good crack at one 87 and think it went in but couldn't see 'cause I had to break away when two 109s came down on me. My birthday nearly ended in disaster after breaking off engagement with the 87. I then went to sea level and came back over the island. I was just about over Luqa when I felt and heard my aircraft being hit, which made me turn steeply to port. A 109 had come up behind me and taken a good squirt at me. There were two large cannon holes in my wing and several machine-gun bullets. I had to land without flaps 'cause the starboard one was all shot away'.

The Kommodore of JG 53, Major von Maltzahn, claimed a fighter shot down and was possibly responsible for the damage to McKay's aircraft. Sgt. Hesselyn was also jumped by a Bf109 as he approached to land with wheels and flaps down, but he was able to retract these and turn steeply, the attacker missing his opportunity; the Messerschmitt climbed away after overshooting, allowing the New Zealander to land safely.

It seems likely that the AA gunners claimed the same aircraft as those attacked by the fighters, for as some 14 Ju87s approached Kalafrana and Hal Far they claimed one, which was reported to have fallen into the sea in flames, one man being seen to bale out. Sgt. Tim Goldsmith was amongst those watching the raid and while there are certain inaccuracies and discrepancies in his account, it nevertheless makes interesting reading:

'Four Hurricanes were up from Hal Far and two (*sic*) Spitfires from Luqa... The 109s were really thick this day, the advance wave had been buzzing around the aerodrome like bees around a hive. The first assault was made by 15 Stukas. They approached from the north over St Paul's Bay, and kept on until they had passed over Mdina. We thought they must have been raiding Luqa when the leader rolled upside down, and then dived like a stone, releasing its bomb to strike into a hill above the 'drome. Jerry seems convinced that we had something valuable hidden in the hill, when actually there was little more valuable than the clothing store in a cave!

'In the excitement of screaming bombs, bursting flak, only one or two spectators noticed the two Spitfires streaking down from the direction of Luqa. There was a flock of 109s after them, and one was attacked and had to break away before reaching the Stukas. The other, who I later heard was Hesselyn, joined the bombers and, attacking from the rear quarter, blew one to pieces. He then moved in behind another and fired a long burst at it. This one flicked over and spiralled earthwards, but both of the crew baled out.'

It seems that Goldsmith had actually seen Nash and Hesselyn (and possibly Plagis) obtaining their victories, but had underestimated the number of Spitfires present. Two Ju87s were actually lost, T6+FN of 8/StG 3 crashing on Delimara Point, with the loss of the gunner, Gefr. Wilhelm Neubauer. The pilot, Uffz. Winfried Günther, managed to bale out and was blown out to sea. A second Stuka from this unit came down in the sea five miles north-east of Valetta. Oblt. Kühn, the pilot, was rescued by an Axis air/sea rescue craft, although the gunner of this machine — Gefr. Helmut Suchlich — was also lost. A third aircraft (from 7 Staffel) was hit and the pilot, Ofw. Kurt Auer, wounded.

From Kalafrana Flt.Lt. Crockett immediately took out seaplane tender ST 338, without permission because he knew it would be refused, and within minutes had picked up Uffz. Günther, who was still struggling to release his

On 1 April 1942 Uffz. Franz Pilz of 5/JG 53 force-landed his Bf109F 'Yellow 12' virtually intact near Paola; he became a prisoner of war. *(NWMA)*

parachute harness. It would appear in this case that Kühn's aircraft was that claimed by Hesselyn, Plagis and the AA gunners, the latter also claiming the aircraft attacked by Nash, while Flt.Sgt. Fletcher also probably attacked one or other of these machines.

The Bf109 claimed by the gunners was actually 'Yellow 12' of 5/JG 53, in which Uffz. Franz Pilz had swooped low over Luqa to strafe the AA batteries. In fact, his aircraft struck its tail wheel against a rubble wall, causing the pilot to lose control; the Messerschmitt belly-landed in a nearby field at Paola, just off the Luqa road, virtually undamaged. Although only slightly injured, Pilz was taken by ambulance from Paola to St Andrews, stopping en route to watch the AA barrage engage yet another formation of raiders; the German pilot was said to have been impressed by the intensity of fire.

During the late afternoon raids, while the fighters were engaged with the Ju87s over Luqa and Hal Far, other Stukas from III/StG 3 attacked what shipping could be found tucked away in creeks in the Grand Harbour. In French Creek the submarine *Pandora*, which had arrived the previous day loaded with supplies and torpedoes, received two direct hits as she lay alongside Hamilton Wharf, still being unloaded. She sank in four minutes, 25 of her crew being killed. In Lazaretto Creek another submarine, *P 36*, suffered a near miss from one of several bombs that fell nearby; she started to take in water, then rolled over, sinking to a depth of about 70 feet. Only two seamen were aboard at the time and both escaped. A third submarine, *Unbeaten*, which was submerged in the same creek, was damaged by a near miss and her torpedo tubes distorted; she would be ordered back to the UK for repairs. Additionally, the minesweeper/drifter *Sunset* was sunk in French Creek, the minesweeper *Abingdon* was damaged in Kalkara Creek, while the oiler *Plumleaf* was further damaged. Three of the ubiquitous tugs — *Ancient, West Dean* and *West* — also sustained varying degrees of damage.

That night a dozen Ju88s returned to attack individually, but at 2145 Plt.Off. Oakes and Sgt. Walsh in Beaufighter X7756 intercepted one, which they claimed to have shot down into the sea. This is believed to have been 3Z+LM of 4/KG 77, in which the Staffelkapitän, Oblt. Otto Bischoff, and his crew were lost; Bischoff would posthumously be awarded the Ritterkreuz. Some 45 minutes later the same crew engaged another bomber, claiming strikes before it evaded them. A third intruder was then encountered, damage being claimed to this also, before the rear-gunner gained hits on X7756's port engine, causing a fire to break out; the starboard engine also stopped, but Oakes managed to make a forced-landing at Luqa, where the aircraft was deemed to be damaged beyond repair. AA gunners claimed one further unidentified aircraft probably shot down.

Thursday, 2 April

Thursday brought a resumption of the heavy assault. At 1010 an estimated 50 Ju88s and Ju87s began crossing the coast under their usual escort cover, again to bomb the Dockyard area and Hal Far. At the latter airfield a Swordfish was damaged and set on fire; on the grass nearby was a depth charge waiting to be loaded aboard. In spite of the danger of imminent explosion, Chief Pty.Off. Bill Bull dashed to the scene and extinguished the fire. He then went to the aid of others tackling another fire near a torpedo workshop, and showing tremendous courage, was instrumental in preventing what could have been a disastrous explosion; it was only by the merest chance that he did not lose his life. CPO Bull had previously led firefighting teams when torpedo-armed Swordfish and Albacores had been set ablaze by exploding bombs, and had also rescued a number of personnel from demolished buildings following raids. His constant display of courage was recognised by the award of the George Medal.

It was the turn of the 126 Squadron pilots to be on duty, four Spitfires being scrambled between 0930 and 0940, with two Hurricanes, one each of 185 and 229 Squadrons. Flt.Lt. Johnston, the Spitfire leader, was unable to start his aircraft and was delayed taking off while he transferred to another. As he caught up with his section, which was being led by Plt.Off. McLeod, Bf109s came flashing down on them and Johnston saw one Spitfire go down in flames. He managed to evade the attackers and, now alone, saw many Ju88s. He attacked one of these from 300 to 100 yards, seeing "a large flash" and what appeared to be smoke from the starboard engine; he was to be credited with its probable destruction. At this point he was again attacked by Messerschmitts, but once more escaped, returning to the airfield where it was established that his Spitfire had been hit more than 20 times.

Two of the four Spitfires had failed to return. Plt. Off. McLeod, one of the unit's Americans, had been hit and slightly wounded, with shrapnel wounds to his left arm and leg; despite weighing a hefty 16 stone, he succeeded in rapidly evacuating AB335/F east of Kalafrana when it started to burn. Having gained the comparative safety of his dinghy, he felt inclined to abandon this when a Messerschmitt pilot persisted in 'buzzing' him, but was soon picked up four miles east of Delimara Point by HSL 128. However, Plt.Off. Winston McCarthy had also been shot down in flames in BP844 — probably the Spitfire Johnston had seen going down — and was presumed killed. It seems that the Spitfires had fallen to Hpt. Wilcke of Stab III/JG 53 — his 36th victory — and Lt. Louis of Stab I/JG 53. The two Hurricane pilots had fared better on this occasion; having avoided contact with the escorting fighters, Plt.Off. Beckitt and Sgt. Pauley jointly attacked and damaged a Ju88 before it made good its escape.

Immediately following this initial engagement, Flt.Lt. Paul Farnes led three more 229 Squadron Hurricanes off at 1000, personally claiming damage to a Ju88 he encountered before the escort intervened. It seems that Bf109s of II/JG 3 formed part of the fighter umbrella, Oblt. Walter Dahl claiming a Hurricane shot down as his 18th victory — although this was not officially credited — and, indeed, Plt.Off. Andrew's BV174 was badly shot up by a Messerschmitt, but succeeded in landing at Luqa without further mishap.

Twenty-six Ju87s and 29 Ju88s were back at 1625, bombing Grand Harbour, Hal Far and Luqa, where an unserviceable Wellington was burnt out. At Kalafrana a hangar and a repair shop were hit and badly damaged, an Albacore under repair being destroyed and another damaged. Six of the escorting Bf109s strafed the schooner *Anna Docoutros* on her way to Gozo and she sank.

Seven 185 Squadron Hurricanes and four Spitfires were scrambled. The Spitfire leader, Sqn.Ldr. Gracie, led his trio after a formation of Ju88s, one of which he claimed probably destroyed. Plt.Off. Graves similarly claimed the probable destruction of a second, while Flt.Lt. Barton damaged a third. Ju87s were engaged by Flt.Lt. Lloyd's Hurricanes but there was only time for a brief clash before the escort came down, hence claims were submitted by Lloyd, Plt.Off. Wigley (Z4942/Y) and Sgt. Tweedale for damaged victims only; Lloyd also damaged a Bf109 as did Plt.Off. Ormrod (Z2698/L), while Plt.Off. Milburn gained strikes on a Ju88, believing that he had probably destroyed it. The defenders suffered no losses in this action. One of the low-flying Stukas was claimed damaged by soldiers manning a machine-gun post. Despite all these claims, only one Ju87 of 9/StG 3 sustained serious damage, the gunner, Fw. Alfons Mundt, being wounded.

Meanwhile, at Takali airfield, Sgts. Tim Goldsmith and 'Dusty' Miller were waiting for a lull between raids to ferry four Spitfires over to Luqa, the Australian later writing:

> 'I cautiously rang the Controller to see if the coast was clear before taking off. Everything was OK and a few minutes later we had landed at Luqa and dispersed our machines (the first two). A car picked us up and drove us with our 'chutes back to Takali for the remaining two machines. Again I rang the Controller and was told to make it snappy and keep low. He rang off before I could get any further particulars. Once more we raced across without wasting time. I landed second (in AB340), and was just turning off the main runway when I saw those nasty grey streamers sizzling across my starboard wing and immediately afterwards a series of flashing explosions on the ground 10 yards away.
>
> 'I twisted my neck around just as a 109 flew over not 20 feet above me. I opened the throttles, and ignoring the taxi-way, taxied across the rough stuff with my tail up, till I reached the dispersal bay. "Dusty" raced across from the next bay, laughing his silly head off, but I was unable to see any humour in the situation for quite some time!'

For more than three months Malta had been almost entirely a Luftwaffe preserve by day, but this situation was about to change. At sunset the 4° Stormo CT began returning to Sicily, where it had been based during November and December 1941, its 10° Gruppo flying into Castelvetrano from Rome/Ciampino with 26 new MC202s, led by Cap. Franco Lucchini. It was followed shortly by the similarly equipped 9° Gruppo. In preparation for the latest assault on Malta, the Aeronautica della Sicilia could now call upon a quite substantial force:

FIGHTERS

4° Stormo CT	MC202
9° Gruppo CT	
73ª Squadriglia, 96ª Squadriglia, 97ª Squadriglia	
10° Gruppo CT	
84ª Squadriglia, 90ª Squadriglia, 91ª Squadriglia	
54° Stormo CT	CR42/MC200/MC202
7° Gruppo CT	
76ª Squadriglia, 86ª Squadriglia, 98ª Squadriglia	
16° Gruppo CT	
167ª Squadriglia, 168ª Squadriglia, 169ª Squadriglia	
377ª Squadriglia Aut CT	CR42/Re2000/MC200

BOMBERS/TORPEDO-BOMBERS

10° Stormo BT	S.79bis
30° Gruppo BT	
55ª Squadriglia, 56ª Squadriglia	
32° Gruppo CT	
57ª Squadriglia, 58ª Squadriglia	
173ª Squadriglia Aut RST	CR25
50° Gruppo BT	Z1007bis
210ª Squadriglia, 211ª Squadriglia	
55° Gruppo BT	BR20M
220ª Squadriglia, 221ª Squadriglia	
4° Gruppo BT/AS	S.84bis
14ª Squadriglia, 15ª Squadriglia	
130° Gruppo Aut AS	S.79sil
280ª Squadriglia, 283ª Squadriglia	
278ª Squadriglia Aut AS	S.79sil

MARITIME RECONNAISSANCE

83° Gruppo RM	Z501/Z506B
170ª Squadriglia, 184ª Squadriglia, 186ª Squadriglia, 189ª Squadriglia	

That night raiders again bombed Luqa, where an unserviceable Wellington (DV412 of 1443 Flight) was burnt out, while at Kalafrana an aircraft repair shop was again hit; an Albacore and Spitfire AB420 (both under repair) were destroyed. At Hal Far another Albacore and a Hurricane were burnt out. During one of the attacks on Hal Far, Flt.Sgt. H.G.W. Cagby removed fifty 40lb bombs from the vicinity of burning aircraft with apparent complete disregard for his own safety, an action for which he was later awarded a BEM.

Friday, 3 April

Good Friday of Easter weekend found the island with few serviceable fighters available. Three major raids were suffered. In the first a Blenheim and a

Beaufighter, both under repair at Takali, were damaged, as was a petrol bowser; AA guns claimed one Ju88 shot down and one damaged. At midday a Hurricane was destroyed at Hal Far, and the Officers' Quarters damaged; AA claimed damage to another Ju88. Four hours later Spitfire AB418 was destroyed at Takali and three others damaged, when a 'rocket bomb' hit the airfield, while at Hal Far another Albacore was damaged and two soldiers killed.

During a lull between raids, General Dobbie and his daughter Sybil paid a visit to the harbour to see for themselves troops unloading cargo from the sunken *Pampas*. Miss Dobbie, with obvious admiration for the soldiers, was to write:

> 'The troops were swimming about in the filthy mess of oil and water in a flooded hold, steering barrels to the side while others winched them out. I saw this day by day but they had been doing this at night too, and did not stop and take cover for any raids.'

Spitfires of 249 Squadron were up to meet one raid, Sgt. Yarra engaging a Ju88 but without tangible success; this was Yarra's last flight with 249 Squadron, for next day he was posted to 185 Squadron to employ his previous experience on Hurricanes advantageously. At the same time Plt.Off. 'Tex' Putnam and Sgt. Tim Goldsmith were posted from that unit to 126 Squadron, due to their earlier experience in the UK on Spitfires.

More raiders appeared during the night of the 3rd/4th, but while two of 1435 Flight's Hurricanes were scrambled and Flg.Off. Rathie intercepted one bomber held briefly in the searchlights, no success was achieved. Possibly the presence of the night fighters frustrated determined attacks on ground targets, for little damage was reported.

Saturday, 4 April

The morning of the 4th opened with an accident at Luqa, when an OADU Wellington (BB512) from Gibraltar collided with another on the ground (Z8575) as it landed; there were no fatalities. When the Luftwaffe put in an appearance, crews of the initial raiders again found themselves opposed only by the guns, but when some of the 14 Ju87s and 25 Ju88s raiding Grand Harbour aimed their bombs at the cruiser *Penelope* as she lay in dock under repair for the damage she had suffered a week earlier, they found a doughty opponent. The ship's gunners claimed one attacker "shot to pieces" by their 4-inch gun, and two others were claimed damaged by short-range weapons. Her victim was undoubtedly Fw. Hans Frank's Ju87 T6+CH of 7/StG 3, only the gunner, Uffz. Georg Gröner, surviving to become a prisoner.

Soon after midday Ju88s bombed *Penelope* again, and the nearby destroyer *Kingston*; the cruiser had suffered minor damage from near misses during the morning attack, but this time escaped relatively unscathed, although many surrounding buildings in Hamrun and Floriana were destroyed during this assault and three civilians killed. A further attack mid afternoon brought bombs on Valetta, where St Paul's Cathedral suffered a direct hit. Finally, as the evening drew on, 60 more Ju88s came in again, covered by many Bf109s; this time four Spitfires and six Hurricanes were available to meet them. However, *Penelope* was hit and further damaged on this occasion, fires breaking out while in Kalkara Creek the previously damaged minesweeper *Abingdon* was now sunk.

Flt.Lt. Macqueen, leading the Spitfires, carried out a stern quarter attack on one Ju88, seeing its starboard engine catch fire. He then shot at the port engine and the bomber turned on its back and dived vertically; although it was claimed shot down this was probably an aircraft of 5/KG 77 which belly-landed at Comiso on return, badly damaged by fighter attack. Another Ju88 was claimed damaged by Plt.Off. Sergeant, who reported an apparent dead rear-gunner following his attack, with the aircraft last seen rolling onto its back; however, this may have been the aircraft under attack by his leader. A third bomber was claimed damaged by Flg.Off. Daddo-Langlois, whose own aircraft (GN-U) sustained one bullet strike from the rear-gunner. One of the Hurricane pilots — Sgt. Potts of 229 Squadron — also claimed a Ju88 damaged.

During one of the day's raids two Bf109 fighter-bombers of 10(Jabo)/JG 53 crashed into the sea, Uffz. Heinz Bross ('White 9') and Ofw. Günther Fronhöfer ('White 2') being lost; it was presumed that they had collided.

Three Italian convoys were now at sea, comprising six merchantmen, seven destroyers and two MTBs. Six torpedo-carrying Beauforts of 39 Squadron from Bu Amud had been despatched to search for them, led by Flt.Lt. J.M. Lander, but these had failed to find their quarry and landed at Luqa when they ran low on fuel. The Beauforts were escorted to the Island by four Spitfires which had been despatched from Luqa to guide them in, Plt.Off. McHan at their head. In the event the Italian vessels all reached Tripoli without interference.

Sunday, 5 April

This morning more Beauforts were due to arrive — on this occasion OADU delivery aircraft from Gibraltar. One of these (AW338) was reported missing, while a second (AW298) crashed as it came in to land at Luqa. The first two raids of the day were again unintercepted, Ju87s hitting the sunken *Abingdon* in Kalkara Creek at 0750, while at midday *Penelope* was further damaged by near-misses from Ju88s. Staffelkapitän Oblt. Georg Graf von Platen bombed the cruiser from 2500 feet, planting his bombs either side of her; one heavy bomb left a huge crater in the dockside.

When 40 Ju88s — including aircraft from KGr 806 — and 15 Ju87s of III/StG 3 attacked under a large fighter escort during the early afternoon, four Spitfires flown by 126 Squadron pilots, and four Hurricanes were scrambled. Plt.Off. John Bisley, an Australian, initially claimed a Ju87 probably destroyed, and a Ju88 damaged but both were later upgraded to confirmed victories; his report of the action read:

> 'I was east of Grand Harbour and followed a Ju88 line astern. I got within 300 yards about three miles out to sea and was not gaining, so I gave one second burst with cannons and observed no results. Turned port back to Grand Harbour at 6000 feet and saw about ten Ju88s in the flak, line astern, and as they came out I went in to attack the nearest from beam, turning to quarter and astern, closing to about 150 yards; rear-gunner did not return fire. I broke to port and noticed black smoke from port engine. I did not follow because about six 109s above. I returned in circles to Grand Harbour and asked Control if there were any more bombers coming in, and they told me there were some Ju87s coming in.
>
> 'I saw two Ju87s which had pulled out of their dives, on my port at same altitude. I turned towards the nearest at 3000 feet and attacked from quarter

> to astern. Rear-gunner fired but ceased after by first burst. I closed in to about 50 yards, firing the whole time and set his engine on fire. He dived to starboard with smoke coming from underneath the engine. I then broke to port and saw a large number of 109s 3-4000 feet, about five miles out to sea, above me. I made for sea level and two 109s dived and attacked me. Had a burst in cockpit which struck right leg (shrapnel wounds to right leg and hand). Shook off 109s after crossing the coast and came in and landed (wheels up) at Takali, with cockpit full of smoke.'

There is little doubt that the Ju87 was an aircraft of 9/StG 3, which crashed in the sea about five miles north of Malta. The pilot baled out and was later rescued, but the gunner (Fw. Christoph Würzer) was lost. Meanwhile, Flt.Lt. Johnston, the Spitfire leader, had sighted what he believed were four Bf109s, but which on investigation turned out to be the four Hurricanes. He then saw Messerschmitts below and dived on the nearest, firing a long burst and seeing a puff of grey smoke from near the engine. A single parachute was observed descending in the area, and Johnston was granted the probable destruction of the German fighter, but almost certainly the parachute contained the pilot of the Stuka shot down by Bisley. On approaching to land, Johnston was fired on by the same Bf109s which had been chasing Bisley, but succeeded in landing safely.

Another of the Spitfire quartet, the American Plt.Off. Putnam, returned having claimed a Ju88 shot down, and the Hurricane pilots also reported meeting an estimated 40 Ju88s and 15 Ju87s, but before they could attack the escort bounced them; Plt.Off. 'Taffy' Andrews of 229 Squadron was seriously wounded in the left arm by a cannon shell. He managed to maintain consciousness despite his severe injury and landed safely at Luqa, but his aircraft (BM964) ran off the airfield due to damage sustained to the brakes, and he was further injured; he was recommended for a Mention in Despatches. Meanwhile, the three 185 Squadron aircraft had pressed home their attacks, Sgt. Tony Boyd (Z2698/L) recording:

> 'Plot 83 plus — 50 Ju88s, remainder 109s. One Hurri shot up before engaged. I attacked two Ju88s — strikes. Dogfight alone with four 109s out over sea. Definitely damaged one. Was attacked in circuit by two 109s, but evaded OK. One bullet through starboard wing and one clipped bottom of seat and parachute cover. Phew!'

The other two Hurricane pilots — Plt.Off. Ron Noble (Z4942/Y), leading the section, and Plt.Off. McKay (GL-Z) — also engaged the bombers, the latter reporting:

> 'The bombers came in over Grand Harbour and we all split up and went in. I think I got one 88 but couldn't see what happened to it 'cause I had to break away when four 109s attacked. I have never seen so many 109s in my life before they went all over the place, even in the circuit. God knows how any of us came back seeing it was twelve to one odds against. There were 83 enemy planes and seven of us. When we landed Ron, Boyd and I split an 88 three ways destroyed.'

One Ju88, M7+JL of 3/KGr 806, crash-landed one mile west of Catania on return, Uffz. Hugo Paul and two of his crew sustaining injuries; they reported, however, having been hit by AA fire. Following this raid, no fighters were available to meet the final attack at 1705, when 28 Ju88s raided Grand Harbour and Jabo Bf109s attacked Takali. During the day the destroyer *Lance* was damaged by two direct hits whilst in the Dockyard, and the Greek submarine *Glaucos* was sunk in French Creek.

With nightfall Sqn.Ldr. Westmacott scrambled in a Hurricane, but as he was vectored onto a Ju88, a glycol pipe burst and he was obliged to give up the chase, and landed at once. At 0300 Flt.Lt. Lander was despatched in one of the 39 Squadron Beauforts to search for a 10,000-ton freighter, sighted earlier by an ASV Wellington, but he was unable to find it. During the night, however, a bomb dropped by an intruding Axis raider gained a hit on another of the unit's Beauforts, N1035 being completely destroyed. The remaining five aircraft departed for Bu Amud next morning.

Monday, 6 April

There was to be only one major — unopposed — raid on Easter Monday, but it was a damaging one. At least 20 Ju87s and 55 Ju88s attacked Grand Harbour and the Dockyard, where a floating crane was sunk and four others damaged. Luqa also came under heavy attack, where five Hurricanes (Z3757, BE349, BE351, BG698 and BG764) and two Spitfires (AB338 and AB454) were damaged beyond repair; at Hal Far several aircraft were slightly damaged, and the Officers' Mess was hit. One Ju88 of 3/KG 54 crash-landed about three miles north of Pozzallo on return, killing Obgfr. Siegried Schmelcher, the pilot, and injuring his crew.

The day did, however, see the arrival of the second flight of 229 Squadron (see Table 4 below), nine Hurricanes flying in from Gambut, as recalled by Plt.Off. Len Malthus, who had failed to complete the earlier flight:

> 'Since we had to fly at deck level to avoid detection and we couldn't do our own navigation at that level, we were given an escort of a Beaufort, and we had to form up on this and fly along with it escorting us.
>
> 'We had been flying for a long time and began wondering when the Beaufort was going to turn to port, because we had to do a dogleg to keep well away from Jerry territory; we had to fly north and then west to get to Malta, and we wondered when the Beaufort was going to make its turn.
>
> 'Suddenly we picked up Malta's frequency on our VHFs, and they told us that we were flying in the wrong direction, and that we were heading directly for Sicily. We couldn't make radio contact with the Beaufort so two or three of us flew alongside, waggled our wings violently and turned away. I suppose we did this four or five times but the Beaufort crew paid not the slightest attention, so we turned off for Malta.

TABLE 4

9 Hurricane IICs of 229 Squadron from Middle East

Flt.Lt. M.A. Beatty	BM985		
Plt.Off. J.H. Nixon		Flt.Sgt. D. Roy	BM964
Plt.Off. K.L. Lee, RNZAF		Sgt. J.R. Pendlebury	
Plt.Off. L.G. Malthus, RNZAF		Sgt. R.J. Lees	BN181
Plt.Off. T.G. Foley, RCAF		Sgt. L.D. Brooks, RCAF	

'We could see Malta from a long way off because there was an air raid going on. As we approached we could see the palls of smoke from the bombing. We landed at Hal Far in the middle of an air raid but got down safely. I never heard any more of the Beaufort — it was possibly shot down or landed in Sicily.'

126 Squadron recorded that nearly all its former Hurricane pilots had now departed, including Sqn.Ldr. Norris, Flt.Lts. Anderson, Davis and Kee, together with several others; the unit also released Sgt. Wilbert Dodd to reinforce 185 Squadron at Hal Far. 249 Squadron received a replacement pilot when Flg.Off. Ron West was transferred from 126 Squadron. There was also some re-shuffling in the Luftwaffe camp, with 6 Staffel of II/JG 3 being briefly detached from Sicily to the Libyan Desert, there to fly with JG 27.

Of this period, LAC Metcalf at Takali confided to his diary:

'This Easter has been one that I'll remember (should I be one of the lucky ones that get away with it!). From dawn to dusk wave after wave of 88s, 87s and other gash kites to make weight have bombed and better bombed. During one lull I bobbed my head above the slit trench and suddenly spotted a fresh wave of 88s coming in over St Paul's. I counted 27 but when the leader put his nose down and started a power-dive straight for my slit trench — what a sensation — I could neither speak nor move! Luckily he came a few feet too low and the bombs went over the top of the trench.

'What a Hell-hole! And still they came, in all their might. God in heaven alone knows what's going to happen next and where this is all going to end. It's a pity we haven't some fighter protection, but what we do have has done wonderful work and each pilot deserves a VC at least. To send the last few up alone would be murder in the first degree. The ack ack boys too are great and I hold my hand out to each of them.

'I'm absolutely disgusted. Last night the BBC announced "Enemy activity over Malta on a reduced scale." I only wish the bloke who read it out had been in the slit trench with me at 6 pm!'

Out to sea to the west, the destroyer *Havock* was making for Gibraltar, carrying many of *Breconshire*'s survivors. During the day she ran aground near Cape Bon, her crew and passengers being interned by the Vichy authorities.

Many intruders were over the Island during the night of the 6th/7th, including seven BR20Ms of the 55° Gruppo BT, which dropped 400 small anti-personnel bombs but little damage was suffered. Two of 1435 Flight's Hurricanes were again on patrol, Sgt. Wood encountering an aircraft believed to have been a Ju88, which he claimed damaged. One of the Beaufighters was also up, Flt.Lt. Coleman and Sgt. Peasley in X7750 engaging a twin-engined aircraft which they took to be a Ju88, and claiming this shot down.

Tuesday, 7 April

Raids on the 7th found the fighters once again grounded. The first raid concentrated on Grand Harbour and the airfields. *Penelope* and *Kingston* were favoured targets, but were not hit, although a small fire was caused aboard the steamship *Golly* in Marsa Creek. At Kalafrana an ASR Swordfish floatplane and a Walrus were both damaged, while Spitfire AB262/B of 249 Squadron (under repair) was rendered irreparable when further damaged. In the water, a whaler and two launches were destroyed, while two refuellers and three tenders were damaged, and various civilian vessels were strafed.

When 69 Squadron's PR Spitfire AB300 returned from a sortie over Sicily, Plt.Off. Coldbeck found the gunners at Luqa not surprisingly rather jumpy, and he was shot-up by the light AA as he came in to land. Neither pilot nor aircraft suffered damage though. Later in the afternoon *Penelope* and *Kingston* were again attacked, and missed, but ammunition lighters in French Creek were hit and blew up. During an evening raid on these same choice targets, *Penelope* was near-missed and suffered a severe shaking, while in Valetta the elegant and stately Opera House was struck by a bomb, as was the Officers' Mess at Kalafrana. AA gunners claimed two Ju88s and a Bf109 shot down, and a Ju88 damaged; but German losses appear to have been nil, with returning aircraft suffering superficial damage only. Italian bombers were again due to resume the attack by night, although adverse weather caused all but one to return early.

Wednesday, 8 April

Following desperate efforts by ground crew, fighters were serviceable in sufficient numbers to offer some resistance on the 8th — not however to the morning raids, three of which were made. The first was the most damaging, *Penelope* suffering some shrapnel wounds from a near miss by a 220kg bomb. At Kalafrana the damaged Swordfish floatplane and Walrus were finished off, and another Swordfish damaged, as were a number of aero engines, a hangar, the torpedo depot, a tender and a refueller.

At last at 1330, as a dozen Ju88s and 21 Bf109s — including some carrying bombs — approached Takali, three Spitfires of 249 Squadron, three Hurricanes of 185 Squadron and four of 229 Squadron intercepted, attacking six of the bombers at 14,000 feet over Kalafrana. The Spitfires dived out of the clouds onto the bombers, which were flying in two vics of three, with Bf109s behind and between them. Flt.Lt. Heppell attacked one bomber, seeing strikes on wings and fuselage, then fired at a second, hitting the cockpit, fuselage and starboard engine, which gave off smoke. He fired a further six-second burst from astern and then broke away due to the attentions of another. A splash was observed in the sea, convincing Heppell that his victim had gone in.

The New Zealander Plt.Off. Jeff West attacked another bomber head-on and saw strikes on the cockpit. He then turned onto the tail of a Bf109 and closed, firing all his ammunition and causing black smoke to appear; this may have been a 6/JG 53 aircraft flown by Lt. Hans Möller which crashed into the sea off Valetta although, reportedly, as a result of AA damage; Möller was later picked up by an ASR craft from Sicily. The third member of the trio, Plt.Off. Harry Kelly, claimed damage to yet another bomber.

Meanwhile, the Hurricane pilots also engaged the Ju88s, Flt.Lt. Lloyd (GL-W) claiming damage to one of these, and to an escorting fighter, while Sgt. Boyd (in HA-S) reported:

> 'Our section of three Hurricanes attacked incoming bombers head-on; I attacked one head-on seeing strikes, then attacked a second from about 100 yards. My tracers entered him from nose to tail (two-seconds), and small pieces like fabric flew off. I made second attack on same aircraft from astern as he dived and poured two-seconds in from astern, definitely striking — claimed damaged.

'Next I saw a Ju88 below 6000 feet and dived vertically on him, shooting from above to astern, 50 to 100 yards, and then a couple more bursts. His starboard engine immediately poured black smoke and must have stopped as he slowed up, but Me109s made me break off. As I looked back there was a large splash. Claim — very probable. Position approximately six miles north of Zonkor Point.

'Note: Flt.Lt. Lloyd noticed a long line of foam in sea looking like a large aircraft going in sea four miles north of Zonkor.'

It seems very likely that both Heppell and Boyd had attacked the same aircraft at the same time — a Ju88 of KüFlGr 606 ditching in the sea after being hit by fighters, the crew later being picked up safely by Axis air-sea rescue craft.

A bigger raid developed at 1500, no less than 57 Ju88s and 26 Ju87s being reported, together with many fighters, with Grand Harbour and Luqa as the targets. Flt.Lt. Heppell again led off three Spitfires, which were joined by nine Hurricanes. Flying AB346/K, Heppell attacked a Ju88 over the harbour at 8000 feet, seeing strikes on the wing roots and tail unit, but at that moment his Spitfire received a direct hit from an AA shell; he was blown out of his aircraft with nothing more serious than gashes to his head and legs, and severe bruising. Despite the suddenness of it all, he managed to get his parachute open, and landed heavily in a bomb crater near Floriana, while the wreckage of the Spitfire crashed into a cemetery at Sliema! Initially it was believed that he had "hit an aerial mine."

Sgt. Boyd — again in HA-S — claimed another Ju88 as probably destroyed, as testified by his subsequent report:

'We caught first raid as it dived on Grand Harbour. I went round barrage to north and attacked one Ju88 coming out. Beam shot, four seconds, 100 yards; stern shot, 150 yards, six seconds. Port engine poured white smoke, then both engines black smoke. Left him in dive just north of Grand Harbour. Me109s made me break off. Strikes observed going in both engines and fuselage. In second wave attacked one Ju88 from below astern. Saw strikes. No other results.'

Other claims were made by Flg.Off. Ron West (of 249 Squadron) for a Ju88 probable, while another was damaged by Plt.Off. Wigley (GL-P), who commented:

'Armed only with .303 Brownings, I merely succeeded in damaging one.'

One Ju88 of 6/KG 77 crash-landed at Comiso, 30% damaged by fighters. During this raid Lt. Kläger of 8/JG 53 claimed a Hurricane shot down for his 12th victory. It is possible that he attacked Boyd's aircraft, and then saw Heppell's Spitfire falling.

At 1715 ten Ju87s raided the Dockyard again, but *Penelope* had just departed, making a dash for Gibraltar. Twenty-five minutes later more than 50 Ju88s attacked, gaining a direct hit on *Kingston*, which was wrecked. *Penelope* was soon under way however, and was narrowly missed by two bombs which fell ten yards to port. More Stukas arrived and attacked her, one of the worn-out barrels of her 4-inch gun exploding and killing two gunners and an officer, and wounding others. Nonetheless, 'HMS Pepperpot' — as she had been nicknamed due to the many holes in her — escaped bombs aimed at her in subsequent attacks at dusk, and headed westward at full steam.

During the day the AA defences made substantial claims for the destruction of three Ju88s, plus one probable and two damaged, and for three Bf109s and one damaged. Two Ju87s of 9/StG 3 were reported missing, although allegedly as the result of a collision, in which Oblt. Helmut Gröss and Fw. Walter Diehm and their gunners were lost.

With the approach of dusk, three of 249 Squadron's Spitfires were again scrambled, this time after an air-sea rescue Do24 of 6 Seenotdienstaffel, which was operating off shore under a screen of Messerschmitts, obviously searching for survivors of the missing aircraft. The flyingboat was seen taxying on the water with six Bf109s overhead and six Ju88s in the general area, Flg.Off. Ron West at once diving to attack the Dornier. Strikes were seen all along the fuselage and the rescue aircraft caught fire, the crew escaping unhurt and later themselves being rescued.

Plt.Off. Kelly, meanwhile, had attacked one of the Ju88s from quarter astern, claiming strikes on the port engine and the cabin, before following West down to attack the flyingboat. As West pulled up from his attack, he was bounced by some of the escorting fighters but succeeded in getting a deflection shot along the fuselage of one of these as it overshot. A patrolling Hurricane pilot apparently reported that he had seen both the Messerschmitt fired at by West, and the Junkers attacked by Kelly, hit the water; consequently both were confirmed as having been shot down, though available Luftwaffe records fail to show the loss of either.

Nocturnal intruders began appearing within two hours of this latter engagement, while both a Beaufighter and a Hurricane were up. At 2045 the Beaufighter crew — Flt.Lt. Hayton and Plt.Off. Josling in X7750 — intercepted a Ju88C night fighter of I/NJG 2 over Safi and shot it up. The pilot of the damaged aircraft, Ofw. Alfred Vogel, attempted to force-land R4+CL at once, but missed the runway and hit a stone wall; the aircraft burst into flames and all four of the crew were killed. The swastika-painted fin panel was salvaged as a souvenir to adorn a wall of the Officers' Mess.

Thursday, 9 April

Initial incursions on the 9th were only small, and not until after midday did a large raid approach the coast, the airfields being the target on this occasion for 40 plus Ju88s, 16 Ju87s and almost 40 Bf109s. At Luqa 20 dive-bombing Ju88s destroyed one unserviceable Wellington and damaged a second, while Ju87s hit Luqa village, where an air-raid shelter suffered a direct hit which killed 23 civilians, including eight members of the Attard family. Grand Harbour was also attacked, the destroyers *Lance* and *Gallant* being the obvious targets.

Over 60 Ju88s and a dozen Ju87s resumed the attacks at 1630. At Takali, which was bombed and strafed by two waves of Ju88s, each a dozen strong, a Maryland was damaged, a Hurricane under repair was written off, and a Beaufighter damaged. Bofors gunners put up a spirited resistance, but one Lewis-gunner was killed.

Ten minutes after the commencement of this attack on Takali, three bombs fell on Mosta Church; one exploded outside the massive 184-feet high dome, doing little damage, while the second hit the right side belfry, damaging part of the stonework before rolling away — unexploded — down to the parvis. Others struck the very foundations of the building, but again none exploded. However, one 500kg missile did penetrate the nine-feet thick dome, bounced twice off the interior wall, but also failed to explode! It then skidded along the floor of the nave and came to a standstill. There were some 300 of the congregation present, but most had scattered to the side chapels and corridors for shelter as the bombs began falling, and none was hurt, even by flying debris! The Maltese believed — and many still do — that it was a miracle!

Mosta Church, famous for its vast dome — the third largest unsupported cupola in the world. A bomb pierced this dome on 9 April 1942 when a service was in progress, but failed to explode. The legend of the 'Miracle of Mosta' was perpetuated thereafter. *(Authors' Collection)*

LAC Jim Somerville, an airman of 249 Squadron, was in the vicinity of the church, and recalled seeing a lady emerging from the building bringing the news that there was an unexploded bomb on the floor of the rotunda. He and two or three soldiers entered the church and proceeded to roll the bomb outside, from where it was taken away, with the other unexploded bombs, on an army pick-up truck. Seconds later Somerville was wounded in the leg by shrapnel from another bomb which went off nearby.

As the bombs were falling two Jabo Bf109s of 10/JG 53 were over the area, flown by Uffz. Dr. Felix Sauer and Gefr. Franz Scheffl, having come in low from Comiso to avoid radar detection and AA fire. Even so, the intense barrage drove them away from Takali — their intended target — and as they passed over Mosta, Sauer saw his partner jettison his bomb, following which he saw what he described as a jet of flame and dust coming out of the dome of the church, causing him to believe that it was Scheffl's bomb which had struck the dome. However, the latter's Messerschmitt was then hit by AA fire, and Scheffl failed to return, Sauer believing that he had ditched in the sea.

To combat this heavy raid two Spitfires and ten Hurricanes — equally drawn from 185 and 229 Squadrons — had scrambled; of the fight, Plt.Off. McKay recorded:

> 'There were ten Hurricanes and two Spitfires against a plot of at least 100, about 50 bombers and the same number of Me109Fs. It seemed futile but we did manage to put a lot of the bombers off their target and then a terrific

dogfight ensued. The dogfight went on for quite some time and we were having trouble getting in to land 'cause there were 109s around trying to get you when you got your wheels and flaps down. I had two bullet holes in the port wing and one through the perspex (of GL-P). I got a Ju88 I think.'

Total claims were made for eight Ju88s damaged; the two Spitfire pilots, Flt.Lt. Barton and Flt.Sgt. Schade, claimed two and one respectively, while other Hurricane pilots claimed four more, one each being credited to Flt.Sgt. Brooks of 229 Squadron, Flt.Lt. Lawrence (GL-W), Flt.Sgt. Fletcher (HA-S) and Sgt. Boyd of 185 Squadron. Tony Boyd (BN118) reported:

'I attacked a Ju88 front port quarter to abeam, 150 yards with three-second burst of cannon, and broke off quickly for the next. My No 2 — Sgt. Tweedale — who watched my attack, saw a stream of pieces fly off the Ju88, which went in a steep dive still streaming pieces. A gun-post observer, who watched the engagement, saw a Ju88 engaged by a Hurricane about same position, and the Ju88 did not pull out of its dive. Claim one Ju88 damaged, or on evidence from gun-post — probably destroyed.'

Left: Grp.Capt. A.B. 'Woody' Woodall, the genial Senior Fighter Controller, who was held in great affection by all Malta's fighter pilots. **Right:** Oblt. Helmut Belser, Staffelkapitän of 8/JG 53, in the cockpit of his Bf109F. Belser was to be III/JG 53's most successful pilot over Malta, claiming eight victories between March and May (his 21st-28th). *(J. Prien via W. Bock)*

However, Sgt. Pauley of 229 Squadron was shot down into the sea in Z3505 by a Bf109, baling out off Grand Harbour, while several other Hurricanes returned with battle damage. Oblt. Belser of 8/JG 53 claimed a Hurricane for his 23rd victory, and Lt. Neuhoff of 7 Staffel claimed two more, his 39th and 40th victories. Flt.Lt. Crockett set out at 1855 to pick up Sgt. Pauley, but spotted a small boat in which he found three Army officers and the slightly wounded pilot, whom they had picked up. All four were transferred to the HSL and the boat was taken in tow to Kalafrana. During the day's engagements the AA had claimed a Ju88 and two Ju87s shot down, as well as a Bf109, plus two more Messerschmitts damaged. No bomber losses are recorded in available Luftwaffe records.

Meanwhile at sea to the west, the cruiser *Penelope* had continued her dash for Gibraltar, but had come under frequent attack. At 0800 two floatplanes —

identified as He115s, but probably Z506Bs or RS14s — circled overhead, although the vessel was flying a huge Italian ensign which had been made by the crew during the night, in a desperate bid to bluff and confuse! This obviously failed to fool the shadowers, for at 1045 three S.79sil torpedo-bombers of 280ª Squadriglia AS attacked, initially simultaneously, after which one came in alone but released from too great a distance; the torpedoes were easily combed. This attack was followed at 1128 by two He111s, which came in at low-level, dropping eight bombs without effect; the gunners claimed to have hit these aircraft repeatedly, but they do not appear to have been seriously damaged. Six minutes later a lone Ju88 released two bombs which fell 50 yards to port.

As the warship came within range of Sardinian-based aircraft, a Z506B was sent to locate it, followed by 14 CR42s of 24° Gruppo, half of them armed with pairs of 100kg bombs, but they failed to find her. At 1330 six more S.79sil approached — this time from 256ª and 257ª Squadriglia — and these fanned out into pairs, *Penelope* only narrowly avoiding one of the torpedoes they launched. One machine-gunned the cruiser as it passed overhead at low-level, and return fire was seen striking its fuselage. As the attack was underway, two S.84 bombers attempted to bomb from higher level, but missed the violently-manoeuvring vessel. Her ordeal was still not over, for at 1500 at least a dozen Ju88s appeared and attacked individually, gaining some near-misses but causing no damage.

Finally, at 1640, a single Ju88 and a lone floatplane — again identified as an He115 — began shadowing, but after about two hours the Ju88 suddenly carried out an attack, and dropped one very large bomb which shook the vessel severely, although the ship's Oerlikon gunner raked the bomber as it swept over; both aircraft then departed. At the end of this traumatic series of assaults, the ship's cat gave birth to three kittens in Captain Angus Nicholl's sea cabin; they were appropriately named 'Bomb', 'Blitz' and 'Blast' in recognition of the events of this day! There were to be no more attacks, and *Penelope* reached Gibraltar at 1600 next day.

Friday, 10 April

The first raid on Malta on Friday came in at 1245 and met no defenders; at Luqa a damaged Wellington was destroyed and two Hurricanes damaged. The bombers returned in great strength at 1745, an estimated 65 Ju88s and 20 Ju87s attacking Grand Harbour, Hal Far and Takali; Admiralty House at Vittoriosa was amongst those buildings demolished in this raid, while off Marfa a fishing boat was strafed and seven of the crew wounded.

To meet this mighty onslaught eight Hurricanes of 185 Squadron had scrambled, led by Flt.Lt. Lloyd, followed by four of 229 Squadron and four Spitfires flown by 249 Squadron pilots. The latter attacked ten Ju88s of III/KG 77, one of which Flt.Lt. Macqueen claimed shot down; two of the crew appeared to bale out but, in fact, the gun position had been blown off the cabin of 3Z+HS, this and the body of the gunner, Uffz. Paul Boger, falling on Takali airfield. This 8 Staffel machine was also claimed by the AA gunners. Of the incident LAC Metcalf wrote:

> 'The rear-gunner of an 88 was shot out of his kite complete with turret and landed roughly 50 yards from our trench. He wasn't greatly disfigured although his neck was broken.'

Meanwhile, Flg.Off. Buchanan dived out of the sun on a Bf109 over St Paul's Bay as it was pulling up after firing at a Hurricane. He fired from long range and rather to his surprise, the aircraft burst into flames and the pilot baled out; he was credited with its destruction. However, Sgt. Horricks of 185 Squadron (BD826/A) reported chasing a Bf109 from 17,000 feet to sea level, four miles north-west of Grand Harbour. He fired a four-second burst and reported that it exploded and burst into flames, the pilot baling out. Sgt. Tony Boyd witnessed the combat, recording:

> 'Terrific odds. We couldn't do much about the bombers. Three Hurricanes lost, remainder shot up, but all pilots safe. Sgt. Horricks got a 109. The best flamer I've seen yet.'

Only one Messerschmitt was lost, the pilot none other than III/JG 53's leading 'Experte', Lt. Hermann Neuhoff in 'Yellow 1' — who now became a prisoner; only the previous evening he had been promoted to lead 6 Staffel in place of Oblt. Belser, the latter resuming command of 8 Staffel. Neuhoff subsequently asked to meet his victor, and was introduced to Buchanan (who has been credited with shooting him down ever since). On the evidence it seems more likely that Neuhoff was actually brought down by Garth Horricks, although Buchanan's fire may have played a contributing part. However the returning pilots of JG 53 believed that Neuhoff had in fact been shot down accidentally by Lt. Werner Schow of 1 Staffel, who had apparently admitted firing at a Messerschmitt in error during the heat of battle. Despite Neuhoff's obvious belief at the time that he had fallen to an RAF fighter, after the war he appeared to subscribe to the Geschwader's view. The unfortunate Schow was killed in Russia later in the year.

Other claims were submitted by Flt.Lt. Lee for a Ju88 probably destroyed and one damaged, and by Plt.Off. Nash (GN-X) for a Ju87 probable; he recorded:

> 'My 87 gave off lots of black smoke when I attacked from just under his tail. Then bounced by six 109s. Got strikes on wings and rear of cockpit from one. Not sorry to get down again today!!'

His attack on the Ju87 would seem to have been successful, for one Ju87 of 8/StG 3 crashed into the sea north of Valetta after being attacked by a fighter, both Uffz. Gerhard Bode and Gefr. Josef Seidl, the gunner, being wounded, although both were later rescued.

Apart from Sgt. Horricks, the rest of the Hurricane pilots had little chance of success, and were overwhelmed by the escorting Messerschmitts, although Flt.Lt. Lloyd (GL-W) claimed damage to a Ju88 before the escort struck. Plt.Off. Phil Wigley in GL-P was one of those who came to grief:

> 'The Malta Hurricane pilots experienced their most arduous day when the enemy attacked with about 80 Ju87s and Ju88s with a very strong escort of 109Fs.
>
> 'I was attacked by several 109s near Luqa at about 500 feet and my Hurricane received hits in the Merlin engine and apparently in the glycol coolant tank, judging by the amount of fumes and hot liquid entering the cockpit. After attempting to land at Hal Far when I was again attacked by a 109 but was warned in time by the Duty Pilot's VHF radio, I baled out at about 400 feet when the engine caught fire over Ghar Lapsi, on the south

Lt. Hermann Neuhoff of 6/JG 53, who was shot down and made prisoner on 10 April 1942 immediately after claiming his 40th victory.

coast of Malta. I landed near the cliff edge about 50 yards from the wreck of my Hurricane, and was immediately greeted by a Maltese army corporal with a Tommy gun who fortunately did not mistake me for a German.'

Wigley's was not the only Hurricane shot down, as witnessed by Sgt. Tim Goldsmith who, from the ground, watched others attacking the bombers:

'Four Hurricanes came in from the beam and attacked. Three of them followed down hill after the bombers, but the fourth seemed unable to keep up with his target. As he slipped further behind, we saw a 109 creeping up behind and below him. Each moment we expected the Hurricane to whip round to meet the danger but he kept on after the 88, until we heard the rattle of the Hun's cannon. The Hurri curved peacefully round to the left, then its nose fell and it went into a crazy uncontrolled dive to the earth, 15,000 feet below, where it crashed and burst into flames on the hill behind Naxxar, on the far side of the aerodrome.

'Poor bugger, said someone, but an excited cheer from one of the Maltese spectators drew our attention to his arm pointing to the sky. A parachute seemed suspended there, as the little figure beneath it swung to and fro like a pendulum, eventually to come to earth near Mosta village.

'It was in the evening that I learned it was Ernie Broad (*Plt.Off. Broad of 185 Squadron in Z3766*). He had been rescued by the army and taken to St Andrew's 45th General Hospital, with his left calf well-filled with shrapnel. I was surprised that Ernie should have got himself caught like that, but very pleased to hear that his injuries were not serious.'

Plt.Off. 'Sonny' Ormrod was obliged to crash-land his Hurricane (BG756) in flames at Luqa, having been shot up by a Bf109 while attacking a Ju87, which was claimed damaged. To reach the aircraft, the Duty Fire Crew, led by Cpl. Hugh Clawson, had to cross the aerodrome whilst Ju88s dived to attack, bombs exploding across their path. On arriving at the scene, Clawson and LAC Eddie Mitchison assisted Ormrod to extricate himself, despite the attempts of Bf109s to strafe, and undoubtedly saved his life; both rescuers were awarded a George Medal.

For 229 Squadron only Sgt. Vidler was able to claim a Ju88 damaged before his own aircraft was attacked and hit by one of the escorts; he crash-landed his damaged machine (BN122) near that of his colleague, Sgt. Pendlebury, whose Hurricane (BN142) had also been badly shot-up.

Against actual losses sustained by the defenders of two Hurricanes shot down and three crash-landed, plus another and a Spitfire damaged, OKW reported that 11 victories were awarded in total, including at least eight to pilots of JG 53, Obfw. Ehrenberger of II Gruppe claiming three Spitfires shot down, raising his personal tally to 24 (11 of which he had claimed over Malta); another Spitfire was claimed by Fw. Alfred Seidl of 8 Staffel (his tenth victory), while Hurricanes were claimed by Lt. Louis of Stab I, Oblt. Quaet-Faslem of I Gruppe, Oblt. Wilfred Pufahl of 7 Staffel (his eighth), and Oblt. Friedrich-Karl Müller of 1 Staffel (his 23rd), who reported:

'I took off at 1735 with three aircraft of 1 Staffel. We undertook a "Freiejagd" and gave cover for bomber formations which were attacking the port and airfields of Malta. We attacked enemy fighters several times without any success. I then attacked a Hurricane coming from the east above the airfield hangar (at Hal Far). After a short burst with MG and cannon the plane burned immediately and went down vertically north of the airfield. Witness from the air: Ofw. Krause.'

From the available evidence it would seem likely that 'Tutti' Müller's victim was Plt.Off. Broad; this was recorded as the 90th victory awarded to 1 Staffel, and the 288th of I Gruppe. The loss of Lt. Neuhoff was a blow to JG 53; he was one of the most successful Luftwaffe fighter pilots to be shot down over Malta during the whole siege. He had claimed 40 victories, 21 of them over Russia, although only four over Malta; the award of his Ritterkreuz was announced shortly after he had gone into captivity. Interrogation obviously uncovered details of his claims, for Plt.Off. Peter Nash noted in his logbook:

> 'Stop Press. Buchanan's 109 was the Hun that got Doug Leggo!'

Saturday, 11 April

During the next few days the defending fighters were not able to achieve much. Early on the 11th an OADU transit Hudson (V9175) crashed on landing at Luqa, one of the crew being killed and the others injured. Only a few hours previously another Hudson had crashed taking off from Luqa, but on that occasion the crew of the 1444 Flight machine (AE524) survived. Soon after midday bombers again attacked Grand Harbour and the airfields, Ju88 3Z+HS of 6/KG 77 being shot down off Marsaxlokk by AA, with the loss of Uffz. Harry Müller and his crew. The AA gunners also claimed a Ju87 shot down and another Ju88 damaged, and indeed, one Stuka of III/StG 3 crash-landed in the sea near Cape Scaramia, and a second crash-landed at San Pietro on return, both reportedly due to engine damage.

During these raids heavy damage was inflicted on the airfields; at Luqa an unserviceable Wellington was destroyed, and another damaged, while two Beauforts, one of which was unserviceable, and a Hurricane were also destroyed. Two Spitfires and a Hurricane were damaged at Takali, while another Hurricane was burnt out at Hal Far, and two others damaged; one of the petrol bowsers was also damaged.

An evening raid by an estimated 50 Ju88s and 20 Ju87s caused further heavy damage. Luck finally deserted the destroyer *Kingston* and she was severely damaged in No 4 Dock by the Stukas of III/StG 3, while a launch was sunk in Grand Harbour. Another unserviceable Wellington was destroyed at Luqa, two others, a Maryland and a PR Spitfire all sustaining damage from debris and shrapnel. Three Hurricanes were damaged beyond repair at Hal Far (two of these being the crash-landed 229 Squadron machines, BN122 and BN142), where an invaluable petrol bowser was set ablaze.

The Italians reported that a Z501 flyingboat (MM35607) of 197ª Squadriglia RM (flown by Mar. Andrea di Fonzo) which had departed Stagnone di Marsala at 0655, was shot down by an aircraft; the Regia Marina observer, Guardia Marina Giorgio Martucciello was posthumously awarded the Medaglia d'Oro. No RAF claims for such an engagement have been found, although a transit Wellington (DV505 of 1443 Flight) was reported down in the sea off the Sicilian coast, from which five prisoners were taken. It is possible the flyingboat had been shot down by the Wellington. Despite the intensity of raids on Malta, transit aircraft continued to fly in from Gibraltar, 56 such machines having arrived safely during the first week of April alone, most continuing on their way to Egypt after refuelling. A few never arrived, some having become lost. On one occasion a Beaufighter was sent out to bring in a Wellington lost over the Ionian Sea, and just within radar range. When eventually the two aircraft made visual contact, the bomber's gunners mistook their twin-engined saviour for a Ju88, and seriously damaged it!

That night (12/13th April), between 1925 and 2230, three bomb-carrying Bf110s of III/ZG 26 escorted by four Bf109s raided Takali. A single Beaufighter was up on patrol, but failed to make contact. At 2030 Hudson AM717 of 24 Squadron arrived from Gibraltar, flown by Flg.Off. J.F.P. Matthews and carrying passengers and mail, to institute a service which would continue every three or four days for the rest of the siege. Refuelled and loaded with return mail and passengers, the transport left again four hours later.

As the Hudson departed, a pair of raiders approached (at 0225) and bombs fell near Rabat and Mtarfa. Flt.Sgt. Miller and Sgt. Tearle in Beaufighter X7752 intercepted one of the intruders over Gozo at 0345, and shot down Cap. Alberto Zampini's BR20M of 55° Gruppo BT, the bomber falling in flames on the little island. The Beaufighter crew reported seeing some of the crew bale out as the Fiat spun earthwards, and Serg. Gianfranco Viola survived to be rescued off Comino islet. Miller later spoke to the rear-gunner, who recalled that so sudden had been the attack, as the Beaufighter's cannon shells began ripping into the bomber, Zampini had called him on the intercom and enquired whether he was testing his guns! The next moment the port engine had burst into flames!

Air Marshal Sir Arthur Tedder on a visit from Egypt on 12 April 1942, is introduced to the newly-arrived pilots of 229 Squadron by Flt.Lt. Paul Farnes (left). The line of pilots includes from left, behind Farnes: Plt.Offs. Lumsden, Nixon, Foley and Carter; Sgts Potts, Lees, Carson, Fullalove, Brooks and Vidler, with whom the Air Marshal is shaking hands. *(Wg.Cdr. P. Farnes)*

Sunday, 12 April

Sunday saw the arrival of Hudson V9093 of 267 Squadron from Egypt, carrying Air Marshal Sir Arthur Tedder, AOC Middle East, for a brief visit to gain first-hand knowledge of Malta's plight. Of this visit, Air Vice-Marshal Lloyd was to write:

> 'There was a raid at Takali as soon as Tedder arrived there, and from the veranda of the Officers' Mess he was able to get an excellent view of the enemy tactics and the encircling patrol of 109s as it closed on the aerodrome below us to dive on every sign of movement. They even made some dives at Tedder as he was standing on the veranda, and a photographer who was

> trying to photograph the Chief and a 109 on the same plate found discretion preferable to valour when he saw another 109 flying straight at him with cannons firing.
>
> 'The visit to Luqa, however, was better timed, as a few minutes before Tedder had arrived there, the Axis had dropped a few more hundred tons of bombs, making it a shambles. Pilots, observers, radio operators, air-gunners and airmen and soldiers were busy moving the stone and filling the holes, all of them as happy as sandboys. I have never seen Tedder so delighted with any scene, and pointing with the stem of his pipe to a group of men who were busy filling holes and then to some of the men surrounding him, as if to add emphasis to his comment, he said — very quietly: "That — is the spirit of Malta."'

Tedder's visit to Hal Far was also interrupted by ground strafing Bf109s, one of which was shot down by Flt.Sgt. H.T. Gibbs, 830 Squadron's senior ground NCO, who was manning a machine gun, as he did at every opportunity. On this occasion his aim was true and he caught Gefr. Horst Gisy's 'White 2' of 4/JG 53 as it swept by. Plt.Off. McKay recalled:

> 'Air Officer Commanding Middle East gave us a pep talk and told us we were doing a magnificent job, but we all wished he would go up in one of our Hurricanes against Me109s that outnumbered us at least ten to one!
>
> 'There was a raid just after the talk and then the 109s started ground strafing. One was firing on its way over the aerodrome when it was hit by ack ack and it went straight in. There was a terrific explosion and huge sheet of flame. The engine rolled at least two hundred yards away from the wreckage. The pilot was more or less swept up.'

Another of the bewhiskered, oil and sweat-stained pilots assembled to meet the Chief, laconically recalled:

> 'When Tedder passed this way we shook him rigid. I thought he was going to get out his wallet and give us ten bob each to buy a new shirt!'

Other AA guns claimed a Ju87 shot down and two Ju88s damaged. Some damage was done to the airfields and a number of aircraft were destroyed or damaged; Hurricane BE562 was burnt out at Hal Far, Spitfire AB347 badly damaged at Takali, and two Wellingtons under repair at Luqa were destroyed. In the harbour the half-submerged *Talabot* was again hit and set on fire, effectively terminating any further salvage work.

During the evening raid another Wellington (DV537 of the OADU) was destroyed at Luqa, this time the AA gunners somewhat optimistically claiming two Ju88s and three Ju87s shot down in the fading light, from the estimated 130 aircraft over the Island. Actual losses included L1+GM of 4/LG 1, flown by Ofw. Waldemar Kremin, and a Bf110 of III/ZG 26; the latter machine, 3U+AT, went down into the sea off the Sicilian coast with the loss of Uffz. Willi Jünger and Fw. Albert Wörner, but it is not known for certain whether this aircraft had participated in the raid.

Monday, 13 April

Only reconnaissance flights bothered the radar operators and controllers at Malta on the 13th, allowing Spitfire and Hurricane maintenance personnel unexpected and uninterrupted valuable working hours, and all a welcome respite from the hitherto continuous bombing. Out to sea off the east coast of Malta, MTBs of the German 3rd Flotilla laid a further 80 mines in the course of three sorties, whilst Luqa received a new Station Commander when Grp.Capt. W.K. Le May OBE, succeeded Grp.Capt. Chick. With darkness the first of 35 raiders began crossing the coast, including six of 55° Gruppo BT's BR20Ms; Grand Harbour, Takali and Hal Far were attacked. Two Beaufighters were on patrol and at 2030 Plt.Off. Daniel's radar operator, Sgt. Gosling, vectored X7750 onto one of the Fiats, a 220ª Squadriglia machine (MM22606), flown by Ten. Luigi Ceccato; the chase was on, the bomber finally being tagged some 15 miles off the Sicilian coast. The burning machine force-landed near Scoglitti, where three of the crew were killed; Ceccato survived with severe injuries, although his second pilot was only slightly hurt.

Tuesday, 14 April

In contrast to recent days, the 14th was to be a day of sustained activity. 'Ultra' intercepts of Italian Naval signals had revealed that three convoys were now at sea. From Malta the submarines *Upholder, Urge* and *Thrasher* of the 10th Flotilla were ordered out to try and intercept the ships known to be departing Naples; while from Bu Amud (Cyrenaica), Blenheims and Marylands of 203 Squadron were briefed to search for the vessels, aided by a single ASV-equipped Wellington of 221 Squadron. The crews were fully aware that should they sight and shadow the ships to the limit of their range, they would be obliged to land on Malta to refuel — probably under attack from the omnipresent Messerschmitts which patrolled around the Island.

The convoy which had put out from Naples comprised the German *Reichenfels* and the Italian *Vettor Pisani*, escorted by two destroyers and a torpedo boat. A third transport — *Ravello* — had departed Taranto with two destroyers, whilst from Brindisi came *Reginaldo Giuliani*, with a destroyer and an MTB. East of Sicily the three groups converged into a single convoy, all heading for Tripoli. Freedom from air assault from Malta was confidently anticipated, given the level of attack the Island had been suffering. Indeed, 70 Ju87 and 60 Ju88 sorties were to be made during the day against Grand Harbour and the airfields in three attacks, whilst Bf109s maintained a continuous patrol over and around the Island, and joined Bf110s and Ju88s in providing cover for the ships.

Searches had begun by single ASV Wellingtons from both Malta and Bu Amud at about four hours before midnight on the previous evening, the Malta Wellington sighting a small convoy at 0030 to the north-east of Sicily, heading northwards; this, however, was not the convoy for which the search was being made. The other Wellington was forced to abandon its task owing to severe electrical storms, the crew having made no sightings.

With the arrival of daylight three reconnaissance Marylands of 203 Squadron departed Bu Amud to continue the search, joined in this task at 0930 by two of the unit's Blenheims. At 1000 one of the Marylands, AH298 flown by Flg.Off. J.B. Halbert, made contact with the main convoy a short distance from the east coast of Sicily, steaming southwards at an estimated ten knots. The crew reported four merchant vessels and five destroyers. The Maryland commenced shadowing and sent reports of progress until fuel shortage forced Halbert to head for Malta. Four miles from the Island AH298 was intercepted and shot down, victim it was believed of a Bf110 or Ju88; there were no survivors.

The cause of the loss of one of 203 Squadron's searching Blenheims — Z7902 flown by Flg.Off. Miles Bowker — has not been ascertained, but it too may have fallen victim to one of the many Luftwaffe fighters active around the convoy. When Sqn.Ldr. J.A.G. Coates, the unit commander, arrived in the area later, he saw hostile aircraft but was not attacked as he took over the shadowing role. He was to continue until late in the day, finally landing back at Bu Amud in the dark with his fuel virtually exhausted.

Meanwhile, an ASV-equipped Beaufort of 22 Squadron had also been sent out, having departed Bu Amud at 0700, with Flt.Sgt. S.E. Howroyd at the controls. He too located the convoy and reported its position, then headed for Malta. As he came in to land at Luqa, a Bf109 appeared behind and sprayed AW282 with cannon fire; the pilot was killed instantly and slumped forward, the Beaufort crashing at once. The other three members of the crew all sustained wounds. Flt.Sgt. Joe Lee, the navigator, later died in hospital.

The first raid on Malta had occurred at 1045, six Ju88s attacking Takali. Immediately thereafter three 249 Squadron Spitfires took off to provide initial protection for a departing Maryland of 69 Squadron, but these were engaged by Bf109s, Plt.Off. Kelly (AB342) claiming one damaged before being shot down himself — probably by Fw. Schmidt of 7/JG 53 for his 5th victory. Kelly baled out from about 800 feet, three miles west of Hal Far, but his parachute failed to open properly and he hit the water very hard, suffering severe bruising. He also became entangled in the shroud lines, and lost his dinghy whilst freeing himself.

Two more Spitfires were at once scrambled to search for him, the two Wests locating him and circling overhead, some two miles offshore. Kelly was seen to be swimming strongly and even found the strength to raise two fingers to his colleagues as they passed overhead at wavetop height! HSL 128 was despatched to the rescue, covered by a pair of 185 Squadron Hurricanes, and Kelly was soon located. As the launch stopped to pick him up, two Bf109s appeared and attempted to attack, but were driven off by the Hurricanes, Flt.Sgt. Fletcher (BN163) claiming damage to one.

Another two Spitfires were off at 1300 to cover Plt.Off. Tom Channon's returning Maryland (BS762), finding it being pursued by fighters. Flt.Lt. Macqueen and Plt.Off. Bob Sergeant attacked at once, jointly shooting down a Bf109 of 8/JG 53 into the sea, and claiming two more damaged; the German pilot was subsequently rescued by the Axis ASR service. In view of the Maryland's narrow escape and the loss of the 203 Squadron aircraft, it was decided that 69 Squadron should suspend all such flights by these aircraft, relying upon the speed and manoeuvrability of its handful of PR Spitfires to complete the reconnaissance required.

While this little action had been underway, six torpedo-armed Beauforts of 39 Squadron and two of 22 Squadron had departed Bu Amud, to strike at the convoy; they were then to fly on to Malta and land, as were the four Beaufighters of 272 Squadron supplied as escort. At the briefing it was stressed that all aircraft were to fly very low, down to 100 feet in the reconnaissance area, while the Beaufighters were to locate the target for the Beauforts, then break for Malta when at the limit of their fuel. Originally it had been intended that nine Beauforts would participate in the strike but at the last moment one 39 Squadron machine developed a fault, and only eight departed, formed into three flights as follows:

X8924	Flt.Lt. J.M. Lander)
N1100	Plt.Off. G. Belfield) 22 Squadron detachment
N1169	Flt.Lt. R.G.W. Beveridge
N1186	Flg.Off. R.B. Seddon
X8923	Flg.Off. D.A.R. Bee
W6505	Flt. Lt. A.T. Leaning
N1002	Flg.Off. S.W. Gooch
N1166	Plt.Off. B.W. Way

The rather inadequate escort of four Beaufighters were led by Sqn.Ldr. Bill Riley, who was actually no longer officially with the squadron, and was employed as a controller at 201 Group whilst waiting to take command of a new Beaufighter unit; he had volunteered to lead the escort. His No 2 was Plt.Off. Stephenson, while Flg.Off. Derek Hammond led the other section with Flt.Sgt. J.S. France on his wing. Due to the speed differential with the Beauforts, these four were obliged to weave overhead, increasing fuel consumption and thereby reducing their range.

By the time the strike force had reached a point 70 miles south-east of Malta the leader, Flt.Lt. Lander, realised that they must have overshot the convoy and turned south-west to continue the search. Twenty minutes into the new heading, Sqn.Ldr. Riley sighted a Bf110 on the same course as the Beauforts, and chased it for 15 minutes without result. On turning to rejoin the formation he sighted what he took to be two more Bf110s at 2000 feet. He climbed to attack and claimed both shot down into the sea. Whilst one of his victims would seem to have been a Zerstörer of III/ZG 26 in which the gunner, Uffz. Rudolf Lenthoff was wounded, the other was actually a Do17Z of the same Gruppe, which was shot down. It was assumed that one of these two aircraft had been responsible for the loss of Flg.Off. Halbert's Maryland. Riley then chased a Ju88 but was only able to damage it before running out of ammunition. These combats led him towards the convoy, which he saw only a few miles away.

The other Beaufighters attacked a Ju88 which appeared to be shadowing the Beauforts, but the combat was indecisive. On climbing to attack this aircraft (which was at about 1000 feet) the crews also spotted the convoy: "It was at this time that the mistake was made which affected the success of the operation." So concurred the subsequent official enquiry into the mission, which was about to turn into a disaster for the gallant torpedo-bomber crews, now 500 miles from their base, for neither Sqn.Ldr. Riley nor Flg.Off. Hammond ascertained whether the convoy had also been seen by the Beauforts before turning towards Malta. Both section leaders apparently thought that the strike force could not have failed to see the convoy and that they were manoeuvring for position to attack. Actually, the Beauforts, flying much lower than their escort — at approximately 40/50 feet — had not sighted and did not do so until about 30 minutes later, owing to the small field of vision at such a low altitude.

The Beauforts, now devoid of escort, pressed on but as they approached the convoy at wavetop height, some 15-20 Bf109s of JG 53, six Bf110s and a number of Ju88s were seen patrolling overhead. The crews were alarmed at the prospect of having to evade the Messerschmitts, particularly the Bf109s, such types not being anticipated so far out to sea — at least 120 nautical miles from Sicily; it seems likely that they were fitted with auxiliary fuel tanks for the purpose. The fighters pounced on the torpedo-bombers as the pilots attempted to line up on their chosen targets — the two largest transports, *Reichenfels* and *Reginaldo Giuliani*.

Flt.Lt. Lander and Plt.Off. Belfield went for the rear ship on the left, attacking from starboard, while Leaning's section made for the same vessel from the port quarter; Beveridge's trio took the rear right-hand transport. Only five torpedoes were launched — three explosions being reported, with much smoke being seen from both ships, while a destroyer was also believed hit — the other three aircraft being forced to jettison when engaged by the escort. In fact, none of the torpedoes struck home and no damage was done to any of the vessels.

As soon as the torpedoes had been released, Plt.Off. Bert Way's aircraft was seen to have lost contact with the others of its section; Way attempted to join up with Lander's section instead, but as he moved closer he was attacked by a Bf109 and shot down. The crew of an escorting Z506B floatplane of 170[a] Squadriglia RM reported being attacked by three 'Blenheims', one of which was then shot down by a Messerschmitt; the Italians had undoubtedly witnessed the demise of Way's aircraft and crew. It seems likely that N1166 fell to Fw. Ludwig Reibel of 1/JG 53, who claimed a Beaufort shot down about 60 miles south-east of Malta, and of this, his 7th victory, reported:

> 'Shortly before reaching the convoy our Gruppe noticed eleven (*sic*) low-flying Bristol Beauforts. We managed to drive them away from our convoy by attacking. I chased three Beauforts flying south-west and attacked the last one. On my second attack the aircraft was leaking fuel from its left side. On my fifth attack there was an explosion on the left side. The aircraft went into the water and crashed. I couldn't see what happened to the crew as I had to follow the other aircraft.'

A desperate race to reach distant Malta was now begun as the remaining Beauforts stayed close above the water, taking violent evasive action. Their chances were slim, but they nearly made it. Malta was almost in sight when Flt.Lt. Robert Beveridge's luck ran out and his aircraft splashed into the sea. This was closely followed by another from his section, flown by Flg.Off. Bob Seddon, whose crippled N1186 ditched some six miles short of the Island. Flg.Off. Derek Bee's aircraft was seen flying low over Malta, endeavouring to line up for a landing, but a Messerschmitt appeared on his tail and shot the Beaufort down into the sea; there were no survivors.

Next to go down was Plt.Off. Belfield's N1100, four Bf109s being seen buzzing around this until it ditched off Zurrieq, the crew taking to their dinghy. A nearby fishing boat which went to pick them up turned back owing to the presence of the Messerschmitts. Two fishermen in another boat disregarded the fighters however, and rescued the crew. In the meantime another boat manned by L/Cpl. Julian Sciberras and Paul D'Amato went out to meet the fishing boat and two of the airmen were transferred to this.

Only three Beauforts now remained, and Flt.Lt. John Lander's aircraft was the next singled out for attack as he made his final dash for safety. His badly damaged aircraft had sustained a twisted wingtip, caused by hitting the sea whilst taking evasive action, and the gun turret was out of action. Dodging some of his pursuers by flying close to Dingli Cliffs, he managed to crash-land on Luqa runway, without hydraulics and with the rudder stripped of fabric over three-quarters of its length; he and his crew escaped injury. Flg.Off. Gooch's machine also got down, badly holed in the fuel tanks and with its hydraulic lines severed, while Flt.Lt. Leaning's W6505 also landed safely; paradoxically, it had escaped even a single bullet hole!

As the Beauforts had approached the Island at 1645, two Hurricanes of 185 Squadron had been scrambled to go to their aid, followed ten minutes later by three more of 229 Squadron. Plt.Off. Wigley recalled:

> 'One Beaufort was spotted too late — it was at sea level and under attack from two Bf109s — and before the Hurricanes could reach it, it was shot down a mile short of the relative safety of Malta. 185 felt badly about the loss of the Beaufort crew so close — unfortunately the Hurricanes had been ordered to climb after take-off and, of course with the benefit of hindsight, a sea-level patrol would have been more appropriate and the Beaufort might have been saved.'

HSL 128 had also been despatched to look for survivors, the Hurricanes subsequently providing cover for this vessel as Bf109s attempted repeatedly to attack it. Wreckage was sighted, amongst which Flt.Lt. Beveridge's body was found and recovered. Messerschmitts again attacked, but the Hurricanes drove them off, although Sgt. Yarra's HA-D was hit and damaged. He was forced to return to Hal Far, where he crash-landed. Two others remained to circle overhead; Plt.Off. Ormrod — even though he was out of ammunition — continued to make dummy attacks on the German fighters until the coast was reached. Inevitably one Bf109 evaded the Hurricanes and raked the launch, Cpl. Timms, the coxswain, being wounded in the thigh and four other members of the crew suffering less serious wounds. Flt.Lt. Crockett took over the wheel and kept '128 under the protection of the cliffs until darkness fell, returning to Kalafrana at 2035.

During the course of these actions the Hurricane pilots claimed damage to three more Messerschmitts, Sgt. Horricks (Z4004) attacking two near Filfla, then a third on which he observed strikes on the underside of the fuselage and wing roots before it rolled over and dived away; other claims were submitted by Sgt. Tweedale (BN163) of 185 Squadron, and Sgt. Lees of 229 Squadron.

The Luftwaffe patrols had enjoyed a field day, and were credited with eight victories. Apparently the crews of III/ZG 26 were credited with two Beauforts, while Fw. Rollwage of II/JG 53 claimed two more in quick succession, just south of Qrendi at 1705 and 1707. Uffz. Glaser of 7 Staffel claimed a Beaufighter for his first victory, but this was possibly a misidentification of a Beaufort, while Oblt. Quaet-Faslem of I Gruppe also claimed a Beaufort, as did Fw. Reibel (as recorded earlier) and Hpt. Michalski, Kommandeur of II Gruppe.

Further bad news was on the way, for at 1547 reports had been received from the submarine *Upholder* that eight British torpedo-carrying aircraft had been observed attacking the convoy — obviously it was in the immediate vicinity at the time. Then — silence! The submarine had, in fact, been spotted by one of the convoy's escorting aircraft, and the destroyer *Pegaso* carried out an immediate, and lethal, attack. *Upholder*'s whole crew was lost, including her illustrious commander, Lt.Cdr. Malcolm Wanklyn VC. This most successful of all Malta's marauders had been credited with sinking 21 vessels (including three opposing submarines) totalling some 128,353 tons.

At Kalafrana that evening HSL 128 was hastily patched up and was off again

 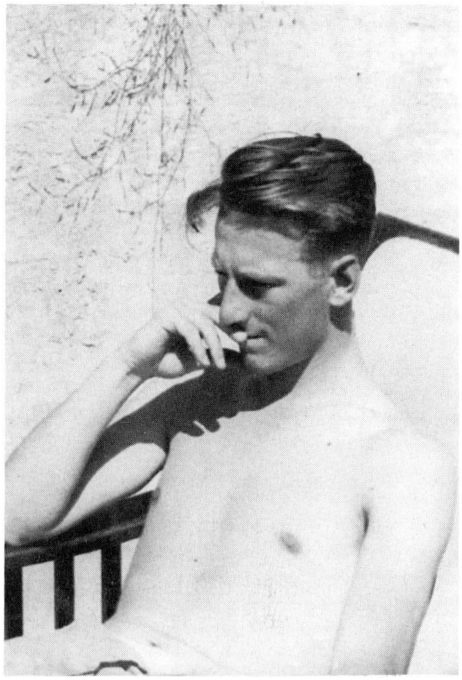

Left: Sqn.Ldr. P.B. 'Laddie' Lucas took command of 249 Squadron when Stan Grant was promoted. He was to lead the unit through some of the toughest battles. **Right:** Plt.Off. (later Flt.Lt.) R.A. 'Buck' McNair of 249 Squadron was a tough Canadian who developed into one of the RCAF's most notable fighter pilots. *(Daddo-Langlois Collection)*

in less than half an hour as it was believed that four Beaufort survivors were in their dinghy under the cliffs of Dingli, but the craft was unable to get to the given location. In the event, only one man was still alive in the sea — Sgt. McGregor, the Canadian navigator from Flg.Off. Seddon's aircraft. Following the ditching, the crew had managed to extricate themselves, although two had been badly wounded. However, their dinghy had been holed, and would not inflate. McGregor, whose back had been peppered with shrapnel, and Sgt. Alex Miller, one of the gunners, decided to swim for the shore. The wounded Seddon and Sgt. Tom Keegan remained with the sinking aircraft, supported by their Mae Wests, in the hope that an ASR craft would spot them and pick them up. They perished, however, as did Miller when exhaustion finally overtook him. Alone, McGregor swam for five hours before finally reaching a rocky cliff edge, from where he was rescued next morning.

During the course of the day the AA defences of the Island had submitted a multiplicity of claims which were far from accurate. Two Ju88s, two Ju87s and two Bf109s were believed to have been shot down, with three more Ju88s, three Ju87s and a Bf109 damaged! In fact they had damaged a Ju88 of KGr 806, but apparently no other bombers were seriously hit! The gunners did, however, manage to shoot down the Bf109 flown by Hpt. Karl-Heinz Krahl, Kommandeur of II/JG 3, as he was making a low-level attack. The Messerschmitt, carrying the arrowhead marking denoting his status ('2 Winkel', in Luftwaffe parlance) crashed, taking the 24-victory Ritterkreuzträger to his death — the second major 'Experte' to be lost in five days. Following Krahl's loss, Oblt. Kurt Brändle of 5/JG 53 was posted to take over command of the unit. Brändle had 30 victories to

Hpt. Karl-Heinz Krahl, Kommandeur of II/JG 3, who was shot down and killed whilst making a strafing attack on 14 April. His aircraft crashed inverted into a stone parapet.

Servicemen inspect the wreckage of Hpt. Krahl's Bf109F on 14 April. *(NWMA)*

his credit, and in turn was replaced as Staffelkapitän by Oblt. Ernst-Albrecht Schultz, a Battle of Britain 'ace' who had been wounded in Russia in July 1941, and who had recently been appointed Stab I/JG 53's Technical Officer.

Following the day's ineffectual and disastrous attacks on the convoy, a single Swordfish and two Albacores were despatched from Malta by night on a follow-up attack. The vessels had been re-located and were being shadowed by an ASV Wellington, and were then over 120 miles off Kalafrana. One Albacore returned early, having lost formation, and then crashed on landing back at Hal Far. The remaining two biplanes failed to find the convoy; on returning to Hal Far the second Albacore also crashed. Fortunately neither crew was injured, while the Axis convoy reached its destination unscathed.

Adverse weather — heavy cloud and high winds — now brought flying to a virtual standstill over Malta and Sicily for the next three days. Reconnaissances by small groups of Bf109s were made each day, but no offensive operations were undertaken. On the 15th General Dobbie received a message from the King:

> 'To honour her brave people I award the George Cross to the Island Fortress of Malta to bear witness to a heroism and devotion that will long be famous in history.'

That evening the Governor relayed this message to the people, emphasising that this was the first (and only) time in British history that such an award had been made to a community.

Saturday, 18 April

The Luftwaffe was back with a vengeance on the 18th, making four raids against the airfields; no fighters were available to intercept them. During the course of an estimated 139 Ju88 and 53 Ju87 sorties, considerable damage was inflicted at Hal Far, where two Hurricanes were destroyed and a Maryland damaged; at Luqa where a small bomb dump was blown up, and to buildings at Kalafrana; three servicemen, two policemen and a civilian were killed, and 16 service personnel and four civilians were injured. AA gunners claimed one Ju88 shot down, and a second and a Ju87 probably so, during the morning attacks.

Luftwaffe records show that a Ju88 of KüFlGr 606 crash-landed in Sicily and was destroyed, Uffz. Heinz Geschlössl (the pilot) and two of his crew escaping unhurt, while an aircraft of 3/KGr 806 crash-landed at Catania but was only slightly damaged; a Bf109 of 9/JG 53 was also reported to have been irreparably damaged following a crash-landing, Uffz. Max Nairz surviving with injuries. During the day a Z501 of 142ª Squadriglia RM crashed into the sea off the Calabrian coast, three survivors (including a Regia Marina observer) reaching the shore; in this case an accident was presumed.

Sunday, 19 April

Again on the 19th no interceptions were made of the three raids; during the morning 23 Ju87s and 30 Ju88s attacked Grand Harbour, Safi and Hal Far, where a Swordfish and an Albacore were damaged, and a Hurricane burnt out: AA gunners claimed a Ju88 shot down, another as damaged and a Bf109 probable. The 1325 raid caused many casualties, the gunners claiming a further two Ju88s shot down and two damaged; and again in the evening the gunners submitted claims for four Ju88s and a Bf109 destroyed, another of the latter and two Ju87s damaged. In fact, two Ju88s failed to return from these attacks — 7T+BH of 1/KüFlGr 606, in which Stfw. Wilhelm Hagen and his crew were lost, and 3Z+KN of 5/KG 77, which crashed in the sea off Sliema Point during the evening raid. The pilot, Lt. Horst Rosenfeldt, and the radio-operator, Obgfr. Rudolf Krizek, survived to be captured. One witness to the demise of the KG 77 machine, Miss May Agius, provided the readers of the *Times of Malta* with this report:

> 'One bomber was split in two with a direct hit and was falling down into the sea. Four white puffs of parachutes hung in the clear cloudless evening sky with four dark figures suspended from them — escaping the very jaws of death and falling towards the blue Mediterranean.
>
> 'The loud cheers of the few spectators brought shelterers up to enquire, and the news — good and welcome news — spread like wildfire from shelter to shelter. In no time there were excited people running to the Sliema front to see one of the enemy pilots (*sic*) who had descended near enough to be within swimming distance. Crowds gathered by the Sliema front railings; men, women and children, all so excited as to forget the still impending danger overhead. The weather's serenity provided the enemy pilot with an opportunity to save his life.
>
> 'There in the distance was the wrecked plane, its wings still floating and bobbing up and down on the tiny waves. A speck on the surface of the water could be seen to be gradually approaching, as the airman made his way to the shore, swimming vigorously, stroke by stroke. And over both wreckage and swimmer swooped down Messerschmitts, making it impossible for a boat to go out to the aid of this representative of a nation of traitors.
>
> 'When the swimmer was near to the shore calls for help were clearly audible and then the bobbing head appealed for mercy, mercy which is never denied a stricken enemy by the British. Soldiers lined the beach ready to help the swimmer, and soon a lifeline was thrown out, to which the man clung for dear life. He was ashore. As rifles were pointed at him he lifted his arms in surrender, and then fell back in a heap on the cold bare and hard rocks of Malta. Two soldiers assisted him to his feet and in their strong grasp he

moved off, with little trace to show for his exhausting swim of at least over two miles.

'As the prisoner was blind-folded, the watching crowd booed with all its might, whistling and booing, and calling upon the soldiers to hand the prisoner over to them. When Maltese anger is once roused it is not easily cooled, and only at bayonet point did the people desist. The soldiers (*Lancashire Fusiliers*) laid the prisoner on a stretcher and carried him into the fort at Ghar-id-Dud (*Sliema*).'

The day had also seen the first operation over the Island by the recently-arrived Italian fighters of 10° Gruppo CT. The Macchis undertook a straightforward acclimatization flight, but during this Serg. Elio Trevisan of 90ª Squadriglia experienced trouble with his oxygen supply, and was obliged to bale out; he was picked up safely. This would prove to be a frequent problem, causing constant unserviceability. After the arrival of the Stormo commander on the 23rd, he would ask Feldmarschall Kesselring if more efficient German equipment could be made available.

At this time, the 54° Stormo CT, which was still based in Sicily for convoy escort duties with its MC200s and CR42s, received a number of photo-reconnaissance MC202/RF aircraft; these were issued to the 76ª Squadriglia of the 7° Gruppo, and would be operated frequently over Malta — flying from Castelvetrano and Pantelleria — to photograph the Island with Kodak 30cm cameras.

TABLE 5

6 Hurricane IICs of 229 Squadron from Middle East

Flt.Lt. R.C. Dafforn DFC	Flt.Sgt. Burleigh	BN636
Plt.Off. T.E. Lawrence, RNZAF	Sgt. N.A. Ganes, RCAF	
Wt.Off. D.F. Corfe	Sgt. G.H. Willcox	

It had now been five days since Malta's dwindling number of fighters had been able to operate, and the situation was truly desperate. Help was once again on the way, however, and during the 19th seven more Hurricane IICs were flown in to Hal Far from Gambut by pilots of 229 Squadron, led by Flt.Lt. R.C. Dafforn DFC (see Table 5 above). Of the long and arduous flight, one of the new arrivals, Plt.Off. Tom Lawrence, a New Zealander, later wrote to his parents:

'We travelled 720 miles over nothing but water hoping we shall strike this very small island which is only 60 miles in circumference. However, as the sun sank slowly behind the horizon — of which I was glad, because we had been flying for about two hours with it in our eyes — there, in the distance, was a column of black smoke and then the outline of the island itself, and a raid was in progress.

'Well, that was no joke! Long-range tanks, which means no manoeuvrability, very little gas left, and the only three aerodromes may be cratered, and feeling exceptionally tired, we came in uneasily. However, with an odd 109 and an 88 still about, we came in and landed. One chappie who landed with me had only five gallons left (about seven minutes flying).

> Another chap went over on his back. They had to get a crane to extricate him, and out he walked with a broken wrist — lucky fellow!'

The injured pilot who had overshot the runway (in BE636) was Flt.Sgt. J. Burleigh, who escaped lightly with a fractured wrist and lacerated face. Flt.Lt. Bob Dafforn had only recently been posted to the squadron at El Firdan, and on arrival at Malta was promoted to command, vice the sick Sqn.Ldr. Kain. He was an experienced operational pilot, having flown with 501 Squadron — as had Flt.Lt. Farnes — in France and the Battle of Britain, when he had been credited with at least six victories.

While this handful of Hurricanes were welcome, more effective help was imminently at hand.

Chapter 4

'WHO SAYS A WASP CAN'T STING TWICE?'

While the delivery of the two initial batches of Spitfires to the Island had brought some relief, it was obvious that the small numbers involved would not allow sustained operations to be maintained for long — as had indeed been the case. On 1 April, Prime Minister Churchill had cabled President Roosevelt:

> 1: Air attack on Malta is very heavy. There are now in Sicily about 400 German and 200 Italian fighters and bombers. Malta can now muster only 20 or 30 serviceable fighters. We keep feeding Malta with Spitfires in packets of 16 loosed from *Eagle* carrier from about 600 miles west of Malta. This has worked a good many times quite well, but *Eagle* is now laid up for a month by defects in her steering gear. There are no Spitfires in Egypt. *Argus* is too small and too slow, and moreover she has to provide fighter cover for the carrier launching the Spitfires and for the escorting force. We would use *Victorious*, but unfortunately her lifts are too small for Spitfires. Therefore there will be a whole month without any Spitfire reinforcements.
> 2: It seems likely, from extraordinary enemy concentration on Malta, that they hope to exterminate our air defence in time to reinforce either Libya or their Russian offensive. This would mean that Malta would be at the best powerless to interfere with reinforcements of armour to Rommel, and our chances of resuming offensive against him at an early date ruined.
> 3: Would you be willing to allow your carrier *Wasp* to do one of these trips provided details are satisfactorily agreed between the Naval Staffs? With her broad lifts, capacity and length, we estimate that *Wasp* could take 50 or more Spitfires. Unless it were necessary for her to fuel, *Wasp* could proceed through the Straits at night without calling at Gibraltar until on the return journey, as the Spitfires would be embarked in the Clyde.
> 4: Thus, instead of not being able to give Malta any further Spitfires during April, a powerful Spitfire force could be flown into Malta at a stroke and give us a chance of inflicting a very severe and possibly decisive check on the enemy. Operations might take place during the third week of April.

The President replied in the affirmative two days later, and while the manner of delivery of more Spitfires was thus being organised, who was to go was also the subject of considerable discussion. The first two batches, whilst effectively reforming existing squadrons upon arrival, had been no more than collections of available pilots brought together in England for the purpose. Grp.Capt. C.A. Bouchier DFC, Deputy Director of Fighter Operations at the Air Ministry, had submitted a memorandum on 27 March, calling for a reversion to the policy of

1941, when the air parties of existing squadrons had been delivered to the Island as units in being.

Bouchier's plan was heeded on this occasion, but it was to be the last time. Despite the many dozens of Spitfire squadrons now operational in the UK, Fighter Command could hardly be expected to part with two of its more experienced units at a time when the new Luftwaffe fighter, the Fw190, was beginning to appear on the other side of the Channel and taking a rising toll of the RAF's Spitfire Vs. There were other considerations too; with the great problems associated with getting shipping to the Island, the ground parties could only hope that at some point they might be re-united with their air echelons.

Pilots of 601 Squadron aboard USS *Wasp*, en route to Malta: Front row, l. to r,: Plt.Off. R.F. Tilley; Plt.Off. W.E. Cripps; Flt.Lt. D.W. Barnham; Sqn.Ldr. E.J. Gracie; Sqn.Ldr. J.D. Bisdee; Flt.Lt. H. Parry; Plt.Off. K.W. Pawson; Flg.Off. C.M. Hone; Plt.Off. R.P.W. Sewell. Middle row: Plt.Off. W.A. Caldwell; Plt.Off. T.W. Scott; Plt.Off. G.M. Briggs; Plt.Off. M.H. Le Bas; 2/Lt. A. Bartleman; Plt.Off. M.R.B. Ingram. Back row: Sgt. G.R. Dickson; Sgt. R. Downing; Sgt. E.G. Shea; Wt.Off. F.H. Belcher; Sgt. F.W. Farfan; Plt.Off. W.J.E. Hagger; Sgt. J.N. McConnell; Sgt. F.S. Howard; Sgt. J.W.L. Innes. *(National Archives, Washington)*

The two squadrons chosen to go aboard the American carrier for the voyage to the besieged Island were both notable Auxiliary Air Force units with enviable records from 1940 — but neither could be said to be more than shadows of their former selves. 601 'County of London' Squadron had been out of the line since June of the previous year. The unit had been withdrawn to East Anglia to exchange its elderly Hurricanes for the first of the American-designed and produced Bell Airacobra fighters to enter service with the RAF. The commanding officer who had led the squadron through the protracted — and subsequently unsuccessful — working-up period to try and make this unusual fighter suitable for use over Western Europe, had been none other than Sqn.Ldr. Gracie, the present commander of 126 Squadron; one of his flight commanders had been 249 Squadron's current CO, Sqn.Ldr. Grant. Finally, in early March, re-equipment with Spitfire Vs had taken place, but almost at once had come orders for overseas — accompanied, it must be added, by the posting of seven of the few experienced pilots to other units.

The unit's present commander, who had arrived at the same time as the Spitfires, was Sqn.Ldr. J.D. Bisdee DFC, a pilot of some considerable skill and experience. John Bisdee had served with 609 Squadron throughout 1940, and by the time he was sent on rest in July 1941 had become a flight commander, with a DFC and at least six individual victories to his credit. He was joined by a new flight commander, Flt.Lt. Denis Barnham, who had also seen recent service with 609 Squadron, where he had been credited with shooting down one of the new Fw190s, The other flight commander was Rhodesian-born Flt.Lt. Hugh Parry. Another new arrival was American Plt.Off. Reade Tilley, who had served with 121 Squadron, the second *Eagle* squadron. Amongst the other pilots, it would be charitable to say that experience was at something of a premium. Indeed, seven of them had no operational experience at all, and a further four had less than 25 hours flying time on Spitfires. Twelve of the 23 had never fired their guns in action. The squadron boasted a truly international flavour — apart from five Britons there were four Canadians, four New Zealanders, four Rhodesians, two Australians, and one each from America, Trinidad, Argentina and South Africa; the latter — 2/Lt. Archie Bartleman — sported the khaki uniform of the South African Air Force.

Pilots of 603 Squadron aboard USS *Wasp* en route to Malta: Front row, l. to r: Plt.Off. G. Murray; Plt.Off. J.W. Forster; Flt.Lt. L.V. Sanders; Flt.Lt. W.A. Douglas; Sqn.Ldr. Lord D. Douglas-Hamilton; Flt.Lt. J.W. Buckstone; Plt.Off. A.C.W. Holland; Plt.Off. N.S. King; Plt.Off. J.G. Mejor. Middle row: Plt.Off. G.B.P. Davis (did not go to Malta); Plt.Off. F.E. Almos; Plt.Off. J.W. Slade; Plt.Off. L.W. Watts; Plt.Off. H.R. Mitchell; 2/Lt. C.J.O. Swales; Plt.Off. O.M. Linton; Plt.Off. C.B. McLean. Back row: Flt.Sgt. J. Hurst; Flt.Sgt. J.E. Otis (did not go to Malta this trip); Sgt. Buckley (did not go to Malta); Sgt. Walcott (defected); Sgt. L.F. Webster. *(National Archives, Washington)*

603 'City of Edinburgh' Squadron was perhaps a little better prepared for its forthcoming ordeal. Flying Spitfires since the early days of the war, the unit had operated as part of the Hornchurch Wing, flying over Europe until December 1941, when it was rested by a move up to Dyce in Scotland. Here the unit was taken over by Sqn.Ldr. Lord David Douglas-Hamilton, an ex-instructor who had only gained his first — and very limited — introduction to operational flying late the previous month! His squadron went to Malta with three Flight

Lieutenants on its strength, but only Flt.Lts. Bill Douglas and Lester Sanders had any worthwhile experience, both having flown on sweeps over Northern Europe. Flt.Lt. John Buckstone had been a ground officer in 1940, and had applied for pilot training, getting in a few sweeps before taking over 'B' Flight. Another 'late starter' in the squadron was Plt.Off. Neville King, Irish cousin of the CO's wife, who had been a policeman in London during the Blitz involved in bomb-disposal duties.

Flt.Sgt. Johnny Hurst had been a very active and aggressive member of the squadron since mid-1941, and while credited with only one confirmed victory, he had also claimed five Messerschmitts probably shot down; he would prove to be a tower of strength on Malta. Another NCO pilot who had just been posted in from 485 Squadron, the all-New Zealand Spitfire unit, was Flt.Sgt. Jack Rae. His record closely resembled that of Hurst, for he had been credited with two confirmed and four probables — all against Luftwaffe fighters. Otherwise the squadron was little better off than 601, no less than nine of its pilots possessing no operational experience at all. It was hardly the most appropriate and well-prepared group of pilots to send into the inferno that was Malta in April 1942!

Like 601 Squadron, 603 included a number of Commonwealth and North American pilots — three Canadians, two New Zealanders, no less than five Americans — as well as Belgian-born Plt.Off. John Georges Mejor, while 2/Lt. Ormonde 'Zulu' Swales (like Bartleman of 601) was also a member of the SAAF; volunteers both, for no SAAF aircrew were obliged to serve north of the African Mediterranean coast at this time (see Table 6 below).

TABLE 6

Operation 'Calendar'

47 Spitfires from USS *Wasp*

Sqn.Ldr. E.J. Gracie — led 1st group

601 Squadron

Sqn.Ldr. J.D. Bisdee DFC	led 2nd group	Plt.Off. W.J.E. Hagger (Rhodesian)
Flt.Lt. D.W. Barnham	BP969/R	Plt.Off. W.A. Caldwell, RNZAF
Flt.Lt. H. Parry (Rhodesian)		2/Lt. A. Bartleman, SAAF BR127
Flg.Off. C.M. Hone (Rhodesian)	BR125/P	Wt.Off. F.H. Belcher, RCAF
Plt.Off. K.W. Pawson		Flt.Sgt. Cleveland
Plt.Off. R.P.W. Sewell, RCAF		Sgt. J.W.L. Innes
Plt.Off. W.E. Cripps, RCAF		Sgt. J.N. McConnell, RNZAF
Plt.Off. T.W. Scott, RAAF		Sgt. G.R. Dickson, RNZAF
Plt.Off. G.M. Briggs, RAAF		Sgt. E.G. Shea, RCAF
Plt.Off. M.R.B. Ingram, RNZAF		Sgt. F.S. Howard (Rhodesian)
Plt.Off. M.H. Le Bas		Sgt. F.W. Farfan (Trinidad)
Plt.Off. R.F. Tilley, RCAF (US)		Sgt. R. Downing

603 Squadron

Sqn.Ldr. Lord D. Douglas-Hamilton	BR190/2A (led 3rd Group)
Flt.Lt. W.A. Douglas	led 4th group

TABLE 6 (Continued)

Plt.Off. L.W. Watts	Flt.Lt. J.W. Buckstone
Plt.Off. J.G. Mejor (Belgian)	Flt.Lt. L.V. Sanders
Plt.Off. O.M. Linton, RCAF	Plt.Off. H.R. Mitchell, RNZAF
Plt.Off. C.B. McLean, RCAF	Plt.Off. N.S. King
2/Lt. C.J.O. Swales, SAAF	Plt.Off. J.W. Slade
Flt.Sgt. J.D. Rae, RNZAF	Plt.Off. A.C.W. Holland BR184/2C
Sgt. J. Hurst	Plt.Off. G. Murray, RCAF (US)
Sgt. L.F. Webster	Plt.Off. F.E. Almos, RCAF (US)
Sgt. C.F. Bush	Plt.Off. D.E. Booth, RCAF (US)
Sgt. Walcott (US) BP958 (defected)	Plt.Off. J.W. Forster

Thus it was that the USS *Wasp* — under Captain J.W. Reeves Jr, USN — arrived on the Clyde at Glasgow, where she berthed in King George V docks. The majority of her bomber and scouting aircraft had been flown ashore to make room in her hangars for the 52 Spitfires, which she began lifting aboard during 12 and 13 April. The Spitfires had been flown from Prestwick to the small grass airfield at Renfrew — which had not previously been used by Spitfires — during the past few days; sadly, during these ferrying operations, two crashed in bad weather and both the ATA pilots, R.A. Porter in AD296 and A. Scott in AD395, were killed. From Renfrew the Spitfires travelled to the docks on RAF Queen Mary transporters, fitted with special cradles for loading aboard the carrier.

To allow maximum space below decks, the 19 Grumman F4F Wildcats of her resident fighter Squadron (VF-71) were secured on deck. The laden carrier sailed on the 14th, escorted by the British battle cruiser *Renown*, and by four British and two US destroyers. Subsequently, as the vessels approached the Straits of Gibraltar, two RN anti-aircraft cruisers — *Charybdis* and *Cairo* — joined what became Force 'W', the armada passing through the Straits in

Spitfire U-2 aboard USS *Wasp*; this aircraft was allocated to 603 Squadron initially, although on arrival on Malta it was to be flown by whichever squadron was on duty. *(National Archives, Washington)*

darkness during the early hours of the 19th, and commenced steaming eastwards into the Mediterranean.

The Spitfire pilots, spared the voyage to Gibraltar in the conditions so graphically described by Sgt. Yarra during the previous month, undertook the whole journey in the relative luxury of the well-appointed *Wasp*. They were looked after with typical hospitality and generosity by their American hosts, as the Spitfires were readied for the forthcoming launch. Aware of the tradition of rum and gin in the Royal Navy, most were surprised to find the US vessel 'dry' — although to many ice cream and Coca-Cola proved an acceptable alternative to palates accustomed to wartime rationing at home.

Aboard the carrier to brief the pilots on their forthcoming flight was Wg.Cdr. John McLean, aided by Sqn.Ldr. Gracie, who had been flown to Gibraltar to lead the Spitfires to Malta. The aircraft in the ship's hangars were all Mark Vcs armed for the first time operationally with the maximum possible armament of four 20mm Hispano cannons and four .303 Browning machine guns. Each was also fitted with a 90-gallon overload fuel tank, and like the earlier deliveries, also featured a Vokes air filter beneath the nose — all of which added to the weight and to the air resistance which inevitably reduced the overall performance. All were painted in the RAF's 'sand and stone' desert camouflage scheme, with blue undersides, but were now to be sprayed dark blue to make them less obvious during the long sea flight; the application of the blue paint was still underway in the hangars as the carrier sailed.

601 Squadron aircraft all featured a number '1' painted on one side of each fuselage roundel, and an individual letter on the other side, while 603 Squadron aircraft sported a number '2' and similar individual letters. This was a most unusual departure from normal RAF identification codes, particularly for squadrons which had carried two-letter codes — UF for 601, and XT for 603 — which had been in use since the outbreak of war.

At 0400 on Monday, 20 April, Operation 'Calendar' began as 11 Wildcats of VF-71 took off to provide air cover while the RAF pilots breakfasted and received their final briefing from Wg.Cdr. McLean. It was decided that the Spitfires would form roughly into four groups — to be led by Sqn.Ldrs. Gracie, Bisdee and Douglas-Hamilton, and Flt.Lt. Douglas — but that they were to proceed in pairs or individually. Hence, at 0545 precisely, Gracie's Spitfire rolled down the deck, dipped out of sight off the bows, and climbed laboriously into the sky; within 61 minutes 47 aircraft — all that could be made serviceable — were in the air and on their way; one of those left behind was Sgt. Joe Otis, one of 603 Squadron's Americans. As if to test their taut nerves even more, a number of the tense pilots — strapped into their cockpits awaiting the launch — witnessed a horrific incident as an RAF mechanic walked into the turning propeller of one of 601 Squadron's aircraft, and was killed outright. Of the flight, Bartleman (BR127/1-N) recalled:

> 'No time to think about take-off — off, and terrible sinking feeling as off the end of the deck; only one circuit of the carrier permitted — when we were to switch over to the long-range tank — and we were ordered to fly on pre-set courses, either singly or in pairs. I flew on my own as I didn't see any other Spits. About half way to Malta, off Cape Bon, when flying at about 12,000 feet, I saw at about 2000 feet below possibly 12 Ju52s flying singly towards Tunisia. Although two machine guns were loaded, these were purely for

defence if attacked — we were ordered not to become involved in combat. When Pantelleria came into view, a new course was set for Malta, and I arrived at about 1030. I had about ten minutes fuel left. About eight Spits had already landed safely.'

Although four Italian submarines were stationed in the area to the south of the Balearic Islands to intercept, only one — *Velella* — spotted the ships, launching an ineffectual attack on a destroyer. With the successful departure of the last of the serviceable Spitfires, *Wasp* and Force 'W' turned back towards Gibraltar, while patrols of four Wildcats were maintained for the rest of the day. Several plots appeared on radar and one 'snooper' was chased but no contact made. At 1117, a message was received from Malta that 46 aircraft had arrived safely, and that one was missing. This was the aircraft flown by one of 603 Squadron's Americans, Sgt. Walcott, who had been with the unit for only a month. He had confided to a Canadian pilot that he had no intention of flying to Malta. Consequently, as the Spitfires began their 660-mile flight, he turned for Algeria (some 55 miles to the south) where he force-landed BP958 in the area to the south of the Atlas mountains. Making contact with the US Consulate, he claimed to be a lost civilian pilot in need of repatriation!

The flight to Malta proved uneventful for the majority of the remainder of the Spitfire pilots, although the Germans were following the course of the whole operation on their radio intercept service; they had decided to attack immediately after the new Spitfires had landed, rather than try to intercept the armed fighters as they flew in. Nevertheless, Messerschmitts were intruding over and around the Island as the new arrivals approached, and as Plt.Off. Reade Tilley noted:

'109s picked up the last flight of the group just before they reached the coast of Malta. Nobody had enough petrol to do more than run some 109s out of the pattern.'

There were no casualties. 601 Squadron landed at Luqa and 603 Squadron at Takali without further incident. Within 20 minutes, however, the Luftwaffe began to appear, which caused Sqn.Ldr. Bisdee to comment:

'Oh, the Battle of Brit all over again!'

The initial intention was that half the new aircraft would go to reinforce 126 and 249 Squadrons, whilst the new units would retain the rest. The events of the next 48 hours soon put an end to these plans, however.

Malta had already experienced one raid that morning when 70 Ju88s and 20 Ju87s attacked Valetta, Hal Far and Kalafrana, Hurricane BE710 of 229 Squadron being destroyed at the airfield and three more of these fighters being damaged. No aircraft were scrambled to intercept this attack, although the AA gunners claimed two Ju88s shot down and one Bf109 damaged.

Meanwhile, as already mentioned, the Axis radar and radio intercept units had picked up the incoming Spitfires, a major effort at once being prepared. During the rest of the day a total of 272 bomber sorties and 223 by escorting fighters were made against the Malta airfields. The first of the new Spitfires had arrived at around 1000 hours, and it was 1230 before the initial attack was plotted coming in, comprising 32 Ju88s and 20 Ju87s. These hit all three airfields but without causing undue damage: at Takali one Blenheim IVF was destroyed, one newly-arrived Spitfire badly damaged, and three Spitfires and one Hurricane slightly damaged. A Maryland was damaged at Luqa, but by a Bofors' shell, while a petrol bowser went up in flames at Hal Far.

With the approach of the raid, 185 Squadron scrambled three Hurricanes, which joined six Spitfires — in the hands of 249 Squadron pilots. One of the latter, Flg.Off. McNair, turned on a Bf109 as it attacked his No 2, Flg.Off. Daddo-Langlois; he saw strikes along the fuselage before it stalled and was seen to dive into the sea south of Delimara. He then attacked a Ju88 and saw strikes on this also, claiming it damaged. The 109 hit by McNair was an aircraft of I/JG 53 which then, in fact, collided with Daddo-Langlois's aircraft (GN-C), knocking off its wingtip. The pilot was seen to bale-out and was later picked up by an Axis ASR craft. Daddo-Langlois noted:

> 'Squirted at Ju87, Ju88 and 109s. Collided with 109 head-on. Pranged on landing. 109 confirmed.'

Sgt. Tayleur carried out a diving attack on another of the escorting fighters, claiming some damage, but a cannon shell hit his own cockpit hood and perspex splinters lacerated his face. Despite bleeding profusely, Tayleur then attacked a Ju87 which he claimed probably destroyed. A further Stuka was attacked by Flg.Off. Ron West, which turned over and was seen to go down five miles south of Delimara; he also claimed damage to a second Ju87 before gaining strikes on a Ju88, another of which Plt.Off. Sergeant damaged.

Two of the Hurricane pilots managed to intercept the Ju88s, Plt.Off. Noble (GL-B) reporting strikes on one, while Sgt. Boyd (Z2698/L) went after a flight of four — he gained strikes on the belly of one from 100 yards; saw strikes on the fuselage and port wing of a second, then hit a third, but this appeared to receive a direct hit by AA and was shot down, two of the crew baling out. Before exhausting his ammunition, he had time to fire at the fourth bomber as it fled south of Hal Far; it was left pouring smoke. The bomber which Boyd believed had been shot down — a machine of Stab III/KG 77 — actually struggled back to Sicily, but two crew members had baled out; Lt. Hans Mayer-Luhmann (the observer) landed near Rabat, having been mortally wounded. He died 15 minutes later. The other member of the crew to bale out was seen to go into the sea, but was not recovered. AA also claimed damage to two more Ju88s.

The Hurricanes then attempted to provide cover for the Spitfires as they came in to land in the face of strafing Messerschmitts, LAC Somerville recalling:

> 'Airmen were encouraged to fire at low-flying enemy aircraft. It had become a habit for enemy aircraft to follow our Spits into Takali when they (*the Spits*) had run out of fuel and/or ammo, with the object of shooting up an easy target. Drill was to collect from the armoury a rifle and belts of .303 machine-gun ammunition — ammo supplies unlimited.
>
> 'Imagine the effect when the 109s saw tracer bullets converging on them from all around Takali — tracers, armour-piercing, incendiaries, the lot! It was not haphazard banging away with guns (the task was taken seriously as the airmen had been advised they were first line of defence should there be an invasion). As a matter of fact two enemy aircraft destroyed were credited to small arms fire at Takali.'

One of the damaged Spitfires attempting to evade the strafers was that flown by Flg.Off. Daddo-Langlois; Sgt. Ray Hesselyn was watching from the ground:

'I noticed one Spit with its wing-tip sheered off. He was flying low down with a bunch of 109s above, and was whistling around the circuit, waiting a favourable moment to come in and land. His damaged wing was plainly visible from the ground. About 18 inches of it was missing, and instead of the usual elliptical section of a Spit wing, it looked rather like the square-cut wing of a 109E.

'Eventually the Spit came in, but was hit. It went running past dispersal when the pilot whipped up his undercart, and skidded the aircraft along on its belly... It came to rest in a cloud of dust. Brennan ran towards it, but the 109s swooped down and started to beat up the aerodrome. Brennan dodged behind some sandbags, and Buck (*Buchanan*) and I ran towards a slit trench.

'Before we could reach it, the 109s were overhead and we had to fling ourselves on the ground. As we did so I saw Raoul Daddo-Langlois leap from the cockpit of the Spitfire and make a bee-line for dispersal. Machine-gun bullets ploughed into the ground all round us, and a cannon-shell burst within a few yards of Buck, but luckily we were not hurt.'

Four-cannon Spitfire Vc in its blast pen; note the solid limestone walls with sandbag topping, and the camouflage sheeting over the wings. *(NWMA)*

It was some hours before the next raid arrived but in the meantime, at 1400, the Italians put in an appearance when 19 MC202s of the 10° Gruppo CT undertook their first mission — a fighter sweep over Malta. Led by Cap. Giovanni Guiducci of 90ª Squadriglia, they were half an hour into their flight when Guiducci and his No 2 (Serg. Magg. Giambattista Ceoletta) collided, both aircraft falling into the sea off Porto Empedocle. Although Ceoletta managed to bale out and was picked up by a fishing boat, Guiducci's aircraft fell in flames and he was killed; the mission was at once aborted. Subsequently Cap. Ranieri Piccolomini was posted in to take over 90ª Squadriglia.

As evening approached radar warned that another big raid was brewing. At 1700 two Spitfires of 249 Squadron took off to provide airfield defence, flying out to sea to enable them to offer cover when the main interception force returned to land. As Flg.Off. Buchanan and Sgt. Hesselyn climbed to 10,000 feet, they skirmished with a number of Bf109s which were approaching ahead of the main force, and were obliged to engage these. Hesselyn got onto the tail of one and attacked, chasing it across the Island and giving a four-second burst as they passed over the coast at St Paul's Bay, the Messerschmitt nosing down and apparently going vertically into the sea. He was then jumped by others but evaded these and fired at some Ju88s, seeing strikes on one. Buchanan, meanwhile, also chased a Bf109, claiming to have shot this down into the sea in the same area — witnessed by Hesselyn — but the two were then attacked by others. An aircraft of I/JG 53 did, in fact, crash into the sea off Valetta, from which the pilot was later rescued by Axis ASR craft.

No other losses appear to have been recorded, but one of their opponents may have been an aircraft of 3/JG 53, in which Lt. Walter Seiz was hurt when he crash-landed on return, although reportedly due to engine failure; a second Messerschmitt from 5 Staffel also crash-landed at Comiso, less seriously damaged. The evening raid was recorded initially at 1715, and was indeed a major affair, including an estimated 64 Ju88s, 25 Ju87s and more than 30 Bf109s, accompanied by an air-sea rescue Do24. At 1720 six Spitfires from Takali flown by 249 Squadron pilots, and six from Luqa flown by 126 Squadron personnel, were scrambled — the latter late getting into the air due to telephone lines being down as a result of the earlier raid.

The 249 Squadron pilots met Bf109s south-west of Gozo at 15-17,000 feet, and then Ju88s which had just attacked their own airfield, Takali. Flt.Lt. Macqueen claimed one bomber shot down into the sea, and Plt.Off. Sergeant a second north of Grand Harbour. He attacked this from dead astern, using all his ammunition as he closed to 100 yards; the port engine caught fire and he last saw the bomber diving away, flaming and smoking, following which he noted a large flash. One of the escorting fighters was claimed shot down by Sgt. Brennan, and was seen to fall into the sea seven miles west of Gozo by Flg.Off. Ron West; Brennan then attacked a Ju88 over Mtarfa, which was also observed — by Flt.Lt. Connell from the ground — to crash into the sea with both engines afire. Return fire from this aircraft hit Brennan's Spitfire (2-W) but he was able to land safely. A second Messerschmitt was claimed as a probable by Flg.Off. McNair, who believed he had shot off most of its tail, while Flt.Lt. Lucas gained hits on a third.

It seems that the bombers were from KüFlGr 606 and KGr 806. One aircraft from the former unit was crash-landed at Catania in a badly damaged condition by Fw. Winfried Böhlen, two of the crew having been wounded, while an aircraft from the latter Gruppe crash-landed at Catania.

Meanwhile, the 126 Squadron Spitfires led by Flt.Lt. Barton had become engaged with Messerschmitts, and suffered badly. Two pilots were lost — the 28 year-old American Plt.Off. 'Tex' Putnum was wounded by a cannon-shell and then collided with a radio mast near Siggiewi, being killed when his aircraft crashed; he may have been hit by Lt. Quaritsch of 8/JG 53, who claimed a Spitfire shot down for his first victory. Flt.Sgt. George 'Ricky' Ryckman, a Canadian from Ontario, was thought to have followed a Ju88 out to sea, where he was jumped by a Bf109; watchers saw a splash in the sea just off the coast where it was believed his aircraft had fallen. Oblt. Klaus Quaet-Faslem of 2/JG 53 reported:

> 'After meeting several Spitfires at a height of 3500 metres, I saw a few Ju88s flying towards Valetta, but these disappeared north. To cover them I got between a group of Spitfires and the Ju88s. (*Over the radio*) I heard a report

> of a Spitfire behind a Ju88 over the sea, and spotted this, but it disappeared in a right turn behind another Ju88 before I could get close enough to open fire. I fired from long range and the Spitfire broke away from the bomber. After I had passed above the Spitfire, I saw it turning towards the Ju88 again. At the same time Lt. Zellot attacked the Spitfire which did a left turn and flew off south towards the island. Lt. Zellot fired at the Spitfire whilst in a turn and hit the fuselage and the top of the right wing. Very soon the plane started swinging and before the pilot could escape, went down into the water leaving a white and blue smoke trail. The aircraft was the latest model of Spitfire with four cannons.'

Lt. Walter Zellot, the successful pilot, added:

> 'I fired at the Spitfire and it tried to escape by doing a left turn towards Valetta. I followed and fired so that pieces of the fuselage flew off. Shortly afterwards I saw a small flame and a light trail of smoke coming from the right side of the motor. Swinging violently from left to right, the Spitfire lost height, fell sideways and crashed down vertically into the water from a height of 300 metres. I couldn't see anything apart from an oil slick where the aircraft had hit the sea.'

Clearly Sgt. Ryckman had been Zellot's 12th victory — the 92nd for 1 Staffel of JG 53, and 291st for I Gruppe of that unit.

Flt.Lt. Johnston had discovered that his radio was not working as he took off, while his engine developed a leak, spraying his windscreen with oil. Alone, he encountered and pursued a single Ju88 over Takali, but was unable to carry out an attack due to his oiled-up screen. Skirmishing with several other aircraft, he headed back towards Luqa where he saw two Messerschmitts strafing, but he managed to avoid these at low level when a tremendous explosion — subsequently ascertained to have been caused by a bomb from a Ju88 — threw his Spitfire upwards, out of control. He baled out at 150 feet, bruising his heel on landing, while the stricken Spitfire crashed near Qormi. The blast from this bomb also bowled over 126 Squadron's Sgt. Crist, who was on the airfield taking pot-shots at strafing Bf109s with a rifle! The only claim the 126 Squadron formation could make was for a single Messerschmitt damaged by Plt.Off. Brooker.

Five Hurricanes (three/185 and two/229) were despatched to patrol over an ASR launch searching for the missing Ryckman, but these ran into a number of Ju88s, making several claims. Sgt. Tweedale (Z4011) claimed to have destroyed two of the bombers but was apparently credited only with their probable destruction, while Flt.Lt. Lloyd (Z2698/L) and 229 Squadron's Sgt. Brooks each claimed damage to two others. Sgt. Yarra, flying one of 126 Squadron's old Hurricanes (HA-D), was obliged to crash-land at Hal Far after his aircraft had been shot-up in this engagement. Of Ryckman there was no sign. Ofw. Ehrenberger of II/JG 53 claimed a Spitfire shot down, and may have misidentified Yarra's Hurricane.

At Takali two Spitfires had been destroyed and three slightly damaged, while two more were damaged at Luqa. The Luftwaffe believed that they had shot down four British aircraft and destroyed five more on the ground during the evening attack. The German claims were very accurate compared to those made by the AA gunners on this occasion — seven Ju88s were claimed shot down, plus

Ofw. Rudolf Ehrenberger of 6/JG 53 in his 'Yellow 4' had raised his total of claims to 25 by 20 April, 13 of them over Malta. *(Kienzle via J. Prien/W. Bock)*

two more and a Bf109 damaged!

Air Vice-Marshal Lloyd had been delayed getting to Takali to welcome the new arrivals due to a bomb splinter puncturing a tyre on his car, but when he did arrive he found many of the new pilots almost speechless at the exhibition of concentrated bombing. He feared that Takali would be unserviceable for three or four days, so severe appeared the damage. But soldiers and airmen worked all through the night and by first light on the 21st the runways had been cleared, filled and rolled, allowing Spitfires which had landed at Luqa or Hal Far to return. Nine other Spitfires remained trapped in their pens by debris, however, and could not be moved for the time being.

The condition of many of the new Spitfires left much to be desired. Many were in a poor state of serviceability, and even after being worked on all night, most were still not ready by morning; guns were dirty and had not been synchronised; most had not been fired since they had been installed; many radios were not working. The AOC was furious and made his feelings known to those responsible. He also complained of the lack of experience of most of the new pilots, his subsequent cable to the Air Ministry emphasising:

> 'Only fully-experienced operational pilots must come here. It is no place for beginners. Casualties up to now have been the beginners.'

One further Spitfire was lost during the day when a long-range photographic-reconnaissance Mark IV failed to arrive at Malta from Gibraltar, en route to Egypt. Owing to technical problems, Sgt. Clifton, RAAF, had force-landed BP907 near Djedeida, Tunisia, setting fire to his aircraft before being captured and interned.

It had in other ways been a good day for 185 Squadron which received the announcement of a number of awards to its pilots — Acting Sqn.Ldr. Rhys Lloyd, Plt.Off. Phil Wigley and Plt.Off. 'Sonny' Ormrod received DFCs, Sgts. Tony Boyd and Garth Horricks received DFMs, whilst the latter was also notified of his commission, as were Flt.Sgts. Jack Fletcher and Eastman.

Tuesday, 21 April

Just before dawn on the 21st six Wellington ICs of 148 Squadron flew in to Luqa from Kabrit (Egypt), via LG104 at El Daba, led by Wg.Cdr. J.D. Rollinson. These carried with them six additional crews and seven specialist groundcrew. The aircraft were hastily dispersed on the Safi Strip, from where it was proposed that each should carry out three sorties each night against Comiso airfield, each crew operating on alternate nights.

Only 27 Spitfires could be made serviceable to oppose the anticipated onslaught on the airfields, the first Axis raid approaching at 0730. An estimated 37 Ju88s and 34 Bf109s began a series of attacks on Grand Harbour, the Docks, Luqa and Takali; in Dockyard Creek the anti-submarine trawler *Jade* was sunk, while an unserviceable Maryland was damaged at Luqa, and a Spitfire slightly damaged at Takali. Ten Spitfires (four/126 and six/249) and five Hurricanes (three/185 and two/229) were scrambled shortly after 0830.

Sqn.Ldr. Gracie (BR125/P) led the 126 Squadron quartet to the north of the Island, waiting for departing bombers. His patience was rewarded when he spotted a section of three Ju88s below, speeding out to sea. Diving onto them from above and astern, he claimed two shot down into the sea in quick succession, reporting strikes on the third before it escaped. Plt.Off. Peck (BR192/W) gained strikes on another before it, too, evaded, and the escorting fighters intervened, one of which Sgt. Goldsmith (BP964/K) claimed shot down:

> 'I was flying No 2, Wombat White Section, to Plt.Off. Peck, when we were jumped by four 109Fs at 18,000 feet. I took evasive action, aileron turning down to about 6000 feet, and about seven miles north of Grand Harbour. Here, one of the four e/a which had followed me down, crossed my nose in a climbing turn to the left, at a range of about 150 yards. I followed him round, opening fire with the four cannons, observing strikes along the top of mainplane and fuselage. After about two seconds, port cannons ceased firing, and I continued firing with starboard guns for two-three seconds. I then saw a large splash on the surface, and the e/a was seen for a few seconds just under the water before disappearing.'

It is likely that the Australian had shot down 'White 6' of I/JG 53, flown by Ofw. Franz Kaiser, who became a prisoner. Goldsmith continued:

> 'A little later another 109F attacked me from astern. I turned sharply starboard, and then when he overshot, I turned back and opened fire with starboard cannon as he climbed. Fired for about six seconds and saw strikes along bottom of fuselage, range 150-200 yards, before breaking off. I was attacked again from behind, and struck in the port wing with a cannon-shell, partially jamming my ailerons. I took evasive action, and the remaining e/a broke off the engagement as I crossed the coast at about 1500 feet near Sliema.'

From this engagement the fourth member of the quartet, Plt.Off. Stan Brooker, failed to return. The Canadian's Spitfire (BP976/O) was shot down into the sea and he was killed, as was 229 Squadron's Sgt. John Fullalove (BN278); his body was later recovered by one of the rescue launches. Two of the Hurricane pilots made claims, two Messerschmitts being reported damaged by Sgt. Finlay (Z2698/L) and Plt.Off. Horricks (BG905/J); the latter also claimed a Ju88 probably destroyed:

Plt.Off. (later Flt.Lt.) Jimmy Peck served with 126 Squadron, subsequently leading the all-American flight in that unit. He was awarded a DFC, and later transferred to the USAAF, flying Spitfires in Tunisia with a US unit in early 1943. *(NWMA)*

> 'I attacked a Ju88 near Takali; saw strikes on nose, fuselage and port wing root — into dive, smoking heavily, last seen below cliff level south of Hal Far.'

The six 249 Squadron Spitfires — two of which were flown by Sqn.Ldr. Douglas-Hamilton and Flt.Lt. Buckstone of 603 Squadron, on their maiden flights from the Island — encountered six Ju88s which had just bombed Luqa. Sqn.Ldr. Grant and Plt.Off. Plagis (AB263) engaged one bomber, Grant attacking first and causing the starboard engine to begin smoking. Plagis then attacked and set the port engine ablaze, and with the rear gunner silenced, the Junkers was last seen diving steeply towards the sea with both engines pouring black smoke; they were credited with its destruction. Plagis also claimed damage to a Bf109, as did Sgt. Hesselyn, while Flg.Off. Buchanan gained strikes on another Ju88. Due to their inexperience of the unique fighting conditions over Malta, both the 603 Squadron pilots had become separated from the others and failed to make contact with the bombers.

A Do24, escorted by seven Bf109s, was soon on the scene, obviously searching for the missing Ofw. Kaiser, while at 1210 the second raid approached — 20 Ju88s, 15 Ju87s and 36 Bf109s being reported, making for Takali, Hal Far and Grand Harbour. At Takali two Spitfires (BP849 and BP874) were destroyed and one damaged. Plt.Off. Peter Nash of 249 Squadron ran across to see if he could help extinguish a burning Spitfire in its pen, but was caught by the blast of an exploding bomb and rendered unconscious for 15 minutes, although otherwise unhurt.

Eight Spitfires were scrambled at 1220 to meet this new attack, Sqn.Ldr. Gracie leading off Sqn.Ldr. Bisdee and Flt.Lt. Barnham of 601 Squadron on their first operation from the Island. They were followed ten minutes later by eight 249 Squadron aircraft from Takali, one of which was being flown by 126 Squadron's Plt.Off. Peck. The initial trio attacked a formation of Ju88s, Barnham in BP955/J gaining strikes on the port engine of one, which he last saw close to the water pouring twin plumes of black smoke. He was then attacked by two Bf109s, but managed to get on the tail of one. Firing a long burst, he saw it pour black smoke and "topple sideways", but more Messerschmitts then appeared and his Spitfire was hit; the engine exploded, issuing clouds of smoke, and the aircraft fell away, although he was able to regain control and crash-landed at Hal Far, under attack by a number of Bf109s as he did so. He was credited with the Ju88 as probably destroyed, and the Bf109 as damaged.

Meanwhile Sqn.Ldr. Bisdee had also attacked a Ju88, damaging its starboard engine, and it was confirmed to have crashed by the crew of an AA battery. So

Left: Lt. Gerd Stamp of I/LG 1 carried out a number of raids on Malta on one occasion crash-landing his damaged Ju88 bomber in Sicily on return. **Right:** Lt. Walter Zellot of I/JG 53 shot down Sqn.Ldr. John Bisdee, commanding officer of 601 Squadron, on 21 April for his 13th victory.

intent on shooting down the bomber was Bisdee that he failed to notice a Messerschmitt closing on his tail. Lt. Walter Zellot of I/JG 53 was part of the escort to the bombers, and he spotted Bisdee's BP954/D:

> 'I noticed a Spitfire firing at a Ju88 from long range. I was flying with Oblt. Tedler about 1000 metres above it. I went down right behind the Spitfire and tried to chase it away with my machine-guns. It would not break away and stayed behind the Ju88, which kept shooting back. I could see that the Englishman was not hitting the bomber hard. I was close enough to fire at the Spitfire from a shallow left turn. At once pieces flew off the aircraft.
>
> 'As he now saw me, he tried to get away by doing a very sharp left turn, but while he was doing so, I had the whole upper side of the aircraft in my sights. I did a right turn and was ready to fire again when I saw a parachute opening. The Spitfire tumbled over and crashed down into the sea. I then saw the parachute floating close to the oil slick which appeared in the water.'

This combat — Zellot's 13th victory — was witnessed by Oblt. Karl-Friedrich Müller and Oblt. Udo Padior of the same unit.

As Sqn.Ldr. Bisdee baled out, the jolt as his parachute opened tore the webbing harness from his shoulders. Only by hooking his leg round one of the loops did he prevent himself falling to his death! He fell into the sea head-first, freed himself from his harness and scrambled into his dinghy. When Sqn.Ldr. Gracie landed alone, having claimed a Ju88 probable and a second damaged, he informed the enquiring 601 Squadron pilots that he considered Bisdee and Barnham had been lost. But soon came news of Barnham's crash-landing at Hal Far and searches were made throughout the rest of the day for the CO who, unbeknown to the searchers, was paddling towards the Island three or four miles to the north. After about six hours Bisdee eventually reached the rocky shoreline beneath the cliffs not far from Hal Far. By chance, he was spotted from the cliff top by an FAA airman, Air Fitter Monck, who scrambled down the rocks and dragged the semi-conscious pilot to safety.

Meanwhile, the combat-experienced pilots of the 249 Squadron formation enjoyed greater success. Sgt. Hesselyn claimed a Ju87 in flames as it was attacking Takali and then took a snap shot at a Bf109, which was hit by his cannon-fire and was also considered shot down. He was then chased down to 2000 feet by another, which Plt.Off. Plagis drove off his tail and claimed probably destroyed; Flg.Off. Buchanan claimed a second Ju87 shot down, while Plt.Off. Watts and Plt.Off. Peck each reported strikes on Messerschmitts. No losses were suffered.

The third and final raid began at 1559, with an estimated 60 Ju88s, 20 Ju87s and 40 Bf109s approaching to attack the airfields and Grand Harbour yet again. The AA gunners put up an intense barrage and claimed two Ju87s and a Ju88 shot down, plus four Ju88s and a Bf109 damaged; however, no losses were actually recorded. Flt.Lt. Barton of 126 Squadron (BR192/W) had taken up Flt.Lt. Parry of 601 Squadron (BR125/P) on a familiarisation flight at 1620, while nine Spitfires of 249 Squadron had been scrambled to intercept the raiders. The first pair encountered one of the Ju88s, which they attacked and claimed to have damaged. At 1645 two of the 249 Squadron aircraft dived on some Bf109s but were then attacked by other fighters, one Spitfire sustaining slight damage. Whilst it was assumed that their attackers had been Messerschmitts, it seems likely that they were in fact engaged by MC202s of 10° Gruppo CT. Twenty-two of these were over Malta on a sweep when Sottoten. Luigi Giannella became separated, and was attacked in error by JG 53 Bf109s, which he managed to evade. He then saw five Spitfires and claimed one shot down.

At 1720 the Spitfires encountered a number of Ju88s and their escorts as they were diving in line astern from 12,000 feet, heading for Filfla after attacking Takali. Flt.Lt. Macqueen claimed one Bf109 shot down and a bomber damaged, but was then set upon by two more Messerschmitts as he came in to land. The first pilot missed his opportunity and the second did not attack, driven away by Bofors fire. Sgt. Brennan claimed to have set fire to a Ju88 over Filfla and was credited with its probable destruction, but was then attacked by a Bf109; a cannon-shell hit his cockpit as he went after a second bomber, and he was attacked repeatedly as he went in to land but was not again hit. Another Junkers was claimed shot down into the sea by Flg.Off. Buchanan, but his aircraft was shot-up in the circuit as he was endeavouring to land; despite the damage he got down safely. Plt.Off. Sergeant's Spitfire was also hit when six Messerschmitts attacked; he went into a spin as his engine cut but was able to regain control at 200 feet, where the engine restarted. Although unable to climb or to fly at more than 140 mph, he landed safely.

It seems probable that 249 Squadron's opponents in this clash were from III/JG 53, 8 Staffel's Oblt. Belser claiming one Spitfire for his 24th victory, Lt. Müller another for his 2nd whilst Fw. Rudolf Schmidt of 7 Staffel recorded his 6th. OKW reported a total of seven aerial victories and nine more aircraft destroyed on the ground. During the day's actions, two Spitfires and a Hurricane had been shot down and six more Spitfires damaged in combat. On the ground the evening attack had taken a heavy toll. Some 150 bombs had struck Takali, and while not rendering the airfield completely unserviceable, had destroyed two Spitfires (BP963 and BP974) and damaged four others. At Luqa no less than five Wellingtons (Z8352, Z8584 and Z9032 of the OADU, Z1178 of 1443 Flight, and Z8892 of the SD Flight) had been destroyed, while two of the newly-arrived 148 Squadron detachment were badly damaged, and would be written-off.

That night Wg.Cdr. Rollinson led five of 148 Squadron's Wellingtons to attack Comiso, but due to very adverse weather conditions only three crews found what they believed to be the correct target. In fact, they bombed Gerbini where three Italians were killed and ten Germans wounded. The other two bomber crews released their bombs near Catania. Amongst the transit aircraft which departed for Egypt under cover of darkness was a Wellington in which Flt.Lt. Connell, Flg.Off. Norm Lee, Plt.Off. Lawrence, three American pilots — Plt.Offs. McHan, Booth and McLeod — and Sgt. Cairns, were passengers; they had been instructed to fly to El Ballah airfield, near Heliopolis, from where they were to collect replacement Hurricanes for 229 Squadron and to ferry them to Malta.

Wednesday, 22 April

When the first raid approached the Island at 0930 on the morning of the 22nd, no more than 17 Spitfires could be made ready for operations. The raiders again headed for the airfields and as a result of the attack on Takali, Spitfire BR129 was destroyed, whilst two soldiers were killed and six wounded. Luqa suffered the destruction of another Wellington, while the AA gunners claimed two Ju88s damaged on this occasion.

First off at 0915 to meet the raiders were four Spitfires, with Flg.Off. McNair (BP968/N) of 249 Squadron leading three inexperienced new arrivals — Plt.Off.

Left: Spitfire T-I, BR290, of 249 Squadron at Takali, with others in the background. *(I. Primmer)*.
Right: 2/Lt. Archie Bartleman of 601 Squadron, seen here in the cockpit of his Spitfire, was a South African from the Orange Free State. *(A. Bartleman)*.

Max Briggs (BP969/R) and Plt.Off. Bill Hagger (BP975/K) of 601 Squadron, and Sgt. Webster (BP973/J) of 603 Squadron — on their first sorties over the Island. They gave chase to a reconnaissance Ju88 — almost certainly Uffz. Wilhelm Schreiber's 3Z+FM of 6/KG 77 — at which all fired. McNair observed many strikes during his attack and was probably responsible for inflicting most of the damage; he recalled:

> 'In a stern attack I saw him burn and spin earthwards.'

The four pilots were jointly credited with its probable destruction, but this aircraft actually failed to return, the crew being lost. Sgt. Webster then engaged one of the two escorting Bf109s, which he claimed to have damaged.

At 1010, seven Spitfires were scrambled — again led by McNair — the three 249 Squadron and four 603 Squadron pilots intercepting 20 Ju88s approaching St Paul's Bay. Flg.Off. Ron West claimed two bombers damaged and Sgt. Brennan another, although he was then attacked by Bf109s and his own aircraft hit in the lower cockpit area, his flying boots being ripped to ribbons by cannon splinters! 603 Squadron's experienced Flt.Sgt. Johnny Hurst engaged a Bf109 of 9/JG 53 which he shot down, the pilot baling out into the sea; he was later picked up by an Axis ASR craft. Plt.Off. Gordon Murray (one of 603's Americans) was seen to break away and pursue a Ju88, but his Spitfire (BP970) was presumed shot down into the sea by Bf109s; he was killed. As he landed back at Takali, Plt.Off. Linton's Spitfire ran through the boundary fence and tipped on its nose, while Plt.Off. Holland, observing this accident, attempted to land short and ran into a bomb crater!

A further big raid at midday was not intercepted, although AA claimed two Ju88s; Takali was cratered and a number of Spitfires under repair were further damaged. When 50 Ju88s and 20 Ju87s appeared at 1730, however, six 126 Squadron Spitfires and two 185 Squadron Hurricanes were up to meet them. The Spitfire leader, Flt.Lt. Barton, claimed one Ju87 shot down with a second as a probable, and a Bf109 damaged, before his own aircraft BR120/T was hit. Plt.Off. Bailey's BR125/P was also hit but he claimed a Ju88 probably destroyed first; his target was almost certainly an aircraft of II/LG 1 which returned damaged by fighter attack. A Messerschmitt was claimed damaged by Sgt. Miller, but Plt.Off. Frank Jemmett was attacked by two more from the beam and was mortally wounded. He belly-landed BP969/R near Rabat; the aircraft slithered into a stone wall and caught fire. Some soldiers attempted to free him but had trouble with the seat harness until Plt.Off. Jeff West arrived and aided them; Jemmett was rushed to hospital, badly burnt, and died shortly after arrival.

The two 185 Squadron pilots also became engaged, Plt.Off. Wigley (Z4942/Y) claiming a Bf109 probably destroyed; his victim was possibly an aircraft of 4/JG 53 which crash-landed at Comiso, 50% damaged. The other Hurricane pilot, Plt.Off. 'Sonny' Ormrod, was lost. He was seen to pursue a Ju88 through the Grand Harbour barrage, but was apparently hit by both AA and by a Bf109, his Hurricane (Z4011/B) crashing into the sea a mile off Valetta; his demise was unwittingly witnessed by his young Maltese friend, Edgar Smith:

> 'The German bombers approached from the east with the Grand Harbour their intended target. A curtain of steel was awaiting them. The gunners let loose well before the first plane flew through it all. It seemed an impossibility to fly through all that inferno and come out in one piece, but through it they came. A Hurricane was flying in pursuit; but the barrage did not distinguish a Hurricane from a Junkers. As I stood watching, on a height, together with a friend, to our horror, the Hurricane came to an abrupt stop and plummeted to earth. My friend and I saw the pilot coming out of the plane and rolling down, with no parachute open. Presumably he was killed instantly.
>
> 'In the evening of that day, Sqn.Ldr. Mortimer-Rose came over to see me and asked: "Have you heard about Sonny?" I was momentarily choked and could not answer.'

HSL 128 went out and searched for one and a half hours for Ormrod, but no trace could be found; after dark the craft again went out when a light was reported at sea, but once more there was no sign of the missing pilot. The ASR crew were particularly distressed by his loss, as he had often flown cover to their launch, and while on such duty lived at the Kalafrana Mess with them. Eventually, many weeks later in September, Ormrod's body was discovered on a rooftop in Cospicua. Of the nine claims recorded by OKW on this date, Hpt. Wilcke, Kommandeur of III/JG 53, claimed a Hurricane as his 36th victory; he may have been Ormrod's victor.

During the evening attack more claims were made by the AA crews, this time for a Ju88 and a Ju87 shot down, with a Ju88 and a Bf109 damaged. Wg.Cdr. Satchell and Sqn.Ldr. Westmacott had set up a machine-gun post above some caves at Takali, and during the two days 21st and 22nd, claimed hits on two Ju88s (one each) and three low-flying Messerschmitts (two by Satchell and one by Westmacott). However, this final raid had again been costly — at Luqa four Wellingtons and a Blenheim were damaged, while three Spitfires (BR180, BR188 and BR204) were destroyed at Takali. Hal Far suffered severe damage to a torpedo store, where a Hurricane was also damaged.

After dark two of the 148 Squadron Wellingtons which had been damaged during the day, but had since been made serviceable, joined one other and set off at 2140 to raid Comiso, the crews subsequently reporting bombs exploding close to the hangars. On return two were refuelled, rearmed and taken over by fresh crews, who made a second such attack in the face of intense AA fire. One aircraft made a third sortie, returning at 0450; some bombs fell near Ragusa.

Thursday, 23 April

Thursday opened with a small early morning fighter-bomber attack, followed at

1035 by a major raid by an estimated 42 Ju88s and 15 Ju87s, directed against the usual targets. At Takali a number of aircraft pens were damaged and two unserviceable fighters — a Spitfire and a Hurricane — were destroyed; a second Hurricane was destroyed at Hal Far. Six Spitfires and half a dozen Hurricanes were scrambled to oppose this raid, Sgt. Tweedale (Z2698/L) of 185 Squadron shooting down a Ju87 — S7+CM of III/StG 3 — over Kalafrana Bay, despite being under attack by Bf109s. Uffz. Jurgen Schwengers ditched the crippled Stuka in Marsaxlokk Bay but it sank at once in 12 feet of water, both members of the crew being drowned. For some time afterwards the wreck could clearly be seen on a calm day, with the body of the pilot still in the cockpit.

Two other Hurricane pilots, Sgt. Dodd (Z2396/D) and Plt.Off. Wigley (Z4011), claimed damage to a Ju87 and a Bf109 respectively, but two aircraft of this unit returned with damage, while Plt.Off. Tilley's Spitfire was also shot-up; Oblt. Belser of 8/JG 53 claimed a Hurricane shot down as his 25th victory. Phil Wigley recalled:

> 'On this occasion it was noticed that several Ju87s jettisoned their bombs in the sea north of Grand Harbour when attacked by the fighters, thus incidentally sparing them from dive-bombing through the Grand Harbour AA barrage. The barrage was a spectacular sight though it must have been a nerve-shattering experience for the Luftwaffe crews who were not lacking in courage — only very rarely did one see a bomber break away from the barrage without attacking.'

During this raid AA gunners claimed four Ju88s shot down. They not only hit Lt. Rolf's Haase's aircraft of 9/KG 77 which belly-landed on return, the pilot being wounded, but also another aircraft of 5/LG 1 which also crash-landed on return with two members of the crew wounded.

The bombers were back at 1555, an estimated 50 Ju88s and 16 Ju87s attacking the airfields and Dockyard. A Spitfire was destroyed at Takali, where three others and three Hurricanes were damaged, while an unserviceable Wellington (ES984 of 1443 Flight) was destroyed at Luqa and another slightly damaged by debris; an Albacore was destroyed at Hal Far, another and a Hurricane sustaining damage. AA claimed a Ju88 shot down and another damaged.

Four Hurricanes and two Spitfires were scrambled, but only the latter managed to intercept, Sqn.Ldr. Gracie (BR120/T) and Flt.Sgt. Schade (BP850/F) of 126 Squadron being credited with two Ju87s shot down — one jointly, the other by Schade, who recorded:

> 'Climbed up sun to the south of the Island, about 26,000 feet and about 15-20 miles out to sea. Called in by Ops about 1605. Dove down onto Takali, passing about 15 Me109s at about 20,000 feet to our starboard (six of these peeled off and followed us). We missed the Ju88s at Takali so made off to the Grand Harbour with the CO. We dove onto the 87s as they were just pulling out of their dive. I was a little behind the CO and to the right. I saw him attack an 87, pulling up at the same time and stalling. As the CO broke away to port I was just in the right position to attack the same 87. I opened fire at about 200 yards, closing in to about 70 yards. I fired about a two-second burst and saw hits then black smoke come out from underneath the e/a.
>
> 'I broke away to port after this and went into a tight, steep turn, coming back at the 87s just in time to catch the second lot diving. I engaged an 87

from quarter-stern from about 200 yards closing to about 50 yards. Hits were observed on the e/a (the plane shook) and black smoke came out of the wing roots. I broke away to port again and joined up with the CO, who made off towards Takali. We dodged a couple of 109s by going in and out of cloud. We eventually landed with Hurricanes as cover.'

During the early evening nine Ju88s and 21 Bf109s made an undisputed raid on Luqa, where another Spitfire was destroyed on the ground. This was the 13th Spitfire to be destroyed in this manner in the last four days, with at least another dozen sustaining debris and blast damage, while a further nine had been shot down or had crash-landed. The situation was again becoming very serious for the defenders.

For the third consecutive night the Wellingtons were out. Two replacement aircraft had flown in during the day and these, with two serviceable survivors of the original detachment, set off to raid Comiso again at 2110. Here, on this occasion, the defences proved particularly effective, the bomber flown by Plt.Off. R.M. Harper being shot down and a second seriously damaged; the Australian Harper and his crew perished when their aircraft (DV573) crashed near Vittoria. On return the two undamaged Wellingtons were refuelled and rearmed, setting out once more with replacement crews at 0110. Both returned, despite heavy defensive fire, and were able to be prepared at once for a third sortie. On this occasion BB483/Q was shot down, crashing near Acate; three of the crew were killed, but Flt.Lt. A.R.H. Hayter (the pilot) and two others survived to become prisoners. Although a few bombs fell near Vittoria railway station during the night, not one fell on Comiso airfield despite the eight sorties made.

Friday, 24 April

Friday opened with a raid on Grand Harbour and the airfields by at least 30 Ju88s and 20 Bf109s, Luqa bearing the brunt of the attack. Here two Hurricanes were destroyed, as was a Wellington of 148 Squadron, while yet another Spitfire was damaged. Four Spitfires of 126 Squadron were scrambled at 0730, followed five minutes later by four Hurricanes of 185 Squadron and two of 229 Squadron, but these could not prevent the Gozo ferry-boat from being strafed by the Messerschmitts; five civilians aboard the vessel were wounded. Flt.Lt. Johnston led his quartet of Spitfires to engage a formation of bombers over Grand Harbour — he attacked one and set both engines on fire before being forced away; Sgt. Crist also claimed a bomber probably destroyed while Sgt. Miller and Sgt. Wally Milner, both on their first operational sorties, claimed damage to two others.

Meanwhile, Flt.Lt. Lawrence (Z4942/Y) and his Hurricane formation became entangled with the escorting Messerschmitts, one of which he claimed damaged; Plt.Off. Fletcher (GL-C) reported gaining strikes on a Ju88 before the escort pounced; Sgt. Boyd (Z2698/L) experienced a successful engagement, recording:

'At 10,000 feet we were attacked by four Me109s. I turned into these and gave the last one a short burst 250 yards from astern. Lost remainder of formation in doing so. Flying alone at 7000 feet (*I was*) attacked by two Me109s (three machine-gun bullet holes in port wing and rudder controls shot away). Took evasive action and fired a (*one*) second burst into one from stern quarter, 100 yards. Observed strikes with tracer.

Six pilots of 185 Squadron pose with a wing panel removed from the wreck of Hpt. Krahl's II/JG 3 Bf109F, shot down on 14 April; from the left are Plt.Off. Yarra, Plt.Off. McKay, Sqn.Ldr. Lloyd, Flt.Lt. Lawrence, Flt.Sgt. Sim, Plt.Off. Broad and a Maltese Operations clerk. *(P. Wigley)*

> 'Saw a pair of 109s diving on a Spitfire. Caught one as he pulled up. Two-second burst, saw strikes from astern on fuselage, two puffs of black smoke from his engine before he "pulled the tit". Proceeded to manoeuvre in a circle with six 109s at 5000 feet near Hal Far. Fired at one pair abeam below. No result. Caught another one at 50 yards from starboard beam. Fired remainder of ammunition. Saw strikes all along fuselage and starboard wing. He pulled up very steeply, rocking from side to side.'

It is possible that the two Messerschmitts which Boyd reported hitting were aircraft of 6 and 7 Staffel, JG 53, which crash-landed at Comiso on return, although both reportedly due to engine failure. During this fight Ofw. Herbert Rollwage of II Gruppe claimed a Spitfire shot down.

The next raid came in at just after 1000 when 26 Ju88s and 14 Ju87s bombed Valetta, although the Dockyard was most probably the intended target. St Luke's Hospital was hit, where one person was killed and three injured; two shelters were also hit, killing four civilians and injuring 13 others; two off-duty RCAF airmen of 148 Squadron — Sgt. Alex Balinson and Sgt. Art Charron — were also killed.

Flt.Lt. Barton (BP973/J2) led off four Spitfires of 126 Squadron to meet the raiders, encountering a number of bombers near Takali. Barton and his No 2, Sgt. Milner (BR176/N), jointly engaged a Ju88 and claimed his shot down, while Sgt. Crist (BP850/F) severely damaged a Ju87; his aircraft then developed a glycol leak and he was forced to crash-land near Siggiewi. As the Spitfires attempted to land, half a dozen Bf109s tried unsuccessfully to strafe them. AA gunners also claimed a Ju88 shot down and two Bf109s damaged. Lt. Josef Einsinger of 5/JG 53 crash-landed his Messerschmitt at Comiso on return; the aircraft was totally destroyed.

A Bf110 of III/ZG 26 crash-landed at Trapani airfield, with Fw. Heinz Richter and his gunner both sustaining injuries. They had possibly been involved in combat with a reconnaissance Blenheim of 203 Squadron, out from Bu Amud. Maryland AH280/Y from this unit had encountered a number of Ju52s over the Mediterranean, but before an attack could be made by Flg.Off. Fox, two escorting Bf110s of III/ZG 26 appeared. The Maryland evaded and managed to escape. However, Blenheim Z7849 from the same unit flown by Flt.Lt. W.R.

Hole, was also in the vicinity and failed to return. It was assumed that this aircraft may have also encountered the Messerschmitts, as was indeed the case, for Uffz. Lauff claimed such an aircraft shot down; there were no survivors.

Watchers on Malta counted 32 Ju88s and 20 Bf109s approaching just after midday, Grand Harbour and the airfields receiving further visits. Only two Hurricanes of 229 Squadron and one from 185 Squadron were available, and during the ensuing skirmish Plt.Off. Nixon of the former unit claimed damage to a Bf109. All three Hurricanes returned safely.

The last raid of the day was made by 34 Ju88s and 15 Ju87s on the three airfields, a single Spitfire being burnt out at Takali. Three Spitfires of 601 Squadron, one of 249 Squadron and four Hurricanes of 185 Squadron scrambled, intercepting the Stukas. Flt.Lt. Barnham (BR975/K) attacked two and claimed one shot down in flames but was then attacked by Bf109s when in the circuit, stalled whilst on approach and crash-landed; he was unhurt apart from his pride. It is possible that his attacker was Lt. Quaritsch of 8/JG 53, who claimed a Spitfire shot down for his second victory.

Sgt. Finlay of 185 Squadron saw 15 Ju87s over Grand Harbour at 10,000 feet, attacking one from 250 to 200 yards, and seeing strikes on its tail and cockpit. He then attacked a second with which he almost collided, again seeing strikes on the engine cowling, then a flash of flame. He was credited with one damaged. Claims for damage to Stukas were also made by two of the Spitfire pilots, Plt.Off. Scott (BP973/J2) and Plt.Off. Le Bas (BR125/P), while Plt.Off. Pete Nash, the 249 Squadron pilot, had suffered engine failure immediately after take off and had crash-landed on the cliff tops near Rabat. Hurricane Z2396/D, flown by Plt.Off. Noble, was hit in the port elevator by a cannon-shell from a Bf109, though he landed safely. AA gunners claimed one Ju88 shot down and two damaged.

Saturday, 25 April

Up to 85 Ju88s and 15 Ju87s were reported attacking Luqa on the morning of Saturday the 25th, a raid which was not opposed by the fighters. The building commonly known as the Poor House (formerly an old people's home now used to billet airmen and soldiers) was hit and an RAF officer seriously injured, while five soldiers of the West Kents were killed and four airmen wounded on the airfield. Bofors gunners scored a hit on a low-flying Bf109 of 5/JG 53, from which Fw. Alexander Kehlbuth baled out and landed in a nearby field to become a prisoner.

Soon after midday a further 80 Ju88s and Ju87s returned, Luqa's Poor House now being totally destroyed, and a Wellington of 148 Squadron badly damaged. St George's Barracks were also hit and 14 soldiers killed, with over a dozen more seriously injured. Bombs also fell on the 4.5-inch HAA gun battery at Spinola, where a dozen British gunners and one Maltese signalman lost their lives. On this occasion six Hurricanes (four/185 and two/229) and three 601 Squadron Spitfires were scrambled at 1225, followed half an hour later by two more of 249 Squadron and two of 603 Squadron; all became heavily engaged.

First in the air were the 601 Squadron trio, who attacked Ju87s near Luqa. Plt.Off. Ken Pawson (BP973/2-J) failed to return, but when the other two pilots — Plt.Off. Hagger and Sgt. Howard — landed, they reported that they believed Pawson had probably shot down two Ju87s and had then seen him being pursued out to sea by four Bf109s. They were later to learn that he had attempted to get

Bofors gun position, with a member of the crew relaxing before the next raid. *(via C. Bassett)*

back to the airfield, but had crashed his damaged aircraft in a field near Naxxar; he subsequently died from his injuries. It would appear that he had been shot down by Ofw. Josef K. Kronschnabel of 9/JG 53 as his ninth victory. Hagger and Howard each claimed a Stuka damaged.

Plt.Off. Wigley (Z2481) led the six Hurricanes to intercept ten Ju88s, ten Ju87s and numerous Messerschmitts, Sgt. Finlay (Z4942/Y) claiming damage to two Ju88s over St Paul's Bay while Sgt. Dodd (Z2396/D) claimed another of these damaged and a Ju87 probable. He engaged the latter as it was coming out of its dive and it disappeared into cloud pouring black and white smoke after a four-second burst. A further Ju88 was claimed damaged by Wigley and a Bf109 shot down by Sgt. Tweedale (Z2698/L). However, Flt.Sgt. Douglas Corfe of 229 Squadron — a 24 year-old who had been wounded in the Battle of Britain — became separated and was attacked by Messerschmitts, being mortally wounded by a cannon-shell before his aircraft was hit by ground fire.

From the ground witnessing the fight were Flt.Lts. Barnham and Parry of 601 Squadron. They were visiting Sqn.Ldr. Bisdee at the Pilots' Rest Camp at St Paul's Bay when Corfe's Hurricane (BE708) was shot down; Barnham graphically recorded:

> 'Two black machines, closely followed by two more, turn fiercely over tree tops and twist away over St Paul's Island; there were five machines arcing there and one is a Hurricane, one of our own aircraft and fighting desperately. The enemy seem to slacken for a moment, their sharp winged Messerschmitts drawing out to sea a little. The Hurricane, seizing the opportunity, dives into the cover of the hills. As it disappears from sight below the hill crests there's a sharp burst of gunfire from the ground. From the ground! It was our own guns firing!
>
> 'With terrible anxiety I watch the Hurricane re-appear. Its huge shape lifts over the skyline with part of its left wing breaking away. Uncontrollable it plunges into rocks; an exploding crimson flame scars the hill, while a smaller black shape, trailing black smoke, bounces on down towards the water; there at the water's edge a second fire breaks out.'

The other four Spitfires, meanwhile — again led by Flg.Off. McNair — had been ordered to join the 601 Squadron section in the attack on the Ju87s, following which Sgt. Brennan (2-E) then engaged a Ju88 over Naxxar but was in turn attacked by six Bf109s. He pulled up into these, and all but one overshot:

> 'I pulled up 30 or 40 feet underneath him. It was point blank range, and every detail of his machine stood out vividly. I could see his markings, his twin radiators, his retracted wheels, even the rivet heads on his fuselage. I gave him a second and a half with all four cannons. The result gave me a terrible fright. His starboard wing snapped off near the fuselage. It folded back, and banged against the fuselage. For a moment I thought it was going to tear away from his machine and come hurtling into my aircraft.'

The Messerschmitt pilot — Uffz. Heinrich Becker of 8/JG 53 — managed to bale out of 7+I and was later rescued by an Axis ASR craft. Sgt. Brennan then attacked a Ju88 from dead astern at 200 yards range and saw this catch fire, reporting that it crashed into the sea in flames (confirmed by ground crews at Takali, who were watching the aerial fight). However, Brennan's Spitfire had taken a number of hits from the rear-gunner of the Junkers and it went out of control. He managed to regain control and headed back to Takali, but here Bf109s were in the circuit and he heard Grp.Capt. Woodhall (the Senior Controller) call for Spitfires to cover the Hurricanes as they attempted to land at Hal Far.

In response to this call for help, Brennan and McNair arrived over Hal Far to keep the Messerschmitts at bay, but as two Hurricanes attempted to land simultaneously, one took the other for a Bf109 and pulled away. The other mistook the Spitfires for Messerschmitts and also hesitated! An irate McNair threatened to shoot down the over-cautious pilots himself if they did not land quickly! When McNair himself landed, he claimed damage to two Bf109s, a Ju87 and a Ju88. However, Brennan reported that McNair had got two confirmed during this sortie, and it is possible that the claims for the two bombers were later upgraded.

The Luftwaffe were back again in the evening, when 57 Ju88s and 24 Ju87s were reported attacking Takali and Luqa from 1740 onwards, damaging airfield buildings. Four Hurricanes of 185 Squadron had been sent off at 1705 to meet the incoming raid, followed 25 minutes later by one more from this unit, two from 229 Squadron and four Spitfires — two each from 126 and 603 Squadrons. Plt.Off. Noble (Z2396/D) of 185 Squadron reported:

> 'Fired at two Ju88s — no results seen. Dogfight with Me109. Cannon-shell in starboard wing. One Me109F destroyed.'

Another pilot of this unit, Plt.Off. Fletcher (Z2698/L), claimed a Ju88 shot down, as did Flt.Lt. Douglas of 603 Squadron, while Sgt. Webster damaged one. Two Ju88s of KGr 806 were indeed hit, Lt. Werner Schrader's 3 Staffel aircraft (M7+LL) crashing near Vittoria on return due to damage, all the crew being wounded or injured. In the second bomber — M7+FK of 2 Staffel — the rear gunner (Obgfr. Herbert Schulz) was killed. A bomber from 5/LG 1 crashed due to engine failure on return to Catania, possibly due to damage sustained in action; Lt. Wolfgang Herkner and one other member of his crew survived with injuries, whilst the other two were killed.

As the two 126 Squadron Spitfires had taken off, piloted by Plt.Off. Peck and Sgt. Goldsmith, the latter's cockpit hood flew off and he returned to land again.

Sgt. (later Plt.Off.) Tim Goldsmith was a high-scoring Australian who served with 126 Squadron, gaining a DFC and DFM. *(L. McAulay)*

Seeing this, Flt.Lt. Johnston took off alone in BR125/P to join Peck but was unable to catch up with him. After sighting several aircraft, Johnston dived to attack some Ju88s but was set upon by several Messerschmitts and became embroiled in dogfights with these. Having evaded his attackers he responded to a radio call to cover Sgt. Webster as the latter crash-landed his damaged Spitfire at Takali, following which he landed safely at Luqa.

One of the two 229 Squadron Hurricanes had also been forced to return early, leaving Sgt. Lucien Brooks alone. It was believed that he had shot down a Ju87 before being attacked by four Messerschmitts over St Paul's Bay. These shot the port wing right off the Canadian's Hurricane (BN182), and he crashed to his death. It seems likely that Brooks and the other 229 Squadron pilot shot down on this day (Flt.Sgt. Corfe) were the victims of Hpt. Wilcke and Oblt. Below of Stab III/JG 53; Wilcke claimed a Hurricane as his 37th victory, and Below a 'P 40' as his sixth.

A resumption of night raids on the Island by the Regia Aeronautica was postponed when a mission by five Z1007bis of 50° Gruppo BT during the night of the 25th/26th was cancelled due to bad weather. From Malta it had been planned to send out 148 Squadron's last two Wellingtons to attack a battleship reported at Messina, but one of these bombers had been badly damaged during the day and Air Vice-Marshal Lloyd ordered the sortie cancelled. Crews of the 148 Squadron detachment were now advised that six Wellingtons would arrive from Egypt — not to stay, but to evacuate all remaining personnel of their unit.

Sunday, 26 April

The AOC was advised that an 'Ultra' intercept of Luftwaffe 'Enigma' traffic indicated that some units of Fliegerkorps II were preparing to leave Sicily. There was little obvious evidence of this immediately however, as 55 Ju88s and some 15 Ju87s arrived from 1430 onwards to attack Kalafrana and Valetta, the Telephone Exchange being amongst other buildings demolished in the city. Six Spitfires (three/601 and three/249) and four Hurricanes (three/229 and one/185) were scrambled. The 601 Squadron trio engaged Ju87s, the New Zealand pair Sgt. Dickson (BP964/X) and Sgt. McConnell (BR192/W) claiming one damaged between them, but their section leader (Plt.Off. 'Pip' Cripps) was hit by fire from a Bf109 — possibly Oblt. Belser of 8/JG 53, who claimed his 26th victory — and was seriously wounded in the foot by a cannon shell. The Canadian managed to bale out, but his parachute only partially opened and he broke his other foot on landing, later dying in hospital from spinal concussion and shock. His Spitfire (BR125/P) crashed in Qormi main street.

The four 249 Squadron aircraft had scrambled five minutes after the 601 Squadron section had departed, but Plt.Off. Nash had returned with an electrical systems failure, leaving Sgt. Ray Hesselyn to lead Plt.Off. Ralph James into action against a number of Bf109s over St Paul's Bay. Hesselyn claimed damage to one Messerschmitt, but was attacked by many others and his own aircraft was hit. He was then warned of Ju87s diving on Takali and engaged one at 8000 feet, firing a four-second burst. The aircraft was seen to catch fire and the crew bale out; two parachutes were observed over Naxxar, and the Stuka seen by witnesses to crash into the sea. Meanwhile James, after attempting to attack Ju88s over Grand Harbour, was also attacked by Bf109s and his Spitfire (BR199) was badly damaged; cannon splinters wounded him in the neck and left leg but he succeeded in belly-landing the aircraft at Takali. Despite his wounds he was able to scramble clear of the wreck and reach a shelter as Messerschmitts swooped down to strafe.

Among the Hurricane pilots, Plt.Off. Horricks of 185 Squadron claimed damage to a Bf109 and Sgt. Lees of 229 Squadron similarly damaged a Ju87, but Sqn.Ldr. Dafforn was attacked as he landed BV163 at Hal Far and he crashed with wounds to his left arm and leg. One more Hurricane and another Spitfire sustained minor battle damage during these actions, while the AA gunners managed to shoot down a Ju88 of 3/KG 54. Hpt. Wilhelm Schmidt's B3+NL was hit whilst flying over Kalafrana, the bomber ditching in the sea. Staffelkapitän Schmidt, although wounded, survived to be rescued by German ASR craft, while his gunner was picked up by a rescue boat from Malta; the other two members of his crew were lost.

That evening, at 1755, four Ju88s and 15 Ju87s returned to bomb Kalafrana and Hal Far, AA claiming two of the former shot down. At the seaplane base two tenders and a dinghy were destroyed and another tender damaged, while two airmen were killed and the slipway cratered.

Since the arrival of the Beaufighter flight to reinforce the night defences, 1435

The latest version of the Junkers Ju87 Stuka, the 'D' model, employed over Malta by III/StG 3. *(E.C. Des Armees)*

Flight had received no new aircraft, and was now very short of Hurricanes. After dark on the 26th, Sqn.Ldr. Westmacott took off in BE347 for an intruder sortie over Catania and Comiso, attacking a train with cannon fire to the south of the former airfield; he saw strikes on this before it took refuge in a tunnel. On return, the Hurricane was refuelled and rearmed, and taken over by Sgt. Jimmy Wood. His brief was to intrude the skies around Gerbini, but as he arrived in the vicinity of the airfield his aircraft was shot down by Flak; he was killed.

The Fleet Air Arm unit was in little better state at this time, and could muster only four Albacores in 828 Squadron and a single 830 Squadron Swordfish. The latter aircraft, which was ASV-equipped, now located three southbound Italian merchant vessels with an escort of three destroyers, steaming 25 miles off Linosa. At 0245 a single Albacore — T9232 piloted by Sub Lt. J.A. Cramp — attacked, the crew claiming a probable hit on a 5000-ton vessel; smoke was seen and intense, accurate Flak experienced, but in fact no damage had been inflicted on the freighter.

Monday, 27 April

Remaining fighter strength was now so reduced that little resistance could be offered to two raids on Monday. During the morning 46 Ju88s and 16 Ju87s were counted in the sky over Luqa, where an unserviceable Wellington was destroyed and further damage inflicted on a previously damaged Wellington and a Maryland. AA gunners blazed away with more than usual effect, shooting down two Ju88s and claiming one more and a Bf109 damaged — 3Z+FM of 4/KG 77 went into the sea with the loss of Uffz. Gerhard Linke and his crew, while L1+GM of 4/LG 1 crashed near Fort St Rocco, close to Kalkara; there were no survivors from Lt. Hans-Georg Witt's crew.

Mid afternoon saw another 35 Ju88s and 21 Ju87s (accompanied on this occasion by five Z1007bis of 50° Gruppo BT and 27 MC202s from the 4° Stormo) raid Luqa, Takali and the Grand Harbour; a Wellington under repair was destroyed at Luqa. In return AA gunners claimed a Ju88 probably destroyed, and in fact caused splinter damage to three of the Italian bombers.

The ASV Swordfish and one Albacore were out after shipping again during the night, searching the Cape Bon-Pantelleria area. At 0045 a southbound 4000-ton cargo vessel was located, escorted by two or three warships some 30 miles off Pantelleria. A torpedo was launched by the Albacore from 500 yards and it was believed that a hit was gained on the merchantman, much smoke being seen.

Tuesday, 28 April

The first scrambles of the day came early on Tuesday, two Spitfires of 126 Squadron and one of 601 going off at 0740. They were followed ten minutes later by four Hurricanes of 185 Squadron, to counter an estimated 43 Ju88s, 20 Ju87s and large fighter escort. Three bombers were seen to detach themselves from the last wave, dive low over Floriana and release their bombs. One struck the dome of the picturesque Church of St Publius. The miracle of Mosta was not to be repeated, for the bomb penetrated into the crypt and exploded, killing about a dozen persons taking shelter, including the Rev. Pawl Portelli; two other bombs also hit the church, which was severely damaged.

The three Spitfires made initial contact with the raiders and dived after the Ju87s, but the 601 Squadron pilot had to break away with engine trouble, and returned to land. Flt.Lt. Johnston (BR192/W) got on the tail of one Stuka, but was attacked by another. He was so surprised, that he thought at first it was a Messerschmitt, or that he was mistaken. He broke away feeling "as if I'd been charged by an outraged ewe!" and to his amazement was pursued in a tight turn by his assailant; he later wrote:

> 'I kept thinking: "the intrepid bastard" — I should like to hear the line he's shooting in his Mess tonight; feel he's justified too!'

Johnston — having evaded his attacker — went after another Stuka, seeing strikes, followed by white vapour, but broke away as Messerschmitts approached. The Hurricanes also attacked the Ju87s, Plt.Off. McKay (Z2396/D) claiming damage to two, although his own aircraft was hit:

> 'A few holes made by some keen 109 types! Hope they don't get anymore practice!'

Plt.Off. Wigley (Z3462) attacked a Ju88 which he claimed damaged, but was set upon by four more Messerschmitts, while Plt.Off. Jack Fletcher was shot down by another near Grand Harbour. The Canadian was seen to bale out of his blazing Z2698/L but apparently pulled his ripcord too soon and the parachute streamed over the tailplane, causing him to fall to his death. On recovery of his body, it was noted that eight panels of the parachute had been ripped out, rendering it useless. Of this action, Flt.Lt. Barnham, who had been watching the battle overhead in the company of Flg.Off. Cyril Hone, wrote:

> 'Two Ju87s have been shot down; burning, they pass over our heads to crash a mile or two behind us... Cyril taps me on the shoulder: "There's a parachute coming down"... Yes, there's the chute looking pink against the deepest blue of all, descending steadily, descending rather fast perhaps... Something's wrong with it; it's only half open, the rest flapping loosely, and the man is not struggling but just looking down past his feet at the ground rushing up to meet him. The parachute appears for an instant in front of a square house in the valley, then disappears.'

The two Stukas Barnham reported seeing shot down may have been the pair engaged by Plt.Off. McKay, although their loss is not shown in available Luftwaffe records. Nor is the Ju88, claimed shot down by the AA gunners, who also reported damaging two others. A little later, as the raid was clearing the Island, three Spitfires of 603 Squadron were sent off, Plt.Off. Jack Slade claiming damage to one of four Bf109 engaged.

Later in the morning a second Canadian Hurricane pilot was killed when Plt.Off. Tom Foley suffered an engine failure while air-testing 229 Squadron's BE565. A friend, 'Skip' McKay, noted in his diary:

> 'He tried to get into the airdrome but just didn't make it and spun just off the boundary; the aircraft turned over and burst into flames. I was quite near at the time and saw it all happen. I rushed down with the airmen to see if we could get him out but it was impossible. I think he was dead and likely never knew his aircraft was burning.'

Another raid at midday was not intercepted, a Wellington being destroyed at Luqa and a damaged Spitfire — BR124 of 603 Squadron — was written off at Takali following further damage. The guns claimed two bombers damaged during the raid.

The fighters were up again to meet the evening raid when 37 Ju88s and 15 Ju87s, escorted by many Messerschmitts and Macchis, arrived to attack the usual targets. Six Spitfires and four Hurricanes had scrambled, Flt.Lt. Barnham leading four of 601 Squadron to attack some of the bombers. He reported seeing one of his flock — 2/Lt. Bartleman (BR116/V), on his first operational flight — knock pieces off a black-painted Ju88. He then became engaged with several Messerschmitts, almost colliding with one, and returned with his own aircraft (BP964/R) hit several times. The American, Plt.Off. Tilley (BR185/Q) attacked a Bf109 on the tail of another Spitfire (believed to have been Barnham's aircraft) and claimed to have shot it down in flames. The guns claimed a further Ju88 shot down, while on the ground an Albacore, two Spitfires and a Hurricane were damaged, and considerable further damage inflicted on airfield buildings.

Wednesday, 29 April

Raids on the 29th proved to be much smaller affairs, but brought heavy fighting nonetheless. Seven Ju88s and eight Bf109s raided Hal Far at 1445, five 126 Squadron Spitfires being led off to intercept by Sgt. Goldsmith, followed somewhat later by four Hurricanes (two/185, two/229). The Spitfires climbed to 20,000 feet, where ten Bf109s were seen and engaged, Plt.Off. Peck (BR116/V) claiming one probable and one damaged. Flt.Sgt. Crist (BR192/W) then attacked a Ju88 which he claimed as probably destroyed, but he was hit and slightly wounded by splinters in the hand and backside, subsequently crash-landing. Crist's aircraft had probably been hit by Fw. Alfred Seidl of 8/JG 53, who claimed a Spitfire as his ninth victory. Tim Goldsmith also attacked a Ju88, but when he opened fire his cannons jammed. He reported seeing Flt.Sgt. Schade (BR185/Q) "hammering" fire into another Junkers, but with a Messerschmitt manoeuvring onto his tail. Goldsmith at once made a dummy attack on this and it sheered away, allowing Schade to continue his attack; he claimed the bomber shot down and, indeed, B3+DH of 1/KG 54 (flown by Lt. Martin Krickl) was reported shot down by a fighter; there were no survivors.

The Hurricanes then appeared and also engaged the bombers, the pilots claiming three damaged; Plt.Off. Noble (GL-C) reported:

> 'Fired cannons at Ju88 formation. Big yellow flash.'

Sgt. Tony Boyd (BD826/A):

> 'Leaders R/T packed up so I led the flight. Very successful interception five

> miles east of Kalafrana at 18,000 feet. Bombs still on. Damaged one Ju88. Upset bombing. Well-strafed by 109s as I touched down. Machine riddled with MG. Armour plate saved my back.'

The third claimant, 229 Squadron's Sgt. Vidler, overshot on landing and his Hurricane (Z2396/D) was damaged.

Six more Ju88s and six Bf109s returned at 1720 to attack Luqa, damaging one Spitfire and some buildings; AA claimed one bomber shot down. At 1845, five Z1007bis raided the same target but their bombs fell wide, and although six Spitfires went up they failed to make an interception. 4° Stormo Macchis were providing escort, led by Cap. Aldo Gon of 73ª Squadriglia. Intense AA fire followed the formation right across the Island, hitting Gon's fighter and causing severe damage, while the pilot was seriously wounded. Nonetheless, despite his wounds, he managed to reach Sicily and force-landed at Agrigento. Command of his squadriglia was assumed by Ten. Giuseppe Oblach.

The day was also marked by two unusual and tragic events. Now almost devoid of an air defence force, Malta had become too precarious a base even for her successful submarine unit, 10th Flotilla, which was ordered to withdraw to Alexandria. *P31* had already departed on the 26th, followed by *Urge* and *P34* next day, while *Una* and *P35* were to leave within the week. Early on the 29th Lt.Cdr. E.P. Tomkinson's *Urge* was running on the surface after departing the Island, when she encountered a convoy off Ras el Hilal, obviously making for Derna. At once the submarine's gunners opened fire on the merchant vessel *San Giusto*, but the ship was being escorted by eight bomb-carrying CR42 fighter-bombers of 3° Gruppo CT and these at once attacked, each dropping two 110kg bombs. *Urge* was hit and sank almost immediately with the loss of all hands; she had been second only to the late Lt.Cdr. Wanklyn's craft in successes, having been credited with the sinking of 74,669 tons of Axis shipping.

On the same day a civilian Cant Z506 floatplane (I-DORA/MM60473) was in flight from Tripoli to Stagnone di Marsala (Sicily), with some 15 crew and passengers on board. En route it passed over an Axis convoy near Kerkenah Island, and was at once attacked by a Bf110 of III/ZG 26 which was providing part of the escort. Two of those aboard were killed in the initial attack, and the floatplane went down in flames to crash into the sea. The whole engagement was witnessed by the crew of Ten. Giuseppe Bertuzzi's CR25 of 173ª Squadriglia RST, which was also part of the escort. It appeared to the horrified watchers that the German pilot, Uffz. Georg Schleich, realised at once what he had done, for he was seen to drop his aircraft's dinghy to the survivors, then apparently deliberately to dive his aircraft (3U+LS) into the sea; pilot and gunner, Uffz. Werner Beck, both perished. Survivors of the floatplane were picked up by the MTB *Castore*, which was accompanying the convoy.

Thursday, 30 April

April ended with two Luftwaffe raids on the 30th, the first by 20 Ju88s, 18 Ju87s and a number of Bf109 fighter-bombers, which raided Hal Far and Luqa just after 1100, a Beaufighter being destroyed at the latter airfield. Four 603 Squadron Spitfires scrambled, followed by four more from 126 Squadron, the former quartet attacking Ju88s over Hal Far. Here, Flt.Sgt. Hurst claimed one shot down but his own aircraft was damaged in return, and Flt.Lt. Buckstone claimed one damaged before one of his cannons jammed. Sqn.Ldr. Douglas-

Hamilton also suffered jamming of one cannon, while both those on Plt.Off. King's aircraft refused to fire; the cause was later ascertained to be faulty 20mm ammunition of American manufacture.

Ten 126 Squadron Spitfires also attacked the Ju88s, newly-promoted Sqn.Ldr. Tony Barton (BR116/V) and Plt.Off. Bailey each claiming one damaged, while Barton also claimed a Bf109 probably shot down. As the 603 Squadron Spitfires returned to Takali the pilots found Messerschmitts once again in the circuit, and one of these attacked Sqn.Ldr. Douglas-Hamilton as he attempted to land. Of the incident, he later recalled:

> 'We became split up, but had re-formed over the aerodrome, and then we had the longest part of the flight waiting to land. Round and round we went, a few feet above the ground, watching the 109s circling above, waiting for the unwary. Suddenly I saw a 109 coming straight for me. He was very low, just above the ground. As I turned I saw his tracer come out...'

Help came from an unusual source, for Wg.Cdr. Satchell was manning his machine-gun post, and recalled:

> 'I was manning a pair of Vickers "K" guns (which I did most days in company with Westmacott and others, who helped with the loading, etc), when a 109 came in behind one of our remaining Spitfires (flown by David Douglas-Hamilton), who had wheels down for landing. I aimed the gun directly at Lord David's aircraft; the deflection of the speed was just right. I fired and had the satisfaction of seeing the 109 pull straight up, stall, and crash on the far side of the airfield. It was very spectacular indeed.'

His victim, Fw. Josef Kroschel of 8/JG 53, managed to bale out just before 'Black 5' crashed and was taken prisoner. This brought Jack Satchell's tally with his twin-Vickers to one confirmed, two probables (a Bf109 and a Ju87) and a dozen damaged (five Bf109s, four Ju88s and three Ju87s) in the last two weeks!

Other such brave men who had been fighting back against the strafers were not always so fortunate. Flt.Sgt. Harry Gibbs of 830 Squadron, who had already accounted for one low-flyer, and possibly a second, was killed at his gun post at Hal Far by another Messerschmitt. He was posthumously awarded a Military Medal for his bravery and success. During this morning's raid, two victories were claimed by the Luftwaffe, Lt. Beckmann of Stab III/JG 53 and Lt. Harder of 7 Staffel each claiming Spitfires, although on this occasion no losses were suffered by the defenders.

The Regia Aeronautica was back at 1620, four Cants of 50° Gruppo BT (escorted by almost two dozen 4° Stormo Macchis) bombing in the Melleiha Bay area. Again six Spitfires took off — and again no interception resulted. An hour later ten Ju88s and 23 Bf109s hit Luqa and Safi, finishing off a damaged Spitfire. AA gunners claimed another Bf109 shot down and one damaged, as well as a Ju88. They were successful in the case of the Messerschmitt, hitting an aircraft of JG 53's JaboStaffel, the pilot of which baled out into the sea. Within the hour an escorted Do24 arrived to pick him up from under the very noses of the defenders.

With air and naval striking forces now virtually non-existent, the defenders too were once again in poor shape. Despite the strong reinforcement of only ten days earlier, no more than seven Spitfires and a handful of Hurricanes remained serviceable. Indeed, as from the 29th, 229 Squadron had effectively ceased to function due to shortage of aircraft, although a number of pilots had returned to Egypt to ferry back a few replacements; these were due imminently but their arrival would hardly effect the state of play. With the hospitalization of the wounded Sqn.Ldr. Dafforn, Paul Farnes had taken over the Squadron:

> 'As there appeared to be no one else available I was promoted to Squadron Leader and made OC 229 Squadron. Thus, after having been posted in disgrace only three months previously — as a Pilot Officer — I found myself a Squadron Leader!'

There had been other personnel changes towards the latter part of the month, for Wg.Cdr. Stan Turner had departed the Island, his place as Wing Commander at Takali being taken by newly-promoted Wg.Cdr. Gracie; command of the latter's 126 Squadron had passed to newly-promoted Sqn.Ldr. Barton. Other tour-expired departees at this time included Sqn.Ldr. Westmacott, Flg.Offs. Winton and Rathie of 1435 Flight and Plt.Offs. Horricks and Eastman of 185 Squadron. The injured Flt.Lt. Heppell and sick Plt.Off. Jeff West of 249 Squadron also left the Island. A number of other notables had departed, albeit on temporary assignment to Gibraltar, from where Sqn.Ldr. Grant, Flt.Lt. Lucas, newly-promoted Flt.Lt. Ron West, Flg.Off. McNair and Flg.Off. Daddo-Langlois assisted with the next Spitfire ferry operation.

Thus, what was to become known as "the cruellest month" came to an end. Although during April there had been 'only' 170 alerts by day compared to 186 in March, these included no less than 3547 incursions by bombers, while at night the sirens sounded no less than 182 times. Indeed, on two days only — when the weather had been particularly bad — had the Island not reverberated to the thud of explosions; 339 civilians and 208 servicemen had been killed in the raids, and 550 more civilians injured. In the three months February to April, a staggering 9867 tons of bombs were estimated to have fallen on the Island; no less than 6727 tons were recorded in April alone.

An indication of the weight of attack suffered by the airfields and other targets can best be given by comparison of the tonnage of bombs received compared with the two previous months:

	February	**March**	**April**
Takali	120	482	841
Luqa	218	486	804
Hal Far	174	347	750
Kalafrana	7	30	196
Dockyard	152	314	3156
Other targets	322	488	980
Total	993	2147	6727

No other month of the siege would approach this intensity and ferocity of attack. At least 22 Spitfires and 19 Hurricanes had been destroyed on the ground during these attacks. The month was marked by one other phenomenon: while March had been a good month for the guns — 28 aircraft claimed shot down — in April the gunners excelled themselves, for once outperforming the fighters. With ammunition supplies restored from the salvage of the ships of convoy 'MW10'; with large numbers of German aircraft over the Island; with nearly two years' of practice behind them; with less defending fighters available; whatever the reason, they claimed 102 victories, 12 probables and 69 damaged during the month, against claims by the fighters for 53 shot down, 29 probables and 118 damaged. As has been illustrated, however, actual Axis losses had been substantially lighter than this. The successes of the defending AA gun crews had not been gained without severe sacrifice however, at least 100 fatalities being suffered during the month, of whom 22 were members of the Royal Malta Artillery.

Bombing had not been the only concern of the authorities during the month however, for on the 21st a reconnaissance Spitfire had returned from Sicily with photographs revealing a large rectangular area, some 1500 yards by 400 yards, which was being marked out near Gerbini airfield. Three days later it had been levelled and was initially believed to be another satellite landing ground. However, two more such areas were then discovered in the same vicinity, parallel to the main runway, each within easy reach of a railway station; at each station new sidings were under construction and all were close to the main rail line from the Messina ferry. It was feared that glider components and troops were about to be assembled. Much equipment had already arrived by rail alongside some of these suspected glider airfields, where sheds were being erected as though to allow assembly to take place. Recorded Air Vice-Marshal Lloyd of his Staff's assessment:

> 'Each airfield was alongside a railway and the gliders, having been packed in Germany, could have been railed non-stop through Italy and over the Messina ferry straight to the fields; once there, they could have been assembled in the dark whilst the towing aeroplane arrived in the evening. On the following morning the gliders could have been over Malta. As each dawn broke I expected the Axis assault and for that reason we would "save" some fighters every afternoon in the hope of impressing the Axis the following morning.'

Governor Dobbie immediately appealed to the Prime Minister for an intervention by UK-based aircraft from Bomber Command to raid the airfields in Sicily. An invasion threat was not, however, taken seriously by the Chiefs of Staff Committee, who were at pains to reassure Dobbie and Lloyd that such could be discounted, certainly for the time being. Their reason was that the 'Ultra' intercepts had indicated that two Gruppen (Ju88s of II and III/KG 77) of Fliegerkorps II were already preparing to withdraw from Sicily to France, and that more units were to follow. There were now urgent calls to strengthen the Luftwaffe in Russia for the forthcoming Spring offensive there, and to support Rommel's planned 'push' in Cyrenaica.

In fact, plans for the airborne/seaborne invasion of Malta had long been prepared by the Axis commanders under the codename Operation 'Herkules', but Hitler was far from enthusiastic — the carnage of Crete was still fresh in his mind — while Rommel appealed for his bid for supremecy in North Africa to be given priority. Mussolini had continued to harbour a desire to conquer Malta — and subjugation of the Island fortress remained the foremost of his tempered demands. Amongst the most ardent supporters of immediate action were Grand-Admiral Erich Raeder, Chief of the German Navy, and Feldmarschall Kesselring — the former's reaction predictable owing to the threat Malta posed to Axis convoys and warships. Kesselring considered Malta was ripe for the plucking following the April blitz. Hitler was not to be convinced however by any of the arguments offered, and made it clear that command of such an operation (should it go ahead) would be left to the Italians, whom he believed were incapable of carrying it through. When Mussolini announced at a meeting towards the end of April, that to complete the plans for such a landing would take the Italians another three months, Hitler felt the point had been proved. To placate Mussolini however, Hitler agreed that he would offer his full support "one day", but first he would give his blessing to Rommel's drive in North Africa. A new timetable was therefore announced; first Tobruk was to be captured in June; then perhaps, Malta in July (see Appendix IV for details of the proposed Operation 'Herkules').

Nonetheless, Churchill had given Dobbie's appeal some thought and seen other advantages inherent; he had written to Air Chief Marshal Sir Charles Portal:

> 'It might be that this would be necessary in order to keep down the attack just before a wave of Spitfires was landed (by us). How would you do it? Could the Wellingtons fly from England to bomb Sicily, land on possibly cratered airfields of Malta, and return home next night, dropping another load of bombs? If not Wellingtons, what other aircraft would you use? It is quite understood that this would be very costly if it had to be done. Pray let me have the best plan possible.'

It is presumed that Portal had little difficulty in dissuading the Prime Minister from authorizing such a hazardous and unlikely undertaking, which could well have ended in disaster.

Even as these deliberations were underway, Dobbie had advised the Prime Minister of Malta's growing crisis — indeed, he reported that the description 'crisis' was not severe enough:

> 'It has now gone beyond that point, and it is obvious that the very worst may happen if we cannot replenish our vital needs, especially flour and ammunition, and that very soon... It is a question of survival.'

This cable had arrived on the 20th, and was followed a few days later by advice that it had been necessary to reduce bread consumption by 25% and that

Spitfire pilots cluster round the nose of a Ju88 shot down over Malta, which has crash-landed on the island. *(NWMA)*

supplies generally would not last beyond mid June.

Not only had the Island to be strengthened and a further convoy planned, but Dobbie's continued leadership of the garrison had seriously to be considered. Reports of the fiasco of the March convoy, of an attitude of growing defeatism, and Dobbie's obvious tiredness and poor health, now caused the Prime Minister to plan a change. The Minister of State in the Middle East (newly-appointed Mr R.G. Casey) was due to travel to Egypt, and the PM charged him with the duty of stopping at Gibraltar and Malta en route. At the former he was to hand to the Governor, Field Marshal Lord Gort VC, a letter advising him that he might be required to take over from Dobbie at short notice. At the second stop he was to assess the situation and report accordingly.

Meanwhile, the Prime Minister had decided that Malta must be held, even at serious naval risk — a decision in which he was supported by the Admiralty — and plans were set in train to send the battleship HMS *Warship* and a force of cruisers through the Suez Canal to fight a convoy through from the east. First, however, he appealed to President Roosevelt for the further use of the carrier *Wasp* to deliver more Spitfires, since the first batch had failed to achieve the longer term change in the situation that had been hoped for:

> 'Without this aid, I fear Malta will be pounded to bits. Meanwhile its defence is wearing out the enemy's Air Force and effectively aiding Russia.'

The President's response to this overstatement of the case was again favourable, and was received even as Churchill was penning his message to Lord Gort. Hence, on the last day of April, the big carrier arrived back at Glasgow to take aboard 50 more Spitfires and a group of reinforcement pilots to fly them. She sailed for Gibraltar three days later (3 May), accompanied by the battle cruiser *Renown*, cruiser *Charybdis*, two British and two American destroyers; Operation 'Bowery' was underway.

The Prime Minister was determined that the momentum should be maintained and he requested the Chief of Air Staff to let him have a programme for the feeding of Spitfires to Malta over an eight-week period — which was to see three further substantial deliveries follow 'Bowery'.

Friday, 1 May

On Malta, May opened with a number of small fighter sweeps. The first of these was intercepted at around mid morning by two Spitfires of 249 Squadron flown by Flt.Lt. Macqueen and Plt.Off. Watts (recently transferred from 603 Squadron), who were advised of the presence of Messerschmitts nearby whilst on an air test near Filfla. Four Bf109s of 6/JG 53, all carrying long-range tanks, were spotted. Giving chase at once, Macqueen and Watts jointly shot down one Messerschmitt, the pilot carrying out a successful ditching in the sea off Cape Scaramia, Sicily; they also claimed two others damaged. Later, while searching for the downed pilot, Fw. Karl Reinhold was obliged to force-land his Do24T flyingboat of Seenotst 6; but despite this mishap, the Messerschmitt pilot was picked up safely by another craft.

Late afternoon saw the appearance of five 50° Gruppo BT Z1007bis over the Island, escorted by 19 MC202s of 9° Gruppo CT, two of which were slightly damaged by AA fire. A lone Bf109 was then reported off the coast, presumed to be on a reconnaissance. Four Spitfires of 603 Squadron had been scrambled at 1700 to intercept the Italian bombers, but these encountered instead a number of Messerschmitts, two of which attacked Flt.Lt. Buckstone and Flt.Sgt. Rae. The latter's Spitfire (BP962/2-R) was hit by cannon fire from Lt. Soukop's aircraft of 6/JG 53 while at 17,000 feet, and with the control column shot away and a slight leg wound, Jack Rae baled out while seven miles out to sea. However, the wind blew him back over the Island, and he eventually came down near Rabat. Meanwhile, Sqn.Ldr. Douglas-Hamilton and Sgt. Bert Mitchell fired at Soukop's aircraft, and Buckstone saw a cannon shell apparently hit the Messerschmitt's tail; it was later reported to have crashed into the sea. In fact Soukop returned safely, and it is believed that this report referred in error to the aircraft shot down that morning by Macqueen and Watts.

On the ground Flt.Sgt. Rae was having problems, for an irate Maltese farmer had approached with a shotgun, believing Rae to be a German as his Mae West was painted with a number of swastikas, actually indicating his earlier score whilst flying from England! Happily his identity was established before injury occurred.

During the morning a Fiat RS14 floatplane — MM35388 of 170ª Squadriglia flown by Ten. Francesco Brera — was reported to have been attacked by an aircraft identified as a Blenheim while some 12 miles south-east of Capo Murro di Porco, Syracuse. Two of the crew were wounded, but the attacker was claimed shot down in return. No record of such an engagement has been discovered in RAF records. It is presumed that the aircraft in question may have been on a delivery flight, and like others, to have been off course.

Night raids were now again becoming a frequent occurrence, and with darkness the approach of 13 raiders was plotted, nine crossing the coast. Luqa and Hal Far were bombed, one of 89 Squadron's night fighter Beaufighters (X7752) being destroyed at the former airfield. Once again, as on many other occasions, Wt.Off. David Bishop's team of RAF bomb disposal volunteers went into action at Hal Far, his work on this night being specifically mentioned in the citation for the George Medal he was later to receive. Of the gallant and sometimes slightly eccentric Bishop, one pilot recalled:

> 'After a bomb raid he would casually saunter across the field and flag all the D/As (delayed-action bombs) he could locate. He used to carry a little swagger stick with him, and while he was examining the bomb and making notes, he would often tap the bomb a few times with his stick, and on some occasions, to show his contempt for the danger, he would take a leak on the bomb! It was quite a performance and we used to enjoy watching it from the safety of our pens or a slit trench. He was eventually awarded the GM, but as far as I was concerned, I would have given him one every week.

Meanwhile, four of 185 Squadron's Hurricanes had been sent off at 2025 to attempt interceptions, Sgt. Boyd (Z5147/C) returning early when the tail trim of his aircraft jammed. Sgt. Jack Yarra (HA-B) attacked a Ju88 which was held in searchlights over the sea just off the coast, and fired a long burst, reporting:

> 'Picked up exhausts, closed and squirted 88 — probably destroyed — disappeared from plot.'

The radar plot had indeed faded some 38 miles north of the Island, and the intruder was considered to have been probably destroyed. However, available Luftwaffe records do not verify this loss.

During the night a Hudson transport, V9227 of 267 Squadron, crashed at

Luqa on arrival from Cairo, although the crew survived unhurt. From Gibraltar came Sunderland W3993/W of 10 RAAF Squadron, carrying Mr Casey, on his way to Egypt (as recorded earlier). Arriving during one of the raids, Flt.Lt. Tom Stokes was obliged to creep along the coast at low level until the dimmed flarepath at Kalafrana could be seen; he alighted with intruders still overhead, whereupon Casey and three other passengers were whisked ashore for the meeting with General Dobbie. The flyingboat was refuelled in less than three hours, allowing Stokes to depart for the return journey before dawn, carrying 14 passengers, most of whom were sick or injured.

Saturday, 2 May

Sqn.Ldr. Bisdee, who had returned to 601 Squadron from convalescence, decided to lead a dawn readiness patrol of four Spitfires on the 2nd. He and two others operated to Takali from Luqa, but Flt.Lt. Barnham was delayed as his aircraft required further work to render it fully serviceable. He followed a little later, landing at Takali just as a lone Ju88 swept in. As Barnham climbed from his Spitfire he was surprised to see everyone else running away from him. He looked up to see the raider diving in his direction, and as he too dashed for cover, was bowled over by the explosion of one bomb, but was unhurt; this raider's other three bombs had been released elsewhere, one falling on the main square at Zejtun, which was crowded with people; 21 were killed and 29 seriously injured.

The afternoon saw a raid by 12 Ju88s on Luqa and Safi, with escort provided by Messerschmitts and Macchis, 18 of the latter from 10° Gruppo CT, which had transferred to Gela airfield only the previous day. A Maryland was damaged and an unserviceable Wellington burnt out, although four Spitfires of 249 Squadron managed to scramble. However, only Flg.Off. Buchanan succeeded in gaining strikes on a Messerschmitt before others drove him and his section away. Later that evening, with the arrival of darkness, three Albacores launched an attack on a convoy of two merchant vessels 14 miles off Lampione. One possible hit was claimed, but one of the attackers failed to return; it is believed the crew survived.

Flt.Sgt. Jack Rae, a New Zealander who arrived with 603 Squadron, but transferred to 249 Squadron soon after arrival. *(Daddo-Langlois Collection)*

Sunday, 3 May

At 1155 on Sunday, seven Ju88s and up to three dozen Bf109s raided Hal Far, damaging two Hurricanes which were on the airfield. Five of 249 Squadron's Spitfires were scrambled. and Plt.Off. Pete Nash (2-C), flying with Plt.Off. D'Arcy Milburn of 185 Squadron (who had been attached to 249) covered the airfield:

> 'D'Arcy and I were 'drome defence section. Came in at 12,000 feet just under 9/10th cloud and jumped four 109s over Hal Far. D'Arcy lost me during subsequent manoeuvres. Chased two and shot the No 2 down at sea level. Was then jumped by two more so came home from five miles west of Kalafrana. Only had port cannon working.'

Milburn claimed a second Messerschmitt as damaged, and Plt.Off. Watts a third. In fact, the German fighters appear to have escaped loss or severe damage on this occasion.

When five Cants bombed at 1355, the crews found no defending fighters up. Bombs fell close to Naxxar where 601 Squadron pilots were now billeted. Flt.Lt. Barnham and 2/Lt. Bartleman, with Plt.Offs. Briggs and Scott, rushed to give aid. Finding a bomb-damaged house from which emanated the sounds of groans, the four pilots began digging with their bare hands. Of the incident, Barnham subsequently wrote:

> 'The last rocks removed, the old man is freed, and we lift him on to a stretcher that has been squeezed through to us... now I'm walking alongside the stretcher for he talks to me and I hold his hand. We pass red-eyed neighbours, who, peering from their doorways, cross themselves as we approach the square where an ambulance is surrounded by an excited crowd. In the ambulance the old man talks to me for a few moments, then, relaxing his grip on my hand, he dies.

Almost two dozen Ju87s from III/StG 3, a dozen Ju88s, bomb-carrying Bf109s, and a strong fighter escort, including 16 MC202s of 9° Gruppo CT, approached at 1740 to attack Hal Far and Luqa again; one more Hurricane was slightly damaged at the former field, a PR Spitfire and a Wellington suffering damage on the latter. Five Spitfires were again scrambled, this time flown by pilots of 603 Squadron: Flt.Lt. Douglas attacked a Ju87, shooting off the cockpit canopy and seeing the gunner slump, apparently dead, over his gun. To his chagrin, he was credited only with a 'damaged'. However, Plt.Off. Slade succeeded in shooting down another Ju87 with his machine guns only, when his cannons refused to fire. Gefr. Karl Haf's S7+JP crashed near Zonqor, only his gunner (Gefr. Fritz Weber) surviving to be taken prisoner. Problems with cannons jamming were becoming ever-more frequent, and on investigation it was discovered that one third of all 20mm cannon rounds in the armouries were misfits.

Monday, 4 May

Monday was to prove a rather costly day. At 1015 six Ju88s and nine Bf109s, some with bombs, raided Luqa and Safi, AA claiming one Messerschmitt shot down. Six hours later in a similar raid on Hal Far, a Swordfish was damaged by debris. Shortly afterwards, the usual five Z1007bis — aircraft of 211ª Squadriglia — covered by five 9° Gruppo CT Macchis and ten Bf109s, came over and bombed Grand Harbour. The Italians reported that three Spitfires attempted to attack the bombers, and that two of these were claimed shot down by Sottoten. Alvaro Querci and Serg. Teresio Martinoli of 73ª Squadriglia, one of which they believed crashed into the sea. They may have attacked Sgt. McConnell's BR187/O, one of four 601 Squadron Spitfires which had taken off; he crash-landed at Luqa after the radiator of his aircraft sustained damage — though reportedly following an attack by a Messerschmitt.

Four 249 Squadron aircraft had also been scrambled, Flt.Lt. Norman Macqueen flying with Plt.Off. Fred Almos, an American 'new boy' as his No 2, with Sgt. Brennan and Plt.Off. Linton on his wing. Paul Brennan recorded:

> 'Caught as we headed upsun, a little south of Gozo. The 109s were everywhere. Linny and I were at once separated from Mac and Almos — the last I saw of Linny was when he was in a vertical dive, skidding and twisting like blazes, with four 109s hotly pursuing him. It seemed to me as if I had been throwing my aircraft about for an hour... when a Hun blundered. He made a belly attack on me, missed and overshot. He was a sitting target. I gave him four seconds. He went into a spin, pouring glycol... Almos called up that Mac was in trouble and wanted to land.'

'White 7', a Bf109F of II/JG 3, at Comiso. Lt. Karl-Heinz Steinicke is about to enter the cockpit. *(K-H. Steinicke via NWMA)*

Brennan claimed a probable, but it was subsequently confirmed as destroyed — his 6th victory. Meanwhile, Linton had escaped his pursuers and had landed safely, but Macqueen and Almos had run into trouble. Having arrived too late to catch the Italian bombers, Macqueen had also apparently suffered an R/T failure and, consequently, was unable to hear warnings of approaching danger. Watchers on the ground saw a Bf109 'bounce' him, but miss and overshoot. The German No 2 — Uffz. Walter Manz of III/JG 53 — then pulled up underneath and gained strikes on Macqueen's aircraft; smoke was seen issuing from the engine of the obviously damaged BR226, but the Spitfire regained formation; spectators were of the impression that the inexperienced Almos had been too close to cover properly his leader's tail from this attack, during which a cannon shell was seen to strike below the cockpit. Probably Macqueen was wounded, although his aircraft remained in formation until it was almost back to base. Suddenly however, it went into a dive and crashed; Macqueen, one of the Island's top-scorers at the time with eight victories, was killed.

The day saw several strafing and bombing attacks by Bf109s, Wellington DV605 being destroyed at Luqa, but on one occasion only did the defending fighters rise to contest them. At 1225 Flg.Off. Buchanan and Sgt. Hesselyn scrambled to provide cover for a returning PR Spitfire, which was being pursued by Italian fighters; the reconnaissance pilot evaded his attackers but crashed on landing, though escaping injury.

No sooner were the 249 Squadron duo airborne than they were warned of two low-flying Bf109s over Hal Far. Unable initially to find these, they then saw a pair — probably the same — being fired upon by AA over Grand Harbour. Catching up with one, Hesselyn opened fire for two seconds before his cannons jammed. The Messerschmitt dived steeply for Takali, and at first it appeared about to crash, but at the last moment it pulled up and flew off northwards. Hesselyn was credited with damaging the fighter, but as it sped away it passed over a bus full of Maltese, which was trundling down the Rabat-Takali road. Thinking they were about to be strafed, the passengers piled out of the bus, seeking cover. One man dived through a window, cracked his skull on the road, and died shortly afterwards from the resultant fracture.

Later in the afternoon a dozen Ju88s attacked Hal Far, where two Hurricanes were destroyed and two more damaged; AA gunners claimed damage to one of the raiders. With the passing of this raid arrived five Hurricane IICs, 229 Squadron's replacement aircraft from Gambut, led in by Flt.Lt. Connell; another would arrive the following evening, in the hands of Plt.Off. McHan. Plt.Off. Tom Lawrence, making his second ferry flight to the Island, noted:

> 'As we came in towards the coast another raid was in progress. However, our boys were up this time and covered us, otherwise we would have definitely had it. A dirty big 88 stooged over the top of me but I knew he wouldn't do anything about it. We all got in OK.'

Whilst these new machines briefly resurrected the Hurricane unit, their presence had little actual effect on the outcome of the present series of air battles being fought in the skies above Malta.

At this time an all-American flight was formed in 126 Squadron, headed by the newly-promoted Flt.Lt. Jimmy Peck. The unit's existing Americans — McLeod, Downs, Tilley and Booth — were joined by Almos from 249 Squadron and McHan from 1435 Flight.

Wednesday, 6 May

With the arrival of the new Hurricanes, Wednesday saw 229 Squadron once again operational, four of the unit's aircraft and four 603 Squadron Spitfires scrambling to intercept ten Ju88s and ten Bf109s at 0945; while two 126 Squadron Spitfires took off to provide airfield defence. The main interceptor force attacked the Junkers, Flt.Lt. Sanders, Plt.Off. Slade and Sgt. Webster of 603 Squadron, and Sqn.Ldr. Farnes of 229 Squadron each submitting claims for bombers damaged. Another Hurricane pilot, Flt.Sgt. David Roy (BM964), also attacked one of the bombers but his engine was hit by return fire and he made for Hal Far, where he crash-landed. The Hurricane collided with a stone-built torpedo store at the far end of the runway, causing large blocks of stone to fly into the air and crash down onto the aircraft. Fortunately for Roy the torpedoes had been removed to the safety of an underground store the night before, and he suffered only slight injuries. Not so lucky was Sgt. Bob Lees (BN181), who failed to return; he was seen to ditch five miles off Benghaisa Point, but when HSL 128 went out to pick him up, only wreckage could be found.

On 6 May Sgt. David Roy of 229 Squadron was obliged to force-land this Hurricane (BM964) at Hal Far, the aircraft skidding into the Royal Navy's torpedo store. *(F.J. Sherlock)*

Meanwhile, the two 126 Squadron Spitfires had been vectored to Hal Far to counter Messerschmitts which were overhead as the Hurricanes went in to land, Flt.Lt. Johnston and Plt.Off. Booth attacking four Bf109s. Johnston reported gaining strikes on one with one cannon only operating, then attacked another while Booth continued the attack on the first; this was last seen flying very slowly, making only gentle turns and was considered unlikely to have reached its base. As Johnston opened fire on another, three cannon shells struck his Spitfire (BR116/V) and it caught fire. It began vibrating violently and he either blacked-out or was knocked unconscious, recovering to find the cockpit full of flames. He managed to bale out and with his legs peppered with shell splinters, temporarily blinded by burns to his face and with severely burnt arms, he landed at Siggiewi, while his Spitfire crashed near Zebbug. He was immediately assisted by soldiers who came running to his aid, and was rushed to hospital.

About midday five Z1007bis and 15 Macchis came over, one fighter being damaged by AA fire, but no other opposition being met. Five Ju88s of KüFlGr 606 raided Hal Far, escorted by a dozen Bf109s and seven MC202s. Bombs also fell on Gozo, where the ferry boat *Royal Lady* was again hit; she broke in two in harbour at Mgarr. The steamship *Franco* was also rendered unseaworthy, one man being killed and three wounded by strafing. AA claimed one of the raiders — a Ju88 — damaged.

That night a BOAC Lodestar arrived from Egypt to inaugurate a new thrice-weekly service to the Island, which would be maintained until midsummer, bringing in vital spares and ammunition and ferrying out transit crews whose aircraft had been destroyed — or women and children waiting to be evacuated. On arrival, Capt. A.P.W. Cane was ordered to stand off 50 miles to the south as a raid was in progress. However, as the alert lasted all night, he was eventually ordered to land during an apparent lull in activity in the middle of it. The aircraft was turned around in 55 minutes, allowing it to get out of the danger zone by first light.

Thursday, 7 May

Italian Intelligence had picked up information that a further reinforcement of Spitfires was imminently due, but had got the day wrong! Hence, throughout the daylight hours of the 7th, pairs of MC202s patrolled off the coast of Malta to prevent the landing of new arrivals but, of course, nothing was to be seen. At 0945, a pair of 229 Squadron Hurricanes went out to search for a missing launch, but were recalled early as two Jabo Bf109s were reported attacking Kalafrana. These had, in fact, strafed and bombed a petrol storage barge (identified as *C-42*), which contained 30,000 gallons of fuel; the craft had been attacked several times in the past but had escaped damage. It was not to be so lucky on this occasion however, for at least one bomb struck home and a fire broke out. The Kalafrana ASR crews assisted in fighting the fire, but an explosion blew two firefighters into the sea — they were rescued with only minor burns. Eventually the fire was extinguished and more than 20,000 gallons of fuel were saved.

Towards evening another five Cants and 15 MC202s approached, more than 20 Bf109s also patrolling over the coast. Six Spitfires of 603 Squadron and eight Hurricanes, four of these flown by 185 Squadron pilots, took off to intercept. Only Sgt. Tweedale (Z2698/L) of the latter unit reported a successful engagement, claiming a Bf109 shot down at 1925.

During the hours of darkness eight raiders crossed the coast, bombs falling on Takali, Zonqor, Hal Far, Mosta and Gzira. Located in Gzira, as in many other areas, were a number of civilian garages and workshops where repairs to aircraft and equipment were carried out under the guidance of RAF technicians from Kalafrana. One such garage was 'Muscat's' where, on this night, a bomb scored a direct hit, extensively damaging the building; three airmen were killed and others injured. At 0800 the following morning, as airmen were clearing away the debris, an unnoticed delayed-action bomb exploded, causing much further damage and killing four of them, including a Maltese; one of the injured later died in hospital.

As a result of Mr Casey's recent visit, Flt.Lt. Stokes of 10 RAAF Squadron returned to the Island from Gibraltar. Sunderland W3993 alighted at Marsaxlokk Bay, carrying the new Governor, Lord Gort and his ADC. They arrived in the middle of a raid, a stick of bombs falling nearby as the party were ferried ashore, causing several of those assembled to meet them to take cover. Gort remained outwardly unmoved, as he continued to appear later when a bomb exploded only 40 yards away as he was being sworn in! His reaction, however, to being informed that Malta was unlikely to hold out for another six weeks, and that his first task might well be to sue for surrender, is not recorded!

Following the brief ceremony, General Dobbie, his wife and daughter — and eight other passengers — embarked on the Sunderland, and at 0315 Stokes taxied out for the return flight. He had difficulty in getting the flyingboat airborne, covering a good mile out to sea before it lifted into the air, after a run lasting two and a quarter minutes! Later, as the Sunderland neared Gibraltar, it overflew the convoy departing for Malta with the latest reinforcement of Spitfires. Within days of arriving in England, Dobbie, who had not enjoyed the best of health and who had been under severe strain and stress, was admitted to hospital for an appendicitis operation.

Friday, 8 May

After several days which had been much quieter than those of late April, Friday brought more activity. An early sortie at 0625 witnessed a single reconnaissance Ju88 and two escorting Bf109s over the coast, bombs falling at Zejtun. Two Spitfires of 126 Squadron intercepted; Plt.Off. Tilley engaged a Messerschmitt 30 miles north of the Island, and claimed to have shot it down. Two hours later six Ju88s of KGr 806 and 15 Ju87s of III/StG 3 with a large escort (including six MC202s from 97ª Squadriglia, 9° Gruppo CT, as close escort and eight 10° Gruppo Macchis as indirect cover) approached the Island, bombs falling at Hal Far, Kalafrana and Luqa, where a reservoir was damaged. In Kalafrana Bay the damaged petrol storage barge, *C-42*, had been moved to confuse further attempts at attack, the older lighter *Edith* replacing her. The ploy apparently succeeded, for now two Jabo Bf109s appeared and bombed *Edith*, one direct hit passing right through her and exploding in the water!

Seven 229 Squadron Hurricanes and four Spitfires flown by 126 Squadron pilots had taken off at 0900, followed by four more Hurricanes of 185 Squadron some 40 minutes later. The first formation made contact, Sgt. Potts of 229 Squadron claiming damage to a Ju88, whilst Plt.Off. Tilley and Plt.Off. Mejor jointly damaged a Bf109. Cap. Lucchini's flight of 10° Gruppo Macchis went to the aid of the Ju87s which were being pursued by five fighters identified as Spitfires, while Cap. Roberto Dagasso's 9° Gruppo fighters engaged others which were attacking the Ju88s. Ten. Luigi Giannella of 10° Gruppo claimed two Spitfires shot down and also reported seeing a German aircraft in difficulties, watching the pilot bale out into the sea near Pozzallo. Two more Spitfires were claimed shot down by Cap. Dagasso and Ten. Ado Bonuti.

The successful RAF pilots were actually those from the 185 Squadron flight which had taken off later; Sgt. Boyd (Z4942/Y) reported:

> 'I led our flight. We jumped six Ju88s out of the sun at 18,000 feet. I got one, both engines, etc. Mixed it with ten Macchi 202s; came down, mixed it with 109s at zero feet. Hit in engine by cannon, glycol tank blew up. Drenched me. Belly-landed Takali.'

There is little doubt that Boyd had shot down M7+KL of 3/KGr 806, flown by Uffz. Gerhard Andrea, which ditched near Pozzallo — possibly the aircraft seen by Giannella; Andrea and his crew were posted missing. Sgt. Wilbert Dodd, meanwhile, attacked a Macchi at 17,000 feet, five miles south of the Island, firing a three-second burst from 100 yards and seeing strikes all over it. He reported that it turned over and went straight down, and it was claimed as probably destroyed. His victim was probably Ten. Giovanni Barcaro, whose aircraft was hit by a 20mm shell; although wounded in the right arm, Barcaro succeeded in reaching his base.

The aggressive Sgt. Tweedale (GL-F) was also mixing it with the escorting fighters, having first attacked a Ju88 which he claimed probably destroyed; he may have attacked the same aircraft as Boyd. When the Messerschmitts intervened he reported shooting down one and probably a second. It seems likely that one of his victims was 'Black 3' of 8/JG 53 which crashed on Marsa racetrack, Uffz. Heinrich Becker baling out and landing safely, although it would seem that this aircraft was also claimed by AA gunners. The aerial battle was being watched by Flt.Lt. Barnham, who recorded that Bofors shells blew the tail off a Messerschmitt as it passed over low down, and it hit the ground "in a pillar of smoke near the brewery chimney". Possibly the gunners hit the fighter after it had been abandoned by Becker following Tweedale's attack. The fourth pilot of the flight, Sgt. Finlay, was attacked whilst approaching to land, being obliged to belly-land BD789 at Takali.

The AA gunners had also been having a successful day, and apart from claiming Becker's Messerschmitt, had shot down one of the Ju87s, S7+HN flown by Fw. Walter Obermailander falling into the sea two miles off St Paul's Bay; neither the pilot nor his gunner, Uffz. Albert Westphalen, survived.

The raiders were back at 1325. Five Ju88s, 18 Ju87s and eight Bf109s attacked Luqa and Takali, while Hal Far was bombed by five Cants, escorted by 16 Macchis. Only a dozen Hurricanes and six Spitfires remained serviceable, and as these were being preserved for the morrow, no fighters rose to intercept. At Takali about half a dozen 603 Squadron pilots were on the airfield. They took shelter in slit trenches, from where they shot at the dive-bombers with rifles. The gunner of one Ju87 put a bullet through Sqn.Ldr. Bisdee's hat without wounding him! Not so fortunate were two of 249 Squadron's pilots, Flt.Lt. Connell and Flg.Off. Buchanan, both of whom were caught in the open, Connell being wounded. On a brighter note, the day was marked by the announcement of the award of the DFC to Flg.Off. McNair, and DFMs to Sgt. Brennan and his close friend, Sgt. Hesselyn.

It was also on this date that two Bf109s of Stab/JG 53 were lost in circumstances which seem to link up with a favourite story emanating from Malta at this time. According to German records the two aircraft had collided, both pilots baling out safely near Agrigento (Sicily). However, 'Y' Service reports gave the RAF cause to believe that they may have been directly responsible, but in a most unlikely way! With the shortage of fighters on Malta, several 'spoofs' had been attempted by Grp.Capt. Woodhall and his fellow controllers, bogus and imaginary squadron radio call signs being interchanged with those of genuine formations, in an effort to confuse their German and Italian counterparts. On occasion, an imaginary formation would be ordered into the air, while a 'leader' whose voice would be well-known to the Axis radio intercept stations, would reply to orders issued from a ground station.

It was felt that these stratagems had on several occasions caused Axis fighter formations to be ordered to remain on high cover, rather than to come down and strafe. The prime example — and decidedly suspect! — would appear possibly to have occurred on this date, however, and Grp.Capt. Woodhall recalled:

> 'On one occasion all our fighter aircraft were grounded in order to try to increase serviceability. The Hun bombers came over in force with quite a large fighter escort. It happened there were several fighter pilots with me in the Operations Room, one of whom was a Canadian with an unmistakable voice. I put him at the microphone at a stand-by radio set and proceeded to give him dummy orders as if he was flying his fighter. This, we suspected, caused a cry of "Spitfeuer Achtung"! to go over the German radio. In any case, two 109s enthusiastically shot each other down without any British aircraft being airborne. This knowledge that the Germans intercepted our orders stood us in good stead. We claimed that Pilot Officer 'Humgufery' shot down the two Huns!'

That night three Hudsons arrived from Gibraltar and one BOAC Lodestar from Cairo, the latter flown by Capt. R.J.W. Barnett to bring in spares. All were quickly unloaded, refuelled and sent off, but as the Lodestar commenced its take-off run, one tyre was punctured by a bomb splinter; the aircraft swung off the runway, crashed and caught fire. Passengers and crew scrambled clear without injury, but the aircraft was a total loss.

Now, however, the arrival of the new Spitfires was imminent. *Wasp* had departed Gibraltar during the night of 7th/8th, with 50 such fighters embarked, she and her escorts now joined by *Eagle* (carrying a further 17 Spitfires) and by nine more destroyers, together forming Force 'W'. Aboard *Wasp* to oversee the operation was Wg.Cdr. McLean, while Sqn.Ldr. Grant and Flt.Lt. Ron West of 249 Squadron were to lead the first two flights; Flt.Lt. Lucas and Flg.Off. McNair of the same unit were on *Eagle* for similar duty, where Wg.Cdr. Stan Turner was in charge of operations. More than half the pilots aboard the two carriers were from Commonwealth countries, of whom at least 25 were members of the RCAF, including four Americans (see Table 7 below). The pilots embarked on *Eagle* were, in fact, a complete flight from 611 Squadron under the command of Flt.Lt. Winfield.

TABLE 7

Operation 'Bowery'

64 Spitfires from USS *Wasp* and HMS *Eagle*

Sqn.Ldr. S.B. Grant	sent to Gibraltar to lead formation — led in first 16 from *Wasp*
Flt.Lt. R. West	sent to Gib to lead formation from *Wasp*
Ft.Lt. P.B. Lucas	sent to Gib to lead flight from *Eagle*
Flg.Off. R.W. McNair	sent to Gib to lead flight from *Eagle*
Flt.Lt. J.P. Winfield	(611)
Flt.Lt. R.H.C. Sly, RAAF	
Flg.Off. R.A. Mitchell	
Flg.Off. J.R. Stoop	
Plt.Off. G.W. Northcott, RCAF	
Plt.Off. E.S. Dicks-Sherwood (Rhodesia)	
Plt.Off. A.S. Yates, RAAF	(611)
Plt.Off. R.H. Turlington	(611)
Plt.Off. W.J. Johnson	(611)
Plt.Off. R.O. Jones, RCAF (US)	(611)
Plt.Off. E.L. Hetherington	(611)
Plt.Off. J.W.P. Baril, RCAF	(611)
Plt.Off. A.R. Boyle	(611)
Plt.Off. J.A. Smith	BR126 X3 — landed back on *Wasp*
Plt.Off. N.R. Fowlow, RCAF	
Plt.Off. L.G. Barlow (Rhodesian)	
Plt.Off. R. Bairnsfather	
Plt.Off. F.J. Sherlock, RCAF	
Plt.Off. A.A. McNaughton, RCAF	
Plt.Off. C.A. King, RCAF	BR248
Plt.Off. D.W. Kent, RCAF	
Plt.Off. J.R. Halford	
Plt.Off. O.W.H. Berkeley-Hill	
Flt.Sgt. F.D. Schofield	
Flt.Sgt. T. Parks, RCAF	
Flt.Sgt. D.A. Bye	(611)
Flt.Sgt. H. Haggas	(611)
Flt.Sgt. B. Butler, RCAF	

TABLE 7 (Continued)

Flt.Sgt. J.W. Williams, RCAF	
Flt.Sgt. R.H. Brown	
Flt.Sgt. W.C. Conway, RNZAF	
Flt.Sgt. J.E. MacNamara, RCAF	
Flt.Sgt. G.H.T. Farquharson, RCAF	
Flt.Sgt. D.G. Reid, RCAF	
Flt.Sgt. L.A. Verroll, RNZAF	
Flt.Sgt. C.N. Valiquet, RCAF	failed to arrive Malta
Flt.Sgt. J.V. Rounsefell, RCAF	failed to arrive Malta
Sgt. R.D. Sherrington, RCAF	killed on take-off from *Wasp*
Sgt. W.R. Irwin, RAAF	
Sgt. D.E. Llewellyn	(611)
Sgt. C.A.M. Barbour	(611)
Sgt. C.E. Graysmark	BP871 (611)
Sgt. L.J. Morsheimer, RCAF	(611)
Sgt. J.W. Patterson	(611)
Sgt. F.R. Johnson, RAAF	(611)
Sgt. J.I. Williamson	
Sgt. K.R. Mitchell, RAAF	Sgt. G. Allen-Rowlandson
Sgt. C.S.G. De Nancrede, RCAF	Sgt. E.D. Moye, RCAF (US)
Sgt. J.C. Gilbert	Sgt. H.J. Fox, RCAF
Sgt. J.C. Gray	Sgt. V. Willie, RCAF
Sgt. K.J. Lusty	Sgt. M.W. Vineyard, RCAF (US)
Sgt. E.T. Brough, RNZAF	Sgt. Shepherd, RCAF
Sgt. E.J. Shaw, RNZAF	Sgt. Bell

NB: One flight of 16 pilots from 611 Squadron, as indicated.

Malta was ready for them this time. Wg.Cdr. Gracie had recently flown back to the Island from London, via Gibraltar. Acting as the AOC's ambassador, he had created such a stir in Whitehall that all demands for better organization were agreed to! On his return to Malta he advised the pilots at Takali of the imminent arrival of reinforcements, and emphasised that he wanted every Spitfire back in the air within 15 minutes of its arrival. That same evening all squadron and flight commanders had met at Mdina to be addressed by Air Vice-Marshal Lloyd and Grp.Capt. Woodhall. The AOC believed that if the aircraft arrived in moderately serviceable condition and in good daylight, it should be possible to turn them round in ten minutes. If this could be achieved, the damage inflicted which had so undermined Operation 'Calendar' could be avoided. Five men were to be allocated to each aircraft pen, plus an experienced pilot to take over the aircraft. Long-range tanks would be removed first, and each pen would contain all that was necessary to rearm and refuel the fighters, the fuel being kept in four-gallon cans protected by sandbags.

Slit trenches were available by every pen, both for the vital stores and for the ground crews. Further supplies and meals would be delivered by lorry to each pen by the Army. Every incoming Spitfire would have a large number/letter combination painted on its fuselage, and each pen had been allocated a specific aircraft so identified, which had to be led in regardless of the situation at the time. Whatever the rank of the new arrival, the Malta pilot in the pen was in command, and was to take over the aircraft at once and get it back into the air with all speed. If the aircraft happened to be damaged, it was to be taxied to repair pens at the rear. The pilot, if not wounded, was to return to the airfield to take over a more junior pilot's aircraft.

Every man due to be on the airfield — gunners, repairmen, debris removers — were all fully briefed. It now remained to be seen if the arrangements would work! In addition to Takali, both Luqa and Hal Far were to be used as landing grounds for the new arrivals. Hal Far was to be a new base for Spitfires, the small airfield only recently having been tested for its suitability to operate this type.

Operation 'Bowery': the 50 pilots selected to fly Spitfires to Malta from USS *Wasp* on the carrier's second sortie into the Mediterranean; six of those present here would not participate in this particular ferry trip for a variety of reasons. 17 more were despatched from HMS *Eagle*: Front row, l. to r: unknown, Plt.Off. J.A. Smith; unknown; Sgt. Willie; Flt.Sgt. D.G. Reid; Sgt. E.J. Shaw; Flt.Sgt. C.N. Valiquet; Sgt. Irwin; unknown; Flt.Sgt. T. Parks; unknown. Second row: unknown; Plt.Off. F.J. Sherlock; unknown; Plt.Off. G.W. Northcott; Flg.Off. J.R. Stoop; Flt.Lt. R.H.C. Sly; Wg.Cdr. Gomez, Engineer Officer; Flg.Off. R.A. Mitchell; Plt.Off. L.G. Barlow; Plt.Off. E.S. Dicks-Sherwood; Plt.Off. J.R. Halford. Third row: unknown; unknown; Sgt. K.R. Mitchell; Plt.Off. C.A. King; unknown; unknown; Plt.Off. A.A. McNaughton; unknown; Plt.Off. D.W. Kent; Plt.Off. N.R. Fowlow; unknown; unknown; Flt.Sgt. B.W. Andrews (did not go this time); Sgt. Shepherd; unknown. Back row: Sgt. C.S.G. De Nancrede; Flt.Sgt. J.W. Williams; Sgt. E.L. Mahar (did not go this time); Flt.Sgt. W.C. Conway; Flt.Sgt. G.H.T. Farquharson; Sgt. H.J. Fox; Flt.Sgt. J.V. Rounsefell; unknown; unknown; unknown; unknown; Sgt. Bell. *(National Archives, Washington)*

Saturday, 9 May

In the pre-dawn, *Wasp* launched 11 F4F Wildcats of her resident fighter squadron (VF-71) to provide Combat Air Patrol, Sqn.Ldr. Grant then taking off in the first Spitfire at 0643. On this occasion the launch was not to be quite so trouble-free. As Sgt. R.D. Sherrington took off — the twenty-third to go from *Wasp* — his aircraft failed to gain sufficient flying speed as the propeller had inadvertently been set in coarse pitch, and it dropped from the flight deck, the airscrew catching the bows as it did so, and crashed into the sea. At once the carrier passed over it, splitting the aircraft in two, and the Canadian pilot was killed.

Another Canadian, Plt.Off. J.A. Smith, got BR126/3-X into the air but found the pump in his long-range tank to be faulty. Against orders and to the

Operation 'Bowery'; Spitfire 3-M being prepared for take-off from USS *Wasp*, with HMS *Eagle* in the background. *(National Archives, Washington)*

After being launched from *Wasp* on 9 May, Plt.Off. Jerry Smith was obliged to return when his long-range fuel tank malfunctioned. He made a successful landing back aboard the carrier without the aid of an arrester hook. *(National Archives, Washington)*

amazement of the crew, Smith turned back and having waited for all aircraft to take-off, and for any unserviceable fighters to be cleared from the deck, he made an approach to land, only to be waved off by the DLO, Lt.Cdr. David McCampbell, as he was too high. He came round once again to make a second attempt and although he was approaching a little too fast, McCampbell waved him to cut the engine, which he did. The Spitfire bumped down on the deck and Smith applied full brakes, taking virtually the full length of the deck to stop; he eventually came to a halt some six feet from the bows!

Once aboard, Jerry Smith requested a replacement tank to be fitted to his aircraft, but was ordered instead to remain aboard and return with the carrier to Gibraltar. Although his performance was somewhat frowned upon by the British authorities, he was heartily congratulated by Lt.Cdr. McCampbell (later to become the US Navy's top-scoring fighter pilot of the war in the Pacific with 34 victories, and the award of the Medal of Honor). That evening Ensign C.H. Gates of VF-71 recorded:

> 'P/O Smith was given a cake and a pair of Navy Wings (my spare pair) by Doug Fairbanks Jr at dinner.'

All other Spitfires — 62 in total, of which 45 were from *Wasp* — got safely airborne, Sqn.Ldr. Grant leading the first 16 from *Wasp* to Takali, while Flt.Lt. R.H.C. Sly, RAAF, led the next batch to Hal Far. The third group from the big carrier went to Luqa led by Flt.Lt. West. Meanwhile, pilots of the two flights from *Eagle* were briefed to land at Luqa and Takali, respectively.

First enemy activity over Malta had occurred at 0720, when a reconnaissance Ju88 and five Bf109s crossed the coast, only the AA guns engaging them. When another Ju88, five Cants, 16 Macchis and up to 45 Messerschmitts appeared two hours later however, nine Hurricanes (six from Luqa and three from Hal Far) took off to provide some protection for the first batch of Spitfires, which were by then imminently due. They were followed by six Spitfires flown by 603 Squadron pilots, both formations seeking to provide maximum cover for Takali.

From near Pantelleria, Sqn.Ldr. Grant advised Malta of his flight's imminent arrival, and half an hour later the 16 fighters arrived over Takali. As the first of the new arrivals appeared, they went in to land at once, the Hurricanes endeavouring to hold the Messerschmitts at bay. As one Spitfire lowered its wheels and went in slow and straight, a Bf109 raced onto its tail, but Sqn.Ldr. Farnes of 229 Squadron was at once on to it, turning violently with it as it attempted to avoid his fire; he claimed some damage and succeeded in driving it away. One of his pilots, Plt.Off. Lawrence, wrote:

> 'I did not engage, but when I was coming into land I was strafed by Messerschmitts. On the point of landing, with wheels and flaps down, I was jumped by 109s. Controller called up other pilots to give me protection for I was helpless, but it was really too late, and the next thing I heard was the Controller let out a groan.
>
> 'Well I thought, I have had it; but I managed to race along to the end of the runway and turned the aircraft with my back to the sea (to take advantage of armour plating, as I knew they would be coming from that direction) and stopped with my head well down in the cockpit. There was a roar and a babble all round me, and I looked up and saw the Messerschmitt climbing for height. Well, I got out of that one alright.'

As the 603 Squadron formation climbed to the south of the Island, led by Flt.Lt. John Buckstone (BP872), they were attacked by Bf109s, and the leader's No 2, Flg.Off. Tony Holland (BR184), reported:

> 'As they passed us, we all fired at them, and John was either hit in their attack or, I think more likely, followed one down too far and too fast. I saw the 109 go into the water with a great dirty splash and John Buckstone's Spitfire hit the water seconds later with a big clean white splash.'

On the strength of Holland's report, a Messerschmitt was credited jointly to Buckstone, Plt.Off. Bert Mitchell and himself, while Flt.Lt. Sanders also claimed one shot down; only one was actually lost — 'Yellow 6' of 6/JG 53, flown by Uffz. Helmut Schierning — while Buckstone was probably shot down by Ofw. Rollwage, who claimed a Spitfire at 1105 south-east of Luqa. A further Messerschmitt was claimed by Takali Bofors gunners, who reported that it went over the airfield in a gentle glide at 500 feet and crashed into the sea a few hundred yards off St Paul's Bay.

All the first batch of Spitfires had got down safely, although harried by Bf109s; a few were refuelled and rearmed in four minutes, the last in seven minutes, with pilots strapped in the cockpits ready to scramble, including Wg.Cdr. Gracie. Of his flight and arrival at Malta, one of the new pilots, Flg.Off. Richard 'Mitch' Mitchell, recalled:

> 'Took off from *Wasp* at 0645 hrs. Landed at Takali at 1030 hrs. The formation leader flew too fast and got his navigation all to hell, so I left them 40 miles west of Bizerta, five miles off the North African coast, and set course for Malta, avoiding Pantelleria and Bizerta owing to fighters and flak being present there. Jettisoned the long-range tank 20 miles west of Bizerta with 20 gallons to spare in main tank. On landing at Takali, I immediately removed my kit, and the machine was rearmed and refuelled. I landed during a raid and four 109s tried to shoot me up. Soon after landing the airfield was bombed but without much damage being done.'

All was going well with the initial refuelling, and at 1055 eleven of the new Spitfires took off, now flown by 249 Squadron pilots and led by Sqn.Ldr. Grant, who had just arrived. The formation almost immediately encountered Messerschmitts, as Plt.Off. Nash (BR108/C-20) recorded:

> 'I was leading D'Arcy (Milburn), Almos and Linton, Sent to Hal Far to deal with 109 trouble. We bounced them at 3000 feet from 15,000 feet. Mine went into the sea off Hal Far. Formed up again and attacked by three 109s. One stuck around above us. Got up to him and gave short burst. Spun down, lots of black smoke, five miles east of Malta.'

Nash was credited with one confirmed and one probable, but Plt.Off. Harry 'D' Arcy' Milburn was shot down and killed as he attempted to land; jumped by four Bf109s at 1000 feet, his Spitfire (BP845) crashed in a field near Safi. Flg.Off. Buchanan engaged a Bf109 at 10,000 feet, five or six miles south-east of Kalafrana, claiming a probable when it dived away streaming glycol but then lost sight of it near the sea.

At 1115, Spitfires were again scrambled, 31 taking the air as more new arrivals approached the Island. Flt.Lt. Ron West, leading his flight to Luqa, attempted to formate on a patrol of Bf109s over Grand Harbour by mistake, a large piece being blown out of his fuselage as a result; he force-landed safely. At least 28 of the new arrivals were still in the air when AA bursts indicated another swarm of Bf109s — estimated at 40 strong — approaching at 12,000 feet, shepherding a dozen Ju88s and five Z1007bis. Their target was Hal Far, which disappeared under a cloud of dust and smoke; two civilians and three soldiers were killed, nine more men wounded, while the airfield was rendered unserviceable for several hours.

Just prior to the attack on Hal Far, Flt.Lt. Ray Sly, an experienced Australian who was due to take command of a flight of 185 Squadron, had landed safely when he saw others of his flight being attacked; he immediately attempted to take off again down-wind to go to their aid, his Spitfire (BR348) striking the top of a dispersal pen and blowing up. Sly was dragged alive from the wreck but died later the same afternoon. Amongst those struggling to avoid the Messerschmitts over Hal Far was Canadian Plt.Off. Johnny Sherlock, who recalled:

> 'As we neared Malta, and which we could see some distance away, we could hear lots of natter on the R/T and we knew the Jerries were waiting for us over the Island. We started a shallow dive some distance west of Malta... we could see Flak all over the Island and by now some of the pilots were yelling that they were out of petrol and were gliding in. In other words, anybody with any petrol was to get the hell out of their way and to cover them as they glided in. P/O Cy King and I were together and he called that he was out of gas and he dropped his wheels and flaps. An Me109, also with wheels and flaps down, flew in front of Cy and he lifted the nose of his plane, took a squirt, and continued to land. I had my wheels and flaps down and when I went around in the circuit I realised many of the planes in the circuit were not Spits.
>
> 'It seemed to me that there were as many Me109s in the circuit as there were Spits. Everybody was yelling: "Spit, break! Break! Watch out behind you! Break," and with that every Spit over the Island would break sharply and practically spin in. I imagine the German R/T was just as hectic. Two or three Spits were on the field or landing path at Hal Far (there was no runway other than a dirt strip and which was marked by flags and empty petrol cans as most of the field was bomb cratered and u/s).
>
> 'I recollect seeing a Spit which appeared to me to have landed, speed up and try to take off again, and then hit a pen and crash. An Me109 was shooting at me at the time and there was so much going on at the same time, your main concentration was to get down safely. Several Me109s were shooting up the field and anything that moved was a target... About the same time I saw another Spit touch down and saw puffs of dust running up to the Spit but a little off to one side. Two Me109s, going flat out, roared along the field, one of them obviously shooting at the Spit. The Spit slowed down but before it came to a stop, the pilot climbed out onto the wing and jumped off, falling ass over teakettle. The Spit came to a stop, swerving slightly, the engine stopping. The pilot had obviously chopped the switches. The pilot of this plane was Sgt. "Tex" Vineyard, a US citizen in the RCAF.
>
> '"Tex" had filled every space on his plane with bottles of Coca-Cola. After a few seconds "Tex", who was possibly thinking more about his Coke than the plane, started out to his plane with the intention of taxying it into the safety of his pen. He had proceeded only a short distance when a D/A

(delayed-action bomb) went off and "Tex", thinking another raid was in progress, scurried back to the pen. "Tex" waited a short time longer and then started out again when several D/As went off very close together. The plane and Coke were, however, finally retrieved intact.'

Only two of this latest batch of Spitfires failed to arrive, and were initially reported to be down in the sea near Lampedusa, where it was believed the pilots had ditched, having presumably exhausted their fuel. However, an Italian account appears to indicate more precisely what had become of Flt.Sgt. Charlie Valiquet, an experienced and aggressive pilot, and Flt.Sgt. John Rounsefell, both members of the RCAF. A Fiat RS14 floatplane of 170ª Squadriglia RM, flown by Sottoten. Luigi Arco, was reported to have been attacked while on patrol by two Spitfires, but was struck only by two bullets. Fire was returned by the dorsal gunner, Av.Sc. Arm. Piero Bonannini, who claimed to have hit one of the fighters, whereupon it collided with the other and both crashed into the sea; neither pilot survived.

Spitfire 3-K being refuelled and re-armed following its arrival from USS *Wasp* on 9 May. Note the use of hand-held petrol cans and primitive filter. *(P. Wigley)*

Throughout the rest of the day the Axis air forces returned repeatedly in an effort to catch the new arrivals on the ground. At 1315, some 15 Ju88s and 18 escorting Bf109s approached, making for Hal Far and Takali. At the latter airfield, AA splinters wounded seven people, but while two motor vehicles were damaged, no aircraft suffered on the ground. A strong formation of 24 Spitfires took off, ten flown by 126 Squadron pilots, eight by 249 Squadron and six by Hurricane pilots of 185 Squadron. In the ensuing scrap, Plt.Off. Graves and Plt.Off. Tilley of 126 Squadron each claimed Ju88s damaged, as did Sgt. Goldsmith:

Scrambled in new Spitfire (BP871). Jumped by 109s but evaded. Attacked Ju88 and left it with starboard engine smoking.'

The 249 Squadron formation could not reach the bombers in time before becoming engaged with the escorting fighters off Dingli, one of which Plt.Off. Nash claimed damaged:

> 'We were scrambled too late to catch the bombers. Saw two 109s below so bounced them. Only one cannon working.'

For the veterans of 185 Squadron, it was for most their first experience of Spitfires, as Phil Wigley recalled:

> 'Most of the pilots had never flown Spitfires before and it had been originally intended that they should not fly them immediately on operational flights. However, the few survivors of 185 were not prepared to accept this decision without protest, and an appeal to Air Vice-Marshal Lloyd soon reversed it — those without Spitfire experience had been shown the cockpit drills by Plt.Off. McKay, who had; the wrecked fuselage of one of the March contingent of Spitfires was used for this purpose.'

Although it was an understandable decision at the time — with the desperate circumstances prevailing — to allow Malta-experienced pilots the opportunity of flying the new machines into action, it would ultimately prove to be a tragically unwise one. Sgt. Tony Boyd (3-J) was one of the six chosen for this initial sortie:

> 'First trip in Spit. Two minutes after take-off was squirting at 88s. No claims. Got on well, wizard machine. Six of us covered remainder in landing at Takali.'

Plt.Off. Ron Noble did not fare quite so well in his first solo in BP980:

> 'Scramble. To cover other Spits landing. Ops said Me109s at 8000 feet but one jumped me at 3000 feet. Pierced side of cockpit with cannon shell and crashed on trying to land at Takali with no flaps, brakes or ASI. Aircraft written off — slight shrapnel wounds in leg and shoulder. He very nearly got me!'

A reconnaissance Ju88 with two Bf109s as escorts which appeared at 1530, caused four 249 Squadron Spitfires to be scrambled, but they did not engage, and patrolled instead off Sicily. As they departed, a dozen 603 Squadron aircraft took off at 1550, followed 30 minutes later by six of 185 Squadron's newly-received Spitfires. They were all up to intercept 18 Ju87s and 20 Bf109s, which approached to raid Luqa and Grand Harbour. Amongst the specific targets attacked by the Stukas was the HAA gun position at St Peter's, one mile from Fort Ricasoli. The attack was carried out by three dive-bombers, two bombs landing directly on No 4 gun causing nine casualties, four of which were fatal. The ammunition stacked around the gun pit was immediately set alight and started to explode, greatly endangering the lives of the wounded lying nearby. Wt.Off. Carmel Caruana, the Battery Sgt.Major, rushed to the scene and started rescuing the wounded, although bombs were still falling on the position, an act for which he was awarded the George Medal.

603 Squadron made initial contact with the raiders but became engaged with the escort, Flg.Off. Holland, Plt.Off. Bert Mitchell and Flt.Sgt. Hurst each claiming Bf109s damaged. The latter's Spitfire was shot up as he came in to land. The 185 Squadron machines then engaged the Ju87s over Grand Harbour, Flt.Lt. Keith Lawrence attacking one which Denis Barnham witnessed from the ground, reporting that it burst into flames and crashed into a field. Probables

were claimed by Plt.Off. Wigley (BR306) and Plt.Off. Ernie Broad (BR294), who also claimed a second damaged, before he was attacked by a Messerschmitt. Reported Tony Boyd:

> 'Six of 185 Squadron set off late. Fired at two Ju87s and one 109, windscreen oiled up. Covered the others again while they landed. Pretty hot time. Lost Sgt. Tweedale. No claims.'

The Squadron had indeed lost Flt.Sgt. Gordon Tweedale, the successful Australian pilot being shot down in BR248 — probably by Lt. Beckmann of Stab III/JG 53, claimed as a Hurricane for his seventh victory. The Spitfire crashed in St Saviour Street, Lija, killing both the pilot and a Maltese soldier, Gunner Seraphim Cauchi. One of the new arrivals, Plt.Off. Cy King, recalled briefly meeting Tweedale, who had been allocated his aircraft:

> 'Tweedale and I stayed in or close to the dispersal pen and I gave him all the "gen" I could on the Spitfire, as all his time had been on Hurricanes. Going over how it handled on the ground, in the air, controls, critical speeds, cockpit drills, everything, getting him to sit in the cockpit while I sat beside him on the wing, then I would get in and show him, as he watched... about 2.30 or 3 all the serviceable Spits were scrambled and Tweedale took off... There were many enemy planes all over the Island, the object to destroy as many of the new arrivals as possible, as was done in April.
>
> 'After a time the Hal Far aircraft began to come back and land in ones and twos and taxied to the widespread dispersal pens. Tweedale did not appear. I waited a long time at the pen with the airmen but no more aircraft landed... So within hours of arriving off the *Wasp*, my aircraft, and the personable Aussie who flew it, were gone.'

Returning from the sortie to Sicily, the 249 Squadron quartet met the Stukas over Grand Harbour as they headed home, Plt.Off. Nash (BR108/C-20) claiming a probable:

> 'Chased recco 88 but unable to find him even over Sicilian coast. Stuck around at 27,000 feet for big raid. Bounced 87s over Grand Harbour. Only one cannon (*working*) again. He went on his back belching black smoke.'

Shortly after the 603 Squadron aircraft had landed, and were being refuelled, some six Ju88s swooped on Takali. Pilots leapt from cockpits and headed for slit trenches; one large bomb exploded 20 feet from one trench crammed with pilots and groundcrew, but no one was hurt, although two Spitfires were riddled with shrapnel. Sgt. Brennan of 249 Squadron twice tried to take-off between raids, but was prevented on the first occasion by a flat tyre, just reaching a trench before the bombs fell. On the second occasion, he was fully strapped in as the Ju88s appeared. He ripped off his straps although in the panic forgot the dinghy cord, which jerked him back and for a few seconds had him suspended on the wingroot of the Spitfire! Once more, he just reached cover before the first bombs exploded. At Luqa another unserviceable Wellington had been burnt out and a Spitfire damaged, but aircraft losses on the ground remained low.

It was now the turn of the Regia Aeronautica, and at 1745 the usual formation of five Z1007bis approached — aircraft of 210ª Squadriglia BT on this occasion — escorted by 16 Macchis, eight from each Gruppo. To meet this threat, 33 Spitfires were scrambled, and 11 of these from 126 Squadron intercepted, led by

Sqn.Ldr. Barton; Barton's single section engaged the escort while Plt.Off. Graves led the rest to attack the bombers. Three Cants were claimed shot down, two by Flt.Sgt. Schade and one by Sgt. Goldsmith, who noted:

> 'Attacked one Cant, leaving him ablaze with pieces falling off.'

Schade also claimed a Macchi damaged, as did Barton and Graves, while Plt.Off. Bisley — recently returned to operations on recovery from his wounds — claimed one shot down. On this occasion enthusiasm seems to have overcome the Spitfire pilots, for only a single Cant was hit. Although badly damaged, it did return, one member of Serg. Giovanni Dal Ponte's crew being killed and two slightly wounded. One of the latter was the dorsal gunner, Av.Sc.Arm. Francesco Melpignano, who claimed one fighter — identified as a 'P-40' — shot down and one probable. The Macchis also all returned, although Ten. Luigi Giannella's aircraft had been hit by a 20mm shell. The Italian pilots were no less optimistic in their claims, Cap. Lucchini, Serg. Ambrogio Rusconi and Serg. Teresio Martinoli all claiming Spitfires shot down, while Magg. Larismont Pergameni claimed one damaged; in fact all Spitfires returned undamaged! Over Takali a lone Messerschmitt was seen circling, obviously seeking a returning Spitfire, and this was attacked and shot-up by Flg.Off. Holland of 603 Squadron.

The last raid of the day occurred during the evening when seven Ju88s and a dozen Bf109s attacked Takali from 1840 onwards. Nine Spitfires of 601 Squadron, eight of 603 Squadron and three of 249 Squadron had all been ordered into the air towards the end of the previous Italian raid, and were still up, several of these making contact with the escorting Messerschmitts. Plt.Off. Max Briggs of 601 claimed a Bf109 shot down as it was strafing, and Plt.Off. Scott another damaged. Similiar claims were submitted by 603 Squadron, with Flt.Lt. Douglas claiming one shot down, and Plt.Off. Slade one damaged. Only one of the bombers was successfully attacked, 601's Plt.Off. Sewell and Sgt. Howard gaining strikes before being forced away.

The day had been almost the success planned for. A total of 61 Spitfires had arrived safely, although of the three aircraft lost during the operation, all the pilots had been killed; in addition, the experienced Flt.Lt. Sly had been killed soon after arrival. In the frantic fighting over the Island during the day, four more had been lost and one damaged in combat, with the loss of three further pilots; and six aircraft had been damaged to some extent on the ground. Nonetheless, with the remaining Spitfires already on the Island, nightfall saw the defenders with at least 50 undamaged aircraft to hand, with another dozen or so repairable, together with the available Hurricanes; the defences had never been in better shape.

The confusion of the fighting had led, however, to some of the greatest overclaiming yet; defending fighter pilots' claims had totalled ten destroyed, five probables and 14 damaged, with the gunners adding claims for another two Ju88s and two Bf109s damaged. Axis losses, despite eyewitness reports to the contrary, appear to have amounted to a single Bf109, with one Z1007bis and one MC202 damaged, causing Phil Wigley to comment:

> 'Some unintentional overclaiming by the RAF and artillery was inevitable in the heat of battle. However, it seems inconceivable that, according to German records, large numbers of Ju88s and the more vulnerable Ju87s could attack Malta from dawn to dusk and be opposed by experienced pilots

in cannon-armed fighters, and by well-practised artillery, without a single Ju88 or Ju87 sustaining any damage, let alone being shot down!!

'This is really straining credibility too far and one feels that the German records may be incomplete in this instance.'

With nightfall 15 raiders approached singly between 0040 and 0150, bombs falling on Luqa and Kalafrana. A Beaufighter of the 89 Squadron detachment, crewed by Flt.Lt. Coleman and Sgt. Peasley, was vectored onto one of the intruders, identified as a BR20. This was claimed probably destroyed, while AA gunners believed they probably shot down a Ju88. Again no Axis losses were recorded, although an ASV-equipped Special Duties Flight Wellington VIII (Z8712), out on a shipping search in the area between southern Sicily and Cape Bon, failed to return; Sqn.Ldr. J.E. Gorringe-Smith and his crew were reported missing.

As a back-up to the successful delivery of the Spitfires, the fast minelayer-cruiser *Welshman* had made an unescorted run from Gibraltar, and crept into harbour at 0525 on the 10th, carrying quantities of AA ammunition, smoke-making cannisters, aero engines, powdered milk, canned meat and dehydrated foodstuffs, as well as 100 RAF technicians to aid in servicing the additional fighters now to hand.

An inquest on Operation 'Bowery' held on the Island considered that the new arrivals did not contain sufficient flight leaders and experienced pilots; in fact, there were only two officers of Flight Lieutenant rank included — Flt.Lts. Phil Winfield and Ray Sly — one of whom (Sly) had already been killed. More than half the new arrivals were NCOs, and many of the others were newly-commissioned Pilot Officers. It was agreed that briefing aboard *Wasp* had not been thorough — pilots did not know the names of others in their sections, and had very little instruction on methods of joining up and flying to Malta. Many did not know the names of the Malta airfields and had no maps of the Island; one section leader had taken his formation to the North African coast before setting course, then followed the coastline towards Malta. Indeed, Flt.Lt. Barnham recorded that he was given the job of interviewing many of the new pilots, the intention being that all with 50 hours or less of operational flying experience should be sent straight back to the United Kingdom, and it does appear that a number of pilots may indeed have been disposed of in this way.

Certainly 611 Squadron recorded that in early July Sgts. L.J. Morsheimer and J.W. Patterson were returned to the squadron as their experience was considered insufficient for conditions on Malta. It was also noted with some acerbity that Plt.Off. J.A.W. Gunn, who had reached Gibraltar in readiness for the flight to Malta, was considered so inexperienced that he was returned forthwith, rejoining the Squadron later in June. "He was not thought capable of facing Messerschmitts over Malta, although he is expected to fight Focke-Wulfs over Europe!" was the irritated comment. However reasonable this response may have seemed,the unit was not aware of the conditions over the Island.

Nonetheless, Prime Minister Churchill was jubilant and cabled his appreciation to the US President, exulting:

'Who says a Wasp can't sting twice?'

No doubt on this occasion the PM can be forgiven the mis-quote in his relief and delight, for it is a bee which cannot sting twice!

Chapter Five

SPRING ATTRITION

On Sunday, 10 May the defenders were ready for the Axis raiders as never before. *Welshman* had delivered smoke canisters, and for the first time a smoke screen was laid over Grand Harbour. Two early morning reconnaissance flights caused Spitfires to be scrambled, during which Plt.Off. Plagis (3-N) of 249 Squadron claimed damage to a Messerschmitt. However, it was 1020 before a major raid approached, some 20 Ju87s and ten Ju88s making for Valetta to attack *Welshman* under a heavy fighter escort. The smoke screen operated and no bombs hit the vessel, but meanwhile 37 Spitfires and 13 Hurricanes had scrambled — an unprecedented reception!

First off at 1040 were 11 Spitfires of 601 Squadron and nine of 126, Flt.Lt. Peck's section of four from the latter unit breaking away to patrol off the Sicilian coast to await returning stragglers. With Sqn.Ldr. Bisdee called away to Valetta, and Flt.Lt. Parry in hospital with 'Malta Dog', Flt.Lt. Barnham was to lead 601 Squadron, but at the last moment he too succumbed to a bout of the 'Dog', so he asked Plt.Off. Briggs to lead instead. This initial force of 20 Spitfires was followed at 1048 by eight pilots of 185 Squadron, newly-mounted on Spitfires, and five minutes later by seven more of 603 Squadron and five of 249 Squadron.

Reports of the hectic action which then developed were illuminating, as 2/Lt. Archie Bartleman (4-A) recalled:

> '601 scrambled and ordered to get to about 30,000 feet into sun — unable to reach this height before raid arrived; on about same level as about 40 Ju87s as

Several pilots of III/JG 53 gained successes during the 10-14 May period. (a) Hpt. Wolf-Dietrich Wilcke, the Gruppenkommandeur, (**top right**) claimed his 38th on 12th. (b) Lt. Jürgen Harder (**opposite page**) was Wilcke's wingman; (c) Lt. Karl-Heinz Quaritsch (**top left**) was one of the unit's most successful pilots over Malta with five claims; (d) Lt. Wolf Schaller (left) and Lt. Hermann Munzert (**above**) with a Bf109F and an Italian officer. *(via J. Prien/W. Bock)*

> they reached the Island. Attacked from abeam — bombs jettisoned and formation broke up. Selected one and fired from about 200-300 yards and closing. No return fire; black smoke seen and it went down vertically. Onto tail of second 87 — again black smoke and it went spinning down; attacked a third and saw pieces fly off, and it fell away.'

As the 249 Squadron flight climbed steeply, they were attacked by Bf109s over Filfla; Flg.Off. Buchanan's section attempted to hold these off while the others went after the Ju87s over Grand Harbour, diving through the AA barrage to get at them. Plt.Off. Peter Nash (BR108/C-20) also claimed two:

> 'Terrific party over Grand Harbour. All the 87s missed the target (two cruisers). Everyone got something. The Stukas stuck! Starboard wing came off one, the other disappeared into smoke screen at 200 feet!'

Sgt. Paul Brennan (3-U):

> '87 attacked — he literally flew apart... his radiator fell off, the air scoop broke away, the pilot's hood whirled off in one piece, and bits of the fuselage scattered in every direction — into the sea off Grand Harbour. Confirmed; another damaged; another 109 and 87 attacked — no results.'

Plt.Off. Johnny Plagis (3-N) claimed a further Stuka shot down north-east of Grand Harbour but had initially experienced difficulty in finding a suitable target:

> 'Flew seven miles out to sea to find Ju87 which didn't have Spit on its tail.'

603 Squadron's commander, Sqn.Ldr. Lord Douglas-Hamilton, did not enjoy quite the same success:

> 'An almost solid cone of AA bursts rose over the harbour. From ground level to about 7000 feet. Into this the Huns were diving. Into it, too, the Spitfires dived, chasing the Huns. It never occurred to any of us that we might just as easily get hurt. In fact, it was with some irritation that I watched an 87 I was making for in front of me blown to pieces by a direct hit.'

He then closed on a Bf109 only to have all his four cannons jam, these remaining so when he subsequently attempted to attack a Ju87. As he approached to land, a Bf109 attacked him from astern but failed to hit his aircraft.

Sgt. Tony Boyd (BR350/3-J) of 185 Squadron also had an exciting time:

> 'Most terrific air battle ever seen here — astounding — plus an appalling barrage. There were about 25 Spits, eight Hurris, 30 Stukas, 15 Ju88s, 20 109s all mixed up in one enormous milling fight. 30 e/a destroyed or damaged in this raid. We lost one Spit. I got 88 probable, 88 damaged. First at 2000-3000 feet over Grand Harbour in five-second burst, 300-200 yards on 88, and large explosion rear of cabin — black smoke poured out and (*he*) nosed down in shallow dive three miles north of Grand Harbour.'

Plt.Off. McKay (BR306) of 185 Squadron, following a successful attack on the Ju88s, commented:

> 'Four cannons certainly blow hell out of an aeroplane!'

Frustratingly for him, Sgt. Hesselyn of 249 Squadron had suffered a flat tyre as he attempted to take off, and was obliged to watch the action from the ground:

> 'The Hun was getting a hiding. I counted 12 opened parachutes drifting towards the sea. They were floating down lazily, presenting a curious contrast to the diving, twisting and turning aircraft. I watched two 109s crash, one by St Paul's Bay, the second at Naxxar. The latter burst into flames as it hit the ground.'

His exuberance was somewhat stifled when it was later realised that the parachutes seen did not actually carry unfortunate German aircrew but parachute mines, released by the Ju88s!

The losses in this action were not confined to the raiders, for Plt.Off. Briggs of 601 Squadron was shot down into the sea in BR282, and killed, while Sgt. Dickson of this unit survived an extraordinary experience. His aircraft (BP960) was hit by an AA shell over Grand Harbour and blown in half. The pilot's seat straps snapped and Dickson was thrown through the perspex hood; nonetheless, he managed to pull his ripcord and fell into the sea about a mile offshore in Marsamxett Harbour.

Rescue was soon on the way to the downed pilot, whose leg had been badly gashed as he was blown out of his aircraft. Despite the presence of many enemy fighters in the vicinity, three small boats put out to pick him up, one crewed by brothers Emanuel and Vincent Nappa, another by Joseph Camenzuli; but it was that manned by Gunner Joseph Azzopardi of the RMA and Tony Saliba, which reached the wounded pilot first. On gaining the shore, Dickson was placed on a makeshift stretcher — a broken door — and carried to an ambulance amidst cheers from the local populace, many of whom had witnessed the whole incident.

Meanwhile, Flt.Lt. Jimmy Peck's 126 Squadron section off the Sicilian coast had also achieved success, engaging a number of Bf109s; Sgt. Tim Goldsmith (BP871) recalled:

> 'Four of us jumped two 109s, but had cannon trouble. I fired 20 rounds at one, saw strikes on wing and fuselage. He dived away. Confirmed as destroyed.'

As the section returned to Malta, Ju87s were engaged and Peck was able to claim one shot down and one damaged.

When the smoke and dust had settled, and the pilots' claims analysed, Malta's claims were put at:

	126 Squadron (4:3:6)
Flt.Lt. Peck	one Ju87 destroyed, one Ju87 damaged, one Bf109 damaged
Plt.Off. Tilley	one Bf109 damaged
Flt.Sgt. Milner	one Bf109 probable
Sgt. Goldsmith	one Bf109 destroyed
Flt.Sgt. Schade	one Ju88 destroyed
Sqn.Ldr. Barton	one Bf109 probable
Plt.Off. Bailey	one Ju87 destroyed, one Ju88 damaged
Plt.Off. Graves	one Ju88 probable, one Ju87 damaged
Flt.Sgt. Cleveland	one Bf109 damaged

	185 Squadron (4:1:2)
Sgt. Boyd	one Ju88 probable, one Ju88 damaged
Flt.Sgt. Dodd	one Ju87 destroyed
Flt.Lt. Lawrence	one Ju88 destroyed
Plt.Off. Broad	one Ju88 destroyed
Plt.Off. McKay	one Ju88 destroyed, one Ju88 damaged
	249 Squadron (4:1:2)
Plt.Off. Nash	one Ju87 destroyed, one Ju87 probable (later upgraded)
Sgt. Brennan	one Ju87 destroyed, one Ju87 damaged
Flg.Off. Buchanan	one Ju87 damaged
Flt.Lt. Lee	one Ju87 probable
Plt.Off. Plagis	one Ju87 destroyed
	601 Squadron (1:2:2)
2/Lt. Bartleman	two Ju87s probable, one Ju87 damaged
Sgt. McConnell	one Ju87 destroyed, one Ju88 damaged
	603 Squadron (1:1:6)
Flt.Lt. Douglas	one Ju87 probable, one Ju87 damaged
Flt.Sgt. Hurst	one Ju87 destroyed, one Ju87 damaged
Flg.Off. Holland	three Bf109s damaged
Plt.Off. Mejor	one Ju88 damaged

Holland and Hurst each had their aircraft slightly damaged by AA shrapnel as they entered the barrage over Grand Harbour. Additionally, the AA defences claimed a Ju87 and a Bf109 destroyed, while Royal Marine gunners also claimed a Stuka shot down to give total claims for the raid of: 17 destroyed, eight probables and 18 damaged.

Ofw. Herbert Rollwage of II/JG 53 reported shooting down a Spitfire just south of Valetta, while observers on the ground reported seeing a Stuka apparently shoot down a Spitfire, the pilot of which was intent on shooting down another of the dive-bombers.

After a minor alert at midday, the Luftwaffe returned at 1400, seven Ju88s covered by at least 30 Bf109s again raiding *Welshman* — and again missing the target. Twenty Spitfires (ten/126, eight/249 and two/601) were scrambled, accompanied by six Hurricanes, but only the 249 Squadron pilots reported decisive engagements. Sqn.Ldr. Grant claimed one bomber shot down in flames, while Flg.Off. Buchanan and Plt.Off. Watts added two more as probables. Sgt. Hesselyn dived on the Ju88s and had just selected a target, when a cannon shell burst in the cockpit of his Spitfire. Splinters tore his helmet, while another shell struck the port wing root. At that moment a Messerschmitt overshot him — probably his attacker — and he fired at this from 20 yards:

> 'My shells struck first on his starboard wing and, as he flew across my line of fire, travelled right across his cockpit and then crashed into his port wing. Pieces flew off him in all directions. He seemed to be cut in half. His machine literally collapsed and went down in bits of varying sizes.'

Despite this graphic description, there were no witnesses and Hesselyn was credited only with a probable. However, it seems likely that his victim was

'Yellow 3' of II/JG 53, from which Lt.Dr. Jorg Heiner baled out into the sea; a launch set out to pick him up and he was rescued unhurt. Two Hurricanes were also slightly damaged in this combat, and it is probable that these and Hesselyn's Spitfire were the three aircraft claimed by three pilots of III Gruppe — Lts. Müller, Quaritsch and Schaller. AA gunners also claimed one Ju88 — possibly the same aircraft as attacked by Sqn.Ldr. Grant.

As evening approached, another raid began to build up on the radar screens, and at 1740 nine 601 and one 126 Squadron aircraft were sent up in readiness. This time it was the turn of the Italians — five Z1007bis from 50° Gruppo BT, heavily escorted by 20 MC202s of 4° Stormo CT and ten Re2001s of 2° Gruppo, approaching at 1810, followed by about 20 Ju87s of III/StG 3 with a large escort of Messerschmitts. More Spitfires were scrambled — seven of 185 Squadron at 1815, eight of 249 Squadron and ten of 603 Squadron at 1835, and then seven of 126 Squadron 15 minutes later, while six Hurricanes were sent up to provide cover for the airfields and returning Spitfires.

The original sections on patrol engaged the Italian formation, Sqn.Ldr. Bisdee leading 601 Squadron against the bombers and attacking Ten. Domenico Robillotta's 211ª Squadriglia Z1007bis (MM23417) which blew up, the wreckage crashing into a field near Kalkara; three of the crew were killed and one injured in the crash, whilst a fifth was seen to bale out and fall into Grand Harbour when his parachute failed to open properly. Sgt. Fernando Farfan (from Trinidad) claimed a second bomber probably destroyed, and Sgt. Innes damaged a third; MM23400 was hard hit and landed at Gela with two members of the crew wounded, one later dying in hospital. Plt.Off. Caldwell (4-H) engaged one of the escort and shot down the Macchi flown by Cap. Roberto Dagasso, commander of 97ª Squadriglia, who was killed.

In return, the Italian fighter pilots claimed six fighters shot down, as well as a Beaufighter, together with two probables and two damaged. Pilots of 4° Stormo claimed three, one by Serg. Teresio Martinoli, another by Ten. Mario Massa (strangely identified as a Defiant), the third jointly by the missing Dagasso, Ten. Emanuele Annoni, Sottoten. Leo Boselli and Serg.Magg. Massimo Salvatore; 2° Gruppo pilots claimed the remainder. Ten. Remo Cazzolli and Mar. Olindo Simionato each claimed one, while a third was shared by Cap. Roberto Fassi and Mar. Antonio Patriarca, the latter also claiming a probable; Ten. Carlo Seganti claimed the Beaufighter — possibly a transit aircraft encountered over the sea — while two Spitfires were reported damaged by Cap. Salvatore Teia and Serg. Giuseppe Baraldi, and another pilot was awarded a probable.

The Spitfires which were scrambled as the raid approached all intercepted the German aircraft in the second wave, claiming between them a Ju87 and two Bf109s shot down, one Ju87 and three Bf109s probable, and six damaged — three of each type. Flg.Off. Mitchell of 603 Squadron recalled:

> 'The CO dived down into the barrage and I followed close on him... I spotted a Ju87 climbing out of the fringe of the barrage and I turned and chased him. I gave him a one-second burst of cannon and he broke off sharply to the left. At that moment another Ju87 came up in front of my nose and I turned into him and let him have it. His engine started to pour out black smoke and he started weaving. I kept the tit pushed hard, and after a further two or three second burst with one cannon I had left, the other being jammed, he heeled over at 1500 feet.'

This Stuka crashed in flames at Senglea and was almost certainly S7+FM of 7/StG 3. Mitchell was then attacked from astern but managed to turn into his assailant, but saw another Messerschmitt ahead; he opened fire and saw black smoke from its engine before running out of ammunition. Two more then attacked him, but he evaded these and landed safely.

One of the last to take-off was 126 Squadron's Sgt. Tim Goldsmith (BP877):

> 'Was orbiting Luqa at approx 8000 feet when two Me109s approached from the north at about the same height, going south. I engaged the second one attacking from the beam to quarter, giving three seconds burst at range 200-150 yards; saw strikes on fuselage. He dived south towards the sea, smoking. I did not see him reappear. This engagement was watched from Luqa by Plt.Off. Bisley and Sgt. Graysmark of 126 Squadron, who both saw a lot of black smoke from the e/a as it disappeared behind the cliffs. It was not seen to reappear.
>
> 'Later engaged one Me109 about eight miles north of St Paul's Bay, same height, head-on from underneath. Fired about six seconds, closing to about 20 feet. Saw many strikes on bottom of fuselage. He dived straight into the sea. No parachute seen.'

However, although it seems that Goldsmith's victim was almost certainly 'White 7' of II/JG 53 flown by Uffz. Erhard Ritterbusch, Luftwaffe records indicate that the loss of this aircraft was caused by a collision with that flown by Lt. Herbert Langer. It seems likely that Ritterbusch's aircraft had been damaged by Goldsmith and had then collided with the other. In the event, both pilots survived, Ritterbusch picked up from the sea at 1945 by HSL 128, which had been sent out to locate a pilot reported down three miles south of Kalafrana. Meanwhile, Langer succeeded in flying his damaged machine back to Comiso, where it crashed on landing and was totally destroyed.

Messerschmitt Bf109Fs of II/JG 53 lined up at Comiso. *(Dr Felix Sauer)*

The only loss suffered by the defenders was BR348 of 603 Squadron, shot down as Plt.Off. Mejor came in to land; he was able to bale out unhurt, and probably fell victim to Ofw. Rollwage of II/JG 53, who claimed his second Spitfire of the day at 1904, south of Valetta.

Apart from those credited to Mitchell and Goldsmith, other claims for this raid were two Bf109s damaged by Plt.Off. Broad and Flt.Sgt. Dodd of 185 Squadron, while for 249 Squadron Plt.Off. Hetherington claimed a Bf109 probable, Plt.Off. Watts one confirmed, and Flt.Lt. West one damaged; Flt.Sgt. Milner of 126 Squadron also claimed one probable Bf109, and Plt.Off. Tilley a Ju87 damaged.

With the end of the day's fighting, a list of preliminary claims for the whole day was drawn up, with the following assessment:

	By fighters	By AA gunners	
Ju87	9: 7: 8	5: 0: 0	
Ju88	3: 4: 3	1: 0: 0	
Bf109	2: 8: 9	1: 0: 1	(including one damaged by rifle fire)
Z1007bis	1: 1: 1		
MC202	1: 0: 0		
	16:20:21	7: 0: 1	

It appears, however, that two 'probable' Bf109s and two 'probable' Ju88s were subsequently upgraded to 'confirmed'. One RAF pilot was reputed to have remarked:

> 'The sea between Malta and Sicily was so full of rubber dinghies and shot down aircraft that it looked like Henley on Regatta Day!'

This had been a serious, meaningful defence — no longer a token effort — and indeed 10 May can justifiably be claimed to have been the turning point. Undeniably there were many months of hard fighting still to come, but never again would the defenders be reduced to mere handfuls of fighters, capable only of 'showing the flag'. How serious had the Axis losses been, therefore? Was it a setback for them? There can be little doubt that the losses had far exceeded anything actually experienced over the Island so far in 1942. However, it would certainly appear that the fighters and gunners had again double-claimed in some cases — particularly against the Stukas — but that being said, Axis losses were on this occasion not so far from those claimed. As has been seen, the Regia Aeronautica's casualties fitted the claims almost to an exactitude; Luftwaffe losses were:-

			I/KG 54
I/KG 54	Ju88	B3+JH	Ditched about 200 miles east of Gozo; rear gunner (Uffz. Georg Hero) lost, other three rescued by Axis ASR
2/KG 54	Ju88	B3+GH	Lt. Johannes Warkalla and crew missing; two seen to bale out reported shot down by AA
2/KG 54	Ju88		65% damaged by fighters
			KGr 806
I/KGr 806	Ju88	M7+DL	Lt. Helmut Kissling and crew missing
2/KGr 806	Ju88	M7+KK	Lt. Anton Schweinsteiger and crew missing

			III/StG 3
7/StG 3	Ju87	S7+GN	Uffz. Gerhard Nicolai/Uffz. Walter Kern shot down one mile north of Valetta; both killed
7/StG 3	Ju87	S7+FM	Uffz. Walter Rastinnes/Uffz. Walter Rauer, shot down north-east of Valetta, crashed at Senglea; both POWs
8/StG 3	Ju87	S7+EM	Uffz. Christian Apmann/Uffz. Heinrich Schäfer, shot down one mile north of Valetta; both killed
8/StG 3	Ju87		Shot down into sea by fighters; crew rescued by Axis ASR craft
			II/JG 53
	Bf109	'Yellow 3'	Lt. Dr. Jorg Heiner, POW
	Bf109	'White 7'	Uffz. Erhard Ritterbusch, POW; reported collided in mid air north of Valetta with Lt. Langer
	Bf109		Lt. Herbert Langer wounded/injured; crashed on return — aircraft totally destroyed; reported collided with Uffz. Ritterbusch

Monday, 11 May

The reduction in aerial activity on Monday was noticeable. Italian fighters were out early, looking for survivors from the previous day's missing aircraft, 4° Stormo MC202s twice escorting Z506B ASR floatplanes without success.

First over Malta at 0725 was a reconnaissance Ju88 with fighter escort. Four Spitfires of 249 Squadron scrambled, but Sgt. Brennan at once force-landed at Luqa with a faulty engine while the remaining three pursued the intruder back towards Sicily. On approaching the coast, eight Re2001s of 2° Gruppo CT (incorrectly identified by the Spitfire pilots as MC202s) were encountered, and one of these was attacked by Plt.Off. Plagis; he reported that it dived into the sea whilst taking evasive action, but no losses were actually suffered by the Italian flight. One of the latter claimed hits on Plagis' Spitfire (3-N), but although his aircraft was not damaged the Rhodesian was fortunate to get back safely; he landed with just three gallons of fuel left.

Up to 15 Ju88s and about 40 Bf109s approached just before 1030 and 23 Spitfires were scrambled, including eight from 249 Squadron and six from 126 Squadron. The 249 Squadron flight was vectored onto a section of three bombers south-east of Kalafrana Bay, but as Plt.Off. Plagis and Flt.Sgt. Williams dived on one, eight Messerschmitts came down on them. Sgt. Brennan (3-N) called a warning and immediately engaged the attackers, becoming involved in an intense struggle during which he gained strikes on one but was almost shot down himself. He yelled over the R/T for help, Plt.Off. Nash and Wt.Off. McLean arriving to chase away his assailants, but at this point Brennan heard that more Bf109s were off Grand Harbour, and gave chase:

'Chased two 109s and caught them about 20 miles north of Gozo. I gave the

> rear one a short burst, but saw no result. He began to turn. I turned inside him, and gave him another very short burst. He could not have been more than ten feet from the water, and suddenly his right wing hit the sea. He catherine-wheeled on his wing-tips and tail once or twice, then blew up.'

Meanwhile, Nash (BR107) had claimed one of the Messerschmitts with which Brennan had previously been engaged:

> 'Got one of them two miles off Grand Harbour — went straight in from 5000 feet. Only fired 20 rounds cannon all from one gun from 50 yards.'

McLean claimed another Bf109 damaged, while Williams believed he had probably destroyed a Ju88. Amongst the 126 Squadron section Sqn.Ldr. Barton claimed a Bf109 probable and Flt.Lt. Peck one damaged; one of the unit's Spitfires was damaged during this engagement and the pilot slightly wounded.

At least one Messerschmitt (Wrk Nr 7282) was shot down in this action, no less a pilot than Maj. Günther von Maltzahn, the Geschwader Kommodore of JG 53, being obliged to bale out into the sea off Valetta; he was probably the victim of Nash. Immediately his loss was known an intensive search was carried out, and he was successfully located towards evening in his dinghy, being safely picked up by a Do24.

Three escorted Ju88s raided Hal Far and Luqa during the early evening, two Spitfires being badly damaged and one slightly so at the latter airfield. Twenty-one Spitfires were scrambled (two/126, seven/185, five/601 and seven/603). Flt.Sgt. Bob Sim of 185 Squadron followed a Bf109 which had dived on some of the Spitfires, and claimed to have hit it with a deflection shot; it flicked over, pouring black smoke, when two 603 Squadron Spitfires came racing in from different directions to attack it. Flt.Lt. Douglas (BP964) opened fire and saw strikes, but then Plt.Off. Bairnsfather (BP991) — a new pilot — misjudged his approach and collided with Douglas' aircraft; both pilots baled out, each having sustained slight injuries. It was reported that the Messerschmitt had crashed into the sea, and was apparently credited to Douglas! Two more Bf109s were claimed

Canadian buddies — Plt.Offs. Johnny Sherlock (left) and Cy King of 185 Squadron, both of whom arrived on 9 May during Operation 'Bowery'. *(J. Sherlock)*

probably destroyed by Sqn.Ldr. Bisdee (601 Squadron) and Plt.Off. Booth (126 Squadron), and two damaged by 185 Squadron pilots, Plt.Off. McKay (BR306/D) and Plt.Off. King. Additionally, Plt.Off. Wigley (BR294/C) of the latter unit claimed a Ju88 damaged, as did AA gunners.

Tuesday, 12 May

Tuesday proved to be a day of more sustained fighter combat, marked as so often on such occasions by some fairly heavy overclaiming on both sides. After an initial abortive attempt by three patrolling Spitfires at intercepting an early morning reconnaissance aircraft, 30 Spitfires and two Hurricanes were off from 1055 to engage six Ju88s and a dozen Bf109s raiding Hal Far, while 20 4° Stormo Macchis carried out a diversionary sweep over the Island.

Immediately after take-off, Sgt. Hesselyn of 249 Squadron discovered that he had no oxygen supply, and signalled Sgt. Brennan accordingly. Consequently, Brennan stayed on his wing, and the pair remained at low altitude. Here they witnessed Plt.Off. Bert Mitchell's 603 Squadron Spitfire (BR127) with a Bf109 on its tail; the Spitfire went into a dive and Mitchell, obviously wounded, was heard to call the Controller (Grp.Capt. Woodhall) over the R/T:

> 'Goodbye, Woody, I've had it.'

Seconds later his aircraft went into the sea at about 300 mph. Hesselyn and Brennan immediately gave chase to his attacker, pursuing it out to sea, the former reporting:

> 'I saw my shells striking the water behind the fleeing 109. I realised I was firing too low. I pulled up the nose of my aircraft, and gave him another quick squirt. This time my shells must have hit him, although I did not see them do so. His speed slackened perceptibly... I throttled back to avoid overshooting him. His speed continued to slacken as we skimmed the sea at about 50 feet. I fired another burst, checked for skid, and gave him another and longer burst. This time I hit him squarely. He flicked over on his back, hung poised for a second, and dropped straight into the drink. I circled around to see if the pilot would get out. He didn't.'

Meanwhile, as Hesselyn was so engaged, Brennan (BP953) was under attack by three others, all of which overshot without hitting him but the first turned for a head-on attack. A cannon shell hit the portside of the Spitfire's armour-glass windscreen, which splintered, some of the splinters hitting Brennan in the left arm; his aircraft flicked over and as a result went into a spin. The Messerschmitt departed, the pilot presumably believing that the Spitfire had been shot down, but Brennan was able to recover control and land at Takali. As Hesselyn returned to Malta, he engaged another Bf109 and "blew half his tail off", but it dived away, covered by two others.

Seven Spitfires of 185 Squadron had now joined the action, Sgt. Yarra (GL-K) reporting:

> 'Engaged 88 — no observed results. Jumped by four 109s; shot down leader, damaged others.'

Plt.Off. Wigley (BR349/3-C) claimed damage to a Ju88, but his own aircraft received a stray bullet through the cockpit hood from the rear gunner. Return fire from another German gunner was thought to be the cause of Flt.Sgt.

Conway being shot down into the sea; he baled out of BR137 and was soon rescued unhurt by HSL 107. One more Ju88 was claimed as a probable by Flt.Lt. Ron West of 249 Squadron, who shared in damaging a second with Plt.Off. Linton.

HSL 107 in St Paul's Bay. *(NWMA)*

It was late afternoon before the next raid developed, and this was reported to comprise four Ju88s and three Z1007s escorted by two dozen Bf109s and MC202s. The Italian bombers were, in fact, S.84s of 4° Gruppo Aut AS, covered by 15 Re2001s of 2° Gruppo CT and 15 MC202s of 4° Stormo CT. Takali was attacked, where two Spitfires were damaged and two airmen wounded. A total of 36 Spitfires and six Hurricanes were ordered off, as recalled by Plt.Off. Johnny Sherlock:

> 'Planes took off from different parts of the field in every direction, and what with the dust and the extreme hurry to get airborne, it was more dangerous at times of take-off than fighting the Jerries.'

In the mad scramble to get off BR136 collided with BR350, but neither Plt.Off. Halford nor Plt.Off. McNaughton was hurt. In the confusion Flt.Lt. Barnham was ordered to land, but in doing so found that his 601 Squadron flight had been left leaderless, so took-off again.

Meanwhile, the two units in the air had been heavily engaged. Plt.Off. Graves of 126 Squadron pursued a Ju88 out to sea and claimed to have probably destroyed it, but the engine of his BP877 was hit by return fire and he was obliged to turn for base. As he crossed the coast at 900 feet, his engine caught fire and he baled out. Another 126 Squadron pilot, Sgt. Bush, was wounded in both legs and belly-landed BR346 at Luqa, crashing through some stone walls at the perimeter of the airfield.

Amongst the 601 Squadron pilots, Sgt. McConnell claimed an MC202 probably destroyed, and Sgt. K.J. Lusty — a new arrival — a Bf109 damaged, but Sgt. Charles Graysmark (BR196) was shot down into the sea and was badly wounded. He managed to get into his dinghy, but had died by the time help arrived. Indeed, Flt.Lt. Barnham and Sgt. Howard later took off to escort HSL

128 out to him, and became engaged in holding at bay four Messerschmitts that attempted to strafe the craft. In consequence, it was believed at the time that Graysmark had been machine-gunned in his dinghy.

Two of the 2° Gruppo Reggianes had been hit — it would appear by McConnell and Lusty — Serg. Mario Marchio subsequently force-landing his burning aircraft near Noto (Syracuse) on the Sicilian coast; he had been seriously wounded, and died a month later from his injuries. Ten. Col. Aldo Quarantotti's aircraft was also hit, and he belly-landed at Catania. Three Spitfires were claimed shot down, two credited to the mortally-wounded Marchio, and one to Cap. Annibale Sterzi, the 358ª Squadriglia commander; three others were claimed as probables and two as damaged.

Reggiane Re2001 '7' of the 358ª Squadriglia, 2° Gruppo Autonomo CT at Comiso. *(N. Malizia)*

Half an hour behind the initial wave of Spitfires had followed eight from 603 Squadron, just in time to catch the Italian bombers over the target area. Two were claimed shot down, one by Plt.Off. Dicks-Sherwood, the other jointly by Flt.Lt. Sanders and Flg.Off. Mitchell. The S.84 (MM23987) flown by Ten. Vinicio Vego Scocco went down before it had released its bombs, and crashed into a garden near Dingli, where one of the crew was found dead near the wreckage; four others were seen to bale out over the sea. Flt.Lt. Barnham saw the parachutists floating down and waved as he flew past, while Sgt. Yarra of 185 Squadron — by now also in the air — noted:

> 'Did some dummy attacks on some Ities coming down in 'chutes. Frightened them.'

The four were seen by watchers on Dingli cliffs to splash into the sea, while Barnham informed Control of their situation and location.

The second S.84 (Ten. Panizzi's MM23955) had been very badly damaged and several members of the crew wounded, but it managed to struggle back to Sicily. One of the escorting Macchi pilots, Serg. Mario Veronesi of 84ª Squadriglia, attacked a Spitfire which was following the damaged Savoia and reported that it force-landed at Luqa (possibly Sgt. Bush of 126 Squadron). The third S.84 was also damaged, while Serg. Teresio Martinoli's Macchi was hit in the tail by a Spitfire, although he was able to claim another shot down. Finally, at 1745, eight 249 Squadron aircraft joined the fighting, Flt.Sgt. Williams claiming a Ju88 damaged and Flt.Lt. Lee a Bf109 damaged, while RAF ground defences at Takali claimed damage to another Messerschmitt.

During the day, Maj. von Maltzahn — apparently having rapidly recovered from his enforced dip in the Mediterranean — claimed a Spitfire for his 62nd victory, and the leading pilots of III/JG 53 claimed no less than nine more — though whether in the morning engagement only is not certain. Four had definitely gone down at that time (although one of these reportedly fell to return fire from a Ju88) and Brennan's aircraft had been damaged, indicating a fair degree of double claiming on this occasion. Hpt. Wilcke of Stab claimed his 38th victory, while Lt. Siegmund Hosnedl of 7 Staffel was credited with his 11th and last victory; next day he suffered an engine failure whilst on a test flight, and crashed to his death near Comiso. Four pilots of 8 Staffel claimed — Oblt. Belser (his 27th), Oblt. Klager (13th), Lt. Quaritsch (4th) and Fw. Seidl (10th), while 9 Staffel pilots were awarded three more victories — Oblt. Götz (his 30th), Lt. Munzert (15th) and Ofw. Stumpf (also his 30th).

There was a sickening conclusion to this day, for when HSL 128 reached the location where the four Italian airmen from the downed S.84 had been seen to splash into the sea, only Serg. Eugenio Rivolta, the second pilot, was to be found. It transpired that the other three had managed to reach the shore at Ta'Zuta (Dingli) where they were spotted clinging to the rocks at the foot of the cliffs. When a rescue unit arrived, however, it was to find that some person or persons unknown had deliberately rolled rocks over the cliff edge onto the helpless airmen, killing all three.

This was not an isolated incident. Many Maltese harboured a particularly deep hatred of the Italians, as recalled by Plt.Off. Sherlock of 185 Squadron:

> 'Another sad memory was when enemy aircrew, especially Italians, were coming down in 'chutes, the Maltese would position themselves accordingly, armed with pitchforks or any other weapon they could find. The enemy had little chance of surviving. It was difficult to blame the Maltese, who had lost homes, relatives, possessions. They had a real interest in the conflict, but to some of us it was still murder to kill an unarmed individual and who might have already been wounded. Several times, if the 'chutes were coming down close to the field, we would run out to try and save the enemy but usually it was too late.
>
> 'We all had big roundels painted on our Mae Wests, but even then there were several narrow escapes from the ever-ready pitchforks!'

Another bizarre incident had allegedly been experienced by Wg.Cdr. Stan Turner, when visiting a tiny cafe in Mdina one day. On enquiring as to what was contained in three large clay pots displayed behind the bar, he was horrified when the bartender opened one and pulled out a severed human head! Apparently it was the head of a German airman who had baled out safely over Malta, but who had then been butchered by a crowd of Maltese!

Whether there was any substance to this story remains debatable. Certainly the following apocryphal tale circulated amongst service personnel — probably for the dubious benefit of new arrivals — ostensibly to encourage them to value their parachutes as parachute silk in wartime was worth a maiden's ransom! It was rumoured that on one occasion a pilot had baled out and had pulled the rip cord, only to find that an old army blanket floated out! John Sherlock continues:

> 'This undoubtedly is a tall story although at the time I think all of us believed this to be true and we became very protective of our 'chutes as we realized

> that we might have to use them on any flight. To embellish the story further, it was rumoured that after this episode, there were quite a few Maltese girls wearing white silk panties, although, again, I did not check into this!'

To the low-flying Messerschmitt pilots any movement on the ground on Malta warranted a burst of machine-gun fire, and many civilians had been killed or wounded in this fashion; buses, ferry boats, fishing boats and rescue launches had all been strafed, so to many Maltese captured aircrew were considered fair game. The war in the air was not always fought in a chivalrous manner, either. More than one British pilot was believed shot in his parachute or in his dinghy, and on one occasion two pilots of 185 Squadron reported witnessing a Messerschmitt pilot strafe and apparently kill one of his own, under the obvious impression that the dinghy contained a British airman. Similarly, a Canadian pilot of 249 Squadron was seen to machine-gun survivors of a shot down Ju88, and there were a number of other such incidents.

That night three raiders crossed the coast, a Beaufighter flown by Plt.Off. Daniel and Sgt. Walsh being scrambled at 2200 to intercept. They were swiftly vectored onto a Ju88 which was claimed shot down in flames.

Flt.Lt. Norman Macqueen (left) and Sgt. Paul Brennan of 249 Squadron "unwinding after a scramble". *(L. McAuley)*

Wednesday, 13 May

The Stukas were back at lunchtime on the 13th, 16 aircraft of III/StG 3, escorted by 26 Bf109s, raiding Hal Far; three Hurricanes on the airfield were hit, BE716 being damaged beyond repair. Eight Spitfires of 249 Squadron and five from 603 Squadron were scrambled, but as Flt.Lt. Ron West's section took off, Messerschmitts swept over and attempted to strafe them, albeit without result.

Sgt. Hesselyn, having escaped this attack, saw another Bf109 pass close by as he was climbing. Turning after it, he failed to gain any strikes, but then saw two more at the same height and got on the tail of the No 2.

Opening fire at 100 yards for two seconds, he reported that it dived straight into the sea, pouring smoke. R/T chatter then reported action over Kalafrana Bay, and on arrival here he spotted another Messerschmitt on a Spitfire's tail:

> 'I went in at once, attacking from the starboard quarter. I could see my shells striking his fuselage. He turned on his back. I turned on mine, firing all the time. He started to go down in a gentle dive, and I kept firing to make sure of him. He crashed into the bay, and as he hit the water Ronnie West's voice came to me over the R/T: "Spit that just shot down that 109, thanks a hell of a lot!"'

One of the Ju87s was claimed damaged by Flt.Sgt. Brown of 603 Squadron, while a Spitfire was slightly damaged — possibly by Ofw. Rollwage of II/JG 53, who claimed a Spitfire just north of Luqa at 1302 for his 20th victory.

As the last light of day rapidly faded, two Macchis were reported patrolling off the coast, and four Spitfires of 126 Squadron were scrambled to investigate. Sgt. Goldsmith (BR244) reported:

> 'Chased two Macchi 202s back to Sicily. Had cannon stoppages after a short squirt from 70 yards.'

Nonetheless, Goldsmith claimed strikes on one of the fleeing fighters, as did Flt.Lt. Peck, and each was credited with one damaged.

Thursday, 14 May

Darkness brought just one raider over Luqa, but here a bomb destroyed Spitfire BR190 in its pen. With the dawn on Thursday another lone reconnaissance Ju88 released some bombs on Sliema, where eight civilians were killed and nine wounded. The first main raid of the day was plotted approaching at 0900, when 28 Spitfires (seven/126, three/185, eight/249, six/601 and four/603) were ordered off to intercept three Ju88s of 1/KGr 806 and a number of Bf109 Jabo, all covered by a large fighter escort. The bombers raided Luqa and Takali, while the fighter-bombers attacked the latter airfield; damage inflicted was minimal.

Flt.Lt. Ron West's section of four from the 249 Squadron contingent saw the Ju88s some 30 miles out and about 1000 feet below their level. West attacked the centre bomber of three, claiming to have shot it down before firing at the port aircraft; this was also attacked by Plt.Off. Linton, and they reported seeing it make off with one engine on fire. West then became involved with one of the escorting Messerschmitts and claimed strikes on this before it evaded and escaped. Sgt. Hesselyn attacked the bomber on the right of the section, seeing strikes along the fuselage and cockpit area, whereupon it blew up. It seems that he and West actually fired at the same aircraft, for apparently only one Ju88 — M7+FH flown by the Staffelkapitän, Hpt. Emil Braun — failed to return. Flt.Sgt. Williams, meanwhile, pursued a Bf109 for some distance but was obliged to break away after registering some strikes. On returning to Takali he belly-landed, having exhausted his fuel.

The pilots of 126 and 185 Squadron also engaged, but as Sgt. Goldsmith recorded:

'Missed out on the bombers, got mixed up with 109s. Gave one a 12 second burst, set it on fire.'

Apart from Goldsmith, Plt.Off. Tilley and Sgt. Boyd (BR349/C) were also each credited with Bf109s shot down and Flt.Lt. Winfield with a probable. Of his combat, Boyd wrote:

'We were attacked by 4 Me109s from above. We climbed into them, circling with them and fired at various ones. I fired 3 seconds at one from port beam below to quarter astern. He streamed white smoke in puffs and then a steady stream. He headed east, slowing up and jerking slightly. I had to break off to avoid others. His glycol tank was obviously hit. In my opinion this e/a could not reach his base, with the loss of glycol, and the fact of a strong headwind against the trip to Sicily.'

Nonetheless, the Messerschmitt did reach Sicily, Lt. Alfred Hammer crash-landing his 4/JG 53 aircraft at Comiso airfield where it was badly damaged and subsequently written-off.

One of 185 Squadron's long-serving pilots, Sgt. Colin Finlay, was seen to be engaged by two Bf109s and his BR291/H was set on fire, crashing into the sea 400 yards off Wied Zurrieq. Finlay was observed to fall clear, but his parachute did not open; two Maltese soldiers — L/Cpl. Julian Sciberras and Pte. Spiro Zammit — at once launched a small boat, reaching the spot in ten minutes. The Messerschmitts were still circling overhead but undaunted they located Finlay and pulled him aboard; sadly, he was found to be dead when they reached the shore. The two soldiers were officially commended for their action; L/Cpl.

Flt.Lt. Denis Barnham of 601 Squadron in the cockpit of his Spitfire after claiming his fifth victory — four German and one Italian. Plt.Off. Mike Le Bas looks on. *(NWMA)*

Sciberras had already been instrumental in attempts to rescue members of a downed Beaufort crew during the previous month.

The next alert sounded soon after midday as three more Ju88s of KGr 806 headed in, escorted by Bf109s, MC202s of 9° Gruppo CT and Re2001s of 2° Gruppo CT; their target was Takali. Seventeen Spitfires and four Hurricanes were sent off, Flt.Lt. Barnham leading a force from 126, 601 and 603 Squadrons to attack the bombers; four 185 Squadron aircraft engaged the Italian fighters, Flt.Sgt. Ferraby (BR294) and Sgt. Boyd attacking eight of these from below. Ferraby put a four-five second burst into one Macchi, which spun away pouring black smoke after he had seen some pieces fall off; he claimed a probable. Boyd's BR349/C was seen to spin out of the fight, however, and it crashed near Takali. One Spitfire was claimed shot down by Mar. Rinaldo Damiani of 9° Gruppo, and two others by Ten. Carlo Seganti and Ten. Leo Venturini of 2° Gruppo. However, Boyd may equally have fallen victim to one of the Messerschmitts; Plt.Off. Reade Tilley watched the fight while his Spitfire was being refuelled:

> 'A dogfight started overhead — some 3 Ju88s came in with 109 escort — Ack Ack going like mad, bursts all over the sky — then I saw a 109 sit on a Spitfire's tail and I heard the brrr of cannon. The Spit rolled over and dived vertically in what appeared to be a controlled evasive manoeuvre, doing a series of aileron turns; there was no smoke trail and apparently he was OK but for some reason I felt he'd had it. Sure enough, he started to pull out too late at a 100 feet, then when it looked as if he would make it, the pilot either died or lost consciousness and ploughed into the deck on the far side of the drome at 300 mph. So at 1305 hours the career of Sgt. Pilot Tony Boyd came to an abrupt and spectacular end — just a terrific explosion and a long sheet of flame.'

Meanwhile, the main force of Spitfires attacked the bombers and claimed all three shot down. Barnham and Plt.Off. Bruce Ingram reported attacking one, which Barnham hit in the port engine and wing, causing a fire; Ingram then attacked and the starboard engine also started to burn, the aircraft falling in flames near Takali. Flt.Sgt. Johnny Hurst of 603 Squadron also reported engaging a Ju88 as it dived on Takali. This crashed on the edge of the runway, although AA gunners also claimed a share in this success. It seems probable that all involved had fired on Fw. Günther Schwerdt's M7+CH, which did indeed crash at Takali. Although the pilot attempted to crash-land the burning bomber, he and his crew perished in the wreck. Amongst the burning wreckage one crew member was seen to be seriously injured, but could not be reached. It was alleged that Wg.Cdr. Gracie drew his revolver and humanely put the man out of his misery.

Flt.Lt. Sanders and Flg.Off. Mitchell of 603 Squadron claimed another Junkers shot down into the sea, Sanders additionally reporting strikes on a Bf109 he attacked; Plt.Off. Dicks-Sherwood of this unit also claimed a bomber, shared with Sgt. Goldsmith of 126 Squadron, who reported:

> 'Scrambled with 601 by mistake. Fired everything at a Ju88 — 150 yards. Set both engines and fuselage on fire; knocked off some lumps.'

Again it would seem that all four pilots attacked the same aircraft, a second Ju88 crash-landing at Catania on return in a badly damaged condition; it was also probably fired on by Flg.Off. Hone (3-R) of 601, who reported:

> 'Knocked glycol out of port engine of Ju88'

The loss of the gallant Australian, Tony Boyd — doyen of the Hurricane pilots — was a sad blow. He, Colin Finlay — also killed that day — Ron Noble, Ian McKay, Joe Beckitt and Phil Wigley were the survivors of the original Hurricane pilots who had flown off the *Ark Royal* to Malta in November of the previous year. All had flown just a few Spitfire sorties — without, it must be added, proper conversion training — prior to their imminent return to the United Kingdom for a well-earned rest; now two of these tired young veterans had been lost in a single day.

Shortly after 1700 a third trio of KGr 806 bombers approached, again under cover of a large fighter escort. Seven Spitfires of 249 Squadron were first off, well in advance of the raider's arrival, and these at once attacked a number of Jabo Bf109s, which had just bombed and strafed Hal Far. Flg.Off. Buchanan claimed one probably shot down, while Flt.Sgt. Harry Fox, an American from New York, called over the R/T that he had also shot one down; moments later however, his Spitfire crashed into the sea, victim of another Messerschmitt — probably an aircraft of III/JG 53. This unit recorded victories over three Spitfires during the day by Oblt. Belser, Lt. Quaritsch and Ofw. Stumpf.

Fifteen more Spitfires from 126 and 601 Squadrons followed at 1730, while six Hurricanes protected the airfields. Flt.Lt. Barnham managed to get on the tail of Uffz. Johannes Prokesch's Ju88 (M7+BL) and put a three-second burst into it which caused the port wing to snap off; the aircraft fell in flames, gyrating like a gigantic catherine wheel, and crashed into the sea. Its demise was witnessed by an AA crew, who also claimed to have shot it down! Returning German crews were of the opinion that this had indeed been their comrades' fate. However, although the pilot and two others of the crew were killed, the observer (Obgfr. Herbert Burger) managed to bale out and subsequently confirmed that a Spitfire had shot down his aircraft, not AA fire. Watching the action from Kalafrana, Phil Chandler later recorded in his diary:

> 'One of them received a direct hit. Smoke poured forth immediately and he did a sharp turn, crossing the path of one of his comrades. This turn was perhaps too much for the stricken machine, for both engines fell out. Then the whole box of tricks fell to pieces. The whole mainplane came off and spun lazily down, leaving a spiral of blue smoke, amid a shower of smaller fragments which continued to flutter down for some minutes afterwards. One got away by parachute.'

Two Bf109s were claimed shot down by Sqn.Ldr. Barton and his No 2, Plt.Off. Tilley, the former adding a second as probably destroyed, and the latter one more as damaged; of the day's intensive fighting, Reade Tilley recalled:

> 'We flew a couple of missions and working closely together bagged several 109s, despite unfavourable odds, getting somewhat shot about in the process.'

The AA defences also claimed damage to a Bf109 and a Ju88, but no other German losses were recorded, although a second Messerschmitt crash-landed at Comiso during the day following combat. In addition to the loss of Flt.Sgt. Fox, one other Spitfire was damaged during this action, and a third suffered some damage on landing.

Friday, 15 May

During the early hours of the 15th two nocturnal raiders — BR20Ms of 264[a] Squadriglia — were reported approaching the Island from the north, the Beaufighter crewed by Flt.Lt. Coleman and Sgt. Peasley being vectored onto one, which they claimed to have shot down. This was undoubtedly Ten. Alessandro Castronovo's machine, which crashed near Palazzo Adriano (Palermo) on return with the loss of all the crew.

Three S.84bis of 4° Gruppo BT, escorted by 30 MC202s of 4° Stormo CT, came over at 0915, the bomber crews briefed to attack barracks at St Paul's Bay (probably Fort Campbell). A dozen Spitfires from 249 and 603 Squadrons were scrambled and engaged the formation shortly after it had bombed; Flg.Offs. Lee and Mitchell each claimed damage to one of the Savoias. The Italians reported that five Spitfires attacked over the target area, Cap. Franco Lucchini claiming one shot down and one damaged. Other Spitfires then came in over Gozo, and three of these were claimed by Ten. Jacopo Frigerio, Ten. Ferruccio Zarini and Serg.Magg. Mario Guerci; the latter and Sottoten. Alvaro Querci also each claimed one damaged. None of the Spitfires were seriously hit however, and 249 Squadron's Flt.Sgt. Verroll was able to get a telling burst into one Macchi (MM7813) which crashed onto the sea, taking the 91[a] Squadriglia commander (Cap. Alberto Argenton) to his death. A subsequent search by an ASR Z506B, protected by 28 of the unit's Macchis, found nothing.

Eleven Spitfires scrambled to intercept a fighter sweep by an estimated 40-50 Bf109s around 1100, Sgt. Gray of 249 Squadron claiming damage to two of these; Plt.Off. Booth of 126 Squadron crash-landed BR229 at Takali having been hit by another Messerschmitt, the Spitfire being written off as a consequence. In mid-afternoon a single reconnaissance Ju88 with a substantial fighter escort approached, two 185 Squadron Spitfires and four from 603 Squadron taking off, the first pair at 1537 and the quartet at 1610. Sgt. Yarra (GL-K) recorded:

> 'Engaged seven 109s, damaged leader; was attacked by four 202s. Shot down one, who collided with his No 2. Fought the remaining two until out of ammo.'

The 603 Squadron section engaged a number of Bf109s of II/JG 53 near Hal Far, Sqn.Ldr. Douglas-Hamilton attacking one head-on. He reported that his fire appeared to cause the port wing of one aircraft to break-off, and the Messerschmitt did about five flick rolls before crashing behind Paola Hill. Lt. Herbert Soukop of 6 Staffel, a member of the German Sudetan minority in Czechoslovakia who had claimed five victories, baled out with his left arm broken by a cannon-shell; unable to properly control his descent, his parachute caught on the roof of a house in a private garden at Zejtun, where he was left dangling in the air. This probably kept him safe from the crowd of angry Maltese who gathered before soldiers arrived to cut him down and take him to hospital. Soukop was later visited in hospital by his victor and several other pilots. During this fight, Sgt. Irwin claimed hits on another Bf109 which was last seen going out to sea, emitting smoke; he was credited with a probable.

Saturday, 16 May

Again it was the Regia Aeronautica which opened the attacks on the 16th, five Z1007bis of 210[a] Squadriglia raiding Takali under cover of 30 Macchis and 15 Messerschmitts, including a number of Jabo. On the airfield one Spitfire was destroyed and another slightly damaged, while two airmen were killed; nonetheless 16 Spitfires succeeded in getting airborne to intercept. At their head once again was Flt.Lt. Barnham of 601 Squadron, although he was again suffering from 'Malta Dog' and had been ordered not to fly; however, with Sqn.Ldr. Bisdee and Flt.Lt. Parry still ill, he decided that he should lead. He ordered Blue Section to take on the bombers while he led his section up to great height to engage the fighter escort, but at 34,000 feet the cold was so intense that one pilot, the South African Bartleman, suffered frostbite to his fingers!

Although given a clear run at the bombers, Blue Section failed to gain any significant success; Flg.Off. Hone (BR125/3-P) and Plt.Off. Hagger jointly claimed one of the Cants probably destroyed, and Sgt. McConnell a Macchi probable. Barnham recorded that Rome Radio subsequently admitted the loss of both a bomber and a fighter during this raid, but this appears not to be the case and no losses have been discovered. Four 603 Squadron aircraft engaged Bf109s, Sqn.Ldr. Douglas-Hamilton and Plt.Off. Northcott each claiming one damaged, but Sgt. Johnson's aircraft was shot up and the Australian crash-landed at Takali. 4° Stormo Macchi pilots claimed four Spitfires shot down, two by Serg.Magg. Massimo Salvatore — one reportedly as it was landing — and one each by Sottoten. Mario Squarcina and Mar. Rinaldo Damiani; one more was claimed by gunners in the bombers.

Early in the afternoon a single Ju88, covered by an estimated 26 Bf109s (including five Jabo) and 15 Re2001s of 2° Gruppo CT, attacked Kalafrana. Six 249 Squadron Spitfires were scrambled at 1440, followed 35 minutes later by five of 126 Squadron. Flg.Off. Buchanan claimed a 'Macchi' shot down, while Sgt. De Nancrede, one of the unit's recently-arrived Canadians, reported gaining strikes on a Messerschmitt; Plt.Off. Plagis (BR176/C-25) and Plt.Off. Nash (BR195) engaged another with greater success — as Plagis recalled:

> 'Peter Nash and I shot down Me109F which came for me.'

Nash was a little more explicit, and noted in his logbook:

Four pilots of the Jabo-Staffel, 10/JG 53, with the tail of one of their Bf109Fs, showing clearly the unit's marking of a bomb falling on Malta. *(Dr Felix Sauer)*

'Damn good party with 109s off Kala(frana) Bay. They attacked in pairs but Plagis and I fixed one from 300 yards. This is the 100th e/a destroyed on Malta by 249 Squadron.'

It would seem they had shot down 'White 6' of JaboStaffel 10/JG 53, although the pilot of this machine, Uffz. Dr. Felix Sauer, believed his aircraft had either been hit by AA fire or that the subsequent explosion in his engine had been caused by a technical problem; he recalled:

'Four Spitfires suddenly appeared. I moved to counter-attack but there was an explosion in the engine, which goes dead. I dived and escaped but there was nothing left to do, so I descend from 3000 metres to 700 metres and take to my parachute.

'My comrades fly round and make me understand that they have seen me, and that they will try to get some help. While baling out I hurt my chin and for a while was stunned. The cold water soon restored my senses. I detached myself from the parachute and inflated my small rubber boat.'

When the 126 Squadron aircraft got into the air, Plt.Off. McHan also claimed damage to a 'Macchi', while Flt.Sgt. Milner's aircraft suffered slight damage. However, four Spitfires were claimed shot down by the Reggiane pilots, one each by Ten. Giorgio Pocek, Ten. Agostino Celentano, Sottoten. Carlo Grillo and Serg.Magg. Guerrino Prodi. In return, Grillo's aircraft (MM7210) was seriously damaged — probably by Buchanan — and force-landed at Comiso.

About one and a half hours later 11 Spitfires were sent off to intercept a Do24 and its Bf109 escort, reported north of Malta and obviously searching for Sauer, who was now about eight miles from Marsaxlokk Bay; he later recalled:

'While it (*the Dornier*) was trying to land, five Spitfires attacked it, though its markings were perfectly visible. This unfair attack was avenged at once; one of the Spitfires was shot down at the same moment. But the rescue aircraft had to turn back as well.'

Sauer's observation was inaccurate, however, for none of the four Spitfires of 603 Squadron which engaged were lost. In fact, Flt.Lt. Sanders and Flt.Sgt. Hurst each claimed a Bf109 probably destroyed, and Flg.Off. Mitchell one damaged. Felix Sauer's ordeal was only just beginning and it would be eight long days before he was rescued (see Appendix VI).

By night eight BR20Ms of 88° Gruppo BT headed for the Island, the first approaching at about 0300; only three actually crossed the coast, and all were claimed shot down in flames by Plt.Off. Daniel and Sgt. Gosling of 89 Squadron. Unusually, on this occasion, the Beaufighter crew's enthusiasm seems to have overcome objectivity for only two of the bombers were hit, and both were able to return to Castelvetrano; all of Cap. Alfredo Sordini's 265ª Squadriglia crew survived unhurt, but in Cap. Ugo Machieraldo's aircraft the radio operator, Mar. Pietro Mercalli, was wounded. There was, however, a further loss during the night at this time, Oblt. Ernst Gragger's Ju88 (B3+FH of 2/KG 54) being shot down in flames at 0332 some 20 miles south of Malta with the loss of the crew. Whilst this loss was recorded as having occurred to AA fire, there was no claim by the gunners, and the aircraft may well have been shot down by Daniel, who identified it as a further BR20.

Uffz. Dr Felix Sauer of 10(Jabo)/JG 53, who was shot down off the coast of Malta on 16 May, drifting in his dinghy for eight days before being rescued. *(Dr Felix Sauer)*

A pair of Fiat BR20M bombers of 220ª Squadriglia, 55° Gruppo Aut BT, which were active by night over Malta during much of 1942. *(Stato Maggiore via N. Malizia)*

Sunday, 17 May

At 0700 on Sunday two Spitfires of 249 Squadron scrambled after a lone reconnaissance Ju88D from 1(F)/122, plotted approaching from the north. They were expertly vectored onto the intruder, and Oblt. Günther Steppmacher's F6+LH was intercepted over Valetta by Flg.Off. Buchanan and shot down into the sea; there were no survivors.

Luftwaffe air-sea rescue aircraft were out early, obviously searching for both Uffz. Sauer and the missing reconnaissance crew. At 0806, five 126 Squadron Spitfires were ordered to intercept these, as were a number of Spitfires from 249 Squadron. As the Spitfires began their take-off run, Sgt. Goldsmith's BP952 ran

In the background can be seen a Dornier Do24T air-sea rescue flyingboat of Seenotstaffel 6 on a Sicilian jetty. In the foreground is a visiting Cant Z506B floatplane of 147ª Squadriglia RST. *(E.C. des Armees)*

into a small hole caused by an unexploded bomb, one wheel being torn away and the wing damaged. The others intercepted an escorted Do24T of Seenotst 6, and this was shot down by Flt.Sgt. Tommy Parks; Obgfr. Wilhelm Kühn (the air gunner) sustained wounds but was rescued with other members of his crew.

Flt.Lt. Winfield claimed one of the escorting Messerschmitts shot down.

It had long been the RAF's policy to attack Axis air-sea rescue aircraft, even those white-painted aircraft emblazoned with prominent Red Cross insignia. This was a decision with which not only Air Vice-Marshal Lloyd concurred, but one which had the approval of Prime Minister Churchill, who later wrote:

> 'We did not recognise this means of rescuing enemy pilots who had been shot down in action, in order that they might come and bomb our civilian population again. We rescued them ourselves whenever it was possible, and made them prisoners of war. But all German air ambulances were forced or shot down by our fighters on definite orders approved by the War Cabinet.'

This decision had been reached during the early days of the Battle of Britain, when a number of such rescue aircraft had been observed flying in the vicinity of British convoys, and it was feared that they were reporting shipping movements; it was also noticed that they were generally armed and amongst the crews captured, there was a noticeable absence of medical orderlies. Air Vice-Marshal Lloyd's reasons for his approval have not been recorded but recent events around Malta would indicate that these included:

(a) retaliation for German attacks on Malta's rescue launches;
(b) it was believed that RAF pilots were not being picked up by Axis aircraft and, indeed, that some British pilots had been deliberately strafed in their dinghies;
(c) that Axis survivors picked up by Malta's launches had proved very useful for interrogation purposes;
(d) finally, that since 1940 the destruction of such aircraft had been Fighter Command's policy in the United Kingdom.

At 1155 six Spitfires of 603 Squadron, and two of 249 Squadron, were scrambled on the approach of a fighter-bomber raid; the pilots of the latter pair of Spitfires

(Plt.Off. Nash and Flt.Sgt. Verroll) each reported shooting down a Bf109, while Verroll claimed another damaged. Only one Messerschmitt was lost however, Lt. Wolfgang Herrmann of 5/JG 53 failing to return in 'Black 8'. A second pilot of this unit baled out over Cape Scaramia, reportedly as a consequence of technical problems. Another Messerschmitt pilot then shot down 20 year-old Peter Nash, who crashed to his death in BR195 near Dingli; the loss of this popular, 11½-victory 'ace' was a hard blow.

Meanwhile, the 603 Squadron pilots had found another of Seenotst 6's flyingboats, which was claimed damaged by Plt.Off. Barlow and Flt.Sgt. Hurst, while Plt.Off. Neville King claimed damage to a Bf109. The Dornier had indeed been hard-hit, and ditched in the sea, where it became a total loss.

During the morning pairs and quartets of MC202s patrolled over and around Malta. One pair (Sottoten. Paolo Berti and Serg. Luciano Perdoni) spotted a small cargo vessel north of Valetta, and attacked this. Another pair, led by Mar. Manlio Olivetti and flying at 10,000 feet, saw a trail of dust at Luqa, which was identified as a Beaufighter taking off. Olivetti dived and attacked, reporting that it exploded; such a loss cannot be verified, however.

An Italian air-sea rescue Z506B of 612ª Squadriglia was out during the evening, protected by 19 Re2001s of 2° Gruppo. Plt.Off. 'Pancho' Le Bas (who was born in Argentina, hence the nickname) led off seven 601 Squadron Spitfires to intercept, the opposing fighters clashing over Takali. Cap. Salvatore Teia and Serg.Magg. Rino Ricci each claimed Spitfires shot down, while one other was claimed as a probable and three more were believed to have been hit. In return, one Reggiane was damaged, as was the floatplane, struck by fire from both a Spitfire and shrapnel from a bursting AA shell. The Spitfire leader, Le Bas, and Plt.Off. A.R. Boyle (a new arrival) each claimed Reggianes probably destroyed, and Wt.Off. Fred Belcher another as damaged, while Plt.Off. Caldwell (3-U) reported shooting down a Bf109. It is believed that Sgt. Stan Howard (BR344) attacked the Z506B but he was then shot up by the escort, his aircraft being hit in the glycol tank. He attempted to reach Luqa, but came in too low and hit a stone wall; the Spitfire cartwheeled across the airfield, shedding its wings and the Rhodesian suffered serious head injuries, from which he died three days later.

Seven more Spitfires from 249 Squadron had by now got into the air and pursued the Italians out to sea, Plt.Off. Plagis (BR176/C-25) firing at one of the fighters, which he identified as an MC202:

> 'Chased a Macchi which strafed Hal Far. Caught him up, fired every round at him 200 yards — and he got away — never forgive myself. Only damaged him.'

Mis-identifying the fleeing fighters as Messerschmitts, Sgt. Paul Brennan reported:

> 'Exchanged shots with some 109s, but without result either side. Shot at by Spit.'

The day was, however, marked by the evening departure of the last of the long-serving Hurricane pilots. Originally intended to fly out two days earlier, they had been delayed by bad weather. Now, at last, they embarked aboard the largest twin-engined aircraft then operating anywhere in the world — the Curtiss-Wright CW 20T*. Apart from the tour-expired Hurricane pilots, a number of the inexperienced arrivals from the last reinforcement flight from *Wasp*, who had been so assiduously weeded out, were aboard for return to the UK.

Curtiss CW-20T transport, G-AGDI 'St Louis', in which a number of the surviving Hurricane pilots of 185 Squadron departed Malta during the night of 17 May. *(R.F. Noble)*

With nightfall the Italian bombers were back, four BR20Ms of 55° Gruppo raiding the Island. One of these was shot down by one of 89 Squadron's Beaufighters (X7750), crewed by Flt.Lt. Hayton and Plt.Off. Josling; Sottoten. Francesco Corallo's aircraft crashed into the sea with the loss of all on board.

Despite all the depredations of the Luftwaffe and the Regia Aeronautica, it had proved possible to maintain a few Special Duties Wellingtons and some Albacores and Swordfish of the RNAS at Luqa and Hal Far, although these had achieved little over the past few weeks. During the night of the 17th/18th however, one of the Wellingtons spotted two 5000-ton vessels with destroyer escort, ten miles off Syracuse; on receipt of this report, four Albacores were despatched on their first operation for some weeks. Unfortunately, two were forced to return early with engine trouble, while the other pair were unable to sight the convoy since the flares carried by the radar-equipped Wellington proved to be faulty. The attack was aborted at that point — a disappointing conclusion to the resumption of activities.

Monday, 18 May

Early on Monday morning, 16 Macchis and eight Re2001s set off towards Malta as cover for a number of Italian MAS (motor torpedo boats) that were operating off the Island. Four 249 Squadron aircraft were ordered to investigate, but at the last moment Sqn.Ldr. Grant's Spitfire became unserviceable. Grant rushed over to Sgt. Brennan's aircraft and ordered him to lead the remaining trio then

*The original prototype of what was later to become famous as the C-46 Commando transport, the CW-20T had been returned to the manufacturer after test by the USAAC in September 1941, and then sold to Britain. Now fitted with 24 seats and long-range tanks, it was in use by BOAC as G-AGDI 'St Louis' and had begun flying a regular night service between Gibraltar and Malta.

A 'gaggle' of Spitfires of 249 Squadron at Takali, 'T-H' in the foreground. *(A. Rogers)*

taking-off; they were soon followed by Flt.Lt. Ron West, who scrambled to bring the flight up to strength, but when he caught up with the others, he allowed Brennan to continue leading. About ten miles east of Zonqor, four fighters — believed to be Macchis — were spotted 2000 feet below and Brennan (BR176/C-25) led an attack on these.

Brennan fired a short burst at one, seeing strikes on the port wing, but this pulled away and flew right across the nose of Sgt. Johnny Gilbert's aircraft. The latter also fired and the Italian fighter fell away, pouring glycol. Brennan, meanwhile, was attacking another:

> 'He promptly went into a vertical dive. I followed him, caught him as he was pulling out of his dive at 2000 feet and, getting dead behind him, gave him a long burst. He hung there for a second, rolled on his back, and hit the sea. As he crashed I saw another aircraft spin into the sea half a mile away. As I thought it might be one of our boys, I called up the others, and Ronnie told me he had just shot down one of the Eyties... The one Johnny had hit force-landed at Zonqor Point, and it was then we learned that the Eyties had not been Macchis, but Reggiane 2001s.'

Their opponents had indeed been four of the 2° Gruppo Re2001s, but despite the specific nature of Brennan's report, the three claims made by 249 Squadron seem only to have been rewarded by one actual Italian loss — presumably that claimed by Gilbert, for Ten. Remo Cazzolli crash-landed near Fort St Leonard on Zonqor Point and became a prisoner (see Appendix VII).

By 0930 the presence of the MAS boats — described as 'Italian E-boats' by the Spitfire pilots — had been spotted and four Hurricanes of 229 Squadron were despatched to attack them. As they were searching, a big Axis fighter sweep began to form up and 18 Spitfires were scrambled to intercept this and to cover the Hurricanes. The latter had just come under attack by Bf109s when five Spitfires of 601 Squadron swept in to the rescue, Plt.Off. Scott claiming one Messerschmitt shot down. At almost the same time Plt.Off. Norm Fowlow was also shot down into the sea off Hal Far in BP993; he managed to climb into his dinghy despite slight wounds. A second Spitfire came under attack and Sgt. McConnell's BR352 was badly hit, the New Zealander's legs being peppered with shrapnel, whilst his shoulder was burned by an incendiary bullet. Nonetheless, he was able to avoid further action and safely returned to Takali.

HSL 128 was at once despatched to pick up Fowlow, four more of 229 Squadron's Hurricanes providing close escort, with two 185 Squadron Spitfires at higher level. Many Messerschmitts were still about, at least 30 being reported,

Ten. Remo Cazzolli of 152ª Squadriglia, 2° Gruppo Aut. CT, who was shot down and taken prisoner on 18 May. *(N. Malizia)*

Remo Cazzolli's Reggiane Re2001 crash-landed near Fort St Leonard, Zonqor Point. *(NWMA)*

and several of these dived on to the 229 Squadron section. One latched on to the tail of Sgt. Jim Pendlebury's Hurricane (BN362) which passed directly over the HSL and was then seen to cartwheel into the sea about two miles ahead. The launch at once made for the point of impact, but found only some wreckage and no trace of the pilot. Plt.Off. Ken Lee fired at the attackers and claimed one damaged, while Plt.Off. Lawrence reported:

> 'Six to eight Messerschmitts dived on us and shot poor old Jimmy down. He went right into the sea.'

Meanwhile, the top cover Spitfires had also become engaged, and Sgt. Yarra (GL-K) shot down Uffz. Johannes Lompa's 4/JG 53 Messerschmitt ('White 3') into the sea, just off Hal Far. Lompa baled out and was seen to come down near Filfla, where he was promptly picked up by the crew of HSL 128. They then continued to search for Fowlow, and about ten miles out from Benghaisa Point another figure was spotted in the sea. On board the launch, assisting the short-handed crew, was 185 Squadron's Plt.Off. Johnny Sherlock, a personal friend of the missing pilot, who recalled:

> 'In view of the shoot-ups on the launch, the crew had no love for Jerries and

sometimes were in no hurry to pick them up. In any event, as we approached a pilot bobbing around in his Mae West, the launch slowed down and one of the crew yelled out: "English?". Upon receiving a negative reply, there were a couple of suggestions as to what he should do and where he should go. The launch started to move away while the downed pilot started to wave furiously. It was at this time I recognized Norm and informed the boat crew that he was Canadian and not English. Everyone thought this was a great joke except Norm.'

Plt.Off. Norm Fowlow of 185 Squadron was shot down on 18 May and baled out into the sea. He was rescued by HSL 128, which also picked up a German pilot who had been shot down during the same action. *(Authors' Collection)*

Uffz. Lompa helped haul the Canadian pilot aboard, warmly shaking his hand, and then both rescued pilots fell into a deep sleep during the short journey back — clearly reaction to their recent experiences.

Meanwhile Yarra's No 2, Sgt. Eric Shaw, had been obliged to return to Luqa when his Spitfire suffered considerable damage at the hands of the remaining Messerschmitts, but Yarra fought on alone, having claimed a second Bf109 as a probable before Shaw's departure. He later noted:

> 'No 2 shot up, returned. Had 12 Me109s to myself. Shot down two and ran out of ammo. Did dummy attacks on remainder until forced to return through lack of fuel. Landed at Takali deadstick.'

By now two other sections of Spitfires had been scrambled to assist. Two from 126 Squadron took off at 1115, some 40 minutes after Yarra and Shaw had departed, followed by three more a further 20 minutes later. The first pair, Flt.Lt. Jimmy Peck and Plt.Off. Rip Jones, encountered six Messerschmitts orbiting over the launch and carried out a 'bounce' on these, each claiming one shot down, while Peck reported hitting another which he considered would fail to make its base. Another Messerschmitt was claimed as a probable by Plt.Off. Bisley, a member of the second section to take off. Finally, at 1145, 249 Squadron sent off five more Spitfires to meet the launch as it returned. These engaged a number of Bf109s, Sgt. Gilbert claiming one shot down, and Sgt.

Gray probably a second.

Towards evening 22 more Messerschmitts were reported approaching the coast, and 14 Spitfires were scrambled. Six of these were from 126 Squadron; Flt.Lt. Peck and Plt.Off. Rip Jones, again flying together, spotted a low-flying Bf109 which they chased and claimed shot down; the crew of an AA battery apparently reported seeing it crash into the sea, while AA gunners also claimed the probable destruction of another such fighter.

Apart from Yarra's victory over Lompa, Malta fighters had thus claimed five further Messerschmitts shot down during the day, plus four probables and one damaged. Aircraft of II/JG 53 were undoubtedly involved in the fight, but this unit's claims are not known. Lt. Jurgen Harder and Uffz. Gerhard Beitz of III Gruppe each claimed a Spitfire, but Beitz was shot down, baling out of his 'Yellow 2' of 9 Staffel into the sea near Filfla. 7 Staffel also lost an aircraft in this engagement off Hal Far, but the pilot was rescued during the afternoon by a Do24T.

It will be recalled that the day's actions opened with the discovery of Italian MAS boats operating within the vicinity of Malta. With the distraction caused by the confused air actions raging overhead, at least two of the Italian craft eventually succeeded — under cover of darkness — in penetrating the coastal defences, but neither sortie achieved its ultimate aim. Ten. di Vasc. Giuseppe Cosulich guided his craft (MTSM 218) into Marsascala Bay, where one of his specially-trained crew dived over the side to inspect beach landing obstacles. However, he wandered too far inland and was later captured when he was unable to re-locate the craft! The other MAS boat (MTSM 214 under the command of Sottoten. di Vasc. Ongarillo Ungarelli) carried aboard a spy, who was disembarked off Dingli Cliffs; his fate will be recorded later. Both operations were connected with the planned invasion of Malta.

Five MC202s of 4° Stormo flew a reconnaissance over the Island during the day, but Sottoten. Vincenzo Fischer experienced engine trouble and was obliged to return early. He crashed whilst attempting to force-land at Gela and was killed. The rest of the flight reported sighting a Beaufighter and two Spitfires, but did not engage. The 'Beaufighter' may have been a transit Beaufort (AW376 of the OADU) which had departed Malta for Egypt, flown by Plt.Off. R.W. Charters. The aircraft developed a fault en route and Charters was forced to ditch off the Libyan coast, losing his life in doing so; the other three members of his crew survived to become prisoners.

Far to the west there had been further aerial action during the day, as a naval force sailed eastwards to undertake Operation 'L.B.' — the delivery of 17 more Spitfires to the Island. These were the backlog of fighters which had remained behind at Gibraltar for one reason or another during recent ferrying operations, and which had all now been made serviceable.

The force comprised the carrier *Eagle* on which were loaded the Spitfires, and also six Albacores as reinforcements for the RNAS at Hal Far. Four Sea Hurricanes of 813F Squadron were embarked for protection duties, but could not be launched until after the departure of the Spitfires as the deck was so crowded. The old training carrier *Argus* was also present to provide some degree of air cover, carrying six Fulmars of 807 Squadron for this purpose. Escort was provided by the cruiser *Charybdis* and seven destroyers. Three Italian submarines were in the area, but only *Mocenigo* was able to manoeuvre to attack; she fired a salvo of three torpedoes at *Charybdis* but without success.

At 0920 that morning (the 18th), a Catalina flyingboat — AJ158/F of 202 Squadron from Gibraltar, flown by Flt.Lt. A.J. Bradley — was heading eastwards to the west of Algiers, when a pair of Vichy French D520s of GC II/3 approached. The Canadian pilot, on spotting the rapidly closing fighters, took his craft down to sea level. The Vichy pilots, however, obviously considered the flyingboat to be within French territorial airspace, whereupon Adjt. Jeannaud and Sgt. Andre attacked; one cannon shell exploded in the cockpit, badly wounding Bradley in the stomach, while the second pilot (Plt.Off. S.G. Sismey) was wounded in the neck. The radio operator immediately sent a signal calling for assistance while Bradley, despite his wounds, succeeded in ditching the crippled craft on the sea about ten miles off Oran.

Seven more D520s of GC III/6 had also scrambled from Maison Blanche airfield to intercept the Catalina. On arrival at the scene of the engagement, Sgt. Michaux was ordered to orbit the ditched aircraft, and await the arrival of a French ship which had been despatched to pick up the crew and to take the flyingboat in tow. Michaux had been circling for some 90 minutes and was beginning to worry about the state of his fuel, when two more fighters arrived to relieve him.

Meanwhile, the destroyer *Isis* had been ordered to break away from the carrier task force and investigate the possibility of rescuing Bradley and his crew. Due to the reported presence of hostile fighters, two Fulmars of Yellow Section, 807 Squadron, were launched from *Argus* to provide cover.

Whilst a patrolling Sunderland (W3983/R) of 10 RAAF Squadron — which was attached to 202 Squadron at Gibraltar — also headed for the area of the ditching, Flt.Lt. R.Y. Powell in Catalina Z2147/C was ordered to depart Gibraltar with a spare pilot aboard (Flt.Lt. A.M. Rushton) with a view to transferring him to the stranded craft, and to evacuating the wounded crew members. In fact *Isis* arrived first, took the crew aboard, and then sank the damaged and abandoned Catalina by gunfire; Bradley's condition was considered sufficiently serious for Powell's Catalina to be signalled to alight nearby, and to evacuate the wounded pilot to hospital as quickly as possible. However, before Powell was able to effect a landing it was necessary for him to jettison the depth charges on board, which caused *Isis* to go to action stations, thinking a submarine was being attacked!

Sunderland 'R' then arrived overhead, the crew observing *Isis* and Powell's Catalina stationary on the water, but at the same time the two GC III/6 Dewoitines appeared and opened fire on the big 'boat. As the attackers remained beyond effective machine-gun range, the Sunderland's gunners did not reply, but *Isis* AA crews opened up and the French aircraft departed.

It was at this point that the two Fulmars appeared, and one crewed by Sub Lt. P.E. Palmer and L/Air. W.A. Taylor at once attacked Lt. Salaun's Dewoitine:

> 'Pieces of fuselage broke off e/a. Smoke issued from underside of fuselage. Flicked over on its back and went down in 30° dive. Hit water and black smoke arose.'

The arrival of the British destroyer and further flyingboats had been reported ashore and three more D520s had at once been despatched by GC III/6, led by one of the unit's leading pilots, Capitaine Leon Richard. On arrival they noticed a lone Fulmar, crewed by Lt. P.R. Hall and Pty.Off.(A) H.W. Nuttall, which turned to face the French trio; Hall later reported:

'Fire from the first e/a penetrated the port side of the pilot's cockpit and engine cowling — coolant tank burst, blinding me... a/c went out of control. No reply from the A/G when told to abandon a/c.'

Philip Hall baled out off Guyotville and was picked up by *Isis*, but Bert Nuttall was lost. The destruction of the Fulmar was credited jointly to Richard, Lt. Satge and Sgt. Chef Farriol; this was the fifth British aircraft which Richard had been involved in shooting down, his four earlier victories over Syria having included another Fulmar.

TABLE 8

Operation 'LB'

17 Spitfires from HMS *Eagle* (pilots believed to have included those listed below)

Sqd.Ldr. W.G. New	
Flg.Off. Daddo-Langlois	had returned to Gibraltar to lead back flight (BR175)
Flt.Lt. R.W. McNair	had returned to Gibraltar to lead back flight
Flt.Lt. P.B. Lucas	BR115
Plt.Off. J.A. Smith, RCAF	BR126/X-3
Plt.Off. N.J. Ogilvie, RCAF	BR163
Plt.Off. J.F. Lambert, RCAF	Plt.Off. J.H. Nicholls
Plt.Off. R.G. Smith	Flt.Sgt. A.W. Varey
Plt.Off. F.D. Thomas	Flt.Sgt. E.L. Mahar, RAAF
Plt.Off. D.G. Newman	Flt.Sgt. K.W.S. Evans
Plt.Off. E.H. Glazebrook, RCAF	Sgt. Braybrooke

NB: All new pilots except Smith were from 130 Squadron

Some hours after this sequence of events, the first of the Spitfires began taking off from *Eagle* at about 1430. They were led in two flights by Flt.Lt. 'Laddie' Lucas (BR115) and Flg.Off. Daddo-Langlois (BR175), both of whom had been flown from Malta to Gibraltar in a 24 Squadron Lodestar for this purpose. The other pilots of this reinforcement were all drawn from 130 Squadron (see Table 8), under the command of newly-promoted Sqn.Ldr. Bill New, with the exception of the Canadian Plt.Off. Jerry Smith who, it may be recalled, had dramatically landed back aboard USS *Wasp* nine days previously. Flying the same aircraft (BR126/3-X), he recorded:

'Perfectly clear day. Could see far into Africa. Flew nearly 400 miles along the coast then cut across Pantelleria. At one point could see Tunis, Sicily, Malta, and far down the coast to Tripoli. Landed in Malta in the middle of a raid but all safe. Trip about 700 miles done in record time. Bags of petrol left.'

Flt.Lt. Lucas — who had spotted, but did not pursue, a Ju88 shortly after the flight commenced — found the trip less halcyon, and annotated his logbook following the three and a half hour flight:

'O! Lord deliver us from such a task again!'

After the last of the Spitfires had left the carrier, the Albacores, fitted with internal long-range fuel tanks, took off just before sunset and the carriers and their escorts turned back to the west. Two hours later the six biplanes appeared overhead and landed back on *Eagle*. All engines had begun to overheat and the pilots had turned back rather than risk carrying on. They had been wise to do so, for subsequent inspection revealed that all air coolers were set in 'Winter' position instead of 'Summer', and in the Mediterranean heat all the aircraft would have been obliged to ditch had they continued towards Malta!

Next day, as the warships retired toward Gibraltar, Axis reconnaissance aircraft continued to search for them. One Fulmar patrol, flying at 1000 feet, reported sighting a Bf110 200 feet above, and Sub Lt. G.P. Magwood attacked this, firing a short burst before it turned away. He gave chase, and was able to get in three more bursts from about 300 yards before it evaded and disappeared, convinced he had inflicted some damage.

The Regia Aeronautica recorded two additional engagements over the Mediterranean during the 18th, but no corresponding entry has been found in British accounts of the day's activities. At 1600, a Z506B floatplane of 186ª Squadriglia RM reported being attacked to the east of Malta by aircraft identified as Blenheims. One of these was claimed shot down into the sea, although the observer in Ten. Tommaso Palermo's aircraft was hit in the right leg by two bullets, and the engineer was also slightly wounded. Some two hours later another Z506B (MM45400) of 144ª Squadriglia RM, flown by Cap. Giuseppe Colli, was attacked by two aircraft identified as 'Skuas', some seven miles north-east of Pantelleria. One of these was also claimed shot down, and was reportedly seen to crash into the sea. It can only be assumed that the British aircraft involved were being ferried by OADU crews, although reports of such actions and subsequent losses have yet to be verified.

In Libya the two armies were both feverishly preparing for a new offensive, and it was likely that whichever could strike first would enjoy a major advantage of initiative. In Russia, too, the Spring thaws were over and new German offensives were getting underway. On both fronts aerial reinforcement was

An impressive line-up of Macchi C202 fighters of the newly-arrived 51° Stormo CT at Gela. *(N. Malizia)*

urgently required, and it was to be Sicily which would be 'plundered' for these. As already mentioned, the Messerschmitts of II/JG 3, and the Ju88s of II and III/KG 77, had departed for Germany and France by the end of April. Now 'Ultra' intercepts indicated that more moves were afoot. In fact, II/JG 3 did not remain in Germany for long but was redeployed to the Eastern front, where it was joined by I/JG 53; meanwhile III/JG 53, I/NJG 2, III/ZG 26 and III/StG 3 — or such elements of these as were still in Sicily — were moved across the Mediterranean to reinforce Rommel's forces in Cyrenaica, and I/KG 54 was to strengthen the units of LG 1 on Crete. Hence, only II/JG 53, KüFlGr 606 and KGr 806, plus the air-sea rescue and reconnaissance elements were to remain in Sicily.

The Regia Aeronautica was also anxious to strenghten its air force in Africa, and 4° Stormo CT was ordered to Libyan airfields. To compensate for this transfer, Sicily was to be strengthened by further units from mainland Italy, and from Rome-Ciampino airfield elements of 155° Gruppo CT from the 51° Stormo CT began moving south; 33 brand-new MC202s, led by Magg Duilio Fanali, would arrive at Gela, its three squadriglie commanded as follows:

351ª Squadriglia	Cap. Riccardo Spagnolini
360ª Squadriglia	Cap. Carlo Miani
378ª Squadriglia	Cap. Bruno Tattanelli

Sixteen Ju87Bs and Rs of 102° Gruppo Tuffatori would also transfer from Italy, but only 13 machines reached Gela airfield accompained by an S.81 transport; the other three Ju87s were damaged in accidents along the way. Formed on 1 May under Cap. Giuseppe Cenni, the unit replaced the recently departed German Stukas of III/StG 3. Its two elements were the 209ª Squadriglia under Cap. Aldo Stringa and the 239ª Squadriglia led by Ten. Sergio Bigoni (soon to be replaced by Ten. Giuseppe Tamborra). These units were not newly formed; the former had previously been part of the 101° Gruppo Ba'T, and the latter a part of 97° Gruppo Ba'T, which had operated over Malta earlier in the war. A few days later, 5° Stormo Tuffatori was formed to control this unit and its sister 101° Gruppo, the latter remaining in Italy. Meanwhile, 59ª and 60ª Squadriglia of 33° Gruppo BT, part of the 9° Stormo BT, arrived at Chinisia with Z1007bis trimotors under the command of Ten. Col. Ercole Savi.

The Messerschmitts of III/JG 53 left for Africa after a very successful period of action against Malta's air force. The unit's illustrious commander, Hpt. Wolf-Dietrich Wilcke, had added four victories to his growing personal score, while the unit's top-scorer had been Oblt. Helmut Belser of 8 Staffel, who had made eight claims. Other successful pilots were Ofw. Werner Stumpf of 9 Staffel with six, and Lt. Karl-Heinz Quaritsch and Lt. Klager (both of 8 Staffel) with five each. Four pilots had each claimed three, including Lt. Jurgen Harder of 7 Staffel and Lt. Hermann Neuhoff, formerly of 7 Staffel, although the latter had since become a prisoner.

British Intelligence considered that even should Rommel strike first, he could hope to achieve little more than to push the British Army back to the Egyptian frontier — quite an accurate assessment as it was to prove. However, it was feared that if he should succeed in taking Tobruk, the next logical step would be for the invasion of Malta to be launched. Such an idea was indeed, still fresh in the minds of the Axis commanders at this time, particularly of Mussolini and his generals.

Tuesday, 19 May

The reduction of Axis strength on Sicily now caused a sudden and most noticeable falling-off in activity over Malta. During the 19th small numbers of Bf109s swept over the Island until mid-afternoon, when three Z1007bis of 50° Gruppo BT approached, escorted by 13 Macchis of 10° Gruppo — on their last raid over Malta — and a corresponding number of Reggianes of 2° Gruppo. Twenty Spitfires were scrambled, ten from 126 and 601 Squadrons intercepting after the bombers had carried out a high level raid on Luqa and Safi, without causing any damage. Plt.Off. Caldwell (3-M) of the latter unit succeeded in shooting down Sottoten. Nicola Falcone's Z1007bis (MM23352), and claimed damage to a second bomber. All three Cants were in fact hit, Falcone carrying out a ditching in the sea; he and his crew were rescued suffering from only minor wounds and injuries. Flg.Off. Hone's Spitfire (3-N) was damaged by a Re2001 but the Rhodesian was able safely to return to Takali.

Two 185 Squadron Spitfires also became engaged in the action, Flt.Lt. Lawrence (GL-B) claiming damage to a MC202, but both Spitfires sustained damage. Reggiane pilots claimed one Spitfire shot down by Ten. Carlo Seganti and a Beaufighter by Mar. Antonio Patriarca, plus five Spitfires damaged. Not yet operational, the newly-arrived Plt.Off. Jerry Smith recorded:

> 'Went to drome at Luqa. Small raid by high-flying Eyties. Located some kit at Naxxar. Meals here are awful. Watched wizard beat up of Takali by Junkers 88s. Nothing hit by bombs. Ack Ack looked wonderful in different coloured streamers. Am now in 601 Squadron.'

The Luftwaffe raid on Takali to which he referred occurred after dark, four Ju88s bombing the dispersal area. Here, in spite of Smith's comments, an unserviceable Spitfire (BR106) of 249 Squadron was burnt out. AA gunners put up a spirited defence, claiming two of the raiders damaged. In the early hours six BR20Ms of 88° Gruppo BT set out to raid Luqa and Hal Far. Two Beaufighters were scrambled, Plt.Off. Daniel (with Sgt. Gosling) intercepting an aircraft which was variously described as a Z1007 or an S.79; it was in fact Ten. Pierino Medesani's 265ª Squadriglia BR20M (MM24141), which was shot down at 0345 and was seen to fall in flames two miles from Xlendi Bay, Gozo, and exploded on impact. The second Beaufighter, crewed by Plt.Off. Oakes and Flt.Sgt. Walsh, picked up contacts but failed to gain any success; two other Italian crews reported being pursued by nightfighters although both escaped unscathed.

Malta's strike force was again in action during the night following the sighting of a small northbound convoy — comprising the transport *Bertani* and three destroyers — some 35 miles off Tripoli, by a Special Duties Wellington crew. Four bombs were aimed at *Bertani* and possible hits were claimed. Meanwhile, at Hal Far, three Albacores were sent out at once to continue the attack. This time the Wellington released its flares successfully at 0015, and two torpedoes were launched by the Naval aircraft. Sub Lt. Reg Elliott (T9142/C) believed that a hit had been gained amidships on one of the destroyers, while the other missile struck the stern of the transport, which had to be towed back to Tripoli.

Wednesday, 20 May

A Z506B floatplane of 612ª Squadriglia was out early on Wednesday, escorted by 14 Re2001s of 2° Gruppo, searching for survivors of the missing BR20M. Ten. Pocek was obliged to return early with engine trouble but near Gozo he reported sighting a lone Spitfire, which he pursued and claimed to have shot down.

The only raid which materialized during the day occurred just before 1600, when half a dozen Jabo Bf109s swept low over Takali, damaging a petrol bowser. When dusk came, Flt.Lt. Price was ordered to take out HSL 107 to rescue a man spotted at the base of Dingli Cliffs who proved to be a civilian, initially identified as 'A. Morelli'. He was, in fact, Carmelo Borg Pisani, a Maltese supporter of Italian fascism who had been trained in Italy for espionage; he had been transported to a point 150 yards off shore two nights previously by one of the MAS boats, as recounted earlier. Complete with radio equipment, pistol, hand grenade and British currency, he paddled ashore in a dinghy only to become stranded! He was later tried by a Maltese Civil Court, found guilty of treason, and hanged (see *Malta: Blitzed But Not Beaten* for further details).

The day also brought news of several awards for Malta's pilots. Within 126 Squadron DFCs were announced for Flt.Lt. 'Tim' Johnston, Flt.Lt. Jimmy Peck and Plt.Off. Reade Tilley, and a DFM for Sgt. Tim Goldsmith, while 249 Squadron was honoured with DFCs for Sqn.Ldr. Stan Grant, Flg.Off. 'Buck' Buchanan and the late Plt.Off. Peter Nash; Sgt. Ray Hesselyn was advised of a Bar to his DFM. There was also the announcement of an 'immediate' DFC for 89 Squadron's Plt.Off. 'Tubby' Daniel.

While Malta had remained fairly quite, a drama had unfolded to the west when an OADU Wellington which had departed Gibraltar, experienced a fate similar to that which had befallen a number of such transit aircraft. When approximately 50 miles from Malta, and with darkness rapdily approaching, Sgt. Harold Bancroft (pilot of Z8589) began to fear that all was not well when the aircraft's instruments began playing up. Although the aircraft was apparently being homed onto the Malta beacon, the impression grew amongst the crew that they were, in fact, flying in a huge circle — possibly due to 'beam-bending' by the Italian CRIRA. While the crew believed that they were off Cape Bon, in retrospect they would seem actually to have been 'guided' to the north of Sicily. When AA fire was seen 10-15 miles away, the crew assumed that they were watching an air raid on Malta, under which circumstance they had been briefed to stand off to the south of the Island until granted permission to land.

At this point the rear gunner, Sgt. Eric Bell, warned of the approach of two shapes in the darkness, which were assumed to be Beaufighters coming to guide them in, but which were probably Ju88Cs of I/NJG 2. One of these promplty opened fire, and believing his aircraft to have been hit in the fuel tank when both gauges indicated empty, Bancroft decided to ditch at once before a second, and probably decisive, attack could be made.

A reasonably successful ditching was accomplished under the circumstances, although Sgt. Reg Hanley (the front gunner) was lost, and Sgt. Arthur Robinson was badly injured. The others, all suffering lesser injuries, reached the safety of the dinghy, into which Robinson was hauled after he had been located in the water with a badly lacerated leg. For six long days and nights they drifted, suffering from exposure, before an aircraft was seen at low altitude. A signal rocket was fired, but seemed to have failed to attract the crew's attention. However, this was not the case, for the crew of the S.79 — for such it was — radioed for help to be sent and later a Z506B flew over the area. This, unfortunately, failed to locate the dinghy, despite two rockets being fired to attract the crew's attention.

Finally they spotted land on the horizon, although the dinghy did not seem to be making towards it. In desperation, Bancroft and Bell decided to swim for it, in a last gasp attempt to get help for Robinson who was by now in a very bad way. Many hours later Bancroft came across a fishing vessel, but was unable to attract attention. Land now lay within sight, however, and with his final strength he reached the rocky shore of Filicudi Island, part of the Lipari group, 25 miles north of Sicily. Help was soon at hand, and the three airmen in the dinghy were rescued, while Bell was discovered washed up on shore; all five men survived as prisoners.

Thursday, 21 May

Meanwhile, dawn at Malta on the 21st brought with it a short, sharp fighter-bomber raid on Hal Far, five Bf109s sweeping in at low-level, bombing and strafing. The defenders were caught unawares, but while two airmen were killed and another seriously wounded, little damage was caused.

A photo-reconnaissance Spitfire of 69 Squadron brought back photographs from Catania indicating the presence of an increased number of Ju88s — in fact 83 compared with 28 spotted on the airfield four days previously! Given the move away from the island, it was surmised that these must have been aircraft in transit, for no increase in attacks on Malta followed.

Soon after midday four Ju88s and ten Bf109s ventured over, ten Spitfires being scrambled. Sgt. Yarra (GL-K) led four from 185 Squadron but as he engaged the bombers, he was shot-up by Messerschmitts, although his aircraft was not badly damaged. One of his section, Plt.Off. Lambert (GL-C), claimed one of the attackers shot down. Four aircraft of 601 Squadron had also scrambled, with Flt.Lt. Barnham at their head. Quite unofficially, Barnham had had the wings of his Spitfire painted with large white spots to enable his section quickly to recognize his aircraft in the air; he had also had the cockpit canopy removed to allow clearer vision. Now, vectored onto the Ju88s at low level, he had just positioned his section for an astern attack when they were pounced upon by Bf109s. One overshot, and Barnham was able to open fire at this before it disappeared from view. A call in his earphones: 'Something's gone in near Filfla', led him to claim this as destroyed. Either he or Lambert of 185 Squadron had shot down Uffz. Ernst-Hans Seidl of II/JG 53, who was killed.

Barnham was then engaged by a number of Messerschmitts and fired at two without observed results. Pursued by five more, he headed low for Takali, only to be greeted by a burst of Bofors fire. On landing, he realised that the white spots on his wings had attracted the attention of the German pilots, and at once arranged for them to be painted out again! Later, when Sqn.Ldr. Bisdee arrived at dispersal, he ordered that the aircraft's cockpit hood be replaced — much to Barnham's chargin.

HSL 128 was sent out when a dinghy was spotted some three miles west of Benghaisa Point. It turned out to contain Uffz. Gerhard Beitz, the 9/JG 53 pilot who had been shot down three days earlier. He had been paddling desperately towards Malta when able to muster sufficient strength, and when rescued was stiff, weary and badly blistered by the sun.

A Special Duties Wellington was again successful in locating a convoy, two 5000-ton transports and two destroyers being reported 70 miles off Cape Turgeunes. A single 250lb bomb was aimed at one of the destroyers, but an effective smokescreen prevented results being observed. Three Albacores were again called in, and at 0210 one made an abortive attempt to launch its torpedo

Spitfire BR246/B of 249 Squadron at Takali. The aircraft has been roughly overpainted locally because the Desert sand and stone camouflage scheme in which most of them were delivered was not favoured by some pilots. *(NWMA)*

through the smoke. The Wellington then made a diving attack, dropping three more bombs while its gunners sprayed a destroyer. A second Albacore lost formation and failed to find the convoy whilst the third, T9142/C flown by Sub Lt. D.J.N. Barnes and Sub Lt. J.J. McCluskey, failed to return.

Friday, 22 May

Not until late on the morning of Friday the 22nd did the first raid approach, when 20 Bf109s crossed the coast, four bombing Hal Far. Eight Spitfires scrambled and four of 249 Squadron intercepted two Bf109s off Kalafrana, Flg.Off. McNair claiming one shot down. A similar number of fighters, reportedly Bf109s and MC202s, patrolled off the coast between 1920-2012, when 14 Spitfires were scrambled; Flt.Sgt. Dodd (GL-E) of 185 Squadron claimed one shot down, and one Spitfire was slightly damaged in return.

Darkness brought a further raid on Luqa and Hal Far by four BR20Ms of 88° Gruppo BT, which were met by an 89 Squadron Beaufighter (X7750), crewed by Flt.Lt. Hayton and Plt.Off. Josling; at 0325 they intercepted Ten. Paolo Veprizchi's MM22722, which fell in flames near Gela; the crew baled out, some of them injured. The same Beaufighter was then vectored onto another bomber, which Hayton claimed probably shot down; this was Ten. Abbarchi's aircraft which returned to Gela in a damaged condition, with two of the crew seriously wounded.

Saturday, 23 May

Saturday morning at 0715 saw a dozen Spitfires of 126 and 601 Squadrons off to intercept five Z1007bis of 50° Gruppo, escorted by 16 Re2001s of 2° Gruppo, approaching to bomb Takali; Bf109s may also have been present. Plt.Off. Tilley claimed one fighter — identified as an MC202 — while Plt.Off. Rip Jones claimed one of the bombers probably destroyed, and Flt.Sgt. Schade also tangled with the escort. He claimed a Messerschmitt probably destroyed and a second as damaged. The 601 Squadron pilots were led by Sqn.Ldr. Bisdee, partially recovered from the 'Dog', flying a Spitfire previously flown by Flt.Lt. Parry who had altered the aircraft's trim tabs. As Bisdee closed on an Italian fighter and opened fire, his port cannon jammed and he found the Spitfire difficult to control. He was pursued by an Re2001, which he was unable to evade, but the Italian pilot flew up alongside him, waved and departed — possibly out of ammunition! Meanwhile, Sgt. McConnell of this unit claimed a Z1007bis probable, while Sgt. Innes claimed a Reggiane shot down and another as damaged.

No Italian aircraft actually fell but two Re2001s were damaged, as was the leading Cant, in which one crewman was mortally wounded and another less seriously hurt. The Reggiane pilots claimed three Spitfires shot down, one by Ten. Giorgio Gasperoni, the other two by several pilots. A fourth was claimed by bomber gunners, and six others were believed to have been hit. In fact, only a single Spitfire suffered damage. Mar. Giovanni Durli, engineer in the 210ª Squadriglia Z1007bis who died of his wounds, was subsequently awarded the Medaglia d'Oro posthumously. Plt.Off. Jerry Smith of 601 Squadron watched the combat from the ground, and reported:

> 'Watched a Macchi (*sic*) firing at a Spit. Spit pilot didn't even know it, but was unhurt. Learned later that Spit pilot was my CO.'

As has been indicated, one of the major effects of the Axis Spring offensive against Malta had been the inability thereby imposed on the British forces to continue their offensive against German and Italian convoys ferrying reinforcement and supplies to Rommel's forces in North Africa. During the past few weeks, 'Ultra' had provided details of no less than 26 Axis shipping movements, but to preserve the security of this code-breaking system there still had to be actual sightings of the convoys before attacks could be mounted. Shortage of reconnaissance aircraft on Malta had resulted in only nine of these convoys actually being spotted; consequently, during April and the first half of May no more than 13 Axis ships were lost throughout the entire Mediterranean. Indeed, by the end of May some 236,500 tons of cargo — mainly military supplies — and 106,500 tons of fuel would have crossed the Mediterranean since the start of February. This was a vast increase in tonnage and every effort was being made to interfere with this traffic, but the fact that recently Malta had not been a secure striking base had rendered this most difficult.

Lack of air support had made even such effort as could be expended at times very costly, as epitomized by the fate of a destroyer force sent out from Alexandria on 11 May. The four warships had been despatched in an all-out bid to intercept and destroy a southbound convoy comprising three merchant vessels and three escorting destroyers, which was heading down the eastern route, along the Greek coastline. Devoid of fighter cover, the Royal Navy force was attacked by Ju88s of I/LG 1 operating from Crete, and three of the destroyers were swiftly sunk. Only *Jervis* weathered the assault, returning to base with 630 survivors from *Jackel, Kipling* and *Lively*.

With reduced activities over the Island however, Malta became once more a base for the resumption of offensive operations. Thus, after dark, the first of ten Wellingtons of 104 Squadron, under the command of Sqn.Ldr. M.H. Young DFC, began arriving at Luqa following the long haul from Egypt. Unfortunately, one of these crashed into a bomb crater on arrival; although the aircraft was a total write-off, the crew escaped unscathed.

A second aircraft (W5554 piloted by Sgt. A.R. Merritt) undershot on landing and hit a stone wall. The front end of the aircraft plunged into a crater and the nose turret broke off; all aboard sustained injuries, the pilot's proving fatal. Six Wellington IC torpedo-carriers of 38 Squadron were then also detached from Egypt, Wg.Cdr. J.H. Chaplin leading these in.

Sunday, 24 May

Sunday morning on Malta was very quite, and it was not until shortly after noon that Plt.Offs. Halford (GL-B) and Ogilvie (GL-C) of 185 Squadron were scrambled and vectored south of Malta to investigate a suspected 'bandit'; 'Buzz' Ogilvie recalled:

> 'I remember we climbed to about 4-5000 feet and we were between the south coast and Filfla. We spotted a Ju88 flying very low over the water in south-easterly direction. Halford indicated to me he was going to make an attack. Of course we didn't have any trouble catching it because of the height we had on it. Halford made his attack; as he was firing he was hit by the rear-gunner and pulled up. I then proceeded to make my attack but because of the speed involved I had to make a considerable allowance — couldn't see whether I was hitting the 88 or not. When I pulled up and looked around, the 88 had disappeared. Halford and I returned to base.'

They were credited with shooting down this aircraft, although no loss was recorded by the Luftwaffe. Just over three hours later, three patrolling Spitfires of 603 Squadron reported encountering three Macchis; two of these were claimed shot down by Plt.Offs. Barlow and Dicks-Sherwood, who also claimed a third damaged. Although Re2001s of 2° Gruppo and MC202s of 54° Stormo patrolled off the Island during the day, none apparently reported any engagements with Malta's Spitfires!

Despite the inauspicious arrival of the Wellingtons of the 104 Squadron detachment, the unit was soon in action. An aircraft of the Special Duties Flight located two merchant vessels, one estimated to be of 5000 tons, the other of 1000

A quartet of 249 Squadron pilots at dispersal; from left, Sgt. Paul Brennan, Plt.Off. Harry Kelly, Flt.Sgt. Jack Rae and Plt.Off. Jimmy James. *(NWMA)*

tons. They were being escorted by two destroyers and were seen 135 miles north-west of Benghazi. The larger vessel was attacked from 700 feet with eight 250lb bombs and a destroyer was also strafed, but no results were observed. Twenty minutes later, three of the 104 Squadron aircraft arrived and bombed from 2000 feet, four bombs being seen to straddle the two transports before well-laid smoke made further observation difficult.

Monday, 25 May

The first day of the new week opened with eight Spitfires of 249 Squadron being ordered off at 1420, followed 40 minutes later by 16 more from 126 and 601 Squadrons. Their opponents on this occasion were three S.84s of 4° Gruppo Aut BT (mis-identified by the Spitfire pilots as Z1007bis), covered by 16 Re2001s as close escort with a dozen Bf109s as indirect cover. The 249 Squadron pilots intercepted first and became entangled with the escort, Flt.Lt. Ron West claiming a Reggiane shot down and Sgt. Brennan reporting strikes on another, while Flg.Off. McNair claimed a Bf109 probably destroyed and Sgt. De Nancrede one damaged.

Flt.Lt. Lee managed to penetrate the fighter screen and fired at one of the bombers, claiming it badly damaged. Flt.Sgt. Goldsmith of 126 Squadron engaged the same bomber and although his own aircraft was hit in the wing and engine, he was able to land safely. The Australian also claimed a Re2001 damaged, subsequently reporting:

> 'Fired at a Cant 1007 (*sic*), left it burning. Also had a dogfight with a Reggiane 2001.'

Sqn.Ldr. Bill New, who was flying with 126 Squadron while gaining experience over the Island prior to taking command of 185 Squadron, also claimed damage to a bomber; Plt.Off. Wally Caldwell (a New Zealander) was shot and killed in BR354, and another Spitfire sustained damage.

2° Gruppo pilots claimed four Spitfires shot down in this action, one each by Cap. Sterzi, Ten. Seganti, Mar. Fabbri and Mar. Patriarca; Cap. Teia, commander of 152ª Squadriglia, claimed another shared with the crew of a bomber. Italian records also show that a further Spitfire was claimed by a Bf109 pilot. No Italian or German fighters were recorded lost or seriously damaged; however all three S.84s were hit, two returning with wounded on board.

Flt.Lt. Ronnie West's latest claim raised his tally to six and he was recommended for a DFC; he was somewhat of a character, as 185 Squadron's Plt.Off. John Sherlock recalled, on the occasion of the latter's visit to 249 Squadron's Mess at Takali:

> 'When I went into the Mess there was a swarthy individual sitting in the hallway, naked except for his shorts and a towel wrapped around his head like a turban. He was sitting crossed-legged and in front of him was a basket with a hunk of rope dangling over the side to represent a snake.
>
> 'This person was swaying back and forth and playing a clarinet, and rather well, too. I stopped and asked the pilot with me as to what the score was. He introduced me to the snake charmer, who was none other than Ronnie West, and who assured me, with a very straight face, that it was just a matter of time until all pilots went just as crazy as he was. After what we had gone through in the past weeks, this was easy to believe!'

Other characters prominent at this time included Wg.Cdr. 'Tiny' Dawson, the diminutive (5′4″) Wing Commander Flying at Hal Far. Although he did not fly on operations with the Spitfires, he was still regularly involved in the series of nocturnal supply-dropping sorties to the agent in Sicily, flying his all-black Hurricane on these occasions. During daytime, he would be seen riding his white horse about the airfield, reins in one hand, fly-swat in the other!

Luqa could also boast an unusual sight for newcomers — 89 Squadron's ace night fighter pilot, Plt.Off. 'Tubby' Daniel, was the proud possessor of a pony and trap and during the day could be seen delivering tools, food and tea, as and when required, to the tireless groundcrewmen as they worked around the airfield. Such antics were appreciated by one and all and provided a much-welcomed relief to the general grimness of the situation.

At dusk six Bf109 Jabo with six more Messerschmitts as escort attacked Hal Far, causing little damage. This raid on Hal Far was immediately followed by another by a dozen Ju88s, which also dropped bombs on Takali and Luqa; at the latter airfield two of the newly-arrived Wellingtons were damaged. Neither force was intercepted, only the AA gunners putting up a defence.

Despite the attack on Luqa, two of 104 Squadron's Wellingtons were despatched to raid the train ferry terminus at Messina, on the north-eastern tip of Sicily. Bomb bursts were seen by the crews east of the citadel, and heavy damage in the area was subsequently admitted. AA gunners claimed one bomber shot down, but while the crews reported accurate fire, both Wellingtons returned safely. A repeat attack was made by seven aircraft next night, again without loss. On this occasion, fires were reported in the railyards and on the ferry slipway, one of which was visible from 35 miles distant.

Tuesday, 26 May

There were no engagements until mid afternoon of the 26th, when eight 603 Squadron Spitfires scrambled, followed by four each from 185 and 249 Squadrons. A fighter sweep by 13 Re2001s of 2° Gruppo was engaged by the 603 Squadron flight. Flg.Off. Mitchell and Plt.Off. Barlow each claimed one shot down, and Flt.Lt. Sanders another damaged. Cap. Annibale Sterzi (commander of 358ª Squadriglia) was shot down, his aircraft going down in a screaming vertical dive to crash in a field near Ghaxaq. He managed to bale out but his parachute failed to open properly, and he fell to his death near Luqa; at least two other Reggianes returned seriously damaged, while one Spitfire was claimed in return by Ten. Giorgio Gasperoni. It would appear that he attacked Sgt. Yarra of 185 Squadron, whose aircraft (GL-B) was shot-up by a Re2001, although the damage was not serious.

The decision had been taken to evacuate some of the battle-fatigued, wounded and sick pilots, since sufficient numbers of acceptable replacements were now available and more were on the way. Amongst the first to depart were two of 601 Squadron's pilots, including the Australian Plt.Off. Scott who had remained in a very distraught state since the loss of his close friend and fellow-contryman, Max Briggs.

Wednesday, 27 May

The last Wednesday in May proved to be relatively quite for the defenders, only four small formations of Bf109s being reported over the Island; no interceptions were achieved by those Spitfires that were scrambled.

Survivors of 229 Squadron prior to departure for Egypt on 27 May, following the unit's brief and costly detachment to the Island. L to r, rear: Flt.Sgt. Carson; Plt.Off. Lee; Plt.Off. Carter. Front: Sgt. Ganes; Sgt Alderdice; Sgt. Potts; Sqn.Ldr. Farnes; Flt.Sgt. Roy; Sgt. Willcox; Sgt. Vidler; Sgt Pauley; Plt.Off. Malthus. *(T.E. Lawrence family via P. Sortehaug)*

With sufficient Spitfires now to hand, the remaining pilots of 229 Squadron were ordered to return to the Middle East. A dozen departed at 0500 in an assortment of Hurricanes, each fitted with long-range tanks, escorted for the first part of the way by Spitfires of 185 Squadron. Sqn.Ldr. Farnes, who led the group, recalled:

> 'Although the weather report was not particularly favourable, bearing in mind that for this long journey we really needed a tail wind, we were nevertheless ordered to leave.
>
> 'I had given strict orders to all pilots that they were not to use their R/T under any circumstances for fear of the enemy obtaining a "fix" on our position. The first part of the journey was flown at sea level to avoid enemy radar at Sicily, then I was instructed to fly at 2000 feet. At this height we were in thick haze and were on instruments for two and a half hours. During this time a Heinkel passed in front of us at a similar height, but there was nothing we could do about it.
>
> 'What was left of the squadron finally landed at Sidi Barrani after four and a half hours flying, and with precious little fuel left, possibly enough for another five or ten minutes flying.'

Three of the Hurricanes — Z2982 flown by Sgt. Norris Ganes, Z4005 flown by Sgt. George Willcox, and BE642 flown by Plt.Off. Ken Lee — failed to arrive; Willcox alone managed to evade capture and returned to the squadron a week later, having apparently been shot down by a MC202 over the coast. The other two also survived crash-landings, as Ganes recalled:

> 'En route I was separated from the squadron, and flew along the coast of North Africa until I ran out of fuel. As we were flying just above the water to avoid radar contract, I crash-landed. Later that day I was picked up by a German patrol.'

Plt.Off. Tom Lawrence of 229 Squadron about to depart for Egypt on 27 May in one of the unit's two-cannon Hurricane IIcs. *(T.E. Lawrence family via P. Sortehaug)*

Lee had experienced electrical problems, neither his R/T nor petrol pump working, and he was therefore unable to transfer fuel from the long-range tanks to the main tank. Deciding to head for the coast, he anticipated making for Tobruk where he hoped to reach British forces. Before breaking away he noticed another aircraft drop out of the formation. En route he met a formation of about half a dozen Ju87s and made an attack on these, but did not observe any results. The rear gunners put up a temendous barrage of fire at him although the Hurricane was not hit. He continued flying towards Tobruk but was forced to crash-land in scrub country about 20 miles west of El Hania when his fuel ran out. He walked westwards for two days and a night, his intention being to steal a boat, but was spotted by Arabs and later that evening was turned over to the Italians (Lee later escaped from the POW camp and reached British lines, for which he was awarded a Mention in Despatches).

Another of the Hurricane pilots, Plt.Off. Malthus, later summed up the reasons for the failure of 229 Squadron to play an effective role on Malta:

> 'In the first place, a Hurricane squadron should never have been sent to Malta at this stage of the blitz. Hurricanes were much slower, and could not cope with the 109s. Secondly, a "green" squadron, with many pilots having little or no operational experience, should never have been chosen.'

The night of the 27th/28th proved eventful; firstly, the crew (Flt.Sgts. Miller and Walsh) of a patrolling Beaufighter of 89 Squadron sighted about 18 E-boats 20 miles south of Malta. Four diving attacks were made and Miller believed that he had obtained strikes on three of the vessels, causing explosions.

While this was going on, an ASV Wellington had spotted two merchant vessels and four escorting destroyers 37 miles off Punto Stilo, and had dropped a stick of five 500lb bombs from 1700 feet. These burst about 50 yards ahead of the transports, which were also machine-gunned from low level. Two more transports and two destroyers were then located 120 miles off Cape Spartivento by another ASV Wellington, which also dropped five 500 pounders to burst on the port side of a 5000-ton vessel, but without observed result. The destroyers replied with accurate AA fire, but the Wellington escaped damage.

Meanwhile, eight bomber Wellingtons from 104 Squadron had been despatched in two waves to attack the Messina ferry. The first found the target completely obscured by a smoke screen, so bombed Catania airfield and Augusta harbour instead. One Wellington was slightly damaged by AA fire. Of the second wave, two returned early with engine trouble and one managed to release its bombs on Messina through a gap in the smoke screen, the other bombing the target by estimation through the smoke; both aircraft returned safely, although the Italian AA defences claimed to have shot down five bombers in the Messina Straits zone during these raids!

Thursday, 28 May

The next days brought little activity over Malta. On Thursday during the late afternoon, four 126 Squadron Spitfires were scrambled on warning that a number of fighters were approaching; two dozen Bf109s, including at least four Jabo, then crossed the coast and attacked Luqa where little damage was done. The 126 Squadron section intercepted and Flt.Sgt. Schade claimed a probable. A further alarm was sounded at 2050, when six raiders approached but did not cross the coast. Four Spitfires were scrambled and chased a number of Ju88s of KGr 806 back towards Sicily, where Bf109s came to their aid. No claims were made, although one Ju88 (M7+MK) failed to return from an intended raid on Luqa; Fw. Friedrich Brehm and his crew were posted missing.

Shortly before midnight, Cap. Cenni led four Ju87s of 239ª Squadriglia on their first operation — a night raid on Gozo, Luqa and Takali. One was obliged to return early but the other three were stalked by a Beaufighter of 89 Squadron, although no contacts were made. This raid was followed by an attack on Takali by nine Z1007bis of 33° Gruppo which similarly escaped interception.

Whilst the Italian Stukas were over Malta, 104 Squadron had despatched six Wellingtons to raid Catania airfield in full-moon visibility, two 4000lb bombs falling on the main runway and other bombs amongst buildings at the north side of the base. Apparently some bombs also fell on nearby Gerbini airfield, where one Italian airman was killed and a second wounded. AA gunners claimed one of the attackers shot down, but all returned, three with slight damage. One returning crew spotted a vessel of 5-6000 tons 15 miles south-east of Catania and when this was reported after landing, Sub Lt. Elliott was sent in a Swordfish (W5900) but found nothing during a four and a half hour sortie.

Meanwhile, two convoys had been located by a 38 Squadron Wellington to the north-west of Benghazi, one comprising six vessels and the other four. Six 250lb bombs were aimed at one ship from 4000 feet but the results were not observed; when five torpedo-carriers were subsequently despatched by the squadron, they failed to find either convoy.

Friday, 29 May

Friday was even quieter for Malta than the previous day, with just two small fighter sweeps and a Jabo raid on Hal Far; there were no interceptions and negligible damage. Four Ju87s of 209ª Squadriglia and four Z1007bis of 33° Gruppo raided the Island after dark, Serg. Gastone Converso's Stuka being intercepted by Beaufighter X7750 crewed by Flt.Lt. Hayton and Plt.Off Josling. Despite sustaining damage to the rudder, port wing and undercarriage, it returned safely.

Catania airfield was again the target for six Wellingtons of 104 Squadron, five of which bombed from 10,000 feet; amongst the bombs dropped were two 4000 pounders. Numerous hits on buildings were reported by the crews and many fires were seen, and a He111 was destroyed on the airfield. One crew reported being approached by two night fighters over the target area, but these then appeared to collide, following which there was a large explosion. One other Wellington had returned early with engine trouble and crashed at Attard, bursting into flames. Four of the crew were killed and one other seriously injured, although the pilot (Sgt. R.J. Hills) escaped with only minor injuries. On returning from the raid, a second Wellington crashed on landing, although the crew in this case escaped unhurt.

Saturday, 30 May

Several small sweeps by German and Italian fighters occurred on Saturday morning; eight Spitfires of 185 Squadron scrambled on the third occasion but made no interceptions. As they returned to Hal Far to land, eight Bf109s followed them in but caused no damage. At 1800 four Spitfires of 185 Squadron, followed by four of 126 Squadron, were ordered off to intercept three S.84s of 4° Gruppo, escorted by 22 Re2001s and a dozen Bf109s; Luqa was the target, where one Spitfire was slightly damaged on the ground.

Flt.Sgt. Ferraby (BP876) of 185 Squadron reported gaining strikes on a Messerschmitt, then attacked a bomber — identified as a Z1007 — which was also attacked by Plt.Off. Bill Johnson, newly-commissioned Plt.Off. Tim Goldsmith, and Flt.Sgt. Milner of 126 Squadron; the tri-motor was claimed destroyed. The other three pilots of 185 Squadron all reported cannon stoppages as they attempted to attack, but Flt.Sgt. Tommy Parks of 126 Squadron also reported gaining strikes on a bomber — probably the same aircraft as that attacked by the others. Only the leading Savoia of the trio had been hit hard, the pilot succeeding in landing his badly damaged aircraft at Catania with one crewman dead and another wounded. Goldsmith reported:

> 'Had a squirt at a BR20 (or something), then attacked a Reggiane. Knocked off his radiator. Landed at Takali as Luqa was u/s.'

No Reggianes were lost but Cap. Roberto Fassi's aircraft apparently suffered engine trouble; despite this handicap, when pursued by two Spitfires he claimed to have shot one down. A second Spitfire was claimed by other 2° Gruppo pilots, who also considered they had damaged 15 more! A reconnaissance Messerschmitt (F6+YH) of 1(F)/122, flown by Lt. Herbert Toula, crash-landed at Catania on return from a sortie and the pilot was injured. It is not known if the aircraft had been damaged during the course of a sortie to Malta.

Two hours prior to midnight saw the first of four Z1007bis of 33° Gruppo BT and four Ju87s of 239ª Squadriglia cross the coast, the raiders approaching singly;

Ten. Giuseppe Tamborra's Stuka failed to return and was reported shot down by AA fire. Beaufighters were sent up, but only Flt.Sgt. Miller and Sgt. Tearle (in V8224) had any success. They were vectored onto one Cant, a 59ª Squadriglia machine flown by Ten. Antonio Errico, which was pursued to within 20 miles of Licata and was claimed destroyed when it was left seriously damaged and on fire. Four crewman baled out into the sea and were lost, but Errico and the second pilot, Serg.Magg. Aldo Endrizzi, stayed with the aircraft and force-landed in a field near Menfi; both were injured.

The Messina ferry was once more the target for three Wellingtons, although again one was obliged to return early with engine trouble. A single 4000lb bomb fell close to the terminus but smoke screens prevented further observations. A delivery Wellington, possibly led astray by CRIRA transmissions, strayed too close to Messina as 104 Squadron's attack was underway, the crew of which probably thought they were witnessing a raid on Malta. The Wellington was fired upon by Messina's AA defences and force-landed near Licata, the crew surviving to be taken prisoner.

Further to the south, off the Libyan coast, an ASV Wellington had found and bombed a 6000-ton transport (with destroyer escort) 165 miles out from Homs. Three Albacores and two Swordfish were despatched to continue the attack — at extreme range — but failed to locate the vessel, while five of 38 Squadron's torpedo-carrying Wellingtons were briefed to attack an 8000-ton cargo ship which had been spotted off Tripoli. Sgt. W.R. Youens claimed to have gained a torpedo hit on the vessel, which was believed to have sunk, although his aircraft was hit by AA fire. Nonetheless, he managed to make the long flight back to the Island, where he landed safely. Youens and his observer, Sgt. G.A.C. Carington, were subsequently each awarded a DFM for this action.

Sunday, 31 May

As a most welcomed change, Sunday morning worshippers were not interrupted, the only alarm sounding just before 1400 when 11 Spitfires were scrambled on the approach of a fighter sweep. There was no contact. Later, four Spitfires were sent out to search for signs of the crew or wreckage of the overdue transit Wellington, the authorities on Malta unaware that they were already in captivity in Sicily.

During the night 209ª Squadriglia despatched a further four Ju87s to Malta, the crews briefed to attack Luqa and Takali. Serg.Magg. Olindo Vigna reported being attacked by a night fighter which he believed to have been a biplane! His aircraft was not hit, nor was that flown by Serg. Guido Savini, who reported being pursued half way back to Sicily.

104 Squadron was able to mount a slightly larger raid in the other direction, six Wellingtons being despatched to bomb the Messina ferry for the fourth time. A very large fire with heavy black smoke was seen, as well as several smaller fires, and it was believed that commercial oil storage tanks had been hit. The raid was considered 'very successful and without doubt considerable damage has been caused.' Messina AA batteries claimed two bombers shot down, both of which were believed to have crashed in the Messina Straits, but again they had been over-optimistic. While Sgt. Curtis' Z8513 did ditch three miles off the coast of Malta on return, the loss was due to engine trouble; the crew were later rescued by HSL 128. A second aircraft (Z8357) went into land at Luqa too

quickly on return since it, too, was suffering engine problems and in so doing collided with two parked delivery Wellingtons and was written off; all three aircraft were damaged, but no personnel were hurt. Sqn.Ldr. Young, the raid leader, was approaching to land when he saw the fire. Displaying great coolness, he avoided the obstructions on the runway and landed safely then, having dispersed his aircraft, he took charge of the flare path and had it moved so that the remainder of the flight were able to land safely.

With the end of another critical month, stock was one again taken in the very different circumstances now prevailing. During the first five months of the year, some 11,000 tons of bombs were estimated to have fallen on the Island, more than three quarters of that total on Luqa, Takali and Hal Far; 520 tons had fallen during May, 75% of that total being dropped during the first eight days of the month. There had been 177 day alerts, 59 of which had developed into raids when bombs fell; 65 more attacks had been made at night.

The balance of claims had swung right back to the fighter pilots who were credited with 122 destroyed, plus one shared with the AA defences, 41 probables and 100 damaged. The guns claimed 14½ destroyed, plus 16 more damaged. Twenty-three Spitfires and two Hurricanes were lost in combat, including two shot down by the Island's own AA guns, and two which collided; 14 pilots had been killed or reported missing. During this more active period for the bombers, 104 Squadron had undertaken 36 sorties, the ASV Wellingtons of Special Duties Flight had undertaken 14, while 38 Squadron's torpedo-carriers had contributed 11 more — all without loss to enemy action; five Swordfish and 29 Albacore sorties had also been carried out by the RNAS unit, at the cost of one aircraft.

Monday, 1 June

June, however, began as quietly as May had ended. At 0935 on the first day of the new month, four Spitfires of 185 Squadron scrambled as part of a force of eight intercepting six Bf109s making a Jabo attack in the Tas-Silc area. Four Messerschmitts were attacked 20 miles east of Zonqor Point, Sgt. Yarra (GL-K) and Plt.Off. Broad (GL-E) each claiming one shot down; two more then bounced the Spitfires and shot down Plt.Off. Andy McNaughton (BP950). The Canadian pilot's body was later recovered from the sea by HSL 128.

During the afternoon Magg. Dulio Fanali led MC202s of the newly arrived 155° Gruppo CT on their first sweep over Malta, but nothing was seen. Darkness brought two Ju88s over in a damaging attack on Hal Far and Luqa, three Wellingtons being peppered by debris. Plt.Off. Daniel's Beaufighter was vectored onto one of the raiders at 2130 and damage was claimed before it disappeared.

A major success was achieved by Malta's night strike force when an ASV Wellington located the 6836-ton Italian *Gino Allegri* 40 miles north of Benghazi, escorted by two destroyers. Four 500lb bombs were released by the Wellington crew, one of which narrowly missed the merchant vessel. On receipt of news of the sighting, an ASV-equipped Swordfish, flown by Sub Lt. C.D. Jacobsen (a New Zealander) with Lt.Cdr. Hopkins operating the radar, set off from Hal Far. He was followed by three Albacores and another Swordfish, all carrying torpedoes. At 0120 contact was made with the convoy, but Lt. Whitfield was obliged to turn away as his Albacore had developed a serious oil leak. The other three strike aircraft went in independently, Sub Lt. Walsh in the Swordfish claiming a hit on the bow of the transport, while Sub Lt. Reg Elliott (T9232) gained a hit amidships:

> 'Two hits of which one was mine. Ship stopped with destroyer alongside after. It was on my run in that I saw a torpedo (with Duplex head) from one of our aircraft (flown by Sub Lt. Cramp) explode just short of the ship. We tended to keep to contact heads after this.'

Gino Allegri sank shortly afterwards with the loss of many of her crew. Meanwhile, Jacobsen's ASV Swordfish had been attacked and damaged by a Ju88C nightfighter of I/NJG 2, and was forced down to sea level. The Naval pilot skilfully managed to evade a second attack, returning to Malta where the aircraft was further damaged whilst landing.

A short while before the RNAS attack got under way, three 104 Squadron Wellingtons had been despatched to attack the submarine base at Augusta, one 4000 pounder falling about 200 yards from the target. Only light and inaccurate AA fire was experienced and none of the Wellingtons were hit.

Tuesday, 2 June

At dawn a delivery Hudson (FH302) crashed on landing at Luqa, the crew surviving unhurt. During the early morning a raid was reported forming up over Sicily, and at 0910 Sqn.Ldr. Lawrence led off six 185 Squadron aircraft, followed by 14 more — drawn equally from 249 and 601 Squadrons — these all climbing out to sea and encountering the incoming force 15 miles east off Kalafrana. The raiders were three S.84s escorted by almost two dozen Re2001s, with 32 MC202s as indirect escort; their target was Safi.

Flt.Sgt. Don 'Shorty' Reid, a newly arrived Canadian in 185 Squadron, claimed damage to one of the bombers, which he identified as a Z1007, and then claimed a Reggiane probably shot down; 2/Lt. Archie Bartleman (BR125/P) of 601 Squadron reported:

> 'Macchis flying top cover for bombing raid — scrambled in time and at 25,000 feet up sun, saw bombers about 5000 feet below, with top cover above and behind; attacked from quarter line astern out of sun — Macchis flying straight and level (at least 12 in formation). Selected victim performed rolls as I closed in — saw shells strike; fell out of control and believed burst into flames and disintegrated; no chute seen'.

Bartleman's opponent was undoubtedly a 2° Gruppo Reggiane and he had probably hit Serg. Giovanni Dringoli's aircraft (MM7216), which was severely damaged in the wing and subsequently belly-landed at Comiso. Ten. Giulio Bartolozzi's 150ª Squadriglia Reggiane was also damaged — possibly by Reid — although two more were claimed damaged by Plt.Off. Hagger of 601 Squadron and Sgt. Moye of 185 Squadron. A further Re2001 was badly damaged when Mar. Patriarca, who had suffered a severe bout of air sickness, force-landed MM7252 on return; however, there is no evidence to suggest that his aircraft had been hit in combat.

The Italians reported being attacked by ten Spitfires, 2° Gruppo claiming two shot down (one each by Mar. Luigi Jellici and Serg. Dringoli) and three more damaged, whilst Cap. Miani of 360ª Squadriglia made the first claim for the new Macchis of 155° Gruppo. One Spitfire actually fell in this action, Plt.Off. Halford ditching BR285 in Kalafrana Bay beside the sunken supply ship

Crash-landed Re2001 '7' of 150ª Squadriglia, 2° Gruppo Aut. CT at Comiso on 6 June. Serg. Giovanni Dringoli, seen here with his aircraft, survived unhurt. *(N. Malizia)*

Breconshire, from which supplies were still being salvaged. He was swiftly rescued by a seaplane tender, following which the wreck of the Spitfire was dragged from the channel before it could sink and was deposited near the sunken Ju87 which had ditched in five fathoms late in April; John Sherlock recalled:

> 'We used to paddle over these two planes — we had dinghies from Ju88s and Me109s — to reach the wreck of *Breconshire*, where we used to try and salvage tinned food. We used to joke about it being a sad day to see a Spit and a Stuka in formation in 30 feet of water; the Ju87 still had the dead pilot in the cockpit.'

The day also saw the arrival of a further Italian unit at Sicily, 116° Gruppo BT with BR20Ms flying into Castelvetrano from the mainland under the command of Ten. Col. Luigi Farbiani. From Sardinia on this date. 274ª Squadriglia undertook the first operational sortie with a new type — the Piaggio P 108B four-engined bomber; two of these machines (MM22007 flown by Cap. Balleta and MM22601 captained by Ten. Sotgia) departed Decimomannu airfield searching the Western Mediterranean — without success — for signs of British Naval units which were again about to head towards Malta from the west.

An ASV Wellington on a shipping search during the night failed to locate a seaborne target, Pantelleria harbour being bombed as an alternative. Five Wellingtons of 104 Squadron were sent further afield; the crews were briefed to attack Cagliari airfield, Sardinia, in support of Operation 'Style', the latest delivery of Spitfires to Malta which was due to commence in the morning. Surprise was achieved by the bombers and scant AA resistance was experienced, although only a few small fires were seen following the attack.

Wednesday, 3 June

There were no actions of note over Malta on Wednesday, but far to the west the cruiser *Charybdis* and five destroyers escorted *Eagle* as she headed towards the launch point, this time carrying 31 Spitfires. Two Italian submarines stationed off Algiers failed to sight the fleet, while at 0645 a patrolling Sea Hurricane of

813F Squadron from the carrier, flown by Sub Lt. Michael Crosley, engaged a shadowing Ju88; Crosley got in a single short burst without apparent result, before it escaped.

TABLE 9

3 June Operation 'Style'

31 Spitfires from HMS *Eagle* (pilots believed to have included those listed below)

Sqd.Ldr. A.R.H. Barton	had returned to Gibraltar to lead back flight
Flt.Lt. J.E. Peck	had returned to Gibraltar to lead back flight
Flg.Off. J.A. Plagis	had returned to Gibraltar to lead back flight (BR295)
Flg.Off. D.H. Smith, RAAF	
Flg.Off. J.H. Menary	BR322 shot down by Bf109s
Plt.Off. D.F. Rouleau, RCAF	BR355 shot down by Bf109s
Plt.Off. J.H. Curry, RCAF	BR232
Plt.Off. F.E. Jones, RCAF	
Plt.Off. H.W. McLeod, RCAF	
Plt.Off. C.R. Scollan	
Plt.Off. G. Stenborg, RNZAF	
Plt.Off. H.C. Charlesworth	
Plt.Off. E.W. Wallace, RCAF	
Wt.Off. C.B. Ramsay, RCAF	
Flt.Sgt. J.H. Ballantyne	
Flt.Sgt. T.F. Beaumont	BR313 shot down by Bf109s
Flt.Sgt. H.D.K. Macpherson, RCAF	BR308 shot down by Bf109s
Flt.Sgt. R.G. Middlemiss, RCAF	
Flt.Sgt. P.L. Terry	
Sgt. H.R. Russel, RCAF	
Sgt. A. Drew	
Sgt. D.K. Parker	
Sgt. L.S. Reid, RAAF	BR320
Sgt. Di Perio	
Sgt. C.P.J. Taylor, RCAF	
Sgt. P.M. Charron, RCAF	

To lead the latest batch of pilots (see Table 9 above). Malta veterans Sqn.Ldr. Barton, Flt.Lt. Peck and Flg. Off. Plagis had been sent back to Gibraltar where they had joined the carrier. All went well with the launch of the Spitfires but on this occasion — for the first and only time — the Luftwaffe managed to intercept, a dozen Bf109s of II/JG 53 taking-off from Pantelleria to claim five Spitfires shot down; four were actually lost, two near Pantelleria and two more near Gozo. Piloting one of the new Spitfires (BR230) in Plagis' flight was Australian Sgt. Len Reid, who recalled:

> 'Near Pantelleria we saw some Messerschmitts sitting out there watching us for five minutes. I could see them getting in position, saw them closing. I

recall 'T' shouting the 109s were attacking. I saw them coming. Plagis suddenly rolled over and dived for the sea. He left the rest of us up there like sitting ducks. Those 109s just flew in behind us and shot 'T' out of the sky. 'T' was alongside me; he was shot, obviously, as the stick came back into his stomach, and I saw him go up, smoke coming out. He was probably dead, and it was a matter of rolling over and diving for the sea. Everybody had to look after himself.

'I had one or two on my tail — tracer bullets flying past but fortunately they didn't hit me — and followed right down to the sea. I remember zig-zagging madly across the water, and in the finish I was on my own. I didn't know where I was, but knew I had to steer a certain course which might bring me to Malta. It did. I was supposed to land at Takali, but landed at Hal Far, as I came in from that direction.'

The four pilots who were lost were Flg.Off. J.H. Menary, an Irishman, Plt.Off. D.F. Rouleau, a Canadian, Flt.Sgt. T.F. Beaumont — a former air-sea rescue pilot recently transferred to fighters — and Flt.Sgt. H.D.K. Macpherson, also Canadian. Upon reaching Malta one Spitfire crashed on landing at Takali, although the pilot escaped unhurt. Aircraft from 249 and 601 Squadrons were scrambled to cover the new arrivals and to search for the missing pilots. Flg.Off. Daddo-Langlois spotted one of the NCOs in the sea off Gozo, orbiting for an hour overhead. Sadly, no help was forthcoming and the pilot drowned. 601 Squadron found only an empty dinghy.

It remains a matter of conjecture whether Intelligence suspected the possibility of interception on this occasion, especially with having sent three particularly experienced Malta pilots to lead the new arrivals in.

On his return to the Island Johnny Plagis learned that he had been promoted Flight Lieutenant and posted to lead a flight in 185 Squadron. Amongst the new pilots was New Zealander Plt.Off. Gray Stenborg, who had claimed four victories whilst flying with 111 Squadron.

Twice during the early afternoon, single photo-reconnaissance Bf109s of 1(F)/122 were despatched to Malta, one pilot briefed to observe and photograph the airfields, the other to check upon shipping at Valetta and Marsaxlokk. Niether was intercepted.

That night a Malta-bound OADU Beaufighter (T4990) approached Lampedusa instead — apparently another RAF aircraft led astray by the CRIRA operators — and here it was fired upon by Italian AA, damaged and forced to ditch; Sgt. Henry Gould and his observer, Sgt. Derek Newbury, were rescued and taken prisoner. The crew reported that the Beaufighter had earlier been pursued by a Spanish CR32 biplane fighter (although incorrectly identified by the captives as a CR42) shortly after departing Gibraltar, when it had overflown Spanish territory.

104 Squadron despatched six Wellingtons to raid Catania airfield once again, but the crews were met by 10/10th cloud over the target area and only one crew released their bombs in the estimated area; in fact, they fell near Augusta. Italian AA gunners, firing at aircraft they could not see, claimed one of the raiders shot down but all returned safely.

Thursday/Friday 4/5 June

With daylight on Thursday (the 4th), Spitfires went out from Malta to search for the missing Beaufighter but found no trace. Two small-scale Luftwaffe fighter sweeps came over, four 185 Squadron aircraft encountering Messerschmitts head-on before being jumped by others from behind; Sgt. Yarra (GL-D) was chased back to base but his aircraft was not hit. Friday (the 5th) was marked only by four small-scale fighter reconnaissances, each by a pair of Bf109s.

Junkers Ju88A bombers being prepared for another attack on Malta. *(E.C. des Armees)*

Saturday, 6 June

The start of the weekend heralded the busiest day for two weeks, and Saturday was to be the blackest of the war for 2° Gruppo CT. At 0445 three Spitfires of 185 Squadron took off on a dawn patrol, but shortly after they had got into the air, radar indicated the presence of at least two 'hostiles', and at 0525 four 249 Squadron aircraft were scrambled. As the latter climbed to gain altitude, the 185 Squadron trio spotted a Ju88 at sea level, 30 miles south-east of Kalafrana; Flt.Sgt. Haggas attacked at once from astern, seeing strikes on the fuselage and a stream of glycol. Flt.Sgt. MacNamara also attacked, reporting strikes, just as the 249 Squadron section approached. Flt.Lt. Lucas, who was leading, later reported that he believed he had seen the bomber fall into the sea.

The 249 Squadron quartet then attacked two more Ju88s, Lucas (BR109/C-30) and Plt.Off. Frank Jones (BR246/C-40) shooting down one, although Lucas' Spitfire was hit by return fire, Plt.Off. Linton (BR111/C-18) and Flt.Sgt. Butler (BR377/C41) jointly claiming the second. Two Ju88s of KüFlGr 606 failed to return, 7T+HK (Uffz. Heinz-Wolf Bartels) and 7T+BL (Lt. Werner Dielas) crashing into the sea with the loss of their crews.

A second scramble was called an hour later, four more 249 Squadron aircraft and 11 from 603 Squadron going off to intercept five 50° Gruppo Z1007bis bombers (two from 210ª Squadriglia and three from 211ª) which attacked Safi, escorted by 24 MC202s of 155° Gruppo and a dozen Re2001s of 2° Gruppo. Wt.Off. 'Chuck' Ramsay (BR352/GL-W) and Sgt. Johnny Gilbert (BR119/C-1) of 249 Squadron each claimed a Reggiane shot down; one, or both, had attacked Ten. Leonardo Venturini of 358ª Squadriglia who radioed that he was about to ditch off Malta, but was lost. Wt.Off. Gray (BR175/C-51) claimed damage to a fighter he identified as a Bf109, while Gilbert and Plt.Off. Watts (BR176/C-25) reported damaging one of the bombers. This was the same aircraft being attacked by 603 Squadron's CO, Sqn.Ldr. Lord Douglas-Hamilton and Plt.Off. Wally McLeod; the latter's aircraft was hit by return fire however and the engine cut, but he landed safely.

Other Reggianes were claimed probably destroyed by Plt.Off. Neville King and Flg.Off. Mitchell of 603 Squadron, while another of the bombers was claimed damaged by Plt.Off. Eddie Glazebrook (who identified it on this occasion as an S.84!). One Cant sustained damage to the fuel tanks and engines, but the bomber crews claimed two Spitfires shot down in return. Another was claimed by Mar. Olindo Simionato of 2° Gruppo, who reported that it fell in flames, while other Reggiane pilots added a probable and reported strikes on many others to add to the tally. A fourth Spitfire was credited to Ten. Giuseppe Bonfiglio of 155° Gruppo, who believed that it crashed into the sea and he also claimed another as damaged.

The day was still young however, and at 0920 an estimated 20 Axis aircraft were reported searching to the east of Malta; in fact, 11 Re2001s were out searching for the missing Venturini, led by Ten. Col. Aldo Quarantotti. They spotted some possible wreckage and oil where his aircraft was believed to have ditched but of the pilot there was no sign. While so engaged and flying low, they were attacked by four 249 Squadron Spitfires which had been scrambled to investigate, Flg.Off. Daddo-Langlois (BR107/C-22) and Plt.Off. Frank Jones (BR246/C-40) each claiming a Reggiane shot down, while Plt.Off. Linton (BR111/C-18) and Flt.Sgt. Butler (BR377/C-41) each claimed one damaged. Recorded Daddo-Langlois:

> 'Section met four Re2001s east of Zonqor. Jones destroyed one. I got one destroyed. Linton and I were jumped by four 109s. Running fight to Kalafrana from 15 miles out. These yellow-nosed boys know their stuff.'

Ten. Arnaldo De Merich of the 152ª Squadriglia, 2° Gruppo Aut. CT with his Re2001. He was shot down and killed in combat with 249 Squadron Spitfires on 6 June. *(S. Teia via N. Malizia)*

Cap. Salvatore Teia's Re2001, '4' of 152ª Squadriglia, 2° Gruppo Autonomo CT, which crash-landed at Comiso following combat with 249 Squadron Spitfires on 6 June. *(S. Govi via N. Malizia)*

Sottoten. Romano Pagliani (left) and Ten. Agostino Celentano of 2° Gruppo Aut. CT, with Cap. Teia's crash-landed Re2001. *(S. Govi via N. Malizia)*

One Reggiane (MM7235 flown by Ten. Arnaldo De Merich) had gone down at once and crashed into the sea, while a second — MM7214 flown by Cap. Teia — had been seriously damaged and belly-landed on return to Caltagirone. During the engagement, the Italians reported that Sottoten. Celentano of 150ª Squadriglia shot down a Beaufighter immediately following De Merich's demise, while two more British aircraft were claimed as probables. Again, no twin-engined aircraft are recorded either as lost or even operating from Malta at this time.

It seems probable that Daddo-Langlois and Linton had been attacked by II/JG 53 Messerschmitts. Four more 249 Squadron Spitfires had scrambled at 1020, Wt.Off. Gray (BR175/C-51) claiming damage to an Re2001, and Flt.Lt. Lucas (BR109/C-30) to a Bf109.

The Italians were back in the afternoon, this time 13 Re2001s and six MC202s escorting a Z506B of 612ª Squadriglia on a search for the missing pilots to the east of Malta. Four 185 Squadron Spitfires were scrambled to intercept at 1605, followed by four more (Blue Section) ten minutes later. The initial section, led by the newly-promoted Flt.Lt. Plagis (BR321/J), chased the Reggianes 40 miles out to sea; he recorded:

> 'Intercepted about 10-12 enemy a/c 30/40 miles east of Malta — joined by another 36 e/a. Reid got one Re2001. Blue Section got "Blood Wagon". I got two Re2001 destroyed. Both pilots baled out!! RIP.'

Flt.Lt. Johnny Plagis of 185 Squadron after claiming his 11th victory on 6 June. *(N.J. Ogilvie)*

Flt.Sgt. 'Shorty' Reid had actually claimed one destroyed and another damaged. Against the three 'confirmed' claims submitted, a further two Reggiane pilots were lost, Ten. Giuseppe Baraldi's MM7228 last being seen trailing black smoke, while Serg.Magg. Aldo Geminiani's MM7223 crashed into the sea; like De Merich, both were members of 152ª Squadriglia. Two weeks later a dinghy containing Geminiani's body was found by the Italian hospital ship *Arno*. On this occasion the 2° Gruppo pilots had only been able to claim a single joint victory against a Spitfire, while a second was claimed by Serg.Magg. Giovanni Del Fabbro, a Macchi pilot of 155° Gruppo's 378ª Squadriglia. One Spitfire was actually damaged in the fight, Plt.Off. Sherlock being forced to crash-land BR109 at Hal Far on return; he was unhurt.

Meanwhile, Plt.Off. Ogilvie had encountered the white-painted, Red Cross-emblazoned Z506B:

> 'I didn't know what the hell to do with this thing. Jerry had been shooting up our rescue launches, and I thought this was fair game. However, I pulled up alongside of it — formating on it almost to within a 100 yards of its right-hand side — indicating to the pilot that I wanted him to turn around and land at Malta.
>
> 'While all this negotiating was going on, someone came up behind and blew it out of the sky. It must have been carrying a tremendous amount of petrol on board. The explosion was tremendous.'

The destruction of Sottoten. Arduino Marega's floatplane (MM45272) was credited jointly to the other three Canadians of Blue Section, Plt.Off. Lambert, and Flt.Sgt. Dodd and Sgt. Russel; there were no survivors.

After dark an estimated 20 bombers crossed the coast, Ju88s included, and bombs fell on Luqa, Takali (where a decoy Hurricane was burnt out and an ambulance slightly damaged) and Dingli. On this occasion four or five flare-dropping aircraft arrived first, releasing several dozen green, white and red flares, which descended quite slowly from 5000 feet over Luqa, the bombers then concentrating their attack. Two Spitfires were sent off but were not able to make any interceptions; AA gunners claimed one Ju88 shot down, although no loss was recorded.

Sunday, 7 June

Four Spitfires of 185 Squadron were scrambled shortly after midday on Sunday the 7th, as part of a force of 11 sent up to intercept 15 Bf109s on a sweep; of his 12th and last Malta victory claim, Flt.Lt. Plagis (BR321/J) noted:

> 'One Me109F destroyed five-seven miles east of Delimara Point — confirmed.'

A second Messerschmitt was claimed probably destroyed by Flt.Sgt. 'Shorty' Reid, although no Luftwaffe losses are recorded on this date. However, records show Lt. Wilhelm Ruge of 5/JG 53 missing in 'Black 3' off Cape Scaramia on the 8th, when no claims for Bf109s shot down were made. It is possible that his loss may have been recorded a day late, and that he was Plagis' victim.

185 Squadron was again involved in the afternoon's action, when eight aircraft were ordered to investigate a further force of fighters approaching the coast. Although the main body of Spitfires failed to make contact, Flt.Sgt. Yarra (GL-N) was obliged to return to base early due to engine trouble and en route was attacked by three Re2001s; turning into these, he claimed to have inflicted damage on two.

Darkness brought another raid, a dozen bombers — Ju88s, Italian Ju87s and Z1007bis — crossing the coast from 2200 onwards. Bombs fell on Luqa, Takali and Hal Far. The crews of the four Cants were briefed to bomb Luqa and Takali; one returned early due to engine trouble whilst another crew reported sighting a prowling night fighter, but was not attacked. For the second consecutive night, AA gunners claimed a Ju88 shot down and, in fact, Uffz. Ernst Schneider's M7+ML of 3/KGr 806 fell into the sea off Wied iz-Zurrieq; there were no survivors.

Monday, 8 June

The Messerschmitts of II/JG 53 accounted for two of Malta's Spitfires during brief skirmishes over the Island during the 8th, Plt.Off. Leslie Barlow (BR231) of 603 Squadron being shot down as nine aircraft of his unit scrambled to intercept a sweep shortly before noon; his aircraft fell into the sea and the Rhodesian was killed. Only Flt.Sgt. Brown managed a passing shot as the Bf109s sped out to sea again, claiming one damaged. During the afternoon, a dozen Spitfires of 249 Squadron were scrambled to intercept a dozen Messerschmitts. Four were encountered, resulting in Flt.Sgt. Butler's aircraft (BR312) sustaining damage; the Canadian crash-landed in a field near Takali and was slightly injured. It is possible that one of these Spitfires fell to Maj. von Maltzahn as his 63rd or 64th victory.

Far to the west, a further Spitfire reinforcement operation was underway — the third in less than a month — as 32 Spitfires were ferried towards the Island aboard *Eagle*. Anti-submarine aircraft from Gibraltar preceded the carrier and her escort — the cruisers *Cairo* and *Charybdis*, and six destroyers — to clear the way. A Sunderland of 10 RAAF (attached to the resident Gibraltar-based 202 Squadron) had detected a surfaced submarine at 0400 on the morning of the 7th; this was undoubtedly the Italian *Veniero*. Flt.Lt. R.W. Marks took his aircraft in to attack, depth charges falling 30 yards abeam as the submarine opened fire with machine guns and its heavy deck gun; the flyingboat's starboard outer engine was hit, forcing Marks to disengage and return to base. Some time later, Flg.Off. R.M. Corrie of 202 Squadron homed in on what was almost certainly the same submarine, the flyingboat crew reporting an oil patch and air bubbles on the surface following their second attack; *Veniero* was reported to have been sunk by air attack south of Sardinia with the loss of all hands.

A reconnaissance Z1007bis of 213ª Squadriglia was despatched from Decimomannu (Sardinia) to search for the ships, but was reported to have been intercepted and shot down by five fighters, identified as 'Spitfires'; Ten. Lamberto Pardini and his crew, with the exception of the W/T operator, were later rescued. The identity of the fighters involved has not been established, and records do not reveal any FAA activity. Nor is the reason known for the loss of a second such aircraft, despatched by 212ª Squadriglia, in which Sottoten. Gaetano Berlinazzo and his crew perished.

Tuesday, 9 June

Early in the morning the Spitfires were launched, the first flight being led by Plt.Off. Reade Tilley who had been flown back to Gibraltar for the task. The flight was made safely and landings began at Takali from 1000 onwards. One aircraft (BR388 flown by Plt.Off. John McElroy) damaged its tail on take-off and subsequently crashed on landing. An angry Wg.Cdr. Gracie, not fully aware of the facts, immediately grounded the luckless Canadian and threatened to have him posted to the Middle East. Of the flight, Australian Flt.Sgt. Colin Parkinson (BR376) recorded:

> 'Took off from Eagle about 7 a.m. Eight of us with an inexperienced flight lieutenant to lead us. His speeds varied from 100 mph to 200 mph. On the way we saw a sub being refuelled by a depot ship just off the coast of Africa. The flight leader was doing one of his usual little tricks of 100 mph when my long-range tank ran out. My kite dropped like a stone; however, I managed to get it going again OK. Jettisoned the tank over Tunis. It took approx four hours to get to Malta where we all landed safely without too much damage to the aircraft; two were pranged.'

The combat experience of a number of the new arrivals was better than had often been the case with previous reinforcements (see Table 10 below). In particular, two former pilots of 41 Squadron had already achieved some success, Plt.Off. Arthur Glen having claimed three victories, while Canadian Sgt. George Beurling had claimed two (one of which may not have been confirmed); 20 year-old 'Buzz' Beurling had already achieved some notoriety, and had not endeared himself to his superiors; with an obvious disregard for discipline, his posting to Malta was seen by some as a last chance for the young extrovert. He, too, experienced an uneventful flight to Malta, as he later recalled:

'The weather was cloudy but we were told to expect excellent visibility at Malta. The Wing Commander had said: "Keep your eyes peeled for Jerries as you come near home. The last time we came down this way the blighters lay in wait between Tunis and Pantelleria and shot down three or four of them. Knocked every one of them into the sea and every pilot killed — just because he didn't keep his eyes peeled!"

'By 0605 the first eight were on the way, leaving the flight deck about two minutes apart. As each plane became airborne it climbed and made left-hand circuits of the carrier until joined by its mates. At 2000 feet they formed up over the ship, then legged for Malta, climbing hard. I went away with the third flight at 0630. Malta came into view at 0950 from 20,000 feet. My gang made Takali, all right side up, at 1030. Right then the war began in earnest for Sergeant Beurling!'

TABLE 10

Operation 'Salient'

32 Spitfires from HMS *Eagle* (pilots believed to have included those listed below)

Unknown Flt.Lt.		had returned to Gibraltar to lead back flight	
Plt.Off. R.F. Tilley, RCAF		had returned to Gibraltar to lead back flight	
Flg.Off. A.C. Rowe, RNZAF		Flt.Sgt. C.H. Parkinson, RAAF	BR376
Flg.Off. J. Smith		Sgt. B.W. Spradley, RCAF (US)	
Plt.Off. C.H. Lattimer, RNZAF		Sgt. G.F. Beurling	BR380
Plt.Off. J.H.R. Paradis, RCAF		Sgt. C.L. Baxter, RAAF	
Plt.Off. J.F. McElroy, RCAF	BR388	Sgt. D.F. Hubbard	
Plt.Off. H. Kelly, RCAF (US)		Sgt. M.E. Tomkins	
Plt.Off. A.A. Glen		Sgt. L.G.C. De l'Ara	
Plt.Off. G.A. Levy-Despas, RCAF (French)		Sgt. E. Budd	
		Sgt. C.E. Mutch, RCAF	
Plt.Off. C.A. Newman		Sgt. A.R. Richardson, RAAF	
Plt.Off. J.L. Hicks		Sgt. C.L. Wood, RNZAF	
Flt.Sgt. B.W. Andrews, RCAF (US)		Sgt. K.H. Davey	
Flt.Sgt. J.A.H. Pinney		Sgt. W. Marshall, RCAF	
Flt.Sgt. I.R. Maclennan, RCAF		Sgt. W. Young, (Rhod)	
Flt.Sgt. R.A. Stevenson			

No sooner were the new Spitfires down when, at 1050, 36 of those already there were ordered off as 16 Bf109s approached. Four 603 Squadron pilots gave chase and Sgt. Webster claimed damaged to one. All then remained relatively quiet until early evening, when three S.84s with a large escort of Macchis and Reggianes raided Takali where an already damaged Spitfire was destroyed on the ground. A total of 22 Spitfires of 126 and 603 Squadron were scrambled, and newly-commissioned Plt.Off. Hurst of the latter unit claimed a bomber damaged, while Plt.Off. Graves of 126 Squadron claimed a Bf109 shot down, and Flt.Sgt. Evans of this unit a Reggiane probable.

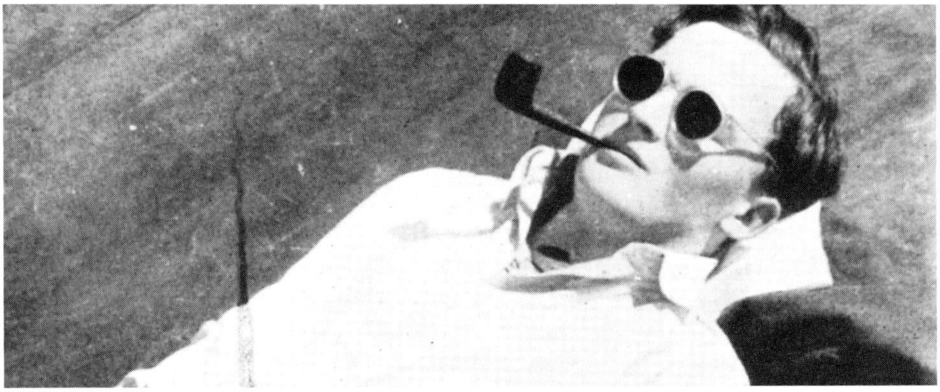

Flt.Lt. Mike Graves of 126 Squadron, relaxing in the spring sunshine. *(NWMA)*

The Macchi pilots of 155° Gruppo in turn claimed three Spitfires shot down, one apiece being credited to Mar. Pasquale Bartolucci and Serg.Magg. Angelo Cerri, the third being claimed jointly by Mar. Lorenzo Serafino and Mar. Aldo Romagnoli; others were believed damaged. Only one Spitfire suffered any damage, the 126 Squadron pilot crash-landing BP869 at Takali.

Having completed her task, *Eagle* and her escorts headed back towards Gibraltar, whilst anti-submarine aircraft continued to scour the sea lanes for submarines. On this occasion it was Catalina Z2143/J of 240 Squadron (attached to 202 Squadron), flown by Flt.Lt. D.E. Hawkins, which successfully attacked a surfaced submarine, the Italian *Zaffiro* being located between Algeria and Cagliari. In spite of heavy AA fire from the craft, Hawkins succeeded in dropping four depth charges, one of which exploded 15 yards from the stern of the craft, whilst his gunners silenced the submarine's forward gun. *Zaffiro* submerged but five minutes later re-surfaced and remained stationary; members of the crew were seen to come on deck, some making gestures of surrender, and were soon forced to abandon the craft as it began to sink by the stern. Hawkins attempted to alight nearby to take prisoners but was met by a heavy swell; the Catalina was badly damaged although it was able to take-off again and reached Gibraltar safely.

Wednesday, 10 June

During Wednesday Malta was to see a sudden increase in its offensive potential, pending an attempt to run major convoys through to the Island. Fifteen Beaufighters of 235 Squadron had been detached from Coastal Command in the United Kingdom and had flown to Gibraltar. Led by the commanding officer, Wg.Cdr. H.J. Garlick, a dozen of these set out for the long flight to Malta, all but one arriving safely; X8076 had been lost en route, ditching 20 miles east of Cape Bon. It is uncertain if this aircraft had been intercepted by Bf109s from Sicily or Pantelleria, but Plt.Off. G.R. Stead and Sgt. J. Cockshott were both lost, the latter's body later being recovered from the sea. Four Spitfires were in the air to cover their arrival and while two Bf109s were seen, no contact was made. The three remaining Beaufighters arrived from Gibraltar over the next few days.

On inspection of the new arrivals, Malta's maintenance crews were shocked at the condition of the Beaufighters' armament, reporting cannons and machine-guns in a very poor state of cleanliness; investigation revealed that the link chutes on five aircraft were not wired up, causing stoppages. The belts were composed of American ammunition of doubtful serviceability, and all were badly made up; it was decided to replace them with belts prepared in Malta. Added to all these time-consuming tasks, enquiries established that few of the pilots knew whether their guns and sights had been harmonised. Ground crews were hard-pressed to make the aircraft fit for operations in the time available.

There was again no contact when 11 Spitfires were scrambled after nine Messerschmitts on a sweep at 0930 but a patrolling minesweeper was attacked, the crew claiming to have shot down one of the German fighters and to have damaged a second. Ten 249 Squadron Spitfires were sent off at 1100 as more Axis fighters appeared, ten Bf109s and MC202s being reported, Wt.Off. Gray (BR309/W) claiming one of the latter shot down. On returning to Takali, Gray undershot as he came in to land and crashed, but suffered only minor injuries.

A little while later an escorted Do24 approached the Island and a dozen Spitfires were ordered off to investigate, three of 249 Squadron making an interception. Wt.Off. Ramsay (BR176/C-25) claimed a Bf109 probable out of a dozen met, while Flt.Lt. Lucas (BR108/C-20) and Plt.Off. Linton reported damaging the flyingboat.

At 1810, eight 249 Squadron Spitfires took off, led by Sqn.Ldr. Grant, to cover the arrival of a formation of nine Beaufort torpedo-bombers of 217 Squadron flying in from Gibraltar, which had radioed that they were under attack by a fighter. Their attacker was identified as a Bf109 but was probably an MC202 of 54° Stormo CT, operating from Pantelleria. One bomber — L9893 — was damaged and Sgt. Denis Norman (the gunner) was killed, while the pilot was obliged to force-land on arrival at Luqa.

Before the 249 Squadron flight could reach them however, the Spitfires were vectored onto an incoming raid, and a dozen more Spitfires (eight/601 and four/185) were scrambled at 1845. The raiders, which reached the Island half an hour later, were five Z1007bis escorted by 27 MC202s and 19 Re2001s; their target was Safi. It appears that Messerschmitts of II/JG 53 were also present. All three Spitfire formations engaged; for 249 Squadron, Sqn.Ldr. Grant (BR176/C-25) claimed an Re2001 shot down (bringing his victory tally to at least nine). This was undoubtedly the machine flown by Serg. Giovanni Dringoli of 150ª Squadriglia; the pilot was believed to have been mortally wounded and his aircraft was seen to crash into the sea. Flt.Sgt. Williams (BR163) claimed a second as damaged — probably Ten. Celentano's aircraft which was badly damaged, but managed to reach base — while Flt.Lt. McNair (BR107/C-22) claimed a Bf109 for his seventh victory; his victim may have been Uffz. Heinrich Sedlmaier of 5/JG 53, who was reported by the Luftwaffe to have been shot down north of Valetta, allegedly by AA; he baled out, wounded, and was subsequently rescued.

Meanwhile, Plt.Off. Percy Sewell of 601 Squadron shot down a 155° Gruppo Macchi flown by Mar. Serafino of 378ª Squadriglia, witnesses on Gozo reporting seeing two fighters — which were obviously those flown by Serafino and Dringoli — crash into the sea about two and a half miles south of Mgarr. In return, 155° Gruppo reported four Spitfires shot down, claimed by Ten. Giobatta Caracciolo Carafa, Ten. Bonfiglio, Ten. Vittorio Bastogi and Serg.Magg. Cerri. In fact, only one Spitfire (BP875) was lost — that flown by Plt.Off. Innes of 601 Squadron; a cannon shell exploded under his seat which fell forward and pinned him against the instrument panel. The Spitfire plunged vertically from 25,000 feet, the speed causing the aircraft to break up, and Innes was thrown out. His parachute opened and he landed safely in the sea, from where he was soon picked up by HSL 107, A second Spitfire (GL-N) of 185 Squadron was struck in the windscreen by return fire from one of the bombers, Flt.Sgt. Yarra sustaining slight injuries to his face caused by splinters of perspex; however, he returned to base without further damage.

The rescue of Plt.Off. Innes by HSL 107 could well have ended in disaster. In the approximate area where the pilot was believed to have come down, a drifting mine was encountered in high seas and Flt.Lt. Price ordered the turret gunner, LAC Joe Maitland, to detonate it at a safe distance with his twin Lewis guns. The gunner had already expended a pan of ammunition, when another member of he crew, LAC 'Ginger' Strickland, spotted a figure in the vicinity of the mine! The launch was cautiously eased towards the downed pilot and he was soon hauled aboard, but the mine was also drawn towards the craft. By using the boathook, LAC Reg Hargreaves gingerly kept it at bay until the launch was clear.

The Beauforts which had arrived under the command of Wg.Cdr. W.A.L. Davies were destined for Ceylon, and were followed to Malta by six others within two days. However, Air Vice-Marshal Lloyd had other plans for the detachment!

Again there was initial disappointment concerning the condition of the Beauforts, as maintenance crews at Luqa were dismayed to find that none of the first nine aircraft to arrive had full torpedo equipment. Although the squadron had been at Gibraltar for a week, no action had been taken to check equipment which, on arrival at Malta, was in such a state of confusion that all had to be removed and refitted. By calling on the Dockyard and other resources, nine aircraft were made serviceable within three days; three others were brought up to operational standards later, but the remaining three could not be made serviceable. Owing to the lack of operational experience amongst the crews themselves, the AOC must have queried whether the unit would be of much use in the anticipated forthcoming actions.

After nightfall (at 2215) a dozen raiders approached the coast, seven of which

A crash-landed Bristol Beaufort torpedo-bomber at Luqa. *(NWMA)*

One of Malta's Matilda infantry tanks, painted with the camouflage scheme specially developed for use on the Island, is used to tow away a crash-landed Beaufort for repair or cannibalisation. *(NWMA)*

crossed it, and bombs fell in the Siggiewi area. Beaufighter V8224/F of 89 Squadron was up and Flt.Sgt. Miller was guided by Sgt. Tearle onto a Ju88, which was probably that (B3+AA) flown by the Staffelkapitän of StabStaffel/KG 54, Hpt. Hans Humburg. The W/T operator was able to get off a message that it was under attack by a night fighter, and witnesses reported seeing 'a big ball of fire falling into the sea one mile to the south of Gozo'. A second Ju88 — 7T+LK of 2/KüFlGr 606, flown by Lt. Gunther Chemnitz — also failed to return; again witnesses reported seeing this aircraft crash into the sea between Wied iz-Zurrieq and Filfla. However, there appears to have been no fighter or AA claim made relating to the demise of this bomber.

Midnight on the 10th/11th brought to a close two full years of air attack on Malta. During this period there had been 2537 air raid alerts, 492 of which had developed into bombing attacks by day, and 574 by night; records indicate that the civilian population had suffered the following casualties:

Killed outright	997	Seriously injured	1493
Died of injuries	218	Slightly injured	1437
Total	1215	Total	2930

During the past week, the Wellingtons of 104 Squadron's detachment had continued their series of nightly raids, albeit without tangible success although whatever their achievement it was obtained without loss. Six aircraft had attempted a raid against Catania airfield on the night of the 4th/5th, but again met very poor weather and only two crews found gaps in the cloud over Syracuse, releasing their bombs there; the other four returned with their cargoes intact. Six aircraft flew further afield on the 5th/6th, raiding Naples where bombs reportedly fell on an industrial area, causing several fires. One 4000 pounder was seen to burst in the centre of the city, but an effective smoke screen prevented more accurate damage assessment. The Messina ferry was again the target for six Wellingtons on the 6th/7th, while seven returned to Cagliari on the 7th/8th, and eight raided Taranto naval base on the 8th/9th, and again next night. A final strike on this target was made by seven bombers on the 10/11th, all these recent attacks having been launched in preparation for the forthcoming convoys. Immediately after this last attack, the Wellingtons returned to Egypt, however, to make room at Luqa for the force of Beaufort torpedo-bombers and Beaufighters which had just arrived.

The Fleet Air Arm crews of the composite 828/830 Squadron had bade farewell to their commanding officer, Lt.Cdr. Hopkins, who had departed on completion of his tour; his place was taken by another observer, Lt.Cdr. A.J.J. Roe. Little shipping had been seen for several nights, but on the 10th/11th an ASV Wellington located three transports and three destroyers some 22 miles off Cape Bon. At once bombs were dropped and one hit was claimed on the stern of the largest vessel, her decks also being raked, by machine-gun fire. Five Albacores were summoned to attack, the convoy being sighted at 0400. Flares were dropped but by the time the aircraft had manoeuvred to attack, the vessels had been lost from sight and were not re-located.

Thursday, 11 June

Thursday was to be a day of limited action, a dozen Spitfires being ordered off at 0940 to intercept six Bf109s on an offensive reconnaissance sortie. Plt.Off. Bisley of 126 Squadron claimed one shot down. During the day Sunderland L5805 of 95 Squadron — which was on detachment from West Africa — crashed into the sea near Malta, apparently as a result of some technical fault; Flg.Off. Jack Pybus and all nine of his crew were lost.

One of the Messerschmitt Bf109Fs which fell during the early summer fighting. *(NWMA)*

By night, raiders were over again and the AA gunners were very active, a Ju88 of KGr 806 being hit; this aircraft belly-landed at Catania on return and the crew survived.

Friday, 12 June

An early morning raid on Luqa developed on the 12th, two Ju88s and 15 Bf109s carrying out the attack; little damage was done to the airfield, while three of the covering Messerschmitts were claimed damaged by Flt.Sgt. Terry of 185 Squadron, Plt.Off. Sewell and Sgt. Lusty of 601 Squadron. Fighters only comprised the next intrusion, eight Bf109s crossing the coast during mid morning. 249 Squadron despatched a dozen Spitfires and 185 Squadron scrambled a further four to meet the threat, and a number of dogfights ensued. Sgt. Beurling (BR176/C-25) opened his Malta account when he claimed to have blown the tail off a Messerschmitt he attacked, but it was not seen to crash and he was credited only with a damaged; Flt.Sgt. Rae (BR254 X-G) was also credited with a damaged, while Flg.Off. Daddo-Langlois (BR107/C-22) recorded:

> 'Found myself alone with three, 15 miles out. Got shot up.'

His aircraft was hit in the tail, wings and fuselage, although he was able to fly it back to base. The 185 Squadron section failed to make contact.

The sailing of the reinforcement convoys was now imminent and a photo-reconnaissance Spitfire (BP908) of 69 Squadron, flown by Sgt. Leslie Colquhoun, was sent over to Taranto to check on the state of the Italian fleet. He brought back evidence of the presence of three battleships, four cruisers, the seaplane carrier *Giuseppe Miraglia*, 20 destroyers, the liner *Gradisca* and 14 smaller vessels. At the seaplane base were identified 13 Z501 seaplanes, 20 Z506B and four Ro43 floatplanes, while on the slipway ashore were nine more Ro43s, one Z506B, two Z501s and a large flyingboat identified as one of the new six-engined Blohm & Voss Bv222s.

More activity occurred with nightfall, four raiders releasing their bombs over Takali and Luqa; at Rabat one civilian was killed and 18 injured. Although two Beaufighters were sent up, they achieved no interceptions but searchlights successfully held two Ju88s for the gunners, who shot down Fw. Kurt Kahle's 7T+KH of 1/KüFlGr 606 and claimed the second damaged.

Chapter 6

THE JUNE CONVOYS

"Somebody didn't see a hole in the landing area!" Spitfire at Takali. *(N.J. Ogilvie)*

Reduced Luftwaffe presence in Sicily and the regular deliveries of Spitfires by aircraft carrier had enabled the defence of the Island to be strengthened greatly by early June. The offensive capabilities available to strike at the ever-vulnerable Axis supply routes were rising once more — but still the problem remained regarding the Island's own supplies. Everything was now critically scarce, especially the bulk essentials — food, aviation spirit and ammunition for the AA guns. Aircraft ammunition and urgently-needed spare parts created somewhat less of a problem, since these could be flown in by transports and flyingboats from Gibraltar and Egypt, or aboard submarines. Of these anxieties, Air Vice-Marshal Lloyd wrote:

> 'Petrol and food were the key items. The one was useless without the other. Food to live; petrol for the fighters in the air... once the Spitfires could not fly again it would be the end of Malta... Petrol and food had to travel along so as to reach the starvation date (August) more or less together.'

Owing to the dire fuel shortage even torpedoes for attacking shipping were in short supply, since these had to be flown in by Wellingtons and 600 gallons of precious petrol were required for each aircraft's return flight to Egypt. There were shortages of most commodities — particularly of petrol for motor transport — while shortage of labour and building materials forced officers and men to sleep in shelters, caverns, dug-outs, or quarries; 300 lived in one underground cavern; 200 in a disused tunnel; 160 in partly-demolished houses near the airfields — there was little comfort and no warmth due to the shortage of coal, coke and paraffin.

There was no beer, spirits or soft drinks; cigarettes and tobacco were scarce, so were razor blades, soap, toothpaste, shaving cream and clothes; the RAF wore mixtures of Air Force grey-blue, Navy blue and Army khaki. However the major cause of concern was the scarcity of food. The civilian population, including many thousands of children, somehow struggled by on meagre rations while the average daily diet for service personnel consisted of:

Breakfast:	1½ slices of poor quality bread with jam
Lunch:	1 slice of bread and bully-beef
Dinner:	2 slices of bread and bully-beef

Margarine was available every two to three days and small quantities of tinned milk, potatoes and vegetables were issued on an irregular basis; tea and sugar were available, but there was no coffee.

Desperation was now evident even amongst senior officers; some aircrew informed the AOC that given the choice of surrender and prisoner-of-war camps, they would prefer to take their chances and fly south into the heart of Africa until their fuel ran out. Others expressed a desire to fly to Vichy-controlled Tunisia and Algeria. Even the new Governor, Lord Gort — as a recipient of the Victoria Cross who had commanded the British Expeditionary Force in France in 1940 until its evacuation from Dunkirk, a man not lacking in fighting spirit — had openly confessed that should things get this far, rather than surrender, he would personally muster a force of volunteers and fight it out in Sicily! It was now many weeks since a convoy had got through and it was becoming vital that an attempt once again be made.

In North Africa the war was going badly for the British and Commonwealth forces. Rommel's offensive at Gazala was on the point of sending the 8th Army reeling back in near-rout. If this occurred, control of the Western Egyptian and Cyrenaican coastal area, along which any convoy from the east would have to sail, would be lost and Malta would once again be totally isolated.

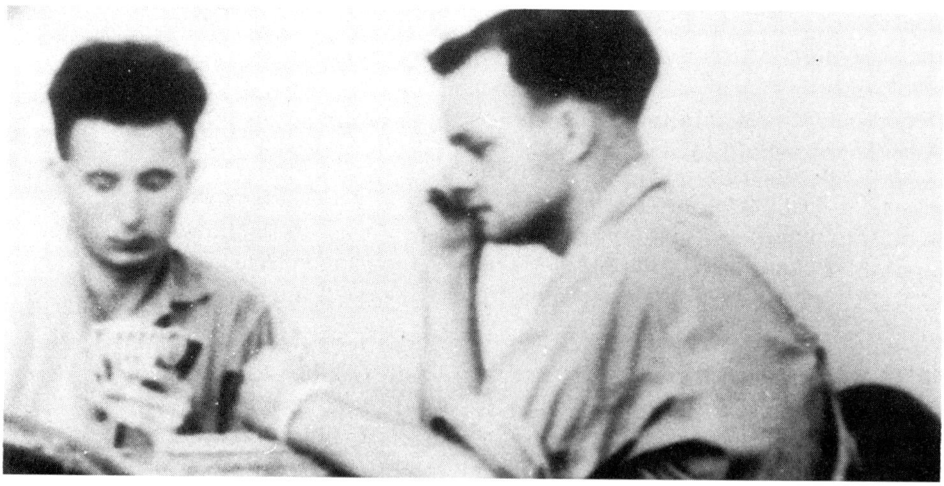

A pair of 185 Squadron's successful Commonwealth pilots playing cards at dispersal. Left is Sgt. Wilbert Dodd (Canadian), with Flt.Sgt. Eric Mahar (Australian). *(L. McAulay)*

The War Cabinet was fully aware of Malta's plight. The Prime Minister became personally and emotionally involved, as his memoirs revealed:

> 'Malta cried aloud for help. The strain was at many points more than could be borne... I was prepared to run serious naval risks to save Malta, and the Admiralty were in full accord. We prepared, and kept the option in hand, to send Admiral Somerville with all his carriers and the *Warspite* through the Canal into the Mediterranean, and to carry a convoy through to Malta, hoping to bring about a general engagement with the Italian Fleet on the way.'

Admiral Sir James Somerville's newly-assembled Indian Ocean Fleet included three armour-decked carriers — *Formidable*, *Indomitable* and *Illustrious* — as well as his flagship, the battleship *Warspite* and a number of cruisers and destroyers. It represented all the Navy could spare from other operational theatres to oppose the all-conquering Japanese forces, who were now at the door of India. Serious risks, indeed, were being considered.

The plan devised to bring relief to the Island was a bold one, given the weakness of the naval forces available to support such a venture. Demands in the Pacific eventually precluded use of Somerville's Fleet and further US involvement, whilst the need to maintain a substantial fleet in the North Atlantic was paramount. Force 'H' (Gibraltar) could provide as main escort only the carriers *Eagle* and *Argus* — the latter little more than useless as an operational vessel — together with the elderly battleship *Malaya*. These capital ships would be supported by the cruisers *Kenya* and *Liverpool*, the anti-aircraft cruiser *Charybdis* (equipped with the first ship-borne W/T and R/T intelligence gathering 'Y' Unit, manned by RN and RAF parties) and eight destroyers; this assemblage was identified as Force 'W'. To provide oiling facilities, the Royal Fleet Auxiliary oiler *Brown Ranger* would accompany the warships, complete with her personal escort of two corvettes, and this group was labelled Force 'Y'.

The close escort (Force 'X'), which would chaperon the convoy right through to Malta, comprised the light AA cruiser *Cairo*, five large Fleet destroyers, four smaller 'Hunt'-class vessels, four minesweepers of 17th Flotilla (due to be based at Malta to replace earlier losses) and six motor launches of 6th Flotilla, which added further minesweeping facility. The convoy to be protected by this force included two British merchant vessels, the 7421-ton *Troilus* and the 5601-ton *Burdwan*; the New Zealand Shipping Co's large (10,350 tons) freighter *Orari*; the Dutch *Tanimbar* (8169 tons); the US *Chant* (5600 tons), and a fast new American Texaco tanker, the 9308-ton *Kentucky*. The five merchantmen carried between them about 43,000 tons of urgent supplies including bombs, aviation fuel, ammunition, wheat and other foodstuffs. The whole force, which was to operate under the codename 'Harpoon', was to be commanded by Vice-Admiral A.T.B. Curteis. Additionally, under cover of the main convoy the Island's old friend, the speedy *Welshman*, was to proceed individually at greater pace crammed full with urgent supplies.

As many submarines as could be assembled were to aid the operation — nine were to patrol off Taranto and south of the Straits of Messina, and four others were to be stationed between Sicily and Sardinia.

Aboard Admiral Curteis' two aircraft carriers were based the following units:–

Eagle	***Argus***
813F Squadron: 4 Sea Hurricanes	807 Squadron: 2 Fulmars
801 Squadron: 12 Sea Hurricanes	813 Squadron: 9 Swordfish
807 Squadron: 4 Fulmars	824 Squadron: 4 Swordfish

It is worth recounting here how 801 Squadron, based in Scotland at the end of May, happened to be available for this operation, as recalled by one of the unit's pilots, Sub Lt. H.E. Duthie:

> 'The departure of 801 for the Med was somewhat of a farce and the reason is still a mystery. It may have been for security or it may have been because most of us had never done a deck landing or perhaps it was just a cock up! Probably the latter!
>
> On a pouring wet day (*27th May*) the squadron flew from Turnhouse to Abbotsinch (*Glasgow*), then a grass airfield, and on that occasion, almost waterlogged. By the greatest of good fortune, all twelve aircraft landed intact, at which time the wings were unbolted; the tails were tied into the backs of an assortment of lorries and the fuselages towed on their own wheels through the streets of Glasgow to Greenock. The wings followed in another assortment of lorries.
>
> On arrival at Greenock, the assorted bits were lifted on to lighters and ferried out to *Argus* in mid Clyde. The single crane on *Argus* was situated aft on a miniscule quarter deck, which had access to the hangar deck and was, I believe, used for fishing seaplanes out of the water in the 1920s. A stoker was provided to work the levers of this crane but the rest of the operation was left in the incapable hands of 801 personnel! Fortunately, some had had previous seamanship experience.
>
> It speaks wonders for Chiefy Merwood (*Chief Air Artificer F.E. Merwood*) and his crews that, after this treatment, all aircraft were able to fly off the relatively short deck of *Argus* (*7 June*), fly for 300 miles or so to Gibraltar, and all land safely. It should also be remembered that most of the ground crews had not been to sea before, and with a large proportion seasick, re-assembled the aircraft on passage.'

With the arrival of the Sea Hurricanes, which were to form part of *Eagle*'s air group, the carrier briefly put to sea on 10 June to fly on her aircraft, a number of the 801 Squadron pilots thus achieving their first deck landings! Owing to the inadequate size of her hangar lift, *Eagle* was unable to stow fully assembled Hurricanes below deck; therefore her deck area had been adapted to allow her to operate her fighters efficiently. 'Red' Duthie offers an insight into the unique method of working fixed-wing Hurricanes in *Eagle*:

> 'The *Eagle* was originally built as a battleship for the Chilean Navy (*built in 1913 as the* Almirante Cochrane*; purchased by the Admiralty in 1918*) and one of the peculiarities of her conversion to an aircraft carrier was the step in her deck. This was about eighteen inches high and more a sloping ramp but, to my knowledge, no one ever caught the first arrester wire because of it.
>
> Aft of the carrier's island were welded five metal channels (outriggers) about six inches wide, and extending about eight feet over the side. When a Hurricane stopped after landing on the arrester wire and was released from the hook, at about the same time a fork about six feet long was clipped to the tail wheel, and the engine stopped by the pilot. Six of the flight deck party then applied themselves to the leading edge of the wing and pushed the aircraft backwards at the run. In the meantime, the flight deck party member on the tail fork was steering it down the nearest vacant channel. On reaching the end of the channel, he flung himself sideways and down into the safety

> nets below, taking the tail fork with him!
>
> This turned the tail wheel sideways which, in theory, stopped the aircraft. The end of the trough was also built up for the same purpose but, believe me, the pilot kept a very watchful eye on the flight deck Petty Officer and, at his sign, jammed on the brakes as hard as he could! We did not ever lose an aircraft over the side but there were some pretty close calls. There are a fair few tail wheel forks lying at the bottom of the Med! After some practice we could land on six Hurricanes with a twenty second landing interval.'

There was to be a second string to the British bow on this occasion however, for even as the 'Harpoon' convoy assembled ready to pass through the Straits of Gibraltar, a second convoy ('MW11') was forming far to the east at Alexandria, Port Said and Haifa. This convoy comprised 11 merchant vessels; the operation designed to get these ships to Malta was to be codenamed 'Vigorous', of which more later.

On Malta the defenders were preparing to play their part in the forthcoming actions. Of the 213 Spitfires which had reached the Island during the past three months, 52 had been shot down and a further 16 had crash-landed due to combat damage, while at least 35 had been written off on the ground during bombing raids; currently just 95 serviceable aircraft remained with the five fighter squadrons. It was planned to provide continuous cover by flights of six Spitfires over each convoy once within range, but to meet this requirement would leave Malta with only a dozen Spitfires available for air defence duties! A number were fitted with conventional long-range fuel tanks, but as there was only a limited supply of these, two dozen Spitfires were fitted with locally-adapted Hurricane 44-gallon long-range tanks. This modification worked well and the tanks proved easily jettisonable. For longer-ranging work, the detachment of 235 Squadron had 14 Beaufighters available; there were also the 15 'shanghaied' Beauforts of 217 Squadron, although only a dozen were fully operational.

To increase the night anti-shipping force, a flight of six Wellington torpedo-carriers from 38 Squadron returned to Malta from El Adem. They joined the remaining seven FAA torpedo-bombers of 828/830 Squadron, three of which were equipped with ASV. To provide reconnaissance, the long-serving 69 Squadron was being brought back up to strength, the three PRU Spitfires, which had been held on the Island during their flights from England, keeping a close watch on Italian naval forces based at Taranto. These were now joined by six twin-engined Baltimores which had flown in from the Middle East during the first half of the month; the latter were to co-operate with the anti-shipping aircraft. Four of the ASV-equipped Wellington VIIIs had also been 'hijacked' to ensure the continuation of the work undertaken for so long by the Special Duties Flight, and to keep the ports of Palermo and Naples under nocturnal surveillance. Finally, the night defence of the Island remained in the hands of five AI Beaufighters of the 89 Squadron detachment.

In preparation for the anticipated blitzing of Malta's airfields, over 700 soldiers stood by with loaded trucks, ready to carry out instant repairs; a further 400 were made available to help maintain the Wellingtons, Beauforts, Baltimores, Beaufighters and Spitfires — the AOC required at least 1000 men available to keep the aircraft in flying condition. It would have been quite impossible to have maintained all the aircraft at immediate readiness, or to ensure a very quick turn round, had it not been for the help of the Army. All work had been stopped at the Command Repair Shops in order to provide a nucleus of skilled tradesmen in the pens for each aircraft, where a complete maintenance crew was always at readiness.

The 'Harpoon' convoy would, in its initial stages, face mainly the Regia Aeronautica. As soon as Intelligence regarding the sailing reached Comando Supremo, the RA would begin reinforcing the units in Sardinia and moving elements of the forces available in Sicily to airfields on the west side of the island.

The Regia Aeronautica's Order of Battle on the eve of operations was as follows:

Aeronautica della Sardegna (Sardinia)

BOMBERS

36° Stormo AS	Decimomannu, 30 S.84, 2 S.79
108° Gruppo AS	
256ª Squadriglia, 257ª Squadriglia	
109° Gruppo AS	
258ª Squadriglia, 259ª Squadriglia	
51° Gruppo Aut. BT	Decimomannu, 9 Z1007bis
212ª Squadriglia, 213ª Squadriglia	
130° Gruppo Aut. AS	Elmas, 12 S.79sil
280ª Squadriglia, 283ª Squadriglia	
46° Stormo BT/AS	Decimomannu, 14 S.79sil
104° Gruppo AS	
252ª Squadriglia, 253ª Squadriglia	
9° Stormo BT	Villacidro, 24 Z1007bis
29° Gruppo BT	
62ª Squadriglia, 63ª Squadriglia	
33° Gruppo BT	Decimomannu, 6 P108B
59ª Squadriglia, 60ª Squadriglia, 274ª Squadriglia Aut. BGR	

FIGHTERS

54° Stormo CT	part Sardinia/part Pantelleria
7° Gruppo CT	29 MC200
76ª Squadriglia, 86ª Squadriglia, 98ª Squadriglia	
16° Gruppo CT	
167ª Squadriglia, 168ª Squadriglia, 169ª Squadriglia	
24° Gruppo Aut. CT	various airfields, 31 CR42, 17 G50bis
354ª Squadriglia, 355ª Squadriglia, 370ª Squadriglia	

RECONNAISSANCE/RESCUE

138ª Squadriglia RM	Olbia/Elmas, 14 Z501/10 Z506B
146ª Squadriglia RM, 188ª Squadriglia RM, 287ª Squadriglia RM	

613ª Squadriglia Aut. Soccorso	Elmas, 2 S.66
65° Gruppo OA	Villacidro, 13 Ro37
28ª Squadriglia OA, 124ª Squadriglia OA	

Aeronautica della Sicilia (Sicily) could boast a further 62 multi-engined bombers and torpedo-carrying aircraft, 15 Ju87 dive-bombers and 129 fighters, as follows:

BOMBERS

10° Stormo BT	S.79
30° Gruppo BT	
55ª Squadriglia, 56ª Squadriglia	
32° Gruppo BT	
57ª Squadriglia, 58ª Squadriglia	
4° Gruppo Aut. BT	S.84
14ª Squadriglia BT, 15ª Squadriglia BT	
50° Gruppo Aut. BT	Z1007bis
210ª Squadriglia BT, 211ª Squadriglia BT	
88° Gruppo Aut. BT	BR20M
264ª Squadriglia BT, 265ª Squadriglia BT	
116° Gruppo Aut. BT	BR20M
276ª Squadriglia BT, 277ª Squadriglia BT	
102° Gruppo Ba'T	Ju87B/R
209ª Squadriglia Ba'T, 239ª Squadriglia Ba'T	
131° Gruppo Aut. AS	S.79sil
279ª Squadriglia AS, 284ª Squadriglia AS	
132° Gruppo Aut. AS	S.79sil
278ª Squadriglia AS, 281ª Squadriglia AS	

FIGHTERS

54° Stormo CT	44 MC200, 23 CR 42, 7 MC202
7° Gruppo CT	
76ª Squadriglia, 86ª Squadriglia, 98ª Squadriglia	
16° Gruppo CT	
167ª Squadriglia, 168ª Squadriglia, 169ª Squadriglia	
155° Gruppo Aut. CT	29 MC202
351ª Squadriglia, 360ª Squadriglia, 378ª Squadriglia	
2° Gruppo Aut. CT	14 Re2001
150ª Squadriglia, 152ª Squadriglia, 358ª Squadriglia	
377ª Squadriglia Aut. CT	3 Re2000, 6 CR42, 1 MC200
Comando Caccia	1 MC200, 1 CR42

RECONNAISSANCE/RESCUE

173ª Squadriglia Aut. RST	3 CR25
612ª Squadriglia Aut. Soccorso	3 Z506B

The Luftwaffe's presence in Sicily remained considerably reduced at this stage, and available for operations in support of their allies over the sea and over Malta, were only the following:

Stab & II/JG 53	27 Bf109F-4
KüFlGr 606, KGr 806	21 Ju88A-4
1(F)/121	Ju88D-1, Ju88A-4, Bf109F-5

Operation 'Harpoon' (12-17 June)

Friday, 12 June

The 'Harpoon' convoy began passing through the Straits of Gibraltar into the Western Basin of the Mediterranean in the early hours of the 12th, to be met by Force 'W' out of Gibraltar. Admiral Curteis had devised a cruising disposition which allowed the carriers and their escorts to operate freely on the port flank; the two columns of merchantmen, each headed by a cruiser, were positioned in the centre and encircled by the destroyers. *Malaya* and four minesweepers brought up the rear; *Malaya*'s Walrus amphibian would also provide ASR capability. This disposition allowed all ships to fire inwards and outwards with freedom.

Italian 'observers' along the Spanish coast had already reported many unlit cargo ships passing through the Strait during the night, followed by the departure of *Eagle*, *Argus* and *Malaya* from Gibraltar. At 0900, a Ju88D from Sicily sighted the ships south of Ibiza, while in the late afternoon the convoy's location was reported by the Spanish freighter *Cabo Prior* as being 60 miles north-north-west of Oran. On receiving news of the sightings Italian submarines were deployed at various stations en route — ten along the Algerian coastline, five in the Lampedusa-Malta region, and another five in the Ionian Sea; a further two, plus six German U-boats, were stationed further eastwards.

Saturday, 13 June

Early on the morning of the 13th, German and Italian aircraft again searched for the convoy, *Cairo's* radar detecting 'bogies' at 0810 approaching to within 16 miles, before disappearing from the screens. Half an hour later a section of patrolling Sea Hurricanes were vectored towards another unidentified aircraft, only to find it was a Swordfish from *Argus* on anti-submarine duty. Shortly before midday, one of the destroyer escorts — *Coltsfoot* — opened fire on the approach of another 'snooper' and claimed a hit on it before it was lost from sight. This may have been the Ju88 onto which two Sea Hurricanes were vectored just after midday. As they headed towards the aircraft to the south-west of the convoy, it was seen to drop an object — which the Naval pilots thought might have been a long-range tank, but may have been a jettisoned bomb — and drew away before the Hurricanes could engage.

Sunderlands, Catalinas and Hudsons from Gibraltar were employed on anti-submarine patrols ahead and to the flanks of the convoy. During the course of one such sortie, Flt.Lt. Powell's Catalina 'F' of 202 Squadron was attacked by a Ju88; the flyingboat's gunners returned the fire, and the Junkers made off in the direction of Tunis. Earlier in the day, a 10 RAAF Squadron Sunderland, attached to 202 Squadron, spotted a large submarine off the Sardinian coast. As Sqn.Ldr. R.B. Burrage manoeuvred his 'boat (W4028) to attack, his gunners began strafing the deck of the submarine — the Italian *Otaria* — when crew members were seen running towards the 4-inch gun; in an exchange of fire one of the submariners was wounded in both legs, while the Sunderland's port inner engine suffered minor damage. Although a salvo of seven 250lb depth charges straddled *Otaria*, she was only slightly damaged and was able to dive and escape.

The first positive steps taken by the Italians to interfere with the convoy's progress proved to be ineffective, for when a formation of six S.79 torpedo-bombers from 130° Gruppo set out from Sardinia to carry out the initial strike, they failed to locate the ships. Similarly, two cruisers and three destroyers of VII Divisione which had sailed from Cagliari in an attempt to intercept *Welshman* — which was in the Cape Bon area, speeding ahead of the convoy — were ordered to put in at Palermo when it was learned that British submarines were also in the area; these warships had also been spotted by one of the fleet's Swordfish. Another of *Argus*'s Swordfish, returning from patrol, crashed on landing. The wreck was promptly pushed over the side, creating some welcome extra space in the carrier's cramped hangar.

First contact between the Naval fighters and Axis reconnaissance aircraft occurred during the early afternoon. Sections of Sea Hurricanes from *Eagle* were on patrol when at 1405 Sub Lts. G.W. Parish and A.G. Blanchard of 801 Squadron were directed visually on to a 'shadower' seen from the carrier. They engaged a Ju88 one mile to port, flying in the opposite direction, and attacked from out of the sun, firing from close range. They could only claim damage before it escaped, reporting that the rear gunner had most probably been killed. It seems likely that this was Hpt. Dr. Nikolaus Büsen's Ju88D (F6+HH) of Libyan-based 1(F)/122 which failed to return from a sea reconnaissance, crashing on the Algerian coast near Algiers; all four of the crew were injured, the pilot later dying from his wounds.

Just over three hours later action stations was sounded again and orders given to scramble the fighters, when a number of 'blips' appeared on the radars. Within 30 minutes no less than five shadowers were within sight; these were all driven away by the fighters but were not engaged for a variety of reasons, the chief of which was the Sea Hurrricane's lack of speed!

At 1930, just when things seemed to have quietened down, Pink Section/813F Squadron were scrambled when another telltale 'blip' appeared on the radar, indicating the approach of yet another 'snooper' some 15 miles distant. Climbing to 3000 feet, Sub Lt. Michael Crosley soon spotted an aircraft low down to the south. He and his leader, Lt. T.J.A. King-Joyce, immediately gave chase; this proved too much for the latter's engine, which effectively 'blew-up', forcing the pilot to break away. With his aircraft streaming black smoke, King-Joyce nonetheless managed a safe landing aboard the carrier, Captain Mackintosh having turned *Eagle* into the wind to assist him. Meanwhile, after a 20 mile chase Crosley closed on the 'bogey' which was in fact a Z1007bis trimotor of 212ª Squadriglia; of his attack, he later wrote:

> 'I could now see the dark exhaust smoke from his three engines passing over the top of my hood as I closed in. I pulled up and made my attack . . . got his underside flying into the centre of the ringsight and pressed the firing button . . . I could see smoke coming from his port side. I continued firing through the smoke, hopelessly in his slipstream by now, until I caught sight of a wing tip so near that I pulled away and downwards.'

With port wing and engine on fire, the Cant fell away, Ten. Gerolamo Piccioni struggling vainly to control the crippled machine before being compelled to ditch. The aircraft floated sufficiently long for all six members of the crew to climb into their dinghy, from which they were later picked up by a British destroyer.

Malta enjoyed a quiet day as the Axis in Sicily prepared to attack the convoy as it came within range, just two reconnaissance Bf109s crossing the coast. In the other direction though, 69 Squadron's PR Spitfires had a busy day photographing airfields in Southern Sicily and on Sardinia, as well as checking harbours on these islands and at Taranto. During the morning one of the reconnaissance Baltimores was on a sortie over the Central Ionian Sea when a Bf110 was observed. Apparently taking the German crew by surprise, the Baltimore carried out an attack during which strikes were seen on the Zerstörer; the Messerschmitt broke away without returning fire.

The only other event of note occurred when a Canadian Beaufighter pilot, Plt.Off. John Doncaster, on completion of an air test, apparently decided to 'beat up' the airfield but stalled in a vertical bank; T5006/P crashed on top of a car being driven by 601 Squadron's Wt.Off. F.K.G. Relton, who was killed together with Doncaster and his observer, Sgt. Webster. A second of the Island's strike aircraft was lost later in the early hours of the morning when Wellington DV418/W of 38 Squadron crashed on take-off, Sgt. P. LeBrocq and his crew escaping injury; three crews had been briefed to attack a convoy located by an ASV Wellington. In the event, the convoy was not found by the remaining two aircraft.

Sunday, 14 June

In the early morning hours of the 14th, under cover of darkness, two Italian submarines — *Giada* and *Uarsciek* — attempted to manoeuvre into positions to make attacks on the convoy but were thwarted by the escort. Depth charges were fired at 0255 when the first threat materialized, more being detonated three hours later. One of the destroyers on the port screen then opened fire on a suspicious object thought to be a submarine, but this turned out to be HMS *Westcott* regaining her position on the screen with the coming of daylight.

With dawn the vessels were coming well within range of the airfields in southern Sardinia, and at 0420 a Z1007bis from the 51° Gruppo's 212ª Squadriglia was despatched on reconnaissance, followed by a second (from 213ª Squadriglia) at 0720. The first sighting of an 'unidentified' aircraft was made at 0555 by the destroyer *Vidette*, but this turned out to be a Catalina out from Gibraltar. However, the flyingboat crew were obviously unsure of the identity of the warship and, having circled the vessel, they apparently decided it was 'unfriendly'; the Catalina came in low and dropped a stick of five depth charges, which fell about 400 yards on the starboard quarter, before making off in haste! Subsequent sightings at 0605 and 0710 proved to be the searching Cants. On the second occasion two patrolling Sea Hurricanes pursued the 'snooper' but failed to make an interception.

With the convoy re-located, strikes were immediately ordered by the Italian command. First into the air was a pair of S.79 torpedo-bombers from the 256ª and 259ª Squadriglia of the 36° Stormo AS, which were to lead a formation of fighter-bombers to the attack. The latter, eight CR42s drawn from all three squadriglie of the 24° Stormo CT led by Cap. Alberto Brondi, set off at 0815, each carrying two 100kg bombs beneath their wings.

Meanwhile, Lt. King-Joyce and Sub Lt. Crosley of 813F Squadron were patrolling over the ships when they were vectored towards a 'shadower' which was spotted some 2000 feet above, silhouetted against cloud; they climbed above the Ju88's port beam and attacked individually as the bomber went into a shallow dive. Lt. Tobias James Alphonsus King-Joyce, a genial Irishman known as 'Spike', went in first. He closed to within 100 yards from astern, firing all the way, and was followed by Crosley:

> 'I pressed the firing button... The shape was wandering into my sight, huge and black, first one side then the other... I finished the entire 12 seconds of ammunition and must have been closer than 100 yards at the end. I saw the de Wilde ammunition hitting his port wing, sparking like firecrackers. Bits of the aircraft flew past me. Or so it seemed — or they might have been the rear gunner's empty shell cases. I was sure I had hit him and mortally wounded him. I saw a burst of smoke from his port wing root again, this time after I had finished firing all my ammunition... The Ju88 flew on in a shallow dive and I found myself easily overtaking him. He had slowed right down to about 160 knots. I was sure he was a "gonner". I didn't wait this time to see him splash.'

This was almost certainly Uffz. Emil Schwarz's Ju88D (F6+EH) of 1(F)/122, which was reported shot down about 120 miles west of Trapani, at about 0830. Next day three of the crew, including the pilot, were found in their dinghy by a British warship, in the area where the 813F Squadron section had clashed with the Junkers. The German airmen, two of whom were seriously hurt and later died from their injuries, apparently confirmed having been shot down by what they estimated to have been four Hurricanes.

An hour later two more Sea Hurricanes, flown by Lt.Cdr. R.A. Brabner (CO of 801 Squadron) and Sub Lt. P.J. Hutton, engaged another 'shadower' which they identified as a 'Breda 88', pursuing this at sea level for over 50 miles and claiming to have inflicted severe damage, part of the starboard rudder and flap being seen to fall away. It seems very probable that this was the 212ª Squadriglia Z1007bis, which had already been attacked by one Hurricane when two and three-quarter hours into its flight, and was then intercepted again 90 minutes later by a reported three Hurricanes. One of the attackers was claimed shot down, but the bomber was hit and returned with a dead gunner and wounded engineer aboard.

Yet another 'snooper' was encountered at 1015 by Sunderland W3994/X, an aircraft of 10 RAAF seconded to 202 Squadron at Gibraltar, which was flying an anti-submarine patrol in support of the convoy. Plt.Off. T.A. Egerton's aircraft was attacked from close range by a Ju88, but the German's fire was rather wayward, only the 'boat's W/T aerial being shot away; the gunners returned fire and the Junkers was reported to have dived away towards the sea, emitting streams of white smoke from one engine.

Even as this engagement was taking place, three pairs of Sea Hurricanes — Red, Green and White Sections of 801 Squadron — were scrambled from *Eagle's* deck, followed by Red Section Fulmars; this latter pair came under the control of *Argus* and were to return to that carrier at the end of their patrol. This was in accordance with *Eagle's* policy to transfer as many Fulmars as possible to *Argus* in order to facilitate the operation and direction of a high (Sea Hurricane) and a low (Fulmar) force. The slow old carrier — affectionately referred to as 'HMS Ditty-Box' by those who served in her — also launched her two Fulmars, identified as Blue Section, in response to radar detecting a small incoming formation.

At 1100 White Section — Lt. F.R.A. Turnbull and Sub Lt. Duthie — were vectored onto this formation, which had now been tentatively identified as approximately ten S.79s; these were without doubt the pair of 36° Stormo aircraft and eight CR42s, the Sea Hurricanes quickly intercepting one of the S.79s at 15,000 feet; the two British pilots failed to observe any other aircraft — the CR42 fighter-bombers were flying at a different height and were some distance behind — but reported that the trimotor intercepted by them had a very polished appearance, with its engine cowlings painted red; they concurred that it must have been either the personal aircraft of a senior officer, or from a training flight! It was, in fact, Ten. Alberto Leonardi's 259ª Squadriglia Savoia; included in the crew of this aircraft was a Regia Marina observer from 287ª Squadriglia RM, Ten. Vasc.Oss. Guglielmo Priorini, whose task it was to identify the ships. But fate was about to take a hand. 'Red' Duthie, flying Z4923/C, recalled:

> 'We made one attack and were turning to come back for another pass, when I looked all around, as was the rule, and spotted six, I think, Ju88s about 10,000 feet, straight above us and heading more or less in the direction of the fleet. We were by then down to about 10,000 feet ourselves. I reported these to Dick (*Lt. Turnbull*) and this transmission was picked up by Fighter Direction and acknowledged. There was no hope of gaining enough height to attack the high formation, so we continued to shoot down the solitary S.79. One small incident I remember very clearly. On the second pass we made a section quarter attack, one from each side, pulling round to astern. I was much too close before breaking away, which was something all too easy to do when one was looking through a reflector gunsight. I had just pushed the stick forwards to break away downwards, when one of the crew jumped from the S.79. He missed my Hurricane by what seemed inches, and I distinctly remember that he was wearing a black flying suit with silver buttons. We later saw his parachute open but never knew whether or not he was picked up.'

By now all three engines were on fire and the bomber splashed into the sea; there were no survivors. The crew of the other bomber reported that five British fighters had attacked their aircraft, and claimed that the gunners shot down two of these in flames! Presumably they had unknowingly witnessed the demise of Ten. Leonardi's flaming bomber from afar.

Meanwhile, at 1025, the CR42 pilots spotted *Argus* and dive-bombed the carrier from about 3000 feet, claiming two hits; *Malaya* was also attacked, as were one or two of the convoy but, in fact, none of the bombs found their mark. After releasing his bombs, Sottoten. Ernani Loddo of 370ª Squadriglia engaged what he described as a biplane floatplane, which he tentatively identified as a cruiser-launched Fairey Seafox, and claimed to have shot it down. The identity of Loddo's opponent remains a mystery, for none of the British ships carried a Seafox on this operation, nor was there a report of a Walrus amphibian, or even a Swordfish, being attacked. He may conceivably have encountered an Ro43 spotter biplane floatplane from one of the Italian ships, although none were reported lost during this day's action.

As one pair of CR42s crossed over *Argus*'s starboard bow to port quarter, they were chased and caught by the Red Section Fulmars, crewed by Lt. A.B. Fraser-Harris/Sub Lt. L. Rowland and Sub Lt. L.P. Twiss/PO(A) R. Holroyd. The Italian pilots could hardly have been keeping a sharp look out, for both were promptly shot down by combined fire from the pursuing Fulmars, Fraser-Harris reporting:

> 'Two CR42s seen 50 miles west of Galite Island — carried out deflection attacks — one crashed in flames and the other baled out, then his aircraft seen to crash.'

Peter Twiss, flying X8768, recalled:

> 'This was the first time I had been in combat with the CR42 and was under the impression that they would outmanoeuvre the heavy Fulmar. No 1 aircraft was shot down by "F.H."; the pilot baled out, his parachute opening O.K. The second was turning inside "F.H.", and with flaps partly lowered, I was able to turn inside the second aircraft and give it a long burst. The pilot turned over his aircraft and baled out.'

The Fiat leader, 26 year-old Cap. Brondi, who was also the commander of 355^a Squadriglia, and Sottoten. Bruno Castro both lost their lives; they were subsequently awarded the Medaglia d'Oro posthumously for their part in the attack. Two other CR42s were obliged to force-land due to fuel shortage at Sidi Hamed, in Tunisia, following the attack. Here, Sottoten. Massimo Suppo and Sottoten. Silvano Dessanti were interned by the Vichy French authorities.

'Red' Duthie, a New Zealander from Auckland who had transferred from the RNZAF on being offered a commission in the FAA, later recalled a rather bizarre anecdote concerning the engagement between the Fulmars and the Fiats:

> 'A story went round concerning the two CR42s destroyed by "Farris" (Fraser-Harris' nickname) and Peter Twiss. This was that the second aircraft shot down was not hit but did some pretty fancy evasive action which ended in a loop. At the top of the loop (it was suggested) the pilot fell out, and it was assumed that in a hurry to take off, he had forgotten to strap himself in!'

To meet the next raid, which began appearing five minutes later at 1105, six Sea Hurricanes (Red, Green and Black Sections/801 Squadron) were up, as well as the Blue Section Fulmars from *Argus*. Their presence was certainly urgently needed, for this was to be the first main Italian attack. Bomber and torpedo-bomber formations were, in order of take-off:

Eight S.79sil from 280^a and 283^a Squadriglia, 130° Gruppo Aut. AS; nine S.84s from 258^a and 259^a Squadriglia, 109° Gruppo AS; ten S.79sil from 252^a and 253^a Squadriglia, 104° Gruppo AS; six S.84s from 256^a and 257^a Squadriglia, 108° Gruppo AS; and finally ten Z1007bis from 62^a and 63^a Squadriglia, 29° Gruppo BT, five of which turned back early.

To escort the bombers, nine MC200s of the 7° and 16° Gruppo CT took off at 0950, followed at 1020 by 20 more plus 19 CR42s of 24° Gruppo CT. Finally, half an hour behind this formation came a further ten Z1007bis bombers from 59^a and 60^a Squadriglia, 33° Gruppo BT.

The torpedo-bombers were spotted first as they approached at low level and swung to the port side of the convoy. About half the attackers came in from this side at 1110, the remainder continuing to circle round to the starboard beam, making their runs some 20 minutes later. At once the Fleet opened up with its formidable anti-aircraft armament, while the two Fulmars launched the initial fighter attack. Lt. Hall and Sub Lt. Palmer closed in on three S.79s and two of these were claimed shot down into the sea, but Blue 1's fighter was hit by return fire; as Hall attempted to return to *Argus* with his damaged aircraft, he was attacked by three of the escorting CR42s, and further damage was sustained. He glided the stricken Fulmar down to carry out a ditching in the sea, the aircraft then being further damaged by Oerlikon fire from HMS *Wrestler*, and crashed. Philip Hall was killed, although his observer, Sub Lt. L.D. Urry, survived and was picked up. Thirty minutes later, Sub Lt. Peter Palmer reported attacking another Savoia but then contact was lost with his aircraft. The Fulmar failed to return and it was assumed Palmer and his observer, Sub Lt. John Ceely, had been shot down.

It is probable that one of the Fulmars' victims was the reconnaissance Z1007bis of 213ª Squadriglia, which had been shadowing the ships for some hours; the crew reported that they had been attacked by fighters, two of which they claimed shot down, one by the gunner, the other by the engineer. The bomber was seriously damaged and force-landed near Carloforte, on the Isola San Pietro, with two seriously wounded crewmen. The other S.79 claimed was probably one of two lost by 104° Gruppo.

Many of the torpedo-bombers managed to evade the few fighters and for the next 20 minutes the ships were subjected to high- and low-level attacks. One S.79 released its torpedo at *Eagle* from about 400 yards range but from a height of about 120 feet; it appeared to enter the water too steeply and probably failed to gain the proper depth to be effective. This aircraft was shot down by *Eagle*'s defences just as it passed clear of her bows. One of the destroyer screen, *Icarus*, steaming ahead of the carrier, brought down a second attacker and *Argus*'s starboard Oerlikon gunners shot down another.

Towards the end of this attack, both *Eagle* and *Argus* were the targets of high-level (12,000 feet) bombing by the Cants of the 29° Gruppo, and both were near-missed. Not so fortunate, a few minutes later, was *Liverpool*; a torpedo penetrated her starboard engine room, effectively putting her out of the action; the damaged cruiser veered off course, her speed dropping to four knots. One of the escorting destroyers was ordered to stand by, and to give any necessary assistance. The convoy did not escape the onslaught, two torpedoes hitting the Dutch *Tanimbar*. The freighter caught fire and blew up ten minutes later; 23 of the crew were lost. The Savoia crews, however, did not find the merchantmen submissive targets, the port Oerlikon gunner aboard *Troilus* shooting down one, while the ship's 12-pounder hit another, which broke in two.

As the Sea Hurricanes attempted to get at the torpedo-bombers, they were engaged by the fighter escort. Green Section claimed two of the fighters shot down — Sub Lt. Godfrey Parish attacked one Macchi when another got on his tail; he succeeded in turning inside this aircraft, probably flown by Serg.Magg. Raimondo Giardini, and shot it down into the sea. He then opened fire on an S.79, which he claimed severely damaged, before being hit in the engine by return fire; Parish successfully force-landed his damaged aircraft on *Eagle*'s deck, much to the consternation of the Captain and Commander Flying!

Meanwhile, Green 2 — Sub Lt. Alan Blanchard — having evaded the

Macchis, became entangled with the nimble CR42 biplanes. He latched onto one, which he reported released a bomb when he attacked, chased it down to sea level and gave it two bursts, following which it dived straight in. This was undoubtedly a 355[a] Squadriglia machine (MM7594), which failed to return; Serg.Magg. Aldo Mazzolani was killed.

The two Sea Hurricanes of Black Section, flown by Lt. Jack Welply and Sub Lt. Mike Hankey, gave chase to a trimotor which they incorrectly identified as a BR20, flying low down at about 150 feet. Welply gave it four long bursts from astern; this was followed by an attack from Hankey and it was last seen trailing smoke 10-15 feet above the waves.

Red Section (Lt.Cdr. Brabner and Lt. L.F. Tickner) engaged a dozen Macchis and several S.79s at 11,500 feet, Brabner reporting:

> 'Attacked an MC200 from astern which spun down and was considered destroyed. Head-on attack on S.79 and hits seen — another attack on different S.79 and explosion in rear of aircraft, and caught fire. Attacked third S.79 and hits seen on starboard wing root — last seen losing height.'

Rupert Brabner, who had fought in the defence of Crete the previous year, was credited with one S.79 shot down, as well as the Macchis — this was probably Serg.Magg. Bombarda's aircraft, which was sufficiently damaged for him to force-land near Bone — plus a second S.79 as probably destroyed; but he lost his No 2 in the action. Lt. Lennox Tickner, regular Royal Navy, known to his colleagues as 'Guns' due to his former vocation as a gunnery officer, was presumed shot down by another MC200.

At the height of the raid, two more Sea Hurricanes — Yellow Section — were launched from *Eagle*, Sub Lts. D.J. McDonald and N.D. Fisher soon finding themselves in the thick of the action. Three trimotors were seen — misidentified as BR20s — the one on the port side being attacked; smoke was seen issuing from it before they were set upon by CR42s. These were evaded and both inexperienced pilots safely returned to the carrier, although Nigel Fisher was fired upon by *Eagle*'s pom-pom crews as he made his first circuit; this somewhat disconcerted him, and it was on his fifth approach that he finally managed to land.

Magg.Pier. Giuseppe Scarpetta, the Macchi leader, claimed a Hurricane and a Defiant (*sic*) shot down. The latter was presumably an incorrectly identified Fulmar, from which he reported the pilot baled out; one of his pilots, Serg.Magg. Magnaghi, also claimed a Hurricane. The 24° Gruppo CR42 pilots claimed two more Hurricanes — one by Sottoten. Moretti, the other shared by Ten. Italo Marchi and Serg. Casalini, and these two pilots were also jointly credited with a probable; two more probables were credited to Serg.Magg. Corti and Serg. Rizzardo. Additionally, gunners in the 108° Gruppo S.84s claimed five Hurricanes shot down and two probables!

What had been the Italian bomber and torpedo-bomber losses in this first attack? The attackers had indeed suffered very severe casualties. The initial eight S.79sil of 130° Gruppo had escaped loss, but the 104° Gruppo formation had been hard hit. The two aircraft of 253[a] Squadriglia flown by Ten. Mario Ingrellini and Ten. Giovanni Vivarelli were both shot down, while three more were badly damaged; Ten. Enrico Marescalchi force-landed his aircraft at Cape Teulada airfield on return, while the commander of 104° Gruppo, Magg. Virginio Reinero, force-landed at Elmas. Ten. Ingrellini and Serg.Magg.

Giorgio Compiani, a 253ª Squadriglia crewman who was killed in one of the returning aircraft, each received posthumous awards of the Medaglia d'Oro.

Losses amongst the S.84s of 36° Stormo were even higher, six aircraft failing to return. In one of these, Ten. Col. Giovanni Farina, the 36° Stormo commander, and Magg. Mario Turba (commander of 109° Gruppo) were lost; while in another, Cap. Paolo Simeoni — commander of 259ª Squadriglia — and his crew were killed. The crews of Ten. Oreste Bedosti, Ten. Angelo Abate and Ten. Angelo Zanelli were also lost, only that of Sottoten. Oliviero Donati being rescued by a Cant seaplane from Sardinia, after seven hours drifting in their dinghy. Awards of the Medaglia d'Oro were made posthumously to Farina and Turba.

Returning S.84 crews claimed hits on a 'Renown-type' battleship, three cruisers and a 10,000-ton steamer, while the air gunners wildly overestimated their actual achievements by claiming nine Hurricanes shot down, plus four probables! Added to this, the S.79 crews believed they had also hit a battleship and two cruisers, and had sunk three steamers!

As the surviving aircraft from the first assault landed, more reconnaissance aircraft were sent off to maintain contact with the convoy, two more Z1007bis, at least two Z506B floatplanes and a Savoia S.66 being deployed by the late morning and early afternoon. The first of the Z1007bis reported being intercepted by a trio of fighters identified as 'Buffaloes', but it escaped. Only two engagements were recorded by the carrier fighters during the afternoon period. The first was at 1320, when two of *Argus*'s Fulmars engaged a 'shadower', identified as a BR20. Sub Lt. Twiss (X8768) claimed many strikes on this before a large calibre bullet struck his propeller spinner, almost forcing the Fulmar to crash into the sea. In spite of his windscreen, and his face, being covered in oil, Twiss safely reached *Argus*.

At 1600, Lt. Fraser-Harris was off again after yet another 'snooper', which was intercepted at low-level; he closed to within 30-40 yards, firing short bursts but the aircraft (identified as an S.84) although streaming smoke was not seen to crash.

Following the damage suffered during the morning attack, the cruiser *Liverpool* turned back, escorted by the destroyer *Antelope*. This pair now became the focus of attack for the Sardinian-based aircraft, as the main convoy moved towards Sicily's zone. A Catalina from Gibraltar, Z2146/B of 240 Squadron flown by Flg.Off. K.J. Riddy, was diverted from its anti-submarine duties and ordered to escort the damaged cruiser.

The first attacks were launched by six CR42s from 24° Gruppo CT, again with 100kg bombs. An hour or so later, eight S.79sil from 104° and 130° Gruppo AS took off from Decimomannu and Elmas, escorted by 14 more 24° Gruppo CR42s, and followed by ten 9° Stormo BT Z1007bis from Villacidro.

At 1705 Flg.Off. Riddy's crew spotted two flights each of five trimotor bombers, accompanied by four CR42s, approaching to attack *Liverpool* from between 6-7000 feet. Ten minutes later a further seven bombers were seen. Displaying great courage and resource, Riddy engaged the bombers and broke up the formation before a co-ordinated attack could develop. Further damage was claimed to the cruiser, but one of the 104° Gruppo S.79s, flown by Ten. Giovanni Giacomello of 253ª Squadriglia, was reportedly hit by AA and Fulmars (unlikely) and was shot down.

Ten minutes later, the Catalina was attacked by four of the CR42s but Riddy skilfully manoeuvred his lumbering flyingboat, enabling his gunners to repel repeated attacks. Nonetheless, Serg. Casalini of 354ª Squadriglia carried out a number of determined attacks, gaining strikes on the 'boat's hull and slightly wounding the W/T operator. The Fiats finally departed some 25 minutes later but not before Serg.Magg. Lorenzo Ramacciotti was obliged to bale out of his fighter due to fuel shortage, and was drowned. Two more CR42s landed in Sicily for similar reasons. Meanwhile, the Catalina continued escorting *Liverpool* and later that evening spotted a dinghy in the sea; on alighting it was found to contain four Italian airmen, survivors of Ten. Giacomello's crew. Another ten 9° Stormo Z1007bis later bombed *Liverpool* again, but without result, while in the dusk a trio of S.79sil from the 3° Nucleo Aerosiluranti made a final — ineffective — attack with torpedoes.

It was, however, now the turn of the air forces in Sicily to enter the fray. During the early evening the remaining overworked carrier fighters were again warned of an incoming raid. Green Section Fulmars from *Argus* and Red Section of Sea Hurricanes from *Eagle* were already in the air at 1815, a further two Sea Hurricanes — Yellow Section — being rapidly scrambled as nine Ju88s from KüFlGr 606 came drifting out of the evening haze to dive-bomb *Argus*; commencing their dives at about 10,000 feet and pulling out at 4000 feet, they appeared to drop three 500lb bombs apiece. The carrier was narrowly missed on the starboard bow, which severely shook the ship but caused no apparent damage to the hull or machinery. Exposed personnel forward were drenched with water but there were no injuries. None of the other ships was attacked.

Meanwhile the Sea Hurricanes were getting amongst the bombers, Red Section (Lt.Cdr. Brabner and Sub Lt. Hutton) forcing two Ju88s to jettison their bombs. Red Leader's subsequent report read:

> 'Attacked Ju88 head-on at 9000 feet — long burst and enemy aircraft jettisoned its bombs and dived away. Another long burst from astern. No results seen.'

Sub Lt. Peter Hutton, following closely on his leader's tail, went after the same aircraft and delivered the 'coup de grace'. He then attacked two more and claimed one of these shot down, and the other probably so. Two bombers were indeed lost — 7T+IL flown by Lt. Gerhard Koopmann and 7T+HL captained by Lt. Artur Penske; there were no survivors (Penske's body was washed ashore at Marsalforn Bay, Gozo, over three weeks later). Three more Junkers were chased and two claimed damaged by Sub Lts. McDonald and Fisher of Yellow Section, both of which were last seen trailing smoke from their engines. From the vantage of *Argus* those following the fortunes of the pair of Fulmars, which were seen flying just above the waves to the south, observed a splash and Green 2 (crewed by Sub Lt. Geoffrey Spalding and L/Air. John Duncan) did not return.

Now came the Sicily-based units of the Regia Aeronautica. At 1830 some 17 Ju87s of the 102° Gruppo Tuffatori's 209ª and 239ª Squadriglia took off from Chinisia airfield, where they had arrived that morning from Gela. Five of the Ju87Bs carried SD 1000kg bombs, while the remainder — all Ju87Rs — carried SD 500kg missiles. The dive-bombers were escorted by 19 MC202s of 155° Gruppo CT, one of which was forced to return early. Fifteen minutes later they were followed by 14 S.79sil torpedo-bombers of 278ª and 281ª Squadriglia, 132° Gruppo Aut. AS, from Castelvetrano, led by the celebrated and skilful torpedo pilot Magg. Carlo Emanuele Buscaglia. They were escorted by 15 Re2001 fighters of the 2° Gruppo Aut. CT from San Pietro di Caltagirone — Ten. Col. Aldo Quarantotti at their head — and seven MC200s of 54° Stormo CT.

As the torpedo-bombers approached the area, crews reported seeing two Ju88s being shot down — obviously the two KüFlGr 606 machines. They arrived over the convoy at 2006. A few minutes before their arrival, the pilot of Fulmar Green 1 from *Argus* — Sub Lt. J.F. Rankin — who was still in the air following the Ju88 attack, announced that his aircraft had been hit by AA fire from the minesweeper *Hebe* and that he was ditching; he and his observer, Midspm. R.G. Armitage, were picked up by the destroyer *Hythe*. A pair of Sea Hurricanes — Brown Section of 813F Squadron — were also in the air at this time, while Pink Section/813F and White Section/801 were in the process of taking-off.

Immediately after take-off, White Section engaged the torpedo-bombers. Lt. Dick Turnbull reported:

> 'Fourteen S.79s seen at 200 feet... attacked rear aircraft and both wheels dropped then burst into flames and into sea following attack by White 2. Attacked two others in same vic... hits seen on both, one starboard engine on fire, but then hit by return fire and oil tank badly holed.'

Lt. Turnbull returned to the carrier with his engine temperature 'off the clock'. Sub Lt. Duthie (White 2, again flying Z4923/C) stayed with the Savoias and used up the rest of his ammunition, claiming two more badly damaged. Their joint victim was undoubtedly Sottoten. Giannino Negri's machine, which reportedly blew up with the loss of the crew, while Sottoten. Moretti crash-landed his badly shot-up S.79 at Castelvetrano and it was totally destroyed; three of his crew had been wounded during the fighter attack.

The four 813F Squadron pilots of Brown and Pink Sections, higher in the sky, were fighting for their lives, almost totally overwhelmed by the 2° Gruppo Reggianes. Both Brown Section aircraft and one of Pink Section were hit, Sub Lt. B.E. Bullivant (Brown 2) baling out at 2000 feet as his fighter fell in flames, after being attacked by what he identified as three BR65s (*sic*); he was picked up by the destroyer *Matchless* after about an hour in the sea. Lt. King-Joyce (Pink 1) had his aircraft badly shot about, forcing him to land down wind on *Eagle* at 2016, while 15 minutes later, Sub Lt. H.R. Spedding (Brown 1) crashed attempting to land his damaged aircraft on the carrier; he was unhurt and the wreckage of his Sea Hurricane was pushed over the side. He had claimed a Macchi shot down, and of his combat recounted:

> 'Saw large formation of bombers twelve miles ahead of the convoy — BR20s (*sic*) with MC200 escort. Attacked rear section when Brown 2 (*Sub Lt. Bullivant*) warned of three Macchis on my tail — turned and head-on attack on the leader — caught fire immediately; attacked by another three and received damage to my radiator... dived away.'

His victim was Mar. Giovanni Treggia's Reggiane, the 152ª Squadriglia pilot baling out into the sea, from where he was later rescued by fishermen.

In their rush to get at the four Sea Hurricanes, which they engaged near Galite Island, the pilots of 2° Gruppo had obviously all attacked together and had vastly overestimated the results of the combat, claiming no fewer than 11 Sea Hurricanes shot down! The Re2001 leader, Ten. Col. Quarantotti claimed two, as did Ten. Agostino Celentano of 150ª Squadriglia; other pilots from this squadriglia claimed two more, one each by Ten. Giorgio Pocek and Ten. Giulio Bartolozzi. For 152ª Squadriglia Ten. Italo Larese Gortigo and Serg.Magg. Albino Fabbri each claimed one, and shared another, while two more were claimed by Mar. Treggia (the pilot who was shot down) and Serg.Magg. Elio Cesaro.

Ten minutes later White Section returned, together with Pink 2, the pilot of which (Sub Lt. Mike Crosley) claimed an S.79 probably destroyed and the possible destruction of a Reggiane. He later wrote:

> 'I saw below me and on my starboard side a light-brown camouflaged fighter aircraft. It looked something like a long-nosed Hurricane, but the colour intrigued me and I dived down on it ... I opened fire at about 300 yards, rather too far I feared. He immediately pulled up in a steep right hand turn. I tried to follow him, but, going much faster, I blacked out hopelessly and he must have flown right through my sights. I have no idea what happened after I "came to" for he was nowhere to be seen.'

Two successful Reggiane Re2001 pilots of 2° Gruppo Aut. CT. at Ciampino; Mar. Olindo Simionato of 150ª Squadriglia (left) and Mar. Giovanni Treggia of 152ª Squadriglia. *(S. Govi via N. Malizia)*

It seems likely this was Mar. Olindo Simionato's Re2001 of 150ª Squadriglia, which force-landed in Tunisia, near Korba; here the aircraft was repaired and Simionato was able to fly back to Sicily a few days later. Meanwhile, Sub Lt. Crosley continued his patrol and encountered "at least four flights of four or five S.79s" — these were, of course, the aircraft from 132° Gruppo, to which the Reggianes were providing escort, and onto which the Sea Hurricanes of 801 Squadron were closing. Crosley continues:

> 'I built up a massive overtaking speed... I turned in... and started my firing run... I rapidly closed the range. However, I was so close by the time I broke away, that the cockpit was dark with the shadows of surrounding Italian aircraft and the air bumpy with their slipstreams. I had no idea whether they were firing at me or not, but I felt that they were and it was very frightening. I had expended all my ammunition in the two attacks apart from a very few rounds, and I certainly wasn't going into the deathtrap again... Just then,

someone from 801 Squadron piped up "Tally Ho" on the radio, and I had a grandstand view of their four (*sic*) going into attack, one after the other. They hacked down one... and the formation ahead completely broke ranks and fell all over the sky.'

At the height of the attack, three S.79s each released a torpedo in the same water at intervals of 5-10 seconds on *Argus*'s starboard bow, at a distance of 2-3000 yards. *Argus* turned to starboard to comb the tracks which were seen to pass down the port side. The two inner tracks were roughly parallel to the carrier's new course and to each other, while the third one was seen converging towards the stern. When first seen the tracks were about four yards apart. Returning Italian crews claimed damage to both *Argus* and *Malaya*, and to have shot down three attacking Sea Hurricanes.

It was at this stage — with no carrier fighters airborne or immediately available — that the 102° Gruppo Ju87 dive-bombers arrived overhead at 11,000 feet, at the very limit of their range. They were at once led down in a dive to 1800 feet by Cap. Cenni. Claims were made for hits on a cruiser with two SD 1000kg bombs, the warship believed possibly sunk, while an unidentified vessel was claimed cut in half, and a second warship probably damaged by four near-misses! They actually achieved no substantial damage to any vessels. Turning for home, the Ju87s were now in trouble due to fuel shortage, Sottoten. Antonio Vecchione ditching his 209ª Squadriglia bomber in the sea just four miles out from the Sicilian coast; he and his gunner were later picked up by a Do24 sent out to search for them. Several others had their engines cut before they could taxi off the runway after landing back at Chinisia.

Over the convoy at 2100, patrols were reinstated by Black Section of Sea Hurricanes and the first four Beaufighters from 235 Squadron, which now arrived from Malta; but at this point the heavy units of Admiral Curteis' Force 'W', which included the carriers, having reached the pre-arranged departure point west of the Sicilian Narrows, turned back towards Gibraltar. Thus there remained *Cairo*, nine destroyers and four minesweepers of Force 'X', under Captain C.C. Hardy, to take the convoy the final 250 miles to Malta. Air defence of the convoy now became the responsibility of the Malta-based Beaufighters, until such a time as it could come within range of the Spitfires.

Perhaps hardly surprisingly, the patrolling Beaufighters were at first fired at by the escorting warships until identification could be made. Then, shortly after 2200, the convoy came under attack from marauding Ju88s, parachute flares being released by these in attempts to illuminate the ships. Although *Cairo*'s radar and R/T were malfunctioning, causing grave concern about her ability to control and co-ordinate patrolling fighters, Beaufighter 'Y' (flown by Sqn.Ldr. A.E. Cook) was vectored onto one bomber which was being fired upon by the guns, and this was attacked; shortly afterwards a glow was seen in the night sky and a burning object was observed falling into the sea by those in the convoy. It was assumed the bomber had been shot down in flames, but the "flaming object" may have been another flare. Whilst a Ju88 from KGr 806, on a night sortie, returned to Sicily in a damaged state following fighter attack, this aircraft may have been the victim of a night fighter Beaufighter (X7750) from Malta, Flt.Lt. Hayton claiming one such bomber shot down about this time.

As the convoy and its protecting Force 'X' continued eastwards, disturbing reports began reaching Captain Hardy of two Italian cruisers and five destroyers steaming out of Palermo, heading in his direction. Further to the west, as he withdrew towards Sardinia, Admiral Curteis received the same reports and whilst he deliberated over sending help to Force 'X', he considered his priority was to protect the returning carriers. The convoy and Force 'X' were thus on their own.

The Italian force comprised the cruisers *Raimondo Montecuccoli* and *Eugenio di Savoia*, and five destroyers of the VII Divisione under Ammiraglio Angelo da Zara, which had earlier failed to find *Welshman*. When the ships had initially been reported by Sqn.Ldr. Messervy's ASV Wellington crew it was not known for certain whether or not they were departing to join forces with Ammiraglio Iachino's fleet from Taranto, which was advancing to intercept the Alexandria convoy (see later), but it soon became apparent they were after the five surviving merchantmen from Gibraltar.

Monday, 15 June

At first light on the 15th, following a relatively uneventful night passing through the Skerki Channel, where the main alarms had come from supposed submarine contacts, Force 'X' had rounded Cape Bon and hugged the Tunisian coast as far as Kelibia; the convoy was now some 22 miles south of Pantelleria. At this point, three Beaufighters arrived with alarming news — they had passed over da Zara's force just 12 miles north, steering a course to intercept the convoy. At 0615 the enemy squadron was in sight, and Captain Hardy ordered Cdr. B.G. Scurfield in *Bedouin* to lead his five Fleet destroyers to engage, whilst *Cairo* and the remaining four Hunt-class destroyers laid smoke screens to protect the merchant vessels; *Cairo* also radioed Malta for help, followed by a second signal 18 minutes later calling for an air strike against the cruisers. Few aircraft were immediately available however, as most of the Beauforts were already away over the Eastern Basin (of which more later), and the Wellingtons had only just returned from night raids elsewhere; whatever was to hand would be sent.

Meanwhile, as expected the out-gunned British destroyers were no match for the Italian cruisers, and soon both *Bedouin* and *Partridge* had been hit and were stationary. However, the RCN's *Ithuriel*, although slightly damaged herself, was able to engage *Raimondo Montecuccoli* and gained two hits on the cruiser at a range of 8000 yards, forcing her to turn away. The other two destroyers, *Marne* and *Matchless* turned their attention to the Italian destroyers, *Vivaldi* sustaining a hit in the engine room.

Up above, as the crews of two relief Beaufighters were observing this gallant naval action, into the area came Ten. Mario Sodi's Ro43 reconnaissance spotter floatplane (MM27147), which had been catapulted from the *Eugenio di Savoia*. This was promptly pounced upon by Sqn.Ldr. W.C. Wigmore and in a one-sided action was shot down into the sea. The observer, Ten. Vasc. Vitaliano Marsigliani was killed. A Ju88 'shadower' was then spotted. Wigmore chased this away, reporting leaving it in a damaged state; the other Beaufighter pilot, Plt.Off. F.A. Cohen, chased two more Ju88 'shadowers' but could not get his guns to fire!

The smoke now began to clear and the Italian cruisers started firing again, but at that point seven Ju88s from I/KG 54 arrived and attacked. The two American vessels took the brunt of this assault, *Chant* being overwhelmed and struck by three bombs, which killed seven of her crew. With smoke billowing from her stern, she gradually dropped behind sinking slowly; her survivors were picked up, however. Witnesses considered that one of the attackers had been shot

With its top wing brightly painted with red stripes in order that the aircraft may easily be spotted from the air if it is obliged to come down on the sea, a Meridionali Ro43 biplane spotter floatplane is launched from the catapult aboard an Italian cruiser. Several of these Regia Marina aircraft were to fall foul of RAF fighters during the June convoy operations. *(Via N. Malizia)*

down. The tanker *Kentucky* suffered a near-miss which damaged her engines and fractured a steam pipe, and she too dropped out of the convoy; the escorting *Hebe* was ordered to go to her aid, and the crippled vessel was taken in tow by the minesweeper.

Troilus also came under attack, and bombs which fell close to the port side severely shook the ship; her gunners opened fire with all weapons as the bombers pulled out of their dives, hitting one which they reported crashed and burst into flames. An officer aboard *Troilus* as part of the RAF reinforcement for the Malta garrison, recounted:

> 'We then sailed past two German airmen floating in the sea who had escaped from their wrecked aircraft. They shouted "Hilfe" (help!) to us, as if we who had nearly lost our lives through them should risk them even further by stopping to save their lives. They were picked up by a warship.'

This latter statement would seem to have been slightly inaccurate, as it would appear that these airmen were not rescued by an escorting vessel. Müller, the pilot, was killed in the crash, his body being recovered from the sea five days later by an Italian MTB. However, the three survivors took to the aircraft's dinghy and were fortunate to be washed ashore at Tigne Point, Malta, after six days at sea.

The two Italian cruisers moved in on the remaining merchant vessels, which had turned north-west to seek shelter in neutral waters. Only *Cairo* and the out-ranged destroyers acted as a barrier. During an exchange of gunfire, *Cairo* was hit amidships by two shells but the damage was not serious. Somewhat to the surprise of Captain Hardy and his officers, the cruisers failed to follow up this success and moved instead to a point to the north of the minefield barrier on the direct approach to Malta, here to await the convoy. With the departure of this naval threat, the latter turned south again. Malta lay 150 miles to the west.

Following this action, the seriously damaged *Bedouin*, which had sustained nine shell hits, was taken in tow by the less badly damaged *Partridge*. However, on the approach of the two Italian cruisers, the latter managed to slip her tow, laid smoke to protect the helpless *Bedouin* and stood off to attract their fire. For almost an hour she endured salvo after salvo, until eventually and inevitably two near misses jammed her rudder; Italian fire was then concentrated on *Bedouin*. When two S.79sil of 281ª Squadriglia arrived, Sottoten. Martino Aichner promptly put his torpedo into the doomed destroyer; she sank within ten minutes, but not before her gunners had defiantly shot down their attacker. Aichner ditched his damaged machine (MM23942) nearby, he and his crew soon being rescued, together with 209 survivors from *Bedouin* including Cdr. Scurfield. The damaged *Partridge* luckily avoided a similar fate and made good her own escape to the west, subsequently reaching Gibraltar.

Throughout mid morning several somewhat confused engagements occurred overhead. Aichner's torpedo-bomber had been one of three aircraft from 281ª Squadriglia which had set out from Castelvetrano to seek the convoy, but had been attacked by the Beaufighters of the early morning convoy patrol which were on their way back to Malta, and all three had been hit. With his aircraft on fire and three of the crew wounded, Ten. Umberto Camera was forced to seek the sanctuary of nearby Pantelleria; the fire substantially abated and the pilot managed to force-land near the fortress-island's airstrip.

Strangely, whilst the Beaufighter crews had reported seeing several bombers, these had been identified as Ju88s, escorted by MC202s and CR42s. Sgt. A.J. Hall in Beaufighter 'L' attacked one bomber, claiming hits on its fuselage before being driven off by fighters. However, Italian fighters known to have been airborne at this time included six Re2001s of 2° Gruppo Aut. CT, operating from Pantelleria, which chased an aircraft somewhat bizarrely identified as a 'Blackburn Roc' to the Tunisian coast, but without result. This aircraft may, in fact, have been Plt.Off. R. Munro's reconnaissance Baltimore from 69 Squadron, the crew of which reported being attacked by an MC202 near Pantelleria at 0929. Sgt. A. Covich, the gunner, claimed to have probably shot this down.

At 1040 the first four Spitfires — flown by Flt.Lt. Winfield, Plt.Off. Goldsmith, and Flt.Sgts. Evans and Farquharson of 126 Squadron — arrived from Malta, each aircraft fitted with a 90-gallon jettisonable overload fuel tank. This allowed for a maximum 60 minutes patrolling over the convoy, at this range. In the event, these arrived too late to catch the Ju88s, but an assortment of other machines came their way.

Tim Goldsmith recorded in his diary that, having found the convoy 160 miles east of Malta, he then passed two Italian cruisers before spotting what he thought was a trimotor floatplane low over the sea heading for Pantelleria. He gave it a three-second burst and it crashed. This was undoubtedly a twin-engined Fiat RS14 (MM35391 '5') of 144ª Squadriglia from Stagnone di Marsla, flown by Ten. Antonio Carnielli, which had taken off at 0825 to relieve another RS14 'shadower'; all aboard perished.

Goldsmith then attacked a bomber, identified as a 'BR20', at 600 feet and shot it down in flames with a three-second burst of fire from his port cannon; two parachutes were observed. Although he appears to have claimed this as his success alone, he was apparently credited with a shared victory with Evans, while Winfield also submitted a claim for a 'BR20' and Farquharson for one damaged.

The bombers encountered were part of a formation of nine S.84s from 4° Gruppo, which were engaged in a high level attack on the convoy, hits being claimed on two steamers. Two of the Savoias fell to the Spitfires, Mar. Aldo Pinna and his crew in MM22504 perishing, whilst three of the crew of MM23986 (flown by the Gruppo commander Magg. Gastone Valentini) baled out into the sea, from where they were later rescued.

On board the latter aircraft a stowaway had been discovered — a technical officer, Sottoten. GArat. Achille Zezon, who had a passion for flying. Now, as the Spitfires attacked, Zezon manned one of the guns but was killed before the bomber crashed into the sea. Valentini and the two other survivors subsequently claimed that Zezon had shot down two of the attackers before his death, one of which allegedly crashed into the sea in flames. In the heat of battle it seems likely the crew had confused Pinna's falling aircraft with that of a Spitfire; Zezon was posthumously awarded a Medaglia d'Oro.

During the return flight to Malta, Goldsmith encountered a fighter which he identified as an MC200 — probably an aircraft from 54° Stormo from Pantelleria — and engaged in a brief fight; he left it streaming oil and apparently claimed its destruction, but there is no evidence of such a loss.

With the departure of the Spitfires, and before their reliefs had arrived, the Ju88s of I/KG 54 returned when 11 aircraft swept in at 1120, attacking in three waves; the freighter *Burdwan* was severely shaken when narrowly missed by a stick of bombs. She came to a standstill, disabled. The prime need was to save such of the ships as remained undamaged and get them to Malta without delay. Consequently, Captain Hardy ordered the destroyer *Badsworth* and minesweeper *Hebe* to stay behind and evacuate the crews of the crippled *Burdwan* and *Kentucky*, then sink both; they were unable to comply with the latter part of this order due to the intensity of air attack, but during the early afternoon the 'coup de grace' was delivered by Ju88s of KüFlGr 606.

Activity over the convoy increased in the late morning, when the strike force from Malta at last arrived. Only two serviceable Beauforts with very inexperienced crews were available, plus four vulnerable torpedo-armed Albacores of 828/830 Squadron. This small formation had departed Malta at 0930 with the benefit of an escort of 16 Spitfires provided by 249 Squadron, but the latter had insufficient range and endurance to escort them the whole way.

Due to their greater speed the Beauforts arrived first. Sgt. J. Fenton, who was in the lead, released his torpedo at a cruiser — probably the damaged *Raimondo Montecuccoli* — from 800 yards; he and his crew were convinced the missile struck home. This attack was closely followed by that of Flg.Off. Frank Minster, who was making his first torpedo drop! Due to inexperience and enthusiasm, he misjudged the distance and closed to 300 yards before dropping, the torpedo passing under the cruiser and failing to explode!

When the Albacores arrived the crews reported seeing a cruiser, or large destroyer, apparently on fire and surrounded by a number of small boats and motor boats. Another cruiser and four destroyers were within sight, as was a floatplane — a Z506B — and two MC200s from Pantelleria. The Albacores approached apparently unobserved, and it was not until about 15 seconds before the first torpedo was dropped that AA fire was experienced. Sub Lt. Cramp (with the CO, Lt.Cdr. Roe, as his observer in T9232) and Sub Lt. J.J. Bromfield both attacked the stationary cruiser. Whilst the crews believed hits had been scored, both apparently missed, as did the torpedo released at the same target by Sub Lt. Horrocks. The strike leader, Lt. B.G. Smith, meanwhile attacked the damaged destroyer *Vivaldi* but similarly failed to achieve success.

As the Albacores pulled away, the two Macchis attacked. One made a diving pass on Harry Horrock's biplane, hitting the lower mainplane and damaging the hydraulics system. The Naval pilot fired back with his fixed front gun, getting in two good bursts and claimed his attacker probably shot down!

Two more Beaufighters headed for the convoy at 1105, although they were driven off by hostile twin-engined aircraft. They were immediately followed by four Spitfires from 601 Squadron; two hours later, as these were approaching the end of their stint, the next raid developed. Under the leadership of Cap. Cenni, ten Ju87s of the 102° Gruppo Tuff. had taken-off at 1150 armed with SD 500kg bombs and heading for the ships at about 12,000 feet, covered by 25 MC202s from 155° Gruppo CT. On sighting the convoy, the Italian Stuka crews dived to 1200 feet to release their loads as the defending Spitfires attacked. Plt.Off. Ingram and Sgt. Allen-Rowlandson jointly claimed one shot down, while Wt.Off. Belcher claimed damage to one of the escorts, which he identified as a Bf109. The extra fuel expended during these actions proved too much for Allen-Rowlandson's aircraft and during the return flight to Malta he was forced to bale-out of BR360 as the engine spluttered; he floated down into the sea some 20 miles short of the Island. Help was soon on its way, however, and within the hour he was picked up by HSL 128.

A second flight of four Spitfires from 601 Squadron, led by 2/Lt. Bartleman, had arrived half an hour after the first and these too became involved with the Stukas. When the Ju87s were spotted below, Bartleman ordered his pilots to jettison their long-range tanks and led them down to attack in line astern:

'I closed in to 100 yards on the rear aircraft and saw strikes — it burst into

Spitfire Vc fitted with a pair of locally-modified Hurricane long-range tanks, as used during sorties flown in support of the June convoy. *(NWMA)*

flames and spun down. No 'chutes were seen. Saw second Ju87 ahead and opened fire, seeing pieces fly off, when I was jolted by a fearful noise — instinctively broke away from contact, and saw several '109's. Headed back for Malta.'

The damage to his Spitfire (UF-G) was minor, just one bullet through the tailplane. The South African's first victim was almost certainly the aircraft flown by Serg.Magg. Gastone Converso and 1° Av.Mot. Enrico Boerci, which was shot down into the sea after the gunner had claimed damage to one attacking Spitfire; the crew were rescued. Plt.Off. Jerry Smith went through the heavy AA barrage to fire at one Ju87, and saw "a huge piece" break off it; he was credited with its probable destruction. He then attacked a fighter — also identified as a Messerschmitt — and left it trailing smoke, heading for Pantelleria; the engine of his Spitfire (BP871) was then hit by AA splinters and he was obliged to withdraw from the action and head back to Malta. Of the other pilots, Flg.Off. Hone was unable to jettison his supplementary fuel tank and was chased away by the fighters before he had a chance to come to grips with the dive-bombers.

Towards the end of this action a third flight of 601 Squadron arrived, Flg.Off. C.R. Scollan claiming one Stuka probably destroyed, but Sgt. Jack McConnell was shot down and killed by the escorting Macchis; his aircraft (BR306) was seen gliding down, followed by a big splash as it crashed into the sea, taking its New Zealand pilot down with it.

Four Stukas were actually badly hit by the fighters during this action, including Converso's aircraft which had been shot down as recorded; a second was forced to ditch about three miles south-east of Pantelleria, the crew of which were seen clinging to the tail section of the sinking aircraft by Mar. Gino Gamberini. Although he dropped his dinghy to the struggling men, neither Mar. Antonio Marchetti (the pilot) nor Av.Sc.Mot. Luigi Grosso, were subsequently found by rescue craft. The aircraft flown by Cap. Aldo Stringa and Mar. Zaccaria Perozzi were both very badly damaged but managed to regain their base at Chinisia; two further Ju87s were damaged by AA fire.

Somewhat optimistically, the returning crews claimed one auxiliary cruiser and two merchant vessels sunk, but they had not in reality hit anything. Meanwhile, the escorting Macchi pilots claimed four of the Spitfires shot down and another as probably destroyed, without loss; claims were: Cap. Carlo Miani, one and one probable; Magg. Dulio Fanali (the Gruppo commander) and Sottoten. Tullio Martinelli, one each, while Mar. Remo Zeda and Mar. Roberto Gaucci jointly claimed another.

At 1245 another of 69 Squadron's Baltimores set off for the Pantelleria area, but AG699 — flown by Sgt. F.W. Baum — failed to return. Italian records noted that a 'Beaufighter' had been shot down off Linosa by German fighters and that Sgt. Baum — reportedly a pilot of German origin from 252 Squadron — was captured; they also recorded that Sgt. W.E. Fincham, Baum's radio operator, was picked up from the sea after being shot down by Flak off Linosa! It seems likely that the Baltimore was actually shot down by Lt. Franz Schiess of Stab/JG 53, who claimed his victim as a Beaufighter — an aircraft of quite similar appearance in many ways to the Baltimore, which would not have been familiar to him.

To the west aircraft from Sardinia continued to seek the elements of Force 'W' now returning to Gibraltar, and during the late morning three S.79sil from the 2°

Nucleo AS sought to attack the warships. These were intercepted at 1315 by two 801 Squadron Sea Hurricanes, Lt. Turnbull and Sub Lt. Duthie sighting two of the Savoias in the distance which, when they spotted the fighters, separated. Rather than each pursue a bomber, both Naval pilots attacked Ten. Lelio Silva's aircraft and with its starboard engine on fire, the aircraft ploughed into the sea with the loss of all aboard. Silva was subsequently posthumously awarded the eighth Medaglia d'Oro to be granted to aircrew for the operations of the 14th and 15th.

The last engagement for the carrier fighters was recorded at 1504, when *Argus* Fulmars intercepted a further S.79sil, which escaped them. An hour earlier however, at 1410, another four Spitfires from 126 Squadron had arrived over the convoy and during their patrol encountered a number of fighters which they identified as Bf109s. One was claimed shot down by Flt.Sgt. Schade, while a further quartet from the same unit — Flt.Lts. Bailey and Rowe, Plt.Offs. Thomas and Wallace — also saw action when they encountered a Z506B, an aircraft ('7') of 288ª Squadriglia. This floatplane had taken off at 1505 on a reconnaissance but reported being attacked by 'ten Hurricanes'; Sottoten. Ugo Cusmano's crew claimed one of the attacking fighters shot down with a second probably so, but the burning Cant was obliged to crash-land on the sea ten miles from Linosa, turning on its side. Despite the Spitfire pilots strafing the machine until it sank, Cusmano and his crew survived their ordeal and were subsequently rescued by a motor fishing boat from Lampedusa.

This section of Spitfires had started out as escort to the three remaining serviceable Albacores which were to carry out a further strike, accompanied by a single Beaufighter of 235 Squadron — X8078 crewed by Sgts. C. Armitage and C.W. Hector — but had become separated. The torpedo-bombers found the retiring Italian warships — reported as two cruisers, two destroyers and two MAS torpedo-boats — at 1655, under an umbrella comprising two Cant floatplanes and an estimated dozen Macchis. The latter were, in fact, nine Re2001s of 2° Gruppo. Lt. W.D. Winterbottom, with the new CO (Lt. W.E. Lashmore) as his observer, led the Albacores in a gentle diving attack out of haze from 3000 feet and all three attacked the same cruiser. No hits were observed but a cloud of black smoke and a column of white steam were seen. Despite the gallantry of these attacks, no damage had actually been inflicted. The second aircraft was flown by Sub Lt. Reg Elliott, who recalled:

> 'I followed Winterbottom down from about 3000 feet to our 50 feet dropping height, and on the way saw about a dozen aircraft circling over the ships — they proved to be Reggiane fighters. We were approaching the rear cruiser on its port quarter, and could see the sea between us bubbling from the falling shot (some call it a "splash barrage"). Winterbottom released his fish and I saw it running. I thought the range a bit too much to get a good sighting so I carried on awhile. It was getting a bit too hot so I released at what I thought was about 1000 yards and turned away relieved at not being hit. It was then I remembered the fighters.
>
> As our range from the cruisers increased so the fighters moved in. I owe my continued existence to my observer Davison, who opened up his rear hood and told me as the fighters turned in to attack. We just turned and dived each time, working our way gradually away. The nearest we got to being shot down was a line of bullets across the tail fin (discovered on

> return). Eventually the fighters left us alone and we could then look towards the cruisers. They were stationary and one had smoke coming from its rear end — we hoped as a result of our attack. At least the Admiral appeared to have had his mind directed away from the convoy, and made no further moves against it.'

Sgt. Armitage's Beaufighter was shot down (his observer losing his life) by the Reggiane leader, Ten. Giorgio Gasperoni, while others shot down the Albacore crewed by Sub Lt. Cyril Casey and Lt. William Paton, both of whom were killed. Once again the 2° Gruppo pilots greatly overestimated the results of the engagement; they identified the attack force as comprising five 'Swordfish' and claimed four shot down, one each by Cap. Teia, Ten. Celentano, Sottoten. Romano Pagliani and Serg. Luigi Battaini.

Sub Lt. Elliott's damaged aircraft (X9029) survived sufficiently for him to engage one of the floatplanes as they departed:

> 'When about half an hour from the cruisers, I saw a Cant Z506 coming head-on to me and slightly below. Davison confirmed the identification so I turned to port and then back to starboard to make a beam to stern attack — we had one front firing machine gun in the Albacore. I think that I managed to damage the Cant but decided to break off as by now I was heading back towards the fighters.'

As the two freighters and their escort made speed towards Malta, the firepower of *Cairo* was greatly supplemented by the arrival from the Island of *Welshman*, armed as she was with six 4-inch guns; the fast minelayer-cruiser, having unloaded her shipment of ammunition with all haste, was now making the run back to Gibraltar. Her reinforcement was in time to help repel the next major assault on the convoy.

The early evening attacks were undertaken by the Luftwaffe; nine Ju88s of KüFlGr 606 and escorting Bf109s were met by a 601 Squadron section at 1800. Plt.Off. Jerry Smith attacked one bomber and saw pieces fall off, but overshot; a Messerschmitt was then engaged but no hits were observed. He soon encountered another Junkers and closed to 50 yards, setting the port engine on fire and seeing pieces fall off; the aircraft dived, turned, and crashed into the sea but the rear gunner hit BR381's radiator. With the engine pouring smoke, Smith turned back towards Malta and baled out into the sea, some 92 miles from the Island; he was indeed fortunate to be picked up within 15 minutes by the destroyer *Blankney* and was returned to Malta next morning, when his flight commander, Flt.Lt. Barnham, who had also flown two sorties over the convoy, noted in his diary:

> 'A few minutes ago Smith, whom we thought was dead, walked in the lounge here. He's been telling us that, over the convoy, he shot down an 88 but his own engine was set on fire. After baling out he was picked up by a destroyer. He's been describing how the deck of his destroyer was already crowded with merchant ship survivors, how they stood as Ju87s and 88s dived on them.'

Flg.Off. Hone also attacked the Ju88s and succeeded in shooting-up one bomber, causing the starboard engine to catch fire. He then "squirted" at three others before being intercepted by one of the escort. By now short of fuel, he put BR122 into a dive only to have the windscreen covered in oil when a seal burst.

A trio of Cant Z1007bis bombers of the 60ª Squadriglia, 33° Gruppo BT of the Regia Aeronautica. Although the best bomber available to the Italians in summer 1942, they were rarely risked over Malta in other than very small and heavily-escorted formations. *(G. Terebinto via N. Malizia)*

So steep was the dive that he 'blacked-out', recovering at 3000 feet to find himself going up! Although he had great difficulty in seeing through the windscreen, he successfully landed at Takali to discover that both wings of the Spitfire were wrinkled from the force of the pullout!

At 1800 four 249 Squadron Spitfires were scrambled, followed by four more from 185 Squadron ten minutes later, and another four from this latter unit at 1840. The first quartet intercepted three Z1007bis and Bf109s over the convoy — still 30 miles out — south-west of Gozo. Flt.Sgt. Williams (BR117/C-22) claimed a Messerschmitt damaged and Flg.Off. John Smith (BR251/C-26) a Cant damaged. One pilot crash-landed BR364 on return but was unhurt and the aircraft only slightly damaged.

The first 185 Squadron section made several claims, Flt.Lt. Ron West (in GL-J) for a Bf109 shot down and a Ju88 probable; Plt.Off. Stenborg (GL-A) claimed another Messerschmitt shot down and two bombers damaged, and Flt.Sgt. Sim claimed a Junkers, while Plt.Off. James (GL-K) "squirted" at two more. A few minutes later the other 185 Squadron section ran into 20 Ju88s and ten Bf109s at 10,000 feet, and lost Plt.Off. Paul Baril who was shot down by a Messerschmitt and baled out of BR353/D; he was also picked up by *Blankney*. Plt.Off. Ernie Broad (GL-R) dived on a bomber but could not gain on it, then found himself on the tail of one of the escort. Firing a two-second burst, he claimed that it poured smoke and crashed into the sea; the pilot was not seen to bale out. Sim was obliged to belly-land GL-E (BR126) following a glycol leak; although it was damaged beyond repair, it would be used for spares.

KüFlGr 606's Ju88s again appeared over the convoy with the last light of this hectic and traumatic day, 12 attacking from out of the setting sun; three or four bombs fell within 30 feet of *Troilus*'s starboard side, the blast and spray blowing bystanders off their feet but causing no serious injuries. A pair of 601 Squadron pilots from the earlier patrol were still over the convoy, Plt.Off. Ingram catching one of the bombers and claiming it shot down.

The final interception occurred in the late evening when four Spitfires of 249 Squadron took off at 2105 to intercept about a dozen unescorted KGr 806 Ju88s heading for the ships, apparently relying on the dusk to protect them. Control ordered the Spitfires to orbit the convoy at 17,000 feet until the bombers came within range, but with dusk rapidly approaching Flt.Lt. Lucas realised the

Spitfire GL-N of 185 Squadron at Hal Far; it had been damaged in combat, subsequently crash-landing with this devastating result. *(N.J. Ogilvie)*

raiders would not be seen against the dark sea and took his section down to lower levels. The Junkers were consequently sighted against the light western sky; two were claimed shot down, one by Lucas (BR377) and Plt.Off. Watts (BR254) jointly, the other by Plt.Off. Frank Jones (BR119). Plt.Off. Linton claimed one more as damaged, as did Lucas; two burst into flames and dived blazing towards the sea. There seems little doubt that these were M7+HL and M7+FK, flown by Uffz. Heinz Kaufmann and Oblt. Kurt Kehrer (the Staffelkapitän) respectively, both of which failed to return. From a third aircraft, the air gunner (Uffz. Heinrich Kalbfeld) baled out into the sea and was lost. Apparently he had panicked and abandoned his aircraft when the Junkers suffered dive-brake failure.

Although the Spitfires had claimed five Bf109s during the day's actions, it seems that only one of these elusive fighters was lost, Fw. Rudolf Schmidt of 7/JG 53 ditching his aircraft in to the sea off the Sicilian coast, apparently due to engine failure; he was later rescued unharmed. Nonetheless, the Spitfires had done their job well — not one merchant ship or escorting warship had been hit while they were providing cover, and a total of 170 sorties had been flown. Although 601 Squadron bore most of the brunt of the action, other units were in the air as much; 603 Squadron, for example, undertook over 40 sorties yet spotted only one enemy aircraft all day — a lone Ju88 in the distance, too far away for an interception! 126 Squadron, on the other hand, flew 42 sorties, its pilots claiming six aircraft shot down.

As the last two merchant vessels made for Grand Harbour, further disaster overtook the ill-fated 'Harpoon' ships. With salvation so close, the escort blundered into a newly-laid minefield. Three destroyers — *Badsworth, Matchless* and the Polish *Kujawiak* — and the minesweeper *Hebe* were damaged, the Polish warship sinking. Even *Orari* sustained damage but was able to gain the dubious sanctuary offered by Grand Harbour, where she and *Troilus* at once began unloading under cover of a smoke screen from smoke-containers brought in by *Welshman* the previous day for this purpose; the cargo was handled by a combined force of civilians and service personnel, including 2500 soldiers. Whilst the supplies delivered were inadequate to replenish the Island's larders — with fuel and food so desperately short — every ounce of the 15,000 tons (which included ammunition and flour) was more than welcome.

Operation 'Vigorous' (June 12-16)

Friday, 12 – Saturday, 13 June

There were nine British merchantmen — *Ajax; Bhutan; Bulkoil; City of Calcutta; City of Edinburgh; City of Lincoln; City of Pretoria; Potaro* and *Rembrandt* — and two Dutch vessels, *Aagtekerk* and *Elizabeth Bakke*, assembled at Alexandria, Port Said and Haifa, under the codename 'Vigorous', and their formidable task was to convey about 72,000 tons of assorted cargo to Malta.

The Mediterranean Fleet had been weakened to a point where no capital vessels at all could be made available for this operation, although support could be expected from the hard-pressed Western Desert Air Force throughout the first leg of the journey. Close escort was provided by a dozen destroyers (from 2nd and 5th Destroyer Flotillas), four corvettes, two minesweepers and two rescue ships. The Fleet was joined by the ancient battleship *Centurion* and although she was nothing more than a sea-going hull normally used as a gunnery target ship, she had been fitted with dummy 15-inch guns in a desperate bluff to deceive the enemy!

Rear-Admiral Vian's covering force comprised eight cruisers of 4th and 15th Cruiser Squadrons, including his flagship *Cleopatra*, 14 destroyers (from 7th, 12th, 14th and 22nd Destroyer Flotillas) and four MTBs to be towed by the merchant ships. Aboard the cruiser *Euryalus* as Fighter Direction Officer was Sqn.Ldr. Westmacott, late commander of the MNFU. On being posted to the cruiser, Westmacott discovered that she was not fitted with VHF radio, and that reception with the existing equipment was very poor; in response to his urgent request for up-to-date equipment, a Type RTD9 VHF unit was immediately installed.

Of immediate threat to the convoy were the Luftwaffe's specialist anti-shipping Ju88s based on Crete — I and II/LG 1, Stab and I/KG 54, and a back-up reconnaissance unit, 2(F)/124. Quantities of the new LT350 'circling' torpedoes were available for use against the convoy, designed to be dropped by parachute in confined spaces ahead of approaching ships where they would perform a slow, circling run. Their subsequent use by aircraft of I/KG 54 — the first time they had been employed operationally — would, however, prove ineffective. As the ships progressed westwards they could also expect to come under attack by German and Italian aircraft based in Libya.

In an attempt to neutralize some of the Luftwaffe's potential, a number of commando raids were launched by Maj. David Stirling's newly-formed Special Air Service (SAS) against airfields in Cyrenaica and Crete on the night of the 13th/14th. Two parties of commandos raided airfields in the Benghazi Sector, three in the vicinity of Derna, and one at Barce. The island of Crete contained two major Luftwaffe bases at Heraklion and Maleme; these, too, were visited, as well as the newly-constructed landing grounds at Tymbaki and Kastelli.

The raids on the Cyrenaican airfields resulted in limited successes and serious losses: a group of 16 Free Frenchmen under Lt. Augustin Jordain, aided by Capt. Herbert Buck and one British NCO, were betrayed and subsequently ambushed at Derna with only the two leaders escaping and no losses to the enemy. Elsewhere, Major Stirling personally led two NCOs to Benina, where it was claimed bombs placed on two Bf110s and three Ju52s all detonated, whilst much machinery and stores were also destroyed.

The sortie undertaken by Capt. Blair Mayne and three NCOs to the Berka satellite landing ground resulted in a gun-fight; only one bomb had been placed on an aircraft when the party was discovered, and one NCO was killed in the retreat. Another all-Free French party of six under Lt. Andre Zirnheld achieved greater success at Berka Main, where 11 aircraft were claimed destroyed and many casualties inflicted on the airfield guards. A further Free French quartet visited Barce but succeeded only in blowing up petrol and supply dumps.

Perhaps the most ambitious raid was that on Heraklion airfield by a small party of four Frenchmen, led by Cmdt. Bergé, and aided by Capt. Lord Jellicoe — son of the famous Admiral. They had been conveyed to Crete by the submarine *Triton* from Alexandria, arriving off Heraklion on the night of the 12th/13th. At least 66 Ju88s were to be seen on the airfield. The following night, as the six men approached the perimeter to commence their sabotage operation, eight Ju88s came in to land followed by a single Blenheim, which apparently made the correct landing signals, then roared across the airfield dropping bombs, before departing as swiftly as it had arrived!

The Blenheim, Z9795 from 14 Squadron flown by Australian Sgt. J.H. Elliott, had filtered in with the returning Junkers, being led to the airfield without difficulty where the flare path was in full operation. Circling aircraft were seen with their navigation lights on as Elliott dived his Blenheim down to 3000 feet, releasing bombs from east to west of the flare path. For all the daringness of the audacious raid however, he succeeded only in severely damaging one bomber, an aircraft of 5/LG 1. Two more Blenheims followed at intervals, while two others bombed Kastelli, but results of these attacks were unobserved.

However, the confusion caused by the Blenheims' appearance allowed the SAS party to gain access to the airfield and soon delayed-action bombs (with two-hour time fuses) were placed on the wings and tailplanes of 16 Ju88s, and on four other aircraft including an Fi156, as well as on a Ju88 about to take-off! More bombs were placed in four trucks and a petrol dump and in crates of aero engines. The commandos got away undetected and rejoined their Greek guide. Capt. Lord Jellicoe and the guide separated from the others to seek a British agent in a nearby village, but misfortune then overtook the Frenchmen when they ran into a German patrol. Caporal Leostic (who claimed to be 18 but was just 14) was killed; Caporal Chef Siebert was wounded and captured, whilst Cmdt. Bergé and Sgt. Mouhot were both taken prisoner. Lord Jellicoe and the guide made good their escape and joined by 25 Cretan patriots, were later picked up by *Triton*. When the time bombs exploded seven of I/LG 1's Ju88As were severely damaged, while two of 2(F)/124's reconnaissance Ju88Ds were so badly damaged that they were deemed irreparable.

The attempted raid on Maleme was called off when it was discovered that the airfield was too well guarded for infiltration, while reconnaissance showed Tymbaki to be vacant. Better success was achieved at Kastelli though, where Capt. George Duncan and two NCOs succeeded in placing their explosive devices on eight aircraft, as well as on six trucks, four bomb dumps and seven petrol dumps; later, intelligence reports suggested that at least 70 military personnel had been killed in the resultant explosions. Eight New Zealanders, who had evaded capture when the island fell the previous year and who had been in hiding ever since, were brought out with the SAS party.

Despite the heroism of these actions, the 'Vigorous' convoy seemed to be ill-fated from the start. Four of the merchant vessels, escorted by the AA cruiser

Coventry and eight destroyers, had departed 36 hours prior to the main sailing as a feint (codenamed 'Rembrandt') designed to draw the Italian fleet to sea early. Late next day (the 13th), as these vessels headed back to Alexandria, a number of Ju88s and 15 Ju87s of II/StG 3 arrived overhead and commenced their dives; *Coventry* was near-missed by sticks of bombs dropped by three Ju88s on either flank, her crew fortunate to escape injury as splinters whined overhead, but *City of Calcutta* was severely shaken. With her plates leaking, caused by the blast of another near-miss, she was ordered to make for Tobruk.

As the attack on the convoy progressed, four Hurricanes of GC 1 'Alsace' — a Free French unit operating from Fuka under RAF control — arrived on the scene. The French pilots observed bombs falling on the convoy and exploding close to *City of Calcutta*, but they failed to spot the attackers in the fading light. The quartet of Hurricanes was soon forced by the rapidly approaching darkness to return to base, those flown by Capitaine Paul Ezanno (the leader) and Sgt-Chef Pierre Leplang force-landing en route; neither pilot was hurt.

No sooner had the main convoy and the rest of the diversionary shipping rendezvoused on the 13th, than *Elizabeth Bakke* began to drop astern, unable to maintain the convoy speed of 13 knots; she was escorted back to Alexandria. Within a few more hours two of the corvettes had been obliged to drop out, while the 6811-ton *Aagterkerk* was also found to be too slow and was ordered to the closest friendly haven, which was now Tobruk. When still some dozen miles out, the old Dutch vessel was discovered, attacked and sunk by an estimated 40 Ju87s and Ju88s, five of her crew being lost. Escorting destroyers put up a spirited resistance, claiming three of the Stukas shot down, although the accompanying corvette *Primula* also suffered damage during the attack. Two of II/StG 3's Stukas were actually reported lost, including S7+HN of 6 Staffel crewed by the Staffelkapitän, Oblt. Anton Ostler, and his gunner, Ofw. Wilhelm Lichenstein.

Sunday, 14 June

By dawn on the 14th the remaining vessels were well into 'Bomb Alley' between Crete and North Africa, the convoy having been shadowed throughout the night. German aircraft almost continuously dropped flares, practically transforming night into day, but no attacks developed. With the coming of daylight, attacks were expected from both north and south, although some escort was provided by elements of the Western Desert Air Force, diverted from the desperate fighting which was underway in the Gazala area.

At 0835 Kittyhawks of 250 Squadron, from their airfield near Mersa Matruh, began a series of patrols over the ships and just over an hour later the first attack by African-based Luftwaffe aircraft was intercepted, as Ju87s and Ju88s approached, escorted by 19 Bf109s of III/JG 53 — the unit which until recently had been operating over Malta. The Messerschmitts attacked at once, Lts. Harder and Quaritsch each claiming a Kittyhawk shot down. Plt.Off F.A. Creighton and Sgt. Webster were lost. The German pilots also reported meeting Hurricanes, two of which were claimed by Oblt. Gotz and a third by Ofw. Stumpf, although one Bf109 was hit and Lt. Hicke was wounded. The Hurricanes were from 238 Squadron, Flt.Lt. M.R. Jenkins and Plt.Off. O.F.A. Oram both being obliged to bale out. The British fighters, however, succeeded in keeping the bombers away from the convoy.

It was now the turn of eight Tomahawks of 5 SAAF Squadron to patrol from

1150 as the convoy passed the stretch of coast between Tobruk and El Adem. Again the Luftwaffe appeared, Ju87s of III/StG 3 attacking under cover of ten Bf109s from I/JG 27 and others from III/JG 53. This time the South Africans were able to get at the bombers, Maj. J.E. Frost and Lt. K.C. Kemsley each claiming one shot down, Kemsley also claiming a second as a probable, before the escorts struck. Lt. L.B. van der Spuy shot down one fighter — it would seem it was that flown by III/JG 53's Lt. Quaritsch who failed to return — but was then shot down himself; he baled out wounded. Frost and Kemsley each claimed Bf109s damaged, but as they turned for base the latter's aircraft was hard-hit and he was obliged to force-land. Two Tomahawks were claimed by Lt. Friedrich Korner and one by Lt. Hans-Arnold Stahlschmidt, both of I/JG 27. The missing Quaritsch, a 13-victory Experte, had claimed five of his successes over Malta earlier in the year.

None of the ships was hit during the Stuka attacks, thanks mainly to the fierce barrage put up by the escorts and the determination of the South African fighters; III/StG 3 reported the loss of S7+FR crewed by Ofw. Gerhard Pantel and his gunner, Uffz. Hermann Riegel, shot down by a fighter.

By the early afternoon the convoy was getting beyond the range of single-engined fighters, and Beaufighters and Hudsons took over patrol duties. Unfortunately, the ships and their air escort were not beyond the range of the German fighters which were based further to the west than were those of the WDAF. Indeed, I/JG 27 and III/JG 53 swiftly moved to Derna to continue their activities. It was to a patrolling Ju88C of I/NJG 2's Derna detachment that the first Beaufighter fell victim however, as six such aircraft from 272 Squadron and three from 252 Squadron took up their patrol areas. T4709/0 of the former unit, crewed by Free Frenchman Flt.Sgt. Jacques Gael and Sgt. F.V. Amos, was seen to fall in flames at 1430, shot down by Lt. Wiedow.

At 1635, ten Messerschmitts of I/JG 27 were off from Derna to escort Ju87s of II/StG 3, followed by nine III/JG 53 aircraft, at about the same time as three 272 Squadron Beaufighters departed from Gambut to commence their convoy patrols. Half an hour later two more aircraft from this unit, and one from 252 Squadron, also set out to cover the convoy and to join a Hudson from 459 Squadron flown by Plt.Off. W. Blackstock. During the next hour two of the Beaufighters and the Hudson (V9022/M) were shot down, the latter by Oblt. Ernst Klager of III/JG 53, the Beaufighters by Lt. Körner and Lt. Karl von Lieres of I/JG 27; none of the RAF crews survived: Sgt. A.E. Cooper, RAAF and Sgt C.C. Ridgway were lost with T3291/A and Sgt. E.R.F. Truby, RCAF and Sgt. K.J. Garrett in T4867/S. It would seem likely that the Beaufighter pilots put up stiff resistance before their demise, as one of the Messerschmitts also failed to return, Lt. Heinrich Hesse of 7/JG 53 baling out of 'White 6' into the sea. One Stuka (S7+GC) fell to ships' AA fire, Uffz. Julius Kuppers and his gunner (Uffz. Johann Kammann) both being killed.

The other 272 Squadron machine of the second patrol, T4841/R flown by Belgian Sgt. Yves Tedesco — an aggressive and successful pilot with four victories to his credit — also failed to return. As twilight approached, Tedesco was warned by *Coventry*'s FDO that two twin-engined 'hostiles' were in the vicinity and almost immediately he encountered a Ju88 emerging from cloud, but only had time for a short burst of cannon fire; he reported seeing a streak of flame from the Junkers before it disappeared from sight again. Control then vectored him onto the second 'shadower' which he saw below, and attacked in a gentle dive; the German gunner opened fire; the Belgian replied, but at once the Beaufighter's starboard engine exploded, the flaming aircraft plummeting into the sea. It was believed, however, that the Beaufighter had been hit by AA fire from the convoy's escort; neither Tedesco nor his navigator (Sgt. Frank Ransom) survived. Meanwhile, Plt.Off. Easton Thwaites, the pilot of the 252 Squadron machine, also encountered a Ju88 and carried out two stern attacks with machine gun and cannon; the Junkers was believed damaged but was lost when its pilot took evasive action, then outpaced the Beaufighter to make good his escape.

Junkers Ju88A-4 coded L1+AM, of 4/LG 1. Lehrgeschwader 1 was a highly-trained unit which specialized in anti-shipping attacks. *(E.C. des Armees)*

During the three hours from 1800-2100 no fewer than seven separate waves of bombers attacked, generally at a strength of about a dozen aircraft per wave. Most were Ju88s of LG 1 and KG 54 from Crete, joined at 1845 by five Z1007bis of 47° Stormo, led by Cap. Carlo Reghini. The convoy was now frequently devoid of fighter escort as the Junkers made their individual dives to 3000 feet before releasing their bombs. The 6104-ton freighter *Bhutan*, lying at the rear of the port column, received much of this attention being struck by at least three bombs in quick succession. She sank within 20 minutes, six of her crew going down with her, although 174 others were picked up by the rescue ships *Antwerp* and *Malines*. A second freighter, *Potaro*, also sustained damage during these attacks while several other vessels were near-missed. The ancient but heavily-armed and armour-decked *Centurion* absorbed several hits, her gunners claiming four of the attackers shot down. However, four torpedo-carrying S.79sil of 41° Gruppo Aut. BT/AS from Derna failed to locate the convoy.

Five more 272 Squadron Beaufighters departed Gambut at 1815, led by Wg.Cdr. Bill Riley who had been attached to this unit from Group Headquarters. As the new escorts took up their station, two Messerschmitts from III/JG 53 appeared overhead, searching for their missing comrade, Lt. Hesse. Oblt. Belser at once dived on Plt.Off. W.B. Roger's aircraft (T4885/F) and shot it down so swiftly that the pilot and his observer, Sgt. G.L. Woolven, later reported that they thought they had been accidently shot down by Wg.Cdr. Riley. This belief was reinforced when Riley returned to claim a Ju88 shot down (raising his victory tally to at least seven). There is little doubt, however, that his victim had indeed been a German aircraft for, apart from the fact that Belser did claim a Beaufighter shot down, two Ju88s were reported lost to fighters or AA and three more were damaged and crash-landed on return to Crete.

The crew of the shot down Beaufighter (Rogers and Woolven) were fortunate to survive the ditching. When their aircraft hit the sea, the observer was able to scramble clear but it rapidly sank, taking the pilot down with it. Unable to open the escape hatch, Rogers resigned himself to his fate until pressure burst open the hatch and he was shot to the surface in an air bubble! At the same time an almost empty fuel tank was ripped from the wing as the aircraft broke up and surfaced nearby allowing Woolven, who was a poor swimmer, to use it as a raft while Rogers pushed him ashore — in a swim that lasted ten hours!

Another of the bombers was claimed during this patrol by 272 Squadron's Sgt. George Tuckwell for his second victory. Tuckwell had been endeavouring to maintain station over the convoy but was constantly fired on by the escorting warships, despite his being in radio contact with *Coventry*, and firing off the correct identification flares. Eventually, finding himself low on fuel, he decided to fly on to Malta but while en route he spotted a Ju88, managed to manoeuvre onto its tail — apparently unseen — and shot it down.

Tuckwell's victim was possibly an LG 1 aircraft flown by Oblt. Gerhard Brenner, from which the crew took to their dinghy; of their subsequent plight, colleague Gerd Stamp recalled:

> 'We shadowed them for several days whilst they were in their dinghy, but the sea was too high and too rough for a landing by a flyingboat. It was terrible not to be able to get them out of the water.'

About a week later the dinghy was recovered but of Brenner and his crew there was no sign; it was assumed they had been washed overboard in heavy sea.

Two other Ju88s from LG 1 crash-landed at Herkalion having sustained fighter or AA damage; Oblt. Helmut Löhnert's Junkers had been heavily damaged, while I/KG 54 also suffered a further loss. Lt. Herbert Knöthe's B3+ML was attacked by a fighter about 70 miles to the west of Crete (probably Wg.Cdr. Riley's victim); the damaged aircraft succeeded in reaching Crete, only to crash on landing at Tymbaki, where it was totally destroyed. The crew perished.

Such was the almost continuous barrage put up by the escorts during the day, particularly during the evening period, that a number of warships now had seriously depleted supplies of anti-aircraft ammunition. Doubt was seriously expressed as to whether sufficient remained to see the convoy through during the final, most dangerous leg of the journey. Worse was to come, for late in the day a reconnaissance Spitfire from Malta spotted a major sortie into the Ionian Sea by a substantial part of the Italian fleet from Taranto.

This sortie included the battleships *Vittorio Veneto* (Ammiraglio Angelo Iachino) and *Littorio* (Ammiraglio Giuseppe Fioravanzo), the latter embarking an R/T and W/T interception unit, as did the cruiser *Garibaldi*. These two ships, and the cruiser *Gorizia*, also carried Luftwaffe FDOs (Fighter Direction Officers). Two other cruisers and a dozen destroyers completed the force, one of the latter (*Legionario*) equipped with German 'Dete' radar apparatus. It was on the personal orders of Mussolini, who had for the first time assumed supreme command of the Italian Navy, that Iachino's fleet had put to sea to challenge the British force.

The report of this foray was a sufficient deterrent to Admiral Vian's small escorting force of British cruisers — they would be quite unable to match the gun power of such formidable adversaries and, reluctantly, at 0200 on the 15th, the convoy was ordered to return to Alexandria.

As the escort vessels turned, six German S-boats of the 3rd MTB Flotilla operating out of Derna — which had been circling the convoy awaiting opportunities to strike — attacked with the benefit of the confusion caused by 40 ships attempting an about-turn manoeuvre. While shadowing aircraft overhead continued to illuminate the scene, Lt. Wüppermann in MTB *S56* seized the opportunity to fire a torpedo at the cruiser *Newcastle*, achieving a hit on her bow which forced her to reduce speed. The captain of *S55*, Lt. Horst Weber, hit another of the escort when *Hasty* took a torpedo amidships; the disabled destroyer was later abandoned and sent to the bottom.

Malta was at once alerted to strike at the new Italian threat and at 2345 five Wellingtons of 38 Squadron, armed with two torpedoes apiece, commenced taking-off from Luqa, from where they were homed to the target area by a sixth ASV-equipped aircraft. On the approach of these bombers the Italians at once made smoke, and only Flg.Off. Michael Foulis (DV544/J) was able to make a couple of runs at the ships; no results of the attack were observed by his crew although the crew of the ASV aircraft reported a red glow in the darkness.

Monday, 15 June

Nine of 217 Squadron's recently-arrived Beauforts were to follow before first light on the 15th, but the unit's aircrew were largely 'green', with little torpedo training and virtually no operational experience. Following take-off at 0415, only five managed to form up in the dark, the other four proceeding independently. After a long and fruitless search, one of the latter, flown by Flg.Off. Arthur Aldridge — one of the few experienced pilots — spotted the long column of big warships in the dawn light. He headed straight in, putting his torpedo into the heavy cruiser *Trento* which came to a halt, on fire, listing and badly damaged. Apparently Italian lookouts had mistaken Aldridge's aircraft as one of their own, the guns opening up only as the Beaufort sped away, although the gunners were fully alerted by the time the main formation arrived shortly afterwards, guided in by the gunfire.

Wg.Cdr. Davies led the first vic of three which, despite intense AA fire, claimed two possible hits on a battleship. Flg.Off. Goodale's aircraft was struck by shrapnel and a small fire started, which was soon extinguished by two members of his crew. From the opposite direction Sqn.Ldr. R.G. Lynn led another pair also to attack one of the battleships, which was believed hit, as was an escorting destroyer. Lt. Ted Strever, SAAF, went after the battleships and their escorts to the north but his aircraft (DD995) was shot-up and his air gunner, Sgt. Bob Gray, wounded; a belly-landing was effected on return to Luqa. Finally, Flg.Off. Bill Stevens, the unit's other experienced pilot on this mission, arrived but his torpedo, aimed at the crippled *Trento* enveloped in the smoke-screen, missed its target. Although crews believed they had achieved hits on various vessels, including both battleships, in fact no additional damage was caused. In return, Italian gunners claimed two of the Beauforts shot down.

The whole attack had been witnessed by Lt. S.L.C. Maydon from the conning tower of his submarine *Umbra*. Amidst all the confusion he went in close to give the stricken cruiser the 'coup de grace', firing two more torpedoes into her considerable bulk; she rolled over and sank taking many of her crew with her, including her captain, Capitano di Vascello Esposito, as well as her Ro43 floatplane (MM27097).

Further strikes were on their way in the shape of a flight of seven USAAF B-24D four-engined, long-range bombers* and two RAF Liberator IIs 160

Squadron from Fayid in Egypt. Following a flight of five and a half hours from Fayid, during the latter stages of which they had overflown Admiral Vian's force — to be greeted by an intense barrage of AA fire resulting in a number of aircraft being peppered with shrapnel — the B-24Ds (led by Major Al Kalberer) accompanied by the two RAF Liberators, arrived over the Italian warships just ahead of another small force of Beauforts from Sidi Barrani. Each aircraft carried a Royal Naval observer to help with identification of targets. Although a number of Ju88s were seen at low level over the convoy — obviously seeking low-flying Beauforts — Kalberer led four of the big bombers down to attack *Littorio*, while the other three of his formation went for *Gorizia*; the two RAF Liberators attacked from low level in an attempt to divert Italian AA gunners. Of the attack, Major Kalberer later reported:

> 'Most of the bombs crashed on the main deck of the big ship, setting fires. The second flight dropped a higher percentage on the cruiser... It was the rare perfect bombing operation. We attained complete surprise and wasted very few bombs. The two ships stopped dead in the water, and the Ju88s climbed after us. We dived to within 10 feet of the waves and made it home untouched, except for the "friendly" damage.'

This statement would not appear to be completely accurate though, for as the bombers sped for home they were seen by two of III/JG 27's Bf109 pilots, who had in the meantime found the missing Lt. Hesse and were circling over his dinghy. Initially identifying the big, slab-sided bombers as "nine four-engined flyingboats", they attacked at 1040, Oblt. Heinecke claiming one shot down into the sea 60 miles off the North African coast! In return, one of the American gunners claimed a Messerschmitt shot down — the first USAAF claim to be made for an Axis aircraft in the Mediterranean area; no Luftwaffe loss was actually suffered.

It would seem that Heinecke — formerly of III/JG 53 — had attacked one of the RAF Liberators, for Sgt. W.J. Wilson's aircraft was hit and badly damaged, the mid-upper gunner being killed; bad weather eventually forced the Australian Wilson to crash-land his ailing machine short of Fayid, fortunately without much further damage to the aircraft or injury to his crew.

Although the bombing was accurate — the three warships being straddled by many near-misses — only one 500lb bomb actually found a target, hitting the *Littorio*'s 'A' turret and killing one member of the crew and wounding 12 others. Little damage resulted apart from shaking one of the battleship's Ro43 spotter aircraft (MM27152) off its launching platform into the sea, while the other Ro43 (MM27160) was damaged.

There was to be a third assault on the Italian force, for 12 Beauforts of 39 Squadron had set out from LG 05 (near Sidi Barrani) shortly after sunrise. They were led by their commanding officer, Wg.Cdr. Mason in DD951, and were to be homed to the area of action by a Maryland of 203 Squadron. Two

---

*The American B-24Ds were part of an original 23-strong force, under the command of Colonel Harry A. Halvorson, that had departed the United States a few weeks previously destined for operations in China, as part of US aid to her new ally. The force had flown from Florida to Brazil, then across the Atlantic to Accra (Gold Coast), where Pan American Airways had a station, and from there across the Central African route to Egypt, via Khartoum. By the time the bombers had arrived in Egypt however, events in China had taken a turn for the worse and they were ordered to remain at Fayid, where they were put at the disposal of RAF ME Command.

Beaufighters of 272 Squadron from Gambut accompanied them as a rather inadequate escort. Spread out in four vics of three, line abreast, the Beauforts — mainly more powerful Mark IIs but led by the CO in an older, slower Mark I — were nearing the limit of their search range without seeing any sign of their quarry, when splashes were noticed in the distance. Believing these to be bomb explosions, the formation headed in that direction, but Mason had been misled. The splashes were as a result of long-range fuel tanks being jettisoned into the sea by five Bf109s of 8/JG 53, which were on their way to Athens/Eleusis airfield in Greece.

The Messerschmitt pilots had spotted what they believed to be 15 Beauforts and Beaufighters heading for Malta and now swept in behind the formation, diagonally from the south-east. By all reports they approached with initial caution. The first the torpedo-bomber crews knew of their presence was when the Beaufort at the far left of the formation, Flt.Lt. C.S. Thomas' AW352, broke in half behind the dorsal turret, the front section of the aircraft plunging into the sea in flames. The remaining aircraft dived for the sea, their throttles wide open. The Messerschmitts followed, 'hosepiping' their fire at the torpedo-carriers and within seconds AW297, positioned on the right and flown by Plt.Off. James Abram, a former Sunderland pilot on his first torpedo operation, crashed into the water. Sgt. Lionel Daffurn's DD974 was so badly damaged by three of the German fighters that he could hardly keep it in the air; with his air gunner, Sgt. Pearson, wounded by shrapnel in both legs and in one hand and arm, Daffurn turned back and eventually managed to crash-land near Sidi Barrani.

Plt.Off. Grant's aircraft (DD949) was also badly hit and his observer, Sgt. Williams, wounded by a cannon-shell. He also turned for land as did two of the flight leaders, Flt.Lts. Taylor and Leaning, both of whom had used excessive fuel in evading their attackers. Meanwhile, Flg.Off. R.C. Hooper's aircraft (DD955) was seen to break away and head in the direction of Malta, but came down in the sea from where the pilot and two of his crew were rescued by an Axis craft; the missing crewman, air gunner Sgt. J. Haining, was picked up separately.

One of the escorting Beaufighters, T4869/J piloted by another Belgian, Plt.Off. Roger Corbisier, was also shot down. It would seem that the Beaufighter fell to the guns of Lt. Beckmann from the Gruppenstab, who was flying with the Staffel. The Staffel pilots over-estimated their success somewhat; they had hit seven Beauforts, shooting down two and causing two subsequently to crash-land, but claimed nine shot down, three by Hpt. Belser (his 34th–36th), two by Lt. Dietrick Kasten (12th and 13th), two by Ofw. Seidl and one each by Lt. Feldkötter and Uffz. Augst.

At around this time, two more Bf109s from III/JG 27 were out looking for Lt. Hesse's dinghy, unaware that two others had already located it. By chance they came upon the other 272 Squadron Beaufighter — Sgt. W.G. Blessing's T4829/V — as it headed back towards North Africa. It was shot down into the sea by Ofw. Rösenberg, the Australian pilot and his observer (Sgt. J.R. Williams) being lost.

Meanwhile, Wg.Cdr. Mason, now with only five of his force of Beauforts remaining, had at last made contact with the 203 Squadron Maryland 'shadowing' the Italian warships. This aircraft led the torpedo-bombers in to attack the capital ships at the same time as the composite formation of Liberators released their bombs from higher level. Two of the Beauforts were hard-hit by AA fire and were forced to release their torpedoes prematurely, but the other three — flown by Wg.Cdr. Mason, Flg.Off. Jepson and Wt.Off. F. Morse — pressed on and made their drops, reporting a hit on the battleship *Littorio*. All had missed, however; what they had seen was the explosion of the bomb dropped by one of the B-24Ds. On completion of the attack, the five aircraft headed for Malta where Sqn.Ldr. Pat Gibbs successfully belly-landed his Flak-damaged aircraft (AW337), and Plt.Off. Dick Marshall collided with a damaged 217 Squadron machine whilst landing his heavily-damaged DD975. Both went up in flames, although Marshall and his crew escaped. Wg.Cdr. Mason was awarded an immediate DFC for his leadership, while Sqn.Ldr. Gibbs received an immediate Bar to his DFC.

Sqn.Ldr. (later Wg.Cdr.) Pat Gibbs, the legendary and inspirational leader of Malta's Beaufort strike force during the decisive attacks of summer 1942 on the Axis supply convoys. *(Authors' Collection)*

Whilst these actions were taking place to the west, other Beaufighters were continuing to provide some cover for the convoy. One pair, flown by Plt.Off. Peter Cobley and Sgt. Bill Knight, encountered an Ro43 biplane spotter

(MM27186) from the cruiser *Gorizia* and shot this down. Cap. Gastone Mezzetti and Ten. Vasc. Arnaldo Pannaria were both killed. The convoy's escort continued to fire at friend and foe alike, and while the Fighter Controller aboard *Coventry* desperately tried to keep the escorting fighters out of harm's way, the situation was very confused. At one stage of the proceedings it became apparent that Cobley was being vectored onto his own shadow, and he retorted with the classic: "Peter was merely chasing Cobley". A second Ro43, MM27127 flown by Serg. Ermanno Tommasini and Ten. Vasc. Benedetto Ferraro, also failed to return at about this time to its mother ship, the cruiser *Garibaldi*; the reason for its loss is unknown.

Another 272 Squadron Beaufighter, which followed at 1020, came across Sottoten. Edoardo Visentin's Z506B floatplane of 171ª Squadriglia out from Augusta, which Sgt. N.J. Cleggett promptly despatched into the sea. Shortly afterwards, a lone S.79 was met by the same crew and in an exchange of fire was claimed damaged. Earlier in this sortie, the Beaufighter had flown over elements of the Italian fleet and making a careful observation, Plt.Off. Gerry Williams (the observer) flashed "Balls!" on his Aldis lamp at the nearest cruiser — which promptly opened fire, albeit very inaccurately! The crew of the shot-down Cant, after some hours in the sea, were heartened to see another Z506B (flown by Ten. Mario Martinelli of 288ª Squadriglia from Taranto) come to their aid, but this was swamped by high seas after alighting; both stranded crews were subsequently rescued by the destroyer *Camicia Nera*.

Following the initial attacks on the Italian fleet by 217 Squadron, during which it was believed both battleships had been hit, Admiral Sir Henry Harwood, Commander-in-Chief, Mediterranean (working closely with Air Marshal Sir Arthur Tedder in Alexandria), ordered Admiral Vian's 'Vigorous' convoy again to turn westwards. Then, at 0830, a signal was received from a reconnaissance aircraft to the effect that the two battleships, with three cruisers and nine destroyers, were still heading for the convoy and were now within 150 miles of intercepting. Admiral Vian was again ordered, for the third time, to reverse course.

Two hours later, with the reports to hand of the claims of the American B-24 crews for hits and near misses on the Italian warships, a further signal was sent to Vian to turn westwards yet again! At 1345, when he received this signal, his ships were under heavy attack by ten Ju87s from III/StG 3, which disabled the cruiser *Birmingham*. Vian realised the battle was lost and that any further attempt to push the convoy westwards would most probably result in the loss of all his ships and their gallant crews, so he ignored this latest order and continued withdrawing to the east. Admiral Harwood finally conceded that Vian — as the man on the spot — must do what he considered best.

To those of the convoy the sky never seemed empty of Axis bombers which continued to appear in small waves of two or three to dive at individual ships. During the early afternoon 35 Ju87s of II/StG 3 arrived on the scene, and soon the destroyer *Airdale* was severely damaged by a number of hits and near-misses which killed 44 of her crew, and she had to be abandoned and sunk by gunfire; *Centurion* was repeatedly hit and *Arethusa* damaged, while the Australian destroyer *Nestor* was so badly holed that she had to be scuttled; three of her crew were lost. Amongst the afternoon attackers was Lt. Sattler of I/LG 1, on his second sortie of the day in L1+NH, who reported a near-miss on the port side of a light cruiser.

272 Squadron from Gambut was again called upon to fly protective sorties as the convoy came within range, but with the loss of seven aircraft and crews in two days' fighting, only a handful of aircraft were available. The squadron diarist sadly noted: "Two of the blackest days in the Squadron's history". Hence only Plt.Off. E.H. Hodgson's Beaufighter was available to patrol between 1500-1900. Help was to hand, however, for 252 Squadron was ordered to make available all its Beaufighters to assist its sister unit, four pairs commencing patrols as from 1400. The ship's gunners continued to give the Beaufighters a hostile reception. When the aircraft flown by 272 Squadron's Sqn.Ldr. C.V. Ogden and his No 2, Plt.Off. Gunnis (of 252 Squadron) arrived to assist, they were almost blasted out of the sky — at which the Beaufighter leader contacted *Coventry* and informed the FDO he was withdrawing.

As soon as the vessels came within range of single-engined fighters, such of these as could be spared were sent out to join the Beaufighters in their task. Towards evening, four Kittyhawks from 250 Squadron arrived and these were over the convoy when six S.79sil from 279ª Squadriglia AS at Derna swept in, joined by four more such aircraft from the 204ª Squadriglia AS from Rhodes. The Kittyhawks attacked, forcing four of the S.79s to jettison their torpedoes; Plt.Off. Percy Copeland (AK955/A) claimed two of the attackers shot down, while Sgt. F.C. De Salvo Hall claimed another damaged. One of the 252 Squadron Beaufighters also engaged the Savoias, Plt.Off. Easton Thwaites (T4831) claiming one of the torpedo-bombers probably destroyed. Ten. Salvatore Annona's aircraft was lost, reportedly having been shot down by two Beaufighters, whilst other crews claimed a destroyer sunk, two cruisers hit and three fighters shot down with a fourth probable! Copeland remained alone over the ships until 2000, when darkness once more fell to protect them.

It was nearly dusk when Ju88s of I/LG 1 and I/KG 54 made their final attack and reported patrolling RAF night fighters with their navigation lights switched on. In an attempt to deceive the ships' gunners Lt. Sattler, now flying L1+AL, switched on his own lights and dived onto a destroyer which he claimed suffered three direct hits on its stern, exploded and sank. The reported 'night fighters' were, in fact, the Beaufighters and Kittyhawks and a single Hudson of 459 RAAF Squadron, which had continued to provide individual aircraft in support of the convoy.

The pilot of this Hudson (V9052/D), Plt.Off. W.G. Cowan-Hunt, reported meeting two Ju88s when flying at 400 feet — one on a parallel course, the other attacking his aircraft from astern. As he took evasive action — with the Hudson almost touching the waves — the turret gunner (Sgt. H.A. Jackson) returned fire, reporting strikes on the Junkers' starboard engine. Cowan-Hunt opened fire on the other aircraft with his front guns as it turned to attack and strikes were seen on its fuselage and starboard engine, which reportedly burst into flames; it was last seen losing height. Another Ju88 was claimed shot down by 252 Squadron's Sgt. B.H. Vickery (T4828), one of the Royal Navy ships apparently confirming his victory.

With these final assaults on his battered convoy underway, Admiral Vian received yet another signal from Alexandria. Reports indicated the Italians had now given up the chase, and were retiring to Taranto. "Now is the golden opportunity to get the convoy to Malta" was the gist of Admiral Harwood's message, but he conceded this would be impractical should fuel and ammunition be causing anxiety. Indeed it was, the majority of the destroyers having just 20%

ammunition remaining, which was considered insufficient for the passage to Malta. The operation was now officially aborted and all ships finally ordered back to Alexandria. The nightmare was not yet over, however, for as the long haul back began, the German submarine *U-205* attacked and sank the cruiser *Hermione* with two torpedoes; 87 of her crew perished. Admiral Harwood later reflected:

> 'Events proved with painful clarity that our air striking force had nothing like the necessary weight to stop the Italian fleet.'

Meanwhile, reconnaissance aircraft from Malta were again searching for the Italian capital ships and their escorts, which were found once more at 1500, heading towards Taranto. On one of these sorties over the Ionian Sea, Baltimore AG715 of 69 Squadron, flown by Plt.Off. A.H. Patrick, failed to return. On board this aircraft as an observer was the squadron's CO, Wg.Cdr. Eric Tennant. There seems little doubt that the aircraft fell victim to one of I/NJG 2's Ju88Cs, Oblt. Albert Schulz claiming an aircraft which he identified as a 'Maryland' for his sixth victory.

Upon the report of the new sighting, a further strike from Malta was ordered by the surviving Beauforts of 217 Squadron, but the crews failed to find anything during the subsequent five and a half hours of night flying. At dusk, five Wellingtons were sent out, ASV equipment again allowing these torpedo-bombers to find their target, but only Plt.Off. O.L. Hawes (DV541/C) was able to penetrate the low cloud and smoke screen to carry out an attack. His target was the slightly-damaged *Littorio*, which was struck by one of his two torpedoes, this time suffering severe damage.

This attack virtually brought to an end the June convoy operations. Although some supplies had got through, the actions were essentially an Axis success, gained at relatively small cost in terms of shipping — one cruiser sunk and several vessels, including one battleship, damaged. In the air, however, losses had been quite heavy. The Regia Aeronautica had suffered as follows:

Sardinia	**Sicily**	**Others**
6 S.84	3 S.79	5 Ro43 (shipboard — including 2 lost aboard ships during air attacks)
6 S.79	3 Ju87	1 S.79 (Rhodes-based)
1 Z1007	1 S.84	
4 CR42	1 Re2001	
1 MC200	3 Z506B	
	1 RS14	

Additionally, Luftwaffe losses by units based in Sicily, Crete and North Africa directly related to these operations included:

Sicily	**Crete**	**North Africa**
4 Ju88	4 Ju88	2 Ju88
1 Bf109		5 Ju87
		2 Bf109

Italian fighter pilots had claimed at least 26 victories and three probables, while their bomber and reconnaissance crews claimed some 18 (!) more, and ships' gunners two. Their German allies had claimed at least 23 more successes, two of them by the night fighters operating by day.

British pilots on the other hand had claimed 45 victories — 19 by Malta-based units, 17 by the carrier pilots and 10 by the North African-based units, including one by the USAAF B-24Ds. Royal Navy and Royal Marine gunners aboard warships and merchant vessels had claimed about 15. Losses had been:

Malta	**Carriers**	**North Africa**
5 Spitfires	3 Sea Hurricanes	7 Beaufighters
2 Baltimores	4 Fulmars	7 Beauforts (incl 3w/o)
1 Beaufighter	1 Swordfish*	2 Kittyhawks
1 Albacore		2 Tomahawks
1 Wellington*		2 Hurricanes
		1 Hudson
		1 Liberator (damaged)

As a consequence of the disappointing results of the convoy operations the Governor, Lord Gort, on the 16th advised the people of Malta:

> Some days ago, two convoys set out, one from the west and one from the east to bring supplies which we need to restore our situation. The Western convoy had to endure severe and prolonged attacks, and only two merchant ships survived the ordeal. They are now in the Grand Harbour... These cargoes are essential for our future and well being. The Eastern convoy, after suffering from prolonged and intense attacks by the Luftwaffe, was ordered to turn back.
>
> I must break to you what the arrival of only two ships means to us. For some time past we have been short of supplies and further privations lie ahead of us... We must stand on our own resources and everyone of us must do everything in his or her power to conserve our stocks and to ensure that best use is made of all the available resources that remain to us... We must make all possible savings in every commodity and stock.'

Despite the convoy operations, losses on the Island had not been severe as a result thereof. However, with the heavy fighting continuing in North Africa, the movement of supplies to the Axis forces there had become more urgent than ever. With Beauforts, Beaufighters, Wellingtons and reconnaissance aircraft still available in some numbers, and with the level of air attack from Sicily remaining muted, Malta was well-placed to resume the offensive against the supply shipping involved.

Tuesday 16 – Friday 19 June

Four Ju88s and a dozen Bf109s crossed the coast at 0645 on Tuesday the 16th, but were engaged by some of the 20 Spitfires which had been scrambled on their approach. One Messerschmitt was claimed shot down by 126 Squadron's Plt.Off. Goldsmith:

> 'Had a dogfight with four 109s about 30 miles north; squirted at one and he dived into the sea. Was attacked head-on and hit in the port wing by cannon

---

* Lost due to accidents, as was one Spitfire recorded above.

> shell. Little damage. Then attacked another 109, but cannons contributed one round between them, so I came home smartly.'

A further fighter sweep by a dozen Bf109s during mid-morning was also met by patrolling Spitfires, 20 of which had been ordered up, including eight of 185 Squadron. Flt.Sgt. Yarra (GL-J) also reported shooting down a Messerschmitt but received a bullet through his engine in return; not so fortunate were two of his squadron colleagues, Flt.Sgt. 'Tex' Vineyard and Flt.Sgt. MacNamara, both of whom were shot down in BR163 and BR320 respectively. Both were able to bale out and were promptly rescued by Spitfire-escorted HSL 128. They were back on dry land within two hours.

Four BR20Ms of 116° Gruppo BT departed Castelvetrano five minutes before midnight, the crews briefed to raid Luqa. One bomber, MM24133 of 277ª Squadriglia, flown by Sottoten. Aldo Ruggeri, was shot down by AA fire and crashed in flames in the village of Zebbug, with the loss of all the crew; slight damage to buildings resulted while nearby precious crops were set on fire by burning debris. Shortly afterwards at Luqa, an ASV-equipped Wellington VIII (HF919) crashed on take-off following engine failure; the pilot and his crew all sustained injuries.

Six Bf109s approached Malta at 1600 on Wednesday the 17th, but two only crossed the coast and 11 patrolling Spitfires of 126 Squadron were ordered to engage; Plt.Off. Goldsmith and Plt.Off. Miller jointly claimed one damaged, as noted by the former:

> 'Wizard interception of 109s but a little low. Later, Dusty and I got in a good squirt at one, hitting him twice. We then chased another back to Sicily.'

Two aircraft, tentatively identified as Ju88s, appeared shortly before midnight and a patrolling Beaufighter (X7642) was vectored onto one, which Flg.Off. Daniel claimed to have shot down. His victim was possibly a BR20M, one of two briefed to bomb Luqa; one crew reported being attacked by a night fighter but succeeded in evading and escaped undamaged.

At 0505 on Thursday the 18th a Fiat RS14 floatplane of 144ª Squadriglia RM set off on a maritime reconnaissance sortie; Sottoten. Luigino Zane and his crew were lost when their aircraft failed to return due to unknown causes. The Luftwaffe also lost one of its 'rare birds' on this date, when a Do17Z of 10/ZG 26 was obliged to ditch in the sea following engine failure; the gunner was injured although he was rescued with the rest of his crew.

Sub Lt. P.A. Jordan was seriously injured and his observer (Sub Lt. R.S. Todd) killed, when their Albacore crashed near Hal Far on the 19th during a test flight. A little later, Wellington HX376 crashed on take-off but on this occasion the crew were unhurt. During the day four delivery Beauforts arrived, two having been damaged by Bf109s of 6/JG 53 — probably flying from Pantelleria — between Linosa and Malta; each aircraft had a wounded crew member aboard. The gunners had fought back and believed they had hit one of the attackers and, indeed, Uffz. Heinz Schumann was lost when 'Yellow 6' crashed into the sea.

In the early hours of the 20th a delivery Hudson (FH248) crashed in a field near Kirkop; the observer was killed, another member of the crew was injured and a third suffered from shock. At dawn a delivery Wellington arrived, having been damaged by MC200s near Pantelleria. None of the crew were hurt and the gunners believed that they might have hit one of their attackers, while Italian pilots claimed to have shot down the Wellington.

Saturday, 20 June

Sqn.Ldr. Keith Lawrence and 'A' Flight of 185 Squadron at Hal Far on 20 June 1942; L to r: Plt.Off. Paul Baril; Flg.Off. John Stoop; Sgt. Len Reid; Plt.Off. Ernie Broad; Flt.Sgt. Peter Terry (sitting on wing); Sgt. 'Tex' Vineyard; Plt.Off. Cy King; Flt.Sgt. Haydn Haggas; Flg.Off. Jones (adjutant); Sqn.Ldr. Lawrence; Flt.Sgt. 'Slim' Yarra (sitting on nose); Flt.Lt. Ron West (i/c 'A' Flight); Flt.Sgt. Bob Sim; Flt.Sgt. 'Mac' MacNamara; unknown; Sgt. Ken Mitchell; Plt.Off. Gray Stenborg. *(C. King)*

A convoy comprising two large merchant vessels with heavy deck cargoes of vehicles was spotted by a 69 Squadron Baltimore (AG746 flown by Plt.Off. Munro), coming out of the Gulf of Taranto during the early afternoon. These freighters were reported to be escorted by three destroyers and were apparently making for Messina. Immediately on receipt of news of this sighting, a strike force of ten Beauforts of 217 Squadron were sent out from Luqa, one of which returned early, whilst two more were delayed taking-off; seven Beaufighters from 235 Squadron were planned to act as escort although only three managed to rendezvous.

A sweep was carried out northward from the southern end of the Gulf of Squillace, doubling back southwards down a leg 15 miles further out, but owing to faulty navigation and ASV difficulties in the leading aircraft, the target was missed. With the benefit of hindsight, it was apparent that the strike came within 10-15 miles of the position of the ships and that the Beaufighter leader, having picked up a probable contact on his radar, failed to direct the strike accordingly; he was later reprimanded for this. In the circumstances, the strike was called off and the aircraft returned to Luqa, but the two straggling Beauforts ran into three Ju88Cs of I/NJG 2 which were on a flight from Catania to Kalamaki, Greece, Lt. Heinz Rökker in R4+PL attacked Flg.Off. Frank Minster's DD959 and made seven attacks before the Beaufort ditched on fire. Minster and his crew taking to their dinghy. Oblt. Hissbach in one of the other Ju88Cs found that his cannons would not fire, and the other Beaufort, skippered by Sgt. Jim Hutcheson, fought off the attackers and made it back to Luqa, the gunner claiming one of the opposing fighters shot down. Rökker's aircraft was hit 25 times during the action, but all three reached Kalimaki. Subsequently, the convoy was found again off the toe of Italy by another 69 Squadron Spitfire and it later put into Palermo harbour.

During the day, both Axis air forces suffered non-operational losses of Sicilian-based aircraft — a reconnaissance Bf109F of 1(F)/122 crashed at Comiso and was badly damaged, while a Z506B (MM45409) of 144ª Squadriglia RM was lost when it was forced to ditch in the sea due to engine trouble; Serg.Magg. Giovanni Zanardi and his crew were rescued.

Just before 1600 three German airmen, survivors of Lt. Müller's I/KG 54 Ju88 shot down six days previously, paddled ashore in their rubber dinghy at Tigne Point, Sliema; they were immediately arrested and transferrred to hospital. After dark the night fighter Beaufighters were active when three bombers were reported over the Island, one of which Flg.Off. Oakes and Flt.Sgt. Walsh claimed shot down just after 2300, identified as a Ju88.

This was to be the final claim by the Beaufighter detachment, its scoreboard now registering 18½ confirmed victories, three probables and four damaged. The detachment departed next day, but was almost immediately replaced by a second detachment. DFCs were awarded to the successful teams of Flt.Lt. Hayton/Plt.Off. Josling (6 victories) and the newly commissioned pair, Plt.Offs. Miller and Tearle (4½ victories), while Flg.Off. Daniel DFC, emerged as the top-scorer with 7 confirmed, and one damaged, 5 of which had been shared with his regular operator, Sgt. Gosling.

Sunday, 21 June

Next morning another convoy was located by one of 69 Squadron's Baltimores (AG746 flown by Plt.Off. Foster) off the Tunisian coast, south of Cape Bon. This comprised the 8326-ton Italian freighter *Rosalino Pilo*, the German 7744-ton *Reichenfels*, and the heavily-armed destroyer *Da Recco*. Between them, the two freighters carried 6563 tons of artillery and ammunition, 638 tons of fuel and lubricants, 376 tons of motor transport, and 393 servicemen.

Nine of 217 Squadron's Beauforts were briefed to attack in three vics of three, respectively led by Sqn.Ldr. Lynn, Flg.Offs. Aldridge and Stevens, with escort provided by six Beaufighters of 235 Squadron. Three of the latter took-off at 1136 to provide close cover, followed five minutes later by the other three as top cover. One Beaufort was forced to return early but the others found the vessels at 1255 almost due west of Malta and some 48 miles from Lampione, under air cover. This was initially identified as comprising a single Ju88 and a single 'S.79' but in fact there were five Junkers, including at least two from 2(F)/122, a ubiquitous Z506B, and two CR25 twin-engined reconnaissance-fighters of the 173ª Squadriglia RST from Palermo, one of which the British pilots had obviously identified incorrectly as a trimotor 'Savoia'.

The CR25s, piloted by Ten. Pietro Rindone and Mar. Fabrizio Dori, engaged a reported six Beauforts and three Beaufighters, Rindone claiming one Beaufort shot down with his front guns, while his gunner claimed a second with the turret machine gun. Dori's crew fired at several without obvious result.

Meanwhile, the close cover Beaufighters (led by Sqn.Ldr. Cook) engaged at once, Flg.Off. Underwood attacking one Ju88 which crashed into the sea with the starboard engine and fuselage on fire. Cook attacked the Italian aircraft that had been seen initially and claimed that he had inflicted damage to the port engine. It dived away in a southerly direction followed by Flg.Off. H. Wood, who then attacked from astern and below; the starboard engine and mainplane reportedly burst into flames and the aircraft was seen to spin into the sea. Since no Italian aircraft was lost, it is possible that Wood had actually attacked the

Ju88 shot down by Underwood, or that the aircraft he saw spinning into the sea was one of the Beauforts. Two minutes later, Underwood spotted a second Ju88 at 1500 feet and attacked, the starboard engine of this aircraft also catching fire. The Junkers appeared to jettison bombs as it glided down to the sea, where it disintegrated.

The high cover trio of Beaufighters also initially spotted one Ju88 and one Italian aircraft; Sqn.Ldr. Wigmore fired at the Junkers but then saw Underwood shoot it down. A second Italian machine was then seen following a Beaufort and Flg.Off. Eyre attacked this, claiming damage. Although none of the Italian aircraft were lost, two 2(F)/122 Ju88s failed to return; Uffz. Heinrich Kramer and his crew of F6+BK (a D-1 sub-type) were killed but the crew of F6+FK (an A-4) survived, although two were wounded, and were picked up by the escorting destroyer.

As the leading vic of Beauforts swept in to make their attack, *Da Recco* put up a wall of fire which shot down the first torpedo-bomber at once; this was probably Sqn.Ldr. Lynn's W6502. As the stricken aircraft hit the sea, its torpedo was seen to come adrift and ricochet into the air and it was believed by watching crews that this hit Sgt. Bill Smyth's aircraft, which also crashed into the sea. Whatever the cause of the loss of AW342 only the Australian navigator, Sgt. Keith Dodd, survived from either machine. He was later picked up by the Italian destroyer, which also rescued Flg.Off. Phillips, the pilot of DD996, the third of the trio shot down.

Whilst Sqn.Ldr. Lynn's section bore the brunt of the escort's wrath, the other five Beauforts got through and claimed four torpedo hits, two on each merchant ship. Flg.Off. Aldridge went for *Reichenfels* and released from 750 yards just as his aircraft was hit by four cannon shells; he was wounded in the right forearm by a splinter and his navigator, Sgt. Vince Aspinall, in the head by another. The starboard aileron control wires were severed but as he was about to ditch his stricken aircraft, Aldridge realised it was still flyable and succeeded in nursing it back to Malta.

Plt.Off. Jim McSharry's aircraft (L9799) came under attack from one of the escorting Ju88s, the Australian pilot suffering a severe wound to his throat. Spotting McSharry's aircraft under attack and despite his own machine's plight, Flg.Off. Aldridge flew over to help, getting close enough to allow his air gunner (Sgt. Bill Carroll) to open fire on the attacker. Smoke was seen to come from the Junkers' port engine before his guns jammed but then a Beaufighter — that flown by Flg.Off. Underwood — arrived on the scene and promptly despatched it into the sea (as already recorded). The badly-wounded McSharry, on his first operational sortie, succeeded with the aid of his navigator in flying back to Malta.

Despite claims that both merchant vessels had been hit, the Italian freighter escaped unscathed. The other ship was not so fortunate, however; *Reichenfels* sustained at least one hit on the port side and was left on fire, the smoke from which was visible some 20 miles away. She later sank without loss, her entire complement of 246 being taken aboard the busy *Da Recco*. The captain of the German freighter reckoned that seven of the Beauforts had been shot down, including the one which had torpedoed his vessel!

With the return of the Beauforts and the coming of darkness, two Albacores and two Swordfish were sent out to continue the attack but these failed to locate the convoy. Three ASV Wellingtons were also despatched to the same general

Arming a 10(Jabo)/JG 53 Bf109F with four 50kg bombs at Gela. *(Dr Felix Sauer)*

area but only one aircraft located the ships; bombs were dropped, one of which was believed to have hit the stern of the merchantman.

From Malta at 1950, four Spitfires of 185 Squadron were scrambled, Flg.Sgt. Yarra (BR387/W) claiming two Bf109s shot down and a Ju88 damaged, as noted in his logbook:

> 'Engaged 4 109s — shot tail off one. Terry shot up. Chased 88 and damaged it — was attacked by 3 109s and shot one down; beat it for home. Met Baltimore and escorted it back to the island.

Flt.Sgt. Terry's Spitfire (BR112/F) was shot-up and he crash-landed, unhurt. Ten minutes later, four more Spitfires went off, Flt.Sgt. Sim (GL-D) also claiming a Bf109 and a second damaged, but Flt.Sgt. 'Pop' Conway's aircraft was hit; the New Zealander, who had apparently baled out on three previous occasions, decided on this occasion to try to get his damaged BR315/T back to Takali but was badly hurt in the crash-landing. Nonetheless, his decision had undoubtedly been the correct one, for subsequent inspection of his parachute showed it to have been riddled by fragments of a cannon shell which had exploded under the cockpit. Despite claims for three Messerschmitts shot down, just one aircraft of 5/JG 53 crash-landed at Comiso in a damaged state.

Two further transit aircraft were reported missing during the day, both Blenheims. One failed to arrive from Gibraltar, the other — a Mark V (BA446) — disappeared whilst on its way from Malta to North Africa. It was assumed both losses were due to technical failure or human error.

Monday, 22 June

The only Axis aircraft to appear in Maltese skies on the 22nd were mainly on reconnaissance, the last being six Bf109s which swept across the coast just before 1930, although these did include a number of Jabo. Bombs fell on Hal Far,

Canadian buddies in 185 Squadron — Don 'Shorty' Reid (left) and 'Buzz' Ogilvie. *(N.J. Ogilvie)*

where the sole surviving Sea Gladiator (N5520) from the ledgendary 'Faith', 'Hope' and 'Charity' days was reported damaged by blast. Flt.Lt. Halford led four Spitfires of 185 Squadron to intercept, Flt.Sgt. 'Shorty' Reid (GL-O) claiming one Messerschmitt shot down, while Flt.Sgt. Ferraby (BR293) pursued another:

> I was diving very steeply down after a 109; didn't look at the speed, but the controls became very hard and it took all my strength to pull out without breaking something! I'd seen tracer going past me and that's what caused me to pull out. Probably just as well or I might have dived in. It was another Spit firing at me. Found out it was Halford firing at me.'

Reinforcements for the Island's strike force and night defences arrived on the 22nd. Five Beauforts of 39 Squadron, led by Sqn.Ldr. Pat Gibbs, flew in from Sidi Barrani to operate with 217 Squadron, while four Wellingtons from 38 Squadron arrived to strengthen the small existing detachment; four more would follow on the morrow — although these were ordered to return to North Africa two days later — while another three arrived on the 27th. Additionally, from Egypt came a second detachment of four night fighter Beaufighters (and six crews), forming 'C' Flight of 89 Squadron. These aircraft were equipped with AI Mk IV radar and would operate in conjunction with the GCI station at St Paul's Bay.

The 'C' Flight detachment comprised:

X7748/C	Flt.Lt. H.G. Edwards and Sgt. J.R. Phillipson
X7716/A	Flg.Off. R.C. Fumerton and Sgt. L.P.S. Bing

X7676/J	Flg.Off. M.C. Shipard and Sgt. D.A. Oxby
X7702/T	Plt.Off. N.E. Reeves and Sgt. A.A. O'Leary

The two spare crews were Flg.Off. H.E. Mitchell and Sgt. J.G. Trebell, and Plt.Off. J. Mck. Ross and Sgt. R.E. Thompson. 'Moose' Fumerton (a Canadian) already had four victories to his credit and Merv Shipard (an Australian) had one, while his radar operator, Sgt. Doug Oxby, was destined to become the RAF's top-scoring operator. When the replaced crews from the original detachment flew back to Egypt two days later in three of their Beaufighters, a fourth aircraft was left behind and was absorbed into the new detachment.

By this stage of the 'electronic' war, means of jamming radar were being put into practice and the Beaufighter crews frequently experienced interference on the AI scopes. However, although frustrated in this manner at times, the new crews continued the successful run of nocturnal victories. Of his Beaufighter night fighter crews — the new arrivals and their predecessors — Air Vice-Marshal Lloyd wrote:

> 'The crews were the most experienced to be found anywhere... Against such a team the Axis raiders in their twos and threes throughout the night had very poor chances of survival.'

Tuesday, 23 June

There was considerable action over and around the Island on the 23rd, starting at first light when a transit aircraft arrived having been intercepted by two Macchis off Pantelleria; the air gunners claimed strikes on both attackers. Soon after, at 0820, a dozen Spitfires of 603 Squadron scrambled to engage six Bf109s, of which Plt.Off. Slade and Plt.Off. Glen each claimed one damaged; one German fighter was reported to have been seen in the sea.

At 1750, a dozen more Spitfires (this time from 249 Squadron) with another eight of 603 Squadron, took-off from Takali — BP980 crashing in the process although without injury to the pilot — to intercept an incoming Italian raid of some size. This comprised three S.84s from the 4° Gruppo BT, escorted by 27 MC202s of 155° Gruppo CT, with indirect support provided by 18 Re2001s of 2° Gruppo CT. The 249 Squadron aircraft went for the bombers — misidentified, as usual, as Z1007s — and Plt.Off. Lattimer fired at the one in the centre, reporting strikes, while Sgt. Baxter shot at two of the Reggianes, claiming that one appeared to 'shake'; 2° Gruppo reported no notable action. Plt.Off. Brennan's Spitfire was damaged by AA shrapnel as he approached the bombers but he was able to land safely. Despite these attacks, the Savoias were able to release their bombs over the Takali area — although the airfield suffered little actual damage; some bombs fell on Mosta, where three persons were killed and six injured.

It was the 603 Squadron pilots who enjoyed greater success on this occasion, Plt.Off. Dicks-Sherwood and Flg.Off. McLeod seeing a dozen Macchis west of Gozo, which they attacked in a dive from 29,000 feet. Dicks-Sherwood saw strikes on the fuselage and starboard wing of one, while McLeod reported strikes on the fuselage of another when he fired a burst at 100 yards. He gave chase to others and finally closed on one from 250 yards astern. After a long dogfight he put in a burst, closing to 25 yards, and claimed and the Macchi dived into the sea from 5000 feet — reportedly "out of panic".

Meanwhile, Plt.Off. Newman and Plt.Off. Ray Smith alternately attacked another Macchi, seeing strikes on the fuselage. Glycol streamed from the port wing root and the cockpit hood flew off. Flt.Sgt. Parkinson (X-N), having been driven away from the bombers by the Macchis, spotted either Newman or Smith apparently getting the worst of the exchange with the Macchi:

> 'I sailed in and the other Spit sailed out. Made one three-quarter head-on attack. The "Ity" flicked and turned away, presenting his tail to me. I was about 200 feet behind with the bead dead on and firing. I saw something break off the fuselage and then the pilot baled out. His kite went into the sea. I circled the pilot whose chute had opened. He looked dead to me so I eventually flew straight at him and then decided he wasn't dead because he started to wave his arms frantically.'

Without doubt they had shot down Mar. Aldo Buvoli of the 360ª Squadriglia, who baled out into the sea; McLeod may also have been attacking this aircraft for it was the only loss reported by the Italians. Apart from the claims for the Macchis, Plt.Offs. Slade and Glen again each claimed 'Bf109s' damaged. One Spitfire (BR385) was shot down, Flg.Off. Mitchell baling out into the sea from where he was picked up by HSL 128 within an hour, thereby becoming the ASR unit's 100th recovery.

Five minutes behind the Takali Spitfires came the Hal Far-based aircraft of 185 Squadron. These also engaged fighters, Flt.Sgt. Vineyard (GL-Z) claiming damage to a 'Bf109'. Two more of 185 Squadron's aircraft were scrambled at 1840 but failed to make contact; Flt.Sgt. MacNamara crashed on landing, although his BR362 was not badly damaged.

The Italian pilots claimed four Spitfires shot down and one more damaged. Sottoten. Giuseppe Riccardi claimed one and two damaged, while the others were credited to Serg.Magg. Giovanni Del Fabbro, Mar. Gino Runci, and the missing Buvoli — his sixth victory — who survived his encounter with the Spitfires, and recounts:

> 'While I was flying in a tight turn, I heard the terrific noise of a burst fired from behind at close range; at that moment I saw the dark shape of an aircraft overtaking me very fast! I was sure my Macchi was hit! In fact, everything began to vibrate. All efforts to control the aircraft were in vain and then sudden warmth came from under the cockpit. Fire! I unhooked the canopy and baled out!
>
> 'The smell of smoke, the noise of the engine and the rush of air stopped, and there I was suspended from my parachute; below me the sea, above the confusion of the battle between the Macchis and the Spitfires. Coming down in the sea, I realised I was north of Gozo, the little Maltese island appearing through the sea mist. The sea was not very calm. From high above it had seemed perfect, but in the water the waves were running. I got out of my parachute, inflated my life-jacket, but at every jolt I drank seawater!
>
> 'Gozo seemed very distant and the waves seemed to push me away. Ninety minutes passed and I was cold, tired and discouraged. Gozo seemed to be getting further and further away. Despite trying to remain still, lying supine on my back, I still continued to swallow seawater. Sunset was now near; I was cold and began to think it impossible that I could survive the night in the sea! I had a presentiment that these were my last hours of life! I tried to resign

Plt.Off. Reade Tilley of 601 and 126 Squadrons; this successful American pilot was awarded a DFC for his services on Malta. *(NWMA)*

myself, but the instinct for life is strong, despite my inability to help myself. I thought of being devoured by sharks!

'While I was being assailed by these dark thoughts, I saw in the distance a sailing boat; it was steering towards me. Driven by a strong wind, it was by me in a few minutes. I could see a woman at the tiller and a man in a strange uniform in the prow waiting to pick me up. In a second I was hauled aboard and laid in the bottom of the boat. Almost exhausted, feelings of unease came over me. I was very cold and I vomited. The man and woman were silent; no word, no sign, only some piercing glances. Probably they had hoped to rescue an English pilot! They remained cold and impassive.

'Before we reached Gozo, to which the sailing boat was heading, I saw another boat, this time a naval motor-launch. This came alongside and "claimed" the survivor. It then headed direct to Gozo.'

During the early morning hours of darkness, one of two patrolling ASV-equipped Wellington VIIIs of the Special Duties Flight located two merchant vessels and two destroyers coming from Naples. At this very moment the Wellington's navigator was taken ill and an attack was not carried out, but the other aircraft was called in, four 500lb bombs being aimed at one of the merchantmen from 1200 feet; a hit was claimed on its stern and a red glow and much smoke was seen.

At around 0730, one of 69 Squadron's reconnaissance Spitfires — BP908 flown by Sgt. Colquhoun — overflew a convoy leaving Palermo harbour; these were the same ships which had taken refuge there following the attacks of the 20th and comprised the 7137-ton *Nino Bixio* and the smaller *Maria Roselli*, with an escort of two destroyers and three torpedo-boats. On receipt of news of this sighting, a force of a dozen Beauforts, including those of the 39 Squadron detachment, were prepared to attack. An escort was provided by 235 Squadron but the lead Beaufighter, flown by Wg.Cdr. Garlick, was forced to return early.

On reaching the convoy, the Beaufort pilots discovered that the escorting destroyers had pulled in much closer to their charges than had been the case when spotted by the Spitfire, and it was necessary to fly through their fire in order to make the drop. Led by Wg.Cdr. Davies and Sqn.Ldr. Gibbs, they pressed on, Gibbs' aircraft (AW300) and Flt.Lt. Leaning's AW240 both being hit, while those of Flg.Off. T.H. Gardiner (DD976) and Sgt. B. Guy (W6518) — both of 39 Squadron — were shot down; Gardiner and his navigator, Sgt. E. Mullins, were picked up by one of the escorts. One more aircraft (L9802 of 217 Squadron) was badly damaged and Sgt. C.J. Nolen, the pilot, was wounded in the leg. Despite considerable loss of blood he continued the run-in and released his torpedo at one of the merchant vessels, claiming a hit, before gamely flying back to Luqa where he crash-landed the damaged aircraft, receiving further injuries.

Although two CR42s, three Z501s (from 184ª Squadriglia) and a Bf109 were seen by the Beaufighter crews, only the Fiats made half-hearted attempts to interfere, both firing at the Beauforts from long range before breaking away. One Beaufighter pilot made an unsuccessful attack on one of the seaplanes, which escaped undamaged, while the others were concerned mainly with strafing the ships to divert the gunners' attention from the torpedo-bombers.

Both the freighters had been hit, *Nino Bixio* returning to Taranto at once, albeit at an agonizingly slow three knots. *Maria Roselli*, reportedly down in the water and smoking from stem to stern, required a tow from two destroyers after emergency repairs had been carried out. A reconnaissance Spitfire later reported that both had reached Taranto, one, evidently badly damaged, having its cargo transferred to another vessel.

When the 252 Squadron Beaufighter which had led the 89 Squadron detachment Beaufighters to the Island the previous day departed to return to North Africa, it led eight Spitfires of 'A' Flight, 601 Squadron to this area. The WDAF still had only one squadron of these fighters at this stage of the war, although others had been promised. The Kittyhawk and Hurricane fighter-bombers, their attentions urgently required for ground support duties, were suffering terrible losses to the high-flying Messerschmitts and Macchis of the Axis and were in great need of help.

Malta's defences had become so strong due to recent deliveries of aircraft, and attacks on the Island had been so much reduced lately, that it was felt one squadron of Spitfires could be spared — particularly as 601 Squadron's ground party had now arrived by sea in the Canal Zone. At the time of departure the squadron had claimed some 25 victories during its stay on Malta, but another was to be added before the balance of the unit — 'B' Flight — followed at the end of the month.

There were a few changes in personnel as the unit prepared to depart. Flt.Lt. Denis Barnham, despite being ill and dispirited, had emerged as the squadron's top scorer with four and one shared victories. However, he had already left for the United Kingdom, tour expired, while recent arrival Plt.Off. Jerry Smith was posted from the unit to 126 Squadron; Smith, who was recovering from both 'Malta Dog' and sand-fly fever, recorded his satisfaction with the change, for 126 Squadron were a "damned good squadron and I'm not sorry to stay, although the old 601 gang were a bloody good lot!".

The new night fighter detachment was swiftly in action when, just before midnight, Flt.Lt. Edwards and Sgt. Phillipson in X7748 intercepted one of 20 bombers plotted approaching the Island from the north. They claimed a Ju88 probably shot down over the sea and were granted a 'confirmed' victory when news of a German aircraft down in the sea reached AHQ. Undoubtedly this was M7+BK of KGr 806, in which Uffz. Herbert Wolenski and his crew were lost during this unit's attack on Luqa. Here a Spitfire was burnt out on the ground but very little other damage resulted. Another Beaufighter crew, Plt.Off. Ross and Sgt. Thompson, chased two other raiders — one as far as Sicily — but without gaining position to attack.

Ironically, the weakening of Malta's defences came at an inopportune moment, for a renewed assault on the Island was in the making. Well-aware of the need to prevent this troublesome base again becoming a hornet's nest, the Axis were seeking to reinforce the Sicilian strike force demanded by Mussolini. Even with a major summer offensive underway in Russia, the Luftwaffe was obliged to rob this front again. Ju88s of Stab, II and III/KG 77 were ordered to the Mediterranean in late June, followed in early July by the Messerschmitts of I/JG 77. After the 'Vigorous' operations of 14 and 15 June, III/JG 53 had again been ordered to return to Comiso but this movement was subsequently revoked, so great was the need for this unit's fighters in Libya.

Wednesday, 24 June

The Regia Aeronautica, too, was reinforcing its Sicilian contingent and on the 24th the HQ flight of 51° Stormo CT (the parent unit of the 155° Gruppo) arrived at Gela, led by Ten. Col. Aldo Remondino, with the unit's second gruppo, the 20° under Magg. Gino Callieri. This latter unit's three squadriglie were:

151ª Squadriglia	Cap. Furio Doglio Niclot
352ª Squadriglia	Cap. Luigi Borgogno
353ª Squadriglia	Cap. Riccardo Roveda

The pilots brought with them 36 brand new MC202s, with which they were extremely keen to enter the fray. At this time, Z1007bis bombers also began arriving to replace the BR20Ms of 88° Gruppo BT.

Having visited Sardinia on the 23rd, where he had presented medals to aircrew based there, Mussolini flew into San Pietro during this day at the controls of his personal S.81. Accompanied by Generale SA Rino Corso

Il Duce Benito Mussolini visited San Pietro airfield on 24 June 1942 to present decorations to personnel of 2° Gruppo Aut. CT. Here Ten. Giorgio Pocek receives his award of the Medaglio d' Argento. *(S. Govi via N. Malizia).*

Fougier, he presented medals to personnel of 2° Gruppo Aut. CT. Medaglia d'Argento awards were made to Ten. Col. Quarantotti, Cap. Teia, Ten. Metellini, Ten. Pocek, Ten. Gasperoni, Ten. Celentano, Ten. Bartolozzi and Sottoten. Pagliani, while di Bronzo awards went to Ten. Larese Gortico, Sottoten. Vichi, Ten. Seganti, Mar Jellici, Mar. Patriarca, Serg.Magg. Fabbri and Serg.Magg. Cesaro.

Aircrew of 102° Gruppo Tuffatori also received awards during the visit, selected personnel being presented with nine Medaglie d'Argento, five Medaglie di Bronzo and 17 Croci di Guerra. Next day six of 2° Gruppo's Re2001s escorted the S.81 as Mussolini flew it back to Grottaglie.

That same night the dive-bomber gruppo despatched three Ju87s over Malta again, in bad weather. After half an hour Cap. Cenni, who was leading, returned to base. The other two failed to receive his message to abort the raid and continued on their way. Sottoten. Fulvio Papalia, new temporary commander of 239ª Squadriglia, and his gunner (Av.Sc. Arm. Pietro Giannini) were intercepted to the north of the Island by Flg.Off. Fumerton and Sgt. Bing in Beaufighter X7716/A soon after 2200, and were shot down. The guns also fired at these intruders and were credited with shooting down a second Ju87 off Mellieha Bay. The night fighters were now well into their stride; next it was the turn of Flg.Off. Mitchell and Sgt. Trebell (X7748/C) at 0130, as seven BR20Ms from 88° Gruppo BT headed for Luqa. Two were forced to turn back early, but the rest reached the target area. As they approached, the 'Servizio Alfa' issued a warning of approaching night fighters, but Ten. Angelo Reseghetti's MM24133 of 264ª Squadriglia was shot down four miles east of Malta by Mitchell.

A little later, six Z1007bis of the 9° Stormo and ten more BR20Ms from the 88° and 116° Gruppo headed for the same target, where the team of Fumerton and Bing were again airborne. Just before dawn Fumerton's fire struck one of the Cants, MM24277 of the 62ª Squadriglia, flown by Cap. Umberto Frigo. It burst into flames and blew up. Owing to the inclement weather conditions, Mitchell and Fumerton both experienced difficulty in correctly identifying their

A Cant Z1007bis of 60ª Squadriglia, 33° Gruppo BT, successfully crash-landed at Chinisia on return from a sortie over Malta. *(G. Terebinto via N. Malizia)*

victims, the former tentatively suggesting a possible four-engined aircraft, perhaps a Ju89! Fumerton thought his opponent to have been a Ju88.

Thursday, 25 June

There was high drama on Luqa airfield in the early morning hours of darkness, when Wellington HX372, returning from an armed reconnaissance, crashed while landing and burst into flames. Despite the danger of the bomb-load going off, a party of five men rushed out and extricated the crew just before one bomb exploded; shrapnel from this severed the leg of one would-be rescuer. Amongst the witnesses was Air Vice-Marshal Lloyd who had to restrain others from entering the inferno to help.

Nothing much happened over Malta on the 25th until the late evening, when nine Bf109s on a fighter sweep approached the coast; at 2010 a dozen Spitfires of 249 Squadron scrambled and these intercepted the Messerschmitts over Gozo. Plt.Off. Owen Berkeley-Hill attacked a section of five, and grey smoke was seen to pour from the fuselage of one which turned over and dived away — it was seen by Sgt. De Nancrede to stream coolant. Berkeley-Hill, recently posted to the squadron, was credited with its probable destruction. Plt.Off. Lattimer (BR108/C-20) attacked another from 100 yards astern, which poured black smoke and apparently went down out of control, then fired on a second from quarter astern and slightly below — he reported that "it blew up in the air". This was undoubtedly an aircraft from 4/JG 53 which crashed into the sea near Gozo, from where the pilot was later rescued by an ASR machine from Sicily. Flt.Sgt. Maurice Tomkins was not so fortunate; he endeavoured to nurse his damaged Spitfire (BR382) back to Takali, as Colin Parkinson noted:

> 'This afternoon I was sitting in my kite ready to take-off when I heard a Spit in a power dive. Looked up and saw it coming down with glycol pouring out. The pilot made for the drome, did a circuit and started to fly across the drome at a low speed. About half-way across his motor cut dead. His wings started to wobble as he lost speed, heading straight for my kite. When almost directly overhead he tried to turn; he stalled at about 60 feet and spun. The aircraft immediately burst into flames. The fire tender was about to approach but the ammo started to go off so they stopped. The kite had nearly burnt itself out before they went near it. I went over to have a look and saw the pilot caught in amongst the wreckage . . . I could smell his clothes burning. It was Flt.Sgt. Tomkins, who sleeps next to me.'

Plt.Off. Harry Coldbeck was one of 69 Squadron's outstanding Spitfire photo-reconnaissance pilots; the New Zealander was awarded a DFC for his work from Malta. *(Daddo-Langlois Collection)*

A photo-reconnaissance Spitfire IV of 69 Squadron; note that the overall blue aircraft carries barely-discernible code letters (LY) indicating its previous owner. *(NWMA)*

With the onset of darkness, two bomb-laden, ASV-equipped Wellingtons and four torpedo-carriers of 38 Squadron went out after a convoy reported off Cape Colonne. Earlier, 69 Squadron's Plt.Off. Coldbeck, flying a Spitfire Vc on this occasion as no PR aircraft was currently serviceable, had sighted a stationary tanker two miles outside Messina harbour. A later sortie showed that it had got underway with an escort of two destroyers and the ASV Wellingtons each located the convoy with the aid of their equipment, the crews aiming their bombs at the tanker but without result. The 38 Squadron crews failed to find the ships and returned with their torpedoes intact.

A delivery Hudson (FH230), at the end of its long flight from Gibraltar, suffered an engine failure as it approached Luqa in the early hours of the morning of the 26th and crashed. The pilot, Flt.Sgt. Docherty, survived with injuries although his crew were killed.

Friday, 26 June

Not until 1800 were six Spitfires of 126 and 601 Squadron scrambled, followed shortly by ten of 603 Squadron and then by eight more from 185 Squadron some 20 minutes later. They were up to intercept a raid comprising five Z1007bis of

33° Gruppo, escorted by 29 MC202s of 155° Gruppo, and 18 Re2001s of 2° Gruppo; the Reggianes were apparently misidentified by the RAF pilots as Bf109s.

Two Macchis were claimed shot down, one by American Plt.Off. John Curry of 601 Squadron (BR301/S) — "down in flames" he noted — the other by Flt.Sgt. Schade (126 Squadron); but Sgt. C.P.J. Taylor's aircraft was badly shot up, the pilot being wounded in the leg by splinters. He managed to land with a dead engine. The 603 Squadron pilots reported meeting Bf109s. Plt.Off. Glen claimed one of these shot down and then damaged a second and gained strikes on one of the Cants. Another bomber was damaged by the combined fire of Plt.Off. Northcott and Sgt. Pinney, while Sgt. Irwin claimed strikes on one of the escorts, also identified as a Bf109. One Spitfire was slightly damaged in return. By the time 185 Squadron entered the fray the raiders had turned for home and only the escort were engaged; one of these — a Reggiane — was claimed shot down by Flt.Lt. Ron West (GL-J) for his eighth and last victory.

None of the Re2001s was lost, but Mar. Gino Runci's 378ª Squadriglia Macchi was shot down, the pilot being seen to bale out; he was not subsequently found. Two Spitfires were claimed by this unit, one each by Cap. Miani and Mar. Zedda, while two of the Reggiane pilots, Cap. Teia and Serg.Magg. Ricci, jointly claimed one more. Other pilots believed they had probably shot down one more and damaged two others.

Although Luqa was the target, where an airman was killed when handling an unexploded bomb, nearby Pieta was also badly hit; here ten civilians were killed and at least another nine seriously injured.

Saturday, 27 June

Four Spitfires of 249 Squadron scrambled during the morning of the 27th, led by Flt.Lt. Daddo-Langlois, and encountered a seaplane identified as a Do24 (which was in fact a Red Cross Z506B) with an escort of a dozen MC202s provided by 51° Stormo. They were searching for Mar. Runci, lost the previous day, and were joined by a number of Ju87s from 102° Gruppo and some Ca 164s.

The Spitfire pilots reported bouncing eight Re2001s 15 miles south-east of Sicily, Flt.Sgt. Rae (BR377/K) claiming one shot down and a second probable, Flt.Sgt. Middlemiss (BR184/S) one and a damaged, and Plt.Off. Verroll (BR295/H) yet another. Apparently three Reggianes were seen in the water within 200 yards of each other, yet Italian records show no losses! In return, Sottoten. Romano Biasiol claimed a Spitfire shot down.

Sunday, 28 June

Between 0300 and 0400, four bombers were reported over the Luqa area, bombs causing much damage to the airfield and runways; a Beaufort was destroyed in its pen and a Baltimore was damaged. To enable incoming delivery aircraft to land the Station Commander, Group Captain Le May, ordered his men to fill in the hole made by an unexploded delayed-action bomb without removing it — and got away with it!

There was not much activity over Malta during the daylight hours of the 28th, only occasional reconnaissance aircraft crossing the coast, but after dark the assault on Malta's airfields continued.

Monday, 29 June

Just after midnight two Ju87s were observed over the Island and one bomb was dropped in the Mellieha Bay area, but the other aircraft, Serg.Magg. Dino Fabbri's Stuka of 239ª Squadriglia, was caught by Flg.Off. Mitchell's Beaufighter (X7676/J) and shot down. The aircraft crashed near Kercem, on Gozo, and the body of the gunner (1° Av. Arm. Riccardo Alasia) was found near the wreckage, while the pilot survived to be taken prisoner.

Two Beaufighters — and two Spitfires of 249 Squadron — took off at 0455 to intercept raiders approaching the coast. Seven of these — Ju88s of KüF1Gr 606 and KGr 806 — crossed; bombs fell on Hal Far, where a Swordfish was destroyed and a soldier wounded, while at Luqa a transit Hudson was damaged beyond repair. Beaufighter X7702/T, crewed by Flg.Off. Fumerton and newly-commissioned Plt.Off. Bing, closed in on one of the raiders. They shot down Lt. Werner Schrader's M7+LL of KGr 806 without opposition, then 7T+IK of the other unit; Uffz. Ernst Tegelmann's gunner, Obgfr. Xaver Röckel, gained hits on the Beaufighter before perishing with his crew as the burning bomber crashed into the sea. The Spitfire pilots saw one of Fumerton's victims fall in flames, the wreckage burning on the water. Ofw. Oskar Plewinski, the wounded navigator of M7+LL, was later picked up from the sea by Axis rescue craft.

At 0855 four Spitfires of 603 Squadron were sent off after eight Bf109s; Plt.Off. C.A. MaC. Barbour was jumped by two and baled out of BR320/K into the sea, about five miles off the coast. HSL 128 sped to his rescue and within the hour he was back on dry land.

Between 2245 and 2330, eight raiders were plotted around the coast, while three Beaufighters were up looking for custom. Sgt. Phillipson soon picked up a contact on his radar screen and led his pilot, Flt.Lt. Edwards, onto Fw. Winfried Pohler's KüFlGr 606 Ju88 (7T+AL), which was shot down into the sea. With eight victories in as many nights, the Beaufighter crews were certainly justifying the AOC's accolade.

Tuesday, 30 June

The only daylight action on the 30th occurred when eight Spitfires of 249 Squadron were sent off to intercept a fighter sweep. After 40 minutes milling around without making contact, the Spitfires were ordered to return. It was then that Bf109s bounced Plt.Offs. Lattimer and Berkeley-Hill, both of whom had their aircraft shot-up, necessitating force-landings at Takali; although both were shaken, neither was hurt.

The 'Taranto' convoy — the ships attacked by the Beauforts a week earlier and forced into Taranto for repairs — appeared ready to put to sea again, joined by a further merchant vessel. Three ASV Wellingtons were despatched to keep an eye on any movement and at 0130, the convoy and its four-destroyer escort was seen in the Gulf of Taranto. Two of the Wellingtons aimed their 4000lb bombs at the leading freighter but no hits were seen.

Five torpedo-armed Wellingtons from 38 Squadron had earlier taken-off from Luqa and these were now homed to the target area. By now an effective smoke screen had been laid, but the largest of the freighters was sighted by three of the torpedo-Wellington crews; only two were able to release their torpedoes, Sgt. Thomson and Flt.Sgt. R.V. Flanagan believing strikes were achieved before both aircraft were hit by light AA fire; Thomson's aircraft was hit in the nose by two cannon shells and the observer was wounded by a fagment. The damaged machine was flown back to Luqa where it belly-landed and was subsequently written off. The victim of their attack — the large freighter — indeed sustained some damage and the convoy returned to Taranto once again.

On the return of the Wellingtons, a number of 'hostiles' were detected approaching, 13 of these crossing the coast just after 0400. Two Spitfires and two Beaufighters were ordered up but on this occasion no interceptions were achieved.

Thus ended June, a month which saw an improvement, even if on a limited scale, in Malta's fortunes. According to the figures issued by Air HQ, the fighters had been credited with 64 confirmed victories, 15 probable and 57 damaged on defensive operations, to raise RAF claims over the Island since June 1940 to 517:195:468; the AA defences had claimed a further 7:0:3 to raise their totals to 218:47:179.

Losses included a dozen Spitfires (but only two pilots), six Beauforts, a Beaufighter, two Baltimores, three Wellingtons and an Albacore. By night, the Wellington IIs of 104 Squadron had launched 57 sorties, dropping 92 tons of bombs during raids on Messina, Augusta, Taranto, Naples, Syracuse, Cagliari and Catania, before their departure for Egypt. The Wellington VIIIs had contributed 35 sorties, and 38 Squadron's torpedo-carrying Mark Vs a further 17; the Beaufort strike force had flown 65 sorties and had launched 33 torpedoes, while the FAA's Albacores and Swordish managed a total of 31 sorties. The four photo-reconnaissance Spitfires of 69 Squadron (BP915 having been added to the unit during the month) had clocked up 56 far-ranging sorties, all without loss.

British Overseas Airways continued to fly limited supplies and stores to Malta with their Whitley V transports, augmented by occasional flights with the CW-20T. However it was 24 Squadron's unarmed Hudson transports of the Gibraltar-Malta shuttle service which regularly arrived with passengers and mail, these undertaking no less than 18 trips to the Island during the month. All these flights were made without loss, even though it was necessary at times for the aircraft to 'stand-off' on arrival in Malta's airspace when air raids were in progress. The only casualty suffered by the shuttle-service during June occurred at the end of the month, and then whilst the aircraft concerned was at Gibraltar.

The circumstance of this loss was unusual, for on the night of 28/29 June, five of the Regia Aeronautica's new Piaggio P 108B four-engined bombers had set out from Decimomannu airfield, Sardinia, to raid Gibraltar. One of these 274ª Squadriglia aircraft was obliged to return early, but Ten. Col. Gori Castellani led the others to release their bombs on the tiny British promontory. One of these scored a direct hit on 24 Squadron's AE533, which was being prepared for the flight to Malta. Fortunately, Plt.Off. E.M. Prchal and his crew were in the Flight Hut at the time and there were no casualties. Eduard Prchal, a Czech and formerly a successful fighter pilot, had flown in France and during the Battle of Britain; he would later be the only survivor of the accident in 1943 which claimed the life of the Polish Prime Minister and Commander-in-Chief, General Wladyslaw Sikorski (and his daughter and members of his staff), coincidentally also at Gibraltar.

The Italian raid was not particularly successful for the crews of the Piaggios, since their engines proved troublesome. More fuel was used than anticipated and two aircraft were obliged to force-land in Spain, both sustaining damage; in addition, Cap. Balletta had to land on the island of Majorca, where he refuelled and then returned to Decimomannu.

A number of decorations and promotions had been announced for the Island's airmen during the month, including: a Bar to DFC for Sqn.Ldr. Barton who now handed over command of 126 Squadron to Sqn.Ldr. Winfield; DFCs to Plt.Offs. Goldsmith DFM, Bisley and Graves, all of the same unit. Within 249 Squadron, Flt.Lt. Lucas was awarded a DFC and was promoted to take over command from Sqn.Ldr. Grant, who was also promoted and left for the Middle East. Flt.Lt. McNair had also left the squadron on completion of his tour, and Daddo-Langlois had been promoted to take his place. With McNair had gone two of the squadron's successful pilots, the inseparable Plt.Offs. Ray Hesselyn and Paul Brennan. 185 Squadron also received a new commander when Sqn.Ldr. Bill New took over at the end of the month, while Flt.Lt. Plagis received a Bar to his DFC.

Amongst awards made to FAA personnel was a DSO to the CO of 828 Squadron, Lt. Haynes, a similar award going to Lt. P.A.S. Downes of 830 Squadron, while Lt. Williamson received a Bar to his DSC. Lt. Head and Sub Lts. W.P. Watson, T.E. Moore and J.C. Morrison each received a DSC, while L/Airmen G.G. Reynolds and P. Watson were advised of DSMs.

Chapter 7

SUMMER SKIRMISHES

Sqn.Ldr. A.R.H. Barton, commanding officer of 126 Squadron (second from left), with three of his Australian pilots from left; Plt.Off. John Bisley, Plt.Off. Tim Goldsmith and Flg.Off. Don Smith. *(I. Primmer)*

The relatively quiet spell which followed the June convoys did not last long. The Regia Aeronautica was now planning a resumption of activities to be launched as the second major Italian assault on the Island, and due to commence on the first day of the new month. Strength in Sicily had been steadily increased, although the contingent in the north-west of the island around Palermo would still play no real part in any action. Here 54° Stormo CT and 10° Stormo BT — the latter with the CR25 twin-engined fighters of 173ª Squadriglia RST attached — would remain involved in convoy-escort duties. Colonnello Giuseppe Gaeta, from his headquarters at Palermo, had been appointed to command the Comando Bombardmento della Sicilia towards the end of June, his task being to control the operations of the eight bomber gruppi. Fighters had also been reinforced — 20° Gruppo CT had arrived at Gela late in the month, with the Stormo headquarters under Ten. Col. Aldo Remondino, the unit's Macchis bringing 51° Stormo CT up to its full establishment.

To support their allies, the Germans had also taken steps to reinforce Fliegerkorps II in Sicily. Stab, II and II/KG 77 returned with their Ju88A-4s from their brief stay at Creil/Rennes and Beauvais/Vannes, in France, to whence they had been despatched to take part in renewed attacks on Southern England. With KüFlGr 606 and KGr 806, this raised to four the number of bomber Gruppen available, backed by the reconnaissance aircraft of 1(F)/121 and by elements of Aüfk1Gr 122, which were operating throughout the Mediterranean area.

Since the only Bf109Fs available to escort this enlarged force were those of

II/JG 53 and elements of the Geschwaderstab, an additional Jagdgruppe was ordered to Sicily from the Eastern Front. I/JG 77 had been operating with great distinction on the Southern Sector of the front but had recently been moved to Rumania, where it had been involved in intercepting B-24Ds of the Halverson Detachment from Egypt (the unit which had attacked Iachino's fleet on 15 June) during the little-known first USAAF bombing attack on mainland Europe, when the Ploesti oil refineries were first raided.

I/JG 77, which arrived at Comiso on 3 July with a tally of around 635 victories, had previously been known as I/(J)LG 2 but had operated with II and III/JG 77 as part of Jagdgeschwader 77 since 1941. The unit's Kommandeur, Major Herbert Ihlefeld, who had been in command since summer 1940, had recently departed to become Geschwaderkommodore of JG 52. He had claimed 103 victories and had been awarded the Ritterkreuz mit Eichenlaub und Schwertern (Knights Cross with Swords and Oakleaves). His place was taken by the similarly-decorated Hpt. Heinz 'Pritzl' Bär, transferred from 12/JG 51, who was credited with 113 victories.

The Gruppe contained a number of other outstanding pilots, notable amongst them Oblt. Fritz Geisshardt, previously Ihlefeld's wingman of many months and now commanding 3 Staffel; Geisshardt had just received the Oakleaves to his Knights Cross, with his score standing at 82. In command of 1 Staffel was Oblt. Siegfried Freytag who would be awarded the Knights Cross on 3 July, having claimed 49 victories in the air and 12 aircraft destroyed on the ground. The unit's 2 Staffel was led by Oblt. Herbert Thurz, about whom little is known.

Amongst the other pilots, Lt. Günther Hannak had claimed 41 victories and was also about to receive his Knights Cross; Ofw. Walter Brandt, the Gruppe's leading NCO pilot, had about 20 victories to his credit, Stfw. Helmut Godert

A trio of Experten of the highest order – Left to right; Oblt. Friedrich Geisshardt (I/JG 77); Maj. Günther von Maltzahn (Kommodore of JG 53) and Hpt. Heinz Bär (Kommandeur of I/JG 77). All wear the Ritterkreuz (Knights' Cross) at their throats.

Lt. Armin Köhler (centre) of I/JG 77 at Reggio, soon after arrival from the Eastern Front, the rudder of his new Messerschmitt Bf109G-2 demonstrating the 11 victories he had claimed there. *(P. Köhler via J-L. Roba).*

about 15, while Lt. Armin Köhler had 11 and the Adjutant, Lt. Heinz-Edgar Berres, had seven — including an American B-24D claimed over Ploesti on 12 June. Other pilots who would later do well included Lt. Eberhard Niese (who already had at least eight victories), Lt. Irving Englisch, Fw. Otto Pöhl, and Uffz. Horst Schlick who had two victories already. This confident, experienced unit soon proved to be a most dangerous adversary for the Malta Spitfires.

Despite the arrival of the convoy survivors, the Island was still desperately short of supplies of all types. The four deliveries of Spitfires during May and June (136 arrived) had done much to resurrect the defences but the departure of 601 Squadron to the Desert, coupled with the gradual attrition, had reduced numbers to levels barely adequate to maintain the four remaining squadrons at strength. Many of the longer-serving fighter pilots were by now tired and weakened by poor food, and by attacks of 'Malta Dog' and sand-fly fever.

Wednesday, 1 July

The afternoon of the 1st saw the new offensive open when ten of 20° Gruppo's MC202 led by Cap. Luigi Borgogno, escorted a Ju88 over the Maltese airfields at 1450, apparently on a reconnaissance. A Staffel of Bf109s from II/JG 53 also participated in the escort, for at 1504 Ofw. Rollwage claimed a Spitfire shot down over St Paul's Bay, the Luftwaffe's only claim of the day. The Italians also reported engaging Spitfires, Borgogno claiming one shot down, while other pilots claimed four damaged.

Their opponents were a dozen Spitfires from 185 Squadron; one flight was led by Sqn.Ldr. New, while Plt.Off. Halford's flight soon became engaged with the escort. Flt.Sgt. 'Shorty' Reid (BR294) claimed a Messerschmitt shot down and a second as damaged, while Plt.Off. Sherlock (BP876) claimed another shot down but was credited only with a damaged; Plt.Off. Charney (BR380) also gained hits on an MC202 but his own aircraft was hit, causing him to crash-land at Hal Far; two more Macchis were claimed damaged by Halford (BR387) and Sgt. Mahar (BR292). Plt.Off. Kent's Spitfire also sustained damage during this action and he, too, was obliged to force-land at Hal Far on return. Johnny Sherlock considered the IO's assessment of his initial claim as somewhat unjust:

'I recollect turning into a couple of Me 109s as they turned in to attack my section... For some reason the leader broke too soon and I got in a lucky deflection shot on his port wing and big hunks flew off. The plane turned over and went straight down, partly on its back. I was involved in further chasing around with his No 2 and other 109s and could not see what happened to the one I hit. There was no doubt, in my mind, that not only was the 109 badly hit but also the pilot had been hit.

'After I landed I reported that I had shot down an Me 109 but admitted I had not seen it go in. When questioned by our I0 about the plane being classed as damaged I became a little sarcastic and suggested that a 109 could not fly back to Sicily with half a wing and a dead pilot. I started to walk away when Ken Charney came in, having landed after I did, his plane being badly shot up. At this time he asked who had shot off the port wing of a 109. I told him I had and asked him if he had seen it go in. He stated he was about 300 feet behind an Me 109, firing when an Me 109 came straight down, passing between him and the plane he was shooting at. This plane was making no recovery efforts, the left wing was mostly missing and the pilot was slumped forward. It was around 5000 feet or less, but Ken did not see it go in as he continued firing at the 109 ahead of him. The I0 mentioned he might raise my claim to probable, and I told him to hell with the claim.'

The next engagement occurred just after 1845 when radar showed approximately 30 aircraft approaching the Island, at least two of which were reported as BR20s; they were in fact two S.84bis of 4° Gruppo BT, their crews briefed to bomb Takali. The escort was provided by 22 Macchis, led by Ten. Col. Remondino, who reported being intercepted by 16 Spitfires before the Island was reached. Remondino personally claimed one shot down, while other 51° Stormo pilots reported hits on six more.

Behind this force came three more S.84bis with an even larger escort, comprising 48 more Macchis from 51° Stormo, plus 15 Re 2001s of 2° Gruppo Aut CT. During the ensuing engagement seven Spitfires were claimed shot down, MC202 pilots claiming four of these, one each by Mar. Ennio Tarantola (20° Gruppo CT), Sottoten. Nicola Longano, Mar. Cesare Ferrazza and Serg. Willy Malagola of 155° Gruppo CT; two more were credited to Reggiane pilots Sottoten. Francesco Vichi and Mar. Luigi Jellici, and one to gunners aboard the bombers. Two Macchis were damaged — those flown by Ten. Giobatta Caraccoilo Carafa and Sottoten. Longano — although both pilots regained Gela without further mishap.

This formation had initially been encountered by a dozen Spitfires of 603 Squadron, the pilots believing their opponents to have included Bf109s. One of these was claimed shot down by Flt.Sgt. Ballantyne, who also reported strikes on a second before his own aircraft (BR367/0) was shot down into the sea; slightly wounded in the neck, the Canadian baled out and was picked up by HSL 107. Flg.Off. Mitchell also claimed a Messerschmitt probably destroyed, while Plt.Off. Hurst believed he had probably shot down one of the bombers; his own aircraft was hit by return fire and by the time he landed the engine had lost all its coolant. Plt.Off. Glazebrook damaged a Macchi, while a Reggiane was claimed by Flt.Sgt. Parkinson, as he later recalled:

'I found an RE fighter with finger trouble. Flew out to one side, recognised it as an RE, flew in behind, gave a long burst, saw strikes, the kite faltered, glycol pouring out and went into a vertical dive. A shower of enemy fighters attacked me so I did a wild dive and escaped them. Last I saw of the RE it was still heading for the drink at about 5 or 6000 feet.'

As soon as the Spitfires landed following the departure of the Italian force, five more from 126 Squadron were scrambled, and engaged a reported six Bf109s, one of which was claimed probably destroyed by Plt.Off. Graves.

So on this first day of the new offensive, Axis claims for ten destroyed, one probable and ten damaged had actually netted one Spitfire shot down and three damaged, whilst RAF claims for four shot down, three probables and eight damaged had, in fact, resulted in damage to just two Macchis! Not a brilliant start!

After dark, the Beaufighters of 89 Squadron's flight were on patrol when seven bombers crossed the coast — bombs fell at Krendi (where seven houses were damaged and a civilian was killed) while others killed two soldiers near Marsaxlokk. Up above at 2230, Flt.Off. Fumerton's X7702/K was guided onto Lt. Paul Volkmann's III/KG 77 Ju88 (3Z+AS), which was shot down in flames into the sea off Ricasoli Point. Three hours later a further six intruders came over Luqa where a Wellington and a Beaufort were destroyed. Although Beaufighters were up there were no interceptions on this occasion; however, a further success was gained just before dawn when Plt.Off. Ross and Sgt. Thompson (X7716/A) engaged another Junkers, reporting "a shower of red flashes" although the bomber was claimed only as probably destroyed. It seems likely that this was an aircraft of 1(F)/122 on an early morning reconnaissance to survey the results of the night's bombing; it crash-landed at Comiso, reportedly hit by fighter attack over Luqa, and was severely damaged.

Thursday, 2 July

Thursday proved a substantially more costly day to both sides as the fighting escalated. Eight Spitfires of 185 Squadron scrambled at 0815, followed by eight of 603 Squadron, on the approach of 18 Bf109s, four of which crossed the coast and were intercepted. Flt.Sgt. 'Shorty' Reid (BR294 of 185 Squadron) claimed one shot down for his fourth victory, while Flg.Off. Mitchell of the other unit gained strikes on a second, but Plt.Off. Hurst in BR184 failed to return. No one saw him go down, except perhaps his victor. Johnny Hurst, 603 Squadron's first pilot to be decorated on the Island, was a sad loss to the squadron. Already with one confirmed and five probable victories on arrival, he had added five more confirmed, one probable and four damaged since April.

Two pilots of 185 Squadron also had their aircraft shot up by Bf109s during this engagement, Plt.Off. Ogilvie force-landing BR468/Z at Takali:

'The radio in my Spitfire had given up, so I didn't hear the call to break formation. And as a result I found myself alone, engaged with six enemy fighters, each trying to do me in. But my intrepidness was of no avail, for my aircraft was suddenly hit with cannon and machine gun fire, the shells blowing a large hole in the fuselage directly behind the cockpit, and the machine gun bullets penetrating the engine, spewing oil and glycol all over myself and my aircraft. The Spitfire shuddered and stalled, then plunged into a dive steaming black smoke and white vapourized glycol.'

Meanwhile Sgt. Dodd, despite shrapnel wounds, managed to return safely to

Hal Far with BP876. However, on landing back at Takali, Flt.Sgt. Reid's port tyre burst and his Spitfire tipped over onto its back; fellow Canadian Johnny Sherlock was amongst those who went to his aid:

> 'I remember helping "Shorty" from under the Spit and thought that had he been any taller, he would have had more than a scratched head and a headache!'

With the return of 'B' Flight's Spitfires, 603 Squadron scrambled 'A' Flight's eight aircraft at 0915, followed five minutes later by a dozen of 249 Squadron, led by Sqn.Ldr. Lucas. About 40 minutes later five Z1007bis of 33° Gruppo BT were seen on their way to bomb Safi and Kalafrana, while their escort of 24 MC202s of 51° Stormo and 15 Re2001s of 2° Gruppo CT tangled with the Spitfires. The Macchi pilots claimed three shot down, one each by Magg. Dulio Fanali and Ten. Giovanni Franchini, the third jointly by several pilots, while seven more were credited to the Reggianes, Serg.Magg. Ricci and Serg. Cesare Di Bert claimed two apiece, and Cap. Teia, Ten. Mettellini and Sottoten. Pagliani each claimed one, the latter sharing a second with 51° Stormo.

Again the Spitfire pilots thought Messerschmitts were present, Plt.Off. Ray Smith (603 Squadron) and Flt.Sgt. Tommy Parks (BR379/V of 249 Squadron) each claiming one shot down, while Sqn.Ldr. Lucas (BR324/R) probably destroyed one more and Plt.Off. McElroy (BR254/G) damaged another. A Macchi was probably destroyed by the combined fire from 603 Squadron's Plt.Offs. King and Glazebrook, although both were hit in head-on attacks and were obliged to crash-land BR345 and BR365 respectively on returning to Takali. Two more of the unit's pilots, Plt.Off. Johnson and Flt.Sgt. Parkinson (X-S) each damaged an Re2001, the latter recording:

> 'Had another scramble, saw some "Ity" bombers but we were jumped before we could attack. I saw a Spit being attacked by an RE, so attacked the RE. Saw strikes under the wing and fuselage, but having no height or speed, I spun off before I had a chance to see if there was any serious result. I came home like a bat out of hell and claimed one RE damaged.'

Sottoten. Giuseppe Riccardi's Macchi of 351ª Squadriglia was shot down into the sea about 18 miles south-east of Valetta, while Serg.Magg. Malagola's aircraft was badly damaged; a number of Reggianes were damaged but all managed to return to Gela.

Several of the Spitfires evaded the close escort and attacked the bombers, but could only claim damage before being forced away. Three pilots of 603 Squadron — Plt.Offs. Ray Smith and Newman, and Sgt. Ken Mitchell — together with Sgt. De Nancrede (BR246/J) of 249 Squadron, jointly claimed damage to one of the Cants, the latter then gaining strikes on another bomber. Wt.Off. Ramsay (BR251/E) also attacked a bomber, both he and De Nancrede then mixing with the escort — thought to be Messerschmitts — each claiming strikes on their opponents before being chased away.

The next raid — by three Ju88s of III/KG 77 escorted by four fighters — was picked up on the radars at 1415; Luqa was the target where two civilians and two soldiers were killed, two others being wounded and a Beaufighter slightly damaged. Eight Spitfires of 185 Squadron and seven more from 249 Squadron were airborne to meet this threat. Two pilots of the latter unit, Plt.Offs. Linton (BR347/Z) and Spradley, were joined by Flt.Sgt. Sim of 185 Squadron in damaging two of the bombers, while Flt.Lt. Daddo-Langlois (BR170/B) pursued the other for 40 miles before being able to shoot it down into the sea; members of Fw. Herbert Leiwelt's crew of 3Z+JT were seen to bale out, this subsequently being recorded as 249 Squadron's 100th victory whilst flying Spitfires. The squadron's Texan pilot, Plt.Off. Harry Kelly (BR184/C) failed to return, presumably shot down by a Messerschmitt of the escort, two of which were claimed by Flt.Sgt. Middlemiss (BR295/H) and 185 Squadron's Sgt. D.K. Parker (BP979); Plt.Off. Ken Charney of this latter unit returned in a slightly wounded condition, his aircraft (BR376) badly shot-up.

Plt.Off. Ossie Linton, another of the many Canadians reaching the Island by mid 1942; he served with 249 Squadron. *(Daddo-Langlois Collection)*

The final attack of the day occurred between 1945 and 2020 when three S.84bis of 4° Gruppo BT, with a close escort of ten MC202s of Cap. Doglio Niclot's 151ª Squadriglia, approached; 18 more Macchis provided indirect support but three were obliged to return early. Seven Spitfires of 249 Squadron had already been scrambled and these were joined by four more from 185 Squadron, the latter pilots enjoying a successful encounter. Flg.Off. Stoop (BP979) shot down one fighter — mis-identified as a Bf109 — which crashed in a field near Mellieha, Serg.Magg. Alberto Porcarelli of 151ª Squadriglia being killed. Meanwhile, Sgt. Haydn Haggas (BR387) carried out a head-on attack on another Macchi, which half-rolled towards the sea; Haggas followed and fired two more bursts, leaving it still diving at 5000 feet. Other pilots confirmed that it dived straight into the sea about two miles off Sliema Point and was undoubtedly Ten. Ennio Cherici's machine, the pilot baling out to be rescued by HSL 107.

Sqn.Ldr. Lucas (BR324/R) claimed another fighter damaged, as did Flt.Sgt. Tommy Parks and Sgt. Len Reid (185 Squadron, flying BR166), all three believing their opponents to have been Bf109s. Sgt. De Nancrede's BR377/K was hit during a head-on attack and crash-landed at Takali. He was probably the victim of Cap. Doglio Niclot, who claimed one Spitfire shot down, while other Macchi pilots claimed a further six damaged.

That night three BR20Ms from 116° Gruppo BT and eight 9° Stormo BT Z1007bis set out to raid the Malta airfields, the Fiats attacking Takali and the Cants Luqa, arriving just after 0100. 'Servizio Alfa' warned the Italian crews of the presence of night fighters but to little avail. One of each type of bomber was shot down, one of them a 'flare-dropper'; the BR20M was flown by Sottoten. Cesare Lusenti. Two Beaufighters were up and each crew claimed a success, while the AA defences claimed a third. Plt.Off. Reeves and Sgt. O'Leary in X7676 reported a conclusive combat at 0100, while an hour later Flg.Off. Fumerton and Plt.Off. Bing (X7716) claimed another bomber shot down in flames about 20 miles north of Gozo, the pilot of this aircraft later being rescued; both victims were initially claimed as Ju88s. Six civilians were killed and eight injured during the raid.

Friday, 3 July

Thirty-six MC202s of 51° Stormo escorted three Z1007bis over Takali in the morning of the 3rd, but while many fighters were encountered — and it was thought possible that three Spitfires had been hit — no casualties were actually suffered by either side and no claims were submitted. However, a Spitfire had been lost when eight of 126 Squadron scrambled at 0830 to meet this raid, Plt.Off. Thomas' BR564 crashing into the sea following propeller malfunction; the pilot was safely picked up by HSL 107.

Shortly after, four more Spitfires of 126 Squadron were scrambled on the approach of further 'hostiles', Plt.Off. McHan leading. The quartet was ordered to climb to 28,000 feet and to await further instructions, but four Bf109s then appeared; the American McHan later recalled:

> 'Something hit my Spitfire (BR465/X) — the engine seemed to explode in front of me. The "ship" was on fire and the "gas" from the cooling unit was streaming into the cockpit. Throwing the hood back would suck the flames outside into the cockpit, and if I turned the ship over, as so many pilots do, the petrol might have spilled to send more flames through the ship. I told our officer on the ground "I'm going to crash-land", but he said: "Bale out". I came down to 15,000 feet straight down, and levelled off. At 10,000 feet I knew the petrol tank might go any second, so I got out, wounded and on fire. I passed out. I remember pulling the ripcord at about 4000 feet, then passing out again. I came to in a hospital.'

The semi-conscious pilot had landed on the roof of a house from which he slid off and hit a wall, then fell to the ground, knocking out two teeth, badly splitting his lip and fracturing his already wounded ankle. When he came to in hospital he found the occupant of the next bed to be a wounded German airman; McHan continued:

> 'They (the hospital authorities) didn't worry about German prisoners escaping — the Huns were afraid of the Maltese who would have been very happy to get hold of them.'

If the day had been relatively uneventful over the Island, it certainly had not been so elsewhere. The Italian convoy which had been forced to seek shelter in

Left: Hpt. Gerhard Michalski who ended 1942 as the Luftwaffe's top-scorer over Malta, poses by the tail of his II/JG 53 Bf109F at Comiso early in July 1942. 43 victory bars can be seen on the rudder of his fighter, 13 of which relate to Russian aircraft claimed during 1941, whilst others in the top row indicate claims made over France and England during 1940. *(via W. Bock)* **Right:** Flt.Sgt. Bob Middlemiss of 249 Squadron, who was one of seven Spitfire pilots brought down on 7 July 1942. He baled out, suffering slight wounds, and was rescued from the sea by HSL 128. *(NWMA)*

Taranto Harbour following attacks by Malta's Wellingtons three days previously — now enlarged to three merchantmen, escorted by three destroyers (*Da Verrazzano, Turbine* and *Euro*) and five MTBs — had re-emerged to make its run to Benghazi. Owing to the shortage of fuel on Malta it had not been possible to keep a standing air reconnaissance over Taranto, and it was due only to the vigilance of a patrolling submarine that the convoy had been sighted the previous evening, hugging the coastline and heading eastwards towards the Greek coast. Although three torpedo-carrying Wellingtons had promptly set out, guided by an ASV-equipped Mk VIII, and located the convoy after a long search off Paxos island, some 20 miles south of Corfu, their attack proved ineffective.

It was now down to the Beauforts, all available aircraft going out at 0700. They failed to locate the convoy however, and were obliged to return to Malta, landing at midday. A PR Spitfire and a Baltimore were then sent out, the latter's crew sighting the convoy 15 miles south of Zante Island. Twelve crews of 217 Squadron and three of 39 Squadron were available for the eight serviceable aircraft, the crews selected commencing take-off at 1830, led by Sqn.Ldr. Gibbs; two aircraft immediately developed faults and failed to start. A further pair were forced to turn back later with engine problems, leaving Gibbs with three 217 Squadron crews and five escorting Beaufighters.

The ships were spotted close to the Greek coast, protected by a crescent of escort vessels out to sea. A direct attack in the face of these was suicidal, so Gibbs led his small formation in over land, turning to attack from the east in the growing dusk. Gibbs and Flg.Off. Stevens selected the largest vessel — *Nino Bixio* — sailing in the centre of the column of three, while Sgt. Russell Mercer (AW240) and Sgt. Jim Hutcheson (L9893) went for that at the rear. The latter pair met a wall of AA fire and both aircraft were shot down with the loss of the crews, despite the Beaufighters strafing the destroyers and torpedo-boats in an attempt to keep down the Flak. Gibbs' aircraft (DD993) was hit in the tail but flew on and finally reached Malta, crash-landing at Luqa at 0100. Later two Beauforts and two Beaufighters were despatched to the area to search for signs of the missing crews, while next day Spitfires and Swordfish were detailed for similar duties, but nothing was sighted.

Nino Bixio had been hit and damaged and was forced to put into a Greek port for repairs. The other two freighters, the Italian *Monviso* and the German *Ankara*, eventually reached Benghazi — but not until 16 days after their original departure from Taranto.

Shortly before the two Beauforts returned, there had been action over the Island when Flt.Lt. Edwards, on patrol in Beaufighter X7748/C, intercepted two flare-dropping Ju88s in quick succession at 0030. He shot down Lt. Oscar Kasimir's M7+GK of KGr 806, which crashed in flames near Qawra Tower, St Paul's Bay. He then chased the second, which he reported dived into the sea whilst attempting to avoid his attacks; this was undoubtedly 3Z+BM of 4/KG 77 flown by Uffz. Luitpold Martin, which also failed to return.

Darkness also provided cover for a single Piaggio P108B four-engined bomber of 274ª Squadriglia to set out from Decimomannu, Sardinia, on the near-800 mile flight to Gibraltar. It is difficult to imagine what success was anticipated for the lone raider but events overtook Cap. Salvatore Balletta's aircraft (MM22601), which not only failed to reach its target but also failed to return. Following a search of the sea along the proposed route, an aircraft's tail wheel was located floating off the Balearics and was assumed to have come from the missing Piaggio; the cause of the loss was unknown.

Saturday, 4 July

Ten Spitfires of 249 Squadron were up to meet the early morning raid on the 4th — three "Z1007s and 14 fighters" being reported approaching the coast just before 0900. The attacking force actually comprised three S.84bis of 4° Gruppo, escorted by 22 MC202s of 51° Stormo led by Ten. Col. Remondino, while 17 more Macchis accompanied them as indirect support. Before take-off Sqn.Ldr. Lucas had briefed his pilots to go for the bombers, each section being instructed to tackle a given target:

> 'Red Section — my section — would take the bomber on the port side; Blue Section, led by Raoul Daddo-Langlois, the one to starboard. Yellow Section, with Jack Rae in the lead, would split into two pairs to cover Red and Blue Sections from the fighters as they went in, and then if they were still disengaged, go for the leading bomber.
>
> 'The squadron went straight through the fighter screen, unseen and unmolested, and closed fast with the bombers... In a few seconds all of us were diving straight for the ground with the fighter cover spreadeagled all over the sky above us. As we pulled out at deck level... three streaming balls of smoke and flames falling slowly from the sky to the south of the Island told the story. All three Cants (*sic*) had been destroyed.'

Lucas (BR324/R) claimed one shot down, another was credited to Rae (BR233/Q), the third falling jointly to Daddo-Langlois (BR170/B) and Flt.Sgt. Middlemiss (BR295/H); one Cant fell in flames near Takali, crashing into a field; the bodies of three crew members were found in the wreckage.

Two 14ª Squadriglia bombers — MM23998 flown by Ten. Raffaele Notari and Serg.Magg. Romolo Cristiani's MM24008 — the latter the aircraft which crashed near Takali, were actually lost; according to the returning crew, one had been shot down by AA fire, while it was believed a second fell in a collision with a Spitfire and crashed into the sea some miles from Marsascala. It was also reported — erroneously — that all members of the crews baled out of these stricken aircraft. The third Savoia was badly damaged by both AA fire and fighter attack but survived to limp back to Sicily, its gunners claiming one Spitfire shot down. Three more Spitfires were credited to the Macchis — one each by Ten. Col. Remondino, Cap. Ricardo Roveda and Mar. Ennio Tarantola, while five others were claimed damaged. Magg. Fanali's indirect escort Macchis then joined in and claimed a further four damaged. Although the Spitfires flown by Daddo-Langlois and Middlemiss were shot-up, both made a safe landing at Takali.

There were three survivors from the bombers including a gunner, Av.Sc. Marc Arduino Perneschi (from MM24008), rescued from the sea by HSL 128; the coxswain, Flt.Sgt. George Head recorded:

> 'This man, when found floating in his Mae West, appeared to be holding in his hand a white handkerchief. When rescued it was found that the "white material" was in fact the remains of his shattered hand, which had been washed clean of blood by the sea water. He had a resigned and pitiful look on his face which simply mirrored the horrors of war.'

No sooner had this raid disappeared from the radar screens than another was plotted. Four Spitfires of 603 Squadron escorting the rescue launch were warned to watch out for fighters, but three Bf109s — this time thought to be Macchis — caught Plt.Off. King unawares, inflicting some damage to his aircraft. The Messerschmitt pilots claimed two Spitfires shot down.

Shortly before 2000 five Z1007bis of 33° Gruppo BT serenely sailed over Malta at 20,000 feet, their substantial escort provided by 20 Macchis of 20° Gruppo led by Magg. Gino Callieri, and ten Re2001s of 2° Gruppo. Eight Spitfires of 249 Squadron were already up to meet this armada, Sqn.Ldr. Lucas again at their head, and were soon joined by a dozen more from 126 Squadron. These made for the bombers, two of which were hit and damaged by Sqn.Ldr. Winfield and Plt.Off. Graves; the latter believed his victim would probably fail to get back. Plt.Off. Jerry Smith wrote:

> 'I had a squirt at three Macchis, one of which was firing at a Spit. Was fired at several times, once by bombers when I raked across them with only one cannon firing. All our chaps got down safely, but only one bomber was probably shot down and one damaged. Pretty poor show, but fun while it lasted.'

Meanwhile, the 249 Squadron Spitfires had become engaged with the escort, Plt.Off. McElroy (BR111/M) claiming a Reggiane probably and Flt.Sgt. de l'Ara (BR254/C) another damaged. Sqn.Ldr. Lucas (BR324/R) had a narrow escape, noting in his logbook:

> 'Shot-up by a 109 and bounced by Reggianes while attacking five Cants!'

The two Cants attacked by 126 Squadron were badly damaged but succeeded in regaining their base; the bomber gunners claimed one Spitfire shot down and one damaged, while the Macchi pilots claimed two more — Serg. Spiridione Giudici and Mar. Pietro Bianchi sharing one and Serg.Magg. Francesco Pecchiari being credited with another — others claiming three probables and two damaged. Three more were credited to the Reggianes — Ten. Seganti, Mar. Jellici and Serg.Magg. Di Bert with one apiece. The Spitfires failed to keep the bombers from crossing the coast and bombs fell at Mosta and Takali, where Beaufighter X7676/J was destroyed.

Saturday, 5 July

The three raids on Malta on the 5th were carried out by small but heavily-escorted formations of Ju88s, the first arriving just after 0715. The bombers headed for Takali where a Spitfire was destroyed on the ground; a number of delayed action bombs were distributed around the airfield, subsequently obliging the pilots of the 20 Spitfires which were in the air to meet the raid, to land at Luqa on return. On the ground frenzied efforts were made to remove all possible equipment from the aircraft before the bombs exploded. In the air only Plt.Off. Halford (BP887) of 185 Squadron made a claim for a Junkers damaged, the escort of a dozen Bf109s and 29 Macchis keeping the others at bay; four of them were claimed damaged by the Italian pilots.

It was late afternoon before the next raid came in, a further trio of Ju88s and 15-20 Messerschmitts being reported. Twenty-two Spitfires of 185 and 603 Squadrons intercepted, Flt.Sgt. Yarra (BR387/W) leading four of the former, claiming a bomber shot down and two of the fighters damaged, one of which he believed probably failed to get back:

> 'Intercepted four Me's. Crawled up on them and fired like hell. Broke off

Plt.Off. Gray Stenborg, a New Zealander in 185 Squadron who claimed seven victories over Malta, for which he was awarded a DFC.

> and spotted nine (*sic*) Ju88s with Me 109 escort. Attacked rear Ju88 amd shot it down. Was chased back by Me 109s; shot up badly — crash-landed.'

His squadron colleague, Plt.Off. Stenborg (BR380), reported that he had shot down two Messerschmitts but the third member of the flight, Flt.Sgt. Haggas, had his own aircraft slightly damaged in the encounter. One further Bf109 was claimed damaged by Flg.Off. McLeod of 603 Squadron.

The third raid of the day comprised just two Ju88s and an escort of ten Bf109s, Takali again being attacked. 603 and 126 Squadrons had aircraft up, these becoming so heavily embroiled with the escort that the bombers escaped interception. Flt.Sgts. Schade and Evans each claimed fighters shot down, the latter claiming one more as probably destroyed. Probables were credited to Flt.Lt. Peck and Plt.Off. Mejor and three were damaged by Sgt. Shepherd, Plt.Off. Wallace — who thought his opponent was an MC200 — and 603 Squadron's Plt.Off. Dicks-Sherwood. None of the Spitfires were hit.

A pair of Junkers Ju87Rs of 102° Gruppo Tuffatori (previously B a'T). The nearest aircraft is MM7082. *(via N. Malizia)*

For the second night in succession Ju87s of 102° Gruppo Tuff raided targets on Malta, escorted to the coast in the dusk on this occasion by 13 MC202s of 51° Stormo. The Stukas were intercepted by patrolling Beaufighters, although all attacks were evaded in the darkening skies. The raid leader, Cap. Cenni, was pursued for some ten minutes before he was able to shake off the night fighter. Sometime later, at around 0400, a dozen more bombers were reported over the Island and one Beaufighter crew, Plt.Off. Reeves and Sgt. O'Leary (X7716), engaged in a very similar combat with a Ju88 to that recently reported by Flt.Lt. Edwards; the crew believed the bomber crashed into the sea whilst taking evasive action. This was not so however, as the aircraft attacked crashed in a field near Zammitello Palace, Mgarr; at least two crew members were found dead near the wreckage of Hpt. Leo Behlau's 3Z+FP of 6/KG 77.

It was possibly this action referred to in a report made by the captain of a

British Overseas Airways Whitley V, when he recalled his arrival in Malta's skies:

> 'It was about half-past two in the morning and black as pitch. The entire Island was covered by cloud down to 800 feet, and I knew that hills reached that height on the Island. We had arrived, of course, in the middle of a blitz. Searchlight beams shot up through the clouds, and I could hear the noise of the anti-aircraft guns in spite of the throb of my own engines. I flew round above cloud for two hours, waiting for instructions. I went in to land six times, and on the first five I was getting ready to touch down when I was hastily ordered up again because of obstructions on the airfield... All the time I kept thinking that we had fighters up over the Island, and that my aircraft could well be mistaken in the darkness for an enemy bomber. The worst moment came when I saw a black object dive at terrific speed just ahead of me, followed a split second later by another. I learned later that the first object was a German bomber, the second a Beaufighter which chased it right into the ground. However, we got down all right in the end.

Monday, 6 July

Double the normal number of Ju88s were sent over just after 0800 on the 6th, as the Luftwaffe stepped up the pace. An estimated 15-20 Bf109s from II/JG 53 comprised the escort. There was little contact between these and the dozen Spitfires of 603 Squadron sent to intercept, although Ofw. Rollwage engaged a Spitfire south-east of Gozo and claimed this shot down at 0837, while in return only Flt.Sgt. Colin Parkinson (UF-N) was able to make a claim:

> 'Our section didn't see the bombers but saw some fighters. An Me 109 swung in to attack a Spit but the Spit turned towards it. They then both went in opposite directions. I put my nose down and went after the 109 with everything pushed. Got to within 150 yards and gave a long squirt... saw strikes and black smoke pour out of the 109. He pulled up slightly and dived steeply. I kept on squirting till my cannon ran out of ammo... Another 109 bounced me but I turned up sun and he lost me... Another kite dived at me and I swung up sun again and did a steep turn on to his tail. It was a Spit.'

Bombs fell on Takali and a Spitfire was badly damaged in its pen. No sooner had the Spitfires landed than 11 more from 249 Squadron were off to meet the next raid — which comprised three Z1007bis of 9° Stormo with 14 Re2001s of 2° Gruppo as close support, and 24 MC202s of 20° Gruppo as indirect support, although three of these were obliged to return early. Yet more Macchis of 151ª Squadriglia, led by Cap. Doglio Niclot, flew a sweep in advance to clear the way for the bombers.

Flt.Lt. Lee led the Spitfires in a head-on attack on the Cants, causing them to jettison their bombs into the sea. Four pilots — Lee (BR379/V), Flg.Off. John Smith (BR295/H), Plt.Off. McLean (BR111/M) and Sgt. Beurling (BR323/S) — claimed hits as they swept past, although none were seriously damaged. 20° Gruppo then engaged the Spitfires, Ten. Francesco Montagnani claiming one shot down but Serg.Magg. Francesco Pecchiari (352ª Squadriglia) was shot down, almost certainly the victim of Beurling. The Canadian reported shooting one Macchi off Flg.Off. Smith's tail, which fell in flames, then engaged another which also tried to get on Smith's tail; this was chased down vertically from

20,000 feet to 5000 feet where it suddenly blew up. Flt.Lt. Lee claimed another — or possibly the same — shot down in flames; it would seem that one of these claims actually related to an Re2001 rather than an MC202.

When the Reggianes engaged the Spitfires, Mar. Olindo Simionato claimed one shot down but the unit lost Sottoten. Romano Pagliani (152ª Squadriglia) who was seen to bale out; it was reported that his parachute failed to open and he was assumed to be mortally wounded. His aircraft crashed on the Island near Zejtun. Five other Re2001s were damaged, including that flown by Ten. Col. Quarantotti, while the Macchis encountered five Spitfires apparently trying to cut off the escape route of the retreating bombers. Cap. Doglio Niclot claimed one shot down, which his No 2 (Mar. Tarantola) reported crashed north of Valetta — this would have been Pagliani's Reggiane he had seen crashing; another Spitfire was claimed by Ten. Michele Gallo, which he believed crashed near St Paul's Bay.

Sgt. Beurling's victories were confirmed by both Flt.Lt. Lee and Plt.Off. Yates, the latter's aircraft (BR246/J) being shot-up, as was that flown by Beurling. In the early afternoon Beurling was called to fly as escort for HSL 128 which went out to pick up survivors and he reported that the two pilots he had shot down earlier were both recovered, but:

> 'One died that night in hospital, badly burned. The other had been hit in the leg by a cannon shell and in the shoulders and arms with machine-gun bullets. The doc had to amputate the leg. The pilot lived.'

However, available records imply that only one of the Italian pilots was picked up from the sea, about three miles out from Kalafrana, by HSL 128; possibly another craft picked up the other or the pilot actually came down on land, as seems more likely in Pagliani's case.

The mid-afternoon raid by five Ju88s and escort, directed at Hal Far and Safi, was challenged by no less than 27 Spitfires from 185 and 603 Squadrons. Aircraft from the latter unit dived onto the bombers, only to be bounced by the escort, but were able to claim two Ju88s shot down by Plt.Offs. Glen and Levy-Despas; one of these was almost certainly M7+ML of KGr 806, flown by Ofw. Peter Wilbertz, who was killed. On interrogation, one member of his crew declared that the aircraft had been hit in the port side and engine by a Spitfire when at 15,000 feet, and had burst into flames; he and two others had managed to bale out. The other aircraft, Oblt. Walter Pruger's 7T+KK of KüFlGr 606, came down in the sea off the Sicilian coast; only the injured W/T operator, Uffz. Walter Pfeifer, was rescued.

Sgt. Irwin and Flt.Lt. Douglas each claimed one of the escorting fighters damaged, although the latter's aircraft was shot-up and crash-landed, while Flt.Lt. Slade's Spitfire was also damaged. 185 Squadron pilots enjoyed greater success, Flt.Sgt. Dodd (BR303) being credited with a Bf109; his subsequent Combat Report read:

> 'Two-second burst at 2000 feet over Delimara — saw two flashes on port wing; second attack and flashes on tail — big flash and lots of smoke — aircraft went down.'

Another fighter was claimed probably destroyed by Plt.Off. Charney (BR380), while Flt.Sgt. 'Shorty' Reid (BR317) also submitted a claim for a probable; four others were claimed damaged by newly-promoted Flt.Lt. Halford in BR387 (two), Plt.Off. Sherlock (BR166) and Sgt. Mahar (BR292). Sgt. Drew (BR119) was credited with a Ju88 shot down, while Sqn.Ldr. New (BR321) also attacked the bombers, believing he had probably destroyed one, and damaged a second; two others were damaged by Halford, and jointly by Reid and Flt.Sgt. Andrews (AB500). The squadron's American pilot, Sgt. Ed. 'Alabama' Moye, was drowned after his Spitfire (BP979) was shot down into the sea. Recalled John Sherlock:

> 'He was my No 2 when we intercepted 30+ Me 109s and six Ju88s. I fired at three yellow-nosed Me 109s at which time I found my No 2 was missing. I did not see him shot down.'

At 1840 a further raid was shown to be approaching, a mass of fighters — 39 MC202s from 155° and 20° Gruppo — escorting four Z1007s of 9° Stormo. These were engaged by 11 Spitfires of 126 Squadron and six from 603 Squadron, Sqn.Ldr. Lord Douglas-Hamilton at their head. Two Australians of the former unit, Plt.Off. Bisley and Flg.Off. Don Smith, attacked the same bomber and were joined by 2/Lt. Swales of 603; Smith, flying BP873, noted:

> 'Flying No 2 to Bisley. Attacked 5 Cants through fighter screen. We both fired at same machine. Confirmed by "Y" Service'.

A second bomber was credited to Sqn.Ldr. Winfield as probably destroyed, while Flt.Sgt. Farquharson damaged another. Sqn.Ldr. Lord Douglas-Hamilton and Plt.Off. Glen also jointly damaged a bomber. Two of the Z1007bis were badly hit and on return to Sicily one ditched in the sea off Cape Passero, and the other landed on fire between Cape Religione and San Pietro, near Pozzallo. The 'Y' Service reported that the pilot of this aircraft had been killed and the observer had flown it back to crash-land.

Meanwhile the fighters had clashed, Plt.Off. Levy-Despas shooting down Sottoten. Adolfo Giovannini's 353ª Squadriglia Macchi into the sea and claiming hits on a second, while Cap. Riccardo Spagnolini was wounded in the leg. This was probably as a result of an attack by Sqn.Ldr. Lord Douglas-Hamilton or Flt.Lt. Bailey, who each claimed a probable; another was believed damaged by Flt.Lt. Douglas, whilst Flg.Off. McLeod's Spitfire (BR845) was hit in return and was further damaged when landing. Ten. Ettore Malosso claimed one Spitfire shot down and others claimed four probables and hits on 15 more!

The final raid of this hectic day occurred at 2030 when three Ju88s of II/KG 77 swept in at low level to bomb Takali, escorted by Bf109s of II/JG 53 and I/JG 77, the latter unit making its first sorties over the Island. Five of 603 Squadron were involved, as were others from 249 and 185 Squadrons, a total of 20 Spitfires taking off. Sqn.Ldr. Lord Douglas-Hamilton led the 603 Squadron flight after the bombers, his guns jamming after a few rounds had been fired; nonetheless, all three bombers were claimed shot down, one by Plt.Off. Glen, another by 2/Lt. Swales and the third shared by Plt.Off. Levy-Despas and Sgt. Irwin; two bombers actually failed to return. Lt. Reinhold Boger's 3Z+JN of 5 Staffel fell into the sea just off Grand Harbour — three survivors later being rescued from their dinghy by HSL 128, two of whom had suffered burns. The other aircraft, of 4 Staffel, ditched in the sea just off the Sicilian coast; none of the crew were hurt.

As if losing two-thirds of its attacking force was not bad enough, this costly raid was rendered even worse when Fw. Toni Engels of I/JG 77 was also shot down into the sea. Claims were submitted for three Messerschmitts, one each by

Plt.Off. Glen (his third claim of the day) and Flt.Sgt. Dodd (BR303) — his second of the day — but it would seem that Engels actually fell victim to Sgt. Beurling, unless the other two were also firing on the same aircraft. Beurling recalled:

'... two Me's dropped on me, but I did a quick wing-over and got onto one's tail. He saw me coming and tried to climb away. I figured he must be about 800 yards away from me when I got him in the sights and let go at him. It was a full deflection shot, and I had to make plenty of allowance for cannon-drop. I gave him a three-second burst, smack on his starboard flank, and got him in the glycol tank. He started to stream the stuff, leaving a long white trail of smoke... I followed my man down to sea level, where he burst into flames and went in the drink.'

Strikes were claimed on two more Bf109s by Sgts. Mahar (BR292) and Drew (BR119), while two Spitfires were damaged in the clash; Ofw. Rollwage of II/JG 53 claimed one shot down north-east of Valetta for his second victory of the day. It would seem other Luftwaffe pilots submitted a number of claims, as OKW assessed the day's Axis victories as 16, of which the Italian units were apparently credited with only five.

During the day the second gruppo of 5° Stormo Tuff arrived at Gerbini, led by the Stormo commander Ten. Col. Guido Nobili. Unlike 102° Gruppo however, 101° Gruppo (208ª and 238ª Squadriglia) was equipped with Fiat CR42 fighter-bomber biplanes. The unit did not, in the event, operate over Malta. After a few shipping escort sorties over Africa-bound convoys, it moved on to North Africa.

Tuesday, 7 July

Another very violent day in retrospect, Tuesday began with a particularly well-recorded raid as a dozen Ju88s headed for Luqa, escorted by 24 Bf109s and 30 MC202s (20 from 20° Gruppo and ten from 155° Gruppo CT). Eleven Spitfires from 249 Squadron and six from 185 Squadron were scrambled to intercept at 0730 and a swirling dogfight commenced, the Messerschmitts and Macchis reacting strongly. Flt.Lt Daddo-Langlois (BR565/U) of 249 Squadron recorded:

'Three of us went for bombers but 109s prevented us getting them. Shot up again. Bob (*Middlemiss*) baled out OK.'

Flt.Sgt. Jack Rae (BR323/S) added:

'... jumped Blue Section from all angles. F/Sgt. Middlemiss shot down — OK, F/Sgt. Parks hit by Flak — OK.'

Sqn.Ldr. Lucas (BR378/V) noted:

'Shaky do with 88s and 109s. Paul and Lint got 109s, Mac a Macchi.'

It was Plt.Off. Paul Brennan's last operational flight of his tour, flying AB562/X-R:

'Scramble. I intercepted six Ju88s with heavy fighter escort. Head-on attack on Ju88. No result observed. Attacked and shot Me 109 down into sea. Damaged another.'

Brennan's victim, his 10th, was seen to go down into the sea in a vicious spiral, a second was claimed by Plt.Off. Linton (BR324/K) and a third by Sgt. Mahar

(BR292) of 185 Squadron, while Flt.Sgt. Dodd (AB469) damaged another; a Macchi was claimed by Plt.Off. McElroy (BR301/UF-S), and Flt.Sgt. Tommy Parks (BR165/Y) damaged a Ju88 but his aircraft was hit by AA fire, which blew its tail off and he baled out. He came down on land near Zebbug with nothing worse than a bruised eye. Two other Spitfires were also shot down. Flt.Sgt. Bob Middlemiss sustained slight injuries when he baled out of BR251/E into the sea, but was seen to scramble into his dinghy, while Flt.Sgt. Dave Ferraby (AB500) baled out to come down near Zebbug also, his Spitfire crashing near Qormi; he recalled:

> 'The first two Spits to take off left a dust cloud right down the track... I took off by myself as close to the dust cloud as I could... My No 2 failed to take off due to dust and I hoped I would be able to join up with some other Spits, but as was often the case, I didn't see a plane in the sky and climbed to 10,000 feet by myself. I can't have kept a good enough look out, because soon there was a loud bang and flames belted into the right side of the cockpit.
>
> 'The hood was open and I pulled the harness release handle and shot half out of the cockpit. I have very long thighs and my knees jammed on the rim of the windscreen. So I had to pull myself back in and straighten my legs. The parachute had caught on the head pad, which stuck out a few inches behind ones head. The plane was going down at about 450 with engine still on — forgot to shut throttle and there was no control from stick. Anyway, got out in the end and pulled rip cord.
>
> 'I much enjoyed floating down and saw a Spit circling me. Turned out it was Dodd, a good pal. Just missed a 10′ wall in a village; 'chute went in over the wall and I landed in a lane. I suppose all the women who gathered round didn't know if I was English or Jerry, but they kept touching my bleeding knees for some reason; burns were just down my right leg from knee down. I'd been flying in shorts and gym shoes!

Luftwaffe claims included one Spitfire by Ofw. Rollwage of II/JG 53 north-east of Zonqor Point at 0747, while Cap. Doglio Niclot and Mar. Tarantola of 51° Stormo CT claimed another jointly, seeing the pilot bale out as the Spitfire went down to crash east of Valetta. Other Italian pilots claimed two probables and two damaged but two MC202s were badly damaged.

Spitfires from 249 Squadron were soon out searching for the missing Middlemiss, covering the sea south and west of the Island; he was located by Plt.Off. Brennan and Sgt. de l'Ara to the east, and was soon on his way back to the Island in the care of HSL 128.

The next raid proved just as costly for the defenders, when Spitfires from 126 and 249 Squadrons clashed with 18 Messerschmitts. Sgt. De Nancrede (BP990/4-0) of the latter unit and Sgt. K.H. Davey (in 126 Squadron's BR566) were both shot down into the sea, from where they were picked up by the hard-working crew of HSL 128. De Nancrede had been attacking a Junkers from below and had seen strikes on its belly and wing roots when the German gunner replied with an accurate burst, hitting his engine. Two other Spitfires were hit and were both obliged to crash-land on return, Plt.Off. Wallace (BR115) sustaining slight wounds while Plt.Off. Hetherington (BR347/Z) escaped unscathed, his aircraft also having been hit by return fire from the Ju88 he was attacking (which he claimed badly damaged).

Left: Plt.Off. 'Sandy' McHan of 126 Squadron was shot down on 3 July 1942, falling victim to a Bf109F, and baling out over Malta. He recovered consciousness to find himself in hospital next to a German airman. *(Mrs Teresa McHan)*. **Right:** Plt.Off. 'Slim' Yarra of 185 Squadron, seen here in his Spitfire 'Ned IV after claiming his 12th victory over Malta on 11 July 1942. *(Authors' Collection)*

On this occasion no less than five Luftwaffe fighters were believed to have fallen to the Spitfires but available records indicate only an aircraft of 4/JG 53 sustaining any serious damage, the pilot of which returned safely to base. Flt.Sgt. Schade claimed two, while Plt.Off. Hicks and Plt.Off. Mejor, who also damaged a Ju88, were credited with one apiece; Flt.Sgt. Rae (BR323/S) reported his victim fell in a head-on attack, the pilot baling out. Plt.Off. Rip Jones reported strikes on one more and a bomber was damaged by Sgt. Richardson.

Yet two more Spitfires fell in the last raid of the day, this time both pilots losing their lives. Twenty-two Spitfires were ordered off to meet five Z1007bis of 9° Stormo as they headed for Luqa, many escorting fighters being reported. There were 35 Macchis, of which 23 were from 155° Gruppo and 12 from 20° Gruppo, and a dozen Re2001s. Possibly Messerschmitts were also involved as indirect support. Some of the Spitfires were able to penetrate the fighter screen to reach the bombers, Flt.Sgt. MacNamara of 185 Squadron claiming two damaged and Plt.Off. Miller of 126 Squadron another, while other sections had been ordered to engage the fighters, as did Flt.Sgt. Yarra (BR387/W):

> 'Intercepted five SM 84s (*sic*) with fighter escort. I took my section down and engaged the fighters — odds six to one. Destroyed two Re2001s. Haggas and Terry both shot down. I was shot up by 109s and had my wing panels shot away. Crash-landed on aerodrome.'

Sgt. Len Reid (AB264) was one of Yarra's section, and noted:

> 'Intercepted 5 SM 84s together with large fighter escort. F/Sgt. Yarra, DFM, F/Sgt. Terry, F/Sgt. Haggas and I engaged the fighters to let our other section get at the bombers; unfortunately F/Sgt. Haggas and F/Sgt. Terry were shot down and killed. Jack (Yarra) got two.'

Flt.Sgt. Peter Terry's Spitfire (BR317) crashed on land killing the pilot, while Flt.Sgt. Haydn Haggas died when BR283 fell into the sea. HSL 128 was sent out once again to look for the missing pilot but all that was found were the mutilated remains of an airman about three miles out from Dingli; some personal belongings were retrieved for identification purposes, then the remains were buried at sea. The Macchi flown by Ten. Fabrizio Cherubini of 353ª Squadriglia also crashed into the sea, obviously one of Yarra's victims, while other pilots claimed five Spitfires badly damaged; one was claimed shot down by Reggiane pilot Mar. Simionato and Messerschmitt pilot may also have claimed, for OKW reported nine Luftwaffe victories during the day's fighting.

One of the Cants — MM23243 flown by Ten. Francesco Antonelli — was hit by AA fire and started to stream smoke before falling out of formation, as recounted by 603 Squadron's Colin Parkinson:

> 'The "Big Five" came over this afternoon. Ack-Ack got one down; two of the crew baled out but shrapnel from the flak blew their 'chutes to pieces. They had to be dug out of a churchyard. Halfway down the bomber blew up. Two more of the crew came out and their 'chutes didn't open.'

The main wreckage crashed onto a house at Siggiewi where an occupant was injured. There were no survivors from the bomber.

There was a celebration in the Takali Mess that evening when 185 Squadron's successful and popular flight commander, Flt.Lt. Ron West was advised of the award of the DFC, a Bar to the decoration rapidly following, as recalled by Plt.Off. Johnny Sherlock:

> 'Ron had been recommended for the DFC, this recommendation going through the Middle East Command, which seemed very slow with all matters dealing with Malta. While waiting for the award to be gazetted, Ron received an immediate award of the Bar. Ron's sense of humour took over and he sewed the small rosette under his wings. He was checked one day by the AOC, who icily demanded what that object was under his wings. Ron, who could keep a very straight face and at the same time look very innocent, stood to attention and advised him that it was a Bar to a DFC. Asked why he was not wearing the ribbon to the DFC, Ron advised him, and quite truthfully, that he had not yet received the DFC but he already had the citation for the Bar. The DFC citation arrived very shortly after what undoubtedly was a very hostile 'phone call from the AOC.'

Shortly after 2215 three bombers were plotted coming in over Malta and two Beaufighters were sent to investigate. Sgt. Oxby, the radar operator in Flg.Off. Shipard's X7642/G soon found some 'trade' and directed his pilot on to Uffz. Walter Mellein's Ju88 of KGr 806. A short burst from the Australian pilot's cannons sent M7+MH blazing into the sea two miles offshore from Mgarr; four members of the crew were seen to bale out but only the wounded W/T operator, Uffz. Herbert Queisser, was picked up by HSL 128 — the craft's 43rd rescue.

Two Albacores and a Swordfish were despatched on a now-rare offensive sortie, the crews briefed to attack shipping in the Straits of Messina where two ammunition ships were known due to arrive. They were to rendezvous with an ASV Wellington which, in theory, was to illuminate the targets while one aircraft (that flown by Lt. Whitfield) was to create a diversion to draw away attention from the others, which were then to attack with torpedoes. In the event, poor visibility frustrated any possible sightings, while intense AA, supported by searchlights, were experienced; one Albacore was shot in the neighbourhood of San Ranieri, Lt. Smith and his observer, Sub Lt. David Walker, scrambling into their dinghy to be rescued at dawn by Italian fishermen. The Swordfish (V4587) was flown by Sub Lt. Reg Elliott, who recalled:

> 'We came into the Straits from the northern end and at about 150 feet. As flak was supposed to be lighter from the Italian mainland we kept nearer to that side. The Albacore (Lt. Smith's aircraft) was just ahead and visible to me, when intense tracer fire enveloped us from the shore. I had no choice but to try and duck under it. Being so low already I hit the sea and fortunately pulled the Swordfish out without damage to the prop. Jess (Sub Lt. Eddie Jess, the observer) complained of getting wet in the back but when we went back to the north end of the Straits, he leant over the side with his torch and could see that our fish was still on but our starboard oleo was up into the wing. We went back in (well over to the Sicilian side this time) and into the harbour. We had flak from the mole and smoke made things tricky, but we could find no ships. As torpedoes were so precious I brought mine back, and then had the job of landing back at Hal Far with its goose-neck flare runway, on my one wheel. It worked without further damage.'

Rather than return with his bomb load intact, the Wellington pilot unloaded his seven 500 pounders in a stick on what appeared to be a warehouse or factory, south-west of Messina harbour; a large fire was observed by the crew as the aircraft departed the scene.

Wednesday, 8 July

Wednesday was to prove another costly day for the defenders with four more Spitfires lost and three pilots killed. The day began with an early morning raid (0730-0800) by seven Ju88s on Luqa, the bombers escorted by Bf109s of I/JG 77 and 21 MC202s of 20° Gruppo. This formation was intercepted by Spitfires from three squadrons, eight from 126 Squadron being scrambled on the approach of the raiders at 0710 to assist a standing patrol of eight from 603 Squadron, while eight more from 249 Squadron were sent off after the attack had commenced.

Flt.Lt. Lester Sanders led his 603 Squadron flight after the bombers but they had to penetrate the fighter screen first. As they dived on to the formation, Sanders and his No 2 (Plt.Off. King) encountered a Messerschmitt, at which both pilots fired, reporting strikes before it dived away. Then, as the bombers sped northwards over Gozo, a lone Ju88 was seen and attacked by Sanders who observed strikes on its fuselage; however, as he closed in, the German rear gunner achieved a direct hit on the Spitfire's armoured windscreen, forcing him to break away.

By now the Spitfires were at sea level and as they turned sharply away from the fleeing bomber, Plt.Off. Neville King's wingtip dipped into the sea and BR198 crashed; the 29 year-old Irishman, a former London policeman, went

Left: Flt.Lt. Lester Sanders of 603 Squadron was shot down by Lt. Heinz-Edgar Berres on 8 July 1942, ditching Spitfire BR108 in Marsalforn Bay, Gozo. *(NWMA)*. **Right:** Lt. Heinz-Edgar Berres, Adjutant of I/JG 77, for whom Spitfire BR108 was his 8th victory and first over Malta.

down with his aircraft.

Two Bf109s of I/JG 77 now latched onto Flt. Sanders' Spitfire and chased him all around Gozo, Lt. Heinz-Edgar Berres gaining a number of telling strikes. With his aircraft streaming glycol, and finding himself too low to bale out, Sanders decided that rather than put the Spitfire down in one of the small stone-walled fields and risk serious injury, it would be wiser to ditch in picturesque Marsalforn Bay, coming down about 100 yards offshore. As BR108 smashed into the sea, Sanders hit his face on the gunsight and collected a black eye but this was the only injury he sustained, and he was able to scramble out before the aircraft sank (see Appendix VIII). The victorious Messerschmitts circled overhead but did not shoot at him.

Help was soon to hand. Four members of the Debono family — Frank, Manuel, Anton and William — had just returned to Marsalforn Bay from an early morning fishing trip for mackerel in their small boat, S132, and were by the quay on the side of the bay when they spotted the Spitfire coming towards them, flying low down in the valley. Within minutes of the ditching, Frank and Anton rowed out and picked up the severely-shaken pilot.

When LAC Metcalf heard the news, he wrote in his diary:

> 'In today's first raid P/O King and F/L Sanders were shot down. King failed to bale out. I nearly cried when I knew because he's the greatest guy I've met yet and that's saying a lot.'

Meanwhile, other pilots of the flight had also closed with the bombers, two being claimed damaged by Plt.Off. Glazebrook, another by Plt.Off. Newman, while one of the escort was similarly claimed damaged by Flg.Off. Mitchell; Flt.Sgt. Ballantyne gained strikes on another Messerschmitt and also admitted firing at a Spitfire, fortunately without hitting it. One of the squadron's Australians, Sgt. F.R. Johnson, was shot-up and wounded in the left arm and leg but succeeded in force-landing BR183 back at Takali. His fellow countryman, Colin Parkinson, who was not flying on this occasion, witnessed some of the fight, and noted:

> 'Was awakened by the sound of gunfire and planes dive-bombing. Went up on the roof and saw Me109 fighters all over the place as low as 2000 feet in some cases. Saw four 109s pass overhead down the sun and dive on four Spits who were flying up sun. The Spits did nothing until the 109s opened fire and one Spit was hit and dived straight for the deck. The other Spits mixed it. Johnson, an Australian, was the pilot shot down. He's OK. The gun panels were shot off, tyres flat, one aileron u/s, flaps u/s, glycol leak. He was wounded in the arm and leg but made a perfect forced landing with wheels down.'

Amongst the 126 Squadron pilots, Flg.Off. Don Smith (BR122) had led a section of three to engage four Bf109s which were spotted above them at 24,000 feet. Smith claimed one probably shot down and this was later confirmed as destroyed, while Sgt. Bush also claimed one shot down. Plt.Off. Jerry Smith saw seven Ju88s but his propeller was giving trouble, and he glided through these and a number of escorting Messerschmitts to force-land at Luqa.

249 Squadron enjoyed more success during this engagement as they too attempted to engage the bombers, only to become entangled with the escort. A Bf109 passed closely above Plt.Off. Hesselyn's aircraft (AB562/X-R) — he pulled up, fired, and saw the Messerschmitt turn on its back and go straight into the sea. Sgt. Beurling (BR128/3-W) got his sights on another and fired a two-second burst; black smoke poured out and he too reported that it went into the sea three miles south of Gozo — confirmed by two Hal Far pilots. Meanwhile, Flt.Sgt. Williams (BR111/M) damaged another while Sgt. Baxter belly-landed his Spitfire (BR295/H) at Takali, although on this occasion not due to combat damage but to lack of fuel.

Mar. Maurizio Iannucci of 352ª Squadriglia claimed one Spitfire shot down during this combat, others claiming one probable and six damaged. Ten. Manlio Biccolini of 378ª Squadriglia was hit and wounded in the neck and leg, his Macchi damaged by a 20mm shell and several machine gun bullets in the tail and wings.

The Luftwaffe was back just after midday, a total of 23 Spitfires intercepting seven Ju88s of II/KG 77 and a dozen escorting II/JG 53 Messerschmitts; the bombers again attacked Luqa where a Beaufort was damaged on the ground. 249 Squadron was in the forefront and broke through the escort to reach the bombers, Plt.Off. Hesselyn (AB562/X-R) gaining strikes on one — causing an engine to catch fire — which he claimed shot down, his 12th and last victory whilst flying over Malta; Flt.Sgt. Williams (BR111/M) reported damaging another, which turned for home. He kept after it, attacking until it crashed in flames off Filfla. One of these was undoubtedly 3Z+GR flown by Oblt. Erich Behr, the Staffelkapitän of 7 Staffel, who was reported lost with his crew. A third bomber was damaged by Plt.Off. Berkeley-Hill (BR324/R), while another was fired at by Sgt. Beurling (BR128/3-W) who reported seeing flames appear from its starboard engine, before being attacked by five Bf109s. He claimed strikes on one which dived vertically for Filfla island with its engine apparently on fire, and was credited with its probable destruction.

Flg.Off. John Smith and Sgt. Johnny Gilbert were also attacking the bombers when a number of Bf109s dived on them. Smith's Spitfire (BR233/Q) caught fire and was then hit by two more Messerschmitts before he could bale out, and blew up. The same fighters then attacked Gilbert's aircraft (BR227/T), which turned on its back and went into the sea off Wied iz-Zurrieq. Both pilots were killed. Beurling was successful in driving off other Bf109s when they attempted to attack Williams, as the latter pursued another Ju88 (which he claimed damaged), but others badly damaged Flt.Sgt. Butler's aircraft; Plt.Off. McLean (BR223/S) damaged one of the Messerschmitts in return.

One of the successful German pilots was again Ofw. Rollwage, who claimed a Spitfire shot down south of Birzebbuga at 1232, the Luftwaffe claiming eight of the 11 Axis victories recorded on this date; the identities of the other claimants are not known.

The last raid of the day was a smaller affair, three Ju88s and 15 Bf109s attacking Luqa and Hal Far at 1940. Sixteen Spitfires were sent up including six from 185 Squadron, whose Flt.Sgt. Dodd reported meeting a Bf109 at 20,000 feet near Dingli. Opening fire, he closed to 50 yards then lost sight of it in the sun; two airmen on the ground reported seeing a Bf109 at about this time streaming glycol and heading for St Paul's Bay, and on the strength of this Dodd was awarded a 'confirmed' victory. Another of the unit's pilots, Flt.Sgt. Yarra, attacked a Ju88 but received two bullets through a propeller blade of his aircraft (BR387/W). AA gunners made one of their now rare claims during this raid, reporting that a Bf109 fell into the sea as a result of their shooting.

Thursday, 9 July

Malta entertained some unusual visitors during the early morning hours of the 9th, when four Halifax bombers from 227 Squadron in Egypt landed at Luqa. Three of the big aircraft had suffered engine failures whilst attempting to climb at full load on the way to attack Tunis. They would return to Egypt within 24 hours.

Shortly before 0900 six Ju88s swept in at low level and carried out a raid on Takali, while the strong escort kept the defenders at bay. Of the 24 Spitfires up, only two pilots managed to engage the bombers. Flt.Sgt. Webster (603) and Sgt. Richardson (126) each claimed damage, although AA gunners did succeed in shooting down Uffz. Herbert Schlitt's 3Z+ET of 9/KG 77 which crashed in flames in Callus Street, Mosta with the loss of all the crew; although several houses were demolished in the crash, there were no civilian casualties.

The pattern of raids differed little to that of previous days — an early morning raid, followed by another around midday and a third during the evening. In fact, the 'midday' raid arrived nearer 1300 when seven Ju88s raided Luqa and the Safi dispersal area, where a Wellington and a Beaufort were destroyed, two more of the latter sustaining damage. Escorting Macchis from 20° Gruppo and Bf109s of I/JG 77 clashed with Spitfires of 126, 249 and 603 Squadrons, Lt. Armin Köhler claiming one Spitfire south-east of Marsaxlokk for his 12th victory, while the Macchis claimed three more badly damaged.

For 126 Squadron Plt.Off. Tilley claimed a Bf109 shot down, and Flt.Sgt. Evans an MC202. This was probably the aircraft of Ten. Francesco Montagnani of 352[a] Squadriglia, who radioed his companions that his aircraft had been hit, and he was attempting to fly back to Sicily when his engine seized; although he was seen to bale out into the sea he was not found. Plt.Off. John Hicks' Spitfire (BR355) of 126 Squadron was shot down and the pilot was killed. 603 Squadron also suffered a loss when their successful 20 year-old French pilot, Plt.Off. Guy Andre Levy-Despas (alias Guy Carlet) was last seen diving after a Ju88 and was killed when BP957 was shot down; he would be posthumously awarded the Legion d'Honneur and the Croix de Guerre. In return, Plt.Off. Northcott damaged a Bf109 and one of the bombers was claimed shot down by two of the 249 Squadron pilots, Plt.Off. McElroy (BR301/UF-S) and Flt.Sgt. Rae (BR323/S), the New Zealander also claiming a Macchi as probably destroyed; another Ju88 was reported damaged by Plt.Off. Paradis (BR128/3-W) whose own aircraft was then attacked and damaged by a Bf109.

Takali was the target for six Ju88s during the evening raid, which approached the coast shortly before 2000 escorted by Bf109s of both II/JG 53 and I/JG 77. Eleven Spitfires of 126 Squadron were first off at 1935, followed five minutes later by eight from 185 Squadron and at 1940 by eight of 249 Squadron; finally at 2000 eight of 603 Squadron were ordered off, making a total of 35 Spitfires to challenge the raiders.

Four of the bombers were claimed shot down; 126 Squadron's Plt.Offs. Tilley and Mejor were credited with one apiece, as was Flt.Lt. Mitchell of 603 Squadron, while the fourth was awarded to AA gunners. Flg.Off. McLeod of 603 claimed the probable destruction of another despite having only one cannon operating, and having been engaged by a fighter which shot away his flaps. Yet another was damaged by the combined fire of four pilots of 126 Squadron — Flt.Lt. Rowe, Plt.Offs. Graves and Miller, and Sgt. Bill Marshall. Two bombers were reported to have crashed into the sea about two miles off Ghar Lapsi, and at least one aircraft from 4/KG 77, 3Z+AM flown by Lt. Friedrich Kleimeier, failed to return while a second from the same unit crash-landed at Comiso.

Although available German records suggest that no Messerschmitts were actually shot down, no fewer than five were claimed — two each by Flt.Sgt. Schade and 185 Squadron's Plt.Off. Stenborg (BR109), the fifth by Flt.Sgt. Parkinson (X-S), who recorded:

> '. . . took off and climbed into the sun over Gozo. Reached about 11,000 feet, turned south-east down sun and reached Malta coast in time to see Ack-Ack bursts over the centre of the Island. Dicks-Sherwood leading. It was our job to prang the bombers. As we drew level with the coastline in a steep dive, I saw a Ju88 underneath with black smoke pouring out of the centre of the fuselage. I rolled on my back and dived after it. At a range of about ten yards I opened fire. The 88 tried to gain height but burst into flames and finally disintegrated. My machine flew right through the falling wreckage. The 88 was a definite goner before I attacked it.
>
> 'I broke away up sun and saw an Me109 weaving in and out among a number of Spits. It was about to give one of them a burst but I got a burst in instead. The 109 continued weaving on its way westward unmolested. I was close behind. It evidently saw me and started to dive. I gave a long squirt and followed it down through light cloud to about 700 feet above the water. The Me continued diving and crashed straight in. I stooged about for another quarter of an hour and then came down to pancake.'

Two more Bf109s were claimed damaged by Flt.Sgt. Evans (126 Squadron) and Plt.Off. Frank Jones (249 Squadron), but 603 Squadron's Flt.Sgt. Jim Ballantyne was shot down for the second time in just over a week, his aircraft (BR364) falling into the sea; the Canadian again successfully baled out and was picked up this time by HSL 128. At least two Spitfires were claimed shot down during this action, one by Lt. Berres of I/JG 77 at 2020, followed by another five minutes later by Ofw. Rollwage, the latter south-west of Dingli.

Friday, 10 July

Nineteen MC202s of 20° Gruppo and six of 155° Gruppo CT, together with Bf109s from JG 53, provided cover for 14 Ju88s raiding Takali on the 10th. Spitfires first engaged when the raiders were still some 20 miles off Malta, then the fighters clashed south of Rabat; Cap. Doglio Niclot and his No 2, Mar. Tarantola, jointly claimed one and Sottoten. Pietro Menaldi another. It would seem their initial opponents were seven Spitfires of 249 Squadron, Plt.Off. Lattimer (BR128/3-W) claiming an MC202 shot down and a Bf109 damaged, while Sgt. Beurling (BR323/S) reported hitting a Messerschmitt "in the belly"; apparently the burst hit the pilot as the aircraft reportedly dived straight into the sea. This was possibly Lt. Hans-Jürgen Frödien of Stab/JG 53, who was reported missing in '< 2' near Rabat, his demise witnessed by 126 Squadron's Plt.Off. Jerry Smith:

> 'Stood on porch watching raid and we saw a long spiral at about 2000 feet — a 109 had been shot up. Pilot baled out. The aircraft came streaking down and crashed straight into rock about 300 yards from us. We could see the markings clearly. Got tail wheel as souvenir.'

Another of 51° Stormo CT's successful Macchi pilots, Mar. Ennio Tarantola, points to the rudder of his MC202 on which he identified his seven claims with small paintings of the aircraft types involved. Sitting on the fuselage of MM9066 '2' of 151[a] Squadriglia, 20° Gruppo, is his mechanic, Mar.Mot. Marcello Boni; they are seen on Gela airfield. *(Achille Vigna via N. Malizia)*

During this combat Mar. Tarantola's Macchi was also badly damaged in the fuselage and fuel tank, but the Italian pilot was able to safely reach base. Seven more Spitfires from 603 Squadron had by now arrived to support those of 249 Squadron, Flt.Sgt. Parkinson (X-S) reporting:

> 'Was scrambled nearly too late. Climbed to about 7000 feet and came round

south of Gozo to the Malta coast and met the Ju's coming out, about 12 of them. Attacked an 88 from beam and astern and strikes on the fuselage, wings and wing roots. Cannons packed up so came home and claimed a damaged.'

Stoppages caused by the faulty American 20mm ammunition being used by the Spitfires at this time were still occurring. One of the Junkers was claimed by Plt.Off. Dicks-Sherwood, and a Bf109 probable by Sgt. Bush; the attacks were then taken up by eight pilots of 126 Squadron as the bombers fled northwards, another being claimed by Flg.Off. Don Smith (BR366):

> 'Made head-on attacks on Ju88 at 1000 feet north-east of Gozo. Hit starboard engine and cockpit. E/A turned back with bombs on. Four Me's escorting broken up. One stayed with the bomber. Chased e/a 35 miles before he "packed-up". Claim Ju88 destroyed, 109 damaged. Reflector sight u/s.'

Cap. Doglio Niclot, leading the 20° Gruppo Macchis, reported meeting four more Spitfires near Gozo. He claimed one shot down, another being shared by Ten. Paolo di Porcia Guacella Brugnera, Mar. Iannucci and Sottoten. Dante Dose, the latter then being shot down, possibly by Smith's flight leader, Flt.Lt. Slade, who claimed a 'Messerschmitt'. None of the Spitfires were lost.

At 1115 eight Spitfires of 126 Squadron, six of 249 Squadron and four from 603 Squadron were scrambled to meet the next raid, comprising six Ju88s with an escort of Bf109s (a Staffel of I/JG 77) and a small number of MC202s. Three pilots of 378ª Squadriglia — Ten. Giovanni Ambrosio, Serg.Magg. Francesco Visentini and Serg.Magg. Giovanni Del Fabbro — jointly claimed two Spitfires in flames but then the latter was shot down and killed, while Visentini was wounded in arm and leg, and baled out; he was rescued from the sea after three hours by a Z506B floatplane. Serg.Magg. Mario Varacca's Macchi was very badly damaged, the pilot sustaining minor splinter wounds to his left eye. A Spitfire was also claimed shot down by Uffz. Horst Schlick, his first victory over Malta; it seems likely that other Messerschmitt pilots made claims.

Flt.Lt. Mitchell of 603 Squadron claimed a Macchi shot down, while 126 Squadron's Flt.Sgt. Milner claimed a Bf109; two Ju88s were also claimed shot down, as Plt.Off. Jerry Smith (AB465) recorded:

> 'Rip Jones and I jumped seven (*sic*) Ju88s and shot down one each. Rip was being fired at by a 109 while firing at the bomber — I wonder he didn't "buy it". Larger raids coming in these days and far too many fighters. Had bloody great dogfight with 109s and Macchis off Gozo. Was shot up thrice. One in head-on attack at fighter, once by bombers, and was hit in oil tank by 88 I got and force-landed at Hal Far while Luqa was being bombed.'

Of the four Ju88s claimed during the two raids, it would appear that only two were actually lost, both from 5/KG 77 — possibly Don Smith and Dicks-Sherwood had fired at the same aircraft during the earlier raid, while Jerry Smith and Jones had similarly attacked the same aircraft during the second raid. In the event three crew of 3Z+LN survived although the pilot, Uffz. Günther Merz, was killed, while Uffz. Joachim Schierz and his crew of the other downed bomber were more fortunate; although all were injured or wounded, they were rescued from the sea off the Sicilian coast.

126 Squadron lost Flt.Sgt. Bernard Reynolds who failed to return in BR244.

Meanwhile, the 249 Squadron flight led by Flg.Off. Eric Hetherington, newly-transferred from 603 Squadron, dived onto a formation of Macchis, one of which Sgt. Beurling (BR323/S) attacked:

> 'The Eyetie went into a steep dive, pulled out and twisted away, rolled and pulled into a climb. Finally he went into a loop at the end of this climb and I nabbed him just at its top. A two-second burst blew his cockpit apart. The pilot baled out in a hell of a hurry. I circled over him as his parachute opened. He seemed to be healthy, so I gave "May Day" on the RT, specifying that the gent was an Italian, not one of our boys.'

It would seem likely that Beurling's victim was Serg.Magg. Visentini. Flt.Sgt. Williams (BR324/R) was credited with a Bf109 and Flt.Sgt. Butler (BR301/UF-S) gained strikes on another; the Messerschmitts were probably from I/JG 77, one of which crash-landed at Comiso, although this was reportedly due to pilot error rather than the result of combat.

It was on this date — a day much more satisfactory to the defenders — that the 51° Stormo pilots first encountered the vibration phenomenon caused by compressibility when diving away from, or after, Spitfires. This was to plague them in coming weeks, and was first manifested when Cap. Carlo Miani suffered such violent vibration that he believed his Macchi had been critically hit in the tail. He baled out over the Sicilian coast, ending up in Scicli hospital, Ragusa, as a result.

Saturday, 11 July

There was a short, sharp raid on Takali by 13 Ju88s between 0925 and 0955 on the 11th, when a petrol bowser was destroyed and a steam roller damaged. Only a few of the dozen pilots of 249 Squadron vectored to intercept them were able to make claims, the large fighter escort — 23 MC202s of 155° Gruppo and 24 Bf109s — successfully warding off attacks. Sqn.Ldr. Lucas (BR379/V) gained strikes on one bomber while Plt.Off. Yates (BR301/UF-S) and Wt.Off. Ramsay (BR111/M) shared in the claimed destruction of a Bf109; Flt.Lt. Daddo-Langlois (BR565/U) also claimed one, apparently an aircraft of Stab/JG 53 which crashed near St Julians; he recorded:

> 'Bounced fighters escorting 12 Ju88s. Got a 109. Pilot baled out on land.'

The uninjured Lt. Heinz Riedel was taken prisoner by soldiers from the nearby Ta' Giorni AA battery.

Ten Ju88s and eight Re2001s of 2° Gruppo made up the afternoon raid which arrived just after 1430, meeting eight Spitfires of 126 Squadron which had scrambled with elements of two other units. Sqn.Ldr. Winfield and Plt.Off. Mejor claimed to have jointly shot down one of the bombers and Plt.Off. Crist damaged another, while other pilots engaged Ten. Col. Quarantotti's Reggianes; one was claimed (as a Macchi) by Flt.Sgt. Farquharson and another damaged by Sgt. Varey, while Plt.Off. Miller and Flt.Sgt. Evans each had their Spitfires shot-up. The Reggiane leader claimed a Spitfire shot down, as did Serg.Magg. Elio Cesaro, and others recorded hits on three more.

Warning of the next raid was received at 1735, eight Spitfires of 126 Squadron being sent off, followed by eight of 185 Squadron at 1750 and eight of 249 Squadron 20 minutes later; but it was not until 1845 that ten Ju88s, 16 MC202s and two dozen Bf109s of I/JG 77 approached the coast, the bombers heading for

Takali. The attack was fairly accurate and one Spitfire (X-S of 603 Squadron) was destroyed in its pen, another two sustaining damage. The defenders reported engagements with Messerschmitts only, three being claimed shot down, one by Flt.Sgt. 'Paddy' Schade — his sixth in a week bringing his total to 12 and one shared, making him the current highest-scorer on the Island; another was credited to Plt.Off. Frank Jones who also damaged a second, while newly-commissioned Plt.Off. Yarra (BR305/N) increased his tally to 12 when he claimed one more:

> 'Scrambled after 40+ plot. Joined up with another Spit. Saw two 109s and attacked one and shot it down (yellow-nosed). Escorted shot-up Spit back to base.'

Two more German fighters were claimed damaged by Plt.Off. Paradis and Flt.Sgt. Tommy Parks but Wt.Off. 'Chuck' Ramsay was shot down in BR111/M, and lost. The badly damaged Spitfire which Yarra reported escorting was Flt.Sgt. de l'Ara's BR347, which crash-landed at Takali, slightly injuring the pilot. Two more Spitfires of 249 Squadron were promptly sent out to search for the missing Canadian pilot, but nothing was sighted.

Seven of the Macchi pilots clashed with the Spitfires, Cap. Doglio Niclot claiming one shot down and another in collaboration with his pilots, while another four were believed hit. Two more Spitfires were credited to the Messerschmitts, one to Oblt. Geisshardt (his 83rd victory) and another to Uffz. Pohlein, the latter reporting his combat over Gozo. That evening, at about 2130, the corpse of a German airman was washed ashore at Marsalforn Bay, Gozo — probably that of a crewman from one of the downed Ju88s.

Earlier in the day one of the remaining Baltimores (AG700) had been despatched to carry out a reconnaissance in the Cape Bon-Lampedusa-

Left: Flt.Sgt. 'Paddy' Schade of 126 Squadron made his 13th claim on 11 July 1942, making him Malta's top-scoring pilot at the time. *(Daddo-Langlois Collection).* **Right:** Plt.Off. Owen Berkeley-Hill, an Anglo-Indian posted to 249 Squadron, who was shot down and killed on 12 July 1942, his Spitfire falling into the sea. *(Mrs Rosamund Hills)*

Kerkenah area; the aircraft failed to return and Sgt. George Corbett and his crew were reported missing. The cause of their demise is unknown.

Sunday, 12 July

Sunday brought little respite from the intensity of the raids, a dozen Ju88s attacking Takali at 1000, the raid coinciding with the arrival of a Sunderland flyingboat. Two Spitfires of 185 Squadron had been sent out to escort this, encountering a number of Bf109s en route, one of which was claimed shot down by Flt.Sgt. Sim (BR321).

Eight Spitfires of 603 Squadron on early morning patrol failed to find the bombers and were eventually ordered back to Takali, as Colin Parkinson recalled:

> 'Taxied into the bay in time to see the crews running like hell for the (so-called) shelters and a flock of Ju88s overhead. Nipped smartly out of my kite and made the world's record for a 200 yard sprint to the surface shelter. One bomb lobbed just at the back of the shelter and shook us all to our underpants. A stick of bombs had fallen along the dispersal pens and punctured my new kite (2-L) in the wings. After inspecting the kite I walked back to dispersal. With a terrific roar a DA (delayed-action bomb) went off 20 yards from my kite. More holes and a rock bashed the spinner. We, B Flight, are left with six aircraft instead of twelve.'

In all, six Spitfires had indeed been damaged. Meanwhile others of 249 Squadron attempted to engage as the bombers raced out to sea again, but were frustrated by the strong fighter escort — 18 Macchis, 16 Reggianes and a dozen Messerschmitts — which prevented them from reaching the bombers. A section from 249 Squadron spotted Ten. Francesco Vichi's 358ª Squadriglia Re2001 about 25 miles north of Gozo, Sgt. Beurling (BR565/U) firing a one-second burst at this, following which the pilot baled out. Apparently this aircraft was also attacked by Flg.Off. Hetherington, as witnessed by Plt.Off. Berkeley-Hill who called over the radio "I saw it, Hether old boy!"; Owen Berkeley-Hill's aircraft (BR324/R) was then attacked by two fighters, reported to be Messerschmitts, and was shot down; the 20 year-old Anglo-Indian, who had joined the RAF two days after leaving school, was killed.

Meanwhile, Cap. Teia of 2° Gruppo had observed a Reggiane in obvious difficulties leave the formation; it was then attacked by a lone Spitfire ten miles from the Sicilian coast and went down vertically; Vichi was seen to bale out, and on return to base Teia reported his observation to Ten. Col. Quarantotti.

Despite bad weather Quarantotti at once led three others of 2° Gruppo to search for the missing pilot, but as they flew low over the sea one was forced to return early with engine trouble. Fifteen minutes later Mar. Patriarca returned to Gela on his own. Neither the Tenente Colonnello nor Ten. Carlo Seganti came back, and it was believed by the Italians that they might have collided; in fact both had been shot down by Sgt. Beurling of 249 Squadron, again flying BR565/U. The Canadian and his section leader, Flg.Off. Hetherington, on returning from the earlier sortie, had volunteered to search for their missing colleague, Berkeley-Hill, when the two low-flying Italian fighters were seen in low cloud. Although misidentifying these as Macchis, they correctly assumed that they were also searching for their own missing pilot. Hetherington climbed to give cover while Beurling pursued one which was lagging:

Ten. Carlo Seganti of 358ª Squadriglia, 2° Gruppo Aut CT with his Re2001, displaying damage suffered in combat with Spitfires over Malta. *(S. Govi via N. Malizia)*

> 'The boys must have been intent on the search for their missing sidekick, for I swear neither had seen me yet. I simply sneaked up behind the tail-ender (*probably Ten. Seganti*) and gave him a one-second squirt. He burst into flames and went down. Without further ado I whipped around on the other lad... I came right underneath his tail. I was going faster than he was; about 50 yards behind. I was tending to overshoot... I closed up to about 30 yards and I was on his portside coming in at about 15° angle. I could see all the details in his face because he turned and looked at me just as I had a bead on him.'

Beurling fired a short burst which apparently decapitated the pilot, adding:

> 'He dived in beside his mate. From the firing of the first shot until both Macchis went down no more than six or seven seconds had elapsed. Things happen fast in this racket.'

Neither Quarantotti nor Seganti survived and each was posthumously awarded the Medaglia d'Oro.

At 1512 a further strike was carried out on Takali by a dozen Ju88s, while Spitfires from 126 and 185 Squadrons engaged the escort, identified as MC202s and Bf109s. Flt.Lt. Charney (BR368) was credited with a Macchi destroyed, Sqn.Ldr. New (BR321) and Plt.Off. Tilley with a damaged apiece, and Plt.Off. Jerry Smith (BR242/A) with a Messerschmitt damaged; Smith later noted in his diary:

> 'Had a smack at a 109 today; damaged him. Later learned that two went into the sea, so he may be confirmed destroyed.'

It was not. One Macchi was damaged, allegedly by AA shrapnel, whilst other Italian pilots claimed hits on two Spitfires.

Although no raiders were reported over Malta during the night, patrols continued to be flown by the Beaufighter crews while others carried out air tests. Flg.Off. Shipard crashed Z7642/G on take-off from Luqa, he and his radar operator, Sgt. Oxby, escaping injury although the aircraft was written-off.

Commanding officer of 2° Gruppo Aut. CT, Ten. Col. Aldo Quarantotti (facing camera, left) briefs his pilots near the tail of one of the unit's Re2001 fighters. After leading the unit in many engagements, he was shot down and killed by Flt.Sgt. George Beurling of 249 Squadron on 12 July 1942, the latter's 11th victory. *(via N. Malizia)*

Ten. Carlo Seganti of the 2° Gruppo Aut. CT's 358ª Squadriglia, became another of Flt.Sgt. George Beurling's victims on 12 July 1942. He is seen here (left) with Cap. Giuseppe Cenni, commander of 209ª Squadriglia, 102° Gruppo Tuffatori, with Cenni's Ju87 in the background. *(S. Govi via N. Malizia)*

Monday, 13 July

An even larger force of bombers — two Staffeln from II/KG 77 comprising 18 Ju88s — were briefed to carry out the early morning raid on Luqa on the 13th, arriving over the airfield at about 0800, where Beaufighter X7694 of the 89 Squadron detachment was destroyed; three persons were killed in the nearby hospital.

Despite a substantial escort of Bf109s plus ten MC202s of 20° Gruppo and six Re2001s of 2° Gruppo, the bombers were engaged. Sgt. Drew of 185 Squadron claimed damage to one Ju88, then 16 more Spitfires — equally drawn from 126 and 603 Squadrons — attacked, Sgt. Varey (126) and Plt.Off. Northcott (603) each claiming a bomber shot down; others were claimed damaged by Flt.Sgt. Farquharson, Sqn.Ldr. Lord Douglas-Hamilton (two) and Flt.Lt. Douglas. For Sgt. Arthur Varey it was his first victory after two months on the Island, for no matter how hard he had tried previously he had been unable to shoot anything down; he later wrote:

> 'Very soon we sighted the bombers flying in a tight formation below us, and hardly had our leader given the word before I was pointing my nose towards them. Down came the Hun fighters, and their tracer bullets came whistling past my wing tips. I twisted and turned, still heading for the bombers. As the last bomber grew larger in my sights, I pressed my gun button and just gritted my teeth as I kept it pressed for six seconds. I could see my bullets hitting him, and almost before I had finished firing both his engines caught fire. I was so excited that I forgot about the two fighters who were still intent on knocking me down, until the sight of their tracers made me instinctively get a move on, and when I did eventually shake them off it was to see my bomber going down in flames. It was my first victory, yet I felt no personal animosity.'

Cap. Doglio Niclot's flight of Macchis clashed with a dozen of the Spitfires, the Italian leader claiming two shot down and another damaged and Ten. D'Amico one more, but two Macchis were lost; Sottoten. Rosario Longo and Sottoten. Pietro Menaldi, both of 151ª Squadriglia, were shot down and killed. One of the Re2001 pilots, Ten. Giorgio Pocek, also claimed a Spitfire. For 126 Squadron, Flt.Sgt. Evans claimed one Macchi and Sqn.Ldr. Winfield a probable, this unit having by now been joined by eight more Spitfires of 249 Squadron which had been scrambled too late to catch the bombers. Flt.Sgt. Rae was credited with a 'Reggiane' and two more damaged, while Plt.Off. McElroy (BR301/UF-S) identified both his victims (one destroyed, one damaged) as Messerschmitts, which were present as part of the escort; it seems both had actually engaged Macchis. Returning alone without ammunition, Cap. Doglio Niclot came across a damaged Ju88 being attacked by two Spitfires and managed to drive them off, then escorted the bomber back to Sicily; the German pilot landed his damaged machine at Gela, 20° Gruppo's base, in order to personally thank Doglio Niclot.

The Spitfires had not escaped unscathed from this encounter, however, for Sgt. Vernon Willie's BR324 of 126 Squadron was shot down into the sea. The Canadian successfully baled out, slightly wounded, some 20 miles out to sea. Help was soon on hand in the guise of HSL 128 and he was on his way back to Malta in little over an hour. Three other Spitfires sustained damage, including BR565/U flown by Sqn.Ldr. Lucas who had been attacked by four Bf109s some 10-15 miles east of the Island; his aircraft was badly shot-up and started to burn but a jammed canopy prevented him from baling out. As he dived down to 14,000 feet the flames and smoke started to subside so he decided to attempt a deadstick landing at the nearest airfield, Hal Far. He successfully landed downwind without flaps and amid a shower of red Very lights, in the path of three Swordfish which were just taking off!

The late morning raid (1125-1155) was an all-German affair, seven Ju88s with Messerschmitt escort raiding Luqa. The attack was effective — a Hurricane and a Beaufort were totally destroyed and three Beaufighters, two Beauforts and a Wellington were damaged. Eight Spitfires of 603 Squadron were too late to prevent the attack but two pilots caught the bombers as they raced northwards,

Sgt. Irwin claiming to have shot one down; the Australian's aircraft was hit by return fire but he got back safely. A second bomber was claimed damaged by Plt.Off. Northcott.

The pilots of 603 Squadron gained greater success during the late afternoon raid (1712-1740) when 15 Ju88s and 15-20 Messerschmitts raided Takali, where a Spitfire was destroyed on the ground and another damaged. Of the 32 Spitfires airborne, only the ten of 603 Squadron were able to engage the raiders over Sliema and off Filfla; these claimed four Ju88s damaged — two by Flt.Lt. Mitchell, one each by Plt.Off. Dicks-Sherwood and Flt.Sgt. Ballantyne, while a Messerschmitt was hit and claimed probably destroyed by Flt.Sgt. Parkinson (EP200/GL-T):

> 'Had a squirt at an Me109 which passed right through my sights.'

Flt.Sgt. Brown also claimed a probable, while a Macchi (sic) was believed to have been damaged by Flg.Off. McLeod before another fighter scored hits which pierced the oil tank on his aircraft, necessitating a forced-landing on his return to Takali.

Elsewhere, seven Spitfires of 249 Squadron searched in vain for the raiders; nonetheless, Plt.Off. Frank Jones was 'jumped' by an unobserved fighter and had his elevator controls shot away, but got down safely.

Before darkness descended, five Beaufighters of 235 Squadron led by Sqn.Ldr. Cook set out to attack a number of F-boats reported some 12 miles off Lampedusa by a PR Spitfire. Whilst these were spotted in rapidly deteriorating light, only three pilots were able to carry out stern attacks from 1500 feet down to 100 feet, without observed results; AA shrapnel hit and slightly damaged Sqn.Ldr. Cook's aircraft. An ASV-equipped Wellington made a further attack some two hours later, four 500lb bombs being dropped, but again, only near-misses were reported.

From Gibraltar several flights of Beauforts set out for Malta; a total of 16 aircraft of 86 Squadron were detailed to arrive before first light, their ultimate destination being Egypt. One aircraft, DD872/V flown by Plt.Off. E.H. Brockhouse RAAF, had developed engine trouble not long after departing Gibraltar and was forced to ditch; the crew were soon rescued and taken back whence they came. The remaining aircraft, led by Sqn.Ldr. J.R. Hyde DFC, reached Malta without further mishap.

Tuesday, 14 July

Following recent heavy losses, including that of the revered Ten. Col. Quarantotti, the 2° Gruppo Aut CT ceased operating for a period of quiet re-groupment while awaiting the arrival of the new commander Magg. Pier Giuseppe Scarpetta, who would arrive in a few days.

The second Italian offensive, though not officially over, was now almost at a standstill. Italian bombers had practically ceased operating and the 'steam' was certainly going out of their fighters. A last raid came in during the morning but it was mainly German in content.

One of the first arrivals at dawn, however, was another Sunderland from Egypt carrying amongst its passengers the new Air Officer Commanding designate, Air Vice-Marshal Keith Park, MC, DFC, previously commander of No 11 Group, Fighter Command, during the Battle of Britain. The flyingboat pilot was ordered to 'stand-off' as an air raid was in progress but having endured

Air Vice-Marshal Keith Park, who took over as Air Officer Commanding on Malta from Air Vice-Marshal Hugh Lloyd on 14 July 1942; he is seen here in the cockpit of one of the Island's Spitfires. *(NWMA)*

this for about 15 minutes, Park ordered his pilot to go in and land as everyone on board was tired, cold and hungry! He was greeted by an irate Air Vice-Marshal Lloyd, who admonished his successor for taking such chances.

New Zealand-born Keith Park, himself a notable fighter pilot during the First War, was very much a fighter pilots' man and his arrival was the cause of much satisfaction amongst the Spitfire pilots on the Island. The abrasive Lloyd — a former bomber commander — whilst an aggressive and charismatic leader, had by no means been universally loved, many of his subordinates feeling that he did not fully understand or appreciate their operating problems. With the new AOC there would be no such reservations, for no one knew better how to handle an air defence against the odds!

Arriving with Park in the Sunderland was Wg.Cdr. J.M. Thompson DFC, a former Battle of Britain squadron commander with at least eight victories, who had been invited by Park to accompany him to Malta with the promise of command of a fighter wing. Park was as good as his word and within days Thompson was posted to take over the Takali Wing.

The next raid approached shortly after 1000, seven Ju88s of KüFlGr 606 attacking Luqa, where one of the invaluable petrol bowsers was destroyed. A large force of Spitfires from all four squadrons — 30 aircraft — were waiting to ward off the attackers. Two bombers were reported shot down — one each by 126 Squadron's Flg.Offs. Rip Jones and Don Smith — having been intercepted over the sea at 15,000 feet; Smith reported diving past the rear of four Messerschmitts of the escort to attack his victim, which spiralled down into the sea after he had shot off its port aileron and had seen the port engine blow up. He recorded that the escort became "extremely savage after the 88 went in" and his Spitfire (BP992) was hit eight times, one bullet hitting his ankle and severing the artery.

While two of the Messerschmitts circled the downed bomber, the other two kept after him; he performed a tight turn onto their tails and at 100 yards tried to fire. However, the Spitfire's hydraulic system had been damaged and the guns would not work. He finally reached the Island — still under attack — and landed without flaps or brakes. Climbing out, he then collapsed unconscious through loss of blood and was rushed to hospital. It would seem likely that either Smith or Jones had attacked Fw. Heinz Geschlössel's bomber — 7T+GK — which failed to return, while a second aircraft from this unit crash-landed at Catania.

Another Junkers was claimed probably destroyed by Flt.Sgt. MacNamara (BR460) of 185 Squadron, while two other pilots from this unit — Plt.Off. Cy King (BR321) and Sgt. Ken Mitchell (BR109) — jointly damaged another and Sgt. Len Reid (BR376) claimed strikes on a third. Plt.Off. Yarra, on his last operational sortie from the Island, also engaged the bombers but his cannons failed to operate. The escorting II/JG 53 Messerschmitts were particularly aggressive, shooting down Flg.Off. Stoop's Spitfire (AB469) into the sea, about 20 miles from the coast. The pilot sustained burns before baling out and HSL 128 rushed to his aid. Two Spitfires of the seven despatched by 249 Squadron were also damaged in this clash, Flg.Off. Hetherington being obliged to force-land BR379/V at Hal Far, while Sgt. Beurling (BR130/2-H) was wounded in the heel by shrapnel from an explosive bullet. He reported that three Bf109s and two Reggianes (sic) had come out of the sun at him from opposite angles, his aircraft sustaining some 20 hits in the wings and fuselage. In return, Flt.Sgt. Williams (BR301/UF-S) damaged one of the German fighters; another was claimed probably destroyed by Plt.Off. Tilley of 126 Squadron, while Flt.Sgt. Parkinson (EP200/GL-T) reported one shot down:

> 'Everything quiet until about 0830. Scrambled up to about 24,000 feet and were bounced by 109s out of the sun. We all became separated so I joined up with another bloke at about 7000 feet. He broke away so I joined up with a nest of two who flew out to sea. We saw two 109s below so we bounced them. I gave one a good squirt and saw burst of cannon shell all over the fuselage and wings. The Me flew level for a few seconds and then did a slow dive down to the sea and right in.'

One of 603 Squadron's Spitfires was damaged in this action. Luftwaffe claims for four Spitfires shot down included one by Ofw. Rollwage and another by Lt. Franz Schiess of Stab/JG 53. Early in the afternoon six Messerschmitts flew over the Island, presumably on reconnaissance, and although seven Spitfires were up no contact was made.

Wednesday 15 — Monday 20 July

As the assault on Malta cooled, stock could be taken. Since the beginning of the month — in just two weeks of concentrated fighting — the defenders had lost some 36 Spitfires destroyed or badly damaged in action, with three more written off in accidents. This represented about 40% of all available fighters with half as many again having suffered damage of a lesser degree. Although losses of pilots — still much more plentiful than were the mounts for them — had been at a much lower level, the rate of attrition of Spitfires was indeed severe. Help was on the way however, for the carrier *Eagle* had sailed again from Gibraltar with a deck cargo of 32 new Spitfire Vcs, to be flown off at dawn on Wednesday the 15th, as Operation 'Pinpoint' (see Table 11 below).

TABLE 11

Operation 'Pinpoint'

32 Spitfires from HMS *Eagle* (one* crashed on take-off and was pushed overboard)

Flt.Lt. A.H.B. Friendship, DFM		
Flt.Lt. G.W. Swannick		
Flg.Off. E.A.C.G. Bruce		
Plt.Off. W.J. Johnson		had returned to Gibraltar to lead back flight
Plt.Off. R.I.A. Smith, RCAF	BR140	Sgt. G. Philp, RNZAF
Plt.Off. J. Lowery, RCAF (US)		Sgt. E.L. Sidey
Plt.Off. V.K. Moody, RCAF		Sgt. J.G. Livingston, RCAF
Plt.Off. G.W. Guthrie		Sgt. H. Roberts, RNZAF
Plt.Off. R.P. Round, RNZAF		Sgt. W. Parks, RAAF
Flt.Sgt. G.A. Hogarth, RCAF		Sgt. C. Weaver, RCAF
Flt.Sgt. H.G. Reynolds, RCAF		Sgt. M.L. McLeod, RNZAF
Sgt. N.L. Pashen, RAAF	EN972	Sgt. D.J. Hartney
Sgt. N.G. Bryden, RCAF		Sgt. I.H. Forrester (Rhod)
Sgt. V.H. Wynn, RCAF (US)		Sgt. T.J. Gunstone
Sgt. N.M. Park, RNZAF	BR464	Sgt. M. Irving Gass
Sgt. W.S. Shewell, RCAF		Sgt. J.E. Otis, RCAF (US)
Sgt. D.F. Ritchie, RCAF		Sgt. J.H. Tanner, RNZAF
Sgt. C.L. Kelly, RNZAF		Sgt. W.B. Knox Williams, RAAF*

The first flight departed without incident but then one aircraft, EP117 flown by Sgt. Bill Knox-Williams (an Australian) crashed into the bridge on take off; the pilot was unhurt but the damaged aircraft had to be pushed over the side to enable those following to take-off. The remaining Spitfires arrived safely, flown in by a predominantly Commonwealth group of pilots including a high proportion of Canadians. One Spitfire had clipped off its wingtip on a 6-inch gun mount on take-off, although the pilot was able to control his aircraft and reached Malta without further event.

Amongst the new arrivals was Plt.Off. Rod Smith, one of the first to land in BR140; Rod was the younger brother of 126 Squadron's Jerry Smith and recorded:

> 'Took off from HM Aircraft Carrier *Eagle*, 500 foot run, at dawn; second off. Flew in first batch of eight to Luqa. We saw Algeria, made landfall at

Tunisia, passed over Tunis; changed tanks in sight of Pantelleria, and landed still in a group — Jerry was at Luqa! Small world!'

Reported his brother:

'Very dull day, windy and dusty. New Spits arrived in the morning and was amazed to find that Rod landed here. He was in AOC's car when I saw him and we had a chat before he left for the Mess.'

Rod Smith would be posted to join his brother in 126 Squadron, together with other new arrivals including Flt.Lt. A.H.B. Friendship DFM, a Battle of France veteran who was not destined long for the Island, and New Zealander Sgt. Nigel Park, who would do well in the coming weeks. Four more Americans were included in this party — Plt.Off. Joe Lowery and Sgts. Joe Otis, Vasseure Wynn

Cap. Antonio Cumbat, commander of the 239ª Squadriglia, 102° Gruppo Tuffatori. *(A. Cumbat via N. Malizia)*

(known to one and all as 'Georgia') and Claude Weaver, the latter of German parentage; he was another who would make many claims in the coming weeks. A further arrival was a single night fighter Beaufighter (V8219) from Egypt, to replace one of those recently lost by the 89 Squadron detachment.

Malta, however, saw little action on this date, although 23 Spitfires were scrambled in mid afternoon when a fighter sweep approached the coast — possibly to reconnoitre the airfields for signs of the new arrivals. Only one engagement resulted when Sgt. Richardson of 126 Squadron clashed with a Messerschmitt, which he initially claimed damaged, although this was later upgraded to 'confirmed'.

To the west, as the Spitfires were flying off *Eagle*, the crew of Sunderland 'O for Orange' of 202 Squadron, out from Gibraltar on an anti-submarine patrol in support of the operation, had spotted a seaplane. They misidentified this as a Cant Z501 which suddenly and without apparent reason alighted on the sea, then burst into flames. Plt.Off. Lawrence took his big 'boat down to sea level and the Italian crew were observed scrambling into their dinghy. Judging the sea to be suitable for a landing, Lawrence alighted nearby and all six crew members of Ten. Cesare Palmieri's Z506B of 146ª Squadriglia were taken aboard and flown to Gibraltar.

Believing that *Eagle* and her escorts might presage another convoy or a sortie into Sicilian waters, 15 Ju87s of the 102° Gruppo Tuff and a supporting S.81 transport were flown to Castelvetrano from Gela early in the afternoon. At 1835 ten Ju87Rs with 500kg bombs and four Ju87Bs with 1000kg bombs, took off to seek a 'suspicious warship' off the Tunisian coast. Three of the shorter-ranging Ju87Bs returned early and the fourth force-landed in Tunisia, but at 2003 the remaining Stukas, led by Cap. Cenni and Cap. Cumbat, spotted the fast *Welshman* on yet another lone dash to Malta.

Shadowing *Welshman* when the Stukas arrived was an S.79 of 10° Stormo BT which had located her, the aircraft now acting as a radio beacon to guide in the dive-bombers; the radio was manned by 102° Gruppo personnel who were aboard for this purpose. The Stukas plummeted down, one hit on the stern and three near-misses being claimed (confirmed by those in the Savoia) but no hits were actually achieved. On return, low on fuel, one Ju87 landed on Pantelleria, one at Trapani/Milo and one force-landed in a field near Castelvetrano, suffering some damage. All returned to Gela next day.

Next morning (Thursday, the 16th) at dawn, Spitfires of 603 Squadron were sent off to protect the vessel from further attack. Colin Parkinson was amongst them:

> 'The *Welshman*, a supply ship which did 47 knots, was being pranged by Ju's off Pantelleria island. We were supposed to patrol and help protect her. She must have made good time during the night because at 6 o'clock she was only 20 miles off!'

It was relatively quiet over Malta during the day, only occasional reconnaissance aircraft and small fighter sweeps causing patrolling Spitfires any concern; there were no engagements. Darkness allowed a few night raiders to cross the coast but only one Beaufighter, crewed by Plt.Off. Ross and Sgt. O'Leary, made radar contact although without further success. A fire then developed in the AI equipment aboard their Beaufighter, following which the aircraft was fired upon by the defences as it approached to land at Luqa.

The Axis were back during the mid-afternoon of Friday the 17th when five Ju88s raided Luqa and Safi, where two Beauforts were damaged. Two dozen Spitfires were up — eight each from 126, 185 and 603 Squadrons — and these claimed four of the 20 escorting I/JG 77 Messerschmitts shot down, with three others damaged; but there were no reports of engagements with any of the 18 MC202s also taking part in this raid. Flt.Lt. Halford (BR321) of 185 Squadron attacked a straggler seen ten miles north-west of Gozo; following two three-second bursts an explosion was seen and a piece fell off the fuselage. It was last seen pouring black and white smoke. A member of his flight, Flt.Sgt. 'Shorty' Reid (BR380) claimed a second plus another damaged, while the newly-arrived American Sgt. Weaver (BR292) was credited with one more. Flg.Off. McLeod (603) also submitted a claim for a Messerschmitt destroyed, two others being claimed damaged by 126 Squadron's Flt.Sgt. Evans and Sgt. Richardson. Wally McLeod later reported of his victim:

> 'The pilot was thrown clear and his 'chute opened. After he had hit the water I circled him and he waved to me, apparently quite cheerfully. So I dropped my dinghy to him to show I had no hard feelings either. He did not make any attempt to climb into the rubber dinghy and the reason became apparent when one of our rescue launches came out to pick him up. He had a cannon shell through his chest.'

This was Fw. Heinz Sauer, who had baled out of 'White 6' about eight miles from Kalafrana. Two Bf109s had actually been shot down, Uffz. Simon Pohlein's 'Yellow 9' falling into the sea off Valetta with the loss of the pilot. Within the hour Sauer was picked up by HSL 128, Flt.Sgt. Head recalling:

> 'This man was badly injured and holding on to a dinghy, just supported by his Mae West. One of the Spitfire pilots (*McLeod*) who had taken part in the engagement came down to sea level and noticed the man's plight. The Spitfire pilot managed to throw his own survival dinghy out of his over-flying plane to Sauer in the water below. Certainly an act of mercy and self sacrifice on the part of the Allied pilot.'

Sadly, despite the efforts to save him, Fw. Sauer had been severely wounded and died soon afterwards in the launch.

Shortly before this raid developed Flt.Sgt. Ian MacLennan had been ordered to fly one of four new Spitfires over to Luqa from Takali, as there were insufficient blast pens available there. He arrived as the attack was underway and found that only one flap was working, as a result of which he landed very hard and almost crashed:

> 'I was soon made aware how valuable such aircraft were in Malta. The airfield was still being shot up, but I ran across the tarmac, and climbed the control tower where the Wing Commander was observing all this. I saluted and said I wanted to report a damaged Spitfire. His reply was, roughly, "Get into a slit-trench, you son-of-a-bitch; I'll deal with you later!" I felt pretty mortified and was told I would have to report to the Air Officer Commanding.'

By night Axis bombers resumed their attacks on the Island, two BR20Ms and two Z1007bis raiding Luqa, while Ju88s of KüFlGr 606 were also active. One of the latter — T7+ZL flown by Fw. Heinz Vollstedt — was chased back to the south coast of Sicily by Plt.Off. Reeves and Sgt. O'Leary in Beaufighter X7702/K, where it was shot down; it crashed near Gela, the pilot losing his life while his three companions were injured.

On Saturday the 18th only one raid was intercepted. The early morning raiders turned back half way across the Malta Strait, although four Messerschmitts sped across the Island. Eight Spitfires of 603 Squadron were airborne and as they broke formation to attempt an interception, Flt.Sgt. Parkinson became separated:

> '(I) dived down at about 380 miles per hour. I tried to pull out of the dive but the stick was loose in my hands. Boy, did I get the twitch. However, by throttling back she lost speed and I gradually regained control. My leader, White 3, is not fit to fly on ops. I will refuse to fly with him again.'

To meet the afternoon raid eight of 249 Squadron scrambled at 1405, followed by eight more from 126 Squadron 15 minutes later. The former chased a single Ju88 — obviously a reconnaissance machine — and 15 escorting Bf109s at sea level, but Plt.Off. 'Chuck' McLean's aircraft (BR323/S) was hit and caught fire. It took the Canadian a full minute to escape from the inferno, by which time he was badly burned about his arms, thighs, groin, chest and face, and was barely able to pull the ripcord of his parachute. On landing in the sea about four miles off Gozo, he was too weak to inflate his dinghy and floated instead in his Mae West — fortunately for only 15 minutes — until HSL 107 came speeding to his aid. The launch had been alerted by Sgt. Bryden, who had witnessed McLean's plight and had circled him on his way down. A second Spitfire was also hit in this encounter and Plt.Off. Lattimer was slightly wounded, but he managed to crash-land BR107 at Takali without further injury.

When the 126 Squadron pilots caught up with the action some ten miles west of the Island, the Smith brothers — Jerry in BR176/Q and Rod in BP952/F — came across the recce Ju88, which appeared to them to be unescorted and they attacked; it was left in a severely damaged condition — flying very slowly, tail low, white smoke pouring from the starboard engine and with the rear gunner apparently out of action. Newly-promoted Flt.Lt. Bill Johnson, leading the flight, claimed damage to one of the escorting Messerschmitts.

The Luftwaffe fighter pilots, from both II/JG 53 and I/JG 77, were credited with three victories, one of which was claimed north of Valetta by Lt. Berres of the latter unit, while a second went to Lt. Schiess of Stab/JG 53. It is believed the other was credited as the 46th victory of II/JG 53's Gruppenkommandeur, Hpt. Gerhard Michalski, for at least his fourth of the month.

The day saw a complete change of command for 249 Squadron, Sqn.Ldr. 'Laddie' Lucas and his flight commanders, Flt.Lts. Raoul Daddo-Langlois and Norman Lee, preparing to leave for the UK. Flt.Lt. Richard 'Mitch' Mitchell was posted in from 603 Squadron to take over command, Flg.Offs. Eric Hetherington and Les Watts being promoted within the unit to take over the flights. 603 Squadron was also about to receive a new commander, Flt.Lt. Bill Douglas taking over from Sqn.Ldr. Lord Douglas-Hamilton, who was promoted to Acting Wing Commander, and became Assistant Station Commander at Takali.

Having had a few days in which to take stock of the situation, Air Vice-Marshal Park now signalled HQ RAF Middle East, advising of his immediate operational needs. Aviation fuel topped the list, followed by aircraft spares and

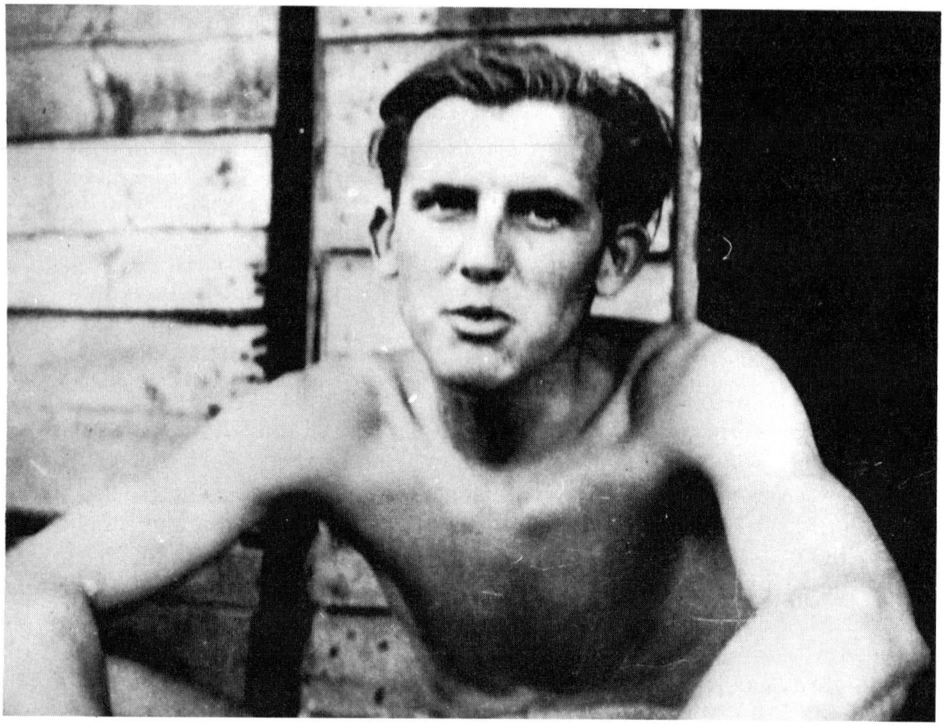

Lt. Franz Schiess of Stab/JG 53 gained his third victory of the month on 18 July 1942 when he claimed a 249 Squadron Spitfire shot down. *(H. Harnisch)*

Flt.Lt. Leslie Watts of 249 Squadron gained several victories during the summer fighting over Malta; he was later to be awarded a DFC. *(Daddo-Langlois Collection)*

experienced fighter pilots. His predecessor, Air Vice-Marshal Lloyd, had similarly expressed disappointment with the 'greenness' of recent arrivals and Park now made it clear that he would accept only pilots with some experience.

As Lloyd had said: "Malta was no place for beginners."

There was but one brief appearance of Axis aircraft on the 19th, when at least a dozen fighters — reported as Re2001s — were encountered by eight Spitfires of 126 Squadron during the afternoon. The Spitfire (BP861) flown by Sgt. Joe Otis, one of the newly arrived American pilots, sustained damage; as he approached Luqa to land, the aircraft suddenly lurched, crashed into a field near Gudja and was totally wrecked; Otis was killed. Another Spitfire was severely damaged during the day when another recent arrival, Sgt. Danny Hartney, flying BR305/N of 185 Squadron on an air test, overshot whilst landing and crashed into a blast pen; the aircraft was ripped into two and the pilot was injured.

Three Ju88 night bombers of I/KG 54 crossed the coast at about 2200, to be pursued by two Beaufighters. Flg.Off. Shipard (with Sgt. Oxby in X7702) caught Lt. Siegfried Sack's aircraft (B3+PH) east of Gozo and shot it down in flames, although his own aircraft sustained some damage in the exchange. The other two bombers were seen to turn away.

With the arrival of dawn on Monday the 20th, radar plotted at least two aircraft approaching the Island, the crews of which were presumably searching for signs of the missing bomber. HSL 107 was performing a similar task, accompanied by six Spitfires as escort. Six miles to the north and 20 miles to the east of Gozo, the rescue craft picked up two Luftwaffe airmen from a raft. They turned out to be Uffz. Albert Mülen and Obgfr. Arthur Blass, and were respectively the observer and gunner from Lt. Sack's aircraft; Sack and his W/T operator were lost.

In the late morning a lone 'bogey' showed up on the radar screens, eight patrolling Spitfires of 185 Squadron being ordered to investigate, while a further four of 603 Squadron were scrambled. When intercepted, the 'bogey' turned out to be a returning PR Spitfire.

Two hours later however, three Ju88s and about 20 Bf109s swept in to attack Luqa. Bombs fell on an RMA Bofors gun position under the command of Lance Sgt. Fedele Zarb — who had recently been awarded a Military Medal — killing Zarb and five of his crew. Eight Spitfires of 185 Squadron were already on patrol to the south-east of the Island as the formation approached, and four of these promptly engaged. Although Sgt. Parker (BR389) reported shooting down one Messerschmitt into the sea 15 miles east of Malta, the Bf109s got the upper hand and shot down Sgt. Hugh Russel, a Canadian from Toronto, who was killed in BR117; his flight commander and fellow Canadian Flt.Lt. Jimmy Lambert (BR460) also fell to their attacks, as Plt.Off. John Sherlock recalled:

> 'J.F. (*Lambert*) was blown out of his cockpit and his 'chute was, fortunately, ripped open which saved his life as he was still unconscious when pulled out of the drink, and his parachute 'D' ring was still unpulled. I fired at a Ju88 and which flew away smoking. I did not see it go down but later someone said they thought they saw a Ju88 go in off Zonqor Point, but it may have been hit by Flak, which was fairly heavy.'

Lambert had come down in the sea not far from the coast, suffering from slight wounds. Two soldiers from the Dorsets rowed out and picked him up, transferring him to the tug *Swona* which had arrived on the scene. By now eight Spitfires of 249 Squadron had been sent to help, engaging both the bombers and their escort but without tangible result, except that Sgt. Wynn's aircraft (BP867/

E) was shot-up by a Messerschmitt, the pilot being slightly wounded in the leg. The German pilots accurately claimed three victories, one by Oblt. Geisshardt of I/JG 77.

There was an attempted repeat raid on Luqa and Safi by three Ju88s at 1645, heavily escorted by at least 18 Bf109s. These were engaged over Dingli by eight Spitfires of 603 Squadron but only Sgt. Irwin was able to claim. He reported seeing 16 of the German fighters in line abreast which he attacked, hitting two, one of which was claimed probably destroyed and the other damaged.

Luftwaffe bombers penetrated Malta's night skies shortly before midnight, their crews briefed to bomb Luqa. Here, one of 69 Squadron's Baltimores was damaged by bomb blast; but the airfield's gunners put up an intense and accurate barrage, shooting down two of the raiders, both aircraft of 8/KG 77. 3Z+FS fell in a field near Kirkop, demolishing a farmhouse. At least three of the crew perished in the wreckage, while Lt. Rolf Haekel's 3Z+CS crashed into the sea. A third Junkers failed to return when the crew of an aircraft of KüFlGr 606 apparently became disorientated; with fuel exhausted T7+GH finally plunged into the sea and Fw. Otto Rutschmann and his crew were reported missing.

Tuesday, 21 July

Tuesday was marked by a number of events of note to the Island. Elements of 86 Squadron which had arrived from Gibraltar with their Beauforts, plus the remaining aircraft and crews of this type already based on the Island, were amalgamated into a new unit, to be commanded by Pat Gibbs, who was promoted to Wing Commander. Gibbs proposed to develop tactics which he had been formulating, involving close liaison with escorting Beaufighters. He considered that all raids launched from Malta should set course due east at 50 feet to avoid being spotted by Axis radar, and should be accompanied by a reconnaissance Baltimore to record results.

This new unit, which included a number of experienced torpedo pilots from the UK who had served before with Gibbs in 22 Squadron, including Sqn.Ldr. Jimmy Hyde (an Australian) and Flt.Lt. D.C. 'Hank' Sharman (a Canadian), was now to undertake its first operation. A Spitfire of 69 Squadron had spotted a large merchant vessel which was the 6339-ton *Vettor Pisani* from Taranto carrying 1000 tons of fuel and 650 tons of mixed cargo — and two torpedo-boats, *Orsa* and *Calliope*, identified as destroyers — off Cephalonia at first light.

At 0955 nine Beauforts (four of 86 Squadron, three from 217 and two of 39) took off led by Gibbs, with an escort provided by six Beaufighters of 235 Squadron. The convoy was sighted just over two hours later eight miles off Cape Geroghambo, and was attacked from dead ahead; eight of the Beauforts succeeded in releasing torpedoes. At least three hits were claimed on the merchantman, from which volumes of brown smoke was observed, and another on one of the 'destroyers', which was believed sunk. Nearly all the aircraft raked the freighter with their machine guns as they swooped over or past. Flt.Lt. Leaning's aircraft was slightly damaged by shrapnel from a bursting AA shell but he managed to get back to Malta safely. The *Vettor Pisani* was hit and in attempting to enter nearby anchorage for sanctuary and repairs, ran aground off Cape Lixuri.

Meanwhile, the Beaufighter crews — down to five after one had been forced to return early — spotted a seaplane, identified as a Do18, at 500 feet. This was a

Z506B of 287ª Squadriglia RM from Sardinia, which had been in the air since dawn shadowing British warships. Sqn.Ldr. Wigmore and Flt.Sgt. Briscoe attacked and claimed strikes, last seeing their opponent diving towards the coast. Sottoten. Luigi Ottolino's crew claimed that they had shot down one of their attackers, but the floatplane (MM45411) was damaged with the co-pilot, observer and gunner all suffering slight wounds.

TABLE 12

Operation 'Insect'

32 Spitfires from HMS *Eagle* (one lost on take-off; another damaged and failed to take-off). Pilots involved believed to have included the following listed below.

Sqn.Ldr. B.J. Wicks, DFC		
Flg.Off. R.O. Jones, RCAF		returned to Gibraltar to lead back flight
Plt.Off. F.E. Jones, RCAF		returned to Gibraltar to lead back flight
Plt.Off. D.G. Newman		returned to Gibraltar to lead back flight
Plt.Off. N.J. Ogilvie, RCAF		(EP197) returned to Gibraltar to lead back flight
Plt.Off. K.C.M. Giddings		Sgt. R.A. Buntine, RAAF
Plt.Off. W.L. Thompson		Sgt. A.H. Scott
Plt.Off. A.R. Stewart		Sgt. J.R. Harmer, RCAF
Plt.Off. W.C. Walton		Sgt. W.H. Walker
Plt.Off. A.D. Owen		Sgt. R.W. Lamont, RCAF
Plt.Off. C. Taylor, RCAF		Sgt. H.J. Smith
Plt.Off. L.G. Bazalgette		Sgt. F.F. Crosswell
Wt.Off. P. Carter, RCAF (US)		Sgt. F.W. Sharpe
Flt.Sgt. C.A. Long		Sgt. R. Hawkins
Sgt. B.C. Peters		Sgt. J.M. Harrison
Sgt. A.J. Tiddy (South African)		Sgt. D.C. Eva
Sgt. W.R. Wilson		Sgt. M.A. Lundy
Sgt. L. Evans	(EP378) lost on take-off	

The warships which the Italians had been shadowing were *Eagle* and her escorts, in the process of making a further delivery of Spitfires (see Table 12 above). To lead the flights were four Malta veterans, Flg.Off. Rip Jones, Plt.Offs. Frank Jones, 'Buzz' Ogilvie and Dudley Newman, all of whom had been flown to Gibraltar, where they joined the carrier. Ogilvie (EP187) recalled:

> 'This time we were launched with greater authority and for two reasons. These new Spitfires had laminated wood hydromatic propellers, giving us much greater acceleration, and also because the desperate Malta diet had reduced our weight considerably!
>
> 'In preparing the course from the *Eagle* to Malta, and not looking ahead to the long haul around Tunisia, off Cape Bon, I decided to shorten the flight by cutting across the so-called neutral land, from its western border at the

Mediterranean to its eastern coast at the same latitude as Malta. The gamble here was no greater in my mind, than the risk of a dog fight with enemy fighters rounding Cape Bon, especially with us carrying 90-gallon belly tanks.

'As we left the east coast of Tunisia on our last leg, I checked my reference point and set course for Malta, being a little south of due east. Here we encountered a dark haze, where we could see straight down but not ahead. About 20 minutes off the east coast of Tunisia, with only the sight of water below, I began to hunger for a little reassurance that I was on the right course. I had visions that I might miss that tiny island of Malta and lead all my followers off into the wild blue yonder.

'So I called fighter control at Malta for a homing vector. At once a socialist democratic Cambridge accent came over the radio, which I didn't recognize: "Oh hello Bullet Blue One, old chap, steer 40°, over and out." At that moment all hell broke loose in my cockpit. I was steering 105°. And with this new course being heard by the members of my following, the tail of every Spitfire twitched nervously, with the pilots no doubt thinking they had a clot for a leader. My God, the winds must have changed drastically, I thought! I must be near the coast of Libya!

'At that moment I got religion again, mentally indicating to the Lord that I would become a monk if He got me out of this one, when fighter control at Malta nearly blew the earphones out of my helmet with: "No, no, no, Bullet Blue One, steer 105°, 105°, over." There was no mistaking that voice. It was Group Captain Woodhall alright... A German fighter controller in Sicily had been up to his old tricks again, trying to home me into Sicily... With Woody's re-assurance, I held my course of 105°, gradually losing height, till we roared over the coast of Malta at 500 feet. We still had plenty of fuel in reserve and had knocked off considerable time taken by other flights.'

A number of the 30 Spitfires aboard had already successfully taken off when another, EP378 piloted by Sgt. Lewis Evans, started to weave, failed to gain sufficient speed, and crashed into the sea; the pilot was lost. Having witnessed this accident, an Australian sergeant pilot apparently panicked when his turn came and also began to weave, his aircraft then ramming a Bofors gun emplacement; neither the gunners nor the pilot were injured. The remaining 28 Spitfires reached Malta safely.

Three more Beaufighter night fighters were also flown in from Egypt to reinforce the detachment of 89 Squadron. The unit's commanding officer, Wg.Cdr. George Stainforth AFC, of Schneider Trophy fame, piloted X7704, the other two (X7671 and X7695) being flown by Flg.Offs. E.F.V. Copsey and G.R. Nottage.

The further new arrivals of Spitfires more than restored the strength of the defences and allowed some changes to be made. At Luqa 1435 Flight was reformed, this time as a day fighter unit with some of the surplus new Spitfires. Initially it was to share messing facilities with 126 Squadron, and was to be commanded by a new arrival from Egypt — a most notable Battle of Britain pilot, Sqn.Ldr. A.D.J. Lovell, DFC and Bar; Tony Lovell already had a dozen victories to his credit and would prove to be a most welcome addition to Malta's strength. Amongst those posted to this new unit were Flt.Lt. Halford, Flt.Sgts. Vineyard and MacNamara from 185 Squadron, Flg.Off. McLeod from 603, and Plt.Off. Lattimer and Sgt. Baxter from 249 Squadron, as well as Flt.Sgt.

MacLennan; Halford and McLeod were to become flight commanders.

Over the Island little was seen of the Axis air forces, the only engagement being noted at about 1600 when eight 126 Spitfires made contact with a similar number of Bf109s off Gozo. Sgt. Varey claimed one probably shot down, while two Spitfires, including Varey's, suffered damage; he recalled:

> 'I was very lucky in a dogfight right over the Island at 25,000 feet. Shells hit my aircraft and stopped my engine. Fortunately, I was able to glide down and land alright, only to find two cannon shells imbedded in the armour plating behind my head.'

Wednesday, 22 July

The night fighter Beaufighters scored again in the early hours of the 22nd, when a solitary intruder was reported over Malta. Two Beaufighters were up and Flg.Off. Shipard was vectored onto the Ju88 just after 0230. His aircraft (X7695) was spotted by the German gunner as he closed in, and was hit and severely damaged (for the second time in consecutive combats) but a burst from the night fighter's heavy armament was sufficient to send the bomber into the sea; two of the crew baled out and were taken prisoner. This was undoubtedly 4U+CK, a Ju88D of 2(F)/123 flown by Lt. Ernst Lischke.

Left: Plt.Off. Noel 'Buzz' Ogilvie of 185 Squadron; note the Canadian Maple Leaf emblem on his Spitfire. *(N.J. Ogilvie)*. **Right:** Flt.Sgt. Don 'Shorty' Reid of 185 Squadron was awarded a DFM for six victories before he was shot down and killed on 22 July 1942 by a Bf109G of I/JG 77. *(Yarra Collection via L. McAulay)*

Fourteen Spitfires from 185 and 249 Squadrons intercepted the late morning raid, when still some 20 miles off Zonqor Point, but two promptly fell to I/JG 77's escorting Messerschmitts. 249 Squadron's French-Canadian, Plt.Off. Jean Paradis (BR128/3-W) — a particular friend of George Beurling — was shot down into the sea; Paradis had just spotted the three Ju88s which formed the nucleus of the raid, when he was bounced. 185 Squadron's Flt.Sgt. 'Shorty' Reid spotted Paradis' Spitfire crash into the sea and orbitted the point of entry; he was seen to engage a Messerschmitt which was believed shot down, before another got onto his tail and shot down BR203/X also; neither Paradis nor Reid survived. It seems likely that the two Spitfires fell to Lt. Berres, who claimed one east of Valetta, and Uffz. Schlick, although other pilots may also have been credited with victories. The American Sgt. Claude Weaver (EP122) of 185 Squadron claimed two of the German fighters shot down in return, but no losses were recorded.

Another raid approached at 1445 when three Ju88s with an estimated 14 Bf109s as escort headed for Hal Far and Kalafrana. Of the 16 Spitfires sent off to intercept, four had to return early, while another four from 185 Squadron were bounced three miles north-east of Zonqor and Flt.Sgt. Mahar's BR109 was shot-up and damaged; as they returned to the Island another was slightly damaged by shrapnel from an exploding AA shell.

By night the reinforced crews of 89 Squadron were in the air as five bombers were reported approaching the coast soon after 2200, but again it was Flg.Off. Fumerton (on this occasion flying with Sgt. Booth as his radar operator in X7702) who was successful. Lt. Leo Skrdla's 3/KGr 806 Ju88 (M7+GL) was intercepted before it reached the Island and was shot down in flames into the sea north of Gozo, its demise being witnessed by Colin Parkinson, amongst others:

> 'Beautiful moonlit night. Ideal for bombing. Sirens went so walked to the Bastion to watch the fun. Saw an 88 go down in flames. Welcome sight.'

Thursday, 23 July

Eight Spitfires of 249 Squadron, led by the new CO, Sqn.Ldr. Mitchell, were the first to be engaged during the mid morning raid on the 23rd when three Ju88s and a dozen fighters — reported as seven Bf109s and five Re2001s — were met at 15,000 feet, heading for Luqa. Diving from out of the sun, through the top cover, Mitchell (BR301/UF-S) shot one bomber down straight into the sea; two more were damaged by Sgt. Beurling (BR135/Z) and Flt.Lt. Hetherington, both of which were left with smoke streaming from their starboard engines. Beurling then engaged a Reggiane which dived on him, and reported blowing off its port wing with a deflection shot, the wreck crashing into the sea.

Two Spitfires of 1435 Flight were flying a protection patrol over minesweepers off the Grand Harbour as the raid swept in. Flt.Lt. Halford attacked a Messerschmitt and saw strikes on its starboard wing; smoke issued and pieces fell off before the Bf109 dived into cloud at 800 feet and Halford was credited with its probable destruction. The bombers blitzed Luqa as they passed overhead, five aircraft sustaining damage on the ground from blast and debris.

249 Squadron was again involved in the afternoon raid — five Ju88s with 15 Bf109s and Macchis being reported; Luqa was again bombed with damage to one Baltimore. Flt.Lt. Watts led his flight after the bombers but the escort kept them busy; a probable was credited to Watts (BR373/N) and Plt.Off. McElroy

(BP976/C) jointly, while the Canadian damaged a second fighter and Plt.Off. Round (BR135/Z) damaged another. 126 Squadron and 1435 Flight scrambled eight Spitfires apiece while 185 Squadron put up another seven, all three units engaging.

The 126 Squadron flight encountered the escorting fighters five miles north-east of Kalafrana, Plt.Off. Downs claiming a Messerschmitt probably destroyed. He later requested this to be upgraded to 'confirmed' on the strength of a remark by his squadron commander, Sqn.Ldr. Winfield, who reported seeing fluorescent dye in the sea near to where the combat took place! Sgt. Varey damaged another and Plt.Off. Tilley damaged a Macchi. A pair from 185 Squadron also engaged the fighters 15 miles east of Zonqor Point, Sgt. Mitchell (BR292) claiming a Macchi damaged, while Sgt. Weaver (EP122) for the second day in succession reported he had shot down a brace of Messerschmitts. Three pilots from 1435 Flight succeeded in reaching the bombers, two being claimed damaged by Sqn.Ldr. Lovell, Flt.Lt. Halford and Flt.Sgt. R.A. Stevenson.

Lts. Berres and Kohler of I/JG 77 each claimed a Spitfire shot down north-east of Valetta, while 151ª Squadriglia reported the loss of Serg.Magg. Bruno Di Pauli who failed to return. It would seem, however, that the Macchi pilot did not fall victim to the Spitfires, for he reported:

> 'As we approached the target, we received a heavy AA barrage. Suddenly, I was hit by an AA shell which damaged both wings, but at first without preventing me from carrying out my job. After we had accomplished our mission, we swiftly headed home, but while the formation went on, my aircraft started loosing speed.
>
> 'I looked back and saw six Spitfires in line astern, following me without firing. I understood that I was in a hopeless state, so broadcast my position but in the confusion of that moment, I said "It's 'Gatto' speaking", and parachuted down.
>
> 'I shot a signal rocket; they (*the Spitfires*) saw me. After one hour, I saw them looking for me again; I shot the two rockets left but they did not make for me, although the rockets made a lot of smoke.
>
> 'The hours went by. However, when the sun was going down, I saw the British aircraft again, at very low level. As I had nothing to let them see me, I started beating the water with my hands, making a lot of foam. I was very lucky; one of them saw me and dived low over my head and the other followed. Finally I saw a launch which came by and took me on board.'

The Italian pilot was picked up from the sea by HSL 128, about five miles east of Kalafrana, and was relieved of his valuables — a gold bracelet, watch and neck chain; these were later returned following a complaint to an interrogating officer, who apparently initially believed that Di Pauli was actually Maggiore Gino Callieri, commander of 20° Gruppo! The confusion had arisen following Di Pauli's emergency radio broadcast when he had used the name 'Gatto'; the message was also intercepted by operators of the RAF's 'Y' Service, to whom the codename 'Gatto' (Cat) was known to refer to Callieri! He had earned this nickname during his air force academy days when he had killed and eaten a cat for a bet!*

During the day, one of the Island's remaining Hurricane IIB's was lost when the engine of Z2825 failed on a test flight. 185 Squadron's Plt.Off. David Kent was killed when the aircraft crashed. A number of the redundant Hurricanes were being test flown prior to their experimental use as fighter-bombers.

Friday, 24 July

It was not until 1015 on the 24th that the first scramble was ordered, eight 1435 Flight Spitfires intercepting up to 20 Messerschmitts escorting five Ju88s of KGr 806, some 30 minutes later. Plt.Off. Lattimer made the unit's first confirmed claim when he reported a fighter shot down. Flt.Lt. McLeod and Sgt. Baxter both claimed probable victories, the latter also claiming one damaged, as did Sgt. Shepherd.

Ten minutes behind them came 16 more Spitfires from 126 and 185 Squadrons, which got through to the bombers. When over Takali at 18,000 feet, Plt.Off. Rod Smith of 126 made a port quarter attack on a Junkers on the left of the formation, firing a six-second burst from 250 down to 50 yards. The port engine burst into flames which quickly spread to the fuselage, one of the crew baling out. The bomber crashed to the south of Luqa, near Qrendi; two of the crew were found dead in the wreckage while the one who baled out landed nearby, slightly injured.

This was possibly the occasion recalled by 89 Squadron's Flg.Off. Merv Shipard. He saw a German airman land about 200 yards away from where his aircraft was dispersed and as he walked towards him, about a dozen Maltese women armed with spades and pitchforks rushed to the scene. The terrified German airman threateningly produced a small pistol from his flying boot, but on seeing Shipard wisely surrendered. Shipard took him into custody and then handed him over to soldiers when they arrived.

Plt.Off. Jerry Smith was also involved in the action, flying BR242/A, and reported:

> 'Got off late on a scramble. Joined the others just as they attacked the bombers. Started to aim at port Ju88, when Rod opened fire — it went down in flames. Moved over to the next one and opened fire, putting port engine aflame. Was hit in glycol (*tank*) and force-landed at Luqa (third time this month). Sgt. Tiddy saw my Ju88 go into the sea.'

For 185 Squadron Plt.Off. Guthrie (EP200/T) and Sgt. Len Reid (AB526) each claimed one of the bombers, the latter recording:

> 'Intercepted four Ju88s together with large fighter escort. Dived straight down on one at a 45° angle, opening up with cannon at 500 yards closing in to 100 yards, giving one long burst. Hit top of cockpit and starboard engine which immediately gave off black smoke and went into a spin. One Ju88 destroyed.'

---

* Other prominent Sicily-based Regia Aeronautica fighter leaders of the period were allotted similar radio codenames, thus:

Ten. Col. Aldo Remondino	'Torino' (his home city)
Magg. Duilio Fanali	'Roma' (his home city)
Cap. Luigi Borgogno	'Borgo'
Cap. Riccardo Roveda	'Rovi'
Cap. Furio Doglio Niclot	'Furio'
Cap. Riccardo Spagnolini	'Pante' (Pantera = Panther)
Cap. Carlo Miani	'Tigre' (Tiger)
Cap. Bruno Tattanelli	'Leo' (Leone = Lion)
Cap. Vincenzo Sant'Andrea	'Marte' (Mars)

A third bomber was credited jointly to Sgts. Weaver (EP122) and Drew (EP139), while Plt.Off. Cy King (BR374) and Sgt. Ken Mitchell (BR292) damaged another, King noting:

> '(I was) Blue Leader. We climbed to 22,000 feet south-east of Kalafrana. Saw the Ju88s going out towards Filfla and went in. I got abeam and astern — fired all my ammo and saw a flash on cabin. One Ju88 damaged & down!'

With the two units attacking jointly, it is apparent that some double-claiming occurred on this occasion; at least one bomber failed to return, Lt. Sepp Hörmann and his crew being reported missing in M7+KH. Apart from the damage to Jerry Smith's aircraft, one other Spitfire sustained slight damage during this action.

The Luftwaffe was back during the late afternoon, five Ju88s raiding Luqa at 1800, where an unserviceable Beaufort was destroyed and two others damaged, as were two Spitfires. Although 32 Spitfires were up only a small number made contact, three pilots of 126 Squadron making claims; Flt.Lt. Slade and Plt.Off. Wallace jointly damaged one of the bombers, while Sgt. Tanner reported strikes on one of the escorting Messerschmitts.

By mid-July the Axis air force's shortage of fuel in North Africa was becoming desperate, a fact confirmed to the British authorities by intercepted 'Ultra' traffic. The air transport system was being brought to a standstill and the fighter force could be used only sparingly. The Panzer Army's need for ammunition and fuel was also becoming urgent. This was partly due to heavy fighting in the past few days, but also as a result of RAF and RN attacks on Axis shipping in the forward area. RAF bombers from Egypt had sunk one small ship (the 766-ton *Max Berendt*) in Tobruk harbour on the night of the 10th/11th, and had gained more success during the following two days. Two large coastal vessels had been brought forward to ply between Mersa Matruh and Tobruk, ferrying fuel, ammunition and other supplies; the fuel-carrying *Brook* (1325 tons) was now sunk by bombs while the slightly larger *Sturla* (1397 tons), also carrying fuel, was initially bombed, then torpedoed and sunk by an MTB, both vessels going down off Matruh. However, one tanker did succeed in reaching Tobruk on the 25th and thus somewhat improved the situation. The Axis front line command considered one ship in Tobruk worth several in Benghazi, and at the beginning of the month tankers and supply ships began sailing to the former port, beyond the range of Malta's strike aircraft.

In a futile effort to help relieve their desperate situation, the Luftwaffe attempted to introduce a fuel ferry service between Crete and Tobruk by using Ju52/3m transport aircraft. One such flight had been intercepted by Beaufighters of 252 Squadron on the 9th but these failed to inflict any damage, while one Beaufighter had been shot down by escorting Bf110s. Better success was achieved two days later when, acting upon Intelligence information, 13 Beaufighters (ten from 272 Squadron and three of 252 Squadron) intercepted about 30 Ju52s over the sea off Tobruk, the escort apparently comprising just one Bf110, a Ju88 and an He111. At least three of the lumbering transports were claimed shot down, with a further one probably destroyed and several others damaged; three Beaufighters were damaged in the action, one crash-landing at base.

Although the Malta-based Beauforts were unable to interfere with convoy traffic along the North African coast, they were again to prove their continuing effectiveness down the Italo-Greek coastlines. At first light on the 24th, Sqn.Ldr. Hyde led off three 86 Squadron crews followed by Flt.Lt. Stevens with three more from 217 Squadron, while 235 Squadron supplied eight Beaufighters as escort; their task was to locate and destroy a convoy reported off Cephalonia earlier in the day by a PR Spitfire. At 0930 the Italian freighter *Vettor Pisani* was seen ten miles off Cape Geroghambro (Cephalonia) — it was she that had been the Beaufort's target three days earlier — with an escort of two destroyers and two torpedo-boats.

The 86 Squadron trio, their Beauforts still sporting the conspicuous green and grey Northern European camouflage, went in relatively high and in tight formation. As they approached, the escort opened up with a violent barrage and in moments all three had been shot down. Hyde's aircraft (AW355/G) was first to be hit and blew up; only the turret gunner, Sgt. Sarene, survived to be picked up from the sea. Debris from this aircraft was believed to have brought down that flown by Plt.Off. D.L. Furphy (AW308/H), who was forced to ditch. His crew scrambled out safely to be taken prisoner, while the gunner in Flt.Sgt. L.C. Thompson's AW356/Z was lost when this aircraft was hit and also forced to ditch moments later; the three survivors were also picked up and were taken into captivity.

Steven's section was more fortunate. They had adopted different tactics, having spread out as they went in low — as previous experience had taught them to do — and all succeeded in releasing their torpedoes at the merchantman, while the escorting Beaufighters strafed. Two hits were claimed on the starboard bow of *Vetor Pisani*, dense smoke and billowing flames erupting from the vessel; down by the bows, she was taken in tow by one of destroyers, stern first and still on fire to the port of Argostoli, where she burnt herself out.

'Blips' which appeared on Malta's radars just after 0100 represented three Ju87s of 102° Gruppo Tuff as they approached the coast in bright moonlight, two Spitfires being scrambled to join Flg.Off. Shipard's patrolling Beaufighter. It was Shipard, however, who gained a 'visual' on one of the Stukas some 15 miles north-west of Gozo shortly after it had dive-bombed Luqa, and fire was exchanged between the two aircraft. Although the Australian noted in his logbook: "No Luck", his burst did, in fact, hit the tail of Ten. Angelo Martini's aircraft; the Italian pilot jettisoned the canopy and warned his gunner to prepare to bale out, but then realised the aircraft was still flyable and returned safely to Gela.

Saturday, 25 July

The main event of the 25th was the return of the Italians to the skies above Malta, when a dozen MC202s of 20° Gruppo and seven of 155° Gruppo joined Bf109s to cover five Ju88s to Luqa and Hal Far during the afternoon. On the latter airfield two Hurricanes (BG719 and BG794) were damaged by shrapnel and debris, while over the target area the Italians reported that six Spitfires were encountered. Two of these were claimed shot down, one by Mar. Tarantola, which he reported crashed near Delimara Point and one east of St Thomas' Bay by Ten. Italo D'Amico; Cap. Doglio Niclot claimed a probable. Four more were claimed damaged, but D'Amico's Macchi was hit five times in the starboard wing.

Plt.Off. Glazebrook, one of eight 603 Squadron pilots scrambled to intercept, claimed a Macchi shot down. His opponent may have been D'Amico or possibly a Bf109 of 2/JG 77, as Ofw. Kurt Görbing was reported missing from a combat sortie in 'Black 6'; the German pilot was located in the sea and was soon rescued by an ASR Dornier from Sicily. Two pilots of 1435 Flight managed to reach the bombers, two of which were claimed damaged by Flt.Sgt. MacLennan and Flt.Sgt. Pinney. One Spitfire was slightly damaged.

It was on this day that Air Vice-Marshal Park issued his 'Fighter Interception Plan'. Until recently, usually out of necessity due to the small numbers of defending fighters available but latterly also out of habit, flight leaders would fly south of the Island to gain height and then attack any enemy seen, usually following bombing attacks; hence, during the first two weeks of July, 34 aircraft had been damaged on Malta's airfields. With the arrival of the new Spitfires sufficient numbers were now available — if not to actually take the fight to the enemy — at least to meet him half-way, and that meant over the Malta Channel. Park issued instructions that raids would be intercepted north of the Island, well out to sea and before the bombers could reach their targets. Of the plan, Park's biographer Vincent Orange later wrote:

> 'The sector controller was to ensure that his first squadron got its height up-sun and then intercepted the enemy's high fighter cover. The second squadron was to intercept the bombers' close escort or the bombers themselves, if unescorted. The third squadron was to make a head-on attack on the bombers about ten miles north of the coast, followed by a quarter attack, to force them to drop their bombs into the sea. If a fourth squadron was available, it would tackle any bombers which broke through the forward fighter screen. The plan had been explained orally to all concerned. It required reliable radar warning and alert pilots. Take-offs must be much quicker than in the past, control must be accurate and clear, and squadrons must obey orders immediately. Wireless discipline must be strict and pilots must not open fire at long range, thereby alerting the enemy and wasting valuable ammunition. Last but not least, sea rescue services must have sufficient high-speed launches and be thoroughly trained in their work.'

This latter point was promptly acted upon for within a few days another launch — HSL 100 — was made available to the ASR unit. The launch was the former Army motor boat *Clive*, which had been repaired after being damaged earlier in the year. With Plt.Off. Houghton in command, HSL 100 was based at Sliema.

Sunday, 26 July

The intensity of the raids was increased on the 26th, raiders which approached at 1038 interrupting Sunday morning Services around the Island; seven Ju88s planted their bombs on Takali, where a Spitfire was burnt out. Other Spitfires intercepted, Flt.Lt. Bill Johnson leading his flight of eight from 126 Squadron after the fleeing bombers, personally claiming one probably destroyed, while others were hit and damaged by Flt.Sgt. Varey (two) and Plt.Off. Downs. A further eight pilots from 1435 Flight tangled with the escort, Sqn.Ldr. Lovell identifying the fighter he damaged as a Macchi.

Shortly after 1400 the bombers were back, five Ju88s bombing Hal Far, where two more Hurricanes (BE428 and BE563) were damaged. Although eight Spitfires of 603 Squadron and four of 1435 Flight were sent after them and their escort, no contact was made. Two hours later more returned — seven Ju88s blitzing Luqa and Safi, where a Spitfire was destroyed and three Beauforts and an ASV Wellington were damaged. Eight Spitfires of 126 Squadron pursued the bombers as they fled northwards over the sea, Plt.Off. Jerry Smith (BP952/F) catching up with one four miles out from Grand Harbour:

> 'Attacked from above but got only one hit. Passed a 109 on way down which Rod squirted at. As I broke over the bombers, was hit in glycol and force-landed at Hal Far while Luqa was being bombed. Rod escorted me down.'

Flg.Off. Rip Jones fared better and claimed one of the bombers shot down about 30 miles out to sea, but as Sqn.Ldr. John Winfield closed in on another his aircraft was hit and he was badly wounded. Despite a massive loss of blood he managed to land safely at Takali, where he was tenderly lifted from the cockpit and rushed by ambulance to hospital. He believed he had been struck by return fire from the Junkers he was attacking but it seems likely he was hit by an unobserved Messerschmitt, as Oblt. Geisshardt of I/JG 77 claimed a Spitfire shot down. Again 1435 Flight was involved, Sqn.Ldr. Lovell gaining hits on one of the escort over Luqa, but it escaped serious damage.

There was yet a further raid over Malta with the onset of darkness, two Ju87s of 239ª Squadriglia and three of 209ª Squadriglia, led by Cap. Cumbat, setting out for Luqa. One was obliged to return early with engine trouble and two others, including Cumbat's, were intercepted by Beaufighters but both evaded and escaped unscathed. The attack was not a success.

The AOC's intention for a more offensive attitude to be adopted was immediately acted upon when three Hurricanes, flown by Wg.Cdr. Dawson and 185 Squadron's Sgts. Weaver and Len Reid (BN408/E), each with two 250lb bombs slung underwing, set off to bomb Gela, taking advantage of the bright moonlight. The sortie was not a success, however. Weaver was unable to locate Gela and returned with his bombs intact, while Reid was unable to reach the designated target owing to heavy fuel consumption and released his bombs in the vicinity of Scicli instead. Consequently, only Wg.Cdr. Dawson actually arrived over Gela and although the two bombs were dropped on the airfield from about 3000 feet, no results were seen. Buildings and M/T were strafed by Dawson, who reported a lack of opposition from the defences.

Monday, 27 July

At 0835 on the 27th eight Spitfires of 185 Squadron were ordered off, followed

Serg.Magg. Faliero Gelli's crash-landed Macchi C202 – '11' of 378ª Squadriglia, 155° Gruppo, 51° Stormo CT – shot down on 27 July 1942 by Flt.Sgt. George Beurling as his 13th victim. *(IWM)*

20 minutes later by six of 249 Squadron and eight of 126 Squadron. All were vectored on to nine Ju88s heading for Takali, but arrived too late to intercept before the Germans completed their bombing. On the airfield two Spitfires were damaged; later, when a delayed action bomb exploded, a further two Spitfires and two Hurricanes were also damaged.

Meanwhile Spitfires, including those of 126 Squadron, were attacking as the bombers headed out to sea on their way home, apparently having lost their Messerschmitt escort; Flt.Lt.Johnson claimed the probable destruction of one and Flt.Sgt. Varey damaged two more. Thirteen Macchis (11 of 20° Gruppo and two of 155° Gruppo), flying as indirect support, moved in to help the bombers; Ten. Mario Mazzoleni pursued one Spitfire down to 1500 feet above the sea and claimed its probable destruction, while other pilots claimed strikes on a further six.

At this moment the 249 Squadron pilots spotted the Macchis and closed in with deadly effect; the indefatigable Sgt. Beurling (in BR301/UF-S) later recalled:

> 'I spotted four Macchis running in line astern and took Number Four. They saw me coming and pulled into a climbing turn to the right. As they did I came up on my man's starboard quarter and let him have a burst. It was a straight deflection shot which went into his engine and radiator. He flicked into a spin, but managed to pull out and crash-landed on Gozo, able to walk away from the mess.'

Whilst Beurling's shooting was deadly accurate, his observation was at fault for Serg.Magg. Falerio Gelli — the pilot of the Macchi — reported that when he pulled out of the spin he was very low and directly over Victoria, the capital of Gozo; he belly-landed his crippled aircraft onto a rocky field, smashing his face into the instrument panel. Eager Gozitan hands pulled the unconscious pilot from the cockpit and he was soon on his way to hospital. Gelli, who had claimed three Spitfires shot down during his tour with 378ª Squadriglia in Sicily, apparently initially disguised his identity, for when Beurling later went to visit him in hospital, he was introduced as 'Cino Valentini'.

Having disposed of Gelli's Macchi, Beurling immediately latched onto another, which was seen to waggle its wings as he closed in and opened fire:

> 'The poor devil simply blew to pieces in the air.'

So died Cap. Furio Doglio Niclot, commander of 151ª Squadriglia. A native of Turin, the 34 year-old was a former test pilot and one of Italy's leading fighter pilots at this stage, having claimed six victories plus three more shared; he was killed instantly. The award of a posthumous Medaglia d'Oro followed.

Adrenalin must have been pumping into Beurling's veins as he moved towards the next Macchi, only to be distracted by a couple of Messerschmitts he spotted below. He immediately half-rolled and pulled up under them, getting in a full burst into the fuel tank of one. He reported that it, too, went down and he still had sufficient ammunition remaining to knock pieces off the wings and tail of the other before it evaded and disappeared from his view.

Other pilots of the 249 Squadron flight were also engaged, apparently with Messerschmitts; Sgt. 'Red' Bryden (EP196) believed his attack killed the pilot of one as it was reported to have dived straight into the sea from 20,000 feet, while Flt.Sgt. Williams (BP976) claimed another. Spitfires of 185 Squadron had by

Most successful of the Regia Aeronautica fighter pilots over Malta in 1942 was Cap. Furio Doglio Niclot, commander of 151ª Squadriglia, 20° Gruppo, 51° Stormo CT. He was shot down and killed on 27 July 1942, another victim of Flt.Sgt. George Beurling. *(via N. Malizia)*

Left: Flt.Sgt. (later Plt.Off.) George 'Buzz' Beurling of 249 Squadron with the rudder and the 'Cat-and-Mice' emblem of 51° Stormo CT, cut from the rear fuselage of the 378ª Squadriglia MC202 shot down on 27 July 1942, which crash-landed on Gozo. *(IWM)*. **Right:** Plt.Off. (later Flt.Lt.) Frank Jones of 249 Squadron before becoming tour-expired. He was awarded a DFC. *(Daddo-Langlois Collection)*

now joined the action, and Plt.Off. Guthrie (AB526) reported seeing some 20 Bf109s five miles off Gozo, one of which he attacked. He gave it an eight-second burst following which smoke was seen gushing from it. Two pilots of his flight, Sgts. Drew and Mitchell, later confirmed having seen an aircraft dive into the sea in the vicinity of the combat. It seems that at least some of the reported

Messerschmitts were in fact Macchis, for two more aircraft of 20° Gruppo were damaged in this fight, Mar. Tarantola being wounded in one arm. Despite his wound he, and the pilot of the other damaged machine, Mar. Sicco of 353[a] Squadriglia, both regained their base safely. Owing to further damage to Takali airfield, the returning Spitfires were ordered to land at Luqa.

Lunch was interrupted at Takali by the approach of five Ju88s of III/KG 77, but the defending fighters prevented them from reaching their objectives. All four squadrons had aircraft up — a total of 25 Spitfires (seven/126, seven/185, six/249 and five/603) — in an attempt to comply with the AOC's latest instructions. It fell to Flt.Lt. Johnson's flight from 126 Squadron to make the suggested head-on attacks on the bombers. These potentially deadly tactics worked ideally on this occasion, three Junkers from 7 Staffel falling into the sea, including that flown by the Staffelkapitän:

3Z+JR	Oblt. Josef Zimmer and crew lost
3Z+BR	Fw. Helmut Heuer and two crew lost; gunner survived as prisoner
3Z+DR	Lt. Günther Bohnet and two rescued; observer lost

An aircraft from 6 Staffel was also hit and the pilot, Ofw. Rudolf Panz, wounded. Flt.Sgt. Varey claimed one while Johnson shared in destroying two, one with Sgt. Bush, the other with Flt.Sgt. Evans; damage to others was claimed by Varey (two) and Sgt. Bill Marshall, while Evans also claimed an escorting Messerschmitt shot down — as did Plt.Off. Bruce Downs, who reported:

> '... I was attacked by three 109s from above and behind — two were firing at long range. I made a quick 180° turn and then the 109s started to break away (two one way, one the other). I got a two-second burst at the last of the two 109s... I saw strikes and the 109 plunged into the sea from a height of 75 feet — one wing hit first and the plane seemed to do a complete cartwheel before it disappeared... No 3 of Red Section observed the crash from several thousand feet above.'

Those on the ground had a grandstand view of the air battle, and Jerry Smith noted:

> 'Watched some of the squadron do a head-on attack on some 88s. Three went down, two in flames.'

To which Colin Parkinson added:

> 'Another bombing raid by Ju88s and 109s. All three bombers shot down before reaching the Island.'

As 126 Squadron efficiently and speedily dealt with the bombers, the 249 Squadron flight battled with the escort, a number of which were spotted circling around the descending parachutes of their countrymen. Flt.Sgt. Williams and Sgt. Bryden dived on these but the former's aircraft (BP976/C) was attacked by another (possibly flown by Lt. Karl-Heinz Preu of Stab/JG 53, who was credited with his fifth victory on this day) and shot up quite badly. Sgt. Beurling (BR301/UF-S) joined the fight and saw two Messerschmitts:

> 'I started chasing one of them around in tight turns and we split-arsed uphill and downdale until he went into a dive to get away. I went along, picked him up in the sights and put a one-second squirt into his glycol tank. He rolled

> over and went into the sea from 1000 feet. During the mix-up I had been on the second Me's tail for a split second, just long enough to give him a quick one. He streamed black, oily smoke from his engine.'

As Williams headed back to Luqa he spotted a lone Bf109 below him which he attacked in a dive — a quick burst and he reported that the Messerschmitt poured flames and went into the sea. It seems likely that Beurling or Williams shot down Lt. Preu, for his aircraft — '< 3' — crashed into the sea and he was killed. With his fourth victory of the day, Beurling had taken his Malta claims to 14 — all achieved during July — and thereby had become the Island's top-scorer, a position he was never to relinquish.

Of the eight Messerschmitts claimed during the day, at least two had undoubtedly been misidentified as records show the combats to have been with Macchis. However, apart from the loss of Lt. Preu, two other Bf109s were shot down by the Spitfires including that flown by Oblt. Freytag, one of the leading pilots of I/JG 77; his aircraft went into the sea, witnessed by watchers on the coast, and HSL 128 was ordered out. However, before a rescue could be effected, a Do24 from Syracuse put down in the water and whisked away — literally from under British noses — one who would have been a prized prisoner; Freytag later recalled:

> 'I was pulled out of the water close to Valetta harbour just as the British rescue launches were coming up.'

Not so fortunate was Uffz. Heinrich Freckmann of 6/JG 53, who was posted missing off Cape Scaramina flying 'Yellow 11'. The only survivor from Fw. Heuer's bomber reached Malta and safety, and may have been the cause of an unpleasant incident recalled by Flg.Off. Shipard of 89 Squadron. Shipard had been relaxing with others at St Paul's Bay when a rubber dinghy came into view, its paddling occupant a German airman who arrogantly spat at a helper who extended a hand; the hand became a fist, and the German was knocked back into the sea. The situation was calmed by the arrival of Maltese police officers, who took the airman away.

Hardly had the various flights of Spitfires landed to refuel and re-arm, when eight of 126 Squadron were scrambled as more enemy aircraft approached the Island. It would seem, however, that these were on a mercy mission searching for survivors of the missing aircraft. Two of the Spitfire pilots sighted a number of Messerschmitts, Flt.Sgt. Evans claiming one probably destroyed and Flt.Lt. Johnson another damaged.

The final raid of the day occurred just before 2000, three Ju88s being escorted to Luqa by Bf109s and ten MC202s of 51° Stormo, the latter led by Ten. Col. Remondino. Again 249 Squadron were involved in the interception, seven from this unit being joined by eight others from 603 Squadron. Only Flt.Sgt. Jack Rae (BR301/UF-S) was able to make any definite claims, when he reported that he probably destroyed a Messerschmitt and damaged a 'Reggiane'. Although the action was centred to the north of the Island, four Spitfires of 126 Squadron had been sent up to provide protection for a Catalina which was was preparing to depart from Kalafrana Bay; the flyingboat was not attacked.

Two hours after this latest raid on the Island, three Hurricanes departed for a further intruder sortie to Sicily, their target on this occasion being Comiso. Wg.Cdr. Stan Turner led this time, again with Sgts. Weaver and Len Reid

(BN408/E). Two of the fighter-bombers dropped their bombs over the south-west corner of the airfield from 4000 feet, experiencing light but accurate anti-aircraft fire; the other Hurricane pilot was unable to release his missiles.

Whilst the Hurricanes were over Sicily, Cap. Cumbat led five Ju87s of 102° Gruppo Tuff from Gela to raid Hal Far. Serg. Giulio Campari's aircraft was intercepted over the sea by a Beaufighter, and although not hit the incident caused the pilot to jettison his bomb into the sea and return to Sicily. Little damage was done at Hal Far as a result of the attack.

Tuesday 28 — Wednesday 29 July

Tuesday the 28th proved another good day for the defenders, but it began badly when eight 1435 Flight Spitfires went off at 0850. They were bounced by Bf109s of II/JG 53, part of a fighter sweep comprising a reported 27 aircraft which included a reconnaissance Bf109F of 1(F)/122; this aircraft force-landed on return to Comiso, possibly as the result of combat damage. Meanwhile, Ofw. Rollwage claimed one Spitfire shot down west of Zonqor Point — possibly the aircraft flown by Flt.Sgt. Brown, who baled out of BR303 into the sea from where he was subsequently rescued. Sgt. Don Hubbard's aircraft (EP189) was also shot-up and it crashed in a field near Kirkop while attempting to approach Luqa; it smashed into a stone wall, ripping off a wing and narrowly missed careering into some parked Beauforts; the pilot was killed.

At 1130, five Ju88s with an escort of 16 Messerschmitts and four MC202s of 51° Stormo were intercepted well north of the Island by 23 Spitfires of 185 and 249 Squadrons, only two of the raiders eventually crossing the coast to attack Hal Far. Pilots of the latter unit reported intercepting three bombers, eight Bf109s and two Re2001s, obviously misidentifying the Italian fighters; there were no conclusive results of the ensuing action in which Sqn.Ldr. Mitchell (BR375/N) claimed one bomber probably destroyed:

> 'I sighted three Ju88s 5/6000 feet below us and dived sharply for them. I attacked first, full beam closing to astern and observed strikes on both mainplanes and fuselage. As I broke away I observed both engines pouring black smoke and the aircraft diving steeply. This was also observed by P/O McElroy, No 3 of my section.'

Flt.Sgt. Rae (BR301/UF-S) and Sgt. Irving Gass (EP196/M) shared the probable destruction of a second of the bombers, Jack Rae reporting:

> 'I carried straight in on the bombers opening fire on the rear one from about 300 yards on the beam closing to almost astern; strikes were observed on the fuselage. I broke down and underneath this E/A. The fire from the rear-gunner ceased before breaking away. I then came up underneath the leading bomber, opening fire for about three seconds from almost dead-astern. E/A commenced smoking from starboard engine and wing root. Sgt. Gass also attacked this E/A observing it smoking before attacking.'

Plt.Off. Yates (BP975/T) damaged one more. Others tangled with the escorting fighters, Flt.Sgt. Tommy Parks (BR131/0) being credited with a Messerschmitt probably destroyed while Sgt. Wynn (BP869/K) and Plt.Off. McElroy (BR135/Z) damaged two more; the latter also claimed a Reggiane damaged. Following behind, 185 Squadron also became involved but only Flt.Sgt. Andrews (EP316) was able to make any claims when he damaged two more Messerschmitts; he gained strikes on the first one, then:

> 'I was forced to break off as another Me manoeuvred for position on my tail. As I still had lots of speed from dive I pulled up sharply and in a four-second burst at 30° astern, I saw cannon strikes on his fuselage behind the cockpit. I was forced to break off by a Spitfire attacking me from out of the sun, and had no time to finish this off.'

In the late afternoon five Spitfires of 185 Squadron were ordered off to patrol to the north of the Island, and were still up at 1710 when 16 more Spitfires took to the air, eight each from 1435 Flight and 126 Squadron. Three Ju88s of II/KG 77 were intercepted at 18,000 feet as they approached Hal Far. The first two were attacked by several pilots and both went down, one in flames and the other trailing white smoke, which developed into a full fire before it hit the sea — there were no survivors from Uffz. Fritz Rottenbecher's 4 Staffel aircraft (3Z+EM) or from that (3Z+BP) flown by Lt. Wolfgang Marzahl of 6 Staffel.

One of the bombers was credited to Plt.Offs. Baril (BR387) and Guthrie (BR321) of 185 Squadron, shared jointly with two pilots of 126 Squadron, Sgts. Tiddy and Nigel Park (BR345/S); the latter fired a four-second burst and saw flames before being forced to break away as a Bf109 closed in on him. Guthrie reported that he carried out a head-on attack on an aircraft which had already been seriously damaged and closed to within 50 yards before it fell in pieces, while Baril thought it fell into the sea off Delimara after he had seen his fire hitting the starboard wing, fuselage and tail.

The second Junkers fell to the combined attacks of five pilots of 126 Squadron — Flg.Off. Rip Jones, Plt.Offs. Thompson, Thomas, Jerry Smith and Flt.Sgt. Farquharson; Smith, who soon discovered that the cannons of his aircraft (BR242/A) had not been loaded, and who then suffered a jammed machine gun, reported:

> 'Turned port into bombers. Fired from 200 yards closing at port 88 — a two or three-second burst and aircraft immediately burst into flames around port engine and front of fuselage. It turned to port and down. I turned into the middle Ju88 and fired a short burst and saw a trail of white smoke... observed the starboard 88 going down almost vertically in flames. Also saw four Spits chasing an 88 at deck level five miles S.E. of Kalafrana, which trailed white smoke, turned to port and crashed into the sea.'

Smith's aircraft suffered a hit in the glycol tank and he was obliged to force-land on return. It would seem that the bomber attacked by 126 Squadron was that which crashed in flames on a Dorset Regiment billet at Tas-Silc; one of the crew was found dead near the wreckage. The third Ju88 was attacked by Plt.Off. Rod Smith:

> 'I took right-hand one and gave 12-second burst at 250-150 yards. Port engine burst into flames, then rest of e/a till engines fell out, wing fell off. All 88s shot down. Action over Kalafrana. E/a went in ½ mile from shore.'

Unbeknown to Rod Smith, this particular bomber was also under attack by three other Spitfires — those flown by Sqn.Ldr. Lovell and Plt.Off. Mejor of 1435 Flight, joined by Wg.Cdr. Stainforth (89 Squadron's commanding officer) who had borrowed one of the unit's Spitfires and come along "for the ride". The Ju88

— 3Z+HP flown by Uffz. Albert Führer — went down close to Kalafrana Bay and two of the crew baled out. The ASR unit commander, Flt.Lt. Crockett, quickly put to sea in seaplane tender ST338 and within seven minutes had picked up Uffz. Gustav Frick (the gunner) and four minutes later the badly wounded W/T operator (Uffz. Karl Bauer) who would undoubtedly have been lost but for Crockett's prompt action. A third member of the crew also survived to become a prisoner.

Of his part in this, his first combat, 43 year-old Wg.Cdr. George Stainforth reported:

> 'After climbing to about 16,000 feet approximately south of Kalafrana, CO (Sqn.Ldr. Lovell) turned and dived on a Ju88 which was then untouched, flying east, followed by the rest of the section. Several Me109s were about, but no other Ju's. Got left 200-300 yards behind on the outside of the turn. An Me109 turned in front of and below me allowing an easy quarter attack from close range. Did not see it go down as I went over the top of it and broke off to keep with my section. After the Spitfire in front (Sqn.Ldr. Lovell) attacked the Ju88, I saw two occupants bale out and the starboard engine began smoking.
>
> 'I made diving quarter attack on it (short burst), then did wide zig-zag to come back for second attack from astern and below. The Hun was flying level after turning north, smoke coming from the starboard engine, both engines running. Opened fire from 200 yards, kept the button pressed until passed a few feet over the top of it. Many strikes observed — fuselage burst into a mass of flames. Nobody else baled out. Did not watch or follow it down, but dived after a Spitfire chasing an Me109 — Sqn.Ldr. Lovell — joined up eventually.'

Still the battle had not quite finished as Sgt. Nigel Park, having shared in shooting down one bomber, then claimed an escorting Messerschmitt shot down. He fired a short burst from about 50 yards as it passed him in a turn and saw strikes right beside the cockpit; it veered away and was seen to go down.

Many on the ground had witnessed the fighting above, but not LAC. Chandler who had more important matters on his mind — his empty stomach! He later wrote in his diary:

> 'While having tea, three bombers came in and Spitfires and ack-ack engaged. Heard a cheer as one kite came down and, a few seconds later, another; but was too busy trying to pinch a bit of bread in the cook's absence to go out. Then came a third cheer! I went to the door of the dining hall and saw an 88 diving and on fire, right above. One of the crew baled out, but his parachute only half opened and he would be lucky to get away with his life. The machine hit some buildings on the other side of the bay and became a huge mass of flames. Finished my tea and was just in time to see one of two more parachutists hit the sea not far out. Watched them brought in. One was said to be about sixteen, and had a hole through his arm.'

This would have been Uffz. Bauer who, during subsequent interrogation, complained that in all his flights over Malta his aircraft had always been detailed to fly on the outside of the bombing formation and thus was the first to be attacked! His gunner, Uffz. Frick, admitted that as a result of their manoeuvrability he considered the Macchis gave better close escort protection than did the Messerschmitts. Although he felt Italian pilots were not up to German standards, he said the Macchis had always afforded him good protection on such flights as he had made with them. One of the prisoners is alleged to have commented, perhaps with tongue in cheek:

> 'Germans at home are becoming impatient at the failure of the Axis to take Malta. It is being suggested that it was time the Japanese took the job in hand!'

The Island had been striking out again as well, for at dawn a reconnaissance Spitfire had found another convoy, this time off Sapienza (Southern Greece). This comprised a large transport, the 5322-ton Italian *Monviso* out from Brindisi making for Benghazi, escorted by the destroyer *Freccia* and torpedo-boat *Calliope*. Wg.Cdr. Pat Gibbs at once led an attack by nine Beauforts — six armed with torpedoes and three with bombs — and six Beaufighters, while one of 69 Squadron's Baltimores — AG734 flown by Plt.Off. Munro — flew at higher level to observe and photograph the result of the attack. The convoy was sighted at midday. While three of the Beaufighters flew as top cover and the other three went in low to strafe the escort, the torpedo-bombers attacked from either beam in flights of three. The merchant ship was seen to be hit on the starboard side and was obliged to accept a tow into the nearby port of Navarino, in a slightly damaged condition. The bomb-carrying Beauforts had, meanwhile, attacked the destroyer but failed to gain any hits.

The convoy had air cover of at least three MC200s (probably from 7° Gruppo CT), a Z506B floatplane and a Ju88, the Macchis attacking as the Beauforts broke away from their respective attacks. Flg.Off. Peter Roper's aircraft (AW302) was badly damaged by one of the fighters, and he was obliged to crash-land on return to Luqa. Some retribution had been gained, however, as the Macchi pilot had overshot, allowing Roper to open up with his fixed wing guns claiming some damage to the fighter before it was lost from sight.

Flt.Lt. Tony Leaning, who was on his last Beaufort sortie before being rested, saw the Z506B ahead of him and was about to attack this when he was driven away by the Macchis. The Beaufighter leader, Wg.Cdr. Ross Shore, also spotted Ten. Gaetano Mastrodicasa's 139ª Squadriglia floatplane — which he identified as a German Blohm & Voss Ha140 — and fired at this, but was chased away by a Ju88. It was just as well that the Cant escaped damage, as two Beauforts were shot down during the attack, one crew owing their subsequent rescue to this Italian aircraft. The first, Wt.Off. R.J. Dawson's AW296, had been hit in the port engine as it approached on its torpedo run and was forced to ditch; three of the crew managed to scramble into their dinghy from which they were picked up by *Calliope* but the navigator, Flt.Sgt. Eric Sutherland, went down with the aircraft.

The crippled Beaufort was seen to ditch by Plt.Off. Munro's Baltimore crew, and the aircraft's dinghy was observed in the sea with the survivors. As the Baltimore turned away, a twin-engined aircraft identified as a Ca310 was encountered and was at once attacked. Closing in from 200 to 50 yards, strikes were seen on the fuselage, wings and engine nacelles of the Italian machine before all guns jammed! Some return fire was experienced but no damage was sustained. Ten minutes later, an unidentified single-engined aircraft — probably an MC200 — appeared and gave chase but was evaded.

The other Beaufort, L9820 flown by Lt. Ted Strever SAAF, was hit in both engines and was also forced to ditch, during which the navigator, Plt.Off. Bill Dunsmore, gashed his arm. All four of the crew managed to get into the dinghy. Shortly afterwards, an MC202 flew over at low level followed half an hour later by Ten. Mastrodicasa's floatplane, which circled then alighted nearby. The Italians motioned them over at which Strever dived into the sea, swimming back with a tow rope.

Once aboard the aircraft the British airmen were given brandy, wine and cigarettes, but the Cant had to be taxied to calmer water before a take-off could be effected. After a two-hour flight it alighted at Prevesa, a Greek mainland harbour just north of the island of Levkas — 139ª Squadriglia's current base. Here they were taken to the Officers' Mess, where they were again generously treated and were given civilian clothes into which to change, and huge plates of macaroni, followed by steak and then more brandy and cigarettes! After weeks of spartan living on Malta and more than 12 hours since their last meal, the food was rapidly devoured. Suitably fed and watered, the prisoners were allowed to play table-tennis in the Mess and to write letters to their next of kin, and were informed that on the morrow they would be flown to Taranto.

That night all four men were allocated rooms in the Officers' Quarters, Strever and Dunsmore sharing one room, Sgts. Wilkinson (the W/T operator) and Brown (the gunner) another. During the night plans were hatched and formulated to attempt to escape at the first opportunity, as it was realised that once in mainland Italy such chances would be remote.

Following a breakfast of bacon, eggs, tomatoes and potatoes, the airmen were taken to the jetty to board another Z506B. This was MM45432 '13', a brand-new machine of 139ª Squadriglia, which would prove to be 'unlucky 13' for the Italian crew! They were seen off at 0940 by many members of the unit, during which photographs were taken. Ten. Mastrodicasa was again the pilot of the Cant, with Mar. Alessandro Chifari as second pilot, Serg. Trento Losi (engineer) and Av.Sc. Marc Antonio Schisano (WOP/AG) as crew, and were joined by Vice-Brigadiere Carabiniere (Police Sgt.) Giulio Scarciella as guard. On arrival at Taranto, the Italian crew were due to start their leave.

Out of consideration for the comfort of their prisoners during the long flight, and the situation they would otherwise find themselves in if the aircraft was forced to come down in the sea, they were not handcuffed. This was to be the Italians undoing, for the Beaufort crew had less than chivalrous intentions towards their undoubtedly chivalrous captors!

After 45 minutes in the air, as the police sergeant's attention began to wander, at a pre-agreed signal Wilkinson suddenly yelled "Spitfire!" and pointed out of the window. In a split second the guard had been floored by a blow to the jaw and his .45 revolver thrown to Strever, sitting near Mar. Chifari, now piloting the aircraft, and flying at about 2000 feet. The sight of the gun caused Chifari to put the plane into a dive; Strever pulled him out of the seat and took over the controls. Ten. Mastrodicasa, meanwhile, who at that particular moment was up at the front of the aircraft, realised what was happening and pulled his Beretta pistol from his pocket. When confronted by the obviously-determined Strever brandishing the guard's .45 however, he quickly capitulated.

While Wilkinson and Brown guarded the five Italians, who were then tied up with their own belts, Strever turned the Cant southwards and Dunsmore searched for maps, none of which could be found; a rough pencil-drawn map of the area was discovered and using this eventually they located Cape Spartivento, on the toe of Italy. Shortly before making this landfall, Sgt. Ray Brown, who was sitting in the gun turret, yelled that an aircraft was formating on them. It was a Ju52 which closed to within 300 yards, both aircraft waggling their wings in greeting, while Brown dipped the guns in salute before the transport aircraft continued on its way. Now that their position could reasonably accurately be assessed, course was set for Malta, some 60 miles distant. At this stage the prisoners were untied and when Mastrodicasa realised the new destination, he protested that it would be impossible to get through because of the threat posed by the Spitfires, but Strever pressed on.

On Malta a section of four Spitfires from 603 Squadron was scrambled, led by Flg.Off. Dicks-Sherwood, to intercept an unidentified 'plot' appearing on the radar screens. Finding the floatplane just above the surface of the sea about ten miles off the coast, and suspecting that it might be about to make a torpedo attack on the harbour, he opened fire. At that very moment Chifari, who had been allowed to take over the controls again, throttled back in preparation for a landing, causing Dicks-Sherwood's burst of cannon fire to churn up the sea some 30 yards ahead of the aircraft; the second Spitfire pilot also missed but Sgt. Bill Young, a Rhodesian (who ironically was a personal friend of Strever's), gained strikes on the port wing with his burst, although the floatplane was able to alight without mishap. Bill Dunsmore took off his singlet and waved as the Spitfire circled, and then flew off towards Malta.

About an hour later HSL 107 arrived to find all nine occupants sitting on the wings, enjoying brandy and wine produced by the Italians, which they had been taking on leave with them! Subsequently the captured Cant floatplane was taken in tow by HSL 107 and eventually brought into St Paul's Bay, while Spitfires patrolled overhead to prevent it from being attacked by any 'snooper' in the vicinity.

This Cant Z506B floatplane, MM45432 '13' of 139[a] Squadriglia RST, was 'hijacked' by Lt. Ted Strever and his Beaufort crew when they were on their way from Greece to captivity in Italy aboard the aircraft on 28 July 1942. It is seen here repainted in RAF colours and in use for air/sea rescue duties. *(via R.C. Jones)*

In their absence, Ten. Mastrodicasa and his crew, plus the unfortunate Carabiniere would be tried by an Italian Court Martial and found guilty of carelessly allowing the enemy to capture their aircraft. Their mistake had been the kindness and consideration they had shown to their prisoners, for which their reward was to be a long spell in a prisoner-of-war camp, whilst Lt. Strever and Plt.Off. Dunsmore immediately received the DFC, and Sgts. Wilkinson and Brown the DFM.

During the previous night (28th/29th), while the Beaufort crew were being entertained at Prevesa, nine Ju87s of 102° Gruppo had again set out to attack Maltese targets. Capitani Cenni, Cumbat and Stringa each led a trio of Stukas to the Island but again very little damage was caused, although returning crews reported seeing large fires at Hal Far and Melliehia Bay following their attacks. There were no interceptions by the Beaufighters.

The following morning (the 29th), seven 249 Squadron Spitfires were scrambled at 0915 to intercept a sweep by a reported 16 Bf109s and four MC202s, which came in after an earlier raid had turned back before reaching the Island. After an initial skirmish, one fighter dived out of the sun on Sgt. Beurling's Spitfire (BR301/UF-S), shooting off the cockpit canopy. The Canadian immediately turned onto the tail of what he believed to be the aircraft which had just attacked him, and from 450 yards fired a one-second burst which hit the engine, fuel tank and cockpit. At once it went down in flames into the sea 500 yards off Sliema Point; his subsequent Combat Report of the action, in the customary clipped style of the day, read:

> 'As Tiger Blue I, attacked 15 Me109s over Grand Harbour. Dogfighting ensued for 15-20 minutes. Made an attack on one e/a from port quarter below; gave a three-second burst cannon and machine gun fire; large pieces of e/a came off, then e/a's gas tank exploded and the aircraft burned. E/a struck the sea 1 mile north of Grand Harbour.'

His victim on this occasion was almost certainly Uffz. Karl-Heinz Witschke of I/JG 77, who was killed in 'Yellow 2'. It seems unlikely, however, that Witschke had been the pilot who attacked Beurling's aircraft, for two claims were submitted by the Luftwaffe, one by Oblt. Geisshardt of I/JG 77, and one by Ofw. Rollwage of II/JG 53. Jerry Smith of 126 Squadron was off duty and witnessed the demise of the Messerschmitt:

> 'Watched a Spit attack a 109 while on the beach bathing. It went down in flames and crashed about half a mile out to sea. Pilot baled out but apparently his 'chute burned because he splashed in shortly after from several thousand feet.'

Meanwhile, another member of the 249 Squadron flight, Sgt. Ernie Budd (EP131/0) reported shooting the fin and rudder off a second fighter, which he believed was another Messerschmitt, and this also fell into the sea. It seems likely that he misidentified his victim, for Serg. Domenico Manini baled out of his Macchi into the sea about three miles south of Marsascala; he was picked up by a minesweeper and taken to Malta. Sgt. Budd's aircraft sustained some damage during the action and crashed on landing at Takali, although he was unhurt.

The day's major activities concluded at around 1800 when seven Spitfires of 185 Squadron were scrambled due to the appearance of a possible hostile 'plot' on the radar screens; this turned out to be three delivery aircraft from the west.

Thursday, 30 July

At 0755 seven of 1435 Flight's Spitfires were scrambled, followed by 16 more from 249 and 603 Squadrons, to meet a reported fighter sweep believed to include approximately 20 Messerschmitts and six Macchis. In fact, there were also three Ju88s present but these did not cross the coast, while the escort included 15 MC202s of 51° Stormo led by Ten. Col. Remondino, as well as Bf109s. The Macchis were undertaking a simulated raid to confuse British radars.

1435 Flight reported being jumped by ten Messerschmitts at 26,000 feet ten miles north of Grand Harbour; but it would seem that the attackers may have been the Macchis, for the Italian pilots claimed two Spitfires shot down, one by Remondino himself, and one jointly by Cap. Bruno Tattanelli, Cap. Egeo Pittoni, Ten. Alberto Volpi, Ten. Giuseppe Bonfiglio, Serg. Magg. Alcide Leoni and Serg. Luigi Berna, while Serg. Magg. Gambari reported seeing two Spitfires crash in flames. Only one Spitfire actually fell, Sgt. Colin Wood (a New Zealander) being killed when his aircraft (EP344) went into the sea off St Paul's Bay. Four Spitfires of 126 Squadron were despatched immediately to search for the missing pilot but nothing was sighted.

Pilots of 603 Squadron reported sighting six Bf109s and six Macchis eight miles north of Zonqor Point — Colin Parkinson (BP989/N-4) later recorded:

> 'Scrambled about 8 a.m. Flew to about 20,000 feet. Intercepted six 109s. I shot one down, hit him in the engine with my first burst, followed him down to about 500 feet and gave a burst from astern at about 50 yards. His port wing fell off and he fell in the sea.'

Somewhat later at 1109, seven Spitfires of 126 Squadron were scrambled to join others from 249 and 603 Squadrons, as another fighter sweep approached at great height. As they climbed over Grand Harbour, two Messerschmitts dived out of the sun and hit the aircraft flown by Sgt. Dave Ritchie, who promptly baled out and landed with nothing worse than a bruised arm. The Luftwaffe was to submit three claims during the day.

Shortly before 1600 at least six Axis fighters crossed the coast at great height, presumably on a reconnaissance sortie, but no contact was made by four Spitfires of 249 Squadron which were up at the time. The Spitfires were actually escorting the captured Cant seaplane from Zonqor to Kalafrana, where it would be repaired, serviced and given new colours. It was intended that from now on it would serve the Island as a rescue craft.

Darkness brought one of the increasingly rare Luftwaffe night raids on the island, four bombers of KGr 806 being plotted crossing the coast from 2145 onwards. Bombs fell in the Naxxar and Birkirkara areas where three civilians were killed and four injured. Eight hours later a delayed-action bomb exploded and killed eight more, injuring 20 others. Only three of the bombers returned to their base, Oblt. Fritz Hermann's M7+FK being caught by Plt.Off. Reeves' Beaufighter (V8219) west of Gozo; two survivors (the W/T operator and the gunner) were later picked up by the Axis air-sea rescue service, while the observer was taken prisoner and Hermann lost his life. 89 Squadron's commanding officer, Wg.Cdr. Stainforth, now returned to Egypt following his brief visit to the detachment. Sadly he and his operator would be killed there in a flying accident two months later.

Friday, 31 July

At 1000 Plt.Off. Gray Stenborg of 185 Squadron took off on an air test in BR321. Warned of hostile aircraft in the vicinity, he encountered three Bf109s, one of which he claimed shot down; he reported:

'I heard Gondor inform the squadron which was airborne that the enemy was at 20,000 feet — I then lost height to 22,000 feet and while flying west saw three Me109s below, flying in a northerly direction. It was a perfect jump so I attacked. I opened fire at the 109 on the right who was lagging farthest behind at 400 yards closing to 50 — bits flew off the aircraft and it burst into flames. The remaining two 109s half-rolled and disappeared.'

This latest claim raised his total to ten, five of them during the month. Although eight Spitfires of 126 Squadron were sent after this small fighter formation, no further contact was made.

A large sweep occurred during the early afternoon, when an estimated 18 Messerschmitts and Macchis were seen. Sixteen Spitfires of 185 and 603 Squadrons were up but had insufficient height to intercept, and were bounced; four Spitfires of the former unit were hit. From a burning EP255 Sgt. J.G. Livingston baled out into the sea, the Canadian being picked up by HSL 128 within the hour, while Sgt. Weaver succeeded in crash-landing his damaged aircraft (EP343) and survived unhurt.

Not so fortunate was the pilot of another aircraft hit in this attack; Flg.Off. Tony Bruce was obliged to bale out of EP137 and despite an intensive search he was not found. It would be the next day before he paddled ashore in his dinghy, exhausted after having covered 15 miles in 15 hours! He complained that although he saw searching Spitfires, including one which came within 800 yards of him, he had no fluorescent with which to attract them, nor a torch or whistle without which he stood little chance of being seen or heard by aircraft or HSL. He also reported that the hand paddles with which the dinghy was equipped were very exhausting, and recommended that any sort of small paddle with a shaft would be preferable.

Close behind 185 Squadron had come the 603 Squadron aircraft, Colin Parkinson recording:

'Scramble at about 3 p.m. Climbed to about 15,000 feet. Two of my section had to land because of engine trouble (*BR562 overshot and was damaged when landing at Luqa*). The CO and myself were left by ourselves. I was keeping watch behind when I saw six enemy aircraft, called up to the CO but he took no notice. I called about six times all told, the Me's were coming too close for comfort. I called up once more and broke up sun and dived to attack. The enemy aircraft were going so fast that I only had them in range for a second. Gave a long burst and saw strikes but no other results. The CO broke also when he saw me.'

The final action of the month occurred shortly after 1800 when an estimated 27 fighters were plotted to the north of the Island. Sixteen Spitfires, eight each from 126 Squadron and 1435 Flight, were sent to investigate and a number of skirmishes broke out some miles out from St Paul's Bay. Plt.Off. Jerry Smith noted:

'Intercepted two squadrons of 109s 20 miles west but couldn't get near them. While flying with Rip (*Flg.Off. Ripley Jones, the American*) one intrepid beggar came up behind us, firing at Rip. I turned into him but he climbed quickly and fired from well out of range. When 15 miles off Sicily a squadron of 109s passed us going back; turned to chase them, but they stooged home.'

Not all the unit were unsuccessful however, Flt.Lt. Johnson claiming a Messerschmitt shot down, and Plt.Off. Thompson an Re2001, although no Italian fighters were apparently engaged on this sweep.

Indeed, this was the end of the Regia Aeronautica's offensive. Generale SA Silvio Scaroni now ordered all further operations by Italian fighters to be suspended due to low serviceability caused by the problems which were being experienced with the Macchi 202s — particularly those which had been built under licence at the Breda factory.

In terms of aircraft losses honours were fairly even for the month, but actual pilot casualties in the RAF units had been relatively low, whilst those amongst Axis aircrew had been quite heavy. Axis bomber losses had been particularly severe, including at least 22 Ju88s and about half a dozen Italian types. The two carrier deliveries of Spitfires had certainly made good attrition, but food and fuel remained the Island's greatest problem.

During the month Spitfire pilots had flown 1780 sorties and had claimed 137½ aircraft shot down; 38 Spitfires had been lost from which almost half the pilots had been saved. There had been 61 Beaufighter sorties (night fighter and strike) during which 13 aircraft were claimed shot down (for no operational loss), while the AA guns were credited with a further 8½ victories. Sixteen armed shipping sorties had been undertaken by the ASV-equipped Wellington VIIIs, and a further ten by the torpedo-carrying Wellington Vs of 38 Squadron, before their departure earlier in the month. The strike Beauforts had suffered the greatest proportional losses, with seven aircraft shot down during 28 sorties.

A number of awards had been made during the month, including a second DFC for Flg.Off. Fumerton, the night fighter pilot, and a DFC for his radar operator, Plt.Off. Bing. The outstanding Sgt. George 'Buzz' Beurling received two DFMs and, at the end of the month, a commission! A belated DFM also came the way of Flt.Sgt. 'Paddy' Schade of 126 Squadron, the top-scoring Malta pilot until eclipsed by Beurling during the closing days of the month. 185 Squadron's New Zealander, Plt.Off. Gray Stenborg received a DFC while two more of the Beaufort pilots were decorated — Flt.Lt. Bill Stevens with the DFC, and Sgt. Nolan with the DFM. Finally, recognition of the invaluable work carried out by the reconnaissance Spitfire pilots of 69 Squadron was acknowledged with the award of a DFM to Sgt. Leslie Colquhoun of that unit.

It is noteworthy that bombing raids had fallen away considerably during the second half of the month, only 19 attacks being made during which 160 tons of bombs were dropped, compared to more than double that tonnage during the initial two weeks of July, when 390 tons had been directed at the Island. Indeed, the bombers had increasingly been conspicuous by their absence, as the focus of Axis effort became devoted to fighter sweeps. On the face of it, Air Vice-Marshal Park's new tactics would appear to have been instrumental in an unacceptable rate of attrition being forced on the Ju88 units. This would cause a resumption of effort by the Axis to force an air superiority battle between the opposing fighters before the bombers could resume their offensive.

Although the lessening in the intensity of raids came as an obvious welcome relief to the Island's population, a further grim reminder of the perilous predicament in which the Maltese found themselves now emerged in the guise of the scourge of all peoples under seige — typhoid. Whilst typhoid in such situations and conditions was often unavoidable, on Malta in July 1942 the epidemic was self-inflicted.

Alarmed by the growing prospect of starvation, the authorities sought ways in which the productivity of the land might be improved. Manure or other fertilisers were almost unavailable, and clearly could not be imported, so permission was granted — against the advice of the Health Department — to utilize defecated human waste as manure, in a very limited way. After a short period the feared consequence manifested itself — an outbreak of typhoid. Almost 1000 cases were reported, 99 of which proved fatal. The experiment was seen to be a complete disaster and was quickly abandoned, but no official heads rolled.

Chapter Eight

OPERATION 'PEDESTAL'

185 Squadron's flight commanders during the summer months of 1942; Flt.Lts John Plagis (left) and Ron West claimed some 18 victories between them. *(N.J. Ogilvie)*

The ending of the second Regia Aeronautica offensive against the Island coincided with preparations to run a further convoy through the Western Mediterranean. The arrival of only two damaged freighters in June had done little to alleviate the ultimate problem facing the defenders — starvation, both in terms of food and fuel.

By now, the overall military situation had changed greatly, and not entirely to the disadvantage of the British. True, Tobruk had fallen soon after the 'Harpoon' and 'Vigorous' endeavours, but the burden thereby placed on Middle East Command to supply and sustain a garrison there had been removed. Indeed, the whole coastline of Cyrenaica and Western Egypt was now in Axis hands. But the grossly extended lines of communications resulting, coupled with the overriding urgency to strengthen and reinforce the Deutsch Afrika Korps at the 'sharp end' at El Alamein, ensured that the imminent threat of invasion of Malta no longer remained a serious proposition — at least in the short term.

The Mediterranean had never been so fertile a hunting ground for the British anti-shipping units — airborne, submarine and coastal forces — be they based at Malta, or in the Nile Delta area. Axis convoys headed now — in greater numbers than ever before — to Tripoli, Benghazi and Tobruk by both the eastern and western routes past the Island. The severe losses already inflicted upon Axis merchant ships was a topic of serious discussion in high places.

Admiral Doenitz commenting:

> 'Even with all the Spanish tonnage and the ships we could seize if we invaded Southern France, even by increasing construction tenfold in Italian shipyards, we could not keep up another Rommel campaign. Malta must be destroyed.'

A feeling also held by Mussolini's Foreign Minister, Count Ciano, who confided to his diary:

> 'This Rommel campaign is becoming sheer madness. Our merchant fleet will not last a year at this rate.'

Rommel clearly agreed but obviously saw the situation from another angle, and wrote:

> 'With Malta in our hands, the British would have had little chance of exercising any further control over convoy traffic in the Central Mediterranean.
>
> 'I have personally warned Marshal Kesselring of the tragic consequences for my lines of communication between Italy and Africa if he does not succeed in establishing air superiority over Malta.'

Malta's potential to disrupt these vital arteries remained as strong as ever — provided that her garrison could be sustained. Clearly a two-convoy attempt on this occasion would be a non-starter, given the Axis domination of the vital stretches of the Eastern Basin, but this would allow the virtue of concentration of forces from the west. The largest naval/air operation yet attempted by the Royal Navy was thus in immediate contemplation.

As July drew to a close the nucleus of this new convoy, to be codenamed Operation 'Pedestal', was forming on the Clyde where 13 fast, modern freighters and a tanker were being loaded with mixed cargoes of urgently-required supplies, totalling in excess of 85,000 tons. The bulk was flour but each ship also carried petrol and aviation fuel, shells and other explosives. This was an essential prerequisite, for to concentrate all stores of one kind in single ships courted disaster, should they then be sunk. These vessels, to come under the overall command of Commodore A.G. Venables (who would sail in *Port Chalmers*) as Convoy WS 21S, were as follows:

Waimarama	(12,843 tons)	*Glenorchy*	(8982 tons)
Melbourne Star	(12,806 tons)	*Port Chalmers*	(8535 tons)
Brisbane Star	(12,791 tons)	*Santa Elisa*	(8379 tons)
Empire Hope	(12,688 tons)	*Rochester Castle*	(7795 tons)
Wairangi	(12,436 tons)	*Almeria Lykes*	(7773 tons)
Dorset	(10,624 tons)	*Deucalion*	(7516 tons)
Ohio (tanker)	(9263 tons)	*Clan Ferguson*	(7347 tons)

Ohio, an American tanker which had been loaned by Texaco to the Ministry of War Transport on her arrival in Britain and now entrusted to the management of the British Eagle Oil & Shipping Co., was re-manned with a hand-picked British crew. Under Captain D.W. Mason, she was loaded with 11,500 tons of kerosene and diesel fuel oils. Two other freighters — *Santa Elisa* and *Almeria Lykes* — were also US-owned but retained their American crews. All the merchantmen were armed for self-defence; some had a single large anti-aircraft gun, ranging from 3-inch to 6-inch calibre and all had 20mm Oerlikons; some also had 40mm Bofors and all were fitted with the relatively ineffective PAC (Parachute and Cable) devise.

The composition of a suitable escort force for this large agglomeration of vessels proved even more complex to arrange. To form Vice-Admiral Sir Neville Syfret's Force 'F', it would incorporate the existing Force 'H' at Gibraltar, strengthened from sources throughout the world. For air cover the faithful *Eagle* and *Argus* were again available, but now they were to be joined by two of the newer armoured Fleet carriers — *Victorious* from the Home Fleet, and *Indomitable*, which returned from the Indian Ocean specially for the operation. 'Big gun' support would be provided by the battleships *Nelson* and *Rodney*, supported by seven light cruisers and 26 destroyers. Within Force 'F', cruisers *Phoebe, Sirius* and *Charybdis* and 15 of the destroyers would escort the capital ships, together forming Force 'Z' (Rear-Admiral A.L.St G. Lyster commanding), while the remaining cruisers — *Nigeria, Kenya, Manchester* and *Cairo* — plus 11 destroyers formed Force 'X' (Rear-Admiral H.M. Burrough), the direct escort, which would stay with the convoy all the way through to the Island.

The possibility of invasion led to the issue of sidearms to pilots. Pilots of 185 Squadron 'go for their guns'; Flt.Lt. Plagis (left), with Plt.Offs Ogilvie, Lambert, Kent and Charney (at rear). *(N.J. Ogilvie)*

Late in the day it was decided to add to Force 'Z' the older carrier HMS *Furious* — not as part of the escort proper since she was preparing to carry to the Mediterranean a further delivery of Spitfires for Malta; her departure had been delayed for reasons that will be described later. Within Force 'X', both *Nigeria*, Admiral Burrough's flagship, and the AA cruiser *Cairo* were fitted with the latest Fighter Direction equipment, staffed by specialist personnel. Additional support for the convoy included two oilers and the tug *Jaunty*, supported by five corvettes, a further pair of destroyers, four minesweepers of 17th Minesweeping Flotilla, seven launches of 3rd Motor Launch Flotilla and, once inside the Mediterranean, the co-operation of the nine available submarines of Malta's 10th Submarine Flotilla.

As these forces prepared for the forthcoming action, it is interesting to ascertain the extent to which the Fleet Air Arm's fighter situation had developed since the previous actions in June. At Gibraltar *Eagle*'s complement remained little changed. She fielded 16 Sea Hurricanes, six of which were stowed on outriggers, together with four additional spares each with one wing removed, stored in the forward hangar. The pilots were essentially those who had done so well in June — Lt.Cdr. Rupert Brabner's 801 Squadron (12 aircraft) and 813F Squadron (Lt. King-Joyce) with four more.

Victorious's air group was still new and fairly inexperienced. She sailed from Scapa Flow for the Clyde, flying on the Sea Hurricanes of 885 Squadron as she did so, but with six aircraft Lt. R.H.P. Carver's new unit was really little more than a flight. Main complement comprised 20 Fulmars — 14 with Lt. E.G. Savage's 809 Squadron and six with Lt. N.G. Hallett's 884 Squadron — plus 12 Albacores of 832 Squadron (Lt.Cdr. W.J. Lucas) for anti-submarine work. Ten of the 809 Squadron pilots had no combat experience at all.

To increase strength, six further Sea Hurricanes of 804 Squadron flew onto *Argus* on 27 July but while landing Lt. C. Walker, the unit's Senior Pilot, crashed over the side and was badly injured. Following this the commanding officer, Capt. Alan Marsh RM, was taken ill and was removed to hospital. Thus the unit sailed with only five pilots, including an inexperienced last-minute replacement, and with no hand at the helm. On arrival in the Biscay area the Sea Hurricanes were transferred to the Spitfire-laden *Furious*, which was carrying only four spare Albacores of 823 Squadron apart from her RAF guests. In the exercise which followed it became clear that the leaderless 804 Squadron pilots were too inexperienced to be committed to the coming adventure, and they were transferred back to *Argus*, which returned them and their aircraft to the United Kingdom.

Indomitable's air group was a different story altogether. After several months of service in the Indian Ocean, this vessel and her escorts passed round the Cape and sailed up to Freetown, re-equipping two of her fighter units en route. These, 800 and 806 Squadrons, had been experienced and successful Fulmar units which had served for long months in the Mediterranean during 1940-41; indeed some of the original pilots still remained, including 800's splendid commanding officer, Lt.Cdr. J.M. 'Bill' Bruen DSC — one of the Fleet Air Arm's true 'greats'. This unit was now equipped with a dozen new Sea Hurricanes.

Lt. R.L. 'Sloppy' Johnston's 806 Squadron, after some months ashore at Ceylon where it had helped repel the second Japanese raid against that island — during which Johnston had claimed one of the raiders shot down — was now composed mainly of replacement pilots. Eleven American-built Grumman Martlet IIs had been provided; the pilots were just getting familiar with these, although they had not had the time to practice operating together as a team; one of the new fighters was lost while landing on, so its strength had already been reduced.

These two units were backed up by ten more Sea Hurricanes of 880 Squadron, an experienced unit which had been the first in the Navy to take these aircraft into action more than 12 months earlier. It was commanded by fiery-tempered, red-bearded Lt.Cdr. F.E. 'Butch' Judd, who was highly thought of by his superiors, but rather feared by his subordinates for his irrascibility. He was supported by a very experienced Senior Pilot, Lt. R.J. 'Dickie' Cork DFC, who had flown with great dash in Douglas Bader's 242 Squadron during the Battle of Britain while on detachment to Fighter Command, and already had five victories to his credit. Aboard *Indomitable* Cork had his own 'private' Sea Hurricane —

Sea Hurricane pilots of the experienced 880 Squadron aboard HMS *Indomitable* just prior to the 'Pedestal' convoy, in August 1942. Left to right: Lt. Dickie Cork DFC; Lt. Cdr. 'Butch' Judd; Lt. Brian Fiddes. *(H. Popham)*

Z4642 — a standard Mark IB but fitted with Mark IC wings complete with 20mm cannons! The air group was completed by Lt.Cdr. D.K. Buchanan-Dunlop's 827 Squadron with 16 more Albacores.

The passage from the Clyde to the joining-up area to the west of Gibraltar proved uneventful for most vessels but was marred on 3 August when an escorting Sunderland (W4025 from 201 Squadron), which was one of the many Coastal Command aircraft in attendance, suddenly and without prior warning appeared out of low cloud and was at once shot down by AA gunners who took it to be hostile. Although the destroyer *Ledbury* raced to the scene, only one member of the crew survived to be rescued.

Never having sought to operate so many air groups together in a single operation, the Navy wisely arranged an exercise prior to the start of the convoy, *Indomitable*, *Eagle*, *Victorious*, *Argus* and their escorts rendezvousing to the west of Gibraltar during the morning of 5 August for Operation 'Berserk', which lasted for three days. The codename proved appropriate, for much confusion reigned as each group sought to orbit and receive direction from their individual carriers. Four of 809 Squadron's Fulmars were written off during the exercise, Sub Lt. C.G. Taylor being lost when he crashed into the sea; wreckage of the aircraft was located but the pilot was not found. Another of 806 Squadron's Martlets was also removed from the serviceability roster, but much of value was learned and as the convoy gathered on the 9th, 68 fighters remained ready for action with four more available as spares.

From the experience gathered during 'Berserk', it was decided to allot the low cover role to *Victorious* due to the slow-climbing performance of her Fulmars, while the other carriers undertook to provide high cover; each vessel would remain responsible for provision of its own protective combat air patrol however. For identification purposes, the wing leading edges and tail fins of all aircraft were painted bright yellow — a choice of colour which in the event was to provide some identification problems.

Thus, as the mighty armada of vessels turned east and began to pass through the Gibraltar Strait at 0200 on 10 August, the scene was set for a great new adventure. But the assemblage of such a convoy could hardly be kept a secret and had already been observed and reported by an Italian agent based in the port of Ceuta, Spanish Morocco, just across the Strait. Had the full extent of the gauntlet the ships would have to run been known to those embarked, the air of confidence which exuded would have been somewhat diminished, for ahead of them, in Sardinia and Sicily, the Axis had amassed over 650 aircraft.

On Sardinia by the 11th were the following forces:

36° Stormo AS		
108°, 109° Gruppo AS (256ª, 257ª, 258ª, 259ª Squadriglia)	13 S.79sil, 18 S.84sil	Decimomannu
130° Gruppo Aut. AS (280ª, 283ª Squadriglia)	13 S.79sil	Elmas
613ª Squadriglia Idrosoccorso	2 Z506B, 2 S.66	Elmas
65° Gruppo OA	11 Ro37	Elmas/Alghero
118ª Squadriglia RM, 146ª Squadriglia RM, 188ª Squadriglia RM, 287ª Squadriglia RM	10 Z501, 18 Z506B	Elmas/Olbia
51° Gruppo RS/BT (212ª, 213ª Squadriglia)	8 Z1007bis	Villacidro
24° Gruppo Aut. CT (354ª, 355ª, 370ª Squadriglia)	27 CR42, 14 G50bis	Monserrato

---

During the evening of the 11th, 115 further aircraft were despatched to the island, of which 111 arrived safely:

From Pisa to Decimomannu came 105° Gruppo AS of 46° Stormo AS (254ª, 255ª Squadriglia), with 12 S.79sil and two transport S.81s, together with a detachment of four S.79sil from III Nucleo Aerosiluranti; from Naples-Capodichino and Rome-Ciampino to Decimomannu came II Nucleo Aerosiluranti with seven S.79sil; from Bari-Gioia del Colle to Villacidro came 32° Stormo BT/AS (38° Gruppo BT with 12 S.84s and 89° Gruppo AS with 12 S.84sil).

From Torino Caselle via Pisa to Decimomannu came 153° Gruppo CT with 21 MC202s, two S.81s and two S.79s (the bombers carrying service personnel and spares); one MC202 crashed on take-off from Pisa and one landed at La Spezia with engine trouble, and crashed; from San Pietro di Caltgirone, Sicily, to Monserrato came 2° Gruppo Aut. CT with 19 Re2001s and one Z506B; one Reggiane (that flown by Cap. Giovanni Bonet, commander of 150ª Squadriglia) force-landed at Castelvetrano and the aircraft was destroyed; the Z506B rescue aircraft which accompanied the flight alighted at Elmas. From Rome-Ciampino to Monserrato came 362ª Squadriglia of 22° Gruppo Aut. CT with 11 Re2001s and one Fiat G12 transport; one Re2001 suffered engine trouble and returned to Ciampino.

From Rome-Guidonia to Villacidro came two experimental S.79 radio-controlled 'flying bombs', and one Z1007bis 'guide'; from Rome-Vigna di Valle to Elmas came two rescue Z506B, and from Brindisi to Elmas one rescue Z506B.

Thus, by the morning of the 12th, Aeronautica della Sardegna could boast a total of 240 front-line aircraft, while in Sicily units were moved where necessary to airfields in the west of the island, and detachments were also despatched to Pantelleria, as follows (numbers shown are for serviceable aircraft):

Pantelleria

132° Gruppo Aut. AS (278ª, 281ª Squadriglia)	14 S.79sil (Magg. Emanuele Buscaglia)
4° Gruppo AS of 7° Stormo (14ª, 15ª Squadriglia)	6 S.84sil (Magg. Gabriele Rivalta)
51° Stormo CT (20°, 155° Gruppo)	27 MC202 (Ten. Col. Aldo Remondino)

Castelvetrano (Trapani)

102° Gruppo Tuff (209ª, 239ª Squadriglia)	14 Ju87B & R (Magg. Giuseppe Cenni)
7° Stormo BT	10 S.84
88° Gruppo BT (264ª, 265ª Squadriglia)	5 BR20M, (Magg. Ugo Machieraldo) 2 CR42 (dive-bombers), 2 S.79 (reconnaissance)

Chinisia (Trapani)

9° Stormo BT: (Ten. Col. Cesare De Porto)

29° Gruppo (62ª, 63ª Squadriglia)	15 Z1007bis	(Ten. Col. Nicola Sacchi)
33° Gruppo (59ª, 60ª Squadriglia)		(Ten. Col. Ercole Savi)

Sciacca (Agrigento)

10° Stormo BT: (Col. Pasquale D'Ippolito)

30° Gruppo (55ª, 56ª Squadriglia)	10 S.79	(Magg. Giuseppe Noziglia)
32° Gruppo (57ª, 58ª Squadriglia)		(Magg. Alberto Capitani)

Palermo Boccadifalco

10° Stormo BT	10 S.79 (reconnaissance)
173ª Squadriglia RST	3 CR25 (maritime patrol)

Stagnone di Marsala (Trapani)

612ª Squadriglia Idrosoccorso	4 Z506B

Additionally 46° Gruppo CT, on its way to Libya via Sicily with 20 CR42s, was temporarily held in case it should be needed. Some 26 other fighters (Re2000s, CR42s and MC200s) of Reparto Volo and 54° Stormo CT were available in flights on Pantelleria and at Palermo Boccadifalco, Reggio Calabria, Castelvetrano and Sciacca for base defence.

The Luftwaffe had sought to reinforce II Fliegerkorps by flying in Ju88s of Stab, I and II/LG 1 from Crete, Ju87s of I/StG 3 from Libya, He111s of 6/KG 26 from Grosseto, Ju88C night fighters of I/NJG 2 and Bf110Cs of 8/ZG 26, both the latter from Libya. Order of Battle had thus become:

Stab and I/KG 54	44 Ju88A	Comiso/Gerbini
Stab, II and III/KG 77	31 Ju88A	Comiso/Gerbini
Stab, I and II/LG 1	28 Ju88A	Comiso/Gerbini
KüFlGr 606	20 Ju88A	Catania
KGr 806	21 Ju88A	Catania
I/StG 3	26 Ju87D	Trapani/Sciacca
6/KG 26	10 He111H	Comiso/Gerbini
1 and 2(F)/122	8 Ju88D,	Catania/Trapani
	4 Bf109F(PR)	Elmas
I/NJG 2	12 Ju88C	Palermo
8/ZG 26	8 Bf110C	Palermo
Stab, II/JG 53	18 Bf109F	Comiso/Gerbini + detach. Pantelleria
I/JG 77	21 Bf109F	Comiso/Gerbini + detach. Pantelleria
6 Seenotdienststaffel	4 Do24T	Syracuse/Augusta

The German contribution on Sicily therefore stood at 255 operational machines which increased the Axis overall strength to a staggering 659 front-line aircraft, of which at least 540 were serviceable and ready to be pitted against the convoy.

Additionally, a fairly substantial naval surface and submarine force was available, as follows:

3ª Divisione Incrociatori pesanti (Heavy Cruiser Division), comprising: *Gorizia* (Admiral Angela Perona); *Bolzano* and *Trieste*, with seven destroyers of 10ª (part) and 11ª Divisione.

7ª Divisione Incrociatori leggeri (Light Cruiser Division), comprising: *Eugenio di Savoia* (Admiral Da Zara); *Muzio Attendolo* and *Raimondo Montecuccoli*, with four destroyers of 10ª (part) and 13ª Divisione, plus the minelaying destroyer *Maloncello* (to mine the Sicilian Channel).

MTBs

2ª Squadriglia	*MS 16, MS 22, MS 23, MS 25, MS 26, MS 31;*
15ª Squadriglia	*MAS 543, MAS 548, MAS 549, MAS 563;*
18ª Squadriglia	*MAS 533, MAS 553, MAS 556, MAS 560, MAS 562;*
20ª Squadriglia	*MAS 552, MAS 554, MAS 557, MAS 564.*

Submarines

Alagi	*Ascianghi*	*Avorio*
Axum	*Bronzo*	*Brin*
Cobalto	*Dessie*	*Dandolo*

Emo	*Giada*	*Granito*
Otaria	*Uarsciek*	*Velella*
Wolframio		

NB: *Dagabur* had been sunk on 11 August.

German Units
MTBs (Schnellboot — S-Boat)

3rd Flotilla: *S 30, S36, S58, S59*

Submarines

U-73, U-205, U-333

NB: *U-331* had been attacked and damaged on the 8th by a Wellington of 223 Squadron from Gibraltar; she managed to reach her base at La Spezia.

On Malta meanwhile, the first few days of August had been fairly quiet although not without event. Whilst the Italians were now appearing only rarely other than by night, the ever-aggressive Messerschmitts continued to arrive overhead on a daily basis, and to take a steady toll of the defenders.

The third day of the month was noted by the formation of an additional new fighter squadron which took on the mantle of the now-defunct 229 Squadron, disbanded after its return from the Island to North Africa some three months earlier. Set up at Takali, the new unit was initially provided with some aircraft and pilots of 603 Squadron, which itself now ceased to operate as a Malta unit. Both 229 Squadron and 1435 Flight would be reinforced up to full squadron strengths following the arrival of the incoming Spitfires, while command of 229 Squadron was assumed by Sqn.Ldr. Bill Douglas. Amongst those initially transferred to this unit had been the SAAF pilot, Lt. Swales, but on the 6th he was posted to 185 Squadron as a flight commander.

To provide added support for the forthcoming convoy operations, aerial reinforcements now began reaching the Island in driblets. The Beaufort force had been increased by the arrival of elements of 86 Squadron, while also from England came the strike Beaufighters of 248 Squadron, Coastal Command, on detachment. The first four had arrived from Gibraltar on the 3rd, led by the commanding officer, Wg.Cdr. J.M.N. Pike DSO, DFC. These were followed by three more next day (including one flown by Sqn.Ldr. D.L. Cartridge DFC, an experienced Coastal strike pilot), another on the 5th, three on the 7th, one on the 8th and four on the 10th. They were joined on the 9th by six more Beaufighters of 252 Squadron from North Africa, led by Sqn.Ldr. A.G. Wincott; five other crews from this unit arrived in one of 117 Squadron's DC-3 transports.

On the 7th meanwhile, three Baltimore IIs and a single Mark I reached Luqa from Egypt, two of them flown by 69 Squadron crews who had been flown over to Africa for this purpose. These were added to the unit's existing establishment of two Baltimores of 'A' Flight, which were soon joined by two Marylands and their crews, on temporary detachment from 203 Squadron at Abu Sueir. The four PR Spitfires of 'B' Flight were supplemented by a two-aircraft, short-term detachment from 2 PRU. The unit also received a new commanding officer when newly-promoted Sqn.Ldr. Adrian Warburton DSO, DFC, returned to Malta for his third term of duty with the squadron; he arrived on the 11th, ferrying one of the 2 PRU Spitfires (BP911).

On this same day a new night fighter Beaufighter (X7840) equipped with new Mark VII AI radar arrived from England, via Gibraltar, for the 89 Squadron detachment. There had been considerable trouble with existing sets during the past month due to susceptibility to jamming, but it was believed that the new set should overcome this problem; a second similarly-equipped fighter (V8268) flew in next day.

That Malta was officially close to starvation was a fact, but Colin Parkinson, now transferred to the new 229 Squadron, provided some interesting insights into the wartime food sources (and indeed Black Market activities) of the civilian population at this time. Parkinson's diary entries over a two-week period noted:

> '"Brown, Brough and myself ate our tinned bacon for breakfast. Very tasty it was too." "A new system of messing and a new cook and caterer — hope we get some good food... lunch at twelve. Food not bad. Collected money to pay the maid. Met a very intelligent Maltese girl who has been to Europe and England... she's going to give me some sugar to make jam." (*At a dance at Queen's Hotel*) "Jeusa usually manages to produce a good brand of whisky for me from some secret corner. Walked round to the Windsor and drank John Collins on the terrace while the moon came up... met Brown and at 10 pm we went to 'Ma Madden's' to scrounge some roast pork which we took to the Mess and ate before going to bed."
>
> '"Walked to Rabat with Brownie to buy some blackberry jam from the 'black market' — 2/– per lb... very nice mutton for dinner." "The girl on the Bastion, Ann, made ten pounds of jam out of some grapefruit and sugar I supplied her with. Gave her half a pound of fruit chocolate. The jam is very nice." "Managed to dig up some bottles of Gordon's Gin, bitters and soda. We sat until about 6 sipping John Collins... Alice went to her pub and I to mine (*to stay after a dance in Valetta*). Managed to talk the doorman into giving me something to eat. Roast pork, salad and pressed meat." "...and went back to the pub for a shower and some lunch. Big eats again." "Had a few drinks at the King's Head bar and tea at Command Fair. Chocolate, stuffed tomatoes and plum duff. Cost about 2/–." "Back to Mess for lunch. Food is becoming less every day." "We get Ovaltine, biscuits and chocolate in the mornings at dispersal now. Back to the Mess for lunch."'

Similar entries appear in the diary of LAC Bill Metcalf; issued rations were insufficient to meet the needs of many and money could work wonders:

> '"I had four dinners at different places at a total cost of 14/9d." "Work from 3 am to 9.30 pm on half a sausage, a slice of bread and a mug of tea without sugar." "Started work at 0300 on a breakfast of one slice of bread, one spoonful of mashed potato and a mug of tea without sugar — our next bite was at 2.35 pm." "The grub isn't fit for pigswill and very scarce." "Out of the last £3.10.0 which I drew, £2.17.4 went on food alone."
>
> 'I've been on a day off today which I spent eating, sleeping and cleaning. I bought 3 lb tomatoes, 3 lb plums, 1 lb of apples and 1 lb of peas, plus 3/8 rotal of bread, and I woofed the lot before tea." "Our bread ration this morning nearly caused a riot amongst the lads. I was disgusted. So much so that during the morning I lost my temper and told Sgt. Jenson what I thought of him. Result: (*my*) two days off stopped."'

Saturday, 1 August

The first day of the month was notable by its lack of aerial activity over Malta; it was not until three hours before midnight that the air raid alarms sounded in earnest, on the approach of three BR20Ms of 88° Gruppo BT, which had set out to raid Luqa. One returned early when the 'Servizio Alfa' warning device alerted the crew to an approaching night fighter, while another was attacked about four miles off Licata but was not hit. A further small force — three Z1007bis of 9° Stormo BT — headed for Luqa within minutes of the Fiats, one of these also returning early when the crew sighted a Beaufighter. The remaining two carried out an attack on Luqa in the face of intense AA fire, but both returned without damage.

Liberators of 159 Squadron were by now staging through Malta en route for Egypt, and Air Vice-Marshal Park — like his predecessor — sought to make good use of any good fortune that came his way. Flt.Lt. J.M.O. Dyer's Liberator (AL579) was soon armed and the crew requested to pay a visit to Navarino Bay (Greece), where a heavily-laden merchantman was reported, before flying on to Egypt. On arrival over the target area there was no sign of the vessel, but four others were seen. However, the four 1000lb bombs were accidentally jettisoned before the ships could be attacked and each fell harmlessly into the sea!

Sunday, 2 August

Three or four bombers plus fighter escort approached at between 20-30,000 feet just after 1400. Twenty-three Spitfires were up by the time the force reached the Island, but only eight of 185 Squadron made contact. Four Bf109s were seen orbiting Gozo at 26,000 feet and these were engaged, Sgt. Weaver (EP139) claiming one as probably destroyed:

> 'I was Green 2 patrolling at 27,000 feet when I noticed an Me109F on the tail of Green 3. I gave the break and turned towards the enemy aircraft. Green 3 broke down and to the right. The enemy aircraft turned slightly my way and I got in a 2 second burst from 200 yards, head-on. I noticed pieces flying off the starboard wing root and hits on the engine cowling and about the cockpit.'

Two Spitfires were lost, however; Plt.Off. James Guthrie in BR362 crashed on the Island and was killed, while New Zealander Sgt. Matt McLeod's BR321 was shot down into the sea; despite a search until dusk no trace of the pilot was found. The jubilant — but unidentified — Messerschmitt pilots accurately claimed two victories.

The Italian night bombers were back at 2130 when two BR20Ms of 88° Gruppo BT set out to raid Luqa; one returned early when the 'Servizio Alfa' gave warning of an approaching night fighter. Twenty minutes later, three Z1007bis of 9° Stormo BT promptly followed the Fiats in raiding Luqa and dropped 18 100kg 'special' bombs. Only light AA fire was experienced while one aircraft was attacked by a night fighter — there was an exchange of fire but no damage sustained by either party.

Monday, 3 August

Twenty-three Spitfires of 185, 229 and 1435 Squadrons were airborne by 1100 as a fighter sweep of 27 Bf109s approached the Island, but the Messerschmitts apparently avoided combat. However, Sgt. Knox-Williams of 1435 Squadron (as it had now become) was bounced by one and shot down in EP331, baling out into the sea; he was rescued by HSL 107 and taken to hospital with superficial facial burns.

The Luftwaffe claimed three victories, possibly including Wellington HX515, a delivery aircraft which failed to arrive at Malta from Gibraltar. It was reported down in the sea 10-20 miles to the south of the Island and although three Beaufighters and an HSL were despatched to the area, only a Very light was seen by one of the aircraft; the crew were not rescued.

Tuesday, 4 August

Four Spitfires of 229 Squadron were off early in the morning to investigate 'hostiles' approaching the Island, and two fighters identified as MC202s were seen east of Zonqor. Lt. Swales attacked one which reportedly smoked heavily, and was last seen flying low over the water; he claimed it as probably destroyed, but there is no apparent record of Italian fighter activity on this occasion.

Soon after lunch eight Spitfires of 126 Squadron were scrambled and joined seven of 229 Squadron to challenge 15 plus Bf109s reported approaching. The former sighted six Messerschmitts and engaged them over St Paul's Bay, resulting in Sgt. Richardson being shot down in BR357; the Australian managed to bale out safely. Fellow-countryman Colin Parkinson of 229 Squadron noted:

> 'I saw a Spit shot down today. It came down like a bat out of hell, pouring glycol, on fire. The pilot baled — it was the "Baron" Richardson, a friend of mine.'

One of two BR20Ms of 88° Gruppo BT which had set out to attack Valetta shortly before midnight, failed to return. The cause of the loss of MM22687 is not known, but Sottoten. Renato Tosi and his crew were reported missing. With a lack of AA claims or night fighter activity, it must be assumed that the technical problems encountered proved insurmountable.

Wednesday, 5 August

An estimated 20 Bf109s of II/JG 53 in two formations approached the coast at 0840, to be met by eight Spitfires of 1435 Squadron; Blue Section engaged three Bf109s of 6/JG 53, one of which was shot down by Flt.Sgt. Pinney, while Green Section patrolled over a Catalina in Kalafrana Bay to prevent it being strafed. Four of 229 Squadron were sent off to search for the downed German pilot but nothing was sighted. Of his combat, Pinney reported:

> 'My section was flying along in south-easterly direction when we were attacked by four 109s, which broke off this attack without firing and passed over our heads, splitting into pairs. I turned and saw another pair of 109s diving down towards us in a south-easterly direction, and completed my turn. I fired a short burst from head-on position, breaking off the attack at less than 50 yards, without observing strikes. On turning again, however, I saw a 109 with glycol pouring from it. This aircraft has been confirmed as destroyed.'

Two hours later eight Bf109s were reported to have crossed the coast while others escorted a seaplane identified as a Do24, which was assumed to have picked up the German pilot shot down by Pinney earlier. Four of 229 Squadron and eight of 126 Squadron were scrambled, four of the latter briefed to patrol over the Catalina in the bay. Red Section saw what they believed was a Do18 on the sea, some 10 miles off St Paul's Bay, with a number of Bf109s orbiting. On the approach of the Spitfires, the seaplane took-off and headed for Sicily; no combat resulted. In fact, it would seem that the formation seen were actually seven 51° Stormo CT Macchis covering a Z506B searching for the missing German pilot, who had baled out into the sea south of Cape Scaramia; he was rescued unharmed. Three Spitfires were seen by the Italians but no action ensued.

The Macchis were back at 1745 when 11 aircraft of 51° Stormo, together with Re2001s and Bf109s, escorted bombers over Malta. Eight Spitfires of 229 Squadron had scrambled on their approach and these intercepted 15 fighters, described as Bf109s and Reggianes, about 20 miles off Comino. Sgt. Irwin reported:

> 'I was flying Blue 3 to Lt. Swales. We were flying due west about 15 miles west of Gozo at 20,000 feet. When Blue 4 reported e/a at 1400 — there were about 15 of them — we swung round to attack and I looked behind to see six Me109s attacking us from behind. Blue Section broke right and I climbed up steeply and lost contact with the rest of the section. I got mixed up in a "do" with three or four Me109s and while circling saw three new e/a enter the scrap from above. One of them attacked me, I skidded sharply to port and throttled back then when the e/a overshot, swung in behind, and fired a 3-second burst from astern at 250 yards.
>
> 'I saw strikes on port wing, forward part of the fuselage and tail. The e/a streamed glycol and black smoke and dived away inverted. At that point I was attacked by his No 2 and was struck by an explosive shell in the starboard magazine. Three or four of my own bullets exploded and I went into a spin from which I was unable to recover until I was right on the water. The enemy aircraft attacked appeared to be a Re2001.'

51° Stormo CT reported engaging two Spitfires south-west of Gozo and claimed both shot down, one by Ten. Vittorio Bastogi and the other shared by Mar. Iannucci and Serg.Magg. Vittorio Iannilli. A third was claimed by one of the Messerschmitt pilots.

Two relatively quiet days followed. In the early hours of the 7th, a Hudson transport of 24 Squadron arrived from Gibraltar carrying amongst its passengers newly-promoted Wg.Cdr. Peter Prosser Hanks DFC, who had gained ten victories in France 1940 and over the Channel the following year; Hanks was to take command of the Luqa Spitfire Wing. Owing to the enforced absence of its wounded commander (Sqn.Ldr. Winfield) 126 Squadron received a new leader in the guise of newly-arrived Sqn.Ldr. Bryan Wicks DFC; he too had served in France, where he had been shot down and had dramatically evaded capture.

Saturday, 8 August

Further action developed when seven Spitfires of 249 Squadron scrambled at 0830, but two were obliged to return early; the remaining aircraft intercepted a formation of eight Bf109s soon after 1000. These were reported to have 'stayed and fought'. Newly-commissioned Plt.Off. Beurling (EN973/T) fired at one as it headed northwards, but was jumped by three more. He claimed that he hit one in the glycol tank and engine with a two and a half second burst, and that it went straight into the sea. This was apparently confirmed by his section leader. Beurling's aircraft was then hit and the engine almost seized; having decided against baling out, he carried out a successful belly-landing in a ploughed, stone-walled field, as he later recalled:

> 'As I came close in over the near wall I put the left wing down to take up the bump and bellied down onto the ground. The wing absorbed the wallop and stopped me cold. The far wall was too near for comfort. I climbed out, unhurt except a superficial cut in one arm.'

Frank Jones (BP869/E), who was leading Blue Section, also claimed a Bf109 shot down:

> 'Six enemy aircraft passed overhead... we turned towards enemy aircraft and saw two more coming down on our tails. I told Blue Section to spiral down to draw enemy aircraft down. I saw e/a attacking Blue 2 Sgt. Budd, and warned him. He broke in front of me followed by the e/a which appeared in front of my nose at less than fifteen yards presenting his belly to me at point blank range. I fired a burst of one second and then was forced to break as I was being fired at myself. Enemy aircraft disappeared and was seen by my No 3 (*Beurling*), to be going down smoking and in obvious distress. I fired a short burst at close range at one other Me109 but saw no results.'

Sgt. Budd claimed damage to one more but his own aircraft (BR131/O) was also hit and damaged, and he sustained shoulder wounds. Despite his injuries, he succeeded in landing safely.

A number of Spitfires of 1435 Squadron were scrambled at 1020 to aid 249 Squadron but Sgt. Clarence Kelly, a New Zealander from Auckland, was reported missing in EP336. His leader, Flt.Lt. Wally McLeod, reported:

> 'Wavy Blue 1 (myself) and Blue 2 (Sgt. Kelly) observed three Me109s pass below us at 10,000 feet. We were at 15,000 feet. We turned into the sun and attacked. I picked out the right hand one who was flying wide. I closed to 250 yards firing a 4-second burst from dead astern. Strikes were observed. Then broke left firing head-on at one of the other two, both of whom had broken right into us. I pulled up and circled to the left, observing my No 2 doing the same. He was some distance behind me and in my opinion did not have an opportunity to fire at the one I had attacked as the other two delivered a head-on attack at him, or at least, were in a position to do so. The one I hit did not seem to do much of anything but stagger along. The two who had broken right continued climbing in a northerly direction after having passed through us.
>
> 'I then informed my No 2 to come home as this was his first engagement on operations, and my starboard cannon had jammed. After looking round for the other aircraft and observing none, I looked down and saw a plane hit the water. There was no parachute. I gave a "Mayday" thinking it might have been my No 2.'

The Luftwaffe reported that 20 Bf109s encountered 30 Curtiss (sic) fighters and claimed three shot down; however Ofw. Rollwage of II/JG 53 correctly identified his opponent as a Spitfire, which he claimed shot down two miles north of Valetta as his 30th victim.

In a bid to establish that Axis seaborne forces were not assembling for an invasion of Malta, pairs of Spitfires were despatched to reconnoitre the Sicilian coastline. One such pair were flown by Plt.Offs. Ogilvie and Sherlock of 185

Ofw. Herbert Rollwage, one of II/JG 53's most successful pilots, garlanded and presented with a bomb-fin plantpot by colleagues to celebrate his 300th operational sortie on 8 August 1942. By this time he had claimed 30 victories, the third of which had not received confirmation.

Squadron, who departed Hal Far at about 1940. They flew at low-level in order to avoid being detected by radar, and when the south-east corner of the island was reached, flew along the beach for about 20 minutes; no suspicious craft or invasion preparations were observed and they flew back to Hal Far in darkness, where a barely discernible flare path had been laid out for them. Notwithstanding this, both landed without mishap.

Sunday, 9 August

At 0950 a total of 22 Spitfires (eight of 229 Squadron, eight of 1435 Squadron and six of 126 Squadron) were ordered off to challenge 19 plus Bf109s as they approached the Island. Blue Section of the former unit engaged three of the Messerschmitts over Filfla at 26,000 feet, one of which was credited to Flg.Off. Dicks-Sherwood; Colin Parkinson noted:

> 'Dicky Sherwood shot down Me (*Messerschmitt*). Beautiful shot. Glycol pouring out.'

Dicks-Sherwood's No 2, Plt.Off. Reynolds, also reported seeing the Messerschmitt on fire but the Rhodesian's own Combat Report was not so conclusive:

> 'I was leading Blue Section. Putting my nose almost vertical I managed to give the leading enemy aircraft a two-second burst, beam attack. Saw strikes slightly forward of cockpit, pieces fell off and enemy aircraft went in northerly direction losing height and streaming glycol (other pilots of 229 Squadron also saw this and were of the opinion the Me was destroyed).'

The 126 Squadron flight reported meeting four Bf109s over St Paul's Bay at 11,000 feet, Sgt. Nigel Park (MK-U) claiming one of these shot down:

'Scrap with four 109s. Got one. One hit me in port wing. Cunning bastard!'

Fifteen Spitfires were scrambled on the approach of a further fighter sweep at 1420, eight of 126 Squadron spotting a number of hostile aircraft but these were not engaged. However, Sgt. Dave Ritchie's Spitfire (BR122) was seen to break formation, turn on its back and go in a shallow dive into the sea; this was the second occasion in under two weeks that the Canadian had been shot down, and he was to spend all night in his dinghy before being rescued next day by HSL 107.

That evening Flt.Lt. Hetherington and Plt.Off. Beurling of 249 Squadron were despatched to search the Sicilian coast for signs of a reported MTB flotilla. Although nothing untoward was sighted, packs of such Italian and German craft were indeed about and would cause havoc when let loose amongst the almost-defenceless convoy, as will be seen.

Monday, 10 August

Plt.Off. Harry Coldbeck was briefed to fly a Spitfire PR sortie to Catania on the morning of the 10th, and was instructed to drop a package as he passed over the airfield. This contained the personal belongings, including family letters, of the captured Cant floatplane crew; the mission was successfully undertaken and the package was dropped from a height of about 3000 feet.

Spitfires of 185 Squadron and 1435 Squadron scrambled to intercept a raid by Ju88s and Bf109s at 1025, attacking these over the Island after they had bombed Luqa. Here one of 248 Squadron's Beaufighters was badly damaged, five others and two Spitfires less seriously so; an airman was killed and an ambulance destroyed. Flt.Sgt. Mahar of 185 Squadron had his aircraft shot-up and he was obliged to crash-land at Luqa, while Flt.Lt. McLeod, Plt.Off. Lattimer and Flt.Sgt. MacLennan of 1435 Squadron each claimed a Bf109 shot down. One dogfight over Kalafrana Bay ended with Uffz. Walter Schmidt's Messerschmitt ('Yellow 9') bursting into flames, from which the badly wounded 6/JG 53 pilot baled out and landed in the sea close by.

Within ten minutes the rescue tender ST338 had reached him and he was soon wrapped in blankets, on his way to hospital — prompt action which undoubtedly saved his life. There is little doubt that Schmidt fell to Wally McLeod's shooting,

Messerschmitt Bf109F 'Yellow 12' of II/JG 53, with jettisonable long-range fuel tank slung beneath the fuselage. *(NWMA)*

as both Lattimer and MacLennan reported combats north of St Paul's Bay. McLeod recorded:

> 'I was Green 1, patrolling at 20,000 feet between Takali and Luqa. We observed the raid off St Paul's Bay and travelling east, cut in behind the bombers. My section singled out several Me109s behind, and attacked. I closed on the left-hand one, firing a four-second burst from 150 yards. Aircraft broke up and pilot baled out.'

Of his first victory claim, fellow Canadian Ian MacLennan reported:

> 'I was Green 3, patrolling at 20,000 feet between Takali and Luqa. As the raid was going out we came down from behind on two Me109s at the rear of the formation. Green 1 (McLeod) took the left, which I observed to go down in flames, and I took the right. I opened fire at close range from slightly below gaining, then had four bursts dead astern. I broke sharply right as I was being bounced. When last seen, he was going down about 45 degrees pouring heavy black smoke. Blue 1 (Lattimer) reports oil patch north of St Paul's Bay, ½ mile offshore, as our attack finished and before he started his.'

Charlie Lattimer's report is an example of how easy it was for pilots to double-claim:

> 'After the main formation of enemy aircraft had left the Island, with Blue 3 I attacked three Me109s who were heading north but turned south-west on observing us. I made a quarter to port head-on attack at one Me109 on the left and gave him a two-second burst with cannon and machine-gun, opening fire at range 250 yards, and closing to follow around with deflection so that after observing strikes — cockpit, wing root and rear of cockpit — I spun to the right and recovered after losing some height. Gondor Control, a few minutes later, reported a parachute coming down 5 miles north-east of St Paul's Bay and requested Gondor Blue to investigate. He stated the victim to be a Hun and requested his captivity. This I consider to confirm my claim to an Me109F destroyed.'

Two Spitfires of 126 Squadron followed at 1145 on a patrol over minesweepers in Grand Harbour, while two others patrolled over HSL 107 departing St Paul's Bay. A Ju88 was seen heading northwards, probably a straggler from the raid intercepted by 1435 Squadron, and Plt.Off. Jerry Smith (BR366) gave chase; he was not seen again. It seems likely that he caught the Junkers, for Fw. Helmut Streubel's 3Z+ET of 9/KG 77 failed to reach Sicily; possibly Smith's aircraft fell to return fire or was, in turn, intercepted by one of the Messerschmitts. His brother Rod was amongst those who searched the sea in vain. At the time of his death he had been credited with three confirmed, one and one shared probables, and four damaged. During these actions the Luftwaffe claimed seven victories for the loss of a single Bf109 and the Ju88.

As Beaufighter X7748 of 89 Squadron's detachment climbed into the night sky just before midnight both engines failed, obliging Flg.Off. Fumerton to ditch in the sea some ten miles off Sliema. On getting into their individual dinghies the operator, Plt.Off. Bing, found that his was holed and he was obliged to cling onto Fumerton's until picked up by HSL 107. The launch had been guided to the area by Plt.Off. Reeves, who had spotted the dinghy's light; no ill effects of the dunking were suffered by the Canadian crew.

With dawn on the 10th the 'Pedestal' convoy had formed up into five columns, the central of which comprised the battleships and operational carriers; the others comprised the merchantmen, each column headed by a cruiser, with further such warships bringing up the rear. The whole convoy was covered by a screen of 21 destroyers. From the very start there were alarms, but the cause of these proved to be patrolling anti-submarine aircraft from Gibraltar which had failed to show recognition signals, or to switch on their IFF devices. Four Sea Hurricanes were scrambled at 0525 but found their 'bogey' to be a Sunderland, which opened fire on them as they closed in to identify it! The gunners aboard the flyingboat were no doubt aware of the fortunate escape of another patrolling Sunderland from Gibraltar two days earlier, when three Vichy D520s of Aeronavale Escadrille 1AC from Port Lyautey attacked and damaged it after it had strayed into French territorial waters.

Sea Hurricanes of 885 Squadron on the deck of HMS *Victorious* on 9 August 1942 as the carrier force steams eastwards. V7506 '7T' in the foreground is parked with its tailwheel on an outrigger, another of which can be seen just beyond it.

Four more Sea Hurricanes which went off at 0645 similarly intercepted a Hudson, but identity was established in good time on this occasion. During the morning *Victorious* launched two surplus Albacores and an unserviceable Fulmar, and these were flown back to Gibraltar.

The first intrusion of note occurred at around 1700 that afternoon, when a French civil LeO H-246.1 flyingboat — F-AREJ flown by Commandant Marceau Meresse, en route from the Vichy zone of France to Algeria — passed overhead. As a non-combatant, the aircraft was not intercepted but the crew, for reasons of their own, "were not playing according to the rules"; they radioed a sighting of the convoy, reporting two battleships, two aircraft carriers, two cruisers, 14 destroyers and 12 transports, and this information was at once conveyed to the Italian Naval Headquarters. The Frenchmen later paid dearly for this unfortunate transgression. Despite this unfriendly action, when two of 806 Squadron's Martlets were scrambled some two hours later and intercepted a Vichy Bloch 174 reconnaissance aircraft of the Armeé de l'Air — out from North Africa to check on the convoy — the British pilots did not attack.

With nightfall a bogus convoy — codenamed 'MG3' — put out from Haifa and Port Said and headed westwards, comprising four merchant vessels, four cruisers and 15 destroyers. The intention was to draw off the Italian cruiser squadron known to be at Navarino, and to hold down Luftwaffe bombers in Crete. The vessels maintained their heading until dusk on the 11th, then struck south into Alexandria. The Axis were not to be so easily fooled, however. Whilst air reconnaissance spotted and reported 'MG3' — and all merchant vessel movement in the Aegean was brought to a halt until further notice — this effort failed to divert a single ship or aircraft back from the Western Basin.

Fully alerted by the report of the French flyingboat, by nightfall the Axis had placed a forward screen of submarines in the area south of the Balearic Islands, comprising the Italian *Brin, Dagabur, Giada, Uarsciek* and *Wolframio*, and the German *U-73, U-205* and *U-333*; these were sharply on the lookout before dawn. Indeed, the German skippers had been urged to penetrate the destroyer screen and attempt to sink the carriers. The first sighting was made at 0438 by Capitano di Corvetta Raffaello Allegri's *Uarsciek*, which reported launching torpedoes without apparent effect.

With dawn on the 11th the 'snoopers' were out seeking the convoy, the first — a Ju88D of 1(F)/122 — being picked up on the escort's radar screens at 0815. Fighter patrols had been in the air since 0630 and Black Section of 880 Squadron were vectored after this intruder, but the German proved very elusive and he managed to report his sighting and make good his escape. Blue Section took over the patrol at 0900, and at 0955 as they were returning to the carrier, Blue 1 and 2 (Lt. Cork and Sub Lt. R.B. Howarth) spotted a Ju88 at 20,000 feet, 2000 feet higher than they were. At once the pilots pulled their Sea Hurricanes into a climb and pursued the intruder for ten minutes, by which time Howarth was close enough to open fire. The Junkers turned away from him allowing Cork to attack, and as the bomber dived away he saw the cowling of the starboard engine fly off, followed by a trail of black smoke as the engine caught fire.

During the initial exchange the rear gunner had hit Cork's cannon-armed Sea Hurricane (Z4642) in the wings, putting the starboard aileron out of use, but now could be seen lying over his gun apparently dead. The Junkers was lost to sight at 200 feet, Cork subsequently being credited with its probable destruction. This was almost certainly an aircraft of 2(F)/122 which returned to Sardinia in a damaged condition with one member of the crew dead and a second wounded; the pilot claimed that his gunner had shot down one of their attackers.

At 1010 the crew of another reconnaissance Ju88 radioed an estimated composition of the convoy as three aircraft carriers, three battleships, 20 cruisers and destroyers and 20 merchantmen. During this period one of *Victorious*'s fighters almost flew into the sea on take-off; the pilot succeeded in landing at once, at which point it was discovered that the engine had been incorrectly assembled! A second Fulmar from 809 Squadron ditched when the port wing suddenly caught fire, apparently as the result of the spontaneous ignition of an old round of incendiary ammunition. The crew were safely picked up by the destroyer *Wishart*. Around noon it was reported that a Spanish airliner had passed over the convoy and — although it was not harassed — it was assumed that the crew would have relayed their observations to the Axis.

The destroyer screen was aware from Asdic soundings that Axis submarines were still in the vicinity, but no firm contacts had been made by midday nor had any torpedoes been sighted. At this stage the convoy had closed to a point where

Operation 'Bellows' could be put into effect, which entailed *Furious* flying off her cargo of Spitfires. This vessel, converted as she had been from a battle cruiser, was probably the third 'battleship' identified by the Axis 'snoopers'. Indeed, her very presence with the convoy had come about to an extent due to her design.

While *Furious* had joined *Ark Royal* in ferrying Hurricanes to the Island on four occasions in 1941, and had carried others to West Africa that year, she had never before launched Spitfires. Consequently, early in August she had slipped out into the Irish Sea from Greenock with a couple of Spitfires aboard for a trial launch. With her went three experienced fighter pilots, Grp.Capt. Walter Churchill DSO, DFC, Flt.Lt. Eric 'Timber' Woods DFC and Plt.Off. Bill Rolls DFM.

After inspecting the ship, they had been concerned as to the prospects, for about one third the way along the deck from the point at which the first of a flight of eight Spitfires would have to take-off, there was a ramp. At the ship's forward end the flight deck ended some way short of the bow, which had originally incorporated a separate, lower flying-off deck at that level. This consequently greatly restricted the potential for an aircraft to 'sink' in front of the carrier as it left the flight deck.

Woods elected to make the initial try. The usual wooden wedges were inserted to hold the flaps open, but chocks were also placed under the undercarriage wheels, and a number of sailors held down the tail with a rope while the pilot ran up the engine to maximum revs. The sudden release of the rope and chocks allowed a certain degree of 'catapult' effect, and the Spitfire shot forward but had hardly any real speed up when it met the ramp. Woods literally had to bounce it off the end of the deck to stay in the air, but as he flew away to land ashore, Churchill and Rolls had to advise the carrier's captain that such a take-off would probably be beyond the capabilities of the average relatively-inexperienced pilot likely to be making the flight.

At that point Rolls recalled having recently flown a Spitfire fitted with a new hydromatic propeller, which had offered a considerably shorter take off run and better climb performance; he suggested that fitting these would probably make all the difference to a take off from *Furious*. On return to Greenock the necessary arrangements were made at high speed, 40 Spitfires being loaded aboard together with 40 of the new propellers (and some 100 groundcrew to fit them) as the vessel sailed for Gibraltar.

A volunteer was called for to make a test launch with an aircraft fitted with the

With its 'slipper' tank beneath the fuselage, a reinforcement Spitfire lifts off from HMS *Furious* to start the long flight to Malta on 11 August 1942. *(P.A.J. O'Brien)*

new propeller, the 'quid pro quo' being that he would then land ashore at Prestwick, and thereby miss the forthcoming operation. As there were no takers, an Australian sergeant was delegated for the task; the take-off proved quite easy and the ship set off southwards, the assembled pilots then being advised by Churchill of their destination.

Now, as the fly-off approached, it was planned to despatch the 38 remaining Spitfires (one having developed a fault) in three flights of eight and two of seven. Grp.Capt. Churchill and Wg.Cdr. Arthur Donaldson DFC, AFC, would lead the first two, Woods and Rolls the next two, and Flt.Lt. Ernest 'Dan' Magruder, a Scot, the fifth (see Table 13 below). The first flight began taking off at 1229. As the Spitfires took to the air, vigilant observers picked up the tell-tale 'blips' on the screens of the Italian-manned Freya radar unit on Lampedusa island, but despite immediate warning to AHQ on Sicily, inexplicably, no action was taken.

TABLE 13

Operation 'Bellows'

38 Spitfires from HMS *Furious* (one* landed on HMS *Indomitable*)

Grp.Cap. W.M. Churchill, DSO, DFC		Sgt. R.J. Roe
Wg.Cdr. A.H. Donaldson, DFC, AFC		Sgt. T.R.D. Kebbell, RNZAF
Flt.Lt. E.N. Woods, DFC		Sgt. J.H. Houlton, RNZAF
Flt.Lt. E.P.F.L.T. Magruder		Sgt. A.B. Stead, RNZAF*
Flt.Lt. G.H.A. Wellum		Sgt. J.F. Yeatman, RNZAF
Lt. K.C. Kuhlman, SAAF		Sgt. J.E. Mortimer, RNZAF
Flg.Off. H.F. Gedge		Sgt. N.D. Sintetos, RCAF (US)
Flg.Off. A.I. Lindsay, RCAF		Sgt. W.R. Whitmore
Flg.Off. P.A. Woodger, RCAF (US)		Sgt. E.H. Francis
Plt.Off. W.T. Rolls, DFM		Sgt. J. Tarbuck
Plt.Off. L. Cheek		Sgt. J.D. Vinall
Plt.Off. L.S. Nomis, RCAF (US)	EP410	Sgt. F.W. Clewley, RAAF
Plt.Off. A.F. Roscoe, RCAF (US)		Sgt. L.P. Garvey
Plt.Off. P.A.J. O'Brien		Sgt. D.G. Guy
Plt.Off. R.B. Park, RAAF		Sgt. R.C. Bolland
Plt.Off. A.R.H. Maynard		Sgt. L.R. Gore
Plt.Off. D.P. Pollock		Sgt. L.H. Swain
Plt.Off. R. Seed		Sgt. C.H. Cornish
Flt.Sgt. E.T. Hiskens, RAAF		
Flt.Sgt. J.G. Sanderson, RAAF	EP517	

As these operations were underway, the Fleet oilers were refuelling some of the destroyers and it was at this point, taking advantage of the general activity, that Kapitänleutnant Helmut Rosenbaum manoeuvred *U-73* within range of the passing procession of major warships. Conforming with an order to leave the merchantmen and seek out the aircraft carriers, he put a salvo of four electrically-impelled torpedoes in rapid succession into the port side of *Eagle*; the first struck under her 6-inch gun mounting, the other three abreast the port wing engine room. She at once took on a list to port, which rapidly became more pronounced; with smoke and steam pouring from her, wracked by internal explosions, she capsized and sank within six minutes. Destroyers *Laforey* and *Lookout* and the tug *Jaunty* rushed to the scene, picking up 68 officers (including Captain Mackintosh) and 862 ratings from her company of 1093, as they leapt into the swirling waters.

All but four of *Eagle*'s complement of aircraft went down with her. Thus, at a stroke, the fighter defences had been reduced by nearly 25% of their strength. The four aircraft which escaped — Sea Hurricanes of 801 Squadron — were up searching for a 'snooper' at the time, Red Section (Lt.Cdr. Brabner and Sub Lt. Hutton) subsequently being instructed to land on *Victorious*, while Yellow Section was ordered to land on *Indomitable*. Owing to a misunderstanding Yellow 2 (Sub Lt. Hankey) also landed on *Victorious*.

The Carrier force underway for Operation 'Pedestal'. From the deck of HMS *Victorious* are to be seen HMS *Indomitable* (with draft screens erected), followed by HMS *Eagle* and an escorting cruiser. One of *Victorious*'s Fulmars is to be seen in the foreground, wings folded.

At 1347 *Furious* resumed despatch of her Spitfires, the final 22 aircraft going off by 1512. As the final flight of Spitfires became airborne, New Zealander Sgt. A.B. Stead discovered that his long-range tank was not feeding through. Initially, the pilots had been told that should they experience problems immediately following take-off, they were to bale out ahead of the nearest destroyer which would pick them up if not too busy! This was greeted with so much adverse comment that it was agreed that should problems arise, a landing could be attempted on the nearest carrier. Sgt. Stead favoured the latter option, and having carried out a low pass over the *Indomitable*, successfully landed at the second attempt. The Naval pilots were reportedly delighted to receive a Spitfire, and were keen to fly it into combat when the time came.

Even as the flying-off was still in progress radar again picked up an intruder. At 1420 what was assumed to have been a specially converted Ju88 (or more probably a pressurized Ju86P of 2(F)/123 from Crete) passed over at such high altitude that it was not spotted visually, the German crew apparently taking photographs of the convoy. Despite the lack of visual contact, the guns opened up a radar-predicted barrage and a section of Martlets from *Indomitable* were despatched to investigate — without success. One of these fighters was forced to ditch 23 miles from the Fleet on return, the pilot being located by a Fulmar, which guided the destroyer *Westcott* to pick him up; ammunition had apparently exploded in one of his wing magazines, causing a fire — the second such occurrence that day!

Meanwhile, realising that the Axis were now fully aware of what was going on, Flt.Off. Rolls decided not to lead his Spitfire flight over the planned route — directly east until off Bizerte, then south-east to Malta, passing Pantelleria to the south — as he anticipated likely interception, particularly from the latter quarter. Instead he headed immediately south-west, which took the flight to the Algerian coast, making landfall at Cape Bougaroni, and passing south of Bone and Tunis. Leading his aircraft in a dive as they passed over the Tunisian coast out over the Gulf of Hammamet, Rolls thus avoided any reaction from the Vichy French. Of this part of the flight one of his pilots, Plt.Off. 'Paddy' O'Brien, recalled:

> 'Some French fighters were spotted well below us but they did not try to intercept. We made our final course alteration at Hammamet with about an hour's flying time left. Shortly after leaving the coast my engine started to splutter. I quickly switched over to the main fuel tanks and it picked up immediately. Gave me a bit of a start... We had to keep a very sharp lookout from now on as the Italian base at Pantelleria came into view on our port side, and soon after Linosa and Lampedusa appeared... We hoped to avoid meeting up with enemy fighters, having no machine guns and we did not want to jettison our long range tanks.'

The Spitfires reached their destination without further event, turning to approach the Island from the south. O'Brien continued:

> 'Our aircraft followed each other around the circuit at Luqa and landed one after the other. My landing was one of the worst I had ever made. I blamed it on fatigue after a three-hour flight. My stomach was sore and my rear end most uncomfortable... I landed with a heck of a thump, fortunately without any damage.'

With her task completed, *Furious* — with an escort of eight destroyers — turned back westwards and headed for Gibraltar to pick up further Spitfires for subsequent delivery.

Three Sea Hurricanes were scrambled from *Indomitable* at 1835 following which Lt.Cdr. Judd, Lt. J.G. Forrest and Sub Lt. S.N. Harris of Black Section/880 Squadron were vectored onto a Ju88 'snooper' flying at 19,000 feet; the three pilots carried out diving attacks from out of the sun and reported that the Junkers dived into the sea at very high speed. This was undoubtedly Uffz. Franz Hronek's F6+FK of 2(F)/122, in which the crew perished. Before its demise, the Junkers' rear gunner (Uffz. Kurt Seiler) managed some accurate bursts of fire at Lt. Forrest's Sea Hurricane, hitting the engine and obliging the pilot to ditch; he was soon located by an 809 Squadron Fulmar and was safely picked up.

Gibraltar now signalled the Fleet that intercepted Axis wireless traffic indicated that a dusk air attack was in preparation. *Indomitable* and *Victorious* turned into wind and launched all available fighters, which climbed to the north, to 20,000 feet. The Luftwaffe had indeed despatched an attack and at 2055 some 30 Ju88s, drawn from the Sicily-based units, dived from 8000 feet, circling the vessels and seeking opportunities to attack. At the same time six He111 torpedo-bombers of 6/KG 26 swept in at wave-top level. The patrolling fighters were unable to spot the attackers from above as the gathering gloom merged them with the darkening sea below, but the guns put up a furious barrage and succeeded in preventing the torpedo-bombers pressing home their attacks, although a few torpedo tracks were spotted and easily avoided.

The Ju88s then attacked; the leading bomber and one other selected *Victorious* as their target and dived from astern. The carrier swung away, all her guns engaging and her crews believing that they had shot down both the bombers, one of which was seen to ditch in a shower of spray; two bombs exploded close alongside but caused no damage. One more Ju88 was claimed by the Oerlikon gunners aboard the tug *Jaunty*, reporting that it spun into the sea with both wings on fire; a Heinkel torpedo-bomber was also claimed shot down. During an attack on the cruiser *Manchester*, bomb splinters damaged her Walrus amphibian in its hangar, whilst aboard Admiral Burrough's flagship *Nigeria*, journalist and broadcaster Anthony Kimmins recorded:

> '... then suddenly a cheer from a gun crew, and away on the port bow a Ju88 spinning vertically downwards with both wings on fire and looking like a giant catherine wheel. More cheers and over to starboard another Ju88 was diving headlong for the sea, with smoke pouring out behind. At about 500 feet the automatic pull-out came into action, and she flattened out and crashed on her belly, with a great splash of water. Against the sunset you could see the parachutes of her crew as they drifted slowly downwards.'

The guns had indeed been effective for M7+DH of KGr 806 failed to return; Lt. Karl-Erich Ritter and his crew were lost. Those that did get back claimed hits had been achieved on a carrier, a cruiser and a merchantman.

The returning Fleet fighters gave chase but were unable to see much in the darkness. Lt. D.B.M. Fiddes and Sub Lt. H.H. Popham from 880 Squadron's Yellow Section, who had been patrolling for almost an hour, attacked one Junkers at 2000 feet at 2110, reporting strikes on the cockpit and starboard engine; Yellow 3 (Lt. J.G. Smith) then joined in and gained further strikes on the fuselage before the bomber broke away at 1000 feet; they were credited with its probable destruction.

Four Fulmars of 809 Squadron, which had been sent to search for possible low-flying Heinkel torpedo-bombers, instead spotted four Ju88s at 10-15,000 feet in the rapidly diminishing light. Three of the Fulmars attempted to attack two of the bombers and although Lt. E.G. Savage, the unit's commander, managed to gain strikes on the engine of one, much to his chagrin the damaged aircraft still outdistanced his Fulmar with apparent ease! Sub Lt. R.J.H. Grose, in an accompanying Fulmar, suffered similar embarrassment as his subsequent report revealed:

> 'I sighted enemy a/c 200 feet above on my port bow. I broke away and made a climbing quarter attack firing a 4-second burst at 400 yards closing to 200. He opened up and drew away. I fired another 3-second burst at 450 yards before I lost him. I am afraid he got home.'

As the Sea Hurricanes and Fulmars returned towards the Fleet between 2145 and 2200, several were by now very low on fuel and it was fast becoming extremely dark. Few of the crews were experienced in night landings, and to add to their difficulties they were continually fired at by the escorting destroyers as they attempted to line up. 880's Yellow Section were particularly low on fuel, and Sub Lt. Popham's engine spluttered to a halt as he approached the nearest carrier — *Victorious* — while she was still out of wind. As a result the Sea Hurricane swung across the deck and collided with another aircraft stowed abaft the island, bursting into flames. Popham escaped unhurt as a deck party, led by the Air Technical Officer, dashed over to extract ammunition from the gun magazines before it could explode. Simultaneously one of the ship's Albacore pilots played a hose on them from the vantage point of an Oerlikon platform to prevent their clothes catching fire. The crash was cleared and the wreck pushed over the side in six minutes, freeing the flight deck for further landings — but few more were to come.

Left: Lt. Dickie Cork DFC, of 880 Squadron, who was credited with six victories during the 'Pedestal' convoy operation. *(J. Pickering)*. **Right:** Sub Lt. Hugh Popham of 880 Squadron, HMS *Indomitable*. *(H. Popham)*

Most of the remaining aircraft had found *Indomitable* and were trying to land on her. Reported Lt. Savage, who had headed *Victorious*'s last patrol by four Fulmars and four Sea Hurricanes:

> 'I now became very anxious about my three companions (*the other Fulmars*) as they had done very few landings, about an hour and a half night flying in the last year, and only three dusk deck landings to prepare them for the coming ordeal. Moreover, we had all become separated in the darkness and were some 20 to 30 miles from the Fleet and I doubted their capacity to find their way home. Owing to the influx of new pilots, I could not have afforded to lose anyone of them, and I consider they showed great fortitude, perseverance and presence of mind in what rapidly became a very unpleasant evening's entertainment. It was a little misty and the darkness soon became that of a cupboard, with neither sea, horizon nor stars and flying had to be done on instruments.
>
> 'The fighter direction staff were, however, still vectoring us cheerfully from place to place, only to be met in each locality with a fresh barrage from the Fleet. This led to the hurried vectoring of more and more fighters to the scene and a consequent intensification of the gunfire as our numbers increased. On these occasions, the danger was usually greater from collision

than from gunfire, as the latter was extremely wild and almost invariably short in range. We were then told to switch on our navigation lights and muster south of the Fleet; this made it much easier for us but led temporarily to a fresh outburst from the guns. Things quietened down for a short while but then someone had the idea that the enemy was copying our tactics and flying about with navigation lights on, and we were fired at once again. Then began the nightmare, completely lost, with orders at times to have navigation lights on, at others to have them off, but always with the same results, being heavily fired on when inadvertently one flew close to a ship. This had now become most unpleasant as the visibility was less than 500 yards and at this range the fire, though still inaccurate, was uncomfortably close.

'Eventually my observer (*Sub Lt. E.N. Frazer*) reported we were over a ship and, as I sheered violently away, concurred almost incredulously that she was not firing at us. Then we looked again, and saw the deck lighting switched on. She proved to be *Indomitable* as her homing light started up and flashed "Ns". There was no sign of our own ship and to wander far away only started a fresh frenzy of fireworks, so we landed. All 809 Squadron landed there and with the exception of the last one, made perfect landings under pitch-black conditions without the aid of bats, as the ones in use were not visible from the air. This I think could not have been done without the aid of the pillar lights, which proved most helpful.'

Indeed, when he realised the problem facing the fighters, Captain Tom Troubridge had pulled *Indomitable* into wind and had taken the risk of turning on lights to allow the Fleet's vital defenders to get aboard. Unfortunately, during the attack on the carrier, a premature detonation in the after 4.5-inch gun turret had severely wounded Lt.Cdr. G.M. Pares, the Deck Landing Officer, and had smashed the illuminated night landing bats. However, by holding a torch in his mouth and others in each hand Lt. S.P. Boddam-Whetham, the deputy DLO, successfully landed-on seven of *Indomitable*'s own Sea Hurricanes, the four 809 Squadron Fulmars and a stray 885 Squadron Sea Hurricane from *Victorious*.

Lt. Jack Smith's Z7055 of 880 Squadron had suffered slight damage in the encounter with the Ju88, and now collided with the Spitfire which had landed on earlier that afternoon; much to the disappointment of the Naval fighter pilots, the Spitfire was considered too badly damaged to be of use and it, and Smith's Sea Hurricane, were unceremoniously pushed over the side. A similar fate awaited the fourth 809 Squadron Fulmar which had smashed its wing against a pom-pom on landing.

Almost joining the wrecks pushed over the side — so the story goes — was the Lieutenant in charge of the starboard aft pom-pom battery, who was allegedly grabbed by the throat by the fiery-tempered commander of 880 Squadron, Lt.Cdr. Judd, when the latter finally landed. Judd had been amongst those floundering around in the night sky, his aircraft, and those of his charges, constantly coming under fire. Even as he had flown slowly up the starboard side of *Indomitable* with his wheels lowered, the offending pom-pom had opened up on him! Under the circumstances, Judd escaped being disciplined for his actions, actions which would only add lustre to his formidable reputation.

Even as the German attack on the convoy had been developing Malta had launched its initial contribution to the action. At 1825 Wg.Cdr. Pike led off 248 Squadron's 11 Beaufighters for a pre-emptive evening strike on Elmas and

Decimomannu airfields, in Southern Sardinia; two Beaufighters were obliged to return early owing to technical defects, but en route the remaining nine passed over three Italian submarines — out from Cagliari and on their way to take up station in the convoy's path. These radioed the alarm to Elmas. On approach, the Beaufighters formed into three sub flights in preparation for the attack, thus:

'C'	Wg.Cdr. J.M.N. Pike
'W'	Plt.Off. D.J. Jay, RCAF
'O'	Sub Lt. J. Maurice, FAA
'A'	Sqn.Ldr. D.L. Cartridge
'E'	Sgt. R.F. Hammond, RAAF
'M'	Sgt. P.J.O. Mueller, RAAF
'N'	Flt.Lt. G.H. Melville-Jackson
'J'	Plt.Off. R.G. Stringer
'V'	Plt.Off. A.P. Wills

The crews found themselves faced with heavy AA fire as they swept over the airfield but nonetheless claimed two S.79s left on fire and six damaged, plus two guns silenced. The formation then flew on to Decimomannu, where they apparently gained complete surprise. Here eight large aircraft were claimed on fire and 16 more seriously damaged. Their claims were fairly accurate; at Elmas an S.79sil of 283ª Squadriglia, 130° Gruppo Aut. AS was destroyed by fire, six more — three from each of the unit's squadriglie — being damaged by bullets and splinters, as were a Luftwaffe Ju52/3m and three Bf109Fs of I/JG 27 in transit. Two Italians and a German airman of 5/KüFlGr 606 were wounded. At Decimomannu four S.79sil — three of 36° Stormo AS and one of 255ª Squadriglia, 105° Gruppo AS — were destroyed, as was a civilian Ca164 biplane, while nine other S.79s were hit and damaged.

A flight of G50bis of 24° Gruppo Aut. CT were in the air — as a result of the prior warning — and these were joined by eight CR42s and some 153° Gruppo CT MC202s. The G50bis pilots gave chase but could not catch the raiders, while two of the biplane fighters managed a brief attack, but without result. AA gunners at Cagliari claimed damage to one Beaufighter but, in fact, all got clear away.

As they headed back towards Malta, the Beaufighter crews saw below them two light cruisers and two destroyers (part of 7ª Divisione Incrociatori) departing Cagliari and heading eastwards. They circled overhead for as long as their fuel would allow, radioing their sighting to Malta, before returning to land at Luqa at 2350. Flt.Sgt. V.S. Lister's crew of Wellington 'O', out from Malta on an anti-submarine patrol, had already spotted and reported four cruisers and eight destroyers (3ª Divisione Incrociatori) heading westwards earlier in the day. At 0130 Lister was out again, keeping an eye on the two bodies of ships and dropping bombs on some of them but without effect.

During the night nine Z1007bis, two S.84s and six BR20Ms from Sicily were despatched to raid Malta, but only nine actually reached their target. From Luqa, heading in the opposite direction, departed four Liberators of 160 Squadron. These had flown in from Egypt for this operation, their crews briefed to bomb Decimomannu, but only two of these actually located and attacked the airfield; a single Wellington was sent to raid Catania as a diversion. Three further Liberators from 159 Squadron had also flown into Luqa from Egypt to raid Navarino Bay (Greece) before flying back to Fayid. One failed to take-off owing to tyre trouble, but Flt.Lt. Dyer (AL544) led the other (AL517 flown by Flt.Sgt. Wilkes) to the target area. Here a direct hit was claimed (by Dyer's crew) on a cruiser moored on the east side of Sphaktina Island — "a terrific explosion" was observed, then white smoke and steam was seen gushing from the vessel. Disappointingly, bombs from Wilkes' aircraft were seen to fall on land.

The two temporarily repaired freighters from the June convoy, *Orari* and *Troilus*, were now despatched from Grand Harbour with an escort of two destroyers (designated Force 'Y') to make a dash for Gibraltar. It was hoped that the general confusion in the Western Mediterranean would allow these vessels an opportunity to reach Gibraltar unmolested, which they eventually did.

Meanwhile during the same night, the Royal Navy submarine *Una* arrived off the south coast of Sicily, near Simeto, to put ashore a seven-man raiding party under Capt. Duncan from the Special Boat Service. The original plan had been to attack Comiso and Gela airfields — the intent to achieve similar success to that of the SAS/SBS raid on Heraklion and Kastelli airfields (Crete) the previous June, the latter raid having also been led by Capt. Duncan. The plan was rapidly revised when it was realised that these airfields were too far inland, and Catania was earmarked for attack instead. However, they ran into an Italian patrol before charges could be laid. Having retreated to the beach, their boat was then intercepted by two fishing boats. Although the raiding party were armed with automatics and hand grenades, they realised that resistance was pointless and surrendered with good grace to the unarmed Sicilian fishermen.

Far to the west — as *Furious* and her destroyer escort raced for Gibraltar — the Italian submarine *Dagabur*, part of the original screen, suddenly appeared on the surface-warning radar screen of the destroyer *Wolverine* just after midnight; Ten. di Vasc. Renato Pecori's craft was spotted on the surface, apparently taken by surprise, and was rammed by the destroyer at speed, sinking at once with all hands.

Nightfall, nonetheless, left the Axis in celebratory mood. They knew that they had sunk *Eagle*, and believed that *Furious* had been withdrawn because of damage inflicted either by *Uarsciek* or *Dagabur*, while damage to one of the other carriers by the evening air raid also seemed a possibility. All efforts were therefore now in hand to prepare the maximum air striking force for the morrow.

Wednesday, 12 August

At dawn reconnaissance aircraft were on their way west and south again, from Sicily and Sardinia. 51° Gruppo RS launched four Z1007bis shortly after 0515, three from 212ª Squadriglia and one of 213ª Squadriglia. Shortly thereafter another from the latter unit followed and behind this came three Z506B floatplanes, one of 146ª Squadriglia and two of 287ª Squadriglia; finally a sixth Z1007bis, again from 212ª Squadriglia, set out. The first of the Z1007bis returned early with technical problems but the remainder maintained their search, and at 0550 Ten. Nilo Rossi (212ª Squadriglia) spotted two destroyers and two merchant vessels steaming west — Force 'Y' out from Malta. It was again one of 1(F)/122's Ju88Ds which made the day's first main sighting

The crew of a reconnaissance Cant Z1007bis of the 176ª Squadriglia RST preparing for a sortie. Note the 'Bacu the Wizard' unit emblem on the fuselage. *(F. Bianchi via N. Malizia)*

however, spotting the convoy at 0620 and reporting its location — 48 miles from Cape Bougaroni.

The first patrol of four fighters — two Fulmars from *Victorious* and two Sea Hurricanes from *Indomitable* — had been launched at dawn. This was soon increased to three sections, totalling a dozen fighters, while all the others were brought to instant readiness; the ships' radars showed many 'blips' denoting searching or shadowing aircraft. Fourteen interceptions of various 'snoopers' were attempted, but only two achieved actual engagements.

With the arrival of daylight the three Fulmars and single Sea Hurricane of *Victorious*'s air group which had landed on *Indomitable* the night before, were flown off to return to their own carrier. Two of the Fulmars each carried one member of the crew of the fourth machine which had been damaged on landing and consequently pushed overboard; these landed at once. The third aircraft — flown by Sub Lts. J.W.D. Stephenson and F. Shutt — was ordered to join two patrolling 884 Squadron Fulmars, crewed by Lt. R.A.F. Churchill and Sub Lt. A. Nunn, and Sub Lt. D.G. Parker and L/Air. A.F. Ferguson.

The patrol was maintained at 2000 feet until 0705, when they were vectored onto a Z1007bis. This was Ten. Lamberto Pardini's 213ª Squadriglia aircraft, the fifth to leave Sardinia and the first of the Italians to find the convoy. Churchill and Parker (in DR724) at once attacked, but Stephenson's guns failed to fire owing to a cracked airline, which had not been spotted due to the aircraft's overnight absence. The fire of the two 884 Squadron Fulmars sufficed however, and the Cant bellied onto the sea in flames, with one member of the crew dead; the survivors would be rescued some 60 hours later by the German *U-205*.

At 0820 two more 884 Squadron aircraft relieved Churchill's section, and at 0900 they were also directed onto a Z1007bis, 20 miles away at sea level. Ten. Pompeo Nespolo's 213ª Squadriglia machine attempted to escape as the two Fulmars, crewed by Lt. S.J. Edwards and Pty.Off.(A) L.F. Barrick, and Sub Lt. W.F.H. Schwenk and L/Air. P.P. Ford, began a stern chase over the Tunisian coast, during which they claimed to have gained strikes on one engine and silenced the rear gunner. The chase was abandoned when Edward's aircraft was hit by return fire, the pilot being wounded in one eye; despite his injury, Edwards flew the damaged Fulmar back many miles to make a safe landing on the carrier. Meanwhile, Nespolo succeeded in reaching Sardinia with his bullet-riddled Cant, where he crash-landed; four wounded members of his crew were rushed to hospital while more than 300 holes were counted in the aircraft! The Italians thought their attackers had been Martlets.

At 0900 a large group of aircraft were detected on the radar screens at a distance of 65 miles, on a bearing of 045° and at a height of 18,000 feet. This was a formation of 24 Ju88s from I and II/LG 1 on their way from Sicily. At once White and Red Sections of 800 Squadron were despatched to intercept 15-20 miles out, while Black and Blue Sections of 880 Squadron were sent off to back up their attack. *Victorious* also launched three Sea Hurricanes, two of 885 Squadron and one of 801 Squadron, followed at 0915 by four Fulmars of 809 Squadron, which got into the air just as the attack developed.

Sea Hurricane '6F' of 800 Squadron about to take off from HMS *Indomitable*, followed by 6H, G, J and C. Also warming up in the background (right) is an 827 Squadron Albacore and (left) a visiting Swordfish.

800 Squadron's Senior Pilot, Lt. W.H. Martyn, led the four Sea Hurricanes of White Section into the bombers at 18,000 feet. He engaged two at once, one of which he claimed to have shot down into the sea. His fire then struck the starboard engine of a second Ju88 which was next attacked by Sub Lt. J.L. Hastings (in Z4056), who shot out the port engine and watched the bomber spiral into the sea, some 20 miles ahead of the Fleet. Martyn's aircraft (V7416) was hit in the engine by return fire and he was obliged to break off the attack, returning to *Indomitable* where he force-landed on the deck.

White 3, Sub Lt. G.W. Roberts flying 'M', engaged another bomber — almost certainly L1+EH flown by Fw. Walter Bastian — reporting both engines bursting into flames and the crew baling out. This was confirmed by witnesses aboard a nearby destroyer, but it seems that this aircraft was also under attack by Red Section aircraft. As Roberts broke away, his aircraft was shot down — he believed by a fighter, but it seems likely that the aircraft had been hit by return fire from the bombers; he was picked up safely by *Pathfinder*, one of the escorting destroyers. One member of the downed bomber's crew, Uffz. Werner Schirmbeck — the airgunner — was plucked out of the sea by the destroyer *Ledbury*, whose captain, Lt.Cdr. Roger Hill, reported:

'Three parachutes seen coming down. One was picked up and found to be a

German, so the other two were left. He (*Uffz. Schirmbeck*) stated that the last raid consisted of German airmen flying Ju88s from Sicily, and that he had been shot down by close-range weapons from the convoy. The most interesting thing about him was that the nails of his boots were made of wood.'

Although the fortunate 22 year-old Schirmbeck, a native of Osnabruck, believed his aircraft had fallen to AA fire, returning crews confirmed that the aircraft had been shot down by fighters; the other three members of the crew perished.

The fourth member of White Section, Sub Lt. F.G. Outwin, attacked one bomber from 10,000 feet down to 3000 feet, making three beam-to-bow attacks and one from below; the starboard engine cowling and parts of the wing were seen to fly off, and the aircraft was last seen losing height and heading for the Tunisian coast.

Red Section claimed two more Ju88s shot down, one by Lt.Cdr. Bruen and the other by Red 4, Sub Lt. A.J. Thomson, who attacked the wingman of the second section of bombers. He saw the port engine burning, following which it turned on its side and dropped away. Thomson's aircraft (V7416) was hit by a cannon shell or heavy machine gun bullet, which shot away part of its engine cowling, but he was able to return safely to the carrier. Sub Lt. J.M. Lucas (V7659) meanwhile followed Bruen in the initial attack, firing at the port aircraft of the leading flight of bombers before breaking away downwards. He then joined with another Sea Hurricane (apparently Roberts of White Section) to attack a single Ju88, which he reported crashed into the sea. The fourth member of Red Section, Lt. H. Muir-Mackenzie flying P3036, reported gaining strikes on the starboard engine of the bomber he attacked and saw pieces of the cowling fly off, but was unable to shoot it down.

As the attack by the 800 Squadron sections ended, 880's Blue Section appeared on the scene and reported a single Ju88 at 4000 feet. All four pilots attacked in turn, Blue 3 (Sub Lt. Howarth in Z4925) attacking head-on, followed by Blue 1 (Lt. Cork in Z4642), Blue 2 (Sub Lt. J.I. Cruickshank) and Blue 4 (Sub Lt. H.L. Cunliffe-Owen); the bomber crashed into the sea and survivors were observed swimming by the wreckage.

Many of the Ju88s had been seen to jettison their bombs when attacked, and only four actually seem to have penetrated the fighter screen to bomb the convoy in shallow dives; it was claimed that a number of torpedo-bombers, believed to be He111s again, also took part but without apparent effect. As the actual bombing attack on the ships was made two further Ju88s were claimed shot down by the Fleet's guns, one by the destroyer *Pathfinder*'s pom-poms, and the other by *Deucalion*'s 4.7-inch gun, although all vessels were blazing away.

Too late to intercept as the raiders headed in, the trio of Sea Hurricanes from *Victorious* now attacked as the bombers broke away. 885 Squadron's commander, Lt. Rodney Carver (encumbered by a fractured arm encased in plaster — the result of an accident), attacked one from astern, firing several bursts before it dived away with its port engine smoking; he then carried out a stern attack on a second, again firing several bursts before it rolled over and dived into the sea. Sub Lt. A.S. Long, his No 2, was attacked by a fighter and his aircraft was damaged. He succeeded in evading his attacker however, and continued towards the bombers, two of which he attacked and claimed damaged. The third member of the trio, 801 Squadron's Sub Lt. Michael Hankey, failed to return and was presumed shot down by fighters or return fire from the bombers. Meanwhile, the 809 Squadron Fulmars had made their way to the west of the barrage, heading round it to the south but arriving too late to catch any of the raiders.

As the attack petered out at around 1015, Blue Section of 880 Squadron spotted a Ju88 — very likely Ofw. Siegfried Fiedler's L1+AP of 6 Staffel — flying slowly towards the Tunisian coast, probably having already suffered damage; it seems very likely that this was the bomber which Sub Lt. Outwin had earlier attacked. Lt. Cork delivered two head-on attacks on this aircraft and reported that it crashed into the sea off the coast, two or three survivors being seen to get out; Cork actually filmed their escape from the sinking aircraft.

At about the same time 880 Squadron's Black Section — which had not been involved in the fight with the bombers — spotted the last of the Z1007bis 'snoopers' at 200 feet. Lt.Cdr. Judd led Sub Lt. Harries into a diving attack on Ten. Vittorio Ottaviani's 212ª Squadriglia aircraft, which continued flying for two or three miles, streaming flames from its engines, before it went down into the sea some 70 miles from Cape Spartivento (Sardinia). Ottaviani had been killed at the start of the attack and Ten. Angelino, the second pilot, made the crash-landing which allowed five members of the crew to escape unhurt; they were picked up next day by a Do24T of Seenotst 6 from Elmas.

As the survivors of the German formation headed for Sardinia to land and refuel, believing that they had sunk a carrier and two merchant vessels, they encountered more trouble. Alerted by the previous evening's surprise attack by the 248 Squadron Beaufighters, the defending fighters of 24° Gruppo Aut. CT were scrambled as the twin-engined aircraft of similar appearance approached. Before the mistake was realised, a patrol of G50bis of 370ª Squadriglia attacked as the Ju88s crossed the coast, two of them being reported shot down by Serg.Magg. Renato Mazzotti and Serg. Enrico Canepa — although it seems probable that both attacked the same aircraft — ironically the only 'successes' these aircraft were ever to achieve in defence of the island! The victim of this tragic mistake was Oblt. Axel Gerlich's L1+GN; he and his airgunner (Uffz. Adam Dotterweich) were killed, the latter baling out but with insufficient height, while the two survivors sustained injuries.

One undamaged Junkers that landed at Elmas to refuel was Uffz. Heinrich Herold's L1+HM of 4 Staffel. The crew reported gaining a near-miss on a large merchant vessel, following which they were pursued for some distance by a fighter identified as a Buffalo — obviously a Martlet — which apparently did not open fire.

Apart from the very accurate claims against 'snoopers', the carrier fighters reportedly claimed eight Ju88s shot down, three probables and at least four damaged during the attack, while the Fleet's AA claimed two more. Actual losses appear to have been seven or eight, including that shot down by the Italian fighters. It seems very likely that White and Red Sections of 800 Squadron attacked at the same time, a degree of double-claiming occurring, whilst the *Victorious* pilots may also have attacked the bombers fired on by the AA gunners. From the details available there seems little doubt that the two bombers attacked by 880 Squadron's Blue Section went down, but the extent to which they had previously been damaged remains uncertain. Similarly, it is possible that the aircraft shot down over Sardinia had also suffered prior damage.

Actual losses of I and II/Lehrgeschwader 1 were:

Junkers Ju88A-4 bombers were very active in attacks on the 'Pedestal' shipping, particularly those of the specialist Lehrgeschwader 1. Seen from the cockpit of another of the unit's bombers, L1+EM of the unit's 4 Staffel heads out over the Mediterranean. *(NWMA)*

1/LG 1	L1+EH	Fw. Walter Bastian and crew missing except airgunner, Uffz. Werner Schirmbeck, who was rescued; shot down by fighters
1/LG 1	L1+OH	Fw. Werner Vogt — all missing; reported shot down by fighters
2/LG 1	L1+YK	Hpt. Werner Lüben — all missing; reported shot down by fighters
5/LG 1	L1+ON	Oblt. Axel Gerlich — pilot and one killed; two others rescued, wounded; reported shot down by Italian fighters
5/LG 1	L1+GN	Oblt. Helmut Deidlauf — all missing
6/LG 1	L1+HP	Lt. Hans-Ernst Hammann — crashed Sardinia, all killed; reportedly shot down by fighters and AA
6/LG 1	L1+AP	Ofw. Siegfried Fiedler — pilot, at least, survived, rescued, believed shot down by fighters
5/LG 1	L1+DN	Aircraft damaged; airgunner, Uffz. Edmund Kühn, killed

As the bomber attack had got under way, enemy submarines again made their presence felt, the destroyers *Laforey, Fury* and *Foresight* launching a depth charge attack from which the Italian submarine *Brin* escaped by diving deeply. Albacores from the carriers continued to undertake anti-submarine patrols, still assisted by flyingboats from Gibraltar which ranged further afield, sweeping ahead of the convoy.

At 0934 the submarine *Giada* (Ten. di Vascello Gaspare Cavallina) was caught on the surface by a Sunderland some 70 miles north-west of Algiers. She was slightly damaged by two depth charges before making good her escape by undertaking a shallow dive. Leakages caused by the attack forced Cavallina to surface again and head for the nearest neutral port (Valencia on the east coast of Spain). At 1345 the submarine was apparently spotted again by a Sunderland which allegedly then dropped four bombs or depth charges. *Giada* suffered a severe buffeting but as the 'boat came in for a second attack, the submarine's gunners held steady and claimed the Sunderland shot down, reporting that it crashed in the sea nearby with a large explosion. No British records to support these actions and to confirm such a loss have been found.

A torpedo-laden Savoia S. 84sil of 256ª Squadriglia, 108° Gruppo, 36° Stormo AS, at readiness on Sardinia's Decimomannu airfield. *(N. Malizia)*

It was now the turn of the Regia Aeronautica in Sardina to try its hand, and a very strong attack was in the making as midday approached. First off from Villacidro at 1110 were ten S.84s of 38° Gruppo BT, led by Magg. Vincenzo Orlando, each bomber armed with two 360kg 'Motorbomba FF'. These weapons — known as 'Mad bombs' — were designed to be dropped vertically by parachute ahead of oncoming shipping. Impact with the water automatically released the parachute and a gyroscopically-controlled motor would start at a depth of ten feet, driving the bomb forward in a spinning motion which left no wake. If no impact with a target was made, it would subsequently self-destruct at the end of a pre-set time fuse.

Fifteen minutes behind this initial formation, torpedo-armed S.79sil started taking off from Decimomannu and Elmas; nine 130° Gruppo aircraft led by Cap. Mario Frongia joined ten more of 36° Stormo led by Magg. Alfredo Zanardi, two of III Nucleo led by Ten. Col. Vittorio Cannaviello, and a single II Nucleo aircraft flown by Cap. Carlo Putti. At the same time 15 of 24° Gruppo's CR42s left Monserrato, led by Magg. Mario Frulla, eight of which were each armed with a pair of underwing 100kg bombs. They hastened ahead of the lumbering trimotors, and had closed up on the leading S.84s by the time the target was approached.

The moment the S.79s had cleared Decimomannu's runway, ten more S.84s thundered into the air at 1130, these 89° Gruppo aircraft led by Ten. Col. Antonio Fadda and all carrying torpedoes. Five minutes later the escorts for the torpedo force took to the air — 14 153° Gruppo MC202s, led by Magg. Andrea Favini, together with nine more S.79sil of 105° Gruppo, led by Ten. Col. Remo Cadringher. It is possible that one more II Nucleo and four more III Nucleo aircraft accompanied this latter formation. After 50 minutes two 259ª Squadriglia

A Savoia S. 79sil bores in through a 'splash' barrage to launch its torpedoes at the British vessels. *(NWMA)*

aircraft from the 36° Stormo formation turned back, but reports suggest that 33 S.79sil and ten S.84sil reached the convoy. Finally, 16 Re2001s of 2° Gruppo departed Monserrato at the same time, led by Magg. Pier Luigi Scarpetta; they were off 15 minutes late as the escort for the 38° Gruppo S.84s, and did not catch them up before the attacks began, with results that were to cost the bombers dear.

Before the first Italian aircraft had left Sardinia, a force of 37 Ju88s from KG 54 and 77 had started taking off from Sicily, the first departing at 0955; all the bombers were in the air by 1030. It would have been impractical to try and provide fighter escort over the distances involved, so early that morning Hpt. Heinz Bär had led 21 Bf109s of a reinforced I/JG 77 to Sardinia. These took off from their temporary airfield at 1145 to rendezvous with the approaching bombers and provide cover for them in the target area.

At 1025 ten more Re2001s from 362ª Squadriglia at Monserrato took off to provide withdrawal support, led by Cap. Germano La Ferla, while at 1230 a reconnaissance Z1007bis of 212ª Squadriglia left Villacidro, in the hands of Sottoten. Gaetano Berlinazzo, to maintain visual contact with the convoy following the attacks. Even as the first aircraft were reaching the target area at 1240, the S.79 'flying bomb' took off, flown by Mar. Mario Badij, who then baled out as arranged. Control was at once assumed by Generale BA Ferdinando Raffaelli (the inventor) in the accompanying Z1007bis 'guide', five of 24° Gruppo's G50bis providing escort for this strange pair.

Finally, at 1305, two specially modified Re2001GVs of the Sezione Speciale — which had just arrived from the Reparto Sperimentale at Furbara (Rome), the Regia Aeronautica's armament experimental centre, took off from Elmas. Flown by Ten. Riccardo Vaccari and Ten. Guido Robone, each aircraft was armed with 50kg fragmentation bombs; it had been originally intended for the Reggianes to each carry a 630kg special armour-piercing bomb, designed for low-level attacks against shipping, but at the last minute faults had been discovered necessitating a change of plan.

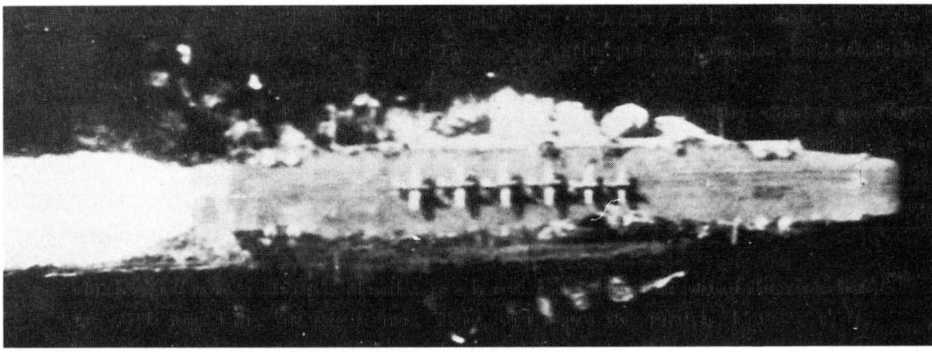

Her decks still loaded with fighters waiting to take off, HMS *Argus* is seen from an attacking Regia Aeronautica torpedo-bomber as it passes close overhead. *(NWMA)*

Meanwhile the defenders had been gathering. At 1055, two Fulmars of 884 Squadron had left *Victorious* to patrol at 10-15,000 feet and at 1130 were ordered to look out for 'bandits'. Two sections of fighters from *Indomitable* were also in the air; 800 Squadron's Green Section of four Sea Hurricanes, led by Lt.Cdr. Brabner of 801 Squadron, was patrolling at 18,000 feet, while 806 Squadron's Orange Section of four Martlets — with Lt. Johnston at their head — were at 15,000 feet. As the raid appeared on the radar screens, 800 Squadron's Red Section was scrambled, Lt.Cdr. Bruen leading them as they gained height to intercept, while from *Victorious* at 1205 four Fulmars of 809 Squadron were also got off as swiftly as possible, followed by four Sea Hurricanes of 885 Squadron. This brought the number of defending fighters in the air to 18.

The pair of 884 Squadron Fulmars (Lt. Hallett/Sub Lt. T.D. Haskey and Lt. F.A.J. Pennington/Pty.Off(A) Barrick) spotted three large formations approaching of what they took to be Z1007bis, about 40 miles out. Making an initial head-on attack, they noted that some of the bombers dropped what appeared to be 'parachute mines' when attacked — obviously 38° Gruppo releasing their Motorbomba. The Fulmars' attacks developed into beam, quarter, then stern chases as the bombers turned for home. The Naval aircrews reported that three bombers fell in flames after their crews had baled out and a fourth was seen with an engine on fire. However, Pennington's aircraft was hit and damaged by return fire, and the remaining bombers drew away gradually due to their superior speed! The pursuit was called off. The two Fulmar crews were subsequently jointly credited with three Z1007bis (sic) destroyed and one probable.

As Green Section raced to the scene of the action four Re2001s were met head-on at 15,000 feet. Sub Lt. R.W. Kearsley turned to get on tail of one as two attempted the same tactic on him; he opened fire and observed a 'flash' on the starboard wing of the one he attacked. Lt.Cdr. Brabner reformed his section and came upon a formation of trimotors flying a few thousand feet below. He reported a mixed formation, about 30 strong and identified as S.79s, Breda 88s — obviously S.84s, misidentified due to their twin tails — and Z1007s, which were similar in appearance to S.84s.

Their attack seems to have coincided with that of the Orange Section Martlets as the bombers closed to 20-30 miles from the leading vessels, which were now 60-80 miles south of Cape Spartivento, and close to Galite Island. Lt.Cdr. Brabner led the attack and reported that he saw pieces fly off one S.79 and then

Martlet AM968 '8M' of 806 Squadron taxies forward to take off from HMS *Indomitable*.

gained strikes on a 'Ba 88'; both aircraft were claimed severely damaged and were apparently credited as destroyed. Sub Lt. Hutton (V7077) claimed an S.79 as probably destroyed, while Sub Lt. J.A. Young made a head-on attack on another Savoia, saw pieces fly off, but then broke away as the convoy's AA barrage opened up. Sub Lt. Bob Kearsley made two attacks on Savoias but saw no result. Meanwhile, the Martlets had also dived in to the attack on trimotors universally identified as S.79s; Lt. N.A. Bartlett (AJ102) saw white smoke stream from one, which then crashed in the sea; Sub Lt. P.D.C. Street (AM998) made three attacks on one of five from which the crew baled out, and Sub Lt. J.A. Cotching (AM968/8-M) hit another in the port engine which caught fire. The bomber fell back from the formation but he had by then run out of ammunition.

Red Section had by now arrived, Lt.Cdr. Bruen attacking one S.84 which had obviously already suffered damage but appeared likely to reach its base. Aided by Sub Lt. Thomson (V7252), he shot it down in flames, two members of the crew baling out. He then attacked an S.79 flying at 25-50 feet above the sea, which had already dropped its torpedo. A stream of petrol appeared from the centre section as he fired, and he saw this bomber crash into the sea. Red 2, Sub Lt. John Lucas in V7659, broke away to attack another aircraft and was not seen again.

Sub Lt. Hutton had become detached from Green Section, and while flying some ten miles north-west of Galite Island he saw below him a fighter which he identified as an Re2000, but was in fact Sottoten. Antonio Bizio's Re2001 of 152ª Squadriglia. Diving apparently unseen out of the sun, Hutton fired from point-blank range, whereupon the Reggiane at once dived straight into the sea and sank. However, Bizio had succeeded in baling out and was picked up by the destroyer *Pathfinder*, which had earlier rescued Sub Lt. Roberts. In the same immediate vicinity at this time Lt. Muir-Mackenzie, one of the Red Section pilots, was climbing to attack an S.84 when he saw four fighters above. Initially he took these to be Hurricanes but then recognised them as hostile, identifying them as MC202s. He fired at close range and saw the cockpit cover of one disintegrate before it dived away towards the sea. This was almost certainly Ten. Giacomo Metellini's Re2001, which was badly damaged. Muir-Mackenzie's aircraft was then hit by tracer bullets from the Fleet, which put three holes in the wing, and he broke away. Three Hurricanes were claimed shot down by the

Torpedo-carrying S. 79sil bombers of the 30° Gruppo Aut.AS's 283ª Squadriglia head out from Elmas, Sardinia, in search of the British convoy.

Reggiane pilots, one each by Serg. Magg. Luigi Battaini, Serg.Magg. Rino Ricci, and Serg. Roberto Di Paolo.

The final engagement with the Italian bombers occurred as the 809/885 Squadron section attempted to intercept. The Fulmar crews had initially seen four Ju88s — the precursors of the German attack — and driven these off. A trimotor identified as a Z1007bis was then seen and was attacked by a Fulmar crewed by Sub Lt. A.McD. Garland and Sub Lt. R.M. Richardson, the pilot reporting:

> 'Made quarter to stern attacks aiming from about 350 to 100 yards. Starboard engine of enemy caught fire and two of the crew baled out. A/c seen to crash into the sea. During the engagement an unknown Hurricane was seen to make one attack from the opposite side.'

The Sea Hurricane pilot was 885 Squadron's Lt. Brian Paterson, whose aircraft had been badly damaged by fighters. Nonetheless he had carried out an attack on the bomber, which he claimed damaged. A Fulmar crewed by Sub Lt. R.D. Wood and L/Air. C.F. Dawson gave chase to another S.79, but was forced to break away by the heavy AA fire. One of the Fulmars was then attacked by two fighters — identified as Bf109s or MC202s — it and its No 2 taking evasive action down to sea level before climbing up to resume their patrol.

The original pair of Fulmars — those flown by Lt. 'Buster' Hallett and Lt. Frank Pennington (a New Zealander) — had meantime also been engaged by half a dozen MC202s and CR42s, two of the latter damaging Pennington's aircraft. His TAG, Pty.Off.(A) Len Barrick, was gravely wounded; despite the severity of his wounds, Barrick continued to give warning of the approach of the Fiats until he fainted. Hallett's aircraft was also forced down from 12,000 feet to sea level. Both aircraft managed to escape however, landing-on at 1230 and 1240 respectively.

What then of the results of this confused engagement? After meeting the initial fighter attacks, the 38° Gruppo S.84s had pressed on until the Fleet opened fire, when they released the Motorbomba which began making five-mile radius circles. On sighting the parachutes going down, the whole Fleet at once began an emergency 45° turn to port and then back on course again to avoid the 'mines'. As they did so, the 24° Gruppo CR42s swept in to bomb and strafe the destroyer screen, near-missing *Lightning* as the torpedo-bombers approached. The 36° Stormo formation had suffered heavily from the fighter attack however — almost certainly attacked by 884 Squadron, and by Green and Red Sections at least.

First to go was a 50ª Squadriglia aircraft flown by Sottoten. Alessandro Della Barba, which broke away with its port engine on fire and failed to return. Then another of this squadriglia's aircraft, that flown by Sottoten. Tullio Dessi, also fell away and went down with one engine ablaze. All the other eight bombers of the formation were hard hit by the fighters, several returning with wounded aboard, and some force-landing short of their airfield as soon as they made landfall at the Sardinian coast. The returning crews believed that their 'mad bombs' had sunk one transport and damaged a destroyer.

The formidable main armament of HMS *Rodney*, one of the battleships accompanying 'Pedestal' convoy, can clearly been seen in this Italian photo, taken by an attacking bomber. Note also the Walrus amphibian which can just be seen, mounted on its catapult on top of the third main turret. *(NWMA)*

As the first of the torpedo force approached, splitting into groups of five or six aircraft to attack, Magg. Zanardi's S.79 was hit by a fighter and the port wing set on fire. The 109° Gruppo commander was seen approaching the battleship *Nelson*, flames streaming back from the engines, but apparently still attempting to line up for an attack. Two torpedoes dropped away — both of which missed — and the Savoia then crashed into the sea. The crew got out safely, but it would be over 50 hours before the survivors were picked up by a German submarine, and Serg.Magg. Marc Pasquale Rombola died of his wounds in the meantime.

The rest of Magg. Zanardi's 36° Stormo formation claimed two transports sunk and hits on a destroyer and probable hits on a carrier, three cruisers and another transport. The bombers' gunners also claimed five Hurricanes shot down and one probable. The remainder of the formation made substantial further claims for hits on vessels, while also claiming another six Hurricanes shot down and one probable. In return, AA fire was reported as being very heavy, five 130° Gruppo and five 105° Gruppo machines being damaged by gunfire, while three more of the latter unit's aircraft were hit by both AA and attacking fighters.

By now the Sicilian-based Ju88s were arriving in force, and there was little but the Fulmars and the odd Sea Hurricane and Martlet available to oppose them. Several bombers were forced to jettison their bombs, but at least a dozen got through the destroyer screen and at 1318 commenced diving attacks on the merchantmen and their escorts. Several near-misses shook both *Rodney* and *Nelson*, while *Cairo* and several of the transports were straddled; Blue Funnel Line's *Deucalion* suffered a direct hit from one bomb which passed through No 5 Hold and out of her side before exploding. Three more near-missed and some of the crew prematurely abandoned ship. However, the freighter was not mortally damaged; members of the crew were rescued and put back aboard, and she proceeded at the reduced speed of eight knots. Escorted by the destroyer *Bramham*, she was ordered to make her way along the inshore route, down the coast of eastern Tunisia.

The remaining Naval fighters sought to harry the Ju88s, but as Lt. Johnston carried out a number of attacks on one — which was reported to have fallen — his Martlet (AJ136) was hit (presumably by return fire). He radioed that he had been seriously wounded, and as he attempted to land the damaged aircraft — without the aid of flaps — on *Indomitable*, the arrester hook missed the wire and the fighter went over the port side, sinking at once. Johnston's victim — and victor — may have been an 8/KG 77 machine (3Z+ES), flown by Oblt. Leopold Lagauer, which failed to return from this raid.

Martlet AM966 of 806 Squadron being readied for a sortie. Note the badge immediately behind the cockpit.

Next on the scene was the S.79 'flyingbomb', crammed with 1000kg of explosives, but the radio guidance system had developed a fault (probably the result of a faulty condenser), and the aircraft failed to respond to signals, droning on southwards until its fuel was exhausted. It subsequently crashed onto the slopes of Mount Khenchela, to the south of Constantine in Algeria, blasting a substantial crater in the rocky mountainside!

By now the original defending fighters had been in the air for over two hours, and these returned to land-on since they were low on fuel. Two Sea Hurricanes had just put down on *Victorious*'s deck at 1324, and three more were seen in the circuit — or so it seemed. Suddenly two of these swept in low and dropped bombs! They were the two Re2001s of the Sezione Speciale, which released their small bombs at the carrier, Ten. Vaccari and Ten. Robone then making good their escape before the AA guns could respond. Watchers on *Indomitable* recorded that two small bombs bounced 'like cricket balls' across the deck and went harmlessly into the sea although, in fact, one broke up on impact flying splinters killing four officers and two ratings.

Meanwhile 809 Squadron's four original Fulmars, having reformed following their initial engagement with fighters, had been vectored to 19,000 feet, attacking one of the bigger formations of Ju88s and causing four of them to jettison their bombs. They had then pursued one, which appeared to be in difficulties, down to sea level but were again attacked by escorting fighters. Evading these, they formed up over the Fleet for a third time to hunt for suspected torpedo-bombers, and on return to their carrier were just in time to meet one of the departing Re2001s. It escaped being attacked because its yellow markings led the pilots to believe it was a Sea Hurricane.

880 Squadron's Blue Section (led by Lt. Cork) went off at 1235, followed by Lt.Cdr. Judd leading off three of Black Section 40 minutes later (the fourth aircraft was delayed taking off, and was then forced to return with low oil pressure). At 1400 the two sections were vectored onto a small formation of wave-skimming, torpedo-carrying He111s of 6/KG 26, escorted by Bf110s of 8/ZG 26. Had the Heinkels been flying higher the Sea Hurricanes would have had a chance to manoeuvre but the torpedo-bombers kept so low that only stern attacks were possible. Judd's aircraft was promptly hit by return fire as he closed to attack, the starboard wing of the Sea Hurricane breaking away and the aircraft crashed into the sea from 500 feet; 'Butch' Judd was lost.

As Cork brought his section in to attack, the ships' guns opened fire, forcing the Sea Hurricanes to pull away; as they did so the escorting Messerschmitts pounced. Sub Lt. John Cruickshank, who continued chasing a Heinkel, was attacked by two and his aircraft fell into the sea, while the Sea Hurricanes flown by Sub Lts. Howarth and Cunliffe-Owen were hit and damaged, both pilots being obliged to return immediately to the *Indomitable*. Only Cork escaped unscathed and he went after one of the aircraft which had shot down Cruickshank; an account of the subsequent action recorded:

> 'Cork saw one of his companions go down into the sea before a Messerschmitt and, turning quickly, managed to get the German in his sights. Trailing smoke, the Messerschmitt climbed to a thousand feet, when the pilot baled out and the aircraft crashed into the sea beside Cork's carrier, whose officers and men cheered as though a goal had been scored in a cup tie.'

Cork, flying his beloved cannon-armed Z4642, reported:

> '110 shot down Blue 2... caught him on top of zoom — port engine caught fire, climbed, pilot baled out and landed ahead of screen. Few holes from 110 in own wing.'

Meanwhile, three 884 Squadron Fulmars (Lt. Churchill/Sub Lt. Nunn; Sub Lt. Parker/L-Air. Ferguson; Sub Lt. Schwenk/L/Air. Ford) had left *Victorious* to patrol at 5000 feet, being diverted to intercept a Z1007bis 'shadower' at 1410; this was Sottoten. Gaetano Berlinazzo's 212ª Squadriglia aircraft, still in the area maintaining visual contact. The Fulmars set off in pursuit, claiming to have shot the intruder down in flames just off the Tunisian coast. However, the section leader's fighter was seen to be hit by return fire and crashed into the sea with the loss of Churchill and Nunn.

It seems they were not alone in their attack on Berlinazzo's aircraft however, for at just this time Cork, alone after his section's fight with the Bf110s, spotted what he believed to be an S.79 flying very low. He made a head-on attack, seeing fire in the cockpit, and reported that the aircraft force-landed in the sea 10-15 miles off the starboard bow of the convoy. No survivors were seen. Clearly he did not see the attacking Fulmars, nor they he, and with the apparent complete lack of cross-checking of claims between the two carriers, he was credited with this victory also. The Cant's gunners succeeded in hitting Cork's aircraft during the attack, two large holes in the wings being added to the damage sustained in the fight with the Messerschmitts.

Sottoten. Berlinazzo had indeed force-landed his aircraft in the sea about 100 miles off the Tunisian coast but he and his crew survived, some wounded, and they were subsequently rescued by the Italian fishing-boat *Vergine di Pompei II*. Despite this loss, visual contact with the convoy was soon resumed by the crew of a 213ª Squadriglia Z1007bis, flown by Ten. Tommaso De Martiis, as well as by the ever-vigilant crews of reconnaissance Ju88Ds.

There followed a gap of nearly three hours before hostile aircraft again appeared in force and at 1652 the first signs were seen on the radars of two large groups of aircraft apparently heading from Sicily to Sardinia. This was the start of a co-ordinated assault planned by II Fliegerkorps and Aeronautica della Sicilia. Between 1505 and 1525, the Italians despatched from Sicily two Z1007bis (one each from 29° and 33° Gruppo BT) and two S.79s, both from 32° Gruppo BT, to search for the convoy; this was spotted by the 29° Gruppo Cant and by one of the S.79s at around 1700. It had originally been the intention to send out torpedo-bombers, dive-bombers and standard bombers under fighter escort, but the impracticality of returning 2° Gruppo Aut CT and its Re2001s from Sardinia in time led to the cancellation of the involvement of the level bombers.

Specially for this action, 13 Ju87s of 102° Gruppo Tuff had moved from Castelvetrano to Pantelleria, led by Cap. Cumbat. Here they had anticipated a full and detailed briefing, but instead an immediate departure was ordered. Because of the range involved, four Ju87B-2s had to be left behind with their larger 1000kg bomb load, Cumbat taking off at 1725 at the head of nine Ju87R-2s, together with an escort of 28 MC202s — 17 drawn from 155° Gruppo and the remainder from 20° Gruppo — led by Ten. Col. Remondino. These were to divide their attention between the Stukas and 14 S.79sil of 132° Gruppo Aut AS — seven each of 278ª and 281ª Squadriglie — led by Cap. Ugo Rivoli. After a few minutes one Ju87 returned early, leaving eight to continue. At virtually the same time 20 Ju87Ds of I/StG 3, led by Hpt. Martin Mossdorf, also took off, escorted by all available Bf109Fs of 8/JG 53 — also flying from Pantelleria; these headed south of the Italians, making for the island of Piana.

As these formations began to be plotted, the RCN destroyer *Ithuriel* spotted the partly submerged conning tower of the submarine *Cobalto* on the port bow, and attacked with depth charges; these brought her to the surface where she was met by gunfire and then rammed at high speed. The Italian craft sank almost at once, but *Ithuriel*'s bows had been damaged and she stopped, picking up three officers and 38 ratings from her victim. Other Axis submarines continued to manoeuvre to try and attack, but without success.

At 1705 it was realised that four potential 'waves' of attackers were gathering, two to the south-east (the German and Italian aircraft from Pantelleria) and two from the north-west. The latter comprised two smaller formations from Sardinia; one made up of eight bomb-carrying CR42s of 24° Gruppo led by Ten. Pietro Andreotti, which were being guided by two 130° Gruppo S.79s and escorted by nine Re2001s of 362ª Squadriglia, led by Cap. Germano La Ferla; the second was formed by eight S.79sil — five of 36° Stormo, two of 130° Gruppo and one of III Nucleo, led by Magg. Giorgio Grossi and escorted by 14 MC202s of 153° Gruppo, all of which had departed their bases around 1645. These latter formations appeared (to the British) to be awaiting the arrival of the forces from the south-east, but they were, in fact, searching for the vessels.

A patrol of Fulmars from 809 Squadron had gone off at 1640, chasing a 'shadower' without success, but the leader then had trouble with his radio and returned to *Victorious*. At once a relief patrol of two 884 Squadron aircraft was sent off at 1730, the second 809 Squadron fighter joining them, as did a single 885 Squadron Sea Hurricane. Meanwhile, Orange Section of 806 Squadron Martlets had been sent off to the west from *Indomitable* to engage the Sardinia formations, but found only a reported six bombers and 20 fighters — in fact the CR42s and Re2001s. Bouncing the formation, Sub Lt. Cotching (AM968/8-M) shot down the 362ª Squadriglia Reggiane of Sottoten. Michele Crimi, who was killed, while Sub Lt. J.B. Madden (AJ102) claimed a probable when smoke was seen and debris flew off the one he attacked. In return, Serg.Magg. Lucio Biagini claimed one of the attackers shot down — identified as a 'P 36 or Buffalo' — but all the Martlets returned unscathed. The two Sardinia formations then withdrew without sighting the ships, although four of the CR42s subsequently came across *Ithuriel*, the damaged destroyer being dive-bombed and narrowly near-missed.

The Pantelleria formations were 'seen' to be splitting up into five separate groups at 1750, while still 50-60 miles out. By now three Martlets, a dozen Sea Hurricanes and six Fulmars were in the air ready for them. At this point the mixed 809/884/885 Squadron formation was vectored towards Cape Servat where an S.79 was intercepted. The 809 Squadron Fulmar crewed by Sub Lt. J.H.O. Nihill and L/Air. W.R. Regan was seen to break away over the top of the bomber, and was obviously hit by the dorsal gunner's 12.7 mm Breda SAFAT, crashing into the sea in flames. The two 884 Squadron Fulmars — flown by Lt. Hallett and Sub Lt. Haskey, and Lt. Pennington and Pty.Off.(A) L.J. Gascoyne — joined by Sub Lt. F.H. Montgomery of 885 Squadron in the Sea Hurricane, kept after the Savoia and reported that it eventually crashed into the sea one mile offshore.

Four more 809 Squadron Fulmars took off at 1820, just getting clear of the Fleet before the attack started, and four more Sea Hurricanes were on the point of departing *Indomitable* at 1830 as the attackers appeared. The Fulmars saw two formations of aircraft which they were advised not to attack (apparently the German and Italian Ju87s), but they were then heavily engaged by fighters — identified as Bf109s or Re2001s — from out of the sun. These shot down the aircraft crewed by Sub Lt. C.J. Evans and L/Air. J. Stewart, while Lt. I.J. Wallace's X8812 was hit in the port wing. The three survivors took violent evasive action down to sea level and escaped further loss. Sub Lt. Hugh Morrison and L/Air. Dawson, finding themselves alone, gave chase to a trimotor leaving the Fleet — which they identified as a Z1007 — but were at once attacked by three more Messerschmitts. Morrison reported:

> 'Enemy a/c dived out of sun. I did steep turn and straightened up to meet attacks. Fired short burst at each. Air Gunner observed enemy a/c on fire and hit sea. Other a/c climbed away as soon as they saw this happen.'

What Morrison's TAG had actually seen was probably their compatriots' Fulmar fall into the sea, for no losses were recorded of Messerschmitts or further Italian fighters. Lt. Cork, again leading Blue Section from *Indomitable*, had seen S.79s and escorting fighters (identified as Re2001s) to the south-east, from 12,000 feet down to sea level. He then spotted the 809 Squadron Fulmars under attack and went to help. Breaking out of the general dogfight, he saw an S.79 very low and gave chase, making three attacks until he ran out of ammunition. He reported that this bomber hit the sea with fire streaming from its cockpit, one man baling out from 50 feet; as he turned to photograph the crew in their dinghy with his gun-camera, he was attacked by two Italian fighters and his Sea Hurricane (he was flying Z7093 as his favourite Z4642 was under repair) was badly shot-up; he reported:

> 'Attacked by Reggiane 2001 at 50 feet, just as I finished all my ammunition on the 79. Several holes through a/c and radiator, rudder half stripped of fabric, port bottom longeron severed.'

Only by skimming the waves was he able to escape but his aircraft was too severely damaged to reach *Indomitable* so he signalled nearby *Victorious*, and landed safely. The engine seized up as he touched down and, as the battered aircraft was considered beyond repair with its radiator practically shot away and the fuselage and wings riddled with bullet holes, it was dumped over the side.

Meanwhile, Lt. Hamish Muir-Mackenzie, flying as Blue 3 in '6-P', also broke out of the dogfight to attack an S.79, reporting damage to its port wing. This aircraft was then attacked by the Fulmars, and he believed that they might have shot it down. Lt. Paterson, one of the 885 Squadron Sea Hurricane pilots, intercepted four of the torpedo-bombers as they closed in, attacking one which was straggling. Closing to 150 yards, he gained hits on the starboard engine which appeared to catch fire. The bomber lost height but return fire then struck the rudder of his aircraft, and he was obliged to break away. Black Section, which had been ordered to the north-west meanwhile, saw nothing.

At 1840 the attack began and Sub Lt. Thomson of 800 Squadron (P5206/7-C) saw below him four light-brown and green Ju87s (almost certainly from 102° Gruppo) at 4000 feet. Diving from 6000 feet, he pulled up underneath and fired a five-second burst into one, which he reported crashed into the sea. The other three jettisoned their bombs and dived away. He was then attacked by a Messerschmitt, and reported:

> 'After attacking Ju87 I was turning away when about seven or eight Me109s came down out of the sun. One attacked me and we got into a tight turn to port. I gave a short burst and he slackened the rate of turn. Then I gave him the rest of the ammunition I had left. Me109 turned over on his back and dived into the sea from about 3-4000 feet. The rest of the 109s were engaged with Martlets and Fulmars. Me109 had yellow nose and leading edge, and yellow or white band round tail. Under side pale. German markings.'

At 1845 the last section of Sea Hurricanes was just getting airborne from *Indomitable* when a dozen I/StG 3 Ju87s suddenly appeared out of the sun from a smokey blue sky, hazy with funnel fumes. Before the guns could be brought to bear, they struck the carrier with two direct hits and three near-misses. Both aircraft lifts were damaged, one being forced above deck level, and the flight deck was put out of action. Six officers and 44 men were killed and 59 more seriously wounded. The off duty Albacore crews of 827 Squadron suffered a number of casualties: Lt. R.B. Park, one of the unit's senior pilots, was killed as were two observers, Sub Lts. G.F. Measures and W.L. Protheroe, while two other observers, Sub Lts. W.A. Davies and C.M. Brown, sustained wounds; Sea Hurricane pilot Sub Lt. Hugo Cunliffe-Owen, of 880 Squadron, was also killed.

Returning Luftwaffe crews reported that the carrier *Wasp* (sic) had been set on fire after six direct hits, a mistake of identity which is believed to have originated due to the lighter paint colours applied to *Indomitable* for her Indian Ocean service. The Italian submarine *Avorio* had also reported the presence of an 'American-looking' carrier.

One of the last pilots off was Sub Lt. Blyth Ritchie of 800 Squadron (V7416), who at once attacked a Ju87 with Lt. Brian Fiddes of 880 Squadron, the latter having also just taken off. Closing to 75 yards, they saw the cockpit hood fly off their target and the aircraft go into the sea. Fiddes then attacked another but was hit by the ships' AA fire, and was forced to ditch at once; he was picked up safely. Five minutes later Ritchie attacked another Stuka:

> 'I saw one Ju87 at 400 feet and chased it for one mile approximately. I did a beam attack at 100 yards and saw part of the cowling fly off, then carried round to astern and closed to 60 yards and saw the gunner double up. It was now smoking and on fire on the starboard side. The starboard wing dropped and it went into the sea from 200 feet.
>
> 'I was flying through the barrage from the Fleet when I saw five aircraft diving from approximately 3000 feet. I climbed to 2000 feet and did a beam attack ending upon the quarter at 50 yards. I saw the pilot's cockpit shatter and the angle of dive changed from 65° to 85° and go straight into the sea. I followed him down but could not continue firing as I had no ammunition left. When the aircraft hit the sea I saw the air gunner begin to climb out. It was later confirmed that the pilot was badly injured but the air gunner was OK.'

Apparently the German crew of this aircraft — believed to have been Uffz. Gerhard and Gefr. Bredenbroker — were rescued from the sea. During the fight Ritchie's own aircraft was hit by one large calibre bullet just behind his headrest, and was peppered with light AA splinters. His claim for the second of the three Stukas was confirmed by witnesses on both *Victorious* and *Indomitable*. Gun crews aboard the *Kenya* and *Charybdis* also believed they had jointly accounted for one.

In the meantime, the three survivors of the four original Fulmars of 809 Squadron had reformed and been joined by two more of their unit, two of 884 Squadron and two Sea Hurricanes of 885 Squadron, the whole formation then being ordered to 10,000 feet at 1857. When they reached 6000 feet, four of the Fulmars were attacked by two MC202s but Sub Lt. D.S. Hill, a New Zealander (with Pty.Off.(A) Gascoyne), made a very spirited attack on these in defence of his No 2, who was lagging. Hill clamed to have shot down the leading Macchi, reporting that it fell with its engine on fire. While this was going on, one of 806 Squadron's patrolling Pink Section Martlets — AM998 flown by Sub Lt. Barry Nation — attacked a bomber identified as a Ju88 (possibly a reconnaissance machine) from out of the sun, and claimed hits on its tail unit before it disappeared from sight.

The aerial assault was virtually over however for at 1850, minutes after *Indomitable* had been hit, Force 'F' turned back for Gibraltar — it had come as far east as planned. Force 'X' and the convoy were now to proceed alone, heading south of due east to pass the Cape Bon peninsula through the Skerki Bank, and then to swing westward, south of Pantelleria.

As the ships took up their new course, those of *Indomitable*'s fighters still in the air came in to land on *Victorious*. Due to the crowding caused by this influx, any seriously damaged aircraft which was not easily repairable was pushed over the side. One Martlet ran out of fuel while waiting to get aboard and ditched, the pilot being picked up by the destroyer *Zetland*. Overhead the remaining Fulmars patrolled until 30 minutes before sunset, the last landing at 2015 — watched, they reported, by Axis fighters up sun which made no attempt to attack.

An S. 79 — aircraft '10' of 58ª Squadriglia, 32° Gruppo, 10° Stormo BT, from Sciacca, Sicily, searches for the convoy in company with another of the unit's aircraft, and under escort by a pair of Messerschmitt Bf110s from III/ZG 26.

What then had the defending fighters actually achieved during this last battle which had netted claims for four or five Ju87s, two fighters and two S.79s shot down and one S.79 probable, plus several damaged? Although a number of the 132° Gruppo S.79s were hit, all returned. The only loss of such an aircraft was that suffered by 32° Gruppo when Cap. Giovanni Mollo's MM22063 failed to return from its reconnaissance. This was probably the aircraft attacked by *Victorious*'s fighters, but may conceivably also have been attacked by Lts. Cork and Muir-Mackenzie.

Given the specific claims made against the Ju87s, what were their losses? 102° Gruppo lost two such aircraft, that flown by Serg. Giulio Cremonesi and 1° Av. Mot. Giovanni Parietti reportedly being shot down by AA and crashing on the stern of the battleship *Rodney*, while Serg. Ugo Casavola and 1° Av. Mot. Giuseppe Calorenna, also members of 239ª Squadriglia, were shot down by a fighter — probably Sub Lt. Thomson of 800 Squadron. I/StG 3 also reported the loss of two Ju87Ds — S7+HL flown by Uffz. Gerhard and CG+SK flown by Uffz. Herbert Gössling — both probably falling to Sub Lt. Ritchie, possibly aided by Lt. Fiddes.

On return to their base on Sicily, 102° Gruppo crews claimed one merchantman sunk and one carrier damaged, while 132° Gruppo AS claimed two merchantmen and a heavy cruiser; they had, in fact, managed only to damage the destroyer *Foresight*. The escorting fighters of 51° Stormo claimed seven victories against fighters identified as Fulmars, Hurricanes and Martlets, these being credited to Magg. Dulio Fanali, Cap. Borgogno, Cap. Spagnolini, Cap. Franchini, Ten. Mazzoleni, Mar. Bianchi and Mar. Gaucci. German fighters apparently also claimed at least seven victories.

By evening the Axis believed that two more carriers had been seriously damaged to add to the supposedly damaged *Furious* and the known sinking of *Eagle*. As soon as *Indomitable* had been hit, *Charybdis* and three destroyers had been despatched to her aid; by 1930 she was able to steam at 17 knots, her fires under control. Within another hour her speed was up to 28 knots.

S. 79 '8' of 58ª Squadriglia, 32° Gruppo, low over the water off the Sicilian coast. *(F. Bianchi via N. Malizia)*

As the last fighters landed on *Victorious*, she carried aboard ten Fulmars, eight Sea Hurricanes and three Martlets available for action — 29 or so less than the number that had been available at dawn. In the two days' fighting seven Sea Hurricanes had been shot down, including one by ships' AA fire, with four pilots killed; three Fulmars had also been shot down with the loss of all three pilots, one observer and two TAGs, and one Martlet had been lost due to enemy action, together with the pilot. A further Martlet and a Fulmar had ditched and at least four badly damaged aircraft had been deemed irreparable and pushed over the side; many others had been damaged. It was considered that the fighters had, during their two days of action, accounted for 39 Axis aircraft shot down and several more probables — as has been seen, about double the actual losses attributable to the fighters. By the end of the day's fighting, *Indomitable* declared her 'score at close of play' to be 28:6:10, thus:

Junkers 88	10	Macchi 202	2
Junkers 87	3	Reggiane 2001	2
Savoia 79	7	Messerschmitt 110	1
Breda 88	2		
Cant Z1007	1		

Whilst under the care of the fighters however, not one merchant ship had been lost, only *Deucalion* suffering damage. Despite the general lack of experience of their pilots, inadequate performance of most aircraft, and general numerical inferiority, they had done extremely well — aided greatly by the excellent radar-directed fighter control, which had generally placed them where they needed to be. One must not overlook the work of the flight-deck parties, seamen who were on duty from dawn to dusk, of whom one *Victorious* pilot wrote:

> 'The maintenance ratings worked like slaves in the cramped space (*of the hangars*). The floors were covered with grease and running with oil and petrol. The heat was intense and they had to work all the time under electric light, taking their food in the hangars as and when they could.'

Just how much the presence of the fighters would be missed was underlined within an hour of their departure.

At 1956 the Italian submarine *Axum* (Ten. di Vasc. Renato Ferrini) fired a salvo of six torpedoes which achieved quite remarkable success. One hit the cruiser *Nigeria*, which was severely damaged, four officers and 48 ratings being killed and two seriously wounded. Rear-Admiral Burrough transferred his flag to the destroyer *Ashanti*. Two more torpedoes struck the AA cruiser *Cairo*, which suffered 23 killed and two badly wounded. Captain Hardy ordered 'Abandon ship!' and all 377 survivors were taken off by the destroyers *Wilton* and *Bicester*, while *Pathfinder* was ordered to sink the stricken vessel with torpedoes; this proved very difficult, and she had to be finished off by gunfire from *Derwent*.

Yet another torpedo from this salvo struck the tanker *Ohio* level with her pump room, the deck on the port side being ripped open and fire spreading rapidly. However, as the blaze took hold, seawater pouring through the huge hole in her side quenched the flames and by 2015 she was under control again. On learning of the damage to *Nigeria* and *Cairo*, Vice-Admiral Syfret ordered *Charybdis* and two destroyers (*Eskimo* and *Somali*) to detach from the Gibraltar-bound Force 'F' to reinforce the remains of Force 'X'.

Just before nightfall the last air attack came in, 30 Ju88s of KG 54, KG 77 and KGr 806 — and seven He111s of 6/KG 26 each carrying two LTF 5b torpedoes — approaching at 2035, with an escort provided by six Bf110s of III/ZG 26 (8 Staffel). They just missed the first attempt to provide air cover from Malta. Six

One of the 'Pedestal' merchantmen, her bows blown off by a torpedo strike, lies stationary in the water. *(NWMA)*

Beaufighters of 248 Squadron had flown out to take over from the carrier fighters, but when on approach they were fired on, the leader decided to abort the mission, returning to Luqa. Without interference from defending fighters therefore, the Luftwaffe bombers moved in on the convoy some 20 miles west of Skerki Bank, attacking in pairs and remaining overhead for 30 minutes. Many vessels were near-missed but then, just after 2035, the Shaw Savill & Albion Co's *Empire Hope*, which had already suffered some damage, was singled out by one Ju88 and sustained two direct hits. She was soon well ablaze when her cargo of cased petrol ignited, and was abandoned. The destroyer *Penn* took aboard all the crew before putting a torpedo into the blazing wreck. Her master, Captain G. Williams, and the 3rd Officer (Mr G.V. Conolly) were each awarded a DSC for their efforts to save the ship.

This was but the start however, for at the same time an He111 torpedoed the ammunition-laden *Clan Ferguson* (Scottish Steamship Co) and at 2102 she blew up violently; despite this, most of her crew managed to escape, including Captain A.R. Cossar; 53 were later picked up by the Italian submarine *Alagi*, which had also fired torpedoes at this freighter. Eleven crew, one gunner and six passengers were lost. Apparently the same Heinkel which had hit *Clan Ferguson* released its second torpedo at Blue Star Line's *Brisbane Star*. Although her bow was blown away, she was able to continue after 20 minutes, though at a much reduced speed. Unable to rejoin the convoy, Captain Riley was ordered to head for the Tunisian coast and hug the coastline. *Wairangi* was narrowly missed by another pair of torpedoes, as was the destroyer *Ashanti* (with Rear-Admiral Burrough aboard), but *Glenorchy* suffered bomb damage.

Some miles behind the convoy came the damaged *Deucalion* and her escorting destroyer *Bramham*. This pair had already been near-missed by two Ju88s when at 2115 two Heinkels appeared on the scene. While the first missed, the second obtained hits with both torpedoes at close range. The freighter's cargo of aviation fuel exploded and several members of the crew were killed; the survivors were taken aboard *Bramham* as the vessel was abandoned.

The German crews returned in triumph, claiming ten merchant ships sunk — eight by bombs and two by torpedoes — and one cruiser hit for the loss of a single Ju88. This was M7+DL of KGr 806, which Lt. Werner Tronicke force-landed in the sea, during which three of the crew (including the pilot) were injured. Bofors gunners on the American *Almeria Lykes* had claimed two attacking Junkers shot down, while Oerlikon gunners aboard the escorting destroyer *Tartar* also claimed strikes on one. The attacks had actually caused the

Another British merchantman in difficulties during Operation 'Pedestal' — seen from an attacking Italian aircraft. *(via N. Malizia)*

loss of three transports, seriously damaged a fourth and damaged a fifth — an outstanding achievement in itself. The remaining vessels were now scattered over many miles — and worse was still to come.

What, however, had Malta's air forces been doing in the meantime? Throughout the day Baltimores and PR Spitfires from 69 Squadron had reconnoitred the Italian harbours and the sea lanes between Sicily and Sardinia, searching for major units of the Italian Navy. At 1000 it had been discovered that elements of 3ª Divisione Incrociatori had left Messina; but heavy cloud prevented their discovery until evening, when Plt.Off. Munro's Baltimore crew spotted a cruiser and five destroyers, shadowing these until nightfall. In fact 7ª Divisione Incrociatori had sailed from Cagliari at 2000 the previous evening as already noted, while the cruiser *Muzio Attendolo* had departed Naples, all these vessels rendezvousing at 1900 that evening (the 12th) in the lower Tyrrhenian Sea. However, the Regia Marina considered the Regia Aeronautica fighter forces inadequate for their escort, and made no attempt to move further south.

Indeed, Malta had prepared a strike force of 15 Beauforts and 15 Beaufighters (as escort) to attack these vessels next day, had they attempted to intervene, but in the event they were not called upon. Two Albacores were held ready for a night torpedo strike, but so dire was the strength of the night striking force at this time that only one Wellington — a patched-up Mark IC (DV542) which had crash-landed on the Island during a transit flight — was available. Plt.Off. Douglas Shepherd, who had no previous operational experience, volunteered to fly this and undertook two raids on Comiso with a volunteer crew, dropping delayed action bombs. On the second sortie his aircraft was hit by Flak and damaged, and as a result it crashed on landing at Luqa; the Australian WOP/AG, Sgt. Harry Fox, was killed and all the others injured. Following the crew's rapid evacuation, the Wellington blew up.

With 15 Beaufighters held ready for the proposed shipping strike next day, and others out attempting to escort the convoy, only four 248 Squadron aircraft and three of 252 Squadron could be made available for a last-light attack on Pantelleria. The flights were to attack separately but one of the 252 Squadron machines was forced to return early and the other two failed to locate the target.

The 248 Squadron flight lost its leader when Flt.Lt. I.U.M. Galloway ditched T5143 in the sea just after take off due to engine failure; the crew were picked up safely. Leadership of the remaining aircraft was assumed by the squadron's Free French Fleet Air Arm pilot, Sub Lt. G.P.R. Weil, he and his section — Plt.Off. P.St.C. Bate and Sgt. R.W. Sebring — arriving over Pantelleria airfield just before dark and catching some of the 132° Gruppo Aut. S.79sil on the ground just after their return from the late afternoon attacks on the convoy. One S.79 was set on fire, and two others and one S.84 were damaged, as was an already-damaged Ju52/3m; 24 drums of aviation fuel were also set on fire. Sottoten. Vittorio Moretti was hit by a bullet and fell, striking his head on a propeller. The blow killed him, while one other Italian airman was wounded.

Over Malta during the mid morning, Blue Section of 185 Squadron was scrambled, the four Spitfires led by newly-promoted Capt. Swales. The section was vectored towards a suspicious aircraft, reported about 60 miles north-east of Zonqor Point, but just then Plt.Off. Ogilvie (EP139) experienced a leaky oxygen valve which caused him to run short, and he was forced to descend very rapidly. On reaching 14,000 feet, Ogilvie sighted an He111 flying at about 4000 feet below, in a north-westerly direction; he recalled:

'I immediately went into attack after notifying Blue 1 of my position. I attacked from above, opening fire at about 200 yards, closing to point-blank range, with a 5-second burst of cannon and machine-gun; saw strikes along fuselage. I finished my ammunition and broke off attack. The attack was continued by Blue 4 (Plt.Off. Sherlock). He found the Heinkel pouring black smoke from its port engine; he made attacks, firing short bursts, and saw e/a turn over on its back from about 3000 feet.

'Swales then made port quarter attack from astern and finished nearly all his ammunition — saw strikes and e/a kept diving, then flew at water level, smoking badly. He followed for about 800 yards when e/a suddenly disappeared — he was convinced it had dived into the sea.'

Plt.Off. John Sherlock recalled a slightly different version of events:

'It was one of those interceptions which worked out perfectly. Zulu (*Swales*) and Buzz (*Ogilvie*) attacked immediately and I pulled up and around in front of e/a, and fired at the perspex nose as the He111 was gliding down, smoking. I merely fired at a "dead duck". The He111 crashed into the sea and I could see no survivors.'

The Heinkel was actually credited to Ogilvie, and was celebrated as the squadron's 100th — all claimed in the defence of Malta. Contemporary records indicated the squadron's full score at this time to be: 100 destroyed (34 bombers, 66 fighters); 50 probables and 129 damaged.

The naval operations of the convoy have been adequately dealt with elsewhere*, and in the light of this only a brief synopsis of the events of the night of the 12th/13th, prior to the resumption of air force involvement at dawn will be given here.

Submarines continued to manoeuvre for targets, and soon after dark *Alagi* released four torpedoes, one of which hit the cruiser *Kenya* and killed three of her crew, but she managed to continue without loss of speed. Another submarine — *Bronzo* — came across the drifting and abandoned *Clan Ferguson* and sent her to the bottom.

At 30 minutes past midnight on the 13th, the motor torpedo boats began attacking the straggling vessels, *MAS 556* claiming one hit and the German *S.59* a hit on a '15,000-ton tanker', which was reported to be in flames. At 0107 two more of the craft, *MS 16* and *MS 22*, fired torpedoes at the cruiser *Manchester*, which was severely damaged. Some of her crew were taken off and she was ordered to head for Gibraltar but later sank, the balance of her crew taking to boats and floats. Over 300 were picked up but the majority were interned in Tunisia by the Vichy authorities, including Lt. C.K. Roberts, her Walrus pilot.

Meanwhile, *MS 26* achieved a hit on the *Rochester Castle*, which was badly damaged but managed to continue at 13 knots. This MTB also reported attacking a cruiser at 0150, the crew believing hits had been gained with both torpedoes. They had, in fact, missed. At the same time *MS 31* put two torpedoes into the bomb-damaged *Glenorchy*; she had previously been engaged by an MTB, which her gunners claimed 'blew up' during an exchange of gun fire, but the Glen Line vessel was now abandoned by her 99 crew and 25 passengers, which included Naval staff for Malta; 108 eventually reached the Tunisian coast aboard two lifeboats, while a further nine on a raft were picked up by an Italian

*The authors recommend Peter C. Smith's book *Pedestal: The Malta Convoy of August 1942.*

MTB, but amongst the seven lost was her master, Captain G. Leslie.

Soon after 0300 the nimble little craft attacked again, *MAS 552* and *MAS 554* simultaneously assaulting *Wairangi*, which suffered one hit but continued on her way. Two more — probably the German *S.30* and *S.59* — attacked *Almeria Lykes*, each crew claiming a sinking. The United States Lykes Brothers Shipping Co's vessel was indeed abandoned as a result of this attack, all 105 of her crew getting away. *MAS 557* attacked the other American vessel, *Santa Elisa*, but her torpedoes missed. Joined by *MAS 564*, the two MTBs then exchanged fire with Cadet Midspmn. Francis Dales, who was manning the bridge Oerlikon, shooting it out with the Italian gunners; three American crewmen were killed but one MTB was reported to have caught fire. It was then that *MAS 564* took advantage of the confused situation and scored a direct torpedo hit, leaving the Grace Line freighter ablaze from end to end; five of her crew were badly burned, but all were rescued by the destroyers *Penn* and *Bramham*.

Finally, at 0508, the Italian MTBs claimed a further success when *MAS 553* reported a hit on another merchant vessel, but this may have been the already mortally wounded *Santa Elisa*. She was to be finished off an hour later when a lone Ju88 located and bombed her; following a severe explosion, she finally sank. Meanwhile, at 0400, six of KG 26's He111s were again out with the dawn on an armed reconnaissance, and two hours into their search located the damaged *Wairangi*, surrounded by survivors in boats and rafts. Two of the German aircraft swept down and released their torpedoes at the stationary vessel — and both missed! Two hours later the destroyer *Eskimo* came on the scene, picking up 79 survivors, but leaving the abandoned, drifting Shaw Saville & Albion Co freighter to her fate. *Wairangi*'s Master, Captain H. Gordon, and the Chief Engineer, Mr A. Chalmers, were each awarded a DSC for their efforts to save their ship. There were several other isolated incidents during the early morning as pairs of Ju88s appeared and attacked damaged or abandoned vessels, but no further sinkings occurred.

Thursday, 13 August

The situation as the first Spitfires — a flight of four led by Wg.Cdr. Hanks — began to appear from Malta therefore, was that *Rochester Castle* was well on her way towards the Island, followed by *Waimarama, Melbourne Star* and the damaged tanker *Ohio*, still making good progress; far behind them came *Port Chalmers*, while *Dorset* was making her own way to the north, and *Brisbane Star* was hugging the Tunisian coastline.

From Malta Wellington VIIIs of 69 Squadron's 'C' Flight, skippered by Flt.Lt. R.S. Le Masurier (HX376/Z), Plt.Off. V.W. Hodnett (HX509/Y) and Flt.Sgt. Lister (aircraft 'O'), had continued to shadow the Italian cruiser division, 'O' dropping flares to illuminate the cruisers whilst 'Y' carried out a bombing attack; these aircraft also sent out spurious radio calls for Liberators to be sent to attack, hoping to bluff listening Italian controllers into believing such bombers were out searching for their ships. But there were no Liberators, despite Malta having been promised the use of such aircraft from the Middle East. However, this ruse may have had some success, for at 0230 the cruisers of 3ª and 7ª Divisione Incrociatori altered course towards the north-east, Admirals Perona and Da Zara totally unhappy with the levels of fighter protection offered to their ships. Almost within striking distance of the convoy, they had turned back.

As the warships started to return to their home bases the Royal Navy submarine *Unbroken* (Lt. Alastair Mars) attacked the 3ª Divisione vessels as they approached Messina, her torpedoes hitting and severely damaging the cruisers *Bolzano* and *Muzio Attendolo*. Although both regained their port, the latter with her bows blown off, neither saw further action.

From early in the day three Beaufighters of 248 Squadron were again out attempting to provide escort, but one failed to find the convoy due to lack of fighter control following the departure or sinking of the cruisers fitted for such duties. The other two patrolled as ordered but were then engaged by a pair of Bf109s; Wg.Cdr. Pike's aircraft was attacked determinedly, the German pilot making five passes but he only succeeded in gaining one strike on the Beaufighter's tail. Not so fortunate were Plt.Off. Jay and Flt.Sgt. McFarlane in T5101/W; a call was heard over the radio to the effect that their port engine had been set on fire and that they were baling out. At 0730 a further flight of five Beaufighters departed to continue the patrols. All were, at one time or another, pursued by Messerschmitts but none were hit. Their attackers may have been aircraft of 2/JG 77 operating from Pantelleria; during the day Fw. Hugo Langer of this unit crashed when taking off from the island's airfield, and was killed.

Amongst the first Axis bombers in the air to resume the attack were eight Ju88s of II/LG 1 led by Maj. Gerhard Kollewe, which lifted off from Gerbini at 0435. These encountered and attacked a number of warships, Uffz. Herold and his crew reporting a direct hit on the stern of a cruiser. At 0810, 12 Ju88s of 9/KG 54 from Catania, led by Oblt. Wolfgang Schultz, found the convoy some 30 miles south-south east of Pantelleria and three of these attacked *Waimarama*. The first missed due to heavy AA fire, but the second gained four hits — three or four bombs falling near the bridge and killing everyone on duty there. The explosion set fire to part of the cargo of petrol — following which the Shaw Savill vessel blew up in a ball of flame, her cargo literally adding fuel to the fire; she sank in seconds. Debris and flames from the explosion engulfed the closely-following *Melbourne Star*, scorching her paintwork and setting fire to her lifeboats. Thus believing their own vessel was on fire, a number of her crew abandoned ship.

Despite the fury of the blast, 33 members of *Waimarama*'s crew were saved — although 87 perished, including Captain R.S. Pearce — many owing their lives to the bravery and persistence of *Ledbury*'s captain, Lt.Cdr. Roger Hill, who ordered his destroyer into the heart of the fire to pick up survivors. He reported:

> '*Ashanti* signalled me to pick up survivors. I went to the scene but did not think it possible that anyone could survive such a terrific explosion and mass of flames, but on approaching, men were seen in the water. Forty-five survivors were picked up, one of whom was dead, including some from *Melbourne Star* who'd jumped over the side.'

Ledbury's whaler was launched, with Commissioned Gunner Charlie Musham in charge, and 22 men were plucked out of the oil and flames. From the destroyer itself, Pty.Off. Charlie Cook dived over the side to rescue a man who was on the edge of the burning mass of oil, while Batman Reg Sida volunteered to go to the aid of another survivor seen on a raft in the middle of the inferno. With a line tied round his middle, Sida reached the stranded seaman and both were hauled to safety.

Watchers on the nearby *Charybdis* reported that a following Ju88 was caught by the blast from the *Waimarama* and disintegrated. A number of the Junkers were hit and damaged, including that flown by Oblt. Schultz, but none appear to

Heinkel He111 torpedo aircraft of II/KG 26 operated from Western Italy against the 'Pedestal' convoy. The fuse has not yet been fitted to the warhead of the torpedo carried by the Loewen Geschwader aircraft. *(E.C. des Armees)*

have been lost.

Next on the scene were eight Ju87s of 102° Gruppo Tuff; five from 209ª Squadriglia and four from 239ª Squadriglia had left Castelvetrano at 0750, again led by Cap. Cumbat, but one had landed on Pantelleria with engine trouble. The others flew on, three B-2s with 1000kg bombs and five type Rs with 500kg missiles, escorted by ten MC202s of 51° Stormo CT. At 0920 they attacked *Ohio* which was near-missed by one bomb, although the Stuka pilots claimed to have sunk her, also claiming damage to a destroyer. Gunners on *Ohio* and the escorting *Ashanti* were constantly in action and claimed two of the attackers shot down. One of them — that flown by Serg.Magg. Oscar Raimondo of 239ª Squadriglia — hit the water obliquely less than 50 feet from *Ohio*, bounced off the crest of a swell and landed flush on the tanker's foredeck; a wing hit the after part of the bridge, and other large pieces were flung all over the ship. The crew perished. *Ohio*'s Gunner Billings was given credit for shooting down the Stuka; an eyewitness reported:

> 'Another destroyer — lying ahead on the port side of the screen — threw all its armaments into liquidating the next Stuka; as did the *Ohio*. Stubbornly the plane flew on, laced and interlaced by crossing threads of tracer; a few hundred feet above the *Ohio*, a sudden burst of flame trailed into a streamer of smoke. Would he be able to pull out? Or would he spiral into the sea? Strangely enough, the pilot did neither. He did not deviate at all from his target. A few seconds more and the plane had crashed into the lower part of the tanker's bridge, on the port side. The streamer of smoke and flames grew into a sheet of fire, into which that end of the bridge temporarily

disappeared. As if that were not enough, another near miss scraped the port side aft, causing a temporary list.'

A further Ju87 of 209[a] Squadriglia, flown by Serg.Magg. Guido Savini, was shot down by Sqn.Ldr. Tony Lovell of 1435 Squadron, the dive-bomber force-landing in the sea with some difficulty. Savini and his gunner, 1° Av. Arm. Nicola Patella, were both thrown out. Claims were also made for Ju87s damaged by Plt.Off. Mejor and Flt.Sgt. Pinney (two), but Flt.Sgt. Bob Buntine (EP197) failed to return. It was later admitted that gunners on *Dorset* had shot down the Australian's Spitfire in flames by mistake, the pilot being lost. Ten minutes later an unidentified trimotor — believed to have been an S.84 — was encountered with an escort of six fighters, the bomber being claimed shot down by Pinney.

There were several other actions reported at this time by the pilots of the Spitfires, which were now out in strength. At 0930 Wg.Cdr. Hanks led off Plt.Off. Thomas and Sgt. J.H. Tanner of 126 Squadron on an escort, but Hanks had to return almost immediately with engine trouble; the remaining two carried on and near the convoy Thomas (AB465) claimed a Ju88 damaged, but John Tanner (EP472) was reported shot down by a Bf109; the New Zealander did not survive. It would seem probable however, that he actually fell victim to an Italian pilot — Magg. Fanali of 51° Stormo claimed a Spitfire during this action; while during a reconnaissance over the Sicilian Channel, Ten. Adriano Visconti of 76[a] Squadriglia claimed two Spitfires shot down over the convoy.

Four 229 Squadron aircraft went out at 1020, Flt.Sgt. Colin Parkinson recording:

'Counted about nine (*sic*) merchant ships, one of which (*Ohio*) was leaking oil very badly and evidently in tow. One of the Beaus went in (*Plt.Off. Jay's aircraft*), the crew baled out but haven't been picked up yet.'

The section leader, Flt.Lt. Northcott, saw two Ju88s, he and Flt.Lt. Magruder giving chase. Northcott closed to point blank range and reported 'masses of strikes', as did Magruder; black smoke was seen pouring from both engines and it was last seen rapidly losing height. They were jointly credited with the bomber's probable destruction. It seems likely that this was an aircraft from 8/KG 77 which returned to Comiso in a damaged condition.

Close behind the 229 Squadron quartet came another four from 126 Squadron, Wg.Cdr. Hanks flying his second complete sortie of the morning as was Sqn.Ldr. Wicks; Plt.Off. Rod Smith and Flt.Sgt. Varey made up the

A Savoia S. 79sil passes over a sinking transport. *(Stato Maggiore via N. Malizia)*

section. They arrived just as a new attack commenced against the surviving ships of the convoy at 1125, carried out by five S.79sil of 132° Gruppo Aut. AS, led by Cap. Ugo Rivoli, and escorted by 14 more 51° Stormo MC202s, again led by Magg. Fanali.

Those aboard the ships reported that the Spitfires became involved with the Macchis while the torpedo-bombers — estimated by them to be at least a dozen strong — swept in to attack, most releasing their missiles from long range due to the heavy AA. One was seen to be hit — possibly by the destroyer *Pathfinder*'s gunners — and crashed into the sea on fire; another was claimed by *Tartar*, while others were believed to have been damaged. Again it would seem that the gunners were firing at aircraft under attack by fighters, for Plt.Off. Rod Smith (in AB465) recorded:

> 'S.79 destroyed. Gave four-second burst. Starboard engine caught fire. Crashed in sea. It was over convoy at 800 feet. Mass of flames.'

Ten. Guido Barani and his crew were lost in the missing bomber. Wg.Cdr. Hanks (EP290) had initially fired at this aircraft, and had observed strikes before Smith had applied the 'coup de grace'. Little had been achieved by the raiders this time, for while one torpedo passed close by *Port Chalmers*, the only one to make contact caught in that vessel's paravane, from where it was subsequently freed and sunk — not without some difficulty.

During the morning attacks, *Rochester Castle* had been severely shaken by three near-misses and had caught fire. Her steering mechanism was damaged, but she managed to continue on her way and the fires were brought under control. Early in the afternoon nine Ju87s of 102° Gruppo went out again, but were not able to locate any of the ships. Fourteen more Stukas from I/StG 3 did, however, find and attack *Dorset* which was hit by one bomb; Captain J.C. Tucket ordered the blazing ship to be abandoned, the crew being picked up by *Bramham* without loss of life.

At about 1445 three flights of I and II/LG 1 Ju88s departed Gerbini to renew their attacks on the convoy, following a brief visit to their temporary base by General Loerzer, when he had decorated a number of LG 1 crews. One flight of bombers roamed to the west of Bizerte, where crews spotted a surfaced submarine and carried out a dive bombing attack. Fortunately their aim was below par for their target was the Italian *Alagi*, whose captain (Ten. di Vasc. Sergio Puccini) successfully manoeuvred to avoid the bombs. Not so lucky was her sister craft *Dessie*, which was similarly attacked by another Staffel of LG 1; the submarine was damaged and eight of her crew wounded, including the captain, Ten. di Vasc. Renato Scandola.

Spitfire pilots continued to report engagements. During a patrol begun at 1350, Flt.Lt. Watts (EP448/F) of 249 Squadron claimed damage to an aircraft identified as a BR20 — probably another Savoia; the crews of two S.79s of 30° Gruppo reported that their aircraft were attacked by fighters, one of 55ª Squadriglia being slightly damaged while the second, from 56ª Squadriglia, escaped when attacked south of Pantelleria by an estimated five fighters. Another 56ª Squadriglia machine was damaged by AA fire from a destroyer at 1250, the bomber landing on Pantelleria where it burst into flames and was destroyed.

A further four of 249 Squadron's Spitfires had followed at 1400 to patrol over the convoy, but from this section Flt.Sgt. Tommy Parks was obliged to bale out of BR246/J when hit by AA fire from the convoy's escorts; he came down in the sea, slightly wounded, and was picked up by a destroyer from which he eventually disembarked in Gibraltar! His unit was not immediately notified of his rescue and Parks had been posted missing for some time before details of his whereabouts were received at Malta. Thurne 'Tommy' Parks was a tough character from Oshawa, Ontario, who had had a number of scrapes with authority, dating back to his departure from Canada, as recalled by his close friend, John Sherlock:

> 'Tommy was a tough hard-nosed kid who didn't know how to step backwards. Tommy took exception at the food served to the Sergeant pilots on board the ship taking him and others to the UK from Canada, and he led a rebellion against the ship's company whom, I believe, were Polish. As a result, this was classed as mutiny and Tommy spent the rest of the trip in the brig, and he ended up at the OTU as a Corporal pilot! He actually joined an RAF squadron as a Corporal but the RAF CO had this rectified in short order.'

Towards the end of the afternoon there were several more engagements. At 1705 Sqn.Ldr. Lovell of 1435 Squadron claimmed an S.84 shot down, while an hour later Flt.Sgt. MacNamara and Sgt. Hawkins of the same unit claimed another S.84, and Flt.Sgt. Scott an S.79. The Italians reported the loss of two of their reconnaissance aircraft during the afternoon, a Z1007bis of 59ª Squadriglia (flown by Ten. Italo Masini) which had departed Chinisia at 1355, and an S.79 (MM21544) of 58ª Squadriglia, in the hands of Ten. Bartolomeo Ferrante, which had lifted off from Castelvetrano at 1632; these undoubtedly fell to 1435 Squadron. Flt.Lt. Wally McLeod claimed damage to a Bf109 which he encountered, while he also shared in probably destroying a Ju88 and damaging a second with Plt.Off. Mejor, Sgt. J.M. Harrison and Sgt. W.R. Whitmore.

A little later (at 1740) three 249 Squadron aircraft encountered a lone reconnaissance Ju88 of 2(F)/122 at about 14,000 feet, some 15 miles east of Linosa, which Flt.Lt. Frank Jones (EP448/F) attacked at once; his head-on pass peppered the nose and wings, while Sgt. Wynn, followingg in BR565/T, gained strikes on the fuselage; Plt.Off. Beurling (EP135/Z) then waded in and shot out the starboard engine; the Junkers (F6+KK) went down in flames 15 miles south of Linosa. Uffz. Hans-Joachim Schmiedgen and the observer were lost, while two others baled out; both were rescued from the sea. Fw. Johann Brenner, who was wounded, was picked up by a Fiat RS14 floatplane.

At 1800 four Spitfires of 126 Squadron patrolled over the convoy at 9000 feet, when three Ju88s of LG 1 were seen about three miles away, commencing their dives from out of the sun. Sqn.Ldr. Wicks (AB465) immediately endeavoured to intercept but by the time he arrived the first had released its bombs and disappeared. The second failed to drop any bombs and climbed away but Wicks engaged the third — L1+BL flown by Uffz. Gerhard Böhr — as it dived on *Ohio*:

> 'I closed with it expending all my ammunition, opening fire at 200 yards, closing to 100 yards. I saw strikes on the starboard mainplane, and a piece dropped off. I then broke away. Red 3, who then attacked the Ju88 states that as I broke away, the starboard engine of the Ju88 started to smoke.'

Red 3 was Plt.Off. Bill Rolls (BP870), newly posted to the squadron, who recalled:

> 'The CO dived down and fired at one of them. I saw smoke coming from it and went in and fired a two-second burst. I saw another Spit dive in front of me so I broke away and dived on a Ju88 from above, firing about three or four seconds of cannon and machine gun. I saw strikes on the port engine and a cloud of black smoke came from it. The aircraft went in a gentle dive as I broke away. I made another attack from about 15° to line astern, and saw a pattern of strikes zig-zag along the fuselage. I ran out of ammo. By this time the 88 was pouring black smoke from both engines, and it dived vertically into the sea.'

Sgt. Tiddy (AB531), who was Red 2, also claimed one of the bombers destroyed. His report reveals:

> 'Red 1 attacked one and I turned to port and attacked another, which was turning to port... I rapidly overhauled and commenced firing at 200 yards. The Ju88 was weaving violently. I observed strikes on the tail and a large piece fell off. I fired another burst and saw strikes on port engine which instantly emitted dense white smoke. I pulled up and attacked again from starboard quarter and saw strikes along the fuselage. I turned for final attack. The Ju88 had stopped weaving, the return fire had ceased and the port engine had failed. It was losing height, gradually turning to port, white smoke still issuing from the engine, at about 1500 feet... In view of the fact that it was losing height in the general direction of Linosa, and a large column of smoke arose from Linosa as I rejoined the section, I claim this as destroyed.'

Finally, at 1925, four more 126 Squadron aircraft were over the ships, again led by Wg.Cdr. Hanks, where two Ju88s were reported attacking. Flg.Off. Rip Jones (BP992) engaged one and saw strikes on top of the fuselage near the rear-gunner's position, but then all his guns jammed! He remained in the bomber's slipstream for a minute trying to get them to fire but was finally forced to abandon the attack. Wg.Cdr. Hanks had flown four convoy protection sorties during the day, totalling in excess of seven hours flying over the sea, cooped up in an uncomfortable cockpit and under the threat of action at almost any time.

A fourth Spitfire had been lost when Sgt. F.W. Clewley, a new Australian pilot in 185 Squadron, crashed BR292 on take off from Hal Far; his vision had been impaired by a dustcloud formed as the leading aircraft took-off. Temporarily blinded, he crashed into a stone-built aircraft dispersal pen. Fred Clewley badly lacerated his chin and suffered concussion, while his aircraft was deemed irreparable and was written off.

During the late afternoon Sqn.Ldr. Warburton carried out a search between Sardinia and Cape Bon, his fifth Spitfire PR sortie in the two days he had been back on Malta; his other flights had ranged from Taranto to Messina and Palermo.

The Regia Aeronautica della Sicilia also reported the non-return of two further S.79sil of 105° Gruppo AS, which had taken off from Chinisia at 1430 as part of a force of six torpedo-bombers on armed-reconnaissance. Splitting into pairs, they had begun a search which had resulted in Cap. Guilio Ricciarini and Ten. Silvio Angelucci finding the destroyer *Ledbury*, which was searching for the cruiser *Manchester*, not knowing she had already been sunk. As Ricciarini's aircraft came in range all the close-range weapons opened up; hit numerous times the Savoia crashed into the sea. Meanwhile, Angelucci managed to release his torpedoes, but his aircraft was also hit and went down in flames; the torpedoes missed. Angelucci and his crew were killed, but Ricciarini had managed to force-land his blazing aircraft in the water and his crew survived, being picked up 21 hours later by a Z506B of 612ª Squadriglia, flown by Mar. Dario Tanassi. Main credit for the destruction of these two aircraft went to L/Seaman Douglas Meakin on the pom-poms, and Oerlikon gunner Able Seaman Arthur James.

Meanwhile, another of the pairs — aircraft of III Nucleo AS led by Cap. Dante Magagnoli — had located *Brisbane Star* in the Gulf of Hammamet; two torpedoes were launched without success, but the British crew — although aware of the presence of the Italian aircraft — were oblivious to the failed attack, having assumed that their presence in French territorial waters had protected them. The 'rules of war' were, however, observed by the crew of another Savoia which arrived sometime later. Having circled three times, the bomber then swept over at mast height, neither side opening fire; the pilot made two further dummy attacks without provoking the ship's gunners to open fire, then departed.

Brisbane Star's Master, Captain Frederick Riley, did not expect to escape being challenged indefinitely, but when signalled from the shore by the Vichy authorities, he delayed his reply sufficiently to allow the vessel to reach open sea. The freighter was then 'shadowed' by a submarine which was assumed to be French, and then confronted by a patrol boat, which fired a warning shot across her bows when she failed to stop. Reluctantly Riley brought her to a halt and two Vichy officers came aboard, but after the consumption of much Scotch whisky he was allowed to continue on his way! On their departure the Frenchmen took with them one badly wounded seaman who was in urgent need of expert medical treatment.

At 1430 the leading elements of the convoy had made contact with an escort force sent out from Malta, and by 1600 the Island was in sight. Just over two hours later *Port Chalmers* (Captain Henry Pinkney), *Rochester Castle* (Captain Richard Wren) and *Melbourne Star* (Captain David Macfarlane) had entered Valetta harbour to the cheers of a wildly enthusiastic and emotional crowd.

Three more vessels were still at sea at this time — *Brisbane Star*, as noted, was limping in from further south and *Dorset* was still afloat — just! It had been hoped that *Bramham* could tow her in, but at 1747 a number of Ju88s appeared again, and one gained a hit which started a large fire. Burning fiercely, the vessel eventually went down at 1900. Finally, there was the vital tanker. Although hit many times and draped with the debris of her unwelcomed guest, with damage deemed so serious that it was thought she would sink at any time, Captain Mason continued heading *Ohio* towards Malta.

Attempts to tow the 30,000-ton weight by the destroyer *Penn* achieved little success, and a second tow-ship was deemed necessary. All that appeared initially was the minesweeper *Rye*; the best this little vessel could do was to try to act as a stabilizer via a cable over the stern, in an attempt to keep the huge vessel from yawing too far to port. Gradually the little group crept along at four or five knots, but at 1835 four more Ju88s evaded the patrolling screen of Spitfires and hit her again with one bomb, starting a fire, while near-misses damaged her rudder. *Penn* and *Rye* were also near-missed, but escaped serious damage. The

Oerlikon gunner on *Ohio*'s lower bridge claimed one attacker shot down, while *Bramham*'s Oerlikon Gunner, Able Seaman Eddie Maddocks, claimed another, but no loss was reported on this occasion. Onwards limped the ships, as welcome darkness finally arrived to cloak them for another night.

Earlier in the day however, there had remained considerable activity over and around the many survivors in the sea. Those from *Clan Ferguson* had been spotted on their rafts towards noon by the Italian submarine *Bronzo*, her commander (Ten. di Vasc. Cesare Buldrini) enquiring in Italian if any wounded were present. On receiving no response he radioed ASR headquarters in Sicily of their position and departed. Two hours later a Do24T arrived and alighted, taking aboard 37 men including several who had been badly burned. With a promise from the German pilot to return, the flyingboat took off again. After a further two hours another Dornier (or the same one) appeared and circled overhead, but declined to alight — probably due to the amount of debris floating in the sea and to the fact that the rafts had now drifted into French Tunisian coastal waters.

At 1900 a Z506B in Red Cross markings approached and did touch down, taking on seven more survivors, whilst an Italian MAS boat then arrived and picked up three officers. The rest finally drifted ashore and were interned by the Vichy authorities. Survivors of other ships were also picked up by various vessels, some being taken to Sicily, some to Tunisia, and some being lucky enough to find themselves aboard Royal Navy warships. Another Red Cross-marked Z506B dropped a life-raft near some survivors of *Manchester*, who were without aid.

It will be recalled that the crew of a 248 Squadron Beaufighter (Plt.Off. Jay and Flt.Sgt. McFarlane) had baled out during the morning, while the crew of a 102° Gruppo Ju87 (Serg.Magg. Savini and 1° Av. Arm. Patella) had ended up in the sea after being shot down. From Malta Wg.Cdr. Jack Satchell had volunteered to take out the captured Z506B to search for the Beaufighter crew, but had found no sign of them, whilst crews of a quartet of 248 Squadron Beaufighters who had sighted their compatriot's dingy were unable to contact SSatchell to direct him to the spot.

Meanwhile, the downed Italians had been lucky; Savini was a non-swimmer, but on coming to the surface following the crash found that the aircraft's dinghy had released directly under his backside, and he was able to climb into it at once! Thrown further away from the crashing Stuka, Patella fortunately was a strong swimmer, but as the sea was running a little high, he was not able to see Savini and the dinghy. Overhead, ignoring his own and his gunner's safety, Serg. Giulio Campari circled and dropped his aircraft's dinghy, but this was carried away by the current and was lost.

To help consolidate his precarious position and to conserve energy, Patella slipped off his shoes, undid his flying overalls and floated on his back, but he was tiring and drifted off into semi-consciousness. Suddenly he was aroused by the sound of an engine — it was another Ju87, flown Cap. Stringa (commander of 209ª Squadriglia), who had refuelled his damaged aircraft on return to Sicily and had taken off again to search for the missing men. On sighting the aircraft, Savini fired off a signal rocket which the searching crew failed to see. Patella did see this however, and with the last of his strength succeeded in swimming over to the dinghy and climbed aboard.

Just before sunset they heard the sound of a whistle, and with some difficulty spotted a head of red hair floating in the sea — it was Flt.Sgt. Ron 'Jock' McFarlane, the Beaufighter observer, afloat in his Mae West lifejacket; of Plt.Off. David Jay DFC, his American pilot, there was no sign. The Scot at once climbed into the dinghy, he and the Italians viewing each other with some astonishment and initial suspicion. Unable to understand each others' language, they communicated by gesture and soon settled down to a necessary fraternisation, sharing the available food and water and discussing as best they could, their youth, the war, Churchill and Mussolini, but above all, their hopes for rescue. For 60 hours they drifted at the mercy of the currents and the elements, until sunset on the 15th, when a Do24T appeared and alighted — to the obvious exultation of Savini and Patella, and the considerable dismay of McFarlane. Even after so long adrift, the Scot attempted to dive out and hide below the dinghy, but he was grabbed by the crew of the German flyingboat and hauled bodily aboard, and into captivity.*

While the day's events had been concentrated mainly upon the area to the south and immediate west of Malta, the Italian units in Sardinia had not remained idle. Reconnaissance aircraft were out looking for vessels returning to the west, these reporting British ships at 0915. Two hours later eight CR42 fighter-bombers and six more of these aircraft which were to act as escort and to strafe, were despatched by 24° Gruppo, guided by a Z506B; they failed to find anything. Six S.79sil followed at 1520, drawn from 280ª and 283ª Squadriglia, led by Ten. Col. Vittorio Cannaviello. The crews reported attacking four destroyers and four unidentified warships, which were actually the damaged cruiser *Nigeria* and her four escorting destroyers. The Italian crews claimed a hit on a cruiser, but none was actually achieved. Finally, between 1715 and 1745, three more S.79sil, ten S.84 bombers, three CR42s and two Re2001GVs (the latter the fighter-bombers of the Sezione Speciale) were despatched, but failed to gain any successes.

Even further west, as Force 'F' approached Gibraltar, the treacherous LeO H-246 flyingboat F-AREJ was spotted making another flight to Algiers. Well aware that it had been this aircraft which had issued the first sighting report of the convoy, the Navy was taking no chances on this occasion. Black Section Sea Hurricanes were vectored onto the flyingboat as it came within range, and Sub Lt. Peter Hutton (V7077) claimed to have shot it down; he identified it incorrectly as a 'Loire 70'. In fact F-AREJ survived his attack, although substantially damaged, as Commandant Meresse recalled:

> 'Dupoy (the co-pilot) came behind my seat, tapped me on the shoulder, and showed me something he had spotted through the side window. Very distinctly, coming right at us to our left side, was a group of four fighters. There was nothing to do but wait so I continued my descent (*to Algiers*) tranquilly. The fighters stayed a short distance behind us, matching their speed with ours.
>
> 'But what had we to fear? For several days they had not shown any hostility to our seaplane and our very conspicuous neutral tricolore. It goes without saying that from the moment we saw those planes our radio stayed completely silent. The planes followed us for some minutes when suddenly they approached square on to our right side, from which I could see the

*In 1987 Nicola Patella visited the United Kingdom where he enjoyed a reunion with Jock McFarlane 45 years on.

leader and one of his wing. As was traditional in our service, I waggled my wings in greeting. At this precise moment I noticed the leader's plane go vertical and begin a turn towards us. Premonition? I don't know, but I pulled back on the four throttles, reducing the motors to a minimum and accentuating my descent and turned to the left. At almost the same instant I heard clearly the dry clack of the bullets hitting our plane from the machine gun burst from the fighters and, curiously, I also smelled the odour of gunpowder.

'Undoubtedly our machine was seriously hurt (later 200 bullet strikes were counted). A quick glance around at my companions told me that not one of us had been touched... yet. At the same time I anxiously looked from one wing to the other, and above all on what could be seen of the engines, astonished at not already seeing the slightest smoke or flames, despite the liquid escaping from numerous places: water from the radiators, and petrol, which must leave behind us a clear vapour trail.

'Dupoy rushed into the cabin and returned a short time later and drew us a picture of the sombre tableau that he had seen: one killed in the attack, the majority of the passengers more or less seriously wounded, including the steward and radio operator.

'My head instinctively shrunk into my shoulders awaiting the 'coup de grace' from our attackers, or to see looming the terrifying conflagration that would engulf us in a few seconds. I increased our nose dive, seeing only our salvation in a crash landing before the irremediable occurred. Immediately after the machine gunning, the radio operator, his main radio being rendered useless, had transmitted the distress signal to Algiers on the standby transmitter... we approached the surface of the sea, heading for the crash-landing; all dumbfounded from having been spared from worse, and from a new intervention from the fighters, which did not return, believing probably they had ruled us out of the count for good.'

The big flyingboat eventually carried out a creditable landing in the sea off Algiers, thus ensuring a proper and decent burial for the four passengers who died of wounds inflicted during the attack, which the Vichy French had considered to be so unjust. On the other hand, the Royal Navy were under no illusion that justice had been done.

For the Fleet Air Arm aircrews there would also be some just rewards. Lt. Dickie Cork was given a DSO for his outstanding performance, having taken the major part in the claimed destruction of six Axis aircraft. Sub Lt. Andy Thomson of 800 Squadron and Lt. Frank Pennington of 884 Squadron each received DSCs, while two TAGs were also decorated — L/Airman C.F. Dawson of 809 Squadron with the DSM, and Pty.Off.(A) Len Barrick of 884 Squadron with the CGM. Eight other pilots and one observer were to be Mentioned in Despatches. Those aboard the carriers who directed, operated and maintained the fighters would not be overlooked; DSCs were awarded to three officers, and DSMs to six NCOs and ratings.

Friday, 14 August

Daybreak on Friday thus found Force 'X' well on its way back towards Gibraltar, while the crippled *Ohio*, surounded by a bevy of destroyers and minesweepers, crawled slowly on round the south to Malta. The gallant *Brisbane*

The Vichy airliner which radioed the presence of the convoy on 10 August 1942, paid the penalty for this transgression on the 13th. The Le0 H-246, F-AREJ, is seen after it had been forced down on the sea in a damaged condition by Sea Hurricanes of 801 Squadron. *(C-J. Ehrengardt)*

Star also limped towards the Island from the south.

The Germans believed that the survivors of the convoy had now reached Valetta and their concern was to inflict the maximum damage on Force 'X', as the two cruisers and five destroyers headed westwards. Throughout the night the retreating warships had been kept under surveillance from radar-equipped Heinkels, and at 0542 three reconnaissance Ju88s of 2(F)/122, 16 bomber Ju88s and a Do24T transferred to Elmas (Sardinia) from Sicily, to resume the assault from there. Meanwhile, 35 more Ju88s began taking off from Sicily between 0433 and 0757 (six of which were obliged to return early with various technical problems), followed by a pair of Bf110s, and then at 0900 by 13 Ju87s, led by a single Ju88 of Stab(F)/122, and finally by two further Ju88 bombers.

Five S.79s from 10° Stormo BT were also sent out at dawn on reconnaissance, the British vessels being spotted 20 miles east of Linosa Island by one of these. However, four Beaufighters of 235 Squadron had gone out individually at 0515 to protect *Brisbane Star*. Flg.Off. Wood (in 'H') found the vessel but then saw a Ju88 which he attacked twice, observing strikes both times. As he was being drawn away from his charge he was obliged to let his quarrie escape; his victim would seem to have been a reconnaissance machine of 1(F)/122, which returned to its base in a damaged condition. Forty-five minutes later Wood spotted an S.79 which appeared about to launch a torpedo from a height of about 220 feet. He did a steep turn to starboard and succeeded in approaching the Savoia from astern. Following a two-second burst, pieces fell off and the fuselage erupted into flames, whereupon it dived into the sea and continued to burn. This was undoubtedly one of the 10° Stormo's reconnaissance bombers flown by Ten. Alfonso Battistini, whose 56ª Squadriglia machine (MM22184) was reported shot down by a Beaufighter. A second of this unit's Savoias crashed on landing at Pantelleria and was burnt out.

Force 'X' first came under attack at 0730, 17 Ju88s seeking to concentrate on the cruiser *Kenya*, which managed to avoid three attacks. AA fire struck 3Z+FM of 4/KG 77, flown by Ofw. Heinz Limmertz, and it crashed into the sea.

The warships were also spotted by a Z1007bis of 51° Gruppo RS from Sardinia at 0910, and at 1115 a force of 15 S.84s from 32° Stormo and eight S.79sil drawn from 109° and 130° Gruppo departed Elmas, while eight more of 132° Gruppo and four of 105° Gruppo took-off from Pantelleria and Castelvetrano to join them in their attacks.

Fifteen Ju88s and 13 Ju87s attacked at 1030, one hit being gained on *Kenya* by one of the latter, but only minor damage resulted; the German crews believed that they had gained hits on both cruisers. One of the Stukas, S7+BL of 3/StG 3 (a Ju87D-3) flown by Uffz. Oskar Bennebach, was shot down by the cruiser's AA, going down north-north west of Philippeville. Two others were hit, one force-landing at Philippeville, the other at Elmas.

From midday onwards the Italian torpedo-bombers swept in, but each formation was broken up by the concentrated AA and while the crews claimed hits on two cruisers, they actually achieved none. At least seven S.79sil were hit and damaged by defensive fire. During the morning's attacks the ships' gunners believed that they had shot down four of the attackers; the two already recorded (3Z+FM of 4/KG 77 and S7+BL of 3/StG 3) were the actual casualties, plus the considerable number that suffered damage.

Further south and east, Italian aircraft from Sicily continued to hunt the remaining convoy survivors, three Z1007bis of 63ª Squadriglia, 29° Gruppo led by Ten. Col. Cesare De Porto bombing *Brisbane Star*. Again the vessel survived and later safely reached Valetta beneath an umbrella of Spitfires. At 0950 however, five Ju87s from 102° Gruppo Tuff (led by Cap. Cumbat) took off from their normal base at Gela, to which the unit had now returned, escorted by 23 MC202s of 51° Stormo, led by Ten. Col. Remondino. They approached *Ohio* at 1050 to find the tanker protected by Spitfires from 229 and 1435 Squadrons.

Sqn.Ldr. Tony Lovell and his No 2, Sgt. G. Philp jointly attacked and shot down one Stuka; Lovell recorded:

> 'As we arrived I saw one Ju87 diving and went for it, overtook it rapidly, opened fire at 300 yards and broke away at 30 yards. I saw strikes all over the engine and fuselage. White smoke poured from both sides. He lost height, smoke stopped and he did a steep turn to port and flew west losing height. I turned back towards the convoy and saw the Ju87 crash into the sea. I claim half share with Sgt. Philp.

Philp, a New Zealander from Wellington, added:

> 'Blue 1 fired and smoke poured from the engine, and as I went in to fire enemy aircraft began to weave. I fired a four-second burst then broke. Looking back I saw the enemy aircraft turn sharply left, losing height, then crash into the sea. Turned and attacked another Ju87 flying north, and fired from about 250 yards range. Fired about two-second burst then had to break off engagement as I was being attacked from the rear by enemy fighter. Saw a few strikes on the Ju87 fuselage but no smoke or flames.'

Flt.Lt. G.W. Swannick (229 Squadron) claimed damage to a third. One Ju87 pilot managed to break through the fighter screen and placed a 500kg bomb alongside the tanker (which the Italians incorrectly identified as a small aircraft carrier); *Ohio*'s great bulk was flung forward, her screws twisted and her rudder smashed. Water gushed in through a great hole in her stern, and her plates began to buckle; the end seemed nigh. But still she hit back — Commissioned

Gunner Charlie Musham, one of *Ledbury*'s heroes during the *Waimarama* rescue operation and who was now in charge of the towing party aboard *Ohio*, manned the Oerlikon and claimed the attacker shot down.

The escorting Macchis came to the aid of their charges, Ten. Caracciolo, Ten. Bonfiglio and Serg.Magg. Giuseppe Mirrione each claiming one Spitfire shot down, while Ten. Italo D'Amico claimed one damaged. No Spitfires were actually lost, and Flt.Sgt. MacLennan was able to shoot down Cap. Egeo Pittoni's 20° Gruppo Macchi, which he incorrectly identified as an Re2001:

> 'Started firing from 150 yards to 25 yards. Saw many strikes all along top of the aircraft. White smoke started pouring out; he turned very slowly to the left, nose slightly up. I closed in to 15 feet or less, firing all over the cockpit and pieces flew off again. His nose dropped and he kept turning slowly to the left, going down, trailing thick white smoke... I claim this aircraft as destroyed as I think the pilot was dead.'

In fact Pittoni was later rescued from the sea by a Do24T of Seenotst 6. Only one Ju87 had actually gone down (probably that claimed jointly by Sqn.Ldr. Lovell and Sgt. Philp), but this was flown by the 239ª Squadriglia's commander, Cap. Antonio Cumbat. He and his gunner, 1° Av. Arm. Michele Cavallo, survived however, and were able to get into their dinghy. Some distance away the downed Macchi pilot, Cap. Pittoni, having successfully baled out, also floated in his dinghy. All three were subsequently rescued, but Cumbat and Cavallo would have a tale to tell as bizarre as that of Savini and Patella on the previous day.

As Cavallo had been wounded in the right arm and chest, Cumbat had decided to force-land his burning Ju87R-5 in the sea rather than bale out. Heading towards Pantelleria, he made a successful ditching, the undercarriage being torn-off and the aircraft settling on its belly. Helping his wounded gunner into the dinghy, Cumbat examined the wound which had been caused by a 20mm shell. Whilst obviously painful, it was not bleeding profusely; Cavallo's chest was torn and his right arm broken but he was initially lucid, though he soon lapsed into a semi-coma, causing Cumbat to fear that the wound might be fatal.

Nothing was to be seen until about 1430 when Cumbat heard the sound of approaching aircraft engines, following which four Beaufighters of 248 Squadron appeared overhead. These spotted the dinghy and circled low, the pilots waving with Cumbat and Cavallo responding. Clearly the RAF crews thought they had found their missing compatriots, Jay and McFarlane!

While three Beaufighters departed, that flown by Sgt. J. Duncan remained overhead for an hour until suddenly attacked and shot-up — by Spitfires! On learning this, 248 Squadron despatched a further Beaufighter, flown by Sub Lt. L. Maurice — a Fleet Air Arm pilot — to continue orbiting the dinghy, together with an escort of three Spitfires. By now the sun was setting and the survivors' hopes of rescue began to recede when over the horizon appeared a Do24T flyingboat, which was being escorted by six 51° Stormo Macchis, led by Ten. Giovanni Franchini. However, the fighters had just reached the limit of their range and turned back before they had sighted the Beaufighter. The crew of the Dornier had, however, seen this aircraft and realizing that they were too late to escape, manoeuvred so as to make clear their intention to alight and execute a rescue. To the amazement of the watching Italians, the Beaufighter actually turned alongside the flyingboat and escorted it to their aid, Maurice having received instructions over the R/T not to attack.

Cumbat and Cavallo could not believe their luck, but in fact the whole flight had been tracked by the Operations Room on Malta on the radar screens. With the departure of the Macchis, 'Ops' had sanctioned the safe conduct of the Dornier in the belief that Jay and McFarlane were about to be rescued, deciding that captivity was better than a possible lingering death at the mercy of the elements. The big flyingboat made a graceful touch-down under the eyes of the Beaufighter crew, took aboard the two delighted Italians (Cavallo would survive his wounds) — and with a gesture of acknowledgement from the German pilot, departed for Sicily! Incidentally, during this operation the ASR Centre at Syracuse (Seenotzentrale Syrakus) performed, and duly celebrated, its 1000th rescue.

Early in the afternoon meanwhile, the last sorties had been launched from Sicily against Force 'X', 30 Ju88s and three He111s going out, followed by three more Ju88s and 14 Ju87s. By now, however, heavy cloud had spread over the area and generally poor visibility protected the ships from further attack, although their pursuers could be seen on the radar screens. Aeronautica della Sicilia had despatched 19 Re2001s (from 2° Gruppo Aut. CT, plus 362ª Squadriglia of 22° Gruppo Aut. CT). These had returned to Sicily from Sardinia that morning to escort the Heinkels, together with four Bf109s, but early in the flight the German fighters turned back. As the weather deteriorated, the Reggianes too began turning back until just three remained with the bombers, flown by Magg. Scarpetta, the commanding officer, Ten. Giorgio Pocek and Sottoten. Isidoro Disint.

Suddenly, at 1515, on the scene came four Spitfires of 126 Squadron which were escorting the captured Cant floatplane, flown by Wg.Cdr. Satchell, still searching for the missing Beaufighter crew, Jay and McFarlane. Spotting the unsuspecting Italian fighters beneath them — and taking them to be Macchis — Flt.Lt. Bill Johnson (BR311) and Sgt. Bill Marshall (BP860) undertook a perfect bounce, shooting all three down into the sea; two fell to Johnson's fire — his 4th and 5th victories — the other to his Canadian No 2; Pocek would later be rescued by a Do24T of Seenotst 6, while Scarpetta — the second commanding officer to be lost by the unit in little more than a month, was subsequently posthumously awarded a Medaglia d'Oro. Johnson recorded:

> 'I was leading Dumbell Yellow Section escorting the Cant out towards Linosa. Just north of Linosa I saw the enemy approaching. They immediately turned round and made off towards Pantelleria. I gave chase with my No 2 after telling Yellow 3 and 4 to stay with the Cant. The enemy made no evasive action until we were almost on top of them, and then the Macchis turned left. I attacked the centre one. They were in line astern. Attacked from port quarter and gave it a burst. I saw the hood come off and the pilot bale out (*almost certainly Ten. Pocek*). I saw my No 2 firing at the first Macchi (*probably Magg. Scarpetta*), which went straight into the sea. I turned round into the third Macchi and gave it a burst, and saw strikes on the wings and fuselage. It turned away streaming oil and climbing, so I climbed right up underneath him and gave him a burst, and he immediately rolled over and went into the sea. The pilot did not bale out.

Sgt. Bill Marshall added:

> 'My leader attacked the centre Macchi. I shot at the last one and saw hits on

the port side of the fuselage. The first Macchi got on my tail and after much manoeuvring, I got in a long burst from astern to port quarter. He rolled over and went in. I saw the middle one's pilot bale out, the aircraft go in, and saw the last aircraft go in as well.'

Meanwhile, of the other two Spitfires escorting Wg.Cdr. Satchell and his five-man crew in the Cant, one developed engine trouble and was obliged to return, leaving only an incensed Plt.Off. Rod Smith to provide protection for the vulnerable floatplane. Shortly after 1530 a section of 229 Squadron Spitfires, flying cover for *Ohio*, spotted the floatplane and Flg.Off. Newman led the other three down into a diving attack. Fortunately for Satchell and his crew, the Spitfires suffered iced-up windscreens which prevented an accurate attack being carried out, and the Cant was not hit!

Following the morning attack by the Italian Stukas, the stricken *Ohio* had taken on more water and was lying dangerously low. The destroyer *Bramham* now closed on her port side and was secured, volunteers from her crew and from amongst survivors of other merchant vessels, going aboard to man portable pumps or to take over the tanker's AA guns. *Penn* then closed on the starboard side and was similarly secured, while *Ledbury* remained attached by cable astern to act as her rudder, this composite 'vessel' creeping on towards Malta surrounded by a trio of alert minesweepers.

The crippled tanker *Ohio*, surrounded by tugs, is towed in sinking condition into Grand Harbour on 15 August 1942. *(NWMA)*

Aware that the tanker was still not in harbour, the Regia Supermarine ordered the submarine *Asteria*, which was hunting for stragglers, to find and attack her. But as his craft had itself been attacked and slightly damaged by British aircraft, the commander did not pursue his search. As *Ohio* neared Malta tugs would later go out to give aid, but in the event it was to be the evening of the 15th before the creaking, waterlogged tanker was at last painfully inched — amidst a tumultuous welcome — into harbour, passing alongside the wreck of another tanker, the sunken *Plumleaf*. Here the two supporting destroyers were cut loose, and the precious fuel she carried was pumped off at once. As her supporting bulk cargo was gradually replaced by water, so the gallant ship, her back broken, settled onto the harbour floor. Her Master, Captain Mason, was later honoured by the award of the George Cross in recognition of his and his crew's tremendous achievement. The masters of the other four surviving ships —

Captains Wren, Macfarlane, Pinkney and Riley — were each awarded a DSO.* Already by the time that *Ohio* arrived, *Rochester Castle*, *Melbourne Star* and *Port Chalmers* had been unloaded, while work on *Brisbane Star* was well advanced — and, amazingly, the great efforts expended to get the cargoes ashore remained inexplicably uninterrupted. No air attacks were launched on the harbour throughout these three days — it would appear that for the time being the Axis bolt was shot!

During this traumatic period of time Malta had not remained entirely raid-free. At 1825 on the evening of the 14th Spitfires of 249 Squadron had been scrambled, the pilots seeing a trio of Bf109s over Hal Far, probably on a reconnaissance. Flt.Sgt. Hiskens (EP706/L) claimed damage to one, but another surprised Flt.Sgt. G.A. Hogarth and shot down his aircraft (EP207), from which he baled out safely into the sea, being rescued by HSL 128.

Statistically, Malta's fighter pilots had flown 414 sorties in support of 'Pedestal' — 389 by Spitfires, including 97 long-range sorties, and 25 by Beaufighters. At least 14 aircraft had been claimed shot down, with a further three probables and nine damaged being credited, for the loss of four Spitfires and one Beaufighter.

That night 15 Italian bombers began taking off from 2100 hours onwards and heading for Malta — six Z1007bis of 7° Stormo BT, four S.84s of 9° Stormo BT and five BR20Ms of 88° Gruppo BT. All but two turned back early, either due to technical troubles or warned of night fighters by the 'Servizio Alfa'. The remaining pair were not so fortunate. An hour before midnight Beaufighter V8219 of 89 Squadron departed Luqa, crewed by Plt.Off. Reeves and Sgt. O'Leary, followed half an hour later by Flg.Off. Fumerton and Plt.Off. Bing in V8268. One of the two bombers to approach the Island — a 9ª Squadriglia S.84 (MM24564), piloted by the commander of 7° Gruppo, Ten. Col. Ivo Ravazzoni, a First War fighter pilot — was intercepted and shot down by Plt.Off. Reeves. He reported:

> 'At approx 2200 hours exhausts of enemy aircraft seen going south. It turned north and we closed to 100 yards and fired. The port engine of the enemy aircraft caught fire immediately and numerous pieces fell off. I skidded the aircraft over and shot at the starboard's engine, and the whole aircraft was enveloped in fire and went into the sea, where it burnt for ten minutes.'

Meanwhile, Flg.Off Fumerton was guided onto the other bomber, Sottoten. Renato Tosi's BR20M of 264ª Squadriglia, and despatched this into the sea also for his 12th nocturnal victory; both Beaufighter pilots tentatively identified their victims as Z1007s. Some 18 hours later, a lone figure was seen in the sea off Gozo, and police set out from Dahliet Qorrot to rescue the man, who turned out to be Ten. Col. Ravazzoni; he was the only survivor from the two downed bombers.

With the conclusion of the 'Pedestal' operations, the Axis command — who had greatly overestimated the number of vessels, both naval and merchant marine, which they had sunk — believed they had achieved a great victory —

*The morning following *Ohio*'s arrival in harbour, an emotional main front page story in the *Times of Malta* read:

> 'Malta feels humble in the presence in her harbours of the Mercantile Marine... If the feelings of the people could be expressed in simple action, Malta's George Cross would be nailed to the mast of every ship in harbour.'

Plt.Off. (later Flt.Lt.) Rod Smith of 126 Squadron, who arrived on Malta to find that his brother Jerry was already there. They frequently flew together thereafter, until Jerry Smith's death in action. *(R.I.A. Smith)*

greater than that in June. Tactically they had enjoyed considerable success, inflicting grievous losses (nine merchant ships sunk with over 300 seamen lost) — but strategically they had failed to prevent the re-provisioning of the Island. More than enough had been despatched in order to be relatively sure of getting something through, and the gamble had paid off. The provisions aboard the four transports — some 32,000 tons — proved sufficient to keep the garrison fed and armed into the autumn, while the arrival of the tanker with her precious life blood for the aircraft and submarines was a major Allied victory. Malta now had food, ammunition, fuel and more Spitfires — she could fight on!

Chapter 9

AUTUMNAL OFFENSIVE

A group of pilots of the Takali Wing in August 1942: from left, Sgt. Stan Shewell; Plt.Off. 'Junior' Moody; Plt.Off. George 'Buzz' Beurling; Flt.Lt. George Swannick; Wg.Cdr. Arthur Donaldson; Plt.Off. Frank Johnson; Sqn.Ldr. Bill Douglas. *(NWMA)*

The success of the 'Pedestal' re-provisioning seemed to take the steam out of Axis activities from Sicily. Despite Rommel's desperate preparations to ready his forces for an offensive before so much British strength built up as to make this impossible, efforts to neutralize Malta faded. True, the Italians were having problems with serviceability, particularly of their fighter aircraft. This was due to deteriorating quality control at the factories, whilst it appeared that the Luftwaffe was taking the opportunity to send some of the long-serving aircrew of II/JG 53, KüFlGr 606 and KGr 806 on extended leave. However, the need to get convoys across to Africa was never greater — particularly so in the case of tankers carrying fuel for the Afrika Korps' Panzers. It was to be against these targets that the Island's striking force was particularly active during the weeks which followed. Over the Island itself, small-scale fighter penetrations proved to be the order of the day.

Saturday, 15 August

At 0645 seven pilots of 1435 Squadron went out to search for their missing colleague, Flt.Sgt. Buntine; they reported attacking a Z506B and an S.84, but made no claims. Eight more aircraft of 185 Squadron were scrambled at 0925, meeting four fighters identified as Bf109s, six miles east of Zonqor. Capt. Swales (EP313) and Sgt. Tarbuck (EP410) claimed one shot down between them, but Tarbuck was then hit by another. Amongst those watching the fight from the ground was newcomer Plt.Off. O'Brien, who recalled:

> 'We could hear and see some 109s mixing it up at about 20,000 feet. Suddenly some fire — a long burst and four short ones, and the next thing we saw was a Spit coming down at a hell of a rate, making bags of noise and with glycol pouring from it. It flattened out of its glide over the sea. It half rolled and went straight down into the drink. Poor bugger, or so we thought, but a few seconds later a parachute appeared.'

Tarbuck was picked up three miles south-west of Benghaisa Point by HSL 128. Five Spitfires of 229 Squadron had also been scrambled but had failed to make an interception; on returning from this sortie, Flt.Sgt. Ballantyne (BR169) collided with a stationary Spitfire (EP517) of 249 Squadron and although he was unhurt, both aircraft were damaged beyond repair.

Fliegerkorps II reported the loss of two Ju88s of II/KG 77 during the day, both to human error. The bombers — 3Z+HN flown by Uffz. Gerhard Albert of 5 Staffel, and 3Z+AP captained by Obgfr. Engelhardt Schimrosczyk of 6 Staffel — became lost whilst out on a maritime reconnaissance mission. Mistaking the lights of Augusta seaplane base for Catania airfield, both machines made 'perfect' wheels-down landings straight into the water; only one man survived from each crew.

Although a dozen Axis ships had been sunk since the middle of June, all had been accounted for during the run along the coast between Tobruk and the front. Owing to the shortage of fuel for her aircraft, Malta had been unable to contribute much during the first half of August, but the arrival of *Ohio* and the other survivors of 'Pedestal' had altered the situation. With fuel supplies now replenished and the Luftwaffe assault diminishing, another sustained attack on Axis shipping became possible. Malta also welcomed the return of a submarine flotilla (initially three craft) and one of these, *Porpoise*, promptly sank the 6070-ton Italian merchantman *Lerici*, which was making for Benghazi. A substantial strike force of Beauforts and crews had been built up over the past few weeks, allowing 217 Squadron to be released for departure to the Far East, its original destination. The 12 crews of 86 Squadron now amalgamated with the ten surviving crews of 39 Squadron, the Beaufort Wing remaining under the overall command of Wg.Cdr. Gibbs.

Until now Beaufort crews had always been detailed for anti-shipping torpedo attacks, but Air Vice-Marshal Park decided to change this policy in view of the high risks; in future the crews for these extremely dangerous missions consisted of volunteers only. Such was the current length of a tour of duty, that few Malta strike crews could expect to survive.

Sunday, 16 August

No action was reported over Malta during the day, the only event of note concerning the Beaufighters of 235 Squadron. Four aircraft from this unit carried out a shipping search during the morning in the vicinity of Linosa and Lampedusa, during which Sqn.Ldr. Wigmore sighted an aircraft which he identified as a Caproni 312 floatplane; he fired two short bursts before realising that it was, in fact, a Red Cross aircraft, whereupon it was allowed to proceed without further hindrance.

Amongst the transit aircraft arriving was Liberator AL531, which was due to fly on to Egypt after refuelling. However the pilot, Sqn.Ldr. McKay, was given the opportunity of making the second leg of the journey via Catania, and that night the airfield was duly bombed from 12,000 feet. Whilst the attack was in progress, the crew reported seeing green flares suspended from parachutes at the same height as their aircraft, but it was not clear whether these had been released by night fighters or fired from the ground.

Monday, 17 August

On Monday morning a further batch of reinforcement Spitfires began arriving, having flown from the carrier *Furious*, which was making a second run from Gibraltar (Operation 'Baritone'). To lead the 32 Spitfires (see Table 14 below) on this occasion were Malta veterans, Flt.Lt. Halford, Plt.Off. McElroy and newly-commissioned Plt.Offs. Ken Evans and Colin Parkinson, all of whom had been ferried to Gibraltar three days previously. Parkinson recalled:

> 'Watched the first eight take off without mishap, the second crowd also. The third bunch were unlucky, one kite taking off, swerved, stalled one wing, and crashed over the side after knocking its tail off. Hit the water on its back and sank immediately.'

TABLE 14

Operation 'Baritone'

32 Spitfires from HMS *Furious* (one lost on take-off and two abandoned). Pilots believed to have included those listed below).

Flt.Lt. J.R. Halford	had returned to Gibraltar to lead back flight
Plt.Off. J.F. McElroy, RCAF	had returned to Gibraltar to lead back flight
Plt.Off. K.W.S. Evans	had returned to Gibraltar to lead back flight
Plt.Off. C.H. Parkinson, RAAF	had returned to Gibraltar to lead back flight
Flg.Off. Davidson, RCAF	Sgt. A.B. Stead, RNZAF
Plt.Off. H.T. Nash, RCAF (US)	Sgt. R.B. Hendry, RNZAF
Plt.Off. J.R. Scott, RCAF	Sgt. A.O. MacLeod, RCAF
Plt.Off. H.G. Reynolds	Sgt. G.W. Turner
Plt.Off. J. Farmer	Sgt. J.S. Hamilton
Plt.Off. J.D. Stevenson, RCAF	Sgt. J.F. Jarrett
Plt.Off. I.F. Preston, RCAF (US)	Sgt. T. Wallace
Flt.Sgt. M.H. Frith	Sgt. R. Miller
Sgt. P.A. Dixon EP573	Sgt. J.G. McGill BR482
Sgt. L.J. McDougall	EP606 — abandoned
Sgt. Sullivan	EP152 — abandoned
Sgt. W.J.A. Fleming	EP194 — lost on take off
Sgt. D.D. MacLean, RNZAF	
Sgt. D.W. Spencer	
Sgt. B. Milligan	
Sgt. Griffin, RCAF	
Sgt. Fuller	
Flt.Sgt. D.L. Rawson (Rhod)	injured — unable to depart

Sgt. W.J.A. Fleming's Spitfire (EP194) struck a signal lamp in the port navigation position as it swerved, and this hit one of the watching pilots, Flt.Sgt. D.L. Rawson (a Rhodesian) breaking his arm. Fleming was lost with his aircraft. Continued Parkinson:

> 'Two other kites (*EP152 and EP606, flown by Sgt. Sullivan and Sgt. L.J. McDougall respectively*) could not get their wheels up after taking off, so the pilots had baled out. They were picked up OK. My section got off the deck OK and set course for Malta. The trip was uneventful. Bags of fuel when we arrived. Had to orbit off the Island while a raid was in progress. One of our section (*Sgt. J.G. McGill in BR482*) crashed at Luqa, and was badly burned.'

Included in the party was the New Zealander Sgt. Al Stead, who had landed on the *Indomitable* when he experienced problems during the previous ferry, while of the 28 new arrivals, seven were immediately posted to 185 Squadron. The influx of reinforcement pilots allowed further releases of tour-expired men, and amongst those leaving the Island at this time were Flt.Lt. Watts and Plt.Off. Linton of 249 Squadron, Flt.Lt. Northcott and Flg.Off. Dicks-Sherwood of 229 Squadron, and Plt.Off. Tilley of 126 Squadron. Another new arrival was Sqn.Ldr. P.M.J. Evans, who flew in from Egypt as a passenger aboard a DC-3 of 117 Squadron to take over 89 Squadron's 'C' Flight from Flt.Lt. Edwards, but on arrival he was taken ill and was immediately transferred to hospital. Two additional AI-equipped Beaufighters (V8263 and X7832) also arrived for this unit.

Shortly before midday 15 Bf109s swept over the Island to be met by an almost equal number of Spitfires (eight/126 and six/185); the 126 Squadron flight failed to make contact, while two of the 185 Squadron aircraft patrolled over Grand Harbour and sighted nothing. The other four, led by Plt.Off. Stenborg, engaged six Messerschmitts over Kalafrana. Sgt. Weaver (BR374) immediately dived to attack and claimed two shot down, and Stenborg one more, but the New Zealander's aircraft (EP457) was also hit and he was forced to bale out; he later recalled:

> 'I was with an American sergeant flying at 31,000 feet. He saw Messerschmitts which I could not, so I told him to attack and I would follow, but as he went down for six Huns, three more followed him up.
>
> 'I shot one down from his tail at point-blank range, but the next minute a great chunk flew off my starboard wing. I heard explosions and the plane shook everywhere and black smoke poured into the cockpit. I began diving out of control at 27,000 feet.
>
> 'I tried to get the hood off, but it would not budge. I tried all ways, while the Spitfire fell 14,000 feet at over 400 miles per hour, and the cockpit filled with smoke. I thought I had had it. It was a horrible feeling; I was expecting the plane to blow up at any moment. But fortunately the hood came off, and I suddenly found myself thrown out. I had seen a German pilot open his parachute at that speed and his harness was ripped off by the force of the sheer speed, so I waited for a while before pulling the ripcord in order to slow up, and then I pulled the cord and landed in the sea.
>
> 'I spent five minutes trying to get free from the parachute and get the dinghy working. That trip shook me to the teeth.'

He came down three miles north-east of Delimara Point and was soon picked up by HSL 128. There is no record of any Luftwaffe loss and these claims, although allowed, must be considered rather dubious. A contemporary of Weaver's noted in his diary:

> 'I'm afraid Weaver has rather disappointed me; he is a bit of a line shooter. It is rather to be expected from a Yank.'

At 0630 on this same day a convoy had departed Naples, sailing via Trapani (Sicily), for Tripoli; the 8300-ton *Rosalino Pilo* — carrying 400 tons of petrol, 1200 tons of ammunition and 1900 tons of other cargo — was escorted by the destroyers *Maestrale* and *Gioberti*. The convoy was not discovered by 69 Squadron until it had passed Pantelleria, when a strike was rapidly ordered. Six torpedo-carrying Beauforts were sent out, led by Flt.Lt. Sharman. These were covered by two Beaufighters of 235 Squadron (flown by Flg.Offs. Wood and Eyre) each armed with four 250lb bombs, and three more of 252 Squadron, whilst eight long-range Spitfires of 126 and 185 Squadrons provided high level fighter protection.

The vessels were located 35 miles west of Lampedusa at about 1600. The five Beaufighters went in to strafe and bomb in the Flak suppression role, attempting to distract the ships' gunners, while the Beauforts (all flown by 86 Squadron crews) split into sections of three and attacked from either side of the transport. As Sharman led his section in for the attack, AA fire from the cargo vessel hit the nose of his aircraft, wounding his navigator, Flt.Sgt. R.G. Kitchen, and causing a fire; despite his wounds, Kitchen crawled forward and extinguished the flames. One of the Beaufighter bombers was seen to gain a hit on the stern of this vessel just as the Beauforts swept in to attack; all released their torpedoes and at least two hits were claimed, one on the starboard quarter, the other port amidships. *Rosalino Pilo* was left stationary, down by the stern and pouring white smoke. The Beaufort gunners sprayed the transport and the escort with machine-gun fire, and so effective was the attack that *Gioberti* was obliged to withdraw and return to Sicily.

The convoy had air cover provided by two CR42s, two MC200s and four MC202s from 54° Stormo CT, in addition to at least four Ju88s. Some of these attempted to intercept the Beauforts, one Junkers attacking Flg.Off. P.K. Roper's aircraft but his gunner (Sgt. Checketts) claimed to have damaged it, while Wt.Off. R.W. Macaskill's gunner similarly reported damaging a 'Messerschmitt' — obviously one of the Macchis. In return, Cap. Pietro Calistri claimed one Beaufort probably destroyed and Serg. Romano one damaged. As the action unfolded at low-level, the covering Spitfires were not ordered down into the fray and consequently failed to engage.

That night the crippled *Rosalino Pilo* was again torpedoed, this time by the submarine *United*, and was sunk. The whole crew less one man was rescued by the tug *Montecristo*, which had sailed from Pantelleria, and the destroyers *Maestrale* and *Maloncello*. The loss of this important freighter, following the sinking of *Lerici* two days earlier, posed a serious threat to the Afrika Korps and caused Rommel to signal Rome that he had sufficient supplies for ten days only, and that he intended his offensive to start in under two weeks. Urgent meetings were held in Rome, where it was decided to sail 20 supply ships to North Africa between 25 August and 5 September. The British authorities would soon be aware of this plan, and of Rommel's predicament, via 'Ultra' intercepts and an all-out effort to interrupt his shipping even further was ordered.

Wednesday, 19 August

A torrential rainstorm next day effectively curtailed flying over the Island, Takali in particular being badly flooded. Nonetheless, half a dozen Spitfires from 1435 Squadron undertook a sweep off the south-east coast of Sicily during the morning, and a repeat of this operation was carried out in the afternoon. On this occasion three of the five Spitfires of 126 Squadron were flown by Grp.Capt. Churchill, Wg.Cdr. Hanks and Sqn.Ldr. Wicks; nothing of interest was seen on either sortie, but the pattern had been set for further such operations.

During the night Flt.Lt. Edwards took Air Vice-Marshal Park up in one of 89 Squadron's Beaufighters to observe the accuracy of the Island's searchlights. Around this time, Sqn.Ldr. Evans was released from hospital and took over command of the detachment from Edwards. In the early hours of the morning, Governor Lord Gort, accompanied by his aide-de-camp Major Lord Munster, departed in one of 267 Squadron's DC-3s for Cairo, where they had been summoned to meet the Prime Minister. The latter had flown to Egypt on his way back from a Moscow meeting with the Russian premier; following the meeting, the Governor and his aide returned to the Island within a few days.

Thursday, 20 August

Thursday was to herald a new era for Malta's fighter pilots — the first official offensive fighter sweep (codenamed Rodeo 1) over southern Sicily; the objective — to draw enemy fighters into the air. Grp.Capt. Churchill (BR379/V) led 18 Spitfires, equally drawn from 229 and 249 Squadrons, but the operation was to be something of an anti-climax, as Plt.Off. Beurling recounted:

> 'We formed up south of the Island and whisked across the water in three layers... we swept into Sicily over Cape Scaramia and took a look at each of the main enemy airfields at Comiso, Biscari and Gela. Not a Jerry stirred. Not a drop of Flak was poured up at us. We rolled along, coming out over Cape Scaramia and beetled home. Nothing much to it, bar the pleasure of sticking your nose into the enemy's country for a change.'

Late on the 19th a new Axis convoy comprising the 7800-ton tanker *Pozarica*, the German steamer *Dora*, two escorting destroyers, *Aviere* and *Camicia Nera*, and two torpedo boats (*Climene* and *Ciclone*) had left Messina for Benghazi. The ships were seen off the toe of Italy early on the 20th by a 69 Squadron Spitfire (BR431 flown by Plt.Off. Colquhoun), and a strike was at once despatched. This comprised ten Beauforts, led by Wg.Cdr. Gibbs (AW296/B), and a dozen Beaufighters of 227 Squadron — a unit newly formed from the survivors of the detachments of 235, 248 and 252 Squadrons still on Malta. Six of the Beaufighters were armed with bombs and the force took-off between 0845 and 0900; two of them were forced to return early, one due to the pilot's sickness, the other owing to engine trouble. As the latter, X8034/H flown by Flg.Off. Eyre, approached Malta, the ailing engine burst into flames and the Beaufighter crashed into the sea south of Kalafrana; only the injured pilot survived to be rescued by HSL 128; his observer, Sgt. C.D. Leslie, went down with the aircraft.

Meanwhile, the strike force had located the convoy, but the tanker was not as heavily laden as had been assumed and was sailing higher in the water. Although several torpedoes were accurately launched at her, these were seen by the crew of a 69 Squadron Baltimore — AG734, flown by Plt.Off. Munro, which

249 Squadron at Takali, August 1942. Front row from left: Plt.Off. Yates; Plt.Off. Moody; Plt.Off. Round; Flg.Off. Lodge (Intelligence Officer); Flt.Lt. Hetherington; Wg.Cdr. Thompson; Sqn.Ldr. Mitchell; Wg.Cdr. Le May (Station Commander); Wg.Cdr. Donaldson; Flt.Lt. Watts; Flt.Lt. Jones; Plt.Off. Seldon (Intelligence Officer); Plt.Off. Lowrey; Plt.Off. Linton; Plt.Off. De Nancrede. Back row from left: Flt.Sgt. Sanderson; Sgt. Gass; Flt.Sgt. Park; Sgt. Wynn; Sgt. Shewell; Sgt. Lamont; Wt.Off. Butler; Plt.Off. Williams; Flt.Sgt. De l'Ara; Flt.Sgt. Beurling; Plt.Off. Roscoe; Plt.Off. Farmer; Flt.Sgt. Hiskens; Sgt. Budd; Plt.Off. Seed; Flt.Sgt. Morgan (ground crew NCO). *(NWMA)*

accompanied the strike to assess the result of the action — to pass underneath and *Pozarica* escaped damage. Wg.Cdr. Ross Shore led his Beaufighters in at low-level and they pressed home their attack on a reported 'cruiser' and other escorts. Plt.Off. Cohen (T4982/U) claimed to have destroyed a vessel variously described as a 'submarine-chaser' or small pilot boat, of about 100 tons, but which may well have been a Flak-ship, as it is believed that nine gunners of I/Flakrgt 46 were killed in this action. The strafing Beaufighters had been effective and many were killed or wounded aboard the warships, particularly on *Camicia Nera*, which was so hard hit that she was permitted to turn back and return to base.

Losses were not light, however. Two Beauforts — AW295/T flown by Plt.Off. R.L. Condon, an Australian on his first operational sortie, and AW341/F flown by Flg.Off. Roper, a Canadian — were both lost, while Beaufighter T4934/S, crewed by Wt.Off. Briscoe and Sgt. Patterson, was shot down by Flak; two other Beauforts were damaged and the observer in AW219 was wounded. It was believed that the two downed Beauforts had probably also fallen to AA fire, although the strike crews had reported seeing single-engined fighters over the convoy.

Wg.Cdr. Ross Shore (X8070/D) and Flg.Off. Wood (X8030/C) jointly claimed a Z501 flyingboat damaged, while the gunner in Sgt. Gordon Head's Beaufort reported gaining hits on an attacking Macchi. Of the action, Wood reported:

> 'After dropping my bombs near the tanker, I sighted the Z501 on the port of the convoy. I attacked from dead astern and strikes were seen on the aircraft. I turned overland but was unable to come round again on the Z501. As I passed out to sea the Z501 was seen to make a very heavy landing in the sea but it did not sink. There was some tracer fire from the enemy aircraft.'

The crew of the seaplane — MM35608 flown by Cap. Gianbattista Corrado of 189ª Squadriglia RM — reported being attacked by three 'Blenheims', one of which they claimed to have shot down, the crew becoming prisoners. Both

Beaufort crews were, in fact, safely plucked from the sea by the escorts to become prisoners, as were Briscoe and Patterson, although Roper's crew drifted in their dinghy almost to the Calabrian coast before they were picked up. Plt.Off. Munro's Baltimore also came under attack from a fighter identified as a Bf109, at which his gunner, Sgt. L. Clayton, fired without visible result.

Friday, 21 August

Following this attack the convoy sailed across the Gulf of Taranto during the night in order to take the safer route down the Greek coast, and early next morning the remaining escort was reinforced by the arrival of the destroyer *Geniere* and torpedo-boat *Pegaso*. Spotted again early on the 21st by 69 Squadron's Sqn.Ldr. Warburton (in Spitfire BR662) and again later by Plt.Off. Colquhoun (flying the same aircraft), another strong strike force was despatched from Malta in the afternoon. This comprised nine torpedo-armed Beauforts, again led by Wg.Cdr. Gibbs, and four bomb-carrying Beaufighters, with nine more as escort, the latter flown by 248 Squadron crews. However, early into the flight, Sgt. Sebring had to return when one of the undercarriage legs of his aircraft refused to remain retracted; he made a safe landing at Luqa.

The vessels were located 12 miles off Paxos island under a substantial air umbrella — at least eight aircraft being seen over the convoy — and the Beaufighters swept in first at 1615, the bombers claiming a hit on a destroyer and two near misses on the tanker. Wg.Cdr. Ross Shore's aircraft (X8033/B) was hit by AA fire just after he had released his bombs although he was able to reach Malta safely; two other bombers were also hit and slightly damaged. Meanwhile, the Beauforts split into three flights of three and attacked the tanker. Gibbs (AW296/B) reported a strike amidships on its starboard side, and the third flight, led by Flg.Off. Grant, gained two more. *Pozarica* was left stationary, belching white smoke and steam, with oil gushing from either side. This was confirmed by the crew of the accompanying 69 Squadron Baltimore — AG751 flown by Sgt. C.J. Shulman. The stricken tanker was subsequently towed to Saiada Bay, Corfu, where she was beached, and the escort headed into port nearby.

One of the Beauforts of the third flight, AW353/V flown by Lt. W.B. Wolfe SAAF, on his first operational sortie, was shot down by Flak. The sea was relatively calm and Wolfe was able to ditch his crippled machine, allowing his crew to scramble to the safety of their dinghy; fishing boats were nearby and the airmen were soon rescued. Another Beaufort (AW305) was also hit by AA fire which wounded the gunner, although the aircraft was able to reach Malta. Not so fortunate was the crew of Beaufighter T5164/O, forced to ditch in the sea off Corfu. Plt.Off. Stanton and his observer, Plt.Off. Bryson, were seen in their dinghy and were later picked up by one of the escorts.

During the attack the Beaufighters had enjoyed a field day with the diverse aircraft which apparently comprised the air cover, but it is clear that the aircraft recognition of the crews left much to be desired! Wg.Cdr. Pike (X8089/H) and Wt.Off. Peter Mueller (T4774/M) shared in claiming a Ju52 shot down, while Sgt. Ron Hammond (T4843/X) claimed a twin-engined type incorrectly identified as a 'Piaggio P32', following a successful engagement with a Ju88; his own aircraft sustained damage but he was able to get back to Malta safely; he reported:

'I sighted a Ju88 about 500 feet above, and approximately 1000 yards away, travelling north. I climbed and opened fire, closing to 150 yards, and when breaking away noticed voluminous white smoke coming from starboard engine. We then manoeuvred into position and delivered attack from dead astern. Flames were then observed coming from his starboard engine and we opened fire again at 2-300 yards. More hits were observed along the fuselage and starboard mainplane, and we closed to about 50 yards and pulled up sharply about 100 feet from the water. When last seen, the Ju88 was in a slight dive with his starboard wing down.

'As we pulled away from the attack on the Ju88, we noticed a P32 (*sic*) at about 1000 feet. We climbed after this and approached him at about 2400 feet and opened fire at his starboard quarter from about 400 yards. Hits were observed on his starboard engine, which burst into flames immediately. He then turned slowly to port and we manoeuvred into position and delivered a second attack from his port quarter. No hits were observed and he turned inside us. We throttled back, manoeuvred into position dead astern, and delivered a third attack. We shot away his port tailfin — large pieces just missing our aircraft — and hits were observed along his fuselage and starboard wing. Oil covered our windscreen, and he was observed spinning out of contol at about 50-100 feet.'

It seems likely that Hammond's German opponent was one of three I/KG 54 aircraft engaged on this escort. The crew of B3+RL claimed damage to a Beaufighter, but their own aircraft had one engine shot out and the observer, Obgfr. Grosch was wounded.

Plt.Off. Wills (T5145/V) also claimed a 'Piaggio P32':

'I saw several enemy aircraft on south-easterly course about to intercept Beauforts at 1000 feet. I did steep climb turn onto the tail of a Piaggio 32 (*sic*) and opened fire at 300 yards dead astern. Enemy aircraft took practically no evasive action and pieces flew off his starboard engine. After my third two-seconds burst, his port engine caught fire and he turned over at 500 feet and dived into the sea.'

Plt.Off. Stringer's X8035/J was hit and the port engine caught fire as he attacked a destroyer but, nonetheless, he was able to fly back to Malta. Meanwhile, Flt.Lt. Melville-Jackson and Plt.Off. Bate (X8083/G) also each claimed twin-engined aircraft shot down, identifying their victims as BR20Ms; possibly they attacked the same aircraft. Reported Melville-Jackson:

'I sighted two enemy aircraft about 500 feet above. I climbed and attacked the second one. I started firing at about 3-400 yards and closed to 100 yards dead astern, at which time I noticed pieces coming off starboard side of aircraft, and also burst of yellow/white smoke from starboard engine. As I broke away, the aircraft dived straight into the sea.'

Melville-Jackson's T5140/N was also damaged during the action and crash-landed at Luqa on return, but there were no injuries. Plt.Off. Peter Bate was flying No 2 to Melville-Jackson, and related:

'I sighted three enemy aircraft circling at 1000 feet to port of convoy. One dived towards 'N'. I then made beam attack on enemy aircraft and fired three-seconds burst and saw several hits. E/a disappeared from view. Then

Strike Beaufighters of 227 Squadron. **From the top:** Ready for operations in its blast pen. A member of the ground crew imagines what action would be like, manning the observer's Vickers 'K' machine gun. Taxying out for a sortie. Victim of air attack, a Beaufighter blazes to destruction. *(All NWMA)*

climbed to 1000 feet and attacked e/a identified as BR20; started attack from beam, finished from quarter to stern, firing five-seconds burst. E/a took no evasive action. As I stopped firing, a large rectangular piece of the aircraft flew off and fell in the sea. Then a small fire developed between the engines. E/a began to break up and then suddenly dived straight into the sea.'

As the Baltimore circled the damaged tanker, the crew taking photographs, three Ju88s appeared below and attempted to climb to attack but were evaded. When off Sicily on the return flight, a Bf110 approached and gave chase but this, too, was evaded. However, on reaching Malta, the Baltimore's engines spluttered and stopped, and Shulman was forced to make a crash-landing between Safi strip and Luqa; AG751 was damaged beyond repair and two of the crew suffered slight injuries.

A further Beaufort was lost during the day, but this was an OADU transit aircraft (DW805) which suffered engine trouble as it approached Malta, and was ditched in the sea one mile off Grand Harbour. The WOP/AG, Sgt. Pritchard, was slightly injured in the crash, but Plt.Off. Moody and his crew took to their dinghy and were soon rescued by HSL 128, which narrowly beat HSL 100 to the scene. Whilst the strike force had been away, 15 Spitfires from 126 and 1435 Squadrons carried out a second offensive sweep over southern Sicily, followed by eight more fighters from 229 and 249 Squadrons during the late afternoon. Again no Axis fighters were drawn up to challenge.

Setting up of 227 Squadron at Luqa under the command of Wg.Cdr. Ross Shore continued during the next few days. On the 23rd most of the 252 Squadron detachment returned to the desert, leaving behind one unserviceable aircraft and four crews, who were to serve temporarily with the new unit. Six Beaufighters and several crews were ferried across from Takali by 248 Squadron, the rest of the detachment's personnel leaving for the United Kingdom within a few days. Meanwhile, the Island's offensive capabilities had been further increased.

The RNAS torpedo-bomber unit was now virtually without aircraft, total strength being just two Swordfish, V4587 and W5896, the latter machine being ASV-equipped, and two Albacores, T9235/W and X8099/A. Aircraft 'W' was a tribute to the skills of the RNAS workshop unit's personnel. The machine had actually been written off earlier following a bombing attack on Hal Far; undaunted by the task they had set themselves the naval team, led by Leading Fitter John Leech, salvaged components from other wrecks and practically rebuilt it. Meanwhile, three of the Naval pilots, frustrated by the lack of action, requested the CO's permission to use some of the redundant Hurricanes dispersed around the airfield. Lt. Lashmore took the request to the AOC, receiving his approval, and a number of Hurricanes were readily supplied to the unit; the three pilots — Sub Lt. Reg Elliott and two New Zealanders, Sub Lts. Ernie Pratt and Colin White — volunteered to fly these on night fighter-bomber sorties over Sicily, following a short conversion course on the type.

BG770 was promptly rendered unserviceable following a crash-landing at Hal Far by Elliott during a practice flight when the undercarriage jammed. Although so few aircraft were unlikely to have much effect on the course of the war, it was felt that any attempt to bait the enemy in their den was worthwhile, particularly as recent reconnaissance of Italian airfields revealed about 150 fighters — Bf109s, MC202s and Re2001s — at Gela, Biscari, Comiso and Pachino, while in excess of 100 Ju88s were counted at Trapani; a further 50 plus Italian trimotors were seen at Castelvetrano, together with about 25 more Macchis.

Having carried out night-flying and dive-bombing practice, the Naval pilots announced they were ready for operations, as recalled by Reg Elliott:

> 'We declared ourselves ready and this was relayed to AVM Park. To our surprise, our first operation was not a night one, but a daylight one. Park had been concerned that the Spitfire sweeps over southern Sicily had not forced the enemy aircraft to engage them, so he thought our three Hurricanes might be the bait.'

Sunday, 23 August

Hence, during the afternoon of the 23rd, the three bomb-laden RNAS Hurricanes set out to raid Gela airfield, escorted by eight Spitfires of 249 Squadron and four of 229 Squadron, the formation led by Grp.Capt. Churchill and Wg.Cdr. Donaldson; the latter had taken command of the Takali Wing from Wg.Cdr. Thompson, who had moved over to lead the Hal Far Wing. One Hurricane (that flown by Pratt) suffered engine trouble shortly before the target area was reached, and the pilot was obliged to jettison his two 250lb bombs and return to Malta. The other two found 10/10th cloud over Gela, White deciding to drop his bombs on a small collection of buildings north-east of the airfield, while Elliott (Z2961) bombed Biscari airfield but results were unobserved. However, Italian reports suggest that four civilians were killed at Gela and three injured. The covering Spitfire pilots spotted two Bf109s but no contact was made. Elliott wrote:

> 'I found some aircraft near a hangar and went for them and then flew out on the deck — I could not see what the result was, but Colin White joined up with me as we crossed the coast and flew in formation with me back to Hal Far. He indicated that one of my bombs had hung up, and was secured by the back clamps of the bomb rack. The controller at Hal Far gave me the option of baling out, having viewed the bomb through binoculars. I decided to land, and unknown to me, the whole aerodrome staff ducked behind shelters! Fortunately the landing was one of my best, and as I got out I noticed the bomb down at an angle so that the spike only just cleared the ground. As it

had been released from the main securing lug it was, of course, primed. I think that had I known, I would have baled out!'

Whilst these attacks were underway, the Spitfires hunted for likely targets but soon Wg.Cdr. Donaldson reported he was experiencing problems with the hydromatic propeller on his aircraft, and the sweep was aborted. The flock escorted their leader safely back to Takali, where a good landing was made.

Monday, 24 August

Two small Axis convoys of empty vessels made the voyage from Tobruk to Piraeus, Greece, without damage, despite air attack from North African-based aircraft; but it was not such prey that the RAF was really after — it was the loaded vessels heading southwards against which their efforts were mainly expended. Indeed, another such convoy was already underway, the fuel-carrying steamers *Istria* (5416 tons) and the smaller *Dielpi* (1527 tons) had departed independently for Piraeus, prior to sailing in convoy for Tobruk, accompanied by two lighters. The operation had only just got going when *Dielpi* and her escorts — the German destroyer *Ermes* and two torpedo-boats — were spotted by Plt.Off. Coldbeck of 69 Squadron (BR665) leaving the Gulf of Taranto during the early afternoon of the 24th. An attack was at once organized.

Within the hour eight Beaufighters, three armed with bombs, and eight Beauforts had departed Luqa, the latter led by Flt.Lt. W. Allsopp. One torpedo-bomber had failed to take off with the others, Sgt. Head discovering that the armourers had neglected to install the turret guns. As he taxied the Beaufort back to the dispersal area to report his aircraft unserviceable, Head was met by his inquisitive commanding officer, who had cycled over to the pen. Wg.Cdr. Gibbs suggested strongly that guns or no guns, the Beaufort should not reduce the capability of the strike force, at which Head realised he had little choice but to take-off and hope to catch up the others. Flying a direct course for the target area, the southern tip of Corfu had just come into view when a lone twin-engined aircraft was spotted, sweeping in from the starboard quarter. It was a Ju88. As it closed in on the tail of the defenceless Beaufort, the main strike formation was seen ahead, and one of the bomber-Beaufighters peeled away to come to Head's aid; the pilot, Sgt. Eric O'Hara (X8083/G), reported:

'I saw a Ju88. I turned to follow and at 300 yards opened fire with cannons and machine guns from slightly above and astern. Tracer was returned from the rear turret of e/a. This soon stopped. I closed in to point blank range and saw strikes on fuselage and port engine. I passed over top of a/c and my observer reported him climbing, on fire. He then dived towards the sea.'

This may have been Obfw. Erich Seefeld's 3Z+NH of 4/KG 77, which was reported missing; none of the crew survived. As the Beauforts swept in to attack *Dielpi*, a Ju88 flying over the convoy was seen to jettison the depth charges it was carrying, only to be fired upon and apparently shot down by the escorting destroyer, although this may have been the aircraft under attack from O'Hara's Beaufighter. The Beaufighters bombed and strafed, Flg.Off. Wood (X8030/C) and Flt.Sgt. G.F. Fargher (X8077/F) each claiming near misses on the steamer, while Flg.Off. Underwood (T5135/W) and Plt.Off. S.O. Laing (T4934/S) reported attacking other Ju88s without result. Sgt. Allen Phillips (X8083/J), an Australian, swept in low to strafe the steamer and a destroyer but was then chased by an aircraft identified as a Bf110, but which was probably one of the Ju88s; his aircraft was not hit. One Beaufort in the third flight, AW290/S flown by Flg.Off. Len Dewhurst on his first strike from Malta, was shot down by Flak; he and his crew perished. An explosion was reported on the starboard side of the steamer but as the attack was made in fading light, this may have been Dewhurst's crashing aircraft. In fact *Dielpi* was only slightly damaged, and she was able to regain the sanctuary of Corfu for repairs.

Apart from the loss of Dewhurst's aircraft, a second Beaufort (DD957) had been badly damaged and, as the pilot struggled home nursing an ailing engine, his aircraft's plot appeared on Malta's radar screens. As a result, Plt.Offs. Beurling and Farmer of 249 Squadron were scrambled from Takali to intercept a suspected 'hostile', encountering instead the crippled Beaufort 40 miles east of Malta. Trailing black smoke, it was escorted back to Malta by the two Spitfires, where it successfully belly-landed.

While the action was taking place over the sea to the east of Malta. Grp.Capt. Churchill and Wg.Cdr. Hanks led another 'Rodeo' over southern Sicily but 25 Spitfires, drawn from 126, 185 and 1435 Squadrons, again failed to bring either German or Italian fighters into the air. Following the return of the Spitfires from Sicily, a further ten of 229 Squadron were scrambled at 1640 from Takali to intercept another 'hostile' reported some 40 miles off Zonqor Point. Recorded Colin Parkinson:

> 'Red Section shot an unescorted Hun bomber down. They don't know what it was. Four of them had a squirt. It finally crashed into the sea in flames. They were given a quarter each destroyed.'

The Squadron tentatively identified the victim of Red Section — Flt.Lt. Magruder, Plt.Off. Nash, Flt.Sgt. Ballantyne and Sgt. Brough — as an "He111 in Italian markings". Magruder reported:

> 'Controller's interception, followed implicitly, was 100% accurate. I led section up sun and attacked from port quarter astern and above. Before I fired, the port side gunner fired at me. I gave a 2½-seconds burst; strikes on nose and port wing root. Second burst; strikes on intersection of fin and tail. Broke away starboard and up and circled round to cover rest of section while they went in to attack. When everyone had finished with enemy, he glided shallowly into the sea, with fire from port engine. No one seen to get out.'

They had, in fact, despatched an S.82 transport, MM60611 of the 45° Stormo Trasporti, which had been flying from Benghazi to Lecce; Ten. Francesco Zavattarelli and his crew were lost.

When night came 69 Squadron sent two of its Wellingtons, flown by Flt.Lt. Le Masurier and Flt.Sgt. Lister, to attack the beached tanker *Pozarica* in Saiada Bay, Corfu. A total of 35 small (45lb) fire bombs were dropped from 3000 feet and a small explosion was seen, but nothing definite could be claimed by the returning crews. *Pozarica* was not, in fact, further damaged in this attack but her days were numbered; later her cargo was to be discharged, following which she was moved to Cattaro for salvage.

Tuesday, 25 August

Activity resumed over Malta on Tuesday where, at 0727, a Baltimore of 69 Squadron (AG697) took off in the hands of Flg.Off. John Foster to search for survivors of Dewhurst's Beaufort crew. This aircraft failed to return, the cause of its loss not being known. HSL 128 was also ordered to search for the Beaufort crew which, as the aircraft had ditched some 100 miles to the south-east of Malta, made this the longest rescue attempt yet undertaken. The launch set out without the comfort of an air escort, and it was three and a half hours before the location was reached, but nothing was found. On the return trip HSL 128 was spotted by a lone Ju88, which circled three times but did not attack, and finally Kalafrana was reached by 1920 — a total of almost nine hours at sea. After refuelling, the same craft departed on a night search for the same crew; although a searchlight was used to illuminate the location area, still nothing was seen. HSL 128 eventually returned home at 1354, the crew having logged a further 16½ hours on operations; the two sorties, totalling 521 miles, used no less than 1500 gallons of precious fuel.

In the meantime, at 1130, ten Spitfires were scrambled by 249 Squadron when at least 30 Bf109s were reported approaching Grand Harbour. Three of these were spotted at 21,000 feet and two promptly turned into the sun and dived on the Spitfires, one getting on the tail of Plt.Off. Reg Round's EN976/C, and shooting it down into the sea; the New Zealander was killed. Rod Smith recalled seeing the demise of his colleague:

> 'He was hit high up and slowly glided in swooping circles, throttled back or engine quit, into the sea off St Julian's Bay, where our Mess was, and where we were swimming. I guess he was killed high up, poor chap.'

185 Squadron had also scrambled eight of its aircraft, Red Section encountering nine Messerschmitts over St Paul's Bay. Sgt. Weaver (BR374) reported an engagement with one over Luqa, which he claimed probably destroyed. During this fighting, a stray bullet hit the ASR Cant moored in Kalafrana Bay, and rendered it temporarily unserviceable.

Another ten of 249 Squadron's Spitfires took off at 1745, together with nine from 229 Squadron, for a sweep over southern Sicily, when they were also to escort three RNAS Hurricanes to raid Biscari. As they took off, one of 229 Squadron's aircraft (X-U with Sgt. Noel Pashen aboard) suffered a burst tyre and was hit by a following aircraft flown by fellow-Australian Sgt. Wally Parks, which burst into flames. Neither pilot was hurt; Pashen wrote in his diary:

> 'On take-off my port tyre blew and I nearly collected the flight commander — then when stopped on the runway another kite took off straight through me — God knows how I got away with it. Result — two aircraft written off — pilots unhurt.'

When just under way the Hurricanes were recalled owing to adverse weather conditions, the pilots being ordered to jettison their bombs in the sea. One experienced a hang-up, but the bomb fell off as Malta was approached on return and fell into the midst of a group of Maltese fishing boats!

Wg.Cdr. Donaldson, the Spitfire leader, decided to carry out the sweep, but as the force headed northwards, 249 Squadron's Flt.Sgt. 'Micky' Butler called out that his aircraft had suffered a malfunction of the hydromatic propeller, similar to that experienced by the Wing Leader two days previously, and that he was going to bale out. Sadly, before he was able to do so, his aircraft (EP695) dived vertically into the sea. The Canadian, a former Blenheim pilot, was killed instantly. Donaldson led his formation over Cape Passero to Comiso, then out again just east of Pozzallo. Two Bf109s were seen but they were too far away to engage.

During the day there were a number of command changes amongst the fighter units, Sqn.Ldr. Bill New of 185 Squadron and Sqn.Ldr. Richard Mitchell of 249 Squadron — at the end of their tours — relinquishing command of their respective units. 185 Squadron's new leader was to be its South African flight commander, Capt. 'Zulu' Swales, now promoted to Major, while 249 Squadron welcomed newly-promoted Sqn.Ldr. 'Timber' Woods. In 126 Squadron, Woods' fellow-newcomer from the *Furious*, Plt.Off. Bill Rolls, was promoted flight commander.

Wednesday, 26 August

Two of the RNAS Hurricanes, piloted by Sub Lts. White and Pratt, set out for Biscari again just before midday with a close escort provided by ten Spitfires of 185 Squadron, and high cover of 16 more from 126 and 1435 Squadrons. Over the target area the Hurricanes dived out of cloud and planted their bombs in the middle of the airfield from 6000 feet, then dived down to strafe buildings, joined by two of 185 Squadron. No aircraft were seen on the airfield, and Pratt's Hurricane (Z4941) was hit twice in the port wing by AA fire as it swept by at low level; an assemblage of 50 or so German soldiers was machine-gunned, the pilots believing they had inflicted considerable casualties.

A trio of Fleet Air Arm pilots who flew Swordfish and Albacore torpedo bombers from Malta throughout much of 1942, and who volunteered to undertake fighter-bomber operations in surplus RAF Hurricanes against the Sicilian airfields during the late summer. At the front, seated, is Sub Lt. Reg Elliott, flanked by Sub Lts. Colin White (left) and Ernie Pratt. *(R.W. Elliott)*

Whilst the sweep was in progress a substantial number of raiders approached Malta although none crossed the coast. Twenty Spitfires were scrambled but only ten of 229 Squadron sighted a pair of Messerschmitts, ten miles north-east of Comino at 27,000 feet, then six unidentified fighters at sea level. One section dived down to investigate and Sgt. Cliff Cornish (BR496) was either shot down or misjudged his height, his aircraft crashing into the sea. Flg.Off. Dudley Newman (EP190) reported that he was orbiting the aircraft in the sea, but also failed to return. It seems that he was bounced by Lt. Franz Schiess of Stąb/JG 53, who claimed a Spitfire shot down on this day. On learning of the two missing aircraft, 1435 Squadron despatched eight more to carry out a search but nothing was sighted. A further search was carried out by five of 229 Squadron, and later by another section from 1435 Squadron, but again no sign of the missing pilots or the wreckage of their aircraft was seen.

Messerschmitt Bf109F of Stab/JG 53 – possibly the aircraft flown by Lt. Franz Schiess.

With trade slackening off over Malta, permission had now been given for 89 Squadron to add a night intruder capacity once more, and to operate over Sicilian airfields and seaplane bases and against shipping. Hence, two Beaufighters were stripped of all special equipment, and at 2035 Flt.Lt. Edwards took off in X7695 with Plt.Off. Ross acting as his observer, on the first such mission. Edwards later reported:

> 'I patrolled off Marsala from 2200 to 2225, watching a flare path on the water. At 2225 an aircraft took off and climbed in a left hand turn. It had a quick-flashing white light on top. I closed in behind it and with full flap managed to stay there. From very close range I gave it two short bursts. Bits came off the wings, tail and hull. It stalled to the right and crashed just south of Marsala in a blaze which lit up the whole town.'

They claimed their victim as a Do18 seaplane but it may possibly have been an Italian craft. Following the attack, Edwards went in low and strafed a motor vessel seen in Marsala harbour. Whilst this action was taking place, the Regia Aeronautica had despatched a small raid against Malta, Cap. Cenni leading nine Ju87s from Gela to attack various targets. Six of the Stuka pilots were briefed to attack Hal Far but the only bombs reported to have fallen on the Island fell in the Madliena area, where Cap. Cenni and his section attacked the radar station located near St Mark's Bay. They claimed it destroyed. However, there was no report of damage whatsoever to 502 AMES. A patrolling Beaufighter pilot sighted two of the Ju87s about 20 miles north of Malta, and an attack was made but no strikes were reported and neither aircraft was hit.

Less than two hours later a dozen Ju88s of III/KG 77 approached and bombs fell in the Luqa, Safi, Gharghur and Paola areas. The AA guns put up an effective barrage, claiming to have brought down one raider and damaged a second. One of the bombers was shot down, but this almost certainly fell victim to the Beaufighter (X7716) crewed by Sqn.Ldr. Paul Evans and Flt.Sgt. Houston, as Evans' report suggests:

> 'I closed in and identified it as a Ju88. I gave a short burst of cannon and machine gun at 150 yards and his starboard engine caught fire. He started to dive — I followed and saw only exhaust flames from port engine. I gave another short burst but missed, owing to violent evasive action. I closed in for a third time to 50 yards and gave a long burst. There were strikes all over and the port engine streamed glycol. About a minute later I saw an aircraft crash on Gozo.'

The 8 Staffel machine (3Z+CS) crashed in a field near Xewkija, where the pilot, Fw. Ernst Klaus, and his radio operator, Uffz. Kurt Klawitter, both survived to be taken prisoner; the other two crewmen were killed.

Thursday, 27 August

The Luftwaffe was back during the morning, eight 126 Squadron Spitfires being scrambled after nine Bf109s over St Paul's Bay. Flg.Off. Wallace (AB332) and Flt.Sgt. Farquharson (BP992) each claimed one damaged. Greater things were afoot, however, for a major strike on the Sicilian airfields had been planned, following the lack of reaction during recent fighter incursions. Just before 1300 ten Spitfires from 185 Squadron headed for Comiso, led by Wg.Cdr. Thompson and Maj. Swales, followed five minutes later by eight from 229 Squadron, led by Grp.Capt. Churchill and Wg.Cdr. Donaldson, bound for Biscari. Finally, Sqn.Ldr. Woods led off a further eight of 249 Squadron five minutes after the departure of 229 Squadron; their target was Gela.

Crossing the coast south-east of Comiso at sea level, Wg.Cdr. Thompson's formation had penetrated inland for about nine miles when eight Ju88s of II and III/KG 77 were encountered, flying at heights between 50 and 500 feet. These had just taken off from the airfield, prior to forming up for a raid on Malta. All Spitfires attacked, and four of the bombers were claimed shot down, with three more probably destroyed, and the eighth damaged; Maj. Swales (EP122/B) reported:

> 'I was leading Red Section. Crossed coast and turned slightly to starboard following Sgt. Weaver, who had sighted a Ju88. The rest of Red Section as well as Blue Section followed me. Weaver closed in on Ju88 which was heading towards us and made an attack on the beam. I, who was about 800 yards behind Weaver, saw him firing and broke away to port making towards Comiso. As I approached the drome I saw a Ju88 at about 300 feet.
>
> 'Closing to line astern, firing in two bursts, closing all the time until cannon ammunition was finished. I saw strikes on the starboard side of fuselage and on starboard mainplane. E/a started to go down as soon as I got in line astern, and when I broke to port at 100 feet, he was still going down... On looking back... I saw great clouds of smoke and flames coming up from the ground.'

Swales then carried out a strafing attack on another Ju88 which was on the airfield, and saw many machine gun strikes; he claimed this damaged. Sgt. Weaver (BR374) commented:

> 'We were going up the valley towards Comiso when I sighted several Ju88s at 100 feet. I reported these and attacked the last one. I fired a four-second burst cannon from 200 yards, noticing a small amount of smoke coming from the port engine. Closing in to 30 yards astern, I fired a further two-second burst cannon and machine gun, noticing strikes on starboard fuselage and mainplane. I manoeuvred for a further attack when it flicked over on its back at about 50 feet, and burst into flames, exploding very violently. (*Credited as destroyed*).
>
> 'Immediately after seeing mine go in, I saw Red 3's (*Lt. Kuhlmann*) Ju88 spin in about 500 yards south of mine, and blow up. I then proceeded to the aerodrome where I saw another Ju88 at 400 feet. I dived under him and pulled up behind, about 40 yards, firing the rest of my cannon. The starboard motor flamed up and he went into a steep dive to the right, burning badly. (*Credited as probably destroyed*).
>
> 'While attacking the second Ju88 I noticed four 109s taking off south to north. I dived into the starboard one and fired about five-seconds machine guns, from 200 yards quarter astern. He crashed straight ahead into a field, north-east of the aerodrome.'

Although forced to land, this 6/JG 53 machine was only slightly damaged; Weaver was however credited with its destruction. Lt. Keith Kuhlmann (EP187) related:

> 'We turned to starboard and I saw Ju88s ahead and another three further to the right, all below 200 feet. Sgt. Weaver attacked one Ju88 from astern and hit the port engine, causing it to smoke badly. I then took a two-second burst from 400 yards and saw it crash and burst into flames on the ground. I do not claim any share in this destroyed aircraft for I consider Sgt. Weaver's attack responsible for its destruction.
>
> 'I then saw another Ju88 to port, and turned towards it. Range approximately 600 yards. The Ju88 turned to port and I was then able to close in to about 200 yards before opening fire. I broke to port at about 70 yards range and my last view of the enemy aircraft was as it dived down to port, with port engine streaming smoke. While firing I observed cannon strikes. No return fire except at the last moment. Sgt. Weaver saw this aircraft strike the ground and burst into flames.'

Sgt. Len Reid (BR380) also claimed a Junkers shot down:

> 'I chased one up and down a valley, just over the tree tops. I was chasing him over the olive groves, in and out. He was doing everything possible to shake me off, but he didn't have the flying speed. I had a lot of trouble catching him. Another 88 shot in front of me, going in the opposite direction — I think somebody else was chasing him. Finally I closed in and gave it two good bursts, saw big red flashes on the back and starboard engine. It immediately went steeply down.'

Flt.Lt. Charney (BR112/X) claimed a probable and a damaged while Wg.Cdr. Thompson (EP685/L) and Sgt. Ken Mitchell (EP553) jointly reported probably destroying another, the latter recalling:

'We caught them taking off and forming up... I can still see my cannon shells going through the 88, which was below me, and exploding on the harsh, rocky terrain underneath.'

EP200, GL-T, a Spitfire of 185 Squadron, is seen after crash-landing near Marina di Ragusa, Sicily, on 27 August 1942 due to Flak damage. Flg.Off. P.A. Woodger, the American pilot, survived unhurt to become a prisoner of war. *(G.F. Cooke via AST)*

The Squadron suffered the loss of Flg.Off. P.A. Woodger when the engine of his Spitfire was hit by light AA fire. The American crash-landed EP200/T near Marina di Ragusa and became a prisoner; the aircraft made a near-perfect belly-landing and was relatively undamaged. Woodger was unfortunately captured before he was able to carry out any demolition work on his machine.

Three Ju88s of 4 Staffel were, in fact, shot down. Oblt. Willy Köhl in 3Z+HM and Uffz. Karl Diestler (3Z+DM) were killed with their respective crews, although Fw. Georg Mayr, captain of 3Z+GM, and his crew survived. Additionally, a machine of 5 Staffel crashed at Modica, Uffz. Heinz Emanuel and two of his crew sustaining injuries, and another (of 8 Staffel) crash-landed on the airfield; the crew escaped. On the airfield, an observer officer of II/LG 1 was killed by the strafing Spitfires; other casualties are not known. A Klemm 35 communications aircraft of II/JG 53 was destroyed on the ground and one of the new Bf109G-2s of the same unit damaged.

Of the 229 Squadron formation, one aircraft was obliged to return early, the remainder eventually crossing the Sicilian coast about six miles east of Gela at 300 feet. Red Section encountered what they took to be a Do217, which had just taken off from Biscari, and this was claimed probably destroyed by Wg.Cdr. Donaldson (AD529) and Flt.Sgt. Ballantyne. It would seem that this aircraft was a Ju88 of 5/KG 77 which crash-landed at Gerbini. Donaldson reported:

'I saw a Do217 (*sic*) bomber about to take off and by the time he was in my sights he was airborne. I chased him for about 20 miles, caught up to 300 yards and opened fire from quarter starboard, closing to astern 100 yards. Strikes all along the fuselage and mainplanes. Black smoke from engine and enemy aircraft turned north, losing speed and height. Then sighted two Me109s so could not see if it actually crashed. It disappeared below a small hill. I was not able to see him hit the ground, but it was obvious that he was a dead duck.'

Red Section then attacked buildings and two water tanks in a railway yard about eight miles north-west of Biscari. Meanwhile, Blue Section made a run from south-west to north-east over Biscari, claiming the destruction of two Ju88s and damaging three unidentified twin-engined aircraft on the ground, as well as a hangar and other buildings. From this section Plt.Off. Colin Parkinson (X-N) recalled:

'As we passed a large town, Vittoria, my leader fired at a tall building. The rest of the section fired also. In the distance on the right I could see a thick, black column of smoke coming from one of the dromes already attacked. I could hear the boys natter as they went in. At last our objective camė into view. Biscari aerodrome. I could see a line of about six bombers on the deck, quite close together. Quarter of a mile from the drome my leader, Group Captain Churchill, was hit by Flak, started to smoke, and then burst into flames, rolled on his back and crashed into the ground. Rather shook me!

'By this time the ground defences had started in earnest. I fired at the line of aircraft on the ground and set one on fire. Attacked the large hangar on the right. After passing over the drome I flew for about five minutes trying to dodge anti-aircraft fire which was coming from every direction, the ground below, the hills all around. I could see a large black column of smoke coming from the drome. Finally managed to dodge into a valley where it was more or less safe. Saw a small train so fired a few rounds at it but didn't notice any strikes.

'As I flew across the coast I was fired at again by anti-aircraft. Fifteen miles off the coast of Sicily, I saw two 109s on the port and above. I looked to the other side and saw another 109 about to attack. I turned into the two and continued to turn. The single aircraft overshot and got in front of me. I shot him down in flames. The other two nearly collided with one another and flew off out of sight.

'Five miles off the coast of Malta I saw a dinghy so orbited until an aircraft came to relieve me. As I flew back to the coast I saw some aircraft in the distance to starboard. Flew over to investigate and saw that three were Spits and that the other two were Macchi 202s. They immediately broke and turned away too fast for me. I found out later that I had no ammunition left anyway.'

Apart from that claimed destroyed by Parkinson, one more of the grounded bombers was claimed in flames by Sgt. Francis. Sgt. Philip Dixon (EP691/A) reported strikes on three more, although his own aircraft was hit and slightly damaged. Dixon, who had arrived only ten days earlier, had been nominated to fly No 2 to Group Captain Churchill, as he recalled:

'I remember him (*Churchill*) as a short stocky man with grey hair, and a rather bouncy manner... following dispersal, he singled me out and said: "Right, keep close, and we'll be all right." We reached Biscari. As we crossed the foremost boundary a shell hit the Group Captain's aircraft (*EP339*) under the port wing root and exploded. He pulled up to the right and over my head, and I did not see him again.

'In front of me was a line of Ju88s and I passed over them firing one long burst with my guns. At the end of the aerodrome I turned to the left and in front of me was a Do217, right on the deck and with black smoke coming from his exhausts as he pushed throttles through the gate. I fired at him, but found I only had machine-gun ammunition left. I followed him for a couple of minutes and fired again, but without results and turned again to resume my flight home.

'About half way to the Sicilian coast there was an explosion in my right wing. It would appear that in my eagerness to fire as much ammunition at the 88s as possible, I had fired in one long burst and had over-heated the guns. The last round that remained in the cannon had gently cooked until this point and then exploded. However, no damage was done to the aircraft.

'On my return, I found a bullet hole in the side of the cockpit, on the left side. Further inspection showed an exit hole about the size of a half crown on the right hand side, and when we ran a rod between the two, we found that the bullet had passed between the control column and myself. It had not touched my thighs, my arm, my stomach or control column, having passed through a space of about nine inches by six inches.'

Left: Plt.Off. Neville Reeves of 89 Squadron, a night fighter pilot who claimed a Ju88 shot down by day whilst escorting Beauforts on an anti-shipping sortie. *(IWM).* **Right:** Portrait of Grp.Capt. Walter Churchill, DSO, DFC, who was shot down by ground fire while leading an attack on Biscari airfield, Sicily, on 27 August 1942. *(RAF Museum).*

Almost simultaneously with the attack on Biscari, the eight Spitfires of 249 Squadron dived on Gela airfield from 300 feet, Red and Blue Sections flying along the west and east dispersal pens respectively. They turned away across the barracks north-west of the aerodrome, re-crossing the coast at 300 feet over Gela town. During the shoot-up of the aerodrome, one Ju88 was claimed destroyed on the ground by Plt.Off. Bob Seed (EP708/U), and an MC202 by Sqn.Ldr. Woods (BP867/E); probables were credited to Plt.Off. Williams (EP706/L) for a Ju87, Sgt. Bryden (EP700/Q) for a Ju88, and Sgt. Shewell (EP338/A) for a Bf109. Finally, a Bf109 was damaged by Flt.Lt. Hetherington (BR373/N). The strike leader, Sqn.Ldr. Woods, reported:

'I was Tiger Leader. We crossed the coast at 300 feet about four miles east of Gela. We approached the aerodrome from the south-east corner and attacked four Macchi 202s parked on the perimeter. I saw strikes all along the fuselage and cockpit, then an explosion. I turned left at 0 feet and attacked a group of soldiers or airmen, killing or wounding them. There were no more suitable targets, so I set course for base. About five miles offshore from Gela, there was a two-masted schooner which Red 3 attacked.'

Buildings and dispersal huts were also strafed and damaged, and it was believed that three airmen working on the MC202 strafed by Woods had been killed. In fact, one airman of 155° Gruppo CT was killed and two of 102° Gruppo Tuff were wounded. For some unexplained reason, one Italian report suggested the attack had been undertaken by Beaufighters, recording that several Regia Aeronautica aircraft were damaged, and a Ju87B of 102° Gruppo Tuff was hit and set on fire. The aircraft had been armed with a 1000kg bomb and three of the unit's ground personnel, led by Ten. Giulio Sutter, rushed over to extinguish the flames before it could explode; the aircraft was, however, destroyed.

One of the effective Italian Scotti 20mm light anti-aircraft guns employed for the defence of most Sicilian airfields. *(F. Bianchi via N. Malizia)*

Seven Spitfires of 1435 Squadron patrolled ten miles off the Sicilian coast at 15,000 feet, to protect the squadrons on their return. No enemy aircraft were sighted. Two aircraft, acting as contact between the Controller, Wg.Cdr. W.R. Farnes, and the main body of the strike, crossed the Sicilian coast at 17,000 feet south of Ragusa and flew inland for 20 minutes, re-crossing the coast at the same point. Both aircraft strafed two small two-masted motor schooners south of Ragusa before returning home. HSL 128, sent out after one of the RNAS Hurricane pilots, Sub Lt. Pratt, spotted a body in the sea, which turned out to be a badly decomposed, unidentifiable Axis pilot. The corpse was weighted down to enable 'burial' at sea, but first it had to be shot to release the body gasses which prevented it from sinking.

Before he was shot down and killed Grp.Capt. Walter Churchill had been seen firing at a Ju88 on the ground. So perished one of the RAF's more illustrious and senior fighter leaders. At the age of 35 he had really been too old for such operations, not being blessed with perfect eyesight or health; indeed he had suffered constantly with sinus trouble and neuralgia whilst flying at height. Nonetheless, he refused to be tied to his desk, and paid the price. 'Buzz' Beurling, who missed the sweep due to a bout of 'Dog', was one of his admirers:

> 'When the war ends, our side should erect a monument over his grave to commemorate a daringly conceived and courageously led raid.'

By this date 'Ultra' had revealed details of the Axis intention to run further supplies to North Africa, including dates of sailings, ports of departure and the routes to be taken. On receipt of this vital information, Liberators from Egypt were despatched to raid the Corinth Canal in southern Greece, through which many of the supply ships would have to pass. These attacks effectively disrupted the programme, and in the light of them, Axis plans were hurriedly re-arranged so that nine fuel-carrying vessels would reach North Africa during a six-day period, commencing on the 28th. Malta was alerted and the Beaufort crews were readied for a period of intense operations.

Friday, 28 August

The first sighting of this new phase occurred almost immediately, when Plt.Off. Coldbeck in a 69 Squadron Spitfire (BR663), once again located the Italian steamer *Dielpi*, now 100 miles north of Derna. Sgt. Shulman was despatched in Baltimore AG735 to shadow and by 1600 a strike force comprised of nine Beauforts, led by Flg.Off. Grant, and ten 227 Squadron Beaufighters had set out, although one of each was forced to return early. At 1840 the steamer and two attendant destroyers or MTBs were sighted, the Beaufighters going in first in an attempt to suppress the Flak. Five of the aircraft were armed with bombs and these attacked the steamer, Wg.Cdr. Ross Shore (X8070/D) and Flt.Sgt. Fargher (X8077/F) each claiming hits; at least one bomb reportedly exploded on *Dielpi*'s stern, while both steamer and escorts were raked by machine gun and cannon fire from low level. Sgt. O'Hara's Beaufighter (X8035/J) was hit and was last seen north-east of the convoy, trailing smoke from its damaged port engine; neither O'Hara nor his observer, Sgt. K. Seddon, survived.

The Beauforts split into three sub flights, and Flg.Off. Grant was seen to gain a hit amidships on *Dielpi*, while Flg.Off. Les Worsdell's crew also reported a successful attack; watching Beaufighter crews reported seeing three torpedo strikes on the steamer. In the event, *Dielpi* blew up and was left blazing from bows to stern, her back broken and decks awash.

At least three Ju88s were seen patrolling over the convoy and these attempted to attack the Beauforts as they broke away, but were driven off by the Beaufighters, one being claimed probably destroyed by Sqn.Ldr. Wigmore (T4666/Y). Plt.Off. Dallas Schmidt (T5150/K), a Canadian on his first operational sortie from Malta, encountered a Z1007bis and despite his own aircraft being hit by return fire, shot down Mar. Carlo Lavezzi's Cant into the sea; only one member of the crew was subsequently rescued. Of the brief combat, Schmidt recounted:

> 'Gave him a short burst and pieces fell off the fuselage and the tail fell off. The second burst set his starboard engine on fire and the third burst set his port engine on fire. The rear gunner of the Cant fired on us the whole time of the engagement. The aircraft was all ablaze when it crashed in the sea.'

The crippled steamer sank soon after 60 of her 67 crew had been rescued by the torpedo-boat *Cascino*. She had been carrying 1500 tons of fuel for the Luftwaffe and her loss was a vital blow to Rommel's hopes of replenishing his rapidly diminishing fuel stocks.

The second steamer, the 5400-ton *Istria*, her cargo including 750 tons of fuel for the Italians and a quantity of MT, was now also on the way by cover of night. But she, too, was found a few miles north-west of Ras el Tin after a five-hour search by one of 69 Squadron Baltimores, AG726 flown by Lt. R. Douglas,

SAAF. During his long flight, Douglas' aircraft was attacked twice, first by two MC202s, then two hours later by four Ju88s; each time he successfully evaded. A number of torpedo-carrying Wellingtons of 38 Squadron were airborne, waiting for a sighting report, and the first of these to be guided to the location at 2300 was captained by Flt.Lt. Michael Foulis; he made a perfect run in the moonlight, launching both torpedoes, one after the other, in the face of an intense AA barrage. The second to be dropped struck home amidships, followed seconds later by the first, which hit the stern. There was a mighty explosion as ammunition stored aboard ignited, with columns of water and debris rising up to 150 feet in the air; the ship sank in four minutes, but 52 of the 58 crew were picked up by the MTB *Pegaso* and an accompanying lighter. Foulis received a Bar to his DFC for this success.

As if the loss of these two vessels was not bad enough for the Axis, a hat-trick of sinkings was achieved with the destruction of the 5463-ton *Manfredo Camperio* 35 miles west of Cape Spada. She was victim of the submarine *Umbra*. Three of the nine fuel-carrying vessels had thereby been sunk on the first day of the desperate operation. As a result, Rommel had no alternative but to restrict his offensive to a local operation aimed at destroying British forces in the Alamein area. Of the promised 2400 tons of fuel required by the Panzers, only 100 tons had arrived, whilst much urgently awaited tank and anti-tank ammunition had also been lost.

With nightfall two RNAS Hurricanes departed Luqa to carry out nuisance raids on Gela and Comiso, Sub Lt. Elliott (Z4941) visiting the former where he dropped his two 250lb bombs on the airfield. Meanwhile, Sub Lt. White (BE110) experienced intense Flak over Comiso, but also succeeded in releasing his bombs on the airfield. Both Hurricanes returned safely.

To complete a successful 24 hours for Malta's offensive forces, Flg.Off. Fumerton and Plt.Off. Bing were off at 2100 in one of 89 Squadron's stripped intruders (X7695), making for Castelvetrano airfield where a beacon and a flarepath were seen. Fumerton made two runs over the airfield but each time the lights were switched off, so he flew out to sea then glided back in from 6000 feet. The lights remained on this time and an aircraft — believed to have been an S.79 — was seen approaching to land and was attacked. Strikes were observed and the aircraft apparently ran off the runway and appeared to crash, but was claimed as damaged only. A second Beaufighter visited Syracuse, where a hangar and vehicles were strafed before accurate light AA fire forced the intruder away. Next day, 89 Squadron would be allocated two coastal strike Beaufighters from 227 Squadron's reserve pool, to enable the unit to expand its intruder capability.

At 1625 on the 28th seven Spitfires of 249 Squadron and nine of 229 Squadron were scrambled, but two of the latter collided in the air and returned at once, both pilots landing safely. Four MC202s were reported above the remaining reduced flight of 229 Squadron, and then four more below, Flt.Lt. Magruder and Sgt. Francis attacking two of the latter, one of which Francis claimed damaged. He then experienced trouble with the hydromatic airscrew on his aircraft (BR488), tried to get back to Takali but had to crash-land on the Naxxar to Mosta road. He was thrown clear, but suffered multiple cuts and abrasions and was taken to hospital. On learning of Francis' difficulties Magruder, the flight leader, turned back to look for him but then disappeared, and when the remainder of the formation returned there was no sign of him or his aircraft

A Spitfire in its blast pen; note the substantial construction of such pens by this time. The stone blocks used were in the main salvaged from bombed buildings. *(C.G. Jefford)*

(BP871). Records indicate that there was no Italian fighter activity on this date, but OKW reported one victory for the Luftwaffe, so the opponents may well have been Messerschmitts, rather than Macchis.

The three RNAS Hurricane pilots carried out a nocturnal intruder patrol over Comiso aerodrome making a bombing run from north to south and diving from 9000 feet. They faced intense AA fire and the results of their attacks were not observed in their haste to get away. Despite the hot reception however, all three returned unscathed. At 0200 Spitfire EP691/A landed at Luqa, with one of 229 Squadron's newly-arrived Americans, Plt.Off. Leo Nomis, in the cockpit. Nomis — intoxicated by the successes achieved by colleagues over Sicily during the past few days, and frustrated at his own inactivity — had 'stolen' the Spitfire from Takali, intent on carrying out a 'one-man' sweep over Sicily! He recalls:

> 'The night was very bright with a full moon. The sortie was diverted about 20 minutes after becoming airborne, by a direct order over the R/T from Fighter Control to return immediately to Luqa — the only base then with an adequate night operations facility.
>
> 'Upon returning to Luqa, I was greeted — after I had alighted from the cockpit — by Wg.Cdr. Grant, and informed that I was, to phrase it kindly, confined to quarters. I was returned to Takali the following morning, under escort, and was further informed that I was grounded and confined to quarters until told otherwise. Everyone at Takali, with the exception of the interrogators, regarded the incident as funny, and such was the state of mind and atmosphere at Malta in those days, no one (except the Inquiry Board) ever asked me why.
>
> 'I soon discovered that I was charged with conducting an unauthorized sortie (at night in a day fighter), unnecessary expenditure of ammunition — I had tested the guns over the sea because we had been having instances of cannon jamming — and unauthorized consumption of petrol.
>
> 'There were several other related charges, but the final upshot of the whole thing was that about three weeks later I received summary disciplinary action through HQ Med. in the form of a transfer to the Middle East. For some curious reason (considering the wretched living and operating conditions at Malta) a transfer to a Western Desert unit was considered being sent to a "punishment" squadron!
>
> 'So, by October, I was packed off to Egypt, flying out in a Dakota and, as

Plt.Off. Leo Nomis, an American member of 229 Squadron, was posted to North Africa in disgrace after he 'stole' a Spitfire with the intention of carrying out an intruder sortie over Sicily, when he became bored with inactivity. *(L. Nomis)*

> it turned out, the "punishment" squadron I was posted to in the Western Desert was the prestigious and high-scoring 92 Squadron, of the Desert Air Force's 244 Spitfire Wing.'

Saturday, 29 August

On this date Plt.Off. Colin Parkinson of 229 Squadron recorded in his diary:

> '"A" Flight came down and took over our machines to do a sweep over Sicily. The CO, Bill Douglas, went with them. All came back OK. Another squadron was jumped and one of our machines was shot down. I think he got back OK. (*Sgt. J.D. Vinall of 185 Squadron did, indeed, crash-land on return with a damaged machine.*) Another was shot down in the sea and I don't think he's been found yet.'

The latter was Plt.Off. Dennis Pollock of 1435 Squadron, who took part in a scramble at 1120 but failed to return in BS160. He was not found in spite of HSL 128 being despatched to the area of battle; only an oil patch was to be seen. However, Flt.Lt. Wally McLeod and Sgt. Scott of this unit each claimed Bf109s shot down in this action, when an estimated 15 Messerschmitts of II/JG 53, including some of the new, more powerful G-2 sub type, were sighted north of St Paul's Bay. Plt.Off. A.R. Stewart and Sgt. W.R. Wilson claimed probables, the latter also damaging one. It is not known who accounted for Pollock, but Fw. Joachim Koelzsch of 4 Staffel was lost in one of the new machines, when 'White 10' crashed into the sea.

Sunday, 30 August

During the morning the 5077-ton tanker *San Andrea* was seen by Flt.Sgt. J.O.

Dalley of 69 Squadron (BR431) in the Gulf of Taranto, close to the Italian coast as it headed for Piraeus (Athens) escorted by the MTB *Antares*. A Baltimore (AG735) of the same unit, flown by Lt. M. Currie SAAF, was despatched to shadow it, and to home in the Beauforts when they arrived. Having studied the reconnaissance report, Wg.Cdr. Gibbs at once organized a strike force, personally leading nine Beauforts out to attack, escorted by 11 Beaufighters, five of which carried bombs. One Beaufort and one of the escort were forced to return early. Owing to the close proximity of the tanker to the coastline, Gibbs had decided the attack would have to be made from landward. The formation flew to the heel of Italy, guided by Gibbs' navigator, Flt.Sgt. John Cresswell. They then climbed to clear the coastal hills and began their run from two miles inland, the crews seeing two men in a rowing boat hastily evacuate their precarious ringside seat!

The convoy had been sighted at 1410, protected by seven MC200s of 7° Gruppo CT, a Ju88 and a Z501. The Beaufighters went in first, bombing and strafing, whilst also attempting to keep the escort at bay. One Beaufort was hit and damaged by Flak as it approached, while those flown by Sgt. Ewan Gillies and Flt.Sgt. Hubert Watlington came under attack from the Macchis. Gillies' gunners, Sgts. G.A. Haynes and L. Smith, claimed one shot down between them, while another was claimed damaged by Watlington's gunners. Wg.Cdr. Gibbs, in the leading machine (AW296/B) unerringly put his torpedo into the tanker, causing a huge explosion, with hatches and superstructure hurtling into the air, through which the following aircraft were obliged to fly. A second torpedo also probably struck home. *San Andrea* drifted out of control, ablaze throughout her entire length; completely burnt out, the wreck subsequently sank. The escorting *Antares* had also been heavily strafed and returned to Taranto with dead and wounded aboard.

The Cant flyingboat was fired upon by three of the Beauforts as the formation withdrew. The gunners aboard the aircraft flown by Flg.Off. Worsdell, Flt.Sgt. Watlington and Sgt. Head, all claimed hits, as did one of the Beaufighter pilots, Plt.Off. Cohen. It was last seen with one float shot away and apparently about to crash into the sea. The lone Ju88 — M7+FL of 1/KGr 806 — was attacked by Plt.Off. Cohen and Plt.Off. Laing, both of whom claimed damage, and by Flt.Lt. Sharman's gunners, Sgts. Roy Gibbons and Mike Wadham. It was claimed probably destroyed but, in fact, the badly damaged Junkers returned to base with a wounded gunner aboard. Despite damage to three of the Beaufighters, all aircraft returned safely to Luqa where the jubilant crews celebrated a highly successful action.

However, the tanker *Giorgio* (4887 tons) and the supply vessel *Unione*, both of which had steamed from Piraeus although not in convoy, safely reached Tobruk on this date. Both survived bombing attacks en route, as did another vessel, *Gualdi*, carrying a further 800 tons of fuel. The arrival of these ships was soured when it was discovered that *Giorgio*'s cargo of 1500 tons of fuel was contaminated and was therefore unusable.

Monday, 31 August

During the morning two more small tankers, *Abruzzi* and *Picci Fassio* (2261 tons), departed Taranto independently, both initially heading for Suda Bay, Crete, with Tobruk as their ultimate destination. The following morning *Abruzzi* was spotted by a reconnaissance Spitfire from Malta (BR665 flown by

'B' Flight of 126 Squadron in late August 1942. Rear row from left: Sgt. D.E. Mortimer; Sgt. H. Roberts; Plt.Off. F.D. Thomas; Sgt. C.F. Bush; Sgt. R.B. Hendry; Flg.Off. E.W. Wallace. Front row from left: Sgt. N.M. Park; Flt.Lt. W.T.E. Rolls; Flt.Sgt. C.A. Long. *(W.T.E. Rolls)*

Plt.Off. Coldbeck) and that night five ASV Wellingtons of 69 Squadron were despatched to attack the tanker, estimated by then to be between Santa Maria di Leuca and Corfu. Four of five destroyers and a steamer — possibly the tanker — were sighted and bombs were dropped. Without the benefit of flares no results were observed, although it would seem that she was hit by one bomb; she was taken in tow by the escorting MTB *Calatafimi*, and eventually reached Ras Halal with her cargo intact.

The second tanker did not escape detection for long and a few hours later, at 0155 on 2 September, an attack was launched by two Wellingtons of 69 Squadron, and bombs aimed by Flt.Sgt. Lister's crew hit *Picci Fassio*. This vessel, carrying 1500 tons of fuel for the Italian army, plus 990 tons of gas oil and 800 tons of paraffin, blew up in one mighty explosion and sank within a few minutes; somewhat surprisingly, 20 of her crew of 33 survived to be rescued from the sea. When another Wellington arrived on the scene, Flt.Lt. Le Masurier reported that as the tanker was seen to be blazing, he proceeded to aim at the escorting destroyers, but missed owing to their violently evasive action. The other Wellington 'H', flown by Plt.Off. R.M. Johnson, failed to return; it is believed that the crew 'missed' Malta on the return flight and, with fuel exhausted, crashed into the sea off the Tunisian coast with the loss of all aboard. Thus, the last attempt to get fuel through to the Afrika Korps while the offensive at Alem el Halfa was underway, failed. Rommel was now forced to cease his offensive in the face of determined defences and such constant air attack, and began withdrawing.

Tuesday, 1 September

Meanwhile, there were no operations of any note by Malta-based units on the first day of the new month, only a couple of accidents in which aircraft were damaged beyond repair — a Spitfire of 185 Squadron was crash-landed at Hal Far by Plt.Off. Cheek, and one of the new Mark VII AI-equipped Beaufighters was written off by Flt.Lt. Edwards. A Hudson transport (V9230) of 24 Squadron crashed on take-off from Luqa the following night, when departing for Gibraltar, but no one was seriously hurt.

Wednesday, 2 September

Four of 249 Squadron's Spitfires took off at 1305 for an offensive reconnaissance over Sicily, passing inland west of Licata 25 minutes later. Macchis from the 51° Stormo were scrambled from Gela to intercept, and near Cape Scalambria one of these, flown by Sottoten. Emanuele De Seta, was seen just before 1600 at 16,000 feet. The Spitfires were at the same height, so they split up and Flt.Lt. Hetherington (EP338/A) made a stern attack from 50 yards, Wg.Cdr. Donaldson (AD529) fired several bursts from 200 yards, and Plt.Off. Farmer (BR373/N) then made a beam to line astern attack, closing to within about ten yards. All three gained hits on De Seta's aircraft and the tail came off as the Macchi went down streaming coolant. The pilot was able to bale out and was picked up safely from the sea.

From Messina the 4301-ton steamer *Monti* departed at 1930, loaded with tanks and motor transport and escorted by three MTBs. Within the hour the convoy had been located, and two Albacores and an ASV Swordfish were ordered off from Malta. Shortly before midnight the Albacores, flown by Sub Lts. Elliott (X9088/A) and G.R. Clarke (T9235/W), swept in to attack the merchant vessel, now some 15 miles north-east of Cape Spartivento. Both torpedoes were released and both struck home, one aft of the funnel, the other aft of the bridge; there was a violent explosion, followed by clouds of black and white smoke, and *Monti* was last seen down by the stern. She was later towed to the Calabrian coast — near Fiumara Condoianni — by one of the MTBs (*Sitori*), where she was beached. Commented Reg Elliott of his part in the attack:

> 'It was illuminated by the flare-dropping Swordfish when we came up on it off Cape Spartivento, and I managed to hit it aft of the mainmast. As I was pulling away after releasing my torpedo, I crossed the stern of the ship, where I could see a gun firing tracer at us, but without hitting us. My observer, a Canadian Sub Lt. Eddie Jess, shouted that he could see the great column of water shoot up where our "fish" had hit. The vessel was subsequently beached, with stern down, just off Spartivento.'

The following night two Albacores were despatched to carry out a further attack on the beached vessel; whilst Sub Lt. Bill Siddall-Simpson (X8099/A) dropped four flares over the target area, Sub Lt. White in T9235/W released his torpedo from the port quarter at 400 yards range. An explosion was seen, with a column of smoke billowing some 60 feet high. Siddall-Simpson's aircraft was armed with six 250lb bombs and three of these were aimed at the steamer, the remainder at a destroyer which was standing by, and which White had illuminated by flares; a bomb was reported to have exploded on the quarter deck of the destroyer. Photographs taken next day by a reconnaissance aircraft showed that *Monti* had a large gap blown in her starboard side, just aft of amidships. Following temporary repairs, she was towed back to Messina.

Meanwhile, a second convoy composed of three small, fuel-carrying and supply-laden steamers — *Padenna* (1589 tons), *Sportivo* (1598 tons) and *Davide Bianchi* (1477 tons) — had sailed from Piraeus on the 2nd, bound for Tobruk. They were under escort by four MTBs, with air cover provided by Bf110s of III/ZG 26 from Kastelli airfield, Crete. These ships were attacked without result during the afternoon of the 3rd by nine Liberators from Egypt. One of the escorting Bf110s, flown by Fw. Günther Wegmann, engaged two of the attacking bombers and claimed damage to one but his own aircraft was hit by return fire which resulted in a crash-landing at Kastelli.

At 2200 these vessels divided into two separate convoys, *Padenna* and two MTBs making their own way southwards. At 0150 (on the 4th) an air attack was made by Egypt-based aircraft on the larger body of vessels, now some 50 miles north-west of Tobruk. *Davide Bianchi*, loaded with 1080 tons of fuel, was struck by a torpedo and set on fire; she subsequently sank. An hour later *Padenna* was torpedoed by the submarine *Thrasher*; she was also full of fuel and suffered a similar fate. Finally, at 0505, one of the MTBs, *Polluce*, was hit and was taken in tow by another but sank two hours later. Only *Sportivo* reached Tobruk, carrying 800 tons of fuel — the first the Axis armies had received for five days.

Saturday, 5 September

There had been little activity over Malta during the past few days, but on the morning of the 5th an incoming plot caused six Spitfires of 249 Squadron to be scrambled at 0855, followed ten minutes later by five of 185 Squadron; one of the former was obliged to return early when the cockpit hood blew off. Four Bf109s were spotted over Grand Harbour at 25,000 feet, then six more at 32,000 feet; the latter were attacked by the 249 Squadron flight, Plt.Offs. Williams (BP867/E) and Giddings (AR488/S) each claiming a damaged. The other flight reported seeing both Messerschmitts and Macchis off Kalafrana, which they intercepted. Flt.Lt. Ken Charney (BR375) attacked one in a half roll, then pulled up and got in a long burst; the fighter turned on its back and dived into the sea about a mile south-east of Kalafrana. Charney believed his victim to have been a Macchi but there seems little doubt that this was actually a Bf109G-2 of II/JG 53, Lt. Hans-Volkmar Müller being reported shot down in 'Black 6' by a Spitfire off Marsaxlokk Bay.

Just as the Spitfire and Naval Hurricane pilots were starting to get a taste for the offensive forays over Sicily, orders arrived from London effectively curtailing such freelance operations. The following notice of explanation was issued by AHQ to all aircrew:

> 'In order to conserve Malta's stock of aviation petrol, the Air Ministry has ordered that offensive sweeps and attacks on enemy land objectives should not be undertaken except when they contribute to the success of attacks on shipping and its escorting air forces. Air Ministry has, however, given instructions for operational training to be re-introduced at Malta so long as it contributes to the success of offensive operations.'

Inspite of these clear instructions, later that morning Wg.Cdr. Donaldson led 19 Spitfires of 229 and 249 Squadrons on a wing sweep to southern Sicily — presumably under the guise of 'operational training' — but only two fighters were seen about 30 miles off Zonqor Point, and these promptly fled. Apparently Donaldson received a mild rebuke from the AOC on his return for his complete disregard of the Air Ministry ruling!

The indefatigable Wg.Cdr. Pat Gibbs was now relieved of his command of the Beaufort Wing at the end of his difficult and exhausting tour of operations; he held the RAF's record of 18 torpedo attacks, half of which he had carried out from Malta, and on this day was advised of the award of the DSO. The citation stated:

> 'He has at all times proved himself to be a leader of exceptional ability and initiative and it is entirely due to his leadership that casualties in his squadron during strikes which he has led have not been higher. His courage and example are of very high order, and prove a source of inspiration to all under his command. He has always displayed the utmost keenness, gallantry and devotion to duty.'

Gibbs had long lived on his nerves, the battle against Rommel's supply convoys becoming almost a personal vendetta; his men followed him blindly into battle, proud to have such an inspiring and gallant leader, but a price was to be paid. On his return to England, he suffered a nervous breakdown, from which he did not fully recover, and he was eventually invalided out of the Service in 1944.

Sunday, 6 September

In the early hours of Sunday, Italian 'Convoy N' sailed from Taranto, the motor cargo vessels *Manara* and *Ravello* being escorted by six destroyers and an MTB. At much the same time, 'Convoy P' left Brindisi, composed of the motor vessel *Sestriera* and the 4700-ton, tank-laden German steamer *Ankara*, escorted by three destroyers and two MTBs. Mid-morning the two convoys met off Cape Santa Maria di Leuca, to become 'Lambado Convoy' and headed for the comparative safety of the Greek coastal waters, before making the dash for Benghazi. This enlarged convoy was soon spotted by Flt.Lt. Mackay's 69 Squadron Baltimore crew, and to attack this formidable armada — identified as four merchant vessels and 11 destroyers — the most powerful strike force possible was put together.

At around 1230, therefore, Flt.Lt. Hank Sharman led off 13 torpedo-armed Beauforts, with a close escort and diversionary force of a dozen Beaufighters from 227 Squadron, six of which were armed with bombs; however, four Beauforts and three Beaufighters were forced to return early, effectively reducing the capability and potency of the strike force by 25% at a single stroke. To provide long-range fighter escort, 89 Squadron's four intruder Beaufighters were also pressed into service as top cover for the whole formation.

Thirty miles south of the Cape two columns of vessels were sighted, with an air umbrella of six Ju88s and a flyingboat. The fighter-bombers at once opened the attack in the face of a formidable curtain of Flak; although bombs were seen falling amongst the ships, no actual hits were observed. The convoy weaved and scattered, the destroyers failing to put up a smoke screen. The Beauforts followed in three flights, sweeping in from the starboard. The defending fighters swarmed all over them despite the efforts of 89 Squadron's Beaufighters; a Ju88 was claimed shot down by Plt.Off. Neville Reeves, possibly M7+HL of 7/KG 54 flown by Lt. Siegfried Philipp; Reeves reported:

> 'Saw a Ju88 and chased it. Squirted and missed. Saw another Ju88, 8-10 miles south of the convoy. Squirted and saw bits off the port engine and starboard wing. Broke away as another Ju88 was shooting from starboard behind. Turned 360° and lost attacker; looked for previous Ju88 which was very near sea level, going slowly, with smoke pouring from both engines, heading for shore. Several single-engined fighters were above so I did not dive to attack again.'

Sqn.Ldr. Evans gained strikes on the fuselage of the flyingboat, which he identified as a Do24, and this was seen to alight near one of the escorting destroyers. Flt.Lt. Edwards reported engaging a Macchi:

> 'As we turned towards the convoy, I saw three single-engined fighters approaching head on, slightly to port. I turned towards them and climbed. I attacked the nearest fighter, firing one long burst from quarter to beam. I saw bursts on the enemy fighter before I passed over the top of it. My last view of the fighter was with its wing vertical, turning away.'

Another Macchi was claimed probably destroyed by Wg.Cdr. Ross Shore (X8030/Q), who gave it a four-second burst from astern. Strikes were seen on its fuselage and pieces appeared to fall off. As it dived away, Sgt. Heath (the observer) gave it a further burst with his hand-held machine gun. Sgt. Phillips (T5050/K) reported engaging a Ju88, and seeing pieces fly off its tailplane before it dived steeply to sea level. Two of the Beaufighters were shot down however, with the loss of Flg.Off. D. de M. Partridge and his observer, Sgt. A.W. Vivian in T4666/Y, and Lt. F.C. Noone SAAF, with Sgt. A.J. Cusworth, a newly-arrived crew, in X8085/A.

The Beaufort attack was not without effect. *Manara* sustained damage from a torpedo strike, resulting in fires breaking out, but the cost was high. Flt.Lt. Sharman's aircraft (AW305/Q) was hit on the run-in when still some distance from the convoy, but despite a burning engine the Canadian, who had flown on the very first Beaufort strike of the war, held course until his machine eventually plunged into the sea. There were no survivors from this; nor from AW280/R, flown by Lt. R.C.B. Evans SAAF, which was also shot down into the sea.

Seeing Sharman's aircraft crash, Flg.Off. Les Worsdell took over the lead, despite being attacked by Macchis, and it was probably his torpedo which caused the damage to the cargo vessel. Meanwhile, Plt.Off. Marshall's AW291 was also shot-up by fighters and his observer, Wt.Off. Huchison, was slightly wounded; Sgt. G.E. Sanderson's machine (AW381) suffered heavier damage, being hit by fighters and AA fire, one of his gunners, Sgt. J.D. Cunningham, being mortally wounded. Yet another Beaufort, Flt.Sgt. Watlington's AW302, was hit by fighters and both air gunners, Flt.Sgt. McEllamy and Sgt. L.H. Tester, suffered wounds; the latter, however, continued greatly to assist his pilot and the damaged machine regained base, as did the other two badly shot-up aircraft.

The Macchis did not get away unscathed, however, for apart from those engaged by the Beaufighters, Plt.Off. Colin Milson's gunner reported one falling into the sea apparently due to his fire. Two others were claimed damaged by gunners aboard Plt.Off. A.F. Izzard's machine and that flown by Wt.Off. R.J. Dawson, the latter also reporting damage to an attacking Ju88.

The damaged *Manara* was escorted to Arilla Bay, Corfu, by the destroyer *Freccia*, where she was beached. Next morning the rest of the convoy was to be attacked by a submarine, although without loss. On the evening of the 7th, the ships again divided, Group 'Ankara' heading for Tobruk under repeated air attack from seven North African-based Liberators of 159 Squadron, during which the destroyer *Fusiliere* was damaged by bombs. Fw. Wegmann of III/ZG 26 was scrambled alone from Kastelli, again making contact with two of the bombers and attacking Flg.Off. Duplex's AL525; the bomber was slightly damaged and the rear gunner, Sgt. A. Warren, wounded. However, Wegmann's aircraft was again hit by return fire, over 50 bullet holes being counted in

3U+AD on its return to Crete. The three remaining transports reached their destinations safely, delivering a combined total of 2500 tons of fuel, 1100 tons of ammunition and other urgently-needed supplies.

Early on the morning of the 6th four pilots of 249 Squadron had been briefed to carry out a reconnaissance of Porto Empedocle, where two 25-ton twin-masted motor vessels were sighted. The Spitfires dropped down to sea level, one pilot gaining strikes on the hull and cabin of one of the vessels, which were, in fact, fishing boats; the other evaded the attack and made for harbour.

Tuesday, 8 September

The second week of the new month was unusually quiet and relatively uneventful for Malta's defences, only the occasional offensive reconnaissance sorties by small groups of high flying Bf109s causing alarm, although on the morning of the 8th two Messerschmitts of I/JG 77 bounced a section of 126 Squadron Spitfires and Sgt. Henry Roberts (AB531) was shot down by Oblt. Geisshardt; he baled out and came down in the sea off Benghaisa Point. HSL 128 set out from Kalafrana before Roberts hit the sea, and he was in the water for only four minutes before being picked up! The delighted New Zealander commented to his rescuers as they fished him out:

> 'A little bit sooner and you could have caught me on the deck and saved me getting wet at all!'

Wednesday, 9 September

It was now the turn of 185 Squadron to lose an aircraft and pilot, when seven Spitfires carried out a sweep over southern Sicily at 0930. Six Messerschmitts and a lone Macchi were seen over Biscari airfield at 18,000 feet, the Italian fighter being attacked and claimed shot down by Capt. Kuhlmann (EP122) after it was seen to be smoking badly as it dived vertically; in fact, the Macchi pilot got down safely, his aircraft having been hit by three cannon shells.

Sgt. Weaver called up to say that he had shot down a Bf109 but that his aircraft was in trouble, and that he intended an attempted landing on the coast. He succeeded in belly-landing BR112/X on the beach at Scoglitti. He had been shot down by Ten. Paolo Damiani of 352ª Squadriglia, who had scrambled from Gela with two others on the approach of the Spitfires. The circumstances of the combat seem to have been contentious, for Colin Parkinson recorded in his diary:

> 'Claude Weaver, DFM, was shot down by Macchis, mainly through disobedience and over-confidence. Dived after a Macchi but was bounced by another two and shot down. Crash-landed in flames (*sic*). He may be alright but I doubt it — kept firing his guns as he went down.'

An airman of 185 Squadron, LAC Ken Cox, recalled the incident in more specific detail:

> 'Weaver's aircraft was hit in the cooling system over Sicily. This he reported to the CO over the R/T. He was told to fly as low as possible towards Malta, land in the sea, and the HSL would be sent out to pick him up. His reply was something like: "You go to hell, they might not find me!" By this time he was over the sea; he turned back and landed on the beach, and a few minutes later waved to some of our aircraft that had escorted him in.'

Sgt. Claude Weaver's Spitfire, BR112/X of 185 Squadron on the beach at Scoglitti, Sicily, on 8 September 1942. *(D. Curcio via N. Malizia)*

Left: Ten. Paolo Damiani of 352ª Squadriglia, 20° Gruppo, 51° Stormo CT, the pilot responsible for shooting down Sgt. Claude Weaver over Sicily on 8 September 1942. *(A.M.I. via N. Malizia).* **Right:** Sgt. Claude Weaver III of 185 Squadron; this American pilot had claimed 10½ victories before he was shot down to become a prisoner. *(Yarra Collection via L. McAulay)*

In fact, the extrovert pilot from Oklahoma City survived unhurt to become a prisoner. His captors were well-aware who they had got, for the able operator of the CRIRA intercept service spoke English well and had followed the exchanges between Weaver and the controller at Malta as the combat progressed. Hence, Weaver was obviously very surprised to be greeted with "Hello Claude, how are you?" by his captors!

During the morning of the 11th, 22° Gruppo Aut. CT, the second unit to be equipped with the Re2001, arrived at San Pietro di Caltagirone from Sardinia to replace the recently departed 2° Gruppo. The new arrivals had been specially trained for fighter-bomber activities. Commanded by Cap. Vittorio Minguzzi, the unit's three squadriglie were:

359ª Squadriglia	Cap. Germano La Ferla
362ª Squadriglia	Cap. Leo Boselli
369ª Squadriglia	Cap. Giovanni Cervellin

Earlier in the month Flt.Lt. H.C. Baker, another Battle of Britain veteran, had arrived to join 229 Squadron; he was an experienced pilot with at least four victories to his credit, and was soon to take command of the unit. Commented Colin Parkinson:

> 'We are going to lose our CO, Bill Douglas. Will be very sorry to see him go. He's been very good to me. We're to have a new one from the Middle East, "Butch" Baker. Seems to be OK.'

Sunday, 13 September

Five Spitfires of 185 Squadron were scrambled at 0800 but the anticipated raid did not materialize. Capt. Kuhlmann was ordered to patrol over Hal Far and was then instructed to allow his new pilots some practice flying. In the course of a practice dogfight between Kuhlmann and Sgt. Lawrence Swain, the latter got into a left-hand spin at 3000 feet, was seen to pull out at 500 feet but then went into a right-hand spin; the Spitfire (BR374) crashed into a field near Safi, and Swain was killed.

This Sunday was the day chosen by Lord Gort to hold the official George Cross award ceremony, which took place in Palace Square, Valetta. Shortage of petrol meant that the numbers attending would not be high, as it was possible to provide only a skeleton bus service. Nonetheless, between 4000 and 5000 people gathered in the square, many having walked long distances to witness Sir George Borg — the Chief Justice — receive the medal on behalf of the people of Malta and Gozo.

The Governor, Lord Gort VC (centre, turned towards camera) conducts the ceremony of presenting the George Cross to the People of Malta and Gozo in Palace Square, Valetta, on 13 September 1942. Chief Justice Sir George Borg (in judicial robes, foreground) receives the award on behalf of the population. *(NWMA)*

Tuesday, 15 September

The Luftwaffe at last returned to the skies over Malta early on the 15th, when nine Spitfires of 249 Squadron were scrambled at 0825 to patrol over Zonqor at 21,000 feet. Three-quarters of an hour later, two Bf109s suddenly dived out of the sun and one Spitfire (BP867/E) was seen apparently performing aerobatics; this was promptly shot down into the sea, Flt.Sgt. Bernard 'Petro' Peters, a pilot reputed to have flown as a volunteer in the Spanish Civil War, perishing. It seems probable that he was the victim of Lt. Heinz-Edgar Berres, Adjutant of I/JG 77, although the Luftwaffe apparently claimed four Spitfires shot down over Malta on this date, including possibly one by Uffz. Horst Schlick of 3/JG 77 for his fifth victory, his third over Malta.

Somewhat later, at 0955, four 229 Squadron Spitfires undertook a reconnaissance patrol when plots on Malta's radar screens showed aircraft approaching southern Italy from the south. These were, in fact, S.82 transports carrying captured survivors of the ill-fated British commando raid on Tobruk. Another survivor who had been fortunate to be rescued by a Royal Navy destroyer when the AA cruiser *Coventry* was sunk during this operation, was Wg.Cdr. Stan Turner, late of Malta, who had been aboard the cruiser as RAF Liaison Officer.

The Savoia transports were not intercepted by the Spitfires, however, which instead sighted eight MC202s, flying in pairs off Cape Scalambria. Flt.Lt. Art Roscoe fired a one-second burst at one, which dived away trailing white smoke from its engine. Plt.Off. John Scott (BR486) turned to attack, but was not seen again, while Sgt. Turner became separated from the others and headed for home; 15 miles north of Gozo, when flying at 4000 feet, he was attacked and shot-up, and had to force-land at Luqa. Two Spitfires of 249 Squadron were immediately despatched to search for Peters and Scott, and at 1215 a dinghy was sighted about 25 miles north of St Paul's Bay; a body was seen face up in the water nearby, dressed in white, but was not considered to be one of the missing pilots.

Flt.Sgt. Ken Evans of 126 Squadron received a DFM for the five victories he was to claim over Malta. *(IWM)*

By the middle of the month transport machines from both the Luftwaffe and Regia Aeronautica were fully employed ferrying troops to North Africa, on average 500 Italians and 270 Germans being flown in daily to reinforce Rommel's advance. Such troop movements were the first priority for the German air transport fleet available to Feldmarschall Kesselring, which totalled some 150 Ju52s and five BV222 flyingboats; during the months of July, August and September approximately 46,000 men and 4000 tons of supplies would be transported across the Mediterranean in this fashion.

Despite this effort however, during the first half of the month only 25% of the Panzer Army's monthly requirements had arrived. Rommel reiterated his demands for a minimum 30,000 tons of supplies during September, rising to 35,000 tons in October, and reinforcements amounting to 5000 men, 2000 vehicles and 70 field guns. To help alleviate the problem of defending the convoys against air and sea attack, Kesselring promised to operate night fighters from Crete as convoy protection. For the remainder of the month, and throughout October, a greater part of the Luftwaffe in the Eastern Mediterranean was thus diverted to convoy escort duties in a sustained effort to reduce shipping losses, which resulted in a high state of fatigue amongst aircrews.

Wednesday, 16 September

During the early evening, at 1745, nine of 249 Squadron's aircraft were again in the air, Flt.Lt. Hetherington and Plt.Off. Beurling engaging eight Bf109s in a series of dogfights for nearly an hour, during which Beurling's Spitfire (EP706/L) received damage to the starboard wing and tail, while Hetherington (BR373/N) claimed one of their opponents damaged.

Thursday, 17 September

This proved to be the busiest day for some time. At 0845 ten Spitfires from 229 Squadron and eight of 126 Squadron were scrambled, pilots of the former unit spotting two aircraft identified as MC202s, going north at 23,000 feet. Flt.Lt. Roscoe fired a two-second burst at one as it turned into the sun, seeing pieces fly off its wings and fuselage. Plt.Off. Farmer attacked the leader of the formation and saw many strikes; both pilots were awarded probables. It seems likely that the Italian fighters were actually Re2001s from 2° Gruppo, for Serg. Luigi Berna of 151ª Squadriglia crashed at Gela on return and was killed, presumably as a result of this combat. Apparently other pilots of 2° Gruppo claimed two Spitfires shot down in this action. As the Spitfires retired, Sgt. Irwin saw two Bf109s and chased one down to sea level, firing a four-second burst and seeing thick grey smoke and one leg of the undercarriage come down; he was credited only with a damaged.

Sqn.Ldr. Wicks led his eight aircraft after an estimated 15 Bf109s seen over Zonqor, but a further eight were then seen below at about 18,000 feet, and these were engaged about 20 miles north-east of Grand Harbour. Plt.Off. W.L. Thompson reported shooting one down, while Sqn.Ldr. Wicks' aircraft was slightly damaged. Thompson's victim was seen to crash into the sea and was undoubtedly 'Yellow 9', a G-2 of I/JG 77, from which a slightly wounded Uffz. Fritz Schneider baled out. Thompson reported:

> Two Me109s tried to jump me from behind, so I broke to left; the 109s overshot on my starboard and did a steep climbing turn to starboard. I gave the rear Me109 six or seven one-second bursts and saw a few strikes, at a range of about 350 yards. I then managed to close into range but could not get a burst in as he rolled on to his back and dived away.
>
> 'I followed him and gave him a one-second burst. He then went into a

51° Stormo CT Macchi C202s from the 351ª Squadriglia, 155° Gruppo, about to take off from Pantelleria. *(G. Franchini via N. Malizia)*

> starboard steep turn, so I gave him two one-second bursts and saw something red fly back from the cockpit. He then flew straight and level and the pilot baled out. I orbited parachute and was jumped by two Me109s but came home as I had no ammunition left.'

Two pilots were detailed to search for the downed pilot, which they did successfully, and after about an hour saw HSL 128 arrive and pick him up.

Whilst the rescue operation was underway, three small formations of aircraft were reported approaching from the north, presumably also searching for the missing pilot. A total of 22 Spitfires were sent up to investigate, and at 1115 several Bf109s and Macchis were seen by the ten patrolling Spitfires of 229 Squadron, about ten miles north of Comino at 25,000 feet. These were engaged, Sgt. Irwin reporting attacking a Messerschmitt head-on, gaining strikes on its fuselage and a wing, following which one of its underwing radiators was seen to fall away. Irwin then attacked a Macchi from astern, seeing strikes on this also, while Sgt. J.L. Sidey claimed another Macchi damaged. However, an unidentified pilot of 1/JG 77 caught Plt.Off. Johnny Farmer off guard and gained a number of telling strikes on his Spitfire (EP663), forcing him into a power dive with his controls shot to pieces. Following a desperate struggle, Farmer managed to bale out at about 450 mph but pulled the ripcord too soon; the jerk of the parachute opening dislocated his shoulders, broke an arm and gave him a slight rupture! He came down in the sea and, fortunately for him, was soon rescued by HSL 107.

During the afternoon Sqn.Ldr. Wigmore led six Beaufighters of 227 Squadron to the Tunisian coastal area to attack an unescorted merchant vessel of about 2000 tons, which had been sighted earlier in the day; five of the Beaufighters were armed with bombs, whilst the other was to deal with a reported air escort. They found the 1237-ton tanker *Carbonia* carrying 320 tons of fuel 30 miles south of Kelibia, proceeding eastwards at about eight knots, and attacked it from mast height. They faced 20mm AA fire from the bridge and Plt.Off. J.D. Moffat's Beaufighter (T5149) was shot down into the sea; neither he nor his observer, Plt.Off. J.F. Dicker, survived. At least one direct hit amidships with a 500lb bomb was achieved by Plt.Off. Schmidt, and there were several near misses; deck cargo was hurled into the sea and the vessel was left stationary with

Ofw. Walter Brandt of 2/JG 77 at Comiso, the rudder of his Bf109G-2 displaying 30 victory bars, 19 of which he had gained on the Eastern Front. *(via W. Bock)*

a list to port, emitting brown and white smoke, and gushing oil from her ruptured plates. She sank shortly afterwards, 32 of her crew being plucked from the sea by MAS boats from Pantelleria. A reconnaissance aircraft next day reported seeing a Z506B circling over widespread wreckage in the sea, with about 40 large packing cases and three upturned ships' boats in the vicinity.

The Italian freighter *Giovanna* had earlier departed Tripoli for Benghazi, but during the morning of the 17th a big explosion had brought the vessel to an abrupt halt, half a mile off the coast in shallow water; it was believed that she had either hit a mine or a torpedo lodged on the sea bed. *Giovanna* was joined by the tanker *Rostro*, also making for Benghazi. The skippers of the two vessels decided to seek the cause of the explosion before progressing further and were both stationary at evening when the submarine *United* came upon the scene, and rapidly despatched both beneath the waves. Only two days earlier the Germans had hinted at an improved supply situation, but the loss of *Carbonia*, *Giovanna* and *Rostro* within such a short space of time must have shaken their new-found confidence somewhat.

Saturday, 19 September

One of 69 Squadron's two New Zealand Spitfire pilots, Sgt. Frank Gillions, was ordered to reconnoitre Sicilian harbours and the island of Lampedusa on the morning of the 19th. Control received a message from him at 1033 but then silence. He had just photographed Castelvetrano and was on his way to Trapani when the engine of AB300 (a jinx aircraft) started to falter, then started smoking heavily. Gillions headed for Malta but had to bale out near Agrigento, and was captured at gunpoint almost straight away. This was the first loss suffered by the reconnaissance Spitfires in the course of some 363 operational sorties flown since the arrival of the aircraft in mid March, although a visiting UK-based Spitfire, briefly attached to the unit, had been lost on operations early the previous year.

During the morning Flt.Lt. Bill Rolls of 126 Squadron took off with his No 2,

Sgt. J.E. Mortimer, to fly an anti E-boat sweep off Sicily. Making landfall east of Cape Scalambria, they flew along the coast to Cape Passero and then towards Syracuse. Suddenly they spotted two white wakes in the sea ahead, which they assumed at first to be E-boats. Turning out to sea, they then swung in to make a head-on attack; Rolls (BR383) recalled:

> 'I was coming in at about 1500 yards when I saw the wake of one stop, and then saw it was a Do24 flyingboat about 15 feet above the water. I opened fire with cannon and machine gun, and at the same time my No 2 opened up on the other, which was a Do18.'

Rolls reported a red-orange glow within the Dornier before it disappeared in a white splash in front of him. Climbing to avoid the column of water, he turned to attack the second aircraft, which had reversed its direction and was taxying fast for land. He fired a short burst into this, then watched Mortimer attack again; more strikes were seen and pieces flew off. When they dived down to look for survivors, only two white disturbed patches were visible on the water; both flyingboats were claimed destroyed. Next day it was noted that Axis aircraft were out over the area in force, and launches were also seen in the vicinity. Radio intercepts by the 'Y' Service led to the view that the aircraft had possibly been carrying German Staff officers for a conference in North Africa, but the identity of these aircraft (and their passengers) has yet to be established.

Four Beaufighters of 227 Squadron were hunting in the opposite direction, having been despatched to attack three small vessels of about 1000 tons, reportedly hugging the coast between Tripoli and Benghazi. Some 24 miles east of Tripoli the vessels were sighted, and Flt.Lt. Underwood led the others in to the attack; seven 500lb bombs were aimed at the ships, and many near misses were seen, while all were raked with cannon fire. One was left stationary, pouring grey smoke from astern, with its wheelhouse collapsed.

Sunday, 20 September

Another tanker — *Leonardo Palomba* — which had departed Palermo for Tripoli by night on the 18th, was near Ras Mahamur by the evening of the 20th. Like the ill-fated *Carbonia*, she had sailed without escort but did, however, carry a special contingent of 25 German Flak gunners of I/Flakrgt 46, equipped with 20mm light anti-aircraft weapons. Shortly after nightfall, the 1110-ton tanker was attacked by gunfire from the surfaced submarine *Unruffled*. The German gunners returned fire and the attack ceased, but in the early hours *Unruffled* suddenly released two torpedoes into the vessel and she sank in minutes. With daylight on the 21st, the Vichy French minesweeper *Ravignan* put out from her Tunisian base and picked up 14 Germans and a lone Italian.

That same evening Beaufighter T5161 of 89 Squadron, crewed by Flt.Lt. Nottage and Flt.Sgt. Holton, visited Castelvetrano but found the airfield covered by a thick haze, so flew south to Empedocle, where a 100-foot vessel was seen about 300 yards offshore. This was attacked, and many strikes were made before the Beaufighter sped out to sea and back to Malta. There were a number of changes within 89 Squadron's Malta detachment at this time, with the arrival of five replacement crews. While Sqn.Ldr. Evans remained in command, Flt.Lt. John Waddingham DFC, took over as deputy from Flt.Lt. Edwards, bringing with him his own radar operator, Plt.Off. A.B. Cumbers DFM; other replacement crews included two Australian pilots — Flg.Off. Charles Crombie and Plt.Off. Ken Gray — with Flg.Off. Michael Kinmonth and Flt.Sgt. Arthur Pring making up the quartet.

The Beaufort unit had also recently received four replacement aircraft and their crews, but three of the pilots had immediately gone down with malaria. Other arrivals about this time included two specially equipped Wellingtons of 162 Squadron from the Middle East, captained by Flg.Offs. R.J. Watson and J.A. Hegman, both New Zealanders. Their task was to provide calibration facilities to Malta's radio and radar installations, and to investigate and jam enemy signals. In a period of 12 nights they would fly eight special sorties over Sicily, Sardinia, Taranto and Tripoli to discover the strength and coverage of the Axis systems. On completion of this survey, Malta was able to route aircraft to achieve maximum surprise and minimum danger of interception.

Monday, 21 September

Sqn.Ldr. Adrian Warburton, continuing his outstanding services with 69 Squadron, undertook a special reconnaissance sortie at 1730 along the Sicilian coast between Marsala and Sciacca. Flying a cannon-armed Spitfire V of 249 Squadron (EP140) on this occasion, he encountered a Do24 at sea level off Agrigento, took some shots at it and claimed to have damaged it.

Tuesday, 22 September

Nine Beauforts and six Beaufighters of 227 Squadron made an attack just as daylight was failing on the 22nd, their target a southbound 6000-ton tanker escorted by three destroyers and three Ju88s, about ten miles west of Antipaxos Island. On the run-in, Flg.Off. A.F. Izzard's Beaufort (AW350) collided with an escorting Beaufighter, the torpedo-bomber crashing into the sea with the loss of the crew; the Beaufighter, T5150/K piloted by Sgt. Phillips, limped back to Luqa where it crash-landed.

As the attack got underway two Beaufighters raked the leading destroyers with cannon fire, causing a small explosion on one, and drawing the Flak away from the torpedo-bombers. The other Beaufighters drove away the Ju88s while the Beauforts attacked the tanker from port and starboard. Eight torpedoes were released, one definite hit and one possible being claimed. An explosion followed by black smoke was visible two miles away. A second Beaufighter (X8061/Q) was damaged by AA fire and crash-landed near Birzebbuga on return; Wg.Cdr. Ross Shore and Sgt. Heath escaped with only slight injuries.

The same night six Wellingtons of 69 Squadron, led by Flt.Lt. Le Masurier, again found the convoy, now some 33 miles south-west of Antipaxos. The destroyers attempted to lay a smoke screen, but this was blown away by the wind. A total of 20 500lb bombs were dropped, a stick of which fell within 10-15 yards of the port side of the tanker, but no results were seen. As Flt.Sgt. J.B. McWilliams completed his bomb run, the rear gunner (Plt.Off. I.C. Cowan) yelled a warning of imminent attack by a Ju88, which he had seen diving on their tail; Cowan had time to fire two bursts as the Wellington made a steep turn to starboard, seeking the sanctuary of cloud. The Ju88 was not seen again. Following this latest attack, the tanker headed for the refuge offered by Patras harbour, little the worse for its experience.

Ju87s of 102° Gruppo Tuff were over Malta again on the 22nd, three attacking the radar station at Salina Bay, while three others attacked Hal Far. Cap. Cenni had for some nights been accompanying these flights in an Re2001, which had been supplied to his unit. He could not explain, however, the loss of Ten. Angelo Martini's aircraft, which failed to return. No claims were made by the defences.

There was further bad news for Rommel and his generals following a highly successful night bombing raid on Benghazi Harbour by North African-based Liberators. The 7949-ton freighter *Apuania* — which had arrived two days earlier from Brindisi as confirmed by 'Ultra' intercepts — was destroyed with most of her cargo, which included 626 tons of ammunition and ten tanks for the Panzer Korps, and 465 tons of bombs for the Luftwaffe. The explosion caused widespread damage to port installations and other ships in harbour. At least three other supply vessels — *Ravello*, *Pertusola* and *Tripolino* — were damaged, as was an MTB.

Wednesday, 23 September

Eight Spitfires of 126 Squadron were in the air when a fighter sweep was reported coming in from the north, an estimated 32 Messerschmitts approaching but not crossing the coast. Ten more Spitfires from 229 and 249 Squadrons were scrambled, but it was the 126 Squadron flight which encountered seven of the fighters 30 miles north of Zonqor Point. Sgt. Nicholas Dimitrios Sintetos, an American newcomer of obvious Greek parentage, claimed one damaged, although his fellow-countryman, Plt.Off. Ian Preston (BR383) was shot down; the Illinoisian, of Scottish ancestry, was killed. He probably fell victim to Ofw. Rudolf Ehrenberger of 6/JG 53, who claimed two Spitfires shot down.

Following a day of intense searching for the crew of the Ju87 lost the previous night, six of the Italian Stukas were back after dark, attacking Hal Far and

Left: Ofw. Rudolf Ehrenberger of 6/JG 53 who claimed at least 13 victories over Malta. **Right:** Plt.Off. Charles Lattimer of 1435 Squadron, a New Zealander awarded the DFC for five victories over Malta. *(K. Lattimer via P. Sortehaug)*

Mellieha Bay; two returned early, but the transmitter for the 'Alfa Servizio' warning system had been damaged and it was not possible to send a night fighter alert to the others. Shortly after midnight two Spitfires of 249 Squadron were scrambled in the bright moonlight, to join two Beaufighters of 89 Squadron in the search for the intruders. Flg.Off. Kinmonth (in Beaufighter V8219) was guided by his AI operator, Flt.Sgt. Edgar, to a point 12 miles due east of Zonqor Point, where a visual sighting of Sottoten. Italo Sciana's jinking Stuka was made. Throttling back to about 100 mph, Kinmonth gave a short burst of cannon which caused an explosion inside the fuselage; pieces were seen to fall off and the wreck plummeted into the sea.

Three other Beaufighter crews were intruding over southern Sicily whilst the Stukas were attacking Malta. Plt.Off. Gray (T5161) visited Trapani, where E-boats and submarines moored in the harbour were strafed, then flew on to Gela and released his two bombs. The Beaufighter was illuminated by a seachlight and fired upon by accurate light AA but was not hit. Flt.Lt. Nottage meanwhile bombed and strafed some flyingboats tethered inside the mole at Syracuse, but did not observe results as the Beaufighter hit a seagull which made it difficult to see through the windscreen. A little later Flg.Off. Crombie and Sgt. Moss in T5165 also went to Syracuse, where a three-engined seaplane — probably a Z506B — was seen and claimed destroyed.

Thursday, 24 September

Thursday turned out to be very quiet over Malta, the only event of interest occurring during a late evening patrol by 16 Spitfires drawn from 229 and 249 Squadrons, when Plt.Off. Beurling spotted an unidentified fighter 15 miles from Cape Scalambria, but this was not engaged. Earlier in the day, a reconnaissance Spitfire had reported a large freighter — possibly the German steamer *Menes* — carrying a deck cargo of 27 trucks. She was hugging the coast ten miles north of Punto Stilo, with an escort of three destroyers and a small naval auxiliary. Despite a report of approaching bad weather, and the onset of darkness, the standby Beaufort flight was briefed to carry out an attack.

Lt. D.P. Tilley SAAF, led off three Beauforts to carry out the unit's first night torpedo strike, but one aircraft returned early with engine trouble. The weather proved to be very bad over the Malta Channel, drastically reducing visibilty; despite this the leader's observer, Sgt. W.C. Stephens, accurately guided the remaining two aircraft to the correct position. An attack was made on the merchantman, the Beauforts approaching from the port bow, but although the torpedoes were seen to be running well, no results were observed; in fact, the vessel was not hit and was seen to put in to Crotone early next morning. Meanwhile, the tanker *Rondine*, running as part of another convoy, had escaped detection and safely reached Tobruk; even so there remained only ten days supply of petrol, restricting Rommel's forces to purely defensive operations.

Friday, 25 September

From Luqa at 1045 on Friday morning three Beaufighters of 227 Squadron set out to locate and attack a minesweeper reported to be between Kuriat Island and Sfax. This was not found, but two miles off Kuriat a Z506B was seen at 300 feet above the sea. This was MM45435 of 197ª Squadriglia RM, searching for survivors from the tanker *Leonardo Palomba* sunk a few days earlier. The Beaufighters attacked at once, Flt.Lt. Underwood jointly shooting down the

Plt.Off. George Beurling, known as 'Buzz' or 'Screwball' in his 249 Squadron Spitfire. On the cowling in front of the cockpit can just be seen two rows each of ten white-edged black crosses, denoting the 20 victories he had claimed by 25 September 1942 – all but two of them over Malta. This disguises the fact that quite a few of these successes were claimed against Italian aircraft! *(via C. Bassett)*

floatplane with Plt.Offs. Carl Johnson and Dick Wills. Although there was an explosion as it hit the sea, machine-gun fire was experienced from the wreck, and one of the Beaufighters dived low and strafed; two of the crew were killed but the wounded pilot, Mar. Attilio Broccaro, and the other three members of his crew were later rescued.

Ten 249 Squadron Spitfires scrambled at 1120, joining two others of 1435 Squadron to intercept a plot reported as 15-20 miles north-east of Grand Harbour; the latter pair sighted about a dozen Bf109s but there was no engagement. The 249 Squadron flight also encountered a dozen Messerschmitts, orbiting 30 miles north-east of Zonqor Point, and attacked from up sun, although only Plt.Off. Beurling (EP706/L) enjoyed any success:

> 'As Tiger White 2, attacked two Bf109s of a formation of 12, from starboard quarter above. Fired 1½-second burst from 300 yards. Enemy aircraft disintegrated.
>
> 'Attacked No 2 aircraft from astern. Two-second burst, 350 yards. E/a emitted black smoke from engine with pieces coming off cowling, then glycol followed afterwards.
>
> 'Attacking third e/a five minutes later, six miles east of previous position, from port quarter, slightly above, 250-300 yards. Fired two-second burst. E/a enveloped in flames, dived vertically, striking the sea. Enemy pilot was seen going down by parachute, and was fired upon by Me109, causing the parachute to stream.'

One of his victims was undoubtedly one of the new G-2s of I/JG 77, the pilot making a safe landfall with his badly shot-up aircraft, but the identity of the pilot seen to bale out is not known. The third aircraft attacked by Beurling had been firing at the Spitfire flown by Plt.Off. Ernie Budd who was unhurt, although Plt.Off. Moody's EP136/P was hit, and he crash-landed at Takali. Two claims for Spitfires were submitted by the Luftwaffe, one by Lt. Berres of I/JG 77, and one for which there was no witness. For some unexplained reason, the German pilots

Sgt. (later Plt.Off.) Ernie Budd of 249 Squadron. *(NWMA)*

thought their opponents to have been American aircraft, while 249 Squadron noted that the German fighter sweeps were getting bigger and tougher — a sign of a new blitz brewing!

Saturday, 26 September

During the morning four Spitfires of 1435 Squadron carried out a reconnaissance of south-east Sicily, and when just south of Syracuse two Bf109s of 2/JG 77 were seen at 20,000 feet. The Spitfires had height advantage and dived on these, Flt.Lt. Wally McLeod shooting down Lt. Karl Eberle's G-2; despite his wounds, Eberle succeeded in baling out and was later rescued from the sea. A Messerschmitt was also claimed probably destroyed by Sgt. Wilson; he may, however, have attacked the same aircraft as McLeod, as suggested by his subsequent report of the action:

> 'I half rolled into one of them and closed to 150 yards, firing a two-second burst from dead astern, closing to 40 yards; saw his tailplane rudder disintegrate into about six large pieces. He half rolled very sharply and went down vertically. I turned right but lost sight of him.'

Two raiders approached the coast at 21,000 feet shortly after 2000, and bombs fell in the sea off Madliena. Two Beaufighters of 89 Squadron attempted to intercept, but Flt.Lt. Waddingham's aircraft (V8268) developed engine trouble, and as he returned to base he was fired upon by AA gunners. He decided to make another circuit of the airfield but crashed near Naxxar; Waddingham and Plt.Off. Cumbers, his operator, were badly burned and were rushed to hospital, where the pilot died from shock.

Meanwhile, another crew — Flg.Off. Crombie and Sgt. Moss in T5165 — were despatched to intrude over Castelvetrano in an attempt to catch the returning bombers. An aircraft was sighted — which they believed to be a Heinkel — and this was claimed shot down.

There was much relief at Tobruk during the morning, when the 4869-ton Italian tanker *Proserpina*, carrying 3500 tons of fuel, arrived safely with two freighters, having survived the perilous journey from Crete despite bomb and torpedo attacks by Allied North African-based aircraft. The German *Menes* also arrived about this time with vehicles and ammunition, but the tanker was to be the last to reach Tobruk, although another convoy was on its way.

The freighter *Francesco Barbaro* (6343 tons) had departed Brindisi for Benghazi, her cargo including 1042 tons of ammunition and 760 tons of rations for the Wehrmacht and Luftwaffe, nine tanks and nine self-propelled guns; she was escorted by a destroyer and two MTBs. Later in the day she had been followed by *Unione* and her escort from Taranto. Early next morning the two convoys joined forces, but as the afternoon wore on an attack was made by the submarine *Umbra*, which put a torpedo into *Francesco Barbaro*. Repeated attempts were made to tow but all to no avail, and she sank in the early hours of the 28th; all but 30 of the 278 men aboard were rescued.

Meanwhile a Wellington of 69 Squadron, HX604/Y flown by Flg.Off. C.K. Fitzgerald, out to attack shipping in the Messina Straits, located *Unione* five miles north-east of Cape Spartivento just after midnight, and bombed in a glide from landwards. One bomb was seen to explode very close to the stern but no damage was observed. A call went out for assistance from the RNAS, the ASV Swordfish and both Albacores being despatched with haste. Within two hours the convoy had been located, one Albacore attacking an escorting destroyer, while Sub Lt. Siddall-Simpson in the Swordfish launched at the freighter; the torpedo struck amidships, followed by a large explosion. The other Albacore failed to sight the vessels and returned with its torpedo intact. The badly damaged *Unione* was taken in tow by the destroyer *Da Varazzano* and reached Navarino safely, where she was beached.

Thus another convoy had failed to get through. During September 11 supply ships had been sunk, containing 20% of the total cargo despatched, but despite these losses, 11,200 tons of fuel, 2500 tons of ammunition and 1806 tons of rations had reached North Africa.

That evening several of the vessels in Tobruk set course for home ports, the steamer *Fougier*, tankers *Nerucci* and the German *Dora* sailing for Piraeus, escorted by the MTBs *Lupo* and *Castore*. Many air attacks by North-African based aircraft were suffered by these vessels during the night, the gunners on *Lupo* claiming one of these shot down.

Of this intensely frustrating and demoralizing period for the Axis, Feldmarschall Kesselring was to write:

> 'The way our convoys were being increasingly molested showed that freedom of movement in the Mediterranean could not be secured by merely defensive action. I could not reconcile myself to this slow ruination in idleness. It was clear to me by the middle of September that an effort must be made to ease our supply situation if only temporarily by an air operation against Malta.
>
> 'I knew the difficulties well enough; the island was fully capable of defending herself and had a substantially strengthened fighter force on hand.

The transfer of British fighter aircraft, taking off from aircraft carriers, was going on apace without our being able to do anything about it. Even though we were able to spot their approach by radar, our fighters always arrived on the scene too late; we just could not overcome the difficulties of getting fast aircraft into the area.

'It followed that as regards comparative strength, the scales had tipped against us, German-Italian formations being so much in demand to shield our convoys. Finally, the British had learnt the lesson of the first air battle of Malta; they had widened their base and achieved the highest degree of protection from bomber attack.'

Nonetheless, in spite of this apparent air of despondency, Kesselring was optimistic and confident about the outcome of such a clash, and showed admirable faith in his men:

'The C-in-C Luftwaffe gave extensive support to the proposed operation; but still every requirement could not be fulfilled. The quality of the formations, however, made up for this to some extent. The fighter wing were old hands at taking on the British, and the bomber formations had years of operational experience. It was hardly possible, however, to place much reliance on the Italian bombers and fighters because their aircraft were obsolescent and the bomber crews had insufficient night operational training.'

Indeed, the Axis air forces were now building up in preparation for an all-out assault on the troublesome Island to the south. There was no longer any question of a possible invasion — the pendulum had swung the other way, and the concern now was for the survival of the Afrika Korps. Despite all Rommel's flashing successes of the summer, the Alem el Halfa battle at the end of August had been a major setback. He was now stalled at Alamein, faced with a massively-strong Allied line, and with 8th Army and the Western Desert Air Force rapidly outstripping him in numbers.

It could only be a matter of time before the new British army commander, Lt.Gen. Bernard Montgomery, launched his own offensive backed by devastating strength. It was absolutely vital, therefore, that the supply route across the Mediterranean be safeguarded from the depredations of Malta's submarines and aircraft, if a disaster was to be avoided.

Thus it was that around the end of September units again began gathering on the Sicilian airfields. From North Africa, Stab and I/KG 54 returned, to join KGr 806 which had been renumbered III/KG 54. III/KG 77 had moved to Crete during September for operations over Eygpt, but this unit also now returned to join II Gruppe and KüFlGr 606, which at this time became a new I/KG 77. II/LG 1 also moved over from Crete to add further strength to the bomber force.

Having spent a busy and very profitable time in South Russia since June, I/JG 53 and the balance of the Geschwader Stab also returned. I Gruppe was now commanded by Oblt. Friedrich-Karl 'Tutti' Müller; he had left the unit earlier in the year when it arrived back in Russia from its first period in Sicily, and had rapidly raised his personal score to 103 whilst serving with I/JG 3, receiving the Knights' Cross with Oakleaves; he returned to his old unit as it moved back to the Mediterranean. His three Staffeln were commanded by Lt. Hans Möller (1 Staffel — 20+ victories), Lt. Erich Thomas (2 Staffel) and Lt. Wolfgang Tonne (3 Staffel). Tonne was an 'Experte' of standing similar to his new Kommandeur,

Lt. Hermann Harnisch of II/JG 53 walks away from his Bf109F, 'Red 9'. *(H. Harnisch)*

victor of 101 combats and recipient of the Knights' Cross with Oakleaves — as was his long-time wingman, Lt. Wilhelm Crinius, whose score had just reached 100. Other prominent members of the Gruppe included Lt. Fritz Dinger (48 victories), who would soon be posted to II/JG 53, Uffz. Heinz Golinski (46 victories) amd Uffz. Marian Mazurek (29 victories).

The force now gathering therefore including seven Kampfgruppen of Ju88A-4s and three Jagdgruppen of Bf109F-4s and G-2s, a most formidable proposition for the defenders, particularly when reinforced by four Regia Aeronautica gruppi CT with the latest fighter types, and five gruppi BT, plus other forces. The Luftwaffe also received reinforcements by elements of KG 100 equipped with He111 bombers to join the night offensive. Order of Battle at about the start of October was thus:

Stab/KG 54	Ju88A-4	Catania
I/KG 54	Ju88A-4	Gerbini
II/KG 54	Ju88A-4	Gerbini
III/KG 54	Ju88A-4	Catania
Stab/KG 77	Ju88A-4	Comiso
I/KG 77	Ju88A-4	Catania/Comiso
II/KG 77	Ju88A-4	Gerbini
III/KG 77	Ju88A-4	Gerbini
II/LG 1	Ju88A-4	Catania
II/KG 100	He111H-6	Catania
Stab/JG 53	Bf109F-4	Comiso
I/JG 53	Bf109F-4/G-2	San Pietro
II/JG 53	Bf109F-4	Comiso
I/JG 77	Bf109G-2	Comiso
I/SchG 2	Bf109F-4 Jabo	Comiso
1(F)/122	Ju88D }	Catania
	Bf109F-5 }	Catania

10(Jabo)/JG 27 and 10(Jabo)/JG 53 had formed 'Jabogruppe Afrika' in August; the Gruppe had then become the nucleus of the newly established I/SchG 2 during September. Additionally, the Bf109G-2s of I/JG 27 would fly into Pachino on 3 October. This unit had been the top-scoring fighter Gruppe in

Die Stern von Malta (The Star of Malta); from the time of his arrival in Sicily until the end of October, Oblt. Siegfried Freytag, Staffelkapitän of 1/JG 77, was to claim 24 victories, raising his personal score to 73. *(via J-L. Roba)*

'Yellow 8', a Bf109F of II/JG 53 in its camouflaged pen on a Sicilian airfield. *(via J-L. Roba)*

Africa, but morale had recently been greatly damaged by the loss during September of three of its leading pilots — the great Hans-Joachim Marseille (158 victories), Hans-Arnold Stahlschmidt (60 victories) and Günther Steinhausen (40 victories). The remaining pilots were tired and demoralized, but despite this there were a number of notable 'Experten' still serving in the Gruppe, including the Kommandeur, Hpt. Ludwig Franzisket (37 victories), Lt. Karl von Lieres (24 victories) and Lt. Hans Remmer (14 victories); several of the unit's pilots were left behind, forming defensive 'Alerte Schwarme' at Fuka in Libya, and on Crete.

Although the Regia Aeronautica della Sicilia looked powerful on paper, the Italians would offer only limited support in the forthcoming battles and their strength was as follows:

	Fighters	
51° Stormo CT	MC202	Gela
20° Gruppo CT		
151ª Squadriglia		

352ª Squadriglia		
353ª Squadriglia		
155° Gruppo CT		
351ª Squadriglia		
360ª Squadriglia		
378ª Squadriglia		
53° Stormo CT	MC202	San Pietro di Caltgirone
153° Gruppo CT		
372ª Squadriglia		
373ª Squadriglia		
374ª Squadriglia		
22° Gruppo Autonomo CT	Re2001	San Pietro di Caltgirone
359ª Squadriglia		
362ª Squadriglia		
369ª Squadriglia		
377ª Squadriglia Autonomo CT		Re2000/CR42/MC200
Nuclei Caccia Notturna (Night Fighter Flight)	CR42/MC200	
	Bombers	
9° Stormo BT	Z1007bis	Chinisia San Giuseppe
33° Gruppo BT		
59ª Squadriglia		
60ª Squadriglia		
10° Stormo BT	S.79	
30° Gruppo BT		
55ª Squadriglia		
56ª Squadriglia		
32° Gruppo BT		
57ª Squadriglia		
58ª Squadriglia		
7° Stormo BT	S.84bis	
25° Gruppo BT		
8ª Squadriglia		
9ª Squadriglia		
88° Gruppo BT	BR20M/Z1007bis	Gela
264ª Squadriglia		
265ª Squadriglia		
102° Gruppo Tuffatori	Ju87B2/R5	Gela
209ª Squadriglia		
239ª Squadriglia		
132° Gruppo Autonomo AS	S.79sil	Gerbini
278ª Squadriglia		

281ª Squadriglia		
173ª Squadriglia RST	CR25/Ca314	Palermo/Boccadifalco

Rescue

612ª Squadriglia Aut. Soccorso	Z506S

Maritime Reconnaissance

83° Gruppo RM	Z501/Z506B/RS14
170ª Squadriglia	
184ª Squadriglia	
186ª Squadriglia	
189ª Squadriglia	
85° Gruppo RM	Z501/Z506B/RS14
144ª Squadriglia	
197ª Squadriglia	

The sea reconnaissance units would be reinforced from time to time by units from Taranto, such as 171ª and 288ª Squadriglia RM.

Despite the obvious strength of the new strike force, the Axis were faced by a greatly enhanced defence. Aircraft on Malta were now protected by well-constructed blast pens, and dispersal had been greatly increased by construction of the Safi strip. Five full squadrons of Spitfire Vs were available with plenty of replacement aircraft and pilots, well-led and well-directed. 89 Squadron's 'C' Flight remained an effective night defence. Strike capability had also grown, represented during the day by the Beauforts of 39 Squadron and the Beaufighters of 227 Squadron, and at night by the torpedo Wellingtons (all of which had now been amalgamated into one flight of 69 Squadron), together with the handful of remaining Swordfish and Albacores of the RN composite unit at Hal Far. This latter unit also continued to operate some Hurricanes, which would be employed mainly to protect the Air/Sea Rescue HSLs and to search for downed pilots. 69 Squadron's other two flights meanwhile continued to provide reconnaissance, the PRU Spitfires operating over Sicily and Italy, whilst the Baltimores ranged over the sea lanes. Since August this squadron had been commanded by its most famous pilot, newly promoted Wg.Cdr. Adrian Warburton. Fighter units were:

Takali Wing	Wg.Cdr. Arthur Donaldson
229 Squadron	Sqn.Ldr. H.C. Baker
249 Squadron	Sqn.Ldr. E.N. Woods
Luqa Wing	Wg.Cdr. Peter Prosser Hanks
126 Squadron	Sqn.Ldr. B.J. Wicks
1435 Squadron	Sqn.Ldr. A.D.J. Lovell
Hal Far Wing	Wg.Cdr. John Thompson
185 Squadron	Maj. C.J.O. Swales

Despite the Axis build-up there followed almost two relatively uneventful weeks before the final blitz on Malta commenced, which allowed an interesting development to progress without interruption. During the past few weeks a number of flying and dive-bombing trials had been carried out from Malta by Spitfires with locally fitted under-wing bomb racks, enabling two 250lb bombs to be carried. Air Vice-Marshal Park had approved the idea and later wrote:

> 'The reason I introduced the Spit-bomber was that the enemy were ignoring our fighter sweeps over his aerodromes in the south of Sicily. I used Hurricane bombers at first and the enemy reacted by sending up his fighters to intercept. As a result of flying trials we found that the fitting of two 250lb bombs to the Spitfire slightly increased the take-off run, and slowed down the rate of climb by about 10%. There was practically no difference in speed at level flight.
>
> 'We designed the bomb gear so that there was no loss of performance when the bombs were dropped. Unlike the Hurricane bomb gear, our Spitfire throws away all external fittings with the exception of a steel rib which protrudes less than one inch from the wing.'

Wg.Cdrs. Hanks and Donaldson were instrumental in testing the Spitfire bomber, the first of which to be so modified — EP201 — had been flown by Hanks on 29 August and had come through the trials successfully; others to follow included BR236 and BR368. Soon other pilots were allowed to practice dive-bombing, amongst whom was Flt.Lt. Rolls:

> "Our Wing Commander Flying had been experimenting trying out a Spitfire with a bomb under each wing. It was a bit of a "Heath Robinson" arrangement and it was a 250lb bomb which was hooked onto a Beaufighter bomb rack. It operated by pulling a piece of string in the cockpit which pulled out two pins holding the bombs in the rack. The danger was if the bomb got caught hooked up on one pin only because the bomb was likely to hit the ground when you landed."

Another of those selected was 229 Squadron's obviously less-enthusiastic Sgt. Noel Pashen, who recorded:

> 'I was selected to do Spit bombing practice. Unfortunately for myself I scored six out of eight hits on a small target (Filfla rock) and so am considered the bomber boy for Sicily — a shaky show.'

September virtually petered out; it had proved the quietest month of the year with only 38 day alerts, and much-reduced night activity. Such action as there had been by the fighters was fairly evenly divided between defensive action against Axis fighter sweeps, and offensive operations over their opponent's bases. Anti-shipping forces had remained very active, however, though not perhaps to quite the same degree as during August. Now, however, the Beauforts — officially gathered under 39 Squadron's banner — would depart for Egypt, their task well done.

Thursday, 1 October

The new month opened on a relatively subdued note — but all on the Island were aware that something was again brewing on Sicily. At first light, HSL 128 — with Flg.Off. Houghton in command — was sent out to search for signs of the crew of a missing Beaufort (DW823), which had departed from Luqa during the night, heading for Egypt. The crew had radioed their plight and had advised

Malta of their proposed ditching about 130 miles south-east of the Island. Poor weather hampered the search and nothing was sighted; on the return of this launch, HSL 100 was despatched to continue looking but again no sightings were made. 69 Squadron sent a Baltimore, and later a Wellington, to search for a possible dinghy from the missing aircraft but both returned without success.

Shortly before 1000 two Spitfires of 1435 Squadron on a reconnaissance patrol south of Cape Scalambria, spotted five Re2001s at 19,000 feet. Sqn.Ldr. Lovell and his No 2 (Sgt. D.C. Eva) dived on them and whilst three dived away, two climbed and circled once before making off towards Sicily; the Spitfires gave chase and Lovell (BS161/U) reported gaining strikes on one. With nightfall Beaufighter T5165 of 89 Squadron intruded over southern Sicily, Plt.Off. Gray releasing his two bombs on Castelvetrano airfield before carrying out a reconnaissance of Sciacca, where the aircraft was greeted by intense light Flak, although it escaped damage.

Friday, 2 October

The day was marked by another minor historical event — the first operational use of bomb-carrying Spitfires — when six of 229 Squadron, led by Wg.Cdr. Donaldson, set out to raid Biscari aerodrome, covered by eight more Spitfires of 185 Squadron; one Spitbomber was obliged to return early but the others carried out their task. No aircraft were seen on the airfield, nor were any tangible results of the bombing observed, but all bombers and escorts returned safely.

Whilst these Spitfires were operating over Biscari, nine more of 249 Squadron patrolled off the southern coast of Sicily to cover the withdrawal. At 1005 two MC202s were sighted going south at 19,000 feet, then two sections each of four Bf109s were spotted. Sqn.Ldr. Woods and Sgt. de l'Ara attacked one of the Macchis, the latter claiming strikes before it evaded and dived away.

During the day a photo-reconnaissance Mosquito (DK320), crewed by Plt.Off. Fred McKay RNZAF, and Flt.Sgt. 'Paddy' Hope, arrived at Luqa following a six-and-a-half hour sortie from RAF Benson (Oxfordshire). During this flight in excess of 800 photographs had been taken over Venice, Trieste, Fiume, Pola, Rome, Littorio aerodrome and Palermo, a performance for which they received a special telegram from the AOC-in-C 16 Group, which read:

> 'Congratulations to P/O McKay and F/S Hope on their very fine reconnaissance on 2/10, which was outstanding in every way.'

By way of a bonus to the news-starved defenders, on board the aircraft were some of the London morning newspapers, which had thus reached Malta by 1100 hours!

Next day McKay set out for North Africa but was forced to turn back due to low cloud; he therefore photographed Palermo instead, before returning to Luqa. The following day he was ordered to fly to Gibraltar, taking photographs of Tunis, Bizerte, Bone and Philippeville en route.

Saturday, 3 October

Such was the calm before the storm that the defenders of Malta were able to relax to a degree; at Luqa an impromptu cricket match was arranged between an RAF team and gunners from the 59th LAA battery, the airmen emerging the victors. Although a lone Beaufighter visited southern Sicily that night delivering two bombs to Castelvetrano airfield, there was no action at all during the daylight hours of the 3rd. Not until the evening did four Wellingtons of 69 Squadron, two with bombs and flares, two with torpedoes, set out to locate and attack a convoy sighted by a PR Spitfire earlier in the day.

Off Cape Santa Maria di Leuca the 6200-ton Italian motor ship *Valfiorita*, bound for Benghazi from Taranto, was sighted with three escorting destroyers. The bomber Wellingtons released flares, then carried out gliding attacks from about 4500 feet, and one of the 1000lb bombs was seen to fall about 150 yards astern of the transport. One of the torpedo-carrying aircraft failed to attack as the target was not sufficiently illuminated, although this did not prevent Plt.Off. W.H. Matthews (HX605/L) releasing his torpedo from about 700 yards; the missile struck home, hitting the tank- and MT-laden *Valfiorita* on the stern, and a red glow was observed amidships. As Matthews pulled the big bomber away, bursting Flak gashed the aircraft, wounding one of the crew, and the damaged Wellington crash-landed at Luqa on return. Meanwhile, the crippled transport was forced to seek refuge and repairs, putting into Corfu harbour.

Sunday, 4 October

The Luftwaffe put in an appearance during the morning, at least 20 Bf109s of I/JG 77 approaching the coast which only a few crossed. Sixteen Spitfires, equally drawn from 185 and 249 Squadrons, were airborne, Red Section of the latter unit encountering four of the intruders at 26,000 feet over Grand Harbour. Before these could be engaged about a dozen more dived out of the sun, attacking in pairs. Sgt. Irving Gass (EP700/Q) who was straggling, was shot down into the sea off Filfla; he did not survive. A second Spitfire (BR379/V) was damaged; seriously wounded, Flt.Sgt. Hogarth struggled back to the Island, only to crash-land in a field near Qrendi as he was approaching to land. The Spitfire skidded into the only building around, where a number of airmen were sunning themselves; no one was hurt apart from the Canadian pilot himself, who was further injured and rushed to hospital, where he died. HSL 128 was sent out to search for Irving Gass, but found only a Mae West and wreckage. One of the Spitfires was shot down by Lt. Berres for his 15th victory.

Wg.Cdr. Ross Shore led off nine 227 Squadron Beaufighters during the early afternoon to attack a convoy reported to be off Cape Santa Maria di Leuca. One

Air Vice-Marshal Keith Park, AOC Malta, visits a Spitfire in a typical sandbag pen in the rear seat of his red MG tourer – a familiar sight to all on Malta. *(IWM)*

Beaufighter — X8063/L flown by Flt.Lt. Underwood — suffered a tail wheel collapse on take off and immediately returned to Luqa, where it crash-landed. A second aircraft then developed engine trouble, and Flt.Sgt. George Fargher was forced to ditch X8039/F in the sea; he was unable to get clear of the aircraft before it sank and was lost, although his observer (Plt.Off. J.F. Briffet) was more fortunate. As he struggled in the sea, his plight was seen by Plt.Off. Schmidt who threw down his dinghy tied to his Mae West, thereby probably saving Briffet's life. Wg.Cdr. Ross Shore decided to call off the strike and ordered Plt.Off. J.M. Bryce to remain circling the dinghy until either a launch arrived, fuel became exhausted or darkness fell. HSL 128 was already on its way to the scene but although a search was conducted until 2230, the dinghy could not be found. Under the circumstances, Flt.Lt. Crockett decided to remain on station until daylight, with the intention of resuming the search then.

69 Squadron despatched a Wellington to continue the search, and 85 miles out from Kalafrana two flashes of light were seen on the sea; flares were dropped but there was no sign of life. Fifteen minutes past midnight one bright light and one yellow light were seen, and although more flares and flame floats were dropped, again nothing was seen. On later reflection it was considered most likely that the lights had come from fishing vessels.

Monday, 5 October

At first light three Beaufighters went out to continue searching for their missing colleagues, the dinghy eventually being sighted about 50 miles off Kalafrana. Sqn.Ldr. Wigmore flew over to where HSL 128 was searching but one engine suddenly seized up, forcing him to ditch X8077/S about two miles from where Briffet was bobbing up and down in his dinghy! Plt.Off. Schmidt circled Briffet's dinghy while Flt.Lt. Underwood circled that containing Wigmore and his observer, until HSL 128 arrived and picked up all three. By the time the launch reached Kalafrana, the crew had been at sea for some 27 hours.

Tuesday, 6 October

Another fighter sweep, estimated to number about two dozen, approached the Maltese coast at 23,000 feet during mid-morning, eight Spitfires of 1435 Squadron being ordered off to join three patrolling machines of 185 Squadron. Eight Bf109s of I/JG 77 were spotted north-east of Zonqor Point, and the 1435 Squadron flight dived on these; they were spotted however, and the Messerschmitts took violent evasive action to escape. Two more were then seen, one of these being attacked by Plt.Off. Lattimer (EN978/O) who claimed it damaged. The other German fighter turned on Sgt. Philp's machine, which sustained slight damage; however, the German pilot was credited with its destruction.

Wednesday 7 — Friday 9 October

The next three days were relatively uneventful for Malta's Spitfire pilots, and no engagements were reported. Two of the PR pilots were despatched to check on the build-up of aircraft on Sicily's airfields, and on Pantelleria, the subsequent reports of Flg.Off. Gubb and Plt.Off. Dalley giving cause for some concern. Their photographs revealed the following:

Comiso 34 Ju88s, 1 He111, 1 Ju87, 1 medium-sized u/i aircraft, 41

	fighters (mainly Bf109s)
Gela	14 Ju87s, 57 fighters including MC202s
Biscari	33 fighters including MC202s
Pachino	30 fighters — believed to be all Bf109s
Catania	41 Ju88s, 6 He111s, 4 Dorniers, 1 Ju87, 1 S.84, 2 Z1007bis, 2 S.79s; 2 Ju52s, 4 Bf109s; 12 u/i fighters; 3 medium-sized u/i aircraft; 3 small u/i aircraft
Gerbini	34 Ju88s, 7 S.79s, 3 Dorniers, 1 He111, 3 small u/i aircraft
Gerbini satellite	4 Dorniers, 1 Ju52, 2 FW58s, 3 medium-sized u/i aircraft
Trapani	21 Ju88s; 11 small u/i aircraft, 3 DFS230 gliders
Sciacca	6 Z1007bis, 28 fighters, 27 S.79s/S.84s, 10 Ca310s
Palermo	12 S.79s/S.84s, 6 Ca310s, 3 S.81s, 6 monoplanes; 6 CR42s, 6 u/i fighters, 18 medium-sized u/i aircraft
Castelvetrano	23 Z1007bis, 10 S.79s/S.84s, 3 BR20s, 13 S.82s, 3 S.81s, 1 small u/i aircraft
Pantelleria	7 S.79s, 1 Ju87, 6 u/i fighters

'Ultra' traffic continued to supply information on Axis shipping movements, resulting in three of Rommel's desperately needed supply vessels being located and sunk on this date. Desert-based strike aircraft torpedoed the Italian *Dandolo* (carrying cargo for the Luftwaffe) off Ras el Tin, while the submarine *Utmost* accounted for the German *Kreta* off Ras Hilal, and another submarine sank the tanker *Lupo* south-east of Djerba island. A further supply vessel, the Italian *Alga* fell victim to submarine attack the next day, although the German *Ankara* did reach Benghazi on the 10th, with the first fuel to arrive for a week. The next Axis ship to be lost, however, had tragic consequences, for the 1055-ton *Loreto* had departed Tripoli with 350 Indian POWs; off Cape Gallo she was torpedoed by the submarine *Unruffled*, and sank with great loss of life.

Monday, 10 October

Monday started badly with the non-arrival from Gibraltar of Beaufort DW824 of the OADU; no reason for its loss nor the fate of its crew is known. Two dozen Axis fighters approached Malta from the north shortly before 0800, some of which crossed the coast. Eight Spitfires of 249 were airborne, one of which was flown by Sqn.Ldr. Mike Stephens, a highly successful fighter pilot with about 15 victories to his credit. He had recently arrived on posting from the Middle East and he was attached to the unit as a supernumerary to gain experience of local conditions.

Four Spitfires of 229 Squadron were also patrolling off the coast, but two of these were forced to return early; the remaining pair sighted about 17 fighters, including MC202s, some 18 miles north-east of Zonqor Point and were then attacked by a number of Messerschmitts. Plt.Off. Hugh Reynolds' aircraft was hit but he succeeded in reaching Takali, where he crash-landed. It seems likely that his attacker was one of the leading German pilots, Oblt. Geisshardt of I/JG 77 claiming a Spitfire shot down for his 88th victory. The Messerschmitts were driven away by three pilots of 249 Squadron, Sqn.Ldr. Stephens (EP706/L) opening his Malta account by claiming one damaged.

At about this time, Plt.Off. Beurling was carrying out an air test on his newly-serviced Spitfire (EP706/L), when Ops reported that two Bf109s had sneaked in at low level and were apparently searching for ground defences on the south-side of the Island. Beurling flew out to sea in a wide arc, sweeping back in close to Filfla, where the two Messerschmitts were seen at about 1000 feet, flying in line abreast:

> 'I dropped in on them. I went down and down, clean under the starboard fellow, and rolled up under him, giving him a quick burst into the engine. He pancaked right smack down on his belly on the island and flipped over onto his back.
>
> 'The other fellow tried to circle away, but I stayed with him. He turned out to sea, then whipped back across Filfla again. As he did I moved onto his starboard quarter and let him have it. The burst caught the gas tank and the "ship" blew up, complete with pilot.'

These latest victories brought Beurling's Malta tally to 21 confirmed, with another shared with two others, and his overall total to 23⅓. A DFC would soon follow to add to the DFM and Bar already awarded.

At 1040 up to 50 aircraft including two Ju88s were reported approaching, some of which crossed over Gozo, where they were intercepted by Spitfires; the bombers jettisoned their bombs, some of these falling on the little Gozitan town of Sannat, where 16 persons were killed and 60 injured. A total of 23 Spitfires from 126, 249 and 1435 Squadrons were up, but only the 249 Squadron flight made contact, initially meeting a dozen Bf109s at 20,000 feet, 15 miles north of Gozo, and attacking head-on. One Messerschmitt was claimed shot down by Plt.Off. 'Jock' Sanderson (BR373/N) for his first victory, his own aircraft sustaining slight damage. He noted:

> 'Gozo bombed. Intrepid! All-in dogfight with 12 Me109s. One Messerschmitt 109F destroyed.'

Another was claimed shot down by Flg.Off. McElroy (EP708/U), who also claimed a second as damaged:

> 'Attacked head-on; enemy aircraft dived to right so turned on their tails. Caught another 109 climbing with two others in line astern. I attacked head-on from above quarter, and fired half-second burst, and observed cannon shells hit leading edge of enemy aircraft's wing. A large piece of wing blew off. I fired at the other 109s, closing from 100 yards to 20 yards, but observed no strikes. I broke right onto another 109, 250 yards line astern, and fired a three-second cannon and machine gun burst, observing hits on engine and wing roots, with heavy black smoke and pieces coming off; the enemy aircraft half rolled, so I followed it down and gained on him in the dive; the aircraft tried to pull out at 5000 feet, so I closed to 200 yards and finished my cannon, observing strikes and glycol. I continued to attack with machine guns down to 50 feet from the sea, 15 to 20 miles south of Sicilian coast; enemy aircraft still diving towards sea, streaming glycol and black smoke.'

Sqn.Ldr. Stephens (EP706/L) was credited with another Bf109 as probably destroyed, having observed strikes on its starboard wing following "a two-second burst with everything I had", while Sgt. Stead (EP199/K) also claimed a probable. Two others were reported damaged by Wg.Cdr. Hanks (BR498 PP-H) and Sqn.Ldr. Woods (AR466/R).

Six Ju88s, with an estimated 25 Messerschmitts and Macchis as escort, were reported coming in from the north at 1600. Eight Spitfires of 229 Squadron, led by Wg.Cdr. Donaldson, encountered the bombers and a dozen fighters about 35 miles north of Gozo. As the Spitfires attempted to engage the bombers, the escort came to their aid, Sgt. Sidey's aircraft being shot-up by what he believed was a Macchi, causing him to crash-land at Luqa on return; two other Spitfires sustained slight damage. Messerschmitts were claimed damaged by Wg.Cdr. Donaldson (AD529) and Sgt. Ron Miller, while Flt.Lt. Roscoe reported shooting one down:

> 'I attacked No 4 of a section of four Me109s in line astern. After breaking off, I was attacked by the leader and he followed me down to 12,000 feet, about 20 miles north of St Paul's Bay. After levelling out, he overshot, which placed me in line astern at 30-75 yards. I gave a three-second burst and observed white and black smoke, strikes, and pieces fly off. He flopped over and dived down. I saw him hit the sea; then Sgt. Miller also observed a "kite" go in the same spot, so it may be the same.'

Fallen eagle – a Messerschmitt Bf109F burns itself out on Maltese soil. *(NWMA)*

A few minutes after midnight five raiders approached, flares being dropped over Mosta and Birkirkara, and incendiaries on Gozo; no damage or casualties resulted. Two Beaufighters were airborne but no contact was made, nor later when two more intruders crossed the coast. Finally, shortly before dawn, a further two raiders tested the defences but these similarly evaded a patrolling Beaufighter.

The increased activity in Malta's skies during the past few days was but a foretaste of what was to follow — and the October blitz was to start in earnest with the coming of the dawn.

Chapter 10

THE LAST BLITZ

In pristine condition, Spitfire Vc BP983 T-B of 249 Squadron. *(NWMA)*

The new blitz opened at 0720 on Sunday morning, 11 October, when seven I/KG 54 Ju88s (escorted by 25 Macchis from 20° and 155° Gruppi led by Magg. Gino Callieri and by four Bf109s) approached the Island, a few bombers crossing the coast to release bombs on Hal Far and Benghaisa Point. Nineteen Spitfires were scrambled (eight/1435, seven/126 and four/229). The first two units intercepted 15-20 miles north-east of Grand Harbour, where the bombers were seen at 25,000 feet, with their escorts 500 feet higher. 1435 Squadron climbed to attack, Plt.Off. Walton (EP714/T) claiming damage to one Junkers, whilst Sgt. J.S. Hamilton (EP259/L) reported gaining strikes on a Messerschmitt.

126 Squadron then engaged the formation, which had descended to 18,000 feet, 11 miles north of Zonqor, and several successful encounters were reported by the RAF pilots. Plt.Off. Jim Stevenson (EP209) shot down a 151ª Squadriglia MC202 into the sea some 30 miles off Cape Scaramia, Sottoten. Urbano Barberini Colonna Sciarra baling out of his stricken aircraft. A second Macchi was claimed damaged by Sgt. Tiddy, whilst Flt.Sgt. Varey claimed a Bf109 probably shot down and a second damaged, and Sgt. Jack Yeatman another damaged. Meanwhile, Sgt. Marshall reported gaining strikes on one of the bombers, while fellow Canadian Flg.Off. Rod Smith (EP330) shot down Uffz

Hermann Müller's Ju88 (B3+YL):

> 'First Hun of Blitz. One of nine (*sic*) Ju88s at 18,000 feet N.E. of Grand Harbour. I gave two six-second bursts from 250 yards and the port engine and wing caught fire; a/c exploded and fell into sea. One of crew baled out and picked up — Uffz. Günther Grams.'

The Macchi pilots returned to submit claims for four Spitfires shot down, Mar. Pasquale Bartolucci and Serg. Dante Testera each reporting that their victims had gone into the sea. The latter shared a second with Ten. Gustavo Castellano, while Mar. Ennio Tarantola reported another shot down in flames. Apart from the loss of Sciarra, Serg.Magg. Angelo Cerri returned with his aircraft damaged in its port wing. One more Spitfire was claimed by the crew of Uffz. Woas' Ju88. The two British squadrons involved suffered no losses, although one Spitfire of each unit was damaged.

Immediately following this fight, HSL 128 was sent out to search for survivors from the Axis aircraft; only Uffz. Grams, the W/Op in the Ju88, was recovered having been sighted ten miles north of Grand Harbour by a 126 Squadron pilot. He had suffered a broken thigh bone. The remains of a German dinghy were also sighted but the three other crew members, one of whom had also been seen to bale out, were not found. The missing Italian fighter pilot had been observed by other members of his unit to be climbing into his dinghy, but subsequent searches by Regia Aeronautica rescue aircraft failed to locate him.

On Malta there was little damage from the opening attack — some buildings and motor transport had been hit at Hal Far but there were no casualties. Amongst those watching from the ground was 185 Squadron's Plt.Off. O'Brien, who was suffering from 'Malta Dog'; he recorded:

> 'The alert was sounded about 8 am this morning and we went up on the roof when the guns started firing. As we've been having only fighter sweeps for the past two months they've been firing only "pointers". However this morning we saw them fire "the real McCoy" and then we saw the bombs going down on Hal Far. It looked as if they had pranged it but we were quite surprised and relieved to find it undamaged. Looks as if Jerry has started his blitzing again — well here's hoping he has!'

Shortly after 1000 the next raid approached, comprising six Ju88s and an estimated 65 fighters. Twenty Spitfires were ordered off (eight/185, six/229, four/1435, two/126), the 229 Squadron flight making initial contact 15 miles north of Comino; but it became entangled with the top cover Messerschmitts, Flt.Lt. Roscoe claiming a probable, and Sgt. Miller one damaged. Minutes later the 185 Squadron aircraft engaged the same formation, which had now reached Luqa; they were similarly held at bay by the escort, and one Spitfire suffered slight damage. The 1435 Squadron quartet attacked next, Sqn.Ldr. Lovell claiming one damaged and Plt.Off. Walton (EP717/D) a probable; he reported:

> 'Red 1 (S/L Lovell) followed on two Me109s which turned to the right ahead. Another Me109 got on Red 1's tail and I turned on him. He started to climb, turning left. I followed giving him all my ammunition. White smoke poured out from him and he turned on his back and dived down.'

Finally, the 126 Squadron pair spotted the bombers just after they had released their bombs over Takali, but were engaged by four Bf109s orbiting over Gozo at

17,000 feet, which were providing withdrawal cover. The bombing caused negligible damage and no casualties.

The third attack of the day began soon after 1330 with the approach of seven more Ju88s — believed to have been from II/LG 1 — and the usual large escort. This time 28 Spitfires were scrambled (eight from each of 185, 229 and 1435 Squadrons, and four of 126 Squadron). The latter section made the initial contact ten miles north of the Island, where they were bounced by Bf109s as they prepared to attack the bombers. One Spitfire was damaged, and crash-landed, although the pilot survived unhurt.

Just before this raid developed Wg.Cdr. Donaldson had been practising dive-bombing, using Filfla as the target. Flying 249 Squadron's BR254/S, he was now able to join up with 229 Squadron Spitfires as they took-off, and led them in a head-on attack on the bombers, personally claiming one shot down; he then claimed strikes on a Messerschmitt, while Flt.Sgt. Ballantyne claimed to have shot down one of these. It is possible that one or both had hit an aircraft of I/JG 77, which crash-landed at Comiso on return due to combat damage. Meanwhile, Plt.Off. Nash claimed damage to what he believed was a Macchi.

As the bombers reached their target, releasing bombs on Takali and Rabat, Flt.Lt. Wally McLeod led the 1435 Squadron flight to engage the top cover Messerschmitts, as AA bursts appeared amidst the bomber formation. Three of the German fighters were claimed damaged in this initial attack by McLeod (BR236/E), Flt.Sgt. MacLennan (EP203/G) and Sgt. Knox-Williams (EN978/O). The Spitfires broke away, but re-engaged after the Junkers had dropped their bombs. They again encountered the escort, three more being claimed damaged by McLeod (whose own aircraft suffered some damage), MacLennan and Sgt. J.F. Jarrett; the latter's aircraft (EP727/N) also sustained damage in return, and he had to crash-land at Takali, suffering slight injuries. Sgt. Kebbell's EP138/K was also hit although he was able to land safely. Meanwhile, four pilots of 185 Squadron patrolling north of St Paul's Bay at 21,000 feet saw a single Ju88 and many fighters over Takali. The Spitfires dived on these and engaged Re2001s near Comino, Plt.Off. Bob Park claiming one damaged.

At Takali and Rabat some civilian casualties were sustained from the bombing, whilst two Spitfires were claimed by I/JG 77, one by Uffz. Schlick over Valetta, the other by Oblt. Freytag for his 69th victory; another was claimed by Lt. Schiess of Stab/JG 53.

The fourth raid proved a rather larger affair, 16 Ju88s taking part on this occasion, escorted by 17 bomb-carrying Re2001s of 22° Gruppo Aut. and 25 MC202s (20/155° Gruppo, five/20° Gruppo), led by Magg. Dulio Fanali. Their main target was the radar station at Salina Bay, but the bombs fell harmlessly in the Mellieha Ridge area. Just before 1700, as this raid was being plotted, 25 Spitfires were scrambled (nine/126, eight/185, eight/229), Wg.Cdr. Hanks (BR498/PP-H) leading the 126 Squadron formation to engage a large number of fighters north of Comino at 27,000 feet. Hanks attacked first, claiming a Bf109F, which he reported crashed into the sea off the Sicilian coast, and later claimed damage to a second as he headed back towards Malta. His victim was possibly Lt. Ewald Schumacher of 4/JG 53, who was killed. Sqn.Ldr. Wicks and Flg.Off. Wallace each claimed a Macchi damaged, while Flt.Lt. Bill Rolls (EN200/Q) claimed two Re2001s:

'I came up under one fighter and delivered one two-second burst, observing pieces fall away from the enemy aircraft. The Re (*Reggiane*) then went over on its back and went down. After being in a dogfight with several aircraft I picked out one for attack and dived from 24,000 feet to 4000 feet towards Sicily; when only 15-20 miles from the Sicilian coast I gave it a burst of two seconds and saw glycol stream from it.'

He later recalled that the pilot of the second Reggiane had baled out, adding:

'Then I saw him flip the aircraft over. He came out and eventually his parachute opened... I circled him as I saw him get in his dinghy... He waved to me as I circled him, but I did not wave back.'

Flt.Lt. Bill Rolls, Battle of Britain veteran and flight commander in 126 Squadron during the October Blitz. *(IWM)*

Two Bf109s then attacked Rolls' Spitfire, gaining a strike on his engine which started to falter. Although some 30 miles out to sea, by carefully nursing his aircraft and with a slice of good luck he was able to get back to Luqa and land safely. However, Sgt. David MacLean (BR183) was shot down into the sea and killed, while Sgt. Nigel Park's MK-M was attacked by a succession of fighters and was damaged. Unable to defend himself as his guns had jammed, Park nonetheless managed to get back to Takali.

Soon after this interception 229 Squadron attacked and split up a formation of 30 fighters some 14 miles north of Gozo, Flt.Lt. Glazebrook and Flt.Sgt. Ballantyne each claiming a Macchi shot down. The Controller (Grp.Capt. Miller) then called in 185 Squadron and Wg.Cdr. Thompson led them to attack fighters between St Paul's Bay and Comino, where three Bf109s were claimed shot down, one each by Thompson (EP122), Sgt. Les Gore (BR375) and Plt.Off. Len Reid (EP186), who reported:

'Attacked a large number of Me109s flying in formation at 20,000 feet. Dived down on them from 24,000 feet and upon breaking up under last two to port, giving one a long burst. It broke up and crashed into sea.'

The Italians reported meeting 25 Spitfires north of Gozo, where Mar. Remo

Wg.Cdr. John 'Tommy' Thompson in his Spitfire JM-T when Wing Leader at Hal Far. *(P.A.J. O'Brien)*

Zedda and Mar. Cesare Ferrazza of 360ª Squadriglia, and Serg. Ferdinando Zanardi of 351ª Squadriglia, each claimed one shot down, both of which were believed to have fallen in flames; others claimed four probables and no less than 21 damaged! Losses included Mar. Romano Pesavento's Reggiane of 369ª Squadriglia, who was shot down and killed after bombing (presumably the victim of Flt.Lt. Rolls), and Serg. Paolo Pedretti of 353ª Squadriglia, who force-landed his Macchi near Gerbini on return. Cap. Italo D'Amico's 151ª Squadriglia Macchi was slightly damaged. It seems that the Messerschmitts present included aircraft from the recently-arrived I/JG 27, Uffz. Walter Timmermann's 'White 7' crashing on Gozo with the death of the pilot — presumably a victim of 185 Squadron.

Soon after these late afternoon actions had ceased and with the onset of dusk, the Luftwaffe launched the strongest bomber formation of the day — but, inexplicably, without escort! Whether the Germans considered the raid would arrive in visibility far too deteriorated to allow the defending Spitfires to operate is unclear, but whatever the reason, the attack proved a costly mistake. Thirty Ju88s from I and III/KG 54 and III/KG 77 approached at 1745, attacking Hal Far and Luqa. Bombs fell at Tarxien and Qormi, where a number of homes were destroyed and civilian casualties suffered; at Luqa, Beaufighter X8078 was burnt out and a 39 Squadron Beaufort, DD993, was damaged beyond repair.

Five Spitfires of 229 Squadron and four of 1435 were airborne at the time of the attack, the latter quartet sighting 15 bombers when they were at 20,000 feet, 20 miles north of St Paul's Bay. Flt.Lt. McLeod (BS161/U) led the Spitfires in for a highly successful stern attack, the Canadian claiming two shot down before his own aircraft was hit by return fire, causing him to crash-land at Takali; two more were claimed by Flt.Sgt. MacLennan (EP717/D), while Sgt. Kebbell (AB264/Z) claimed a fifth; the fourth member of the flight, Sgt. R.J. Roe (AR470/Q), reported gaining hits on two more, while MacLennan damaged another; afterwards he reported:

> 'I climbed and delivered a stern attack, diving down and opening fire from about 100 yards. Return cross-fire was inaccurate. Strikes were observed on the fuselage, also white sheets of flame and pieces flew off, then aircraft caught fire. As I broke off, I observed three parachutes come out. I then attacked another Ju88 over the Island from very close range and saw strikes

on wing, also on fuselage. I broke upwards and lost him. Attacked another approximately south-east of the Island, this time attacking from astern and above.

'Flak and return fire was fairly intense and accurate, both of which hit me, I got strikes all over the fuselage and port engine cowling flew off. I broke away, attacked again but was out of ammunition. The Ju88's port engine caught fire and it spread rapidly and the Ju88 went down into sea, flaming.'

Half an hour later the 229 Squadron pilots saw nine Ju88s, about 15 miles north of Grand Harbour, coming south at between 12-15,000 feet: Wg.Cdr. Donaldson led them in a head-on attack, personally claiming one probably destroyed; two others were claimed damaged by Flt.Sgt. Ballantyne and Plt.Off. Nash, while Plt.Off. Parkinson (EP691/A) probably destroyed another:

'I could see the Ack-Ack going up and the search lights. Decided to wait off Zonqor Point to try and catch an odd bomber on the way home. I was lucky. I caught a glimpse of one at 10,000 feet, about 2000 feet below. Dived in to attack; was fired at by rear gunner who I put out of action with my first burst. Made about two more attacks and finally the Ju88 caught fire. Followed it down to about 1000 feet where I lost sight of it while trying to manoeuvre for another attack. It probably dived into the sea.'

Although two of the attacking Spitfires were claimed shot down by bombers' gunners, the raiders had indeed been hard hit during these interceptions; two failed to return and two more were seriously damaged. One of the latter was Uffz. Johann Schmitt's B3+JK of 2/KG 54, the pilot recalling:

'We approached the Island at 7000 metres and while heading towards the harbour area, my radio operator cried out "Fighters! Fighters!". Three Spitfires, flying at higher altitude, dived and opened fire on my aircraft, killing the observer (*Uffz. Hermann Schulte-Rebbelmund*) in his seat on my right, and wounding the radio operator. As the engines were running rough, I did an emergency dive, released the bombs and turned back towards Sicily with one of the engines on fire.

'When some 300 metres away from Catania airfield, the gunner (*Uffz. Walter Wutz*), who was uninjured, jumped out of the aircraft. I stopped the engine to prevent the fire from spreading and crash-landed in a field. Luckily I escaped with injuries to my head and legs only. Italian civilians took the radio operator and me out of the aircraft and we were driven to hospital at Catania; my radio operator (*Uffz. Franz Vanis*) died whilst being operated upon. I was the sole survivor.'

Luftwaffe losses in this raid were:

I/KG 54

1/KG 54	Ju88A B3+MH	(Oblt. Palliardi); aircraft damaged; observer (Uffz. Horst Lenz) killed
2/KG 54	Ju88A B3+DB	Lt. Hans Scheller and crew lost
2/KG 54	Ju88A B3+JK	Uffz. Johann Schmitt — pilot injured; crew killed
3/KG 54	Ju88A B3+DL	Lt. Günther Wittenberg and crew lost

III/KG 54

9/KG 54	Ju88A B3+CT	Fw. Wilhelm Ohrt killed; crashed at Comiso

following mid-air collision over the airfield with Ju88 (B3+GR, Lt. Wittkausky) which landed safely.

	III/KG 77	
Ju88A	40% damaged	

At the conclusion of the day's hard fighting the Governor, Lord Gort, sent a message of congratulation to AHQ, which read:

> 'Well done. The Spitfires have produced a fine opening score.'

To which the AOC responded:

> 'All ranks of RAF are grateful for your message of congratulations. Spitfires have won the toss and will keep up their hard hitting until the match is won.'

All was not yet over, however, for with darkness came the night bombers. Three approached the coast initially, although only one released bombs, one of which fell near Valetta. AA guns engaged and three patrolling Beaufighters attempted to intercept, but without success. Shortly after midnight, a lone raider flew over Luqa at 21,000 feet, releasing flares and delayed action bombs. This time Beaufighter V8219, crewed by Flg.Off. Shipard and Sgt. Oxbey, was vectored onto the intruder as it departed for Sicily. Shipard fired three bursts with cannon and machine-gun, commenting:

> 'One He111 probably destroyed. Rear gunner caught a packet.'

One of 89 Squadron's most successful night fighting teams to serve on Malta was the partnership of Flg.Off. Merv Shipard (right) and his radar operator, newly commissioned Plt.Off. Doug Oxby. *(M. Shipard via L. McAulay)*

He had almost certainly attacked a Ju88 of 7/KG 77 flown by Fw. Rudi Kühn; this bomber crashed into the sea off Ragusa following an attack by a night fighter and the crew, all wounded, baled out. The same Beaufighter team made three more patrols that night. On the last, some four hours later, they did, indeed intercept an He111 which was claimed shot down in flames into the sea, nine miles north of Malta. This may well have been 6N+HH of 7/KG 100.

Monday, 12 October

The day was again one of major raids and five were experienced between dawn and dusk. Operations were intense throughout the day and both sides sustained considerable casualties.

Raid 1

From 0620 two formations of seven and eight Ju88s respectively — believed to be from III/KG 54 — approached, escorted by about 25 fighters. Eight of 185 Squadron intercepted the first wave before reaching the Island, Capt. Kuhlmann (EP187) claiming one Bf109 destroyed and Sgt. Vinall (EP139) one Ju88 damaged.

Left: Sqn.Ldr. Mike Stephens, who flew with 249 and 229 Squadrons during the October fighting, claiming seven victories. *(M.M. Stephens)*. **Right:** Wg.Cdr. Arthur Donaldson DSO, DFC, and Bar, AFC, on recovery from his wounds. *(IWM)*

Four of 229 Squadron engaged the same wave, and one Ju88 was seen to jettison its bombs when attacked. Flt.Lt. Glazebrook claimed one Ju88 probable and Flt.Sgt. Ballantyne one Ju88 damaged. Despite interception, some bombers reached Takali and Luqa and bombed, and several aircraft were damaged at the latter airfield. Ten of 249 Squadron attacked as the bombers left the Luqa area, and Sqn.Ldr. Woods (AR466/R) claimed one Ju88 probable and a Bf109 damaged, while Sgt. Stead (EP199/K) damaged a second; he then reported shooting down another, which Sqn.Ldr. Stephens (AB377/E) had previously attacked. Stephens, meanwhile, had engaged yet another fighter, also claiming this shot down. Finding himself alone following the action, he attempted to join up with a second Spitfire but was bounced by a lone Bf109. The engine of his Spitfire seized after being hit:

> 'After my engine cut I had plenty of time to transmit for a fix before baling out. I spent a long time in the water floundering around, as the air bottle in my dinghy was flat, but eventually managed to climb aboard and finish inflating it with the bellows. I had a grand stand view of quite a number of combats during which I saw four aircraft shot down. I was quite confident throughout that I should be picked up by our Air/Sea Rescue service, which was quite magnificent. Eventually I was rescued by a seaplane tender (*ST 280*), since all the ASR boats were already out. There was quite a swell and I was as sick as a dog after I had been picked up.'

Meanwhile, surviving Ju88s of the second wave swept in to bomb Hal Far, where one Spitfire was burnt out. One more Spitfire and two Hurricanes were slightly damaged. This formation had already suffered heavily from attacks by six of 126 Squadron north of Grand Harbour — one Ju88 had been hit and had turned for Sicily, while four were claimed shot down. Escorting 51° Stormo Macchi pilots reported seeing many parachutes over the target, and one Italian pilot claimed a Spitfire damaged, but their attacks did not appear to deter the Spitfires from going for the bombers. However, Sqn.Ldr. Bryan Wicks — the CO in BR377 — failed to return, while Flt.Lt. Rolls (BR498/PP-H) claimed one Ju88, Sgt. Park (BR311/L) two more, and Flt.Sgt. Long yet another:

Park:

> 'Went into some Ju88s. Got two.'

Rolls:

> 'I saw one of the Ju88s I had fired at diving down and I put a final burst into it and it almost fell to pieces... I followed to 4000 feet and thought I saw two bale out. I did not see what happened to the others I had hit, I was too busy getting out of the mass of aircraft flying around... I saw Ju88s burning and going down all over the place.
>
> 'I had reached the outside of the melee when I saw a Spitfire going down. I flew up to it and saw it was my CO. He was injured by the looks of it. I watched him bale out and saw his chute open... After what seemed ages he hit the water and his Mae West was supporting him, but there was no sign of life. I circled him but got no response... I gave five fixes but was attacked by Re2001s from 2000 feet. I called up the HSL and directed it to the parachute in the waters.'

Long:

> 'I picked out the outside starboard Ju88 and gave him three quick bursts of cannon fire of about two seconds each, opening at approximately 250 yards and closing to almost zero yards. I saw flashes and the top engine cowling fell away. I went directly over the top of it and broke away to port... I saw the Ju88 was dropping behind the others and diving slightly.
>
> 'I turned towards it and saw the Ju88's dive increasing and flames from his starboard wing. Before I could get within range his starboard wing fell away and he went straight down into the sea.'

Four of 1435 Squadron then joined the fight. Sgt. Knox-Williams (EN978/O), Plt.Offs. Stewart and Lattimer shared one Ju88 damaged, but were then attacked by Bf109s. Two Spitfires were hit and damaged, including that flown by Knox-Williams; meanwhile, Plt.Off. Owen (BP873/Y) claimed one of the attackers damaged. 8 Staffel of KG 54 lost four aircraft during the raid.

HSL 128 was sent out to search for Sqn.Ldr. Wicks but instead located an empty German dinghy. Fifteen minutes later Uffz. Max Zettelmaier, a pilot of 8/KG 54, was found in the water. Then two more Luftwaffe airmen, Uffz. Otto Kobszinowski (W/Op in Zettelmaier's aircraft) and Uffz. Gerhard Lang (W/Op in Lt. Ingo Menny's Ju88) were picked up during the next 20 minutes, but Wicks was not found.

Raid 2

0910: seven Ju88s and 12 MC202s of 153° Gruppo crossed the coast. Bombs fell on Luqa — where some aircraft were damaged — and at Takali without causing damage. The formation had been intercepted on the way in — about 30 miles north of Gozo — by eight of 229 Squadron led by Wg.Cdr. Donaldson (AD529), who shared in the destruction of a Ju88 — believed to be an aircraft from III/KG 54 — with Plt.Off. Reynolds; the pilot was seen to bale out. A second bomber was claimed damaged by Flt.Lt. Glazebrook, while Plt.Off. Parkinson (X-O) recorded:

> 'The whole Wing intercepted a mixture of Ju88s and Breda 205s (*sic*) about halfway to Sicily. We dived into attack from beam astern. I picked out a Breda, fired, only my machine guns worked. Cannons were u/s. Came back to drome disgusted.'

He and Plt.Off. Nash each claimed one Italian bomber damaged, and Flt.Sgt. Ballantyne claimed an MC202 destroyed. Italian fighters claimed one Spitfire shot down and five damaged during two attacks.

Nine of 249 Squadron engaged the indirect escort comprising II/JG 53 Bf109Gs, stepped from 21,000 to 30,000 feet. Flg.Off. McElroy (AR488/S) reported:

> 'I got my sights on one and let him have it fair and square and then engaged another. But the Jerries had had enough and they broke off and headed for home.'

He was credited with shooting one down, but his own aircraft sustained much damage. Sgt. Stead (EP199/K) claimed one Bf109 damaged, Plt.Off. Sanderson (BP869/Z) another damaged and Flt.Sgt. Hiskens (EP135/Z) one probable. One of the bombers was claimed probably destroyed by Hiskens and Sgt. de l'Ara (EP338/A).

Four of 126 Squadron attacked the remaining bombers 15 miles north of Gozo, Plt.Off. Bazalgette and Flt.Sgt. Bush each claiming one damaged, whilst Flg.Off. Wallace reported:

> 'I picked out the leading Ju88 and gave him a two to three second burst of cannon and machine-gun fire on the nose, and then I had to break away. One minute later, Red Section also intercepted the enemy, but found only five Ju88s. Owing to this confirmation and the vulnerability of the nose of the Ju88 (containing the pilot and observer), I claim one Ju88 destroyed.'

Somewhat circumstantial!

Two of 126 Squadron then attacked the same formation north-west of Filfla after they had dropped their bombs. Sgt. Park (BR311/L) claimed one Ju88, while his leader, Flt.Lt. Rolls (BR498/PP-H), claimed two MC202s; he was credited with one and one probable:

> 'At first I thought they had not seen me because they made no attempt to take avoiding action, or so I thought and when we were in range to open fire they suddenly pulled up in the steepest climb I had ever seen an aircraft do from straight and level flight. I knew that when they had height they would half roll down on us which they did, but before they started to turn over for the roll, I did a steep turn and as they came down we were behind them.
>
> 'It was easy. We were nicely in position and I fired at one of a pair and it blew up. I followed the other one who had turned round by now and was trying to get on my tail.'

Just off Gozo, he made further attacks and reported gaining strikes on another. On return to Luqa he was advised that two Macchis had been reported down in the sea off Gozo, but no such losses were actually suffered.

1435 Squadron spotted the second wave — six Ju88s and close escort (a dozen MC202s of 153° Gruppo) with Bf109s as indirect escort, 15 miles north of Grand Harbour, and these were attacked at 20,000 feet just after they had crossed the coast. Flt.Sgt. MacLennan (EP203/G) claimed one Bf109 shot down, but Sgt. Kebbell (BR368/I) was shot down by another over St Julians's and baled out. He landed safely in Valetta with slight bruises, while his Spitfire fell into Spinola Bay.

Takali was attacked by the Ju88s, where eight of 185 Squadron intercepted, but were held at bay by Bf109s. Sgt. John Vinall (EP139) was shot down into the sea and killed; his body was later washed ashore at Dingli. Wg.Cdr. Thompson (EP122) claimed one Bf109 damaged, and Plt.Off. Len Reid (EP186) reported:

> 'Climbed to 15,000 feet over the island. Six 88s reported to starboard. Attacked and dived on one at 10,000 feet; observed strikes and left it smoking.'

Raid 3

Eight Ju88s approached at midday, covered by ten MC202s of 51° Stormo and 20 Bf109s. They were intercepted south of the Sicilian coast and the survivors turned back. Eight of 249 Squadron and seven of 229 Squadron initially attacked the formation — head-on — led by Wg.Cdr. Donaldson (AD529):

> 'I was leading 229 Squadron with 249 Squadron as high escort... I sighted eight Ju88s escorted by 30 plus fighters, 5 miles south of Gela, coming south... made a head-on attack on leading Ju88. No hits were observed. I broke up(wards) and did a stall turn and turned into a Ju88 which I singled out. I made an astern attack from 200 to 80 yards. Port engine smoked and burst into flames. Aircraft dived vertically and four parachutes opened out, and aircraft crashed into the sea in flames.
>
> 'I then saw an Me109F and got on his tail. I fired a two-second burst and he burst into flames and crashed vertically into the sea. No parachute. This was witnessed by P/O Sanderson. I was then attacked by an unseen aircraft and hit in rear fuselage by one bullet. A stray bullet from the Ju88 also hit my oil

cooler but the engine enabled me to regain base.

'It was the most spectacular sight I have ever seen. The whole sky was filled with enemy aircraft in severe trouble! I saw three flaming Ju88s and another three flaming Me109s, and counted no less than ten parachutes descending slowly, three of them from the Junkers I had shot down.'

Plt.Off. Colin Parkinson (EP691/A) added:

> 'Long before we were within range the bombers started to panic. I closed to within a few yards firing head-on; could see shell bursts all over him. Put front gunner out of action. Both engines were smoking. Went into a spiral dive. In the meantime I was attacked by three 109s. One overshot me so I turned into him and gave him a burst which hit the engine and pilot. The Me109 went down in a series of wide barrel rolls, burning and smoking. Crashed into sea.'

In all, the two squadrons claimed four bombers and four fighters shot down, two bombers and one fighter probably shot down, and two bombers and three fighters damaged in this engagement, all without loss. At that stage six of 1435 Squadron led by Flt.Lt. Wally McLeod joined the fight about 40 miles north of Grand Harbour, attacking seven Bf109s seen flying at 25,000 feet. McLeod describes the action:

> 'I closed to point blank range on the right Me109, breaking upwards after the attack. Strikes were observed, but he tried to get on the tail of my No 2 who was, at this time, in front of him. I attacked again, from astern, 200 yards, observing several explosions of cannon on the port wing root. The Me109 flicked over on to its back and then straightened out.
>
> 'I closed in again, firing from 250 yards, observing strikes behind the cockpit, and pieces fly off. The Me109 flicked on to its back and went straight down. I broke as his friends were attacking me and after a few turns to shake them off, saw a large green patch directly below, where an aircraft had gone in.
>
> 'The one I attacked was, I believe, the leader of the formation, as he rocked his wings after my section attacked and the other Me109s formated on him.'

Although the unit added two more damaged claims to McLeod's victory, Sgt. Knox-Williams EN978/O was shot down into the sea — possibly by Hpt. Michalski, Kommandeur of II/JG 53, who claimed his 47th victory during the day. As soon as it was safe to do so, Sub Lt. Elliott took-off in Hurricane BN110 to search for Knox-Williams. He sighted him about 12 miles north-east of Grand Harbour, and one of the HSLs was directed to pick him up.

Claims during this action by the RAF were:

229 Squadron

Wg.Cdr. Donaldson	one Ju88 and one Bf109
Flt.Lt. Glazebrook	one Ju88
Plt.Off. Parkinson	one Bf109, ½ Ju88 probable
Plt.Off. Nash	½ Ju88 probable
Flt.Sgt. Ballantyne	one Bf109 and one damaged

249 Squadron

Flg.Off. McElroy	(AR488/S)	one Ju88
Flt.Sgt. Hiskens	(EP135/Z)	one Ju88
Sqn.Ldr. Woods	(AR466/R)	one Bf109, one Ju88 damaged
Flt.Sgt. de l'Ara	(EP338/A)	one Ju88 probable, one damaged
Plt.Off. Sanderson	(EP340/M)	one Bf109 probable
Plt.Off. Yates	(EP199/K)	one Bf109 damaged
Plt.Off. Lowrey	(EP206/L)	one Ju88 damaged

1435 Squadron

Flt.Lt. McLeod	(AR420/Q)	one Bf109
Sgt. Knox-Williams	(EN978/O)	one Bf109 probable
Flt.Sgt. MacLennan	(EP203/G)	one Bf109 damaged
Sgt. Roe	(EP259/L)	one Bf109 damaged

It seems that several of the combats with fighters were, in fact, with MC202s rather than Bf109s. The 51° Stormo pilots reported meeting 30 Spitfires, claiming two shot down and three damaged; one was shared by Ten. Agostino Cigala Fulgosi and Ten. Plinio Sironi, the other by seven pilots, including Magg. Fanali. Fulgosi was slightly wounded in the left leg, while Mar. Remo Zedda's Macchi sustained a damaged propeller.

Raid 4

1446-1510: radar plots indicated up to 45 fighters departing Sicily. Ten MC202s of 51° Stormo, 13 of 153° Gruppo and eight Bf109s escorted 13 Re2001s of 22° Gruppo; the Italians reported being attacked by 15-20 Spitfires, ten miles from Malta, and claimed two probables and nine damaged. Twenty-three Spitfires were airborne (nine/126, six/229, eight/185), Wg.Cdr. Hanks (BR498/PP-H) leading four of 126 Squadron to engage many Messerschmitts at 23,000 feet:

> 'I saw 18 enemy aircraft (mostly Me109s) in three vics of six aircraft in close formation at 23,000 feet. I dived to attack the right-hand section and immediately saw four of six Me109s on our tails. I gave the order to break right and as I broke, went into a violent spin and recovered at 20,000 feet. I weaved around preparatory to climbing up and saw one Me109 at 15,000 feet going towards Sicily. I dived to attack, opening fire from 250 yards closing to point blank range, giving approximately four-second burst (port cannon u/s), and observed strikes on the fuselage and cockpit followed by thick smoke and flames. The enemy aircraft went through cloud shedding pieces and burning fiercely.'

Hanks' victim may have been Lt. Wilhelm Scheib's 'White 12' of 1/JG 77; the rest of the formation turned back. One Macchi of 51° Stormo was also hit by one cannon shell in the port wing during this engagement.

Raid 5

At about 1530 an estimated 57 aircraft approached, including five Ju88s. These were intercepted half way to Malta, initially by eight of 1435 Squadron led by Sqn.Ldr. Lovell (AR470/Q), who recalled:

> 'While closing in rapidly on the starboard bomber I fired a two-second burst

Wg.Cdr. Prosser Hanks' personal Spitfire, BR498 PP-H, in its blast pen at Luqa. *(NWMA)*

> from a range of 300 to 50 yards and large pieces flew off, and flames came from the starboard engine. I then broke away sharply. P/O Walton and F/Sgt. Scott witnessed the aircraft on fire.'

The unit's other claims were a Ju88 probably destroyed by Plt.Off. Walton (EP140/P) and Sgt. Hawkins (EP259/L); an Re2001 reported shot down and a second damaged by Flt.Sgt. Scott (EP203/G), who also claimed a Ju88 probable; Flt.Sgt. Ron Stevenson (EP209/B) failed to return, however.

Eight of 229 Squadron then arrived and attacked the escort, Sgt. Miller claiming what he thought was a Macchi, and a second as damaged, whilst strikes were reported on Messerschmitts by Sqn.Ldr. Baker and Flt.Lt. Roscoe; the latter recalled:

> 'After our initial attack on the escorting fighters, a 109 made a quarter attack on me from slightly above. The first thing I felt was a blow to my right shoulder — no pain at all. I immediately and instinctivly broke hard right, realizing what a fool I was to not have watched my tail properly. At the time the Spit was in good shape, just minus a few minor bits and pieces with the engine running fine. The 20mm shell passed through me, through the lower instrument panel and out, missing the petrol tank in front of me.
>
> 'As the 109 was still on my tail, and I felt disinclined to engage in a prolonged dogfight, I risked a mid-air collision by pulling the throttle all the way back kicking on a 'yard' of right rudder. The sudden deceleration of my aircraft forced the 109 to detour around me to port. It was at this point that we exchanged glances in passing. As the 109 went by I applied full power and left rudder, and from almost point-blank range and dead astern I let him have it. He went down immediately.
>
> 'I headed directly for Malta as I only now began to realize that I had been badly hit. The Spitfire was flying OK and the engine purring. About halfway to the Island I was bounced again by a lone 109. He must have been on his way back to Sicily, and below me as I had been watching my tail above and behind as best I could, but I never saw him until I was hit. Another wild break, a few turns and he was gone. Now, however, I was in real trouble. I had been hit in the engine and cooling system. All the engine instruments I had left went off the clock, smoke came pouring out of the engine room accompanied by strange clanking noises and lots of vibration.

'As I crossed the coast I decided to try and bale out. A crash-landing in the countryside was not recommended, too much rock and stone. I released the Sutton harness, rolled the Spit over on her back, and pushed the stick forward. Nothing, I didn't budge! I righted the aircraft and continued on towards Takali. The unproductive manoeuvre had cost me altitude and I was so low that I was doubtful I'd ever get there. But the good old reliable Merlin kept chugging along on a few cylinders, spewing smoke, keeping the badly mauled Spitfire barely flying.

'The last thing I remember was praying, cursing and hoping until at the edge of the field I hit the top of a blast pen — and arrived!'

Flt.Lt. Art Roscoe of 229 Squadron was shot down and severely wounded on 12 October 1942. *(A. Roscoe)*

Colin Parkinson noted matter-of-factly:

> 'Roscoe was shot down and crash-landed at Takali. His kite was on fire. He was shot through the shoulder and weak from loss of blood; was thrown out of aircraft unconscious. Broken shoulder, probably broken arm, cuts on face. Otherwise OK.'

Despite the danger of exploding ammunition and petrol tanks, two medical orderlies — LAC Cliff Jenkins and AC1 George Poppleton — ran to the burning wreckage of BR464 and succeeded in extricating the semi-conscious pilot, who was rushed to hospital there to recover from his wounds and injuries. His rescuers were each awarded the BEM for their actions.

During these engagements, the 51° Stormo Macchi pilots had claimed a further two victories against the ten Spitfires they reported meeting — one by Serg.Magg. Giovanni Gambari, the other shared by Magg. Fanali and Serg. Serafini; the unit suffered no loss. It is probable that Bf109s from I/JG 27 were again involved, this unit claiming four Spitfires shot down north of Malta during the day, one each by Hpt. Ludwig Franzisket (his 39th), Lt. von Lieres (26th), Oblt. Josef Schlang and Fw. Paul Becker. It would seem that two of the Messerschmitt claims related to shooting down Flt.Lt. Roscoe's Spitfire.

Conclusion of action at dusk on the 12th indicated a considerable victory for the defenders, who had claimed 27 confirmed victories (12 Ju88s, 11 Bf109s, three MC202s and one Re2001), plus 13 probables and damaged, for the loss of seven Spitfires (three pilots killed) and six more damaged. OKW had reported 15 victories for the Axis, but the Luftwaffe put it at seven in combat, plus four probables and seven damaged, plus two on the ground by Ju88s. Six individual Luftwaffe claims and four by the Italians have tentively been identified.

So far as losses are concerned, those suffered by the German bombers seem to have been close to claims; yet again, however, fighter losses fell far below the casualties believed to have been inflicted.

Luftwaffe fighter losses

4/JG 53	Bf109G-2	(White 10)	Gefr. Georg Gunkel FTR
5/JG 53	Bf109G-2	(Black 7)	Uffz. Paul Stroehla FTR
1/JG 77	Bf109G-2	(White 12)	Lt. Wilhelm Scheib FTR
Stab/JG 53	Bf109G-2	Lt. Wolfgang Dreifke injured in 100% crash due to engine trouble	

Luftwaffe bomber losses

I/KG 77			
1/KG 77	Ju88A	3Z+BH	Shot down by fighters — crash-landed; three of Uffz. Franz Jaeger's crew killed
2/KG 77	Ju88A	3Z+GK	Shot down by fighters; Uffz. Willi Schael's crew lost
III/KG 77			
7/KG 77	Ju88A		Shot down by fighters — crashed at Gerbini; Oblt. Albert Paetz (pilot) injured; observer killed; air gunner baled out over the sea and was lost
7/KG 77	Ju88A		Crash-landed Comiso, 80% damaged; Fw. Karl Fellhöfer (pilot) and two others wounded
9/KG 77	Ju88A		Crash-landed Comiso — Ofw. Kurt Wöhl (pilot) and one other killed; two others wounded
III/KG 54			
7/KG 54	Ju88A	M7+FR	Shot down by fighters; Lt. Fritz Oelmann's crew lost
8/KG 54	Ju88A	B3+KS	Shot down by fighters; Lt. Ingo Menny's crew lost apart from one survivor. Maj. Kurt Stein, Gruppenkommandeur, aboard as observer, also lost
8/KG 54	Ju88A	B3+FT	Shot down by fighters; Uffz. Max Zettelmaier's crew; two POWs

8/KG 54	Ju88A	M7+DR	Shot down by fighters; Obgfr. Rudolf Pauli's crew lost
8/KG 54	Ju88A	M7+GS	Crash-landed; three of Fw. Hans Hertz's crew wounded/injured; one died
9/KG 54	Ju88A	M7+FT	Crash-landed; Uffz. Ulrich Seuber's crew all wounded/injured
9/KG 54	Ju88A	B3+ES	Air gunner wounded
II/LG 1			
	Ju88A		Crash-landed near Cape Passero; crew unhurt
	Ju88A		15% damaged by fighters
		Regia Aeronautica	
51° Stormo	MC202		damaged; Ten. Cigala Fulgosi slightly wounded
	MC202		damaged
	MC202		damaged

Night raiders again appeared, two crossing the coast at 1945, although their bombs fell into the sea north of Grand Harbour and St Paul's Bay. A Beaufighter was up, but failed to make contact due to the AI being jammed by Axis interference. Four more bombers approached within the hour, three crossing the coast; bombs fell at Benghaisa Point and into the sea. Two Beaufighters were airborne this time, and although Flg.Off. Gray's AI was jammed for a second time, Flg.Off. Shipard in X7840 was vectored onto 6N+AH, a Heinkel of 5/KG 100; his operator (Flt.Sgt. Oxby) obtained a head-on contact, and the bomber was seen to jettison its bombs as Shipard opened fire. It went down at once, Ofw. Wilhelm Schuck's crew failing to survive.

At least eight more raiders passed over Malta between 2330 and 0315, but caused little damage. Three Beaufighters patrolled but no contacts were made, and a frustrated Flg.Off. Gray and his operator, Sgt. Mould, experienced further jamming problems. The final raid was made by a trio of 33° Gruppo BT Z1007bis, whose bombs fell in the Kalafrana area. Avoiding interception, the aircraft returned to Sicily but over their base at Castelvetrano, a Beaufighter crewed by Flt.Sgt. Pring and Wt.Off. Phillips was waiting. Sottoten. Adelmo Canini's bomber — which Pring thought to be a returning Heinkel — was shot down as it approached to land and fell in flames over its own airfield, with the loss of the entire crew.

Tuesday, 13 October

Tuesday continued as Monday had left off, with the first raid coming in early in the morning.

Raid 1

At 0635 eight Spitfires of 185 Squadron scrambled as a plot — comprising seven Ju88s of II/LG 1 under an umbrella of some 30 Messerschmitts — appeared on the radar screens. The Spitfires were bounced halfway between Malta and Sicily by five forward cover Bf109s, and two were slightly damaged. It is believed that

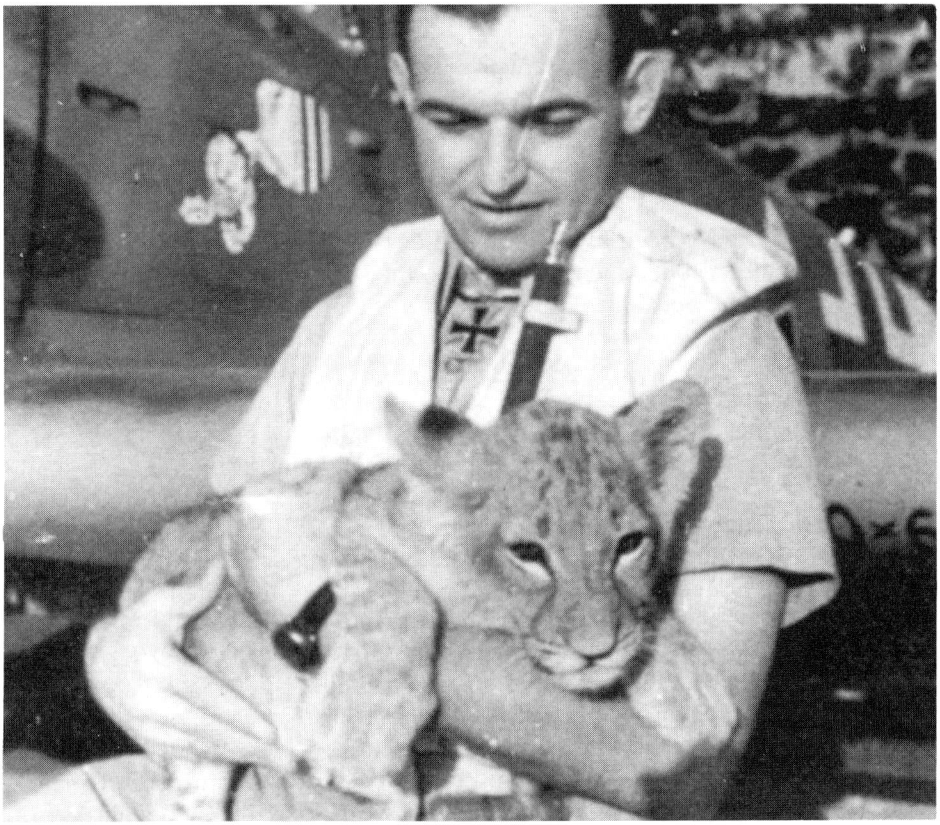

Hpt. Heinz Bär, Gruppenkommandeur of I/JG 77, with the unit mascot in front of his Bf109G-2. *(Authors' Collection)*

Hpt. Heinz Bär of I/JG 77 claimed both as shot down, one at 0658 five miles south of the Sicilian coast, and another 17 minutes later north of Marsaxlokk Bay. In return, Maj. Swales (EP685) and Plt.Off. Maynard (EP343) claimed two Messerschmitts damaged, and Flt.Lt. Charney (BR375) one probably shot down.

Eight of 249 Squadron intercepted the bombers three miles north of St Paul's Bay. While most were kept at bay by the escorts, Plt.Off. Beurling (BR173/D) successfully evaded and dived on the bombers:

> 'As Tiger Red 3 I attacked eight Ju88s, taking a straggler from slightly above to the right with a two-second burst of cannon and machine guns. Pieces came off the starboard wing. I broke away to port and down and saw one Me109 closing in from port above. I broke left and then turned onto him 50 yards line astern, and fired a one and a half second burst of cannon and machine guns. Enemy aircraft burst into flames.
>
> 'A second Me109 came down from starboard quarter above as enemy aircraft pulled out ahead at 250/300 yards. I gave him a four-second burst with machine guns, observed no strikes but pilot baled out. At this time I saw first enemy aircraft strike the sea.'

The remaining bombers reached Luqa, where two civilians were killed. As they left, Beurling was able to get on the tail of one, catching it about eight miles north of Zonqor:

> 'I attacked a Ju88 from starboard quarter above, 300 yards, with cannon and machine guns, two-second burst, and observed strikes on roots of starboard wing, and black, oily smoke poured out. I gave it the remainder of my ammunition into the fuselage. Enemy aircraft did a diving turn to the right, striking the sea.'

This appears to have been Fw. Anton Wilfer's L1+KP which was reported shot down over Valetta, but which crashed into the sea just off the coast. Other 249 Squadron claims were:

Plt.Off.Seed	(AR488/S)	one Ju88 probable, one Bf109 damaged
Flt.Lt. Hetherington	(AR466/R)	one Ju88 damaged
Plt.Off. Giddings	(EP338/A)	one Ju88 damaged
Sgt. Shewell	(EP135/Z)	one Ju88 damaged

Plt.Off. Al Yates crash-landed his damaged EN954 at Takali, the Spitfire skidding into the building housing the Squadron Armoury, but he was unhurt.

Eight of 1435 Squadron and two of 185 Squadron intercepted the remaining bombers as they headed north, catching them at 13,000 feet; Plt.Off. Walton (EP140/P) claimed one shot down, and Plt.Off. Pinney (BR591/R) reported damage to another, then probably destroyed a Bf109. Both 185 Squadron pilots claimed, Plt.Off. Maynard and Flt.Sgt. Mahar (EP696) each reporting strikes on bombers they attacked.

Two RNAS Hurricanes went out at 0730, searching for survivors; the Luftwaffe also sent one Do24 under fighter escort. Four of 126 Squadron were scrambled to patrol, but nothing was seen.

Raid 2

During mid-morning six Ju88s of III/KG 77 escorted by 28 MC202s of 153° Gruppo and 36 Bf109s of I/JG 77 approached. Sixteen Spitfires of 126 and 1435 Squadrons scrambled and attacked half way to Malta, led by Wg.Cdr. Hanks. 1435 Squadron went after the bombers, while 126 Squadron engaged the escort. Claims were:

1435 Squadron

Sgt. Hawkins	(EP259/L)	one Ju88
Wg.Cdr. Hanks	(BR498/PP-H)	one Ju88 damaged
Sgt. Sharpe	(EN968/H)	one Ju88 damaged
Flt.Sgt. Scott	(EP612/B)	one Bf109, two Ju88s damaged
Sgt. Eva	(EP714/T)	two Ju88s damaged, one Bf109 damaged

126 Squadron

Wt.Off. Farquharson		one Bf109 probable
Plt.Off. Thompson		one Bf109 damaged

The Italian fighter pilots reported seeing one Ju88 being shot down by Spitfires and two men bale out, one falling into the sea between Comino and Gozo. This was undoubtedly Lt. Gustav Duvenhörst's 3Z+ET of 9/KG 77, which failed to return. The Macchi pilots also claimed one Spitfire probably destroyed and two damaged, whilst Lt. Berres of I/JG 77 claimed another; one 126 Squadron aircraft was badly damaged, although the pilot landed safely. The surviving bombers raided Luqa, bombs falling on the Safi dispersal area. AA gunners claimed damage to one raider.

Following this attack seven of 249 Squadron were scrambled to meet the next incursion, but this turned out to be an ASR search for the missing KG77 crew. During a lull, an RNAS Hurricane also searched for the three Spitfire pilots lost the previous day, but while unidentified wreckage was seen 15 miles east of Grand Harbour, no dinghies were found.

Raid 3

Six Ju88s, 25 MC202s of 51° Stormo and 40 Bf109s of I/JG 77 approached early in the afternoon. Eight of 185 Squadron intercepted 25 miles north of Zonqor, but the top cover Messerschmitts shot down Sgt. Alex MacLeod (EP316) — who was killed — and damaged a second Spitfire, one of which was probably the 70th victim of Oblt. Freytag.

Eight of 229 Squadron then intercepted the bombers off Kalafrana Bay as they were flying north-west at 20,000 feet, and attacked before they could bomb: Sgt. Miller claimed one Ju88 damaged, while Sqn.Ldr. Baker and Flt.Sgt. Bye each claimed a Bf109 damaged. Two Spitfires were hit, Bye crash-landing BR293 at Takali; Plt.Off. Turner also crash-landed, both pilots surviving uninjured. Bombs fell near Luqa, causing little damage, although two soldiers were wounded.

Two of 185 Squadron and eight of 126 Squadron pursued as the bombers departed and engaged them between 12,000-17,000 feet, north of Zonqor. Maj. Swales (EP685) of 185 Squadron recorded:

> 'When we reached a position roughly south-west of Benghaisa Point, I led Blue 3 in on the bombers, making an attack from beam to line astern. I fired a two second burst and observed strikes on a Ju88's starboard engine and mainplane. First white smoke then black smoke started coming from this engine. I broke off and climbed away as the Me109s were attacking. The smoking Junkers was falling back from the formation, so I attacked it again, firing from beam to quarter. I observed two strikes on the right side of the fuselage. I broke again and attacked again, going from quarter to line astern, giving about a one and half second burst, but saw no results.'

Swales was credited with shooting down this aircraft, but it was also attacked by 126 Squadron's Flt.Sgt. Varey and seems almost certainly to have been the II/LG 1 machine which crash-landed at Comiso, badly damaged. Flg.Off. Rip Jones of 126 Squadron claimed an escorting Messerschmitt shot down and Wt.Off. Farquharson a probable, while Flg.Off. Rod Smith (EP573) was credited with an MC202, which he initially identified as a Bf109:

> 'Gave two three-second bursts of slight deflection and astern over Luqa. Hit him in engine and fuselage both times. Big flash of flame. Fell smoking into mouth of Sliema Bay.'

He had in fact shot down an aircraft of 352ª Squadriglia, flown by Mar. Maurizio Iannucci, who was killed. Other pilots in the Italian formation reported that the missing pilot had shot down a Spitfire before his demise, and they claimed damage to five more.

Raid 4

Seven Ju88s, 30 MC202s drawn equally from 51° Stormo and 153° Gruppo and 42 Bf109s approached, and were intercepted 20 miles north of Gozo by eight of 249 Squadron. Five of the escort were claimed shot down, two of the Messerschmitts being credited to Sqn.Ldr. Woods (AR466/R); a Macchi was claimed jointly by Sqn.Ldr. Stephens (EP338/A) and Flt.Sgt. de l'Ara (BR565/T), while Flt.Sgt. Hiskens (EP135/Z) claimed another, and Flg.Off. McElroy (EP340/M) reported shooting down an Re2001 (sic). The bombers were also attacked, Sgt. Stead (BP869) claiming one damaged, and Sqn.Ldr. Stephens one destroyed, as he later recalled:

> 'We saw Ju88s and escorting fighters among AA bursts, flying south near Filfla. I dived after them through AA and they turned east. I attacked one Ju88, hitting the starboard engine which began to smoke nicely, but then disengaged as the Macchis were after me. This Ju88 was seen from Qrendi Strip by the Squadron Adj to be diving from about 1000 feet with his starboard engine in flames.
>
> 'I then attacked two more Ju88s and was closing in on them when I was warned to break, which I immediately did and a 109 flashed by. I then attacked an MC202 observing strikes on starboard side of engine. P/O Nash of 229 Squadron watched these attacks and saw aircraft crash and the pilot bale out after I was forced to break away.'

Indeed, eight of 229 Squadron had joined the battle after bombs had fallen on Qrendi, Plt.Off. Nash claiming a Ju88 shot down and Wg.Cdr. Donaldson reporting strikes on a second. Donaldson's Spitfire (AD529) was then hit and damaged, and he was forced to crash-land at Takali. Flt.Sgt. Ballantyne, whose aircraft had been shot-up by a Bf109 did likewise, while Sgt. Miller's aircraft received a hole in one wing.

As the Axis force headed homewards eight of 1435 Squadron pursued them, Sgt. Whitmore (EN968/H) claiming a bomber about eight miles north of Zonqor Point, and Flt.Lt. Wally McLeod (BR236/E) a Macchi; two others were claimed damaged by Sgts. Philp (EP612/B) and Knox-Williams (EP714/T), while one of the unit's Spitfires was slightly damaged.

During this fight 153° Gruppo lost two Macchis, Cap. Enzo Radini and Ten. Felice Mezzetti both being reported missing. Radini had baled out badly burned, and was later picked up six miles south-east of Delimara by HSL 128. The Italians claimed two Spitfires as probables and seven others damaged. Apart from the claims of Bär and Berres already recorded, I/JG 77 made at least four more claims during the day, one each by Oblt. Geisshardt, Lt. Köhler, Uffz. Frank and Uffz. Hempfling.

Despite the substantial numbers of claims submitted during the day for Bf109s, none appear to have been recorded as lost or badly damaged — in stark contrast to the Italian fighters, where losses bear some reasonable resemblance to the number of claims made. With the close of hostilities for the daylight hours, Sqn.Ldr. Mike Stephens was posted to command 229 Squadron as Sqn.Ldr. Baker was unwell. Within this unit, Colin Parkinson was elevated to flight commander at the same time.

During the day, about 110 miles off Sapienza, a Baltimore of 69 Squadron had located two southbound merchant ships of 6-7000 tons each, escorted by six destroyers and two low-flying aircraft. Undaunted by the weight of the daylight

Left: Oblt. Siegfried Freytag of 1/JG 77 claimed his 70th victory on 13 October 1942. **Right:** Fw. Heinz Golinski of 3/JG 53 was shot down and killed on 16 October 1942 immediately after gaining his 47th victory. He probably fell to 1435 Squadron's Canadian flight commander, Flt.Lt. Wally McLeod.

attack on Malta, three Wellingtons from the same unit were prepared for a night strike, one armed with torpedoes, the others with bombs. As soon as darkness fell they went off but only one of the bombers succeeded in finding the convoy. An attack was made, but the bombs were seen to fall harmlessly into the sea between the ships.

Two hours before midnight ten raiders approached Malta, although only four crossed the coast and bombs fell ineffectively around Hal Far. As these raiders were coming in, Flg.Off. Crombie and Sgt. Moss headed for Catania in Beaufighter T5161, where they spotted three aircraft with lights on in the landing circuit. Despite his cannons jamming, Crombie claimed one shot down, which he identified as an He111. On their return, Flg.Off. Gray and Sgt. Mould were ordered to patrol near Gerbini in X8030, and here they saw the flarepath lit up. They saw a bomber land — again identified as a Heinkel — and shot it up on the ground. They remained on station for a further hour, when another such bomber was seen approaching. Diving on this, Gray opened fire just as it touched down, but intense light Flak prevented the result of their attack being observed.

Although attacks continued unabated for several more days, already the mini-blitz was effectively over, for the Axis Command had now accepted that it was failing in its intended aim. Feldmarschall Kesselring later revealed:

'The assault in the middle of October had not the success we hoped for; I broke it off on the third day because, especially in view of the expected landings (*the Anglo-American landings in French North-West Africa*), our losses were too high.

'The surprise had not come off, and neither had our bomber attacks against their air bases. Instead, the battle had to be fought against enemy fighters in the air and their bomb-proof shelters on the ground.'

Flt.Lt. Colin Parkinson, a successful Australian with 229 Squadron, who became a flight commander. *(P. Dixon via NWMA)*

Indeed during the last three days and nights, 16 Ju88s, two He111s and a Cant Z1007 had failed to return from raids on Malta, and nine further Ju88s had either crashed or crash-landed on return, or had otherwise sustained serious damage. Sixty-eight members of their highly-trained crews had been lost, a crippling rate of attrition to the fairly small forces involved, and which could not for long be sustained without major reinforcement.

The Spitfire pilots owed much of their current success to the skills of the various fighter controllers. Prominent amongst these were Grp.Capt. J.D. Miller, who had commanded a Hurricane squadron early in the war, Wg.Cdr. W.R. Farnes, Wg.Cdr. J.F. Griffiths (former Station Commander of Hal Far) and Sqn.Ldr. R.F.G. Lea, whilst Sqn.Ldr. J.G. Chamberlain and Flt.Lt. Crawford normally controlled noctural operations. They played no small part in the successes achieved. Plt.Off. Philip Dixon of 229 Squadron recalled:

> 'It was remarkable how on many occasions the controllers were able to interpret their plots to such a high degree that they could differentiate between an ordinary fighter formation and a fighter-bomber formation. The information that we were given by the controllers was, of course, invaluable and very reassuring, both from the point of knowing where your enemy was coming from, and what he was using in the way of aircraft; further it was also heartening to know that you would probably be plotted if you had to force-land in the sea.'

Wednesday, 14 October

Raid 1

At least eight Ju88s with a high escort of some 40 fighters stepped up to 28,000 feet approached soon after 0700, the majority crossing the coast. Twenty-nine Spitfires (nine/126, eight/185, four/229 and eight/249) were airborne, and at 0720 the 229 Squadron section engaged the bombers at 18,000 feet just north of Grand Harbour.

Wg.Cdr. Donaldson (BR130/S) led a head-on attack and saw strikes on one bomber, but was attacked from astern by a Bf109. Bullets smashed the cockpit and engine, splinters hitting him in the face, body, arms and legs; two fingers of his shattered left hand were severed, and blood was splashed all around the cockpit. Reluctant to bale out — as the sight of all the blood led him to believe he might pass out and drown — he managed to control his Spitfire in a glide back to Takali with his good hand, and to effect a highly creditable belly-landing. Even before the aircraft stopped, a fire tender was alongside and he was dragged free and rushed to hospital. From here he despatched a message to Takali, requesting that somebody look into the cockpit of his aircraft to see if they could find his wedding ring!

249 Squadron then engaged over Grand Harbour, carrying out a stern attack as the bombers headed for Takali, a probable and two damaged being claimed. Meanwhile, 185 Squadron became involved with the escorts north of St Paul's Bay, three Messerschmitts being claimed damaged while one Spitfire suffered damage in return:

249 Squadron

Sqn.Ldr. Woods	(AR466/R)	one Ju88 probable
Flt.Sgt. de l'Ara	(BR565/T)	two Ju88s damaged

Plt.Off. Sanderson (AR488/S) noted:

> 'Large party of Me109s kept us very busy. Hottest fight yet. Hit in wing.'

185 Squadron

Wg.Cdr. Thompson	(EP122)	one Bf109 damaged
Plt.Off.Reid	(EP521)	one Bf109 damaged
Plt.Off. O'Brien	(BR375/A)	one Bf109 damaged

'Paddy' O'Brien recorded:

> 'We sighted them above St Paul's Bay and turned for them. Some silly buggers in Spits jumped us from the sun and we all broke up. Sods! I went with the W/C and we joined the dogfight around the bombers which were going out. I climbed up-sun to try and pounce something and entered a dogfight about 20 miles out.
>
> 'A 109 pooped at me and I broke. Then I saw some tracer over my port wing and I broke again. Quite a flap! Had a duel with a 109. He attacked and I turned into him. He squirted head on and hit me with one shot. I turned after him and spun firing off my guns by mistake. Got real scared as I saw the tracer (my own) and felt the kite shuddering like hell (3000 feet only).
>
> 'I squirted at him more in anger than in hope, and missed (range 400 yards

Plt.Off. 'Paddy' O'Brien of 185 Squadron with his GL-A at Hal Far. *(P.A.J. O'Brien)*

plus). He made another attack on me and I got around onto his tail and squirted again (4-5 seconds). I saw strikes on his fuselage around the cockpit and some thick black smoke. He didn't stay to play any more but headed off home. I did not follow. I felt bloody relieved to see him go. This was my first really hectic dogfight and I was rather shaken! A near thing. Came back with four bullet holes.'

Bombs fell on Takali, doing little damage but temporarily rendering the airfield unserviceable; there were two civilian casualties. Eight of 126 Squadron pursued the departing raiders, but top cover Messerschmitts attacked them. Flt.Lt. Rolls (BR498/PP-H) dived the formation to port and attacked the bombers head-on:

'I saw my cannon shells hit the leading aircraft; its port engine blew up and the aircraft went down. The others had also opened up at the other bombers and although it was only a couple of seconds firing, several of the bombers had been hit and the formation broke up in chaos. We pulled up above the formation and attacked the fighters which were in a turn and broken formation.

'I soon ran out of ammunition and went down on the deck to see what had happened and I saw a Spitfire hit the water and a couple of Ju88s were floating half submerged. I could see above me two other Ju88s smoking and coming down.'

Sgt. Nigel Park (MK-A), having shot down another bomber, added:

'I was jumped by two Me109s. I turned quickly to avoid their attack which was on my rear starboard quarter and after a couple of turns, got onto an Me109's tail. I closed in without opening fire to about 100 yards when he changed his turn and I gave him a three-second burst from dead astern. He went into a steep dive and went straight into the sea. I circled the spot but there was no sign of any crew.'

Two more bombers were claimed damaged by Flt.Sgt. Bush and Sgt. Hendry, while Flg.Off. Wallace reported shooting down a Bf109. Rolls had seen a Spitfire (AB489, believed flown by Flt.Sgt. Long) striking the sea, probably shot down by Lt. Berres of I/JG 77, who claimed one north-east of Valetta during this raid. Two other Spitfires were damaged. The downed pilot was spotted in his dinghy — 12 miles out from Kalafrana — by one of the searching RNAS Hurricane pilots, Sub Lt. Pratt, and was soon picked up.

Raid 2

Shortly after 1000 seven Ju88s of I/KG 54 approached, escorted by 45 Bf109s of I and II/JG 53, I/JG 77 and I/JG 27, and 29 MC202s of 51° Stormo, led by Ten. Col. Remondino. Eight of 1435 Squadron initially intercepted 20 miles north of Grand Harbour, three Ju88s being claimed damaged by Flt.Lt. Wally McLeod (BR236/E), Flt.Sgt. MacLennan and Sgt. Whitmore (EP322/A). McLeod then pursued the raiders across the Island and claimed one shot down after it had released its bombs.

Five of the Macchi pilots reported engaging five Spitfires, two being claimed shot down by Serg.Magg. Giuseppe Mirrione and Mar. Tarantola, while three more were claimed damaged. Sgt. Bill Knox-Williams (AR470/O) and Sgt. Ronnie Roe (EP203/G) were both lost and were never found — they may have fallen to the Italians. Another Spitfire was damaged, and only Sgt. Whitmore was able to claim strikes on a Messerschmitt in return. The Italians reported that one bomber was seriously damaged in the initial attack, and was escorted back to Sicily by two of their number.

Wg. Cdr. Thompson (EP122) led eight of 185 Squadron to intercept the bombers over Kalafrana, but could not prevent an attack on Hal Far and Safi, though little damage resulted. Thompson noted:

> 'I dived vertically on two 88s and attacked the starboard one. I opened fire with my cannons and machine guns at 200 yards closing to 50 yards, and saw cannon strikes which caused the enemy aircraft to burst into flames in the middle of the fuselage. Confirmed by ground observation from Luqa.'

This was probably Lt. Hasso Holst's B3+AA of I/KG 54 which was reported shot down into the sea off Malta, and which may also have been the aircraft claimed by McLeod of 1435 Squadron. Three others were claimed damaged by Plt.Off. Cheek (EP696), Capt. Kuhlmann (EP712) and Sgt. Tarbuck (AB532), Cheek also claiming a probable. Two more KG54 Ju88s crash-landed on return to Sicily, one 3 Staffel aircraft coming down at Pachino, near Syracuse, while M7+JT of 9 Staffel bellied-in near Pozzalo, Fw. Georg Thiel being killed.

The Spitfires pursued the attackers out to sea and engaged the escorts in a series of dogfights, during which one Spitfire was slightly damaged. In return Kuhlmann claimed a Bf109 shot down and a second damaged, while Tarbuck claimed another damaged. Plt.Off. Len Reid (EP722) was also successful:

> 'Climbed to 20,000 feet out from the island — again broken up by Me109s... Saw three Me109s diving on Spits below, gave the last one a good burst from quarter astern and it hit the sea. After breaking away got in a burst at Ju88 from below. Observed strikes under belly.'

Eight of 229 Squadron also intercepted the raiders as Hal Far was attacked. Sgt. Brough claimed one Ju88 shot down in a head-on attack, and another was damaged jointly by Flt.Lt. Glazebrook and Plt.Off. Nash, while strikes on two others were reported by Sgt. Lundy. The escorting fighters attacked and Nash's EN979 was shot down into the sea. The Texan got out with a fractured upper jaw

Survivors of the October Blitz — 'A' Flight of 185 Squadron seen late in October 1942. Front from left: Flg.Off. 'Paddy' O'Brien; Wg.Cdr. Thompson; Capt. Keith Kuhlmann; Plt.Off. Len Reid, Rear row from left: Sgt. 'Red' Walker; Sgt. Jim Tarbuck; Plt.Off. Len Cheek; Sgt. Jim Gunstone. *(P.A.J. O'Brien)*

and other facial injuries, and was soon picked up by HSL 128. Plt.Off. Philip Dixon's AR471 was also badly shot-up but he got down safely, although the aircraft was deemed to be irreparable:

> 'We had gone in after some 88s and I had seen two 109s attacking us from above and to the left. I turned into them as they started firing and they veered off. By this time I was on my own so bearing in mind the adage never fly straight, I was gently weaving, watching out on each side and to the rear: my attention was caught by the sight of one of the 88s in the bomber force being set on fire, and I must have relaxed my attention for a moment. The next thing I knew there was a bang from the rear of the aircraft, a smell of cordite and I felt a sting above my flying boot.'

On its return to Takali, Dixon's aircraft was found to have holes in each tailplane, obviously caused by cannon shells, one of which had then exploded in the fuselage whilst the other passed straight through, also holing the starboard wing; the control cables and trimming-gear wires were severely damaged.

One of the Bf109s was claimed probably destroyed by Sgt. Francis, whilst several claims were made in return by the Axis pilots, Lt. von Lieres and Fw. Becker of I/JG 27 each recording victories north of Valetta; Mar. Tarantola, Serg. Luigi Santuccio and Serg. Serafini all claimed Spitfires shot down over the Island, although Tarantola's Macchi suffered serious damage and he was subsequently obliged to bale out near the Sicilian coast.

Raid 3

Twenty-two Spitfires were up to meet the next raid at 1310, when at least seven Ju88s approached, accompanied by the usual strong escort. Seven 126 Squadron aircraft intercepted initially at 20,000 feet, 15 miles north-east of Zonqor; while Flt.Sgt. Bush was able to claim damage to one of the bombers, Sgt. Nigel Park (MK-A) found that his guns had apparently frozen, and he was obliged to dive away to a lower altitude. Here, the warmer air seemed to resolve the problem and he was able to attack a Bf109 at 10,000 feet, which he claimed to have shot down — the second time he had claimed three in one day.

Meanwhile, Sqn.Ldr. Stephens led eight 229 Squadron Spitfires to engage the raiders before they could reach the coast. Attacking at 17,000 feet, they reported encountering Italian fighters, Stephens claiming an Re2001 shot down, and Flt.Lt. Parkinson (X-V) a Macchi. Stephens went on to claim damage to a Ju88, but two of the Spitfires sustained minor damage during this engagement.

249 Squadron flight commanders; Flt.Lts. John McElroy (left) and Eric Hetherington at Takali. *(NWMA)*

At about the same time seven more Spitfires from 249 Squadron were led into the attack just south of Zonqor by Flt.Lt. Hetherington (AR466/R), who personally claimed one bomber probably destroyed, while two more were damaged by Plt.Off. Giddings (EP388/A) and Sgt. Bryden (BR254/E) before Messerschmitts from I and II/JG 53 intervened. In the ensuing series of dogfights, Giddings claimed one shot down, Sgt. Wynn (BR373/N) one probable and Plt.Off. Williams (EP340/M) two damaged. It was Plt.Off. Beurling (BR173/D) who once again stole the show however, though this time at a cost:

> 'As the action opened I spotted five fighters pulling up high, as if to get ready to dive on "Giddy" (*Giddings*) and "Hether" (*Hetherington*). I called into the mike and we soared up to 24,000 feet, just as the five Me's got there. The "Schmitts" promptly peeled off and dived... and away we went, right among the bombers... We each picked a Ju. I took the one on the starboard rear position of the V and gave him a two-second burst from starboard. He burst into flames and went headlong toward the sea.
>
> 'As I nabbed the bomber, "Hether" came whipping just under me, diving away from eight Me's on his tail. I went down in a hurry with them, right past my flamer, and lashed into the leading Hun, just as he was going to let "Hether" have it. As I passed the burning bomber the rear gunner took a shot at me, peppering the port side of my fuselage and the port wing. I picked up about 30 bullet holes, I guess. Explosive bullets were snapping through

the cockpit and one nicked the left middle finger of my throttle hand. Another stabbed my left forearm.

'I'd picked up two Me's on my own tail and still had "Hether" to worry about... I took a long shot from about 450 yards from above and to port. I got the bastard in the engine and he dove for the sea, streaming smoke and shedding pieces... one of the Me's on my tail riddled my port wing like a sieve and put a couple of bullets through the perspex hood, right over my head, while the other "Schmitt" blasted my starboard wing full of holes.

'A call for help came over the RT... My own position was right above Kalafrana, so I rolled over and had a look down, to see a swell melee going on below. I went down vertically, hitting almost 600 mph in my riddled crate and at 14,000 feet pulled up under a Messerschmitt, just as he was all set to pot "Willie the Kid" (*Williams*). I gave the Hun a two-second burst and blew his whole left wing off at the root. He flicked over, and that was that.

'Just as I shot Willie's pal down, another Me nailed me from behind. He got me right in the belly of the Spit. A chunk of cannon shell smashed into my right heel. Another went between my left arm and body, nicking me in the elbow and ribs. Shrapnel spattered into my left leg. The controls were blasted to bits... I threw the hood away and tried to get out, but the spin was forcing me back into the seat... The engine was streaming flame by this time, but somehow I managed to wriggle my way out of the cockpit and out onto the port wing, from which I could bale into the inside of the spin... At about 1000 feet I managed to slip off.'

Plt.Off. Bob Seed had seen Beurling's predicament and followed him down; now, as Seed circled the wounded pilot who was struggling to get into his dinghy, he called Control and requested that a rescue launch be sent out immediately. Within 20 minutes HSL 128 had arrived, and Flt.Sgt. George Head — the coxswain — was subsequently able to record another side to Beurling's rebellious and obstinate character:

'Immediately on gaining the deck of the launch he was very, very concerned with the fact that he could not find his bible. This small volume was quickly located and handed to him whereupon he became more composed, and explained that it had been given to him by his mother and under no circumstances would he fly without it. In the launch on the way back to base he told the crew that he would be flying again that afternoon but it was obvious to the crew that this would not be so. Beurling had a nasty dull blue closed wound in the heel which indicated a possible bullet lodged deep in the flesh.'

A piece of cannon shell had indeed penetrated Beurling's right heel, and this effectively ended his participation in Malta's defence. Although not the easiest of men to live and fly alongside, the Canadian's outward fearlessness and undeniable success had proved an inspiration to many of the other pilots, and he was hero-worshipped by many of the ground personnel. His three final claims had raised his personal total to 27 and one shared, all but one whilst flying with 249 Squadron from the Island.

One Messerschmitt of I/JG 53 was damaged in this action, the wounded Ofw. Josef Ederer crash-landing his 2 Staffel machine at San Pietro, where another I Gruppe aircraft was damaged when it was rammed by a landing Macchi. Three

II Gruppe aircraft were reported to have been damaged in landing accidents at Comiso.

Raid 4

A successful early interception of the afternoon raid caused the majority of the eight Ju88s to jettison their bombs before reaching the coast. However, the Spitfire pilots overclaimed wildly on this occasion. As the bombers approached, escorted by no fewer than 44 Bf109s and 31 MC202s — the latter drawn from 51° Stormo and 153° Gruppo — ten 126 Squadron pilots, with Wg.Cdr. Hanks leading, were the first to attack shortly after 1630. No less than five of the bombers were initially claimed shot down, including one by Flg.Off. Rod Smith (BR471):

> 'We made a head-on attack and slightly to the right, then turned right and attacked from the stern. Many Me109s were also observed in the vicinity. I flew across and attacked the left-hand, rear Ju88 from astern at 250 yards range. I gave two six-second bursts and the port engine and wing caught fire. The Ju88 dived to the port and I saw it crash into the sea.'

(In his logbook, Smith claims this aircraft only as damaged, so it would appear that the claim was subsequently downgraded.)

A second was claimed by Plt.Off. Bill Thompson:

> 'I chose the port Ju88 which was in a left-hand turn jettisoning its bombs. I came underneath him and chased him out to sea. He was doing half steep turns to left and right. I was able to draw in to 100 feet underneath him and delivered a starboard quarter attack, giving him a full one and a half second burst, and observed strikes on the underside of the fuselage, wing root and starboard engine; he rolled onto his back in a clockwise half roll downwards, and I was about to follow him when I hit his slipstream and blacked out. When I recovered control I saw the Ju88 going straight down into the sea.'

Another was claimed by Sgt. Bill Marshall:

> 'With a steep turn to port I found myself within 50 yards of a Ju88 which was turning to port. Closing to 30 yards, I opened fire, seeing strikes on the port engine and cockpit and large pieces fly off the cockpit and engine. I saw the Ju88 dive into the sea just short of Grand Harbour. As I turned away I saw an Me109 hit the sea off St Paul's Bay.'

Two more Ju88s were credited to Sgt. Phil Charron and Flt.Sgt. Varey, the latter claiming a second as probably destroyed and a third damaged; Sgt. Tiddy also claimed a probable. In all, it was believed that damage — at the least — had been inflicted on all eight bombers, with five, possibly seven, shot down!

As 126 Squadron was attacking from astern in this manner, seven more Spitfires from 229 Squadron struck the same formation head-on over Mosta. Sgt. Ron Miller claimed one bomber shot down and one damaged, while others were claimed damaged by Sqn.Ldr. Stephens and Plt.Off. Johnson. The scattered survivors now turned out to sea, at which point they were pursued and engaged by a further eight aircraft from 185 Squadron, Flt.Sgt. Mahar claiming yet another bomber shot down north of Grand Harbour, and Sgt. Guy one damaged. AA gunners also engaged as the force reached the coast, and were credited with sharing in the destruction of one Ju88.

Wg.Cdr. Peter Prosser Hanks, Luqa Wing Leader; on his right can be seen Sqn.Ldr. Blair White who took command of 185 Squadron at the end of October 1942. *(NWMA)*

Several of the Spitfire pilots had become engaged with the escorts, Wt.Off. Farquharson of 126 Squadron claiming a Messerschmitt shot down, while Sgt. Guy claimed one probably destroyed and Wg.Cdr. Hanks (BR498/PP-H) a Macchi damaged.

In a final analysis of the claims, squadron Intelligence Officers concurred that seven Ju88s had been shot down and an eighth probably so. The attacking bomber force had been estimated at ten strong and it was thought that although two had escaped, both had suffered damage.

On this occasion no Spitfires were lost, although one Macchi pilot (Mar. Cesare Ferrazza) reported shooting down one which he believed had crashed into Salina Bay. The aircraft attacked may well have been a returning 69 Squadron photo-reconnaissance Spitfire (BP910); Flg.Off. Gubb, a recently-arrived pilot, reported being attacked by an MC202 but evaded this by throwing his aircraft into a steep turn, a tactic which allowed him to escape without suffering any damage.

During the day Luftwaffe fighter pilots claimed 19 victories, 12 of them credited to pilots of I/JG 77 — including that already recorded by Lt. Berres — two by Oblt. Freytag (his 71st and 72nd) and one by Hpt. Bär, while two had been claimed by I/JG 27 and five by JG 53, one of these the first claim for Lt. Wilhelm Esser of 5/JG 53. Six more claims were made by the Italians, and another by the crew of a Ju88 (probably Beurling). Actual casualties had been five Spitfires shot down, one crash-landed, and seven more damaged.

Two Beaufighters patrolled to the north of the Island shortly before midnight when ten bombers approached, all but one turning back before reaching the coast. The lone intruder dropped its bombs in the Mosta area, causing little damage and no casualties, but managed to evade the night fighters. AA gunners put up a fierce barrage, shrapnel damaging Flg.Off. Crombie's Beaufighter!

About three hours later another lone raider crossed the coast, and bombs fell on Takali and in the Ghain Tuffieha area. Flg.Off. Shipard and Flt.Sgt. Oxby were airborne in V8219, and located the bomber — an He111 of II/KG 100 — at 12,500 feet ten miles east of Malta. Diving from 15,000 feet, Shipard lowered the Beaufighter's undercarriage to reduce his closing speed and avoid overshooting, and fired from astern. 6N+EH blew up and crashed into the sea, showering its victor with burning debris. Maj. Horst Röbling, the Gruppenkommandeur, and his crew of three were all killed.

Thursday, 15 October

Raid 1

Six Ju88s swept in to bomb Luqa during the morning. Although 28 Spitfires were airborne, they failed to intercept the raiders prior to their arrival over the Island. Sqn.Ldr. Lovell led eight of 1435 Squadron to engage over Kalafrana as the bombers were pulling out of their dives. Plt.Off. Walton (EP140/P) claimed one shot down, while Flt.Sgt. Scott (BP873/Y) claimed an escorting Messerschmitt.

Eight more Spitfires from 249 Squadron, which had been ordered to patrol north of Zonqor Point, were attacked by Bf109s before the bombers were sighted. These were fended off however, Sgt. Wynn (BR373/N) claiming one shot down. The bombers were then seen coming away from Kalafrana, Plt.Off. Moody (EP135/Z) claiming one, Plt.Off. Williams (EP340/M) reporting a probable, and Plt.Off. Giddings (BP966/V) a damaged.

As the raiders fled out to sea they were pursued by four 229 Squadron aircraft, which forced them down to 3000 feet. Five miles out, a number of 1435 Squadron Spitfires joined the chase. Sqn.Ldr. Stephens kept after two of the Junkers for 35 minutes, finally managing to claim one shot down, but he was then attacked by six Bf109s; although able to claim one of these also, his own aircraft (BR562) was hit and badly damaged. He escaped at low level, passing through the Grand Harbour barrage to crash-land at Takali. One of the 229 Squadron pilots, Sgt. Noel Pashen (X-V), claimed damage to a fighter identified as an Re2001.

Flt.Lt. Rip Jones led eight 126 Squadron Spitfires to join the fray, but these were bounced by a number of Bf109s north of Zonqor and four of the Spitfires were hit. Wt.Off. Gordon Farquharson baled out of BR176 into the sea with a splinter wound in his heel, while Flt.Sgt. Varey recorded:

> 'I was very lucky in a dogfight right over the Island at 25,000 feet. Shells hit my aircraft and stopped my engine. Fortunately, I was able to glide down and land alright, only to find two cannon shells embedded in the armour-plating behind my seat.'

The other two Spitfires suffered only minor damage. Before he was hit, Varey had been able to claim one of the attackers shot down, as did Flt.Lt. Jones. It seems likely that both had actually fired at the same aircraft — one of II/JG 53's new Bf109G-2s flown by none other than the Gruppenkommandeur, Hpt. Michalski, who was shot down off Marsaxlokk Bay; two other Messerschmitts were claimed damaged by Plt.Off. Thompson and Sgt. Charron. HSL 128 was soon out to rescue Farquharson from the sea, whilst a Do24 from Syracuse picked up Michalski.

Raid 2

Soon after 1000 eight Ju88s and eight Jabo Bf109s — probably from the newly-formed I/Schlachtgeschwader 2 — were escorted towards the Island by 25 MC202s of 51° Stormo, possibly with more Bf109s acting as high cover. The presence of intercepting Spitfires caused the bombers to turn back before reaching Malta, whilst the Jabo were engaged out at sea by seven Spitfires of 249 Squadron and eight of 1435 Squadron. Several were seen to jettison their bombs as they crossed the coast, one or two of these falling at Mellieha where one civilian was killed and two injured.

Before the Spitfires could attack they were bounced by other Messerschmitts. Flt.Sgt. 'Red' Bryden of 249 Squadron had his leg broken by a cannon shell which penetrated the cockpit of BR254/E; in great pain, he managed to bale out into the sea. Plt.Off. Moody's EP135/Z was also hit, although he managed to return to Takali where he crash-landed. Both pilots may have been victims of I/JG 77's Oblt. Geisshardt, who claimed two Spitfires shot down on this day. Sgt. Wynn (BR373/N) was able to claim strikes on one of the attackers. The 1435 Squadron pilots engaged six Messerschmitts 20 miles north of Comiso but no claims were made, although Plt.Off. Lattimer's BR591/R was damaged. It seems likely that one of the fighter-bombers was hit during these encounters, for such an aircraft crash-landed at Comiso on return. Subsequently HSL 128 was again sent out, the crew finding Bryden clinging to his partially inflated dinghy an hour after he had been shot down.

Meanwhile, Wg.Cdr. Hanks (BR498/PP-H) had led four 126 Squadron Spitfires to the north of Zonqor, where two Bf109s were seen at 4000 feet, with a third at sea level. These were chased northwards for 15 miles or so, Flt.Lt. Rod Smith going after the one flying at the lower level. As he closed on this another Messerschmitt attacked him from behind, but was apparently shot down in its turn by Wg.Cdr. Hanks; this was probably Fw. Gerhard Stockmann of 2/JG 53, who was wounded and came down in the sea south of Sicily. Flt.Sgt. Varey reported srikes on another while Smith was able to nurse his damaged Spitfire (BR471) back towards Malta where he baled out opposite the Sliema Point Battery; a launch promptly put out and picked him up.

Raid 3

Midday found the Island's radar screens alive with 'blips' as about 50 fighters approached from the north. Patrolling Spitfire pilots reported that they appeared to be escorting ASR aircraft; nonetheless eight 185 Squadron aircraft engaged four aircraft — identified as MC202s — found orbiting at 4000 feet about 35 miles east of Malta, with a pair of Bf109s circling above. Maj. Swales ordered his section to attack the Macchis, two being claimed shot down by Flt.Lt. Charney (AB532) and Flt.Sgt. Mahar (EP722), while two others were damaged by Swales (EP122) and Sgt. Garvey (EP521).

At higher level eight Spitfires of 229 Squadron provided cover but while several Messerschmitts were seen at the same height, no contact was made. However, at this point another aircraft dived on them and opened fire. Flt.Lt. Glazebrook immediately fired back, gaining strikes on the engine of what he took to be the attacker, before realising it was a Spitfire — none other than that flown by Wg.Cdr. Thompson! The latter recalled a "hell of a bang" as four Spitfires flew over the top of his formation, and his engine began to smoke; he had to crash-land at Hal Far, and on inspection one shell was found to have hit his engine, while a second had entered the fuselage just behind the cockpit!

Flt.Lt. Eddie Glazebrook of 229 Squadron who accidentally shot down Wg.Cdr. Thompson, the Hal Far Wing Leader, on 17 October 1942. *(P. Dixon via NWMA)*

The eight 1435 Squadron aircraft were still airborne as an estimated 30 more fighters, about seven of them carrying bombs, then swept in. Seven more 249 Squadron aircraft and eight from 126 Squadron were scrambled to meet this new threat, the former unit meeting the Jabo five miles north of St Paul's Bay at 20,000 feet. Four were seen to jettison their bombs immediately and turn away, but the remaining three were harried as they attempted to attack Takali, all their missiles falling wide of the target; no claims were submitted however. The other two units both engaged in indecisive encounters, but an attempted attack on five more Jabo seen over Filfla was thwarted by further misidentification, as Sgt. Nigel Park recorded:

'Were just going in on 109 bombers when we were jumped by four Spitfires.'

Raid 5

Six Ju88s were back mid-afternoon, escorted by 30 Messerschmitts of I/JG 53 and 31 Macchis of 51° Stormo and 153° Gruppo. Sqn.Ldr. Woods led 249 Squadron to attack head-on off Kalafrana, as the formation approached from north-east of Zonqor, when once again bombs were seen to be jettisoned into the sea. Claims were:

Flg.Off. McElroy	(BR373/N)	one Ju88, one Ju88 damaged
Plt.Off. Sanderson	(EP448/F)	one Ju88 probable
Plt.Off. Yates	(AR488/S)	one Ju88 probable
Sgt. Stead	(EP338/A)	
Sqn.Ldr.Woods	(AR466/R)	one Ju88 damaged
Flt.Sgt. Carter	(BP869/Z)	one Ju88 damaged

Flt.Lt. John McElroy, a Canadian member of 249 Squadron who was awarded a DFC. In 1948 he flew for the Israelis and shot down at least one RAF Spitfire! *(Daddo-Langlois Collection)*

The escorting Messerschmitts attempted to come to the rescue, but one was claimed shot down by Woods and a second probably so by Stead. However, McElroy's aircraft was badly shot-up and he was slightly wounded in one leg by shrapnel. With the aircraft diving out of control and the cockpit full of smoke, he decided it was time to jump but then discovered that the hood was jammed shut.

Struggling to regain control, he managed to level out and reach Takali, where he crash-landed. Of the action, Sqn.Ldr. Woods reported:

> 'I sighted 10 (*sic*) Ju88s with about 30 fighters escort at about 19,000 feet, flying south. We turned towards them and I led my section down in a quarter head-on attack. I opened fire at about 400 yards, firing cannon and machine guns. I saw strikes on the leader and his No.2 who was echeloned to port of him. I turned to starboard and came underneath another Ju88 and opened fire at about 100 yards and saw strikes on the belly. I received no return fire but was forced to break off and down as an Me109 was attacking me from the stern.
>
> 'I found myself in the middle of about 20 Me109s, one of which broke to port and up, right in front of me. I opened fire at about 100 yards, gave it a two-second burst and saw no strikes but the engine started to smoke and then burst into flames. At this point I stalled and spun down.
>
> 'I came out of my spin behind and below the bombers and climbed up after them, four of which jettisoned their bombs into the sea. Two Ju88s were smoking badly from both engines and four Spitfires were attacking the remainder from all angles, and as I climbed up I saw strikes on practically all the bombers. The bombers started to dive down and I dived down on one who was struggling, and opened fire at about 200 yards; both cannons jammed but I exhausted my machine guns, closing to point blank range and silencing the rear gunner.'

A second Spitfire was shot down however, and Flt.Sgt. Edwin Hiskens (EP340/M) was lost; the 21 year-old Australian almost certainly fell as the 30th victim of Uffz. Marian Mazurek of 1/JG 53, who reported:

> 'Before the Ju88s were able to drop bombs, they were attacked by 6-8 Spitfires. I followed them immediately and fired my MG from a far distance. I managed to place myself in a good shooting position behind a Spitfire. As I came closer I started to fire with all my weapons out of a left turning. After that the plane tumbled down without control and hit the sea 15 kilometres from La Valetta and sank.'

This action, recorded as the 344th victory for 1 Staffel and the 1214th for I Gruppe, was witnessed and confirmed by Mazurek's 'Rottenflieger' (wingman), Uffz. Heinz Loch.

Other units now engaged, 185 Squadron encountering three escorted Ju88s diving from 13,000 feet over Delimara, Plt.Off. Len Cheek (EP696) claiming one shot down; Sgt. Tarbuck (AB532) claimed damage to a Bf109, while two of the unit's Spitfires suffered slight damage in return. Eight 229 Squadron Spitfires also intercepted bombers over Kalafrana, one being claimed damaged by Flt.Lt. Glazebrook, while Sgt. Francis reported strikes on a Macchi. Leading the Italian fighters, Magg. Luigi Borgogno claimed one Spitfire shot down and a second probably so, his pilots reporting strikes on seven more.

From this attack one Ju88 of 3/KG 77 — 3Z+CL flown by Uffz. Herbert Gross — failed to return, probably shot down by McElroy of 249 Squadron and Cheek of 185 Squadron. A 4 Staffel aircraft returned to Comiso badly shot-up by Spitfires and crash-landed. During this raid AA gunners claimed to have hit one Junkers which was then believed to have been shot down by a Spitfire. This may have been L1+DN of 5/LG 1, which was reported damaged by Flak over Luqa;

Sqn.Ldr. Eric 'Timber' Woods, commanding officer of 249 Squadron, ruefully inspects combat damage to the propeller of his Spitfire. *(Authors' Collection)*

one of the gunners, Obgfr. Robert Becker, baled out, landing in the grounds of a technical school near Birkirkara and becoming prisoner.

As the raid faded away three Spitfires lifted off from Luqa for the short hop to Hal Far. In EP318 was Air Vice-Marshal Park, literally on a flying visit, accompanied by Wg.Cdr. Thompson and Plt.Off. Len Reid.

Darkness brought almost continuous alarms throughout the night but few raiders actually crossed the coast, and the bombs dropped caused little damage. AA guns engaged but no interceptions were made, although an aircraft was reported by one night fighter crew to crash north of Cape Passero at about 0300. No Axis loss was recorded however, and this may well have been a transit aircraft.

Friday, 16 October

Raid 1

Eight Ju88s with the usual large escort approached early in the morning, 23 Spitfires from 126, 185 and 1435 Squadrons intercepting about 15 miles north of

Zonqor. A number of bombers were seen to jettison their bombs into the sea as the Spitfires closed in. One claim was submitted by Flt.Lt. Bill Rolls (BR498/PP-H) of 126 Squadron who, of his 16th victory, recorded:

> 'The bombers started a shallow dive and I gave order for head-on attack. I chose the leader of the formation and gave a three-second burst and hit the starboard engine. He immediately started to smoke and he did a steep turn to port, glycol coming from the engine. The rest followed him and jettisoned bombs in St Paul's Bay. The last I saw of the leader he was going down very steeply. The whole action was seen from the shore and F/O Shipard and F/O Gray and several others who were on Balluta Buildings saw this Ju88 crash into the sea, about 10 miles east of Grand Harbour.'

Other claims were:

	185 Squadron	
Capt. Kuhlmann	(EP187)	one Ju88 probable
Plt.Off. Reid	(EP343)	one Ju88 probable
Plt.Off. O'Brien	(EP523)	one Ju88 damaged
	1435 Squadron	
Sgt. Harrison	(EP140)	one Ju88 damaged

One or two bombers did get through though, bombs falling on Sliema and St Julian's causing some damage to property and injuring 13 civilians. On this occasion the escorting Messerschmitts attacked with great determination and inflicted quite severe casualties. Flg.Off. Ed Wallace (BP992), a 6′6″ tall Canadian who had been serving with 126 Squadron since the early summer, and Sgt. Bill Wilson (EP718/S) of 1435 Squadron were both shot down and killed, while Sgt. Whitmore of 1435 Squadron was slightly injured when he crash-landed his damaged aircraft (BP873/Y) at Hal Far; Flt.Sgt. MacLennan's BP860/X was also hit and he too crash-landed on return.

One of these Spitfires fell to the sharp-shooting Uffz. Mazurek of 1/JG 53, witnessed by Lt. Hans Roehrig of 3 Staffel, some ten miles north of Valetta; recorded Mazurek:

> 'After the Ju88s bombed they were attacked by eight Spitfires. Coming out of the sun and doing a left turn I attacked one Spitfire. The plane lost parts of the motor and cockpit. It went down in a black smoke trail which then disappeared as the Spitfire went vertically down into the sea.'

In return for these losses, Sgt. Nigel Park (MK-J) of 126 Squadron claimed one of the Messerschmitts shot down:

> 'We were at about 12,000 feet, 12 miles north of Grand Harbour, when my No.2 was jumped by three Me109s. I called to him to break, which he did, and as the leading Me109 turned towards me I took a two-second burst at him from 250 yards to 150 yards. I saw strikes, one on his motor and one on wing root. I turned into the other two which made off. Capt. Kuhlmann of 185 Squadron followed the one I had damaged and saw it go into the sea, 12 miles north of Zonqor. He later phoned through confirmation.' (*It is possible that Kuhlmann actually saw one of the missing Spitfires crash*).

Sgt. Nigel 'Tiger' Park (left), a successful New Zealander with 126 Squadron, enjoys a mug of 'char' with Flg.Off. Eddie Wallace, a Canadian. Wallace was lost on 16 October 1942, and Park nine days later. *(IWM)*

Other claims were:

1435 Squadron

Plt.Off. Owen	(EP332)	one Bf109 probable, one Bf109 damaged
Flt.Lt. McLeod	(EP541)	one Bf109 damaged

185 Squadron

Sgt. Gore	(BR109)	one Bf109 damaged
Sgt. Tarbuck	(AB532)	one Bf109 damaged

During this raid a Spitfire was again claimed shot down by the crew of Uffz. Woas' 2/KG 54 Ju88.

A Bf109 of I/Sch1G 2 crash-landed at Comiso on return and may have been involved in one of these combats. Throughout the engagement 249 Squadron patrolled up sun, 20 miles north-east of Zonqor, in order to intercept any Axis high cover but saw nothing. Flt.Lt. Crockett and his crew carried out searches in ST338, going six miles south-west of Delimara Point where an aircraft had been seen to fall; only wreckage could be found however.

Raid 2

There was a short lull before raiders again approached, but these proved to be only three Bf109s, which crossed the coast presumably on reconnaissance. Eight Spitfires of 229 Squadron patrolled between Kalafrana and Zonqor, but saw nothing. A further Axis formation then followed, but appeared to be making a sea search and did not approach the Island.

Hardly had this plot disappeared from the radar screens than about 60 aircraft were detected coming in from the north, which included at least seven Ju88s, preceded by a large fighter sweep. Six 1435 Squadron Spitfires engaged first, encountering nine Bf109s some ten miles north of Zonqor but without decisive results. The bombers meanwhile penetrated the defensive screen and attempted to dive-bomb Hal Far, being intercepted near Kalafrana by eight aircraft of 229 Squadron. However, only Flt.Sgt. Ballantyne and Plt.Off. Reynolds were able to report strikes on two of the Ju88s, before a swarm of Messerschmitts fell upon them. Sgt. Francis claimed one of these shot down, but Sgt. Lundy's BP989 was hard hit and the pilot baled out into the sea opposite the Blue Grotto; he was soon rescued by Maltese fishermen, having suffered only minor injuries.

Plt.Off. Reynolds' Spitfire (BP860) was also badly shot-up by the Messerschmitts, but he managed to carry out a creditable landing; his misfortune had been witnessed by Plt.Off. Dixon, who recalled:

> 'I saw a Spitfire approaching; he rocked his wings and he drew alongside me at about 200 yards off to my left... As I looked further left and craned round hard behind, I saw a 109 coming up behind him. I shouted "Break!" into my microphone but as I did so a whole series of flashes appeared around the cockpit of the other aircraft; I had never seen anything like it before. The propeller stopped and the aircraft literally seemed to stand still or stop in the air. It fell away and began to spiral down.
>
> 'I, by this time, had pulled up and left to try and get over and round back onto the tail of the 109, but he pushed his nose down and got away. I saw the other aircraft spiralling down below me and gave a "Mayday" signal in case he went into the sea. I then lost sight of him and continued to weave my way round the sky and gradually made my way back to Takali where I landed. I was quite convinced that whoever had been in the aircraft had either been killed or crashed into the sea.
>
> 'It transpired that the other pilot was Hugh Reynolds. The flashes I had seen had not, in fact, gone through the cockpit but into the back of the engine, fortunately missing the petrol tanks. However, he managed to spiral down and made a forced landing without an engine, at Luqa, completely unhurt. We celebrated that evening with orange juice!'

Reynolds was probably the latest victim of Uffz. Mazurek of 1/JG 53, who claimed his second victory of the morning at about this time, while flying 'White 11':

> 'After dropping bombs the Ju88s were attacked by 8-10 Spitfires. After the attack I noticed two other Spitfires above the fighter group. I managed to go up into the sun unnoticed and placed myself behind the enemy. From a close distance I fired with all my weapons at the left plane. It went down showing a dark smoke trail, turning again and again and burned when it hit the sea 3 km south of Hal Far.'

From the details of Mazurek's and Dixon's accounts, it seems very likely that the former had indeed attacked Reynolds' aircraft, but after watching it spiral down had then seen Lundy's stricken machine hit the sea.

Meanwhile six more Spitfires, this time from 249 Squadron, had attacked the bombers as they were going into their dives over Hal Far. Flt.Sgt. de l'Ara (BR565/T) claimed one shot down, Sqn.Ldr. Woods (AR466/R) and Flg.Off. McElroy (EP132/F) each claiming one damaged. Bf109s then attacked, inflicting damage to Woods' aircraft, although Plt.Off. Lowery (EP201/V-F) claimed one of these shot down. Another Messerschmitt — possibly that flown by Fw. Golinski of 3/JG 53 — was seen to shoot down Flt.Sgt. Peter Carter's EP338/A, which fell into the sea with the loss of the pilot. Heinz Golinski ('Yellow 1'), victor of 46 combats in Russia, had been seen by other JG 53 pilots to shoot down one Spitfire. He was then attacked and killed by another, his aircraft falling into the sea. His victor was probably Flt.Lt. Wally McLeod, who spotted a lone Messerschmitt at 15,000 feet over Luqa as 1435 Squadron trickled back to their airfield. He reported shooting this down three miles north of Hal Far, but was then attacked by another, which caused serious damage to his EP541/Q, and he crash-landed at Luqa on return. A posthumous award of the Ritterkreuz to Golinski was announced during the following month.

Three Hurricanes flown by RNAS pilots made searches for the various missing pilots and covered an area six miles north of Grand Harbour and one mile west of Filfla. All that was spotted, however, were Spitfires of 229 Squadron orbiting oil patches off Kalafrana, where Sgt. Lundy was waiting to be picked up. As Sub Lt. Pratt approached in his Hurricane (BE110), a Spitfire broke away from the formation and attacked his aircraft. His starboard wing was damaged before he was able to evade, and before his assailant realised his mistake.

Raid 3

At about 1300 35 Bf109s, including a number of Jabo, undertook a hit-and-run attack which saw bombs fall harmlessly near Mqabba and Mellieha. Patrolling Spitfires of 126 and 185 Squadrons sighted six Messerschmitts near Comino, but were unable to intercept.

Raid 4

The bombers were back three hours later. Seven Ju88s of KG 77 accompanied by 42 MC202s and 40 Bf109s, including at least six Jabo, crossed the coast in six waves. The Spitfires were late in making contact on this occasion and consequently Luqa was bombed, Beaufighter X8081 of 89 Squadron being damaged beyond repair, and a second suffering from blast effects. Takali was attacked by the Jabo, the airfield being rendered temporarily unserviceable and two civilians were injured.

Seven 1435 Squadron Spitfires then attacked the Ju88s and 20 escorting fighters — incorrectly identified as Re2001s — two miles north of St Paul's Bay. Three bombers were claimed damaged by Plt.Off. Walton (EP140/P), Sgts. Eva and Fuller, one Spitfire being hit in return.

Flt.Lt. Hetherington led eight 249 Squadron aircraft in a head-on attack just after the bombers had crossed the coast on their way home. Flg.Off. McElroy was bounced by a Bf109 before he could engage the bombers and he was again obliged to crash-land at Takali, while Plt.Off. Sanderson (EP132/F) claimed a Messerschmitt shot down; in his logbook he recorded:

> 'Had a scrap with some 109s. Got a squirt at one. One Me109F destroyed.'

Other claims were:

Plt.Off. Williams	(AR488/S)	one Ju88
Sgt. Wynn	(EP177/E)	one Ju88 probable
Flt.Lt. Hetherington	(BR565/T)	one Ju88 damaged
Plt.Off. Budd	(EP459/X-P)	one Ju88 damaged

Seven more Spitfires from 229 Squadron also attacked head-on at about the same time, Sgt. Ron Miller gaining strikes on two, one of which he considered probably destroyed, but his own aircraft was considerably damaged by return fire. Flt.Lt. Parkinson claimed damage to another:

> 'We made head-on attacks on about seven Ju88s. I very nearly collided with one on my right side. Saw strikes along wings, both engines and cockpit. Starboard engine cowling came off.'

Maintenance in the open — Spitfire EP436 V-S of 1435 Squadron undergoing an engine service in its pen. *(C.G. Jefford)*

Whilst this attack was under way ten more Spitfires from 126 Squadron swept in from the flanks, catching the bombers over the Island. Sgt. Charron claimed one shot down, while two others were reported damaged by Sgts. Tiddy and Roberts. Assessment of the three-squadron attack reached the conclusion that, of the eight Ju88s believed to have comprised the formation (there were actually seven), two had been shot down, two probably so, and the remaining four all damaged. In fact Fw. Rolf Pester's 3Z+HH failed to return, a second Junkers crash-landed on arrival at Comiso after suffering severe damage, and was destroyed, while a third returned with one engine shot-out (possibly by Parkinson). Witnessing the raid from Takali, LAC Bill Metcalf recorded:

> 'We were just sitting down to tea when a big Ju88 came diving over the billet with a Spit firing at him. He hit the drink about ½ mile out.'

Some of the 126 Squadron pilots became engaged with the escorts, Sgt. Marshall claiming a Bf109 probably shot down, while Sgt. Tiddy claimed one damaged and Flt.Lt. Rip Jones a Macchi damaged. The Italian pilots reported engaging 12-15 Spitfires and claimed four shot down, Serg. Dante Testera being credited with two of these, the third being shared by Ten. Bonfiglio and Cap. Giovanni Franchini. The fourth was credited jointly to Ten. D'Amico, Ten. Beniamino Spadaro and Mar. Ferruccio Vignoli.

As the attackers departed Flt.Lt. Crockett again set out in ST338 as two men had been sighted in the sea five miles south-east of Delimara Point. Both were located and picked up. They were Uffz. Anton Wallenberger (observer) and Uffz. Otmar Wehner (gunner), who had baled out of Pester's blazing I/KG 77 bomber; both were suffering from burns.

Luftwaffe fighter pilots were credited with eight Spitfires shot down during the day, one of them by Lt. Remmer of I/JG 27. With the four Regia Aeronautica claims and that made by the KG 54 Ju88 crew, this gave a total of 13 for the day against an actual loss of four Spitfires shot down, five crash-landed and three damaged.

The defenders had noticed that Axis tactics had changed during the day. Many formations were now attacking on a wide front and approaching from several directions simultaneously. While several raids had thereby got through, they had failed to inflict much damage on the airfields. As daylight faded, Air Vice-Marshal Park despatched a message to the Spitfire squadrons:

> 'Grand work fighter boys. Your magnificent fighting in the last five days is being watched not only in Malta but by the RAF on other fronts as well, as well as by our Russian allies. Although heavily outnumbered last May, the Malta Spitfires came out on top and I am confident that you will win the second Battle of Malta. Some of the enemy bomber squadrons have already shown they cannot take it. Keep it up and in a few days the other German bombers will throw in the sponge.
>
> 'Replacement pilots and Spitfires are on the way but there is still some stiff fighting to finish the job. Good luck to you and good shooting.'

The AOC did not forget the hard-working maintenance personnel either and sent congratulations to them, but added:

> 'Your part in the present Battle for Malta greatly appreciated but serviceability of Spitfires continues to fall. You can and must get it up again. Where you have worked hard you must work harder and faster. Give the fighter boys Spitfires and they will drive the Hun out of the sky.'

Saturday, 17 October

The early hours of Saturday saw the welcome arrival from Gibraltar of a Hudson carrying a number of replacement fighter pilots, as promised by Park. Daylight brought a resumption of the attacks after a fairly quiet night.

Raid 1

At 0645 some 50 raiders were plotted approaching, including seven Ju88s, the formation flying at between 18,000 and 31,000 feet. Five Spitfires of 249 Squadron at 22,000 feet encountered two Bf109s which were orbiting ten miles east of Zonqor, 3000 feet higher. The British fighters climbed to attack but the Messerschmitts maintained their height advantage and avoided combat. Meanwhile, Sqn.Ldr. Lovell led four 1435 Squadron aircraft in a head-on attack on the four leading bombers, 12 miles north-east of Zonqor; Lovell (EP612/B) gained strikes on one, but did not make a claim as it was then attacked and shot down by another Spitfire. The victor was from 126 Squadron, eight more Spitfires from this unit being led by Wg.Cdr. Hanks (BR498/PP-H) in an attack which resulted in claims for three bombers shot down. Hanks, Plt.Offs. Thompson and Stevenson claimed one apiece, while Flt.Sgt. Varey and Sgt. Yeatman claimed two more probably destroyed; Varey also claimed one of the escorting Messerschmitts shot down, but one Spitfire suffered slight damage.

As Flt.Lt. Rip Jones closed rapidly on the leading Junkers, he was either hit by return fire or misjudged his speed, for EP341 collided head-on with Maj. Heinrich Paepcke's 3Z+AC; the Kommandeur of II/KG 77 and Jones were both killed instantly, though three other members of the German crew were seen to

Left: Sqn.Ldr. Tony Lovell, 1435 Squadron's outstanding commanding officer. **Right:** Flg.Off. Charles Crombie, the successful Australian night intruder pilot with 89 Squadron. *(Authors' Collection)*

bale out. Returning bomber crews reported that the Spitfire pilot appeared to have deliberately rammed the bomber, KG 77 subsequently being credited with a 'ramming' victory as the Spitfire had been seen to go down.

Two further bombers were shot down during 126 Squadron's attack, both machines of 6 Staffel. Lt. Franz Koechling and his crew were lost in 3Z+KP, although the other crew survived their crash and were later rescued by Axis ASR craft. The remaining bombers jettisoned their bombs in the sea and turned back. The raiders were spotted leaving by eight patrolling 185 Squadron pilots, who were at 21,000 feet over Kalafrana Bay, but they were too far off to intercept. However, three fighters identified as MC202s were seen below and one of these was claimed damaged by Flt.Lt. Charney (AB532).

During the remainder of the morning Spitfire patrols were constantly alerted as small groups of aircraft appeared over the sea south of Sicily, but all were apparently seeking the missing crews and none approached or were engaged.

Raid 2

The midday raid was precisely ten minutes late, but when it did appear it comprised eight Ju88s of II/LG 1, nine Jabo Bf109s from I/JG 27 and a heavy escort provided by 41 Bf109s and 31 MC202s, the latter from 51° Stormo and 153° Gruppo. Again the Spitfires were late getting off and by the time they had intercepted, the attacking force had reached the Comino-St Paul's Bay area. Despite vigorous attempts to intercept all the diverse groups of attackers, the Jabo could not be prevented from raiding Takali. Little damage was sustained however, although bombs also fell on Mosta where three civilians were killed and six injured. The Junkers released their bombs in the Birkirkara area, where several houses were demolished or damaged. AA gunners reported gaining strikes on one Ju88 and two Bf109s.

Two Ju88s were claimed shot down by the Spitfire pilots, one by Sgt. Tiddy of 126 Squadron and the other by Plt.Off. Giddings (AR488/S) of 249 Squadron, and it seems that both fell. L1+YC crashed into the sea off Valetta. On board was the Gruppenkommandeur, Maj. Gerhard Köllewe, who baled out with the rest of the crew but was lost, as was the observer, as will be recounted later. There were no survivors from Lt. Ottokar Fritscher's L1+CP of 5 Staffel, which went into the sea about 12 miles south-east of Sicily. Italian pilots had watched as the pilot struggled in vain to keep the aircraft flying on one engine whilst the other belched flames. The gunner in another Junkers of 4 Staffel was wounded when his aircraft came under attack over Luqa. Other claims were made for a Ju88 probable by Plt.Off. Seed (BP866/Q) of 249 Squadron, while Flt.Lt. Charney (EP467), Plt.Off. Bob Park (EP187) and Sgt. H.J. Smith — all of 185 Squadron — each reported strikes on aircraft attacked, Park claiming damage to two bombers.

Maj. Köllewe and Maj. Paepcke were notable bomber leaders, recipients each of the Knights' Cross and Oakleaves, Paepcke being awarded the latter posthumously; it was proving a bad day for the Luftwaffe bombers.

The escorting Messerschmitts and Macchi pilots were doing their utmost to frustrate the Spitfires, Lt. Berres of I/JG 77 claiming one Spitfire shot down near Luqa, whilst a second was claimed by Ten. D'Amico of 51° Stormo. Sgt. Ron Miller of 229 Squadron was lost in BP955/A — possibly Berres' victim — and two 185 Squadron aircraft and one of 126 Squadron were damaged, Sgt. Len Garvey (EP521) of the former unit crashing when his engine cut as he approached to land. Fortunately, Wg.Cdr. Thompson and Flg.Off. Lindsay were on the scene in seconds, and were able to extricate Garvey from the blazing wreck before he was seriously burned.

Three Messerschmitts were claimed shot down in this fight, one each by Flt.Lt. Hetherington (BR565/T) and Plt.Off. Giddings (BR488/S) of 249 Squadron, and the other by Flt.Lt. Parkinson (X-V) of 229 Squadron. Plt.Off. Budd (EP201/V-F) claimed a probable and Plt.Off. Bob Park one damaged. Recalled Colin Parkinson:

> 'CO's kite u/s. Lead squadron. Some of the boys had the twitch; I had a hard job to keep them together. Someone spoilt my interception of Ju88 by breaking down across the squadron. Managed to get them all together again and dove to attack. 109s shadowed us all the way in. Attacked bombers and fighter escort. I shot a 109 down. Pilot baled out. Hell of a mix up for a minute or two. Sky was full of blokes who had baled out. Saw various a/c in flames and diving into sea. Came back to drome to land.
>
> 'Just approaching the runway when a stick of bombs fell just near drome. I saw three 109s going like bats out of hell. Pulled wheels and flaps up, closed hood and chased them out to sea. Couldn't catch them. Saw "Dusty" Miller in his chute so decided to orbit.
>
> 'Three 109s attacked me from 3000 feet. I broke into them and gave one a squirt but I missed. They buggered off anyhow, which was the main thing. "Dusty" landed in the drink. I saw rescue launch so directed it to him. Escorted launch for a while and landed with 10 gallons of petrol.'

On landing, Parkinson discovered that sadly it was not Sgt. Ron Miller — who had shown such a fine fighting spirit during the last few days — in the rescue launch, but a German airman. HSL 128 had been ordered out to pick up survivors from a Ju88, three of whom had been seen to bale out as the aircraft crashed seven miles east of Delimara Point; this was Maj. Paepcke's bomber from the earlier raid. At first, only an empty dinghy had been found, but then Obgfr. Erwin Seibt was seen in the water; five minutes later Ofw. Walter Borner was also found. The search was continued for an hour and a half and eventually the third member of the crew, Fw. Ewald Futterknecht, was discovered.

Left: Maj. Heinrich Paepcke, Kommandeur of II/KG 77, who was killed on 17 October 1942 when his Ju88 was in head-on collision with a Spitfire flown by Flt.Lt. Ripley Jones of 126 Squadron, who was also killed. **Right:** Maj. Gerhard Kollewe, Kommandeur of II/LG 1, holder of the Ritterkreuz mit Eichenlaub (Knights' Cross with Oakleaves), who was shot down and killed on 17 October when his Ju88 fell victim to Spitfires of 126 and 249 Squadrons.

Two more Germans were then spotted and picked up, both survivors from Maj. Köllewe's aircraft. On being pulled aboard, the W/Op, Ofw. Martin Assum, claimed that a Spitfire had swooped on the defenceless airmen in the sea and machine-gunned Köllewe and the observer (Fw. Bernhard Mahler) both of whom had been killed. A number of Bf109s were seen during the early afternoon, obviously searching for the missing aircrew, but no contact was made with patrolling Spitfires.

Three RNAS Hurricanes also undertook searches — Sub Lts. Elliott, White and Pratt* patrolled a semi-circular area from St Paul's Bay to Kalafrana, six to ten miles out to sea. One pilot saw the HSL rescue the two survivors of Köllewe's crew ten miles north-west of Delimara, while Elliott (BN408) directed the vessel to a parachute in the sea three miles east of Zonqor Point, but no survivor was seen .

Raid 3

During mid afternoon about 60 Bf109s, including at least ten Jabo, approached from several directions at great height. Some crossed the coast and bombs fell in the St Paul's Bay area without causing any damage. Thirty Spitfires were in the air and a flight from 1435 Squadron was bounced out of the sun, about 15 miles north of Comino; EP259 was badly shot-up, although Plt.Off. Stewart was able to get back to base and crash-land. 249 Squadron was also bounced, but on this occasion the seven Spitfires managed to avoid any damage. 185 Squadron was over the Island in two sections, the topmost being attacked by a pair of Bf109s. Wg.Cdr. Thompson's EP343 was hit and the hydraulic system was damaged; he, too, managed to reach base where he was obliged to put the aircraft down on its belly. A second Spitfire, flown by Capt. Kuhlmann, received some damage to one wingtip during this action.

Luftwaffe claims for the day totalled ten; apart from Berres' victory, it is known that Hpt. Bär of I/JG 77 claimed a Spitfire south-east of Valetta and Lt. Schiess of Stab/JG 53 another, while Oblt. Freytag of I/JG 77 had taken his tally to 73 by this date. During the day the 22° Gruppo CT transferred its Re2001s to Gela, although 369ª Squadriglia was detached to Pantelleria, where it would be joined next day by the similarly-equipped 2° Gruppo CT.

On Malta, it was now the turn of the Marine Rescue Section to receive the AOC's plaudits:

> 'The AOC sends personal congratulations to the Air/Sea Rescue Unit on their fine achievements during the recent Battle of Malta when they made 36 trips and rescued 12 British and 16 enemy pilots (*sic*). All pilots and aircrews are grateful for your efficient Air/Sea Rescue Service.'

Indeed, to date since the beginning of the year, the Unit had rescued more than 100 airmen of whom about 40 were Germans or Italians; ten bodies had also been recovered from the sea. Flt.Lt. George Crockett, the commander, subsequently received an MBE in recognition of his unit's achievements.

About 15 bombers approached Malta soon after 1800, most crossing the coast to release bombs in the Kalafrana and Birzebbuga areas. At Kalafrana a hangar was damaged by incendiaries but there were no casualties. Three of 89 Squadron's Beaufighters were airborne, although only that flown by Flt.Lt. Nottage and Flt.Sgt. G.V. Holton located a raider and pursued it for 50 miles before it was lost. Single raiders crossed the coast after midnight and again at 0330, but without causing damage.

Flg.Off. Crombie and Sgt. Moss were despatched in Beaufighter T5161 to patrol over Catania airfield during the evening. At 1940 whilst orbiting at 5000 feet, they spotted an aircraft 4000 feet below them, which they identified as a Heinkel; it was in fact a Ju88 of I/KG 54, which Crombie attacked head-on. B3+UL blew up at once and crashed on the runway, only the gunner surviving from Uffz. Adolf Hoffmann's crew.

---

*All three of the RNAS Hurricane pilots would be decorated for their performances on Malta, although only Pratt and White were still there by the end of the month; both would continue to fly Hurricanes on a variety of missions. On one occasion (3 December) White's aircraft was 'intercepted' by a Ju88 which overshot, allowing him to inflict some damage before it was lost from sight; three days later Pratt was again attacked by Spitfires — on this occasion by aircraft of 185 Squadron whose pilots had mistaken the Hurricane's twin underwing fuel tanks for seaplane floats! Believing, therefore, that it was an Italian machine, the Spitfires opened fire at the Hurricane before realising their mistake; Pratt crash-landed at Hal Far on return. Early in the new year (19 January, 1943), while flying a Spitfire, Pratt crashed into the sea off Malta and was lost.

The shipping offensive continues...

Unlike other occasions when Malta had come under sustained attack, the Island's offensive activities had not during this period been curtailed and while the defences had been so heavily involved, other operations had continued. Daily, Spitfires of 69 Squadron's photo-reconnaissance Flight were out, primarily checking the Axis air strength present on Sicilian airfields, but also to reconnoitre the sea lanes and the harbours for convoys both to north and south.

During the night of the 13th/14th three Wellingtons of 69 Squadron were sent to attack a convoy earlier reported by one of the unit's Baltimores, seen moving south through the South Ionian Sea. At 2015 one of the bomber crews spotted two merchant vessels of 6-7000 tons and five destroyers, and released two 1000lb bombs at these but saw no strikes. The other two Wellingtons failed to find the target and brought their loads back with them.

Next morning (the 14th) a Spitfire on an early sortie spotted some vessels south of Malta. Three Beaufighters were despatched by 227 Squadron at 1017, and at 1130 these located what they believed to be a single merchantman of an estimated 1-2000 tons, escorted by a destroyer — actually the German steamer *Trapani* and the large Italian MTB *Medici*; these vessels were 26 miles off Homs and were under escort by MC202s.

The trio attacked at mast height into a deadly hail of fire from the MTB, only Plt.Off. Bryce managing to release his bombs, which overshot. Plt.Off. Tom Freer's bombs refused to drop free and despite seeing Sqn.Ldr. Underwood's X8030/Q shot down in flames, he made a second run. The surviving pair then made off towards Malta, but Bryce was obliged to ditch his badly damaged machine (X8091/X) in the sea, four miles from the scene of the action. On reaching Luqa, Freer's X8082/H suffered a hydraulic failure and crashed on landing, although neither he nor his navigator was hurt.

The Beaufighters had been accompanied by Wg.Cdr. Warburton in PR Spitfire BR665, to observe and photograph the results of the attack. Seeing Bryce and his navigator, Sgt. S.W. Cole, scramble into their dinghy, he circled *Medici* in an effort to guide it to the downed airmen. In so doing he was — not surprisingly — fired on by the MTB and was attacked by six of the escorting Macchis. Having succeeded in evading one persistent fighter which got on his tail four times, he noted that *Medici*'s captain had apparently understood the Spitfire's actions, for the craft now headed for the dinghy, and Bryce and Cole were picked up. For this completely unselfish act, Warburton was awarded a second Bar to his DFC. However, the crew of the other Beaufighter, Sqn.Ldr. Peter Underwood and his navigator (Flt.Sgt. Ivor Miller) were lost.

At dusk a Wellington VIII of 69 Squadron set off to seek out another westbound convoy which had been spotted to the south-east of the Island, and this was followed about an hour later by an ASV Swordfish and two Albacores from Hal Far. The Naval aircraft located the quarry first, reporting a single 7000-ton transport and two escorts identified as small destroyers, 78 miles off Homs, shortly before 2200. In fact, the convoy comprised the 8670-ton Italian steamer *Amsterdam* — which was carrying fuel oil amongst her cargo — escorted by the destroyer *Bombardiere* and two MTBs. The Swordfish dropped flares and aided by this illumination the Albacore piloted by Sub Lt. Clarke attacked *Amsterdam* on the starboard bow from 500 yards. A torpedo hit was claimed when both pilot and observer saw a large flash following the attack, and in fact the ship was hit on the stern. Light AA fire riddled the Albacore, which returned with holes in its mainplanes, fuselage and petrol tank; the second Albacore did not attack as it was unable to manoeuvre into a favourable position.

On receipt of news of this sighting and attack, 69 Squadron despatched four further Wellingtons — two ASV-equipped and armed with bombs, the other two armed with torpedoes — which were sent off at 2325. Even as the pilots struggled to get these heavy-laden aircraft into the air, their colleague had also located the Axis vessels, finding the transport and a single escort stationary on the water. The crew at once attacked, releasing two 1000lb bombs from 4000 feet, but they failed to obtain hits. By the time the four following aircraft arrived a fairly effective smoke-screen had been laid and although a torpedo was launched from 1100 yards, and two more 1000 pounders were dropped, no result was observed.

With daybreak one of the unit's Baltimores — AG755/B piloted by Flt.Lt. Mackay — was sent out to re-locate the crippled *Amsterdam*, and she was photographed about 30 miles off Misurata under tow (by the MTB *Circe*), moving very slowly and now with low-level air cover provided by a number of Ju88s and single-engined fighters. One of the latter gave chase to the Baltimore which managed to evade without being damaged.

A further check on her progress was made in the afternoon, and thereafter she was regularly observed; she eventually reached the Libyan coast and was beached at the head of the wharf at Homs. On the night of the 17th/18th, a Swordfish and an Albacore were despatched from Hal Far to attack the vessel, but the former (V4587 flown by Sub Lt. Elliott) returned early with engine trouble. The Albacore — X9088 flown by Sub Lt. Pratt — attacked in bad light, the crew releasing a torpedo, but failed to see any effects. In the event *Amsterdam* was torpedoed again during the afternoon of the 23rd by the submarine *Umbra*, the hulk settling on the bottom where it would remain.

Meanwhile a further convoy had been spotted west of Malta by Wg.Cdr. Warburton in one of 69 Squadron's omnipresent Spitfires during the afternoon of the 18th, and as soon as darkness fell the attackers went off. Their targets comprised the tanker *Panuco* and three cargo vessels — *Capo Orso*, *Beppe* and *Titania*, which had departed Naples the day before, with an escort of six destroyers and five torpedo-boats under the codename 'Convoy D'. The convoy's presence was known to the British via 'Ultra' intercepts and plans were put into action for the strike, submarines also moving into position.

First off into the squally rainstorms which prevailed as evening fell was an ASV Wellington, to locate and shadow the convoy which was now approaching Lampedusa. This was soon followed by an ASV Swordfish (W5896), two torpedo-carrying Albacores and a similarly-armed Swordfish, but these failed to find the convoy and attacked instead a 4-5000 ton vessel sighted 38 miles off Pantelleria, which was probably the German steamer *Ankara* making for Benghazi. The strike Swordfish did not attack, the pilot deciding to retain his torpedo in the hope of finding the convoy. The other two released their torpedoes, one crew reporting a hit on the stern of the merchantman which was last seen apparently going round in circles; in fact the vessel was not damaged.

Four Wellingtons of 69 Squadron were also despatched to search for the convoy, led by Lt. W.S. Clark SAAF. Three of these made contact at 2140, 50 miles off Punta Stilo; a tanker, two destroyers and an unidentified escort vessel were reported and an attack was carried out. A torpedo was released which was thought to have struck the tanker's bow, but the two 1000lb and four 500lb bombs dropped by the other two failed to achieve any hits. Considerable heavy and light Flak was encountered, and one Wellington sustained a hit in one wing by a 20mm shell.

Next day (the 19th) a Spitfire of 69 Squadron (BR431 flown by Flt.Lt. Coldbeck) again found 'Convoy D' now steaming off Lampedusa. Two Baltimores were despatched to shadow the ships, one of which (Sgt. Shulman's AG734/D) was intercepted by an unidentified fighter during the course of this duty, but nearby cloud cover enabled the reconnaissance aircraft to escape attack. With the re-sighting of the convoy a major operation was laid on for Malta's strike force at nightfall. Meanwhile however, the submarine *Unbending* struck at 1450, firing two torpedoes at *Beppe*; she avoided one but the other struck home lethally and she sank. The other missile hit the escorting destroyer *Da Vararzzano*, which was abandoned by her crew and also sank. By the time an ASV Wellington had been despatched from Luqa to shadow, the convoy had thus already been seriously depleted.

At 1935 Sub Lt. Reg Elliott, flying the ASV Swordfish W5896 — which also carried the CO, Lt. Lashmore — set off at the head of another Swordfish and two Albacores, all armed with torpedoes. They were followed 40 minutes later by four Wellingtons of 69 Squadron, two with torpedoes and two with bombs. Within 90 minutes, the Naval crews had located the convoy 53 miles off Lampedusa. Two 6000-ton cargo ships and five destroyers were reported. The weather was poor with considerable cloud, and the escorts were laying a smokescreen which partially obscured the vessels. Lashmore ordered the strike force to attack independently, but in fact all three torpedo-carriers went for the 5397-ton *Titania* on the port flank. Elliott recalled:

> 'We located the convoy south of Lampedusa and Lashmore directed me into position for my flare dropping. One of the torpedo-carriers hit a merchantmen.

Sub Lt. Bill Siddall-Simpson carried out a gliding approach from the port beam and released his torpedo. He noted a large explosion as he flew away, but this seems likely to have been the result of Sub Lt. D.C. Scott's attack. Scott and his observer, Sub Lt. D.J. Hanson, reported that their torpedo struck the vessel amidships. On seeing the explosion and resultant smoke from this attack, Sub Lt. Pratt also attacked *Titania* as the others disappeared from view into the smoke screen, but he missed. Apparently at about the same time as Scott's success, the submarine *Unbroken* reported torpedoing a merchantman. It would seem both Albacore and submarine had attacked *Titania*, although only one hit was recorded by the Italians. In the event, the stricken vessel was taken in tow by the destroyer *Ascari*, but was torpedoed again at 0720 the following day by the submarine *Safari* and sank.

The Wellingtons arrived at 2305, spotting three destroyers with the vessels, and dropped a torpedo, two 1000lb and four 500lb bombs. A hit was claimed with one of the bigger bombs by Plt.Off. W.J. Martin's crew, and a cloud of black smoke issued forth from one of the transports.

As soon as the RN aircraft landed back at Hal Far a second sortie was prepared. Two fresh crews were to participate but the CO retained his crew and that of Scott/Hanson; the four aircraft set out again at 1245. By now the weather was extremely bad with large masses of thick cloud, and heavy rain squalls. Despite the ASV aircraft experiencing considerable jamming of its signals from the African coast, the convoy was re-located at 0300, 76 miles from Tripoli. Elliott again dropped flares and Scott immediately sighted the tanker and went in for the kill, his torpedo striking *Panuco* amidships. Sub Lt. White also released at another vessel but missed, while the third crew failed to find a suitable target. Of this attack Elliott recalled:

> 'This time the ASV was not very good and, worried that the convoy would be missed, we dropped single flares at intervals to lead the other aircraft in, and then gave a full illumination. In the ensuing attack Scott hit the tanker; he was awarded an immediate DSC for his night's work. I got back after another 4 hrs 45 mins of night instrument flying — a total of 9.05 hrs — and next day I could hardly see out of bunged up eyes.'

Fires broke out aboard the tanker and she was abandoned by her 100-strong crew. However, after some time the fires died down and the captain with 20 volunteers re-boarded her; given a tow, she eventually reached Tripoli.

A further trio of Wellingtons had gone off at 0105, two with bombs and one with torpedoes. A stationary transport and its escort were seen by two of the crews at 0310 some 60 miles from Lampedusa, although the torpedo-carrier was unable to launch because of the evasive action the ships then took. The bomber released two 1000 pounders, but the crew saw no results.

Little activity at sea was apparent for the next three days, but on the 22nd another tanker was spotted off Cephalonia by a Spitfire. Three ASV Wellingtons were again despatched by 69 Squadron, but a severe electrical storm caused the crews to give up the sortie and return to base.

Despite Kesselring's suspension of the bombing assault against Malta, the Island was not yet spared further attack. Just as the end of daylight bombing raids over England in September 1940 had brought several weeks of fighter sweeps and pin-prick fighter-bomber attacks — designed to draw up the British fighters for destruction in the air — this now became the pattern for Malta.

Sunday, 18 October

The first raid came in at 0640, eight Spitfires of 126 Squadron and eight of 185 Squadron scrambling to meet approximately 50 fighters which approached at 0700. They were reportedly escorting seven bombers which had apparently turned back 15 miles north of Zonqor. Six Messerschmitts bounced the 185 Squadron flight five miles north-east of Grand Harbour, although these were evaded; Plt.Off. Len Reid (EP722) reported:

> 'Jumped by several 109s; broke left and was able to get in a good squirt at one from a quarter line astern from above. Observed strikes and flashes over top of cockpit and engine.

The Messerschmitt attacked by Reid had been lining up to shoot at the Spitfire flown by Plt.Off. O'Brien, who later noted in his diary:

> 'Some 109s came up sun of us and around behind us. Someone gave a break and I went to the left... A 109 came right up my tail but I turned in time. Len Reid took a squirt at it and claimed a damaged.

A dozen Bf109s in two separate groups were encountered by the 126 Squadron pilots five miles east of Zonqor, Sgt. Mortimer claiming one shot down. This was possibly Uffz. Heinrich Fankenberger's G-2 of 4/JG 53, which crashed in the sea off Cape Scaramia; the injured pilot was rescued by Axis ASR craft. Meanwhile, Sgt. Nigel Park's EP345/X had been badly shot up, the New Zealander crash-landing on return and suffering slight injuries.

Thirty-five Messerschmitts, including a number of Jabo, raided mid-morning and bombs dropped on Takali without causing damage or casualties. The attack was over before interception could be achieved, but eight Bf109s were seen by pilots of 229 Squadron — and another four by 1435 Squadron; none could be engaged, however. Within 20 minutes another 15 fighters swept in to attack Luqa, again with little effect.

At 1355 an estimated 20 Bf109s were reported, six of 229 Squadron and three of 126 Squadron being scrambled. Fifteen minutes later, the latter trio were bounced by six Messerschmitts four miles south-west of Comino but evaded these. A few minutes afterwards, a lone Bf109 was seen at 7000 feet over Gozo flying northwards, and Sgt. Tiddy dived from 10,000 feet to shoot it down into the sea off Dahlet Qorrot. The pilot was seen to bale out and this was undoubtedly the aircraft flown by Uffz. Karl Könning of 3/JG 27, who failed to return. At around the same time the 229 Squadron pilots spotted two more Bf109s heading west at 23,000 feet, about two miles south of Gozo, although only Sqn.Ldr. Stephens was quick enough to get in a burst at one, claiming some damage.

Up to 75 fighters, Jabo included, crossed the coast in small groups at great height between 1545 and 1700. A number of bombs fell on Luqa, where a Wellington was slightly damaged, and in the Gharghur area. Although 38 Spitfires were airborne only two of 1435 Squadron were able to get near enough to engage, Sgt. Hamilton (AB264/Z) claiming strikes on one Messerschmitt. As the Spitfires returned to land, Plt.Off. Jim Stevenson's AB332 of 126 Squadron went out of control and crashed in a field near Gharghur. The Canadian pilot was killed.

The night of the 18th/19th was marked by six alerts, when a total of 13 bombers crossed the coast; anti-personnel bombs and incendiaries fell in the Birkirkara, Hamrun, Floriana and Dockyard areas. Three Beaufighters of 89 Squadron were ordered off but Flg.Off. Crombie's X7702 ran into a bomb hole and suffered slight damage. Flg.Off. Gray and Sgt. Mould located a Ju88 which took evasive action and was lost from sight. Half an hour later the same crew chased a He111 but were unable to engage.

The 89 Squadron detachment had received a new commander — Sqn.Ldr. D.S. Pain AFC — and a number of replacement crews during the past few days. Soon after 1900 one of the new crews, Flg.Off. Vic Lovell and Flt.Sgt. R. Lilley, set off in V8259 to patrol over southern Sicily. Forty-five minutes later, when over Gerbini aerodrome, an aircraft with landing lights on was spotted orbiting at 1500 feet. This was almost certainly Fw. Hermann Gerdes' 8/KG 77 bomber. Lovell chased it round the circuit and opened fire, seeing strikes on the fuselage, but then lost sight of it. The Ju88 was in fact very badly damaged and crash-landed, the crew all suffering wounds or injuries.

Monday, 19 October

0625-0652: 15 plus fighters and Jabo attacked Hal Far where two Hurricanes were slightly damaged. Eight of 1435 Squadron scrambled and saw six Bf109s

over Kalafrana at 0635. They dived on these from 10,000 feet, Flt.Sgt. Scott (EP203/G) claiming one damaged.
0957-1018: 15 MC202s of 51° Stormo, 23 of 153° Gruppo and 19 Bf109s escorted three Re2001 fighter-bombers to attack the Gharghur area. Twenty-three Spitfires were airborne. At 0948, 1435 Squadron saw five fighters identified as Re2001s over St Paul's Bay at 20,000 feet and dived to attack, Plt.Off. Walton (BR236/E) claiming one probable. This was most likely Serg. Ferruccio Serafini's Macchi which was damaged, the pilot being wounded in both hands; none of the Reggianes were hit. Macchi pilots claimed one Spitfire probably shot down and one damaged.
1322-1541: Some 20 fighters crossed the coast and Attard was bombed. Eight of 185 Squadron intercepted, Capt. Kuhlmann (EP722) and Sgt. T.J. Gunstone (EP471) each claiming a Messerschmitt damaged, but Kuhlmann's Spitfire was damaged and he crash-landed on return to Hal Far.

The next two raids were not intercepted despite large numbers of Spitfires being airborne, although little damage was caused at Luqa and Mosta where a few bombs fell. I/JG 77 now began ferrying their Messerschmitts to Pantelleria, but two of these crash-landed on arrival; a further aircraft of 2 Staffel was badly damaged on the airfield due — according to Luftwaffe records — to sabotage!

This somewhat frustrating day was to end with better success for the defenders, for as dusk settled in 40 unescorted Ju88s from II/LG 1 and III/KG 77 approached in two formations. It was still light enough, however, for a standing patrol of three Spitfires from 249 Squadron to spot the KG 77 aircraft 25 miles out to sea as they approached from the west. The Spitfires were joined by two 89 Squadron Beaufighters, whereupon a number of the bombers were seen to jettison their loads and turn back. Flt.Sgt. de l'Ara (EP201/V-F) then led in his section to intercept the other formation, which was encountered 15 miles east of Malta and again bombs were jettisoned, as de l'Ara recorded:

> 'Whenever I manoeuvred my section nearly within range of a bomber in these groups, they would jettison their bombs and dive into cloud. I was vectored onto one bomber which I recognised as a Ju88, about 400 yards ahead, and crossing my starboard bows. I brought my section round behind it. The top gunner fired at me at about 200 yards, but I had closed to about 150 yards and fired a three or four second burst at the port motor.
>
> 'The engine gave a flash, caught fire and streamed a considerable amount of black smoke. The gunner stopped firing and I noticed a glow inside the cockpit, then I broke right to avoid ramming. Immediately I broke, my No 2 opened fire from astern. The e/a turned slightly to the right, then flicked over and spun left into cloud.'

Only three bombers had in fact crossed the coast and it was one of these — 3Z+GS flown by Uffz. Gerhard Demuth — which fell to de l'Ara and Sgt. Stead (EP520/V). Bombs fell near Luqa and Hal Far but caused no material damage. Amongst those watching the fight from the ground was 89 Squadron's Flg.Off. Crombie, who related:

> 'The Ju88s are still in formation and are just starting to open up and dive on the drome now. One has been hit, a Spit got him and one engine is on fire. Two of the crew have baled out. Christ, here come the bombs also. The Ju88 that was hit has just hit the ground and blown up about a mile from here. Three of the crew are coming down in parachutes.'

Another eyewitness at Luqa wrote:

> 'One was circling my own station, eventually putting her nose down and diving straight for us. I ran, only to find everyone else running in the opposite direction, which is rather complicating. About a hundred feet from the deck she levelled out, crashing 500 yards away. I think that it was the pilot's unlucky day for his 'chute never opened and I remember him flashing past my eyes to disappear in a cloud of dust fifty yards distant.

Meanwhile, the Beaufighter crewed by Flt.Sgt. Pring and Wt.Off. Phillips pursued a fleeing II/LG 1 Ju88 north-eastwards and shot it down. This was undoubtedly Oblt. Ernst Neuffer's aircraft (L1+DN) which crashed into the sea, but the pilot did not believe he had been shot down; his aircraft's demise, he suggested, was due to other causes:

> 'It was at eight o'clock in the evening, 150 km north-east of Malta. The aircraft was not shot down. It happened as a result of sabotage. But I will not say anything about it. I do not know exactly what happened. I had severe injuries to my head, legs and back. I woke up in hospital in Malta.'

However, his radio operator, Uffz. Fritz Hinterberg, was able to recall the incident in greater detail:

> 'By the time we approached Malta it was almost dusk and we received a radio message that British night fighters were ordered to attack us. We were on top alert but all of a sudden it did happen. A detonation and the right engine was on fire; the propeller of the right engine could not be controlled, and we went into a curve on one engine to try to skid on touching the water.
>
> 'Fortunately, the action taken was successful and we got out into the rubber dinghy — which was automatically inflated — alongside the body of the plane. The sea calmed down and we were alone in the rubber dinghy. Four long days, battered by storms and high waves. Once we fell overboard but luckily managed to climb into the dinghy again. Unfortunately, we lost all of the boat's equipment and foodstuffs. On 23rd we saw land. It was Malta. But still it was not until midday that some warships came out of the harbour and probably discovered us, as very shortly an English rescue boat reached us and pulled us up from the water.
>
> 'Oblt. Neuffer, who was the commandant and chief pilot of the aircraft, was severely wounded. His backbone was fractured and what was not discovered and treated medically was a fracture of his skull.'

They were rescued by HSL 128 which had been sent to investigate, Neuffer swiftly being conveyed to hospital where he would remain for some considerable time.

For his leadership during the evening interception, Flt.Sgt. Louis de l'Ara — a former Spitfire test pilot — was awarded an immediate DFM. A number of other awards were forthcoming at this time, honouring half a dozen of the recently successful fighter pilots: DSOs were announced for Wg.Cdr. Donaldson and Plt.Off. Beurling. The latter award evinced some surprise and sharp comment, not everyone considering that the award of a medal normally associated with outstanding leadership was appropriate. Sqn.Ldr. Mike Stephens received a second Bar to his DFC, while Flt.Lt. Art Roscoe, Flt.Lt. Colin Parkinson and Flg.Off. John McElroy were each awarded the DFC.

At this time the Regia Aeronautica had intended to reintroduce night raids by the Ju87s of 102° Gruppo Tuff, since the Gruppo was now in the throes of receiving replacement aircraft for its worn-out equipment. However, the 'new' aircraft proved to be almost equally-worn ex-Luftwaffe machines, still bearing the markings of their previous ownership! During the night of the 19th/20th two of these prepared to take-off from Gela for the first sorties of their new mini-offensive, in the hands of two of the most experienced Italian Stuka pilots, Cap. Cumbat and Cap. Cenni. As Cumbat lifted his aircraft off the runway, the engine cut and the Ju87 crashed and overturned. Cumbat was only slightly hurt but his gunner, 1° Av. Mot. Giuseppe Lentella, was seriously injured; the mission was cancelled.

After the Blitz — a quartet of Spitfire leaders are seen, from left: Sqn.Ldr. 'Timber' Woods of 249 Squadron; Sqn.Ldr. Mike Stephens of 229 Squadron; Wg.Cdr. Arthur Donaldson, recuperating from his wounds; Flt.Lt. Colin Parkinson of 229 Squadron. *(M.M. Stephens)*

Tuesday, 20 October

Tuesday morning brought with it heavy rain and further sporadic raids but few interceptions. Indeed, the only one of note occurred shortly after 1100 when 25 fighters raided Safi strip and Luqa under cloud cover, four bombs being dropped. Eight 1435 Squadron Spitfires were scrambled, but Red Section was jumped by four Bf109s from 20,000 feet and one Spitfire was slightly damaged.

By night, for the first time in weeks, no alerts were sounded; the blitz was clearly at an end, and a rush of congratulatory messages followed.

From GOC Troops, Malta to AOC:

> 'On what appears to be the conclusion of the first phase of the renewed enemy air offensive on Malta, all ranks of the Army send their heartiest congratulations to their comrades of the Royal Air Force on their magnificent achievement.'

To which Air Vice-Marshal Park replied:

> 'All ranks of RAF Malta greatly appreciate your messages of congratulations of the recent success of our fighter defences. We are very grateful for the

> assistance of our comrades in the Army in keeping our aerodromes working at high pressure. The Spitfire squadrons are especially grateful for the helpful co-operation of the A/A batteries in the engaging and breaking up of enemy formations that crossed our coast. In spite of the evening bombing of our aerodromes in the past ten days, we have carried out more attacks on his shipping than during the previous ten days.'

Park backed up the latter statement with a signal to the RNAS at Hal Far:

> 'Grand work. Congratulations on your brilliantly successful attacks on enemy convoy on the night 19th/20th October. This will teach the Hun to try and put Malta aerodromes out of action as attempted in his recent Blitz.'

Wednesday, 21 October

Heavy rain rendered Takali unserviceable for the second consecutive day, whilst fighter incursions continued unabated:
0703-0735: 15 plus Messerschmitts were reported over at 20,000 feet, Jabo bombing Safi and Gudja without effect. Eight of 1435 Squadron encountered four over Kalafrana at 6000 feet and Flt.Sgt. Scott (EP621/N) claimed one probable.
0930-1030: About 35 German and Italian fighters attacked Luqa and Safi, two dozen MC202s of 51° Stormo and three 22° Gruppo Re2001s taking part. Eight of 126 and eight of 1435 Squadrons were airborne, the latter engaging a similar number of Macchis at 23,000 feet over St Paul's Bay. Plt.Off. Walton (EP209) claimed one shot down, but no Italian losses were reported. At Safi strip Beaufighter X8081 of 89 Squadron was damaged.

Three further raids between 1125 and 1600 were not intercepted. The night remained quiet until about 0430 when four hostile plots were noted approaching from the north. Only one bomber crossed the coast, bombs falling harmlessly into the sea north-east of Grand Harbour. Flt.Sgt. Pring and Wt.Off. Phillips of 89 Squadron were vectored onto this intruder which they identified as a He111, and attacked at 22,000 feet. Pring was able only to claim damage before the aircraft evaded him and was lost to sight. The bomber was in fact one of three BR20Ms from 88° Gruppo BT and had been hard hit; as it neared its base at Gela, Sottoten. Salvatore Macanda ordered his crew to bale out. In the confusion, two jumped without their parachutes and were killed. The bomber crashed on houses in the nearby town of Niscemi, killing the second pilot and many civilians, whilst Macanda and the remainder of his crew were injured.

Thursday, 22 October

Fifteen fighters, including some Jabo, crossed the coast at a great height at 0715 and, taking advantage of cloud cover, dropped bombs in the Birkirkara and Hamrun areas; some damage resulted and there were several civilian casualties. Patrolling Spitfires did not make contact on this occasion.
0955-1030: At least ten Messerschmitts, two dozen Macchis and three Re2001 fighter-bombers raided the Takali and Mosta areas, causing little damage. Sixteen Spitfires of 249 and 1435 Squadrons were airborne, Red Section/1435 climbing to 25,000 feet over Comino to be bounced by two MC202s, one of which Flt.Lt. Wally McLeod (BS161/U) claimed shot down. The eight 249 Squadron aircraft then met 14 fighters at 24,000 feet north of Grand Harbour, following these in a dive, and claimed as follows:

Flt.Lt. McElroy	(EP708/U)	Bf109
Plt.Off. Lowery	(EP201/V-F)	
Plt.Off. Sanderson	(EP199/K)	MC202
Sqn.Ldr. Woods	(AD529)	Bf109 probable, Bf109 damaged
Sgt. Stead	(EP520/V)	Bf109 damaged, MC202 damaged

It seems that either Sanderson or McLeod had attacked Ten. Mario Mazzoleni's Macchi, causing severe damage; it crash-landed near Marina di Ragusa on return. Italian pilots claimed damage to three of the Spitfires.
1130-1220: 25 fighters raided all three airfields. There were no interceptions by eight patrolling Spitfires of 126 Squadron, although Bofors gunners claimed one of the raiders shot down.
1512-1610: 60 German and Italian fighters, including 30 MC202s of 51° Stormo and three bomb-carrying Re2001s, approached the coast with about half crossing in cloud cover. Bombs were dropped at Luqa. Two dozen Spitfires from 126, 229 and 1435 Squadrons scrambled, the latter unit engaging MC202s and Re2001s north of St Paul's Bay, where the Reggianes were seen to jettison their bombs in the sea. Plt.Off. Walton (EP612/B) and Flt.Sgt. Brown (EP332/A) each claimed two Macchis damaged, and the Italian pilots claimed five Spitfires hit in return. Ofw. Herbert Rollwage of II/JG 53 reported shooting down a Spitfire just off the east coast of Malta for his 31st victory, but no British aircraft were lost on this occasion.

With evening, a further batch of awards were announced, including DSOs for Wg.Cdr. Peter Prosser Hanks and Sqn.Ldr. Tony Lovell, Bars to DFCs for Sqn.Ldr. 'Timber' Woods and Flt.Lt. Wally McLeod, a DFC for Flt.Lt. Eddie Glazebrook and a DFM for his fellow Canadian, Flt.Sgt. Ian MacLennan. On a more sombre note, members of the 89 Squadron detachment received news of the deaths of two of the earlier detachment. Flt.Lt. Gil Hayton DFC and Flg.Off. Peter Oakes both lost their lives as a result of HMT *Laconia*, on which they were returning to the United Kingdom, being torpedoed and sunk off the West African coast on 12 September; another of the unit's Malta veterans, Plt.Off. 'Dusty' Miller DFM, was rescued by a Vichy cruiser from Dakar where he was interned, as was Plt.Off. Norman Josling, Hayton's navigator; although they had been in a lifeboat for six days before rescue, they were more fortunate than the occupants of another lifeboat, which included Hayton and Oakes.

Most of this boat's equipment had been washed away, and there were three gallons only of fresh water to meet the requirements of the 51 survivors who had clambered aboard. The water was rationed stringently, supplemented by drinking blood from fish that were caught for food, but the occupants gradually grew weaker. On the 17th night a merchant vessel passed within 400 yards of the boat without seeing it. A few days later torrential rain fell enabling the water supply to be topped up, but by then only nine were still alive, four of whom were even then too far gone to recover. On the 36th and 37th days aircraft flew overhead, and on the next day (20th October) a trawler accompanying a convoy picked up the four occupants — the only ones left from the original 51; neither Hayton nor Oakes had survived the ordeal.

Friday, 23 October

Friday saw a continuation of the fighter-bomber raids, which achieved negligible success:

0637-0736: About 35 Bf109s approached Malta in two swift raids, the first just after 0630; bombs fell in St Paul's Bay and near Mosta and Mtarfa. Bofors gunners put up an intense barrage and claimed two low-level raiders shot down, and indeed 'Black 12' of 5/JG 53 crashed near Mgarr, Uffz. Heribert Wagner being killed. A section of 185 Squadron intercepted Bf109s diving on Dingli and Sgt. Ray Saunders (EP467), on only his second operational flight with the squadron, shot down Obgfr. Rudolf Hagen of 4/JG 53, who baled out of 'White 8' into the sea off Gozo; he was picked up by a rescue craft from Malta. Flt.Lt. Charney (EP471) claimed a second damaged.

Flg.Off. Alec Lindsay's Spitfire (EP685) was hit and was seen to dive from 20,000 feet, minus its tail unit, to crash into a field near Dingli. The pilot was killed. Initially it was assumed that he had been shot down by Messerschmitts but later it transpired that his was the second fighter claimed shot down by the Bofors batteries.

1010-1036: 30 fighters raided Takali but bombs fell wide, mostly into Mosta where houses were damaged and one civilian injured. Sixteen Spitfires were airborne, and eight of 229 Squadron intercepted about a dozen Bf109s over Dingli without success. Sgt. Marshall of 126 Squadron encountered five Bf109s over St Paul's Bay at 23,000 feet, and claimed strikes on two. Afternoon incursions were not intercepted.

Saturday, 24 October

The opposing fighters clashed over Malta with rather more severity than of late. An early attack on Takali damaged a Spitfire and wounded three airmen, while one of the raiders was believed to have been brought down by small-arms fire; no interceptions were made.

1300-1340: 15 fighters and fighter-bombers attacked Takali but all bombs missed their intended targets. Eight Spitfires of 185 Squadron were scrambled and Black Section spotted ten Bf109s diving over Dingli, but were unable to catch them. Minutes later, this section was bounced by other Messerschmitts and Sgt. Ray Saunders was shot down and killed, EP467 crashing into a field near Rabat.

During the afternoon at least 40 Messerschmitts and Macchis approached, these being intercepted about 25 miles north of the Island at 1610 by seven Spitfires of 249 Squadron. Attacking head-on, Plt.Off. Giddings (BR565/T) claimed one Macchi shot down and a second probably so, whilst Plt.Off. Williams (EP520/V) shot down a Messerschmitt — almost certainly an aircraft of 6/JG 53. The pilot baled out near Comiso and was rescued by an Axis ASR craft. Ken Giddings reported:

> 'I attacked one gaggle of Macchis in line astern, when the last three rolled onto their backs and dived down. I fired at the No 3 aircraft of the remainder with cannon and m/g for about 3 seconds. Glycol poured from it and there was a violent explosion around the cockpit and the fuselage broke up. I then fired a long burst at the No 4 of the formation and saw a thick stream of glycol pour from it. At that moment I was forced to break away and aileron turned down to 2000 feet. In my dive an e/a streaming black smoke crashed into the sea. This was probably the 109F claimed by Tiger Blue 1 (*P/O Williams*).'

A section of 126 Squadron spotted two Macchis over Filfla at 20,000 feet but were unable to close. However, seven 229 Squadron aircraft engaged eight

Bf109s five miles south of Kalafrana, climbing to attack them when they were themselves attacked from the sun. Sgt. Bud Milligan's EP716 was hit and the pilot was wounded in the leg; he crash-landed on return. Plt.Off. 'Sandy' Goodyear, a new arrival, was also attacked; his aircraft (BP955/A) suffered a hole through one wing, but he managed to return safely.

Line-up of X-coded Spitfires of 229 Squadron at Takali. *(M.M. Stephens)*

Air Vice-Marshal Park had been promising his pilots that help was on the way, and during the day two Hudsons arrived from Gibraltar carrying a number of replacement fighter pilots. The day also brought confirmation of a well-deserved and long-overdue award of the DFC for 249 Squadron's Flt.Lt. Eric Hetherington.

Sunday, 25 October

Two fighter-bomber raids on Takali were the main features of Sunday, during one of which a Bf109 Jabo — 'White 14' of the recently-arrived I/Schlachtgeschwader 2 — had a wing shot off by Bofors gunners and spun into the ground in flames, Oblt. Richard Eckhardt being killed. Spitfires of 126 and 229

Messerschmitt Bf109G-2 'White 2' of II/JG 53 at the butts, having its guns tested and aligned. *(E.C. des Armees)*

Squadrons engaged other raiders, newly-promoted Flt.Lt. Rod Smith (BR311/L) of the former unit reporting:

> 'Bounced four 109s from 24,000 feet; 4-second burst — flash from cockpit and pieces off — dived into sea — confirmed by rest of section and 'Y' Service.'

Flt.Lt. Colin Parkinson of 229 Squadron attacked another:

> 'Had a squirt at a 109... Hit him in the wings, cannon fire — he got away.'

There is little doubt that Smith's victim was another I/SchG 2 machine, Uffz. Willi Diepenseifen's 'White 16' being shot down into the sea with the loss of the pilot.

At 1435 a total of 15 MC202s from 153° Gruppo escorted three Re2001s to Takali, whilst ten 51° Stormo Macchis undertook a sweep as indirect support. An hour later both units reported engagements with Spitfires. Serg. Serafini of 51° Stormo claimed one shot down, while four of the unit's other pilots (Ten. Manlio Biccolini, Sottoten. Plinio Sironi, Serg.Magg. Giovanni Gambari and Serg.Magg. Paolo Pedretti) shared a second with Ten. Gianni Rossini of 153° Gruppo. Cap. Roveda, the 51° Stormo formation leader, claimed a third as a probable.

Amongst the units engaging the Italians was 'B' Flight of 126 Squadron, led by Flt.Lt. Rolls, who also reported meeting Messerschmitts. Rolls' own Spitfire (BR345/S) was hit during the engagement but he got down safely. On landing, however, he discovered that Sgt. Nigel Park was missing in BR311/L:

> 'I was told by one of the pilots that he had seen Parky's aircraft hit the sea and he thought he had seen a parachute coming from it. Someone else had seen a Spitfire crash into the sea, but that it went down with the pilot still in it. I hastily rang the Air-Sea Rescue and they told me they had the information but it would take some time to get there and it would be getting dark soon.
>
> 'I rang Operations to ask permission to go out and search for Parky or to protect him if he was in his dinghy... we took off to that area which we searched for almost an hour and as it was getting dark, we had to return to base and leave it to the Air-Sea Rescue.'

Park was not located and it seems likely that he went down with his aircraft. It was, however, believed that he had accounted for a Messerschmitt before he fell, and he was awarded a victory accordingly. Bill Rolls personally made the appropriate entry in the New Zealander's logbook to raise his total to ten and one shared.

It seems fairly certain that Messerschmitts were involved in this action, Lt. Alfred Hammer of II/JG 53 claiming one Spitfire shot down — his first victory after flying 306 sorties and being engaged in 80 combats over the Island since 12 December, 1941! Whether he or the Italians — or both — were responsible for Park's demise is not known; at the end of the year the award of a DFM for the missing pilot was belatedly announced.

During the day the first two long-range Spitfire Vcs arrived safely on Malta in the hands of Flt.Lt. J.H. Burgess and Flt.Sgt. L.G. Pow RCAF, following a five and a quarter hour flight direct from Gibraltar. Each aircraft was fitted with a 170-gallon jettisonable slipper tank beneath the belly, together with an extra

Long-range Spitfire! A Spitfire Vc fitted with a huge 170 gallon slipper tank is seen here about to depart Gibraltar to undertake the 1,000 mile flight to Malta non-stop. *(NWMA)*

29-gallon tank in the rear fuselage, and a larger than normal oil tank. Only two machine guns were fitted but despite being well-overweight on take-off, both aircraft got airborne in 800 yards. On arrival the Spitfires were to revert to normal standard, being stripped of the special equipment and fitted with full cannon armament*. One non-arrival was Beaufort DW834 of the OADU, in transit to the Middle East, which failed to reach Malta and was believed to have been intercepted and shot down by Axis fighters.

Monday, 26 October

The first day of the new week saw 35 Axis aircraft approaching at 0655, but about half the force turned back upon being intercepted, the rest attacking Takali without tangible result. Three Spitfires of 249 Squadron engaged six Bf109s about 20 miles south of Scalambria, but were bounced by four more which were evaded. Eight 1435 Squadron aircraft, led by newly-arrived Flt.Lt. Blair White, were jumped by six more Messerschmitts 25 miles north of St Paul's Bay but evaded with minor damage only to Flt.Sgt. Hamilton's EP140/P. A second section from this unit intercepted seven Bf109s going south over St Paul's Bay, and Plt.Off. MacLennan (BR591/R) claimed one shot down. Two RNAS Hurricanes were sent out, finding a body in a partially inflated dinghy 8-10 miles north of Gozo. An HSL was called out to investigate.

An estimated 35 Messerschmitts approached on a sweep just after 1030, the first wave being intercepted 25 miles out to sea by eight 126 Squadron Spitfires. After breaking up the main formation of Jabo, Flt.Lt. Rolls (BR345/S) and his No 2 patrolled off Filfla at 16,000 feet, seeing a pair of Bf109s diving down from over Luqa, which they pursued. At 8000 feet, one turned to starboard and Rolls fired; it went down pouring black smoke from the side of the engine. At 4000 feet, he fired again, hitting the starboard wing with cannon fire, whereupon it went into a vertical dive at 2000 feet. At this point he overshot and pulled up, firing at a second Messerschmitt with machine guns only. Initially he claimed

*During November and December 15 more similarly-equipped Spitfires departed from Gibraltar, all but one reaching their destination safely (EP724 failed to arrive at Malta having departed Gibraltar on 14 November.)

only a probable, but this was later upgraded to 'destroyed' when the crash of a machine in the vicinity of his combat was reported — his 17th and last victory. Of his action, Rolls later wrote:

> 'I picked out one on the wing and with my first burst of cannon, blew it out of the sky and within a couple of seconds was turning into a second one. I started to fire at it and was so intent on hitting it, that I did not see one behind me. I managed to lose it...'

He may well have been attacked by Ofw. Rollwage of II/JG 53, who claimed a Spitfire some ten miles north of Valetta at this time as his 32nd victory; no RAF losses were sustained during this particular engagement.

An afternoon raid by almost 40 Messerschmitts, including six Jabo, was engaged initially by eight Spitfires of 1435 Squadron, Plt.Off. Walton (EP188/G) claiming one shot down north of St Paul's Bay. This was possibly an aircraft of I/SchG 2 from which the pilot baled out, and who was later rescued from the sea by Axis ASR craft. Sqn.Ldr. Lovell chased the fighter-bombers across the Island, attacking and claiming damage to one as they dived, while bombs fell harmlessly near Birzebbuga.

Tuesday, 27 October

The fighter-bombers were back early, continuing their series of largely ineffective raids:

0700: 24 fighters and fighter-bombers crossed the coast and bombs fell near Takali. Eight 249 Squadron Spitfires engaged and two raiders were claimed damaged over Dingli by Sqn.Ldr. Woods (BR529/D) and Plt.Off. Moody (AR466/R).

1015: Six Jabo escorted by about 60 Bf109s and MC202s attacked Luqa, where one Spitfire was damaged on the ground. Eight of 126 Squadron and eight of 229 Squadron attempted to intercept without success, while Bofors gunners claimed one Messerschmitt probably shot down into the sea.

PM: Three of 249 Squadron aircraft engaged 40 plus fighters, some of which jettisoned bombs when attacked. Flt.Lt. McElroy (EP708/O) claimed one damaged, but BR529/D was damaged during the engagement and Sgt. G.D. Cameron suffered a slight head injury; he crash-landed near Takali.

Several days of relative quiet were to follow, during which there were a number of changes amongst the Luftwaffe units in Sicily. Around the 26th I/JG 27 returned to Africa, having claimed seven Spitfires over Malta for the loss of two of its Bf109Gs. Next day III/JG 53 arrived from the Desert once again in order to release I/JG 77, which was to move to the battlefront. Here it was planned that the whole of JG 77 should replace the tired and depleted Gruppen of JG 27.

Even as these changes were taking place and the attacks on the Island were petering out, the war of the convoys had resumed — though initially involving units based in Africa, rather than from Malta. On the 25th a small supply vessel had succeeded in reaching Tobruk, only to be attacked twice and damaged by 47 Squadron Beauforts from Gianaclis. Late that same afternoon a convoy of two freighters and one tanker, escorted by four destroyers, was seen by the crew of a reconnaissance aircraft north-east of Benghazi. Wellingtons and Liberators were sent out to attack during the night, but without success. Baltimores shadowed the vessels until noon on the 26th, when Liberators again attacked — again without success.

By the 27th the ships were in range of the Beauforts at Gianaclis. Five 47 Squadron aircraft accompanied by four bomb-carrying Bisleys of 15 SAAF Squadron, and escorted by Beaufighters from 252 and 272 Squadrons, were sent to attack. Flak was intense but the Italian tanker *Proserpina*, carrying 888 tons of fuel for the Luftwaffe, 2500 tons for the German army and 1165 tons for the Italians, was set on fire. She burned for several hours before she finally sank. During the attack, one Bisley collided with the tanker's mast and crashed, whilst a second was shot down and a Beaufort was seen to crash nearby. On the return flight, another Beaufort and Bisley collided and went into the sea, raising losses to five.

The covering Beaufighters encountered five He111s of II/KG 100 (apparently from Sicily) north-east of Sidi Barrani. Plt.Off. Al Smith of 272 Squadron claimed one shot down for his fifth air victory, whilst Sgt. Stan Kernaghan of 252 Squadron claimed a second (also his fifth victory); the other three were claimed damaged, Plt.Off. G.G. Pattearson reporting the one he attacked was last seen on fire, with one engine out of action.

At dusk three torpedo-carrying Wellingtons of 38 Squadron were sent out after the same convoy. The Italian motor vessel *Tergestea*, which was carrying 1000 tons of fuel and 1000 tons of ammunition, was hit and blew up; one Wellington was shot down and a second was damaged. Near Crete meanwhile, another tanker — the 2388-ton *Arca* — was torpedoed and sunk by a Royal Navy submarine.

During the night of the 26th/27th, three of Malta's resident Wellingtons of 69 Squadron were sent to attack shipping off Antipaxoi, which had been reported earlier by a PR Spitfire. One returned early with faulty radar, whilst a second sighted the convoy then lost it again. The other aircraft, HX604/X skippered by Plt.Off. Matthews, attacked a vessel believed to have been a tanker under escort by two destroyers, bombing from 4000 feet. Although no results were observed, one hit was in fact achieved. The Wellington was damaged by AA fire but was able to return safely to Luqa, despite developing serious engine trouble.

Two nights later (the 28th/29th) three more 69 Squadron Wellingtons were despatched at 1845 to locate and attack another convoy seen earlier off the Greek coast by a Baltimore crew. Two of the three aircraft carried torpedoes and the third bombs, but the latter soon suffered engine trouble, jettisoned its bombs in the sea and returned to Luqa, where it was destroyed in a crash-landing; the crew survived.

The two torpedo-carriers meanwhile had located the Italian vessels 20 miles out from Navarino two hours before midnight — this was 'Convoy J' which had departed Taranto for Benghazi. It comprised the 2552-ton tanker *Luisiano*, carrying 1460 tons of fuel, the motor vessel *Etiopia* of 2153 tons (with a cargo of aviation fuel), two destroyers and a torpedo-boat. Plt.Off. Matthews (again flying HX604/X) gained a direct hit on *Etiopia* causing a vivid explosion, following which she was forced to put into Navarino for repairs. Although not sighting this vessel, the pilot of HX565/W, Plt.Off. Harry Donkersley RAAF, did spot the tanker and hit her amidships with a torpedo; *Luisiano* was soon ablaze from stem to stern and sank shortly afterwards. Both pilots received DFCs for their part in the action.

These were to be the last successes for Malta-based aircraft prior to Montgomery's victory at Alamein. But it is interesting to note that *Etiopia* subsequently reached Tobruk after having been repaired, there to be bombed and set on fire on 6 November with the loss of 341 tons of aviation fuel that was still aboard. On that same date, the 6424-ton tanker *Portofino* was also set on fire by RAF attack on Benghazi.

Meanwhile, on the first day of the new month, Wellingtons and Beauforts from Africa torpedoed the 1464-ton *Tripolino* (carrying 440 tons of rations and 318 tons of ammunition) off Derna, and the smaller German steamer *Ostia* (57 tons of rations and 52 tons of ammunition). Next day, Beauforts of 39 Squadron attacked two Italian naval auxiliaries, sinking the 1976-ton *Zara* and damaging the 1987-ton *Brioni*. These latest sinkings meant that 44% of all Axis cargoes despatched to North Africa during the month of October had been lost; 17 vessels each with a displacement of 500 tons or more had been sunk, totalling some 54,804 tons. General Montgomery signalled 201 Group, RAF:

> 'I would like to express my thanks for the way in which No 201 Group are assisting to make easier the task of the Eighth Army. Recent attacks carried out against enemy ships so vital to his effort were a wonderful achievement. I would be grateful if you would convey to those responsible our gratitude for operations carried out which must be epics against ships at sea.'

As a consequence of these latest sinkings, and in response to the ever-more desperate pleas for supplies being received from Rommel, Kesselring ordered the Luftwaffe to transport fuel to North Africa "day and night down to the last crew and the last aircraft". By midnight on 2 November the British were aware of this via 'Ultra' intercepts and were able to conclude correctly that these losses — particularly the sinking of three tankers in the last few days — would seriously undermine Rommel's ability to continue resisting Montgomery's offensive.

Thursday, 29 October

Whilst all remained fairly quiet in the skies over Malta, the day was marked by the arrival of the final carrier-borne reinforcements for the Island, under the codename Operation 'Train' (see Table 15 below). Newly-commissioned Plt.Offs. Mahar and Ken Mitchell were two of the four Malta veterans who had been returned to Gibraltar to lead in the new aircraft. Included amongst the new arrivals was Flg.Off. Howard Crafts RNZAF, who had recently shot down a Ju88 whilst flying a Spitfire from Gibraltar, the only such claim by a Gibraltar-based fighter aircraft (see Appendix IX).

The carrier *Furious* had again departed from Gibraltar, loaded with 32 new Spitfires in addition to her own small air group. The latter was notably different, for it included eight Seafire IB and IIC fighters of 801 Squadron — the first of the navalised version of the Spitfire to see operational service aboard ship. They were accompanied by nine Albacores of 822 Squadron.

Twenty-nine of the Spitfires aboard were launched during the morning, all reaching Malta safely, but between 1000 and 1120 more than 40 Bf109s approached the Island in an effort to intercept the delivery aircraft, about half of these crossing the coast. AA opened fire and 27 resident Spitfires were scrambled, but no engagements or claims were recorded on either side. However two of the Spitfires sent off crashed on take-off. Sgt. Wally Parks of 229 Squadron struck a steam roller with the wing of EP329, crashing sideways into a dispersal pen. The Australian sustained severe injuries to face and head, also breaking his left arm and leg; he failed to regain consciousness and died

TABLE 15

Operation 'Train'

29 Spitfires from HMS *Furious* (pilots believed to have included those listed below).

Plt.Off. H.G. Reynolds	had returned to Gibraltar to lead back flight
Plt.Off. E.L. Mahar	had returned to Gibraltar to lead back flight
Plt.Off. K.R. Mitchell	had returned to Gibraltar to lead back flight
Flg.Off. H.A. Crafts, RNZAF	EP404
Flg.Off. J.J. Lynch, RCAF (US)	
Plt.Off. J.R. Mowbray	Sgt. D.A. Piggott, RNZAF
Plt.Off. W.B. Randall	Sgt. C.D. Leeming
Plt.Off. M.J. Reid	Sgt. M.J. Costello
Plt.Off. Dawkins	Sgt. G.D. Billing
Plt.Off. N.D. Harrison, RNZAF	Sgt. W.A. Laing
Flt.Sgt. J.N. Miller	Sgt. J.D. Thorogood
Flt.Sgt. M.B. Zobell, RCAF	Sgt. G.R. Nadon, RCAF

about 30 minutes later.

Minutes later Spitfire AR488/S of 249 Squadron collided with a truck which had just delivered building materials to the airfield, crashed and was destroyed. Plt.Off. Giddings broke his wrist and several small bones in his arm, while Emanuel Grech, one of those unloading the lorry, was killed instantly and Michael Zerafa was seriously injured.

Meanwhile, on completion of her task, *Furious* and her escorts had turned back westwards. During the afternoon two Seafires were just landing-on from a patrol when a Ju88, which had managed to approach undetected, appeared and released a salvo of bombs, all of which missed their intended target. 801 Squadron's CO, Lt. Robert MacDonald-Hall, pulled up the undercarriage of his aircraft and gave chase, but the 30-gallon slipper tank with which the Seafire was fitted would not jettison, and he could not get closer than 300 yards to the fleeing bomber as a result. He fired all his ammunition at the intruder, reporting seeing strikes along its fuselage before it escaped.

Shortly before sunset MacDonald-Hall was in the air again when a Ju88 shadower was reported and then sighted, he and Sub Lt. Parish giving chase. They pursued the Junkers down to sea level but could not close to less than 400 yards on this occasion, and although both fired long bursts, no results could be observed — a disappointing conclusion to the first Seafire combats.*

With no action for Malta's defenders for 48 hours, the end of the 29th month of the siege allowed stock to be taken. Although losses of Spitfires had been high, pilot casualties had not. Moreover new arrivals both from *Furious* and in Hudsons from Gibraltar were about to allow numbers of time-expired 'old hands', together with some of the wounded, to be given a welcome rest. The defenders were in good heart.

Arrivals from Operation 'Train' — the last of the reinforcement flights — pose with one of their Spitfire Vcs, still fitted with its 90 gallon slipper tank. Plt.Offs. Al Laing (left) and Jerry Billing have just flown in from HMS *Furious*. *(R. Caruana)*

The month's claims were listed as:

Type	Day fighters	AA
Ju88	49: 31: 67	1: 0: 2
Bf109	58: 26: 72	6: 1: 2
MC202	17: 3: 18	
Re2001	2: 2: 2	
BR20	0: 0: 3	
u/i bomber		1: 0: 0
Total	126: 62: 162	8: 1: 4

The month's claims for each Wing were assessed as:

Luqa Wing:	57½: 22: 63
Takali Wing	56½: 31: 69
Hal Far Wing:	12 : 9: 29

In addition, the night fighters of 89 Squadron's 'C' Flight were credited with 6:1:2 for the month.

Saturday, 31 October

During the evening 24 tour-expired or wounded fighter pilots, including Wg.Cdr. Donaldson and Plt.Off. Beurling, together with ten civilians (two of

*Lt. Robert MacDonald-Hall had served with distinction with 806 Squadron during 1941, flying Fulmars from HMS *Indomitable* and Egypt, having amassed a total of four or five victories (see *Air War Over Yugoslavia, Greece and Crete 1940-41*, by the authors). Sadly, as *Malta: The Spitfire Year 1942* was going to press, he was killed when the helicopter he was piloting crashed near his home in Essex.

them young children) who were to be evacuted, boarded a Liberator transport — AL516 of 511 Squadron — bound for the UK via Gibraltar. The aircraft had arrived from Alexandria carrying, amongst others, Sqn.Ldr. Tommy Smart DFC, who was to take command of 229 Squadron.

After refuelling, the Liberator took-off at 0300, arriving over Gibraltar in the midst of a violent storm, low on fuel. Flt.Lt. R. Walton, the pilot, overshot the runway landing two-thirds along its length; because the runway terminated in the sea, he opened the throttles in an attempt to go round again. With insufficient speed the aircraft stalled, flopped into the sea about 100 yards off the runway, broke its back and sank like a stone. Although Walton and his navigator were injured in the crash, the whole crew escaped; but not all the passengers were so fortunate, many being trapped in the rear half of the fuselage when it broke away. Of the ten civilians aboard, eight were drowned or died of injuries — including the children — and the survivors were both injured.

Five pilots were drowned, including Flt.Lt. Eddie Glazebrook and Plt.Off. John Williams, two of the more successful fighter pilots. Flt.Lt. Eric Hetherington was seen conscious and apparently not in difficulties when rescuers arrived; he suggested they help others first, but seconds later he died, presumably from internal injuries.

Despite his wounded foot encased in plaster, George Beurling managed to get out and was picked up from the sea. Wt.Off. Farquharson, also with a foot in a cast, saved himself by clinging to the broken leg of another pilot who had managed to seize a piece of floating wreckage.

Wg.Cdr. Donaldson recalled:

> 'The passengers were all in the bomb bay . . . sitting on parachutes or anything comfortable they could find. Next to me was a beautiful Maltese girl called Bella; she had a son of about one year with her and she was going home to join her husband, an FAA pilot.
>
> 'I can remember a loud noise as we hit the sea. We were all thrown forward, not being strapped in and everything was chaos. In no time we hit the sea bed. I can remember seeing above me there was a small crack which looked lighter; this turned out to be where the aircraft had broken its back.
>
> 'I simply fought my way up through the broken hull to the surface . . . there seemed to be literally hundreds of men swimming out to the position of the wreck and soon someone got hold of me and pulled me towards the shore.'

Another survivor, Flt.Sgt. Arthur Varey, remembered:

> 'We touched down at Gibraltar, seemingly halfway down the runway and the pilot, realizing that he could not make it, opened up the engines to go round again. Unfortunately he hadn't sufficient power and we ploughed into the sea.
>
> 'There were a lot of us in the bomb bay. I was temporarily knocked out and vaguely remember scrambling through the torn fuselage and swimming valiantly to the shore, only realizing afterwards that I was in full uniform with my belt and ammunition strapped round my waist. I recall that "Screwball" Beurling was alongside me, and I did not realize until we got ashore that he had one leg in plaster.'

Flt.Lt. Roscoe was also amongst the survivors, and graphically recalls:

> 'As dawn was breaking I went aft to the waist gun position where there were two gunners at the wide open ports. Beurling came aft and joined me. The gunners produced a thermos of hot coffee and we stayed there for the rest of the flight.
>
> 'As we crossed the end of the runway on final approach we could see out of the gun ports that we were way too high, and as yards and yards of runway went by we felt sure the pilot would go round again for another approach. He didn't however, and the wheels touched down hard somewhere near the end of the runway. Power was applied and the big plane struggled to get airborne again but it was too late now to go round again.
>
> 'The gunners yelled at us to brace for a crash-landing, and I grabbed on to something solid. With an almighty whack the Liberator hit the water, and the deceleration was so sudden we were thrown into the corner of the compartment, suffering minor cuts and bruises. My arm was in a sling and all this jostling didn't make it feel any better.
>
> 'The aircraft had stopped now and was fast filling with water; we were up to our waist in water in no time. Flt.Sgt. Bye of 229 Squadron appeared in the waist compartment, bleeding badly from head cuts. I found a loose life raft, inflated it, and helped Bye out of the gun port and into the raft. I exited the aircraft myself at this time.
>
> 'Beurling was in the water near me and offered to help me with my arm being in the sling, but I told him I was OK and he swam off toward shore. I was a good swimmer but didn't trust my bad arm. The aircraft had settled to the bottom of the shallow bay, resting on the extended undercarriage, with the wing just awash. I climbed onto the wing and tried to help others up.
>
> 'Some of those in the water were all right, others dying or already dead. Some souls were still in the bomb bay, either killed by the impact, or unable to get out and drowned. The army put rafts out from shore and soon we were all taken off, drenched and cold, many suffering from shock.'

A full list of those involved in the accident is shown in Appendix X.

Sunday 1 — Thursday 5 November

On Malta, the first day of the new month was marked by a single scramble by four Spitfires of 1435 Squadron at 1205 to investigate a raid which did not materialize. As Rhodesian Plt.Off. Russell Wright's aircraft became airborne, his engine failed and he was fatally injured when attempting to carry out a subsequent crash-landing.

Next day (the 2nd) at 1340, up to two dozen fighters and Jabo crossed the coast at great height and although four Spitfires of 249 Squadron were up, no sightings were made. A number of Spitfires of 185 and 229 Squadrons were on a training flight however, and four of these were bounced by Bf109s diving from 28,000 feet but there were no casualties. Bombs were dropped on Luqa by a single Jabo although a second would-be raider was shot down by ground fire from RAF defences. The Messerschmitt — 'Yellow 3' of I/SchG 2 — blew up and crashed near Kirkop. Its pilot, Ofw. Heinrich Slany, was killed.

Just over two hours later another fighter sweep approached the coast but only six crossed. 126 and 229 Squadrons each had eight aircraft in the air but failed to make contact. Five more from 249 Squadron were bounced from out of the sun by two Messerschmitts, Sgt. W.B. Weir's EP448/F sustaining some damage and the pilot suffering slight wounds; he crash-landed at Takali on return.

At 1335 on Tuesday (the 3rd) seven Spitfires of 185 Squadron were scrambled on the approach of a Jabo raid directed at Luqa, intercepting a trio of MC202s as they turned away to the east. Chasing these down to 10,000 feet, Sgt. Gunstone claimed to have shot down one into the sea seven miles north of Grand Harbour. No Italian losses were recorded. A Jabo raid on Hal Far two hours later destroyed a Spitfire in its blast pen. Although seven Spitfires were airborne, they failed to make contact.

Within 1435 Squadron, the recently-commissioned Ian MacLennan was promoted to flight commander, taking over from Flt.Lt. White who was himself promoted to command 185 Squadron, where Maj. Swales was being rested.

It was 1435 Squadron which was sent off again on the 5th, four Spitfires engaging an equal number of Bf109s during the middle of the afternoon, one of which was claimed damaged by Flt.Lt. Burgess north of St Paul's Bay.

Darkness brought with it a single raider, bombs falling into St Paul's Bay. As the Z1007bis turned away, it was intercepted by a Beaufighter (T5161) flown by Sqn.Ldr. Pain who shot it down in flames into the sea two miles west of Gozo, for his fifth nocturnal victory. Two of the crew managed to bale out, one of whom — Sottoten. Antonio De Sancti — was admitted to Victoria Hospital, Gozo, in a serious condition.

Fighter-bomber! Spitfire T-N (believed to be BR373) of 249 Squadron, armed with a 250lb bomb under each wing. *(R. Caruana)*

The news from Africa was good for the Allies however, for the previous day Montgomery's forces had at last broken through at Alamein, and it was becoming clear that the Afrika Korps was in full retreat — a great victory was in prospect. But more was afoot, for next day 16 Beaufighters of 272 Squadron flew in to Takali from North Africa, followed by six Wellingtons of 104 Squadron, which went to Luqa. They had come to lend support to a major Allied invasion of French North-West Africa — Operation 'Torch' — which was due to commence only two days hence. Indeed, the newly-arrived Wellingtons were to launch their first attack on the Sardinian airfields at Decimomannu and Elmas, after dark on the 7th.

Friday 6 — Saturday 7 November

Over Malta on the 6th, five Spitfires of 229 Squadron were sent off at 1025 but were bounced by Bf109s, which slightly damaged Flt.Sgt. Edwards' aircraft. Two of 126 Squadron's aircraft, one flown by Flt.Lt. Rod Smith, fought an estimated 12-15 Messerschmitts at 22,000 feet over Grand Harbour for 25 minutes, albeit without obvious result. Next day, feeling ill, Smith reported sick and was hospitalized for a month.

Meanwhile at 1230, a Fiat RS14 floatplane (No 7) of 170ª Squadriglia RM took off from Augusta on reconnaissance. After 25 minutes, when 37 miles from Cape Bon, the aircraft was attacked by two twin-engined machines identified as Blenheims, Sottoten. Vittorio Pruneri's crew claiming to have shot down one of these. It would seem that these were transit Beaufighters en route to Malta, but no record of such an engagement has been discovered.

When darkness came on the 7th, six 104 Squadron Wellingtons commenced take-off for the operation against Decimomannu and Elmas airfields (Sardinia), but Flg.Off. S.C. Morrison's machine crashed near Rabat and caught fire, he and his crew perishing. One of the remaining five bombers returned early with engine trouble whilst the others failed to locate their targets due to haze.

As the bombers headed for Sardinia, two Beaufighters of 89 Squadron were ordered to patrol over western Sicily. At 2015 Flg.Off. Crombie and Sgt. Moss (in T5165) sighted a twin-engined aircraft — identified as a Ju88 — flying at 50 feet about three miles off Cape Granitola. Diving on this from 500 feet, Crombie reported shooting it into the sea. However, the other Beaufighter (T5161 flown by Sqn.Ldr. Pain and Sgt. J.V. Briggs) failed to return. It was thought that their aircraft may have collided with balloon cables at Marsala. The loss of a Ju88 cannot be confirmed from Luftwaffe records, therefore there exists the possibility that Crombie may have inadvertently shot down Pain's aircraft; in the event, Pain and Briggs survived as prisoners.

This latest victory awarded to the night fighters gave a Grand Total credited to the fighters from June 1940 to 7 November 1942, of:

863½ confirmed: 316 probables: 814 damaged

Luftwaffe losses over Malta attributable to fighters and AA defences — according to German records — for the period 19 December 1941 to 7 November 1942, were as follows:

Type	Lost	Damaged (30-60%)	Damaged (5-30%)
Ju88	161	21	18
Ju87	17	2	1
He111	3	0	0
Do17	1	0	0
Do24	0	0	1
Bf109	64	3	4
Bf110	3	0	0
Total	249	26	24

NB: The numbers of aircraft admitted damaged in relation to those reported lost appear to be grossly out of proportion. By comparison, during the early part of

1941 (10 January to 31 May), the Luftwaffe admitted the loss of 55:8:15 to Malta's defences.

Luftwaffe fighter claims over Malta during this period were officially recorded as:

Unit	Number	Period
Stab JG 53	35	December 1941 — May 1943
I/JG 53	29	December 1941 — May 1942
II/JG 53	159	December 1941 — May 1943
III/JG 53	61	January 1942 — May 1943
I/JG 77	99-103	July 1942 — October 1942
I/JG 27	7	October 1942
II/JG 3	6	January 1942 — April 1942
I/NJG 2	11	December 1941 — April 1942
III/ZG 26	7	December 1941 — April 1942

NB: The 284 victories of JG 53 include about 30 claimed during December 1941, and may include a few claimed over Malta during the Tunisian campaign. The victories of I/NJG 2 include three by night; five were claimed during December 1941, one by night.

In the period covered by this book — 1 January to 7 November 1942 — records would suggest that a total of 45 Hurricanes and 148 Spitfires were lost in the air, of which only a handful were due to accidents; at least a further 16 Hurricanes and 66 Spitfires force-landed or crash-landed, mainly as a result of combat, while at least 59 Hurricanes and 5 Spitfires were 'destroyed' on the ground, the majority having sustained irreparable damage during bombing attacks on the airfields; many of those which crash-landed, as well as those written-off on the ground, were stripped of re-usable parts as lack of spares always constituted a problem.

It was estimated that 13,750 tons of bombs had fallen upon the Island since the beginning of the year, during which 1104 Maltese had lost their lives, while 75% of the houses in Valetta had been destroyed or damaged. In addition, 403 soldiers had been killed during the raids of 1942, including 74 Maltese, while 104 RAF ground personnel had also lost their lives during this period.

On Sunday 8 November 1942, British and American troops went ashore at Oran and Algiers, and on the Atlantic coast of Morocco; a new phase of the war had begun. With Rommel's forces in flight towards Western Cyrenaica, the Axis High Commands suddenly had to consider securing Tunisia to prevent the Afrika Korps being caught in a trap. At once forces based in Sicily had to be swung onto this new front, and within days units which had been flying over Malta were transferred to airfields around Tunis.

There would still be occasional sorties flown by the Luftwaffe into the skies over Malta and much hard fighting to come, but essentially the siege was over. Malta was now more than ever a forward striking base to interdict not only the supply routes to Tripoli and Benghazi, but also the newer, closer ones to Cape

Bon. Before November was out Convoy 'Stonehenge' arrived from Alexandria, no longer under threat from Axis air power in North Africa — or even to any great extent on Crete. Four merchant vessels, escorted by five cruisers and 17 destroyers, would reach the Island with damage only to a single cruiser having been sustained. 35,000 tons of vital supplies would be delivered.

During the next six months Malta's Beaufighters and Spitfires played havoc with Axis air transports attempting to carry supplies to the increasingly beleaguered forces in Africa. The anti-shipping units would also have an essential part to play during this period. A detailed account of operations by the Island's air forces from 8 November 1942 to 13 May 1943, has already been given in *Fighters Over Tunisia* (Christopher Shores, Hans Ring and William N. Hess; Neville Spearman, 1975). With the expulsion of the Axis from North Africa, Malta became the major base for the assault by air on Pantelleria and Sicily, and eventually for the invasion of Sicily itself.

By August 1943, just one year after the great 'Pedestal' supply convoy had been fought through, Malta was on the point of becoming a backwater of the war. But hers had been the glory for so long.

Air Chief Marshal Sir Arthur Tedder, later Lord Tedder, was to write:

> 'I hope the lessons of Malta will not be forgotten. I trust that never again shall our unpreparedess lead to our men having to face such odds or be stretched so near to the ultimate limit of endurance.'

Such a statement can only be followed by the timeless reminder:

> War does not determine who is right — only who is left.'

Chapter 11

AFTERMATH

There can be no doubt that after October 1942 the long siege had ended — and on a note of success for the defenders. However, as with the Battle of Britain at the close of 1940, the questions must remain — when fairly posed — how great and complete had been the apparent victory, and how far had the fighting ended as a result of events elsewhere?

As in 1940, the actual figures show that the margin between attackers shot down and losses amongst the defending fighters was far closer than was popularly thought at the time. As in September 1940 over Southern England, the defending fighters over Malta in October 1942 had inflicted painfully severe losses on the opposing bomber force. Indeed, these losses had been sufficiently severe for Feldmarshall Kesselring to call a halt to further daylight attack. As in 1940, however, the defenders were still losing more of their own aircraft to the opposing escort fighters than they were being able to shoot down in return — although that was not apparent to them at the time. What is very clear now is that throughout 1942 the level of overclaiming against the elusive Messerschmitts was every bit as high as it had proved to be on most other fronts from 1940-1943. After that date the wider availability and use of gun cameras greatly improved the accuracy of claim confirmations.

In the whirling confusion of fighter versus fighter combat, it was extremely easy for several pilots to fire at the same aircraft and each believe that he had been the sole victor, or to believe that damage was more conclusive than had been the case; or yet again, to have looked down a moment later to see an aircraft — or even a bomb — splashing into the sea and to have believed this to be proof of his own success. The detailed reports on many of the engagements recorded in the preceding chapters will have given many clues to such events, whilst there is little doubt that some over-enthusiastic and eager pilots tended to take a more optimistic view of the results of their attacks than did others. Around an island such as Malta, confirmation of claims always proved difficult, as so many aircraft either fell into the sea, or were assumed to have done so; there were few available wrecks to check and count.

For the Germans and Italians, operating 60 miles from their bases and entirely over hostile territory, the situation was even more difficult and fraught with opportunities for error. It is noteworthy that over Malta even the usually meticulous Luftwaffe fighter pilots tended to run up a higher proportion of overclaiming than over, say, Western Europe or the North African Desert, where checking from wrecks or ground witnesses was much easier.

The October claims of the Malta-based RAF fighters afford a particularly good opportunity to consider this phenomenon. During the week of the main blitz (11th to 17th) claims made against Ju88s — the predominant bombers —

amounted to 53 'confirmed' and 27 'probables' by day and night. Actual losses totalled 34 Ju88s destroyed and 13 fairly seriously damaged. Thus, actual losses represented 64% of confirmed claims — a creditably accurate proportion. Against the Italian escort fighters claims were made for 11 MC202s and three Re2001s 'confirmed', with three and one respectively as 'probables'. Actual losses appear to have totalled five Macchis and one Reggiane destroyed, with six of the former recorded as damaged. Here the percentage of actual losses to confirmed claims deteriorates to just under 43%. However, claims against Bf109s amounted to 45 'confirmed' and 16 'probables', whilst recorded losses were 12 destroyed and five damaged. This indicates an accuracy level of 'confirmed' claims of about 26.5% — or less than one in four! One consoling fact to emerge was that the night fighters, had, as ever, proved reliably accurate in their one-to-one engagements, claiming four bombers shot down and one 'probable' during this same period against actual Axis casualties of four destroyed and one damaged.

During this period 43 Spitfires were shot down (23) or crash-landed (20), while 39 more were damaged. Thus, whilst it was thought that almost twice as many opposing fighters had probably been shot down as had been lost, in fact more than twice as many Spitfires had been lost as had Axis fighters! The good news for the defenders had been that from the total number of Spitfires lost, only a dozen pilots had been killed while a further seven had survived with wounds or injuries of varying seriousness; 24 were unhurt.

Malta's continued survival as a base for interdiction of Axis supplies played a major part in aiding the success of the British operations in North Africa, whilst the need for the Luftwaffe and Regia Aeronautica to maintain substantial air forces on Sicily, and to a lesser extent on Sardinia and Crete, went far to ensure that they were unable to wrest air superiority from the Western Desert Air Force. Put in global context however, its air battles can hardly be credited with the degree of importance and effect — particularly in denying the Eastern Front — that were claimed for them at the time.

Above all, Malta was evidence that by 1942 the Germans had become overstretched militarily with too many fronts to support. Each time the Luftwaffe came close to neutralizing the Island completely, the greater demands of other fronts led to dispersion elsewhere before the job could be done, whilst the Regia Aeronautica, despite the undoubted bravery of many of its airmen, simply emphasised the inadequacy of its equipment in undertaking such a task.

Just as the demands of the Balkans and the forthcoming invasion of Russia caused the removal eastwards of the greater part of the Luftwaffe in 1941 — ending the blitz on England and effectively preventing any resumption of the daylight assault — so too did the Russian venture take the Germans away from Sicily again at the critical moment in April-May 1942. On at least two occasions during mid 1942 the invasion of Malta had seriously been considered by the Axis forces, but after October the option no longer remained. Before any new assault could be considered, the success of Montgomery's Alamein offensive in Egypt and, above all, the Anglo-American invasion of French North Africa, required an almost total diversion of resources in Sicily to this new danger area. Indeed, the substantial reinforcement of the Luftwaffe to meet the threat in Tunisia, which was now a reality, underlines what could well have been directed against Malta had the German High Command increased its priority as a target.

It is no reflection at all upon the courage, fortitude and achievements of both the defenders and population of Malta that the full force of the still-mighty Luftwaffe was not unleashed upon the Island in 1942. It does need to be borne in mind however, that in substance the whole of the October blitz amounted to no more than the equivalent of a single busy day in the Battle of Britain, and much less than one of the USAAF 8th Air Force's great forthcoming raids on Germany. Rarely was more than the equivalent of a single Geschwader (wing) of fighters and a Geschwader and a half of bombers committed to Sicily at any one time, whilst RAF strength never rose above a strengthened wing of fighters. Malta was marked by the ferocity of the fighting, the endurance of the participants and the sustained nature of the battle, rather than by the size of the forces engaged.

The inability, for whatever reason, of the attackers to subdue the stubborn defence; the determination of the British to sustain that defence at almost any cost, and the consequent continued ability of the resident submarines and strike aircraft to affect Axis strength and ability in North Africa — that was what the Malta epic was all about. And above all, it was the story of the fighter pilots.

The Fighter Aces

Malta was to be a breeding ground for fighter aces*. As has been recorded, it had great 'stars', whilst veterans of earlier battles were able to chalk up further successes here — as the legendary George Beurling once enthusiastically exclaimed: "Malta was a fighter pilot's paradise". The air battles over Malta also provided experience for many pilots who went on to greater successes in combat and leadership over Tunisia, Italy, Western Europe, and even the Far East.

In other theatres the advantages enjoyed during the early years of the war by the Luftwaffe fighter pilots, coupled with the German system whereby they were retained at the front for much longer periods (often out of necessity), ensured that the victory totals attributed to the leading pilots tended to be much greater than those of their British or American (or Russian) counterparts. Not so over Malta however, for here many Germans felt they encountered the most difficult conditions they were to experience anywhere during the war.

The defenders' greatest exponent was beyond doubt George Beurling, whose total over the Island had reached 26⅓ by the time he was shot down and wounded. The Canadian Beurling had no close rivals, but nine other pilots had been credited with ten or more victories — three Australians, two New Zealanders, a Rhodesian, an American, another Canadian and a Malayan-born Englishman. They were followed by a considerable number (34) of pilots with claim totals between five and nine, including six of 89 Squadron's night fighters.

RAF and Commonwealth Fighter Pilots credited with at least five victories whilst flying from Malta, 1 January – 7 November 1942

Name	Squadron	Malta claims	Total for War
Plt.Off. G.F. Beurling, DSO, DFC, DFM+	249 Sqn	26⅓	30⅓
Flt.Sgt. P.A. Schade, DFM	126 Sqn	12½	12½

*The term ace used herewith denotes a pilot credited with at least five 'confirmed' victories.

Flt.Lt. H.W. McLeod, DFC+	603/1435 Sqns	12	20
Plt.Off. A.P. Goldsmith, DFC, DFM	185 Sqn	11¾	15¾
Plt.Off. R.B. Hesselyn, DFM+	249 Sqn	12	21½‡
Plt.Off. J.W. Yarra, DFM	185 Sqn	12	12
Flt.Lt. J.A. Plagis, DFC+	249/185 Sqns	11	15
Flt.Sgt. C. Weaver, DFM	185 Sqn	10½	12½‡
Flt.Sgt. N.M. Park, DFM	126 Sqn	10¼	10¼
Plt.Off. V.P. Brennan, DFC, DFM	249 Sqn	10	10
Plt.Off. P.A. Nash, DFC	249 Sqn	9½	11½
Flt.Lt. C.H. Parkinson, DFC	603/229 Sqns	8½	8½
Flt.Lt. N.C. Macqueen, DFC	249 Sqn	8	8
Flt.Lt. J.F. McElroy, DFC	249 Sqn	8	11½‡
Flt.Lt. R.W. McNair, DFC	249 Sqn	7¾	15¾‡
Flt.Lt. R.O. Jones	126 Sqn	7½	7½
Flt.Lt. W.T.E. Rolls, DFC+, DFM	126 Sqn	7½	17†
Flg.Off. G.A.F. Buchanan, DFC	249 Sqn	7	7½
Plt.Off. G. Stenborg, DFC	185 Sqn	7	14⅓‡
Sqn.Ldr. M.M. Stephens, DSO, DFC++	249/229 Sqns	7	22†
Plt.Off. R.F. Tilley, DFC	601/126 Sqns	7	7
Plt.Off. G.R. Tweedale, DFM	185 Sqn	7	7
Flt.Lt. R. West, DFC+	249/185 Sqns	7	7
Flt.Lt. I.R. MacLennan, DFM	1435 Sqn	6	7
Flt.Sgt. D.G. Reid, DFM	185 Sqn	6	6
Flt.Lt. R.I.A. Smith, DFC	126 Sqn	6	13‡
Flt.Sgt. A.W. Varey, DFM	126 Sqn	6	6
Flt.Lt. F.E. Jones, DFC	249 Sqn	5·83	5·83
Plt.Off. J.H.E. Bisley, DFC	126 Sqn	5½	6½
Flt.Sgt. W.G. Dodd	185 Sqn	5⅓	6⅔
Sqn.Ldr. R.A. Mitchell, DFC	603/249 Sqns	5⅓	5⅓
Flt.Sgt. J.H. Ballantyne, DFM	603/229 Sqns	5¼	5¼
Flg.Off. E.S. Dicks-Sherwood, DFC	229 Sqn	5	6½
Flt.Sgt. K.W.S. Evans, DFM	126 Sqn	5	5
Plt.Off. J. Hurst, DFC	603 Sqn	5	6
Flt.Sgt. A.H. Scott, DFM	126 Sqn	5	5
Sqn.Ldr. E.N. Woods, DFC	249 Sqn	5	10⅔‡

RAF and Commonwealth Night Fighter Pilots credited with at least five victories whilst flying from Malta, 1 January — 7 November 1942

Name	Squadron	Malta claims	Total for War
Flg.Off. R.C. Fumerton, DFC+	89 Sqn	8	14†
Flg.Off. E.G. Daniel, DFC	89 Sqn	7	7
Flg.Off. M.C. Shipard, DFC	89 Sqn	6	13‡
Flt.Lt. G. McL. Hayton, DFC	89 Sqn	5	5
Plt.Off. N.E. Reeves, DFC	89 Sqn	6	16‡
Flt.Lt. H.G. Edwards, DFC	89 Sqn	5	6

NB: Ranks shown were those attained by November 1942; decorations shown were those awarded in recognition of performances whilst flying from Malta, with the exception of the five indicated thus†. These pilots had been decorated for service prior to Malta, then received further awards for their Malta performances. Additionally, the pilots indicated thus‡ received further awards for actions later in the war.

The Luftwaffe's top-scorer was Gerhard Michalski of II/JG 53, whose total during the Malta operations, up to November 1942, reached 26. This tally was closely followed by I/JG 77's Siegfried Freytag, who achieved his successes during a much shorter period, gaining for himself the accolade 'Die Stern von Malta' ('The Star of Malta'). From within his own Gruppe, Michalski was followed by Herbert Rollwage with 20 victories, and Rudolf Ehrenberger with between 13 and 16. Beyond that however, only four other Luftwaffe pilots are believed to have claimed between 10 and 15 victories.

Provisional listing of Luftwaffe Top-Scoring Fighter Pilots over Malta

Name	Unit	Over Malta	Victory numbers	Total for War
Hpt. Gerhard Michalski	II/JG53	26	23-47	73
Oblt. Siegfried Freytag	I/JG77	24	50-73	102
Ofw. Herbert Rollwage	5/JG53	20	12-31	80-85
Ofw. Rudolf Ehrenberger	6/JG53	16	13-28	49
Ofw. Walter Brandt	2/JG77	14	21-34	42
Maj. Günther von Maltzahn	Stab/JG53	14†	51-64	68
Lt. Heinz-Edgar Berres	I/JG77	11	8-19	52
Lt. Franz Schiess	Stab/JG53	10	15-24	67
Oblt. Fritz Geisshardt	3/JG77	9	83-91	102
Oblt. Helmüt Belser	8/JG53	8	21-28	36
Lt. Fritz Dinger	4/JG53	6	13-18	67
Ofw. Walter Stumpf	9/JG53	6	26-31	48
Lt. Ernst Klager	8/JG53	5	10-14	18
Lt. Karl-Heinz Quaritsch	8/JG53	5	1-5	13
Uffz. Horst Schlick	I/JG77	5	3-7	34
Lt. Joachim Louis	Stab/JG53	5‡	1-5	21
Lt. Herbert Soukop	6/JG53	5	1-5	5
Hpt. Heinz Bär	I/JG77	4	114-117	220
Lt. Günther Hannak	2/JG77	4	42-45	47
Hpt. Wolf-Dietrich Wilcke	III/JG53	4	33-36	162

†Maj. Maltzahn claimed three of his 14 victories over Malta in December 1941
‡Lt. Louis claimed one of his five victories over Malta in December 1941

Amongst the Italians, despite the limited firepower of their aircraft, a number of pilots had done well. Top-scorer over Malta for the Regia Aeronautica was Teresio Martinoli of the 4° Stormo CT, who added three more victories to the five he had claimed during the closing months of 1941. In the same unit Franco Lucchini, one of the great Italian fighter pilots of the war, claimed two more to raise his 1941-42 total over Malta to four and two shared. The most successful Italian pilot of 1942 however, had been the 51° Stormo's Furio Doglio Niclot with six and three shared, followed by Ennio Tarantola with five and three shared. Most successful Re2001 pilot had been 2° Gruppo Aut. CT's Agostino Celentano with five, three other pilots in this unit claiming four apiece.

Top-Scoring Regia Aeronautica Fighter Pilots over Malta, 1942

Name	Squadron	Score
Cap. Furio Doglio Niclot	151ª Sq/20° Gr/51° St	6+3 shared
Mar. Ennio Tarantola	151ª Sq/20° Gr/51° St	5+3 shared
Ten. Agostino Celentano	150ª Sq/2° Gr Aut	5
Serg. Magg. Rino Ricci	152ª Sq/2° Gr Aut	4
Ten. Carlo Seganti	358ª Sq/2° Gr Aut	4
Mar. Olindo Simionato	150ª Sq/2° Gr Aut	4

High-Scoring Regia Aeronautica Fighter Pilots over Malta, 1941-42
(not included in above list)

Serg. Teresio Martinoli	73ª Sq/9° Gr/4° St	8 (5 in 1941)
Mar. Aldo Buvoli	360ª Sq/155° Gr/51° St	6 (5 in 1941)
Cap. Franco Lucchini	84ª Sq/10° Gr/4° St	4+ 2 shared (2 in 1942)

Despite the ferocity of the fighting, losses amongst the more notable pilots had not been unduly severe. Indeed, throughout 1942 the Luftwaffe had lost but five of its aces, only one of whom was a high scorer over Malta; three of these (Hpt. Karl-Heinz Krahl, Fw. Hans Schade and Fw. Heinz Golinski) were killed, while the other two (Lt. Hermann Neuhoff and Lt. Herbert Soukop) had become prisoners. However, three of the Luftwaffe's leading pilots — Maj. Günther von Maltzahn, Hpt. Gerhard Michalski and Oblt. Siegfried Freytag — had been shot down into the sea during combat off the Malta coast, from which each had been successfully recovered. Of its ace pilots, the Regia Aeronautica had lost Cap. Furio Doglio Niclot killed, whilst Mar. Aldo Buvoli had become a prisoner.

During 1942 the defenders had lost 109 fighter pilots in action, eight of whom were ace pilots; Flt.Sgt. Nigel Park of 126 Squadron had been the most successful of those killed (the others were Grp.Capt. Walter Churchill — although none of his victories were claimed whilst flying from Malta — Plt.Off. Peter Nash, Flt.Lt. Rip Jones, Flt.Lt. Norman Macqueen, Flt.Sgt. Gordon Tweedale, Flt.Sgt. Don Reid and Plt.Off. Johnny Hurst). Additionally, Flt.Sgt. Claude Weaver had become a POW. Also, Plt.Off. J.W. Williams lost his life in the Liberator crash at Gibraltar on 1 November.

The remainder of the war and its immediate aftermath was to take a very much greater toll of the Malta veterans however, so that relatively few of those who achieved 'acedom' survived to become senior citizens, be they Allied, German or Italian. In order to complete the picture, a brief synopsis (in chronological order) is set out below, nation by nation, of what Fate had in store for some of the more successful pilots whose actions are recorded in the preceding chapters.

As already recorded, Flt.Lt. G.McL. Hayton DFC, the successful New Zealand night fighter, had been lost (death officially reported as having occurred by 20/10/42*) when the ship (HMT *Laconia*) in which he was returning to England had been sunk off the West African coast on 12/9/42. Flt.Lt. L.V. Sanders DFC, who had survived ditching BR108 in Marsalforn Bay, Gozo, returned to England where he was killed in a flying accident on 23/10/42. Before the year was out (10/12/42), Plt.Off. J.W. Yarra DFM, was shot down and killed by fire from a Flakship off the Dutch coast.

1943 brought a spate of accidents. Flt.Lt. E.B. Mortimer-Rose DFC (having dropped rank to return to operations) now a flight commander in 111 Squadron in Tunisia, collided with his Wing Leader and crashed to his death (28/1/43). Sqn.Ldr. A.R.H. Barton DFC & Bar was killed in a flying accident on 4/4/43, whilst an instructor in England, while on 6/5/43 Flt.Lt. H.G. Edwards DFC, having added one more night victory to make his total six, died in a crash with the new 108 Squadron to which he had been transferred in Egypt.

The Australian Flg.Off. V.P. Brennan DFC, DFM, had returned to his native country, but there he too was killed in an accident (13/6/43). By the mid part of that year, many pilots were well into their second or third tours of operations. Wg.Cdr. A.C. Rabagliati DFC & Bar, who had raised his total to at least 17 and one shared (all but six of these successes claimed over Malta during 1941-42) had become Wing Leader at Coltishall. Although usually flying Spitfires, he borrowed a Typhoon to lead the one unit (197 Squadron) in his wing so equipped on a sweep to the Dutch coast on 6/7/43. His aircraft was hit by AA fire and as he headed back across the Channel, he was obliged to ditch in the sea; he was not recovered. Only four days later Flt.Lt. W.R. Daddo-Langlois was lost. After a period as a photo-reconnaissance pilot in England, he had flown a Spitfire out to North Africa, from where he had been posted to command a flight of 93 Squadron in time for the invasion of Sicily. Flying from Malta again on 10/7/43, the day of the invasion, he led an attack on some Ju88s and was heard to say that he had got one, when his aircraft was struck by AA fire from the Allied vessels offshore; he crash-landed on the beach, sustaining a serious skull fracture. As he was ferried, deeply unconscious, by lighter to a hospital ship, another bombing attack commenced during which the lighter was sunk, and he was lost.

Flt.Lt. J.D. Rae DFC & Bar rejoined 485 Squadron, RNZAF, and added five and one shared before going down in France on 22/8/43 to become a POW. Battle of Britain veteran Sqn.Ldr. R.C. Dafforn DFC, one of the tallest men in the RAF, had recovered from his wounds and became Chief Flying Instructor at Sutton Bridge Central Gunnery School, but whilst on an air firing exercise on 9/9/43, his Spitfire crashed and he was killed. New Zealander Flt.Lt. Gray Stenborg DFC had joined 91 Squadron in England in mid 1943, claiming three and one shared German fighters in a month to raise his score to 14⅓, but on 24/9/43 he was shot down and killed. Flt.Lt. R.B. Hesselyn DFM & Bar, another New Zealander, was now a flight commander with 222 Squadron, and added a further nine and one shared victories to his tally. Three of these — all Bf109s — were claimed on 3/10/43 but during that engagement he was shot down in flames,

*The dates are given British style.

baling out wounded in the legs. He did survive as a POW, escaping once — only to be recaptured — and made several other attempts for which he would be awarded an MBE; a DFC was gazetted a few days after he went down.

Plt.Off. A.M.O. Pring DFM had been posted from Egypt to India where a new night fighter squadron was being formed for the defence of Calcutta. Here he shot down three Japanese bombers in one night, but on 6/12/43 a major daylight raid on the city developed, and he was one of several night fighter pilots who scrambled in Hurricanes to intercept; he was shot down and killed by Japanese fighters. Wg.Cdr. E.N. Woods DFC & Bar had continued to fly from Malta during the Tunisian operations, claiming a further three and two shared victories. Following the invasion of Italy, Woods and his No 2 (the CO of 126 Squadron) collided over the Adriatic on 16/12/43 and both were lost.

With the capitulation of the Italians in September 1943, Sgt. Claude Weaver DFM escaped from captivity and returned to the United Kingdom. Commissioned, he joined 403 Squadron, RCAF and rapidly added two further victories to his total, but failed to return from a sortie over France on 28/1/44; the award of a DFC was announced in March. The tough and revered Wg.Cdr. E.J. Gracie DFC returned to operations as a night fighter pilot, commanding first 23 and then 169 Squadron, flying Mosquitoes; he failed to return from a bomber support sortie over Germany during the night of 15/2/44.

On 8/3/44, Flg.Off. J.H. Ballantyne DFM, RCAF was shot down by Flak over France whilst flying with 403 Squadron, and was killed. After leaving Malta, Flt.Lt. J.E. Peck DFC had transferred to his native USAAF, and had flown Spitfires in Tunisia with the 52nd Fighter Group, adding a further victory to his tally. Posted back to England, he was demonstrating a P-38 fighter when he crashed and lost his life on 12/4/44. Two days later (14/4/44), the Fleet Air Arm's hero of Operation 'Pedestal', Lt.Cdr. R.J. Cork DSC, DFC was similarly killed in an accident in a Corsair fighter at Trimcomalee, Ceylon; he had recently been promoted Wing Leader of 15 RN Fighter Wing on HMS *Illustrious*.

The Normandy Invasion of 6 June 1944 was to be followed by several further losses of ex-Malta personalities. Flt.Lt. I.R. MacLennan DFM, now a flight commander in 401 Squadron, force-landed on one of the invasion beaches on 7/6/44 and became a POW. Not so fortunate was Sqn.Ldr. E.G. Daniel DFC. The night fighter pilot had commanded first a special trials Typhoon night operations flight, and then a special flight of the Fighter Interception Unit equipped with Tempests for the night interception of the new V-1 missiles; he shot down three of these but as he attacked one on 5/7/44 it blew up, the blast sending his aircraft out of control into the sea.

Flt.Lt. M.R.B. Ingram DFC had continued to fly with 601 Squadron after its departure to the Desert, and by the end of 1942 he had at least five and four shared victories to his credit. On his second tour he was posted to 152 Squadron in Sicily (in 1943), adding another victory and a shared to his total before being posted to India, where he became squadron commander. Leading the unit in to Imphal in July 1944 he crash-landed, breaking his nose; he was taken to hospital where he contracted malaria and died on 11/7/44.

Meanwhile, after a period as an instructor in England, Flg.Off. P.A. Schade DFM joined 91 Squadron; he was killed in a mid-air collision whilst with this unit on 31/7/44. Sqn.Ldr. H.W. McLeod DFC & Bar had taken command of 443 Squadron, RCAF, in 2nd Tactical Air Force, rapidly increasing his score during the early summer of 1944 to become the RCAF's top-scorer with 20 victories, for which he received a DSO. However he was seen to attack nine Bf109s over the Nijmegen area on 27/9/44, and did not return; he was found dead in the wreckage of his Spitfire a few days later. Another Canadian pilot, Flt.Lt. P.M. Charron DFC, was to claim five victories over Western Europe while flying with 412 Squadron, RCAF, to add to the two he had claimed whilst on Malta; on 19/11/44 he led four Spitfires to attack a large formation of German aircraft, but was shot down and killed.

Following his successful leadership of 249 Squadron, Wg.Cdr. R.A. Mitchell DFC & Bar became a Mosquito intruder pilot with 605 Squadron on his return to England, claiming the destruction of six aircraft on the ground and sharing one aerial victory with this unit. He was reported missing in action on the night of 17-18/3/45. Another of the night fighters, Flt.Lt. R.A. Miller DFC & Bar, continued to operate in his specialist role as part of 2nd TAF, claiming three further victories in 1944. Posted from 604 Squadron to the Fighter Experimental Flight at Ford, he was lost during the night of 26-27/4/45 when his Mosquito was shot down by Flak over Austria. Sqn.Ldr. L.W. Watts DFC served with 616 Squadron from mid 1943 to the closing weeks of the war, flying Gloster Meteor jets when the unit became the first to convert to these. Flying over Germany on 29/4/45 he collided with his No 2 and crashed to his death — the last of the wartime casualties.

Watts' loss was by no means the end of flying-accident deaths amongst the Malta veterans however. On 17/8/45 Wg.Cdr. A.D.J. Lovell DSO & Bar, having led Wings on Malta and Corsica, raising his total to 19 and five shared, was killed in a crash while stunting a Spitfire at Old Sarum. Nine days later (26/8/45), Sqn.Ldr. C.A. Crombie DSO, DFC died of injuries sustained in an aircraft accident. The Australian had brought his night intruding tally to six and three probables before the end of 1942, and had then been posted to India. One night in January 1943 he shot down two Japanese bombers, but his Beaufighter was hit by return fire and he had to bale out. He survived the remainder of the war in the Far East, only to die within days of the Japanese surrender.

Returning to England after leave in Canada, Flt.Lt. George Beurling had transferred to the RCAF. Joining 412 Squadron, RCAF, he claimed two further victories during late 1943 to raise his ultimate total to 30⅓, but he was then posted to a training job as he had not been able to settle down to squadron discipline and methods. Constantly at odds with authority, he was — incredibly — released before the end of the war, rather than being offered the useful role for which he longed. He drifted for some time, and was then recruited to fly for the Israelis in 1948. Taking off in a Norseman transport from Rome on 20/5/48, the aircraft blew up as it climbed away, he and his passenger being killed; sabotage was suspected.

Sqn.Ldr. N.E. Reeves DSO, DFC, having increased his score to nine, returned to the UK and had become another of the Bomber Support night fighters in 100 Group in 1944, adding seven further victories with 239 Squadron and the Bomber Support Development Unit. He remained in the RAF after the war and was killed in a flying accident in a Meteor 4 on 27/1/49. Flt.Lt. G.E. Horricks DFM had gained two further victories over Italy with 417 Squadron, RCAF, during 1943-44. He left the RCAF after the war but rejoined in 1951, and was killed in a Harvard trainer on 1/7/51.

Apart from the fighter pilots, Wg.Cdr. Adrian Warburton DSO & Bar, DFC & two Bars, the outstanding reconnaissance pilot, had continued to operate from Malta, shooting down a Ju88 whilst flying an armed Spitfire to add to the many victories he and his crew had gained in their Maryland in 1940-41; records credit him with participating in nine air victories, plus three destroyed on the ground. In early 1943 the Spitfire Flight of the enlarged 69 Squadron became 683 Squadron, Warburton remaining in command until October of that year; he was then given command of the newly-formed 336 PR Wing in Tunisia, but injured his back in a motoring accident. On recovery he returned to the UK and was attached to the US 7th Photo-Recce Group as Liaison Officer. Unable to keep out of the cockpit for long, he persuaded the American CO to let him fly one of the unit's F-5Bs (the PR version of the P-38 Lightning) on a sortie over Germany on 12/4/44. His and one other F-5B were to land in Sardinia on completion of their tasks, but Warburton failed to arrive. The wreckage of an F-5B was later discovered in Sicily, but the cause of this loss remains unknown.

And what of the other prominent fighter pilots? Several saw no more action, or undertook roles which did not again provide opportunity for involvement in aerial combat. Others were to see action once more to a greater or lesser degree.

Sqn.Ldr. A.P. Goldsmith DFM joined the Australian Spitfire Wing in the Darwin area in 1943, and here he was credited with four Japanese aircraft destroyed. He died in 1961. Sqn.Ldr. H.A.S. Johnston DFC & Bar recovered from his burns and commanded 165 and 66 Squadron later in the war, claiming two further victories. He died in 1967, while Grp. Capt. R.W. McNair DSO, DFC & two Bars succumbed to illness in 1971. Having subsequently commanded 126 Wing in 2 TAF, he had added eight further victories to his Malta tally.

Others who continued to gain further successes included Sqn.Ldr. K.L. Charney DFC & Bar, who later flew with 602 and 132 Squadrons of 2nd TAF, claiming a further five victories, while Sqn.Ldr. J.A. Plagis DFC & Bar commanded first 64 Squadron and then 126 Squadron — one of the Malta units which had returned to the UK for the Normandy Invasion. With these units he also claimed five further victories before ending the war as Wing Leader of a Mustang Wing. Intriguingly, during the closing stages of the European war his Wing apparently clashed with Russian fighters over Berlin, when a number of the latter were believed to have been shot down!

Flt.Lt. W.C. Walton DFC added two further victories in late 1942 before he departed Malta; Flt.Lt. J.H.E. Bisley DFC claimed one further victory against Japanese raiders over Northern Australia in 1943, whilst Sqn.Ldr. J.H. Curry DFC, 601 Squadron's American pilot, claimed five further victories with the unit in North Africa. He then commanded 80 Squadron until 3/44 when he was shot down by Flak over Italy to become a POW. Flt.Lt. E.S. Dicks-Sherwood DFC also went to North Africa where he claimed two more successes. Amongst the pilots who later flew Spitfires over Western Europe, the Canadians were particularly successful. Sqn.Ldr. R.I.A. Smith DFC & Bar flew with 412 Squadron and then commanded 401 Squadron, claiming seven further victories and sharing in the destruction of the first Me262 jet by the RCAF. Sqn.Ldr. G.W. Northcott DSO, DFC was also credited with seven more with 402 Squadron, while Sqn.Ldr. W.G. Dodd DFC gained one and one shared with 402 Squadron. Flt.Lt. J.F. McElroy DFC & Bar flew with 421 and 416 Squadrons, adding three and one shared; later, during 1948-49 he flew Spitfire IXs for the Israelis, claiming at least two aircraft shot down, including one RAF-flown Spitfire 18!

Sqn.Ldr. D.H. Smith DFC led 453 Squadron, RAAF, and gained two further victories, while Flt.Lt. A.A. Glen DFC rejoined 41 Squadron where he was also credited with two more victories. Wg.Cdr. P.B. Lucas DSO & Bar, DFC, on returning to the UK, commanded 616 Squadron and gained one further victory before becoming Wing Leader at Coltishall following the death of Wg.Cdr. Rabagliati; during his third tour of operations he commanded Mosquito intruders of 613 Squadron. Wg.Cdr. W.A. Douglas DFC & Bar claimed three further victories with 611 Squadron and was then promoted to lead the Coltishall Wing, succeeding Wg.Cdr. Lucas.

Amongst the night fighter pilots, Flt.Lt. M.C. Shipard DFC & Bar claimed six more victories over Algeria and Tunisia by early 1943. Wg.Cdr. Fumerton DFC & Bar returned to Egypt to claim two more before the end of 1942, then another while leading 406 Squadron, RCAF, in Europe in 1944, to become the Canadians' most successful night fighter. Sqn.Ldr. G.B.S. Coleman DFC was also to add one victory in Egypt before spending some months with 272 Squadron as an intruder pilot. He resumed night flying in late 1945 in Italy, finishing with seven victories.

One other who deserves mention was 185 Squadron's Flt.Sgt. M.W. Vineyard, who returned to his native USA to join the US Navy. Flying Grumman F6F Hellcat fighters with Squadron VF-2 aboard the aircraft carrier USS *Hornet* during the Philippines Campaign of mid 1944, he claimed six Japanese aircraft shot down, including four in one day.

Luftwaffe

It will have been noted that early in November 1942 III/JG 53 — a unit which had done extremely well over Malta earlier in the year — had returned to Sicily from North Africa. When it had departed Sicily in late May it had done so 'tail high', but it came back a very different unit. No sooner had it reached Africa than its illustrious and long-serving Kommandeur, Hpt. Wolf-Dietrich Wilcke, was posted to the Eastern Front where he joined JG 3. His place was taken initially by Hpt. Erich Gerlitz from I/JG 27, and then by Oblt. Franz Götz from 9 Staffel. The period in Africa had proved very successful in terms of victories, but losses had been far from light; 14 pilots had been killed or posted missing; three more were known to be prisoners, and a further seven had been badly wounded.

Of those who had previously done well over Malta, most were gone. Lt. Karl-Heinz Quaritsch had rapidly raised his total to 12, but was then shot down during the convoy operations of 14 June, as already recounted. Five days later Oblt. Helmut Belser, commander of 8 Staffel, was killed in a take-off accident at Tripoli with his score at 36; on 26 June Lt. Erich Beckmann of the Gruppenstab was killed on the ground during an RAF bombing raid on Sidi Barrani, his total at nine. Lt. Wolf Schaller had been shot down and captured on 17 June, but was released four days later with the fall of Tobruk. No sooner back with his unit, he claimed his ninth victory on 12 July, but was then shot down again and killed by a British fighter. July also brought two further losses of notable pilots, Lt. Ernst Klager having fallen to a Kittyhawk over El Alamein on the 3rd to become a POW after 18 victories, whilst on the 13th Lt. Rudolf Müller was shot down and killed with his score at eight.

On 31 August Ofw. Josef Kronschnabel gained one victory at the start of the Alem el Halfa battle, raising his total to 12, but was then shot down by AA fire to become a prisoner. A month later Ofw. Alfred Seidl, who had been claiming fast and hard, reached 23 victories but was then shot down in combat with a

Spitfire; although he was able to save himself by parachute, he was badly wounded; he would not return to the unit until April 1943, by which time he had been commissioned. Finally, on 13 October Ofw. Werner Stumpf, by then the unit's top-scoring pilot with 47 victories, was brought down and killed by AA fire; he was awarded a Ritterkreuz (Knight's Cross). In the Desert he had claimed 15 further victories, a level of success equalled only by one of the few surviving 'Experten', Lt. Jürgen Harder, who now returned to Sicily at the head of 7 Staffel with a score of 29.

Even as the unit returned to Sicily, Lt. Herbert Munzert (19 victories) was posted to I/JG 53. He did not last long with I Gruppe and was shot down in combat with B-17s over Tunisia on 31/1/43 without having added to his score. He later died of the wounds suffered in this engagement. Another of the Gruppe's successful pilots, Lt. Herbert Schramm (39 victories), had been posted to Germany to a training job in early 1942.

Subsequently, Jürgen Harder would be moved to take over I/JG 53 during 1943. He later became Kommodore of JG 11 in January 1945, receiving the Ritterkreuz and Eichenlaub (Oakleaves), and amassing a victory total of 64. He was killed in a crash on 17/2/45. Wolf-Dietrich Wilcke also failed to survive the war; holder of the Schwerter (Oakleaves with Swords to the Knight's Cross), he was shot down and killed by P-51s over Germany on 23/3/44. Franz Götz survived, however. He led the Gruppe for two years before becoming Kommodore of JG 26 in January 1945; he ended the war with a Ritterkreuz and 63 victories. Amongst his ten victory claims in the Desert had been three flown by ex-Malta Spitfire pilots of 601 Squadron (Flt.Lt. W.J.E. Haggar and Wt.Off. F.H. Belcher on 6 July, and Flg.Off. C.E. Hone on 22 July; the latter survived, though wounded).

It has been possible to compile a breakdown of the Gruppe's pilots who operated over Malta — very few of whom survived the war — to provide a more detailed insight into the make-up of this talented unit.

Unit and name	Total on arrival in Sicily	Claims over Malta	Final score	Date of loss
Stab III/JG 53				
Hpt. Wolf-Dietrich Wilcke	32	4	162	23.3.44 +
Oblt. Friedrich Below	5	1	6	24.5.42 +
Lt. Erich Beckmann	5	2	9	26.6.42 +
Lt. Kurt Lauinger	0	1	1	18.3.42 POW
Lt. Walter Hicke	0	0	5	
Uffz. Horst Schlüter	0	0	1	30.6.42 +
7 Staffel				
Oblt. Wilfred Pufahl	7	1	12	30.12.44 +
Lt. Jürgen Harder	10	3	64	17.2.45 +
Lt. Hermann Neuhoff	37	3	40	10.4.42 POW
Lt. Siegmund Hosnedl	10	1	11	13.5.42 +
Lt. Heinrich Hesse	0	0	0	
Fw. Rudolf Schmidt	4	2	9	4.8.44 +

Uffz. Paul Glašer	0	1	1	
Uffz. Walter Manz	0	1	8+	25.1.45 +
Uffz. Josef Fankhauser	0	0	0	20.3.42 +
Uffz. Klaus Dyck	0	0	0	5.7.42 +
Gefr. Fritz Fischer	0	0	0	25.3.42 +
8 Staffel				
Oblt. Hans-Joachim Heinecke	16	2	28+	
Oblt. Helmut Belser	20	8	36	19.6.42 +
Lt. Herbert Schramm	38	1	42	1.12.43 +
Lt. Karl-Heinz Quaritsch	0	5	8	14.6.42 +
Lt. Rudolf Müller	0	3	7	13.7.42 +
Lt. Ernst Klager	9	5	18	3.7.42 POW
Fw. Hans Schade	12	1	13	1.4.42 +
Fw. Alfred Seidl	7	3	33	
Fw. Josef Kröschel	0	1	1	30.4.42 +
Fw. Heinz Rahlmeier	0	0	0	10.3.42 +
Uffz. Heinrich Becker	0	0	0	8.5.42 Pow
Uffz. Ernst-Hans Seidel	0	0	0	21.5.42 +
9 Staffel				
Oblt. Franz Götz	29	1	63	
Lt. Hermann Munzert	13	2	20+	6.2.43 +
Lt. Wolf Schaller	5	1	9	12.7.42 +
Ofw. Werner Stumpf	25	6	48	13.10.42 +
Ofw. Heinz Hipper	7	1	8	22.2.42 +
Ofw. Josef Kronschnabel	8	1	13	31.8.42 POW
Fw. Walter Schwartz	0	0	0	22.2.42 +
Uffz. Max Nairz	1	1	9+	
Uffz. Gerhard Beitz	0	1	1	18.5.42 POW
Uffz. Heinz Herkenhoff	6	0	0	12.6.42 +

By far the longest-serving German fighter unit in Sicily had been II/JG 53, but sadly the records of this important Gruppe did not survive the end of the war, and less information is available regarding its operations over Malta then of any other of those involved. It had certainly produced three of the four top-scorers over the Island, two of whom were to survive the war. Gerhard Michalski became an Oberstleutnant — Kommodore of JG 4 — with 73 victories and the Ritterkreuz with Oakleaves. Although shot down six times, he was never badly wounded, but his luck finally ran out in February 1946 when he was killed in a motoring accident.

Herbert Rollwage fought on over Tunisia and Sicily, but was badly wounded in combat on 10/7/43, spending many months in hospital. Back in action during the early months of 1944 and now on Home Defence, he was to raise his total to about 85. Awarded a Ritterkreuz in April 1944, he was finally commissioned in August, but in December was posted to an operational training unit as an instructor. He survived both the war, and most of his fellow members of II/JG 53.

The Gruppe's third successful pilot, Rudolf Ehrenberger, also continued to operate over Tunisia, Sicily and Italy, returning to Home Defence with this unit in September 1943. He fell to US P-47s over Wittenberg on 8/3/44 with his score at 49, and was posthumously awarded a Ritterkreuz the following month. Lt. Fritz Dinger of 4 Staffel had achieved six victories over Malta during the spring to raise his total to 18, but at the end of June he was posted to I Gruppe in Russia, where he rapidly added 30 more victories to his tally. In October he rejoined II Gruppe as Kapitän of his old Staffel, receiving a Ritterkreuz in December whilst operating over Tunisia. On 27/7/43, with his score at 67 — 25 of them over Mediterranean countries — he was killed by bomb splinters during an air raid on his airfield in Italy.

Amongst the other pilots in II/JG 53, few had shone. Lt. Herbert Soukop was a POW, whilst Lt. Alfred Hammer, who had finally gained a single victory over Malta, followed a similar course to that of Ehrenberger, his skill slowly but steadily growing. He too was wounded during February 1944, but returned to action in August, finishing the war as Gruppenkommandeur of IV/JG 53 with a total of 26 victories. Lt. Wilhelm Esser was to claim one victory over Tunisia, but then crashed and fractured his skull. On recovery he claimed two more in Sicily and four on Home Defence.

The Geschwader Kommodore, Günther von Maltzahn, had seen little action over the Island after May 1942, having claimed 14 victories by that time — at least three of them during December 1941. He subsequently led the unit during the Tunisian fighting, where he raised his total to a final 68. In October 1943 he left JG 53 to become Luftwaffe fighter commander (Jafu) in Italy for the remainder of the war. He was to die of cancer in 1953. Franz Schiess, most often his wingman, gained great success over Tunisia where he claimed over 20 victories. By 2/9/43 — now Staffelkäpitan of 8/JG 53 — with his score at 67 and having been awarded a Ritterkreuz, he was shot down and killed over Italy when in combat with US P-38s.

Of the pilots of I/JG 53 — who had appeared over Malta early in 1942, and again briefly in October — Friedrich-Karl Müller had performed brilliantly in the East, where he claimed 100 of his 140 victories, 50 of them in a single month! Awarded a Ritterkreuz and Oakleaves, he returned to Italy in late 1943 as deputy Kommodore of JG 53, before taking command of JG 3 in Germany. He crashed fatally at Salzwedel on 29/5/44. Kurt Brändle had made two claims over Malta but when Hpt. Krahl, Kommandeur of II/JG 3, had been lost on 14/4/42, he was posted to that unit to replace him. On the unit's return to Russia he was to claim many victories, reaching a total of 151 by July 1943 and receiving the Ritterkreuz with Oakleaves. On Home Defence thereafter, he brought his final score to 180, but was shot down and killed by P-47s on 3/11/43.

Klaus Quaet-Faslem did not claim again during the October return to Sicily, and the following month he was posted to Germany to lead I/JG 3. He flew into the ground whilst returning from a sortie on 30/7/44 and was killed, his 49 victories bringing the posthumous award of the Ritterkreuz. One prominent pilot of this unit during October had been Marian Mazurek, who had raised his personal tally to 32. He was not, however, to add to his total during the Tunisian fighting, and was killed whilst intercepting B-26s over Sicily on 9/6/43.

I/JG 53 had been accompanied to Russia in May 1942 by II/JG 3, at least four of whose Malta veterans were to shine later. Joachim Kirschner, who had claimed his first successes over the Island, gained great success over Southern Russia during 1943, and later commanded IV/JG 27 in Greece. Recipient of the Ritterkreuz and Oakleaves, and credited with 188 victories — 167 of them in the East — he was shot down on 17/12/43 by P-47s of the US 57th Fighter Group and baled out over Yugoslavia. Here he was captured and shot by partisan forces. Walther Dahl also received the Ritterkreuz and Oakleaves and claimed 128 victories, 77 of them in Russia. He became a leading exponent of the heavy defence units — the Sturmgruppen — during 1944, and towards the end of the war became Inspecteur der Tagdjäger (Inspector of Day Fighters), surviving the fighting.

Although he claimed only one victory over Malta, Fw. Leopold Münster's tally had reached 51 by 21/12/42 when he was awarded the Ritterkreuz. Posted back to Germany on Home Defence, he ran his total to 95 before being shot down and killed on 8/5/44, by which time he had been commissioned. Twenty of his victories had been claimed in the West, including 15 four-engined bombers; the award of the Oakleaves was announced following his death. The operational career of Uffz. Franz Schwaiger ran parallel to that of Münster; he similarly gained only one victory over Malta, but had amassed 53 victories at the time of the award of the Ritterkreuz on 29/10/42. Commissioned, he returned to Germany where he was shot down and killed by a P-51 on 24/4/44, his total then standing at 67.

Possibly the outstanding unit to operate over Malta was I/JG 77 — during its brief detachment to Sicily from June to late October 1942, its pilots were credited with at least 99 victories. The Gruppe continued to serve with great distinction in Libya and Tunisia, where it was joined by the remainder of the Geschwader. Siegfried Freytag, having brought his score to 73 whilst operating over Malta, raised it further to 92 in North Africa, becoming Kommandeur of II/JG 77 in April 1943. Shot down and wounded over Sicily by P-38s during July 1943, he returned to the unit later on Home Defence, claiming his 100th victory during December 1944. In April 1945 he was posted to the Me262 jet-equipped JG 7, ending the war with a score of 102 and a recommendation for the Oakleaves, which was never granted. He disappeared after the cessation of hostilities.

The Gruppe's second-most successful pilot, Walter Brandt, claimed three more in North Africa before being shot down and wounded on 14/1/43, losing a leg as a result; he received the Ritterkreuz. He returned to action with I/JG 3 in early 1944 on Home Defence, ending the war with a total of 42 victories. Heinz-Edgar Berres became the Adjutant of the Gruppe and achieved considerable success over North Africa and Sicily. He fell to Spitfires over the latter island whilst escorting Ju52/3m transports on 25/7/43, his score standing at 53. A posthumous award of the Ritterkreuz followed. Friedrich Geisshardt achieved his 100th victory over North Africa soon after arrival there, but in December 1942 he was posted to Western Europe as Kommandeur of III/JG 26. With two more victories to his credit, he was shot down whilst attacking bombers on 5/4/43 and died next day.

After four victories over Malta, Günther Hannak had been posted during September 1942 to command I/JG 4 in Rumania. In early 1943 he returned to Italy to lead III/JG 27, but during a reconnaissance on 5/5/43 he was forced to ditch near Malta due to engine trouble, and became a POW. The Ritterkreuzträger had claimed a total of 47 victories up to this point, 35 of them in Russia. It has recently come to light that Hannak's first three victories had been claimed over Crete during April and May 1941, a fact not recorded in *Air War for Yugoslavia, Greece and Crete, 1940-41*, another book by the same authors in this series. The Gruppenkommandeur, Heinz Bär, had not achieved a great deal over Malta, but in North Africa he emerged as a very high scorerwith 61 victories in 6½ months. Ill and exhausted, he was rested for a period, but returned to action in 1944, first with JG 1 and then at the head of JG 3 on Home Defence. In 1945 he flew Me262 jets, becoming one of the top-scorers on these with 16 claims, to raise his final total to 220 — one of the most successful of all Luftwaffe pilots against the Western Allies. A very colourful and popular character, he lost his life in a light aircraft crash on 28/4/57.

Of the Gruppe's other pilots operating over Malta, several went on to do well, including Eberhard Niese with a final score of 43 when killed on 19/2/45, Johen Schennel with 38, Otto Pohl with 20 by the summer of 1943, and Irving Englisch, who had claimed 10-15 when killed on 24/12/44. Two survivors were Armin Köhler, who ended the war with a Ritterkreuz and 40 victories, and Horst Schlick, whose tally reached 34. Franz Niederhagen, who gained his first victory over Malta, was to claim about 14 more over Tunisia and Italy before being shot down and killed on 30/1/44.

Mention must be made of one of the leading Zerstörer pilots of III/ZG 26 — Günther Wegmann — who continued to fly over the Mediterranean area in his unit's Bf110s until mid 1943, claiming 15 victories. He subsequently became one of the first operational jet pilots on the Me262, gaining six more successes. On 18/3/45 he was shot down by a B-17 which he was attacking and lost a leg as a result, but survived to see service in the post-war Luftwaffe.

Regia Aeronautica

Amongst the more notable Italian pilots, Furio Doglio Niclot, top-scorer of 1942, had been killed, as had Carlo Seganti — both posthumous recipients of the Medaglia d'Oro — whilst Aldo Buvoli was a prisoner. Ennio Tarantola — who had claimed one victory in Spain in 1938 — had flown Ju87s earlier in the war, when he had been credited with sinking HMAS *Waterhen* off the Libyan coast as a dive-bomber pilot in June 1941. He resumed fighter operations in North Africa in late 1941, and following operations against Malta, subsequently flew in Sardinia in 1943. He then flew with the air force of the RSI, claiming his final victory over Northern Italy in April 1944 to raise his total to ten and four shared, but was shot down and badly wounded.

The two leading surviving Re2001 pilots, Rino Ricci and Olindo Simionato, gained no further victories but both survived the war. Amongst the 51° Stormo pilots, Dulio Fanali (who had also served in Spain) continued to lead the unit in Tunisia and Sardinia, having raised his total to at least 14 by the time of the Armistice of September 1943. Aldo Remondino, another veteran of Spain, also survived the war. Ferruccio Serafini, who had gained two victories over Malta, claimed seven more flying from Sardinia, but on 22/7/43 he collided with his victim and was killed. He received a posthumous Medaglia d'Oro. Carlo Miani added four further victories with the RSI in 1944 to the three claimed over Malta; he survived the war.

Many of the pilots of 4° Stormo also went on to achieve considerable success, and this unit included amongst its ranks several of the Regia Aeronautica's top-scorers. Franco Lucchini claimed at least 15 and 12 shared over North Africa during two periods operating there, to add to five over Spain and his Malta successes. Shot down and wounded in the Desert on 24/10/42, he rejoined the unit on recovery but after claiming his final victory over Sicily on 5/7/43, he was shot down and killed. Teresio Martinoli, after his successes over Malta in 1941-

42, claimed many further victories over North Africa and Italy, raising his score to 22 and 14 shared by September 1943. Re-mustering to the Co-Belligerent Air Force, he was to shoot down a single Luftwaffe aircraft in November 1943, but on 25/8/44 he was killed in a flying accident at Naples; he was awarded a Medaglia d'Oro posthumously.

Massimo Salvatore had claimed two shared in 1941, to which he had added two and one shared during 1942. He claimed another over North Africa, followed by three and one shared over Sicily and Italy during 1943. Luigi Giannella on the other hand, had claimed only one over Malta, but went on to add 13 and two shared over Africa and Sicily.

Despite the ferocity of the fighting, Malta had not proved a costly campaign in terms of the leading fighter pilots involved. Those who had flown and achieved success there seemed fated however, and as already recorded, few survived the war.

Nonethless, some 120 fighter pilots of the British Commonwealth did lose their lives during the defence of Malta in 1942 (up to 7 November). A further ten lost their lives ferrying Spitfires to Malta from the carriers, while 19 members of the Fleet Air Arm were lost defending the convoys.

Additionally 35 members of Beaufighter crews perished, mainly in defence of the convoys. Luftwaffe records reveal that 55 German day and night fighter pilots were killed whilst flying from Sicily against Malta and the convoys, while 39 Italian fighter pilots similarly perished. The names of those who paid the supreme sacrifice are recorded below.

RAF and Commonwealth Fighter Pilots lost in the defence of Malta, 1 January — 7 November 1942

January

22	Sgt. Donald Thomas Neale		242 Sqn (H)
25	Plt.Off. John Kingsley Russell		126 Sqn (H)
27	Plt.Off. Alexander Stuart Mackie		1435 Flt (H)

February

4	Plt.Off. John Graham Kenelm Hulbert		249 Sqn (H)
	Sgt. Hugh John McDowall		249 Sqn (H)
	Plt.Off. Basil William Main	C	126 Sqn (H)
9	Plt.Off. James Robert Alexander Stuart		249 Sqn (H)
12	Flt.Lt. George Allen		605 Sqn (H)
15	Plt.Off. Peter Lowe		605 Sqn (H)

22	Sqn.Ldr. Ronald Ivor Chaffe		185 Sqn (H)
23	Plt.Off. Thady Brian MacNamara		242 Sqn (grd)
24	Plt.Off. Donald Allen Tedford	US	126 Sqn (H)

March

1	Plt.Off. James Dinsmore Tew Jr	US	242 Sqn (H)
	Sgt. Ray Vernon Harvey, RCAF	C	242 Sqn (H)
5	Plt.Off. Marcus William Terence Kidson		242 Sqn (H)
10	Sgt. John Milburn Mayall, RAAF	A	126 Sqn (H)
	Plt.Off. Kenric Newton Lathrop Murray, RAAF	A	249 Sqn (S)
17	Flt.Sgt. Ian Maxwell Cormack		249 Sqn (S)
18	Plt.Off. Harold Mitchell Fox		249 Sqn (S)
	Sgt. George Frank Robert Mulloy		126 Sqn (H)
20	Plt.Off. Douglas Cecil Leggo	R	249 Sqn (S)
21	Flt.Lt. Cecil Harman Baker		126 Sqn (grd)
	Plt.Off. William Cardy Hollis Hallett		126 Sqn (grd)
	Plt.Off. Edward Earl Streets	US	126 Sqn (grd)
	Flg.Off. John Charles Mortimer Booth		249 Sqn (grd)
	Plt.Off. James Joseph Guerin, RAAF	A	249 Sqn (grd)
22	Plt.Off. Philip McLauchlin Allardice		185 Sqn (H)
31	Plt.Off. Archibald Cooper Steele		185 Sqn (H)

April

2	Plt.Off. Winston McCarthy, RCAF	C	126 Sqn (S)
20	Plt.Off. Hiram Aldine Putnam, RCAF	US	126 Sqn (S)
	Plt.Off. George Albert Jack Ryckman, RCAF	C	126 Sqn (S)
21	Plt.Off. Stanley Frederick Brooker	C	601 Sqn (S)
	Sgt. John Kenneth Fullalove		229 Sqn (H)
22	Plt.Off. Gordon Murray, RCAF	US	603 Sqn (S)
	Plt.Off. Frank James Jemmett		601 Sqn (S)
	Plt.Off. Oliver Ogle Ormrod, DFC		185 Sqn (H)
25	Plt.Off. Kenneth William Pawson		601 Sqn (S)
	Wt.Off. Douglas Frederick Corfe		229 Sqn (H)
	Flt.Sgt. Lucien David Brooks, RCAF	C	229 Sqn (H)
26	Plt.Off. Walter Ephraim Cripps, RCAF	C	601 Sqn (S)
27	Plt.Off. James Edward Wood		1435 Flt (H)
28	Plt.Off. John William Spencer Fletcher, RCAF	C	185 Sqn (H)
	Plt.Off. Thomas Gordon Foley, RCAF	C	229 Sqn (H)

May

4	Flt.Lt. Norman Carter Macqueen, DFC		249 Sqn (S)
6	Sgt. Robert John Lees		229 Sqn (H)
9	Plt.Off. Harold Ashton Milburn		249 Sqn (S)
	Plt.Off. Gordon Russell Tweedale, DFM, RAAF	A	185 Sqn (S)
	Flt.Lt. John Walter Buckstone		603 Sqn (S)
10	Plt.Off. George Maxwell Briggs, RAAF	A	601 Sqn (S)
12	Plt.Off. Herbert Robert Mitchell, RNZAF	NZ	603 Sqn (S)
	Sgt. Charles Edward Graysmark		601 Sqn (S)
14	Plt.Off. John Livingstone Boyd, DFM, RAAF	A	185 Sqn (S)
	Sgt. Colin Vernon Finlay		185 Sqn (S)

	Flt.Sgt. Harold Joseph Fox, RCAF	US	249 Sqn (S)
17	Plt.Off. Peter Alfred Nash, DFC		249 Sqn (S)
18	Sgt. James Richards Pendlebury		229 Sqn (H)
20	Sgt. Frank Stanley Howard (wounded 17th)	R	601 Sqn (S)
25	Plt.Off. Walter Alexander Caldwell, RNZAF	NZ	601 Sqn (S)

June

1	Plt.Off. Andrew Albert McNaughton, RCAF	C	185 Sqn (S)
8	Flg.Off. Leslie George Barlow	R	603 Sqn (S)
15	Sgt. Jack Nock McConnell, RNZAF	NZ	601 Sqn (S)
26	Flt.Sgt. Maurice Ernest Tomkins		249 Sqn (S)

July

2	Plt.Off. John Hurst, DFC		603 Sqn (S)
	Plt.Off. Harry Kelly	US	249 Sqn (S)
6	Flt.Sgt. Edwin Dewitt Moye, RCAF	US	185 Sqn (S)
7	Flt.Sgt. Peter Clifford Terry		185 Sqn (S)
	Flt.Sgt. Haydn Haggas		185 Sqn (S)
8	Flg.Off. Neville Stuart King		603 Sqn (S)
	Flg.Off. John Smith		249 Sqn (S)
	Plt.Off. John Carlton Gilbert		249 Sqn (S)
9	Flg.Off. Guy Andre Levy-Despas, RCAF	F	603 Sqn (S)
	Plt.Off. John Longton Hicks		126 Sqn (S)
10	Flt.Sgt. Bernard Walter Reynolds, RCAF	C	126 Sqn (S)
11	Plt.Off. Charles Benn Ramsay, RCAF	C	249 Sqn (S)
12	Flg.Off. Owen William Hugh Berkeley-Hill		249 Sqn (S)
19	Flt.Sgt. Joseph Edward Otis, RCAF	US	126 Sqn (S)
20	Plt.Off. Hugh Robert Russel, RCAF	C	185 Sqn (S)
22	Plt.Off. Donald George Reid, DFM, RCAF	C	185 Sqn (S)
	Plt.Off. Joseph Hubert Roger Paradis, RCAF	C	249 Sqn (S)
23	Flg.Off. David William Kent		185 Sqn (S)
28	Sgt. Donald Frank Hubbard		1435 Sqn (S)
30	Sgt. Colin Lethbridge Wood, RNZAF	NZ	1435 Sqn (S)

August

2	Plt.Off. James William Guthrie		185 Sqn (S)
	Sgt. Matthew Leonard McLeod, RNZAF	NZ	185 Sqn (S)
8	Sgt. Clarence Lloyd Kelly, RNZAF	NZ	1435 Sqn (S)
10	Plt.Off. Jerrold Alpine Smith, RCAF	C	126 Sqn (S)
13	Flt.Sgt. Robert Athol Buntine, RAAF	A	1435 Sqn (S)
	Flt.Sgt. John Harold Tanner, RNZAF	NZ	126 Sqn (S)
25	Flg.Off. Reginald Pearson Round, RNZAF	NZ	249 Sqn (S)
	Flt.Sgt. Basil Butler, RCAF	C	249 Sqn (S)
26	Flg.Off. Dudley Gerald Newman		229 Sqn (S)
	Sgt. Clifford Harry Cornish		229 Sqn (S)
27	Grp.Capt. Walter Myers Churchill, DSO, DFC		(S)
28	Flt.Lt. Ernest Pendleton Francis Louis Tarcisius Magruder		229 Sqn (S)
29	Plt.Off. Dennis Patrick Pollock		1435 Sqn (S)

September

13	Flt.Sgt. Lawrence Harold Swain		185 Sqn (S)
15	Flt.Sgt. Bernard Charles Peters		249 Sqn (S)
	Plt.Off. John Richard Scott, RCAF	C	229 Sqn (S)
23	Plt.Off. Ian Fraser Preston, RCAF	US	126 Sqn (S)

October

4	Flt.Sgt. Murray Irving Gass		249 Sqn (S)
	Flt.Sgt. George Alexander Hogarth, RCAF	C	249 Sqn (S)
11	Flt.Sgt. David Derek MacLean, RNZAF	NZ	126 Sqn (S)
12	Sqn.Ldr. Bryan John Wicks, DFC		126 Sqn (S)
	Sgt. John Douglas Vinall		185 Sqn (S)
	Flt.Sgt. Ronald Alfred Stevenson		1435 Sqn (S)
13	Flt.Sgt. Alexander Owen MacLeod, RCAF	C	185 Sqn (S)
14	Flt.Sgt. William Bedlington Knox Williams, RAAF	A	1435 Sqn (S)
	Sgt. Ronald John Roe, RNZAF	NZ	1435 Sqn (S)
15	Wt.Off. Edwin Tytler Hiskens, RAAF	A	249 Sqn (S)
16	Flg.Off. Edward Wilson Wallace, RCAF	C	126 Sqn (S)
	Wt.Off. Peter Carter, RCAF	C	249 Sqn (S)
	Sgt. William Renton Wilson		1435 Sqn (S)
17	Flt.Lt. Ripley Ogden Jones	US	126 Sqn (S)
	Flt.Sgt. Ronald Miller		229 Sqn (S)
18	Flg.Off. James Douglas Stevenson, RCAF	C	126 Sqn (S)
23	Flg.Off. Alec Ian Lindsay		185 Sqn (S)
24	Sgt. Raymond Harold Saunders		185 Sqn (S)
25	Plt.Off. Nigel Manfred Park, RNZAF, DFM	NZ	126 Sqn (S)
29	Flt.Sgt. Walter Parks, RAAF	A	229 Sqn (S)

November

1	Plt.Off. Russell Albert Wright	R	1435 Sqn (S)

(H) denotes killed whilst flying Hurricane; (S) denotes killed whilst flying Spitfire; (grd) denotes killed whilst on the ground.
Nationality of pilot is British, except where stated otherwise.
A — Australian; C — Canadian; F — French; NZ — New Zealander; R — Rhodesian; US — United States.
NB: In a number of cases, promotion was announced after the death of the pilot concerned.

RAF and Commonwealth Fighter Pilots lost ferrying Spitfires to Malta, 1942

9 May	Sgt. Robert Donald Sherrington, RCAF	*Wasp*
	Flt.Sgt. Charles Napoleon Valiquet, RCAF	*Wasp*
	Flt.Sgt. John Vaughan Rounsefell, RCAF	*Wasp*
	Flt.Lt. Raymond Harold Charles Sly, RAAF	*Wasp*
3 June	Flg.Off. James Howard Menary	*Eagle*
	Plt.Off. David Francis Rouleau, RCAF	*Eagle*

	Flt.Sgt. Hugh Douglas Kingsley MacPherson, RCAF	*Eagle*
	Flt.Sgt. Thomas Francis Beaumont	*Eagle*
21 July	Sgt. Lewis Evans	*Eagle*
17 Aug	Sgt. William Joseph Alexander Fleming	*Furious*

RAF and Commonwealth Beaufighter Strike and Night Fighter aircrews lost in defence of Malta and Malta-bound convoys, 1942

January		
18	{ Plt.Off. Cyril Hardwick Beet	252 Sqn
	Sgt. Jack Victor Gardner }	
February		
15	{ Sgt. Clive Herbert Mulholland, RNZAF	252 Sqn
	Sgt. Daniel Francis Keane }	
	{ Flt.Sgt. Granville Andrew Jackson, RCAF	252 Sqn
	Sgt. Alan Alfred Largent }	
June		
13	{ Plt.Off. John Phipps Doncaster, RCAF	235 Sqn
	Sgt. William White Webster }	
14	{ Flt.Sgt. Jacques Gael (French)	272 Sqn
	Sgt. Frederick Vincent Amos }	
	{ Sgt. Alan Ernest Cooper, RAAF	272 Sqn
	Sgt. Cecil Charles Ridgway }	
	{ Sgt. Ernest Frederick Robson Truby, RCAF	272 Sqn
	Sgt. Kenneth James Garrett }	
	{ Sgt. Yves Charles Tedesco (Belgian)	272 Sqn
	Sgt. Frank Ransom }	
15	Plt.Off. Roger Leon Hermann Corbisier (Belgian)	272 Sqn
	Sgt. William Christie McLeish	
	{ Sgt. Wilson George Blessing, RAAF	272 Sqn
	Sgt. John Raymond Williams }	
	Sgt. Charles William Hector (observer)	235 Sqn
August		
13	Plt.Off. David Joseph Jay, DFC, RCAF (pilot)	248 Sqn
19	Sgt. George Donaldson Leslie (observer)	227 Sqn
27	{ Sgt. Eric O'Hara	227 Sqn
	Sgt. Kenneth Seddon }	
September		
6	{ Lt. Frederick Owen Noone, SAAF	227 Sqn
	Sgt. Albert John Cusworth }	
	{ Flg.Off. Dennis de Montfort Partridge, RAAF	227 Sqn
	Sgt. Anthony William Vivian }	
17	{ Plt.Off. John David Moffatt	227 Sqn
	Plt.Off. John Stuart Dicker }	
27	Flt.Lt. John Waddingham, DFC (pilot)	89 Sqn

October

4	Wt.Off. George Pass Fargher, RCAF (pilot)	227 Sqn
14	{ Sqn.Ldr. Peter Louis Underwood, DFC	227 Sqn
	{ Flt.Sgt.Ivor Reginald Miller	

Fleet Air Arm Fighter Pilots/Aircrew lost in the defence of Malta-bound convoys, 1942

May

18	Pty.Off. (A) Herbert William Nuttall	807 Sqn *Argus*

June

14	Lt. Philip Roderick Hall	807 Sqn *Argus*
	{ Sub Lt. Peter Edward Palmer	807 Sqn *Argus*
	{ Sub Lt. John Thomas David Ceely	
	{ Sub Lt. Geoffrey Spalding	807 Sqn *Argus*
	{ L/Air John Brown Duncan	
	Lt. Lennox Frederick Tickner	801 Sqn *Eagle*

August

12	Sub Lt. Michael Hankey	801 Sqn *Eagle*
	Sub Lt. John Michael Lucas	800 Sqn *Indomitable*
	Lt. Robert Louis Johnston	806 Sqn *Indomitable*
	Lt.Cdr. Francis Elton Christopher Judd	880 Sqn *Indomitable*
	Sub Lt. John Imlay Cruickshank	880 Sqn *Indomitable*
	Sub Lt. Hugo Leslie Cunliffe-Owen	880 Sqn *Indomitable*
	{ Lt. Robert Alec Farquhar Churchill	884 Sqn *Victorious*
	{ Sub Lt. Alan Nunn	
	{ Sub Lt. John Harry O'Caroll Nihill	809 Sqn *Victorious*
	{ L/Air Walter Richard Regan	
	{ Sub Lt. Charles John Evans	809 Sqn *Victorious*
	{ L/Air John Stewart	

Luftwaffe Fighter Pilots lost during the offensive against Malta and Malta-bound convoys, 1 January — 7 November 1942

January

3	Uffz. Werner Mirschinka	4/JG 53
17	Lt. Felix-Dieter Schleif (Ju88C pilot)	4/NJG 2
18	Lt. Herbert Haas (Ju88C pilot)	I/NJG 2
26	Lt. Peter Laufs (Ju88C pilot)	I/NJG 2

February

7	Ofw. Otto Göthe	6/JG 53
13	Lt. Karl-Heinz Ponec	II/JG 3
16	Lt. Robert von Keudell (Ju88C pilot)	4/NJG 2

22	Uffz. Walter Schwartz	9/JG 53
	Ofw. Heinz Hipper	9/JG 53
23	Gefr. Otto Butschek	10/JG 53
28	Lt. Hans-Günther Haumann (Bf109E pilot)	III/ZG 26
March		
9	Oblt. Heinz Schulz (Ju88C pilot)	I/NJG 2
10	Fw. Heinz Rahlmeier	8/JG 53
14	Uffz. Heinz Blum	3/JG 53
20	Uffz. Josef Fankhauser	7/JG 53
	Uffz. Michael Beikiefer	6/JG 3
21	Lt. Hans Hufnagel (Bf110 pilot)	9/ZG 26
23	Uffz. Hermann Katthagen	10/JG 53
April		
1	Fw. Hans Schade	8/JG 53
	Uffz. Gerhard Kitzenmaier	5/JG 53
4	Uffz. Heinz Bross	10/JG 53
	Ofw. Günther Fronhofer	10/JG 53
8	Ofw. Alfred Vogel (Ju88C pilot)	3/NJG 2
12	Gefr. Horst Gisy	4/JG 53
	Uffz. Willi Jünger (Bf110 pilot)	9/ZG 26
14	Hpt. Karl-Heinz Krahl	II/JG 3
29	Uffz. Georg Schleich (Bf110 pilot)	8/ZG 26
30	Fw. Josef Kröschel	8/JG 53
May		
9	Uffz. Helmut Schierning	6/JG 53
15	Lt. Siegmund Hosnedl	7/JG 53
17	Lt. Wolfgang Herrmann	5/JG 53
21	Uffz. Ernst-Hans Seidel	8/JG 53
June		
8	Lt. Wilhelm Ruge	5/JG 53
19	Uffz. Heinz Schümann	6/JG 53
July		
6	Fw. Toni Engels	1/JG 77
10	Lt. Hans-Jurgen Frodien	Stab/JG 53
17	Fw. Heinz Sauer	1/JG 77
	Uffz. Simon Pohlein	3/JG 77
27	Lt. Karl-Heinz Preu	Stab/JG 53
	Uffz. Heinrich Freckmann	6/JG 53
29	Uffz. Karl-Heinz Witschke	3/JG 77
August		
13	Fw. Hugo Langer	2/JG 77
29	Fw. Joachim Koelzsch	4/JG 53
September		
5	Lt. Hans-Volkmar Müller	5/JG 53
October		
11	Uffz. Walter Timmermann	I/JG 27

	Lt. Ewald Schumacher	4/JG 53
12	Lt. Wilhelm Scheib	1/JG 77
	Gefr. Georg Gunkel	4/JG 53
	Uffz. Paul Stroehla	5/JG 53
16	Uffz. Heinz Golinski	3/JG 53
18	Uffz. Karl Könning	3/JG 27
23	Uffz. Heribert Wagner	5/JG 53
25	Oblt. Richard Eckhardt	3/SchG 2
	Uffz. Willi Diepenseifen	3/SchG 2
November		
2	Ofw. Heinrich Slany	3/SchG 2

Regia Aeronautica Fighter Pilots lost during the offensive against Malta and Malta-bound convoys

April		
20	Cap. Giovanni Guiducci	90ª Sq, 10° Gr., 4° St.
May		
10	Cap. Roberto Dagasso	97ª Sq., 9° Gr., 4°St.
12	Serg. Mario Marchio (wounded — died June)	358ª Sq., 2° Gr., Aut.
15	Cap. Alberto Argenton	91ª Sq., 10° Gr., 4°St.
18	Sottoten. Vincenzo Fischer	84ª Sq., 10° Gr., 4° St.
26	Cap. Annibale Sterzi	358ª Sq., 2° Gr., Aut.
June		
6	Ten. Arnaldo De Merich	152ª Sq., 2° Gr., Aut.
	Ten. Giusppe Baraldi	152ª Sq., 2° Gr., Aut.
	Serg. Magg. Aldo Geminiani	152ª Sq., 2° Gr., Aut.
10	Serg. Giovanni Dringoli	150ª Sq., 2° Gr., Aut.
	Mar. Lorenzo Serafino	378ª Sq., 155° Gr., 51° St.
14	Cap. Alberto Brondi	355ª Sq., 24° Gr., Aut.
	Sottoten. Bruno Castro	355ª Sq., 24° Gr., Aut.
	Serg.Magg. Aldo Mazzolani	355ª Sq., 24° Gr., Aut.
	Serg.Magg. Raimondo Giardini	7ª Gr., 54° St.
26	Mar. Gino Runci	378ª Sq., 155° Gr., 51° St.
July		
2	Sottoten. Giuseppe Riccardi	351ª Sq., 155° Gr., 51° St.
	Serg.Magg. Alberto Porcarelli	151ª Sq., 20° Gr., 51° St.
6	Serg.Magg. Francesco Pecchiari	352ª Sq., 20° Gr., 51° St.
	Sottoten. Romano Pagliani	152ª Sq., 2° Gr., Aut.
	Sottoten. Adolfo Giovannini	353ª Sq., 20° Gr., 51° St.
7	Ten. Fabrizio Cherubini	353ª Sq., 20° Gr., 51° St.
9	Ten. Franco Montagnani	352ª Sq., 20° Gr., 51° St.
10	Sottoten. Dante Dose	20° Gr., 51° St.
	Serg.Magg. Giovanni Del Fabbro	378ª Sq., 155° Gr., 51° St.
12	Ten. Francesco Vichi	358ª Sq., 2° Gr., Aut.
	Ten. Col. Aldo Quarantotti	2° Gr., Aut.

	Ten. Carlo Seganti	358ª Sq., 2° Gr., Aut.
13	Sottoten. Rosario Longo	151ª Sq., 20° Gr., 51° St.
	Sottoten. Pietro Menaldi	151ª Sq., 20° Gr., 51° St.
27	Cap. Furio Doglio Niclot	151ª Sq., 20° Gr., 51° St.
August		
12	Sottoten. Michele Crimi	362ª Sq., 22° Gr., Aut.
14	Magg. Pier Giuseppe Scarpetta	2° Gr., Aut.
	Sottoten. Isidoro Disint	150ª Sq., 2° Gr., Aut.
September		
17	Serg. Luigi Berna	151ª Sq., 20° Gr., 51° St.
October		
11	Sottoten. Urbano Barberini Colonna Sciarra	151ª Sq., 20° Gr., 51° St.
	Mar. Romano Pesavento	369ª Sq., 22° Gr., Aut.
13	Mar. Maurizio Iannucci	352ª Sq., 20° Gr., 51° St.
	Ten. Felice Mezzetti	373ª Sq., 153° Gr., Aut.

Appendix I

FIGHTER UNITS BASED ON MALTA 1942

Unit	**Aircraft**	**Commanding Officer**
126 Squadron	Hurricane II	Sqn. Ldr. S.C. Norris
	Spitfire Vc	Sqn. Ldr. E.J. Gracie
		Sqn. Ldr. A.R.H. Barton
		Sqn. Ldr. J.P. Winfield
		Sqn. Ldr. B.J. Wicks
185 Squadron	Hurricane II	Sqn. Ldr. S.A.D. Pike
		Sqn. Ldr. P.R. McGregor
		Sqn. Ldr. R.I. Chaffe
		Sqn. Ldr. E.B. Mortimer-Rose
		Sqn. Ldr. R.M. Lloyd
		Sqn. Ldr. K.A. Lawrence
	Spitfire Vc	Sqn. Ldr. W.G. New
		Maj. C.J.O. Swales
		Sqn. Ldr. B.E.G. White
229 Squadron	Hurricane II	Sqn. Ldr. D. Kain
		Sqn. Ldr. R.C. Dafforn
		Sqn. Ldr. P.C.P. Farnes
	Spitfire Vc	Sqn. Ldr. W.A. Douglas
		Sqn. Ldr. H.C. Baker
		Sqn. Ldr. M.M. Stephens
242 Squadron	Hurricane II	Sqn. Ldr. W.G. Wells
249 Squadron	Hurricane II	Sqn. Ldr. H.J.S. Beazley
		Sqn. Ldr. P.S. Turner
	Spitfire Vc	Sqn. Ldr. S.B. Grant
		Sqn. Ldr. P.B. Lucas
		Sqn. Ldr. R.A. Mitchell
		Sqn. Ldr. E.N. Woods
601 Squadron	Spitfire Vc	Sqn. Ldr. J.D. Bisdee
603 Squadron	Spitfire Vc	Sqn. Ldr. Lord D. Douglas-Hamilton
		Sqn. Ldr. W.A. Douglas
605 Squadron	Hurricane II	Sqn. Ldr. S.E. Andrews
		Flt.Lt. D.W.A. Stones (temp)
1435 Flight	Hurricane II	Sqn. Ldr. I.B. Westmacott
1435 Squadron	Spitfire Vc	Sqn. Ldr. A.D.J. Lovell
89 Squadron	Beaufighter	Flt.Lt. G. McL. Hayton
Detachment		Flt.Lt. H.G. Edwards
		Sqn. Ldr. P.J.M. Evans
		Sqn. Ldr. D.S. Pain

Appendix II

RAF FIGHTER SQUADRON CODE LETTERS, MALTA 1942

In the past there has been considerable confusion regarding the system of identification letters applied to fighters serving on Malta. A brief synopsis has therefore been prepared in an effort to give some guidance and assistance to those with an interest in such matters.

At the start of 1942, Hurricanes present on Malta were generally painted with a two-letter squadron code and an individual aircraft letter, similar to other units both in the United Kingdom and in North Africa. Since aircraft were becoming increasingly scarce, they were frequently pooled and it became quite normal for the pilot of one squadron to fly sorties within a brief time-scale in aircraft carrying two or three different sets of identification letters.

In January the codes in use were:

HA	126 Squadron	LE	242 Squadron
GL	185 Squadron	UP	605 Squadron
GN	249 Squadron		

By March, as the first Spitfires arrived, all remaining Hurricanes had been amalgamated into 126 and 185 Squadron, whatever letters they carried. The Spitfires went to 249 Squadron, and these too were painted with the 'GN' code.

However, when 601 and 603 Squadrons flew off USS *Wasp* in April, they carried a new form of coding — 601 Squadron aircraft bearing the number '1' forward of the fuselage roundel on the starboard side, and a letter aft ('1-A', '1-B' etc), whilst 603 Squadron machines were marked with the number '2' and individual letter. In the apparent rush to get the job done in time, it would appear that some machines were marked the opposite way round — letter fore, number aft! Further Spitfire deliveries during May carried similar schemes, batches being numbered '3' and '4', although the majority of the 9 May delivery aircraft were coded 'C' ('C-1', 'C-2' etc, up to at least 'C-51'). With little time available for re-painting, these Spitfires therefore went into action carrying such non-standard markings.

In May, 185 Squadron received its first Spitfires to replace the few surviving clapped-out Hurricanes, and these soon received the code 'GL'; by June, all the unit's aircraft were correctly coded, while 249 Squadron was starting to re-code its aircraft with the single letter 'T'. Both 601 and 603 Squadrons started repainting their aircraft — 'UF' for the former (the unit's UK code), single 'X' for the latter (although 'XT' had been its UK code).

By August, 126 Squadron had begun to apply 'MK' to its Spitfires, and when 229 Squadron was resurrected from the disbanded 603 Squadron, it took over the latter unit's 'X' coding, while the newly-formed 1435 Squadron adopted a single 'V'. Therefore, by the late summer, while there were still exceptions (for example, although 601 Squadron had departed for the Western Desert in June, at least three aircraft of that unit — UF-N, UF-R and UF-S (BR301) — remained on the island, serving with 603 and 249 Squadrons), units were by and large operating with the following identification letters:

MK	126 Squadron	T	249 Squadron
GL	185 Squadron	V	1435 Squadron
X	229 Squadron		

Deliveries of Spitfires by carrier during 1942 had been:

Date	Carrier	Carried	Arrived	Lost
7 March	HMS *Eagle*	16	15	
21 March	HMS *Eagle*	16	9	
29 March	HMS *Eagle*	7	7	
20 April	USS *Wasp*/HMS *Eagle*	50	46	1
9 May	USS *Wasp*/HMS *Eagle*	64	60	3
18 May	HMS *Argus*/HMS *Eagle*	17	17	
3 June	HMS *Eagle*	31	27	4
9 June	HMS *Eagle*	32	32	

15 July	HMS *Eagle*	32	31	
21 July	HMS *Eagle*	30	28	1
11 August	HMS *Furious*	38	37	
17 August	HMS *Furious*	32	29	3
29 October	HMS *Furious*	31	29	
Total		396	367	12

Appendix III

ESTABLISHMENT OF THE FIRST RDF* (RADAR) STATION — 241 AMES AT DINGLI

A decision was made in 1938 that an RDF station was to be erected in Malta. 241 AMES under Flt.Sgt. James, with six specialist wireless and electrical mechanics, was despatched in January 1939, as recalled here by one of the party — Corporal (later Flt.Lt.) Reg Townson:

'For a number of years, the RDF stations were known as "Air Ministry Experimental Stations" for security reasons, this being abbreviated to AMES, and the station sent to Malta was numbered 241. In its original form, 241 AMES consisted of an MB.1 transmitter manufactured by Metropolitan-Vickers, serial number 1 of the RM.2 receivers made by Cossor (each housed in its own Leyland prime-mover), separate receiver and transmitter antennae mounted on 70-foot high, telescopic masts made by Merryweather and, also in the transmitter vehicle, a Meadows-engined generating set.

'The site already chosen for 241 AMES was on Dingli Cliff, where there was a spot height of 817 feet and erection of the station started as soon as the equipment arrived, the crew being accommodated in the RAF barracks at Marsamxett, and travelling daily to Dingli by taxi but, even then, completing the last few hundreds of yards eastwards from the RN Signal Station on foot, along a track studded with outcrops of rock.

'It soon became clear that Mussolini had designs on Mare Nostrum and would fall in behind his German master, so we needed to be at Dingli full-time, and commandeered a house in the village. Buildings of local stone were erected to house the equipment, and ease our heating and ventilation problems, while in the fullness of time, a domestic building was put up and RAF Station Dingli was born. Before this, we had made the best of having the original vehicles and equipment in use, though there was one hectic period of 48 hours, when our transmitter Merryweather was blown over in a gale; even then, it was tough enough to have been repaired and re-erected, except that the bottom section was shattered across a cable drum standing on edge at the base of the tower. A 60 foot telegraph pole was erected by 'Works and Bricks' (AMWD); we combed RAF and Naval stores for components to adapt to our requirements, and a new transmitter array was in operation in just under two days, during which time there was, regretfully, an increase in civilian casualties.

'On the operational front, we earned a few signals of congratulations from the AOC, as Malta's use as a staging post for ferrying aircraft to the Middle East was increasing in proportion to the inevitable lessening of aircrew experience, and a blacked-out Malta was not the easiest place to find in the dark. The UK briefing before departure warned of misleading enemy radio signals and, indeed, on one occasion, HQ Med was obliged to give approach instructions to a lost aircraft in plain language instead of the usual verifiable code. On another occasion, it was a saddening experience for us to watch "blips" disappear from our A-scope when carrier-borne Hurricanes were made to fly off at too-great a range from the Island (see pages 86/87 *Malta: The Hurricane Years, 1940-41*).

'Flt.Sgt. Jimmy James became ill, spent a short time in the RN Hospital at Bighi and had to return to England. That left me in charge with a total technical strength of nine to operate the equipment as well as keep it running for as many of the 24 hours a day as possible. It is of interest to note that 242 AMES, when it arrived from the UK, was commanded by a Flight Lieutenant (C.S. Jones) and had a total strength of about 45.

'As well as looking after 241, we found there was little or no knowledge at HQ Med of making the best use of the information we were able to give, and the organization was autocratic rather than efficient. For example, the original plotting table in the War Room used range rings and bearing lines from Dingli, rather than a grid; it needed a Flight-Sergeant (or above) to put plots on the table (as opposed to the young ladies who were doing the same job in the UK), and no lesser a mortal than a Wing Commander could be trusted to control the situations as they arose, regardless of the Branch in which they normally operated.

'The Controllers wasted valuable time by having the Duty Signals Officer come from his office to operate the R/T, instead of talking directly to the pilots and, when Dingli was joined by three low-looking stations — COLs — in other locations on the Island, the original idea from HQ Med was that the COLs should pass their plots to Dingli for conversion to Dingli's range and bearing, regardless of the delay this would cause, rather than change the plotting-table map. In fairness, it must be stressed that we had the advantage of being involved in the evolution of a reporting system in the UK, and when problems of logistics arose, HQ Med was first-class, as witness, for example, the night we lost the transmitter mast, the way buildings were provided to replace our original vehicles and, subsequently, how a Filter Room was provided, to be followed by a bomb-proof War HQ.

'Even so, there was a clear need for training on the operational uses of RDF, particularly on the part of the would-be Controllers, some of whose mistakes could fairly be described as monumental. Fighter pilots were not briefed (at least in the early days) that a detection system was in operation, and so were left sitting in their cockpits in the open, which one can only assume was the next best thing to being on standing patrol — a clear impossibility with only three or four serviceable aircraft. One particular mistake by a Controller caused the deaths of several personnel at Luqa, when an early-morning raid by a single Ju88 was tracked by RDF, skirting the Island to the south-east, where it "faded" in a known blind area. By this time, we had a Filter Room in operation, which had the air raid warning sounded but, a little later, declared "All Clear", despite the Filter Room keeping the plot on the table, since the Flight Sergeant in charge at the time knew of the blind area to the south-east, and realised that the "hostile" might have proceeded south towards North Africa or could have turned west towards Malta.

'Tragically, the latter was the case. The official version which came later, ascribed the tragedy to the gap in the RDF cover, which was only partly true, and the real blame fairly belonged on one particular pair of shoulders. Similarly, the same Controller was responsible for failing to warn St Paul's Bay (where Sunderlands were based), in spite of a 25-mile track pointing straight there (see page 162 *Malta: The Hurricane Years, 1940-41*). To make matters worse, he apologised — on an "open" telephone line — that the failure to give any warning was "due to a fault in our RDF system", at a time when security about the very existence of RDF was supposed to be paramount! In case it is assumed that I am only quoting hearsay evidence, let me add that both the incidents described involved me.

'The position in which we, as "Other Ranks", found ourselves was decidedly unusual in that we shouldered great responsibility by operating the "early warning" system in an important theatre, without the authority to back up what we were doing. At one stage, we were visited by Wg.Cdr. John Tester, the Chief Radio Officer, Middle East Command, who was a "radar" man to the core, and to whom we could unburden ourselves without fear of, for example, being court-martialled for insubordination, as could well have happened had we spoken in similar vein to some of the senior staff at HQ Med.

'The next significant event on the operational front was a visit by Flg.Off. John Findlay, a Scientific Officer and specialist in operations work, who went into the history of every raid on the Island to date, from every possible angle, returned to England, and paid a subsequent visit for a further study. Changes certainly followed the Findlay visits and, whether or not a direct consequence, Air Vice-Marshal Hugh Lloyd arrived to take command, and the change in attitude was seen. In August (1941) I went down with dysentery, and the doctors at Mtarfa Hospital decided I should be sent home.'

---

*RDF was the name originally given to the system of radio-location developed by Watson-Watt, Bainbridge-Bell and others. Its progress into a method of detecting the approach of enemy aircraft in the time of war is well-documented, and needs no repetition here.

Appendix IV

OPERATION 'HERKULES': THE PROPOSED AXIS INVASION OF MALTA — 15 AUGUST 1942

Initial plans for a possible invasion of Malta were drawn up by Mussolini's generals as far back as 1936, at the height of the Italian empire-building period. With the outbreak of hostilities between Great Britain and Italy in 1940, Malta was considered a 'target of extreme importance' and would have been ripe for plucking, but the generals could not agree upon a plan of action. By early 1941 the Germans had arrived at Sicily, with Feldmarshall Kesselring and Grand-Admiral Raeder championing the cause, but Hitler would respond with only:

> 'I shall do it one day!'

However, by early 1942 the German military machine had achieved great success in the Middle East, with little Malta ostensively the only obstacle to Axis domination of the Central Mediterranean area of operations. It was during this period that the latest proposal of invasion was put forward by General Kurt Student — conqueror of Crete. His plan was enthusiastically accepted by the Axis representatives at the conference, which included not only top German and Italian commanders but Admiral Abe of the Imperial Japanese Navy, and Colonel Shinizu of the Imperial Japanese Army Air Force.

General Student was himself to command the force, which was to comprise the 'Brigade Ramcke' (Maj-Gen Bernhard Ramcke's 7th Division Fallschirmjager), one Italian airborne division ('Folgore'), one Italian infantry division ('La Spezia'), one German tank regiment and, if required, one German mountain division. Five hundred Ju52s and a dozen Me323s would be made available, plus 300 DFS 230 gliders, each capable of carrying ten men, and 200 of the newer-design Gotha 242 gliders, able to carry 25 fully-armed men. To provide escort for this force it was estimated that the Luftwaffe would have available 216 fighters, the Regia Aeronautica a further 222; the Italians would also be able to commit more than 470 bombers, torpedo-bombers and assault aircraft, while the Germans could offer a further 200 such machines. In excess of 30,000 men were available for the airborne landings alone — equivalent to the whole Malta garrison — and a further 70,000 were earmarked to follow by sea. The Regia Marina would have available five battleships, four heavy cruisers and 21 destroyers, 14 submarines, as well as MTBs, minesweepers and landing-craft. Student commented:

> 'It was an impressive force, five times as strong as we had against Crete.'

Student proposed:

Phase 1

A reinforced battalion was to be landed in the area of Qrendi. Its task was to form a bridgehead about two small bays, at Torri Zurrieq (between Wied iz-Zurrieq and Blue

Grotto) and Hagra S-Sewda (west of Ghar Lapsi). AA positions within the area and a suspected airfield were to be captured. This force, in gliders towed by Ju87s, was to leave Sicily just before dawn and to approach the south of Malta from a westerly direction. At a point about 20 miles south of Malta (a U-boat was to surface to indicate this point) each aircraft and its glider was to turn to port so that they would approach the Island in line abreast from a southerly direction; this way the whole unit could be landed simultaneously, and the AA defences would not be able to concentrate on individual aircraft. Up to and during this manoeuvre the aircraft were to fly at between 11,500 and 13,000 feet; as soon as the turn had been completed, the gliders were to be cast off. The Ju87s were to go on and dive-bomb AA sites etc, and then immediately the gliders were to come in and land. The bridgehead was to be held by one battalion for six hours.

Phase 2

At Zero Hour+6, parts of an Italian Division ('La Spezia') and a German tank regiment were to land from the sea in the bridgehead already established; and at the same time an Italian parachute division ('Folgore'), strengthened by Ramcke's parachute brigade, were to drop in certain areas north-west of the bridgehead. This airborne force was to capture Mdina and Rabat at once.

Phase 3

An attack by the seaborne troops eastwards from the original bridgeheads. They were to capture two airfields — Hal Far and Safi; and then go on to capture the harbours of Marsaxlokk and Birzebbuga. At the same time the airborne troops were to form a defensive line, running approximately from the coast at Ghar Bitija (south of Dingli) up to Il Qattara (north-west of Takali), and then down to Kirkop. These airborne troops were particularly charged with preventing the British from using the airfields at Luqa and Takali. During this phase, if they were considered necessary by the Commander, a German mountain division could be landed from Ju52s on an airfield captured during the first phase.

Phase 4

The remainder of the 'La Spezia' Division was to land in the harbours captured during Phase 3; when this was completed the attack on Valetta itself was to be carried out. The 'La Spezia' Division and the German tank regiment were to advance from the south and capture the small peninsulas pointing at Valetta from the south-east. At the same time the airborne forces were to advance from the west and capture Sliema, north of Valetta. Then the two forces were to join up at the base of the Valetta peninsula, cut it off and capture it. Once Valetta was captured it was considered that no further resistance could be organized on the Island.

But it was not to be. At the beginning of June General Student was ordered to Hitler's HQ in East Prussia. The Fuhrer listened to Student's report, admitted the likelihood of a successful bridgehead should the invasion go ahead, but then damningly declared;

> 'But what then? I guarantee what will happen. The Gibraltar squadron will leave port at once, and the British fleet will come steaming from Alexandria. Then you will see what the Italians will do. At the first radio reports they will go running back into their Sicilian harbours — warships, transports and all. And you and your paratroops will be left sitting on the Island alone! I forbid you to return to Italy! You will stay in Berlin.'*

That, in effect, was the end of any serious threat of invasion. As with the abandoned invasion of England in 1940, the golden chance of success had been there for the taking. Had Student's plan been carried out against Malta in August 1942, in all probability it would have been a resounding success. Without fuel for its Spitfires, or food for its

*As quoted in *The Luftwaffe War Diaries* by Cajus Bekker.

people, the means for Malta's defenders to have put up a sustained resistance would have been denied.

Hitler had twice hesitated when he should have struck. Even more so than had been the case in 1940, the Royal Navy had in effect won a truly significant victory without a shot being fired!

Appendix V

ITALIAN AND GERMAN VESSELS SUNK OR DAMAGED AT PALERMO HARBOUR AS A RESULT OF ATTACK BY WELLINGTONS OF 37 SQUADRON ON THE NIGHT OF 2/3 MARCH 1942 (AND SUBSEQUENT EXPLOSION OF THE DAMAGED *CUMA* THE FOLLOWING DAY)

Merchant vessels		
Cuma (German)	6600-ton steamer	sunk
Ruhr (German)	5945-ton steamer	sunk
Securitas	5365-ton steamer	heavily damaged; sank
Le Tre Marie	1085-ton steamer	heavily damaged
Ida Orlando	235-ton steamer	heavily damaged
Tricolore	179-ton tanker	heavily damaged
Sicilia	146-ton tug	heavily damaged
Gino Allegri	6835-ton steamer	lightly damaged
Sabbia	5787-ton steamer	lightly damaged
Sirio	5622-ton steamer	lightly damaged
Honestas	4959-ton steamer	lightly damaged
Assunta De Gregori	4219-ton steamer	lightly damaged
Etruria	2633-ton steamer	lightly damaged
Marte	2502-ton tanker	lightly damaged
Una	1431-ton steamer	lightly damaged
Giuseppina	735-ton steamer	lightly damaged
Salvatore	716-ton tug	lightly damaged
Ustica	403-ton steamer	lightly damaged
Raffio	360-ton steamer	lightly damaged
Ist	336-ton steamer	lightly damaged
Giuseppe Bertolli	283-ton steamer	lightly damaged
Epomeo	243-ton motor ship	lightly damaged
Albina	223-ton steamer	lightly damaged
Lussino	222-ton steamer	lightly damaged
Arno	208-ton steamer	lightly damaged
Andrea Sgarallino	146-ton pontoon	lightly damaged
Trinacria	141-ton tug	lightly damaged
Vettor Pisani	130-ton steamer	lightly damaged
Linotii	99-ton steamer	lightly damaged
Liliana	72-ton steamer	lightly damaged
Michelino	38-ton tug	lightly damaged
Maria Concetta	27-ton motor fishing craft	lightly damaged
Orazio	25-ton motor fishing craft	lightly damaged
Madonna Di Porto Salvo	23-ton tug	lighty damaged
La Nuovo Annunziata	22-ton motor fishing craft	lightly damaged
San Domenico	22-ton motor fishing craft	lightly damaged

Warships		
Frecchia[1]	destroyer	heavily damaged
Partenope	torpedo-boat	heavily damaged
Abba	torpedo-boat	lightly damaged
Folgore[2]	destroyer	lightly damaged
Maloncello	destroyer	lightly damaged
Vivaldi	destroyer	lightly damaged

[1]*Frecchia* was heavily damaged on the night of the 3/4 when *Cuma* exploded.
[2]*Folgore* was damaged during the raid and again when *Cuma* exploded.

CAPTAINS OF THE 37 SQUADRON WELLINGTONS INVOLVED IN THE RAID ON PALERMO HARBOUR, 2/3 MARCH

First Raid	
Z9111/D	Sqn.Ldr. E.E.C. Tomkins (overshot on return)
Z9038/H	Flg.Off. M.S. Blyth
DV421/W	Flg.Off. C.P.T. Halliwell
W5646/R	Flg.Off. E.H.G. Nesbitt
X9938/Z	Flt.Sgt. J. Morrison, RCAF
Z1043/L	Flt.Sgt. J.R. Vallance
X9886/G	Flt.Sgt. F. Ellison
Z8731/J	Sgt. B. Steward
DV453/U	Sgt. L.G. Fuller, RAAF
DV483/Y	Sgt. G de L. Carver
Second Raid	
DV421/W	Flg.Off. C.P.T. Halliwell
W5646/R	Flg.Off. E.H.G. Nesbitt
X9938/Z	Flt.Sgt. J. Morrison, RCAF
Z1043/L	Flt.Sgt. J.R. Vallance
Z8731/J	Sgt. B. Steward
DV453/U	Sgt. L.G. Fuller, RAAF

Appendix VI

MEDITERRANEAN ODYSSEY

Uffz. Dr Felix Sauer of 10/JG 53 — a 30 year-old teacher of biology and chemistry at a German High School in civilian life — who was shot down on 16 May, spent eight long days at sea in his rubber dinghy before being rescued; on his return to Sicily he recalled the nightmarish adventure:

Day 1

'The sea is empty. In the distance Malta appears on the skyline. Will there be someone else to look for me? And then my comrades are back again, this time with two rescue aircraft, and with them they have plenty of protection. But dusk is setting in. My comrades fly past hardly 10 metres above my head. In order to attract their attention I fire my whole supply of signal rockets, but they fail to find me. For a while they fly to and fro, but when it is dark they disappear to the north.

'Night is falling. The sea is calm. I start to check on my supplies: three bars of caffeine-chocolate — they will hardly be of any use as they make you thirsty; some Pervithin lozenges; the aluminium container of a Leica film filled with sugar, but not a drop of drinking water! While checking my provisions, the breeze blows me towards the coast. At the same time I am able to observe a night bombing attack on Malta.

'Later I notice two small boats approaching and scanning the waves with the fingers of their searchlights. Apparently the English are looking for me, but I rather trust my comrades; better wait for the uncertain chance of rescue in a friendly country than to march into certain captivity. Therefore I lie down flat in my boat, without moving, so that the enemy can not see me. At that moment a wave of bombers arrives from the north and the small boats switch off their seachlights and disappear.

Day 2

'The morning dawns. The sun has just risen when another rescue plane appears. It passes within a distance of 50 metres without discovering me. The breeze takes me south but Malta is still in sight. I try to divert myself, watching the duels between English and Axis fighters. It is a fascinating fight which lasts all day. At dusk I catch sight of the small island of Filfla. The breeze caries me away from Sicily and takes me to the south of Malta.

'Who is coming along over there? Apparently five English torpedo-boats. There is now no choice left... it will be better to attract their attention. During the day I discovered one left-over signal rocket in the folds of the boat. When the English units have come up to a distance of five kilometres I give the signal, but they disappear towards Marsaxlokk Bay, leaving huge waves behind them. It is highly improbable that they should not have noticed me. Actually they were in a great hurry.

'And yet the English did see me! One hour later — it is already night — two small boats turn up, searching the waves with their lights. They even approach very closely. I shout at the top of my voice, again and again, but the boats depart without having discovered me.

'I deliberate: My comrades have given me up; the English did not find me. Who will be left to help me now? Leave apart the fly buzzing around me all day long (most probably it will be asleep now, perched on one of my shoulders like a chicken in a coop); leave aside also my companion, the sea-gull. The breeze may be of use to me now. At the moment it blows from the south. If it continues like that I might find myself west of Malta tomorrow, and near the shore. And someone would be sure to see me.

'I carry with me a yellow silk cloth — serving as a flag-signal — and a telescopic metal tube, extendible like a photographer's stand. The piece of cloth fixed to the rod is used to enhance visibility. I, however, use it as a sail. I put up the rod like a mast, fixing it to one foot with a strap. One side of the sail I tie to the rod, the other I hold in my hand. I also manage to stretch out fairly comfortably in the boat, so as to hold out as many hours as possible. Thank God I do not feel very thirsty yet. Slowly the breeze carries me north again.

Day 3

'At last another day dawns. Over there, those might be the mountains of Sicily. And that peak over there must be Mount Etna. If the breeze would remain as strong but, alas, the breeze shifts and takes the tiny boat back south. Gone the hope to reach Sicily. But Africa is not so far away. I drop a scrap of paper into the water, and watch it drift away and estimate its relative speed. Adding the probable speed of the waves, I conclude — quite philosophically — that, given this speed, I might reach Libya in four days. But, hard to believe, the wind changes again. It is blowing from the west now — where would I land following this direction? Most probably in Crete. Excellent! I will now try to reach Cete. It is a long way off, but in seven days, maybe...

Day 4

'Slowly the dreaded thirst is setting in, the kind of thirst you can not resist. In the morning — the sea had been calm during the night — I find that a little steam has condensed on the boat — dew — many tiny drops. With a bit of gauze I collect these tiny traces of the precious water, and manage to quench my tormenting thirst. I will be able to manage till tomorrow.

Day 5

'Next morning: the big disappointment — the waves kept the boat moving during the night — not a trace of dew. Never mind — there will be something else. I have an idea — it might work. I remember that in salines, they use twigs to facilitate the condensation of salt. I might help myself in a similar way. Instead of twigs I take a bit of gauze, fill the shell of a signal flare with sea water, put the gauze inside and expose the shell to the sunlight. When the salt condenses the remaining water might be drinkable, but after two trials I have to state that this test does not work. The salt has condensed but the water tastes bitter, as before.

'And what if I drink salt water? Actually, the main thing is to avoid the salty taste in the mouth, for it produces the feeling of thirst. The sugar! It might serve as an antidote. I swallow three shell cases of sea water and add a little sugar... might be worse, but the interior burning is quenched. Three shells of sea water with some sugar in the morning, three in the evening, that's the magic formula. I feel I may be able to manage like that.

Days 6 and 7

'On and on I drift — eastwards — in absolute solitude. Far away four Spitfires pass, and then six German transports. Those are the only meetings. I begin to realise — from one hour to the next — that I am losing strength. The probability of rescue is fading away but hope does not leave me. My comrades — for certain — will no more go up to search for me. Nor will the English come back. The sea is not a highway where a good Samaritan passes every day. But there is still the Almighty who knows everything, and who also knows that spot with the shipwrecked in his tiny boat.

'On the back of my wife's photograph I start my last letter to her, continue it on a scrap of cardboard and then on a bit of paper I dig from my pocket. Those are rather shaky pencilled signs, giving utterance to my last thoughts, but my wife will be able to read those signs some day — even if they are disfigured by salty waves:

> "Dearest, I'll have to die unless a miracle happens. I know it. Die of thirst and hunger, alone in the wide ocean. But I don't believe that God should abandon he who fights for his home, his country and for his just cause, and this firm faith gives me strength. I shall be able to hold out another three days.
>
> "You must not think that I am talking this way because my intelligence is already troubled. No, I am fully conscious. And you know me. I believe that, at the end of these three days, the miracle will happen. If God wills otherwise, I am also happy to die for my country.
>
> "You know, at night, I watch the same stars which are shining at home. And then I feel quite close to you. I may have only a

short while left, and yet, my soul is still strong. And in the evening I pray to God, as you will do in our dear home."

'Now and again, I look up from my paper and see, still circling around, the faithful fly and the white sea-gull, those two dear friends that have given me much consolation.

Day 8

'Dawn of the new day. I know this is my last sun. I may yet see it set, but never again will I see it rise from the dark of night to spell light and hope to this earth. Unless...! But down south, there is something. It is not water; these are not dolphins, nor clouds, nor a mirage. A mirage would not have such solid, geometrical outlines. A miracle!

'A big boat is moving straight towards me, as if obeying a secret command. This is something hard to believe and yet, I am not overwhelmed. In my heart of hearts, at the very root of my faith, I felt and knew that this *must* happen. And that is why I was able to carry through. With a last effort I raise the little sail, so that they may discover me more easily. But there is no need for that. Aboard the boat — the torpedo-boat *Turbine* — the alarm had been given. By now I am able to recognize the flag: red-white-green. Hurrah!

'Those are friends. When I am taken aboard, helpless, hardly able to move, I burst into tears. When taken ashore, I am a changed man already, thanks to the kind and extremely devoted care of my Italian comrades. I am still feeling weak, and hardly able to keep on my feet.'

Whilst recovering in hospital from his ordeal, Uffz. Sauer was presented with the Iron Cross 1st Class for his 90+ flights over Malta. Following four weeks' convalescence, he returned to his unit but soon afterwards was posted back to Germany, where he joined JG 104; he remained with this training unit until the war's end, having been commissioned.

Appendix VII

SHOT DOWN OVER MALTA

These are the words of Tenente Remo Cazzolli:

'18 May 1942: eight Re2001s left Caltagirone in pairs for a raid over Malta, a sweep in support of Assault Motor Launches (MTBs) of the Regia Marina. I was leader, with Sottotenente Romano Pagliani as my wingman. That morning — so nice and bright — a big dogfight began over the Island between the Re2001s and Spitfires. There were many Spitfires and few Re2001s, so when I ordered my pilots to break formation and engage, I found myself surrounded by Spitfires!

'As I opened fire, I saw before me in planform, like a cross, a Spitfire. I took aim and fired, seeing a long, black trail — possibly a sign that I had hit him.

'Minutes passed slowly like the years of youth; suddenly there was a terrible noise like thunder and my engine stopped; it was the fire of 20 mm cannon, which overwhelmed my senses. An instant of infinite fear followed the realisation — my Re2001 was shot down!

'I realised at once the situation, and my face was covered with blood (I still bear the sign of those injuries to this day); by instinct I sought to open the cockpit canopy, but it was stuck, a shell having struck behind the seat armour and crushed the canopy forward against the windscreen.

'I thought it was the end. I was in an aircraft with no power, a radiator shot away, a shattered aileron fluttering, with the earth of Malta coming up inexorably to meet me!

I tried to recover control. I do not know what condition the tail of the aircraft was in, but that aircraft seemed to have a life of its own; it would not kill me!

'I saw a rock flush in the sea, there was an indescribable crash, and I passed out.'

Following his crash, Remo Cazzolli was transferred to Mtarfa Hospital where he was wrapped in a plaster cast from head to foot, suffering many fractures and contusions. Although very small in stature, he proved of strong constitution, making a remarkable recovery after some two months confined to bed. During this period he befriended a fellow patient, Oblt. Hans Rottmann of KG 54, who had been shot down in his Ju88. When he was fit to move, Cazzolli, still partially in a cast, left Malta with a group of other prisoners aboard a ship for Britain. On arrival he was sent to a POW camp in Scotland, but at once he began to make plans for an escape, despite his poor physical condition:

'I had a crazy desire to "beard" the English after what they had done to me. I wanted to fly and fight again.'

One night in September 1942 Cazzolli, still plastered heavily, with Oblt. Hans Haussen and Tenente Vascello Ciollaro (commander of the submarine *Glauco*) escaped during an informal party in the camp. Hoping to get across to neutral Eire, to reach the Italian Embassy in Dublin, they walked by night and hid by day until they reached Glasgow, by which time they all had the appearance of three tramps. Realizing that their escape attempt was futile, tired and hungry, they decided to surrender. Because he spoke English well, the small and youthful Cazzolli approached a police officer in the dark, and humbly stated: "I am an Italian pilot escaped from prison camp; I want to surrender me."

Looking down at this small bundle of rags, topped by a boyish face, the policeman, in a bored manner, advised him: "Get to your home... boy!" Cazzolli insisted, but the constable just became more irritated, until finally Haussen and Ciollaro showed themselves. Possibly then recalling news of the escape of three officer prisoners, he took them in.

On return to the POW camp, Cazzolli was found to be in such a bad state that he was transferred to London, where he remained for a month. The capital was frequently being bombed at this time, and unable to go to shelter whilst bombs exploded nearby, Cazzolli found it "worse than combats over Malta!"

By Christmas 1942 his condition was worse, and he was progressively becoming paralysed. He was moved again to hospital where he was seen by a delegation of Red Cross doctors from Switzerland, who recommended repatriation. The British agreed to his exchange for an RAF prisoner. On 24 April 1943 therefore, he returned to Italy via Lisbon, Portugal, and was hospitalized in the "Instituto Rizzoli' in Bolgna, where he finally made a good recovery under the care of a famous orthopaedic specialist, Professor Delitala.

Appendix VIII

AWAITING TRANSFER

Although not strictly a part of the Malta story, the following incident involved two Spitfire pilots — a New Zealander and a Canadian — both of whom were at Gibraltar awaiting posting to Malta. This account has been provided by New Zealand aviation historian and researcher, Paul Sortehaug.

Flg.Off. Howard Crafts, RNZAF (Spitfire EP444) and Flt.Sgt. L.L. Gerner, RCAF (Spitfire EP787) were on patrol on 11 October 1942 from Gibraltar, when they were vectored onto a 'bogey'. Crafts later recalled:

'We intercepted this Ju88, which was on a photographic-reconnaissance, about 30 miles east of the Rock. I had Sgt. Gerner, a Canadian boy, as No 2 to me; we chased it for 100 miles — we couldn't catch it. In the end it got right down on the deck and it was just as fast as us.

'We were flying right on the deck, so I sat behind the Ju88 and I switched on cannons only, and started to poop at him. After a while he started to weave and we caught up, and by the time I did catch up I had no cannon shells left, so I fired the machine guns and shot out one engine. I called Gerner, and he stuck in behind, but what happened I don't know.

'I think probably it was his engine overheating rather than return fire — I reckon I knocked the gunner out. He was sitting in behind the Ju88 at reasonably short range — he wasn't firing — the next thing was his glycol spewed out. I screamed at him to get out. I said get up, get up high, quick. And he pulled up. I said now straighten out and talked him all the way.

'I think he must have flapped because he just didn't get out; he was 50 feet off the deck and flew straight into the sea. It was a terrifying thing for me because I saw it all.'

Despite Crafts' comments, Gerner was officially listed as having been shot down by return fire from the Ju88, his aircraft crashing into the sea off Cape Sacritif, Spain; he did not survive. Crafts continued:

'I claimed a "damaged" first of all, but then there was a very nice English chap whom I'd met in Gibraltar — who was literally a spy — I'm not kidding! He was in and out of Spain all the time — he was Secret Service. He came back two weeks after (the combat) and told me: "I've got good news for you, boy, that 88 you plonked, or had a go at, its down on the beach at Melilla. Two crew dead." The pilot had turned and headed for North Africa, but didn't make it though. So I got a destroyed out of that.'

The aircraft involved was a Ju88D-1 of 2(F)/122 from Trapani, Sicily, coded F6+KK (Werknr. 430319); which did crash-land at Melilla, Spanish Morocco; Uffz. Kurt Schneider, the wireless operator and Ofw. Walter Muller (the gunner) were both injured.

Appendix IX

SPITFIRE Vc BR108

Pride of place in the Air Hall at the National War Museum in Valetta is taken by the front section of the wreckage of Spitfire Vc BR108. This was recovered from the seabed of Marsalforn Bay, Gozo, by members of the RAF Subaqua Club in 1973, and was the aircraft ditched by Flt.Lt. Lester Sanders of 603 Squadron on 8 July 1942, as recorded in Chapter Seven.

BR108 was built by Vickers-Armstrongs (Supermarine) Ltd in early 1942, its maiden flight taking place at High Post Aerodrome on 3 March; it was flown to 8 Maintenance Unit five days later, then to 47 Maintenance Unit on 23 March. From here — in company with others — it was partially disassembled, crated and loaded aboard the freighter *Empire Heath*, destined for Gibraltar. Here it was reassembled, test flown, allocated the code 'C-20' and loaded aboard the USS *Wasp* on 7 May, from where it was flown to Malta two days later.

BR108 was issued to 249 Squadron, retaining the code markings 'C-20' until about 19 June, when it was re-coded 'T-W' ('T' being 249 Squadron's identification letter, 'W' the individual aircraft identification letter). Finally, at the beginning of July, BR108 was transferred to 603 Squadron and was presumably re-coded once more — possibly as 'X-W' ('X' being 603 Squadron's identification letter. Known operational flights were:

249 Squadron	**Pilot**	**Action**
9 May	Plt.Off. P.A. Nash	Bf109 destroyed
		Bf109 probable
	Plt.Off. P.A. Nash	Bf109 damaged
	Plt.Off. P.A. Nash	Ju87 probable

10 May	Plt.Off. P.A. Nash	Scramble
	Plt.Off. P.A. Nash	2 Ju87s destroyed
12 May	Plt.Off. P.A. Nash	Scramble — hit steamroller when taxying-in on return; damaged
6 June	Flt.Lt. P.B. Lucas	Scramble
	Flt.Lt. R.W. McNair	Scramble
8 June	Sqn.Ldr. S.B. Grant	Shipping patrol
	Sgt. R.B. Brennan	Scramble
10 June	Flt.Lt. P.B. Lucas	Scramble
	Flt.Lt. P.B. Lucas	Scramble
	Flt.Lt. P.B. Lucas	Scramble
11 June	Sqn.Ldr. S.B. Grant	Scramble
12 June	Flt.Lt. P.B. Lucas	Scramble
	Flt.Lt. P.B. Lucas	Scramble
16 June	Flt.Sgt. M.E. Tomkins	Scramble
19 June	Flt.Lt. P.B. Lucas	Scramble
20 June	Flg.Off. J. Smith	Scramble
21 June	Flt.Lt. P.B. Lucas	Scramble
	Flt.Lt. P.B. Lucas	Scramble
24 June	Flg.Off. R. Daddo-Langlois	Scramble
25 June	Plt.Off. C.H. Lattimer	Bf109 destroyed, Bf109 probable
28 June	Flg.Off. J. Smith	Scramble
29 June	Wt.Off. C.B. Ramsay	Scramble
	Wt.Off. C.B. Ramsay	Scramble
603 Squadron		
8 July	Flt.Lt. L.V. Sanders	Ju88 damaged, Bf109 probable shared with Plt.Off. N.S.King

BR108 was then shot down by Lt. Heinz-Berres of I/JG 77, and ditched in Marsalforn Bay, Gozo, from where the slightly injured pilot was rescued by Maltese fishermen.

Although initially located by members of RAF Luqa's Subaqua Club in 1968, the wreckage of BR108 would remain on the seabed for a further five years.

Appendix X

THE CRASH OF LIBERATOR AL516 OF 511 SQUADRON AT GIBRALTAR ON NIGHT ON 31 OCTOBER/1 NOVEMBER, 1942

There follows a list of all those involved on that fateful night:

The crew

Flt.Lt. R. Walton (pilot) injured
Plt.Off. E.J. Saunders (2nd pilot) unhurt
Plt.Off. G.W.R. Frampton (navigator) injured
Sgt. E.J. Booker (flight engineer) unhurt
Flt.Sgt. I. Watson (WOp) unhurt
Flt.Sgt. J. McCulloch (WOp) unhurt

NB Flt.Lt. Walton and Sgt. Booker were survivors from a Liberator which had been shot down off Norway in February 1942, and had returned to the United Kingdom after an arduous journey across Norway into Sweden.

There were 34 passengers (24 air force and 10 civilians) of whom 14 were killed (of 10 civilians, 8 were killed and 2 injured).

Those who lost their lives:

Flt.Lt. E.L. Hetherington, DFC	Mr & Mrs E.J. Rowe
Plt.Off. J.W. Williams, RCAF, DFC	Mrs E.P. Sheldon
Flt.Lt. E.H. Glazebrook, RCAF, DFC	Mrs M.B. Hucklebridge
Flt.Sgt. C.E. Mutch, RCAF	Mrs W.G.S. Aston & child
Sgt. K.H. Davey	(family of FAA officer)
Sgt. D.W. Spencer	Mrs K.N. Chase & child

Injured

Mrs D.W. Spencer (wife of Sgt. Spencer)	Mrs J. Neighbours

Air force survivors (passengers)

Wg.Cdr. A.H. Donaldson DSO, DFC, AFC	Plt.Off. L.S. Reid, RAAF
Flt.Lt. A.F. Roscoe, DFC	Plt.Off. C.F. Bush
Flg.Off. F.R. Johnson, RAAF	Wt.Off. G.H. Farquharson, RCAF
Flg.Off. A.S. Yates, RAAF	Flt.Sgt. D.A. Bye
Plt.Off. G.F. Beurling, DSO, DFC, DFM	Flt.Sgt. A.W. Varey
Plt.Off. C.A. McC. Barbour	Flt.Sgt. L.G. Pow, RCAF
Plt.Off. J.G.W. Farmer	Flt.Sgt. E.L. Mahar, RAAF
Plt.Off. J.A.H. Pinney	Sgt. K.R. Mitchell, RAAF
Plt.Off. F.D. Thomas	Sgt. F.W. Clewley, RAAF

Appendix XI

LORD GORT VC

Early November (1942): during a night raid a petrol dump near Hamrun was hit, and a large fire broke out. Governor Lord Gort was soon on the scene and proceeded to help remove petrol cans from a block which was already on fire; the can he was carrying burst into flames and he was quite badly burned. He had his burns dressed at Hamrun civil hospital but refused to be hospitalized, and despite great pain, continued to carry out his duties. The burns took weeks to heal, but worse was to follow. Some 20 years earlier, Gort had developed a cancerous growth in his lip, and this now flared up again. On the last day of the year his condition forced him to go to London for treatment; the disease would cause his premature death in 1946.

BIBLIOGRAPHY

Publication **Author** **Publisher**

'*Spitfires over Malta*' Plt.Off. Paul Brennan DFC, DFM, Plt.Off. Ray Hesselyn DFM & Bar, and Henry Bateson Jarrolds, 1943

'*Malta Spitfire*' Flg.Off. George F. Beurling DSO, DFC, DFM, and Leslie Roberts Oxford University Press, 1943 (Republished by Arms & Armour Press)

'*Tattered Battlements; A Malta Diary* A Fighter Pilot *Peter Davies, 1943 (Republished by William Kimber with the author identified as Sqn.Ldr. H.A.S. Johnson, DFC)*

'*One Man's Window*' Dennis Barnham William Kimber

'*Warburton's War*' A. Spooner William Kimber

'*In Full Flight*' A. Spooner William Kimber

'*Spitfire Strike*' Flt.Lt. W.T.E. Rolls DFC, DFM, AE William Kimber

'*Pedestal; the Malta Convoy of August 1942*' Peter C. Smith William Kimber

'*Hero; the Buzz Beurling Story*' Brian Nolan Penguin Books

'*Air Battle for Malta: the Diaries of a Fighter Pilot*' Lord James Douglas-Hamilton, MP Mainstream Publishing

'*Against All Odds*' Lex McAulay Hutchinson Australia

'*Malta; Blitzed but not Beaten*' Philip Vella The National War Museum Association

'*Night Strike from Malta*' Kenneth Poolman Janes

'*Briefed to Attack*' Air Marshal Sir Hugh P. Lloyd Hodder & Stoughton

'*British Naval Action*' Ray Sturtivant Arms & Armour

'*Sea Flight*' Hugh Popham William Kimber

'*They Gave me a Spitfire*' Mike Crosley

'*Five Up*' Laddie Lucas Sidgwick & Jackson

'*Out of the Blue*' Laddie Lucas Hutchinson

'*Sir Keith Park*' Vincent Orange Methuen

'*The Seafire*' David Brown Ian Allan

'*Carrier Operations in World War II*' David Brown Ian Allan

'*Aircraft Carrier*' Norman Polmar Macdonald

'*Fighter Squadrons of the Royal Air Force*' J.D.R. Rawlings Macdonald

'*Fighters over the Desert*' Christopher Shores & Hans Ring Neville Spearman

'*The Second World War; Vol. 4, The Hinge of Fate*' Winston S. Churchill The Educational Book Co Ltd

The Luftwaffe War Diaries' Cajus Bekker Macdonald

'*Ritterkreuzträger der Luftwaffe; Band 1: Jagdflieger*' Ernst Obermaier Verlag Dieter Hoffmann

'*Chronik des JG-53 Pik-As; Band I*' Jochen Prien Flugzeug Dokumentation

'*Storia degli Aerosiluranti Italiani*' Gen. Carlo Unia Edizioni dell'Ateneo/Bizzarri, Rome

'*Quelli del Cavallino Rampante*' Gen. Antonio Duma Edizione dell'Ateneo, Rome

'*Guerra attraverso l'etere nel teatro Mediterraneo*' Gen. Giuseppe Garello Giorgio Apostolo Editore, Milano

'*Il Radar; la Guerra Aerea – Attacco-Difesa – Organizzazione terrestre*' Nino Arena Edizioni Mucchi, Modena

'*La Regia Aeronautica – Vol 1°, 2°, 3° and 4°*' Nino Arena Edizioni Stato Maggiore Aeronautica, Rome

'*Inferno su Malta*' Nicola Malizia Edizioni Mursia, Milano

'*Il 5° Stormo*' Gen. Giuseppe Pesce & Nicola Malizia Edizioni Mucchi, Modena

'*Gli Stuka della Regia Aeronautica*' Alberto Borgiotti & Cesare Gori Edizioni Mucchi, Modena

'*Il 51° Stormo Caccia*' Nicola Malizia Edizioni Bizzarri, Rome

'*Il Caccia Re2001*' Sergio Govi Giorgio Apostolo Editore, Milano

INDEX

Personnel — I, Allied

Abram, Flg.Off. J., 39 Sqn 355
Alderdice, Sgt. 229 Sqn *294*
Aldridge, Flg.Off. A.H., 217 Sqn 353, 363, 364
Allardice, Plt.Off. P.M., 185 Sqn 121, 132, 137, 665
Allen, Flt.Lt. G., 605 Sqn 80, 664
Allen-Rowlandson, Sgt. G., 601 Sqn 241, 341
Allsopp, Flt.Lt. W., 86 Sqn 529
Almos, Plt.Off. F.E., 603/126 Sqns *197*, 199, 234, 235, 245
Alpe, Flt.Sgt. C.T., 242 Sqn 58
Amos, Sgt.F.V., 272 Sqn 350, 668
Anderson, Flt.Lt. A.G.S., 126 Sqn 42, *43*, *49*, 58, 112, 113, 151, 171
Andrews, Flt.Sgt. B.W., 185 Sqn 242, 310, 394, 437
Andrews, Plt.Off., E. 229 Sqn 155, 165, 169
Andrews, Sqn.Ldr. S.E., 605 Sqn 16, 27, 80, 90, 673
Armitage, Sgt. C., 235 Sqn 343, 344
Armitage, Midspm R.G., 807 Sqn 334
Armour, Mr Peter, BOAC 69
Aspinall, Sgt. V., 217 Sqn 364
Asquith, AC J., Luqa 110
Aston, Mrs W.G.S., Civilian 687

Bader, Grp.Capt. D.R.S 87, 451
Bailey, Flt.Lt. J., 126 Sqn 156,212, 226, 255, 343, 394
Bairnsfather, Plt.Off. R., 603 Sqn 240, 261
Baker, Flt.Lt. C.H., 126 Sqn 47, 52, *81*, 125, 134, 665
Baker, Sqn.Ldr. H.C., 229 Sqn 552, 568, 589, 595, 596, 673
Baker, Sgt. S.R., 18 Sqn 36
Ball, Capt. A. *42*, 43
Balinson, Sgt. A.B., 148 Sqn 216
Ballantine, Sgt. R., 69 Sqn 62
Ballantyne, Flt.Sgt. J.H., 603/229 Sqns 302, 382, 401, 404, 412, 518, 530, 536, 578, 579, 581, 583, 585, 587, 596, 615, 651, 655
Bancroft Sgt. H.G., OADU 287-8
Barbour, Plt.Off. C.A.McC., 603 Sqn 241, 376, 687
Barfoot, Cpl., Takali 82
Baril, Plt.Off. J.W.P., 185 Sqn 240, 345, *362*, 438
Barkas, Cpl. T., Takali 130
Barlow, Plt.Off. L.G., 603 Sqn 240, *242*, 276, 291, 293, 308, 666
Barnes, Sub Lt. D.J.N., RNAS 289
Barnes, Flt.Lt. L.D., 126 Sqn 29, 31, *49*, 91
Barnett, Capt. R.J.W., BOAC 239
Barnham, Flt.Lt. D.W., 601 Sqn *196*, 197, 198, 209, 210, 217, 218, 223, 224, 232, 233, 238, 248, 251, 252, 263, 264, *268*, 269, 270, 272, 288, 344, 371
Barrick, PO(A) L.F., 884 Sqn 476, 483, 485, 509
Bartleman, 2/Lt. A. (SAAF), 601 Sqn *196*, 197, 198, 200, *212*, 224, 233, 252, 256, 272, 300, 341-2
Bartlett, Lt. N.A., 806 Sqn 484
Barton, Sqn.Ldr. A.R.H., 126 Sqn 156, 165, 176, 204, 210, 212, 216, 226, 227, 250, 255, 261, 270, 302, 378, *379*, 654, 673
Bate, Plt.Off. P.St C., 248 Sqn 497, 525
Bates, Sgt. T.H., 185 Sqn 121
Bateson, Sqn.Ldr. J.A., 22 Sqn 128
Baum, Sgt. F.W., 69 Sqn 342
Baxter, Sgt. C.L., 249/1435 Sqns 310, 367, 401, 424, 428
Bazalgette, Plt.Off. L.G., 126 Sqn 423, 585
Beatty, Flt.Lt. M.A., 229 Sqn 170
Beaumont, Flt.Sgt. T.F., USS *Wasp* 302, 303, 668
Beazley, Sqn.Ldr. H.J.S., 249 Sqn 27, 46, 50, 70, 85, 87, 673
Beckitt, Plt.Off. J., 605 Sqn *40*, 76, 132, 143, 147, 159, 164, 270
Bedford, Sub Lt. F., RNAS 90
Bee, Flg.Off. D.A.R., 39 Sqn 114, 186, 187
Beet, Plt.Off. C.H., 252 Sqn 46, 668
Belcher, Wt.Off. F.H., 601 Sqn *196*, 198, 276, 659
Belfield, Plt.Off. G., 22 Sqn 186, 187
Bell, Sgt. E.S., OADU 287-8
Bell Sgt., USS *Wasp* 241, *242*
Berchamps, Sgt., 249 Sqn 127
Bergé, Cmdt (FF), SAS 348
Berkeley-Hill, Plt.Off. O.W.H., 249 Sqn 240, 373, 376, 401, *407*, 408, 666
Beurling, Plt.Off. G.F., 249 Sqn 309, 310, 315, 392, 393, 395, 401, 402, 404, 406, 408, 409, 410, 414, 426, 433, *434*, 435, 436, 443, 446, 460, 461, 463, 504, *517*, 522, 523, 530, 539, 554, 560, *561*, 561, 573, 574, 593, 603, 604, 606, 629, 641, 642, 643, 650, 656, 687
Beveridge, Flt.Lt. R.G.W., 39 Sqn 186, 187, 188
Billing, Sgt. G.D., 185 Sqn 640, *641*
Billings, Gnr, *Ohio* 501
Bing Plt.Off. L.P.S., 89 Sqn 366, 372, 376, 386, 446, 464, 515, 541
Birse, Sub Lt. S.W., 821 Sqn 117
Bisdee, Sqn.Ldr. J.D., 601 Sqn *196*, 197, 198, 200, 201, 209, 210, 218, 232, 239, 252, 257, 262, 272, 288, 289, 290, 673
Bishop, Wt.Off. D., Bomb Disposal 231
Bisley, Plt.Off. J.H.E., 126 Sqn 156, 168, 169, 250, 258, 280, 315, 378, *379*, 394, 651, 657
Blackburn, Plt.Off. C.A., 126 Sqn 58
Blackstock, Plt.Off. W., 459 Sqn 350
Blakeley, Sub Lt. J.B., RNAS 90
Blanchard, Sub Lt. A.G., 801 Sqn 325, 330
Blessing, Sgt. W.G., 272 Sqn 355, 668
Boarman, LAC C., Luqa 111
Bocock, Flt.Lt. W., 95 Sqn 90
Boddam-Whetham, Lt. A.P., HMS *Indomitable* 473
Bold, Sgt., OADU 36
Bolland, Sgt. R.C., 185 Sqn 468
Bolton, Sgt. G.S., 126 Sqn 133, 134, 145
Bone, Sgt. D.T., 18 Sqn 33
Booker, Sgt. E.J., 511 Sqn 686
Booth, Plt.Off. D.E., 603/126 Sqn 199, 211, 235, 236, 262, 271
Booth, Flg.Off. J.C.M., 249 Sqn 134, 665
Booth Plt.Off. , 21 Sqn 61
Booth, Sgt. J.J., 89 Sqn 426
Bosley, Flg.Off. J.E., 69 Sqn 86
Bouchier, Grp.Capt. C.A., Air Ministry 195, 196
Bowker, Flg.Off. M.B., 203 Sqn 185
Boyd, Flg.Off. C.I.L., 37 Sqn 100, 111
Boyd, Sgt. J.L., 242/185 Sqns 50, 51, 93, 94, 103, 112, 116, 121, 160, *161*, 161, 169, 172, 173, 176, 178, 202, 206, 215, 216, 224, 238, 248, 249, 254, 256, 268, 269, 270, 665
Boyle, Plt.Off. A.R., 601 Sqn 240, 276
Brabner, Lt.Cdr. R.A., 801 Sqn 327, 331, 333, 451, 469, 483
Bradley, Flt.Lt. A.J., 202 Sqn 282
Brady, Sgt. J.M., OADU 43
Branch, Sgt. A.T., 249 Sqn 47, 91
Braybrooke, Sgt., HMS *Eagle* 283
Brennan, Plt.Off. V.P., 249 Sqn 109, *116*, *124*, 151, 203, 204, 211, 212, 219, 234, 239, 249, 254, 256, 260, 261, 262, *266*, 276, 277, 278, *291*, 292, 367, 378, 395, 396, 651, 654, 686
Briffet, Plt.Off. J.F., 227 Sqn 572
Briggs, Plt.Off. G.M., 601 Sqn *196*, 198, 212, 233, 250, 252, 255, 293, 665
Briggs, Sgt. J.V., 89 Sqn 645
Briscoe, Wt.Off., 235/227 Sqns 423, 523, 524
Broad, Plt.Off. E.C., 185 Sqn 143, 146, 147, 152, 180, *216*, 249, 256, 259, 299, 345, *362*
Brockhouse, Plt.Off. E.H., 86 Sqn 412
Bromfield, Sub Lt. J.J., 828/830 Sqn 341
Brooker, Plt.Off. S.F., 126 Sqn 205, 207, 665
Brooks, Flt.Sgt. L.D., 229 Sqn 170, 176, *182*, 205, 220, 665
Brough, Sgt. E.T., 603/229 Sqn 241, 457, 530, 601
Brown, Sgt. A.R., 217 Sqn 441, 442
Brown, Sub Lt. C.M., 827 Sqn 492
Brown, Sub Lt. J.M., 826 Sqn 54
Brown, Sub Lt. P.F.C., 815 Sqn 100
Brown, Flt.Sgt. R.H. (also 1435 Sqn), 603 Sqn 241, 267, 308, 412, 437, 457, 632
Bruen, Lt.Cdr. J.M., 800 Sqn 451, 478, 483, 484
Bruce, Flg.Off. E.A.C.G., 185 Sqn 415, 445
Bryce, Plt.Off. J.M., 227 Sqn 572, 623
Bryden, Flt.Sgt. N.G., 249 Sqn 415, 419, 433, 435, 538, 603, 608
Bryson, Plt.Off., 248 Sqn 524
Buchanan, Flg.Off. G.A.F., 249 Sqn 87, 116, 117, 145, 152, *152*, 160, 178, 181, 203, 204, 208, 210, 211, 232, 235, 239, 245, 254, 256, 270, 272, 273, 274, 287, 651
Buchanan-Dunlop, Lt.Cdr. D.K., 827 Sqn 452
Buck, Capt. H., SAS 347
Buckley, Sgt., 603 Sqn *197*
Buckstone, Flt.Lt. J.W., 603 Sqn *197*, 198, 199, 208, *225*, 231, 245, 665
Budd, Plt.Off. A.E., 249 Sqn 310, 433, 461, *523*, 561, *562*, 616, 620
Bugden, L/Air W.H., 826 Sqn 54
Bull, CPO W., Hal Far 164
Bullivant, Sub Lt. B.E., 813F Sqn 334
Buntine, Sgt. R.A., 1435 Sqn 423, 502, 517, 666
Burgess, Flt.Lt. J.H., 1435 Sqn 635, 644
Burleigh, Flt.Sgt. J., 229 Sqn 193, 194
Burrage, Sqn.Ldr. R.B., 10 RAAF Sqn 324
Burrough, Rear-Adm H.M., Force X 450, 471, 495, 496
Buscall, Sub Lt. J., 821 Sqn 92
Bush, Flt.Sgt. C.F., 603/229 Sqns 199, 263, 264, 401, 405, 435, *545*, 585, 600, 603, 687
Butler, Flt.Sgt. B., 249 Sqn 240, 304, 305, 308, 402, 406, *523*, 531, 666
Bye, Flt.Sgt. D.A., 603/229 Sqns 240, 595, 643, 687

Cagby, Flt.Sgt. H.G.W., Hal Far 166
Cahill, Grp.Capt. C.A., Luqa 40
Cairns, Sgt. A.G., 249 Sqn 91, 211
Caldwell, Plt.Off. W.A., 601 Sqn *196*, 198, 257, 276, 286, 292, 666
Cameron, Sgt. G.D., 249 Sqn 637
Cameron, Sgt. G.R., 21 Sqn 61, 74
Cameron, Sgt., 69 Sqn 35, 50, 75
Campbell, Flt.Lt. G.L., 272 Sqn 144
Campbell, Flg.Off., 203 Sqn 54
Cane, Capt. A.P.W., BOAC 236
Capes, Sub Lt. A.W.A., RNAS 29
Carington, Sgt. G.A.C., 38 Sqn 298
Carpenter, Flt.Lt. J.M.V., 126 Sqn 16, 39, 64, 71
Carroll, Sgt. W.R., 217 Sqn 364
Carson, Flt.Sgt. R.L.K., 229 Sqn 155, *182*, *294*
Carter, Plt.Off. D.J., 229 Sqn 155, *182*, *294*
Carter, Wt.Off. P., 249 Sqn 423, 610, 615, 667
Cartridge, Sqn.Ldr. D.L., 248 Sqn 456, 474
Carver, Lt. R.H.P., 885 Sqn 451, 478
Casey, Sub Lt. C., 828/830 Sqn 344
Casey, Mr R.G., Minister of State for ME 230, 232, 237
Cassidy, Flt.Lt. E., 1435 Flt. 64
Cayley, Lt.Cdr. R.D., HMS *Utmost* 48
Ceely, Sub Lt. J., 807 Sqn 330, 669
Chaffe, Sqn.Ldr. R.I., 185 Sqn 90, 91, 92, 93, 665, 673
Chalmers, Mr. A., *Wairangi* 499
Chamberlain, Sqn.Ldr. J.G., Controller 598
Chandler, LAC O.P., Kalafrana 58, 270, 439
Channon, Plt.Off. T.M., 69 Sqn 81, 185
Chaplin, Wg.Cdr. J.H., 38 Sqn 291
Chapman, Sub Lt. S.W., 815 Sqn 100
Charlesworth, Plt.Off. H.C., 601 Sqn 302
Charney, Flt.Lt. K., 185 Sqn 381, 382, 385, 393, 409, *450*, 535, 547, 593, 608, 619, 620, 633, 657
Charron, Sgt. A.E., 148 Sqn 216
Charron, Sgt. P.M., 126 Sqn 302, 605, 608, 617, 656
Charters, Plt.Off. R.W., OADU 281
Chase, Mrs. K.N., Civilian 687
Checketts, Sgt., 86 Sqn 521
Cheek, Flg.Off. L., 185 Sqn 468, 545, 601, *602*, 611
Chick, Grp.Capt. J.S., Luqa 64, 184
Churchill, Lt. R.A.F., 884 Sqn 476, 488, 489, 669
Churchill, Grp.Capt. W.M., Takali 467, 468, 522, 528, 530, 534, 537, *538*, 539, 653, 666
Churchill, Mr Winston, Prime Minister 154, 195, 229, 230, 251, 275, 318, 508, 522
Clark, Sub Lt. N.V., 828/830 Sqn 95
Clark, Lt. W.S. (SAAF), 69 Sqn 624
Clarke, Sub Lt. G.R., 828/830 Sqn 546, 623
Clawson, Cpl. H., Luqa 180
Clayton, Sgt. L., 69 Sqn 524
Cleggett, Sgt. N.J., 272 Sqn 357
Cleveland, Flt.Sgt., 601/126 Sqn 198, 255
Clewley, Sgt. F.W., 185 Sqn 468, 505, 687
Clifton, Sgt., OADU 206
Coakley, Sgt. K., 21 Sqn 39
Coates, Sqn.Ldr. J.A.G., 203 Sqn 185
Cobley, Plt.Off. P.C., 272 Sqn 356, 357
Cockshott, Sgt. J., 235 Sqn 311
Coffin, Plt.Off. H.M., 126 Sqn 32, *49*, *64*, 77, 96, 97, 112, 122
Cohen, Plt.Off. F.A., 235/227 Sqns 337, 523, 544
Coldbeck, Flt.Lt. H.R., 69 Sqn 172, *374*, 374, 463, 529, 540, 545, 625
Cole, Sgt. S.W., 227 Sqn 623
Coleman, Flt.Lt. G.B., 89 Sqn 171, 251, 271, 658
Colquhoun, Sgt. L.R., 69 Sqn 128, 316, 370, 446, 522, 524
Condon, Plt.Off. R.L., 86 Sqn 523
Connell, Flt.Lt. W.C., 126/249 Sqns 90, 97, 111, 117, 118, 121, 151, 152, 204, 211, 235, 239
Conolly, Mr. G.V., *Empire Hope* 496
Conway, Flt.Sgt. W.C., 185 Sqn 241, *242*, 262, 263, 365
Cook, PO C., HMS *Ledbury* 500
Cook, Sqn.Ldr. A.E., 235 Sqn 336, 363, 412
Cook, Plt.Off. L.E., 59 Sqn 43
Cooper, Sgt. A.E., 272 Sqn 350, 668

Copeland, Plt.Off. P., 250 Sqn 358
Copp, Sgt. W.E., 126 Sqn 78
Copsey, Flg.Off. E.F.V., 89 Sqn 424
Corbett, Sgt. G., 69 Sqn 408
Corbett, Lt.Cdr. J.W.S., 826 Sqn 54
Corbisier, Plt. R. (Belg), 272 Sqn 355, 668
Corfe, Wt.Off. D.F., 229 Sqn 193, 218, 220, 665
Cork, Lt. R.J., 880 Sqn 451, *452*, 466, *472*, 478, 479, 488, 489, 491, 493, 509, 655
Cormack, Flt.Sgt. I.W, 249 Sqn 109, 125, 655
Cornish, Sgt. C.H., 229 Sqn 468, 533, 666
Corrie, Flg.Off. R.M., 202 Sqn 309
Cossar, Capt. A.R., *Clan Ferguson* 496
Costello, Sgt. M.J., 249 Sqn 640
Cotching, Sub Lt. J.A., 806 Sqn 484, 490
Covich, Sgt. A., 69 Sqn 339
Cowan, Plt.Off. I.C., 69 Sqn 558
Cowan-Hunt, Plt.Off. W.G., 459 Sqn 358
Cox, LAC K., 185 Sqn 550
Coxon, Sub Lt. C.R., 828/830 Sqn 47, 55, 60, 97
Crafts, Flg.Off. H.A., 185 Sqn 639, 640, 684, 685
Cramp, Sub Lt. J.A., 828/830 Sqn 222, 300, 340
Crawford, Flt.Lt., Controller 598
Creighton, Plt.Off. F.A., 250 Sqn 349
Cresswell, Flt.Sgt. J., 39 Sqn 544
Crichton, Plt.Off. J.M.S., 126 Sqn *49*, 50, *70*, 112, 151
Cripps, Sgt. R.A., 252 Sqn 144
Cripps, Plt.Off. W.E., 601 Sqn *196*, 198, 221, 665
Crist, Flt.Sgt. E.A., 126 Sqn 156, 205, 215, 216, 224, 406
Crockett, Flt.Lt. G.R., ASR 27, 162, 176, 188, 439, 572, 614, 617, 622
Crombie, Flg.Off. C.A., 89 Sqn 557, 560, 563, 597, 607, *619*, 622, 627, 628, 645, 656
Crosley, Sub Lt. R.M., 813F Sqn 302, 325, 327, 335
Crosswell, Sgt. F.F., 249 Sqn 423
Cruickshank, Sub Lt. I.J., 880 Sqn 478, 488, 669
Cumbers, Plt.Off. A.B., 89 Sqn 557, 562
Cunliffe-Owen, Sub Lt. H.L., 880 Sqn 478, 488, 492, 669
Cunningham, Admiral Sir Andrew, C-in-C Med Fleet 24
Cunningham, Sgt. J.D., 86 Sqn 549
Currie, Lt. M. (SAAF), 69 Sqn 544
Curry, Plt.Off. J.H., 601 Sqn 302, 375, 657
Curteis, Vice-Admiral A.T.B., Force 'W' 319, 324, 336, 337
Curtis, Sgt., 104 Sqn 298
Cusworth, Sgt. A.J., 227 Sqn 549, 668

Daddo-Langlois, Flt.Lt. W.R., 185/249 Sqns 87, 96, *116*, 116, 120, *147*, 154, 168, 202, 203, 227, 283, 303, 305, 306, 316, 375, 378, 385, 388, 389, 395, 406, 419, 654, 686
Dafforn, Sqn.Ldr. R.C., 229 Sqn 193, 194, 221, 227, 654, 673
Daffurn, Sgt. L., 39 Sqn 355
Daggs, Flt.Lt., 10 RAAF Sqn 87
Dalley, Plt.Off. J.O., 69 Sqn 543, 544, 572
Daniel, Flg.Off. E.G., 89 Sqn 110, 266, 273, 286, 287, 293, 299, 361, 363, 651, 655
Davey, Sgt. K.H., 126 Sqn 310, 396, 687
Davidson, Flg.Off., HMS *Furious* 519
Davies, Lt. V.N.S., FAA 56
Davies, Sub Lt. W.A., 827 Sqn 492
Davies, Wg.Cdr. W.A.L., 217 Sqn 313, 353, 370
Davis, Flt.Lt. C.C.H., 249/126 Sqn 15, 50, 70, 171
Davis, Plt.Off. G.B.P., 603 Sqn *197*
Davison, 803 Sqn 343, 344
Dawkins, Plt.Off. , 249 Sqn 640
Dawson, L/Air. C.F., 809 Sqn 485, 490, 509
Dawson, Wg.Cdr. H.L., Hal Far 57, 77, 293, 432
Dawson, Wt.Off. R.J., 217 Sqn 440, 549
Deffontaine, Plt.Off. C. (Belg), OADU 98
de l'Ara, Flt.Sgt. L.G.C., 249 Sqn 310, 389, 396, 407, *523*, 570, 585, 588, 596, 599, 615, 627, 629
Delcour, Plt.Off. C. (Belg), OADU 88
De Nancrede, Sgt. C.S.G., 249 Sqn 241, *242*, 272, 292, 373, 384, 385, 396, *523*
De Salvo Hall, Sgt. F.C., 250 Sqn 358
Dewhurst, Sgt. J.S., Luqa 111
Dewhurst, Flg.Off. L., 86 Sqn 530
Dicker, Plt.Off. J.F., 227 Sqn 555, 668
Dickinson, Sqn.Ldr. H.B.H., Bomb Disposal 79
Dickson, Sgt. G.R., 601 Sqn *196*, 198, 221, 255
Dicks-Sherwood, Flg.Off. E.S., 603 Sqn 240, *242*, 264, 269, 291, 367, 391, 403, 405, 412, 441, 462, 520, 651, 657
Di Perio, Sgt., 601 Sqn 302
Dixon, Lt. G., RN 150
Dixon, Plt.Off. P.A., 229 Sqn 519, 537, 598, 602, 615
Dobbie, Miss Sybil, Governor's daughter 167, 237
Dobbie, General W.G.S., Governor 82, 149, 153, 154, 167, 191, 228, 229, 230, 232, 237
Docherty, Flt.Sgt., OADU 374
Dodd, Sgt. K., 217 Sqn 364
Dodd, Flt.Sgt. W.G., 126/185 Sqn 156, 171, 214, 218, 238, 256, 259, 289, 308, *318*, 383, 393, 395, 396, 402, 651, 657
Donaldson, Wg.Cdr. A.H., Takali 468, *517*, *523*, 528, 529, 531, 534, 536, 546, 547, 568, 569, 570, 575, 578, 581, *583*, 585, 586, 587, 596, 599, 629, *630*, 641, 642, 687
Doncaster, Plt.Off. J.P., 235 Sqn 326, 668
Donkersley, Plt.Off. H., 69 Sqn 638
Donohue, Sgt., 38 Sqn 54
Douglas, Sqn.Ldr. W.A., 603/229 Sqns *197*, 198, 200, 219, 233, 250, 256, 261, 393, 394, 411, 419, 456, *517*, 543, 552, 658, 673
Douglas, Lt. R. (SAAF), 69 Sqn 540, 541
Douglas-Hamilton, Wg.Cdr. Lord D., 603 Sqn/ Takali *197*, 197, 198, 200, 208, 225, 226, 231, 254, 271, 272, 304, 394, 411, 419, 673
Dowland, Wg.Cdr. J.N., 69 Sqn 28, 37, 38
Downes, Lt. P.A.S., 830 Sqn 378
Downing, Sgt. R., 601 Sqn *196*, 198
Downs, Plt.Off. B., 126 Sqn 235, 427, 431, 435
Drew, Sgt. A., 185 Sqn 302, 394, 395, 410, 429, 434
Drummond, Air Marshal Sir Peter 68, 69
Dukes-Smith, Flt.Lt. H.F., 21 Sqn 39
Duncan, Capt. G., SAS 348, 475
Duncan, Sgt. J., 248 Sqn 512
Duncan, L/Air. J., 807 Sqn 333, 669
Duncan, Flt.Lt., OADU 59
Dunkerley, Sub Lt. E.D., 821 Sqn 117
Dunsmore, Plt.Off. W., 217 Sqn 441, 442
Duplex, Flg.Off. E.A., 159 Sqn 549
Durrant, Sgt., 69 Sqn 86
Duthie, Sub Lt. H.E., 801 Sqn 320, 328, 329, 334, 343
Dyer, Flt.Lt. J.M.O., 159 Sqn 458, 475

Eastman, Plt.Off. D.E., 185 Sqn 92, 120, 142, 143, 149, 157, 206, 227
Eden, Mr. Anthony, Foreign Secretary 23
Edgar, Flt.Sgt. A.J., 89 Sqn 560
Egerton, Plt.Off. T.A., 10 RAAF Sqn 327
Edwards, Flt.Lt. H.G., 89 Sqn 366, 371, 376, 388, 391, 520, 522, 533, 545, 549, 557, 651, 654, 673
Edwards, Lt. S.J., 884 Sqn 476
Edwards, Flt.Sgt., 126 Sqn 645
Elliott, Sgt. J.H., 14 Sqn 348
Elliott, Sub Lt. R.W., 828 Sqn 286, 296, 300, 343, 344, 399, 528, *532*, 541, 546, 587, 621, 624, 625, 626
Elliott, Sub Lt. W.E.F., 830 Sqn 55
Ellis, Lt. H.M., 826 Sqn 54
Ellis, Sgt. R.J.F., 185 Sqn 89
Ellison, Flg.Off. F., 37 Sqn 124, 680
Etchells, Flt.Sgt. F.A., 249 Sqn 41, 42, 46, 47, 52, 91
Eva, Sgt. D.C., 1435 Sqn 423, 570, 594, 616
Evans, Sub Lt. C.J., 809 Sqn 490, 669
Evans, Plt.Off. K.W.S., 126 Sqn 283, 310, 339, 340, 391, 402, 404, 406, 411, 418, 435, 436, 519, *553*, 651
Evans, Sgt. L., HMS *Eagle* 423, 424, 668
Evans, Sqn.Ldr. P.M.J., 89 Sqn 520, 522, 534
Evans, Lt. R.C.B. (SAAF), 86 Sqn 549
Eyre, Flg.Off., 235/227 Sqns 364, 521, 522
Ezanno, Capitaine Y.P.E.H. (FF), GC 1 349

Farfan, Sgt. F.W., 601 Sqn *196*, 198, 257
Fargher, Wt.Off. G.F., 227 Sqn 529, 540, 572, 669
Farmer, Plt.Off. J.G.W., 229 Sqn 519, 530, 554, 555, 687
Farnes, Sqn.Ldr. P.C.P., 229 Sqn 155, 158, 164, *182*, 194, 227, 235, 244, *294*, 294, 673
Farnes, Wg.Cdr. W.R., Controller 539, 598
Farquharson, Wt.Off. G.H.T., 126 Sqn 241, *242*, 339, 340, 394, 406, 411, 438, 534, 594, 595, 606, 607, 608, 642, 687
Featherstone, Plt.Off. G., OADU 157
Fenton, Sgt. J., 217 Sqn 340
Ferguson, L/Air. A.F., 884 Sqn 476, 488
Ferraby, Flt.Sgt. D.L., 249 Sqn 108, 109, 118, 269, 297, 366, 396
Fiddes, Lt. D.B.M., 880 Sqn *452*, 471, 492, 493
Fincham, Sgt. W.E., 69 Sqn 342
Findlay, Flg.Off. J., SO, ME 677
Finlay, Sgt.C.V., 185 Sqn 112, 207, 218, 238, 268, 270, 665
Fisher, Sub Lt. N.D., 801 Sqn 331, 333
Fitzgerald, Flg.Off. C.K., 69 Sqn 563
Flanagan, Sgt. R.V., 38 Sqn 376
Fleming, Sgt. W.J.A., HMS *Furious* 519, 520, 668
Fletcher, Plt.Off. J.W.S., 185 Sqn 102, 112, 127, 143, 147, 152, 159, 160, 163, 176, 185, 206, 215, 219, 223, 665
Foley, Plt.Off. T.G., 229 Sqn 170, *182*, 224, 665
Ford, L/Air. P.P., 884 Sqn 476, 488
Forrest, Lt J.G., 880 Sqn 470
Forrester, Sgt. I.H., HMS *Eagle* 415
Forster, Plt.Off. J.W., 603 Sqn *197*, 199
Foster, Flg.Off. J.H.P., 69 Sqn 363, 530
Foulis, Flt.Lt. M., 38 Sqn 353, 541
Fowlow, Plt.Off. N.R., 603 Sqn 240, *242*, 278, 279, 280, *280*
Fox, Flt.Lt. E., 21 Sqn 63
Fox, Sgt. H., Luqa 497
Fox, Flt.Sgt. H.J., 249 Sqn 241, *242*, 666
Fox, Plt.Off. H.M., 249 Sqn 109, 126, 134, 270, 665
Fox, Flt.Lt., 203 Sqn 216
Frampton, Plt.Off. G.W.R., 511 Sqn 686
France, Flt.Sgt. J.S., 272 Sqn 186
Francis, Sgt. E.H., 229 Sqn 468, 537, 541, 602, 611, 615
Fraser-Harris, Lt. A.B., 807 Sqn 329, 332
Frazer, Sub Lt. E.N., 809 Sqn 473
Frecker, Flg.Off. A.D., 252 Sqn 110
Freer, Plt.Off. T., 227 Sqn 623
Friendship, Flt.Lt. A.H.B., 126 Sqn 415, 416
Frith, Flt.Sgt. M.H., 229 Sqn 519
Frost, Maj. J.E. (SAAF), 5 SAAF Sqn 350
Fullalove, Flt.Sgt. J.K., 229 Sqn 155, *182*, 207, 665
Fuller, Sgt. L.G., 37 Sqn 100, 101, 102, 680
Fuller, Sgt., 1435 Sqn 519, 616
Fumerton, Flg.Off. R.C., 89 Sqn 366, 372, 373, 376, 383, 386, 426, 446, 464, 515, 541, 651, 658
Furphy, Plt.Off. D.L., 86 Sqn 430

Gael, Flt.Sgt. J.A. (FF), 272 Sqn 350, 668
Galloway, Flt.Lt. I.U.M., 248 Sqn 497
Ganes, Sgt. N.A., 229 Sqn 193, *294*, 294
Gardiner, Flg.Off. T.H., 217 Sqn 370
Gardiner, Sgt. W.N., 242 Sqn 50, 93, 94, 102
Gardner, Sgt. J.V., 252 Sqn 46, 668
Garland, Sub Lt. A.McD., 809 Sqn 485
Garlick, Wg.Cdr. H.J., 235 Sqn 311, 370
Garrett, Sgt. K.J., 272 Sqn 350, 668
Garthwaite, Lt. W.F.C., 828/830 Sqn 96
Garvey, Sgt. L.P., 185 Sqn 468, 608, 620
Gascoyne, PO(A) L.J., 884 Sqn 490, 492
Gass, Sgt. M.I., 249 Sqn 415, 437, *523*, 571, 667
Gee, Flg.Off. D.J.R., 59 Sqn 44
Gedge, Flg.Off. H.F., 185 Sqn 468
Gerner, Flt.Sgt. L.L., Gibraltar 684, 685
Gibbons, Sgt. R., 86 Sqn 544
Gibbs, Flt.Sgt. H.T., 828/830 Sqn 183, 226
Gibbs, Wg.Cdr. R.P.M., 39 Sqn 356, *356*, 366, 370, 387, 388, 422, 440, 518, 522, 524, 529, 544, 547, 548
Giddings, Plt.Off. K.C.M., 249 Sqn 423, 547, 594, 603, 607, 620, 633, 640
Gilbert, Sgt. J.C., 249 Sqn 241, 278, 280, 304, 402, 666
Gillies, Sgt. E., 86 Sqn 544
Gillions, Sgt. F.R., 69 Sqn 556
Gillingham, Lt. A., 828/830 Sqn 96
Glazebrook, Flt.Lt. E.H., 603/229 Sqns 283, 305, 382, 384, 401, 430, 579, 583, 585, 587, 601, 608, *609*, 611, 632, 642, 687
Glen, Plt.Off. A.A., 603 Sqn 309, 310, 367, 368, 375, 393, 394, 395, 658
Goldsmith, Plt.Off. A.P., 185/126 Sqns 87, 93, 146, 152, 162, 165, 167, 179, 207, 219, *220*, 224, 247, 250, 255, 258, 267, 269, 274, 287, 292, 297, 339, 340, 360, 361, 378, *379*, 651, 657
Gomez, Wg.Cdr., USN *Wasp* *242*
Gooch, Flg.Off. S.W., 39 Sqn 186, 188
Goodale, Flg.Off., 217 Sqn 353
Goodyear, Plt.Off. H.K., 229 Sqn 634
Gordon, Capt. H., *Wairangi* 499
Gore, Sgt. L.R., 185 Sqn 468, 579, 614
Gorringe-Smith, Sqn.Ldr. J.E., SD Flt 251
Gort, Field Marshal Lord, Governor 154, 230, 237, 318, 360, 522, 552, *552*, 582, 687
Gosling, Sgt. D., 89 Sqn 110, 184, 273, 286, 363
Gould, Sgt. H., OADU 303
Gracie, Wg.Cdr. E.J., 126 Sqn/Takali 133, *135*, 136, 141, 150, 165, *196*, 196, 198, 200, 207, 209, 210, 214, 227, 241, 245, 269, 309, 655, 673
Grant, Plt.Off. J.G.M., 1435 Sqn *49*, 61
Grant, Flg.Off. K.R., 39 Sqn 54, 355, 524, 540
Grant, Wg.Cdr. S.B., 249 Sqn 106, 107, *107*, 109, 110, 117, 120, *124*, 125, 148, 149, 159, 160, 196, 208, 227, 240, 242, 244, 245, 256, 257, 277, 287, 312, 378, 542, 673, 686
Graves, Plt.Off. M.A., 126 Sqn 133, 142, 143, 145, 146, 165, 247, 250, 255, 263, 310, *311*, 378, 383, 389, 403
Gray, Wt.Off. J.C., 249 Sqn 241, 271, 280, 281, 304, 306, 312
Gray, Flg.Off. K.J., 89 Sqn 558, 560, 570, 592, 597, 613, 627
Gray, Sgt. R., 217 Sqn 353
Graysmark, Sgt. C.E., 601 Sqn 241, 258, 263, 264, 665
Greenhalgh, Wg.Cdr. J., Blenheim Wg 26
Greet, Sub Lt. T.H., 821 Sqn 100
Gridley, Plt.Off. R.V., 69 Sqn 38
Grieve, Plt.Off. J.G.C., 21 Sqn 73
Griffin, Sgt., HMS *Furious* 519
Griffith, LAC T., ASR 71
Griffiths, Wg.Cdr. J.F., Controller 598
Grose, Sub Lt. R.J.H., 809 Sqn 471
Guerin, Plt.Off. J.J., 249 Sqn 109, 134, 665
Gubb, Flg.Off. A.W., 69 Sqn 572, 606

Hadden, Cpl. R., 69 Sqn 128
Haggas, Flt.Sgt. H., 185 Sqn 240, 304, *362*, 385, 391, 397, 398, 666
Hagger, Plt.Off. W.J.E., 601 Sqn *196*, 198, 212, 217, 218, 272, 659
Haines, Sgt., 69 Sqn 52
Haining, Sgt. J., 39 Sqn 355
Halbert, Flg.Off. J.B., 203 Sqn 184, 186
Hale, Sgt. H., 242 Sqn 112, 125
Halford, Flt.Lt. J.R., 185/1435 Sqns 240, *242*, 263, 291, 300, 366, 381, 390, 393, 394, 418, 424, 426, 427, 519
Hall, Sgt. A.J., 235 Sqn 339
Hall, Lt. P.R., 807 Sqn 156, 282, 283, 330, 669
Hallett, Lt. N.G., 884 Sqn 451, 483, 485, 490
Hallett, Plt.Off. W.C.H., 126 Sqn *78*, 112, 116, 134, 665
Halliwell, Flg.Off. C.P.T., 37 Sqn 95, 124, 680
Hamilton, Flt.Sgt. J.S., 1435 Sqn 519, 576, 627, 636
Hammond, Flg.Off. D.H., 272 Sqn 144, 149, 186
Hammond, Sgt. R.F., 248 Sqn 474, 524, 525
Hancock, Sgt. G., 21 Sqn 61
Hankey, Sub Lt. M., 801 Sqn 331, 469, 478, 669
Hanks, Wg.Cdr. P.P., Luqa 460, 499, 502, 503, 505, 522, 530, 568, 569, 574, 578, 588, *589*, 594, 605, *606*, 606, 608, 618, 632
Hanley, Sgt. R.K., OADU 287
Hanson, Sub Lt. D.J., 828/830 Sqn 625
Hardeman, Sqn.Ldr. W.R., Bomb Disposal 79
Hardy, Capt. C.C., Force 'X' 336, 337, 338, 340, 495
Hargreaves, LAC R., ASR 313
Harmer, Sgt.J.R., 185 Sqn 423
Harper, Plt.Off. R.M., 148 Sqn 215
Harries, Sub.Lt. S.N. 880 Sqn 470, 479
Harrington, Capt. J.C., BOAC 69
Harris, Grp.Capt. S.H.V., Luqa 26, 64
Harrison, Sgt. J.M., 1435 Sqn 423, 504, 613
Harrison, Plt.Off. N.D., 1435 Sqn 640
Hartney, Sgt. D.J., 185 Sqn 415, 421
Harvey, Sgt. R.V., 242 Sqn 51, 99, 665
Harwood, Admiral Sir Henry, C-in-C, ME 357, 358, 359
Haskey, Sub Lt. T.D., 884 Sqn 483, 490
Hastings, Sub Lt. J.L., 800 Sqn 477
Hawes, Plt.Off. O.L., 38 Sqn 359
Hawkins, Flt.Lt. D.E., 202 Sqn 311
Hawkins, Sgt. R., 1435 Sqn 423, 504, 589, 594
Haynes, Sgt. G.A., 86 Sqn 544
Haynes, Lt. G.M., 828 Sqn 28, 82, 86, 378
Hayter, Flt.Lt. A.R.H., 148 Sqn 215
Hayton, Flt.Lt.G.McL, 89 Sqn 110, 118, *119*, 129, 174, 277, 289, 297, 336, 363, 632, 651, 654, 673
Head, Sgt. G., 86 Sqn 523, 529, 544
Head, Flt.Sgt. G., HSL 128 389, 418, 604
Head, Lt. R.D., 828/830 Sqn 137, 378
Heath, Sgt., 235/227 Sqns 549, 558
Hector, Sgt. C.W., 235 Sqn 343, 668
Hedger, L/Air. S., 828/830 Sqn 47
Hegman, Flg.Off. J.A., 162 Sqn 558
Hendry, Sgt. R.B., 249 Sqn 519, *545*, 600
Heppell, Flt.Lt. P.W.E., 249 Sqn 107, 109, 110, 115, 121, 125, 172, 173, 127
Hesselyn, Plt.Off. R.B., 249 Sqn 109, *116*, 117, 118, 132, 159, 160, 161, 162, 163, 202, 203, 204, 208, 210, 221, 235, 239, 254, 256, 257, 262, 267, 287, 378, 401, 651, 654
Hetherington, Flt.Lt. E.L., 249 Sqn 240, 259, 396, 406, 408, 414, 419, 426, 463, *523*, 538, 546, 554, 594, *603*, 603, 604, 616, 620, 634, 642, 687
Hicks, Plt.Off. J.L., 126 Sqn 310, 397, 403, 666
Hill, Sub Lt. D.S., 809 Sqn 492
Hill, Sqn.Ldr. R., Luqa MO 111
Hill, Lt.Cdr. R., HMS *Ledbury* 477, 500
Hillary, Sub Lt. G.L., 828/830 Sqn 125
Hills, Sgt. R.J., 104 Sqn 297
Hiskens, Wt.Off. E.T., 249 Sqn 468, 515, *523*, 585, 588, 596, 611, 667
Hodgson, Plt.Off. E.H., 272 Sqn 358
Hodnett, Plt.Off. V.W., 69 Sqn 499
Hogan, Capt. G., 1/Hants 153
Hogarth, Flt.Sgt. G.A., 249 Sqn 415, 515, 571, 667
Holdsworth, Sub Lt. M., 828/830 Sqn 95
Hole, Flt.Lt. W.R., 203 Sqn 216, 217
Holland, Flg.Off. A.C.W., 603 Sqn *197*, 199, 212, 245, 248, 250, 256
Holland, Sgt., 39 Sqn 114
Holroyd, PO(A)R, 807 Sqn 329
Holton, Flt.Sgt. G.V., 89 Sqn 557, 622
Hone, Flg.Off. C.M., 601 Sqn *196*, 198, 223, 270, 272, 286, 342, 344, 659
Hooper, Plt.Off. R.C., 39 Sqn 355
Hope, Flt.Sgt. P., RAF Benson 570
Hopkins, Lt.Cdr. F.E.H., 830 Sqn 28, 35, 55, 141, 299, 315
Horricks, Plt.Off. G.E., 185 Sqn 56, 92, 121, 142, 149, 158, 178, 188, 206, 207, 221, 227, 656
Horrocks, Sub Lt. H., 828/830 Sqn 341
Houghton, Flg.Off. J.S., HSL 100/HSL 128 431, 569
Houlton, Sgt. J.H., 185 Sqn 468
Houston, Sgt. M., 21 Sqn 71
Houston, Flt.Sgt. J.K., 89 Sqn 534
Howard, Sgt. F.S., 601 Sqn *196*, 198, 217, 218, 250, 263, 276, 666
Howarth, Sub Lt. R.B., 880 Sqn 466, 478, 488
Howe, Flt.Sgt. D.J., 605 Sqn 99
Howroyd, Flt.Sgt. S.E., 22 Sqn 185
Howson, Sub Lt. P., 828/830 47
Hubbard, Sgt. D.F., 1435 Sqn 310, 437, 666
Huchison, Wt.Off., 86 Sqn 549
Hucklebridge, Mrs M.B., Civilian 687
Huggins, Plt.Off. P.A., 40 Sqn 34
Huggins, Plt.Off. R., 113 Sqn 39
Hulbert, Plt.Off. J.G.K., 249 Sqn 32, 71, 664
Hunton, Sgt. C.L., 185 Sqn 89
Hurst, Plt.Off. J., 603 Sqn *197*, 198, 199, 212, 225, 248, 256, 269, 273, 276, 310, 382, 383, 651, 653, 666
Hutcheson, Sgt. J., 217 Sqn 362, 387
Hutchinson, Capt. C., Convoy MW10 140, 141, 151
Hutton, Sub Lt. P.J., 801 Sqn 327, 333, 469, 484, 508
Hyde, Sqn.Ldr. J.H., 86 Sqn 412, 422, 430

Ibbotson, Flt.Sgt. J., 21 Sqn 71
Ingram, Plt.Off. M.R.B., 601 Sqn *196*, 198, 269, 341, 345, 655
Innes, Plt.Off. J.W.L., 601 Sqn *196*, 198, 257, 290, 312, 313
Irwin, Sgt. W.R., 603 Sqn 241, *242*, 271, 375, 393, 394, 412, 422, 460, 554
Izzard, Flg.Off. A.F., 86 Sqn 549, 558

Jackson, Sgt. G.A., 252 Sqn 83, 85, 668
Jackson, Sgt. H.A., 459 Sqn 358
Jackson, Lt. J.D., 826 Sqn 54
Jackson, Sgt., 69 Sqn 41
Jacobsen, Sub Lt. C.D., 828/830 Sqn 299, 300
James, A/Sea A., HMS *Ledbury* 506
James, Plt.Off. R.W., 249 Sqn 141, 221, *291*, 345
James, Flt.Sgt., 241 AMES 675
Jarrett, Sgt. J.F., 1435 Sqn 519, 578
Jay, Plt.Off. D.J., 248 Sqn 474, 500, 502, 507, 508, 668
Jefferson, Sqn.Ldr. T.A., 107 Sqn 33
Jellicoe, Capt. Lord, SAS 348
Jemmett, Plt.Off. F.J., 126 Sqn 212, 213, 665
Jenkins, LAC C., Takali 590
Jenkins, Flt.Lt. M.R., 238 Sqn 349
Jenson, Sgt. 457
Jepson, Flg.Off. A.O.S., 39 Sqn 54, 356
Jess, Sub Lt. E., 828/830 Sqn 399, 546
Johnson, Plt.Off. F.R., 603/229 Sqns 229, 241, 272, 384, 401, *517*, 605, 687
Johnson, Sgt. C.E., OADU 157
Johnson, Plt.Off. C.L., 227 Sqn 561
Johnson, Plt.Off. R.M., 69 Sqn 545
Johnson Flt.Lt. W.J., 126 Sqn 240, 297, 415, 419, 431, 433, 435, 436, 446, 513, 657
Johnston, Flt.Lt. H.A.S., 126 Sqn 133, 142, 143, 145, 146, 151, 156, 164, 169, 205, 220, 223, 236, 287
Johnston, Lt. R.L., 806 Sqn 451, 483, 487, 669
Jones, Flt.Lt. C.S., 242 AMES 676
Jones, Flt.Lt. F.E., 249 Sqn 302, 304, 305, 346, 404, 407, 412, 423, *424*, 461, 504, *523*, 651
Jones, Flt.Lt. R.O., 126 Sqn 240, 280, 281, 289, 397, 405, 414, 423, 432, 438, 445, 505, 595, 607, 617, 618, *621*, 651, 653, 667
Jones, Sgt. R.S., 53 Sqn 36
Jones, Flt.Sgt. OADU 36
Jordain, Lt. A. (FF), SAS 347
Jordan, Sub Lt. P.A., 828/830 Sqn 361
Josling, Plt.Off. N.H., 89 Sqn 110, 118, *119*, 174, 277, 289, 297, 363, 632
Judd, Lt.Cdr. F.E., 880 Sqn 451, *452*, 470, 473, 479, 488, 669
Kain, Sqn.Ldr. D., 229 Sqn 155, 158, 194, 673
Kay, Flg.Off. J.K., 126 Sqn 47, *49*, 52, 78
Keane, Sgt. D.F., 252 Sqn 668
Kearsley, Sub Lt. R.W., 800 Sqn 483, 484
Kebbell, Sgt. T.R.D., 1435 Sqn 468, 578, 580, 586
Kee, Flt.Lt. E.H.C., 242/126 Sqns 50, *51*, 58, 102, 112, 116, 171
Keegan, Sgt. T.B., 39 Sqn 189
Kelley, Plt.Off. P., 69 Sqn 40, 157
Kelly, Sgt. C.L., 1435 Sqn 415, 461, 666
Kelly, Plt.Off. H., 249 Sqn 172, 173, 185, *291*, 310, 385, 666
Kemp, Flt.Lt. N.L.D., 242 Sqn 50, 112, 125
Kemsley, Lt. K.C., 5 SAAF Sqn 350
Kennedy, Plt.Off. G.A., OADU 99
Kernaghan, Sgt. S.J., 272 Sqn 638
Kent, Plt.Off. D.W., 185 Sqn 240, *242*, 381, 427, *450*, 666
Kerrison, Sub Lt. R.E.F., 828/830 Sqn 14, 35
Kidson, Plt.Off. M.W.T., 242 Sqn 102, 103, 665
Kimmins, A., Journalist 471
King, Plt.Off. C.A., 185 Sqn 240, *242*, 246, 249, *261*, 262, *362*, 414, 429
King, AC G., ASR 71
King, Plt.Off. N.S., 603 Sqn *197*, 198, 199, 226, 276, 305, 384, 389, 399, 400, 666
Kinghorn, Sub Lt. D., 828/830 Sqn 60, 97
King-Joyce, Lt. T.J.A., 813F Sqn 325, 327, 334
Kinmonth, Flg.Off. M.W., 89 Sqn 558, 560
Kitchen, Flt.Sgt. R.G., 86 Sqn 521
Knight, Sgt. W., 272 Sqn 356
Knox Williams, Flt.Sgt. W.B., 1435 Sqn 415, 458, 578, 585, 587, 588, 596, 601, 667
Kozlowski, Flt.Sgt. S.J., 37 Sqn 111
Kuhlmann, Maj. K.C., 185 Sqn 468, 535, 550, 552, 583, 601, *602*, 613, 622, 627

Laidler, Sub Lt. P.F., 828/830 Sqn 55
Laing, Sgt. W.A., 229 Sqn 640, *641*
Laing, Plt.Off. S.O., 227 Sqn 529, 544
Lambert, Flt.Lt. J.F., 185 Sqn 283, 288, 308, 421, *450*
Lamont, Sgt. R.W., 249 Sqn 423, *523*
Lander, Flt.Lt. J.M., 39 Sqn 168, 170, 186, 187
Langston, Plt.Off. S.A., 203 Sqn 54
Largent, Sgt. A.F., 252 Sqn 668
Lashmore, Lt. W.E., 830 Sqn 343, 528, 625
Lattimer, Plt.Off. C.H., 249/1435 Sqns 310, 367, 373, 376, 404, 419, 424, 428, 463, 464, *559*, 572, 585, 608, 686
Lawrence, Sqn.Ldr. K.A., 185 Sqn 90, *94*, *97*, 143, 176, 215, *216*, 248, 256, 286, 300, *362*, 673
Lawrence, Plt.Off. T.E., 229 Sqn 193, 211, 235, 244, 279, *295*
Lawrence, Plt.Off. , 202 Sqn 417
Lea, Sqn.Ldr. R.F.G., Controller 598
Leaning, Flt.Lt. A.T., 39 Sqn 114, 186, 187, 188, 355, 370, 422, 440
Le Bas, Plt.Off. M.H., 601 Sqn *196*, 198, 217, *268*, 276
LeBrocq, Sgt. P., 38 Sqn 326
Lee, Flt.Sgt. J., 22 Sqn 185
Lee, Plt.Off. K.L., 229 Sqn 170, 279, *294*, 294, 295
Lee, Flt.Lt. N.W., 249 Sqn 109, *116*, 127, 149, 156, 159, 178, 211, 256, 264, 271, 292, 392, 393, 419
Leech, A/Fitter J., Hal Far 528
Leeming, Sgt. C.D., 229 Sqn 640
Lees, Sgt. R.J., 229 Sqn 170, *182*, 188, 221, 235, 665
Leggett, Flg.Off. P.G., 249 Sqn 47
Leggo, Plt.Off. D.C., 249 Sqn 109, 129, 134, 181, 665
Le Masurier, Flt.Lt. R.S., 69 Sqn 499, 534, 545, 558
Le May, Grp.Capt. W.K., Luqa 184, 375, *523*
Leostic, Caporal (FF), SAS 348
Leplang, Sgt.-Chef P. (FF), GC 1 349
Lerwill, Sqn.Ldr. G.F., 18 Sqn 33
Leslie, Sgt. C.D., 227 Sqn 522, 668
Leslie, Capt. G., *Glenorchy* 499
Lester, Plt.Off. H.C., 605 Sqn *40*, 80, 90, 127
Levy-Despas, Plt.Off. G.A. (FF), 603 Sqn 310, 393, 394, 403, 666
Lilley, Flt.Sgt. R., 89 Sqn 627
Lindsay, Flg.Off. A.I., 185 Sqn 468, 620, 633, 667
Linton, Plt.Off. O.M., 603/249 Sqns *197*, 199, 212, 234, 245, 263, 267, 304, 305, 306, 312, 346, 384, *385*, 395, 520, *523*
Lister, Flt.Sgt. V.S., 69 Sqn 474, 499, 530, 545
Livingston, Sgt. J.G., 185 Sqn 415, 445
Llewellyn, Sgt. D.E., 601 Sqn 241
Lloyd, Air Vice-Marshal H.P., AOC, Malta 25, *25*, 29, 35, 40, 57, 64, 66, 68, 88, 98, 128, 136, 148, 150, 154, 159, 182, 206, 221, 228, 241, 248, 275, 313, 317, 367, 373, 398, 413, 420, 421, 677
Lloyd, Flt.Lt. R.M., 185 Sqn 79, 91, 92, 94, *94*, *97*, 149, 165, 172, 173, 177, 178, 205, 206, *216*, 673
Long, Sub Lt. A.S., 885 Sqn 478
Long, Flt.Sgt. C.A., 126 Sqn 423, *545*, 589, 600
Longworth, Sgt. A., 59 Sqn 43
Louttit, Cpl. D., Takali 48
Lovell, Sqn.Ldr. A.D.J., 1435 Sqn 424, 427, 431, 432, 438, 439, 502, 504, 511, 512, 568, 570, 577, 588, 618, *619*, 632, 637, 656, 673
Lovell, Flg.Off. V.C., 89 Sqn 627
Lowe, Plt.Off. P.D., 605 Sqn 85, 664
Lowery, Plt.Off. J., 249 Sqn 415, 416, *523*, 588, 615, 632
Lowrey, Sqn.Ldr. W.E.M., 69 Sqn 86
Lucas, Sub Lt. J.M., 800 Sqn 478, 484, 669
Lucas, Sqn.Ldr. P.B., 249 Sqn 87, *89*, 96, 111, *116*, 116, 120, 121, *189*, 204, 227, 240, 283, 304, 306, 312, 345, 346, 378, 384, 385, 388, 389, 395, 406, 411, 419, 658, 673, 686
Lucas, Lt.Cdr. W.J., 832 Sqn 451
Lumsden, Plt.Off. A.S.C., 229 Sqn 155, *182*
Lundy, Sgt. M.A., 229 Sqn 423, 601, 616
Lusty, Sgt. K.J., 601 Sqn 241, 263, 315
Lynch, Flg.Off. J.J., 249 Sqn 640
Lynn, Sqn.Ldr. R.G., 217 Sqn 353, 363, 364

Lyster, Rear-Adm. A.L.St.G., Force Z 450

McCarthy, Plt.Off. W.F., 249 Sqn 164, 665
Macaskell, Sgt. A.J., 22 Sqn 128
Macaskill, Wt.Off. R.W., 86 Sqn 521
McCluskey, Sub Lt. M.J., 828/830 Sqn 289
McConnell, Sgt. J.N., 601 Sqn 196, 198, 221, 234, 256, 263, 272, 278, 290, 342, 666
McCulluch, Flt.Sgt. J., 511 Sqn 686
McDonald, Sub Lt. D.J., 801 Sqn 331, 333
McDonald, Sgt., 69 Sqn 35, 50, 75
MacDonald-Hall, Lt. R., 801 Sqn 640, 641
MacDougall, Wg.Cdr., Hal Far 26
McDougall, Sgt. L.J., 1435 Sqn 519, 520
McDowall, Sgt. H.J., 249 Sqn 71, 664
McEllamy, Flt.Sgt., 86 Sqn 549
McElroy, Flt.Lt. J.F., 249 Sqn 309, 310, 384, 389, 396, 403, 411, 426, 437, 519, 574, 585, 588, 596, *603*, 610, *610*, 611, 615, 616, 629, 632, 637, 651, 657
Macfarlane, Capt. D., *Melbourne Star* 506, 515
Macfarlane, Flt.Lt. , 37 Sqn 99
McFarlane, Flt.Sgt. R., 248 Sqn 500, 507, 508, 512, 513
McGill, Sgt. J.G., HMS *Furious* 519, 520
MacGregor, Plt.Off. A.N.C., 126 Sqn 78
McGregor, Sqn.Ldr. P.R., 185 Sqn 29, 30, 76, 673
McGregor, Sgt., 39 Sqn 189
McGrorie, Plt.Off., 40 Sqn 41,45,51
McHan, Plt.Off. R.E., 1435 Flt/126 Sqn 90, 121, 125, 152, 168, 211, 235, 273, 386, *387*
Mackay, Flt.Lt. R.C., 69 Sqn 52, 548, 624
McKay, Plt.Off. F., RAF Benson 570
McKay, Plt.Off. I., 185 Sqn 46, 72, 75, 76, 80, 90, *94*, *97*, 98, 115, 116, 127, 151, 159, 160, 161, 162, 169, 175, 183, *216*, 223, 224, 248, 254, 256, 262, 270
McKay, Sqn.Ldr., OADU 518
Mackie, Plt.Off. A.S., 1435 Flt 61, 62, 664
Mackintosh, Capt. L., HMS *Eagle* 109, 325, 469
McLean, Plt.Off. C.B., 249 Sqn *197*, 199, 260, 261, 392, 402, 419, 579
MacLean, Sgt. D.D., 126 Sqn 519, 667
Maclean, Plt.Off. I., 252 Sqn 144
McLean, Wg.Cdr. J.S., USS *Wasp* 200, 240
McLeish, Sgt. W.C., 272 Sqn 668
MacLennan, Flt.Lt. I.R., 1435 Sqn 310, 418, 424, 425, 431, 463, 464, 512, 578, 580, 586, 588, 601, 613, 632, 636, 644, 651, 655
MacLeod, Sgt. A.O., 185 Sqn 519, 595, 667
McLeod, Plt.Off. D.W., 126 Sqn 133, 134, 145, 149, 164, 211, 235
McLeod, Flt.Lt. H.W., 603/1435 Sqns 302, 304, 367, 368, 391, 394, 403, 412, 418, 424, 428, 461, 463, 464, 504, 543, 562, 578, 580, 587, 588, 596, *597*, 601, 614, 616, 631, 632, 651, 655
McLeod, Sgt. M.L., 185 Sqn 415, 458, 666
McNair, Flt.Lt. R.W., 249 Sqn 87, *106*, 126, 129, 151, 152, *189*, 202, 204, 211, 212, 219, 227, 239, 240, 283, 289, 292, 312, 378, 651, 657, 686
MacNamara, Flt.Sgt. J.E., 185/1435 Sqns 241, 304, 361, *362*, 368, 397, 414, 424, 504
Macnamara, Plt.Off. T.B., 242 Sqn 94, 665
McNaughton, Plt.Off. A.A., 185 Sqn 240, *242*, 263, 299, 666
Macpherson, Flt.Sgt. H.D.K., USS *Wasp* 302, 303, 668
Macqueen, Flt.Lt. N.C., 249 Sqn 109, 110, 116, 126, 134, 141, 143, 157, 168, 177, 185, 204, 211, 230, 231, 234, *266*, 651, 653, 665
McSharry, Plt.Off. J., 217 Sqn 364
McWilliams, Flt.Sgt. J.B., 69 Sqn 558
Machin, Sgt. A.G.G., 252 Sqn 144
Madden, Sub Lt. J.B., 806 Sqn 490
Maddocks, A/Sea E., HMS *Bramham* 507
Magruder, Flt.Lt. E.P.F.L.T., 229 Sqn 468, 502, 530, 541, 666
Magwood, Sub Lt. G.P., 807 Sqn 284
Mahar, Plt.Off. E.L., 185 Sqn *242*, 283, *318*, 381, 394, 395, 426, 463, 594, 605, 608, 639, 640, 687
Maher, Sub Lt. A.D., FAA 56
Main, Plt.Off. B.W., 126 Sqn 47, 50, 71, 664
Maitland, LAC J., ASR 313
Malcolm, Flt.Lt. A.S., 252 Sqn 82, 85
Malthus, Plt.Off. L.G., 229 Sqn 155, 170, *294*, 295
Manley-Cooper, Lt.Cdr. N.C., 821 Sqn 117
Mansell, Flt. Steward V., BOAC 69
Marks, Flt.Lt. R.W., 10 RAAF Sqn 309
Mars, Lt.A., HMS *Unbroken* 500
Marsh, Capt. A.E. (RM), 804 Sqn 451
Marshall, Plt.Off. R.S.O., 217 Sqn 356, 549
Marshall, Sgt. W., 126 Sqn 310, 403, 435, 513, 579, 605, 617, 633
Martin, Plt.Off. W.J., 69 Sqn 625
Martyn, Lt. W.H., 800 Sqn 477
Mason, Wg.Cdr. A.J., 39 Sqn 354, 355, 356
Mason, Capt. D.W., *Ohio* 449, 506, 514
Matthews, Flg.Off. J.F.P., 24 Sqn 181
Matthews, Plt.Off. W.H., 69 Sqn 571, 638
Maurice, Sub Lt. J., 248 Sqn 474, 512
Mayall, Sgt. J.M., 126 Sqn 47, 116, 665
Maydon, Lt. S.L.C., HMS *Umbra* 353
Maynard, Plt.Off. A.R.H., 185 Sqn 468, 593, 594
Mayne, Capt. B., SAS 348
Meakin, L/Sea D., HMS *Ledbury* 506
Measures, Sub Lt. G.F., 827 Sqn 492
Mejor, Plt.Off. J.G. (Belg), 603 Sqn *197*, 198, 199, 238, 256, 258, 391, 397, 403, 406, 438, 502, 504
Melville-Jackson, Flt.Lt. G.H., 248 Sqn 474, 525
Menary, Flg.Off. J.H., USS *Wasp* 302, 303, 667
Merritt, Sgt. A.R., 104 Sqn 291
Mercer, Sgt. R., 217 Sqn 387
Merwood, Chief Air Artificer, F.E., 801 Sqn 320
Messervy, Sqn.Ldr., SD Flt. 337
Metcalf, LAC W., Takali 17, 34, 48, 82, 94, 171, 400, 457, 617
Middlemiss, Flt.Sgt. R.G., 249 Sqn 177, 302, 375, 385, 388, 389, 395, 396, 397
Milburn, Plt.Off. H.A., 185/249 Sqns 149, 165, 233, 245, 665
Miller, Sgt. A., 39 Sqn. 189
Miller, Flt.Sgt. I., 227 Sqn 623, 669
Miller, Grp.Capt. J.D., Controller 579, 598
Miller, Flt.Sgt. J.N., 185 Sqn 640
Miller, Sgt. R., 229 Sqn 519, 577, 589, 595, 596, 605, 617, 620, 667
Miller, Plt.Off. R.A., 89 Sqn 110, 111, 182, 295, 298, 314, 363, 632, 656
Miller, Plt.Off. W.L., 126 Sqn 133, 165, 212, 215, 361, 397, 403, 406
Milligan, Sgt. B., 229 Sqn 519, 634
Milner, Flt.Sgt. W.H.L., 126 Sqn 133, 215, 216, 255, 259, 273, 297, 405
Milson, Plt.Off. C.H., 86 Sqn 549
Minster, Flg.Off. F., 217 Sqn 340, 362
Mitchell, Flg.Off. H.E., 89 Sqn 367, 372, 376
Mitchell, Plt.Off. H.R., 603 Sqn *197*, 199, 231, 245, 248, 262, 665
Mitchell, Plt.Off. K.R., 185 Sqn 241, *242*, 362, 384, 414
Mitchell, Sqn.Ldr. R.A., 603/249 Sqns 240, *242*, 245, 257, 258, 264, 269, 271, 273, 293, 305, 368, 382, 383, 401, 403, 405, 412, 419, 426, 437, *523*, 532, 575, 651, 656, 673
Mitchison, LAC E., Luqa 180
Moffat, Plt.Off. J.D., 227 Sqn 555, 668
Monck, Air Fitter, FAA 210
Montgomery, Lt.Gen. B., C-in-C, 8th Army 564, 639, 644, 649
Montgomery, Sub Lt. F.H., 885 Sqn 490
Moody, Plt.Off. V.K., 249 Sqn 415, *517*, *523*, 561, 607, 608, 637
Moody, Plt.Off., OADU 527
Moon, Plt.Off. H.H., 249 Sqn 56, 91
Moore, Sgt. A.C., 69 Sqn 81
Moore, Sub Lt. T.E., 828/830 Sqn 378
Morrison, Sub Lt. H., 809 Sqn 490, 491
Morrison, Sub Lt. J.C., 828/830 Sqn 378
Morrison, Flg.Off. S.C., 104 Sqn 645
Morrison-Jones, Plt.Off. C.R., 242 Sqn 58, 112, 116
Morsheimer, Sgt. L.J., 611 Sqn 241, 251
Morse, Wt.Off. F., 217 Sqn 356
Mortimer, Sgt. J.E., 126 Sqn 468, *545*, 557, 627
Mortimer-Rose, Sqn.Ldr. E.B., 185 Sqn 94, *94*, 131, 132, 143, 147, *147*, 213, 654, 673
Moss, Sgt. R.C., 89 Sqn 560, 563, 597, 622, 645
Mouhot, Sgt. (FF), SAS 348
Mould, Sgt. M.T.St.J., 89 Sqn 592, 597, 627
Mowbray, Plt.Off. J.R., 229 Sqn 640
Moye, Sgt. E.D., 185 Sqn 241, 300, 394, 666
Mueller, Sgt. P.J.O., 248 Sqn 474, 524
Muir-Mackenzie, Lt. H., 800 Sqn 478, 484, 491, 493
Mulholland, Sgt. C.H., 252 Sqn 83, 84, 668
Mulholland, Wg.Cdr.N.G., 458 Sqn 88
Mullins, Sgt. E., 217 Sqn 370
Mulloy, Sgt. G.F.R., 242 Sqn 118, 125, 127, 665
Munro, Plt.Off. R., 69 Sqn 339, 362, 440, 497, 522, 524
Munster, Maj.Lord, ADC 522
Murray, Plt.Off. G., 603 Sqn *197*, 199, 212, 665
Murray, Plt.Off. K.N.L., 249 Sqn 109, 116, 117, 134, 665
Musham, Mr. C., HMS *Ledbury* 500, 512
Mutch, Sgt. C.E., 249 Sqn 310, 687

Nadon, Sgt. G.R., 229 Sqn 640
Nash, Plt.Off. H.T., 229 Sqn 519, 530, 578, 581, 585, 587, 596, 601
Nash, Plt.Off. P.A., 249 Sqn 107, 109, 116, 149, 156, 159, 160, 161, *161*, 162, 163, 178, 181, 209, 217, 221, 233, 245, 248, 249, 254, 256, 260, 261, 272, 276, 287, 651, 653, 666, 685, 686
Nash, Wg.Cdr. R.R., 37 Sqn 99, 100, 128
Nation, Sub Lt. B.H., 806 Sqn 492
Neale, Sgt. D.T., 242 Sqn 16, 51, 664
Neighbours, Mrs. J., Civilian 687
New, Sqn.Ldr. W.G., 185 Sqn 283, 292, 378, 381, 394, 409, 532, 673
Newbury, Sgt. D., OADU 303
Newman, Plt.Off. C.A., 185 Sqn 310
Newman, Flg.Off. D.G., 603/229 Sqn 283, 368, 384, 401, 423, 514, 533, 666
Nicholl, Capt. A., HMS *Penelope* 177
Nicolls, Flt.Lt. V., ASR 71, *72*
Nicholls, Plt.Off. J.H., 601 Sqn 283
Nielsen, Cpl. T., ASR 71
Nihill, Sub Lt. J.H.O., 809 Sqn 490, 669
Nixon, Plt.Off. J.H., 229 Sqn 170, *182*, 217
Noble, Plt.Off. R., 605/185 Sqns *40*, 76, 90, 102, 116, 117, *118*, 121, 143, 147, 152, 159, 169, 202, 217, 219, 224, 248, 270
Nolan, Sgt. C.J., 217 Sqn 370, 446
Nomis, Plt.Off. L.S., 229 Sqn 468, 542, *543*
Noone, Lt. F.C. (SAAF), 227 Sqn 549, 668
Norman, Sgt. D.W., 217 Sqn 312
Norris, Sqn.Ldr. S.C., 126 Sqn *26*, 27, 47, 77, 112, 115, 171, 673
Northcott, Flt.Lt. G.W., 603 Sqn 240, *242*, 272, 375, 403, 410, 412, 502, 520, 657
Nottage, Flt.Lt. G.R., 89 Sqn 424, 557, 560, 622
Nunn, Sub Lt. A., 884 Sqn 476, 488, 489, 669
Nuttall, PO(A) H.W., 807 Sqn 282, 283, 669

Oakes, Flg.Off. P.G., 89 Sqn 110, 163, 164, 286, 363, 623
O'Brien, Plt.Off. P.A.J., 185 Sqn 468, 470, 518, 577, 599, *600*, *602*, 613, 626
Ogden, Sqn.Ldr. C.V., 272 Sqn 358
Ogilvie, Plt.Off. N.J., 185 Sqn 283, 291, 307, *366*, 383, 423, *425*, *450*, 461, 497, 498
O'Hara, Sgt. E., 227 Sqn 529, 540, 668
O'Leary, Sgt. A.A., 89 Sqn 367, 386, 391, 417, 419, 515
Oram, Plt.Off. O.F.A., 238 Sqn 349
Ormrod, Plt.Off. O.O., 605/185 Sqns *40*, 68, 76, 80, 98, 102, 112, 117, 132, 149, 157, 165, 180, 188, 206, 213, 665
Osborne, LAC A., Hal Far 158, 159
Otis, Sgt. J.E., 603 Sqn *197*, 200, 415, 416, 421, 666
Outwin, Sub Lt. F.G., 800 Sqn 478, 479
Owen, Plt.Off. A.D., 1435 Sqn 423, 585, 614
Oxby, Flt.Sgt. D.A., 89 Sqn 367, 409, 421, 582, *582*, 592, 607

Pagdin, Sub Lt. J.S., 821 Sqn 92
Page, Capt. H., BOAC 104
Pain, Sqn.Ldr. D.S., 89 Sqn 627, 644, 645, 673
Palliser, Flt.Lt. G.C.C., 249/605 Sqns 16, 37, *38*, 64
Palmer, Flg.Off. F.R.W., 1435 Flt 57
Palmer, Sub Lt. P.E., 807 Sqn 156, 282, 330, 669
Paradis, Plt.Off. J.H.R., 249 Sqn 310, 403, 407, 426, 666
Pares, Lt.Cdr. J.M., HMS *Indomitable* 473
Parish, Sub Lt. G.W., 801 Sqn 325, 330, 640
Park, Air Vice-Marshal Keith, AOC Malta 412, *413*, 413, 419, 420, 431, 446, 458, 518, 522, 528, 569, *571*, 612, 618, 630, 631, 634
Park, Flt.Sgt. N.M., 126 Sqn 415, 416, 438, 439, 462, *545*, 579, 584, 586, 600, 603, 609, 613, *614*, 627, 635, 651, 653, 667
Park, Plt.Off. R.B., 185 Sqn 468, 620
Park, Lt. R.B., 827 Sqn 492, 578
Parker, Sub Lt. D.G., 884 Sqn 476, 488
Parker, Sgt. D.K., 185 Sqn 302, 385, 421
Parker, Sgt. G.B., 69 Sqn 41, 126
Parkinson, Flt.Lt. C.H., 603 Sqn 309, 310, 368, 373, 382, 384, 392, 398, 401, 403, 404, 408, 412, 414, 417, 419, 426, 435, 444, 445, 457, 459, 462, 502, 519, 520, 530, 537, 543, 550, 552, 581, 585, 587, 590, 596, *598*, 603, 617, 620, 629, *630*, 635, 651
Parks, Flt.Sgt. T., 126/249 Sqn 240, *242*, 275, 297
Parks, T. 384, 385, 395, 396, 407, 437, 503, 504, *523*
Parks, Flt.Sgt. W., 229 Sqn 415, 531, 639, 667
Parrish, Plt.Off. D.F.W., 21 Sqn 79
Parry, Flt.Lt. H., 601 Sqn *196*, 197, 198, 210, 218, 252, 272, 290
Partridge, Flg.Off. D de M, 227 Sqn 549, 668
Pashen, Sgt. N.L., 603/229 Sqns 415, 531, 569, 607
Paterson, Lt. B., 885 Sqn 485, 491
Paton, Lt. W., 828/830 Sqn 344
Patrick, Plt.Off. A.H., 69 Sqn 359
Pattearson, Plt.Off. G.G., 272 Sqn 638
Patterson, Sgt. J.W., USS *Wasp* 241, 251
Patterson, Sgt., 227 Sqn 523, 524
Pauley, Sgt. J.B., 229 Sqn 155, 158, 160, 164, 176, *294*
Pawson, Plt.Off. K.W., 601 Sqn *196*, 198, 217, 665
Paxton, Sgt. T.G., 30 Sqn 45
Pearce, Capt. R.S., *Waimarama* 500
Pearson, Sgt., 39 Sqn 355
Peasley, Sgt. R.W., 89 Sqn 171, 251, 271
Peck, Flt.Lt. J.E., 126 Sqn 133, 134, 143, 145, 149, 156, 207, 208, 209, 210, 219, 220, 224, 235, 252, 255, 261, 267, 280, 281, 287, 302, 391, 655
Pendlebury, Sgt. J.R., 229 Sqn 170, 180, 279

Pennington, Lt. F.A.J., 884 Sqn 483, 485, 490, 509
Peters, Sgt. B.C., 249 Sqn 423, 553, 667
Pettitt, Sub Lt. R.H., 828/830 Sqn 29
Phillips, Sgt. A.J., 227 Sqn 529, 549, 558
Phillips, Wt.Off. C.T., 89 Sqn 592, 629, 631
Phillips, Plt.Off. 217 Sqn, 364
Phillips, Sgt. S., 21 Sqn 71
Phillipson, Sgt. J.R., 89 Sqn 366, 371, 376
Philp, Sgt. G., 1435 Sqn 415, 511, 512, 572, 596
Piggott, Sgt. D.A., 126 Sqn 640
Pike, Wg.Cdr. J.M.N., 248 Sqn 456, 473, 474, 500, 524
Pike, Sqn.Ldr. S.A.D., 185 Sqn 27, 29, 673
Pike, Sgt., 69 Sqn 157
Pinkney, Capt. H., *Port Chalmers* 506, 515
Pinney, Plt.Off. J.A.H., 603 Sqn 310, 375, 431, 459, 502, 594, 687
Plagis, Flt.Lt. J.A., 249/185 Sqn 109, 116, 125, 130, 143, 148, 156, 159, 160, 161, 162, 163, 208, 210, 252, 254, 256, 260, 272, 273, 276, 302, 303, 307, *307*, 308, 378, *448*, *450*, 651, 657
Pollock, Plt.Off. D.P., 1435 Sqn 468, 543, 666
Popham, Sub Lt. H.H., 880 Sqn 471, 472, *472*
Poppleton, AC1 G., Takali 590
Portal, Air Chief Marshal Sir Charles 229
Porter, Mr. R.A., ATA 199
Potter, Plt.Off. A., 69 Sqn 38
Potts, Sgt. R.V., 229 Sqn 155, 158, 168, *182*, 238, *294*
Pow, Flt.Sgt. L.G., Ferry Pilot 635, 687
Powell, Flt.Lt. R.Y., 202 Sqn 282, 324
Powell-Shedden, Wg.Cdr. G.F., Wg Cdr Ops 66, 149, 150, 154
Pratt, Sub Lt. E.F., 828/830 Sqn 528, 532, *532*, 539, 601, 616, 621, 622, 624, 625
Prchal, Plt.Off. E.M., 24 Sqn 377
Preston, Plt.Off. I.F., 126 Sqn 519, 559, 667
Price, Flt.Lt., ASR 287, 313
Pring, Flt.Sgt. A.M.O., 89 Sqn 558, 592, 629, 631, 655
Pritchard, Sgt., OADU 527
Protheroe, Sub Lt. W.L., 827 Sqn 492
Putnam, Plt.Off. H.A., 185/126 Sqns 167, 169, 204, 665
Pybus, Flg.Off. J., 95 Sqn 315

Rabagliati, Wg.Cdr. A.C., Takali 26, *26*, 44, 46, 47, 56, 61, 76, 77, 84, 85, 111, 112, 120, 654, 658
Rae, Flt.Sgt. J.D., 603/249 Sqn 198, 199, 231, *232*, *291*, 315, 375, 388, 395, 397, 403, 411, 436, 437, 654
Ramsay, Wt.Off. C.B., 249 Sqn 302, 304, 312, 384, 406, 407, 666, 686
Randall, Plt.Off. W.B., 229 Sqn 640
Rankin, Sub Lt. J.F., 807 Sqn,334
Ransom, Sgt. F., 272 Sqn 351, 668
Rasmussen, Sgt. N.E., 69 Sqn 86
Rathie, Flg.Off. P., 1435 Sqn 85, 167, 227
Rawson, Flt.Sgt. D.L., 249 Sqn 519, 520
Reeves, Flt.Lt. J.S., 40 Sqn 88
Reeves, Plt.Off. N.E., 89 Sqn 367, 386, 391, 419, 444, 464, 515, *538*, 548, 651, 656
Regan, L/Air W.R., 809 Sqn 490, 669
Reid, Flt.Sgt. D.G., 185 Sqn 241, *242*, 300, 305, 308, *366*, 381, 383, 384, 393, 394, 418, *425*, 651, 653, 666
Reid, Plt.Off. M.J., 185 Sqn 640
Reid, Plt.Off. L.S., 185 Sqn 302, *362*, 385, 398, 414, 428, 432, 436, 535, 579, 586, 599, 601, *602*, 612, 613, 626, 687
Relton, Wt.Off. F.K.G., 601 Sqn 326
Revell, LAC, Takali 48
Reynolds, Flt.Sgt. B.W., 126 Sqn 405, 666
Reynolds, L/Air G.G., 828/830 Sqn 378
Reynolds, Plt.Off. H.G., 229 Sqn 415, 462, 519, 573, 585, 615, 640
Richards, Flg.Off. R., 59 Sqn 43
Richardson, Sgt. A.R., 126 Sqn 310, 397, 402, 417, 418, 458
Richardson, Sub Lt. R.M., 809 Sqn 485
Riddy, Flg.Off. K.J., 240 Sqn 382
Ridgway, Sgt. C.C., 272 Sqn 350, 668
Rignall, Sgt. G.D.S., 252 Sqn 83
Riley, Capt. F., *Brisbane Star* 496, 506, 515
Riley, Wg.Cdr. W., 201 Grp. 186, 351, 352
Ritchie, Sub Lt. B., 800 Sqn 492
Ritchie, Sgt. D.F., 249/126 Sqns 415, 444, 463
Rivers, Sub Lt. B.N., 828/830 Sqn 137
Robb, Sgt. D.J., 605/185 Sqn 137, 149
Roberts, Lt. C.K., HMS *Manchester* 498
Roberts, Sub Lt. G.W., 800 Sqn 477, 478, 484
Roberts, Sgt. H., 126 Sqn 415, *545*, 550, 617
Roberts, Sub Lt. T.D., 828/830 Sqn 55
Robinson, Sgt. A.A., OADU 287-8
Roe, Lt.Cdr. A.J.J., 828/830 Sqn 315, 341
Roe, Sgt. R.J., 1435 Sqn 468, 580, 588, 601, 667
Rogers, Plt.Off. W.B., 272 Sqn 351, 352
Rollinson, Wg.Cdr. J.D., 148 Sqn 207, 211
Rolls, Flt.Lt. W.T., 126 Sqn 467, 468, 470, 504, 532, *545*, 556, 557, 569, 578, 579, *579*, 580, 584, 586, 600, 613, 635, 636, 637, 651
Roper, Flg.Off. P.K., 86 Sqn 440, 521, 523, 524
Roscoe, Flt.Lt. A.F., 229 Sqn 468, *523*, 553, 554, 575, 577, 589, *590*, 590, 629, 642, 687
Ross, Plt.Off. J.McK., 89 Sqn 367, 371, 383, 417, 533
Ross Shore, Wg.Cdr. D., 227 Sqn 440, 523, 524, 527, 540, 549, 558, 571, 572
Rouleau, Plt.Off. D.F., USS *Wasp* 302, 303, 667
Round, Plt.Off. R.P., 249 Sqn 415, 427, *523*, 531, 666
Rounsefell, Flt.Sgt. J.V., USS *Wasp* 241, *242*, 247, 667
Rowe, Flt.Lt. A.C., 126 Sqn 310, 343, 403
Rowe, Mr & Mrs E.J., Civilians 687
Rowland, Sub Lt. L., 807 Sqn 329
Roy, Flt.Sgt. D., 229 Sqn 170, 235, *236*, *294*
Rushton, Flt.Lt. A.M., 202 Sqn 282
Russel, Sgt. H.R., 185 Sqn 302, 308, 421, 666
Russell, Plt.Off. J.K., 126 Sqn 31, 46, 58, 59, 664
Ruston, Sqn.Ldr. P., OADU 69
Ryckman, Flt.Sgt. G.A.J., 126 Sqn 156, 204, 205, 665

Sanders, Flt.Lt. L.V., 603 Sqn *197*, 198, 199, 235, 245, 264, 269, 273, 293, 399, *400*, 400, 654, 685, 686
Sanderson, Sgt. G.E., 39 Sqn 549
Sanderson, Plt.Off. J.G., 249 Sqn 468, *523*, 574, 585, 586, 588
Sarene, Sgt., 86 Sqn 430
Satchell, Wg.Cdr. W.A.J., Takali 26, *27*, 29, 56, 70, 84, 85, 121, 122, 131, 213, 226, 507, 513, 514
Saunders, Plt.Off. E.J., 511 Sqn 686
Saunders, Sgt. R.H., 185 Sqn 633, 667
Savage, Lt. E.G., 809 Sqn 451, 471, 472
Schade, Flt.Sgt. P.A., 126 Sqn 156, 176, 214, 224, 250, 255, 289, 296, 343, 375, 391, 397, 403, 407, *407*, 446, 650, 655
Schmidt, Plt.Off. D.W., 227 Sqn 540, 555, 572
Schofield, Flt. F.D., 601 Sqn 240
Schwenk, Sub Lt. W.F.H., 884 Sqn 476, 488
Scollan, Plt.Off. C.R., 601 Sqn 302, 342
Scott, Mr. A., ATA 199
Scott, Flt.Sgt. A.H., 1435 Sqn 423, 504, 543, 589, 594, 607, 627, 631, 651
Scott, Sub Lt. D.C., 828/830 Sqn 625, 626
Scott, Plt.Off. J.R., 229 Sqn 519, 553, 667
Scott, Plt.Off. T.W., 601 Sqn *196*, 198, 217, 233, 250, 278, 293
Scurfield, Cdr. D.G., HMS *Bedouin* 337, 339
Sebring, Sgt. R.W., 248 Sqn 497, 524
Seddon, Sgt. K., 227 Sqn 668
Seddon, Flg.Off. R.B., 39 Sqn 186, 187, 189, 540
Seed, Plt.Off. R., 249 Sqn 468, *523*, 538, 594, 604, 620
Selkirk, Wg.Cdr. W.R., 21 Sqn 37, 63, 71
Sergeant, Plt.Off. R.A., 249 Sqn *124*, 127, 143, 168, 185, 202, 204, 211
Sewell, Plt.Off. R.P.W., 601 Sqn *196*, 198, 250, 312, 315
Sharman, Flt.Lt. D.C., 86 Sqn 422, 521, 544, 548, 549
Sharpe, Sgt. F.W., 1435 Sqn 423, 594
Shaw, Sgt. E.J., 185 Sqn 241, *242*, 280
Shaw, Sgt. T.G., 252 Sqn 144
Shea, Sgt. E.G., 601 Sqn *196*, 198
Sheldon, Mrs. E.P., Civilian 687
Shepherd, Plt.Off. D.G., Luqa 497
Shepherd, Sgt., 126/1435 Sqn 241, *242*, 391, 428
Sherlock, Plt.Off. F.J., 185 Sqn 240, *242*, 246, *261*, 263, 265, 279, 292, 301, 307, 381, 384, 394, 398, 421, 461, 498, 504
Sherrington, Sgt. R.D., USS *Wasp* 241, 242, 667
Shewell, Sgt. W.S., 249 Sqn 415, *517*, *523*, 538, 594
Shipard, Flg.Off. M.C., 89 Sqn 367, 398, 409, 421, 425, 428, 430, 436, 582, *582*, 592, 607, 613, 651, 658
Shirley, LAC N., 69 Sqn 44, 75, 128, *129*, 129
Shulman, Sgt. C.J., 69 Sqn 524, 540, 625
Shute, Sub Lt. C.V., 828/830 Sqn 55, 125
Shutt, Sub Lt. F., 809 Sqn 476
Sida, Batman R., HMS *Ledbury* 500
Sidey, Sgt. E.L., 229 Sqn 415, 555, 575
Siddall-Simpson, Sub Lt. W., 828/830 Sqn 546, 563, 625
Siebert, Caporal Chef (FF), SAS 348
Sim, Flt.Sgt. R.J., 185 Sqn 109, *216*, 261, 345, *362*, 365, 384, 408
Sintetos, Sgt. N.D., 126 Sqn 468, 559
Sismey, Plt.Off. S.G., 202 Sqn 282
Slade, Flt.Lt. J.W., 603 Sqn *197*, 199, 223, 233, 235, 250, 367, 368, 393, 405, 429
Slater, Lt. R.W., 828/830 Sqn 35, 55
Sluggett, Plt.Off. C.F., 242 Sqn 58
Sly, Flt.Lt. R.H.C., USS *Wasp* 240, *242*, 244, 246, 250, 251, 667
Smart, Sqn.Ldr. T., 229 Sqn 642
Smith, Plt.Off. A.C., Takali 94
Smith, Plt.Off. A.I., 272 Sqn 638
Smith, Lt. B.G., 828/830 Sqn 341, 399
Smith, Flg.Off. D.H., 126 Sqn 302, *379*, 394, 401, 405, 414, 657
Smith, Sgt. H.J., 185 Sqn 423, 620
Smith, Flg.Off. J., 249 Sqn 310, 345, 392, 402, 666, 686
Smith, Plt.Off. J.A., 601/126 Sqn 240, *242*, 242, *243*, 244, 283, 286, 290, 342, 344, 371, 389, 401, 404, 405, 409, 415, 416, 419, 428, 429, 432, 435, 438, 443, 445, 464, *516*, 666
Smith, Lt. J.G., 880 Sqn 471, 473
Smith, Sgt. L., 86 Sqn 544
Smith, Plt.Off. R.G., 603 Sqn 283, 368, 384
Smith, Flt.Lt. R.I.A., 126 Sqn 415, 416, 419, 428, 432, 438, 464, 502, 503, 514, *516*, 531, 576, 595, 605, 608, 635, 645, 651, 657
Smyth, Sgt. W.D., 217 Sqn 364
Somerville, Admiral Sir James, Indian Ocean Fleet 319
Somerville, LAC J., Takali 135, 175, 202
Spalding, Sub Lt. G., 807 Sqn 333, 669
Spedding, Sub Lt. H.R., 813F Sqn 334
Spencer, Sgt. D.W., Luqa 519, 687
Spencer, Mrs. D.W., Civilian 687
Spooner, Flt.Lt. A., SD Flt 28, 53, 63
Spradley, Plt.Off. B.W., 249 Sqn 310, 384
Sprott, Seaman C, HMS *Upright* 75, *76*
Spuy, Lt. L.B. van der, 5 SAAF Sqn 350
Stainforth, Wg.Cdr. G.H., 89 Sqn 424, 438, 439, 444
Stammwitz, Flt.Sgt. H., Takali 130
Stanton, Plt.Off., 248 Sqn 524
Stead, Sgt. A.B., 249 Sqn 468, 469, 519, 520, 574, 583, 585, 596, 610, 627, 632
Stead, Plt.Off. G.R., 235 Sqn 311
Steadman, Plt.Off. D. *49*
Steel, Sqn.Ldr. F.J., 40 Sqn 45
Steele, Plt.Off. A.C., 185 Sqn 30, 92,*93*, 112, 113, 116, 125, 151, 157, 665
Stenborg, Plt.Off. G., 185 Sqn 302, 303, 345, *362*, *390*, 391, 403, 444, 446, 520, 651, 654
Stephens, Sqn.Ldr. M.M., 249/229 Sqns 573, 574, *583*, 584, 596, 603, 607, 627, 629, *630*, 651, 673
Stephens, Sgt. W.C., 86 Sqn 560
Stephenson, Plt.Off. A.P., 272 Sqn 45, 186
Stephenson, Sub Lt. J.W.D., 809 Sqn 476
Stevens, Flg.Off. W.J., 217 Sqn 353, 363, 387, 430, 446
Stevenson, Flg.Off. J.D., 126 Sqn 519, 576, 618, 627, 667
Stevenson, Lt. J.R.O., 828/830 Sqn 14, 63
Stevenson, Flt.Sgt. R.A., 1435 Sqn 310, 427, 589, 667
Stewart, Plt.Off. A.R., 1435 Sqn 423, 543, 585, 622
Stewart, L/Air J., 809 Sqn 490, 669
Stewart, Sqn.Ldr. R.R., 21 Sqn 73
Stickley, Wg.Cdr. L.J., 40 Sqn 28
Stirling, Maj. D., SAS 347
Stokes, Flt.Lt. T.V., 10 RAAF Sqn 232, 237
Stones, Flt.Lt. D.W.A., 1435 Flt/605 Sqn 57, 68, 70, *89*, 90, 96, 99, 103, 112, 127, 673
Stoop, Flg.Off. J.R., 185 Sqn 240, *242*, *362*, 385, 414
Story, Sgt. A.W., 53 Sqn 43
Street, Sub Lt. P.D.C., 806 Sqn 489
Streets, Plt.Off. E.E., 126 Sqn 31, 91, *93*, 134, 665
Strever, Lt. E.T., 217 Sqn 353, 440, 441, 442, *442*
Strickland, LAC, ASR 313
Stringer, Plt.Off. R.G., 248 Sqn 474, 525
Stuart, Plt.Off. J.R.A., 249 Sqn 77, 664
Sullivan, Sgt., HMS *Furious* 519, 520
Sumray, LAC H., Luqa 111
Sutherland, Sgt. E., 86 Sqn 440
Sutherland, Flt.Sgt. J.R., 185 Sqn 30, 91, 92, 125
Swales, Maj. C.J.O., 603/229/185 Sqns *197*, 198, 199, 394, 456, 459, 497, 498, 517, 532, 534, 568, 593, 595, 608, 644, 673
Swain, Sgt. L.H., 229 Sqn 468, 552, 667
Swannick, Flt.Lt. G.W., 229 Sqn 415, 511, *517*
Swithinbank, Sub Lt. M., 828/830 Sqn 74
Syfret, Vice-Admiral Sir Neville, Force 'H'/Force 'F' 109, 450, 495

Tanner, Sgt. J.H., 126 Sqn 415, 429, 502, 666
Tarbuck, Sgt. J., 185 Sqn 468, 517, 601, *602*, 611, 614
Tayleur, Sgt. J.L., 249 Sqn 109, 121, 124, 125, 202
Taylor, Flt.Lt. A.M., 39 Sqn 53, 54, 55, 114, 355
Taylor, Plt.Off. C., HMS *Eagle* 423
Taylor, Sub Lt. C.G., 809 Sqn 452
Taylor, Sgt. C.P.J., 601 Sqn 302, 375
Taylor, L/Air W.A., 807 Sqn 282
Tearle, Plt.Off. F.J., 89 Sqn 110, 111, 182, 298, 314, 363
Tedder, Air Chief Marshal Sir Arthur, AOC, ME *182*, 182, 183, 357, 647
Tedesco, Sgt. Y. (Belg), 272 Sqn 350, 351, 668
Tedford, Plt.Off. D.A., 249 Sqn 50, 70, *95*, 96, 665
Tennant, Wg.Cdr. E., 69 Sqn 41, 359
Terry, Flt.Sgt. P.L., 185 Sqn 302, 315, *362*, 365, 397, 398, 666,

Tester, Wg.Cdr. J., CRO, ME 676
Tester, Sgt. L.H., 86 Sqn 549
Tew, Plt.Off. J.D., 242 Sqn 37, 99, 665
Thwaites, Plt.Off. E., 252 Sqn 83, 351, 358
Thomas, Flt.Lt. C.S., 39 Sqn 355
Thomas, Plt.Off. F.D., 126 Sqn 283, 343, 386, 438, 502, *545*, 608, 687
Thomas, Shenton, Governor of Singapore 153
Thomas, Sub Lt. R.A., 828/830 Sqn 74
Thompson, Flg.Off. A.R.F., 1435 Flt 33, 68
Thompson, Wg.Cdr. J.M., Takali/Hal Far Wings 413, *523*, 528, 534, 535, 568, 579, *580*, 586, 599, 601, *602*, *609*, 609, 612, 620, 622
Thompson, Flt.Sgt. L.C., 86 Sqn 430
Thompson, Flt.Lt. P.D., 185 Sqn 57, 58, 64
Thompson, Sgt. R.E., 89 Sqn 367, 371, 383
Thompson, Plt.Off. W.L., 126 Sqn 423, 438, 446, 554, 594, 605, 618
Thompson, Sgt., 38 Sqn 55, 376
Thomson, Sub Lt. A.J., 800 Sqn 478, 484, 491, 493, 509
Thornton, Plt.Off. W.A., 22 Sqn 128
Thorogood, Sgt. J.D., 185 Sqn 640
Tickner, Lt. L.F., 801 Sqn 331, 669
Tiddy, Sgt. A.J., 126 Sqn 423, 428, 438, 505, 576, 605, 617, 620, 627
Tilley, Lt. D.P. (SAAF), 86 Sqn 560
Tilley, Plt.Off. R.F., 601 Sqn *196*, 197, 198, 201, 214, 224, 235, 237, 238, 247, 255, 259, 268, 269, 270, 287, 289, 309, 310, *369*, 402, 403, 409, 414, 427, 520, 651
Timms, Cpl., ASR 188
Tipton, Plt.Off. J., 40 Sqn 30
Todd, Sub Lt. R.S., 828/830 Sqn 361
Tomkins, Sqn.Ldr. E.C.C., 37 Sqn 100, 101, 680
Tomkins, Flt.Sgt. M.E., 249 Sqn 310, 373, 666, 686
Tomkinson, Lt.Cdr. E.P., HMS *Urge* 225
Townson, Cpl. R., 241 AMES 675
Trebell, Sgt. J.G., 89 Sqn 367, 372
Troubridge, Capt. T., HMS *Indomitable* 473
Truby, Sgt. E.R.F., 272 Sqn 350, 668
Tucket, Capt. J.C., *Dorset* 503
Tuckwell, Sgt. G.A., 272 Sqn 144, 352
Turlington, Plt.Off. R.H., USS *Wasp* 240
Turnbull, Lt. R.F.A., 807 Sqn 328, 334, 343
Turner, Plt.Off. G.W., 229 Sqn 519, 553, 595
Turner, Wg.Cdr. P.S., 249 Sqn/Takali Wg. 87, 91, 96, 110, 115, 121, 126, 227, 240, 265, 436, 553, 673
Tuttle, L/Air, W.P., 828/830 Sqn 137
Tweedale, Sgt. G.R., 185 Sqn 90, 112, 113, *135*, 165, 176, 188, 205, 214, 218, 237, 238, 249, 651, 653, 665
Twiss, Sub Lt. L.P., 807 Sqn 329, 332

Underwood, Sqn.Ldr. P.L., 235/227 Sqns 363, 364, 529, 557, 560, 572, 623, 669
Urry, Sub Lt. L.D., 807 Sqn 330

Valiquet, Flt.Sgt. C.N., USS *Wasp* 241, *242*, 247, 667
Varey, Flt.Sgt. A.W., 126 Sqn 283, 406, 410, 411, 425, 427, 431, 435, 502, 576, 595, 605, 607, 608, 618, 642, 651, 687
Venables, Cmdr. A.G., Convoy WS 21S 449
Venn, LAC H., Takali 130
Verroll, Plt.Off. L.A., 249 Sqn 241, 271, 276, 375
Vian, Admiral Sir Philip, Force 'B' 83, 138, 139, 140, 141, 144, 148, 347, 352, 354, 357, 358
Vickery, Sgt. B.H., 252 Sqn 358
Vidler, Sgt. N.L., 229 Sqn 155, 180, *182*, 225, *294*
Vinall, Sgt. J.D., 185 Sqn 468, 543, 583, 586, 667
Vineyard, Flt.Sgt. M.W., 185/1435 Sqns 241, 246-7, 361, *362*, 368, 424, 658
Vivian, Sgt. A.W., 227 Sqn 549, 668

Waddingham, Flt.Lt. J., 89 Sqn 557, 562, 668
Wadham, Sgt. M., 86 Sqn 544
Walcott, Sgt., 603 Sqn *197*, 199, 201
Walker, Lt. C., 804 Sqn 451
Walker, Sub Lt. D., 828/830 Sqn 399
Walker, Flt.Lt. R.G.M., 69 Sqn 37, 44
Walker, Sgt. W.H., 185 Sqn 423, *602*
Walker, Plt.Off., 69 Sqn 44
Wallace, Flg.Off. E.W., 126 Sqn 302, 343, 391, 396, 429, 534, *545*, 578, 585, 600, 613, *614*, 667
Wallace, Lt. I.J., 809 Sqn 490
Wallace, Sgt. T., HMS *Furious* 519
Walsh, Sub Lt. S.M.P., RNAS 35, 299
Walsh, Sgt. J., 89 Sqn 110, 163, 266, 286, 295, 363
Walton, Flt.Lt. R., 511 Sqn 642, 686
Walton, Plt.Off. W.C., 1435 Sqn 423, 576, 577, 589, 594, 607, 616, 627, 631, 632, 637, 657
Wanklyn, Lt. M.D., HMS *Upholder* 48, 188, 225
Warburton, Wg.Cdr. A., 69 Sqn 14, 28, 35, 37, 44, 46, 47, 81, 100, 101, 128, *129*, 456, 505, 524, 558, 568, 623, 624, 656, 657
Warren, Sgt. A., 159 Sqn 549
Watlington, Flt.Sgt. H.F., 39 Sqn 544, 549
Watson, Flt.Sgt. I., 511 Sqn 686
Watson, Sub Lt. J.A.K., 821 Sqn 100
Watson, L/Air P., 828/830 Sqn 378
Watson, Sgt. R.J., 69 Sqn 81
Watson, Flg.Off. R.J., 162 Sqn 558
Watson, Sub Lt. W.P., 828/830 Sqn 378
Watts, Flt.Lt. L.W., 603/249 Sqn *197*, 199, 210, 230, 231, 233, 256, 259, 304, 346, 419, *420*, 426, 503, 520, *523*, 656
Way, Plt.Off. B.W., 39 Sqn 186, 187
Weaver, Sgt. C., 185 Sqn 415, 417, 418, 426, 427, 429, 432, 436, 445, 458, 520, 521, 531, 534, 535, 550, *551*, 551, 651, 653, 655
Webster, Sgt. L.F., 603 Sqn *197*, 199, 212, 219, 220, 235, 310, 402
Webster, Sgt. W.W., 235 Sqn 326, 668
Webster, Sgt., 250 Sqn 349
Weil, Sub Lt. G.P.R. (FF), 248 Sqn 497
Weir, Sgt. W.B., 249 Sqn 643
Wells, Wg.Cdr. W.G., 242/126 Sqns/Takali 27, 101, 102, 125, 126, 136, 673
Wellum, Flt.Lt. G.H.A., HMS *Furious* 468
Welpy, Lt. J.A., 801 Sqn 331
West, Plt.Off. J.G., 249 Sqn 87, *106*, 121, 172, 213, 227
West, Flt.Lt. R., 1435 Flt/249/185 Sqns 112, 116, 171, 173, 174, 202, 204, 212, 227, 240, 244, 245, 259, 263, 266, 267, 278, 292, 345, *362*, 375, 398, *448*, 651
Westcott, Sgt. J.A., 185 Sqn 32
Westmacott, Sqn.Ldr. I.B., 1435 Flt 27, 47, 57, 61, 62, 74, 76, 77, 96, 111, 170, 213, 222, 227, 347, 673
White, Flt.Lt. B., 69 Sqn 37, 44, 52, 74
White, Sqn.Ldr. B.E.G., 1435 Sqn *606*, 636, 644, 673
White, Sqn.Ldr. C.A., 21 Sqn 61
White, Sub.Lt. C.T., 828/830 Sqn 528, 532, *532*, 541, 546, 621, 622, 626
White, Sgt. F., 39 Sqn 114
White, Plt.Off. J.C., 22 Sqn 128
Whitfield, Lt. P.C., 828/830 Sqn 86, 90, 299, 399
Whitmore, Sgt. W.R., 1435 Sqn 468, 504, 596, 601, 613
Wicks, Sqn.Ldr. B.J., 126 Sqn 423, 460, 502, 504, 522, 554, 568, 578, 584, 667, 673
Wigley, Plt.Off. P., 185 Sqn 76, 80, 85, 89, 99, 121, 132, 137, 143, 149, 157, 165, 173, 178, 179, 188, 206, 213, 214, 218, 223, 248, 249, 250, 262, 270
Wigmore, Sqn.Ldr. W.C., 235 Sqn 337, 364, 423, 518, 540, 555, 572
Wilkes, Flt.Sgt., 159 Sqn 475
Wilkinson, Sgt. J.A., 217 Sqn 441, 442
Willcox, Sgt. G.H., 229 Sqn 193, *294*, 294
Williams, Flt.Lt. E., Luqa 111
Williams, Flt.Lt. E.J.A., 69 Sqn 41
Williams, Capt. G., *Empire Hope* 496
Williams, Sgt. J.R., 272 Sqn 355, 357, 668
Williams, Plt.Off. J.W., 249 Sqn 241, *242*, 260, 261, 264, 312, 345, 401, 402, 414, 433, 435, 436, *523*, 538, 547, 603, 604, 607, 616, 633, 642, 653, 687
Williams, Sgt. 39 Sqn 355
Williamson, Sgt. J.I., USS *Wasp* 241
Williamson, Lt. R.L., 828/830 Sqn 82, 378
Willie, Sgt. V., 126 Sqn 241, *242*, 411
Willis-Richards, Flg.Off. J., 458 Sqn 88
Wills, Plt.Off. A.P., 248 Sqn 474, 525
Wills, Plt.Off. R.A., 227 Sqn 561
Wilson, Sgt. A.S., 185 Sqn 68, 102, 149
Wilson, Sub.Lt. J.F., 828/830 Sqn 45, 63
Wilson, Sgt. W.R., 1435 Sqn 423, 543, 562, 613, 667
Wilson, Sgt. W.J., 160 Sqn 354
Wincott, Sqn.Ldr. A.G., 252 Sqn 456
Winfield, Sqn.Ldr. J.P., 126 Sqn 240, 251, 268, 275, 339, 340, 378, 389, 394, 406, 411, 427, 432, 460, 673
Winterbottom, Lt. W.D., 828/830 Sqn 343
Winton, Flg.Off. D., 1435 Sqn 62, 227
Wolfe, Lt. W.B. (SAAF), 86 Sqn 524
Wood, Sgt. C.L., 1435 Sqn 310, 444, 666
Wood, Flg.Off. H., 235/227 Sqns 363, 510, 521, 523, 529
Wood, Sgt. J.E., 1435 Flt 61, 102, *103*, 171, 222, 665
Wood, Sub.Lt. R.D., 809 Sqn 485
Woodger, Flg.Off. P.A., 185 Sqn 468, *536*, 536
Woodhall, Grp.Capt. A.B., Controller 106, 160, *176*, 219, 239, 241, 262
Woods, Sqn.Ldr. E.N., 249 Sqn 467, 468, 532, 534, 538, 539, 568, 570, 574, 583, 588, 596, 599, 610, 611, *612*, 615, *630*, 632, 637, 651, 655, 673
Woolley, Seaman F., HMS *Upright* 75, *76*
Woolven, Sgt. G.L., 272 Sqn 351, 352
Wootton, Flt.Lt. R.J.S., 69 Sqn 86
Worrall, Plt.Off. T.C. *64*
Workman, Plt.Off. F.J., 21 Sqn 71
Worsdell, Flg.Off. L., 86 Sqn 540, 544, 549
Wren, Capt. R., *Rochester Castle* 506, 515
Wright, Plt.Off. R.A., 1435 Sqn 643, 667
Wynn, Sgt. V.H., 249 Sqn 415, 416, 417, 421, 437, 504, *523*, 603, 607, 608, 616

Yarra, Flt.Sgt. J.W., 249/185 Sqns 106, 107, 108, 109, 133, 134, 136, 167, 188, 200, 205, *216*, 231, 262, 264, 271, 279, 280, 281, 288, 293, 299, 304, 308, 313, 361, *362*, 365, *387*, 390, 397, 398, 402, 407, 414, 651, 654
Yates, Plt.Off. A.S., 249 Sqn 240, 393, 406, 437, *523*, 588, 594, 610, 687
Ydlibi, Sgt. A., 252 Sqn 144
Yeatman, Sgt. J.F., 126 Sqn 468, 576, 618
Youens, Flt.Sgt. W.R., 38 Sqn 298
Young, Sub.Lt. J.A., 801 Sqn 484
Young, Sqn.Ldr. M.H., 104 Sqn 290, 299
Young, Sgt. W., 603 Sqn 310, 442

Zirnheld, Lt. A. (FF), SAS 348
Zobell, Flt.Sgt. M.B., 185 Sqn 640

Maltese
Agius, John, Civil Servant 153
Agius, May, Journalist 192
Attard family, Civilians 174
Azzopardi, Gnr. Joseph, RMA 255
Borg, Sir George, Chief Justice 552, *552*
Borg Pisani, Carmelo, Fascist 287
Camenzuli, Joseph, Civilian 255
Caruana, Wt.Off. Carmel, RMA 248
Cauchi, Gnr. Seraphim, RMA 249
D'Amato, Paul, Civilian 187
Debono brothers, Civilian 400
Gili, V., Police Constable 79
Grech, Carmela, Civilian 63
Grech, Emanuel, Civilian 640
Gridley, Doris, Wife of RAF officer 38
Izett, Gnr. W., RMA 38
Meli, J., Police Constable 79
Mifsud, Mary, Civilian 29
Nappa brothers, Civilians 255
Porteli, Rev. Pawl, Church of St Publius 223
Saliba, Tony, Civilian 255
Sciberras, L/Cpl Julian, RMA 187, 268, 269
Smith, Edgar, Civilian 213
Spiteri family, Civilians 29
Zammit, Pte. Spiro, RMA 268
Zarb, L/Sgt. Fedele, RMA 421
Zerafa, Michael, Civilian 640

Others
Dales, Cadet Midspmn. F., American, *Santa Elisa* 499
Fairbanks Jr. Douglas, American, Actor 244
Gates, Ensign C.H., American, USS *Wasp* 244
Griffiss, Lt.Col. T., American, USAAF 105
Halvorson, Col. H., American, Halforce 354
Kalberer, Maj. A., American, Halforce 354
McCampbell, Lt.Cdr. D., American, USS *Wasp* 244
Reeves, Capt. J.N., American, USS *Wasp* 199
Roosevelt, Franklin, American, President 195, 230
Sikorski, Gen. W., Polish, Polish C-in-C 377
Vooght, Capt. J.F., Dutch, *Clan Campbell* 142

a) Italians

Squ. Grp. St. Type
Abate, Ten. Angelo 257ª 108° 36° AS, 332
Abbarchi, Ten. Loris 265ª 88°– Aut. BT, 289
Agnello, Cap. Edoardo 173ª – – Aut. RST, 21
Aichner, Sottoten. Martino 281ª 132°– Aut. AS, 339
Alasia, 1° Av. Arm. Riccardo 239ª 102° 5° Ba'T, 376
Allegri, Cap. di Corv Raffaello, *Uarsciek*, 466
Ambrosio, Ten. Giovanni 378ª 155° 51° CT, 405
Andreotti, Ten. Pietro – 24° – Aut. CT, 490
Angelino, Ten. Mario 212ª 51° – Aut. BT/RS, 479
Angelucci, Ten. Silvio 255ª 105° 46° AS, 505, 506
Annona, Ten. Salvatore 204ª 41° – Aut. AS,
Annoni, Ten. Emanuele 96ª 9° 4° CT, 257
Antonelli, Ten. Francesco 60ª 33° 9° BT, 398
Arco, Sottoten. Luigi 170ª 83° – RM, 247
Argenton, Cap. Alberto 91ª 10° 4° CT, 271, 671

Badij, Mar. Mario, S.79 flyingbomb, 482
Baldassare, Cap. Antonio 144ª 85° – RM, 21
Balletta, Cap. Salvatore 274ª – – Aut. B.G.R., 301, 377, 388
Baraldi, Serg. Giuseppe 152ª 2° – Aut. CT, 257, 307, 671
Barani, Ten. Guido 278ª 132° – Aut. AS, 503
Barberini Colonna Sciarra, Sottoten. Urbano 151ª 20° 51° CT, 576, 672
Barcaro, Ten. Giovanni 97ª 9° 4° CT, 238
Bartolozzi, Ten. Giulio 150ª 2° – Aut. CT, 300, 335, 372
Bartolucci, Mar. Pasquale 360ª 155° 51° CT, 311, 577
Bastianelli, Ten. Felice 184ª 83° – RM, 21
Bastogi, Ten. Vittorio 351ª 155° 51° CT, 312, 460
Battaini, Serg. Magg. Luigi 152ª 2° – Aut. CT, 344, 485
Battistini, Ten. Alfonso 56ª 30° 10° BT, 510
Beccaria, Magg. Francesco – 16° 54° CT, 20
Bedosti, Ten. Oreste 259ª 109° 36° AS, 332
Beneforti, Magg. Albert – 7° 54° CT, 20
Bergamini, Ammiraglio Carlo – – – –, 84
Berna, Serg. Pier Luigi 151ª 20° 51° CT, 444, 554, 672
Berti, Sottoten. Paolo 84ª 10° 4° CT, 276
Berlinazzo, Sottoten. Gaetano 212ª 51° – Aut. BT/AS, 309, 482, 488, 489
Bertuzzi, Ten. Giuseppe 173ª – – Aut. RST, 225
Biagini, Serg. Magg. Lucio 359ª 22° – Aut. CT, 490
Biancardi, Cap. Cesare 60ª 33° 9° BT, 21
Bianchi, Mar. Pietro 352ª 20° 51° CT, 390, 494
Biasiol, Sottoten. Romano 360ª 155° 51° CT, 375
Biccolini, Ten. Manlio 378ª 155° 51° CT, 401, 635
Bigoni, Sottoten. Achille 287ª – – RM, 157
Bigoni, Ten. Sergio 239ª 102° 5° Ba'T, 285
Biundo, Sottoten. Girolamo 220ª 55° – Aut. BT, 129
Bizio, Sottoten. Antonio 152ª 2° – Aut. CT, 484
Blengini, Cap. Antonio 186ª 83° – RM, 21
Boerci, 1° Av. Mot. Enrico 209ª 102° 5° Ba'T, 342
Bombarda, Serg. Magg. Olimpio 86ª 7° 54° CT, 331
Bonannini, Av. Sc. Arm. Piero 170ª 83°– RM, 247
Bonet, Cap. Giovanni 150ª 2° – Aut. CT, 453
Bonfiglio, Ten. Giuseppe 351ª 155° 51° CT, 305, 312, 444, 512, 617
Bonfiglio, 1° Av. Mot. Vito 280ª 130° – Aut. AS, 140
Boni, Mar. Mot. Marcello 151ª 20° 51° CT *404*
Bonuti, Ten. Ado 97ª 9° 4° CT, 238
Borgogno, Cap. Luigi 352ª 20° 51° CT, 371, 381, 428, 494, 611
Boselli, Cap. Leo 97ª 9° 4° Aut. CT, 257, 551
Boselli Cap. Leo 362ª 22° – Aut. CT, 257, 551
Brera, Ten. Francesco 170ª 83° – RM, 231
Broccaro, Mar. Attilio 197ª 85° – RM, 561
Brondi, Cap. Alberto 355ª 24° – Aut. CT, 326, 329, 671
Buldrini, Ten. di Vasc Cesare, *Bronzo*, 507
Buscaglia, Magg. Carlo Emanuele – 132° – Aut. AS, 334, 454
Buvoli, Mar. Aldo 360ª 155° 51° CT, 14, 368, 653, 663

Cadringher, Ten. Col. Remo – 105° 46° AS, 481
Calistri, Cap. Pietro 76ª 7° 54° CT, 521
Callieri, Magg. Gino – 20° 51° CT, 371, 389, 427, 576
Calorenna, 1° Av. Mot. Giuseppe 239ª 102° 5° Ba'T, 493
Camera, Ten. Umberto 281ª 132° – Aut. AS, 339
Campari, Serg. Giulio 239ª 102° 5° Ba'T, 437, 507
Canepa, Serg. Enrico 370ª 24° – Aut. CT, 479
Canini, Sottoten. Adelmo 59ª 33° 9° BT, 592
Cannaviello, Ten. Col. Vittorio – 3° Nucleo AS, 481, 508
Capitani, Magg. Alberto – 32° 10° BT, 21, 454
Caracciolo, Carafa, Ten. Giobatta 360ª 155° 51° CT, 312, 382, 512
Carnielli, Ten. Antonio 144ª 85° – RM, 339
Casalini, Serg. Renato 355ª 24° – Aut. CT, 331, 333
Casavola, Serg. Ugo 239ª 102° 5° Ba'T, 493
Castellani, Ten. Col. Gori 274ª – – Aut. B.G.R., 377
Castellano, Ten. Gustavo 351ª 155° 51° CT, 577
Castro, Sottoten. Bruno 355ª 24° – Aut. CT, 329, 671
Castronovo, Ten. Alessandro 264ª 88° – Aut. BT, 271
Cavallina, Ten. di Vasc Gaspare, *Giada*, 480
Cavallo, 1° Av. Arm. Michele 239ª 102° 5° Ba'T, 512, 513
Cazzolli, Ten. Remo 152ª 2° – Aut. CT, 257, 278, *279*, 683, 684
Ceccato, Ten. Luigi 220ª 55° – BT, 184
Celentano, Ten. Agostino 150ª 2° – Aut. CT, 273, *306*, 312, 334, 344, 372, 653
Cenni, Cap. Giuseppe – 102° 5° Ba'T, 285, 296, 336, 341, 391, 410, 417, 443, 454, 533, 558, 630
Ceoletta, Serg. Magg. Giambattista 90ª 10° 4° CT, 203
Cerretti, Sottoten. Claudio 146ª – – RM, 157
Cerri, Serg. Magg. Angelo 351ª 155° 51° CT, 311, 312, 577
Cervellin, Cap. Giovanni 369ª 22° – Aut. CT, 551
Cesaro, Serg. Magg. Elio 152ª 2° – Aut. CT, 335, 372, 406
Cherici, Ten. Ennio 353ª 20° 51° CT, 385
Cherubini, Ten. Fabrizio 353ª 20° 51° CT, 398, 671
Chifari, Mar. Alessandro 139ª 82° – Aut. RM, 441, 442
Ciano, Count Galeazzo, Foreign Minister, 449
Cigala Fulgosi, Ten. Agostino 360ª 155° 51° CT, 588, 592
Ciollaro, Ten. di Vasc, *Glaucio*, 684
Colli, Cap. Giuseppe 144ª 85° – Aut. RM, 284
Compiani, Serg. Magg. Girogio 253ª 104° 46° BT/AS, 331, 332
Converso, Serg. Gastone 209ª 102° 5° Ba'T, 297, 342
Corallo, Sottoten. Frabcesco 220ª 55° – Aut. BT, 277
Corrado, Cap. Gianbattista 189ª 83° – RM, 523
Corti, Serg. Magg. Ferruccio 354ª 24° – Aut. CT, 331
Cosulich, Ten. di Vasc Giuseppe, MTSM 218, 281
Crabbia, Serg. Antonio – 160ª – Aut. CT, 61
Cremonesi, Serg. Giulio 239ª 102° 5° Ba'T, 493
Crimi, Sottoten. Michele 362ª 22° – Aut. CT, 490, 672
Cristiani, Serg. Magg. Romolo 14ª 4° 7° BT, 389
Cumbat, Cap. Antonio 239ª 102° 5° Ba'T, 416, 417, 432, 437, 443, 489, 501, 511, 512, 513, 630
Cupini, Col. Ranieri – – 10° BT, 21
Cusmano, Sottoten. Ugo 288ª – – RM, 343

Dagasso, Cap. Roberto 97ª 9° 4° CT, 238, 257, 671
Dal Ponte, Serg. Giovanni 210ª 50° – Aut. BT, 250
Damiani, Ten. Paolo 352ª 20° 51° CT, 550, *551*
Damiani, Mar. Rinaldo 97ª 9° 4° CT, 269, 272
D'Amico, Ten. Italo 151ª 20° 51° CT, 430, 512, 580, 617, 620
D'Auria, Col. Giovanni – – 9° BT, 21
David, Ten. Giuseppe 377ª – – Aut. CT, 21
da Zara, Ammiraglio Angelo, *Eugenio di Savoia*, 337, 455, 499
De Caterina, Cap. Gerardo 58ª 32° 10° BT, 21
Del Fabbro, Serg. Magg. Giovanni 378ª 155° 51° CT, 307, 368, 405, 671
Della Barba, Sottoten. Alessandro 50ª 38° 32° BT/AS, 486
Dell'Anna, Ten. Andrea 279ª 131° – Aut. AS, 139
De Merich, Ten. Arnaldo 152ª 2° – Aut. CT, *305*, 306, 307, 671
De Martiis, Ten. Tommaso 213ª 51° – Aut. BT/RS, 489
De Porto, Ten. Col. Cesare – – 9° BT, 21, 511
De Sancti, Sottoten. Antonio 265ª 88° – Aut. BT, 331
De Seta, Sottoten. Emanuele 353ª 155° 51° CT, 546
Dessanti, Sottoten Silvano 354ª 24° – Aut. CT, 329
Dessi, Sottoten. Tullio 50ª 38° 32° BT/AS, 486
Di Bert, Serg. Cesare 150ª 2° – Aut. CT, 384, 390
di Fonzo, Mar. Andrea 197ª 85° – RM, 181
Di Paolo, Serg. Roberto 152ª 2° – Aut. CT, 485
Di Pauli, Serg. Magg. Bruno 151ª 20° 51° CT, 427
di Porcia Guacella Brugnera, Ten. Paolo 352ª 20° 51° CT, 405
Disint, Sottoten. Isidoro 150ª 2° – Aut. CT, 513, 672
Doglio Niclot, Cap. Furio 151ª 20° 51° CT, 371, 385, 386, 392, 393, 396, 404, 405, 407, 411, 428, 430, 433, *434*, 653, 663, 672
Donati, Sottoten. Oliviero – – 36° AS, 332
Dori, Mar. Fabrizio 173ª – – RST, 363
Dose, Sottoten. Dante 352ª 20° 51° CT, 405, 671
Dringoli, Serg. Giovanni 150ª 2° – Aut. CT, 300, *301*, 312, 671
Durli, Mar. Mot. Giovanni 210ª 50° – Aut. BT, 290

Endrizzi, Serg. Magg. Aldo 59ª 33° 9° BT, 298
Erasi, Cap. Massimiliano 278ª – – Aut. AS, 21
Errico, Ten. Antonio 59ª 33° 9° BT, 298
Esposito, Cap. de Vasc *Trento*, 353

Fabbri, Mar. Albino 152ª 2° – Aut. CT, 292, 335, 372
Fabbri, Serg. Magg. Dino 239ª 102° 5° Ba'T, 376
Fabriaini, Ten. Col. Luigi – 116° – Aut. BT, 301
Fadda, Ten. Col. Antonio – 89° 32° BT/AS, 481
Fagnani, Col, Tarcisio – – 54° CT, 20
Falcone, Sottoten. Nicola 211ª 50° – Aut. BT, 286
Fanali, Magg. Dulio – 155° 51° CT, 285, 299, 342, 384, 389, 428, 494, 502, 503, 578, 588, 590, 663
Farina, Ten. Col. Giovanni – – 36° AS, 322
Fassi, Cap. Roberto 150ª 2° – Aut. CT, 257, 297
Favini, Magg. Andrea – 153° – Aut. CT, 481
Ferrante, Ten. Bartolomeo 58ª 32° 10° BT, 504
Ferrari, Ten. Libero 30ª 76° – OA, 21
Ferraro, Ten. Vasc Benedetto *Garibaldi*, 357
Ferrazza, Mar. Cesare 360ª 155° 51° CT, 382, 580, 606
Ferrini, Ten. di Vasc Renato *Azum*, 495
Festa, Cap. Valentino 76ª 7° 54° CT, 20
Fioravanzo, Ammiraglio Giuseppe 'Littorio', 352
Fischer, Sottoten. Vincenzo 84ª 10° 4° CT, 281, 671
Fougier, Gen. S.A. Rino Corso, General Staff, R.A. 371, 372
Franchini, Cap. Giovanni 351ª 155° 51° CT, 384, 494, 512, 617
Francine, Cap. Alfredo 189ª 83° – RM, 21
Francione, Cap. Alfredo 197ª 85° – RM, 21
Franco, Cap. Mario 55ª 30° 10° BT, 21
Frigerio, Ten. Jacopo 97° 9° 4° CT, 271
Frigo, Cap. Umberto 62ª 29° 9° BT, 372
Frongia, Cap. Mario 283ª 130° – Aut. AS, 481
Frulla, Magg. Mario – 24° – Aut. CT, 481

Gaeta, Col. Giuseppe, Bombardamento della Sicilia, 379
Gallo, Ten. Michele 151ª 20° 51° CT, 393
Gambari, Serg. Magg. Giovanni 378ª 155° 51° CT, 444, 590, 635
Gamberini, Mar. Gino 209ª 102° 5° Ba'T, 342
Garfagnoli, Cap. Pietro 167ª 16° 54° CT, 21
Gasperoni, Ten. Giorgio 358ª 2° – Aut. CT, 290, 293, 344, 372
Gaucci, Mar. Roberto 360ª 155° 51° CT, 342, 494
Gelli, Serg. Magg. Faliero 378ª 155° 51° CT, *432*, 433
Geminiani, Serg. Magg. Aldo 152ª 2° – Aut. CT, 307, 671
Geymet, Cap. Eugenio 59ª 33° 9° BT, 21
Giacomello, Ten. Giovanni 253ª 104° 46° AS, 332, 333
Giannella, Sottoten. Luigi 84ª 10° 4° CT, 211, 238, 664
Giannini, Av. Sc. Arm. Pietro 239ª 102° 5° Ba'T, 372
Giardini, Serg. Magg. Raimundo – 16° 54° CT, 330, 671
Giosue, Ten. Alfio 612ª – – Aut. Socc., 22
Giovannini, Sottoten. Adolfo 353ª 20° 51° CT, 394, 671
Giudici, Serg. Spiridione 353ª 20° 51° CT, 390, 671
Gobbi, Cap. Edoardo 170ª 83° – RM, 21
Gon, Cap. Aldo 73ª 9° 4° CT, 225
Gostini, Cap. Saverio 98ª 7° 54° CT, 20
Grillo, Sottoten. Carlo 150ª 2° – Aut. CT, 273
Grossi, Magg. Giorgio – 130° – Aut. AS, 490
Grosso, Av. Sc. Mot. Luigi 239ª 102° 5° Ba'T, 342
Guerci, Serg. Magg. Mario 73ª 9° 4° CT, 271
Guiducci, Cap. Giovanni 90ª 10° 4° CT, 203

Iachino, Ammiraglio Angelo, *Vittorio Veneto*, 138, 140, 337, 352
Iannilli, Serg. Magg. Vittorio 353ª 155° 51° CT, 460
Iannucci, Mar. Maurizio 352ª 20° 51° CT, 401, 405, 460, 595, 672
Ignaccolo, Magg. Giovanni – 76° – OA, 21
Ingrellini, Ten. Mario 253ª 104° 46° BT/AS, 331

Jellici, Mar. Luigi 150ª 2° – Aut. CT, 300, 372, 382, 390
Juzzolino, Ten. Emilio 280ª 130° – Aut. AS, 140

La Ferla, Cap. Germano 359ª 22° – Aut. CT, 482, 490, 551
Larese, Gortigo, Ten. Italo 152ª 2° – Aut. CT, 335, 372
Larismont Pergameni, Magg. Antonio 97ª 9° 4° CT, 250
Laudano, Cap. Giovanni 40ª 76° – OA, 21
Lavezzi, Mar. Carlo 63° 29° 9° BT, 540
Lentella, 1° Av. Mot. Giuseppe 239° 102° 5° Ba'T, 630
Leonardi, Ten. Alberto 259ª 109° 36° AS, 328
Leoni, Serg. Magg. Alcide 351ª 155° 51° CT, 444
Lisardi, Cap. Luigi 168ª 16° 54° CT, 21
Loddo, Sottoten. Ernani 370ª 24° – Aut. CT, 328
Longano, Sottoten. Nicola 360ª 155° 51° CT, 382
Longo, Sottoten. Rosario 151ª 20° 51° CT, 411, 672
Losi, Serg. Trento 139ª 82° – Aut. RM, 441
Lottero, Cap. Antonio 169ª 16° 54° CT, 21
Lucchini, Cap. Franco – 10° 4° CT, 14, 165, 238, 250, 271, 652, 653, 663
Lusenti, Sottoten. Cesare 276ª 116° – Aut. BT, 386

Macanda, Sottoten. Salvatore 264ª 88ª – Aut. BT, 631
Machieraldo, Magg. Ugo – 88° – Aut. BT, 273, 454
Magagnoli, Cap. Dante – 3° Nucleo AS, 505
Magnaghi, Serg.Magg. Carlo 98ª 7° 54° CT, 331
Malagola, Serg. Willy 360ª 155° 51° CT, 382, 384
Malosso, Ten. Ettore 151ª 20° 51° CT, 394
Manini, Serg. Domenico 378ª 155° 51° CT, 443
Marasco, Cap. Massimo 57ª 32° 10° BT, 21
Marchetti, Mar. Antonio 239ª 102° 5° Ba'T, 342
Marchi, Ten. Italo 355ª 24° – CT, 331
Marchio, Serg. Mario 358ª 2° – Aut. CT, 264, 671
Marega, Sottoten. Arduino 612ª – – Aut. Socc, 307
Marescalchi, Ten. Erico 253ª 104° 46° BT/AS, 331
Marietta, Sottoten. Gaetano 280ª 130° – Aut. AS, 140
Marini, Cap. Giulio 279ª 131° – Aut. AS, 139
Marsigliani, Ten. Vasc Vitaliano, *Eugenio di Savoia*, 337
Martinelli, Ten. Mario 288ª – – RM, 357
Martinelli, Sottoten. Tullio 360ª 155° 51° CT, 342
Martini, Ten. Angelo 209ª 102° 5° Ba'T, 430, 559
Martinoli, Serg. Teresio 73ª 9° 4° CT, 234, 250, 257, 264, 652, 653, 663, 664
Martucciello, GM Oss Giorgio 197° 85° – RM, 181
Masini, Ten. Italo 59ª 33° 9° BT, 504
Massa, Ten. Mario 73ª 9° 4° CT, 257
Mastrodicasa, Ten. Gaetano 139ª 82° – Aut. RM, 440, 441, 442
Mazzolani, Serg.Magg. Aldo 355ª 24° – Aut. CT, 331, 671
Mazzoleni, Ten. Mario 378° 155° 51° CT, 433, 494, 632
Mazzotti, Serg.Magg. Renato 370ª 24° – Aut. CT, 479
Medesani, Ten. Pierino 265° 88° – Aut. BT, 286
Melpignano, Av.Sc.Arm. Francesco 210ª 50° – Aut. BT, 250
Menaldi, Sottoten. Pietro 151ª 20° 51° CT, 411, 672
Mercalli, Mar. Pietro 265ª 88° – Aut. BT, 273
Metellini, Ten. Giacomo 152ª 2° – Aut. CT, 372, 384, 484
Mezzetti, Ten. Felice 373ª 153° – Aut. CT, 596, 672
Mezzetti, Cap. Gastone, *Gorizia*, 357
Miani, Cap. Carlo 378ª 155° 51° CT, 285, 300, 342, 375, 406, 428, 663
Minguzzi, Cap. Vittorio – 22° – Aut. CT, 551
Mirrione, Serg.Magg. Giuseppe 351ª 155° 51° CT, 512, 601
Mollo, Cap. Giovanni 58ª 32° 10° BT, 493
Montagnani, Ten. Francesco 352ª 20° 51° CT, 392, 402, 671
Monterumici, Sottoten. 204ª 41° – Aut. AS, 148
Moretti, Sottoten. Giorgio 354ª 7° 54° CT, 331
Moretti, Sottoten. Vittorio 278ª 132° – Aut. AS, 334, 497
Mussolini, Benito, El Duce, 228, 229, 285, 352, 371, *372*, 508
Muti, Ten.Col. Ettore – 41° – Aut. AS, 144

Negri, Sottoten. Giannino 278ª 132° – Aut. AS, 334
Nespolo, Ten. Pompeo 213ª 51° – Aut. BT/RS, 476, 477
Nobili, Ten.Col. Guido – 101° 5° Ba'T, 395
Notari, Ten. Raffaele – 14ª 4° 7° BT, 389
Noziglia, Magg. Giuseppe – 30° 10° BT, 21, 454

Oblach, Ten. Giuseppe 73ª 9° 4° CT, 225
Olivetti, Mar. Manlio 96ª 9° 4° CT, 276
Orlando, Magg. Vincenzo – 38° 32° BT/AS, 481
Ottaviani, Ten. Vittorio 212ª 51° – Aut. BT/AS, 479
Ottolino, Sottoten. Luigi 287ª – – RM, 423

Paccalegna, Sottoten. Giulio 170ª 83° – RM, 85
Pagliani, Sottoten. Romano 152ª 2° – Aut. CT, *306*, 344, 372, 384, 393, 671, 683
Palermo, Ten. Tommaso 186ª 83° – RM, 284
Palmieri, Ten. Cesare 146ª – – RM, 417
Panizzi, Ten. 14ª 4° 7° BT/AS, 264
Pannaria, Ten. Vasc Arnaldo, *Gorizia*, 357
Papalia, Sottoten. Fulvio 239ª 102° 5° Ba'T, 372
Pardini, Ten. Lamberto 213ª 51° – Aut. BT/AS, 309, 476
Parietti, 1° Av. Mot. Giovanni 239ª 102° 5° Ba'T, 493
Patella, 1° Av. Arm. Nicola 209ª 102° 5° Ba'T, 502, 507, 508, 512
Patriarca, Mar. Antonio 358ª 2° – Aut. CT, 257, 286, 292, 300, 372, 408
Pecchiari, Serg. Magg. Francesco 352ª 20° 51° CT, 390, 392, 671
Pecori, Ten. di Vasc Renato, *Dagabur*, 475
Pedretti, Serg. Magg. Paolo 353ª 20° 51° CT, 580, 635
Pegna, Cap. Oscar 284ª 131° – Aut. AS, 139
Pellegrini, Sottoten. Vasc Emilio 170ª 83° – RM, 85
Perdoni, Serg. Luciano 84ª 10° 4° CT, 276
Perneschi, Av. Sc. Marc Arduino 14ª 4° 7° BT, 389
Perona, Ammiraglio Angelo, *Gorizia*, 84, 455, 499
Perozzi, Mar. Zaccaria 209ª 102° 5° Ba'T, 342
Pesavento, Mar. Romano 369ª 22° – Aut. CT, 580, 672
Piccinini, Gen. B.A. Mario, OC fighters, Sicily?
Piccioni, Ten. Gerolamo 212ª 51° – Aut. BT, 326
Piccolomini, Cap. Ranieri 90ª 10° 4° CT, 203
Pinna, Mar. Aldo 15ª 4° 7° BT/AS, 340
Pittaluga, Cap. Vincenzo 63ª 29° 9° BT, 21
Pittoni, Cap. Egeo 353ª 20° 51° CT, 444, 512
Pocek, Ten. Giorgio 150ª 2° – Aut. CT, 273, 286, 335, *372*, 372, 411, 513
Politi, Cap. Bruno 86ª 7° 54° CT, 20
Porcarelli, Serg.Magg. Alberto 151ª 20° 51° CT, 385, 671
Priorini, Ten. Vasc. Oss Guglielmo 287ª – – RM, 328
Prodi, Serg.Magg. Guerrino 150ª 2° – Aut. CT, 273
Pruneri, Sottoten. Vittorio 170ª – – RM, 645
Puccini, Ten. di Vasc Sergio, *Alagi*, 503
Putti, Cap. Carlo – – 2° Nucleo AS, 481

Quarantotti, Ten.Col. Aldo – 2° – Aut. CT, 274, 305, 334, 372, 393, 406, 408, 409, *410*, 412, 671
Querci, Sottoten. Alvaro 73ª 9° 4° CT, 234, 271

Radini, Cap. Enzo 373ª 153° – Aut. CT, 596
Raffaelli, Gen. B.A. Ferdinando, S.79 flyingbomb, 482
Raimondo, Serg.Magg. Oscar 239ª 102° 5° Ba'T, 501
Ramacciotti, Serg.Magg. Lorenzo 354ª 24° – Aut. CT, 333
Ranieri, Ten. Gugliemo 279ª 131° – Aut. AS, 139
Ravazzoni, Ten.Col. Ivo – – 7° BT/AS, 515
Reghini, Cap. Carlo 261ª 106° 47° BT, 351
Reinero, Magg. Virginio – 104° 46° BT/AS, 331
Remondino, Ten.Col. Aldo – – 51° CT, 371, 379, 382, 388, 389, 428, 436, 444, 454, 489, 511, 601, 663
Reseghetti, Ten. Angelo 264ª 88° – Aut. BT, 372
Riccardi, Sottoten. Giuseppe 351ª 155° 51° CT, 368, 384, 671
Ricci, Serg.Magg. Rino 152ª 2° – Aut. CT, 276, 375, 384, 485, 653, 663
Ricciarini, Cap. Giulio 255ª 105° 46° AS, 505, 506
Rindone, Ten. Pietro 173ª – – Aut. RST, 73, 363
Rizzardo, Serg. Angelo 354ª 24° – Aut. CT, 331
Rivalta, Magg. Gabriele – 4° 7° BT/AS, 454
Rivoli, Cap. Ugo – 132° – Aut. AS, 489, 503
Rivolta, Serg. Eugenio 14ª 4° 7° BT/AS, 265
Robillotta, Ten. Domenico 211ª 50° – Aut. BT, 257
Robone, Ten. Guido, Sezione Speciale, 482, 488
Romagnoli, Mar. Aldo 351ª 155° 51° CT, 311
Romano, Serg. Cesare 168ª 16° 54° CT, 521
Rombola, Serg.Magg. Marc Pasquale – 109° 36° AS, 486
Rossi, Ten. Nilo 212ª 51° – Aut BT/RS, 475
Rossini, Ten. Gianni 372ª 153° – Aut. CT, 635
Roveda, Cap. Riccardo 353ª 20° 51° CT, 371, 389, 428, 635
Ruggeri, Sottoten. Aldo 277ª 116° – Aut. BT, 361
Runci, Mar. Gino 378ª 155° 51° CT, 368, 375, 671
Rusconi, Serg. Ambrogio 91ª 10° 4° CT, 250

Sacchi, Ten.Col. Nicola – 29° 9° BT, 454
Salvatore, Serg.Magg. Massimo 97ª 9° 4° CT, 257, 272, 664
Sant'Andrea, Cap. Vincenzo 359ª 22° – Aut. CT, 428
Santuccio, Serg. Luigi 351ª 155° 51° CT, 602
Savi, Magg. Ercole – 33° 9° BT, 21, 285, 454
Savini, Serg. Guido 209ª 102° 5° Ba'T, 298, 502, 507,
508, 512
Scalia, Sottoten. Giovanni 280ª 130° – Aut. AS, 140
Scandola, Ten. di Vasc Renato, *Dessie*, 503
Scarciella, Vice-Brig Giulio, Carabiniere, 441
Scaroni, Gen. D.A. Silvio, OC fighters, Sicily, 20, 446
Scarpetta, Ten.Col. Pier Giuseppe – 2° – Aut. CT, 331, 412, 482, 513, 672
Schisano, Av.Sc. Marc Antonio 139° 82° – Aut. RM, 441
Scianca, Sottoten. Italo 209ª 102° 5° Ba'T, 560
Seganti, Ten. Carlo 358ª 2° – Aut. CT, 257, 269, 286, 292, 372, 408, *409*, 409, *410*, 653, 663, 672
Selano, Cap. Aligi 62ª 29° 9° BT, 21
Serafini, Serg. Ferruccio 378ª 155° 51° CT, 590, 602, 628, 633, 663
Serafino, Mar. Lorenzo 378ª 155° 51° CT, 311, 312, 671
Sicco, Mar. Alessandro 353ª 20° 51° CT, 435
Silva, Ten. Lelio – 2° Nucleo AS, 343
Simeoni, Cap. Paolo 259ª 109° 36° AS, 332
Simionato, Mar. Olindo 150ª 2° – Aut. CT, 257, 305, *335*, 335, 393, 398, 653, 663
Sironi, Ten. Plinio 378ª 155° 51° CT, 588, 635
Sodi, Ten. Mario, *Eugenio di Savoia*, 337
Sondalini, Cap. Ettore 205ª 41° – Aut. AS, 138
Sordini, Cap. Alfredo 265ª 88° – Aut. BT, 273
Sotgia, Ten. 274ª – – Aut BGR, 301
Spadaro, Ten. Beniamino 151ª 20° 51° CT, 617
Spagnolini, Cap. Riccardo 351ª 155° 51° CT, 285, 394, 428, 494
Squarcina, Sottoten. Mario 73° 4° CT, 272
Sterzi, Cap. Annibale 358ª 2° – Aut. CT, 274, 292, 293, 671
Stringa, Cap. Aldo 209ª 102° 5° Ba'T, 285, 342, 443, 507
Suppo, Sottoten. Massimo 354° 24° – Aut. CT, 329
Sutter, Ten. R.S. Giulio – 102° 5° Ba'T, 539

Tamborra, Ten. Giuseppe 239ª 102° 5° Ba'T, 285, 298
Tanassi, Mar. Dario 612ª – – Aut. Socc, 505
Tarantola, Mar. Ennio 151ª 20° 51° CT, 382, 389, 393, 396, 404, *404*, 428, 430, 435, 577, 601, 602, 653, 663
Tattanelli, Cap. Bruno 378ª 155° 51° CT, 285, 444
Teia, Cap. Salvatore 152ª 2° – Aut. CT, 257, 276, *306*, 306, 344, 372, 375, 384, 408
Testera, Serg. Dante 353ª 20° 51° CT, 577, 617
Tommasini, Serg. Ermanno, *Garibaldi*, 357
Tosi, Sottoten. Renato 264ª 88° – Aut. BT, 459, 515
Tourn, Ten. Giorgio 204ª 41° – Aut. AS, 148
Treggia, Mar. Giovanni 152ª 2° – Aut. CT, 334, 335,
335
Trentadue, Serg. Arm Vito 173ª – – Aut. RST, 73
Trevisan, Serg. Elio 90ª 10° 4° CT, 193
Turba, Magg. Mario – 109° 36° AS, 332

Ungarelli, Sottoten. di Vasc Ongarillo, MTSM 214, 281

Vaccari, Ten. Riccardo, Sezione Speciale, 482, 488
Valentini, Magg. Gastone – 4° 7° BT/AS, 340
Varacca, Serg.Magg. Mario 378ª 155° 51° CT, 405
Vecchione, Sottoten. Antonio 209ª 102° 5° Ba'T, 336
Venditti, Magg. Gennaro – 85° – RM, 21
Venturini, Ten. Leonardo 358ª 2° – Aut. CT, 269, 304
Veprizchi, Ten. Paolo 264ª 88° – Aut. BT, 289
Vergo Scocco, Ten. Vinicio 14ª 4° 7° BT/AS, 264
Vernesi, Cap. Vezio 115° 76° – OA, 21
Veronesi, Serg. Mario 84ª 10° 4° CT, 264
Vichi, Sottoten. Francesco 358ª 2° – Aut. CT, 372, 382, 408, 671
Vigna, Serg.Magg. Olindo 209ª 102° 5° Ba'T, 298
Vignoli, Mar. Ferruccio 151ª 20° 51° CT, 617
Vimercati, Ten. Lionello 607ª 149° 44° SAS, 69
Viola, Serg. Gianfranco 220ª 55° – BT, 182
Visconti, Ten. Adriano 76ª 7° 54° CT, 502
Visentin, Sottoten. Edoardo 171ª – – RM, 357
Visentini, Serg.Magg. Francesco 378ª 155° 51° CT, 405, 406
Vivarelli, Ten. Giovanni 253ª 104° 46° BT/AS, 331
Volenterio, Cap. Pietro 56ª 30° 10° BT, 21
Volpi, Ten. Alberto 378ª 155° 51° CT, 444

White, Sottoten. Normanno 205ª 41° – Aut. AS, 138

Zampini, Cap. Alberto 220ª 55° – BT, 182
Zanardi, Magg. Alfredo – 109° 36° AS, 481, 486
Zanardi, Serg. Ferdinando 351ª 155° 51° CT, 580
Zanardi, Serg.Magg. Giovanni 144ª – – RM, 363
Zanchi, Ten.Col. Adalberto – 83° – RM, 21
Zane, Sottoten. Luigino 144ª – – RM, 361
Zanelli, Ten. Angelo 257ª 108° 36° AS, 332
Zappi, Ten. Spartaco 221ª 55° – Aut. BT, 115
Zarini, Ten. Ferruccio 73ª 9° 4° CT, 271
Zavattarelli, Ten. Francesco – – 45° SAS, 530
Zedda, Mar. Remo 360ª 155° 51° CT, 342, 375, 579, 580, 588
Zezon, Sottoten. GArat Achille 15ª 4° 7° BT/AS, 340

Ahrens, Fw. Claus, 2/KG 54 73
Alex, Uffz. Rudolf, 3/KGr 806 121
Albert, Uffz. Gerhard, 5/KG 77 518
Andrea, Uffz. Gerhard, 3/KGr 806 238
Apmann, Uffz. Christian, 8/StG 3 260
Assum, Ofw. Martin, II/LG 1 621
Auer, Ofw. Kurt, 7/StG 3 162
Augst, Uffz. Hans, 8/JG 53 355
Augustin, Fw. Herbert, 3/KGr 806 144

Bär, Hpt. Heinz, I/JG 77 380, *380*, 482, *593*, 593, 596, 606, 622, 652, 662, 663
Bartels, Uffz. Heinz-Wolf, KuFlGr 606 304
Bastian, Fw. Walter, 1/LG 1 477, 480
Bauer, Uffz. Karl, II/KG 77 439
Bayerlein, Oberst Fritz, CoS, Afrika Korps 18
Beck, Uffz. Werner, III/ZG 26 225
Becker, Oblt. Gerhard, 6/KG 77 113
Becker, Uffz. Heinrich, 8/JG 53 219, 238, 660
Becker, Fw. Paul, I/JG 27 590, 602
Becker, Obgfr. Robert, 5/LG 1 612
Beckmann, Lt. Erich, Stab III/JG 53 226, 249, 355, 658, 659
Behlau, Hpt. Leo, 6/KG 77 391
Behr, Oblt. Erich, 7/KG 77 99, 401
Beikiefer, Uffz. Michael, 6/JG 3 126, 130, 670
Beitz, Uffz. Gerhard, 9/JG 53 113, *113*, 281, 288, 660
Below, Oblt. Freidrich, Stab III/JG 53 220, 659
Belser, Oblt. Helmut, 8/JG 53 110, 122, 159, *176*, 176, 211, 214, 221, 265, 270, 285, 351, 355, 652, 658, 660
Bennebach, Uffz. Oskar, 3/StG 3 511
Berres, Lt. Heinz-Edgar, I/JG 77 381, *400*, 400, 404, 419, 426, 427, 553, 561, 571, 595, 596, 601, 606, 620, 652, 662, 686
Beyschlag, Maj. JG 53 *58*
Biemer, Oblt. Walter, 5/KG 77 39
Bischoff, Oblt. Otto, 4/KG 77 163
Blass, Obgfr. Arthur, KuFlGr 606 421
Blum, Uffz. Heinrich, 3/JG 53 120, 670
Bode, Uffz. Gerhard, 8/StG 3 178
Boger, Uffz. Paul, 8/KG 77 177
Boger, Lt. Reinhold, 5/KG 77 394
Böhlen, Fw. Winfried, KuFlGr 606 204
Böhmer, Oblt. Otto, 6/JG 53 110
Bohnet, Lt. Günther, 7/KG 77 435
Bohr, Uffz. Gerhard, LG 1 504
Borner, Ofw. Walter, II/KG 77 621
Bösch, Ofw. Heinz, 7/KG 77 77, 79
Brändle, Oblt. Kurt, II/JG 53, II/JG 3 189, 661
Brandt, Ofw. Walter, I/JG 77 380, *556*, 652, 662
Braun, Hpt. Emil, I/KGr 806 267
Bredenbroker, Gefr, I/StG 3 492
Brehm, Fw. Friedrich, KGr 806 296
Brenner, Oblt. Gerhard, I/LG 1 352
Brenner, Fw. Johann, 2(F)/122 504
Bretschneider, Uffz. Hans, 7/StG 3 146
Bross, Uffz. Heinz, 10/JG 53 168, 670
Burger, Obgfr. Herbert, I/KGr 806 270
Büsen, Hpt. Dr. Nikolaus, 1(F)/122 325
Butschek, Gfr. Otto, 10/JG 53 94, 670
Buttstadt, Uffz. Wolfgang, 4/JG 3 135, 136

Camler, Uffz. Emil, 9/ZG 26 132
Chemnitz, Lt. Günther, 2/KuFlGr 606 314
Christl, Hpt. Georg, III/ZG 26 19
Claus, Uffz. Georg, III/StG 3 149
Crinius, Lt. Wilhelm, 3/JG 53 565
Cruger, Maj. Arved, Stab/KG 77 140

Degenhardt, Uffz. Albert, 2/KuFlGr 606 102, *103*
Dahl, Oblt. Walther, II/JG 3 164, 662
Damaske, Lt. Hermann, 3/KGr 806 144
Dammbrück, Lt. Eberhard, 8/KG 77 72
Deidlauf, Oblt. Helmut, 5/LG 1 480
Demuth, Uffz. Gerhard, III/KG 77 628
Diehm, Fw. Walter, 9/StG 3 174
Dielas, Lt. Werner, KuFlGr 606 304
Diepenseifen, Uffz. Willi, 3/SchG 2 635, 671
Diestler, Uffz. Karl, 4/KG 77 536
Dinger, Lt. Fritz, I/JG 53, II/JG 53 565, 652, 661
Dotterweich, Uffz. Adam, 5/LG 1 479
Dreifke, Lt. Wolfgang, Stab/JG 53 591
Dronke, Oblt. Wolfhelm, 5/KG 77 61
Duvenhörst, Lt. Gustav, 9/KG 77 594
Dyck, Uffz. Klaus, 7/JG 53 660

Eberle, Lt. Karl, 2/JG 77 562
Eckhardt, Oblt. Richard, 3/SchG 2 634, 671
Ederer, Ofw. Josef, I/JG 53 604
Ehehalt, Uffz. Hermann, 1/KuFlGr 606 90
Ehler, Uffz. Horst, 1/KuFlGr 606 118
Ehrenberger, Ofw. Rudolf, II/JG 53 180, 205, *206*, 559, *559*, 652, 660, 661
Einsinger, Lt. Josef, 5/JG 53 216
Emanuel, Uffz. Heinz, 5/KG 77 536
Engels, Fw. Toni, I/JG 77 394, 395, 620
Englisch, Lt. Irving, I/JG 77 381, 663
Esser, Lt. Wilhelm, 5/JG 53 606, 661

Fankenberger, Uffz. Heinrich, 4/JG 53 627
Fankhauser, Uffz. Josef, 7/JG 53 129, 660, 670
Feldkötter, Lt. Friedrich, 8/JG 53 355
Fellhöfer, Fw. Karl, 7/KG 77 591
Fiedler, Ofw. Siegfried, 6/LG 1 479, 480
Fischer, Lt. Ernst, 8/KG 77 56
Fischer, Gefr Fritz, 7/JG 53 660
Fischer, Fw. Max, Stab II/JG 3 148
Frank, Fw. Hans, 7/StG 3 167
Frank, Uffz., 3/JG 77 596
Franzisket, Hpt. Ludwig, I/JG 27 566, 590
Freckmann, Uffz. Heinrich, 6/JG 53 436, 670
Freesman, Lt. Fritz, 2(F)/122 61
Freytag, Oblt. Siegfried, 1/JG 77 380, 436, *566*, 578, 595, *597*, 606, 622, 652, 653, 662
Frick, Uffz. Gustav, II/KG 77 439
Frickmann, Uffz. Arno, 7/ZG 26
Fritscher, Lt. Ottokar, 5/LG 1 620
Frodien, Lt. Hans-Jürgen, Stab/JG 53 404, 670
Fronhöfer, Ofw. Günther, 10/JG 53 168, 670
Führer, Uffz. Albert, II/KG 77 439
Futterknecht, Fw. Ewald, II/KG 77 621

Geisshardt, Oblt. Fritz, 3/JG 77 380, *380*, 407, 422, 432, 443, 550, 573, 596, 608, 652, 662
Gerdes, Fw. Hermann, 8/KG 77 627
Gerhard, Uffz., I/StG 3 492, 493
Gerlich, Oblt. Axel, 5/LG 1 479, 480
Gerlitz, Hpt. Erich, I/JG 27, III/JG 53 658
Geschlossel, Fw. Heinz, KuFlGr 606 192, 414
Giessubel, Fw. Vincenz, 2/NJG 2 85
Gisy, Gfr. Horst, 4/JG 53 183, 670
Gläser, Uffz. Paul, 7/JG 53 188, 660
Godert, Stfw. Helmut, I/JG 77 380
Golinski, Fw. Heinz, 3/JG 53 565, *597*, 615, 616, 653, 671
Görbing, Ofw. Kurt, 2/JG 77 431
Gösch, Uffz. Rudolf, 6/KG 77 119
Gossling, Uffz. Herbert, I/StG 3 493
Göthe, Ofw. Otto, 6/JG 53 75, 669
Götz, Oblt. Franz, 9/JG 53 *113*, 265, 349, 658, 659, 660
Graggar, Oblt. Ernst, 2/KG 54 273
Grams, Uffz. Günther, I/KG 54 577
Grassmann, Uffz. Heinrich, 8/KG 77 99
Gröner, Uffz. Georg, 7/StG 3 167
Grosch, Ogfr., I/KG 54 525
Gröss, Oblt. Helmut, 9/StG 3 174
Gross, Uffz. Herbert, 3/KG 77 611
Gunkel, Gfr. Georg, 4/JG 53 591, 671
Günther, Uffz. Winfried, 8/StG 3 162

Haas, Lt. Herbert, 4/NJG 2 16, 45, 669
Haase, Lt. Rolf, 9/KG 77 214
Habicht, Oblt. Peter, 8/ZG 26 92
Haekel, Lt. Rolf, 8/KG 77 422
Haf, Gfr. Karl, III/StG 3 233
Hammann, Lt. Hans-Ernst, 6/LG 1 480
Hammer, Lt. Alfred, II/JG 53 268, 635, 661
Hagen, Obgfr. Rudolf, 4/JG 53 633
Hagen, Stfw. Wilhelm, 1/KuFlGr 606 192
Hannak, Lt. Günther, I/JG 77 380, 652, 662
Harder, Lt. Jürgen, 7/JG 53 127, 226, *252-3*, 281, 349, 659
Harnisch, Lt. Hermann, III/JG 53 *565*
Haumann, Lt. Hans-Günther, III/ZG 26 99, 670
Haussen, Oblt. Hans, POW 684
Heeman, Lt. Klaus, III/StG 3 149
Heinecke, Oblt. Hans-Joachim, 8/JG 53, III/JG 27 79, 86, 354, 660
Heiner, Lt. Dr. Jorg, II/JG 53 257, 260
Heinze, Hpt., JG 53 *58*
Heipe, Obfw. Wilhelm, 3/KGr 806 125
Hempfling, Uffz. Hans, 3/JG 77 596
Herberg, Lt. Klaus-Dieter, I/KG 54 127
Herkenhoff, Uffz. Heinz, 9/JG 53 660
Herkner, Lt. Wolfgang, 5/LG 1 219
Hermann, Oblt. Fritz, KGr 806 444
Hermann, Fw. Hubertus, 7/KG 77 128
Hero, Uffz. Georg, I/KG 54 259
Herold, Uffz. Heinrich, 4/LG 1 479, 500
Herrmann, Lt. Wolfgang, 5/JG 53 276, 670
Hertz, Fw. Hans, 8/KG 54 592
Hess, Oblt. Günther, 6/JG 53 112
Hesse, Lt. Heinrich, 7/JG 53 350, 351, 354, 355, 659
Heuer, Fw. Helmut, 7/KG 77 435, 436
Hicke, Lt. Walter, III/JG 53 659
Hinterberg, Uffz. Fritz, II/LG 1 629
Hipper, Ofw. Heinz, 9/JG 53 91, 660, 670
Hissbach, Oblt., I/NJG 2 362
Hitler, Adolf, Reich Chancellor 158, 228, 229, 678, 679
Hoffmann, Uffz. Adolf, I/KG 54 622
Holst, Lt. Hasso, I/KG 54 601
Hörmann, Lt. Sepp, KGr 806 429
Hosnedl, Lt. Siegmund, 7/JG 53 265, 659, 670
Hronek, Uffz. Franz, 2(F)/122 470
Hufnagel, Lt. Hans, 9/ZG 26 132, 670
Humburg, Hpt. Hans, Stab/KG 54 314

Ihlefeld, Maj. Herbert, I/JG 77 380

Jager, Uffz. Franz, 1/KuFlGr 606
Jaeger, Uffz. Franz, 1/KG 77 591
Janzik, Lt. Hermann, 3/KG 54 143
Jennerich, Uffz. Adolf, 7/JG 53 120
Jesek, Lt. Heinz, KGr 806 100
Jung, Hpt. Rolf, 4/NJG 2 19, 34
Jünger, Uffz. Willi, III/ZG 26 39, 99, 183, 670

Kahle, Fw. Kurt, 1/KuFlGr 606 316
Kaiser, Ofw. Franz, I/JG 53 207, 209
Kalbfeld, Uffz. Heinrich, KGr 806 346
Kaminski, Maj. Herbert, I/JG 53 19, *58*
Kammann, Uffz. Johann, III/StG 3 350
Kasimir, Lt. Oscar, KGr 806 388
Kasten, Lt. Dietrich, III/JG 53 355
Katthagen, Uffz. Hermann, 10/JG 53 142, 670
Kaufmann, Uffz. Heinz, KGr 806 346
Kehlbuth, Fw. Alexander, 5/JG 53 99, 217
Kehrer, Oblt. Kurt, KGr 806 346
Kern, Uffz. Walter, 7/StG 3 260
Kesselring, Feldmarschall Albert, C-in-C, South 22, 130, 193, 228, 553, 554, 563, 564, 597, 626, 639, 648
Keudell, Lt. Robert von, 4/NJG 2 88, 669
Kipfmuller, Lt. Walter, 1/KuFlGr 606 143
Kirschner, Lt. Joachim, 5/JG 3 151, 661
Kissling, Lt. Helmut, I/KGr 806 259
Kitzenmaier, Uff. Gerhard, 5/JG 53 160, 670
Kläger, Lt. Ernst, 8/JG 53 127, 129, 173, 265, 285, 350, 652, 658, 660
Klaus, Fw. Ernst, 8/KG 77 534
Klawitter, Uffz. Kurt, 8/KG 77 534
Kleimeier, Lt. Friedrich, 4/KG 77 403
Klötzer, Uffz. Hartmut, 7/JG 53
Knöthe, Lt. Herbert, I/KG 54 352
Kobsczinowski, Uffz. Otto, 8/KG 54 585
Koechling, Lt. Franz, 6/KG 77 619
Koelzsch, Fw. Joachim, 4/JG 53 543, 670
Kohl, Oblt. Willy, 4/KG 77 536
Köhler, Lt. Armin, I/JG 77 *381*, 381, 402, 427, 596, 663
Kollewe, Maj. Gerhard, II/LG 1 500, 620, *621*
Könning, Uffz. Karl, 3/JG 27 627, 671
Koopman, Lt. Gerhard, KuFlGr 606 333
Koretschek, Gefr. Eugen, ErgSt/StG 1 82
Korner, Lt. Friedrich, I/JG 27 350
Krahl, Hpt. Karl-Heinz, II/JG 3 19, 116, 189, *190*, *191*, *216*, 653, 661, 670
Kramer, Uffz. Heinrich, 2(F)/122 364
Krause, Ofw. Helmut, 1/JG 53 180
Kreig, Oblt. Rolf, KuFlGr 606 135
Kremin, Ofw. Waldemar, 4/LG 1 183
Krickl, Lt. Martin, 1/KG 54 224
Krizek, Obgfr. Rudolf, 5/KG 77 192
Kron, Obgefr Heinrich, ErgSt/StG 1 79
Kronschnabel, Ofw. Josef, 9/JG 53 218, 658, 660
Kröschel, Fw. Josef, 8/JG 53 226, 660, 670
Kruger, Oblt. Kurt, II/KG 3 att'd I/KG 54 120
Kuhn, Uffz. Edmund, 5/LG 1 480
Kuhn, Fw. Rudi, 7/KG 77 583
Kuhn, Obgfr. Wilhelm, Seenotst 6 275
Kuhn, Oblt., 8/StG 3 162, 163
Künzi, Uffz. Walter, 6/KG 77 113
Kuppers, Uffz. Julius, III/StG 3 350

Lagauer, Oblt. Leopold, 8/KG 77 487
Lang, Uffz. Gerhard, 8/KG 54 585
Lange, Lt. Max, 10/JG 53 141
Langer, Lt. Herbert, II/JG 53 258, 260
Langer, Fw. Hugo, 2/JG 77 500, 670
Langermann, Ofw. Werner, 10/JG 53 141
Lauff, Uffz. Friedrich, 7/ZG 26 217
Laufs, Lt. Peter, 4/NJG 2 16, 60, 669
Lauinger, Lt. Kurt, Stab III/JG 53 126, 659
Lenthoff, Uffz. Rudolf, III/ZG 26 186
Lenz, Uffz. Horst, 1/KG 54 581
Leps, Uffz. Martin, 4/KG 77 160
Leiwelt, Fw. Herbert, III/KG 77 385
Lichtenstein, Ofw. Wilhelm, II/StG 3 349
Lieres, Lt. Karl von, I/JG 27 350, 566, 590, 602
Limmertz, Ofw. Heinz, 4/KG 77 510
Linke, Uffz. Gerhard, 4/KG 77 222
Lischke, Lt. Ernst, 2(F)/123 425
Loch, Uffz. Heinz, 1/JG 53 611
Loerz, Oblt. Herbert, 7/KG 77 80
Loerzer, Genllt Bruno, II Fliegerkorps 19, 503
Löhnert, Oblt. Helmut, I/LG 1 352
Lompa, Uffz. Johannes, 4/JG 53 279, 280, 281
Louis, Lt. Joachim, Stab/JG 53 59, *60*, 113, 164, 180, 652
Luben, Hpt. Werner, 2/LG 1 480

Mächer, Uffz. Edmund, 6/JG 3 61
Mahler, Fw. Berhard, II/LG 1 621
Maltzahn, Maj. Günther von, Stab/JG 53 16, 19, 57, *58*, 58, 59, 80, 85, 162, 261, 265, 308, *380*, 652, 653, 661
Manz, Uffz. Walter, 7/JG 53 234, 660

Marseilles, Oblt. Hans-Joachim, I/JG 27 566
Martin, Uffz. Luitpold, 4/KG 77 388
Marzahl, Lt. Wolfgang, 6/KG 77 438
Mayer-Luhmann, Lt. Hans, Stab III/KG 77 202
Mayr, Fw. Georg, 4/KG 77 536
Mazurek, Uffz. Marian, 1/JG 53 565, 611, 613, 615, 661
Meister, Obgfr Günther, I/KG 54 93
Mellein, Uffz. Walter, KGr 806 398
Menny, Lt. Ingo, 8/KG 54 585, 591
Merz, Uffz. Günther, 5/KG 77 405
Michalski, Hpt. Gerhard, II/JG 53 188, *397*, 419, 587, 607, 608, 652, 653, 660
Mirschinka, Uff. Werner, 4/JG 53 32, 669
Möller, Lt. Hans, 6, 1/JG 53 172, 564
Mossdorf, Hpt. Martin, I/StG 3 489
Mulen, Uffz. Albert, KuFlGr 606 421
Müller, Lt. Freidrich, KuFlGr 606 33
Müller, Oblt. Friedrich-Karl, I/JG 53 180, 210, 564, 661
Müller, Lt. Hans-Volkmar, II/JG 53 547, 670
Müller, Uffz. Harry, 6/KG 77 181
Müller, Lt. Heinz-Karl, 9/KG 77 147
Müller, Lt. Herbert, I/KG 54 113
Müller, Uffz. Hermann, I/KG 54 338, 363, 576, 577
Müller, Lt. Rudolf, 8/JG 53 137, 257, 658, 660
Müller, Ofw. Walter, 2(F)/122 685
Mundt, Fw. Alfons, 9/StG 3 165
Münster, Uffz. Leopold, II/JG 3 91, 662
Münzert, Lt. Hermann, 9/JG 53 99, *253*, 265, 659, 660

Nairz, Uffz. Max, 9/JG 53 91, *113*, 192, 660
Neubauer, Gefr. Wilhelm, 8/StG 3 162
Neuffer, Oblt. Ernst, II/LG 1 629
Neuhoff, Lt. Hermann, 7/JG 53, 6/JG 53 *126*, 127, 129, 176, 178, *179*, 180, 285, 653, 659
Nicolai, Uffz. Gerhard, 7/StG 3 260
Nicolay, Uffz. Waldemar, 1/KuFlGr 606 47
Niederhagen, Fw. Franz, I/JG 77 663
Niese, Lt. Eberhard, I/JG 77 381, 663

Obermailander, Fw. Walter, III/StG 3 239
Oelmann, Lt. Fritz, 7/KG 54 591
Ohrt, Fw. Wilhelm, 9/KG 54 581
Ostler, Oblt. Anton, II/StG 3 349

Padior, Oblt. Udo, I/JG 53 210
Paepcke, Maj. Heinrich, II/KG 77 618, 620, 621, *621*
Paetz, Oblt. Albert, 7/KG 77 591
Palliardi, Oblt., I/KG 54 581
Pantel, Ofw. Gerhard, III/StG 3 350
Panz, Ofw. Rudolf, 6/KG 77 435
Paul, Uffz. Hugo, 3/KGr 806 169
Pauli, Obgfr. Rudolf, 8/KG 54 592
Penske, Lt. Artur, KuFlGr 606 333
Pester, Fw. Rolf, I/KG 77 617
Pfeifer, Uffz. Walter, KuFlGr 606 393
Pfeiffer, Uffz. Heinz, 5/LG 1 157
Philipp, Lt. Siegfried, 7/KG 54 548
Pilz, Uffz. Franz, 5/JG 53 *163*, 163
Platen, Oblt. Georg Graf von 168
Plewinski, Ofw. Oskar, KGr 806 376
Pohl, Fw. Otto, I/JG 77 381, 663
Pohler, Fw. Winfried, KuFlGr 606 376
Pohlein, Uffz. Simon, 3/JG 77 407, 418, 670
Polenz, Fw. Otto, III/ZG 26 39
Ponec, Lt. Karl-Heinz, Stab II/JG 3 81, 669
Preu, Lt. Karl-Heinz, Stab/JG 53 59, 435, 436, 670
Prokesch, Uffz. Johannes, I/KG 806 270
Pruger, Oblt. Walter, KuFlGr 606 393
Pufahl, Oblt. Wilfred, 7/JG 53 180, 659

Quaet-Faslem, Oblt. Klaus, I/JG 53 180, 188, 204, 661
Quaritsch, Lt. Karl-Heinz, 8/JG 53 204, 217, *253*, 257, 265, 270, 285, 349, 350, 652, 658, 660
Queisser, Uffz. Herbert, KGr 806 398

Raab, Oblt. Hermann, 10/JG 53 103
Raben, Uffz. Heinrich, 5/JG 3 61
Raeder, Grand-Admiral Erich, C-in-C, German Navy 228, 677
Rahlmeier, Fw. Heinz, 8/JG 53 115, 660, 670
Ramcke, Maj-Gen. Bernhard, Brigade Ramcke 677, 678
Rastinnes, Uffz. Walter, 7/StG 3 260
Rauer, Uffz. Walter, 7/StG 3 260
Reibel, Fw. Ludwig, 1/JG 53 187, 188
Reimers, Obfw. Gustav, 3/KGr 806 152
Reinhold, Fw. Karl, Seenotst 6 230
Remmer, Lt. Hans, I/JG 27 566, 617
Richter, Fw. Heinz, III/ZG 26 216
Riedel, Lt. Heinz, Stab/JG 53 406
Riegel, Uffz. Hermann, III/StG 3 350
Ritter, Lt. Karl-Erich, KGr 806 471
Ritterbusch, Uffz. Erhard, II/JG 53 258, 260
Röbling, Maj. Horst, II/KG 100 607
Rockel, Obgfr. Xaver, KuFlGr 606 376
Roehrig, Lt. Hans, 3/JG 53 613
Rökker, Lt. Heinz, I/NG 2 362
Rollwage, Ofw. Herbert, II/JG 53 33, 188, 216, 256, 258, 267, 381, 392, 395, 396, 402, 404, 414, 419, 437, 461, *462*, 632, 637, 652, 660
Rommel, Feldmarschall Erwin, C-in-C, Afrika Korps 17, 18, 19, 55, 158, 228, 229, 285, 318, 517, 521, 540, 545, 548, 554, 559, 564, 573, 639, 646
Rosenbaum, Kaptltn, *U-73* 468
Rosenberg, Ofw. Heinrich, 9/JG 27 355
Rosenfeldt, Lt. Horst, 5/KG 77 192
Rosenkranz, Oblt., Luftnachrichten Regt 200 22
Rothmann, Lt. Johannes, I/KG 54 152
Rottenbecher, Uffz. Fritz, 4/KG 77 438
Rottmann, Oblt. Hans, KG 54 684
Ruge, Lt. Wilhelm, 5/JG 53 308, 670
Rutschmamm, Fw. Otto, 8/KG 77 422

Sack, Lt. Siegfried, I/KG 54 421
Sattler, Lt. Georg, I/LG 1 95, 357
Sauer, Uffz. Dr. Felix, 10/JG 53 141, 155, *155*, 175, 273, *274*, 680, 681, 682, 683
Sauer, Fw. Heinz, I/JG 77 418, 670
Schade, Fw. Hans, 8/JG 53 116, 159, 160, 653, 660, 670
Schael, Uffz. Willi, 2/KG 77 591
Schäfer, Uffz. Heinrich, 8/StG 3 260
Schaller, Lt. Wolfgang, 9/JG 53 *113*, *253*, 257, 658, 660
Scheffl, Gfr. Franz, 10/JG 53 175
Scheib, Lt. Wilhelm, 1/JG 77 558, 591, 671
Scheller, Lt. Hans, 2/KG 54 581
Schennel, Fw. Johen, I/JG 77 663
Schierning, Uffz. Helmut, 6/JG 53 245, 670
Schierz, Uffz. Joachim, 5/KG 77 405
Schiess, Lt. Franz, Stab/JG 53 *58*, 58, 59, 95, 96, 342, 414, 419, *420*, 533, *533*, 578, 622, 652, 661
Schimrosczyk, Obgfr. Engelhardt, 6/KG 77 518
Schirmbeck, Uffz. Werner, 1/LG 1 477, 478, 480
Schlang, Oblt. Josef, I/JG 27 590
Schleich, Uffz. Georg, III/ZG 26 225, 670
Schleif, Lt. Felix-Dieter, 4/NJG 2 44, 669
Schlick, Uffz. Horst, I/JG 77 381, 405, 426, 553, 578, 652, 663
Schlitt, Uffz. Herbert, 9/KG 77 402
Schlüter, Uffz. Horst, 8/JG 53 659
Schmelcher, Obgfr. Siegfried, 3/KG 54 169
Schmidt, Fw. Rudolf, 7/JG 53 185, 211, 346, 659
Schmidt, Uffz. Walter, 6/JG 53 463
Schmidt, Hpt. Wilhelm, 3/KG 54 98, 221
Schmiedgen, Uffz. Hans-Joachim, 2(F)/122 504
Schmitt, Uffz. Johann, 2/KG 54 581
Schneider, Uffz. Ernst, 3/KGr 806 308
Schneider, Uffz. Fritz, I/JG 77 554
Schneider, Uffz. Kurt, 2(F)/122 685
Schnez, Oblt. Viktor, KGr 806 31, 58
Schow, Lt. Werner, 1/JG 53 178
Schrader, Lt. Werner, 3/KGr 806 219, 376
Schramm, Lt. Herbert, 8/JG 53 80, 659, 660
Schreiber, Uffz. Wilhelm, 6/KG 77 212
Schuck, Ofw. Wilhelm, 5/KG 100 592
Schulte-Rebbelmund, Uffz. Hermann, 2/KG 54 581
Schultz, Oblt. Ernst-Albrecht, I/JG 53 191
Schultz, Oblt. Wolfgang, 9/KG 54 500
Schulz, Oblt. Albert, I/NJG 2 359
Schulz, Oblt. Heinz, I/NJG 2 111, 670
Schulz, Obgfr. Herbert, 2/KGr 806 219
Schumacher, Lt. Ewald, 4/JG 53 578, 671
Schumacher, Oblt. Hans, I/KG 54 50
Schümann, Uffz. Heinz, 6/JG 53 361, 670
Schwaiger, Uffz. Franz, II/JG 3 662
Schwarz, Uffz. Emil, 1(F)/122 327
Schwartz, Uffz. Walter, 9/JG 53 91, 660, 670
Schweinsteiger, Lt. Anton, 2/KGr 806 259
Schwengers, Uffz. Jürgen, III/StG 3 214
Schwerdt, Fw. Günther, I/KGr 806 269
Sedlmaier, Uffz. Heinrich, 5/JG 53 312
Seefeld, Obfw. Erich, 4/KG 77 529
Seibt, Obgfr Erwin, II/KG 77 621
Seidel, Fw. Ernst-Hans, 8/JG 53 288, 660, 670
Seidl, Fw. Alfred, 8/JG 53 180, 224, 265, 355, 658, 660
Seidl, Gfr. Josef, 8/StG 3 178
Seiler, Uffz. Kurt, 2(F)/122 470
Seiz, Lt. Walter, 3/JG 53 120, 204
Seuber, Uffz. Ulrich, 9/KG 54 592
Skrdla, Lt. Leo, 3/KGr 806 426
Slany, Ofw. Heinrich, I/SchG 2 643, 671
Sommer, Ofw. Hermann, 4/NJG 2 54
Soukop, Lt. Herbert, 6/JG 53 74, 231, 271, 652, 653, 661
Spies, Hpt. Walter, II/JG 53 19
Spix, Obgfr. Hans, 1(F)/122 143
Stadermann, Lt. Waldemar, 6/KG 77 84
Stahlschmidt, Lt. Hans-Arnold, I/JG 27 350, 566
Stahnke, Fw. Karl-Heinz, 4/KGrzbV.500 39
Stamp, Lt. Gerd, II/LG 1 143, *209*, 352
Stein, Maj. Kurt, III/KG 54 591
Steinhausen, Obfw. Günther, I/JG 27 566
Steinicke, Lt. Karl-Heinz, II/JG 3, *234*
Steppmacher, Oblt. Günther, 1(F)/122 274
Stockmann, Fw. Gerhard, 2/JG 53 608
Stockmann, Fw. Hans, 2/JG 53, 112, 113
Streubel, Fw. Helmut, 9/KG 77 464
Stroehla, Uffz. Paul, 5/JG 53 591, 671
Student, General Kurt 158, 627, 678
Stumpf, Ofw. Werner, 9/JG 53 113, *113*, *122*, 122, 127, 265, 270, 285, 349, 652, 659, 660
Suchlich, Gefr. Helmut, 8/StG 3 162

Tegelmann, Uff. Ernst, KuFlGr 606 376
Thiel, Fw. Georg, 9/KG 54 601
Thomas, Lt. Erich, 2/JG 53 564
Thurz, Oblt. Herbert, 2/JG 77 380
Timmermann, Uffz. Walter, I/JG 27 580, 670
Tonne, Lt. Wolfgang, 3/JG 53 564
Toula, Lt. Herbert, 1(F)/122 297
Tronicke, Lt. Werner, KGr 806 496

Vanis, Uffz. Franz, 2/KG 54 581
Vogel, Ofw. Alfred, I/NJG 2 174, 670
Vogel, Uffz. Wolfgang, 6/JG 3 84
Vogt, Fw. Werner, 1/LG 1 480
Volkmann, Lt. Paul, III/KG 77 383
Vollstedt, Fw. Heinz, KuFlGr 606 418

Wagner, Uffz. Heribert, 5/JG 53 633, 671
Wallenberger, Uffz. Anton, I/KG 77 617
Warkalla, Lt. Johannes, 2/KG 54 259
Weber, Gfr. Fritz, III/StG 3 233
Weber, Lt. Horst, MTB *S55* 353
Wegmann, Uffz. Benedikt, 5/JG 53 102
Wegmann, Fw. Günther, III/ZG 26 43, 547, 549, 663
Wehmeyer, Lt. Alfred, III/ZG 26 39, 80
Wehner, Uffz. Otmar, I/KG 77 617
Westphalen, Uffz. Albert, III/StG 3 239
Wicklaus, Lt. Rudolf, 4/JG 3 149
Wiedow, Lt. Georg, 4/NJG 2 54, 350
Wilbertz, Ofw. Peter, KGr 806 393
Wilcke, Hpt. Wolf-Dietrich, Stab III/JG 53 19, *58*, 164, 213, 220, *253*, 265, 285, 652, 658, 659
Wilfer, Fw. Anton, II/LG 1 594
Witschke, Uffz. Karl-Heinz, I/JG 77 443, 670
Witt, Lt. Hans-Georg, 4/LG 1 222
Witt, Fw. Herbert, 5/KG 77 135
Wittkausky, Lt., III/KG 54 582
Woas, Uffz., 2/KG 54 577, 614
Wittenberg, Lt. Günther, 3/KG 54 581
Wöhl, Ofw. Kurt, 9/KG 77 591
Wolenski, Uffz. Herbert, KGr 806 371
Wörner, Uffz. Albert, III/ZG 26 39, 183
Wuppermann, Lt., MTB *S56* 353
Würzer, Fw. Christoph, 9/StG 3 169
Wutz, Uffz. Walter, 2/KG 54 581

Zellot, Lt. Walter, I/JG 53 205, *209*, 210
Zettelmaier, Uffz. Max, 8/KG 54 585, 591
Zielke, Uffz., 8/JG 53
Zimmer, Oblt. Josef, 7/KG 77 435

c) Vichy French

Andrea, Sgt., GC II/3, 282
Dupoy, Air France, 508
Farriol, Sgt. Chef, GC III/6, 283
Jeannaud, Adjt., GC II/6, 282
Meresse, Cmdt. Marceau, Air France, 465, 508
Michaux, Sgt., GC III/6, 282
Richard, Cte. Leon, GC III/6, 282, 283
Salaun, Lt., GC III/6, 282
Satge, Lt., GC III/6, 283

d) Japanese

Shinizu, Colonel, Imperial JAAF, 677
Abe, Admiral, Imperial Japanese Navy, 677

Air Force Units

I) Allied

RAF Units

201 Group 68, 144, 186, 639
Hal Far Wing 528, 568, 580
Luqa Wing 568, 606
Takali Wing 413, *517*, 528, 568
11 Squadron 53
14 Squadron 53, 123, 139, 348
18 Squadron 16, 28, 33, 36, 37
21 Squadron 37, 39, 50, 60, 63, 70, 73, 79, 89, 92
22 Squadron 128, 185, 186, 422
24 Squadron 181, 283, 377, 460, 545
37 Squadron 88, 90, 91, 95, 99, 100, 101, 102, 110, 111, 113, 115, 118, 120, 123, 127, 139, 679, 680
38 Squadron 53, 54, 55, 139, 291, 296, 298, 299, 326, 353, 366, 374, 376, 377, 446, 541, 638
39 Squadron 52, 53, 114, 155, 168, 170, 185, 354, 366, 370, 387, 422, 518, 568, 569, 580, 639
40 Squadron 13, 16, 28, 30, *32*, 41, 44, 88, 123
47 Squadron 637, 638
53 Squadron 36
55 Squadron 52
59 Squadron 36, 43, 44
69 Squadron 26, 28, 33, 37, 41, 47, 52, 62, 75, 81, 85, 88, 113, 124, 125, 126, *129*, 157, 158, 172, 185, 288, 316, 326, 342, 359, 362, 363, 370, *374*, 374, 377, 422, 440, 446, 456, 497, 499, 522, 524, 529, 530, 540, 544, 545, 548, 556, 558, 563, 568, 570, 571, 572, 596, 623, 624, 625, 626, 638
70 Squadron 114, 123
86 Squadron 412, 422, 430, 456, 518, 521
89 Squadron 110, 231, 251, 273, 277, 289, 293, 295, 296, 313, 321, 366, 370, 383, 410, 417, 424, 425, 428, 436, 438, 444, 457, 464, 520, 522, 533, 538, 541, 548, 557, 560, 562, 568, 570, *582*, 616, *619*, 622, 627, 628, 631, 632, 645, 651, 668
95 Squadron 90, 315
104 Squadron 28, 34, 37, 139, 291, 293, 296, 297, 298, 299, 300, 301, 303, 313, 377, 644, 645
107 Squadron 28, 33, 37
108 Squadron 139
113 Squadron 37, 39
117 Squadron 456, 520
126 Squadron 10, 15, *15*, 16, 26, *26*, 27, 29, 31-2, 39, *42*, 42-3, 46-7, *49*, 50, *51*, 56-8, *64*, *67*, *70*, 70-1, 77, *78*, *81*, 90-1, *93*, 94, *95*, 97, 104, 112, 115, 117, 122, 124-6, 134, *135*, 136, 141-3, 145, 149, 150-1, 156, 164, 167, 171, 196, 201, 204-5, 207, *208*, 209-10, 214-6, 219, *220*, 223-7, 235-8, 247, 249, 252, 255, 257-8, 260-4, 267, 269, 270-4, 280-1, 286, 289, 292, 296-7, 310-1, *311*, 315, 339, 343, 346, 360-1, *369*, 371, 374-5, 378, *379*, 383, 386, *387*, 389, 391, 394, 396-7, 399, 401-6, *407*, 409-11, 414-9, 421, 424-5, 427-9, 431-3, 435-6, 438, 444-6, 459-60, 462-4, 502, 504-5, 513, *516*, 520-2, 527, 530, 532, 534, *545*, 550, *553*, 554, 556, 559, 568, 574, 576-8, *579*, 584-6, 588, 594-5, 599, 600, 602, 605, 607-8, 612-3, *614*, 616-20, *621*, 626-7, 631-7, 643, 645, 650-1, 653, 664-7, 673-4
127 Squadron 123
138 Squadron 32
148 Squadron 123, 139, 207, 211, 213, 217, 221
159 Squadron 458, 475, 549
160 Squadron 353, 474
162 Squadron 558
185 Squadron 13-4, 27, 30, 32, 39, 46, 56-7, 64, 80, 90-2, 94, *94*, 96-8, *97*, 102-3, 110, 112, 115-7, *118*, 121, 125-7, 131, *135*, 136-7, 142-3, 146-8, *147*, 151, 159-60, *161*, 164-5, 167, 169, 171, 175, 177-8, 180, 185, 188, 202, 205-7, 212-4, *216*, 217, 219, 221, 223-4, 231, 233, 237-8, 246-9, 254, 252, 256, 259, 261, *261*, 262, 264-9, 271, 278, *280*, 286, 288-9, 291-4, 297, 299-300, 304, 307, *307*, 308, 312, 315-6, *318*, 344, *346*, 361, *362*, 365-6, *366*, 368, 374-5, 378, 381, 383-5, *387*, 390, *390*, 393-8, 402-3, 406, 408-9, 414, 418, 421, 424, *425*, 426-8, 432, 435, 437-8, 444-5, *448*, *450*, 456, 458, 461, 463, 497, 505, 517, 520-1, 530-2, 534, *536*, 547, 550, *551*, 552, 568, 570-1, 577-80, 583, 586, 588, 592, 594-5, 599, *600*, 601, *602*, 605, 608, 611, 612-4, 616, 619-20, 622, 628, 633, 643-4, 651, 665-7, 673-4
201 Squadron 452
202 Squadron 282, 309, 312, 324, 327, 417
203 Squadron 52, 53, 54, 155, 184, 185, 216, 354, 355, 456
217 Squadron 312, 353, 356, 357, 359, 362, 363, 387, 422, 430, 518
221 Squadron 184
227 Squadron (Halifax) 402
227 Squadron (Beaufighters) 522, *526*, *527*, 527, 540, 541, 548, 555, 557, 558, 560, 568, 571, 623, 668, 669
229 Squadron (Hurricanes) 155, 158, 160, 164, 168-70, 172, 175-7, 180-1, *182*, 188, 193, 201, 205, 207, 211, 215, 217-8, 220-1, 224-7, 235, *236*, 237-8, 244, 278-9, 294-5, *294*, *295*
229 Squadron (Spitfires) 456-60, 462, 502, 511, 514, 518, 520, 522, 527-8, 530-1, 533-4, 536, 541-3, *543*, 547, 552-5, 559-60, 568-70, 573-4, 576-81, *583*, 583, 585-9, *590*, 595-9, *590*, 595-6, *598*, 598-9, 601-2, 605, 607-8, *609*, 611, 614-7, 620, 627, *630*, 632-5, *634*, 637, 639, 642-3, 645, 651, 665-7, 673-4
230 Squadron 68
235 Squadron 312, 336, 343, 362, 363, 370, 412, 422, 430, 510, 518, 521, 522, 668
238 Squadron 349
240 Squadron 312, 332
242 Squadron 10, 16, 27, *30*, 33, 37, 42, 47, 50, 56, 57, 58, 71, 77, 84, 87, 93, 94, 99, 101, 102, 110, 111, 112, 116, 121, 124, 125, *160*, 451, 664, 665, 673, 674
248 Squadron 456, 463, 473, 479, 496, 497, 500, 507, 512, 522, 524, 525, 668
249 Squadron 15-6, 27, 31-2, 37, *38*, 41-2, 46-7, 50, 56-8, 70-1, 77, 87, 91, 94-5, 104, *106*, 110, *115*, *116*, 120, *124*, 127, 129, 131, 134, 136-7, 141, 145-6, *147*, 148, 152, *152*, 158-60, *161*, 167, 171-5, 177, 185, *189*, 196, 201-4, 207-11, *212*, 217, 221, 227, 230, 232-5, 239-40, 245, 247-50, 252, 254, 256-7, 259-60, 262-4, 266, *266*, 267, 270-1, 273-8, *278*, 280, 286-7, *289*, 289, *291*, 292-3, 300, 303-6, *305*, *306*, 308, 312, 315, 340, 344, 367, 373, 375-6, 378, 384-5, *385*, 388-9, 392, 394-6, *397*, 399, 401-8, *410*, 411, 413-4, 419, *420*, 421, 424, 426, 433, *434*, 435-7, 443-4, 460-1, 463, 503-4, 515, 518, 520, 522, *523*, 527-8, 530-2, 534, 538, 541, 546-7, 550, 552-4, 558-62, *561*, *562*, 568, 570-1, 573-4, 578, *583*, 583, 586, 588, 593-6, 599, *603*, 603, 607-11, *610*, *612*, 614-6, 618, 620, *621*, 622, 628, *630*, 631, 633-4, 636-7, 640, 643, *644*, 650-1, 664-7, 673-4, 685
250 Squadron 13, 349, 358
252 Squadron13, 45, 82, 84, 88, 110, 123, 139, 144, 342, 350, 351, 358, 370, 429, 456, 497, 521, 522, 527, 638, 668
267 Squadron 182, 231, 522
272 Squadron 45, 139, 143, 149, 185, 350, 351, 352, 355, 357, 358, 429, 638, 644, 668
511 Squadron 642, 686
601 Squadron 10, *196*, 196, 198, 200-1, 217-9, 221, 223, 233-4, 250, 252, 255-6, 257, 261-3, 267, *268*, 269-70, 272, 276, 278, 286, 288-90, 292, 300, 303, 312, 326, 341-2, 345-6, *369*, 370-1, 374-5, 381, 651, 659, 665-6, 673-4
603 Squadron 10, 128, *197*, 197, 198, 200-1, 208-10, *212*, 217, 219, 223-6, 230, *232*, 235, 237, 239, 245, 248-50, 252, 254, 257-8, 261-2, 264, 266-7, 269, 271-3, 275-6, 291, 293, 304-5, 308, 310, 346, 367, 374-6, 382, 384, 389-94, 398-9, *400*, 402-8, 410-12, 414, 417-9, 421-2, 424, 430, 435-6, 442-5, 456, 651, 665-6, 673-4, 685
605 Squadron 10, 27, 33, 37, *38*, *40*, *46*, 64, 68, 77, 80, 85, 89, *89*, 90, 96, 97, 99, 102, 112, 125, 212, 664, 673, 674
1435 Squadron 458, 459, 461-4, 502, 504, 511, 517, 522, 527, 530, 532-3, 539, 543, *559*, 561-2, 568, 570, 572, 574, 576-8, 580, 585-6, 587-8, 594, 596, *597*, 601, 607-8, 612-4, 616, *617*, 618, *619*, 622, 627-8, 630-2, 636-7, 643-4, 651, 666-7, 673-4

3 Squadron, RAAF 138
5 Squadron, SAAF 349
10 Squadron, RAAF 87, 232, 237, 309, 324
15 Squadron, SAAF 638
458 Squadron, RAAF 88
459 Squadron, RAAF 350

1435 Flight 27, 47, 56, 57, 61, 68, 84, 85, 102, *103*, 110, 111, 118, *119*, 167, 171, 221, 222, 227, 235, 424, 426, 427, 428, 431, 432, 437, 438, 443, 444, 445, 456, 664, 665, 673
1442 Flight 107, 109
1443 Flight 166, 181, 211, 214
1444 Flight 181
SD Flight 14, 28, 31, 35, 53, 63, 211, 250, 291, 321, 370

Fleet Air Arm units

800X Flight 60
800 Squadron 451, 477, *477*, 478, 483, 491, 492, 669
801 Squadron (Sea Hurricane) 319, 320, 325, 327, 329, 334, 343, 451, 469, 477, 478, 479, 483, 493, 509, 669
801 Squadron (Seafire) 639, 640
804 Squadron 451
806 Squadron 451, 452, 483, *484*, *487*, 490, 641, 669
807 Squadron 109, 156, 281, 282, 319, 669
809 Squadron 451, 452, 466, 470, 471, 473, 477, 479, 483, 485, 488, 490, 491, 509, 669
812 Squadron 109
813 Squadron 319
813F Squadron 109, 281, 302, 319, 325, 327, 334, 451
815 Squadron 100
821 Squadron 92, 100, 117, 123
822 Squadron 639
823 Squadron 451
824 Squadron 319
826 Squadron 52, 54, 55
827 Squadron 452, 492
828 Squadron 14, 28, 47, *75*, 90, 92, *104*, 117, 137, 158, 222, 315, 321, 340, 378
830 Squadron 14, 28, 47, 158, 183, 222, 226, 315, 321, 340, 378
832 Squadron 451
880 Squadron 451, *452*, 446, 470, 471, *472*, 473, 477, 478, 479, 488, 492, 669
884 Squadron 451, 476, 483, 486, 488, 490, 509, 669
885 Squadron 451, *465*, 473, 477, 478, 483, 485, 490, 491, 492

Miscellaneous

2 PRU 28, 37, 40, 456, 457
15 OTU 124, 128
21 OTU 88
OADU 23, 30, 36, 43, 84, 88, 90, 96, 98, 113, 124, 157, 158, 167, 168, 181, 183, 281, 284, 287, 303, 573, 636
BOAC 26, 69, 104, 239, 277, 392
GC I 'Alsace' (FF) 349
Halvorson Detachment 354, 380
Squadron VF-71 (USN) 199, 200, 242, 249

Radar Units

241 AMES 24, 675
242 AMES 24, 676
501 AMES 24
502 AMES 24, 533
504 AMES 24
521 AMES 24

ASR Craft

HSL 100 43, 527, 570
HSL 107 27, 71, 75, 86, 99, 114, 117, 120, 127, 263, *263*, 287, 382, 385, 386, 421, 442, 464, 555
HSL 128 16, 27, 34, 71, 127, 164, 185, 188, 213, 235, 258, 263, 264, 265, 279, *280*, 288, 299, 361, 368, 376, 389, 392, 396, 398, 404, 411, 414, 418, 427, 445, 515, 518, 521, 522, 527, 531, 539, 543, 550, 555, 569, 571, 572, 585, 596
HSL 129 27, 56, 71, *72*
ST 338 86, 162, 439, 463, 614, 617

II: Axis

a) Regia Aeronautica

Squadriglie (where individually specified)

8ª Squadriglia (25° Gr., 7° St. BT/AS) 567
9ª Squadriglia (25° Gr., 7° St. BT/AS) 515, 567
14ª Squadriglia (4° Gr., 7° St. BT/AS) 166, 323, 389, 454
15ª Squadriglia (4° Gr., 7° St. BT/AS) 166, 323, 454
28ª Squadriglia (65° Gr., Aut. OA) 22, 323
30ª Squadriglia (76° Gr., Aut. OA) 21
40ª Squadriglia (76° Gr., Aut. OA) 21
50ª Squadriglia (38° Gr., 32° St. BT/AS) 486
55ª Squadriglia (30° Gr., 10° St. BT) 21, 166, 323, 454, 503, 567
56ª Squadriglia (30° Gr., 10° St. BT) 21, 166, 323, 454, 503, 510, 567
57ª Squadriglia (32° Gr., 10° St. BT) 21, 166, 323, 454, 567
58ª Squadriglia (32° Gr., 10° St. BT) 21, 166, 323, 454, *493*, *494*, 504, 567
59ª Squadriglia (33° Gr., 9° St. BT) 21, 285, 298, 322, 329, 454, 504, 562
60ª Squadriglia (33° Gr., 9° St. BT) 21, 285, 322, 329, *344*, *373*, 454, 567
62ª Squadriglia (29° Gr., 9° St. BT) 21, 322, 329, 372, 454
63ª Squadriglia (29° Gr., 9° St. BT) 21, 322, 329, 459, 511
73ª Squadriglia (9° Gr., 4° St. CT) 166, 225, 234, 653
76ª Squadriglia (7° Gr., 54° St. CT) 20, 166, 193, 322, 323, 502
84ª Squadriglia (10° Gr., 4° St. CT) 166, 264, 653, 671
86ª Squadriglia (7° Gr., 54° St. CT) 20, 166, 322, 323
90ª Squadriglia (10° Gr., 4° St. CT) 166, 193, 203, 671
91ª Squadriglia (10° Gr., 4° St. CT) 166, 271, 671

96ª Squadriglia (9° Gr., 4° St. CT) 166
97ª Squadriglia (9° Gr., 4° St. CT) 166, 238, 257, 671
98ª Squadriglia (7° Gr., 54° St. CT) 20, 166, 322, 323
115ª Squadriglia (76° Gr., Aut. OA) 21
118ª Squadriglia RM 453
124ª Squadriglia (65° Gr., Aut. OA) 22, 323
138ª Squadriglia RM 22, 322
139ª Squadriglia (82° Gr., Aut. RM) 440, 441, *442*
142ª Squadriglia RN 192
144ª Squadriglia (85° Gr., Aut. RM) 21, 284, 339, 361, 363, 568
146ª Squadriglia RM 22, 157, 417, 453, 475
150ª Squadriglia (2° Gr., Aut. CT) 300, *301*, 306, 312, 323, 334, *335*, 335, 453, 653, 671, 672
151ª Squadriglia (20° Gr., 51° St. CT) 371, 385, 392, *404*, 411, 427, 433, *434*, 554, 556, 576, 580, 653, 671, 672
152ª Squadriglia (2° Gr., Aut. CT) *279*, *305*, *306*, 307, 323, 334, 334, *335*, 393, 484, 653, 671
167ª Squadriglia (16° Gr., 54° St. CT) 21, 166, 322, 323
168ª Squadriglia (16° Gr., 54° St. CT) 21, 166, 322, 323
169ª Squadriglia (16° Gr., 54° St. CT) 21, 166, 322, 323
170ª Squadriglia (83° Gr., Aut. RM) 21, 85, 166, 187, 231, 247, 568, 645
171ª Squadriglia RM 85, 357, 568
173ª Squadriglia Aut. RST 21, 73, *74*, 166, 225, 323, 363, 379, 454, 568
184ª Squadriglia (83° Gr., Aut. RM) 21, 166, 370, 568
186ª Squadriglia (83° Gr., Aut. RM) 21, 56, 83, 284, 568
188ª Squadriglia RM 22, 322, 453
189ª Squadriglia (83° Gr., Aut. RM) 21, 166, 523, 568
197ª Squadriglia (85° Gr., Aut. RM) 21, 181, 560, 568
204ª Squadriglia (41° Gr., Aut. AS) 358
205ª Squadriglia (41° Gr., Aut. AS) 138, 144
208ª Squadriglia (101° Aut. Ba'T) 395
209ª Squadriglia (102° Gr., 5° St. Ba'T) 285, 297, 298, 323, 333, 336, *410*, 432, 454, 502, 507, 567
210ª Squadriglia (50° Gr., Aut. BT) 62, 166, 249, 272, 290, 304, 323
211ª Squadriglia (50° Gr., Aut. BT) 62, 166, 233, 257, 304, 323
212ª Squadriglia (51° Gr., Aut. BT) 22, 44, 309, 322, 325, 326, 327, 453, 475, 479, 482, 488
213ª Squadriglia (51° Gr., Aut. BT) 22, 309, 322, 326, 330, 453, 475, 476, 489
220ª Squadriglia (55° Gr., Aut. BT) 86, 166, 184, *274*
221ª Squadriglia (55° Gr., Aut. BT) 62, 166
235ª Squadriglia (60° Gr., 41° St. BT) 36
238ª Squadriglia (101° Gr., Aut. Ba'T) 395
239ª Squadriglia (102° Gr., 5° St. Ba'T) 285, 296, 297, 323, 333, 372, 376, 416, 432, 454, 493, 501, 512, 567
252ª Squadriglia (104° Gr., 46° St. BT/AS) 322, 329
253ª Squadriglia (104° Gr., 46° St. BT/AS) 322, 329, 331, 332
254ª Squadriglia (105° Gr., 46° St. BT/AS) 453
255ª Squadriglia (105° Gr., 46° St. BT/AS) 453, 474
256ª Squadriglia (108° Gr., 36° St. AS) 22, 177, 322, 326, 329, 453, *481*
257ª Squadriglia (108° Gr., 36° St. AS) 22, 177, 322, 329, 453
258ª Squadriglia (109° Gr., 36° St. AS) 22, 322, 453
259ª Squadriglia (109° Gr., 36° St. AS) 22, 322, 326, 328, 332, 453, 481
264ª Squadriglia (88° Gr., Aut. BT) 271, 323, 454, 515, 567
265ª Squadriglia (88° Gr., Aut. BT) 273, 286, 323, 454, 567
274ª Squadriglia Aut. BGR 301, 322, 377, 388
276ª Squadriglia (116° Gr., Aut. BT) 323
277ª Squadriglia (116° Gr., Aut. BT) 323, 361
278ª Squadriglia (132° Gr., Aut. AS) 21, 138, 139, 166, 323, 333, 454, 489, 567
279ª Squadriglia (131° Gr., Aut. AS) 139, 323, 358
280ª Squadriglia (130° Gr., Aut. AS) 22, 139, 140, 166, 177, 322, 329, 485, 508
281ª Squadriglia (132° Gr., Aut. AS) 323, 333, 339, 454, 489, 568
283ª Squadriglia (130° Gr., Aut. AS) 22, 166, 322, 329, 453, 474, *483*, 508
284ª Squadriglia (131° Gr., Aut. AS) 139, 323
287ª Squadriglia RM 22, 42, 157, 322, 328, 423, 453, 475
288ª Squadriglia RM 343, 357, 568
351ª Squadriglia (155° Gr., 51° St. CT) 285, 323, 384, *555*, 567, 580, 671
352ª Squadriglia (20° Gr., 51° St. CT) 371, 392, 401, 403, 550, *551*, 567, 595, 671, 672
353ª Squadriglia (20° Gr., 51° St. CT) 371, 394, 398, 567, 580, 671, 672
353ª Squadriglia (20° Gr., 51° St. CT) 371, 394, 398, 567, 580, 671, 672
354ª Squadriglia (24° Gr., Aut. CT) 22, 322, 333, 453
355ª Squadriglia (24° Gr., Aut. CT) 22, 322, 329, 331, 435, 453, 671
358ª Squadriglia (2° Gr., Aut. CT) 264, *264*, 293, 304, 323, 408, *409*, *410*, 653, 671, 672
359ª Squadriglia (22° Gr., Aut. CT) 551, 567
360ª Squadriglia (155° Gr., 51° St. CT) 14, 285, 300, 323, 368, 567, 580, 653
362ª Squadriglia (22° Gr., Aut. CT) 453, 482, 490, 513, 551, 567, 672
369ª Squadriglia (22° Gr., Aut. CT) 551, 567, 580, 622, 672
370ª Squadriglia (24° Gr., Aut. CT) 22, 322, 328, 453, 479
372ª Squadriglia (153° Gr., 53° St. CT) 567
373ª Squadriglia (153° Gr., 53° St. CT) 567
374ª Squadriglia (153° Gr., 53° St. CT) 567
377ª Squadriglia Aut. CT 21, 166, 323, 567
378ª Squadriglia (155° Gr., 51° St. CT) 285, 307, 312, 323, 375, 401, 405, *432*, 433, 567
607ª Squadriglia (149° Gr., 44° St. SAS) 69
612ª Squadriglia Aut. Socc 22, 276, 286, 307, 323, 454, 506, 568
613ª Squadriglia Aut. Socc 22, 323, 453

Gruppi (where no squadriglie specified)
2° Gruppo Aut. CT 257, 260, 263, 264, 269, 272, 276, 278, 286, 289, 291, 292, 293, 297, 300, 304, 305, *306*, 307, 323, 334, *335*, 339, 344, 367, *372*, 372, 375, 382, 384, 389, 392, 406, 453, 482, 489, 513, 551, 554, 622, 653, 671, 672
3° Gruppo (6° St. CT) 225
4° Gruppo (7° St. BT/AS) 166, 263, 271, 292, 297, 323, 340, 367, 382, 385, 388, 454
7° Gruppo (54° St. CT) 20, 166, 193, 322, 323, 329, 440, 515, 544, 671
9° Gruppo (4° St. CT) 165, 166, 230, 233, 238, 269
10° Gruppo (4° St. CT) 14, 165, 166, 193, 203, 210, 232, 238, 286
16° Gruppo (54° St. CT) 20, 166, 322, 323, 329
20° Gruppo (51° St. CT) 371, 379, 381, 389, 392, 394, 395, 397, 399, 402, 404, 405, 410, 411, 427, 433, 435, 489, 512, 567, 576, 578, 671
22° Gruppo Aut. CT 453, 551, 567, 578, 588, 622
24° Gruppo Aut. CT 22, 176, 322, 326, 329, 331, 332, 453, 474, 479, 481, 482, 486, 490, 508
25° Gruppo (7° St. BT) 567
29° Gruppo (9° St. BT) 21, 289, 322, 329, 330, 454
30° Gruppo (10° St. BT) 21, 166, 323, 454, 489, 505, 567
32° Gruppo (10° St. BT) 21, 166, 323, 454, 489, 493, 567
33° Gruppo (9° St. BT) 21, 285, 296, 297, 322, 329, *344*, *373*, 375, 384, 389, 454, 567, 592
38° Gruppo (32° St. BT/AS) 453, 481, 482, 483, 485
41° Gruppo Aut. BT/AS 148, 351
46° Gruppo CT 454
50° Gruppo Aut. BT 62, 166, 220, 222, 226, 230, 257, 286, 289, 304, 323
51° Gruppo Aut. BT 22, 322, 326, 453, 475, 511
55° Gruppo Aut. BT 62, 111, 115, 118, 129, 166, 171, 182, 184, *274*, 277
65° Gruppo Aut. OA 22, 323, 453
76° Gruppo Aut. OA 21
83° Gruppo Aut. RM 21, 166, 568
85° Gruppo Aut. RM 21, 568
88° Gruppo Aut. BT 273, 286, 289, 323, 371, 372, 454, 458, 459, 515, 567, 631
89° Gruppo (32° St. BT/AS) 453, 481
97° Gruppo Aut. Ba'T 285
101° Gruppo Aut. Ba'T 285, 395
102° Gruppo (5° St. Ba'T) 285, 323, 333, 336, 372, 375, *391*, 391, 395, 417, 430, 437, 443, 454, 489, 493, 494, 501, 503, 507, 511, 539, 558, 567, 630
104° Gruppo (46° St. BT/AS) 322, 329, 330, 331, 332
105° Gruppo (46° St. BT/AS) 453, 481, 486, 505, 511
108° Gruppo (36° St. AS) 22, 322, 329, 331, 453
109° Gruppo (36° St. AS) 22, 322, 329, 332, 453, 486, 511
116° Gruppo Aut. BT 301, 323, 361, 372, 386
130° Gruppo Aut. AS 22, 138, 166, 322, 325, 329, 331, 332, 453, 474, 481, 486, 490, 511
131° Gruppo Aut. AS 323
132° Gruppo Aut. AS 323, 333, 335, 454, 489, 494, 497, 503, 511, 567
149° Gruppo SAS 13, 14
153° Gruppo CT 453, 474, 481, 490, 567, 585, 586, 588, 594, 596, 605, 610, 619, 628, 635
155° Gruppo (51° St. CT) 14, 285, 299, 300, 304, 305, 307, 312, 323, 341, 367, 371, 375, 382, 394, 395, 397, 404, 406, 408, *410*, 410, 412, 430, 433, 489, 539, 567, 576, 578
160° Gruppo Aut. CT 61

Stormi (where no gruppi specified)
4° Stormo CT 14, 165, 166, 222, 225, 226, 257, 260, 262, 263, 271, 272, 281, 285, 652, 663
5° Stormo Ba'T 285, 395
7° Stormo BT 454, 515, 567
9° Stormo BT 30, 34, 62, 285, 322, 332, 333, 372, 386, 392, 394, 397, 454, 458, 515, 567
10° Stormo BT 21, 166, 323, 379, 417, 454, 510, 567
32° Stormo BT/AS 453, 511
36° Stormo AS 22, 138, 322, 326, 328, 332, 453, 474, 481, 486, 490
45° Stormo SAS 530
46° Stormo BT/AS 322, 453
51° Stormo CT 14, 285, 371, 375, 379, 382, 386, 388, 391, *404*, 406, *404*, 436, 437, 444, 454, 460, 494, 501, 502, 503, 511, 512, 546, 566, 584, 586, 588, 590, 592, 595, 596, 601, 605, 608, 610, 619, 620, 628, 631, 632, 635, 653, 663
53° Stormo CT 567
54° Stormo CT 14, 20, 69, 73, 166, 193, 291, 312, 322, 323, 334, 340, 379, 384, 454, 521

Other formations
Aeronautica della Sicilia 323
Aeronautica della Sardegna 322
Comando Caccia (Reparto Volo) 323
2° Nucleo AS 333, 342, 343, 453, 481
3° Nucleo AS 453, 481, 490, 506
Nuclei Caccia Notturno 567
Sezione Speciale 482, 487, 508

b) Luftwaffe

Stab (Staff Flights where specified)
Stab/JG 53 *16*, *19*, *57*, *58*, 59, *60*, 80, *95*, 96, 113, 126, 127, 162, 239, 261, 324, 342, *380*, 404, 406, 414, 419, *420*, 435, 455, 533, *533*, 565, 578, 591, 622, 646, 652, 670
Stab III/JG 53 220, 226, 249, 265, 659
Stab/KG 54 30, 314, 455, 564, 565
Stab/KG 77 20, 371, 379, 455, 565
Stab III/KG 77 140, 202

Staffeln (where specified)
1/LG 1 480
2/LG 1 480
4/LG 1 183, 222, *351*, 479, *480*
5/LG 1 157, 214, 219, 348, 480, 611
6/LG 1 480
ErgSt/StG 1 79, 82
2/NJG 2 85
3/NJG 2 670
4/NJG 2 19, 34, 35, 44, 54, 60, 92, 669
4/JG 3 135, 149
5/JG 3 61, 151
6/JG 3 61, 126, 130, 171
3/StG 3 511
6/StG 3 349
7/StG 3 146, 162, 167, 258, 260
8/StG 3 162, 178, 260
9/StG 3 165, 169, 174
Seenotst 6 20, 113, 174, 230, *275*, 275, 276, 455, 479, 512, 513
6/KG 26 455, 470, 488, 495, 499
7/KG 26 43
8/ZG 26 92, 455, 495, 670
9/ZG 26 132, 670
10/ZG 26 361
10(Jabo)/JG 27 565
1/JG 53 102, 178, 180, 187, 205, 564, 611, 613, 615
2/JG 53 102, 112, 204, 564, 604, 608
3/JG 53 204, 564, *597*, 613, 615, 670
4/JG 53 32, 183, 213, 268, 279, 373, 397, 543, 578, 591, 627, 633, 652, 669, 670, 711
5/JG 53 71, 99, 102, 160, *163*, 163, 189, 204, 216, 217, 276, 308, 312, 365, 591, 606, 633, 652, 670, 671
6/JG 53 71, 74, 75, 99, 110, 172, 178, *179*, *206*, 216, 230, 231, 245, 271, 361, 436, 459, 463, 535, 559, *559*, 633, 652, 669, 670
7/JG 53 102, 120, 129, 176, 180, 185, 188, 211, 216, 226, 265, 281, 285, 346, 350, 659, 670
8/JG 53 79, 86, 110, 115, 116, 121, 122, 137, 159, 173, *176*, 176, 178, 180, 185, 204, 211, 214, 217, 219, 221, 224, 226, 238, 265, 285, 355, 489, 652, 658, 660, 670
9/JG 53 91, 99, 113, *113*, *122*, 122, 192, 212, 218, 265, 281, 285, 288, 652, 660, 670
10(Jabo)/JG 53 82, 94, 100, 101, 103, 141, 145, 155, *155*, 168, 175, 226, *272*, 273, *274*, *365*, 565, 670, 680
1/KG 54 224, 259, 581
2/KG 54 73, 117, 259, 273, 581, 614
3/KG 54 143, 170, 221, 581, 601
7/KG 54 548, 591

8/KG 54 585, 591, 592
9/KG 54 500, 581, 592, 601
1/JG 77 380, *566*, 588, 591, 670, 671
2/JG 77 380, 431, 500, *556*, 562, *597*, 628, 652, 670
3/JG 77 380, 553, 652, 670
4/KG 77 117, 205, 222, 388, 394, 403, 438, 510, 511, 529, 536, 620
5/KG 77 39, 61, 117, 135, 168, 192, 394, 405, 518, 536, 620
6/KG 77 84, 113, *114*, 119, 125, 173, 181, 212, 391, 435, 438, 518
7/KG 77 77, 80, 128, 401, 435, 583, 591
8/KG 77 56, 72, 99, 177, 422, 487, 502, 534, 536, 627
9/KG 77 147, 214, 402, 464, 591, 594
5/KG 100 592
7/KG 100 583
1(F)/122 143, 274, 297, 303, 324, 325, 327, 363, 383, 437, 455, 466, 475, 510, 565
2(F)/122 20, 61, 363, 364, 455, 466, 470, 504, 685
2(F)/123 469
2(F)/124 347, 348
4/KGrzbV 500 39

1/KuFlGr 606 89, 118, 143, 192, 316
2/KuFlGr 606 102, *103*, 313
3/KuFlGr 606 125, 128
5/KuFlGr 606 474
1/KGr 806 259, 267, 544
2/KGr 806 70, 219, 259
3/KGr 806 121, 143, 152, 169, 192, 219, 238, 308, 425

Gruppen (where Staffeln not specified)
I/LG 1 91, 95, 116, 123, 129, 136, *209*, 290, 347, 348, 357, 358, 455, 477, 479, 503
II/LG 1 143, 212, 347, 455, 477, 479, 500, 503, 536, 564, 565, 578, 592, 595, 619, *621*, 628, 629
I/NJG 2 16, 45, 111, 118, 130, 174, 285, 287, 300, 350, 359, 362, 455, 646, 669, 670
I/SchG 2 565, 608, 614, 634, 635, 637, 643, 671
II/JG 3 19, 61, 81, 84, 85, 91, 116, 148, 171, 189, *190*, *234*, 285, 646, 661, 669, 670
I/StG 3 455, 489, 491, 493, 503
II/StG 3 20, 349, 350, 357
III/StG 3 20, 146, 148, 149, 151, 163, 168, 181, 183, 214, *222*, 233, 238, 252, 260, 266, 285, 350, 357
III/ZG 26 19, 39, 41, 43, 52, 80, 92, 99, 130, 131, *133*, 181, 186, 188, 216, 225, 285, *493*, 495, 546, 549, 646, 663, 670
I/JG 27 350, 474, 565, 580, 590, 601, 602, 606, 617, 619, 627, 637, 646, 658, 670, 671
III/JG 27 354, 355, 662
I/JG 53 19, *58*, 59, 102, 164, 180, 188, 191, 202, 204, 205, 207, *209*, 210, 285, 564, 565, 565, 603, 604, 609, 611, 646, 659, 661
II/JG 53 19, 31, 32, 33, 59, *62*, 71, 73, 99, 102, 128, 180, 188, 205, 216, 256, 257, 258, *258*, 260, 267, 271, 281, 285, 288, 302, 306, 308, 312, 380, 381, 392, 394, 396, *397*, 401, 403, 414, 419, 437, 443, 455, 459, 461, *462*, *463*, 517, 536, 543, 547, *565*, 565, *566*, 585, 587, 601, 603, 607, 632, *634*, 635, 637, 646, 652, 660, 661
III/JG 53 19, *58*, 79, 99, 116, 120, *126*, 127, 129, 159, 164, 176, 178, 211, 213, 234, *252*, *253*, 257, 265, 270, 281, 285, 349, 350, 351, 354, 371, 637, 646, 652, 658
I/KG 54 20, 50, 93, 100, 101, 113, 115, 116, 126, 127, 130, 151, 152, 259, 285, 337, 340, 347, 352, 358, 363, 421, 455, 525, 564, 565, 576, 580, 581, 601, 617, 622
II/KG 26 *501*
III/KG 54 564, 565, 580, 581, 583, 591
I/JG 77 371, 380, *380*, *381*, 394, 399, *400*, 402, 403, 404, 405, 406, 418, 419, 422, 426, 427, 432, 436, 443, 455, 482, 550, 553, 554, 555, 561, 565, *566*, 571, 572, 573, 578, *593*, 593, 594, 595, 596, 601, 606, 620, 622, 628, 637, 646, 652, 662, 686
I/KG 77 120, 123, 159, 564, 565
II/KG 77 20, 39, 73, 84, 100, 116, 118, 123, 128, 129, 130, 159, 160, 163, 228, 371, 379, 394, 401, 410, 438, 455, 518, 534, 564, 565, 618, *621*
III/KG 77 20, 56, 100, 115, 116, 130, 177, 228, 285, 371, 379, 383, 384, 435, 455, 534, 564, 565, 580, 582, 594, 628
II/KG 100 565, 607, 638
Aüfklgr 122 379, 510
KuFlGr 606 20, 47, 100, 126, 128, 130, 135, 142, 173, 192, 204, 236, 285, 304, 324, 333, 334, 340, 343, 345, 376, 379, 393, 413, 418, 422, 455, 517, 564
KGr 806 20, 31, 79, 97, 100, 101, 126, 130, 135, 168, 204, 219, 238, 259, 269, 270, 285, 296, 315, 324, 336, 371, 376, 379, 388, 393, 398, 428, 444, 455, 471, 495, 496, 517, 564

Geschwadern (where Gruppen not specified)
LG 1 285, 351, 352, 504
JG 27 144, 171
JG 53 25, 46, 47, 186, 211, 404, 606, 616, 646
KG 54 72, 351, 482, 495, 618, 684
KG 77 46, 72, 482, 495, 595, 616, 619

Other formations
Luftflotte 2
II Fliegerkorps 19, 22, 61, 79, 83, 92, 127, 138, 228, 379, 455, 489
XI Fliegerkorps 158
'Freya' radar 23, 24
'Dete' radar 352
Operation 'Hercules' 228, 229
Kampffliegerschule 1
I/Flakrgt 46 557
Luftnachtrichtenregt 23, 200

c) Vichy French

Fighter units
GC II/3 282
GC III/6 282
Aeronawafe Esc 1AC 465

Naval Units and Ships

a) Allied

Codenames
Operation 'Baritone' 519
Operation 'Bellows' 467, 468
Operation 'Berserk' 452
Operation 'Bowery' 230, 240, *242*, 243, 251, *261*
Operation 'Calendar' 198, 200, 241
Operation 'Crusader' 18
Operation 'Harpoon' 319, 321, 322, 324, 448
Operation 'Insect' 423
Operation 'LB' 281, 283
Operation 'Pedestal' 449, 465, *469*, *472*, *480*, *486*, *495*, *496*, *501*, 515, 517, 518, 647, 655
Operation 'Picket I' 133, 138
Operation 'Picket II' 156
Operation 'Pinpoint' 415
Operation 'MF8' 122
Operation 'Rembrandt' 349
Operation 'Salient' 310
Operation 'Stonehenge' 647
Operation 'Style' 301, 302
Operation 'Torch' 644
Operation 'Train' 639, 640, *641*
Operation 'Vigorous' 321, 347, 348, 357, 371, 448
Ultra 29, 34, 35, 37, 39, 52, 111, 113, 158, 184, 221, 228, 429, 521, 539, 639
Y Service 24, 79, 239, 394, 427, 557

Naval Forces
Force 'B' 83, 84
Force 'F' 450, 495
Force 'H' 109, 319, 450
Force 'K' 46, 57, 77, 83, 138, 141
Force 'W' 199, 201, 240, 324, 336
Force 'X' 319, 336, 337, 450, 493, 495, 509, 510
Force 'Y' 475
Force 'Z' 450

Naval Units
2nd Destroyer Flotilla 347
3rd Motor Launch Flotilla 450
4th Cruiser Squadron 347
5th Destroyer Flotilla 347
6th MTB Flotilla 319
7th Destroyer Flotilla 347
10th Submarine Flotilla 48, 91, 128, 184, 225, 450
12th Destroyer Flotilla 347
14th Destroyer Flotilla 347
15th Cruiser Squadron 347
17th Minesweeper Flotilla 319, 450
22nd Destroyer Flotilla 347

Aircraft carriers
HMS *Argus* 109, 134, 156, 281, 282, 319, 320, 324, 325, 327, 328, 329, 330, 332, 333, 334, 336, 343, 450, 451, 452, 669, 674
HMS *Ark Royal* 14, 270, 467
HMS *Eagle* 103, 108, 109, 133, 134, 156, 195, 197, 240, *242*, *243*, 244, 281, 283, 284, 301, 302, 310, 311, 319, 320, 324, 325, 327, 330, 331, 333, 415, 417, 423, 450, 451, 452, 468, 469, *469*, 475, 494, 674, 675
HMS *Formidable* 319
HMS *Furious* 450, 451, 467, *467*, 468, 469, 470, 475, 494, 519, 532, 639, 640, *641*, 675
HMS *Illustrious* 319, 655
HMS *Indomitable* 319, 450, 451, *452*, 452, 468, 469, *469*, 470, 472, 473, 476, *477*, 477, *484*, 487, 488, 490, 491, 492, 493, 494, 520, 641, 669
HMS *Victorious* 450, 451, 452, *465*, 465, 466, 469, *469*, 470, 471, 472, 473, 476, 477, 479, 483, 487, 488, 490, 491, 492, 493, 494, 495, 669
USS *Wasp* (American) 195, *196*, *197*, 198, *199*, 200, 201, 230, 239, 240, *242*, 242, *243*, 244, 245, *247*, 249, 251, 277, 283, 492, 674, 685

Battleships
HMS *Centurion* 347, 351, 357
HMS *Malaya* 109, 319, 324, 328, 336
HMS *Nelson* 450, 486, 487
HMS *Rodney* 450, 487, 493
HMS *Warsprite* 230, 319

Battlecruiser
HMS *Renown* 230

Cruisers
HMS *Arethusa* 357
HMS *Birmingham* 357
HMS *Cairo* (AA) 309, 319, 324, 336, 337, 338, 344, 450, 487, 495
HMS *Carlisle* (AA) 45, 83, 141
HMS *Charybdis* 230, 281, 301, 309, 319, 450, 492, 494, 495, 500
HMS *Cleopatra* 77, 79, 140, 347
HMS *Coventry* (AA) 349, 350, 352, 357, 358, 553
HMS *Dido* 122
HMS *Euryalus* 122, 140, 141, 347
HMS *Hermione* 109, 359
HMS *Kenya* 319, 450, 492, 498, 510, 511
HMS *Liverpool* 319, 330, 332, 333
HMS *Manchester* 450, 471, 498, 505, 507
HMS *Newcastle* 353
HMS *Nigeria* 450, 471, 495, 508
HMS *Penelope* 83, 138, 140, 142, 167, 168, 171, 172, 173, 176, 177
HMS *Phoebe* 450
HMS *Sirius* 450

Minelayer-cruiser
HMS Welshman 251, 252, 256, 319, 325, 337, 344, 347, 417

Destroyers
HMS *Airdale* 357
HMS *Antelope* 332
HMS *Ashanti* 495, 496, 500, 501
HMS *Badsworth* 340, 346
HMS *Bedouin* 337, 339
HMS *Bicester* 495
HMS *Blankney* 344, 345
HMS *Bramham* 487, 496, 499, 503, 506, 507, 514
HMS *Coltsfoot* 324
HMS *Decoy* 79
HMS *Derwent* 495
HMS *Eridge* 142
HMS *Eskimo* 495, 499
HMS *Foresight* 480, 494
HMS *Fortune* 77
HMS *Fury* 480
HMS *Gallant* 174
HMS *Hasty* 353
HMS *Havock* 45, 171
HMS *Hythe* 334
HMS *Icarus* 330
HMS *Isis* 282, 283
HMS *Jackel* 290
HMS *Jervis* 290
HMS *Kingston* 167, 171, 172, 173, 181
HMS *Kipling* 290
HMS *Laforey* 469, 480
HMS *Lance* 171, 174
HMS *Ledbury* 452, 477, 500, 505, 512, 514
HMS *Legion* 138, 150
HMS *Lightning* 486
HMS *Lively* 290
HMS *Lookout* 469
HMS *Maori* 79
HMS *Marne* 337
HMS *Matchless* 334, 337, 346
HMS *Nestor* 357
HMS *Partridge* 337, 339
HMS *Pathfinder* 477, 484, 495, 503
HMS *Penn* 496, 499, 506, 514
HMS *Somali* 495
HMS *Southwold* 142, 145
HMS *Tartar* 496, 503
HMS *Vidette* 326
HMS *Westcott* 326, 470
HMS *Wishart* 466
HMS *Wolverine* 475
HMS *Wrestler* 330
HMS *Zetland* 493
HMS *Zulu* 83
HMAS *Waterhen* 663
HMCS *Ithuriel* 337, 489, 490
Kujawiak (Polish) 346

Submarines
HMS *P 31* 225
HMS *P 34* 225
HMS *P 35* 225
HMS *P 36* 84, 86, 133, 163
HMS *P 38* 82, 91
HMS *P 39* 101, 150
HMS *Pandora* 163
HMS *Porpoise* 518

HMS *Thrasher* 184, 547
HMS *Triton* 348
HMS *Umbra* 69, 353, 541, 624
HMS *Una* 225, 475
HMS *Unbeaten* 48, 163
HMS *Unbending* 625
HMS *Unbroken* 500, 625
HMS *United* 520, 556
HMS *Unruffled* 557, 573
HMS *Upholder* 48, 184, 188
HMS *Upright* 75, 76
HMS *Urge* 184, 225
HMS *Utmost* 48, 573
HMS *Safari* 625
Glaucos (Greek) 171
Sokol (Polish) 128

Miscellaneous
HMS *Abingdon* (minesweeper) 163, 167, 168
HMS *Breconshire* (auxiliary) 57, 83, 138, 140, 141, 142, 145, 148, 149, 150, 151, 154, 171, 301
HMS *Hebe* (minesweeper) 334, 338, 340, 347
HMS *Jade* (anti-submarine trawler) 207
HMS *Primula* (corvette) 349
HMS *Rye* (minesweeper) 506
HMS *Sunset* (minesweeper/drifter) 163
HMT *Laconia* (transport) 632
RFA *Brown Ranger* (oiler) 319
RFA *Plumleaf* (oiler) 148, 150, 163, 514

Tugs
Ancient 145, 148, 150, 163
Beryl 145, 151
Jaunty 450, 469, 471
Robust 148, 151
Swona 151
West Dean 163
West 163

Convoys
MF 3 45
MG 3 446
MW 9 86
ME 10 83
MW 10 138, 227
MW 11 321
WS 21S 449

Allied merchant vessels
Aagtekerk (Dutch) 347, 349
Ajax 45, 83, 347
Almeria Lykes (US) 449, 496, 499
Bhutan 347, 351
Brisbane Star 449, 496, 499, 506, 509, 510, 511, 515
Bulkoil 347
Burdwan 319, 340
Cape Hawke 107, 108, 109
Chant (US) 319, 337
City of Calcutta 45, 83, 347, 349
City of Edinburgh 347
City of Lincoln 347
City of Pretoria 347
Clan Campbell 82, 138, 141, 142
Clan Chattan 82, 83
Clan Ferguson 45, 83, 449, 496, 498, 507
Deucalion 449, 487, 495, 496
Dorset 449, 499, 502, 503, 506
Elizabeth Bakke (Dutch) 347, 349
Empire Heath 685
Empire Hope 449, 496
Franco 236
Glengyle 46, 57
Glenorchy 449, 496, 498
Golly 171
Kentucky (tanker, US) 319, 338, 340
Melbourne Star 449, 499, 500, 506, 515
Ohio (tanker, US) 449, 495, 499, 501, 502, 504, 506, 507, 509, 511, 512, 514, *514*, 515, 518
Orari 319, 346, 475
Pampas 138, 142, 145, 148, 149, 150, 153, 154, 167
Port Chalmers 449, 499, 503, 506, 515
Potaro 347, 351
Rembrandt 347
Rochester Castle 449, 498, 499, 503, 515
Rowallan Castle 57, 82, 83
Santa Elisa (US) 449, 499
Talabot 138, 142, 145, 148, 149, 150, 153, 154, 157, 183
Tanimbar (Dutch) 319, 330
Thermopylae (Norwegian) 45
Troilus 319, 330, 338, 345, 346, 475
Waimarama 449, 499, 500, 512
Wairangi 449, 496, 499

Miscellaneous
Anna Dacoutros (schooner) 165
C-42 (petrol storage barge) 237, 238
Edith (lighter) 238
Royal Lady (Gozo ferry boat) 126, 236
Antwerp (rescue vessel) 351
Malines (rescue vessel) 351
S132 (fishing boat) 400

Army units
8th Army 564
4/Buffs 66
2/Devons 66
1/Hampshires 153
11/Lancashire Fusiliers 193
8/Manchesters 66
2/Royal Irish Fusiliers 66
2/Royal West Kents 66, 217
SAS/SBS 347, 348, 475
59th LAA Battery 570

b) Axis

i) Italian

Codenames
CRIRA (radio interception) 23, 24, 36, 43, 88, 157, 287, 298, 303
Servizio Alfa (warning system) 24, 386, 458, 515, 560

Naval units
3 Divisione (heavy cruiser) 455, 474, 499
7 Divisione (light cruiser) 455, 474, 499
10 Divisione (destroyer) 455
11 Divisione (destroyer) 455
13 Divisione (destroyer) 455
2 Squadriglia (MTB) 455
15 Squadriglia (MTB) 455
18 Squadriglia (MTB) 455
20 Squadriglia (MTB) 455
VII Divisione (destroyer) 337
13th Cruiser Squadron 52

Battleships
Caio Duilio 52, 84
Littorio 138, 140, 352, 354, 356, 359
Vittorio Veneto 352

Cruisers
Bolzano 455, 500
Eugenio di Savoia 337, 455
Garibaldi 352, 357
Giovanni Delle Bande Nere 138, 140
Gorizia 138, 352, 354, 357, 455
Muzio Attendolo 455, 497, 500
Raimondo Montecuccoli 337, 340, 455
Trento 138, 353
Trieste 455

Destroyers
Ascari 625
Aviere 522
Bombardiere 623
Camicia Nera 357, 522, 523
Carabiniere 84, 86
Da Noli 74
Da Recco 363, 364
Da Varazzano 387, 563, 625
Euro 387
Folgore 101, 680
Freccia 101, 549, 680
Fusiliere 549
Geniere 524
Gioberti 520
Legionario 352
Maestrale 520
Maloncello 101, 455, 520, 680
Pegaso 188
Premuda 74, 82
Usodimare 92, 115
Vivaldi 101, 337, 341, 680

Submarines
Alagi 455, 496, 498, 503
Ascianghi 455
Asteria 514
Avorio 455, 492
Axum 455, 495
Brin 455, 466, 480
Bronzo 455, 498, 507
Cobalto 455, 489
Dagabur 456, 466, 475
Dandolo 134, 455
Dessie 455, 503
Emo 456
Giada 326, 465, 466, 480, 481
Granito 456
Moncenigo 134, 281
Otaria 325, 456
Uarsciek 326, 456, 466, 475
Velella 201, 456
Veniero 309
Wolframio 456, 466
Zaffiro 311

MTBs
Abba 101, 680
Antares 544
Calatafimi 545
Calliope 36, 422
Cascino 35, 540
Castore 225, 563
Ciclone 522
Circe 91
Climene 522
Lupo 563
Medici 623
Orsa 68, 69, 422
Partenope 101, 680
Pegaso 524, 541
Polluce 115, 547
Sitori 546
Turbine 387
MS 16 455, 498
MS 22 455, 498
MS 23 455
MS 25 455
MS 26 455, 498
MS 31 455, 498
MAS 533 455
MAS 543 455
MAS 548 455
MAS 549 455
MAS 552 455, 499
MAS 553 455, 499
MAS 554 455, 499
MAS 556 455, 499
MAS 557 455, 499
MAS 560 455
MAS 562 455
MAS 563 455
MAS 564 455, 499
MTSM 214 281
MTSM 218 281

Convoys
Convoy 'Lambado' 548
Convoy 'D' 624, 625
Convoy 'J' 638
Convoy 'M 43' 34
Convoy 'N' 548
Convoy 'P' 548
Convoy 'T 18' 52

Merchant vessels
Abruzzi (tanker) 544
Albina 679
Alga 573
Allegri 113
Amsterdam 623, 624
Apuania 559
Arca (tanker) 638
Ariosto 82
Arno 679
Assunta de Gregori 679
Beppe 624, 625
Bertani 286
Brook 39, 429
Capo Orso 624
Carbonia (tanker) 555, 556, 557
Dandolo 573
Davìde Bianchi 546, 547
Delia 36
Dielpi 529, 530, 540
Epomeo 679
Etiopia 638
Etruria 679
Fougier 563
Francesco Barbaro 563
Gino Allegri 101, 299, 300, 679
Giordani 111, 113
Giorgio (tanker) 544
Giovanna 556
Giuliani 113, 125
Giuseppe Bertolli 679
Giuseppina 679
Gradisca (liner) 316
Gualdi 544
Guilio Giordani 45
Honestas 679
Ida Orlando 679
Ist 679
Istria 529, 540
Leonardo Palomba (tanker) 557, 560
Lerici 111, 113, 518, 520
Le Tre Marie 679
Liliana 679
Linotii 679
Loreto 573
Luciano Manara 115
Luisiano (tanker) 638
Lupo (tanker) 573
Lussino 679
Manara 548, 549
Manfredo Camperio 541
Maria Roselli 370
Marte (tanker) 679
Monginevro 52, 100

Monreale 113
Monti 546
Monviso 52, 55, 74, 388
Napoli 68, 69
Nerucci (tanker) 563
Nino Bixio 113, 370, 387, 388
Padenna 546, 547
Panuco (tanker) 624, 626
Perla 35
Pertusola 559
Picci Fassio (tanker) 544, 545
Portofino (tanker) 639
Pozarica (tanker) 522, 523, 524, 530
Proserpina (tanker) 563, 638
Raffio 679
Ravello 52, 111, 113, 184, 548, 559
Reginaldo Giuliani 184, 187
Rondine (tanker) 74, 560
Rosalino Pilo 363, 520
Rostro (tanker) 556
Sabbia 679
Salona (ex-Yugoslav) 125
San Andrea (tanker) 543, 544
San Giovanni Battista 63
San Giusto 225
Securitas 101, 679
Sestriera 548
Sirio 679
Sportivo 546, 547
Tergestea 628
Titania 624, 625
Tricolore (tanker) 679
Tripolino 559, 639
Una 679
Unione 111, 113, 544, 563
Ustica 679
Valfiorita 571
Vettor Pisani (1) 52, 184, 422, 430, 679
Vettor Pisani (2)

Fishing vessels
La Nuova Annunziata 101, 679
Maria Concetta 679
Orazio 679
San Domenico 679
Vergine di Pompei II 489

Miscellaneous
Andrea Sgarallino (pontoon) 679
Arno (hospital ship) 307
Brioni (auxiliary) 639
Giuseppe Miraglia (seaplane carrier) 35, 316
Madonna di Porto Salvo (tug) 679
Michelino (tug) 679
Montecristo (tug) 520
Salvatore (tug) 679
Sicilia (tug) 679
Trinacria (tug) 679
Victoria (liner-cum-troopship) 35, 52, 54, 55
Zara (auxiliary) 639
Zuri (patrol vessel) 39

Vichy French
Lillois (coaster) 44

Others
Cabo Prior (Spanish merchant vessel) 324

ii) German

Naval units
3rd MTB Flotilla 41, 129, 284, 352, 456

Destroyers
Ermes 529

MTBs
S.30 456, 499
S.36 456
S.55 353
S.56 353
S.58 456
S.59 456, 498, 499

Submarines
U-73 456, 466, 468
U-205 359, 456, 466, 476
U-331 456
U-333 456, 466
U374 48

Merchant Vessels
Achaja 73, 125
Ankara 388, 548, 573, 624
Atlas 82
Cuma 100, 101, 679
Dora 522, 563
Kreta 573
Max Berendt 429
Menes 560, 563
Ostia 639
Reichenfels 184, 187, 363, 364
Ruhr 101, 679
Sturla 429
Trapani 623

Places

Malta
Attard 130, 134, 135, 628
Birkirkara 134, 444, 575, 612, 619, 627, 631
Birzebbuga 402, 558, 622, 637, 678
Boschetto 134
Benghaisa Point 71, 126, 235, 279, 288, 518, 550, 576, 592, 595
Blue Grotto 615, 677, 678
Comino islet 182, 460, 533, 555, 578, 579, 594, 616, 619, 622, 627, 631
Cospicua 124, 213
Delimara Point 57, 85, 91, 99, 121, 126, 129, 146, 162, 164, 202, 308, 392, 430, 438, 520, 596, 611, 614, 621
Dingli/Cliffs 24, 36, 117, 187, 189, 248, 264, 265, 276, 281, 287, 308, 398, 402, 404, 422, 586, 633, 675, 676, 678
Dockyard 72, 89, 158, 160, 164, 170, 173, 207, 214, 216, 313, 627
Filfla 50, 71, *72*, 73, 89, 91, 93, 103, 116, 125, 188, 211, 279, 291, 314, 401, 402, 412, 462, 569, 571, 574, 578, 596, 609, 633, 636, 681
Floriana 100, 167, 173, 233, 627
Fort Campbell 271
Fort Ricasoli 248
Fort St Leonard 278, *279*
Fort St Rocco 222
French Creek 150, 163, 170, 172
Ghain Tuffieha 607
Ghar Bittija 678
Gharghur 534, 627, 628
Ghar id-Dud 193
Ghar Lapsi 24, 178, 403, 678
Ghaxaq 293
Grand Harbour 23, 29-30, 41, 46, 48, 57, 75, 79-81, 89, 96, 100, 102, 117, 125, 128-9, 141-5, 148-52, 154, 156-7, 159-60, 163, 165, 167-71, 173-4, 176-8, 181, 184, 192, 204, 207, 209-10, 213-5, 217, 221-3, 233, 235, 245, 248-9, 252. 254-7, 260-1, 346, 360, 394, 426, 432, 443-4, 464, 475, 514, 520, 527, 531, 547, 554, 561, 571, 576-7, 581, 584, 586-7, 592, 595, 599, 601, 605, 607, 613, 616, 626, 631, 644-5
Gudja 421, 631
Gzira 29, 134, 237
Hagra S-Sewda 678
Hal Far 13, 26-9, *30*, 30, 33, 37, 41, *46*, 47-8, 50-2, 55-6, 58-60, 62, 65-6, 68-73, *75*, 77-8, 79-80, 87, 90, 92, 95-6, 100-1, 110, 112-8, *114*, 121, 126-7, 130-2, 135, 137, 145-6, *147*, 155, 157-8, 160, 162-7, 170-1, 177-8, 180-1, 183-5, 191-3, 201-2, 205-6, 214, 216, 219, 221, 225-6, 231, 233, 235-9, *236*, 242, 244-7, 249, 261-2, 266, 270-1, 276-8, 281, 286, 288-9, 293, 297, 299, 303, 307-8, *346*, 361, *362*, 365, 376, 381, 392, 399, 401, 411, 414, 426, 430-2, 437-8, 443, 462, 505, 515, 528, 552, 558-9, 568, 576-7, *580*, 584, 597-8, *600*, 601, 609, 612-3, 615-6, 622-5, 627-8, 631, 644, 678
Hamilton Wharf 163
Hamrun 129, 167, 627, 631, 687
Il Qattara 678
Kalafrana/Bay 26-7, 32, 34, 39, 50, 52-3, 56, 58, 68-72, 76, 84, 89, 100, 114, 118, 121, 125, 130, 142-3, 145, 149, 151-2, 164, 166, 171-2, 176, 188, 191, 201, 208-10, 213-4, 221, 225, 232, 237-8, 245, 251, 259-60, 267, 270, 272-3, 289, 300, 304, 384, 392, 426, 436, 439, 444, 459, 463, 520, 522, 531, 547, 550, 572, 592, 595, 601, 604, 607, 610-11, 614-16, 619, 621-22, 628, 631, 634
Kalkara Creek 163, 167, 168, 222, 257
Kirkop 361, 422, 437, 678
Lascaris 24
Lazaretto Creek 128, 163
Lija 249
Luqa 13, 26, 28-33, *32*, 35, 37, 39-41, 43-8, 50, 52-3, 56, 62, 65-6, 73, 75-7, 80-1, 84, 86-8, 90, 94-6, 100-2, 110-3, 115, 118-9, 120, 121, 123-4, 126-8, 130, 136-8, 145-6, 148, 150-1, 157-8, 162-9, 172-4, 178, 180-1, 183-5, 187, 201-2, 204-8, 211, 213-5. 217, 219-20, 222, 224-6, 231-4, 238-9, 242, 244-5, 248-9, 251, 259-61, 263-4, 267, 277, 286, 289, 290, 293, 297-300, 308, 312-6, *313*, 353, 361-2, 370-3, 375-7, 383-4, 386, 388, 390, 395, 397, 399, 401-2, 409-11, 413, 415-8, 421-2, 424, 426, 428-32, 435-7, 440, 456, 458, 460, 463-4, 474-5, 496-7, 524, 527, 529, 531, 534, 542, 544, 546, 553, 558, 568, 571-2, 575, 579-80, 582-3, 585-6, *589*, 593, 595, *606*, 607, 611-2, 616, 620, 623, 625, 627-32, 637-8, 643-4, 676, 678, 686
Madliena 24, 562
Manoel Island 41, 79, 101, 110, 129
Marfa 126, 177
Marsa 150, 171, 238
Marsascala 281, 399, 443
Marsamxett Harbour 13, 41, 255, 675
Marsaxlokk Bay 57, 76, 99, 102, 148, 149, 151, 181, 214, 237, 273, 303, 383, 402, 547, 593, 602, 628, 681
Mdina 162, 241, 265, 678
Mellieha/Bay 226, 372, 376, 385, 443, 560, 578, 608, 616
Mosta 48, *93*, 103, 130, 134, 135, 174, *175*, 175, 180, 223, 237, 367, 390, 402, 541, 605, 607, 619, 628, 631, 633
Mqabba 616
Mtarfa 182, 204, 633, 684
Naxxar 110, 130, 180, 218, 219, 221, 233, 255, 444, 541, 562
Niscemi 631
Paola 80, 123, *163*, 163, 271, 534
Pembroke Ranges 102
Pieta 375
Qawra Tower 388
Qormi 77, 91, 116, 205, 221, 396, 580
Qrendi 63, 129, 383, 428, 571, 596, 677
Rabat 61, 103, 128, 134, 135, 182, 202, 212, 217, 231, 235, 316, 404, 457, 578, 633, 645, 678
Ras Hanzir 150
Ricasoli Point 383
Safi 76, 101, 112, 113, 123, 174, *192*, 207, 226, 232, 233, 245, 286, 300, 304, 384, 392, 418, 422, 431, 527, 534, 552, 568, 595, 601, 630, 631, 678
Salina Bay 24, 558, 578, 606
San Anton 81
Saqqajja 135
Senglea 259, 260
Siggiewi 39, 43, 102, 204, 216, 314, 398
Sliema 72, 123, 124, 129, 135, 173, 192-3, 207, 363, 385, 412, 431, 443, 464, 595, 608, 613, 678
Spinola/Bay 217, 586
St Andrews 163
St Julians 129, 406, 531, 586, 613
St Mark's Bay 553
St Paul's Bay 72, 132, 162, 171, 178, 204, 218, 220-1, 239, 255, 259, *263*, 271, 366, 381, 388, 392, 436, 442, 444, 445, 459-60, 462, 464, 534, 553, 575, 578-80, 592-3, 599, 605, 609, 613, 616, 619, 621-2, 628, 631-3, 636-7, 644, 676
St Peter's 248
St Thomas' Bay 430
Ta'Giorni 406
Takali 13, 17, 26-7, *27*, 31-4, *31*, 47-8, 50-1, 56-8, 61, 65-6, 70-1, 76-7, 80-1, 87-9, 94, 96, 102-3, 107, *108*, 109-10, 115, 117-9, 120, 123, 125, 127-8, 130-1, *133*, 134-7, *135*, 151-2, 159, 165, 167, 169, 170, 172, 175, 177, 181-5, 201-2, 204-7, 209-17, *212*, 219-22, 224, 226, 232, 235, 237-9, 241-2, 244-5, 247-8, 250, 262, 264, 267, 269, 271-2, *278*, 280, 286-8, *289*, 292-3, 296-9, 303, 308-12, 316, *317*, 345, 365, 367, 373, 376, 384, 386. 388-92, 394, 398, 401-2, 404, 406-9, 412-3, 418-9, 428, 432-3, 435, 443, 456, 464, *517*, 522, *523*, 527, 529-30, 541-2, 561, 568, 573, 577-80, 583, 585-6, 590, 594-6, 599-600, 602, *603*, 607-9, 611, 615, 617, 619, 627, 631, 633-5, *634*, 637, 644, 678
Tarxien 80, 580
Tas-Silc 24, 157, 299, 438
Tigne Point 38, 124, 134, 338, 363
Valetta 29, 32, 71, 81, 86, 90, 96, 118, 123, 129, 130, 144, 158, 162, 172, 178, 201, 204, 205, 213, 216, 221, 252, 256, 259, 260, 261, 274, 276, 303, 312, 384, 395-6, 418, 426-7, 436, 459, 461, 506, 511, 552, *552*, 578, 586, 594, 601-2, 611, 613, 620, 637, 646, 678, 685
Vittoriosa 123, 177
Wied is-Sewda 91
Wied iz-Zurrieq 126, 268, 308, 314, 402, 677
Zabbar 121
Zammitello Palace, Mgarr 391
Zebbug 130, 236, 361, 396
Zejtun 129, 232, 237, 271, 393
Zonqor Point 137, 142-3, 173, 233, 237, 278, *279*, 299, 305, 421, 426, 437, 444, 459, 497, 517, 530, 547, 552, 554, 559, 560-1, 572-3, 576, 594-6, 603, 607-8, 610, 613-14, 618, 621, 626-7
Zurrieq 84, 187, 677

Gozo 24, 41, 63, 77, 101, 110, 120, 126-7, 149, 151, 165, 182, 204, 215, 234, 236, 259, 271, 286, 296, 303, 312, 314, 333, 345, 367-9, 373, 376, 386, 392, 399, *400*, 401, 403, 405, 407, 418-9, 421, 425-6, 433, *434*, 434, 444, 458, 460, 515, 552, *552*, 553, 574-5, 577, 579-80, 585-6, 594, 596, 627, 633, 636, 644, 685, 686
Dahlet Qorrot 515, 627
Jordon Lighthouse 41
Kercem 376
Marsalforn Bay 333, *400*, 400, 407, 685, 686
Mgarr 236, 398, 633
Nadur 41
Sannat 574
Victoria 433, 644
Xewkija 534
Xlendi Bay 151, 286

Sicily

Acate 215
Agrigento 81, 115, 225, 454, 556, 558
Augusta 14, 20, 21, 61, 83, 296-300, 303, 377, 455, 518, 645

Biancavilla 81
Biscari 522, 528, 536, 537, *538*, 538, 550, 570, 573
Caltagirone 306, 683
Cape Gallo 573
Cape Granitola 645
Cape Passero 61, 86, 394, 531, 557, 592, 612
Cape Peloro 98
Cape Religione 394
Cape Scalambria 546, 553, 560, 570, 636
Cape Scaramia 181, 230, 276, 308, 436, 460, 522, 576, 627
Capo Murro di Porco 231
Carini 71
Castelvetrano 20, 21, 33, 34, 56, 62, 69, 88, 138, 165, 193, 273, 301, 333, 334, 339, 361, 417, 453, 454, 455, 501, 504, 511, 528, 541, 556, 557, 563, 570, 573, 592
Catania 13, 19, 20, 21, 44, 45, 48, 57, 61, 62, 76, 79, 81, 83, 92, 95, 111, 124, 127, 128, 130, 135, 138, 140, 143, 157, 169, 192, 204, 211, 219, 222, 264, 269, 288, 296, 297, 303, 314, 315, 362, 377, 414, 455, 463, 475, 500, 518, 519, 565, 573, 581, 597, 622
Chinisia San Giuseppe 21, 285, 336, 342, *373*, 454, 504, 505, 567
Comiso 15, *15*, 19, 20, 44, 46, 57, *58*, 61, 62, 64, 70, 72, 99, 117, 120, 125, 128, 147, 152, 160, 168, 173, 175, 204, 207, 211, 213, 215, 216, 222, *234*, 259, *259 264*, 265, 268, 270, 273, 300, *301*, *306*, 363, 365, 371, 380, 383, 403, 406, 436, 455, 475, 497, 502, 522, 528, 531, 534, 535, 541, 542, *556*, 565, 572, 578, 581, 591, 595, 604, 608, 611, 614, 617, 633
Della Correnti 88
Donna Fugata 99
Donnalucata 155, *155*, 157
Gela 19, 20, 21, 44, 68, 102, 130, 141, 232, 257, 281, *284*, 285, 289, 333, 371, 379, 382, 384, *404*, 408, 417, 418, 430, 432, 437, 475, 511, 522, 528, 533, 534, 536, 538, 541, 554, 560, 566, 567, 573, 586, 622, 630
Gerbini 20, 44, 62, 117, 211, 222, 228, 296, 395, 455, 500, 503, 536, 565, 567, 573, 580, 597, 627
Licata 68, 298, 546
Magnisi 36
Marina di Ragusa *536*, 536
Marsala 21, 22, 533, 558, 645
Messina 52, 84, 91, 98, 221, 228, 293, 296, 298, 314, 319, 362, 374, 377, 399, 497, 505, 546, 563
Modica 68, 88, 536
Monte Erice 23
Monte San Pallagrino 23
Monte Etna 60, 61, 70, 74, 681
Noto Bay 56, 264
Pachino 98, 528, 565, 572, 601
Palazzo Adriano 71, 271
Palermo 20, 23, 52, 68, 70, 71, *74*, 100, 101, 102, 115, 271, 321, 325, 336, 362, 363, 370, 379, 455, 505, 557, 570, 573, 679, 680
Palermo/Boccadifalco 44, 73, 454, 455, 568
Porto Empedocle 203, 550, 557
Porto Palo 23
Pozzallo 170, 238, 394, 532, 601
Prizzi 71
Punto Stilo 296. 560, 624
Ragusa 213, 406, 539, 583
San Pietro di Caltagirone 19, 135, 181, 334, 371, *372*, 394, 453, 551, 565, 567, 604
San Ranieri 399
Santa Cruse 99
Santa Flavia 71
Santa Maria di Licodia 81
Santa Stefano Quisquina 71
Scalea 70
Scoglitti 91, 184, 550
Sciacca 21, 61, 138, 454, 455, 558, 570, 573
Scicli 406, 432
Simato 475
Stagnone di Marsala 181, 225, 339, 454
Syracuse 20, 36, 88, 99, 103, 264, 277, 314, 377, 436, 455, 513, 541, 560, 562, 601, 608
Taermina 74
Trapani 20, 21, 23, 61, 74, 98, 216, 327, 417, 454, 455, 520, 528, 556, 560, 573, 685
Villa Correnti 88
Vittoria 215, 219, 537

Elsewhere
Abu Suier, Egypt 110, 456
Alamein, *see* El Alamein
Alem el Halfa, Libya 545, 564
Alexandria, Egypt 13, 18, 57, 68, 81, 138, 144, 148, 290, 321, 347, 348, 349, 352, 358, 359, 466, 647
Alghero, Sardinia 22, 453
Algiers, Algeria 282, 301, 325, 480, 509, 646
Antipaxoi, Greece 558, 638
Argostoli, Greece 16, 430
Athens, Greece 139, 355
Atlas Mountains, Algeria 58
Barce, Libya 347, 348
Bardia, Libya 52
Bari, Italy 453
Benghazi, Libya 24, 45, 52, 53, 292, 296, 299, 347, 388, 429, 440, 448, 518, 548, 556, 557, 559, 563, 571, 573, 624, 637, 638, 639, 646
Benina, Libya 47, 48, 52, 347
Berka, Libya 45, 53, 54, 348
Bizerte, Tunisia 245, 470, 503, 570
Bone, Algeria 43, 231, 570
Brindisi, Italy 30, 184, 440, 453, 548, 559, 563
Bu Amud, Libya 114, 168, 170, 184, 185, 216
Buerat-el-Hsum, Libya 29, 68, 73
Cagliari, Sardinia 301, 314, 325, 377, 474, 497
Cairo, Egypt 25, 40, 60, 105, 117, 148, 232
Calato, Rhodes Island 123
Candia, Crete 123
Cape Bon, Tunisia 36, 37, 50, 63, 64, 74, 81, 128, 171, 200, 222, 251, 287, 315, 325, 337, 363, 407, 423, 424, 493, 505, 645, 646, 647
Cape Bougaroni, Tunisia 470, 476
Cape Colanne 374
Cape Gerogh'ambro, Greece 422, 430
Cape Lixuri, Greece 422
Cape Matapau, Greece 24
Cape Sacritifi, Spain 685
Cape Santa Maria di Leuca, Italy 545, 548, 571
Cape Servat 490
Cape Spada, Crete 541
Cape Spartivento, Italy 296, 441, 546, 563
Cape Spartivento, Sardinia 479
Cape Teulada, Sardinia 331
Cape Turgeunes, Tunisia 74, 288
Carloforte, Isola San Pietro 330
Catanzaro, Italy 62
Cattaro, Italy 530
Cekhira, Tunisia 59
Cephalonia, Greece 422, 430, 626
Ceuta, Spanish Morocco 453
Constantine, Algeria 487
Corfu Island, Greece 32, 91, 387, 524, 529, 530, 545, 549, 571
Corinth Canal, Greece 540
Crete 138, 139, 144, 158, 228, 285, 290, 331, 347, 348, 349, 351, 352, 359, 429, 455, 466, 469, 544, 546, 550, 554, 563, 564, 638, 677, 682
Crotone, Italy 14, 560
Cypus 123
Decimomannu, Sardinia 22, 44, 301, 309, 322, 332, 377, 378, 388, 453, 474, *481*, 481, 644, 645
Dekheila, Egypt 60
Derna, Libya 24, 45, 46, 60, 225, 347, 350, 358, 540, 639
Djedeida, Tunisia 206
Djerba, Tunisia 92, 573
Edcu, Egypt 123
El Adem, Libya 53, 54, 60, 92, 96, 100, 117, 321, 350
El Agheila, Libya 52
El Alamein, Egypt 448, 541, 564, 638, 644
Eleusis, Greece 139, 355
El Daba, Egypt 207
El Firdan, Egypt 155
El Hania, Libya 295
Elmas, Sardinia 23, 44, 138, 157, 322, 323, 331, 332, 453, 473, 474, 479, 481, 482, 510, 511, 644, 645
El Zauir, Libya 63
Eolie Islands 140
Fayid, Egypt 354, 475
Filicudi Island 288
Fiumara Condoianni, Italy 546
Fiume, Italy 570
Fuka, Egypt 349
Gaddura, Rhodes 148
Galite Island 128, 329, 334, 483, 484
Gambut, Libya 138, 139, 143, 144, 149, 155, 193, 235, 350, 351, 355, 358
Gazala, Libya 56, 318, 349
Gianaclis, Egypt 638
Gibraltar 23, 36, 37, 40, 43, 46, 59, 62, 68, 69, 72, 76, 88, 90, 92, 98, 103, 105, 106, 107, 108, 109, 115, 123, 133, 157, 158, 168, 171, 176, 177, 181, 199, 200, 201, 206, 227, 230, 237, 239, 241, 244, 251, 277, 282, 283, 287, 302, 303, 309, 310, 311, 312, 313, 317, 319, 321, 324, 326, 327, 332, 336, 337, 339, 342, 344, 365, 374, 377, 388, 412, 415, 417, 422, 423, 450, 451, 452, 456, 457, 459, 460, 465, 467, 470, 475, 480, 495, 498, 504, 508, 509, 519, 546, 570, 573, 618, 634, 635, *636*, 636, 639, 640, 642, 678, 684, 685, 686
Grosseto, Italy 455
Grottaglie, Italy 372
Guidonia airfield (Rome) 36
Gulf of Gabes 61, 79
Gulf of Hammamet 470, 506
Gulf of Squillace 362
Guyotville, Algeria 283
Halfaya, Egypt 52
Haifa, Palestine 321, 347, 466
Hassani, Greece 139
Heliopolis, Egypt 211
Heraklion, Crete 138, 139, 144, 347, 348, 352, 475
Homs, Libya 50, 298, 623, 624
Ibiza, Spain 324
Isola San Pietro 330
Kabrit, Egypt 207
Kalamaki, Greece 362
Karamanli Mole (Tripoli), Libya 51
Kastelli, Crete 347, 348, 475, 546, 547, 549
Keliba, Tunisia 555
Kerkenah Island 36, 37, 39, 50, 225, 407
Korba, Tunisia 335
Kuriat Island 35, 92, 560
Lampedusa Island 13, 24, 45, 92, 125, 128, 132, 247, 303, 324, 343, 407, 468, 470, 518, 520, 556, 624, 625, 626
Lampione Island 79, 232, 363
La Spezia, Italy 453, 456
Levkas Island, Greece 441
Lindos, Rhodes Island 123
Linosa Island 222, 342, 343, 361, 470, 504, 505, 510, 513
Lipari islands 288
Littorio, Italy 570
Maison Blanche, Algeria 282
Majorca 377
Maleme, Crete 347, 348
Marcellinara, Italy 62
Maritza, Rhodes Island 123
Martuba, Libya 24
Melilla, Spanish Morocco 685
Mersa Matruh, Egypt 349, 429
Milas, Turkey 123
Misurata, Libya 29, 35, 624
Monserrato, Sardinia 22, 453, 481, 482
Mount Khenchela, Algeria 487
Naples, Italy 30, 68, 88, 138, 184, 314, 321, 370, 377, 453, 497, 520, 624
Navarino, Greece 440, 458, 466, 475, 563, 638
Olbia, Sardinia 22, 322, 453
Oran, Morocco 282, 324, 646
Pantelleria 19, 20, 21, 22, 23, 24, 35, 37, 40, 43, 47, 69, 73, 77, 79, 81, 83, 90, 98, 111, 114, 131, 134, 156, 193, 222, 245, 283, 289, 301, 302, 310, 312, 322, 337, 339, 340, 342, 361, 367, 416, 417, 454, 455, 470, 489, 490, 493, 497, 500, 501, 503, 510, 511, 512, 513, 520, *555*, 556, 572, 573, 622, 624, 628, 647
Paxos Island, Greece 387, 524
Philippeville, Algeria 511, 570
Piana Island 489
Piraeus, Greece 529, 544, 546, 563
Pisa, Italy 453
Pola, Italy 570
Port Lyautey, Morocco 465
Port Said, Egypt 321, 347, 466
Prevesa, Greece 441, 443
Ras Mahamur, Tunisia 557
Ras el Hilal, Tunisia 225, 545, 573
Ras el Mahedia, Tunisia 68
Ras el Tin, Tunisia 540, 573
Reggio di Calabria, Italy 44, *381*, 455
Rettimo, Crete 139
Rhodes Island 122, 138, 148, 358
Rome, Italy 52, 158, 165, 272, 285, 453, 482, 520, 570
Saiada Bay, Corfu 524, 530
Santa Maria di Leuca, *see*Cape Santa Maria di Leuca
Sapienza, Greece 440, 596
Sfax, Tunisia 560
Shallufa, Egypt 90
Sidi Barrani, Egypt 45, 294, 354, 355, 638
Sidi Hamed, Tunisia 329
Sirte, Libya 29, 53
Skerki Bank/Channel 337, 493, 496
Sollum, Egypt 52
Sousse, Tunisia 69, 81
Sphaktina Island, Greece 475
Suda Bay, Crete 544
Suez Canal, Egypt 230, 319, 371
Taranto, Italy 35, 81, 84, 138, 184, 314, 315, 319, 321, 326, 337, 352, 357, 358, 362, 370, 376, 377, 387, 388, 422, 441, 505, 524, 529, 544, 548, 558, 563, 568, 571, 638
Tobruk, Libya 18, 82, 117, 229, 285, 295, 349, 350, 429, 448, 518, 529, 544, 546, 547, 549, 553, 560, 563, 637, 639
Torino Caselle, Italy 453
Trieste, Italy 570
Tripoli, Libya 14, 24, 30, 34, 35, 41, 44, 50, 51, 52, 55, 59, 63, 69, 72, 74, 75, 94, 95, 96, 99, 100, 114, 125, 128, 157, 168, 184, 225, 283, 286, 298, 448, 556, 557, 558, 573, 626, 646
Tunis, Tunisia 283, 309, 310, 324, 402, 416, 470, 570, 646
Tymbaki, Crete 139, 347, 352
Valencia, Spain 480
Valle Inviolata (Rome) 23
Venice, Italy 570
Villacidro, Sardinia 22, 322, 323, 332, 453, 481, 482
Zaezis, Libya 61
Zante Island, Greece 387
Zuara, Libya 29, 50, 61